Did you know? Apparently the reading comprehension rate of Japanese youth is among the highest in the world. Isn't that terrific? I mean, isn't that great? And do you know why that is? Even among the Japanese, the ones with the best reading comprehension are those who read manga. Isn't that terrific news? Seriously. Isn't it très magnifique? (←French style)

– Eiichiro Oda, 2002

· AUTHOR BIOGRAPHY ·

Eiichiro Oda began his manga career in 1992 at the age of 17, when his one-shot cowboy manga *Wanted!* won second place in the coveted Tezuka manga awards. Oda went on to work as an assistant to some of the biggest manga artists in the industry, including Nobuhiro Watsuki, before winning the Hop Step Award for new manga artists. His pirate adventure *One Piece*, which debuted in *Weekly Shonen Jump* magazine in 1997, quickly became one of the most popular manga in Japan.

ONE PIECE: BAROQUE WORKS 22-23-24

SHONEN JUMP Manga Omnibus Edition
A compilation of the graphic novel volumes 22–24

STORY & ART BY EIICHIRO ODA

English Adaptation: Lance Caselman
Translation: JN Productions
Touch-up Art & Lettering: Vanessa Satone (graphic novel volumes 22–23),
Primary Graphix & Hudson Yards (graphic novel volume 24)
Additional Touch-up: Rachel Lightfoot (graphic novel volumes 22–23)
Design: Shawn Carrico (Omnibus edition), Sean Lee (graphic novels)
Editors: Megan Bates (Omnibus edition), Yuki Murashige (graphic novels)

Printed in the U.S.A.

Published by VIZ Media, LLC
P.O. Box 77010
San Francisco, CA 94107

10 9 8 7 6 5 4 3 2
Omnibus edition first printing, February 2014
Second edition, February 2016

www.viz.com

www.shonenjump.com

SHONEN JUMP MANGA

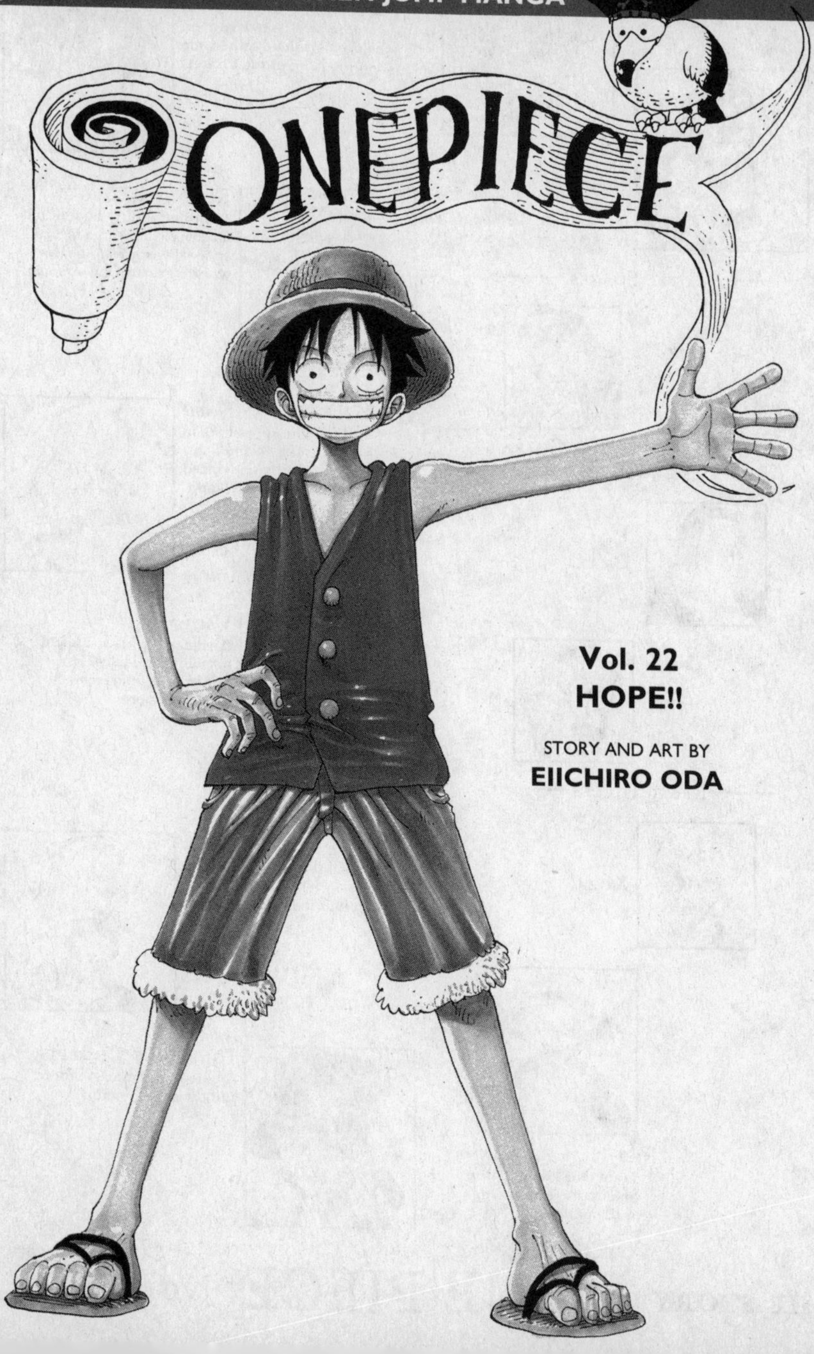
ONE PIECE

Vol. 22
HOPE!!

STORY AND ART BY
EIICHIRO ODA

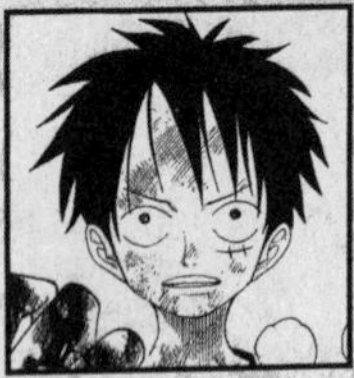

MONKEY D. LUFFY
Boundlessly optimistic and able to stretch like rubber, he is determined to become King of the Pirates.

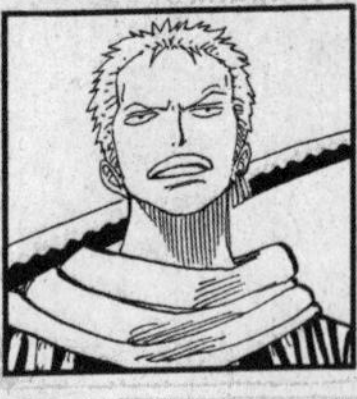

RORONOA ZOLO
A former bounty hunter and master of the "three-sword" style. He aspires to be the world's greatest swordsman.

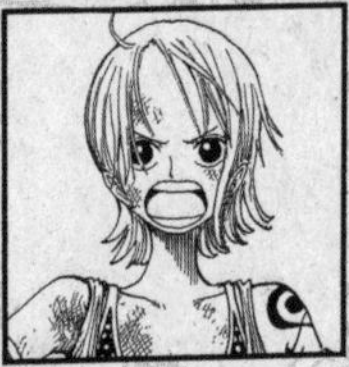

NAMI
A thief who specializes in robbing pirates. Nami hates pirates, but Luffy convinced her to be his navigator.

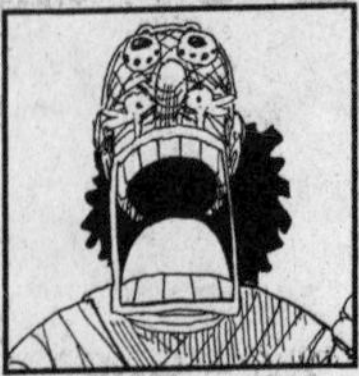

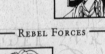

USOPP
A village boy with a talent for telling tall tales. His father, Yasopp, is a member of Shanks's crew.

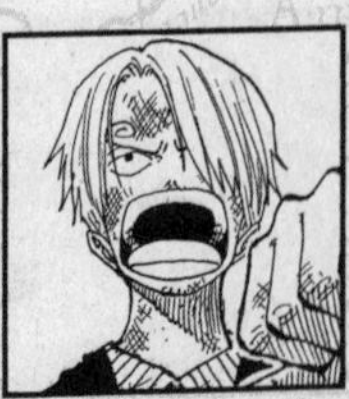

SANJI
The kindhearted cook (and ladies' man) whose dream is to find the legendary sea, the "All Blue."

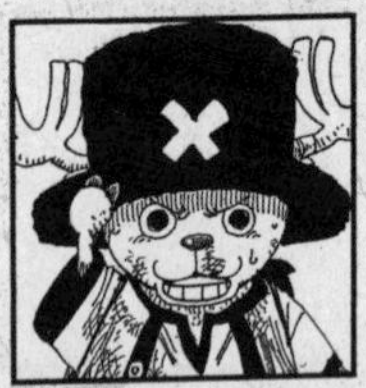

TONY TONY CHOPPER
A blue-nosed man-reindeer and the ship's doctor.

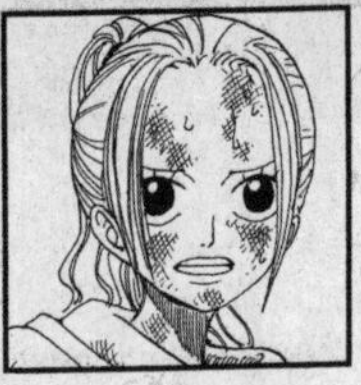

VIVI

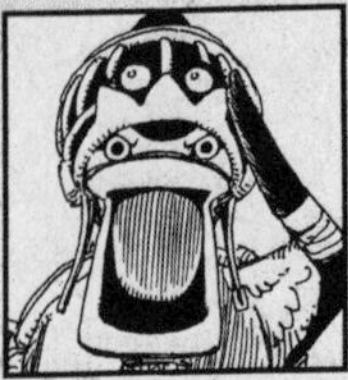

KAROO

ROYAL FORCES

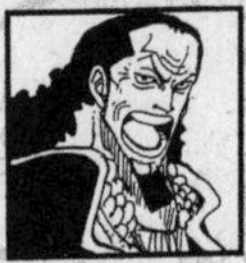

NEFELTARI COBRA (KING OF ALABASTA)

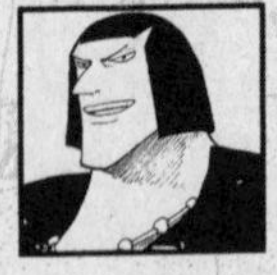

CHAKA

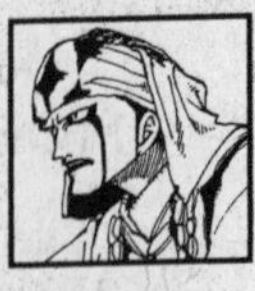

PELL

REBEL FORCES

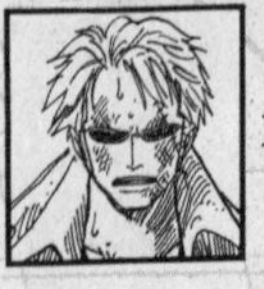

KOZA

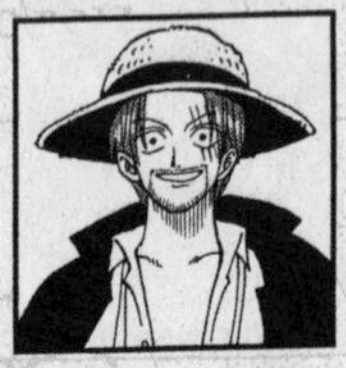

"RED-HAIRED" SHANKS
A pirate that Luffy idolizes. Shanks gave Luffy his trademark straw hat.

THE STORY OF ONE PIECE · VOLUME 22 ·

Baroque Works

Navy

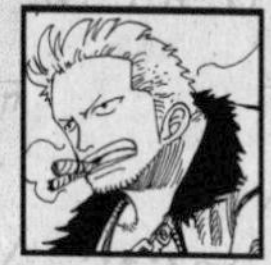

Captain Smoker

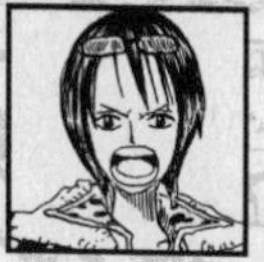

Tashigi

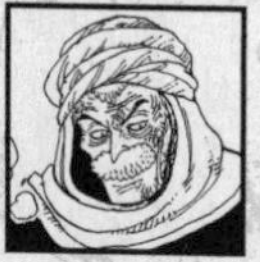

Toh-Toh

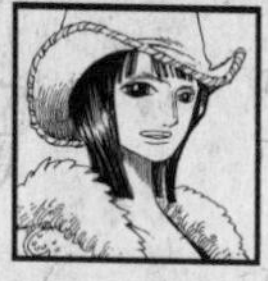

Ms. All Sunday (Nico Robin)

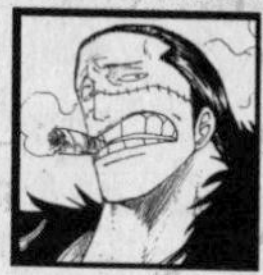

Mr. Zero (Sir Crocodile)

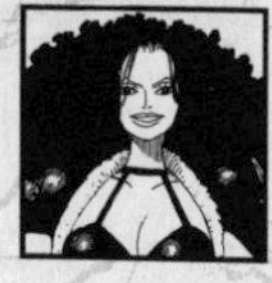

Ms. Doublefinger

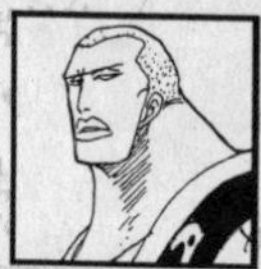

Mr. 1

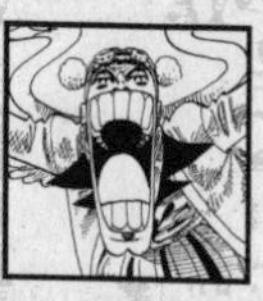

Mr. 2 Bon Clay

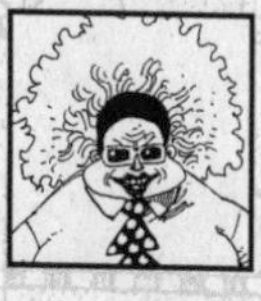

Ms. Merry Christmas

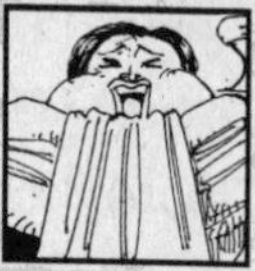

Mr. 4

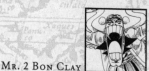

Monkey D. Luffy started out as just a kid with a dream—and that dream was to become the greatest pirate in history! Stirred by the tales of pirate "Red-Haired" Shanks, Luffy vowed to become a pirate himself. That was before the enchanted Devil Fruit gave Luffy the power to stretch like rubber, at the cost of being unable to swim—a serious handicap for an aspiring sea dog. Undeterred, Luffy set out to sea and recruited some crewmates: master swordsman Zolo, treasure-hunting thief Nami, lying sharpshooter Usopp, the high-kicking chef Sanji, and the latest addition, Chopper—the walkin' talkin' reindeer doctor.

Luffy and crew fight to help Princess Vivi save her war-torn and drought-ravaged kingdom from the evil Sir Crocodile and his secret criminal organization, the Baroque Works. Having finally reached the royal palace in Alubarna, Vivi devises a plan to end the civil war, only to be thwarted by the sudden arrival of Sir Crocodile, who reveals his true objective—to get his hands on the most destructive weapon of the ancient world, the Pluton! But first he intends to put an end to the rebellion himself by blowing up everyone near the palace, regardless of whose side they're on! With Luffy half-dead in the Alabastan desert and the rest of the crew taking on the Officer Agents in the streets of Alubarna, can anyone stop this fiend from realizing his evil plan?

BAROQUE WORKS

ONE PIECE

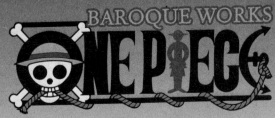

Vol. 22
Hope!!

CONTENTS

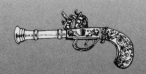

Chapter 196:
1

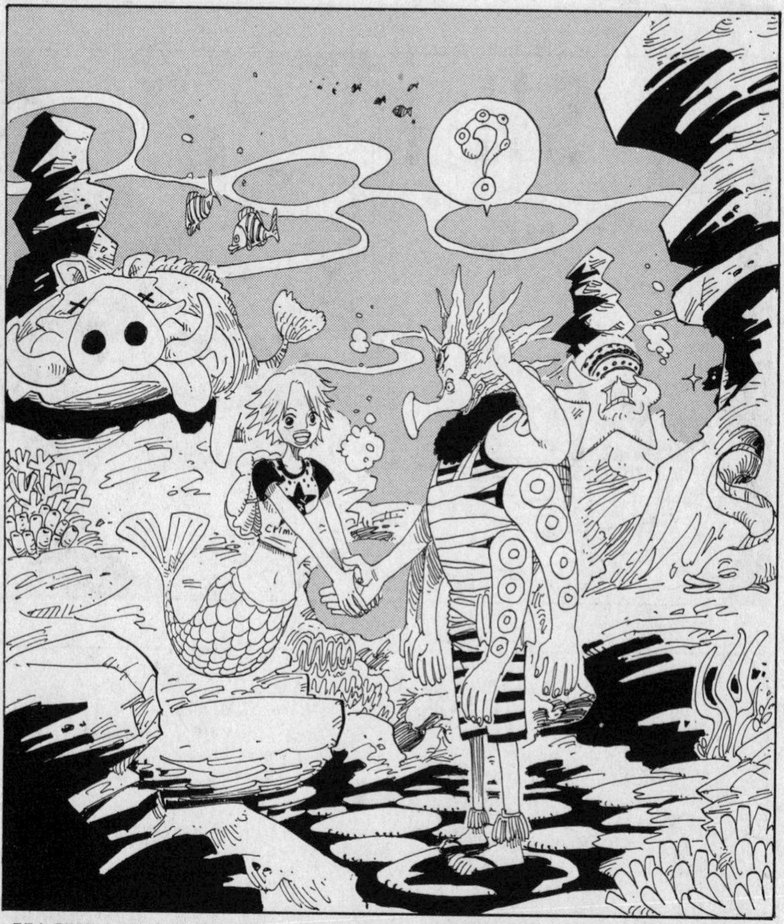

HACHI'S WALK ON THE SEAFLOOR, VOL. 13: "A SHADOW DRAWS NEAR HACHI, WHO SAVES SOMEONE WHO HAD BEEN EATEN BY A FISH, WHO HAD ALSO ALMOST BEEN EATEN BY A FISH"

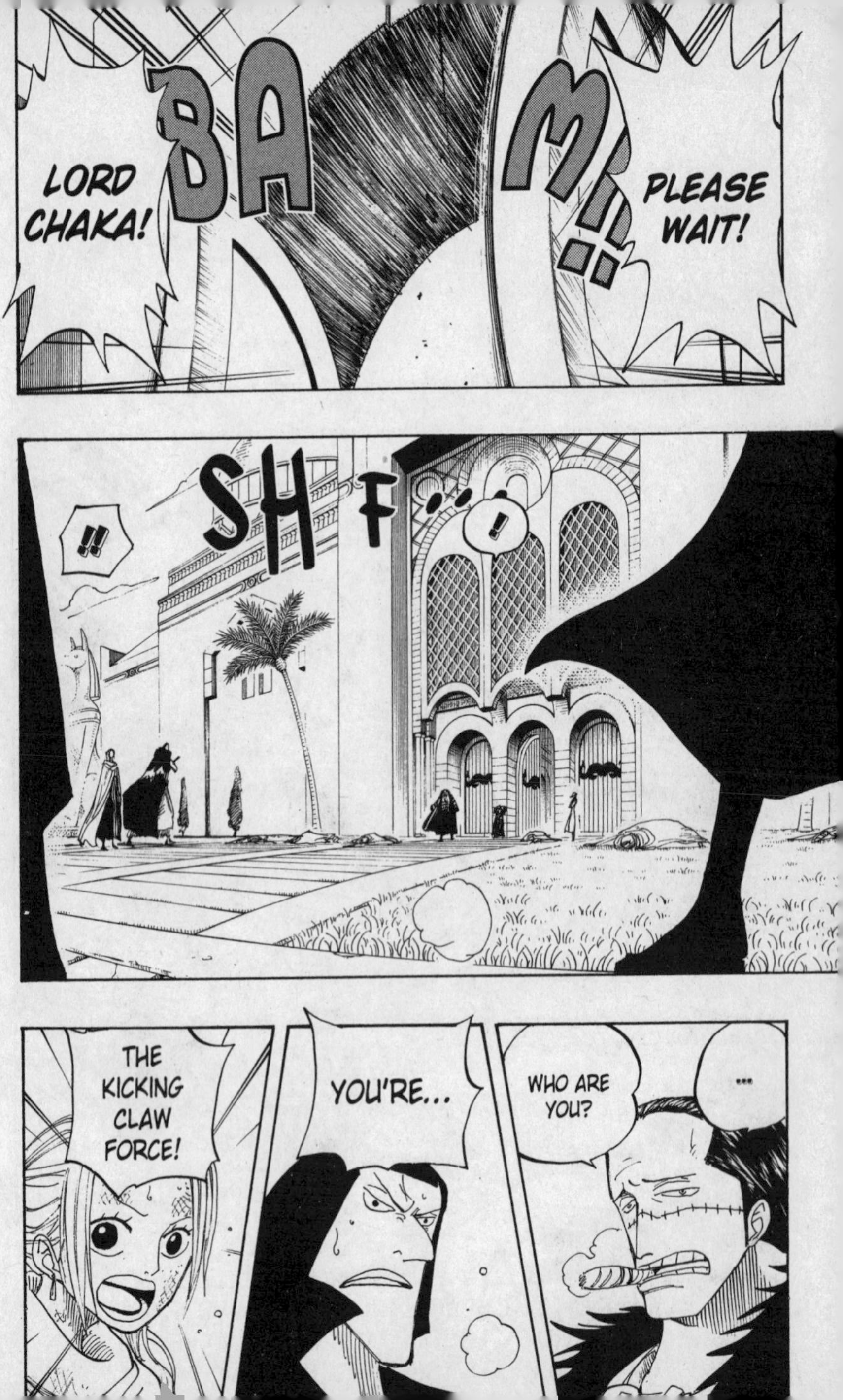
PLEASE WAIT!
BAM!!
LORD CHAKA!
...!
SHF
!!
...
WHO ARE YOU?
YOU'RE...
THE KICKING CLAW FORCE!

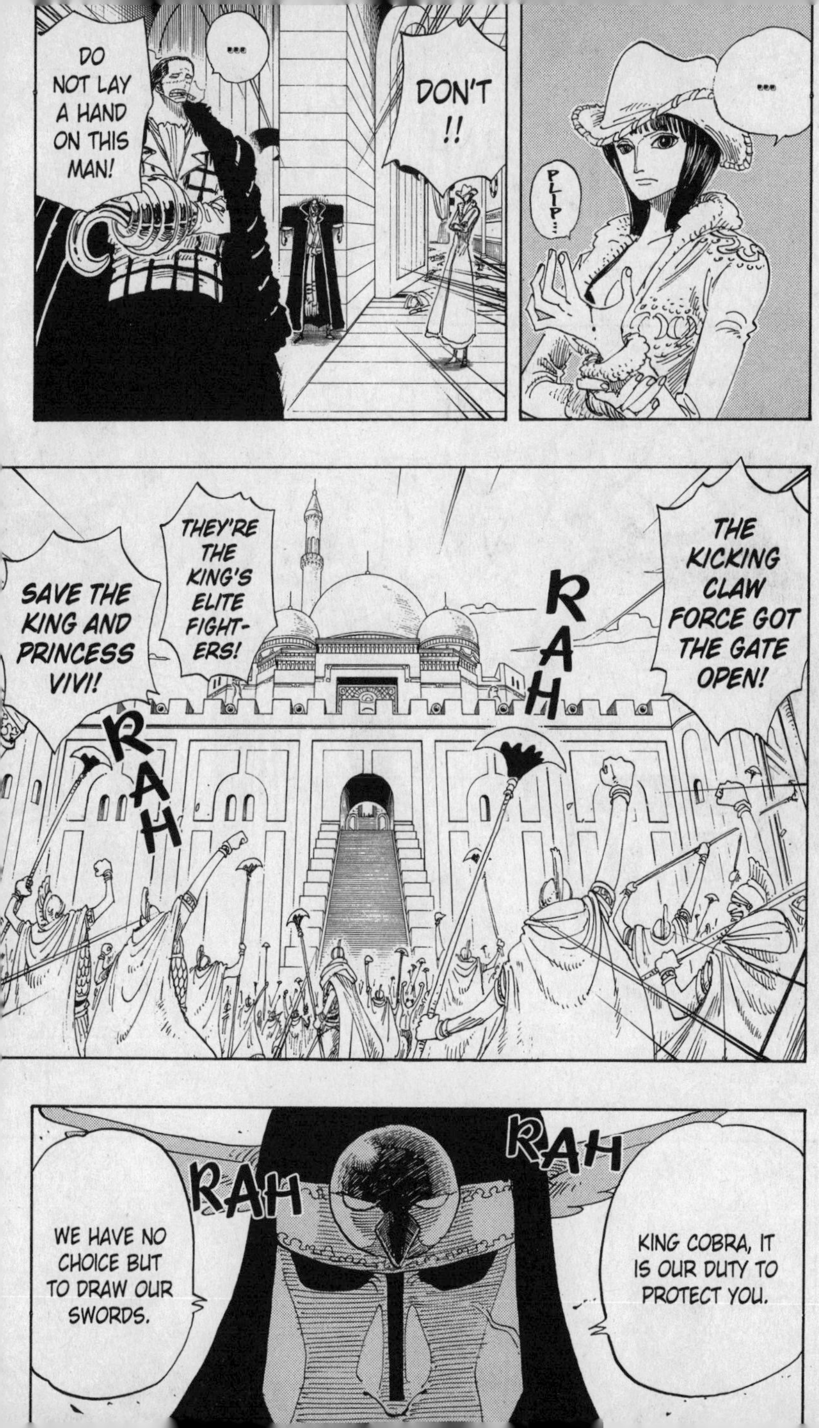
...
PLIP...
DON'T !!
...
DO NOT LAY A HAND ON THIS MAN!
THE KICKING CLAW FORCE GOT THE GATE OPEN!
RAH RAH
THEY'RE THE KING'S ELITE FIGHTERS!
SAVE THE KING AND PRINCESS VIVI!
RAH RAH
RAH
KING COBRA, IT IS OUR DUTY TO PROTECT YOU.
RAH
WE HAVE NO CHOICE BUT TO DRAW OUR SWORDS.

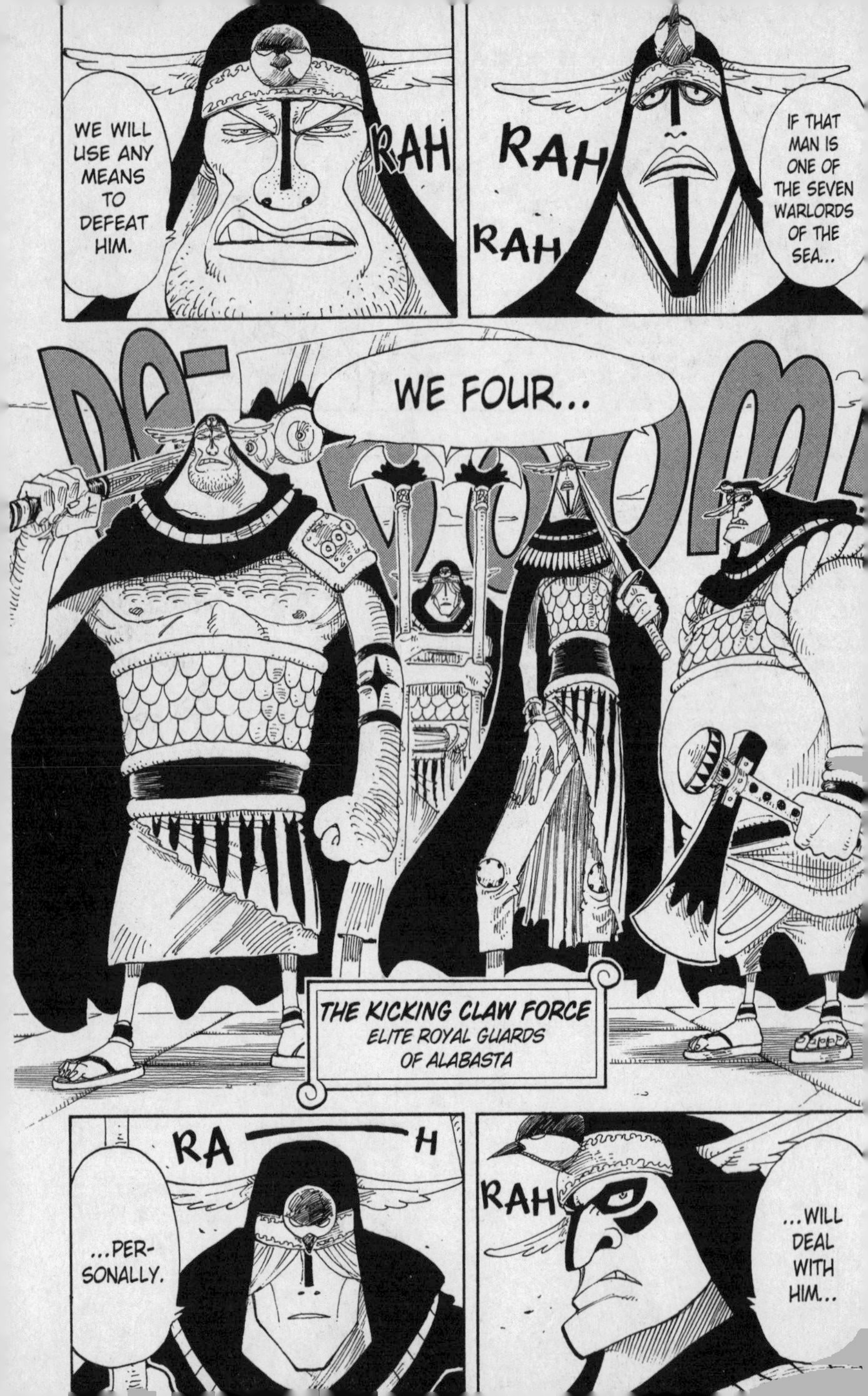

RAH
RAH
IF THAT MAN IS ONE OF THE SEVEN WARLORDS OF THE SEA...
RAH
WE WILL USE ANY MEANS TO DEFEAT HIM.
DE-
DOM
WE FOUR...
THE KICKING CLAW FORCE
ELITE ROYAL GUARDS OF ALABASTA
RAH
...WILL DEAL WITH HIM...
RA—H
...PER-SONALLY.

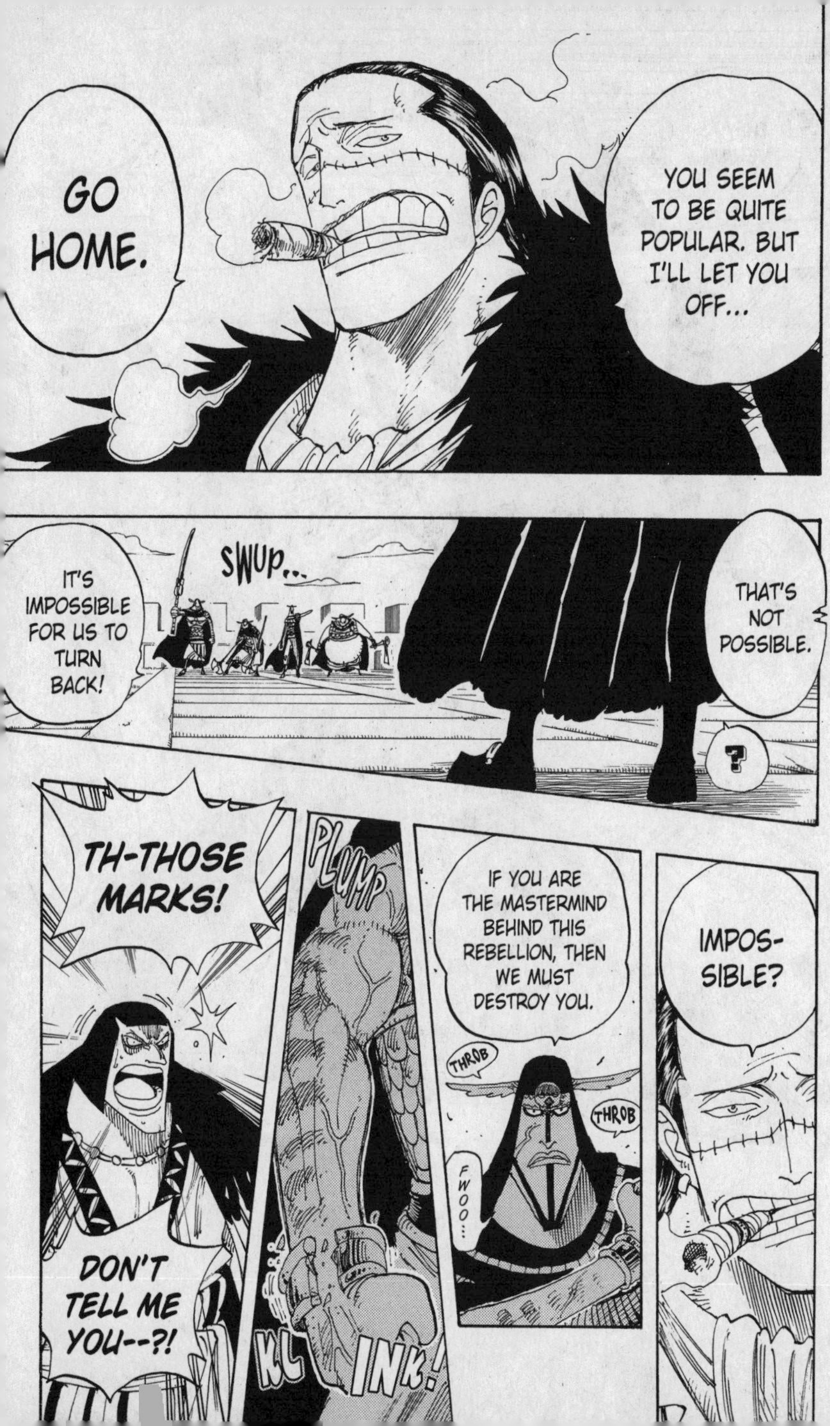
YOU SEEM TO BE QUITE POPULAR. BUT I'LL LET YOU OFF...
GO HOME.
THAT'S NOT POSSIBLE.
?
SWUP...
IT'S IMPOSSIBLE FOR US TO TURN BACK!
IMPOS-SIBLE?
IF YOU ARE THE MASTERMIND BEHIND THIS REBELLION, THEN WE MUST DESTROY YOU.
THROB
THROB
FWOO...
PLUMP
KL INK!
TH-THOSE MARKS!
DON'T TELL ME YOU--?!

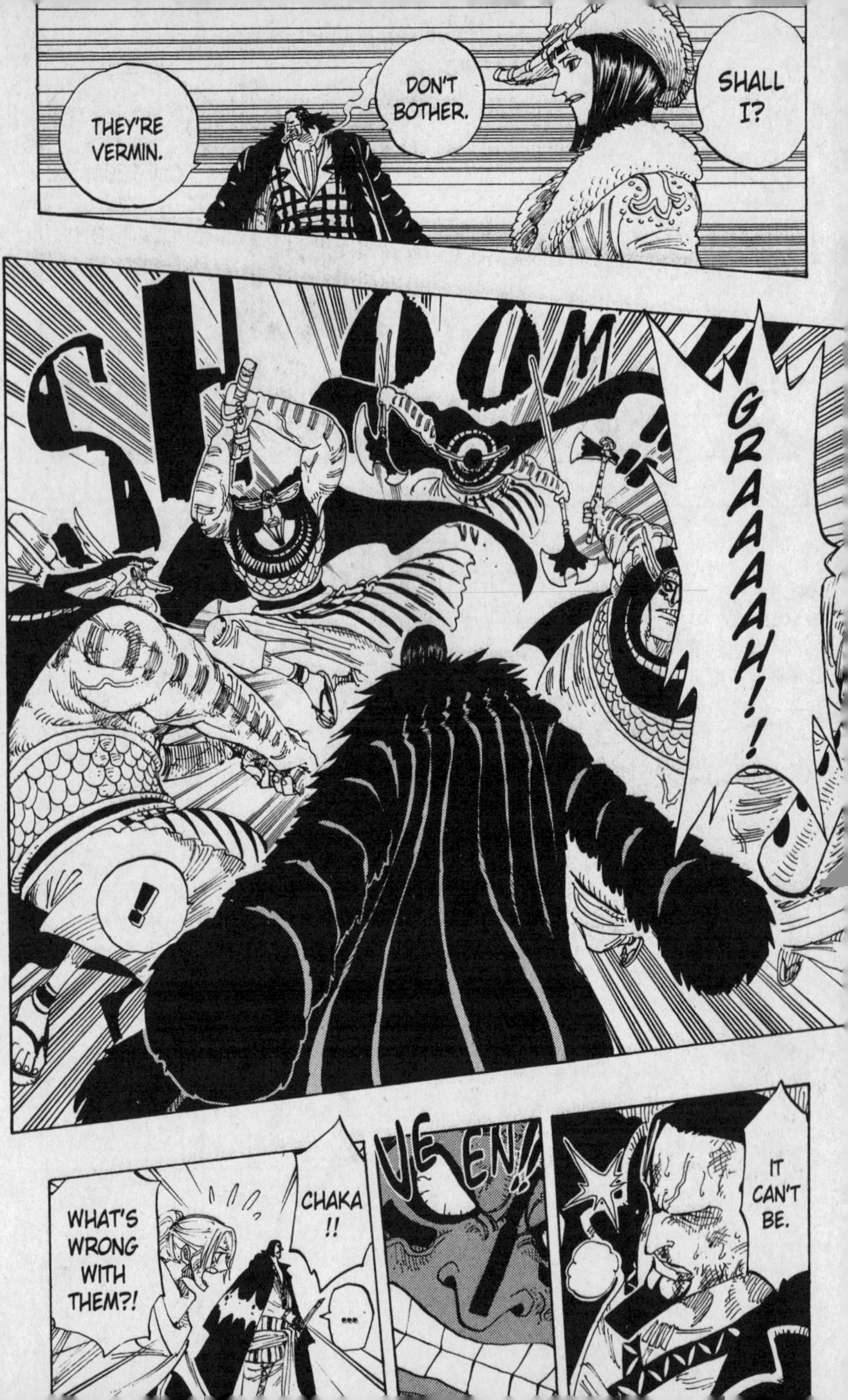
SHALL I?
DON'T BOTHER.
THEY'RE VERMIN.
GRAAAAAH!!
SHOOM
!
IT CAN'T BE.
VEEN
CHAKA!!
...
WHAT'S WRONG WITH THEM?!

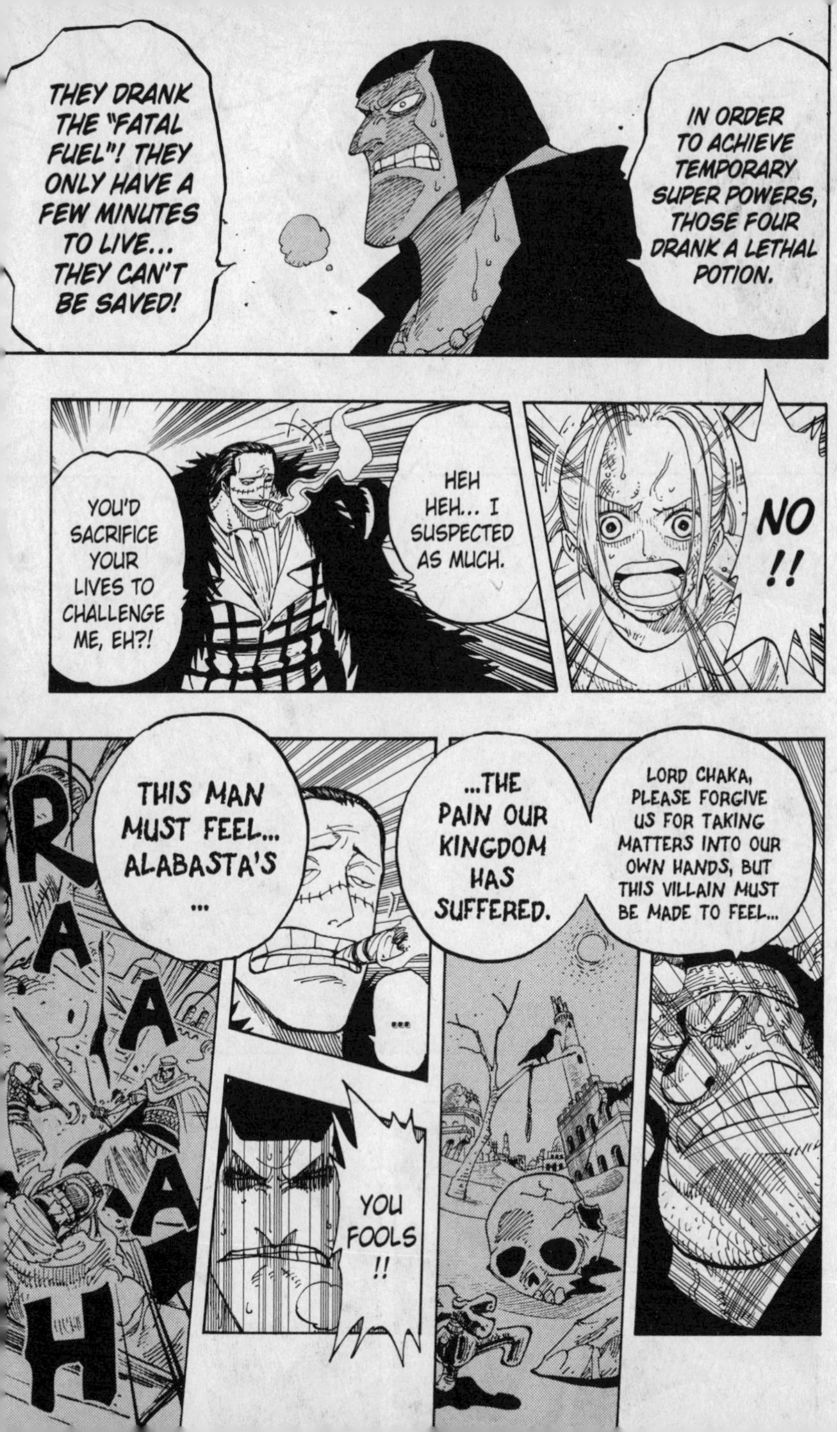
IN ORDER TO ACHIEVE TEMPORARY SUPER POWERS, THOSE FOUR DRANK A LETHAL POTION.
THEY DRANK THE "FATAL FUEL"! THEY ONLY HAVE A FEW MINUTES TO LIVE... THEY CAN'T BE SAVED!
NO!!
HEH HEH... I SUSPECTED AS MUCH.
YOU'D SACRIFICE YOUR LIVES TO CHALLENGE ME, EH?!
LORD CHAKA, PLEASE FORGIVE US FOR TAKING MATTERS INTO OUR OWN HANDS, BUT THIS VILLAIN MUST BE MADE TO FEEL...
...THE PAIN OUR KINGDOM HAS SUFFERED.
THIS MAN MUST FEEL... ALABASTA'S ...
...
YOU FOOLS!!
RAAAH

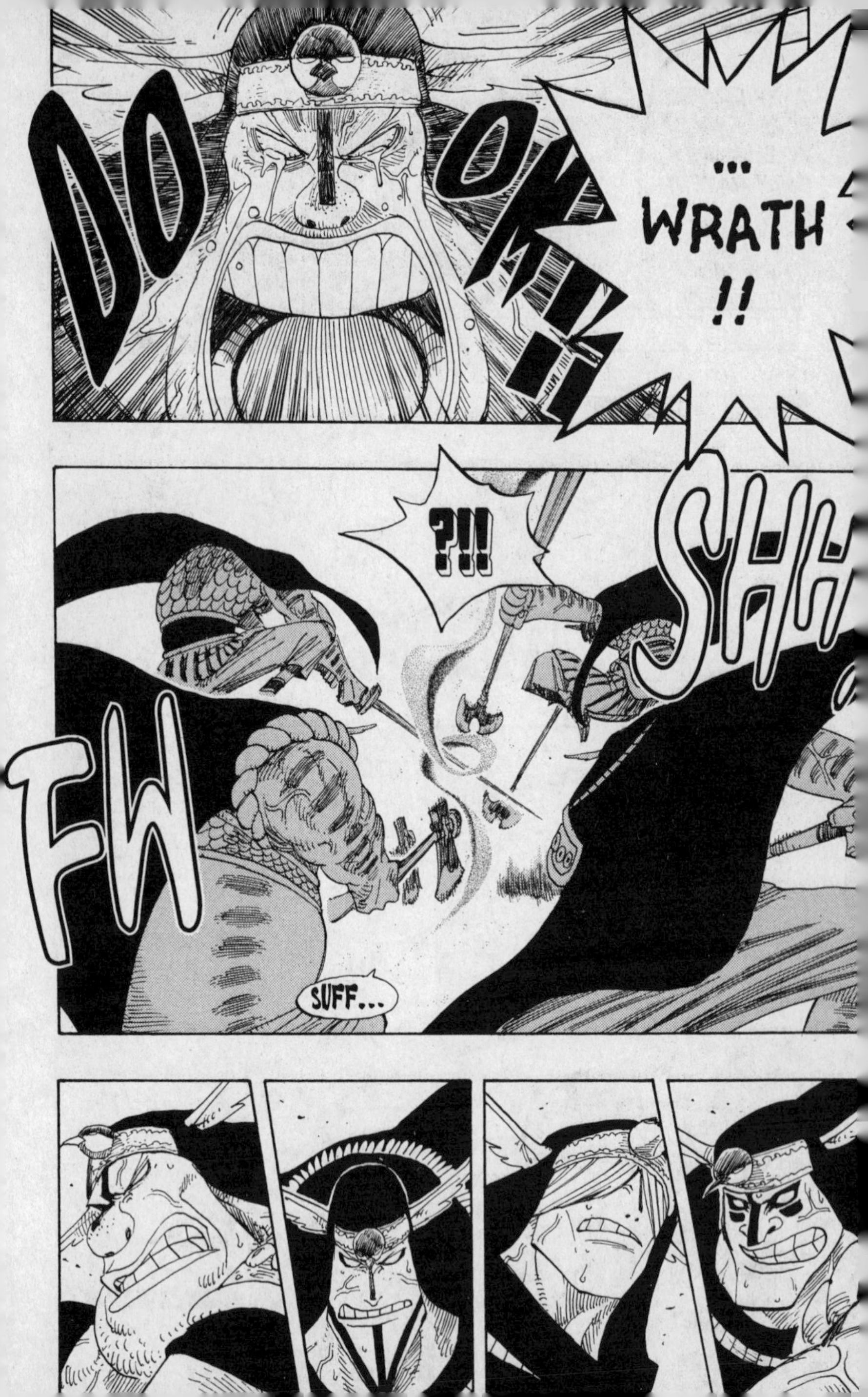
... WRATH !!
DOOOM
?!!
SHH
FW
SUFF...

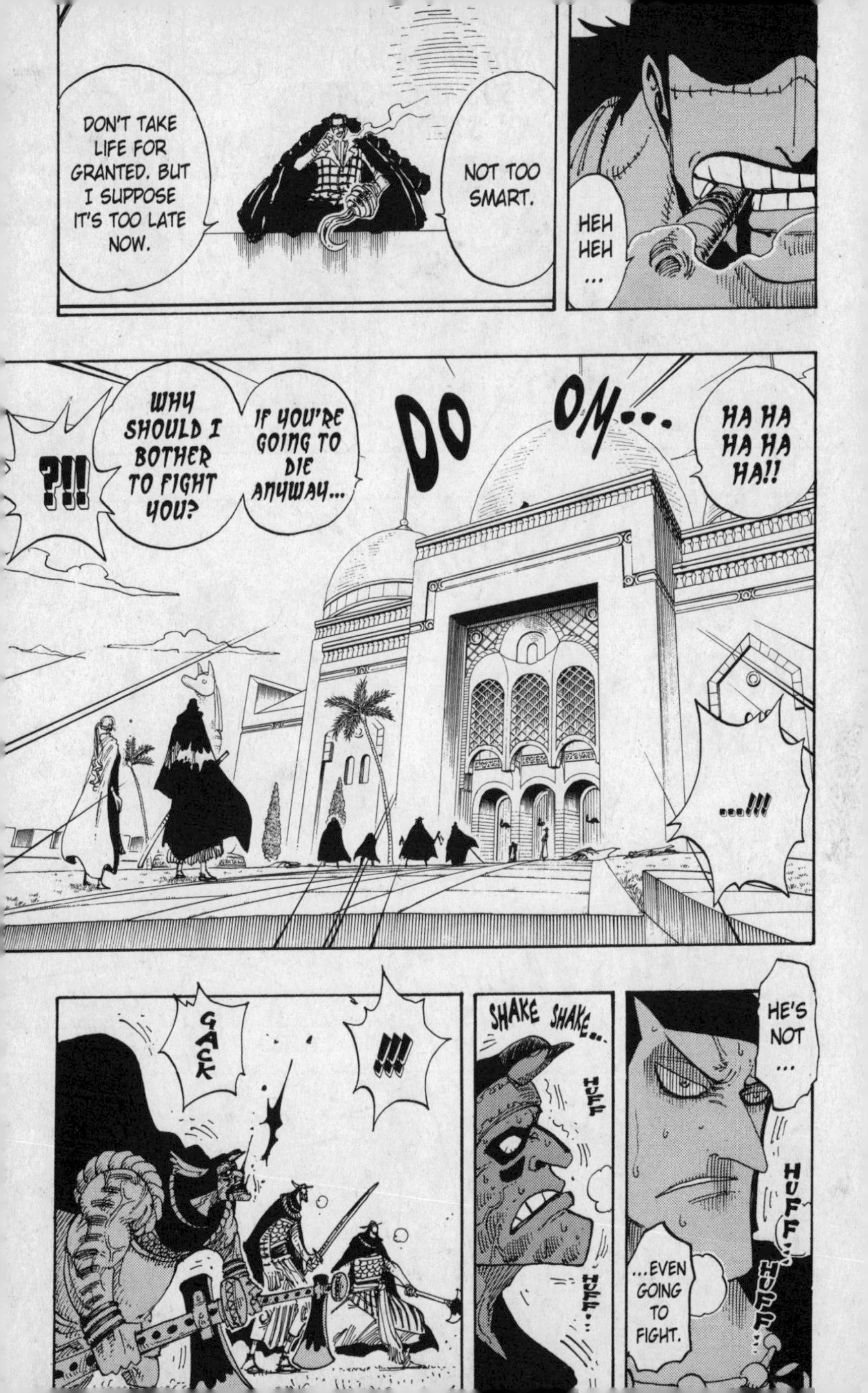
HEH HEH ...
NOT TOO SMART.
DON'T TAKE LIFE FOR GRANTED. BUT I SUPPOSE IT'S TOO LATE NOW.
HA HA HA HA HA!!
DO OM...
IF YOU'RE GOING TO DIE ANYWAY...
WHY SHOULD I BOTHER TO FIGHT YOU?
?!!
...!!!
HE'S NOT ...
HUFF
...EVEN GOING TO FIGHT.
HUFF...
SHAKE SHAKE...
HUFF
HUFF...
!!!
GACK

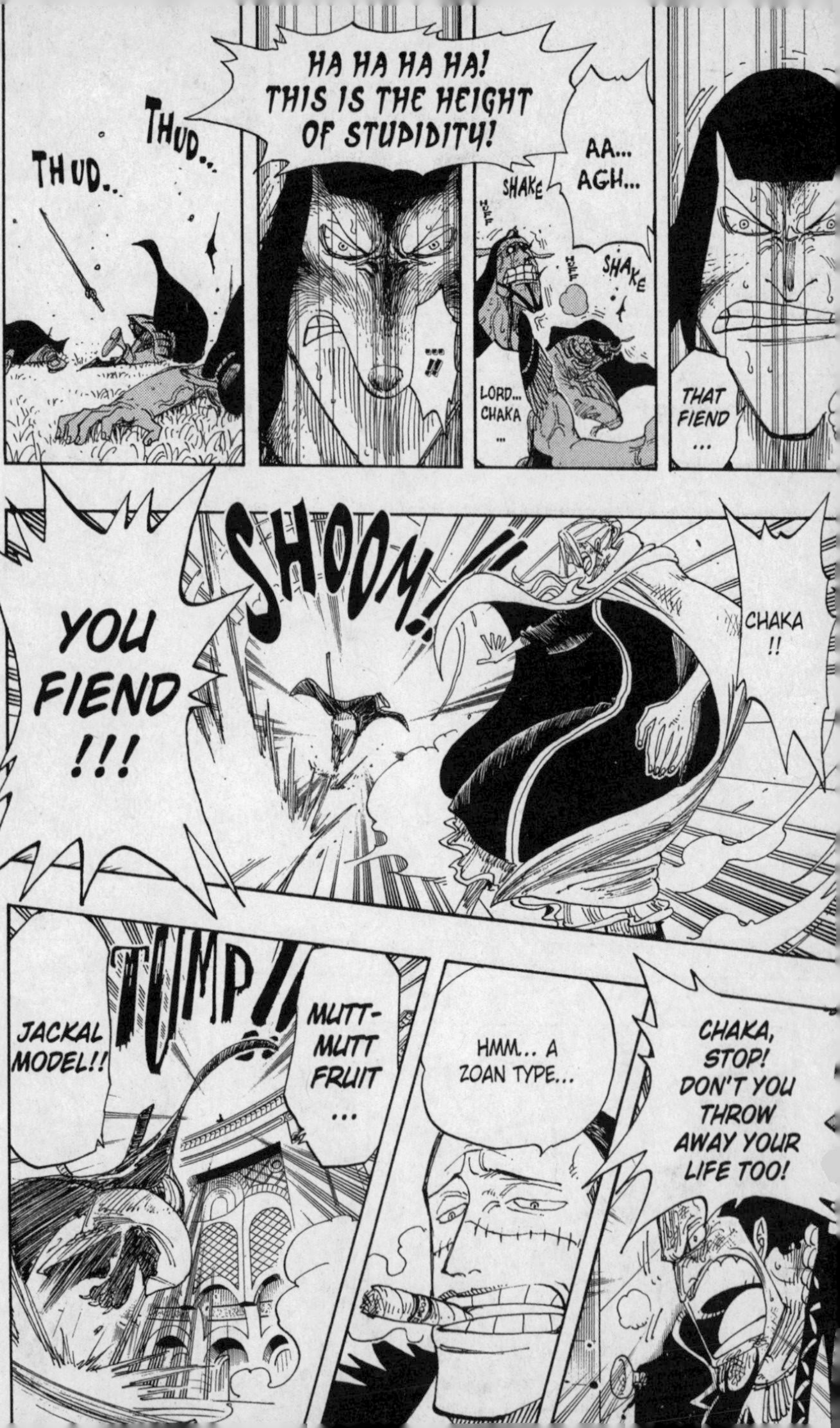
THAT FIEND ...
AA... AGH...
SHAKE
HUFF
HUFF
SHAKE
LORD... CHAKA ...
...!!
HA HA HA HA! THIS IS THE HEIGHT OF STUPIDITY!
THUD...
THUD...
CHAKA !!
SHOOM!!
YOU FIEND !!!
CHAKA, STOP! DON'T YOU THROW AWAY YOUR LIFE TOO!
HMM... A ZOAN TYPE...
MUTT-MUTT FRUIT ...
TUMP!!
JACKAL MODEL!!

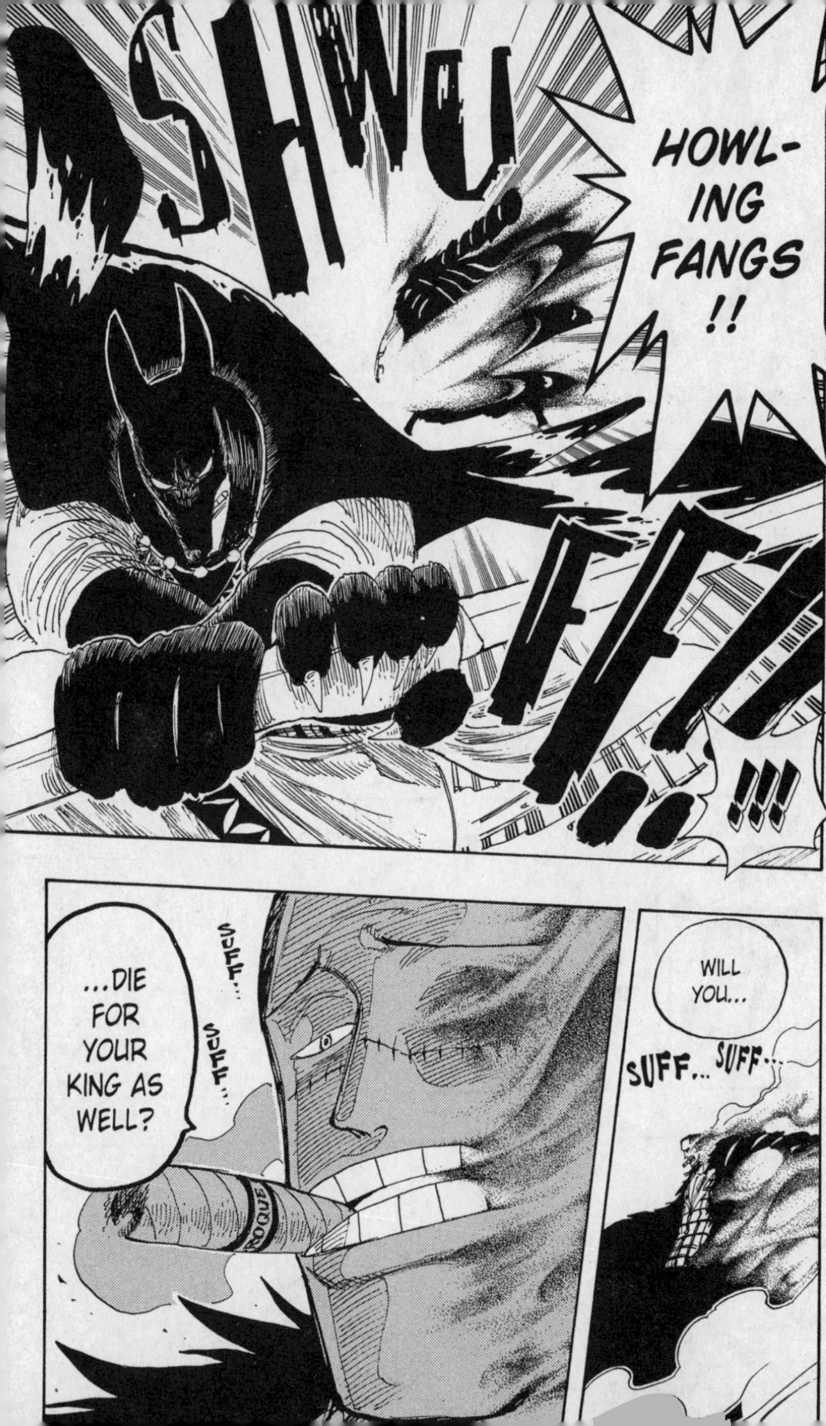
HOWL-
ING
FANGS
!!
WILL
YOU...
SUFF... SUFF...
SUFF...
SUFF...
...DIE
FOR
YOUR
KING AS
WELL?
CROQUE

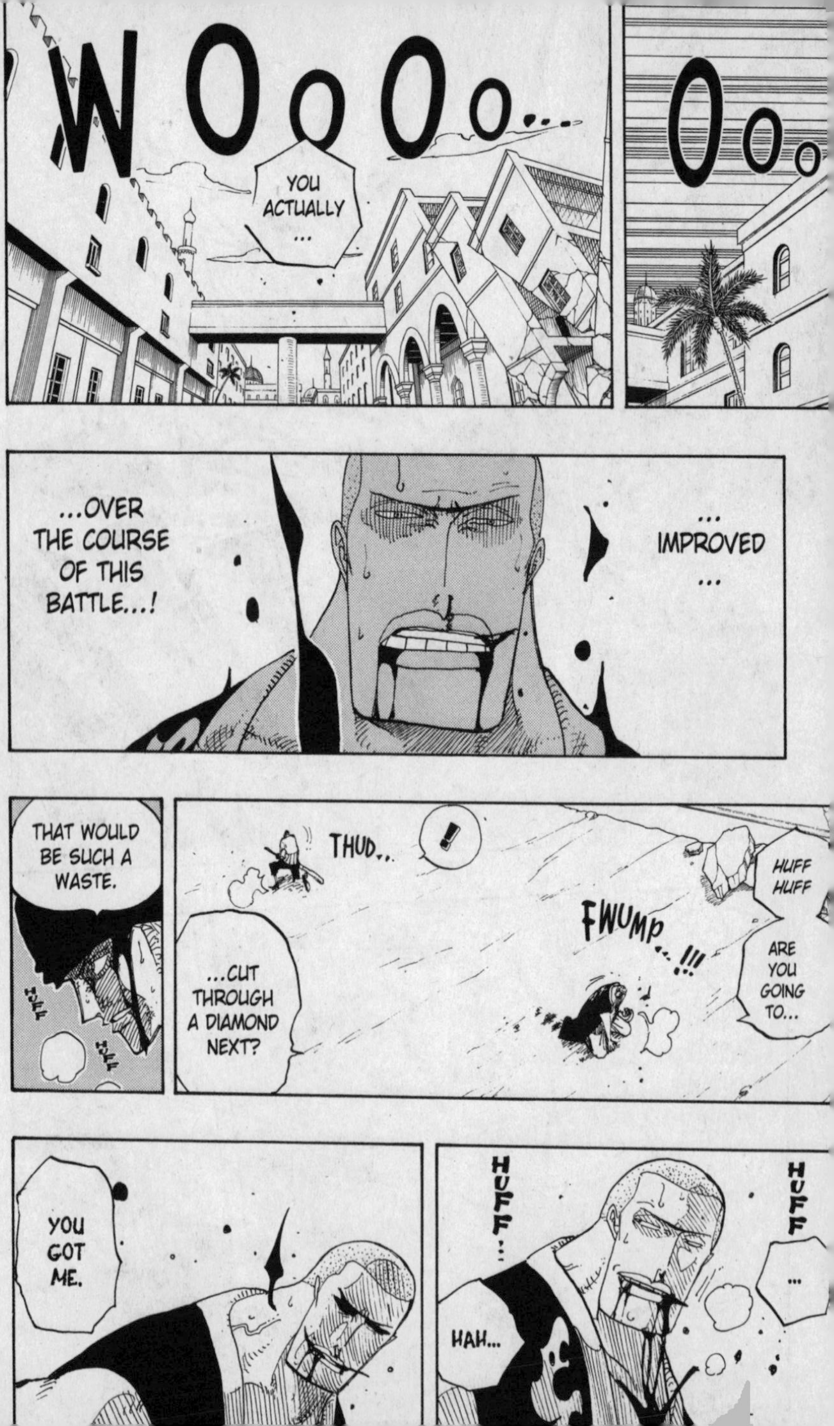

WOOOOO... OOO
YOU ACTUALLY ...
... IMPROVED ...
...OVER THE COURSE OF THIS BATTLE...!
HUFF HUFF
ARE YOU GOING TO...
FWUMP...!!!
!
THUD...
...CUT THROUGH A DIAMOND NEXT?
THAT WOULD BE SUCH A WASTE.
HUFF
HUFF
HUFF
HUFF...
...
HAH...
YOU GOT ME.

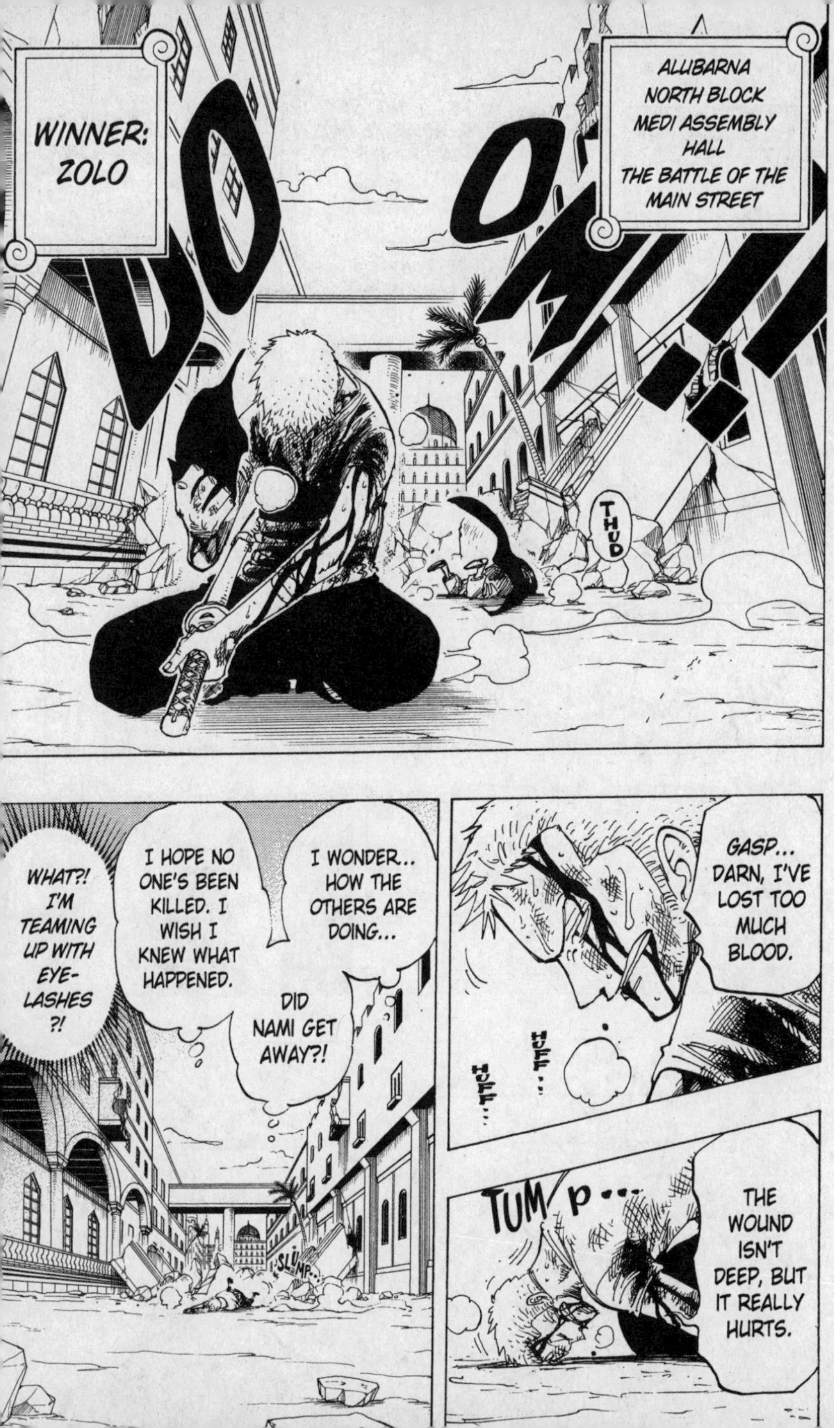
ALUBARNA NORTH BLOCK MEDI ASSEMBLY HALL THE BATTLE OF THE MAIN STREET
DOOM!!
WINNER: ZOLO
THUD
GASP... DARN, I'VE LOST TOO MUCH BLOOD.
HUFF...
HUFF...
TUMP...
THE WOUND ISN'T DEEP, BUT IT REALLY HURTS.
I WONDER.. HOW THE OTHERS ARE DOING...
I HOPE NO ONE'S BEEN KILLED. I WISH I KNEW WHAT HAPPENED.
WHAT?! I'M TEAMING UP WITH EYE-LASHES?!
DID NAMI GET AWAY?!
SLUMP...

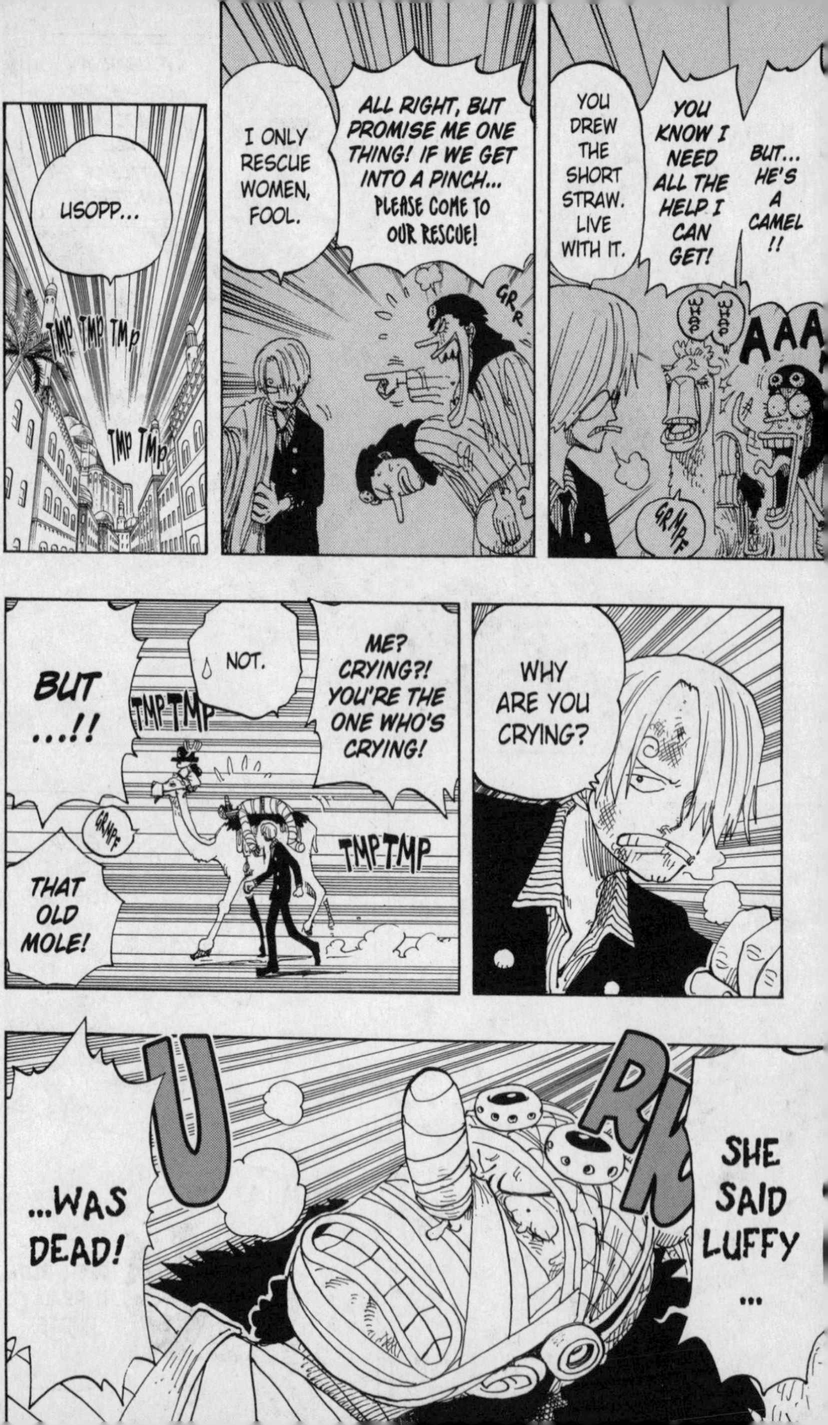
BUT... HE'S A CAMEL !!
YOU KNOW I NEED ALL THE HELP I CAN GET!
YOU DREW THE SHORT STRAW. LIVE WITH IT.
WHAP
WHAP
AAA
GRNPF
ALL RIGHT, BUT PROMISE ME ONE THING! IF WE GET INTO A PINCH... PLEASE COME TO OUR RESCUE!
I ONLY RESCUE WOMEN, FOOL.
GRR
USOPP...
TMP TMP TMP
TMP TMP
WHY ARE YOU CRYING?
ME? CRYING?! YOU'RE THE ONE WHO'S CRYING!
NOT.
BUT ...!!
TMP TMP
GRNPF
TMP TMP
THAT OLD MOLE!
SHE SAID LUFFY ...
...WAS DEAD!
U
RK

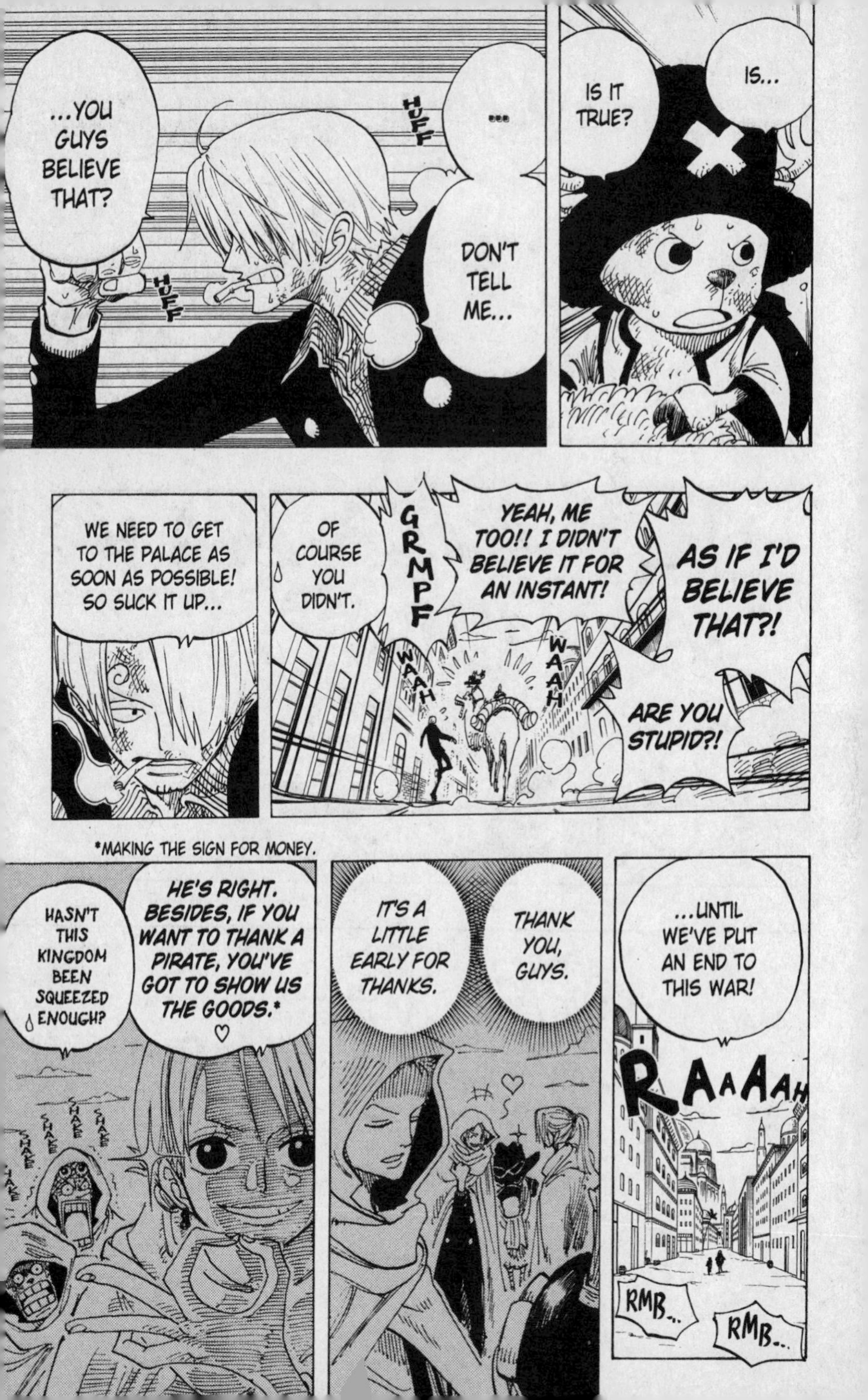
IS...
IS IT TRUE?
...
DON'T TELL ME...
HUFF
HUFF
...YOU GUYS BELIEVE THAT?
AS IF I'D BELIEVE THAT?!
YEAH, ME TOO!! I DIDN'T BELIEVE IT FOR AN INSTANT!
ARE YOU STUPID?!
GRMPF
OF COURSE YOU DIDN'T.
WAAAH
WAAAH
WE NEED TO GET TO THE PALACE AS SOON AS POSSIBLE! SO SUCK IT UP...
...UNTIL WE'VE PUT AN END TO THIS WAR!
RAAAAH
RMB...
RMB...
THANK YOU, GUYS.
IT'S A LITTLE EARLY FOR THANKS.
HE'S RIGHT. BESIDES, IF YOU WANT TO THANK A PIRATE, YOU'VE GOT TO SHOW US THE GOODS.* ♡
HASN'T THIS KINGDOM BEEN SQUEEZED ENOUGH?
SHAKE
SHAKE
SHAKE
SHAKE
*MAKING THE SIGN FOR MONEY.

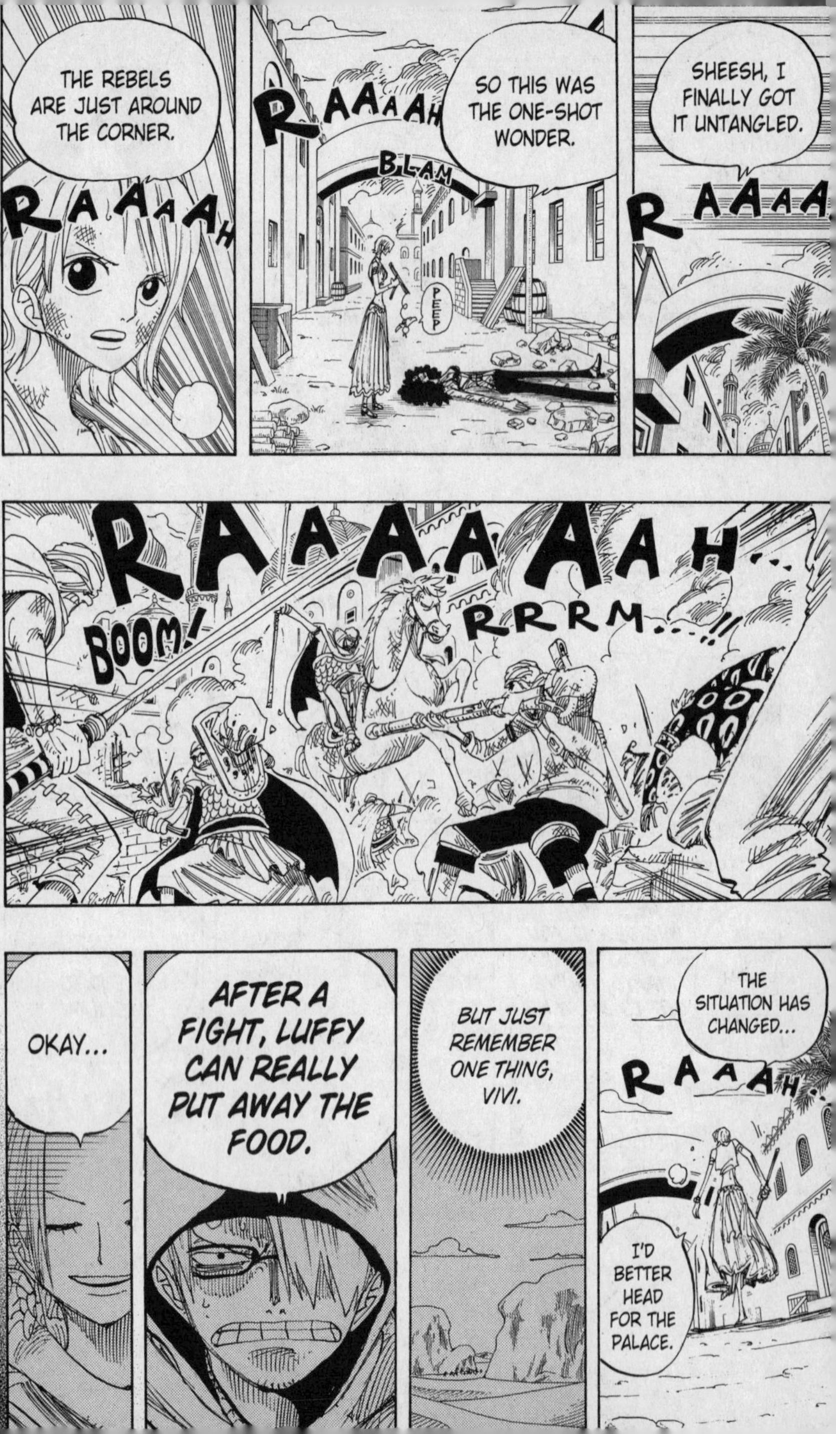
SHEESH, I FINALLY GOT IT UNTANGLED.
RAAAA
SO THIS WAS THE ONE-SHOT WONDER.
RAAAAH
BLAM
PEEP
THE REBELS ARE JUST AROUND THE CORNER.
RAAAAAH
RAAAAAAH...
RRRM...!!
BOOM!
THE SITUATION HAS CHANGED...
RAAAH...
I'D BETTER HEAD FOR THE PALACE.
BUT JUST REMEMBER ONE THING, VIVI.
AFTER A FIGHT, LUFFY CAN REALLY PUT AWAY THE FOOD.
OKAY...

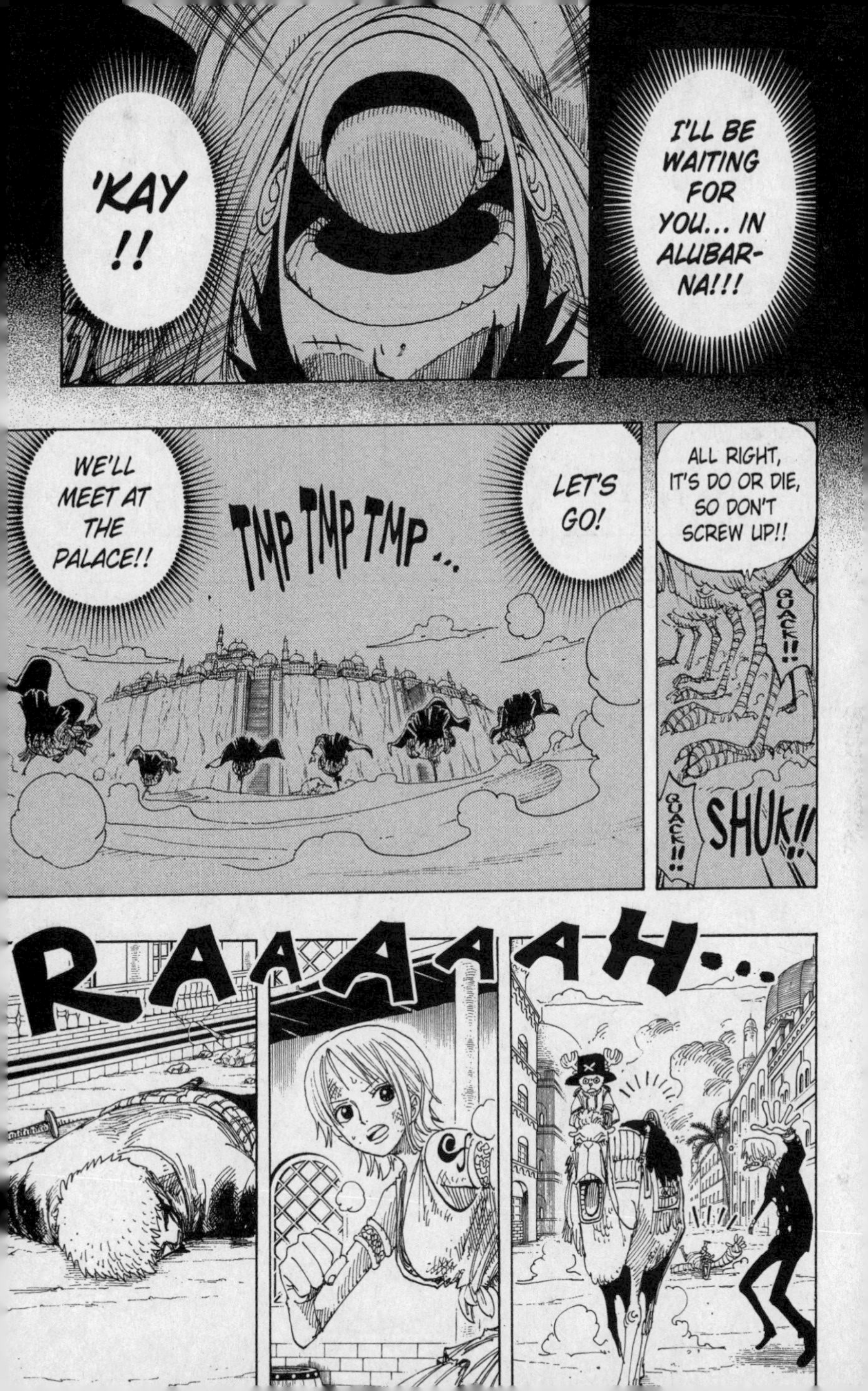
I'LL BE WAITING FOR YOU... IN ALUBAR-NA!!!
'KAY!!
ALL RIGHT, IT'S DO OR DIE, SO DON'T SCREW UP!!
GUACK!!
SHUK!!
GUACK!!
LET'S GO!
TMP TMP TMP...
WE'LL MEET AT THE PALACE!!
RAAAAAH...

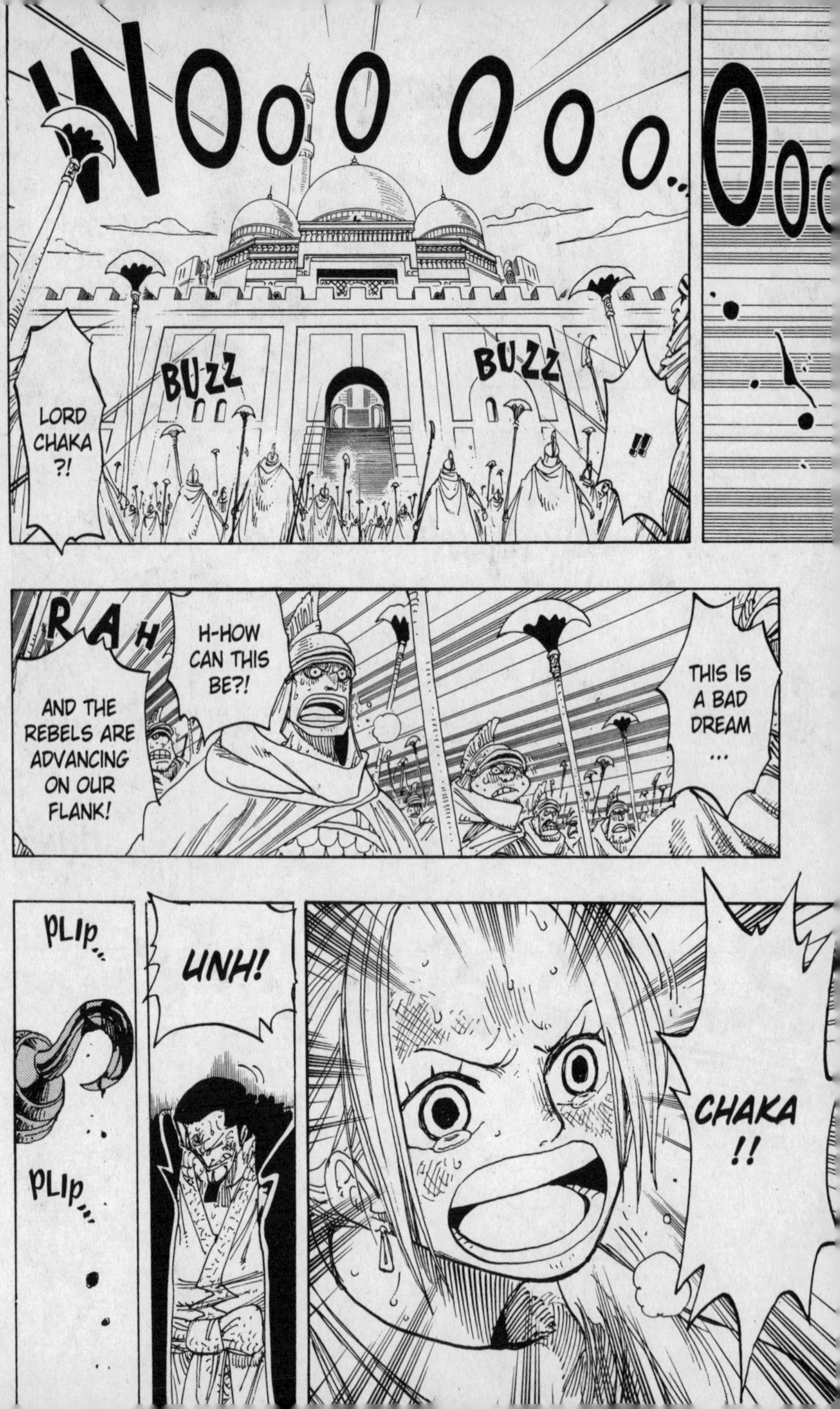
WOOOOOOO...OOO
!!
BUZZ
BUZZ
LORD CHAKA ?!
THIS IS A BAD DREAM ...
H-HOW CAN THIS BE?!
RAH
AND THE REBELS ARE ADVANCING ON OUR FLANK!
CHAKA !!
UNH!
PLIP...
PLIP...

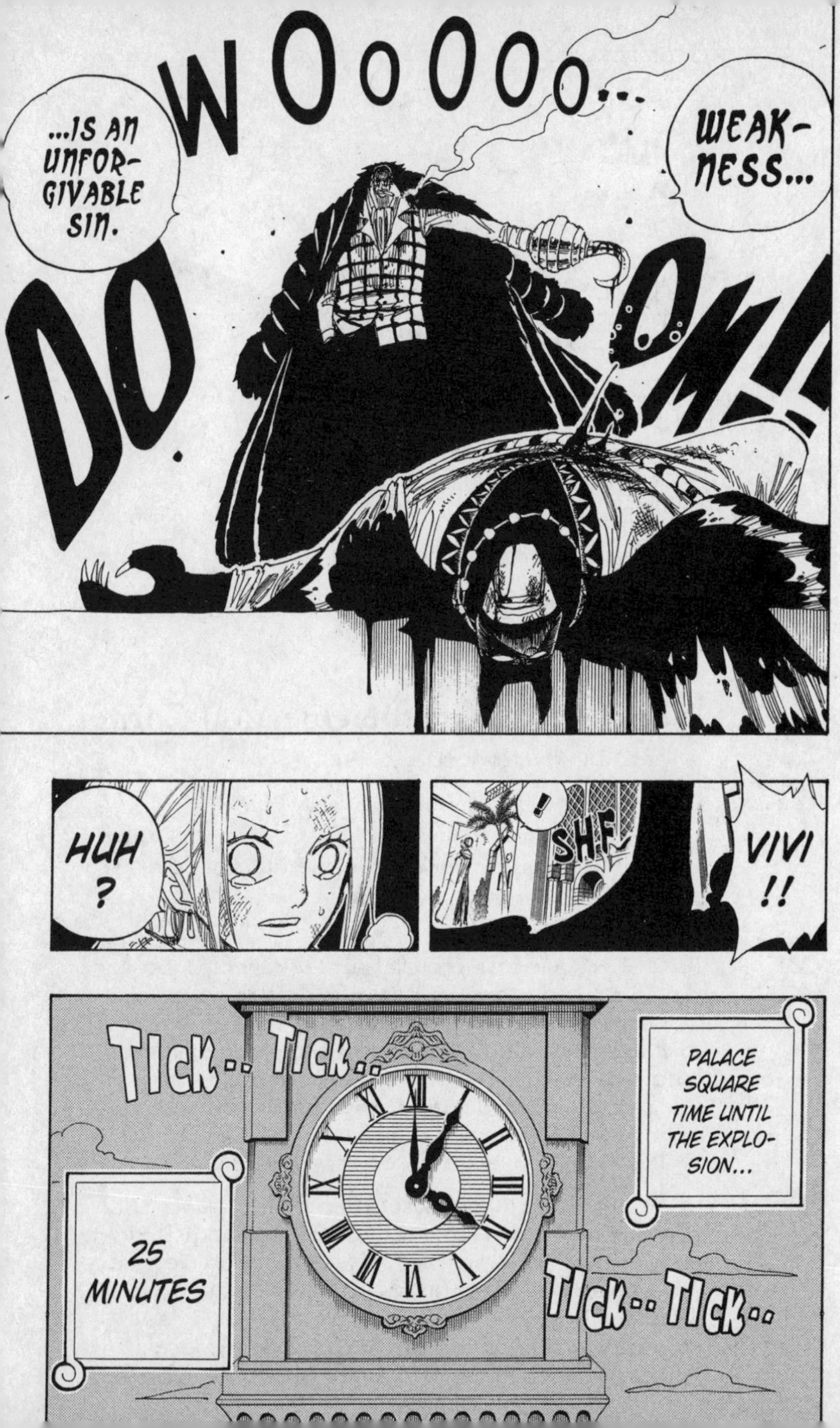
WEAK-NESS...
DOWOOOOO...
DOON!!
...IS AN UNFORGIVABLE SIN.
VIVI !!
!
SHF
HUH ?
PALACE SQUARE TIME UNTIL THE EXPLOSION...
TICK.. TICK..
TICK.. TICK..
25 MINUTES

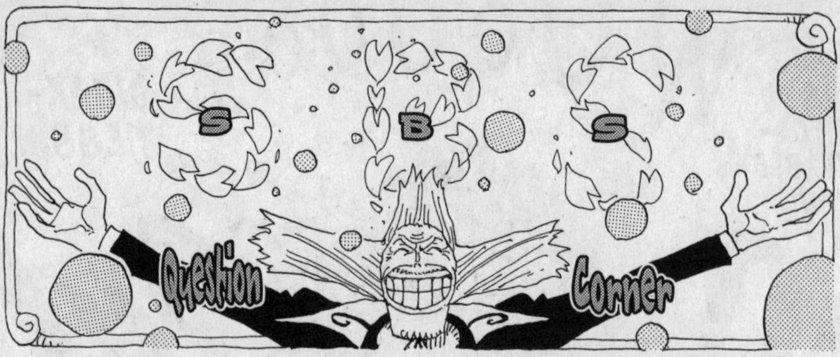
S
B
S
Question
Corner

Reader: Just now, I came upon a person in strange glasses lying in the street. So I bought him a beef bowl for lunch. Out of gratitude, he gave me an unusual ring with a sheet of instructions that read "How to Hypnotize People." So, since you've been having trouble lately getting the Question Corner started, I'm going to hypnotize you to help it go more smoothly.
Are you ready? Look closely at the ring. When I say "One, two, djanko!" you will begin the Question Corner immediately, no matter what.
Here I go. ♡ One, two, djanko!

Whoa! Let's start the Question Corner!

Oda: Whaat?! Did you hypnotize yourself?!

Reader: Oda Sensei! I love, love, love, love, love *One Piece!*
I go to the store every day to see if the latest volume has arrived. The waiting is agony! So would you list the dates when *One Piece* hits the stores?! Please!
--White Cat Pirates

Oda: Huh? That's a lot of trouble, but I understand. So for the sake of you fans that buy the graphic novel, I'm going to reveal the release schedule. Please note it in your calendars. *One Piece* comics are released in the following cycle: two months, two months, three months. So after three months, you'll know when the next two volumes will be released. Got that?*
[*This release schedule is for Japan. –Ed.]

Oda: Oh yes, I forgot. There was an error in Volume 21. I found it myself and I wanted to tell you about it right away. In the title drawing for the Question Corner I drew Crocus and Laboon again, like I did in Volume 18. Oh well. I must've had Crocus fever in Volume 21. Am I repentant? Yes, yes. (←I say this as I pick my nose.) Anyway, we'll continue in the next Question Corner.

Chapter 197: THE LEADERS

KANJI ON CLOTHING SAYS "DEEP" -- ED.

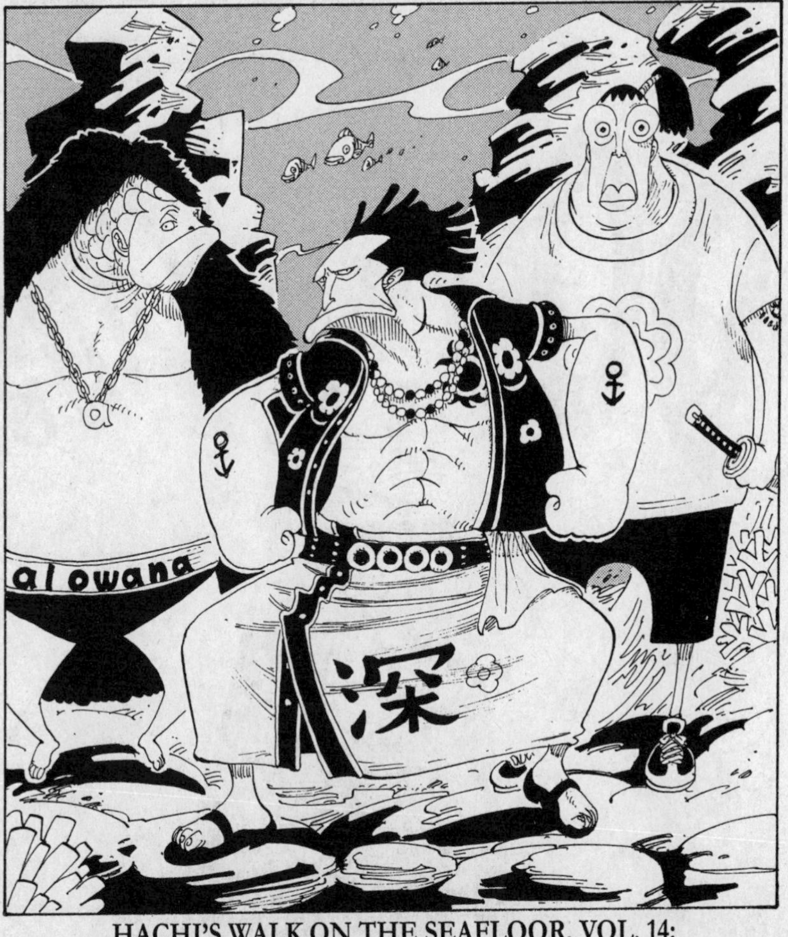
alowana
深

HACHI'S WALK ON THE SEAFLOOR, VOL. 14:
"THE MACRO FISHMAN PIRATES ON THE SCENE"

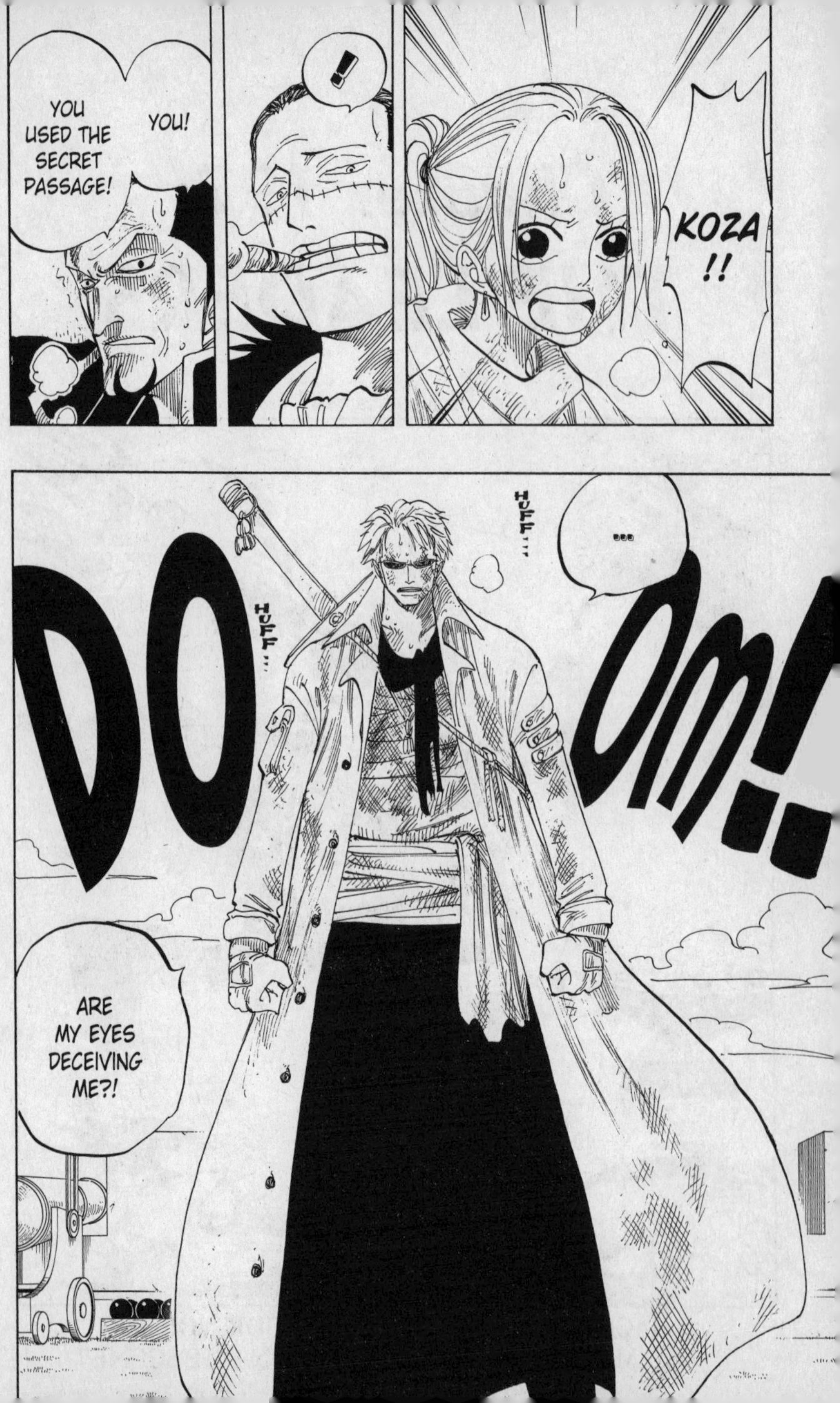
KOZA!!
!
YOU!
YOU USED THE SECRET PASSAGE!
...
HUFF...
DOOM!!
HUFF...
ARE MY EYES DECEIVING ME?!

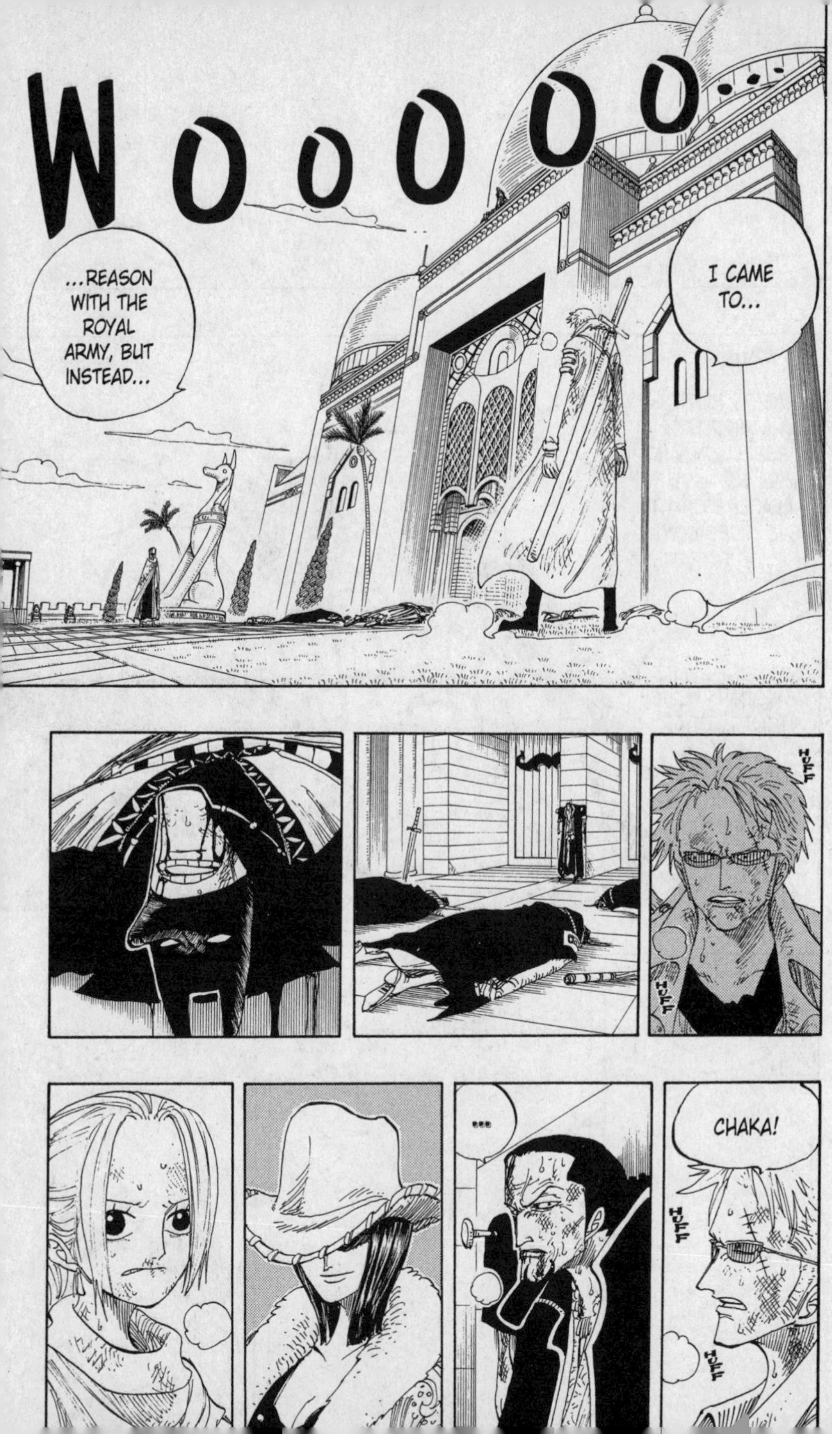
WOOOOOO...
I CAME TO...
...REASON WITH THE ROYAL ARMY, BUT INSTEAD...
HUFF
HUFF
CHAKA!
HUFF
HUFF
...

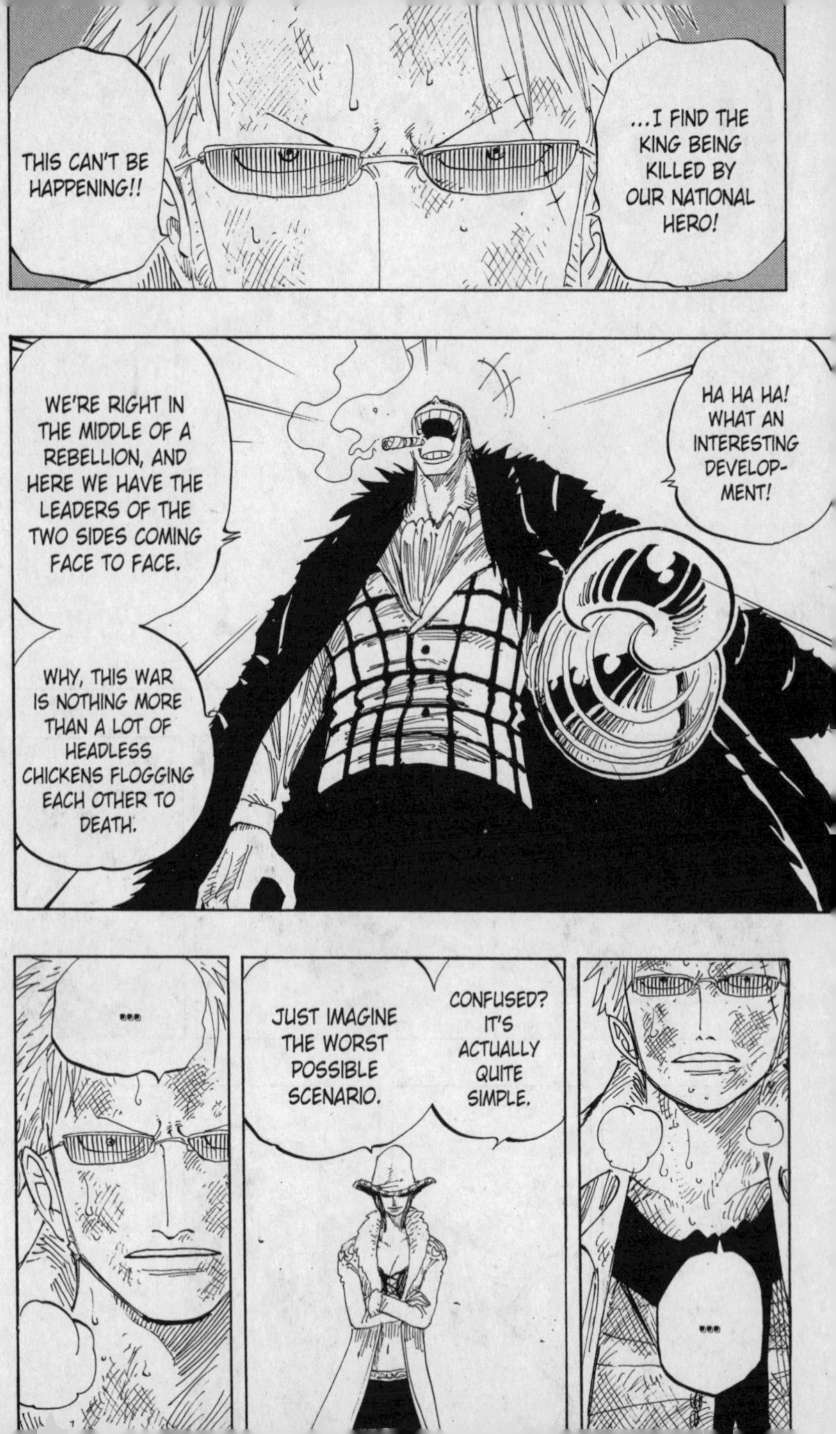
...I FIND THE KING BEING KILLED BY OUR NATIONAL HERO!
THIS CAN'T BE HAPPENING!!
HA HA HA! WHAT AN INTERESTING DEVELOP-MENT!
WE'RE RIGHT IN THE MIDDLE OF A REBELLION, AND HERE WE HAVE THE LEADERS OF THE TWO SIDES COMING FACE TO FACE.
WHY, THIS WAR IS NOTHING MORE THAN A LOT OF HEADLESS CHICKENS FLOGGING EACH OTHER TO DEATH.
...
CONFUSED? IT'S ACTUALLY QUITE SIMPLE.
JUST IMAGINE THE WORST POSSIBLE SCENARIO.
...

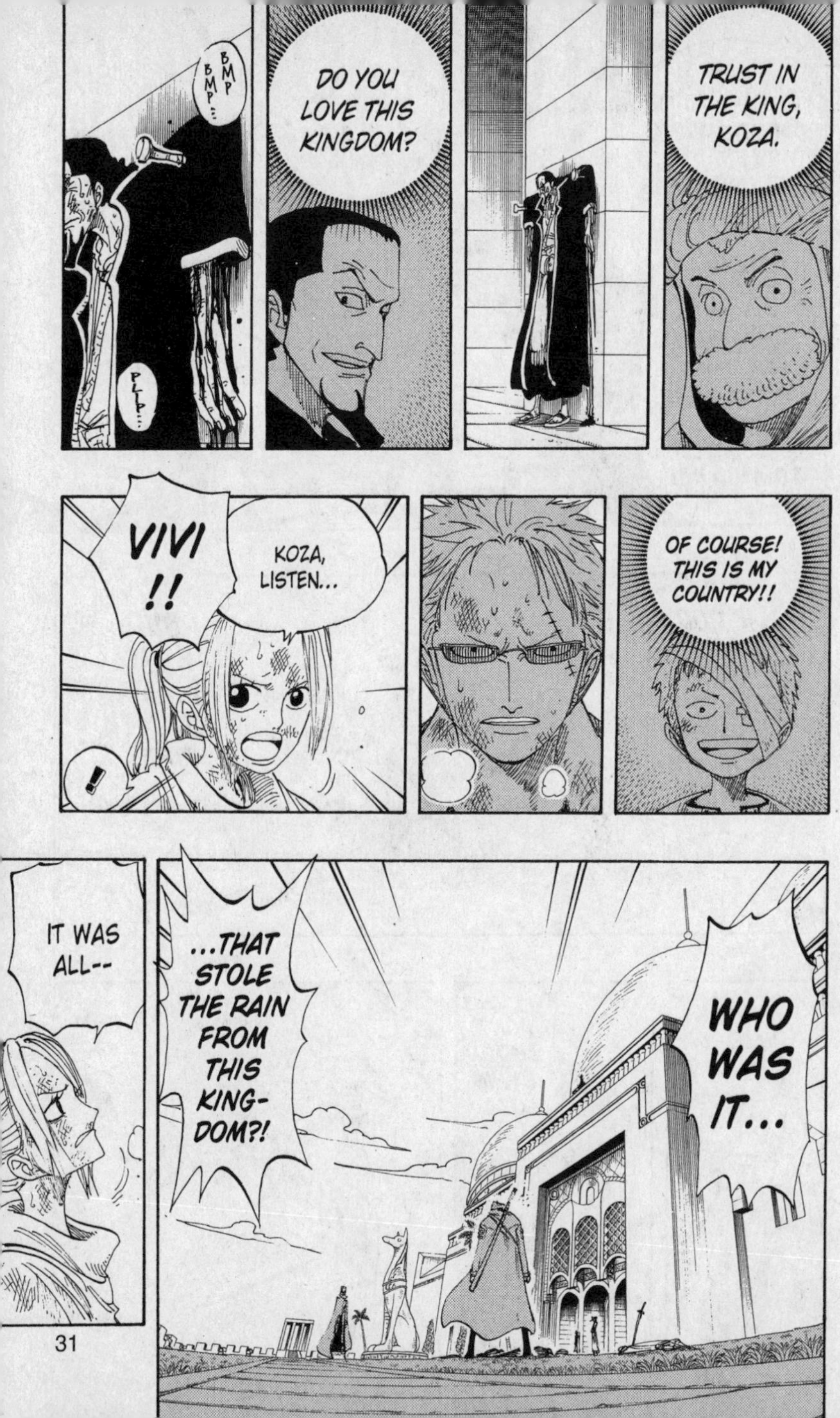
TRUST IN THE KING, KOZA.
DO YOU LOVE THIS KINGDOM?
BMP BMP...
PLIP...
OF COURSE! THIS IS MY COUNTRY!!
KOZA, LISTEN...
VIVI !!
!
WHO WAS IT...
...THAT STOLE THE RAIN FROM THIS KING-DOM?!
IT WAS ALL--

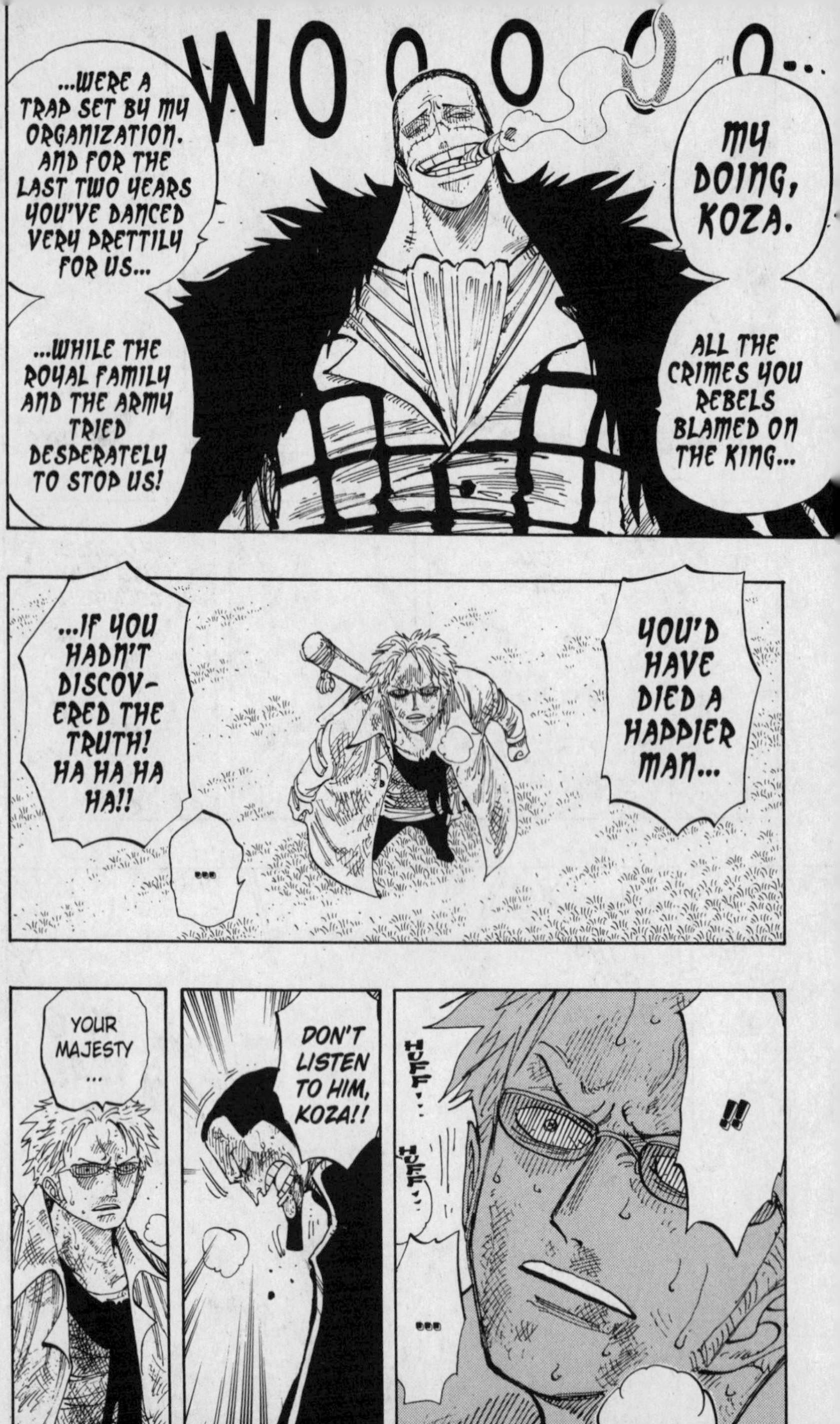
WOOOOO...
MY DOING, KOZA.
ALL THE CRIMES YOU REBELS BLAMED ON THE KING...
...WERE A TRAP SET BY MY ORGANIZATION. AND FOR THE LAST TWO YEARS YOU'VE DANCED VERY PRETTILY FOR US...
...WHILE THE ROYAL FAMILY AND THE ARMY TRIED DESPERATELY TO STOP US!
YOU'D HAVE DIED A HAPPIER MAN...
...IF YOU HADN'T DISCOVERED THE TRUTH! HA HA HA HA!!
...
HUFF... HUFF...
!!
...
DON'T LISTEN TO HIM, KOZA!!
YOUR MAJESTY ...

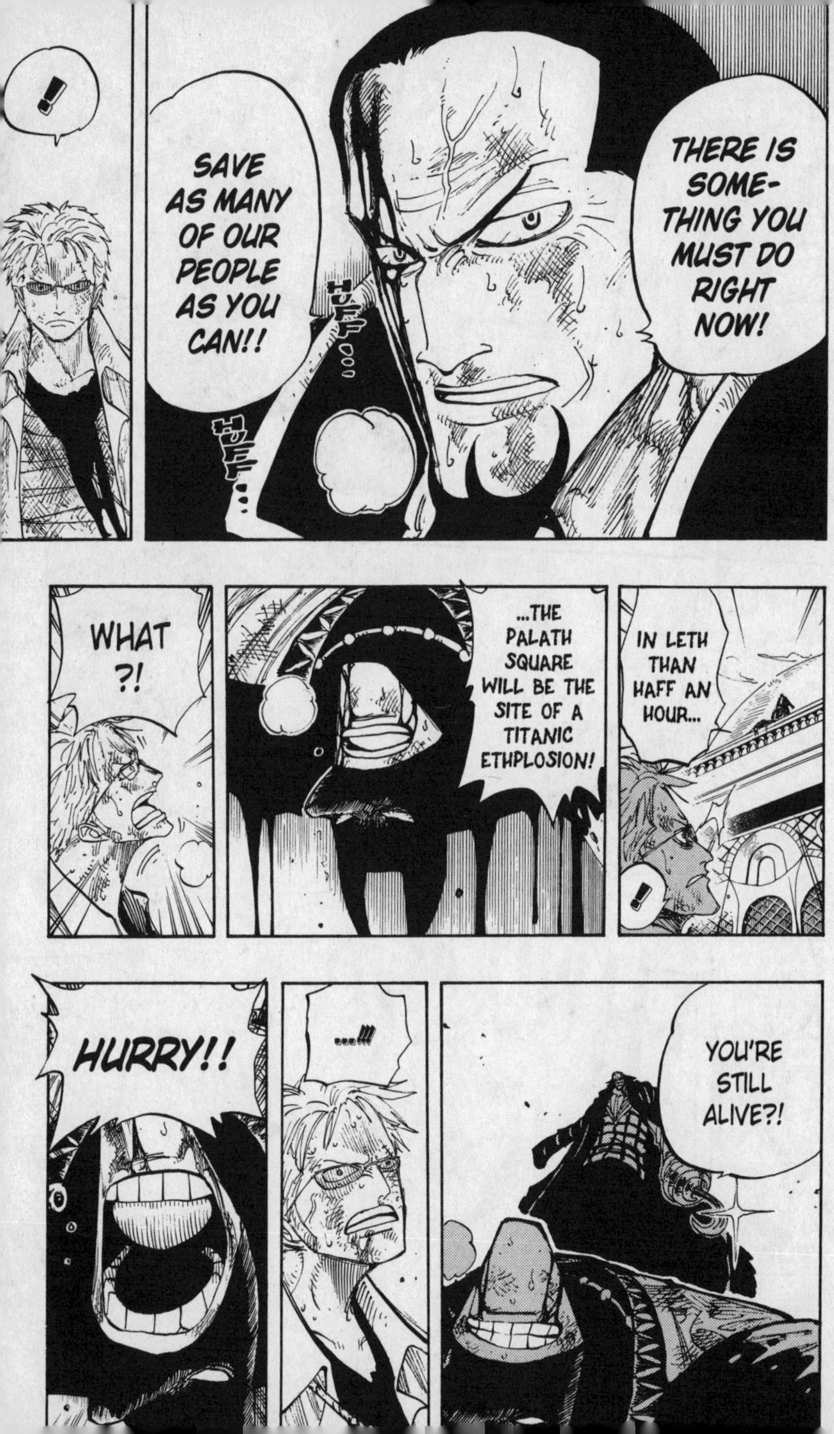
THERE IS SOME-THING YOU MUST DO RIGHT NOW!
SAVE AS MANY OF OUR PEOPLE AS YOU CAN!!
HUFF...
HUFF...
!
IN LETH THAN HAFF AN HOUR...
!
...THE PALATH SQUARE WILL BE THE SITE OF A TITANIC ETHPLOSION!
WHAT ?!
YOU'RE STILL ALIVE?!
...!!!
HURRY!!

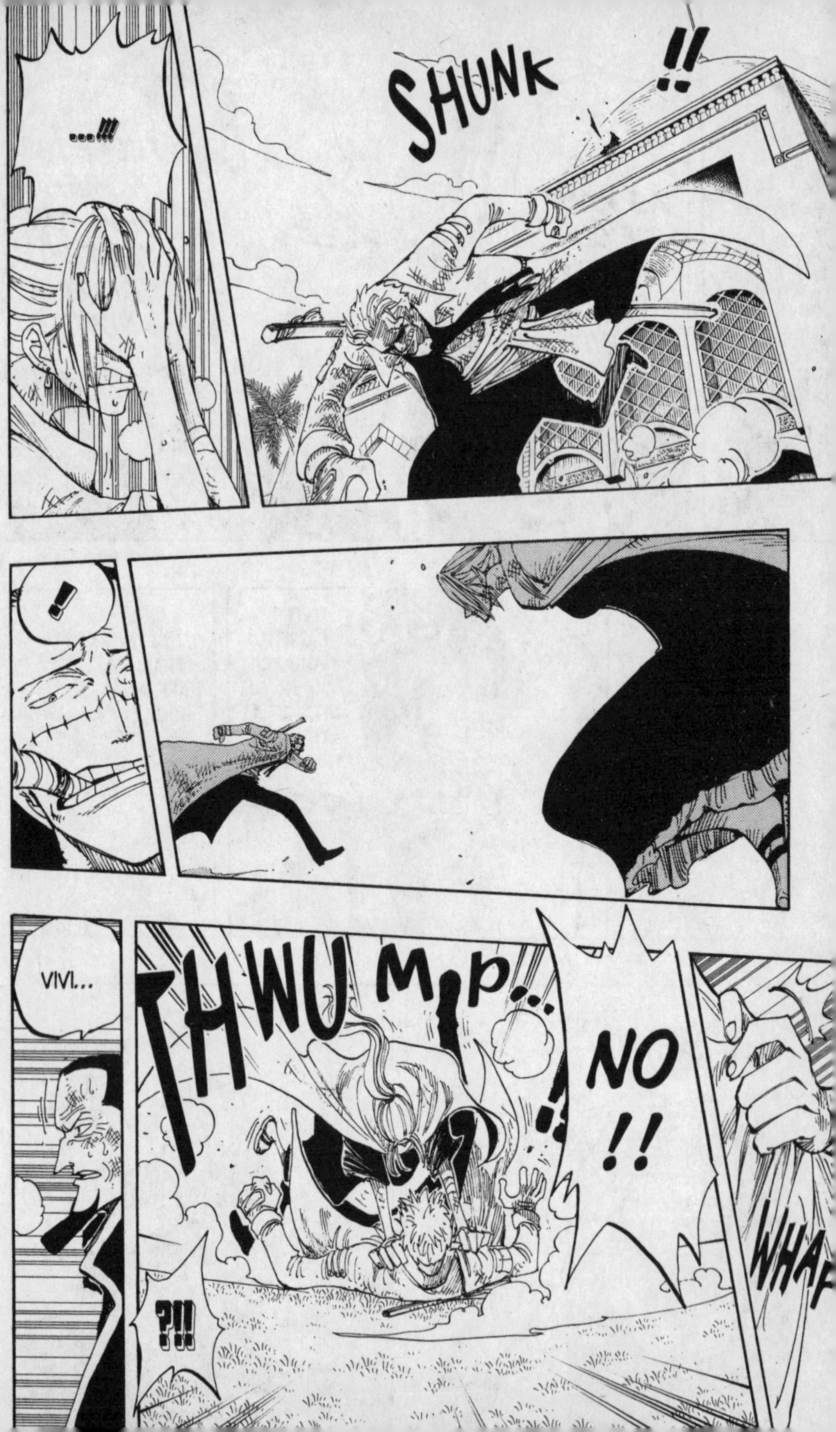
SHUNK!!
...!!!
!
WHAP
NO!!
THWUMP...
?!!
VIVI...

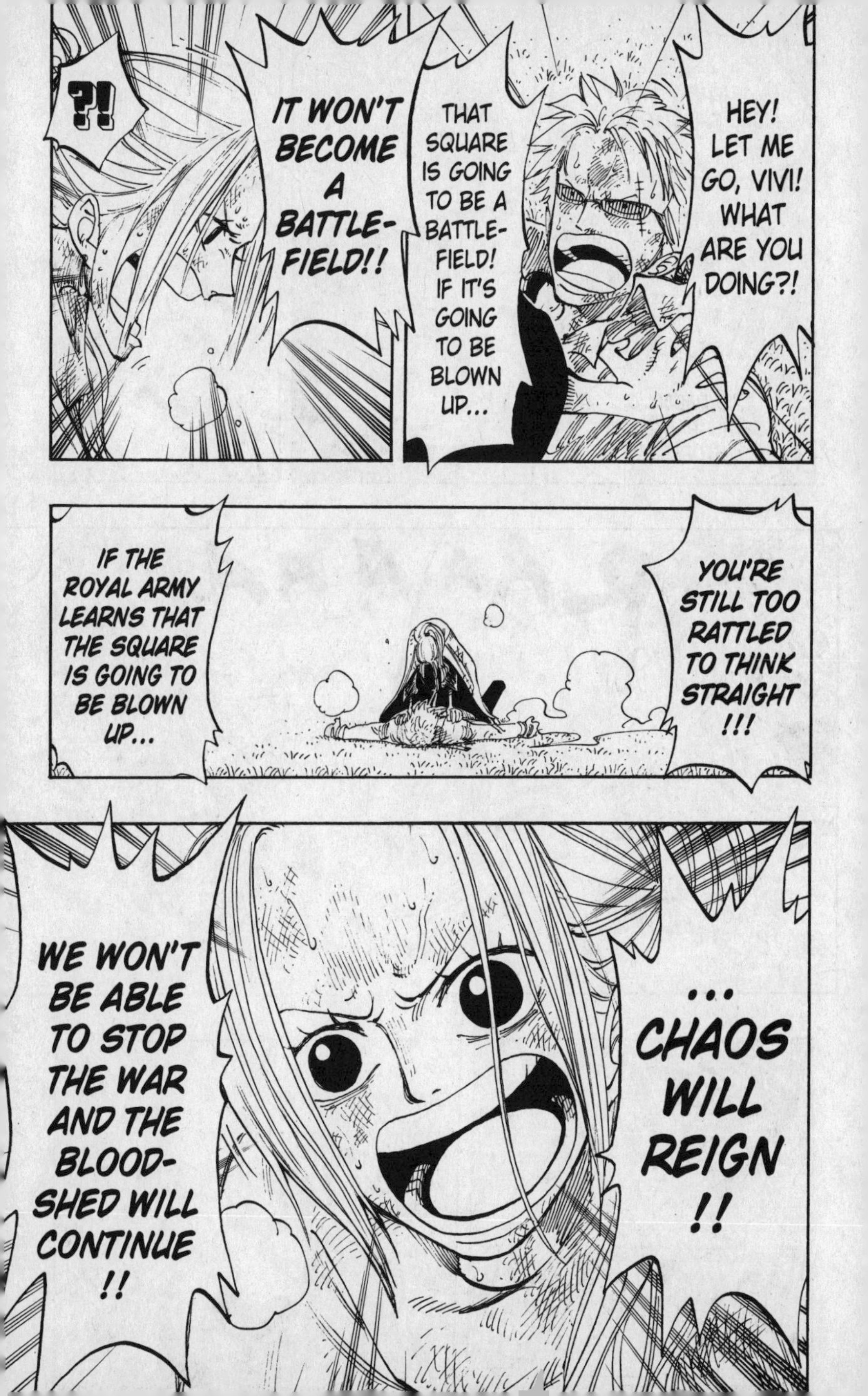
HEY! LET ME GO, VIVI! WHAT ARE YOU DOING?!
THAT SQUARE IS GOING TO BE A BATTLE-FIELD! IF IT'S GOING TO BE BLOWN UP...
IT WON'T BECOME A BATTLE-FIELD!!
?!
YOU'RE STILL TOO RATTLED TO THINK STRAIGHT!!!
IF THE ROYAL ARMY LEARNS THAT THE SQUARE IS GOING TO BE BLOWN UP...
...CHAOS WILL REIGN!!
WE WON'T BE ABLE TO STOP THE WAR AND THE BLOOD-SHED WILL CONTINUE!!

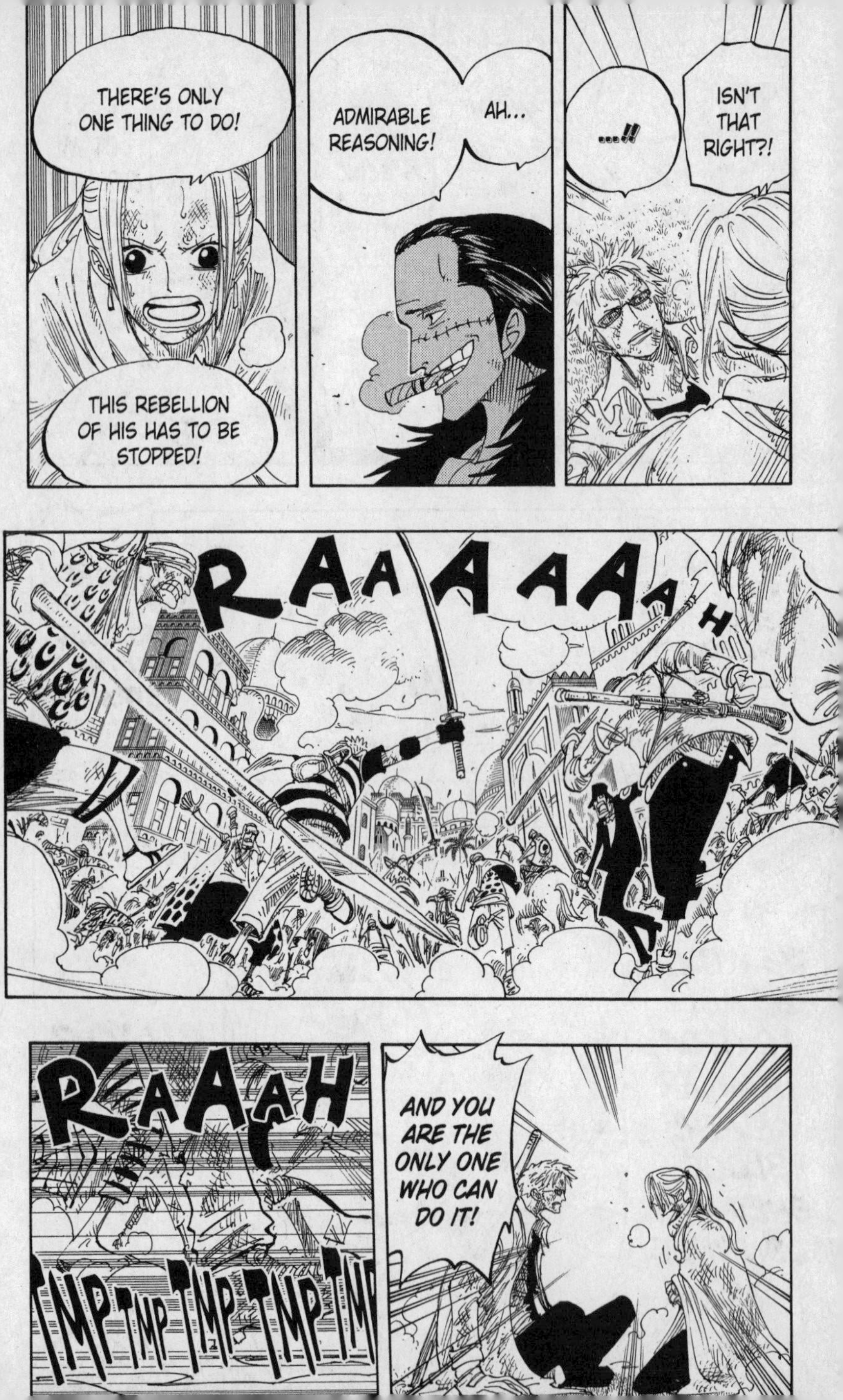
ISN'T THAT RIGHT?!
...!!
AH...
ADMIRABLE REASONING!
THERE'S ONLY ONE THING TO DO!
THIS REBELLION OF HIS HAS TO BE STOPPED!
RAAAAAAAH
AND YOU ARE THE ONLY ONE WHO CAN DO IT!
RAAAH
TMP TMP TMP TMP TMP

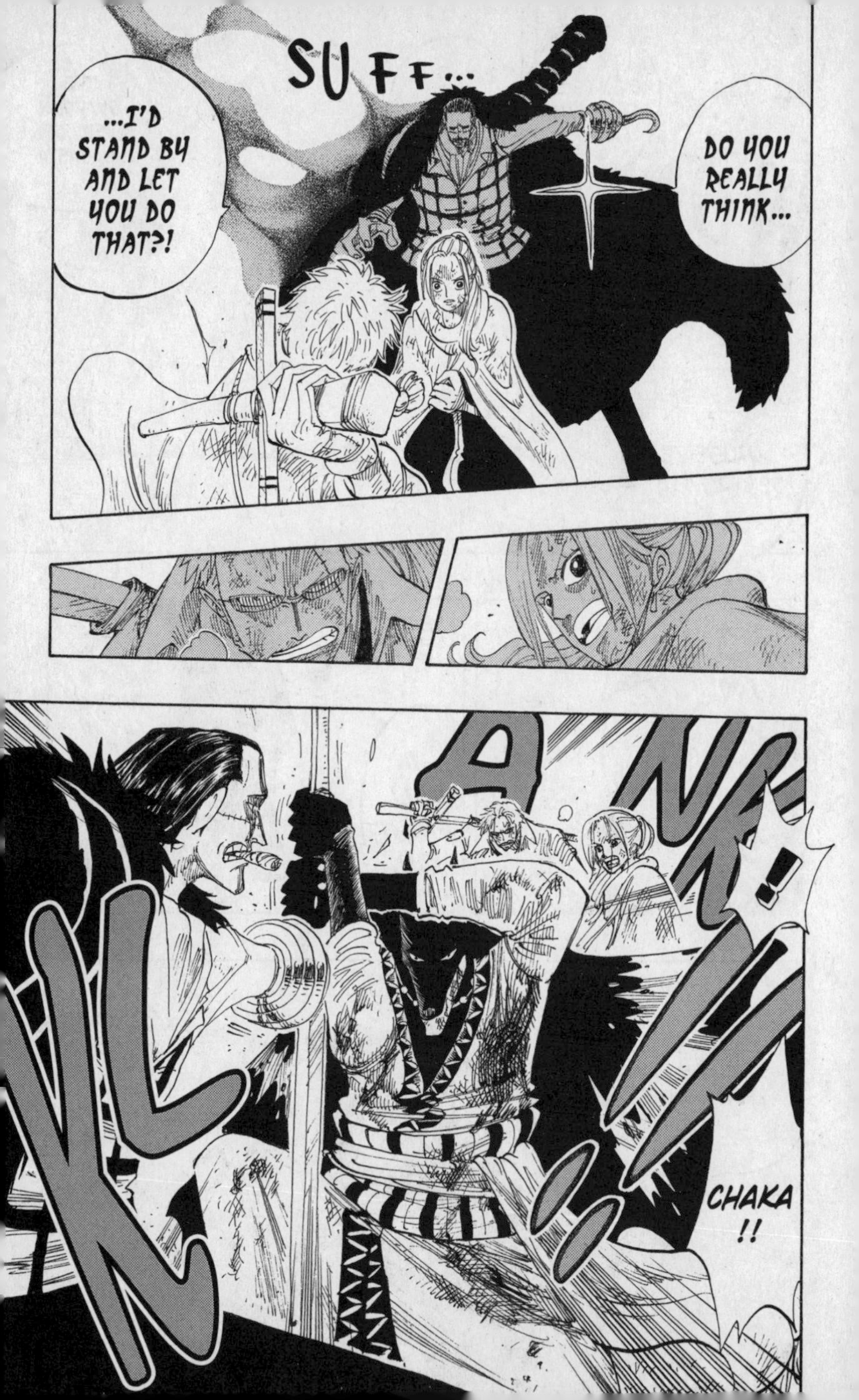
SUFF...
DO YOU REALLY THINK...
...I'D STAND BY AND LET YOU DO THAT?!
KLANK!
CHAKA!!

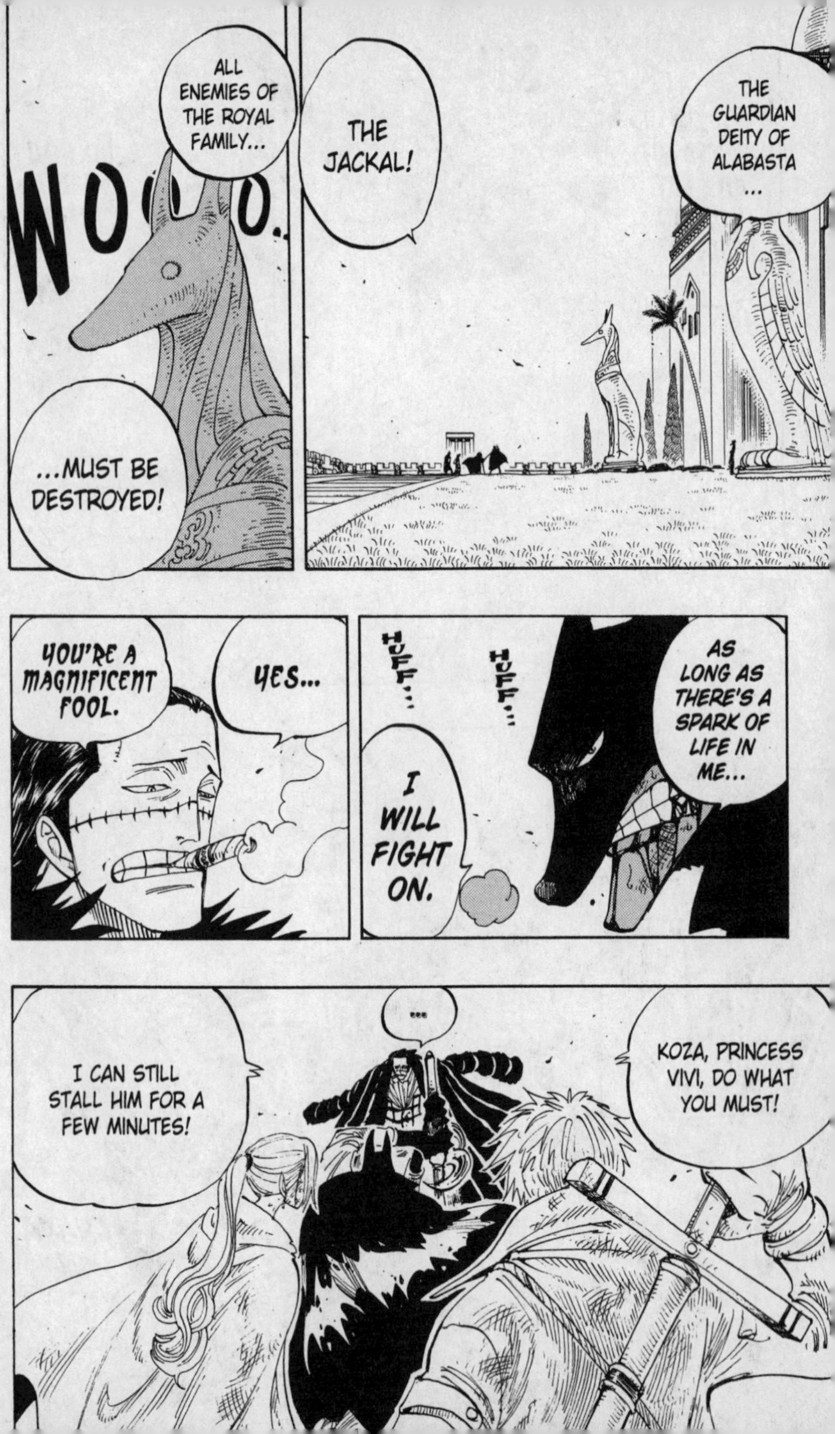
THE GUARDIAN DEITY OF ALABASTA ...
THE JACKAL!
ALL ENEMIES OF THE ROYAL FAMILY...
WOOO..
...MUST BE DESTROYED!
AS LONG AS THERE'S A SPARK OF LIFE IN ME...
HUFF...
HUFF...
I WILL FIGHT ON.
YES...
YOU'RE A MAGNIFICENT FOOL.
KOZA, PRINCESS VIVI, DO WHAT YOU MUST!
...
I CAN STILL STALL HIM FOR A FEW MINUTES!

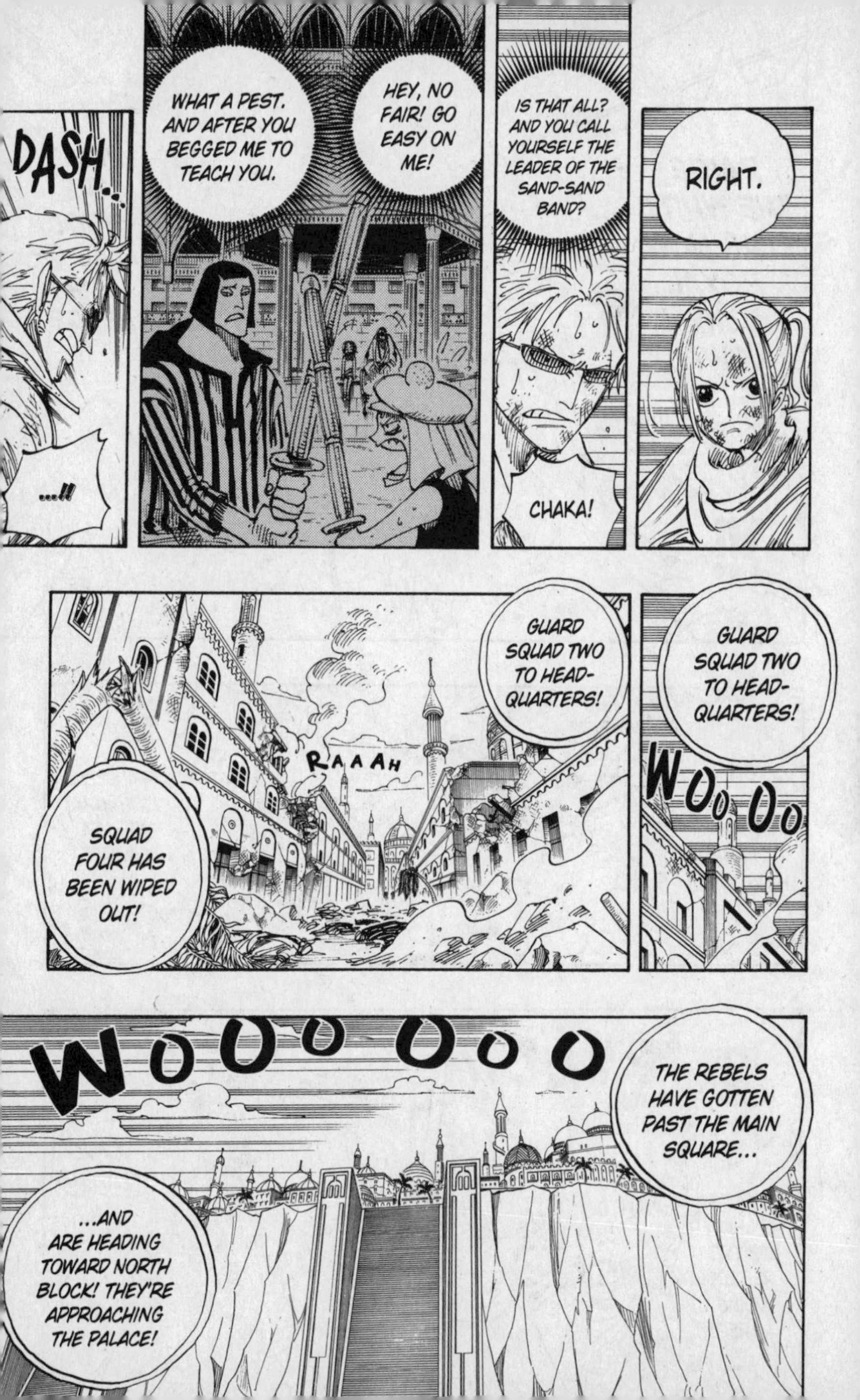
RIGHT.
IS THAT ALL? AND YOU CALL YOURSELF THE LEADER OF THE SAND-SAND BAND?
CHAKA!
HEY, NO FAIR! GO EASY ON ME!
WHAT A PEST. AND AFTER YOU BEGGED ME TO TEACH YOU.
DASH...
...!!
GUARD SQUAD TWO TO HEAD-QUARTERS!
WOOOO
GUARD SQUAD TWO TO HEAD-QUARTERS!
RAAAH
SQUAD FOUR HAS BEEN WIPED OUT!
THE REBELS HAVE GOTTEN PAST THE MAIN SQUARE...
WOOOO OOO
...AND ARE HEADING TOWARD NORTH BLOCK! THEY'RE APPROACHING THE PALACE!

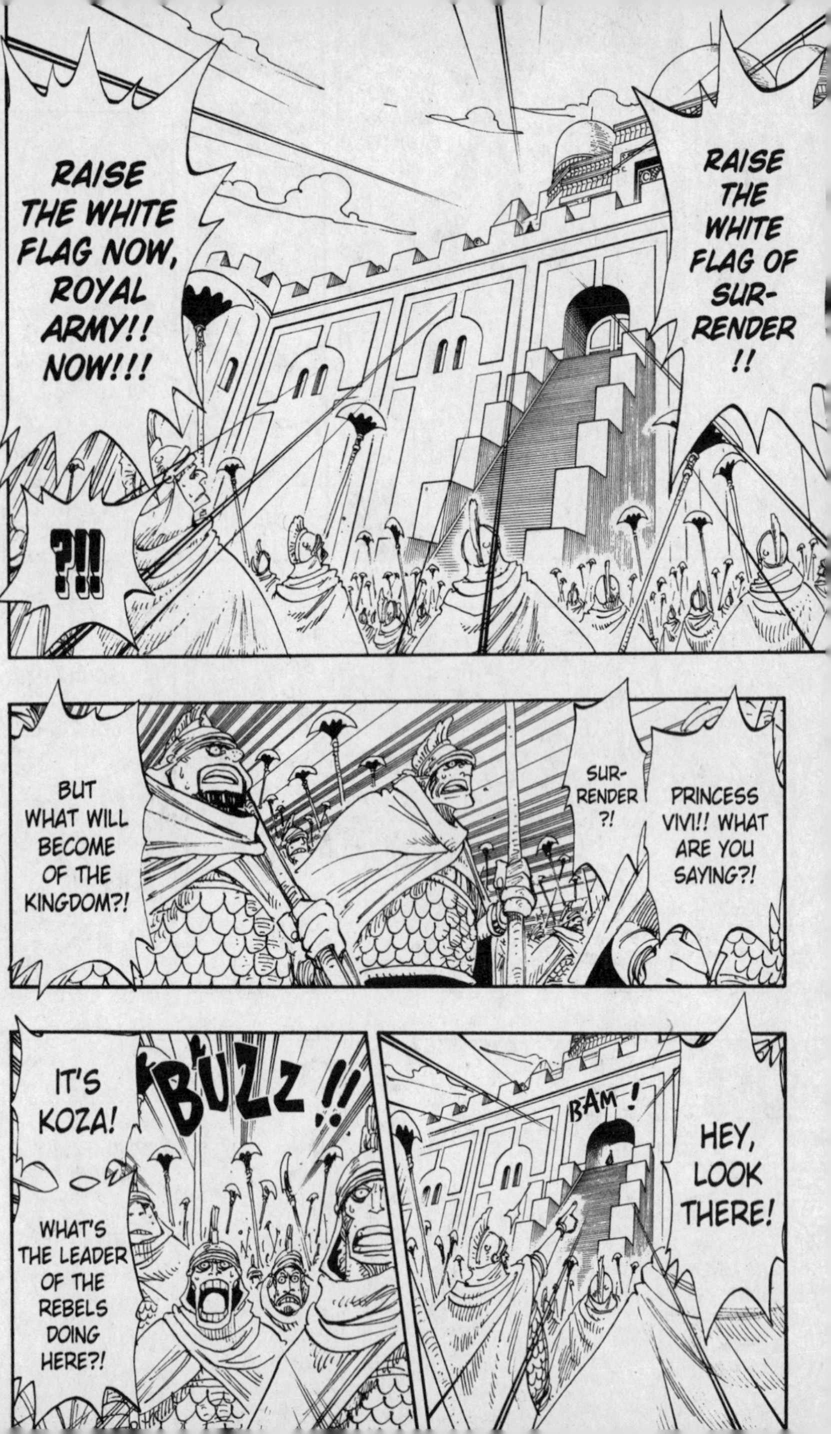
RAISE THE WHITE FLAG OF SUR-RENDER!!
RAISE THE WHITE FLAG NOW, ROYAL ARMY!! NOW!!!
?!!
PRINCESS VIVI!! WHAT ARE YOU SAYING?!
SUR-RENDER?!
BUT WHAT WILL BECOME OF THE KINGDOM?!
BAM!
HEY, LOOK THERE!
BUZZ!!
IT'S KOZA!
WHAT'S THE LEADER OF THE REBELS DOING HERE?!

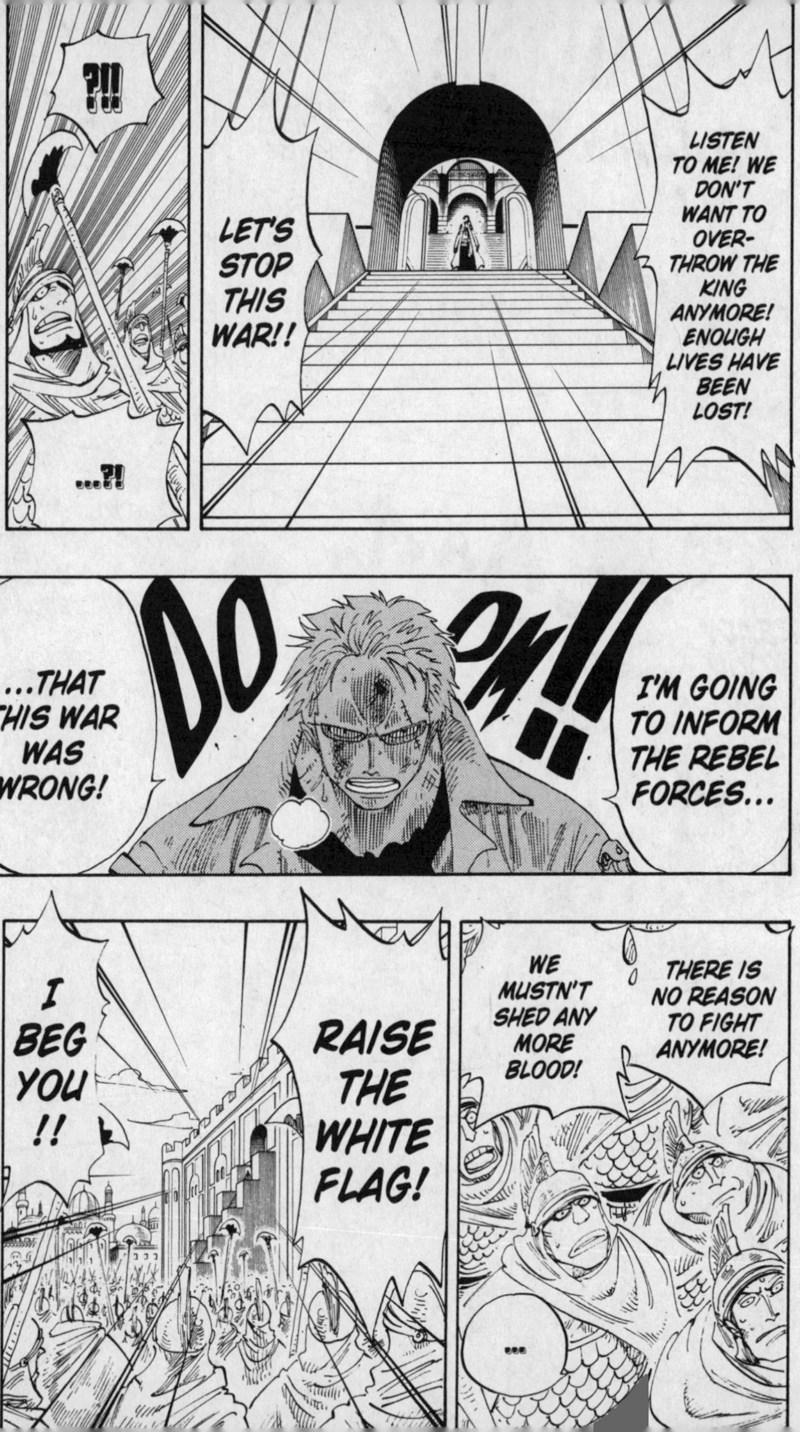
LISTEN TO ME! WE DON'T WANT TO OVER-THROW THE KING ANYMORE! ENOUGH LIVES HAVE BEEN LOST!
LET'S STOP THIS WAR!!
?!!
...?!
I'M GOING TO INFORM THE REBEL FORCES...
DOOM!!
...THAT THIS WAR WAS WRONG!
THERE IS NO REASON TO FIGHT ANYMORE!
WE MUSTN'T SHED ANY MORE BLOOD!
...
RAISE THE WHITE FLAG!
I BEG YOU!!

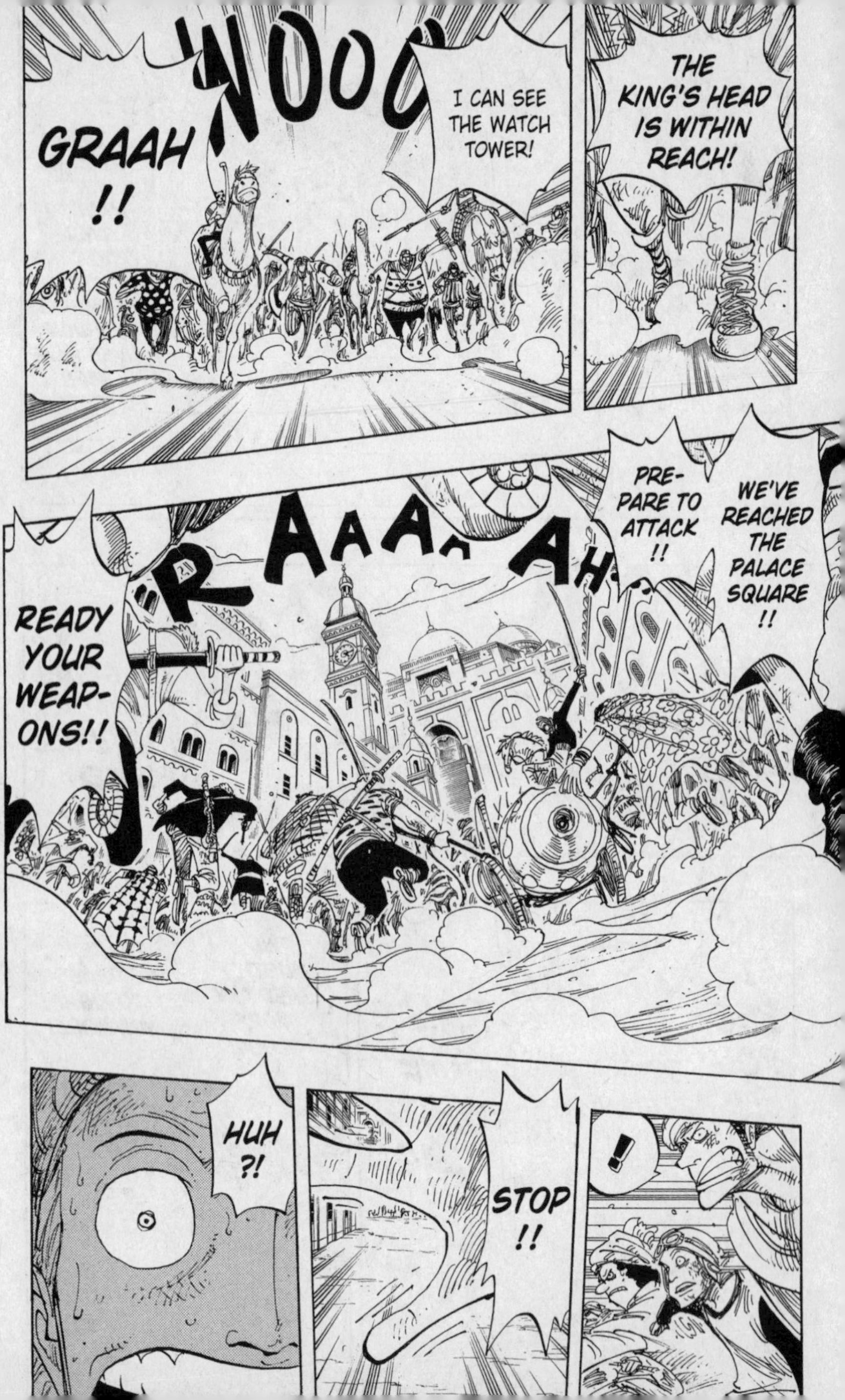
THE KING'S HEAD IS WITHIN REACH!
I CAN SEE THE WATCH TOWER!
WOOO
GRAAH!!
WE'VE REACHED THE PALACE SQUARE!!
PRE-PARE TO ATTACK!!
RAAAAH
READY YOUR WEAP-ONS!!
!
STOP!!
HUH?!

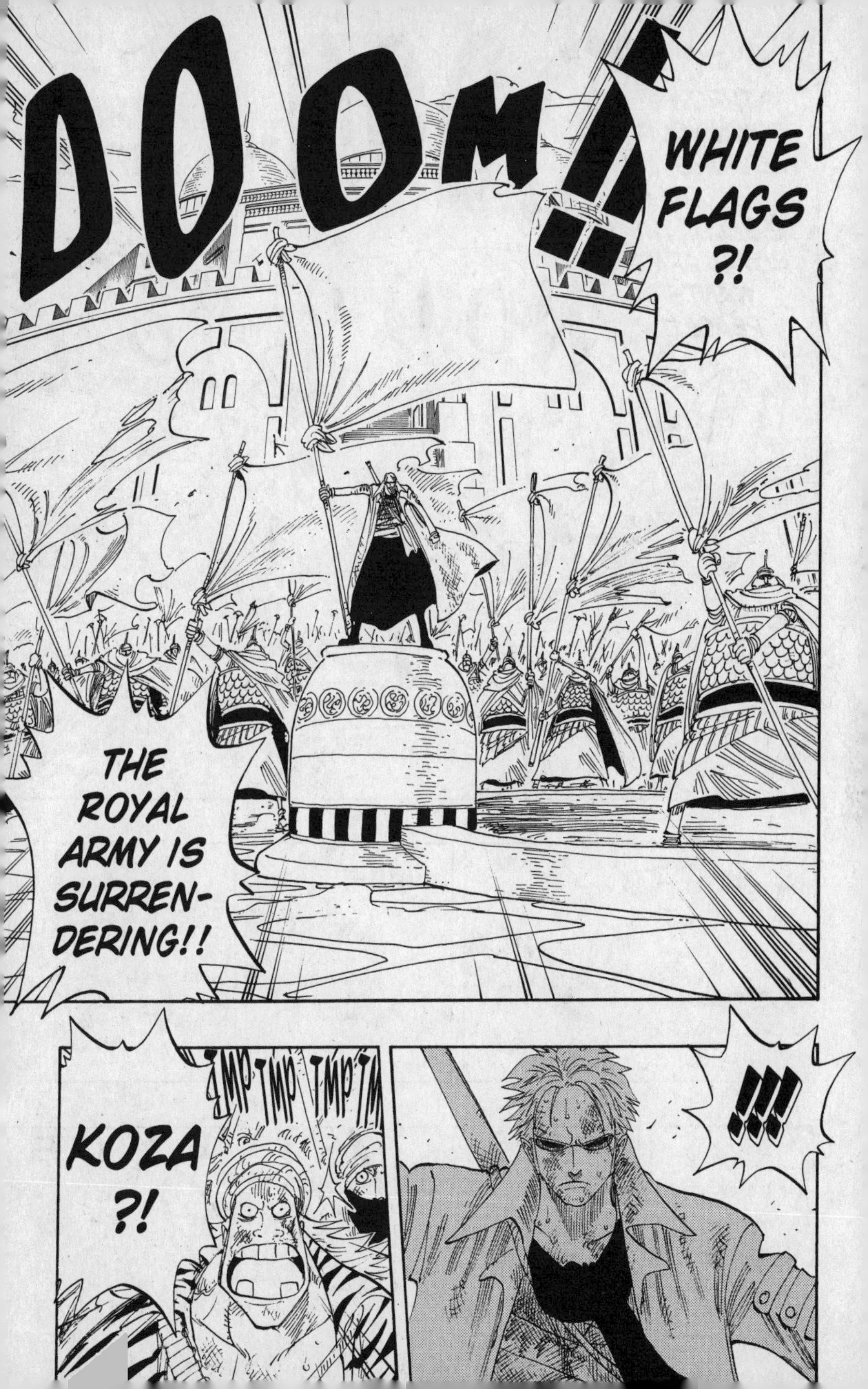
DOOM!!
WHITE FLAGS ?!
THE ROYAL ARMY IS SURREN-DERING!!
!!!
TMP TMP TMP
KOZA ?!

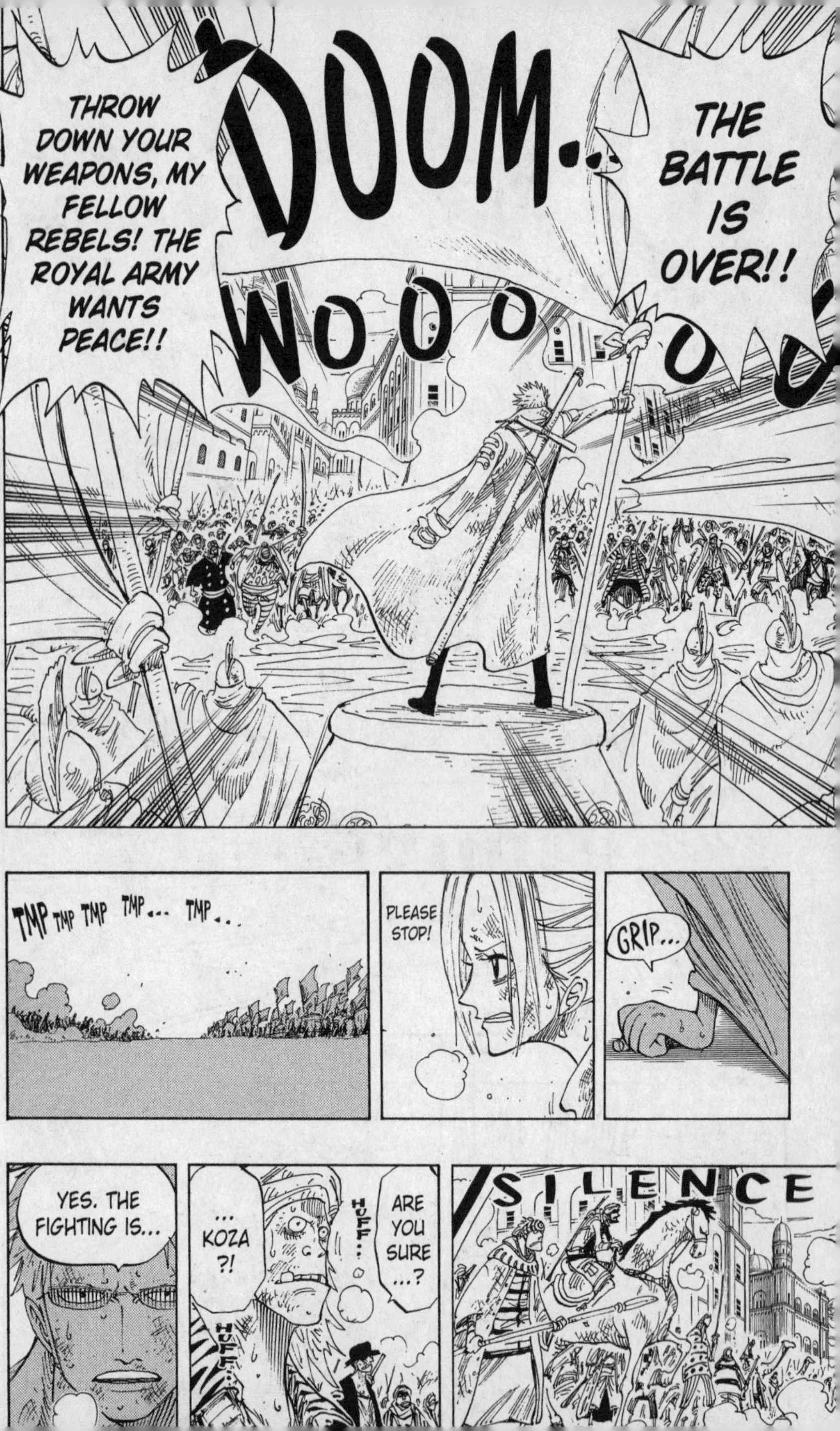
THE BATTLE IS OVER!!
DOOM..
WOOOOO
THROW DOWN YOUR WEAPONS, MY FELLOW REBELS! THE ROYAL ARMY WANTS PEACE!!
GRIP...
PLEASE STOP!
TMP TMP TMP TMP... TMP...
SILENCE
ARE YOU SURE ...?
HUFF...
... KOZA ?!
HUFF...
YES. THE FIGHTING IS...

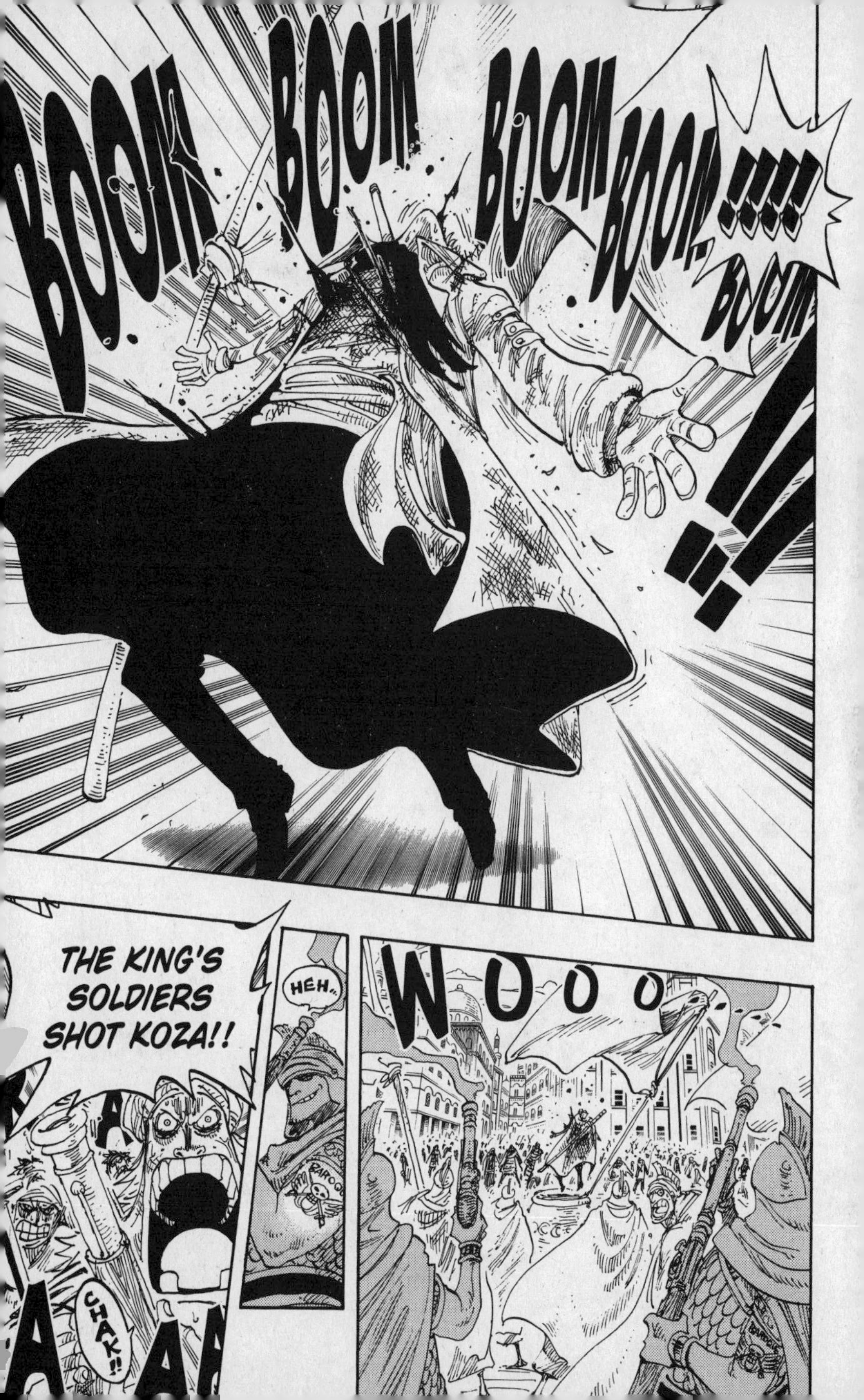
BOOM
BOOM!!!!
BOOM
BOOM
BOOM
WOOO
HEH...
THE KING'S SOLDIERS SHOT KOZA!!
CHAK!!

Chapter 198: 4:15 P.M.

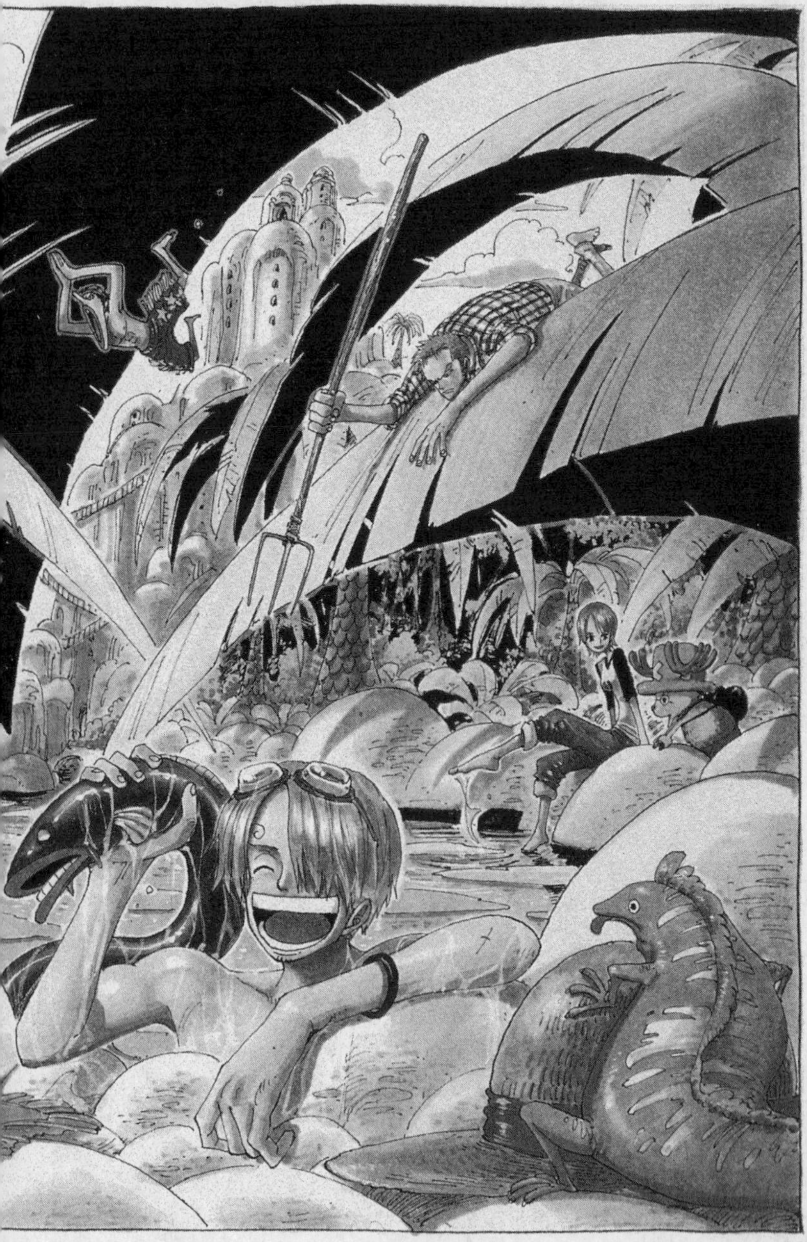

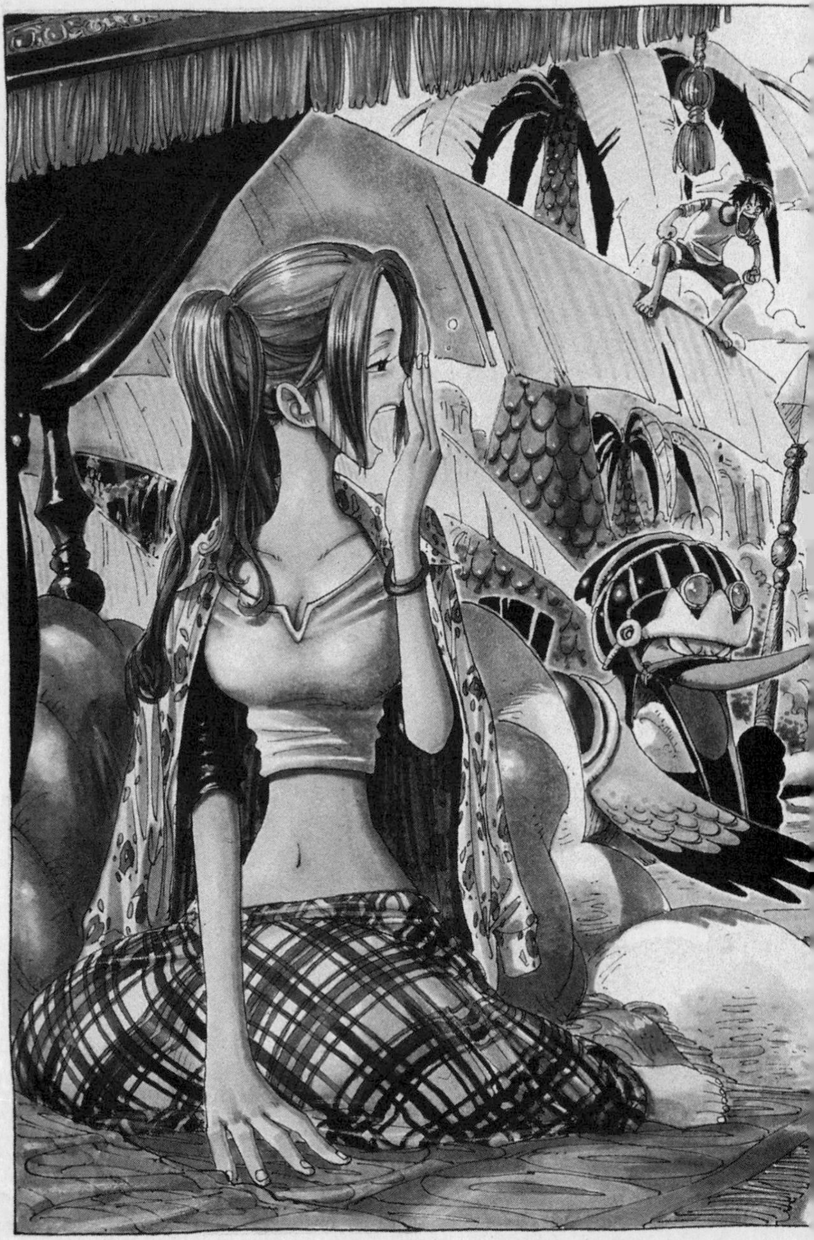

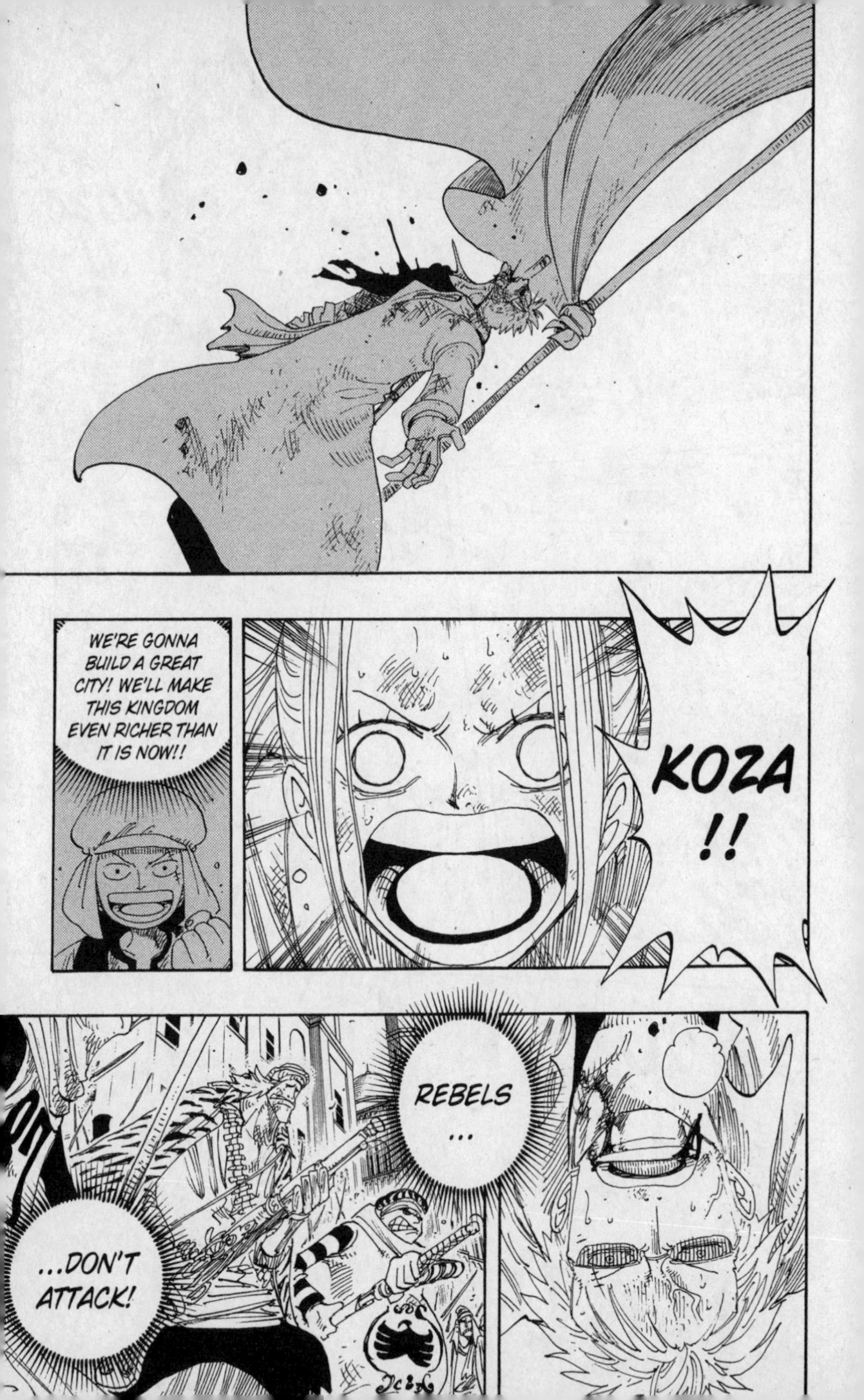
KOZA!!
WE'RE GONNA BUILD A GREAT CITY! WE'LL MAKE THIS KINGDOM EVEN RICHER THAN IT IS NOW!!
REBELS...
...DON'T ATTACK!

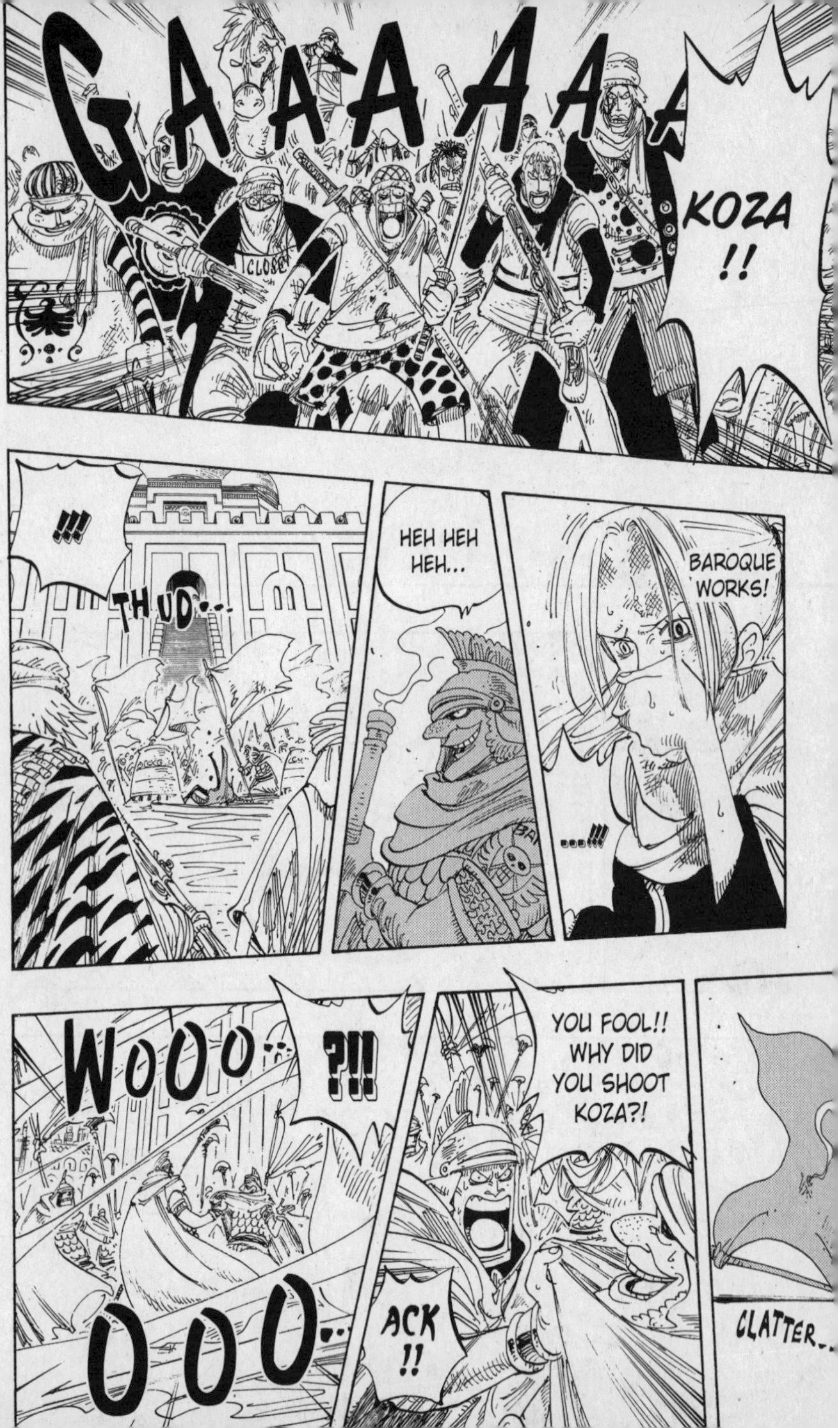
GAAAAAA
KOZA !!
BAROQUE WORKS!
...!!!
HEH HEH HEH...
!!!
THUD...
CLATTER...
YOU FOOL!! WHY DID YOU SHOOT KOZA?!
ACK !!
?!!
WOOO
OOO...

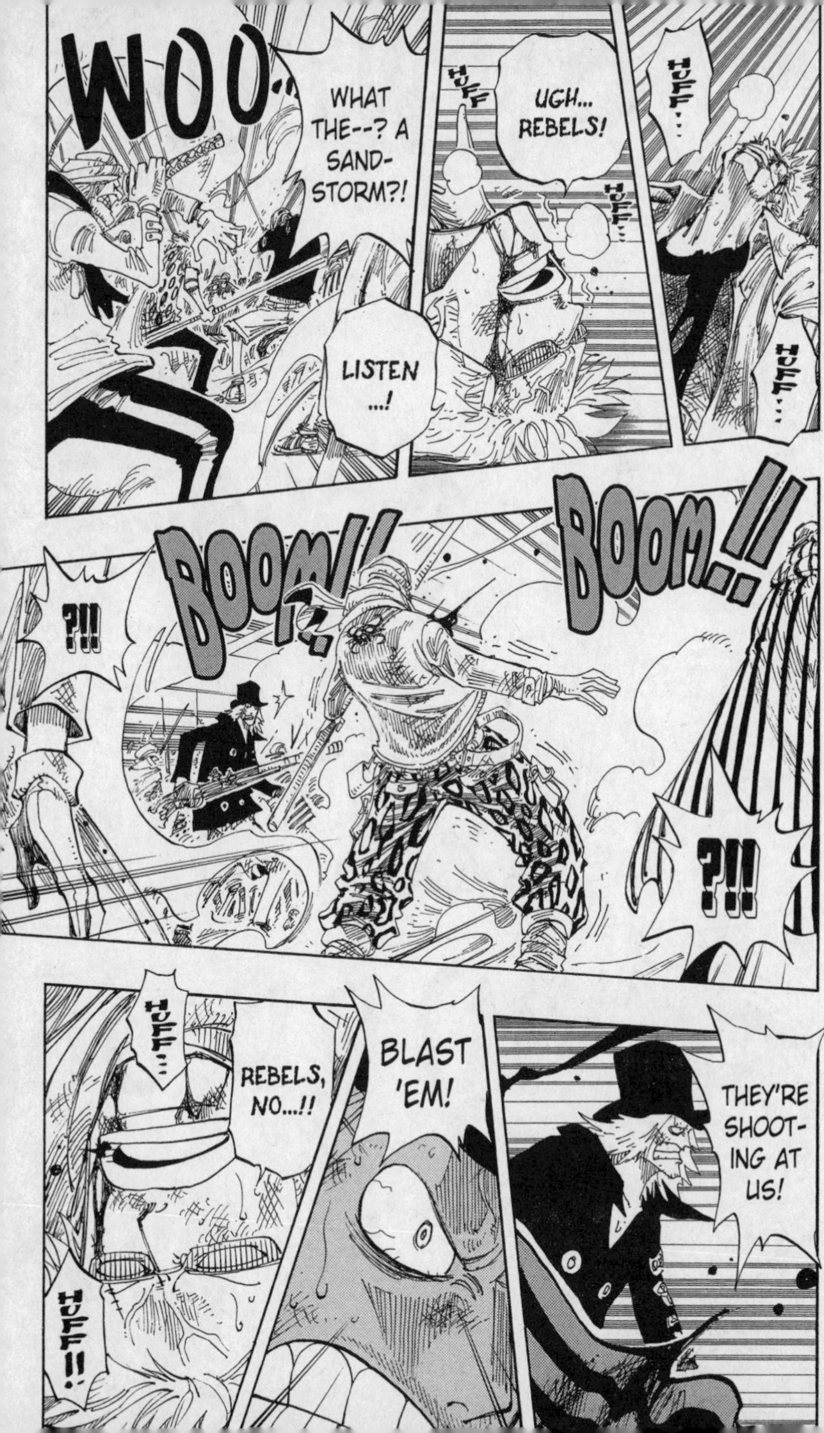
HUFF...
HUFF...
HUFF
UGH... REBELS!
HUFF...
LISTEN ...!
WOO...
WHAT THE--? A SAND-STORM?!
BOOM..!!
BOOM..!!
?!!
?!!
THEY'RE SHOOT-ING AT US!
BLAST 'EM!
HUFF...
REBELS, NO...!!
HUFF!!

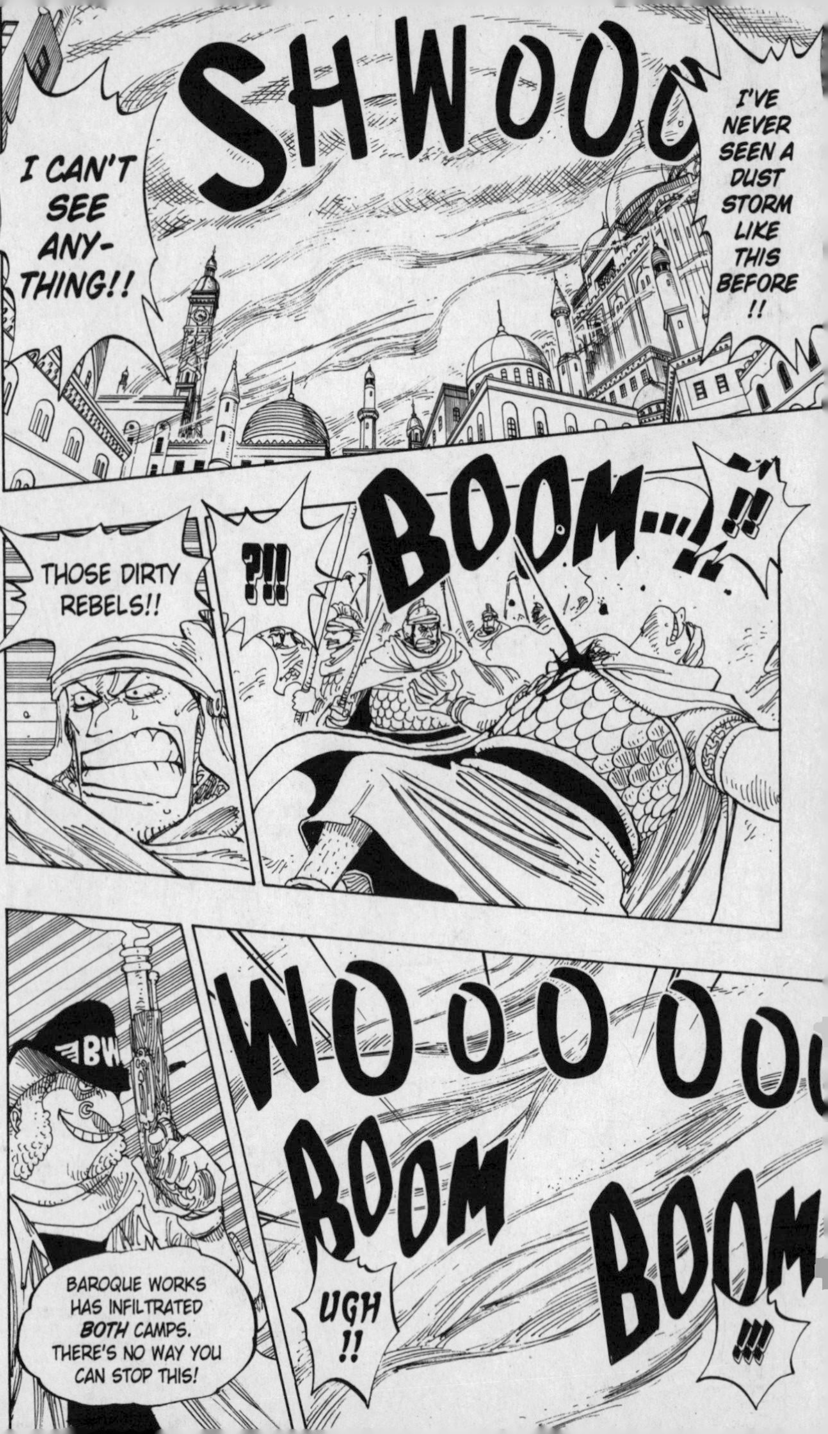
I'VE NEVER SEEN A DUST STORM LIKE THIS BEFORE!!
SHWOOO
I CAN'T SEE ANY-THING!!
BOOM...!!
?!!
THOSE DIRTY REBELS!!
BOOM!!!
WOOOOOO
UGH!!
BOOM
BAROQUE WORKS HAS INFILTRATED *BOTH* CAMPS. THERE'S NO WAY YOU CAN STOP THIS!

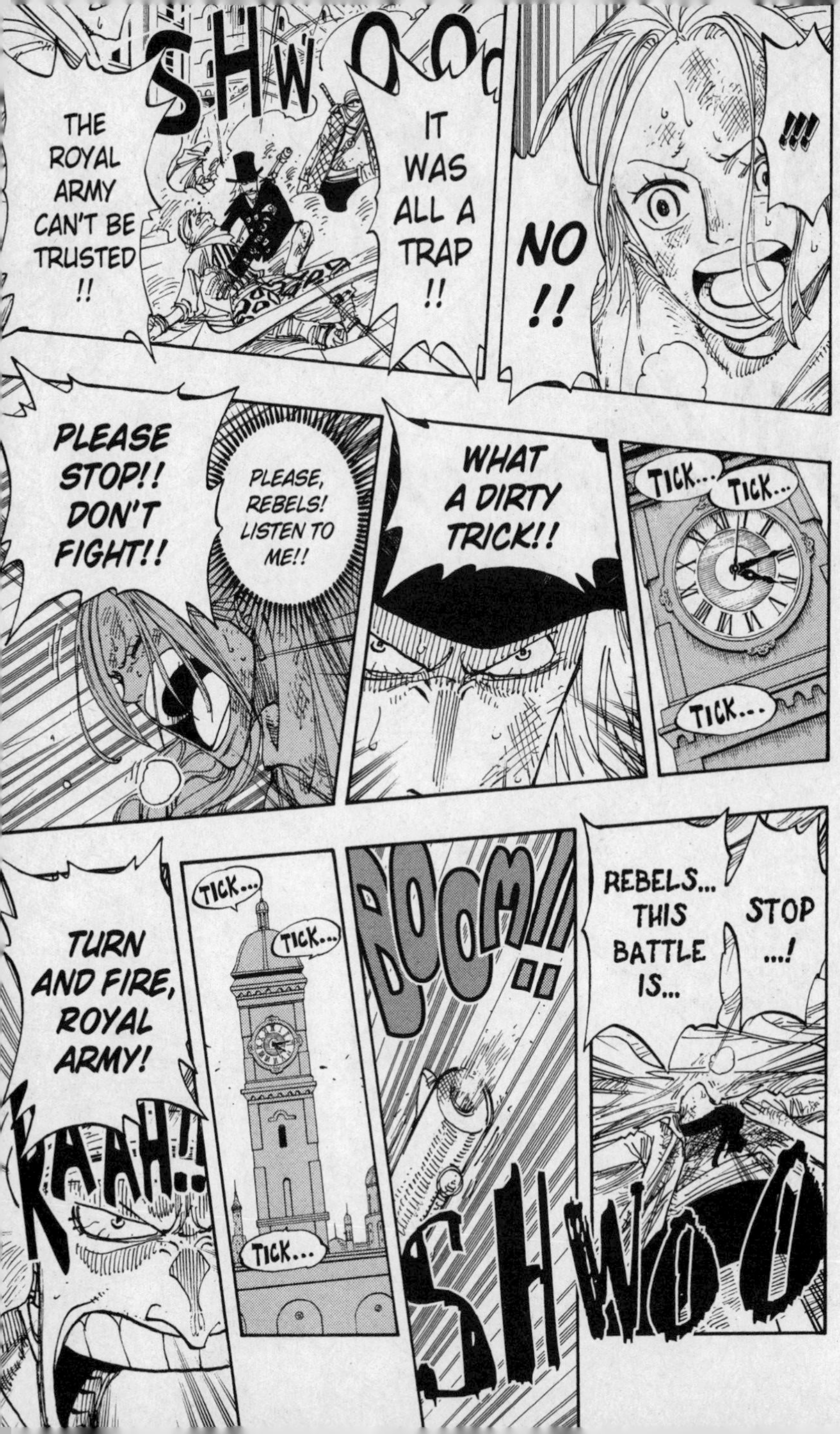
!!!
NO !!
SHWOOO
IT WAS ALL A TRAP !!
THE ROYAL ARMY CAN'T BE TRUSTED !!
TICK...
TICK...
TICK...
WHAT A DIRTY TRICK!!
PLEASE, REBELS! LISTEN TO ME!!
PLEASE STOP!! DON'T FIGHT!!
STOP ...!
REBELS... THIS BATTLE IS...
SHWOOO
BOOM!!
TICK...
TICK...
TICK...
TURN AND FIRE, ROYAL ARMY!
KAAH!!

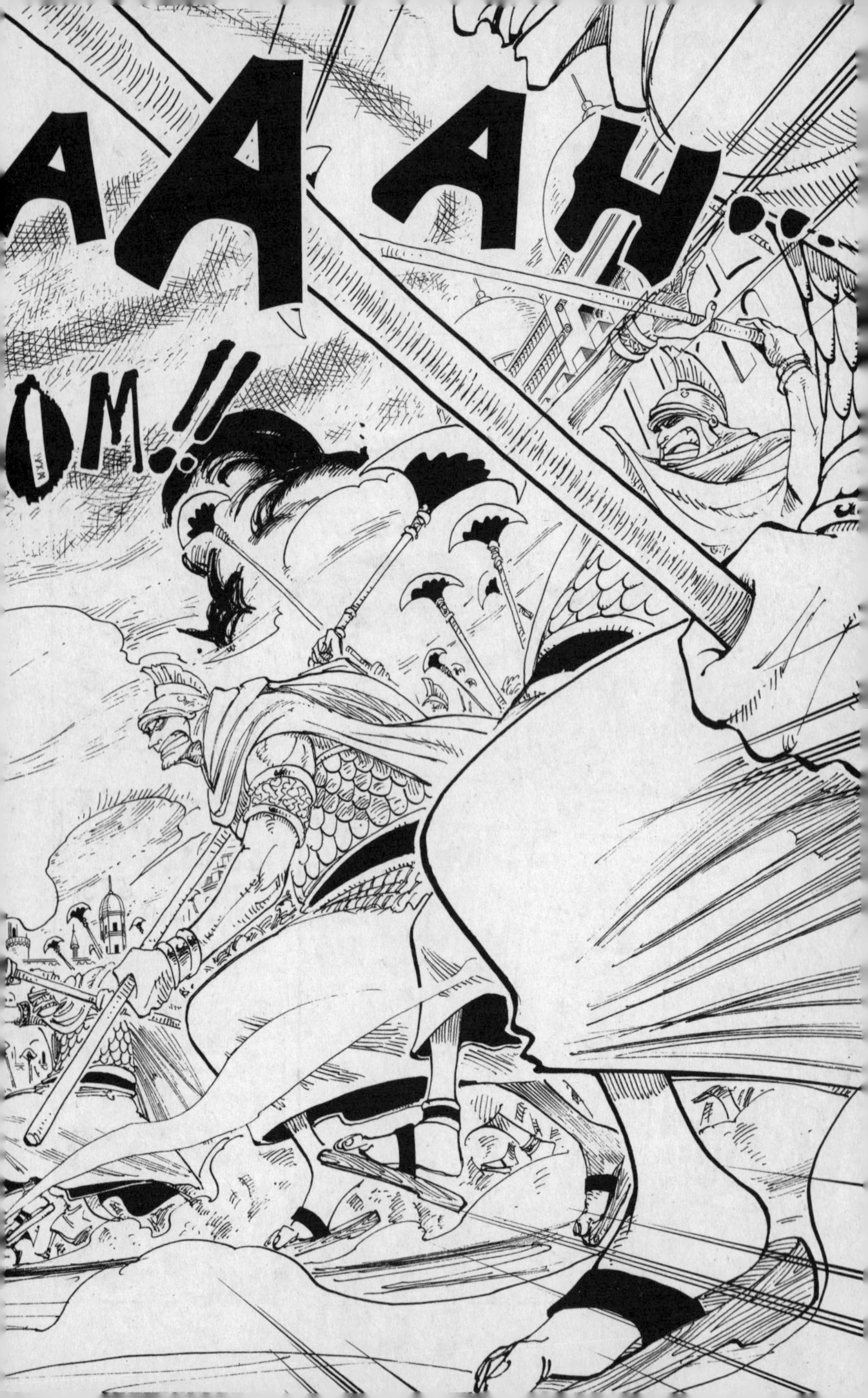
AAAH...
OM!!

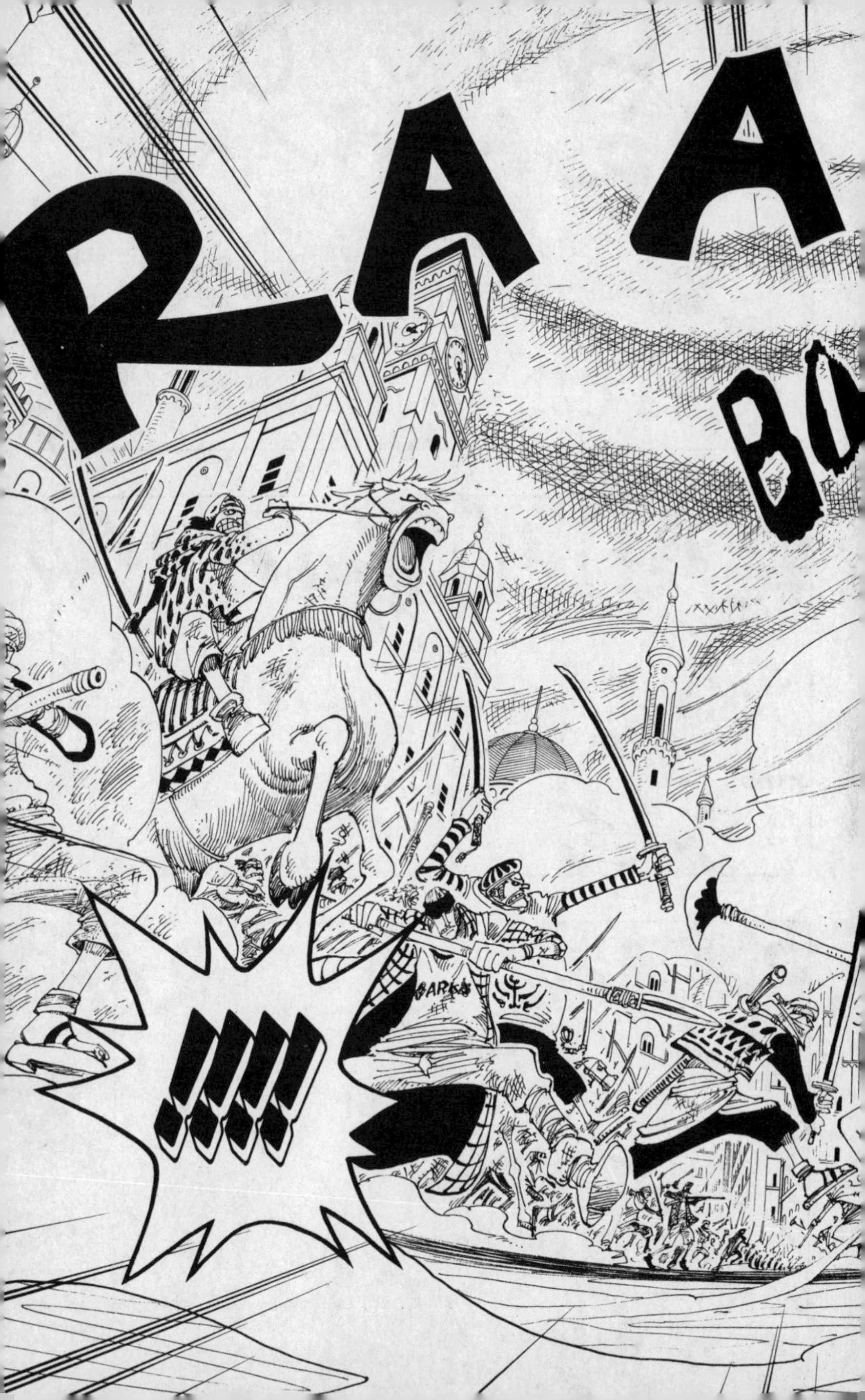
RAA
BO
!!!!!

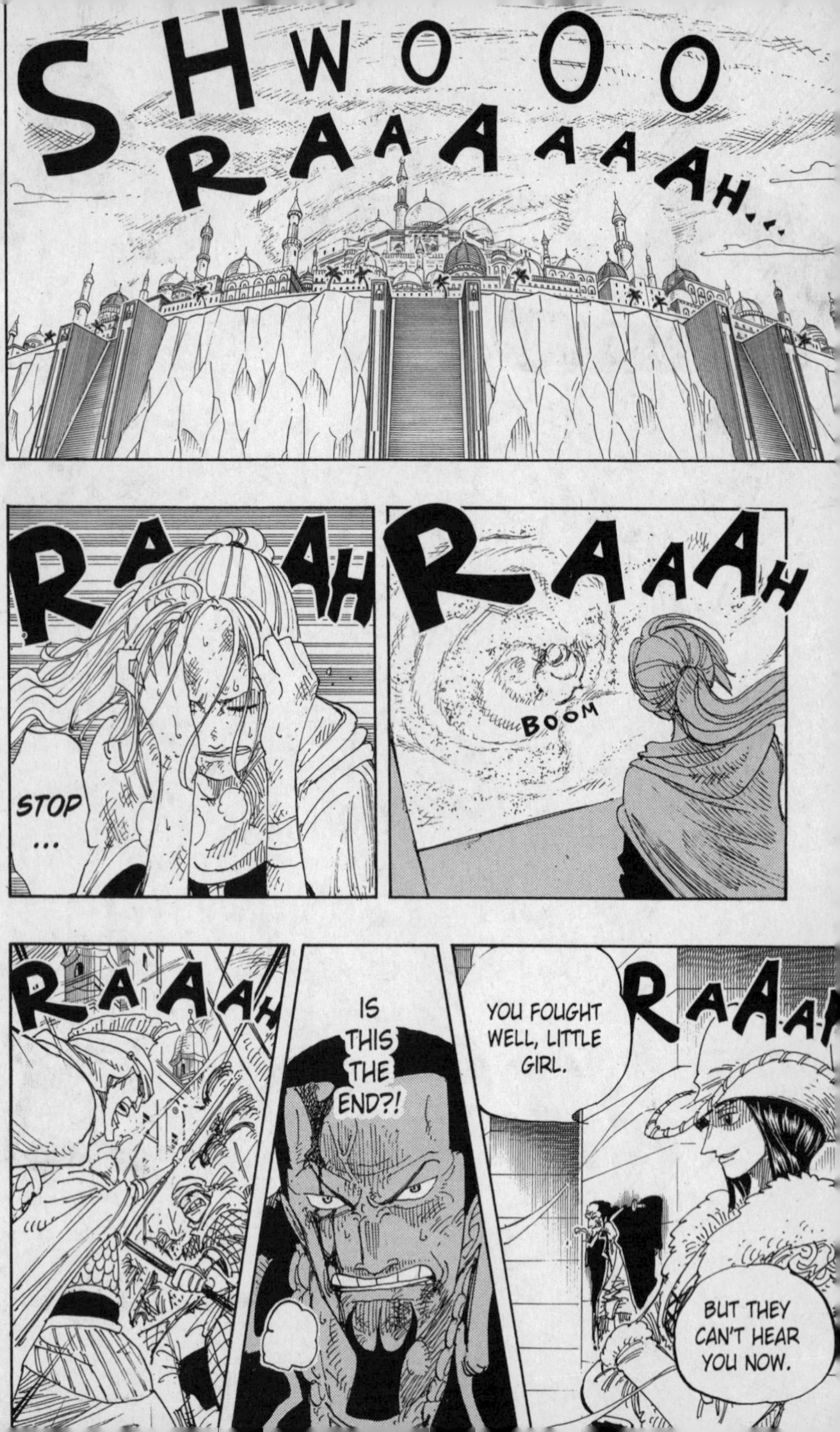
SHWOOO
RAAAAAAH...
RAAAH
BOOM
RAAH
STOP ...
RAAA
YOU FOUGHT WELL, LITTLE GIRL.
BUT THEY CAN'T HEAR YOU NOW.
IS THIS THE END?!
RAAAH

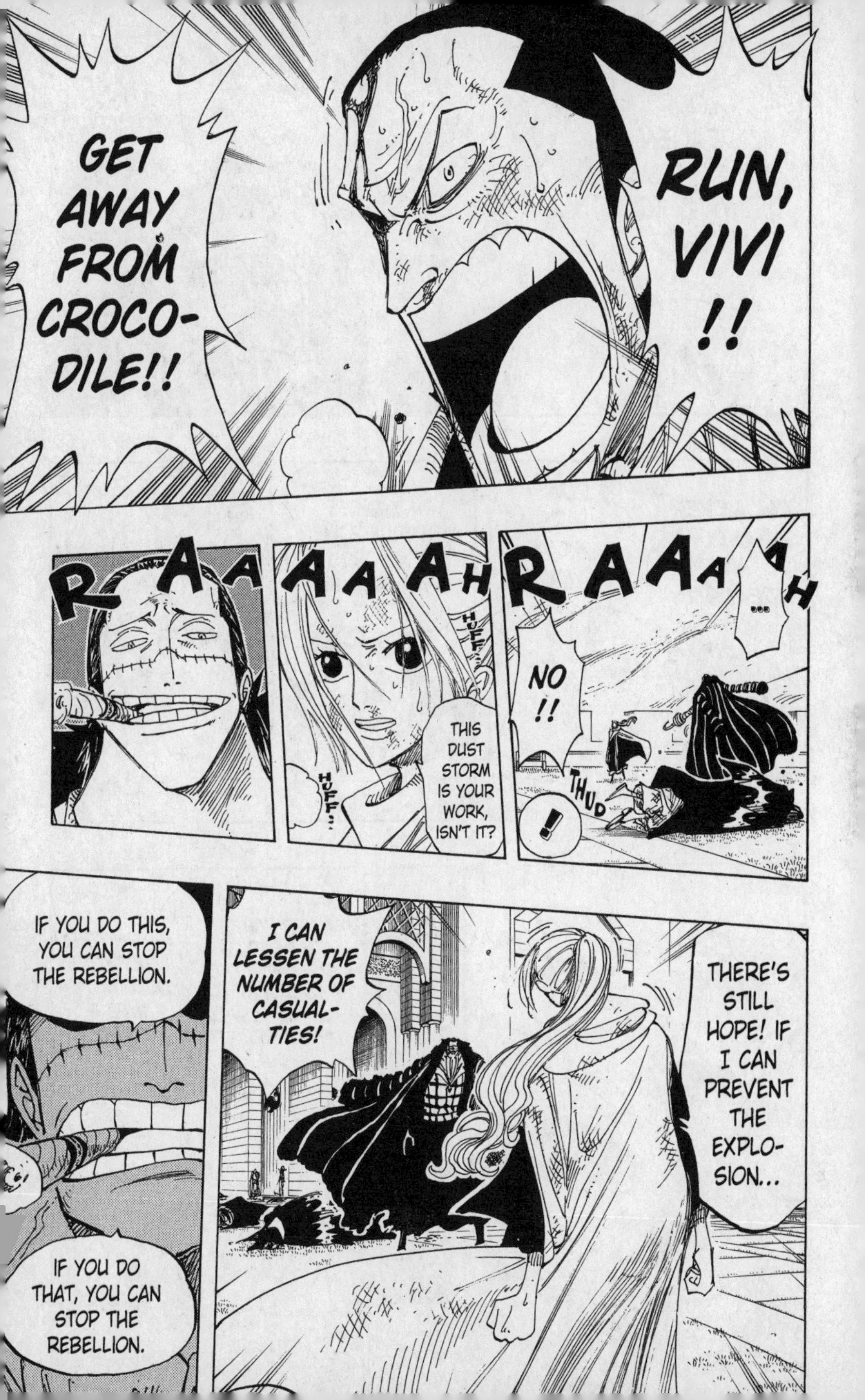
RUN, VIVI!!
GET AWAY FROM CROCO-DILE!!
RAAAAAHRAAAAAH
...
NO!!
THUD
!
HUFF HUFF
THIS DUST STORM IS YOUR WORK, ISN'T IT?
HUFF HUFF
THERE'S STILL HOPE! IF I CAN PREVENT THE EXPLOSION...
I CAN LESSEN THE NUMBER OF CASUAL-TIES!
IF YOU DO THIS, YOU CAN STOP THE REBELLION.
IF YOU DO THAT, YOU CAN STOP THE REBELLION.

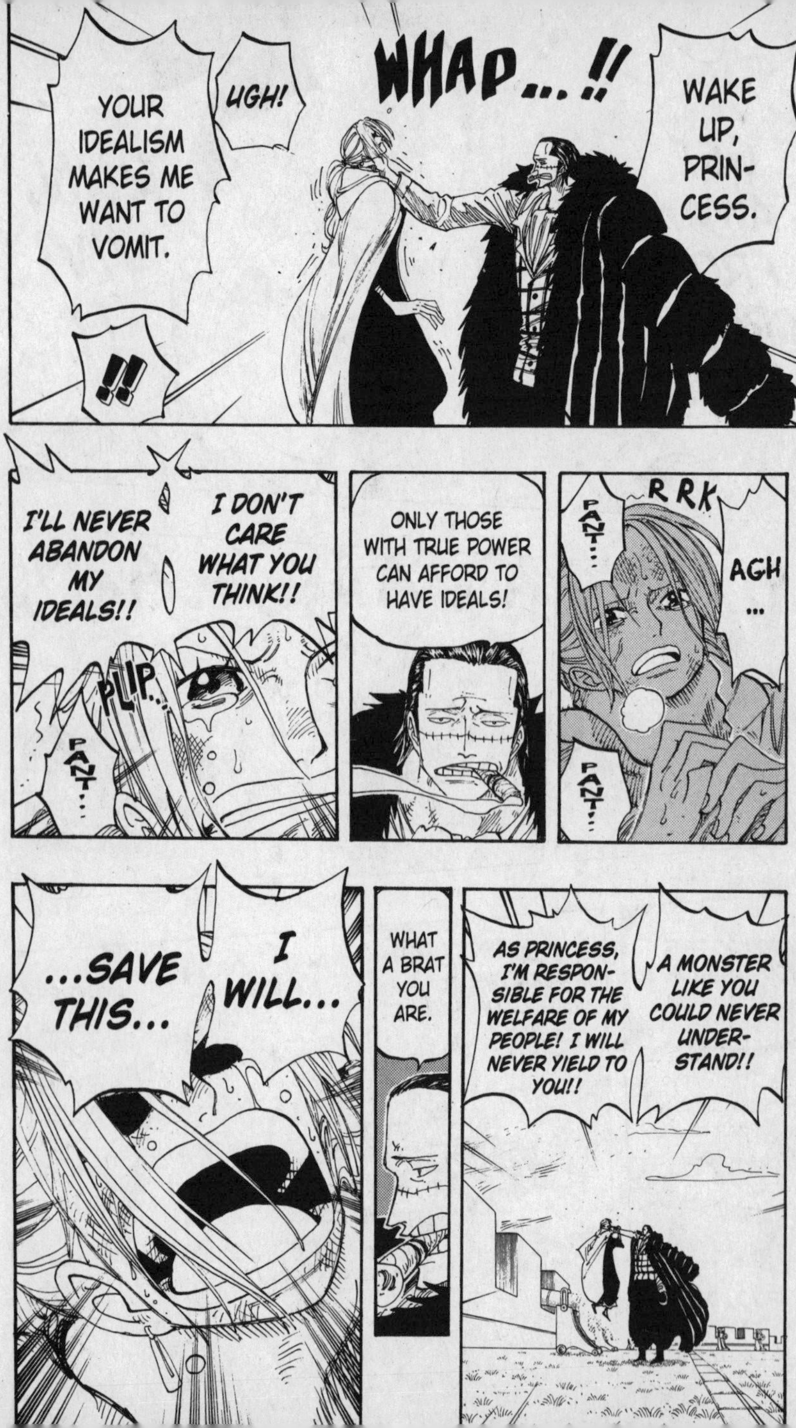
WAKE UP, PRINCESS.
WHAP...!!
UGH!
YOUR IDEALISM MAKES ME WANT TO VOMIT.
!!
RRK
PANT...
AGH...
PANT...
ONLY THOSE WITH TRUE POWER CAN AFFORD TO HAVE IDEALS!
I DON'T CARE WHAT YOU THINK!!
I'LL NEVER ABANDON MY IDEALS!!
PLIP...
PANT...
A MONSTER LIKE YOU COULD NEVER UNDERSTAND!!
AS PRINCESS, I'M RESPONSIBLE FOR THE WELFARE OF MY PEOPLE! I WILL NEVER YIELD TO YOU!!
WHAT A BRAT YOU ARE.
I WILL...
...SAVE THIS...

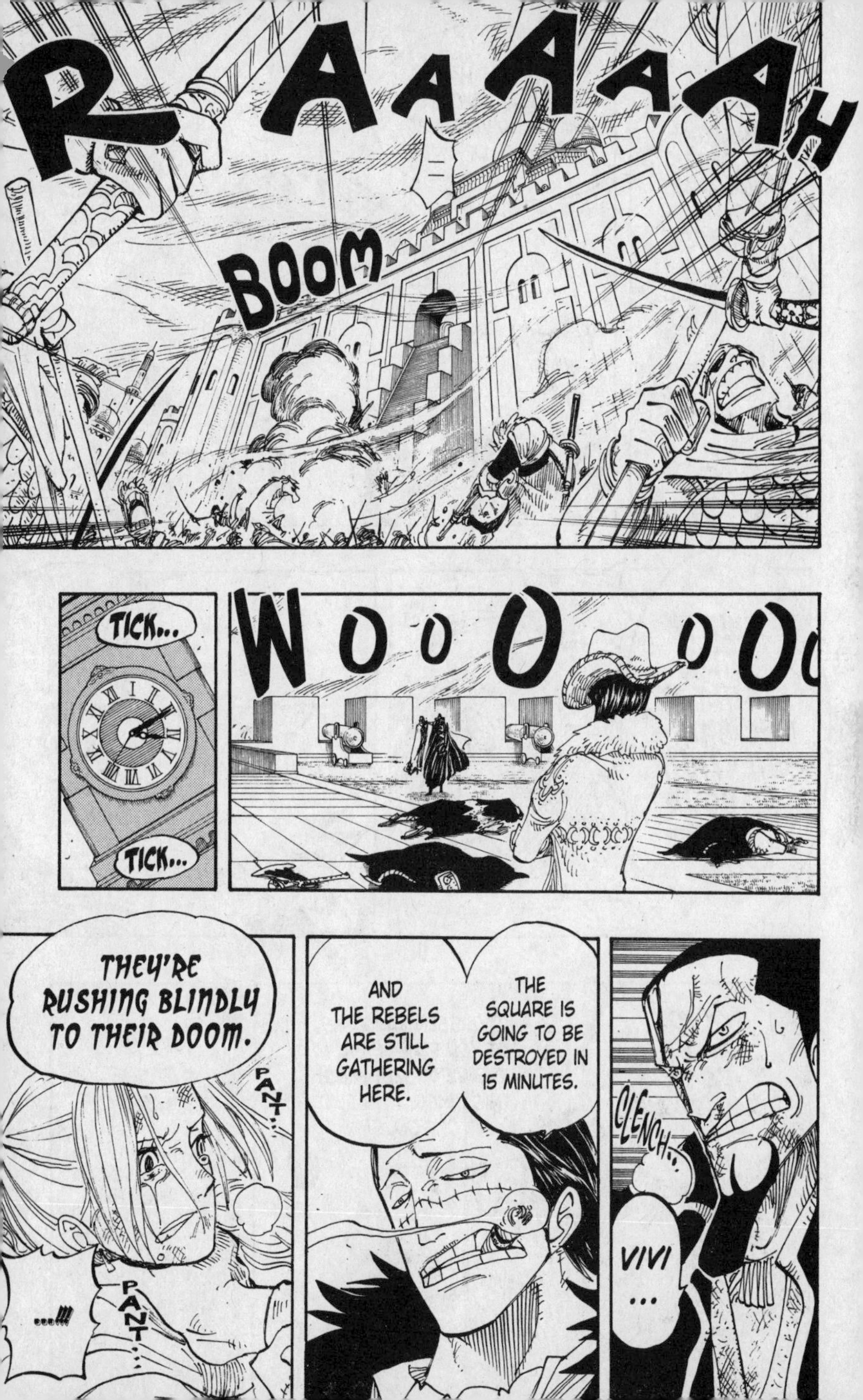
RAAAAAH
BOOM
WOOOOOO
TICK...
TICK...
CLENCH...
VIVI ...
THE SQUARE IS GOING TO BE DESTROYED IN 15 MINUTES.
AND THE REBELS ARE STILL GATHERING HERE.
THEY'RE RUSHING BLINDLY TO THEIR DOOM.
PANT...
...!!!
PANT...

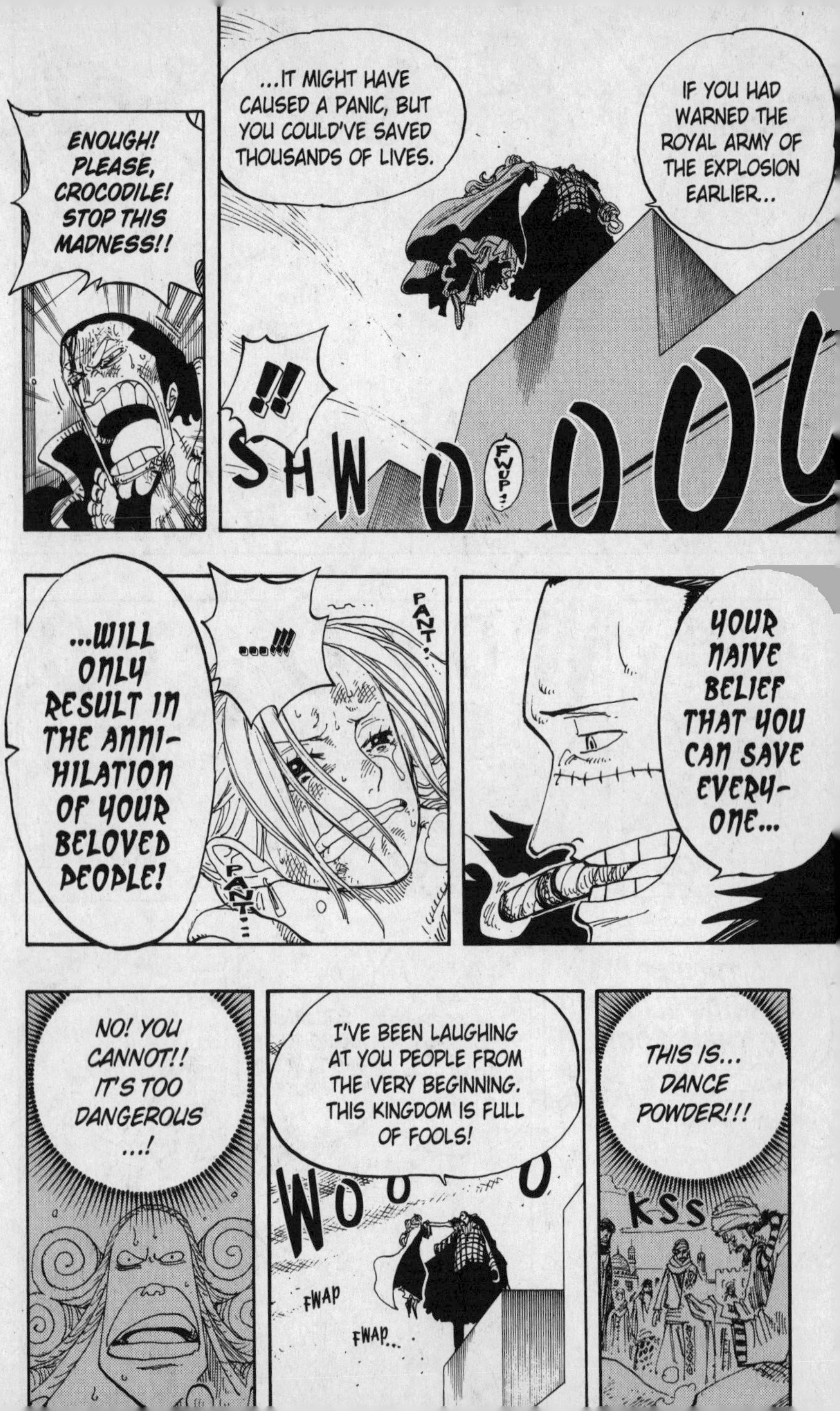
IF YOU HAD WARNED THE ROYAL ARMY OF THE EXPLOSION EARLIER...
...IT MIGHT HAVE CAUSED A PANIC, BUT YOU COULD'VE SAVED THOUSANDS OF LIVES.
!!
SHWOOOOO
FWUP!
ENOUGH! PLEASE, CROCODILE! STOP THIS MADNESS!!
YOUR NAIVE BELIEF THAT YOU CAN SAVE EVERY-ONE...
...WILL ONLY RESULT IN THE ANNI-HILATION OF YOUR BELOVED PEOPLE!
...!!!
PANT...
PANT...
THIS IS... DANCE POWDER!!!
KSS
I'VE BEEN LAUGHING AT YOU PEOPLE FROM THE VERY BEGINNING. THIS KINGDOM IS FULL OF FOOLS!
WOOOO
FWAP
FWAP...
NO! YOU CANNOT!! IT'S TOO DANGEROUS ...!

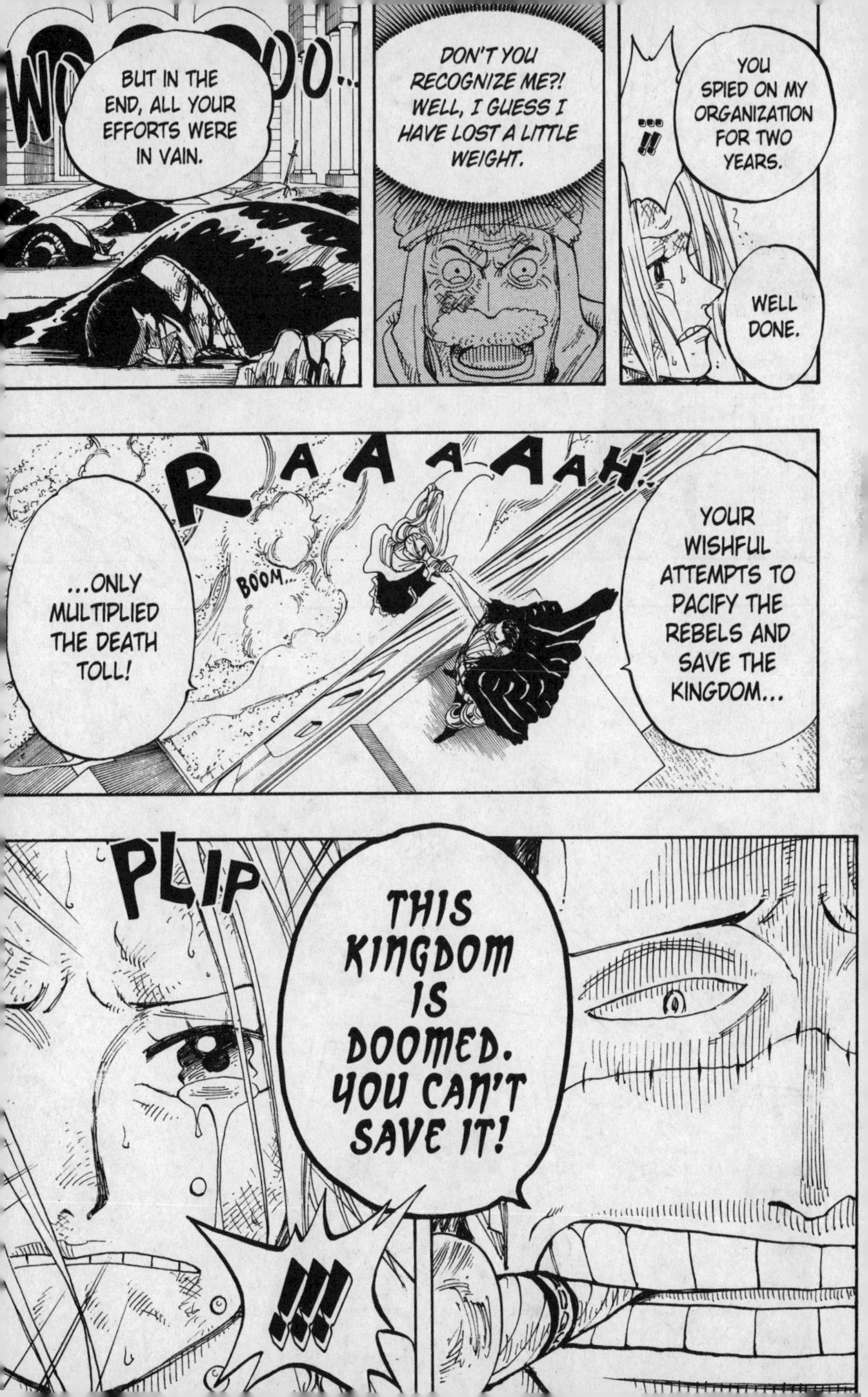
...!!
YOU SPIED ON MY ORGANIZATION FOR TWO YEARS.
WELL DONE.
DON'T YOU RECOGNIZE ME?! WELL, I GUESS I HAVE LOST A LITTLE WEIGHT.
BUT IN THE END, ALL YOUR EFFORTS WERE IN VAIN.
RAAAAAH..
YOUR WISHFUL ATTEMPTS TO PACIFY THE REBELS AND SAVE THE KINGDOM...
BOOM...
...ONLY MULTIPLIED THE DEATH TOLL!
THIS KINGDOM IS DOOMED. YOU CAN'T SAVE IT!
PLIP
!!!

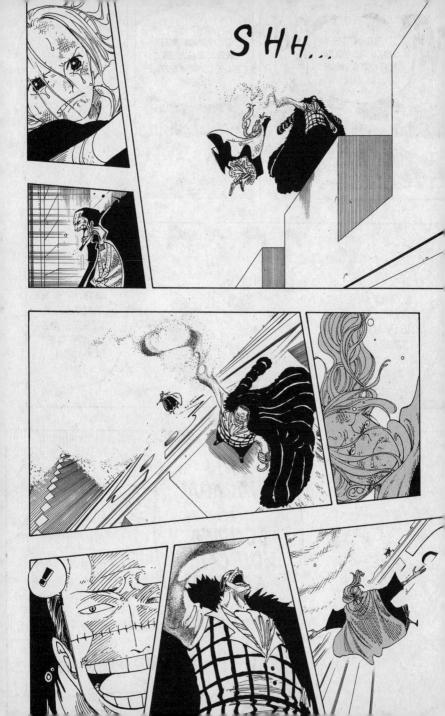

SHH...

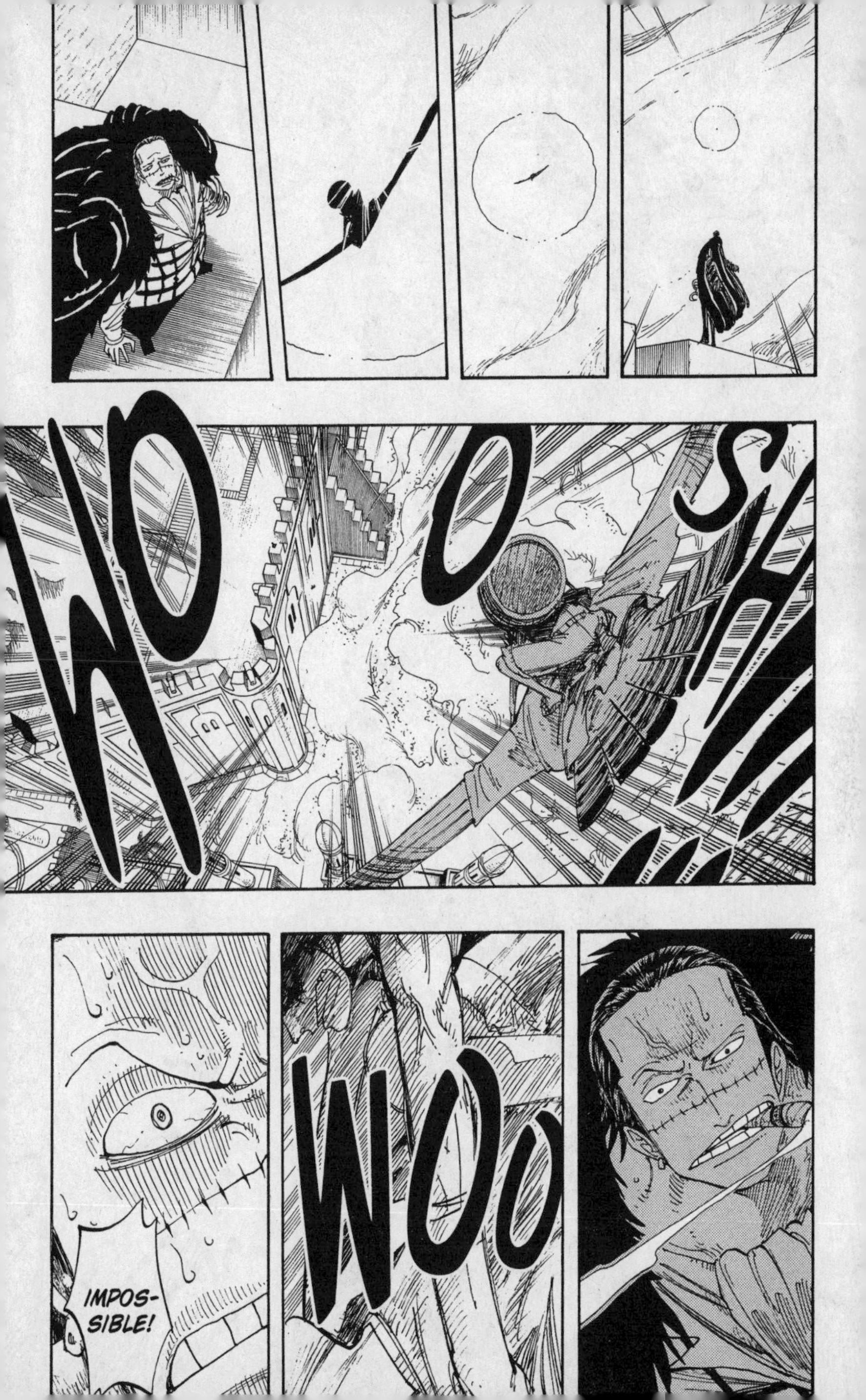

WHOOSH
WOOO
IMPOS-
SIBLE!

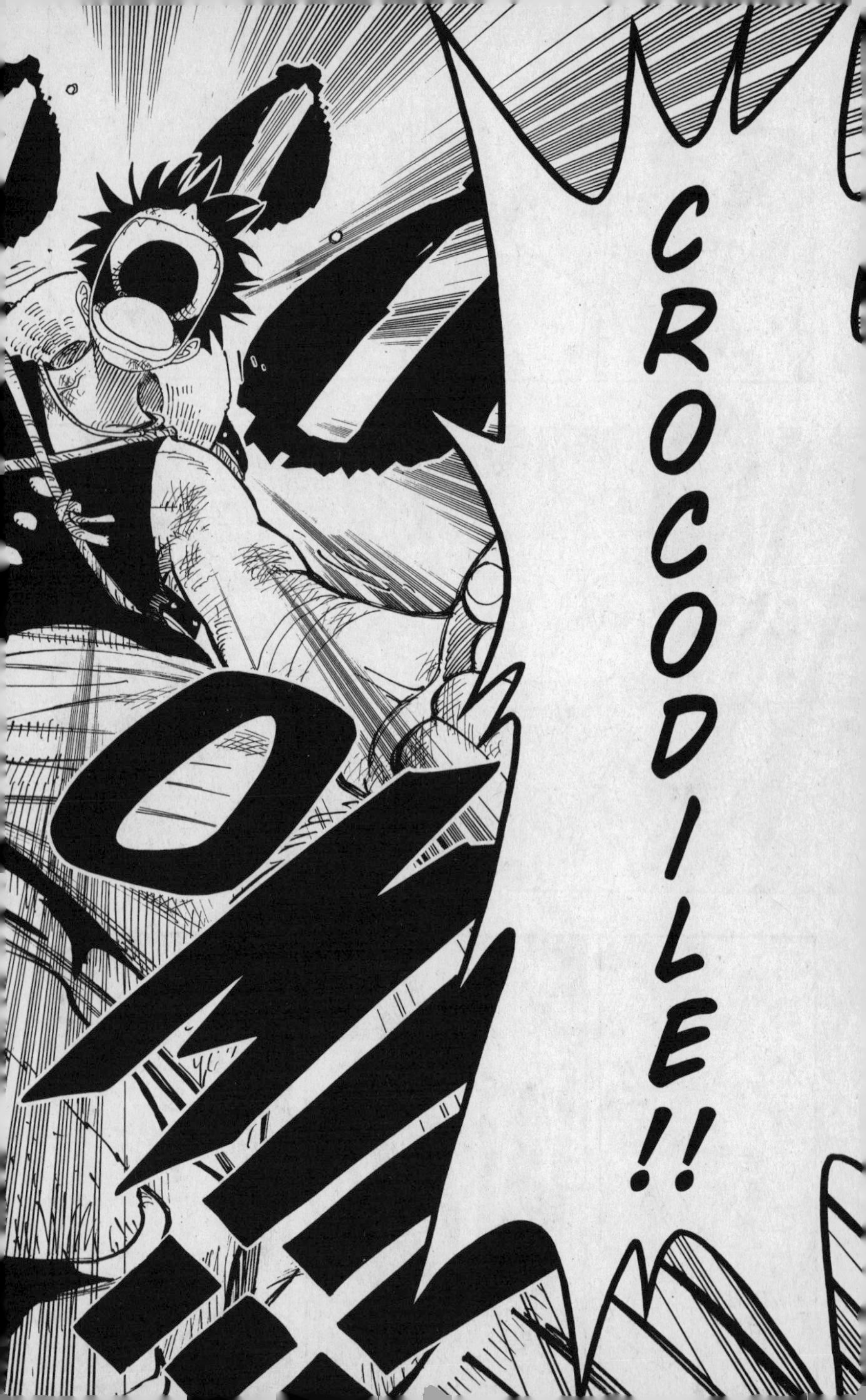
CROCODILE!!

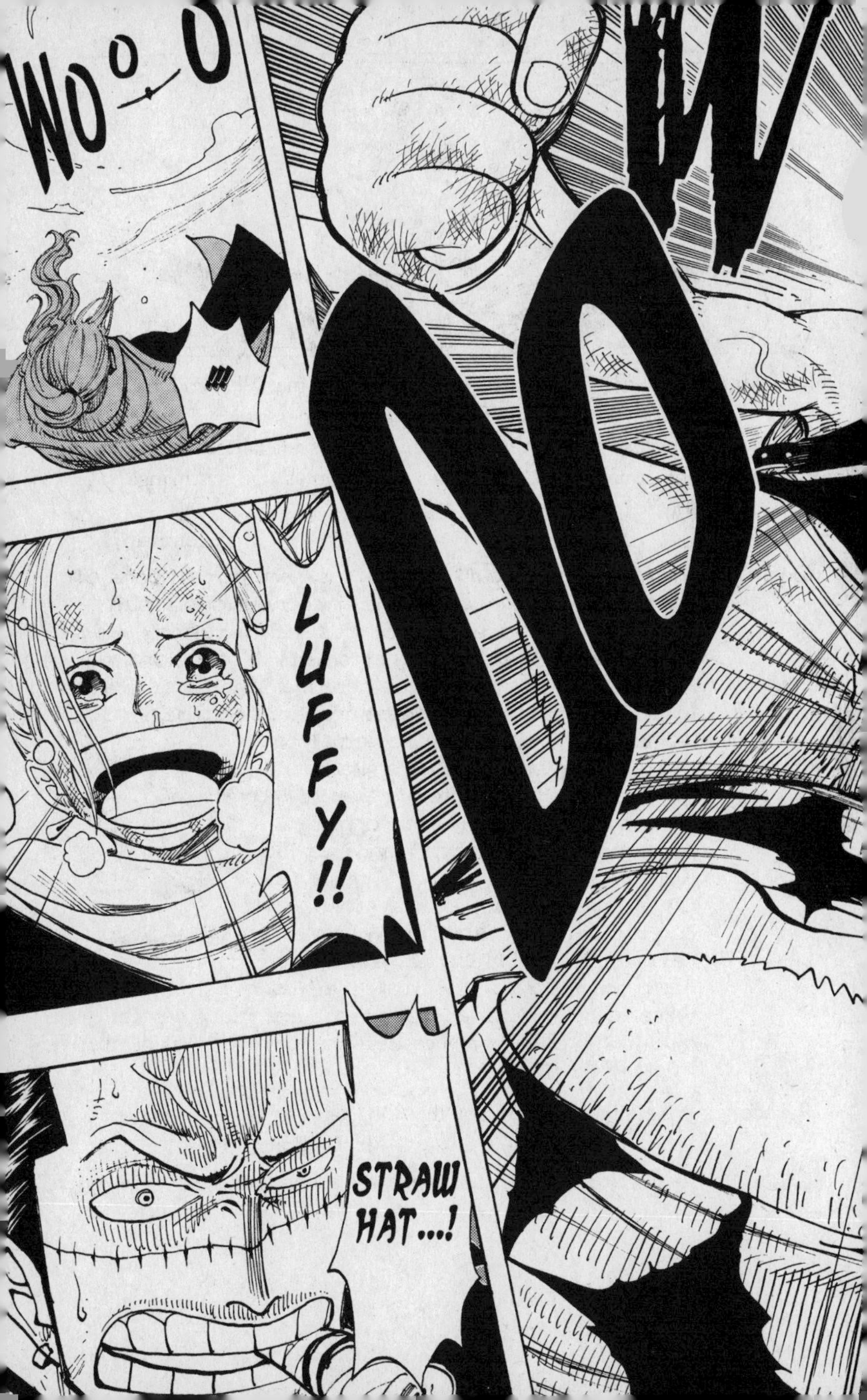
WOOO
!!!
LUFFY!!
STRAW HAT...!

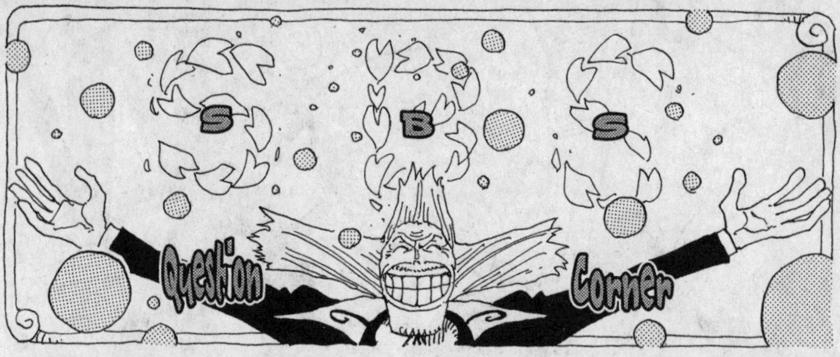
S B S
Question Corner

Reader: Oda Sensei, something's been bothering me. What country are Luffy and the others from? In my sociology class we learned that Japanese pirates were called *wakô*. Is this a Japanese translation or something, or is "pirates" a special term used in this manga? Please tell me.

--Kuroman

Oda: Well, first of all, Luffy and his crew are not citizens of any country. And I won't make any conclusions about their ethnicity. As for *wakô*, let's see. Historically, *wakô* were pirates. *Wakô* mostly attacked in boats along the Korean peninsula and the Chinese mainland. Once in a while our history books mention "sending soldiers to Korea." These soldiers were actually pirates. They went there to pillage. They were bad guys. The *Murakami Suigun* ("Water Army") terrorized and controlled the Seto Inland Sea. They were pirates too. They had a real impact on Japanese history, though most people don't know much about them. I once researched the difference between the *wakô* and the *suigun*. Actually the *suigun* were sometimes called *wakô*, so there really wasn't much difference. In any case, there were lots of pirates in Japan.

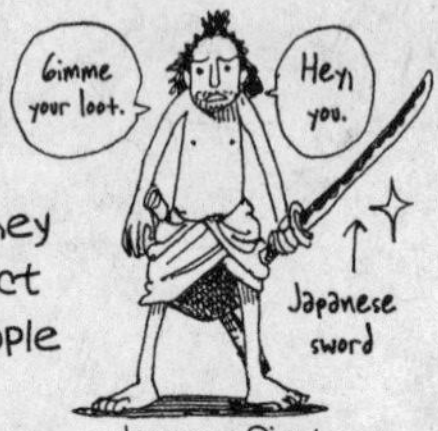
Gimme your loot.
Hey you.
Japanese sword

Japanese Pirate (as I picture him)

Reader: What is the speed limit on the "Oh Come My Way" Way?

--Mr. Tsu Bon Curry

Oda: The speed limit is 300 fake eyelashes an hour.

Chapter 199:
HOPE!!

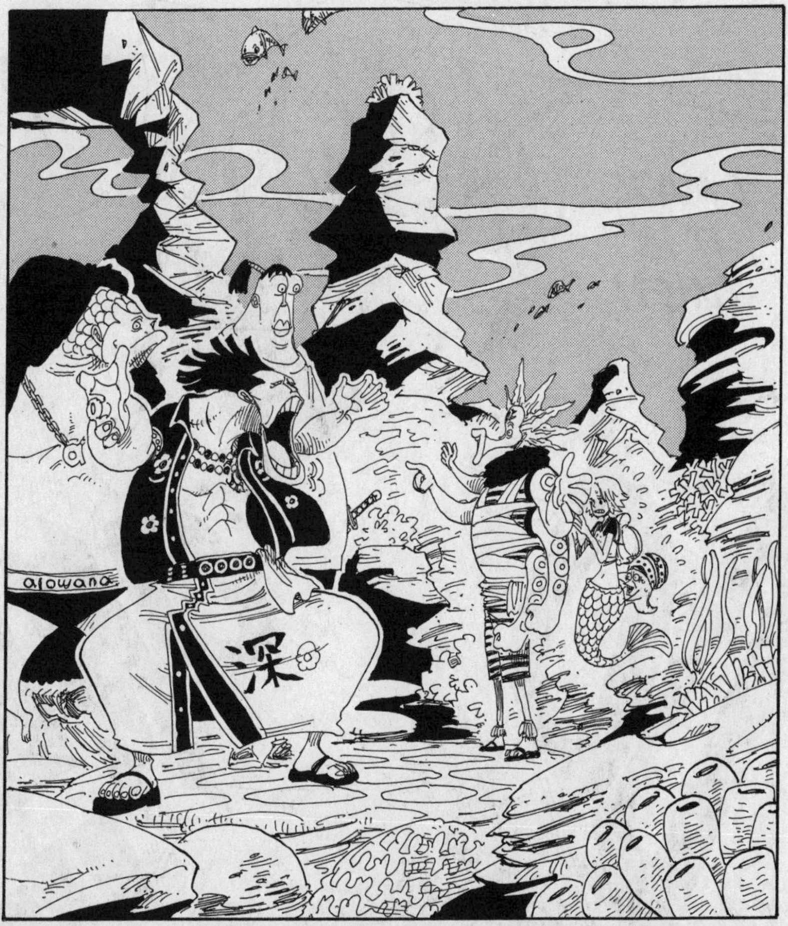
aiowana
深

HACHI'S WALK ON THE SEAFLOOR, VOL. 15:
"A REUNION WITH OLD COMRADES"

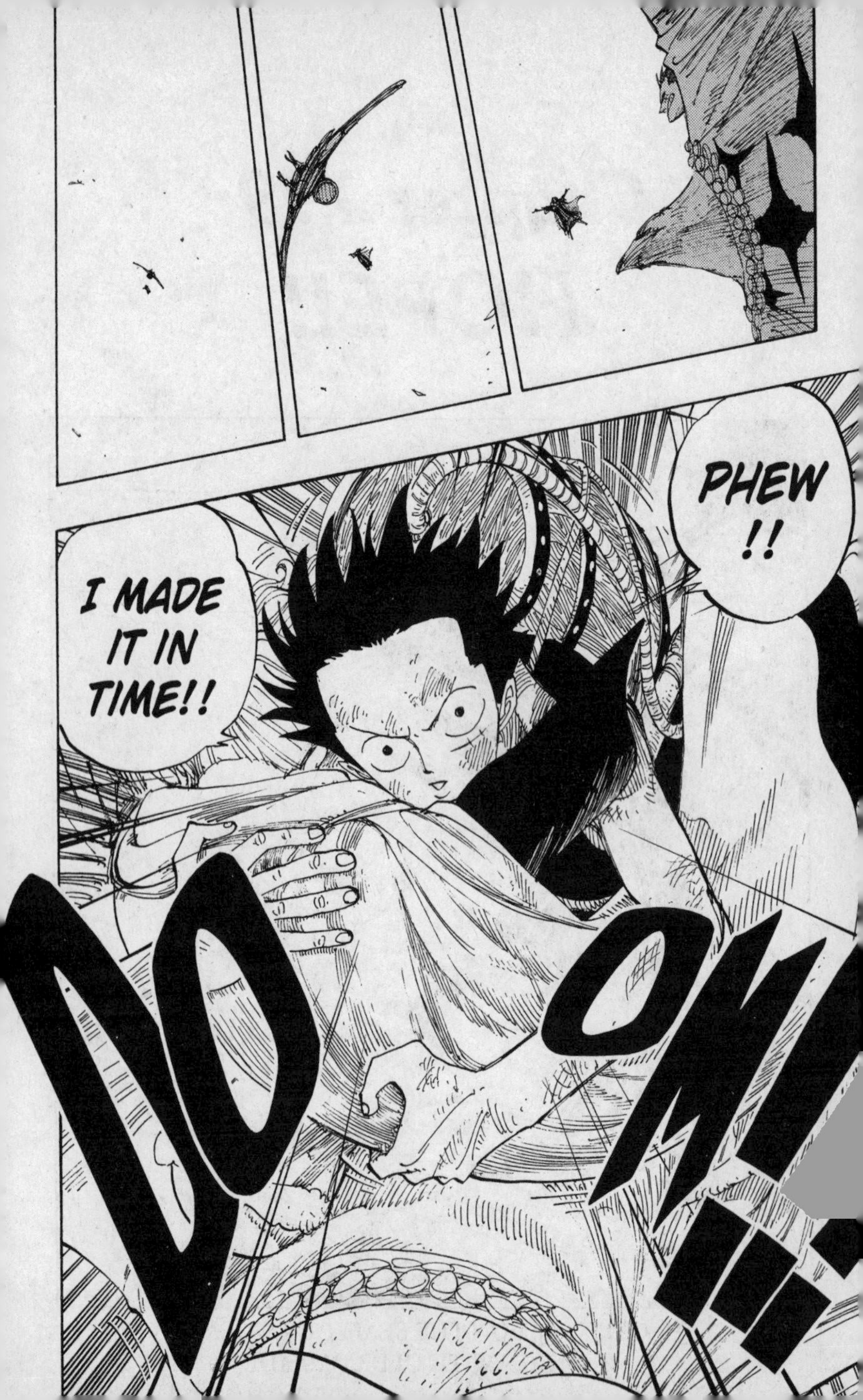
PHEW!!
I MADE IT IN TIME!!
DOOM!!

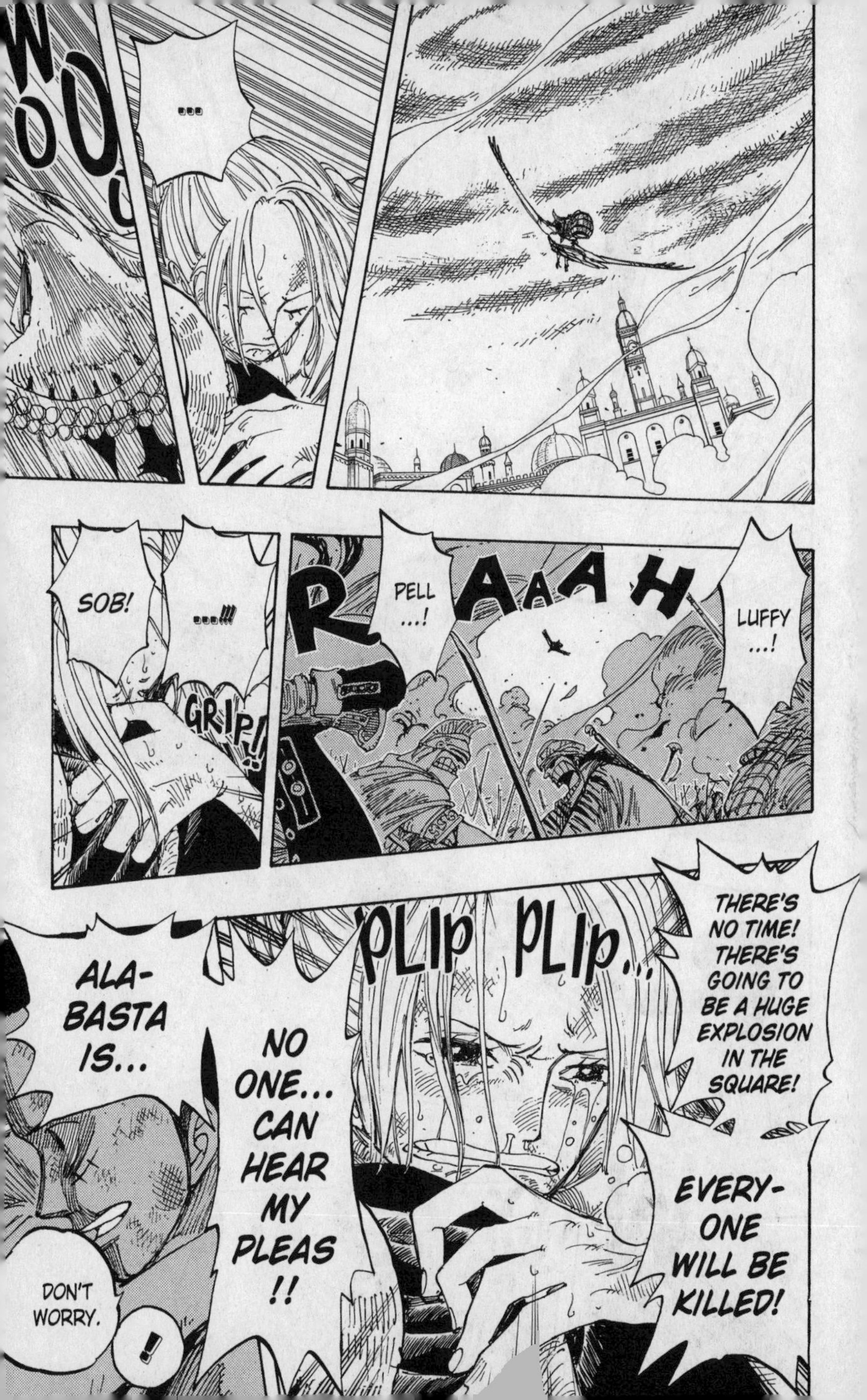

...
WOO
LUFFY ...!
RAAAH
PELL ...!
...!!!
SOB!
GRIP!!
THERE'S NO TIME! THERE'S GOING TO BE A HUGE EXPLOSION IN THE SQUARE!
PLIP PLIP...
EVERY-ONE WILL BE KILLED!
NO ONE... CAN HEAR MY PLEAS!!
ALA-BASTA IS...
!
DON'T WORRY.

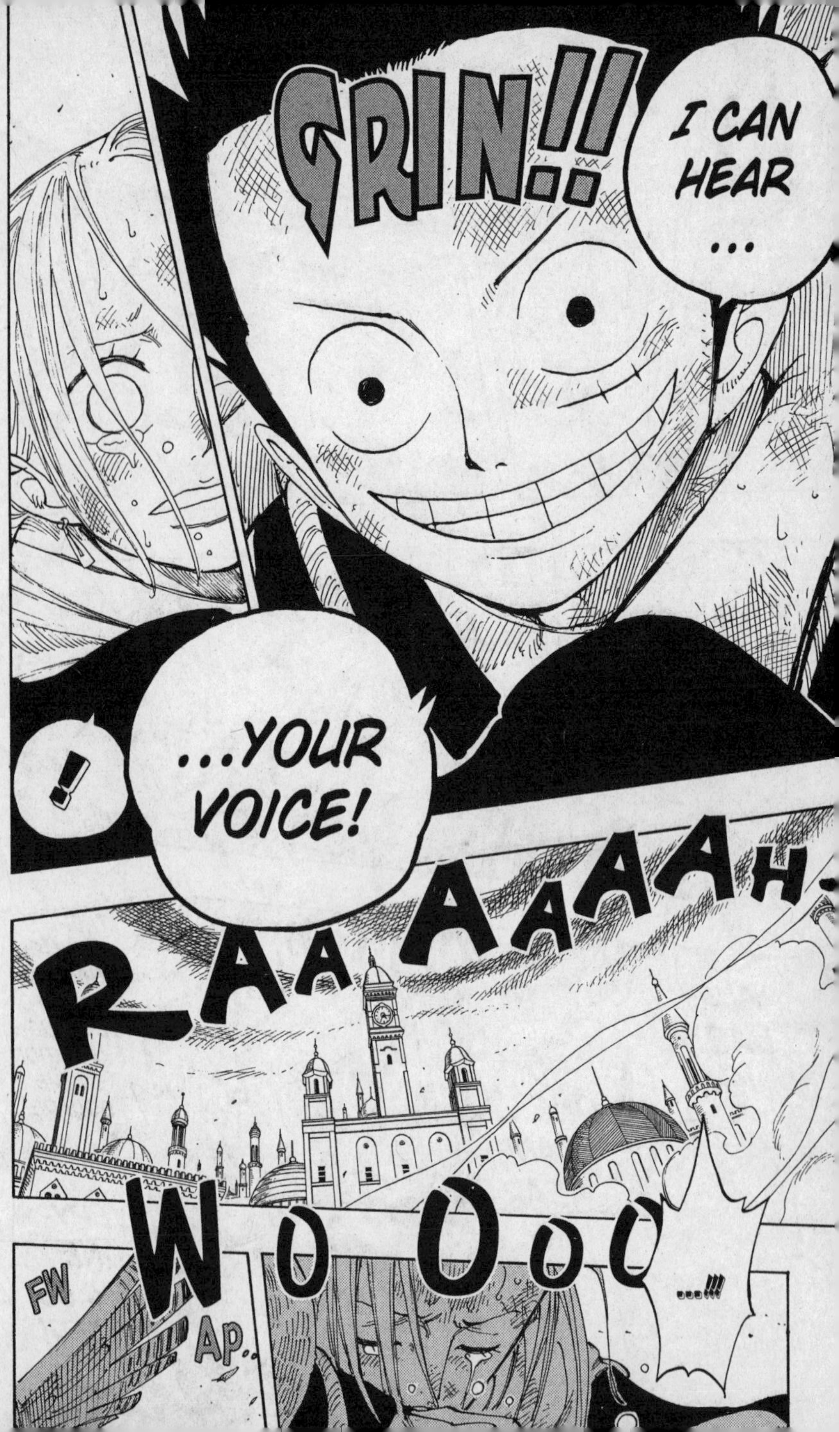
I CAN HEAR ...
GRIN!!
...YOUR VOICE!
!
RAAAAAAH-
WOOOO...!!!
FWAP..

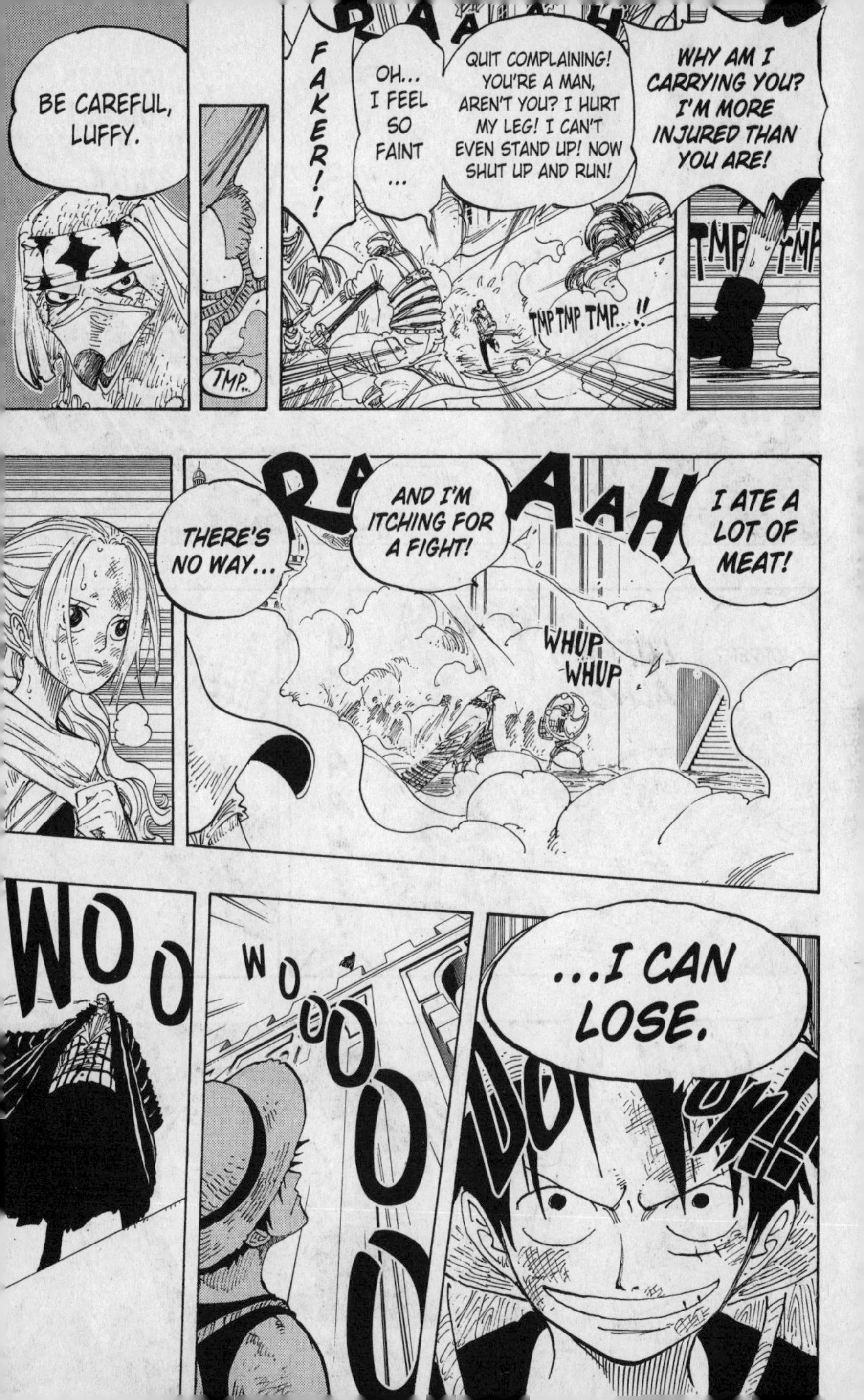
WHY AM I CARRYING YOU? I'M MORE INJURED THAN YOU ARE!
TMP TMP
RAAAH
QUIT COMPLAINING! YOU'RE A MAN, AREN'T YOU? I HURT MY LEG! I CAN'T EVEN STAND UP! NOW SHUT UP AND RUN!
OH... I FEEL SO FAINT ...
FAKER!!
TMP TMP TMP...!!
TMP...
BE CAREFUL, LUFFY.
I ATE A LOT OF MEAT!
RAAAH
AND I'M ITCHING FOR A FIGHT!
THERE'S NO WAY...
WHUP WHUP
...I CAN LOSE.
WOOOOOO
WOO

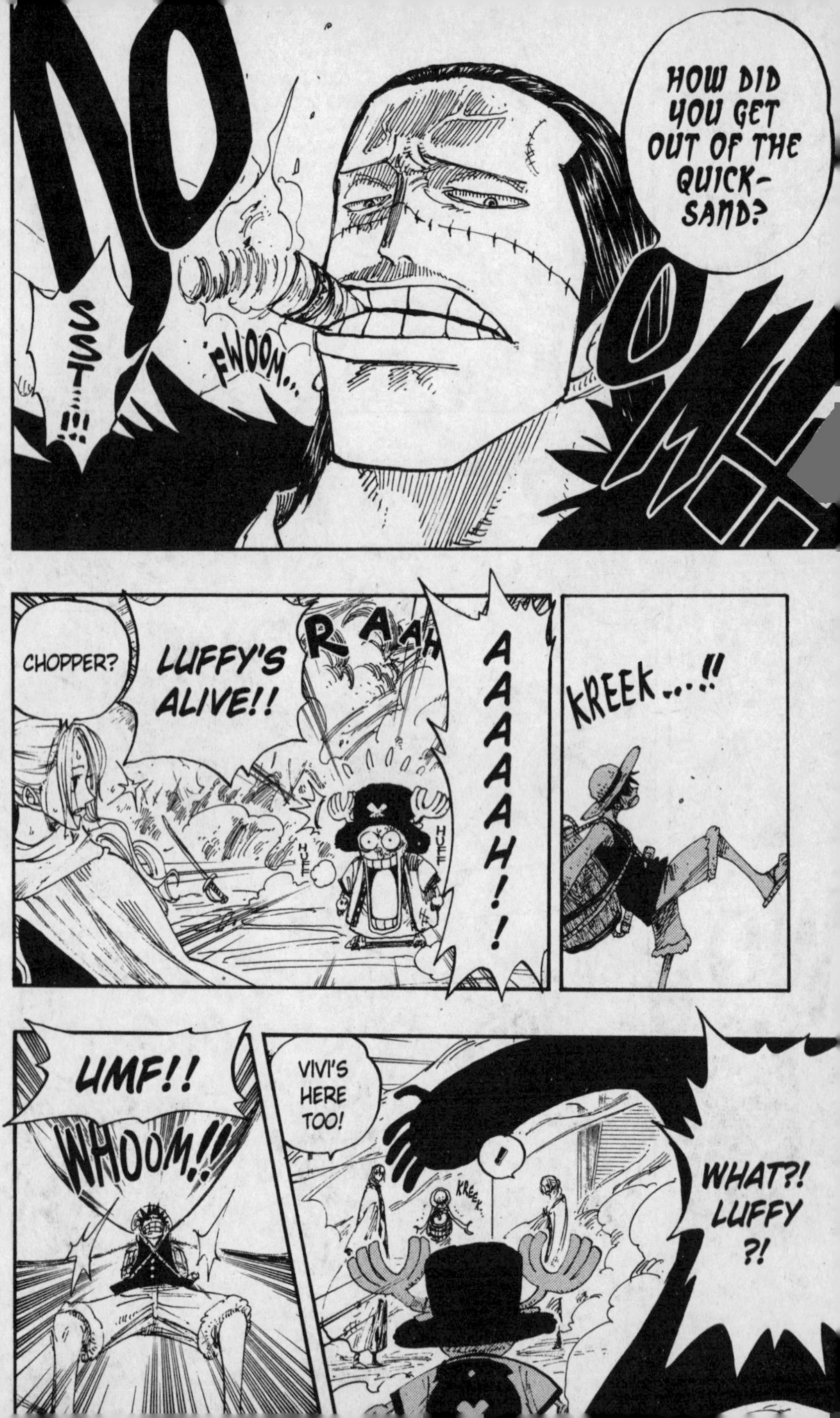
HOW DID YOU GET OUT OF THE QUICK-SAND?
FWOOM...
SSST...!!!
KREEK...!!
AAAAAAH!!
RAAH
HUFF
HUFF
LUFFY'S ALIVE!!
CHOPPER?
WHAT?! LUFFY ?!
!
KREEK...
VIVI'S HERE TOO!
UMF!!
WHOOM!!

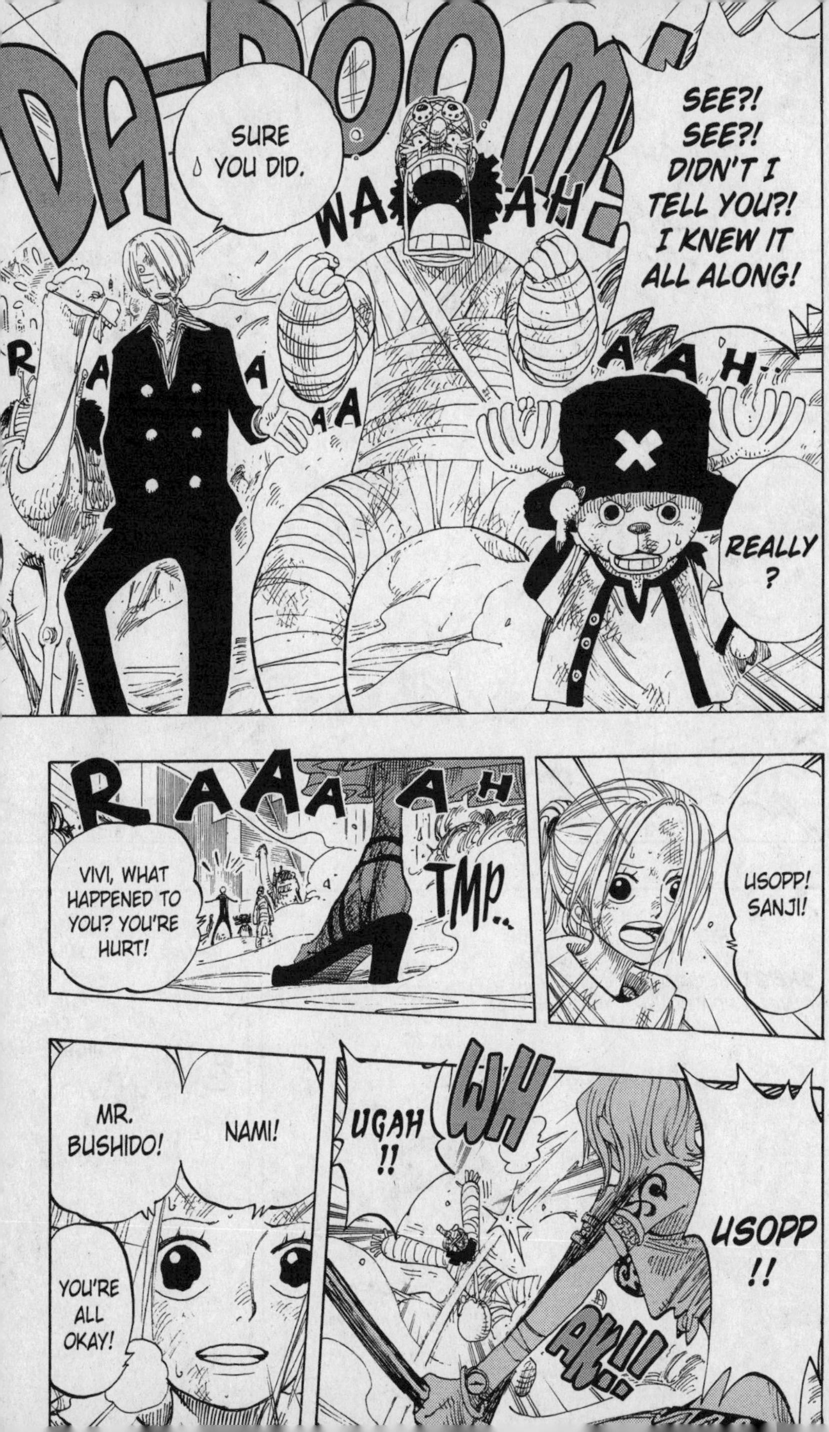
DA-DOOM!
SEE?! SEE?! DIDN'T I TELL YOU?! I KNEW IT ALL ALONG!
WA AH!
SURE YOU DID.
AAH..!
REALLY?
RAAAA
USOPP! SANJI!
RAAAAH
VIVI, WHAT HAPPENED TO YOU? YOU'RE HURT!
TMP...
WH
USOPP!!
UGAH!!
AK!!..
NAMI!
MR. BUSHIDO!
YOU'RE ALL OKAY!

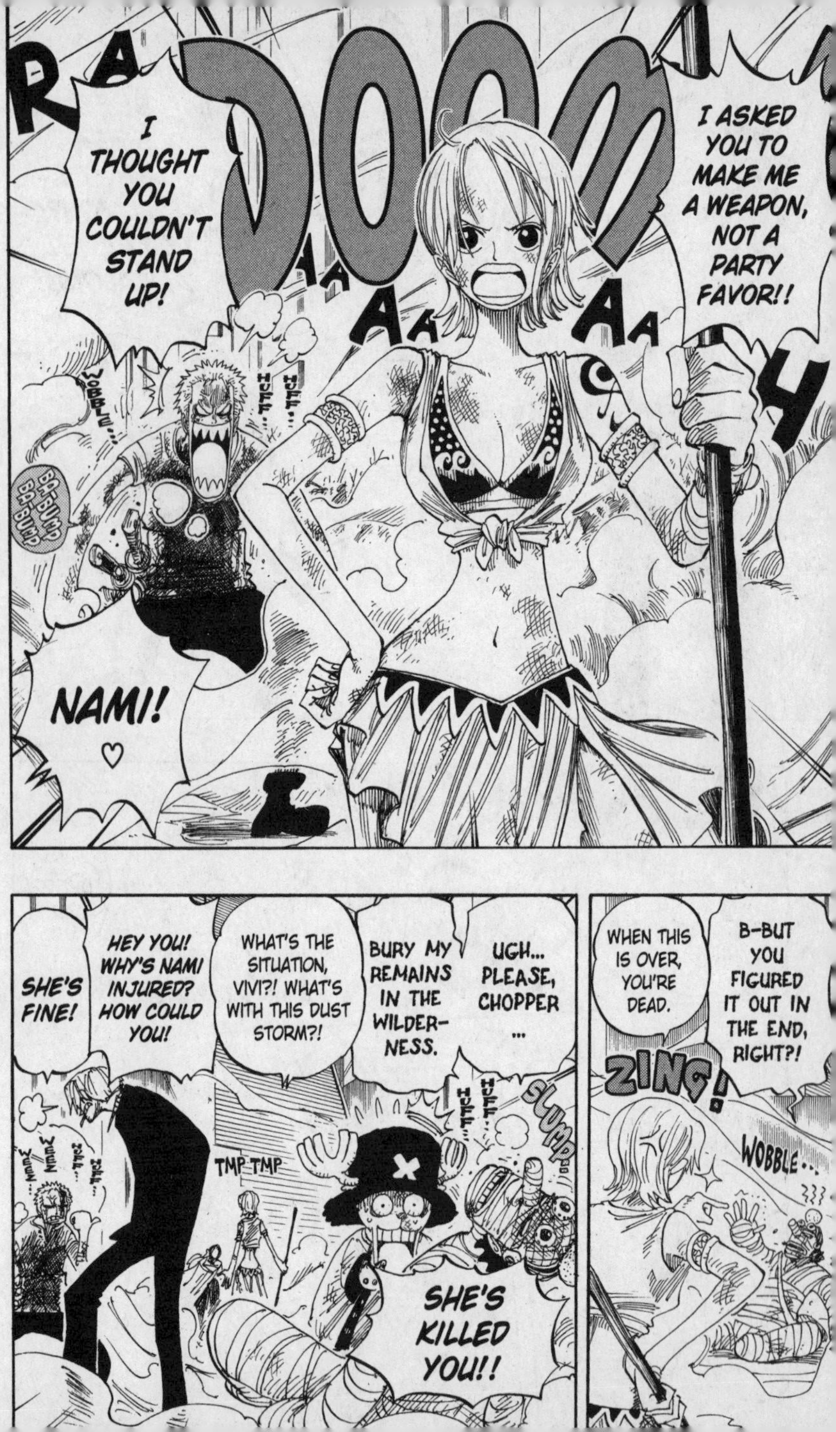
I ASKED YOU TO MAKE ME A WEAPON, NOT A PARTY FAVOR!!
I THOUGHT YOU COULDN'T STAND UP!
HUFF... HUFF...
WOBBLE...
BA-BUMP BA-BUMP
NAMI! ♡
B-BUT YOU FIGURED IT OUT IN THE END, RIGHT?!
WHEN THIS IS OVER, YOU'RE DEAD.
ZING!
WOBBLE...
UGH... PLEASE, CHOPPER ...
BURY MY REMAINS IN THE WILDER- NESS.
SLUMP
HUFF... HUFF...
WHAT'S THE SITUATION, VIVI?! WHAT'S WITH THIS DUST STORM?!
HEY YOU! WHY'S NAMI INJURED? HOW COULD YOU!
SHE'S FINE!
TMP TMP
HUFF... HUFF...
WEEN WEEN...
SHE'S KILLED YOU!!

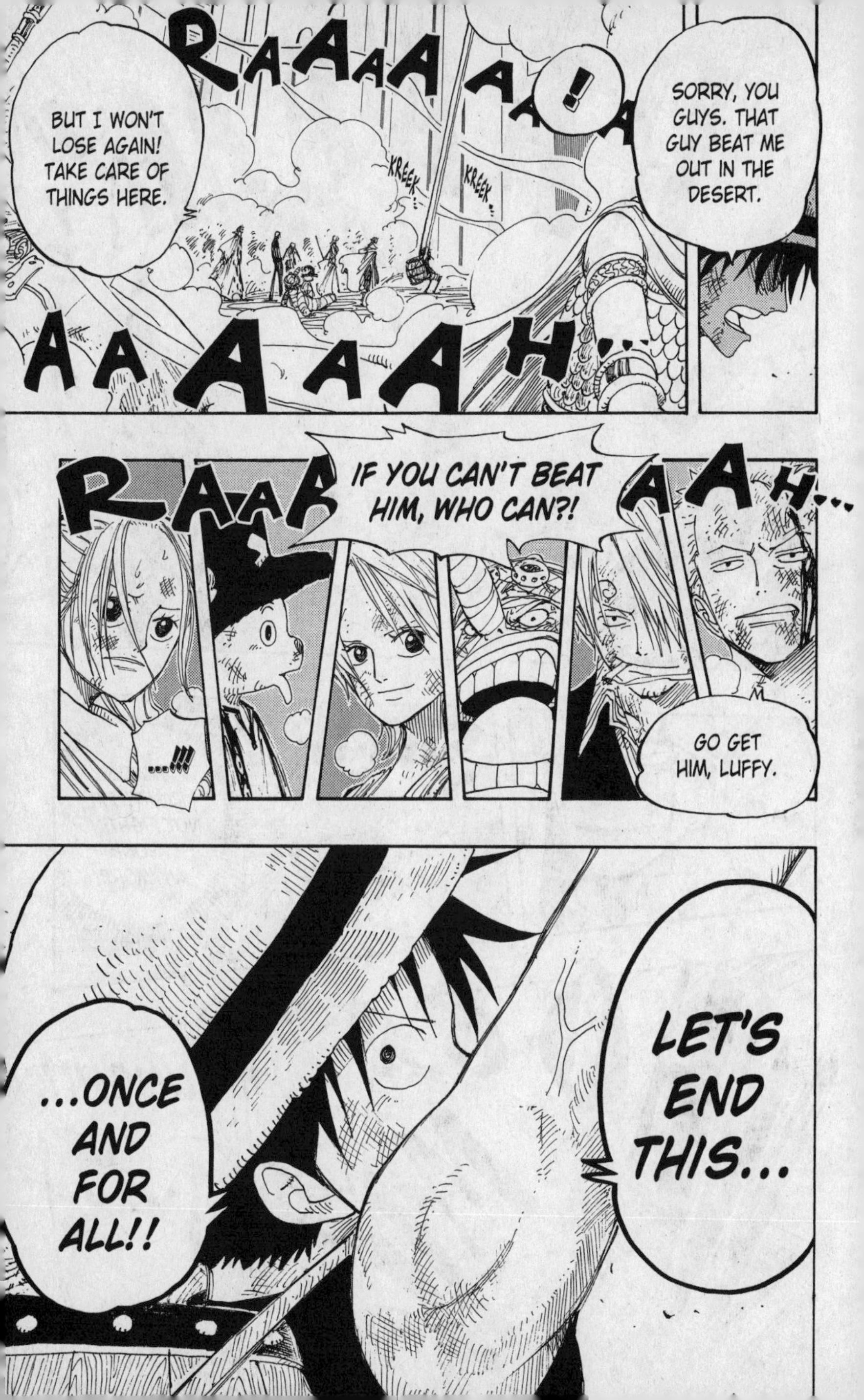

SORRY, YOU GUYS. THAT GUY BEAT ME OUT IN THE DESERT.
RAAAAAAA!
KREEK
KREEK
BUT I WON'T LOSE AGAIN! TAKE CARE OF THINGS HERE.
AAAAAAH...
RAAAAAH...
GO GET HIM, LUFFY.
IF YOU CAN'T BEAT HIM, WHO CAN?!
...!!!
LET'S END THIS...
...ONCE AND FOR ALL!!

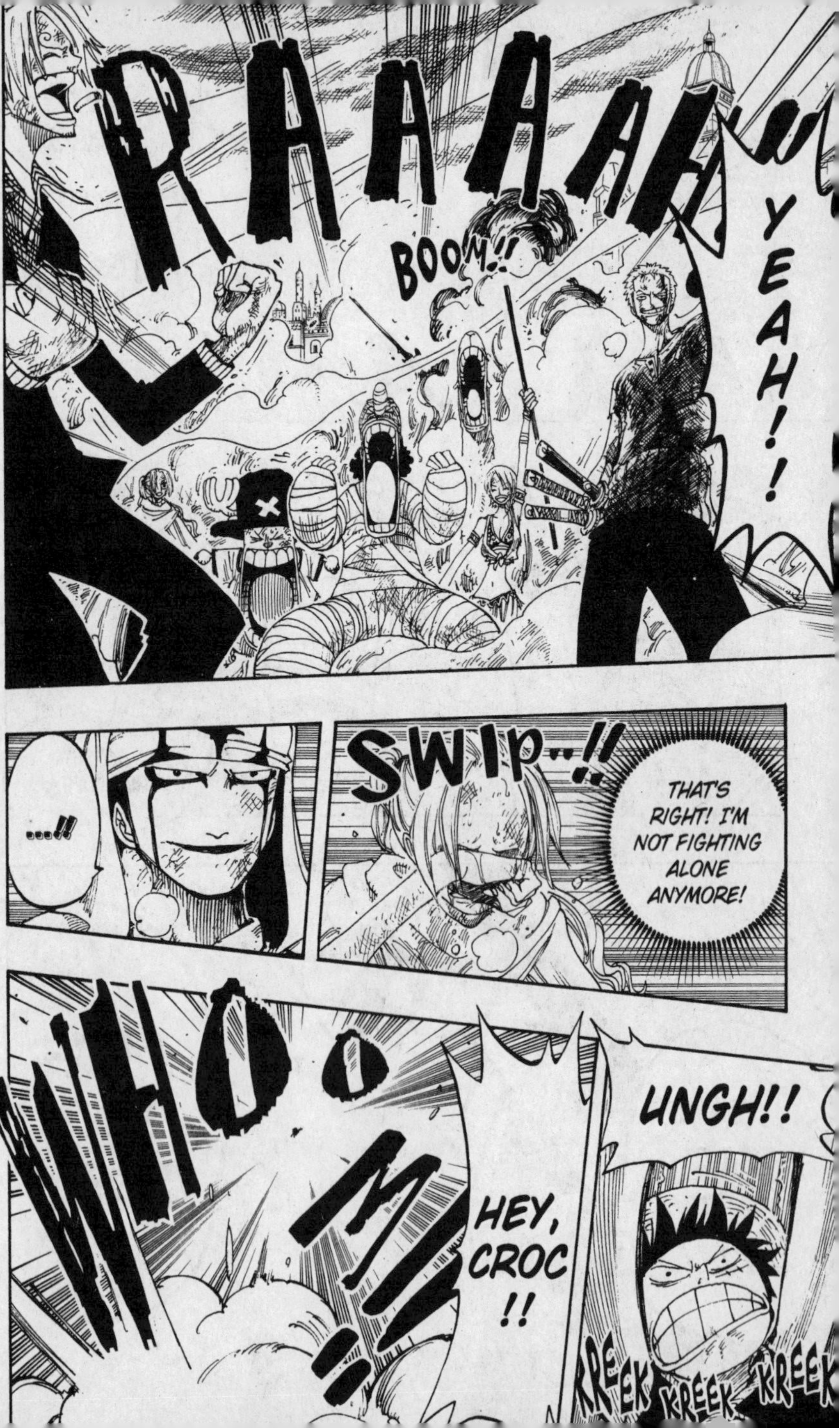

RAAAAH
YEAH!!
BOOM!!
THAT'S RIGHT! I'M NOT FIGHTING ALONE ANYMORE!
SWIP..!!
...!!
UNGH!!
KREEK KREEK KREEK
HEY, CROC!!
WHOOM!!

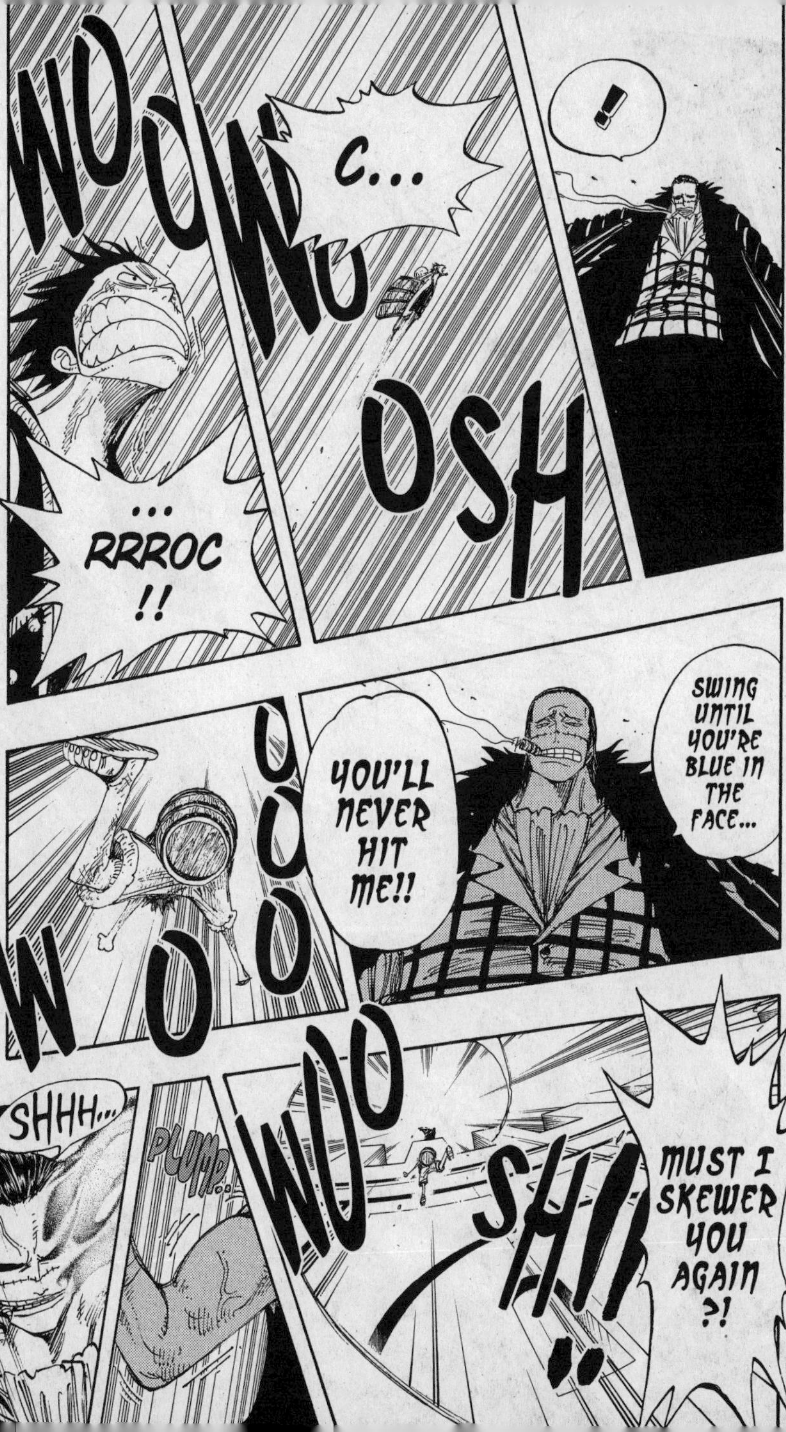
!
C...
WOOOSH
...RRROC!!
SWING UNTIL YOU'RE BLUE IN THE FACE...
YOU'LL NEVER HIT ME!!
WOOOOOO
MUST I SKEWER YOU AGAIN?!
WOOSH!!
SHHH...
PLUMP..

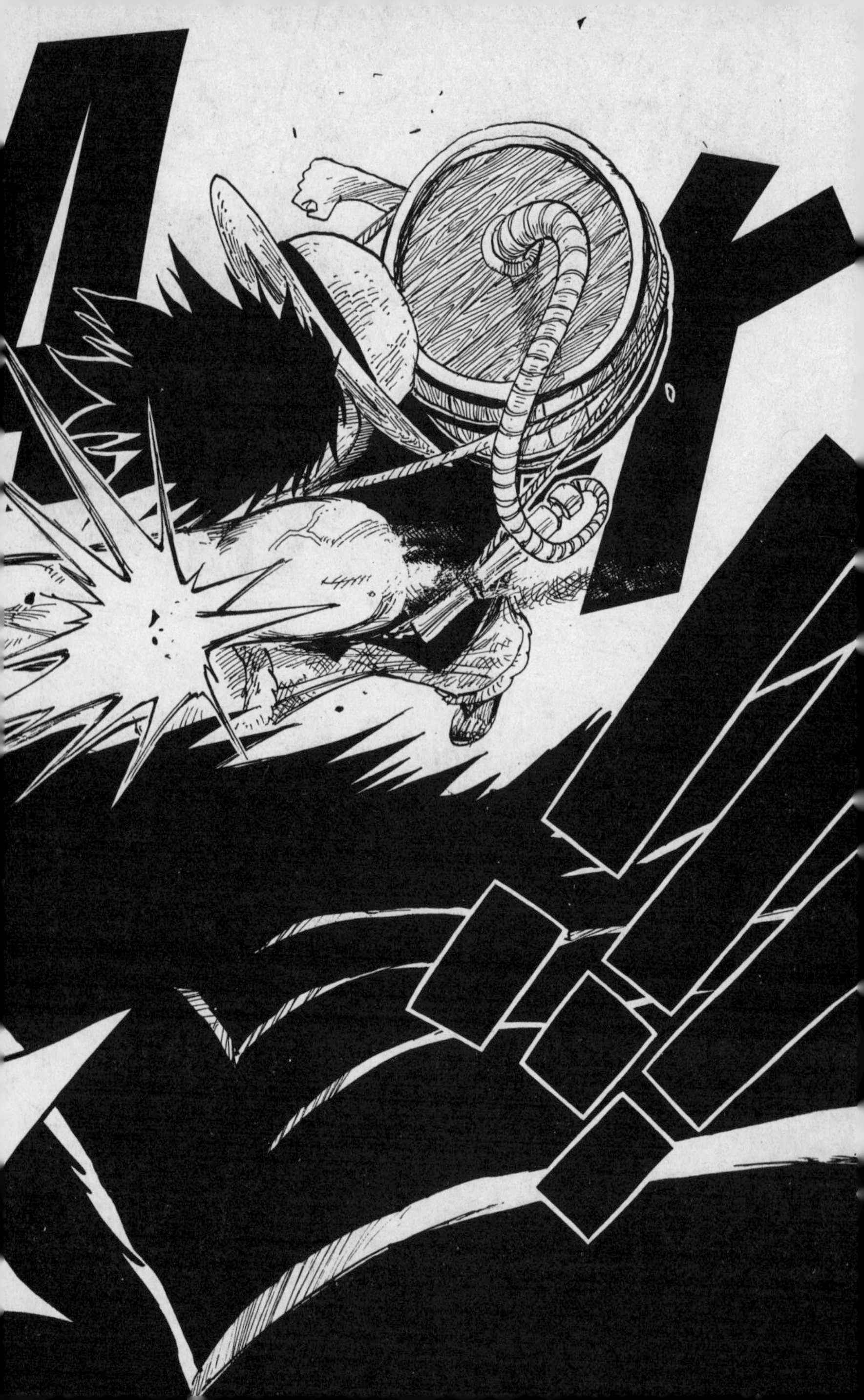

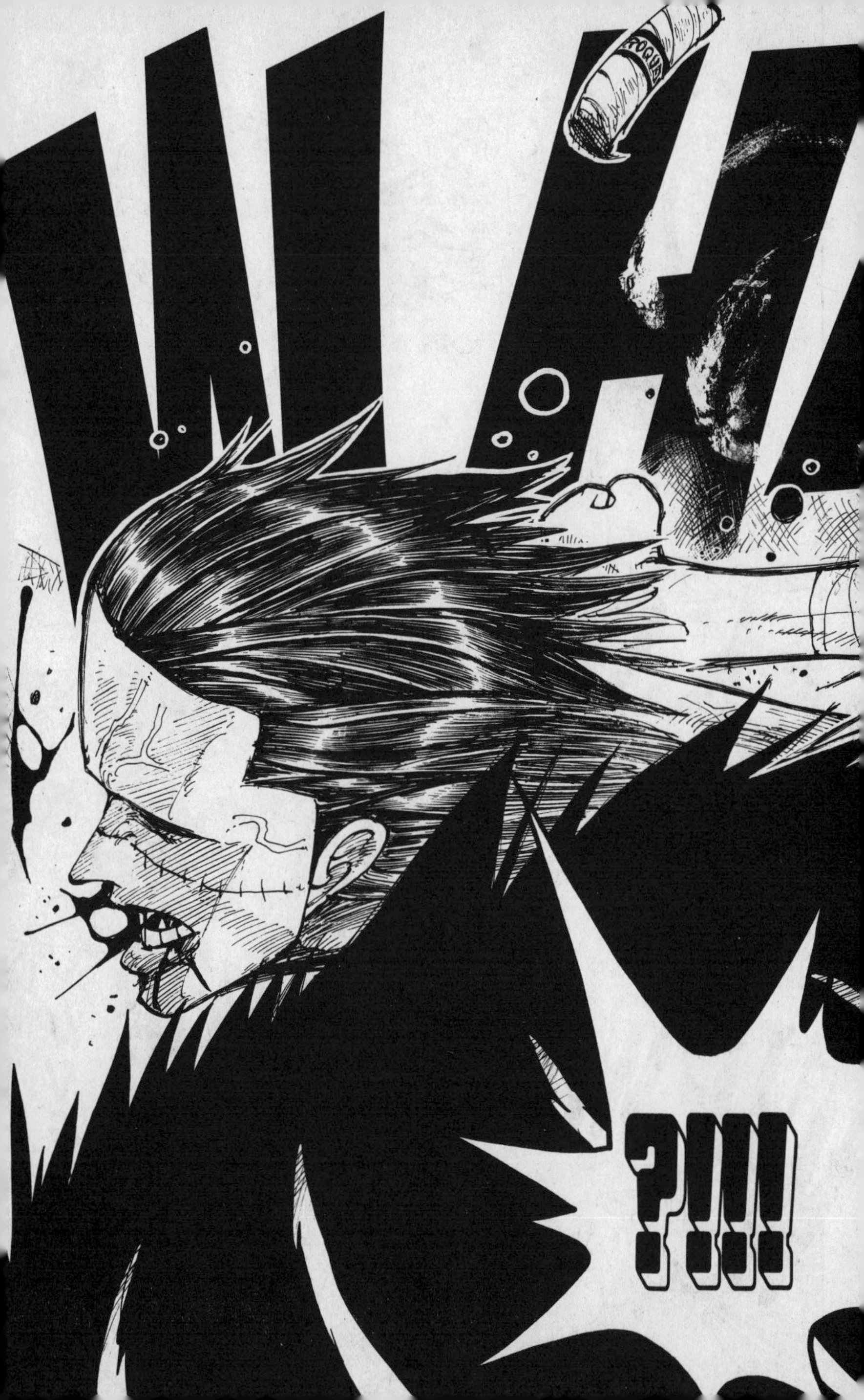
?!!!

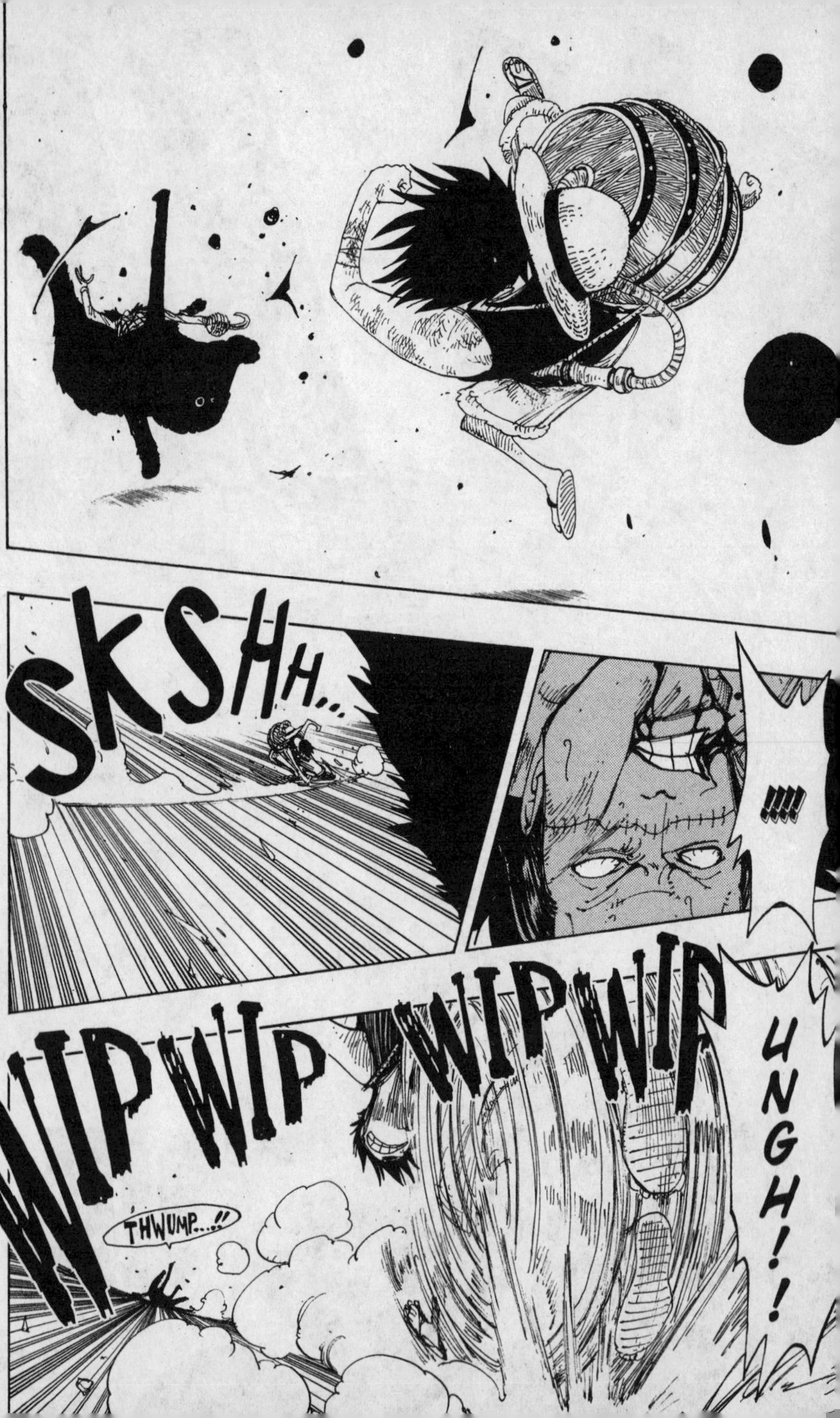
!!!!
SKSHH...
UNGH!!
WIP WIP WIP WIP
THWUMP...!!

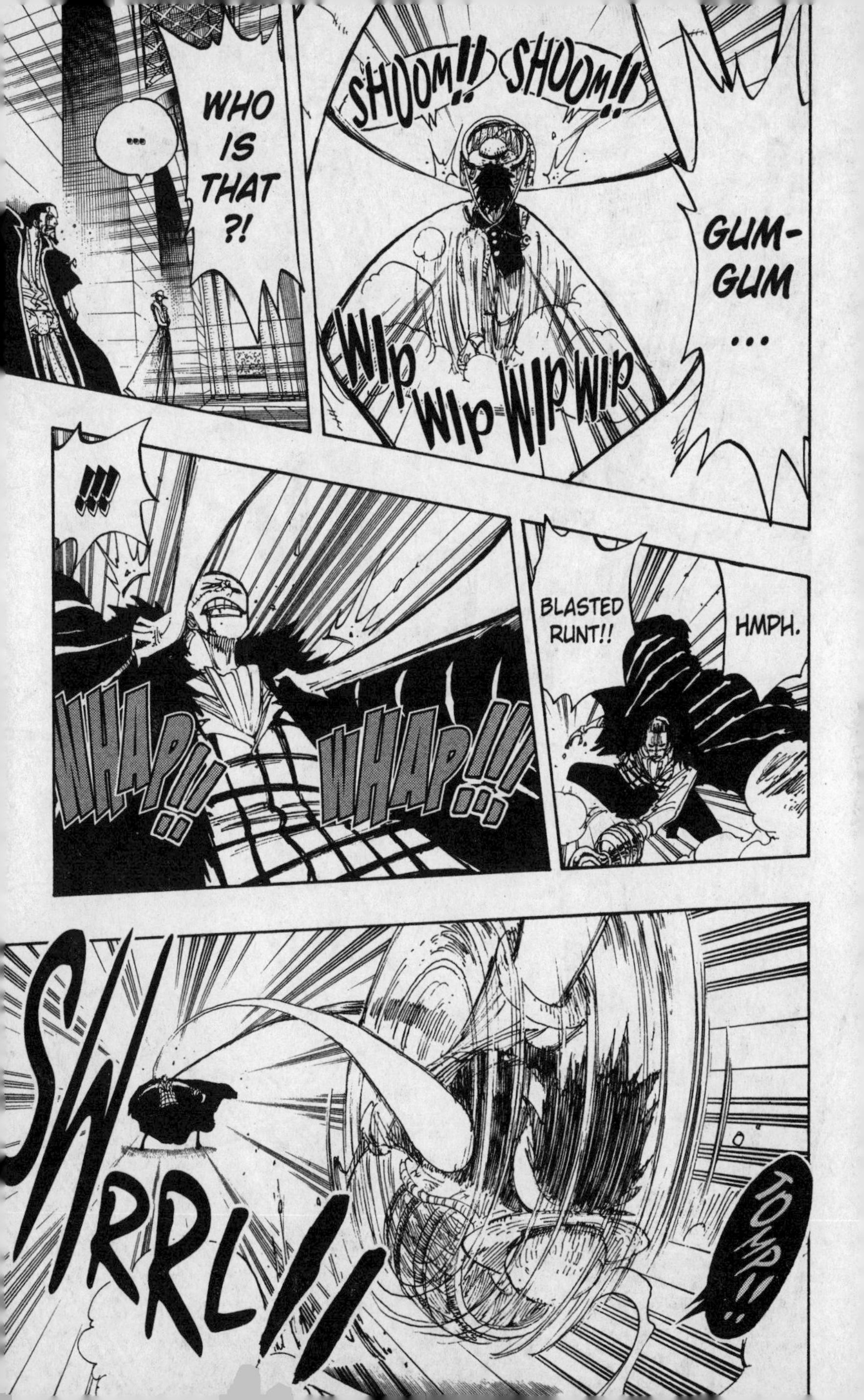
SHOOM!!
SHOOM!!
GUM-GUM...
WIP WIP WIP WIP
WHO IS THAT?!
...
HMPH.
BLASTED RUNT!!
!!!
WHAP!!!
WHAP!!!
TOMP!!
SWIRRL!!

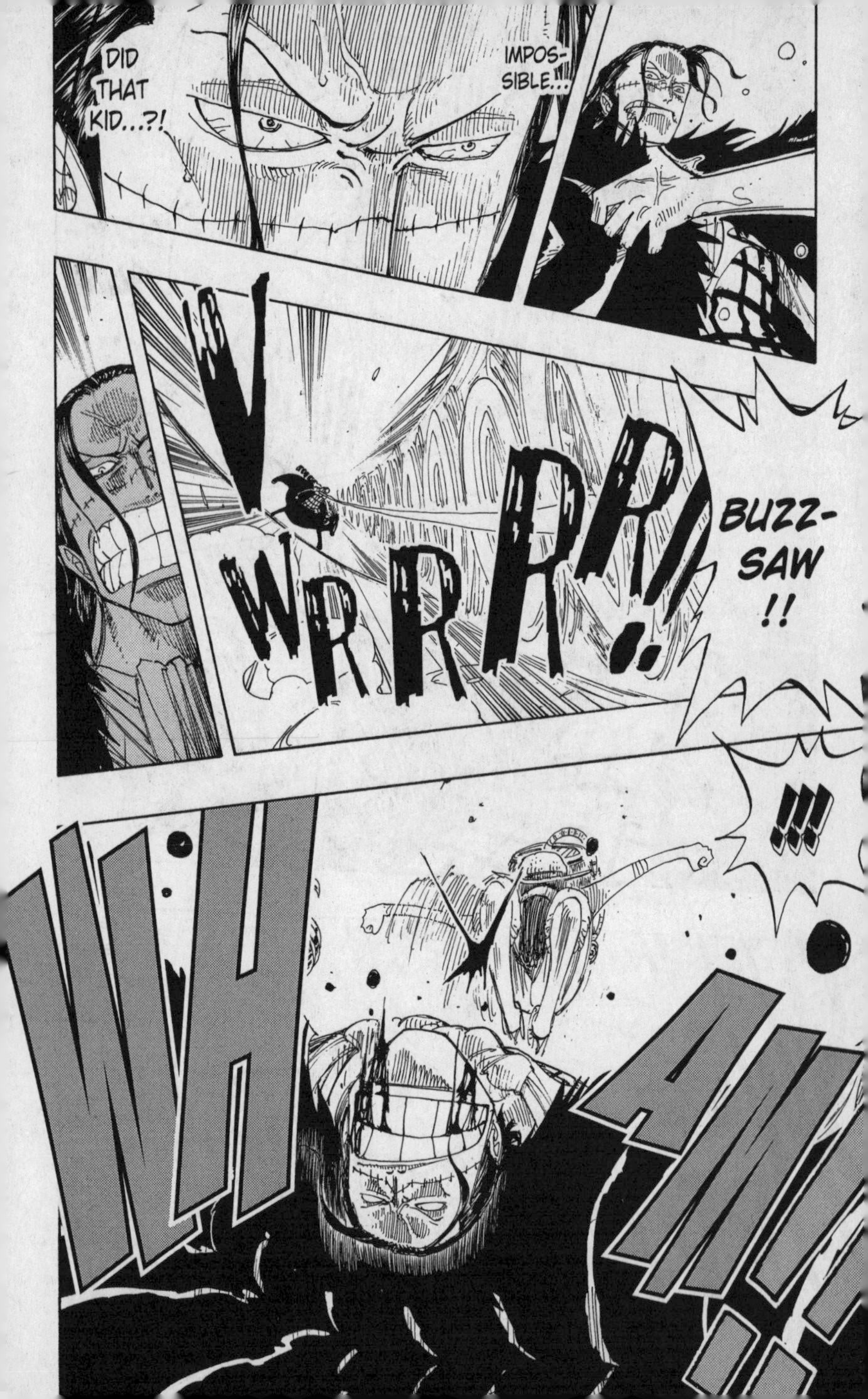
IMPOS-
SIBLE...
DID
THAT
KID...?!
BUZZ-
SAW
!!
!!!

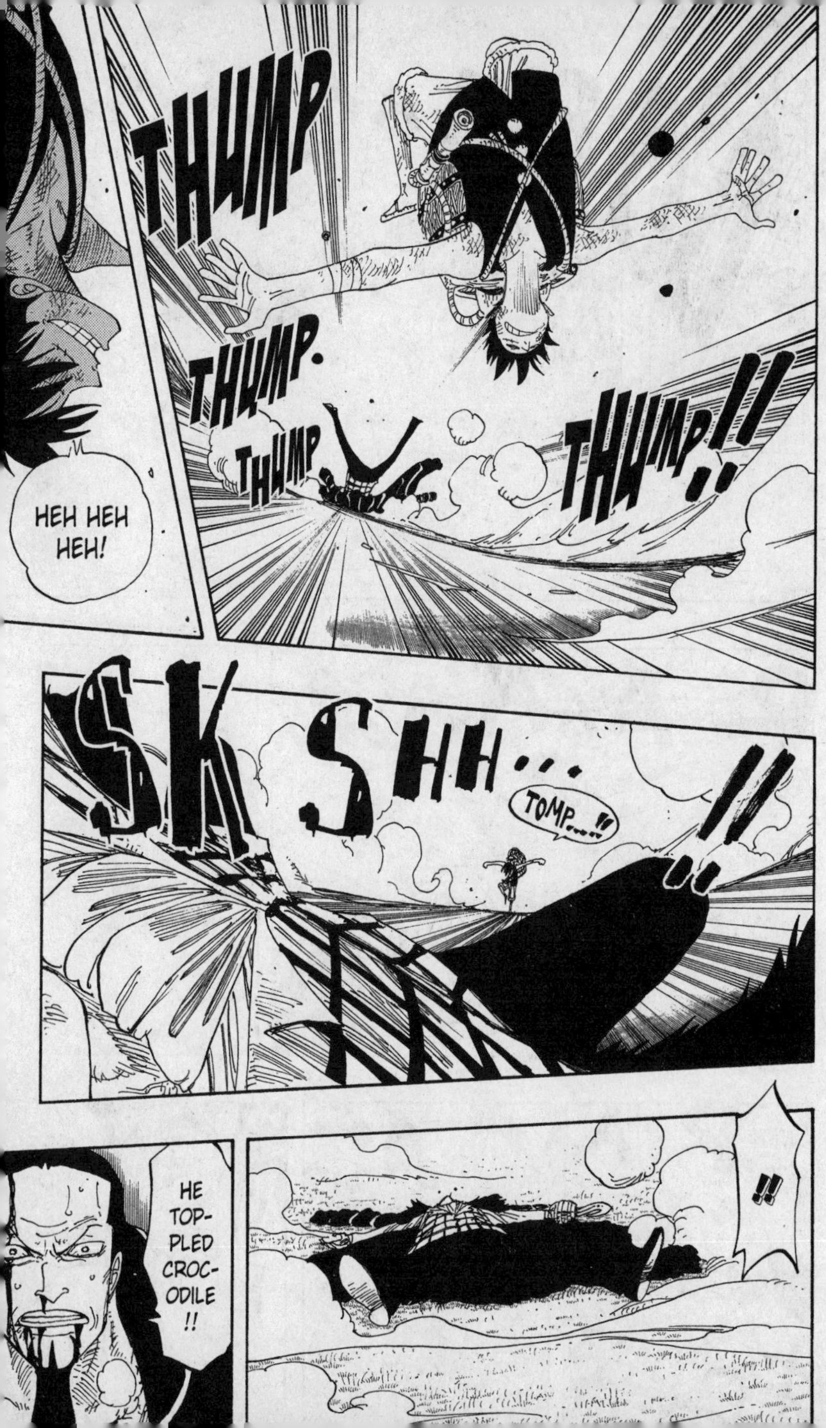
THUMP
THUMP.
THUMP
THUMP!!
HEH HEH HEH!
SKSHH...!!
TOMP...!!
!!
HE TOP-PLED CROC-ODILE!!

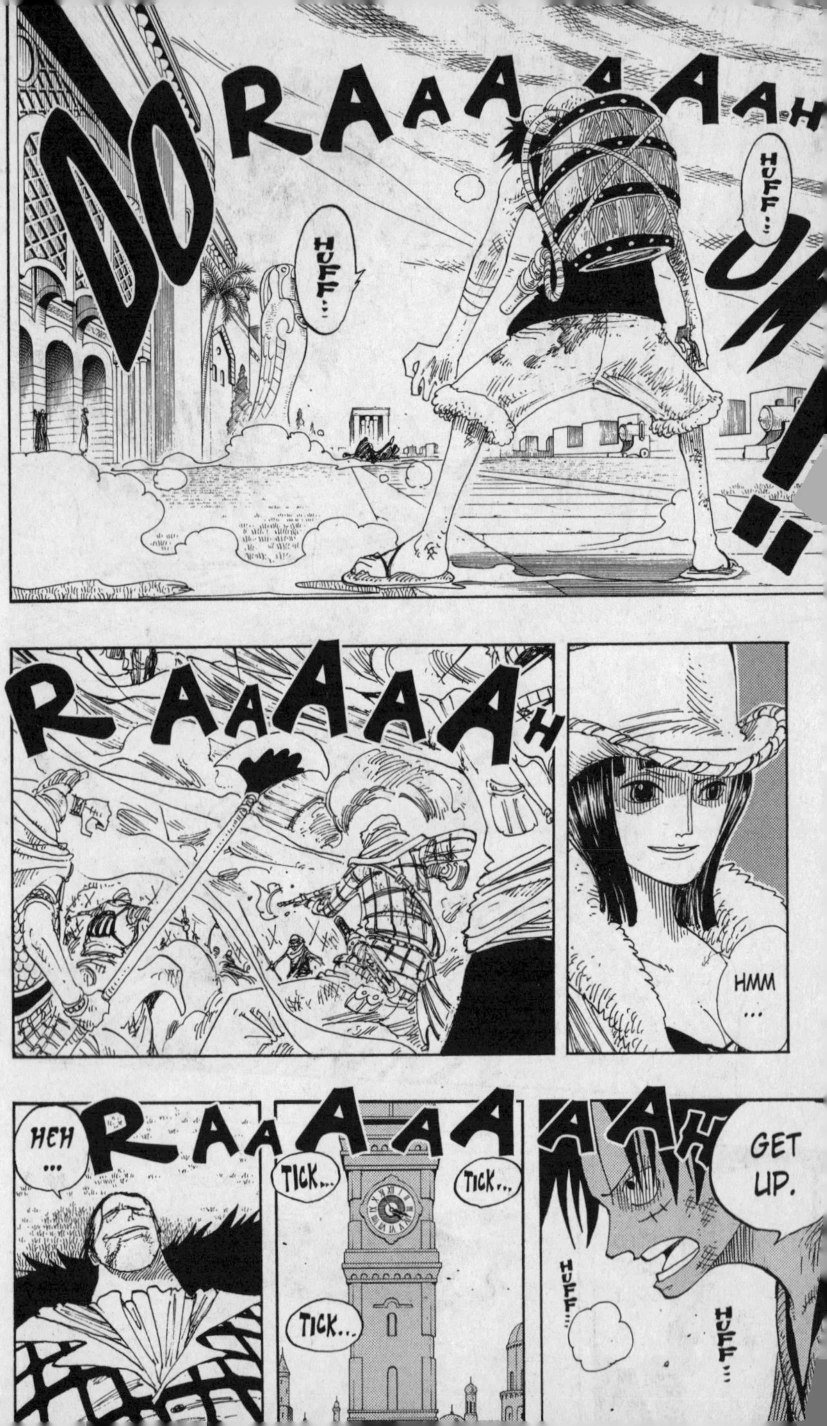
DORAAAAAH
HUFF...
HUFF...
HMM...
RAAAAAH
RAAAAAAAAH
GET UP.
HUFF...
HUFF...
TICK...
TICK...
TICK...
HEH...

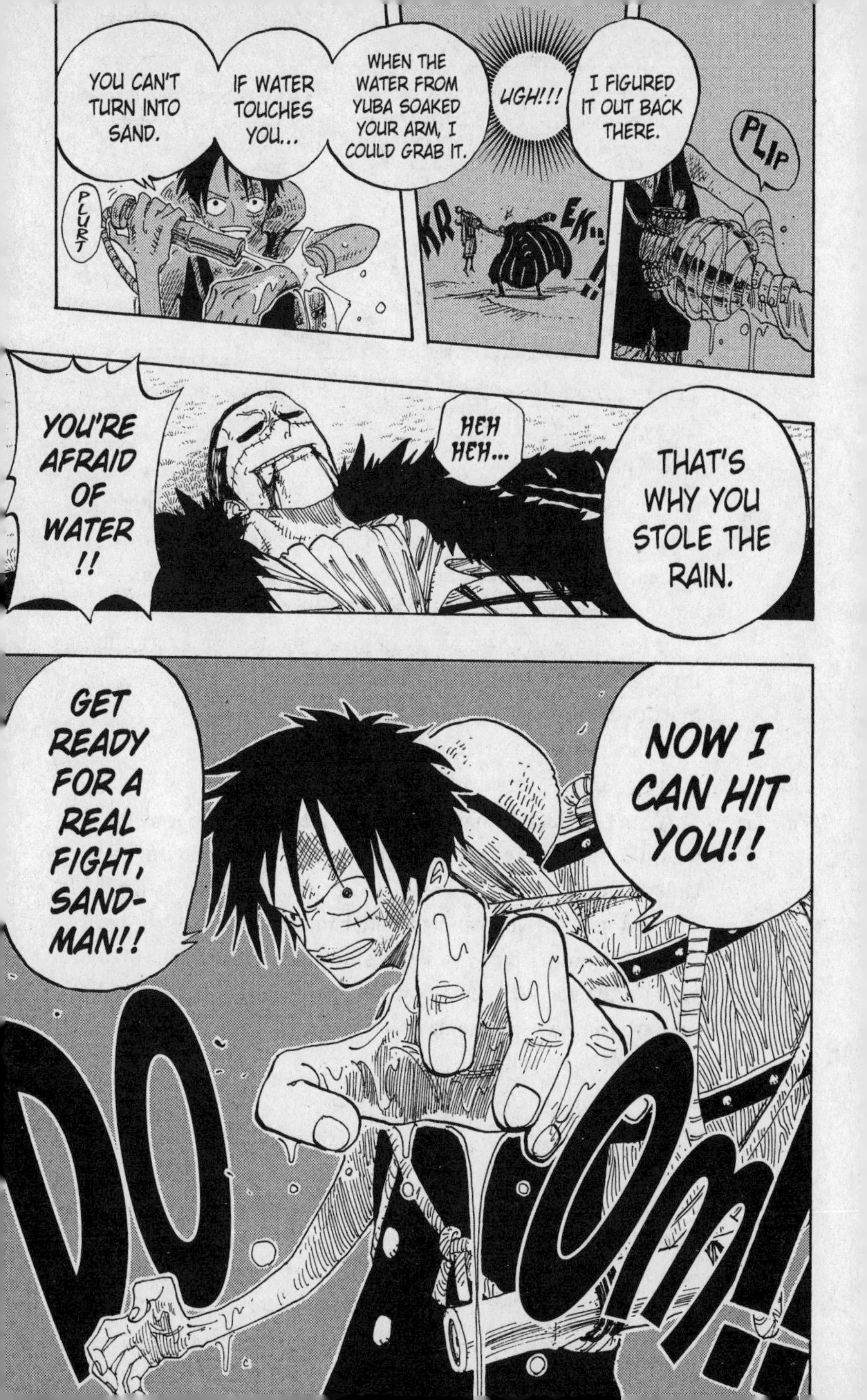

I FIGURED IT OUT BACK THERE.
PLIP
UGH!!!
KR-EK!!
WHEN THE WATER FROM YUBA SOAKED YOUR ARM, I COULD GRAB IT.
IF WATER TOUCHES YOU...
YOU CAN'T TURN INTO SAND.
PLURT
THAT'S WHY YOU STOLE THE RAIN.
HEH HEH...
YOU'RE AFRAID OF WATER!!
NOW I CAN HIT YOU!!
GET READY FOR A REAL FIGHT, SANDMAN!!
DOOM!!

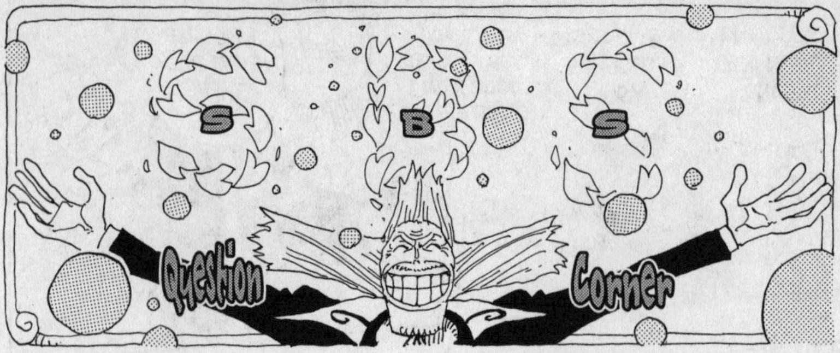
S B S
Question Corner

Reader: The town on the other side of the tunnel was very strange.

Oda: Okay, let's continue.

Reader: Hey, Mr. Bon Clay! Yeah, you! You brag about your dancing too much! Your *port de bras* stinks! Get it right! And your toe shoes aren't even tied properly! The ribbons go around your ankles… Your **ankles!** They should go two centimeters higher. And your Swan Arabesque--ha! You're not raising your leg correctly! You won't be ready to attempt an attitude turn for at least another hundred years.
Start over from the beginning! And shave your legs!
--Studied Ballet for Ten Years

Oda: Hmm... Well, I called him. Here he is.

Mr. 2: **This ain't no joke!! Shave my legs?! Never! If I shaved my legs, I'd be nothing! My leg hair is what makes me unique! Unless you're saying you want to get rid of me! Is that it?! Oh, and you say you studied ballet for ten years? Well, isn't that something?! But I've been studying my Oh Come My Way Karate for 20 years! Got any complaints?! If you do, I'll be happy to give you some free lessons! I'll twirl and twirl and twirl! Yes I will!**

Oda: Okay, enough of that ham-bone.

Reader: Hello, Oda Sensei! My name is Enari. Why does Vivi always pull on Usopp's nose?

Oda: Well... Let's say there's a pot in front of you. What part of it would you grab? You'd grab the handle, right? You'd grab the part that sticks out. I guess that's the reason. It's probably the easiest place to grab. Right? I guess it just works.

Chapter 200:
WATER LUFFY

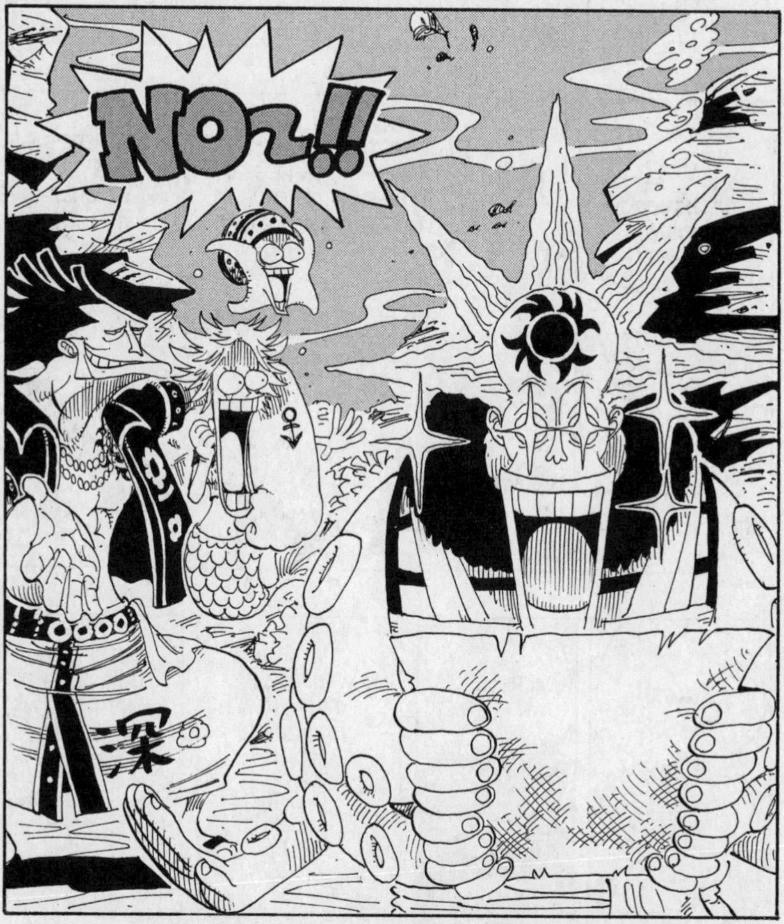
NO~!!

HACHI'S WALK ON THE SEAFLOOR, VOL. 16:
"CAMIE'S SURPRISE! A DEAL WITH THE FISH-MEN FOR THE OCTOPUS FRITTER MAP"

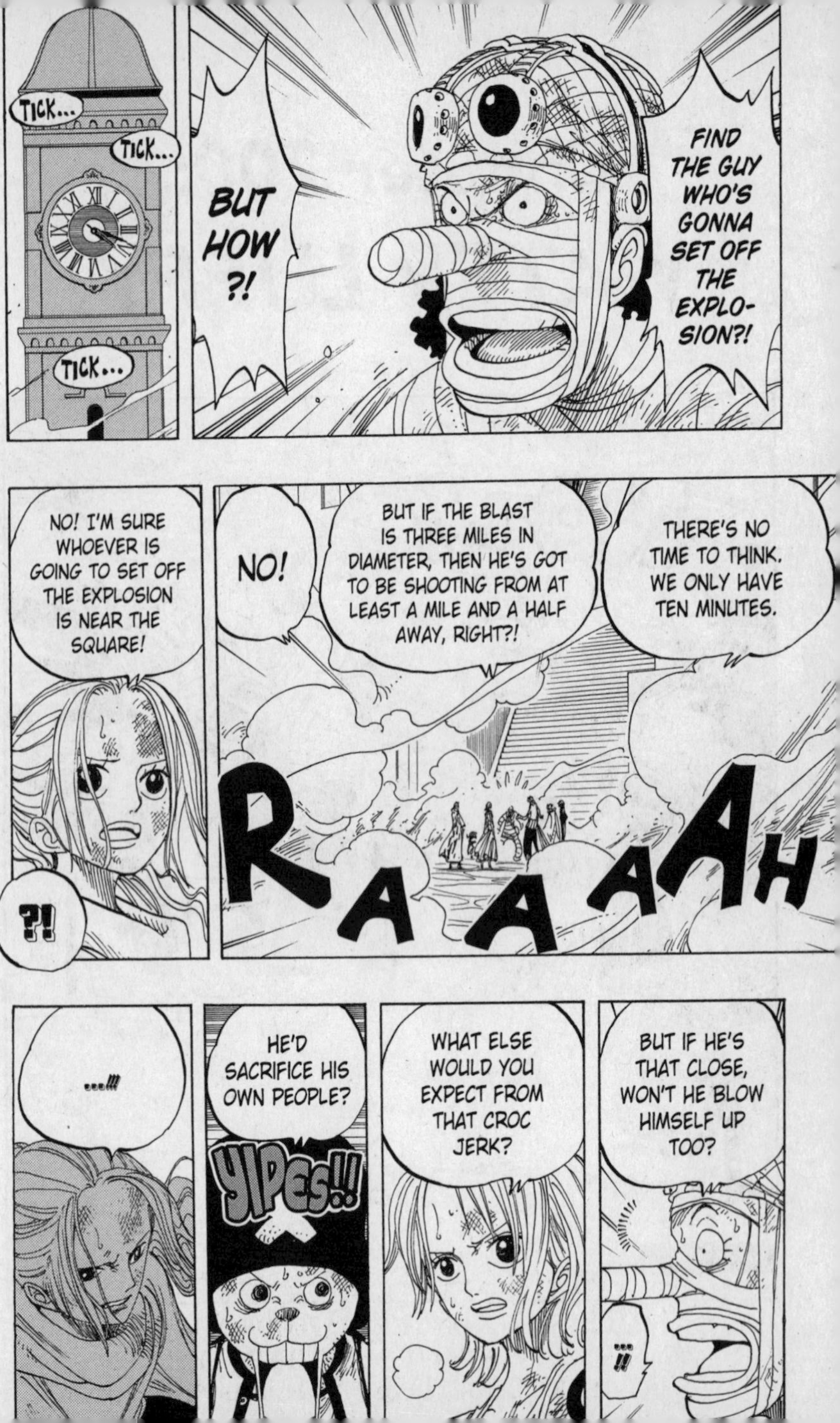

FIND THE GUY WHO'S GONNA SET OFF THE EXPLOSION?!
BUT HOW?!
TICK...
TICK...
TICK...
THERE'S NO TIME TO THINK. WE ONLY HAVE TEN MINUTES.
BUT IF THE BLAST IS THREE MILES IN DIAMETER, THEN HE'S GOT TO BE SHOOTING FROM AT LEAST A MILE AND A HALF AWAY, RIGHT?!
NO!
RAAAAAH
NO! I'M SURE WHOEVER IS GOING TO SET OFF THE EXPLOSION IS NEAR THE SQUARE!
?!
BUT IF HE'S THAT CLOSE, WON'T HE BLOW HIMSELF UP TOO?
...!!
WHAT ELSE WOULD YOU EXPECT FROM THAT CROC JERK?
HE'D SACRIFICE HIS OWN PEOPLE?
YIPES!!!
...!!!

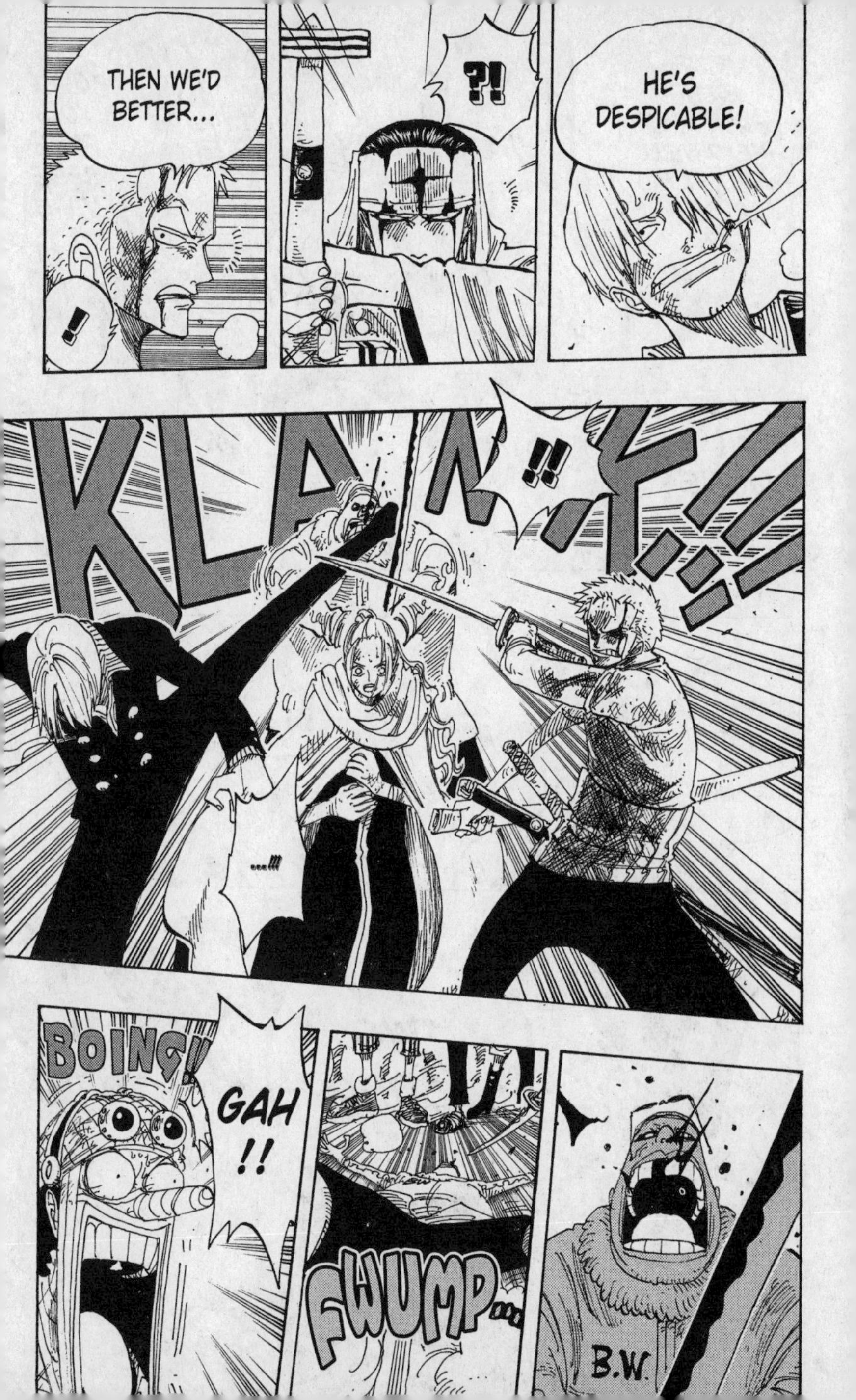
HE'S DESPICABLE!
?!
THEN WE'D BETTER...
!
KLANK!!
!!
...!!!
B.W.
FWUMP...
BOING!!
GAH !!

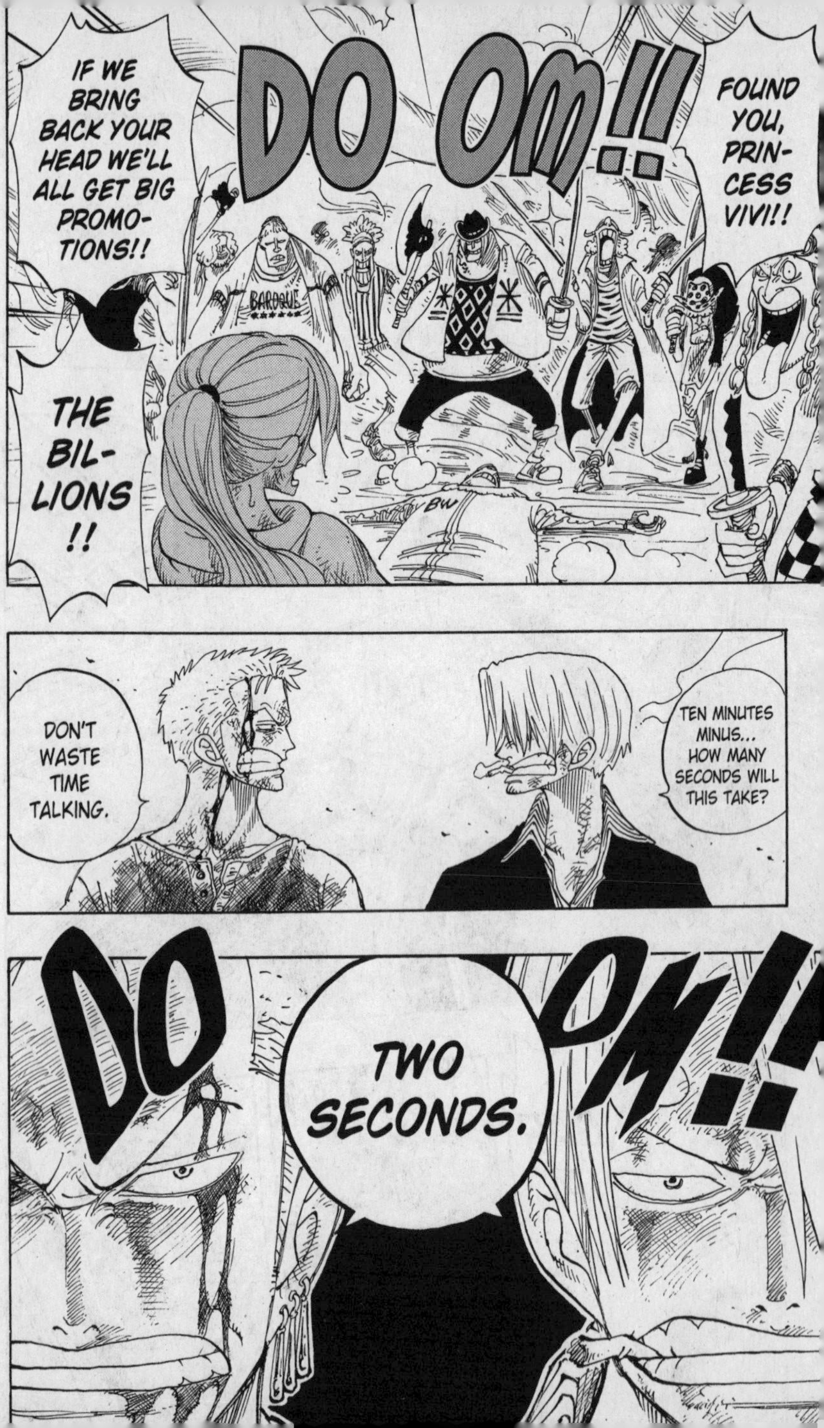
FOUND YOU, PRINCESS VIVI!!
DO OM!!
IF WE BRING BACK YOUR HEAD WE'LL ALL GET BIG PROMOTIONS!!
THE BILLIONS!!
BAROQUE
BW
TEN MINUTES MINUS... HOW MANY SECONDS WILL THIS TAKE?
DON'T WASTE TIME TALKING.
DO OM!!
TWO SECONDS.

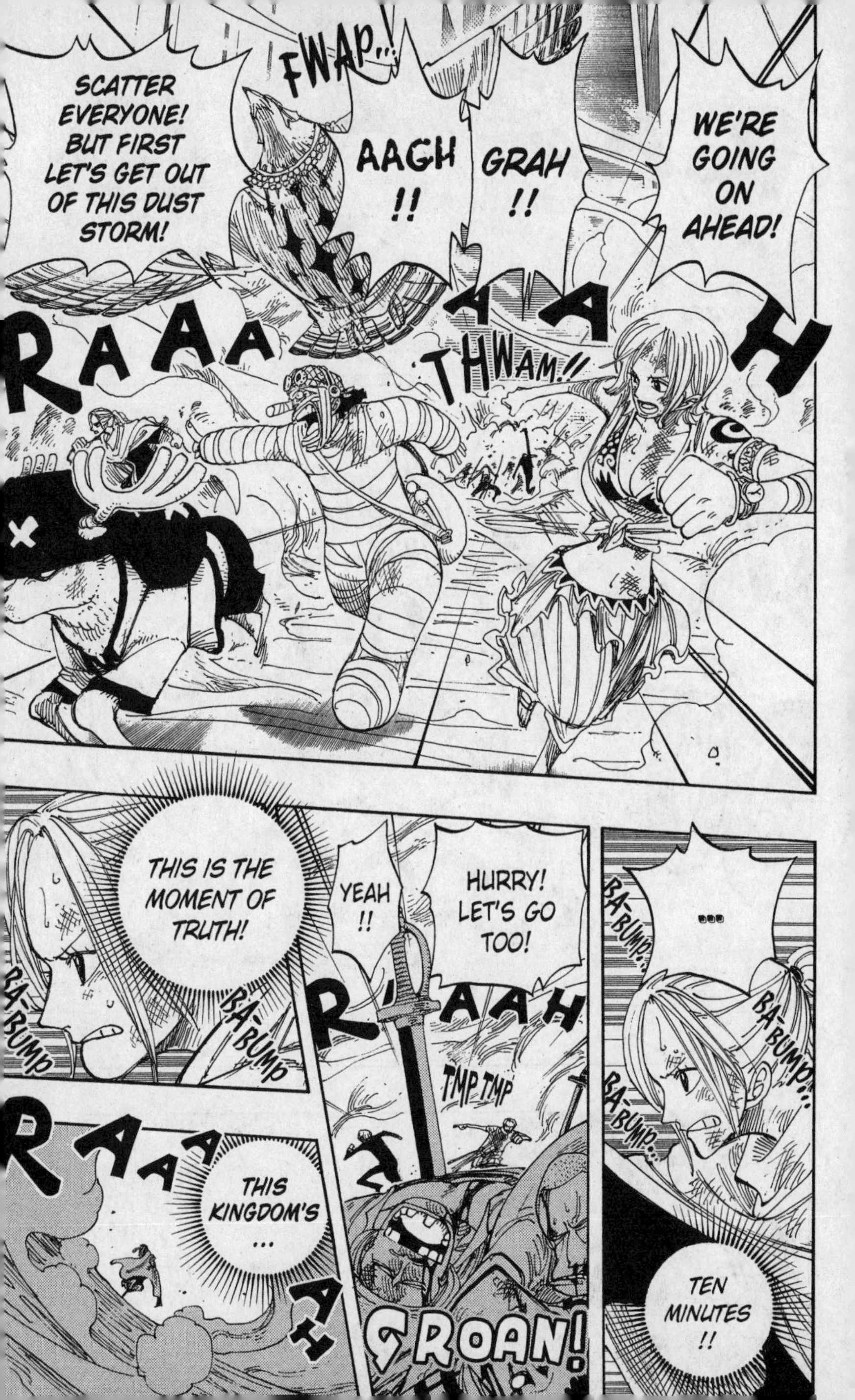
WE'RE GOING ON AHEAD!
GRAH!!
AAGH!!
FWAP..!
SCATTER EVERYONE! BUT FIRST LET'S GET OUT OF THIS DUST STORM!
RAAAAAAH
THWAM!!
...
BA-BUMP..
BA-BUMP...
BA-BUMP...
TEN MINUTES!!
HURRY! LET'S GO TOO!
YEAH!!
RAAAH
TMP TMP
GROAN!
THIS IS THE MOMENT OF TRUTH!
BA-BUMP
BA-BUMP
RAAAAH
THIS KINGDOM'S ...

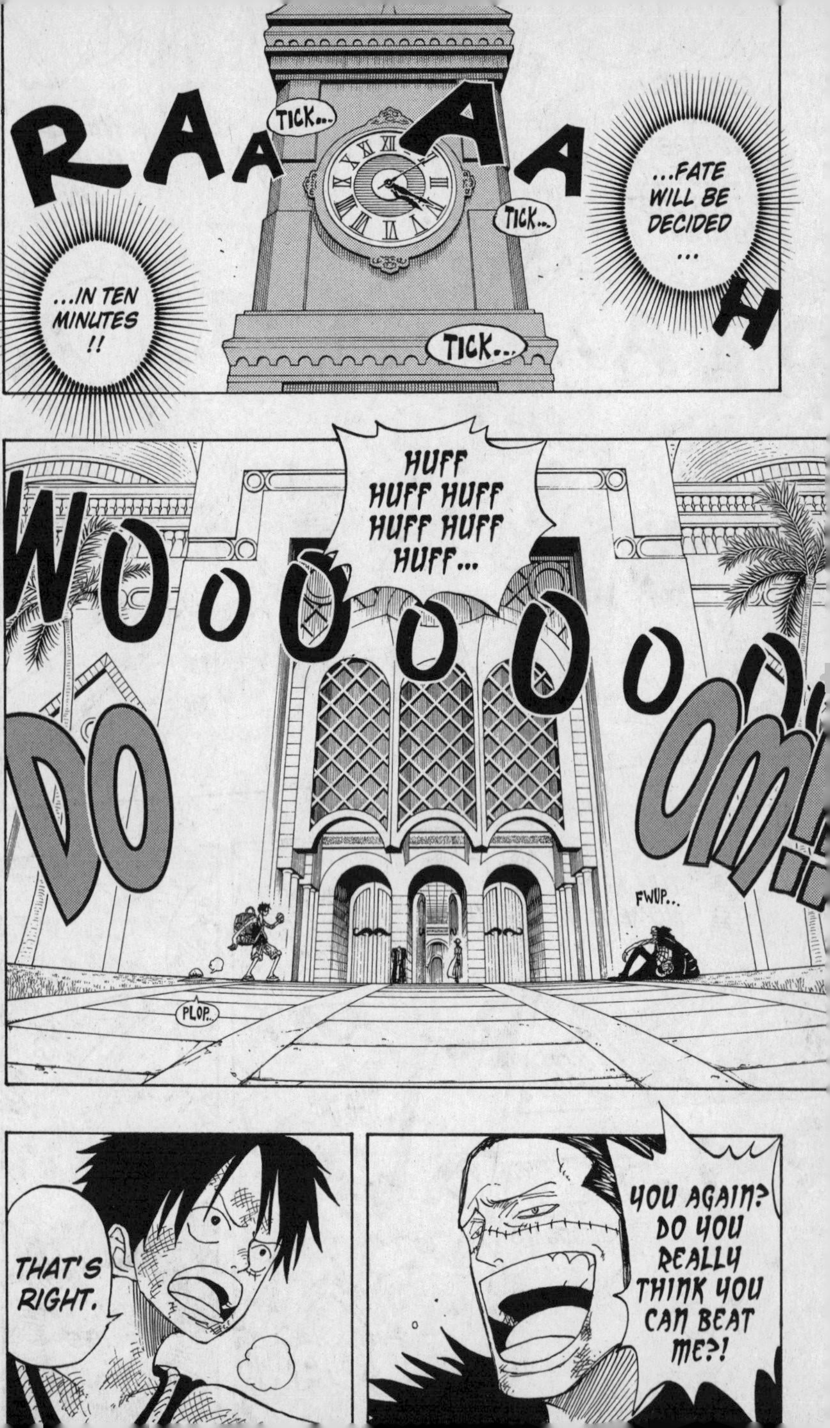
...FATE WILL BE DECIDED ...
RAAAAAH
TICK...
TICK...
...IN TEN MINUTES !!
TICK...
HUFF HUFF HUFF HUFF HUFF HUFF...
WOOOOOOOOM
DOOOM!!
FWUP...
PLOP...
YOU AGAIN? DO YOU REALLY THINK YOU CAN BEAT ME?!
THAT'S RIGHT.

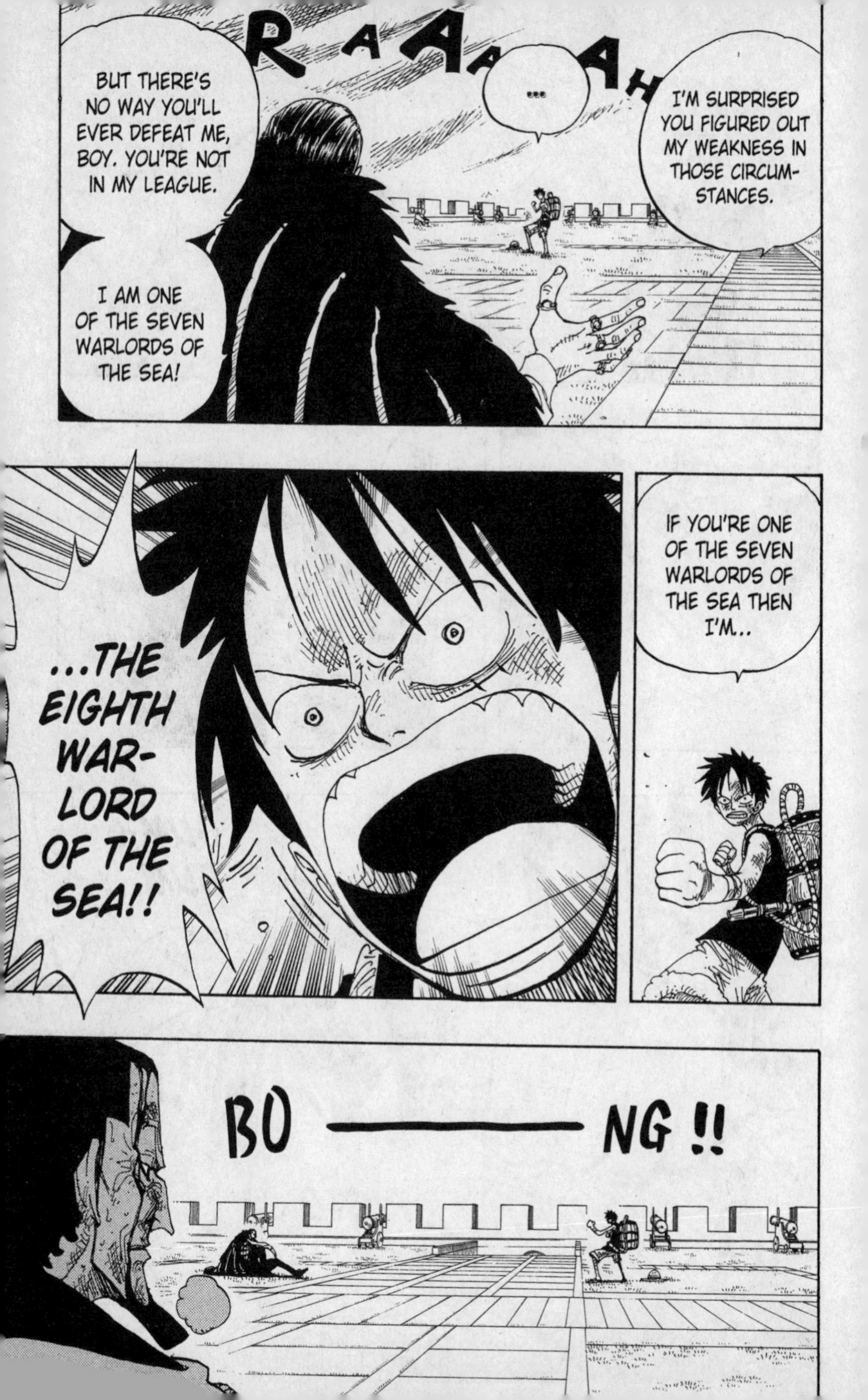
I'M SURPRISED YOU FIGURED OUT MY WEAKNESS IN THOSE CIRCUM-STANCES.
...
RAAAAH
BUT THERE'S NO WAY YOU'LL EVER DEFEAT ME, BOY. YOU'RE NOT IN MY LEAGUE.
I AM ONE OF THE SEVEN WARLORDS OF THE SEA!
IF YOU'RE ONE OF THE SEVEN WARLORDS OF THE SEA THEN I'M...
...THE EIGHTH WAR-LORD OF THE SEA!!
BO——NG!!

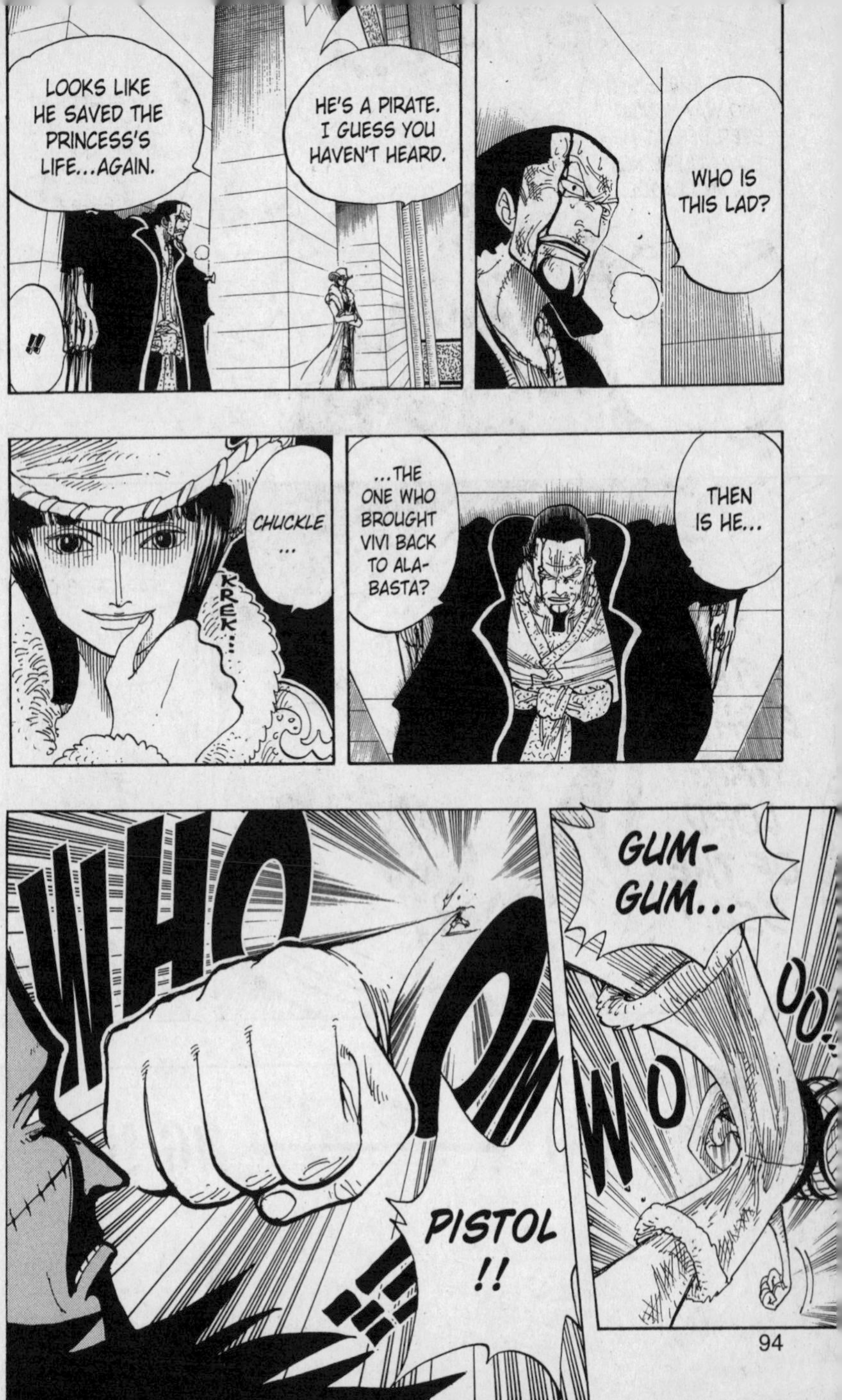
WHO IS THIS LAD?
HE'S A PIRATE. I GUESS YOU HAVEN'T HEARD.
LOOKS LIKE HE SAVED THE PRINCESS'S LIFE...AGAIN.
!!
THEN IS HE...
...THE ONE WHO BROUGHT VIVI BACK TO ALA-BASTA?
CHUCKLE ...
KREK..
GUM-GUM...
WOOOO..
WHOOM
PISTOL !!

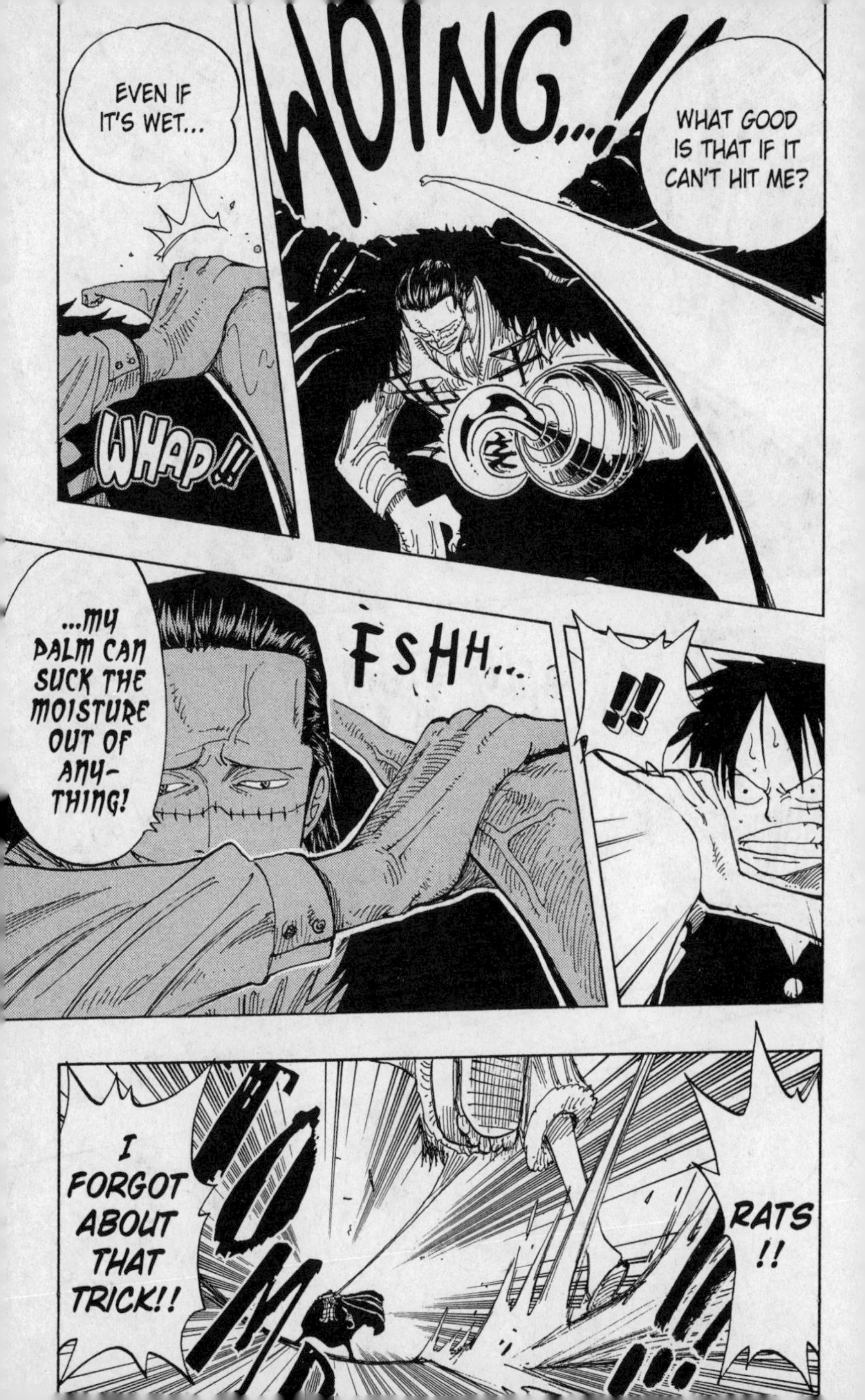
WOING...!!
WHAT GOOD IS THAT IF IT CAN'T HIT ME?
EVEN IF IT'S WET...
WHAP!!
!!
FSHH...
...MY PALM CAN SUCK THE MOISTURE OUT OF ANY-THING!
RATS!!
I FORGOT ABOUT THAT TRICK!!

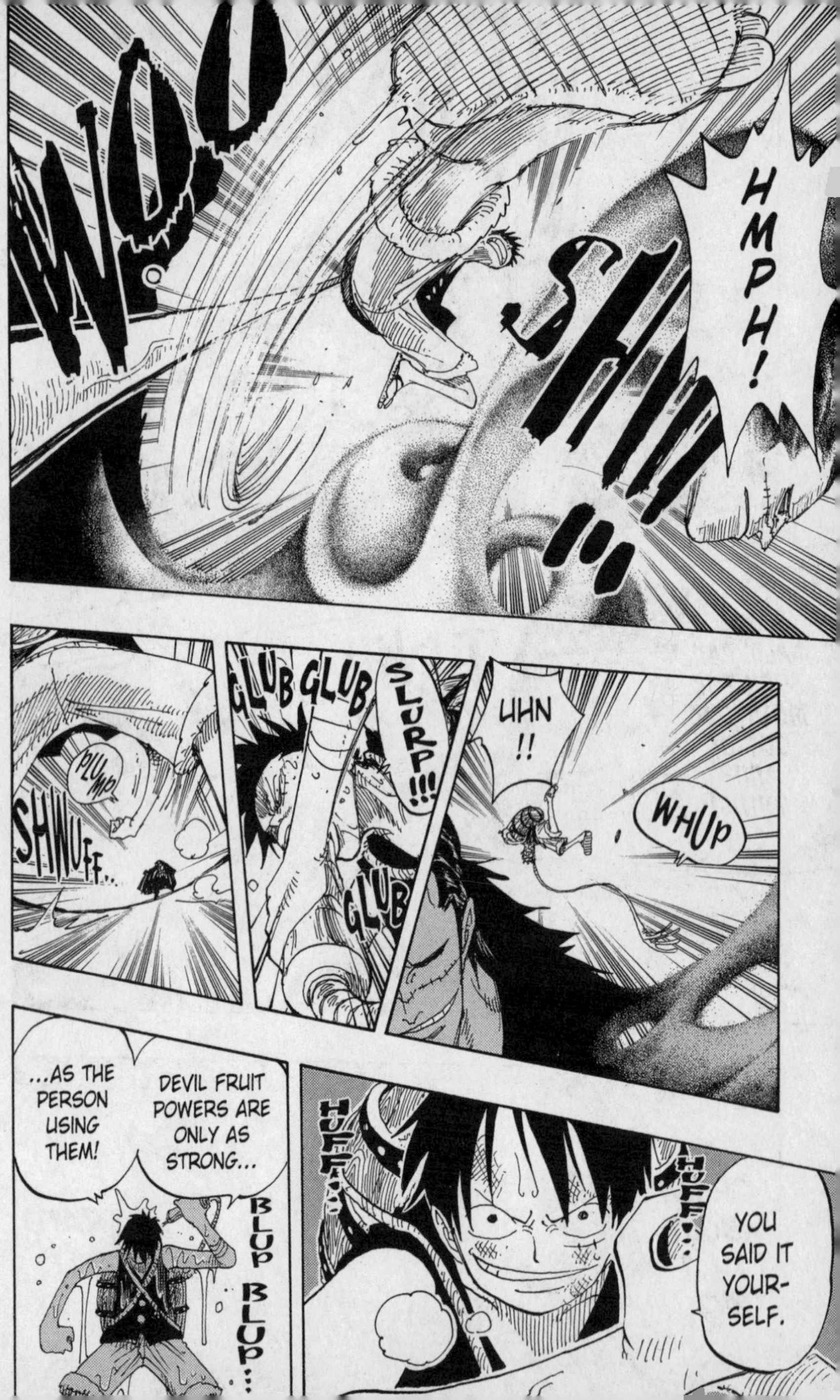
HMPH!
UHN !!
WHUP
SLURP!!!
GLUB GLUB
GLUB
PLUMP
SHWUFF...
HUFF...
HUFF...
YOU SAID IT YOURSELF.
DEVIL FRUIT POWERS ARE ONLY AS STRONG...
...AS THE PERSON USING THEM!
BLUP BLUP...

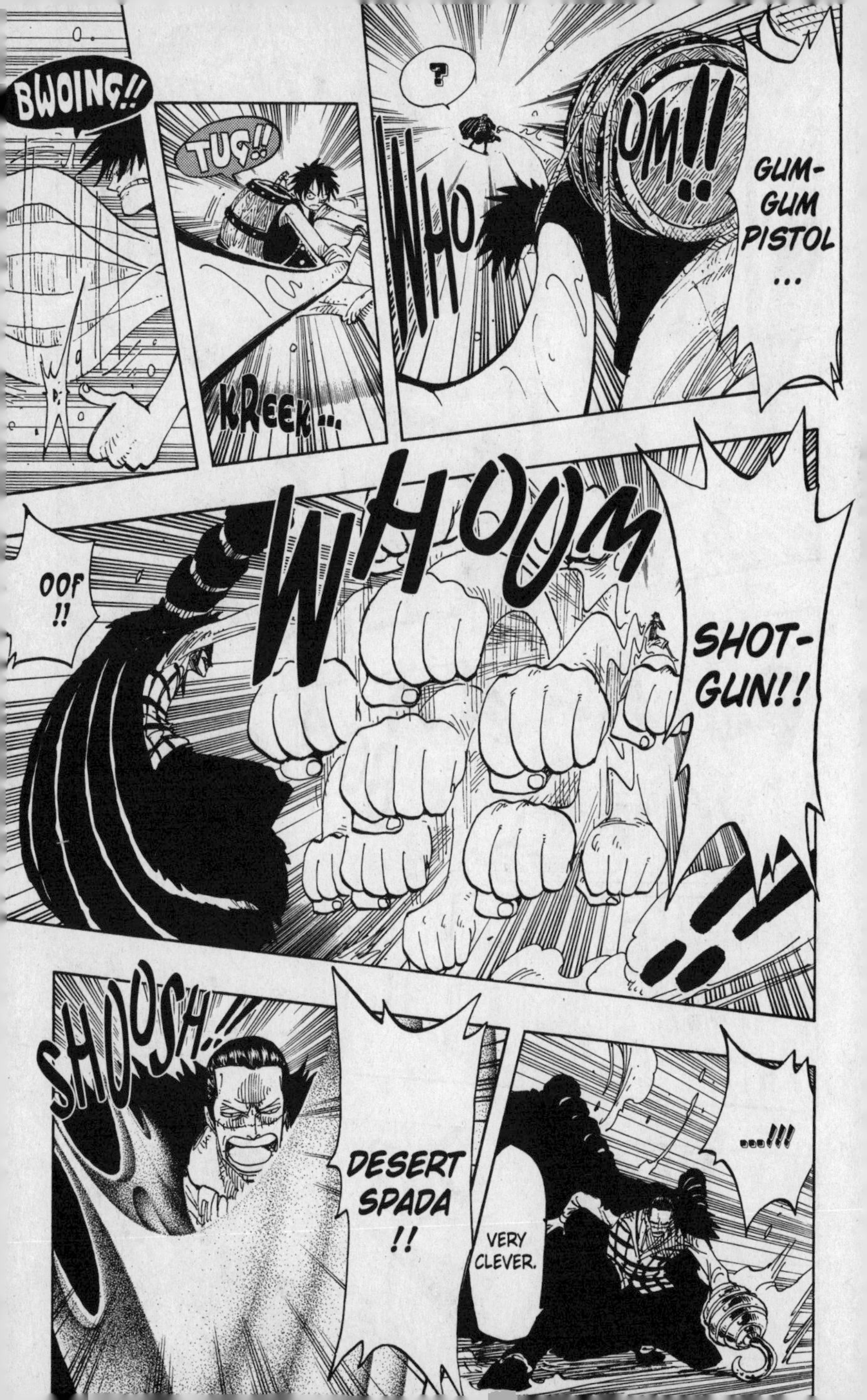
GUM-GUM PISTOL ...
?
WHO OM!!
TUG!!
KREEK ...
BWOING!!
SHOT-GUN!!
!!
WHOOM
OOF !!
...!!!
VERY CLEVER.
DESERT SPADA !!
SHOOSH..!!

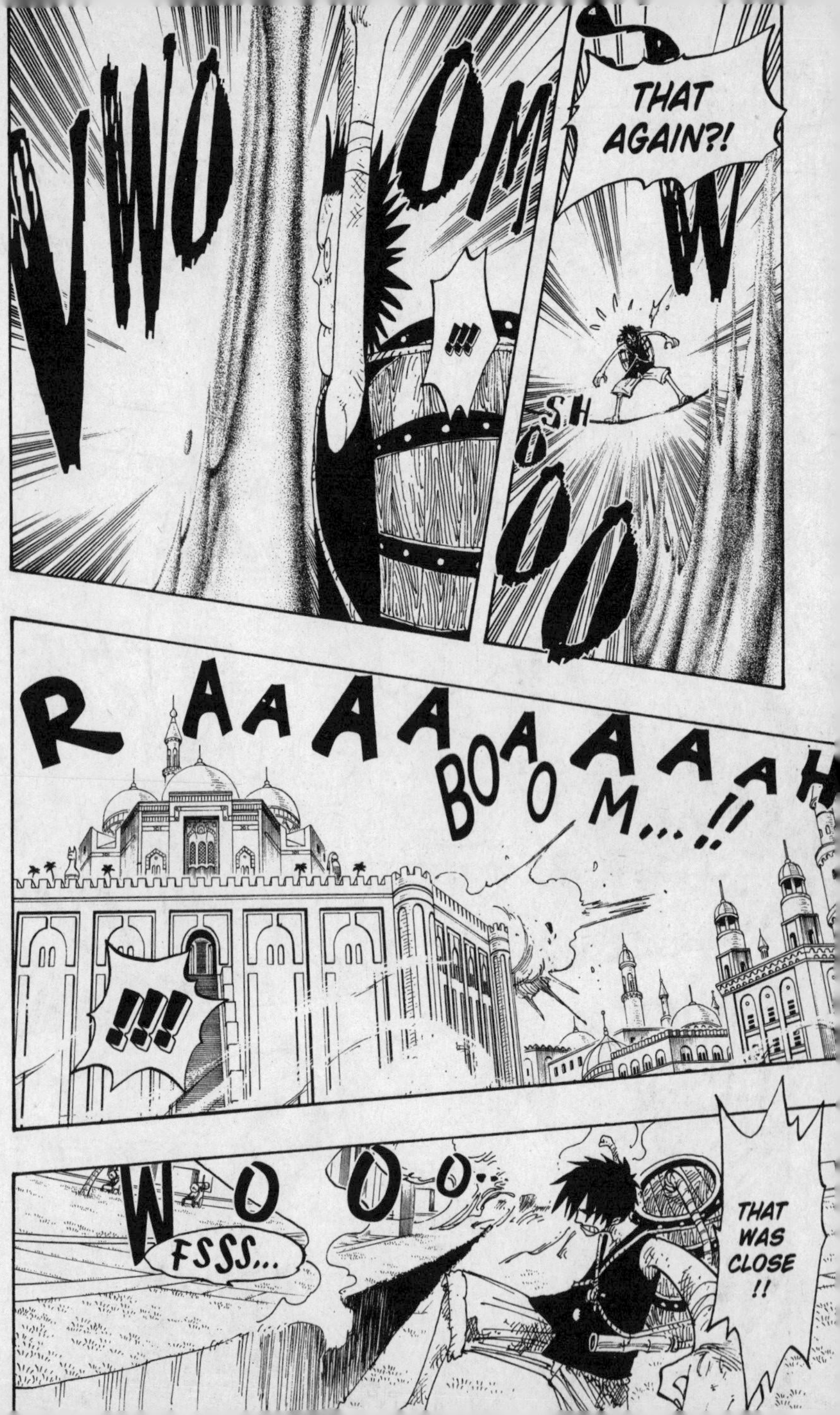
THAT AGAIN?!
SHOOOO
VWOOOMW
!!!
RAAAAAAAH
BOOM...!!
!!!
THAT WAS CLOSE !!
WOOO
FSSS...

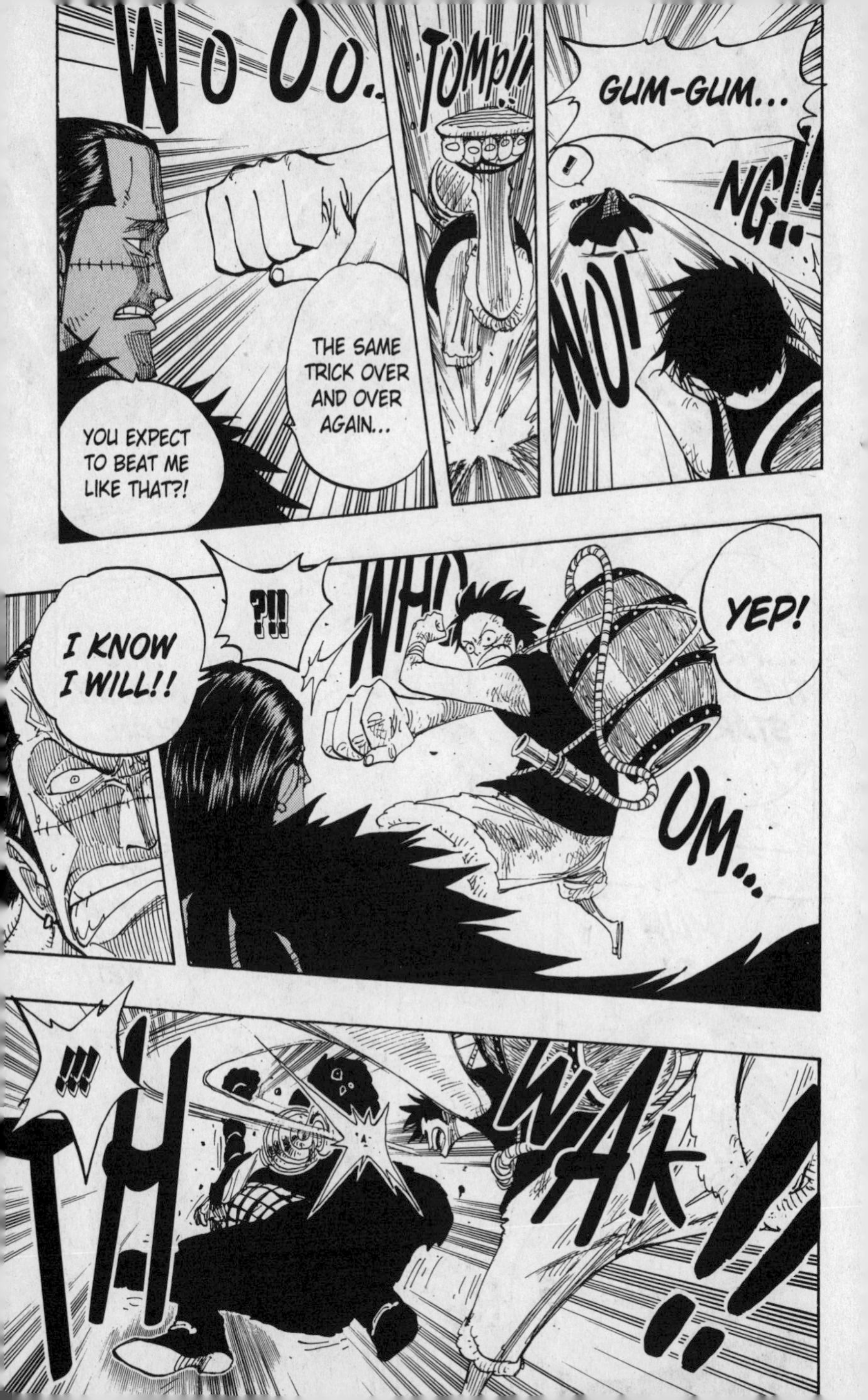

GUM-GUM...
!
WOI
NG!!
TOMP!!
WO OO..
THE SAME TRICK OVER AND OVER AGAIN...
YOU EXPECT TO BEAT ME LIKE THAT?!
YEP!
WHO
OM...
?!!
I KNOW I WILL!!
WAK!!
!!!
TH

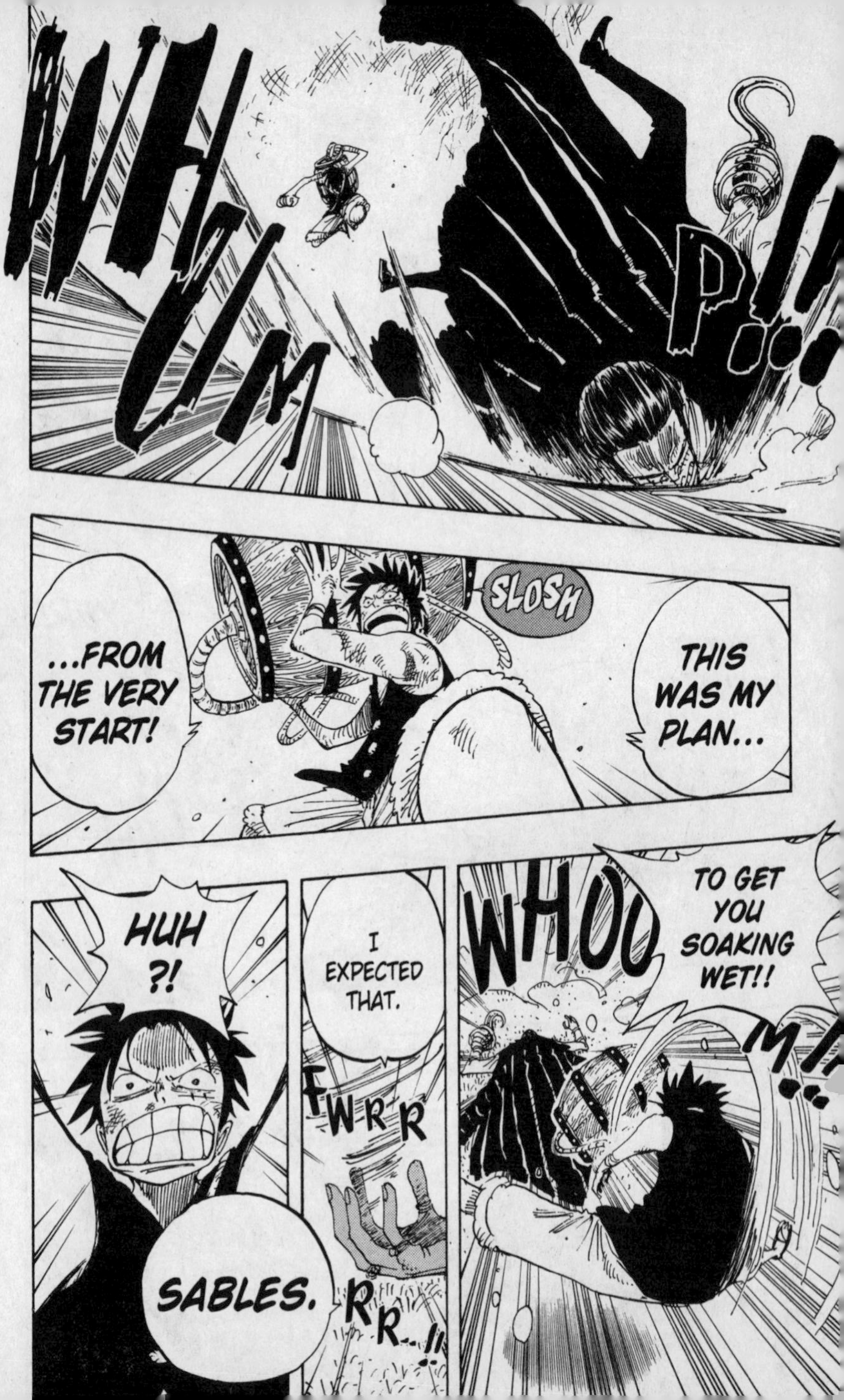

WHUMP!!
THIS WAS MY PLAN...
SLOSH
...FROM THE VERY START!
TO GET YOU SOAKING WET!!
WHOOM!!
I EXPECTED THAT.
FWRRR
HUH?!
SABLES.
RRR!!

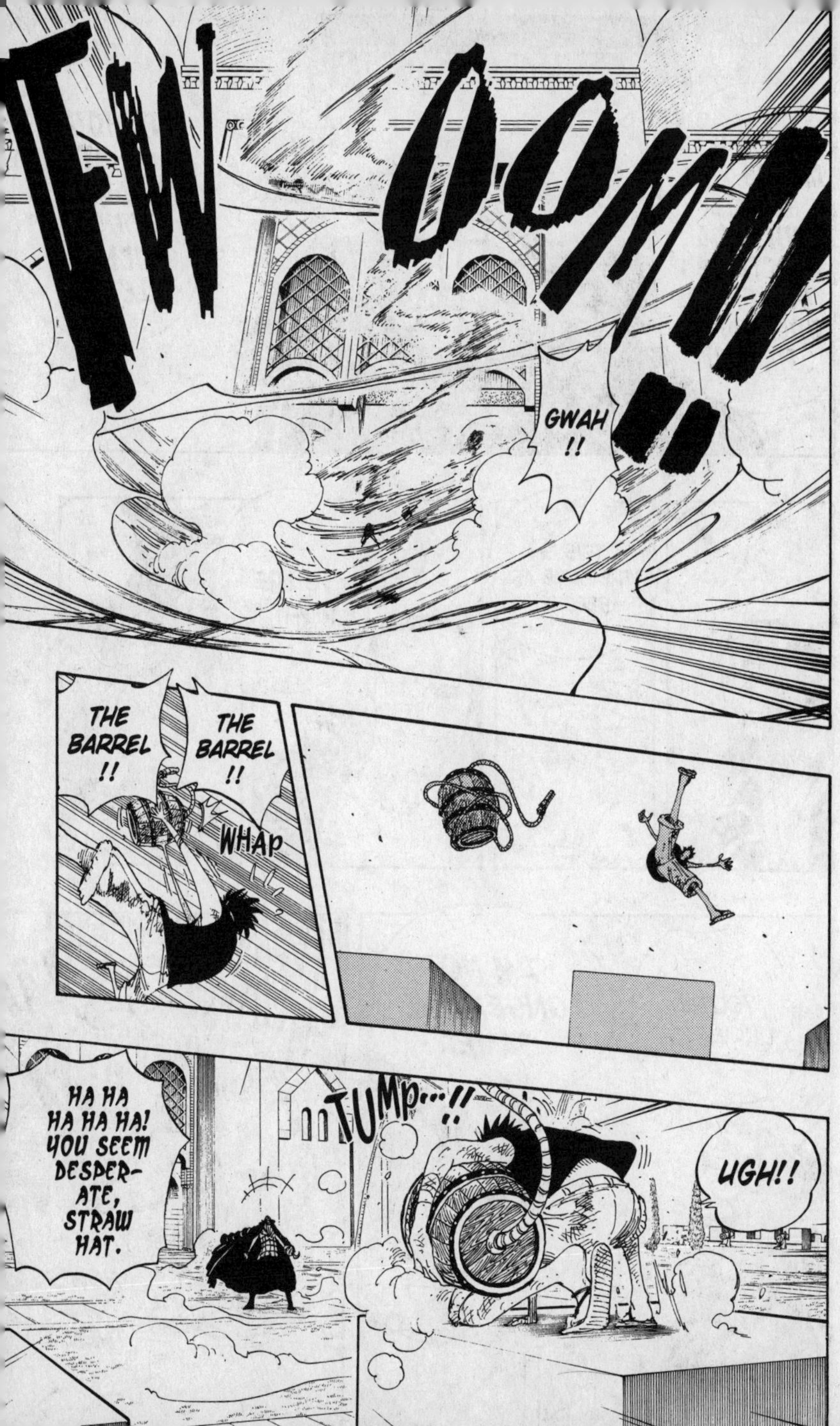
FWOOM!!
GWAH!!
THE BARREL!!
THE BARREL!!
WHAP
UGH!!
TUMP...!!
HA HA HA HA HA! YOU SEEM DESPERATE, STRAW HAT.

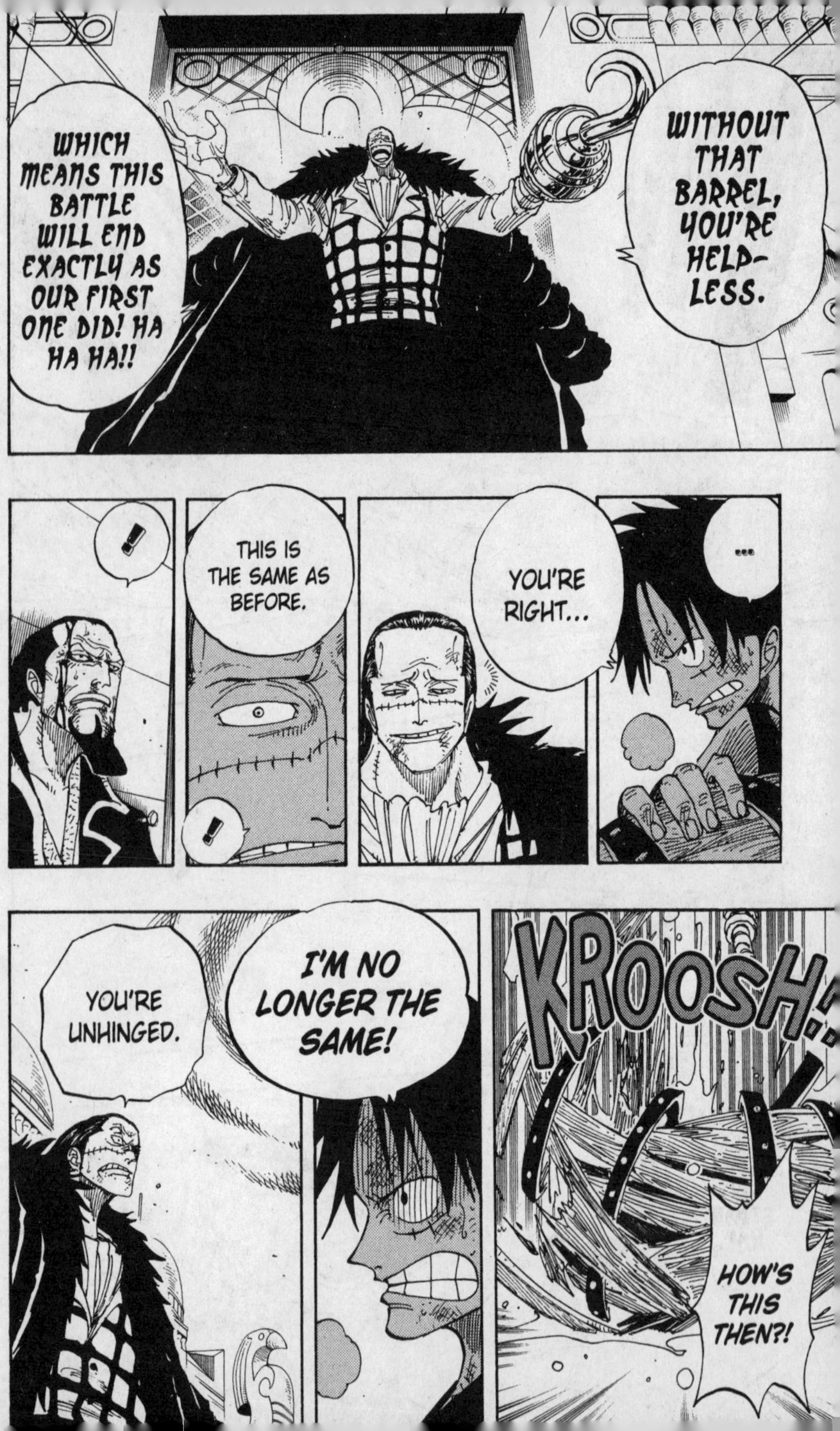
WITHOUT THAT BARREL, YOU'RE HELP-LESS.
WHICH MEANS THIS BATTLE WILL END EXACTLY AS OUR FIRST ONE DID! HA HA HA!!
...
YOU'RE RIGHT...
THIS IS THE SAME AS BEFORE.
!
!
KROOSH!!
HOW'S THIS THEN?!
I'M NO LONGER THE SAME!
YOU'RE UNHINGED.

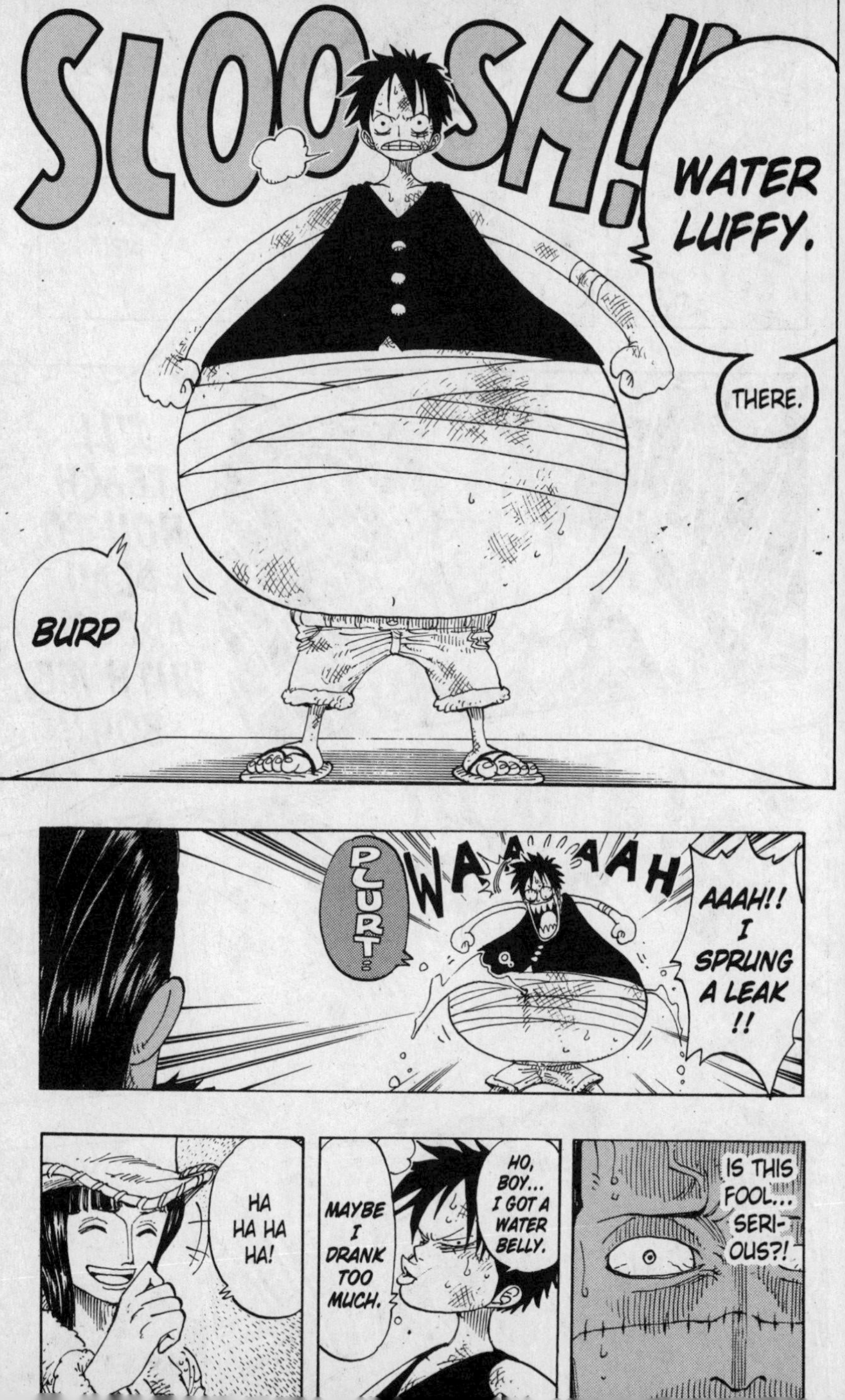
SLOOSH!!
WATER LUFFY.
THERE.
BURP
AAAH!! I SPRUNG A LEAK !!
WAAAAAH
PLURT!
IS THIS FOOL... SERI-OUS?!
HO, BOY... I GOT A WATER BELLY.
MAYBE I DRANK TOO MUCH.
HA HA HA HA!

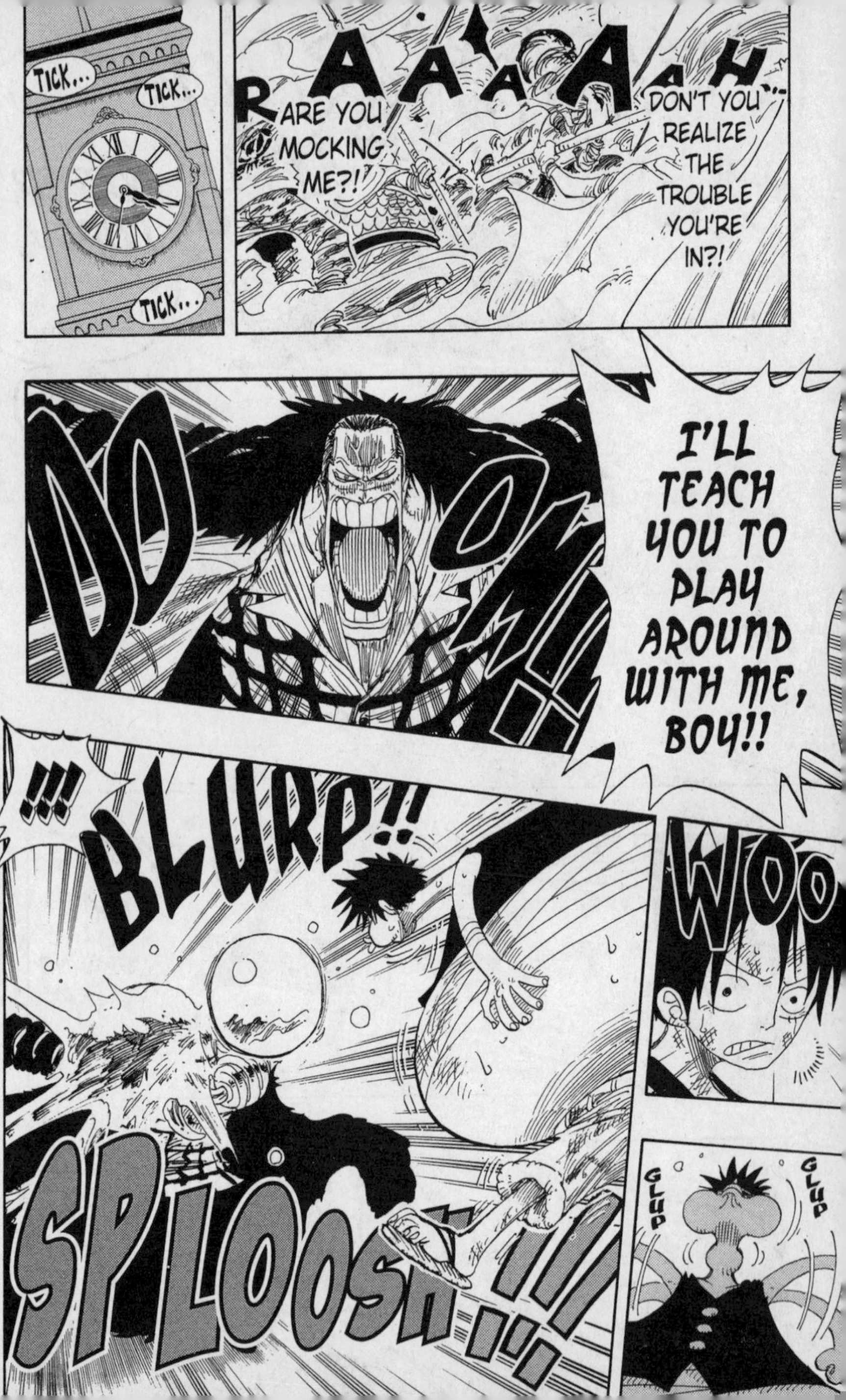
RAAAAAH
DON'T YOU REALIZE THE TROUBLE YOU'RE IN?!
ARE YOU MOCKING ME?!
TICK...
TICK...
TICK...
I'LL TEACH YOU TO PLAY AROUND WITH ME, BOY!!
DOOM!!
WOO
GLUP
GLUP
!!!
BLURP!!
SPLOOSH!!!

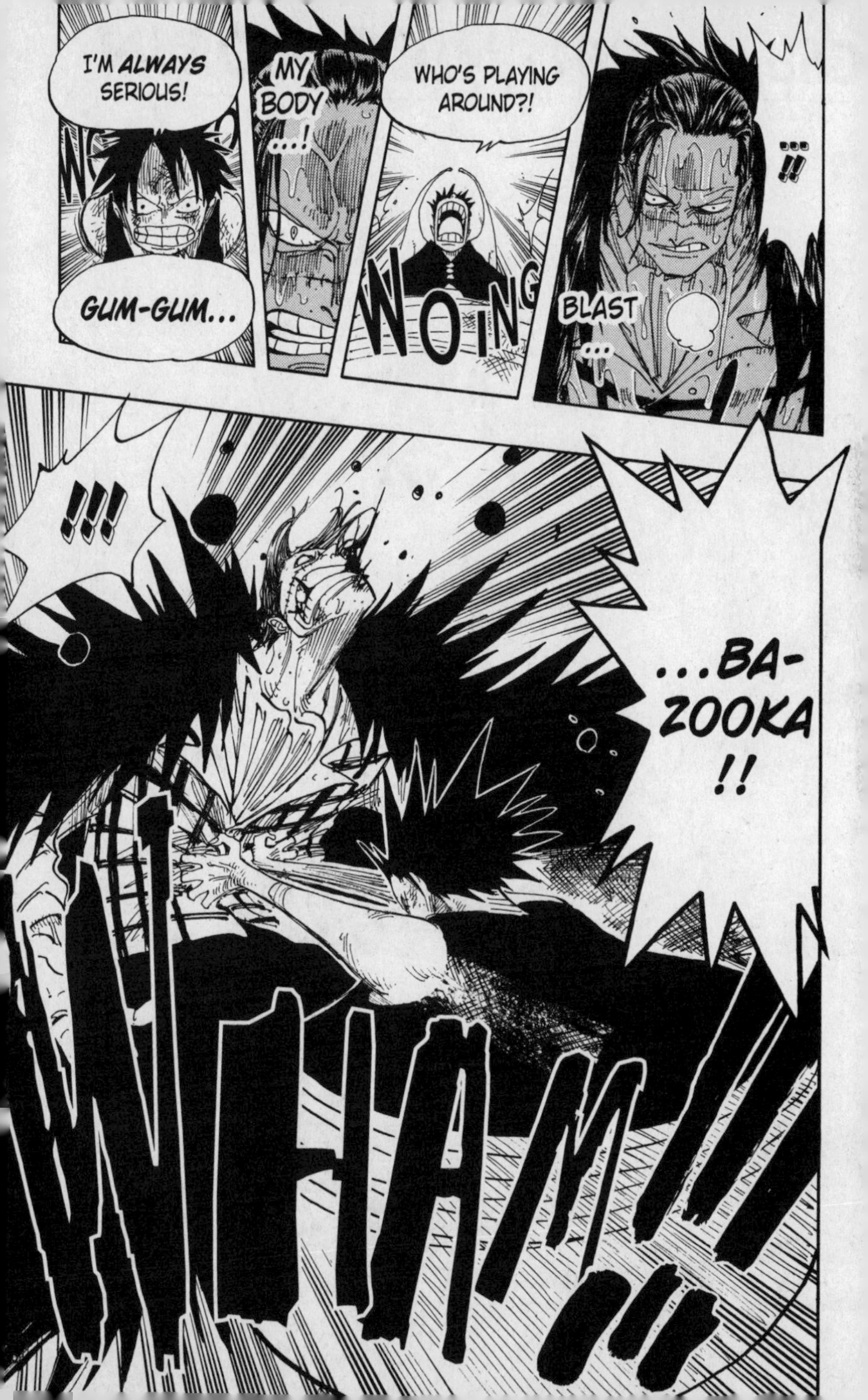
..!!
BLAST...
WHO'S PLAYING AROUND?!
WOING
MY BODY ...!
I'M ALWAYS SERIOUS!
GUM-GUM...
...BA-ZOOKA!!
!!!
WHAM!!

Chapter 201: NICO ROBIN

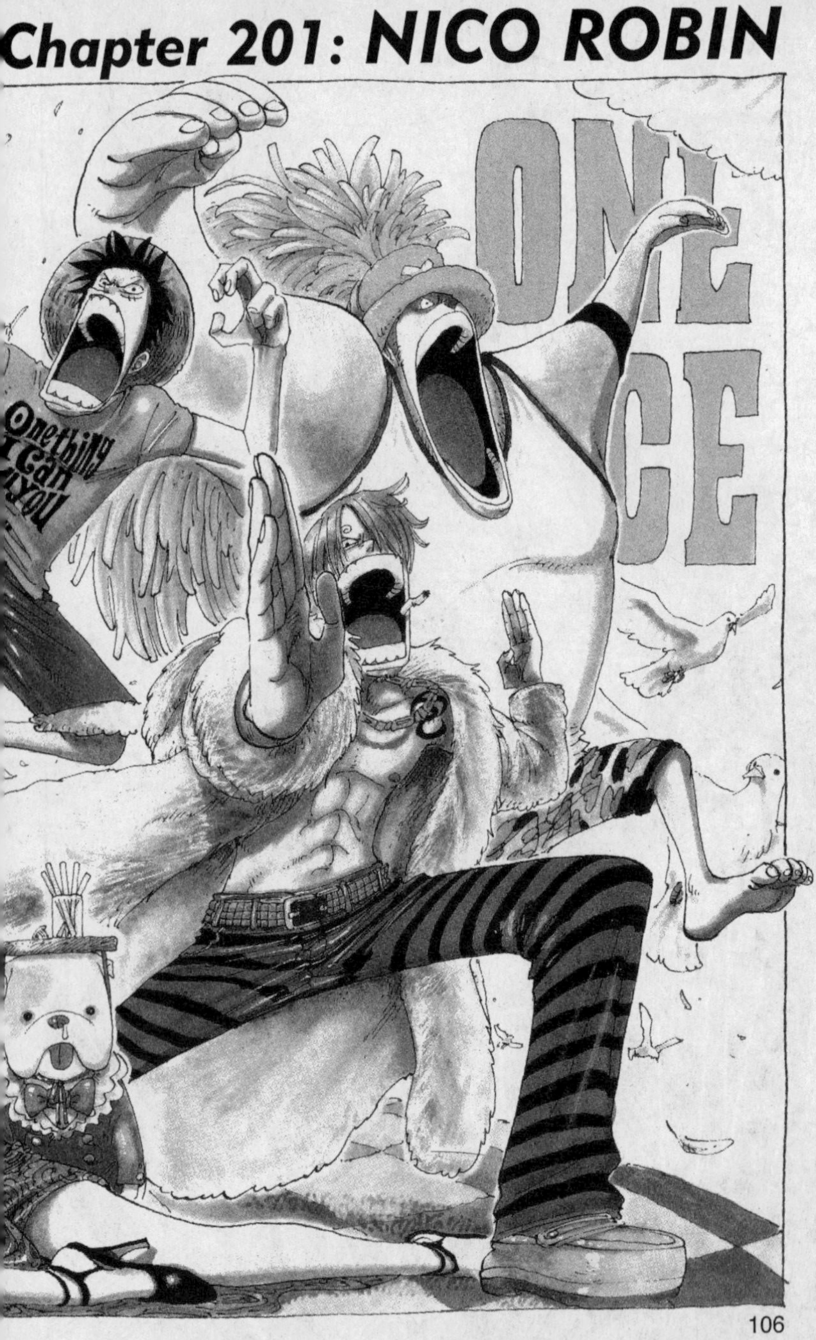
One thing
I can

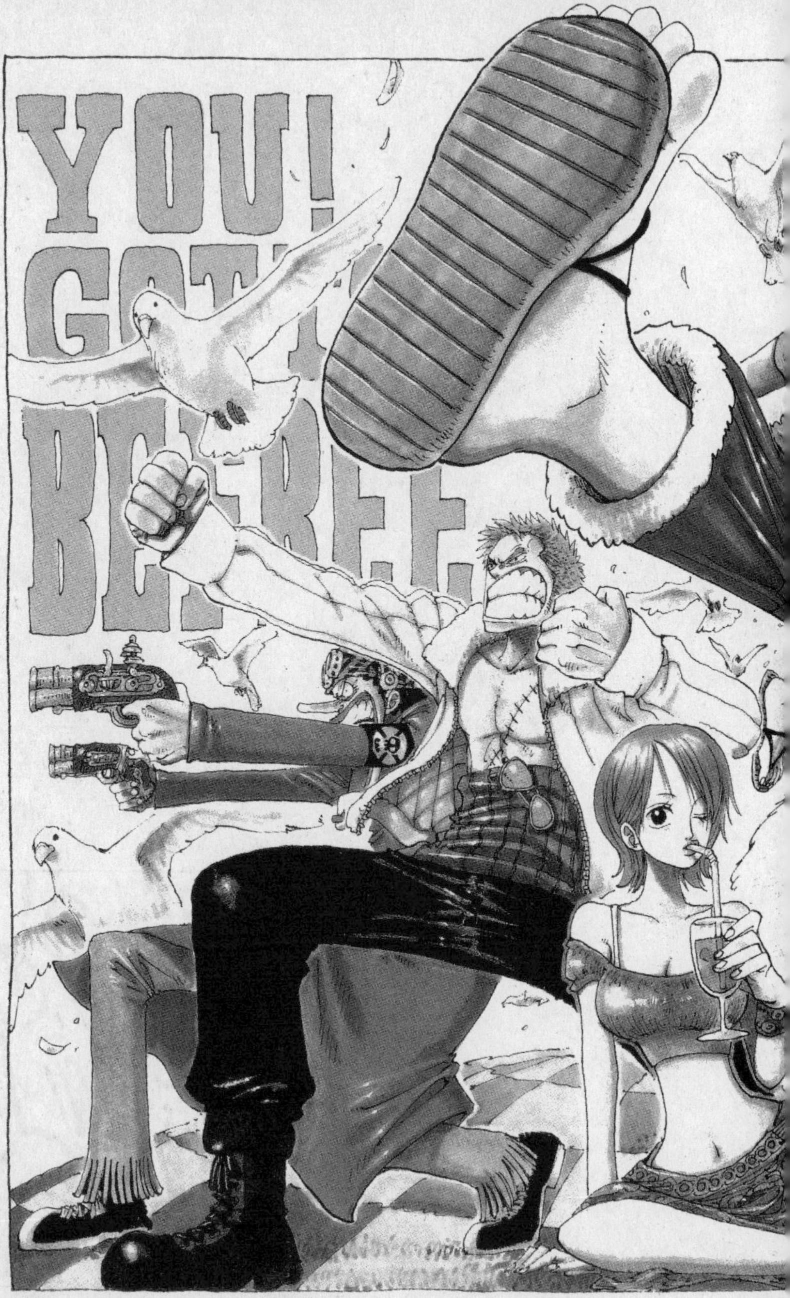
YOU!

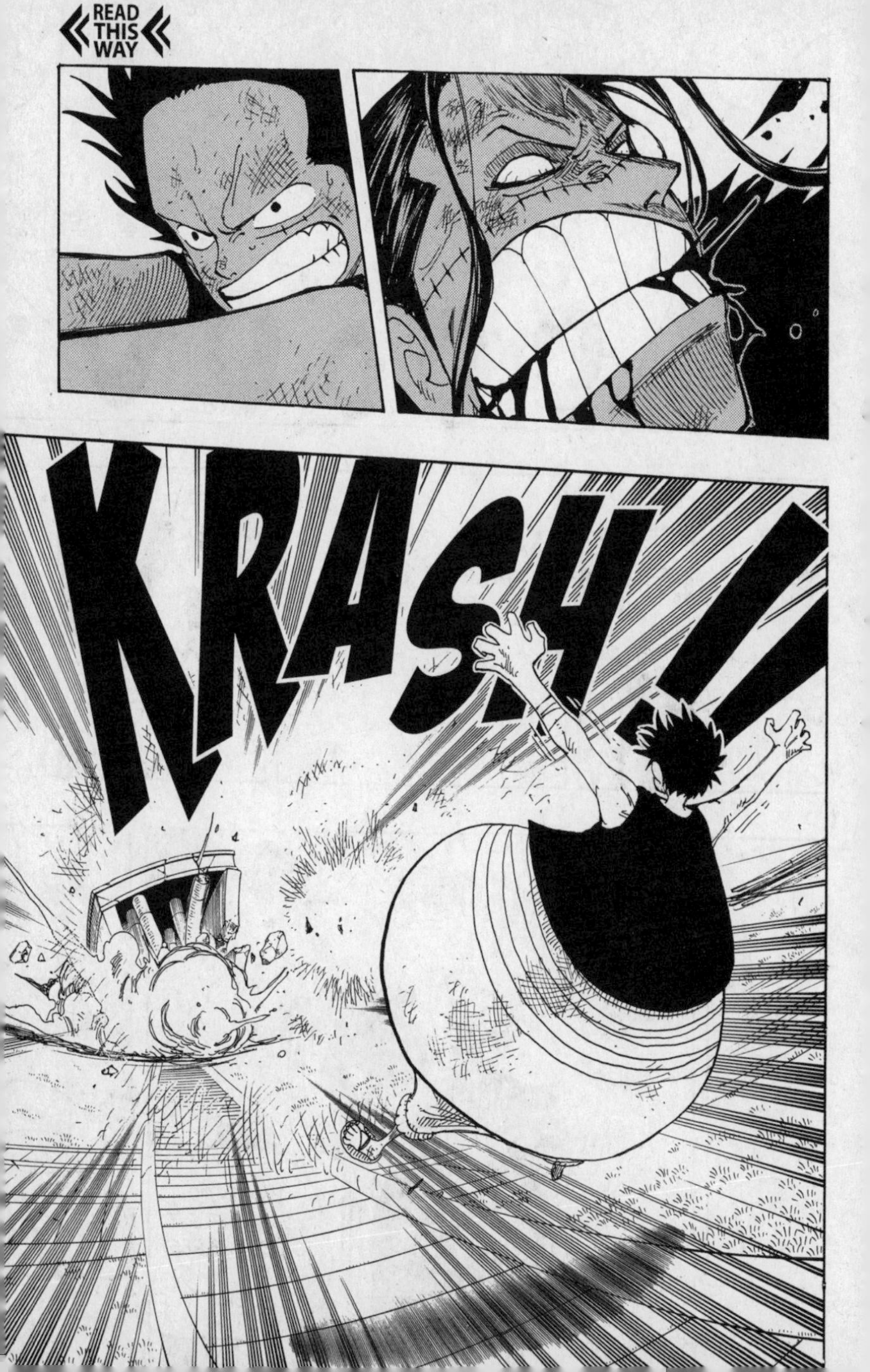
READ THIS WAY
KRASH!!

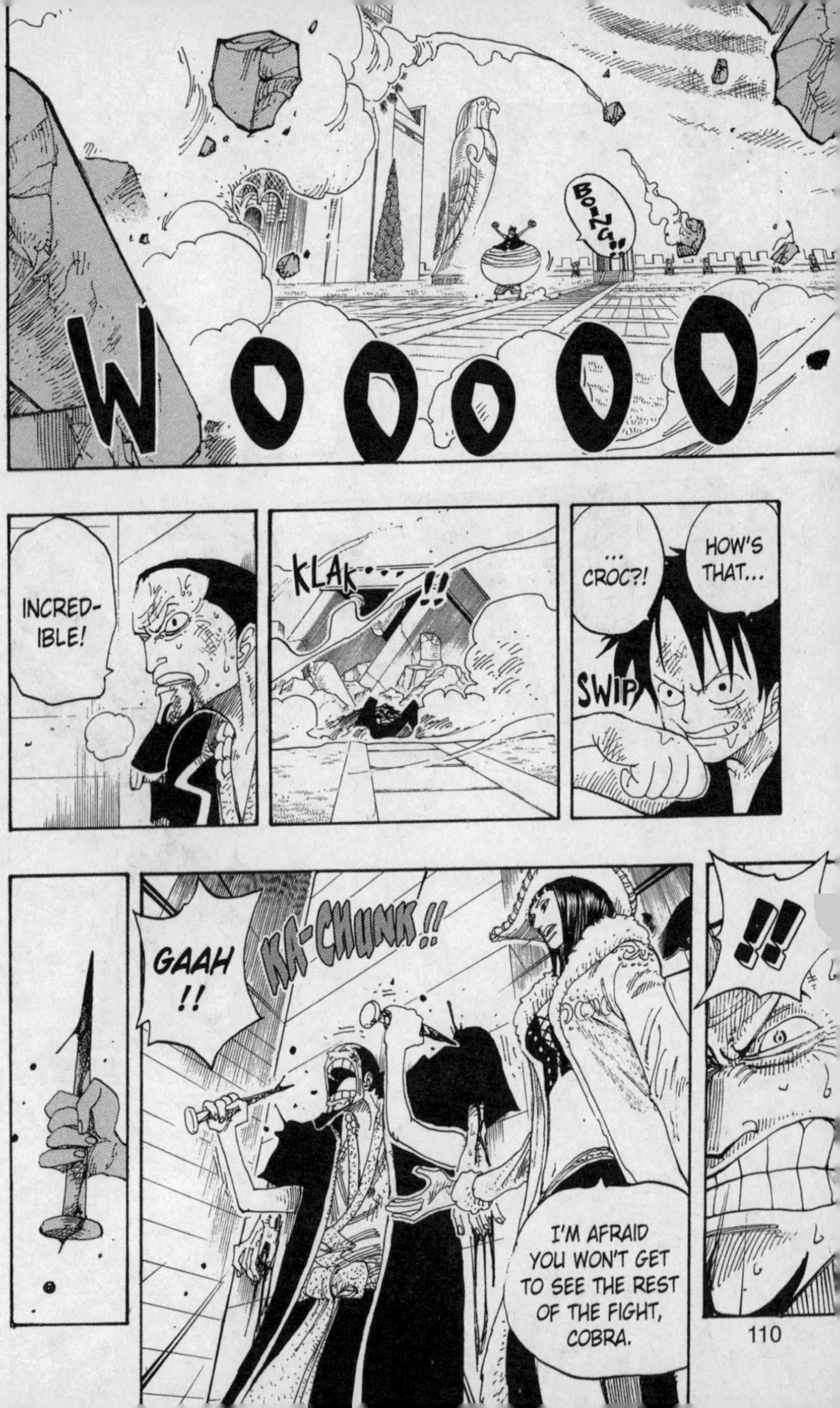
BOING!!
WOOOOOO
HOW'S THAT...
...CROC?!
SWIP
KLAK...!!
INCRED-IBLE!
!!
KA-CHUNK!!
GAAH!!
I'M AFRAID YOU WON'T GET TO SEE THE REST OF THE FIGHT, COBRA.

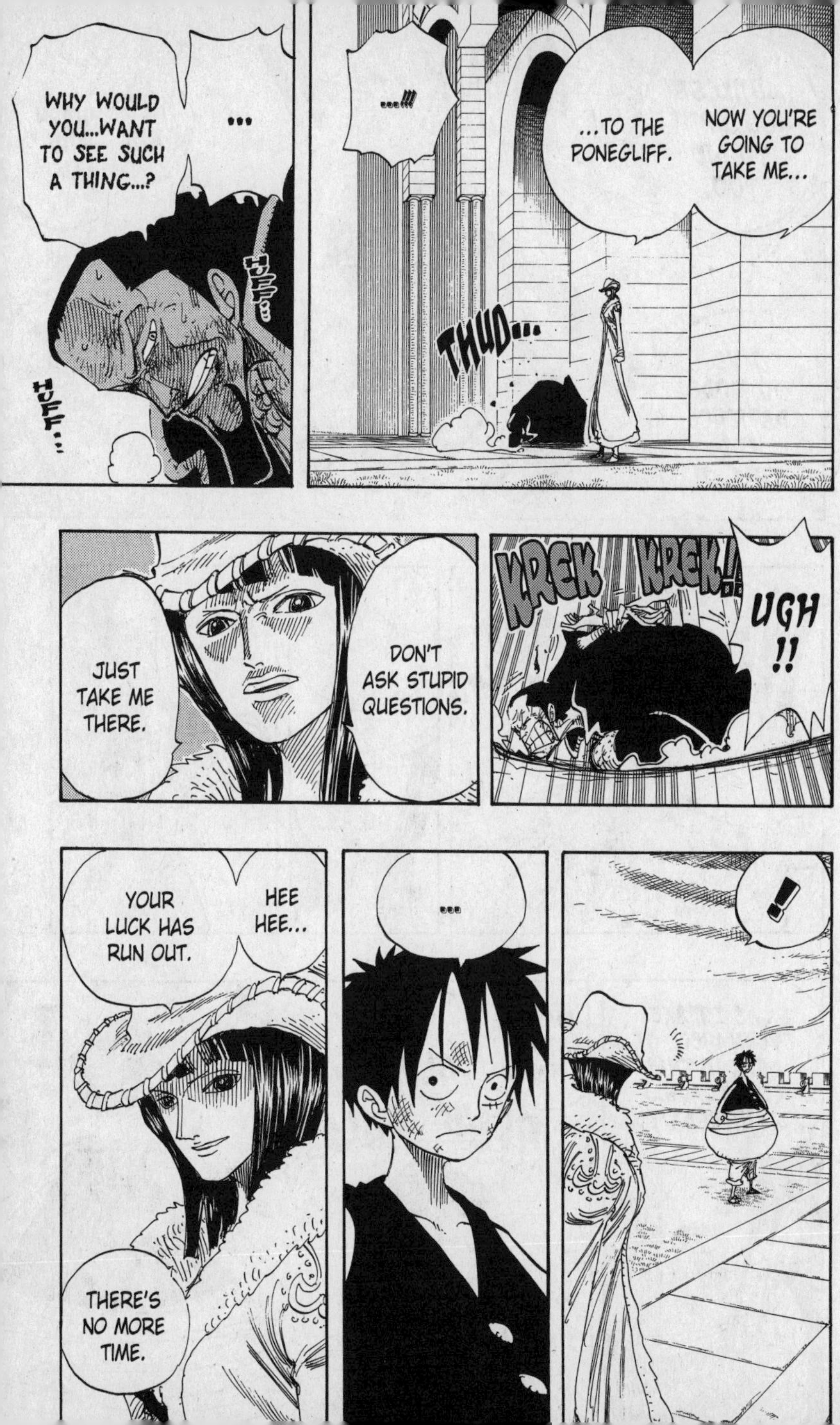
NOW YOU'RE GOING TO TAKE ME...
...TO THE PONEGLIFF.
...!!!
THUD...
...
WHY WOULD YOU...WANT TO SEE SUCH A THING...?
HUFF...
HUFF...
KREK KREK!!
UGH !!
DON'T ASK STUPID QUESTIONS.
JUST TAKE ME THERE.
!
...
HEE HEE...
YOUR LUCK HAS RUN OUT.
THERE'S NO MORE TIME.

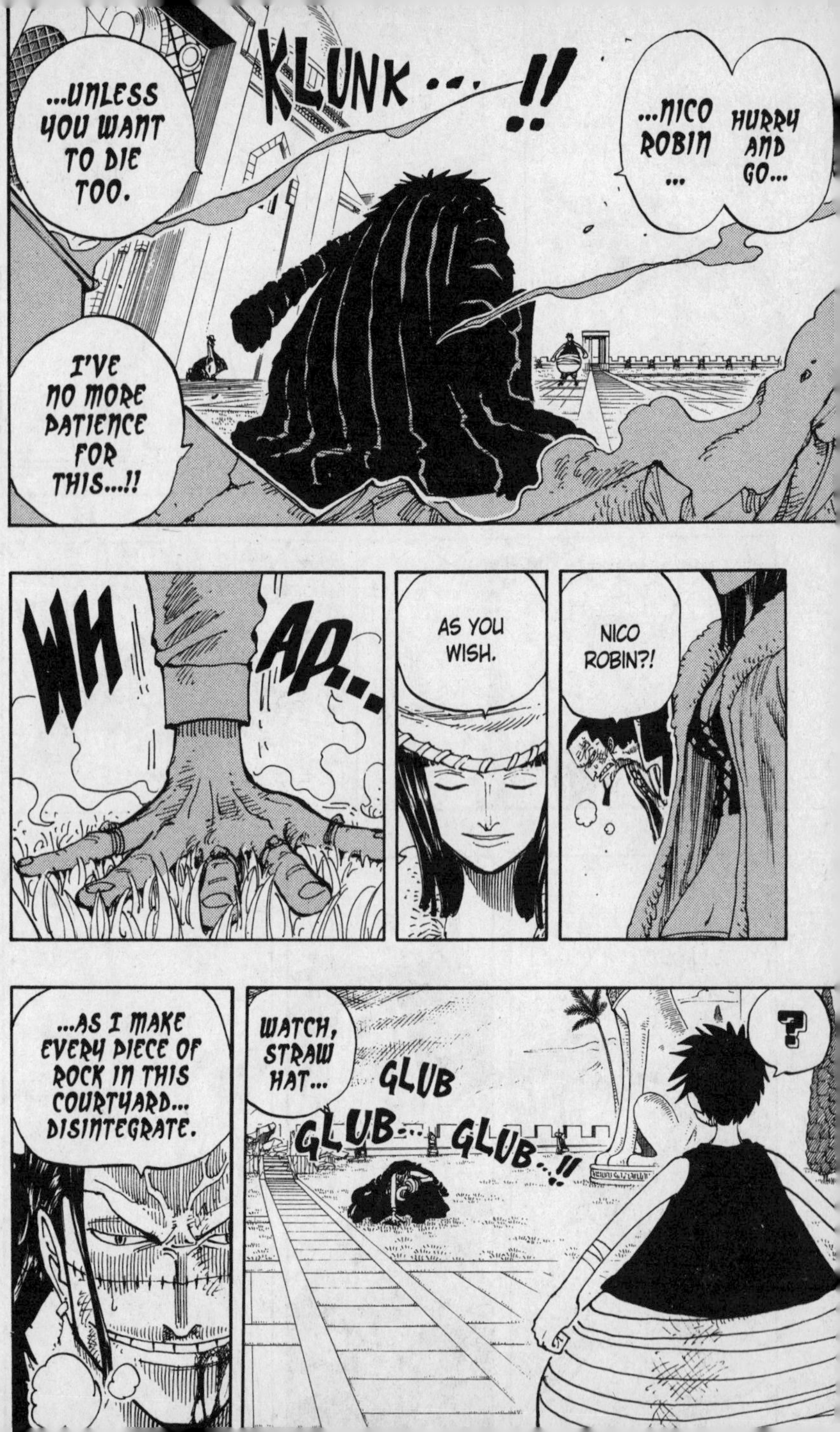
...NICO ROBIN ... HURRY AND GO...
KLUNK...!!
...UNLESS YOU WANT TO DIE TOO.
I'VE NO MORE PATIENCE FOR THIS...!!
NICO ROBIN?!
AS YOU WISH.
WHAD...
?
WATCH, STRAW HAT...
GLUB
GLUB... GLUB...!!
...AS I MAKE EVERY PIECE OF ROCK IN THIS COURTYARD... DISINTEGRATE.

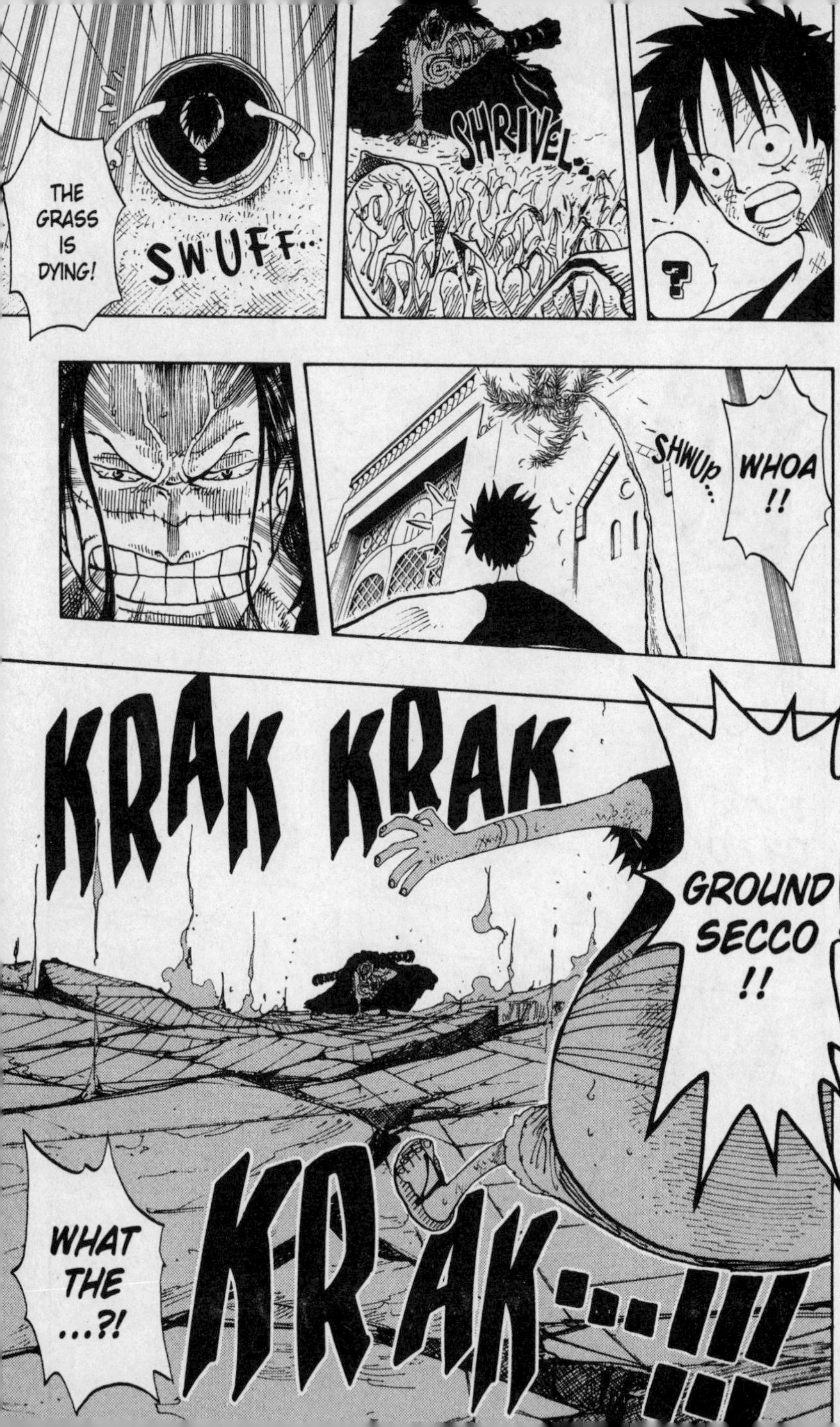
?
SHRIVEL...
SWUFF...
THE GRASS IS DYING!
WHOA!!
SHWUP...
GROUND SECCO!!
KRAK KRAK
WHAT THE ...?!
KRAK...!!!

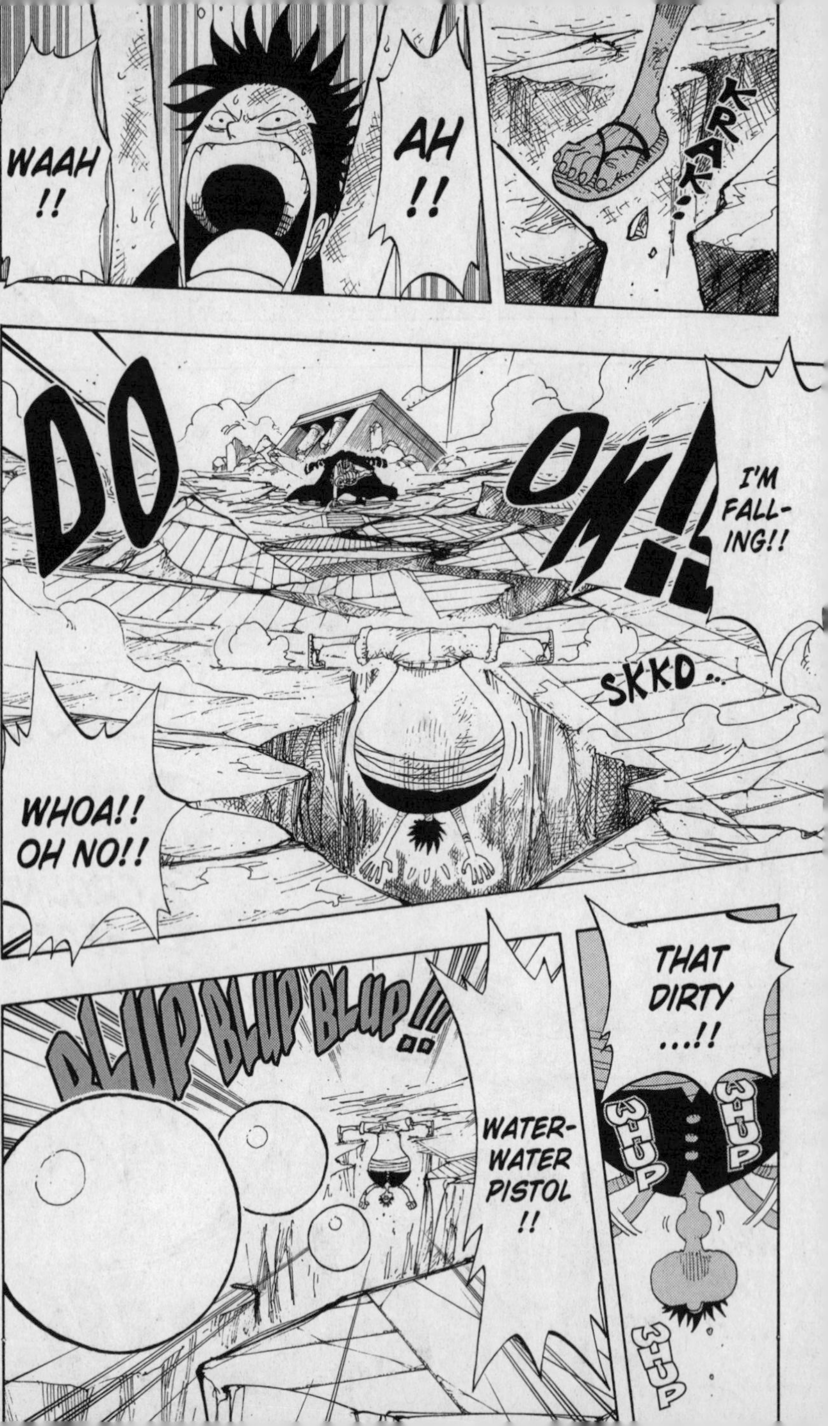
KRAK!!
AH !!
WAAH !!
DO ON!!
I'M FALLING!!
SKKD...
WHOA!! OH NO!!
THAT DIRTY ...!!
HUP HUP HUP
HUP
WATER-WATER PISTOL !!
BLUP BLUP BLUP!!!

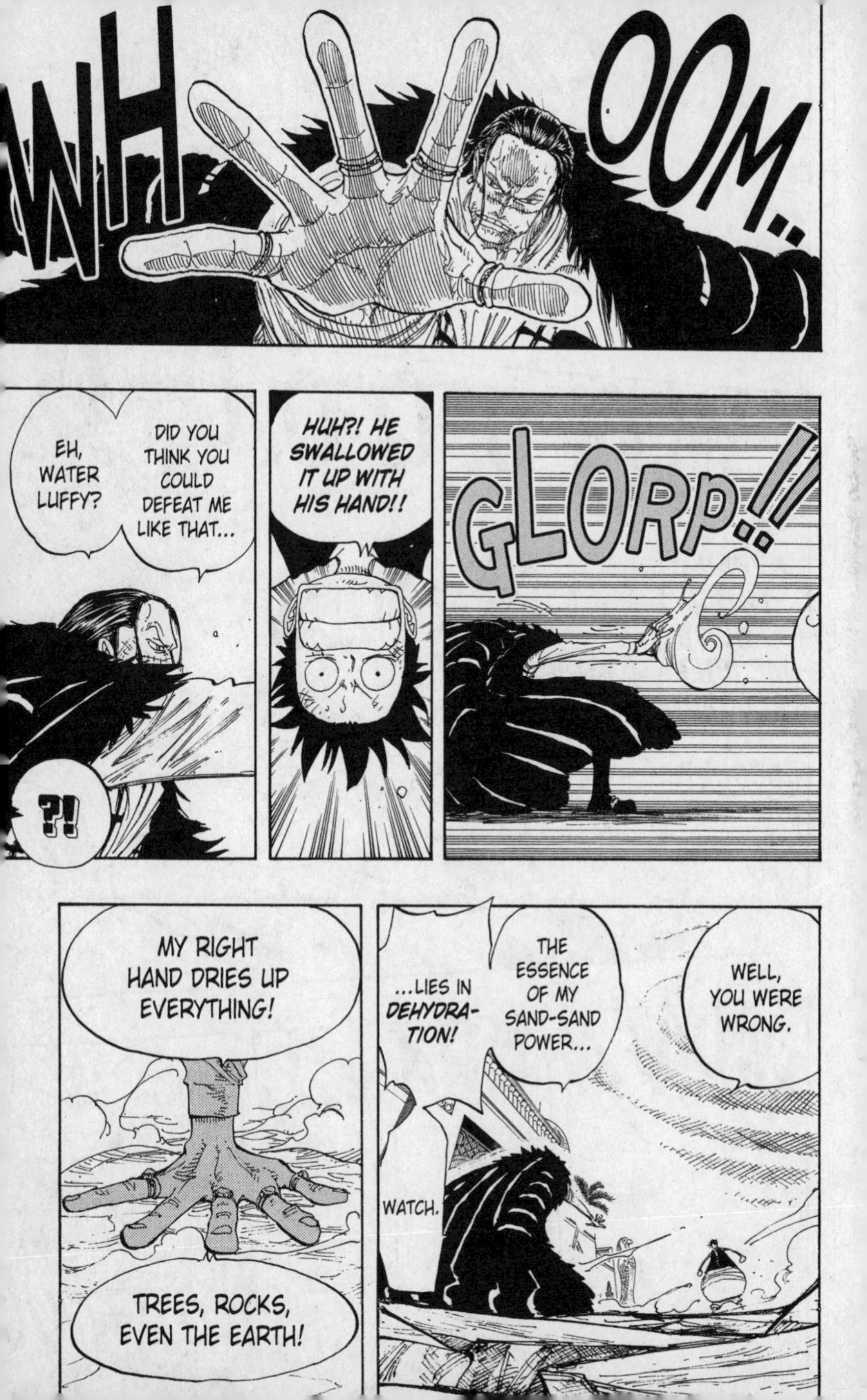
WHOOM..
GLORP!!
HUH?! HE SWALLOWED IT UP WITH HIS HAND!!
DID YOU THINK YOU COULD DEFEAT ME LIKE THAT...
EH, WATER LUFFY?
?!
WELL, YOU WERE WRONG.
THE ESSENCE OF MY SAND-SAND POWER...
...LIES IN DEHYDRATION!
WATCH.
MY RIGHT HAND DRIES UP EVERYTHING!
TREES, ROCKS, EVEN THE EARTH!

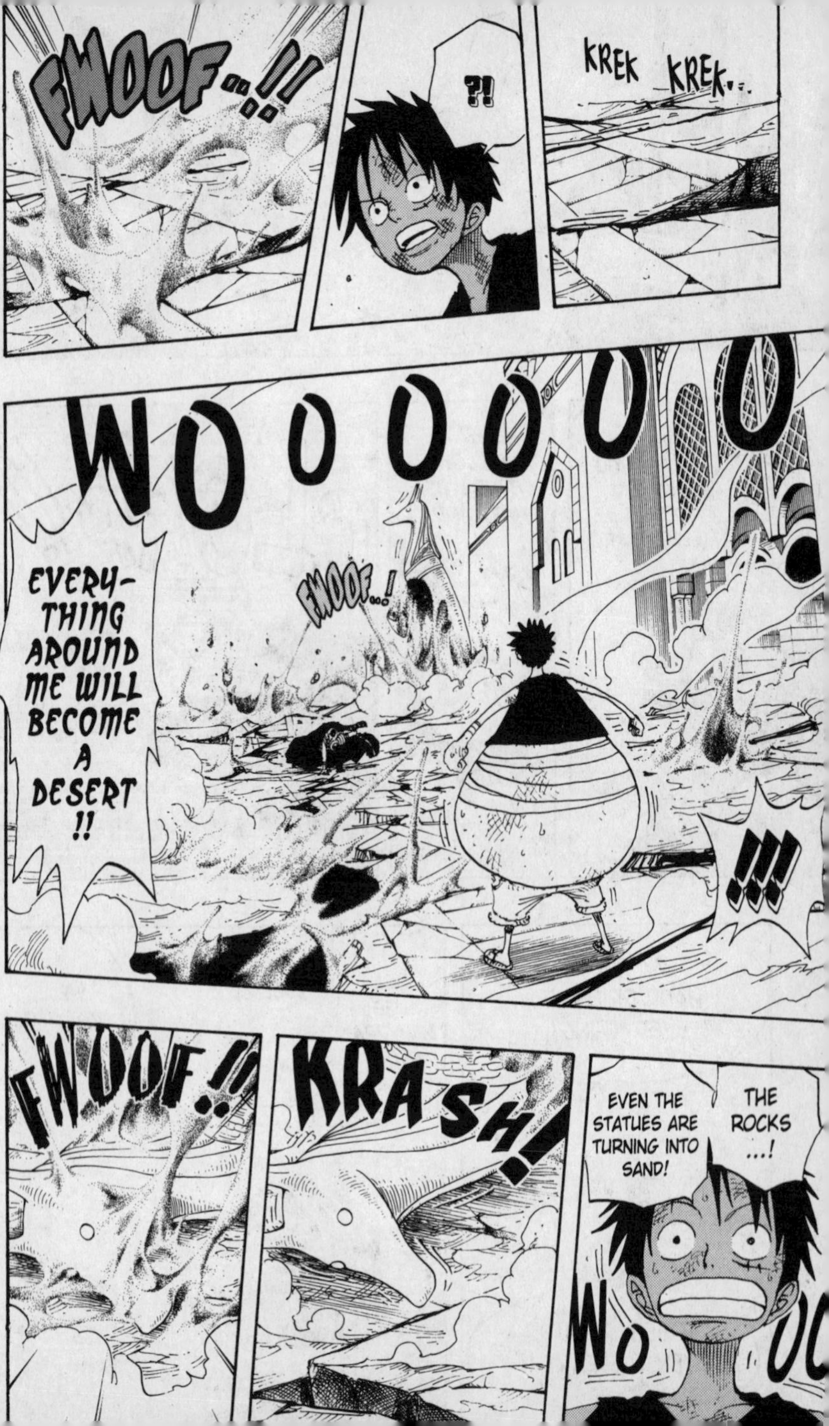
KREK KREK...
?!
FWOOF...!!
WOOOOOOO
!!!
FWOOF...!
EVERY-THING AROUND ME WILL BECOME A DESERT !!
THE ROCKS ...!
EVEN THE STATUES ARE TURNING INTO SAND!
WOOO
KRASH!
FWOOF..!!

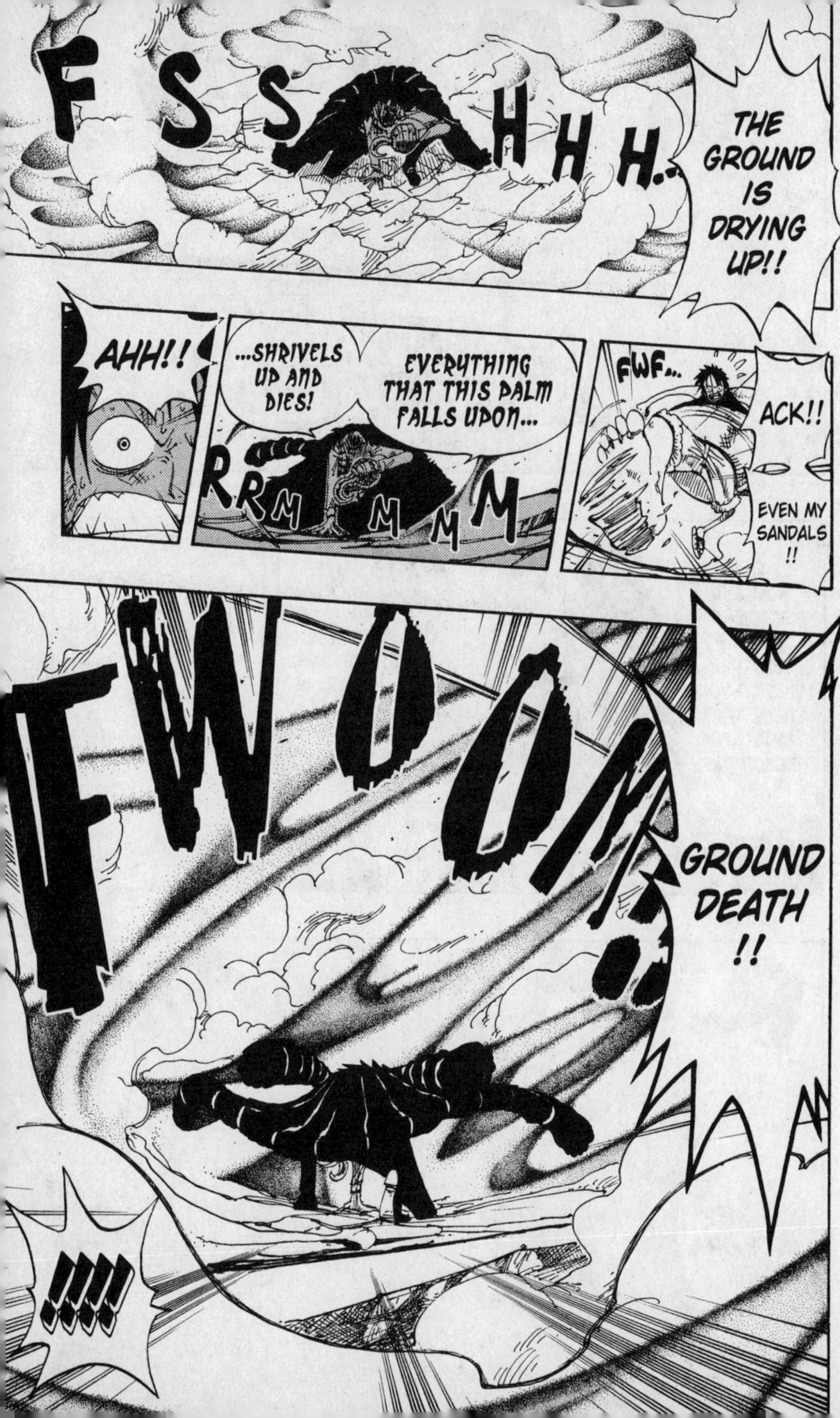
THE GROUND IS DRYING UP!!
FSSHHH...
ACK!!
FWF...
EVEN MY SANDALS!!
EVERYTHING THAT THIS PALM FALLS UPON...
...SHRIVELS UP AND DIES!
RRMMMM
AHH!!
GROUND DEATH!!
FWOOM
!!!!!

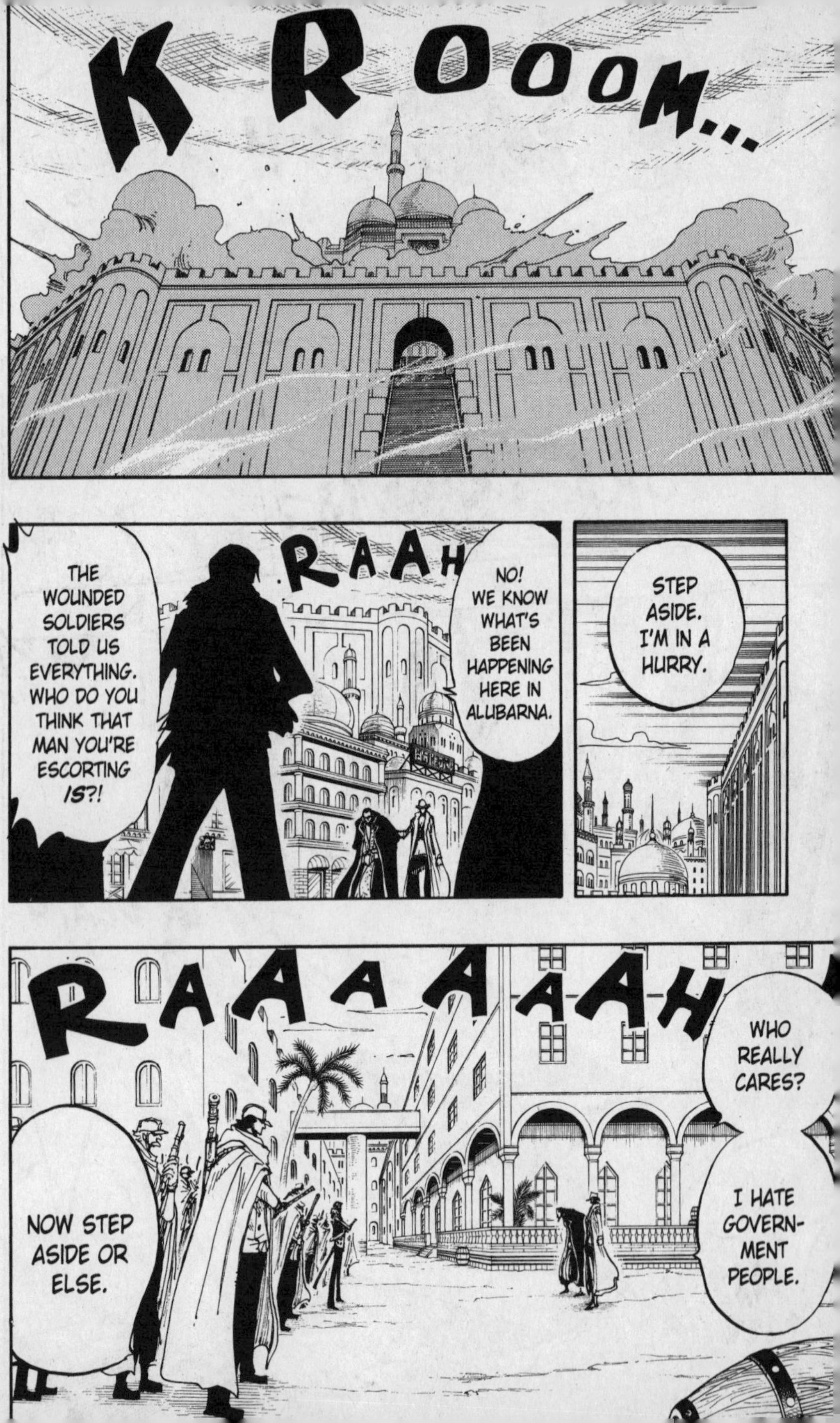
KROOOM...
STEP ASIDE. I'M IN A HURRY.
NO! WE KNOW WHAT'S BEEN HAPPENING HERE IN ALUBARNA.
RAAH
THE WOUNDED SOLDIERS TOLD US EVERYTHING. WHO DO YOU THINK THAT MAN YOU'RE ESCORTING *IS*?!
RAAAAAAH
WHO REALLY CARES?
I HATE GOVERNMENT PEOPLE.
NOW STEP ASIDE OR ELSE.

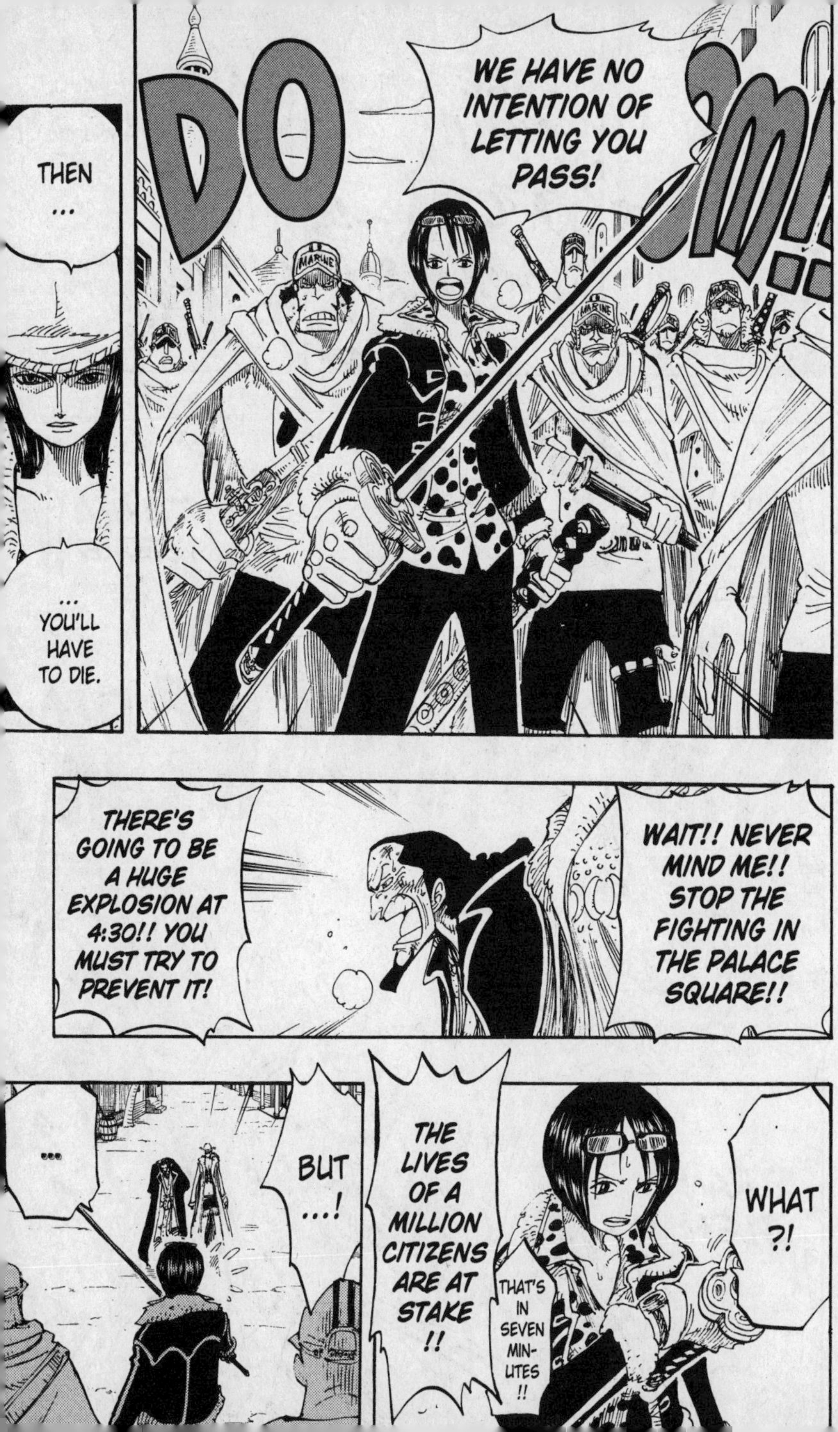
DOOM!!
WE HAVE NO INTENTION OF LETTING YOU PASS!
THEN ...
... YOU'LL HAVE TO DIE.
WAIT!! NEVER MIND ME!! STOP THE FIGHTING IN THE PALACE SQUARE!!
THERE'S GOING TO BE A HUGE EXPLOSION AT 4:30!! YOU MUST TRY TO PREVENT IT!
WHAT ?!
THAT'S IN SEVEN MIN-UTES !!
THE LIVES OF A MILLION CITIZENS ARE AT STAKE !!
BUT ...!
...

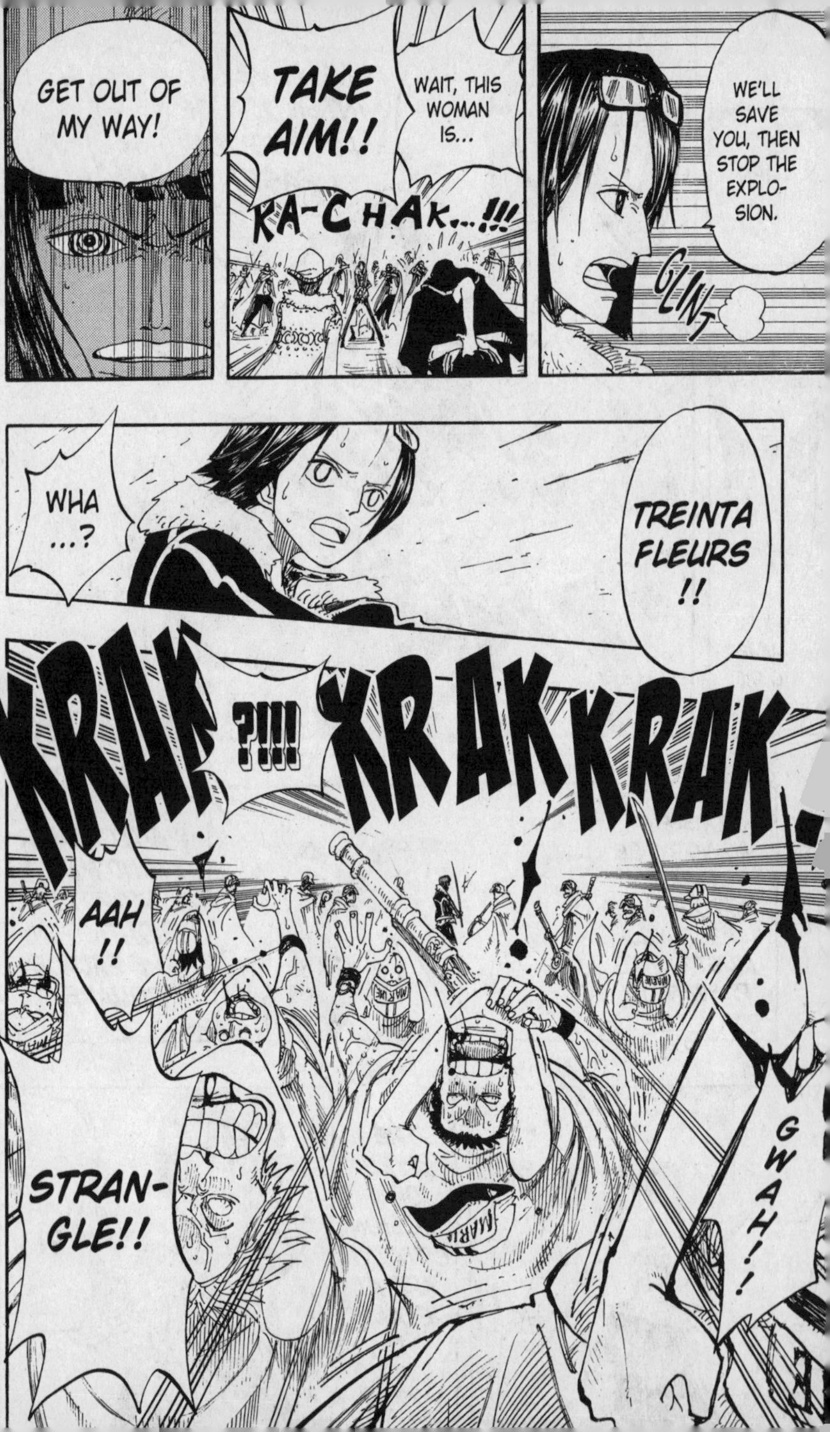
WE'LL SAVE YOU, THEN STOP THE EXPLOSION.
GLINT
WAIT, THIS WOMAN IS...
TAKE AIM!!
KA-CHAK...!!!
GET OUT OF MY WAY!
TREINTA FLEURS!!
WHA...?
KRAK KRAK...
KRAK
?!!!
KRAK
GWAH!!
AAH!!
STRANGLE!!

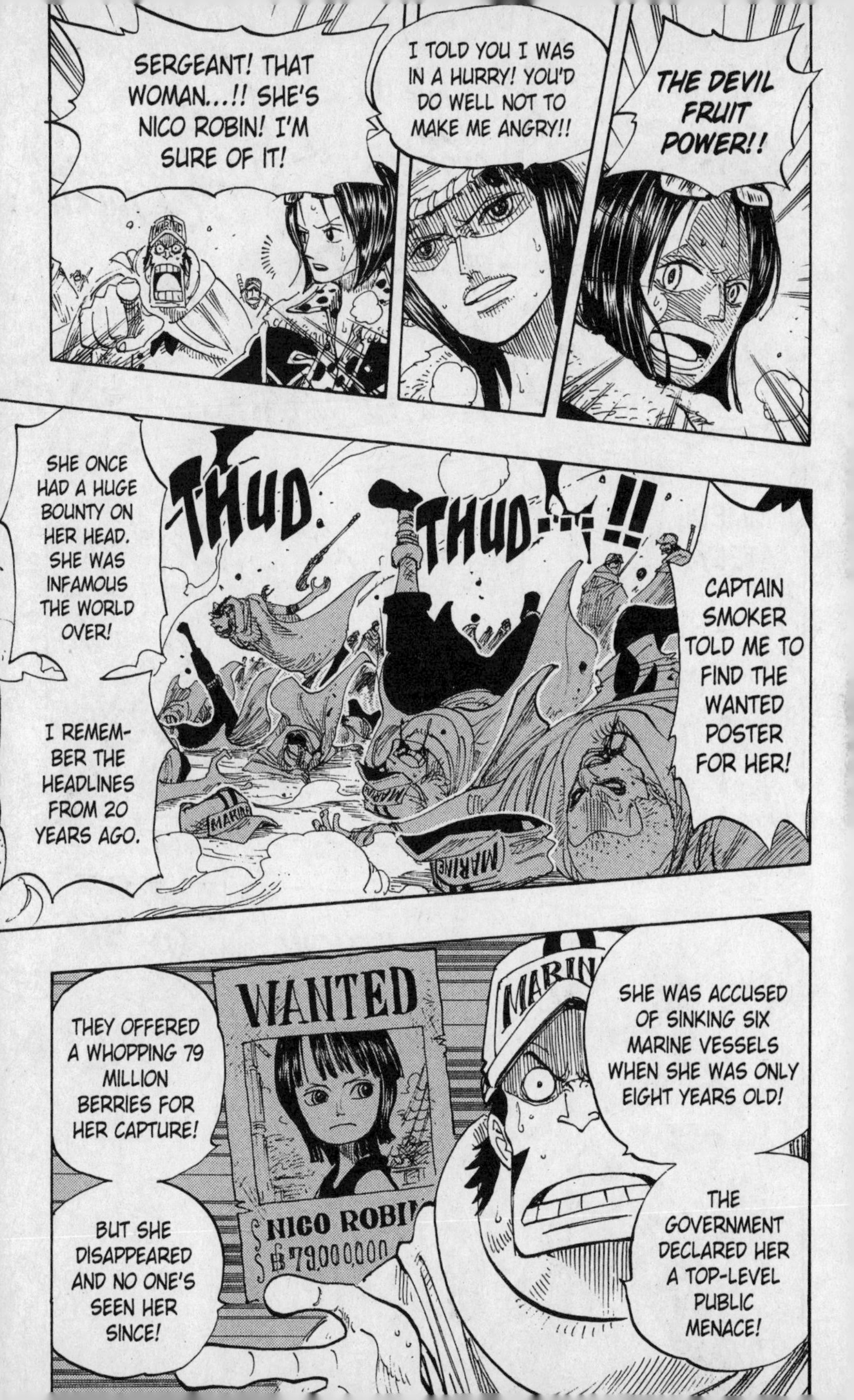
THE DEVIL FRUIT POWER!!
I TOLD YOU I WAS IN A HURRY! YOU'D DO WELL NOT TO MAKE ME ANGRY!!
SERGEANT! THAT WOMAN...!! SHE'S NICO ROBIN! I'M SURE OF IT!
THUD...!!
THUD.
CAPTAIN SMOKER TOLD ME TO FIND THE WANTED POSTER FOR HER!
SHE ONCE HAD A HUGE BOUNTY ON HER HEAD. SHE WAS INFAMOUS THE WORLD OVER!
I REMEMBER THE HEADLINES FROM 20 YEARS AGO.
SHE WAS ACCUSED OF SINKING SIX MARINE VESSELS WHEN SHE WAS ONLY EIGHT YEARS OLD!
THE GOVERNMENT DECLARED HER A TOP-LEVEL PUBLIC MENACE!
WANTED
NICO ROBI
฿79,000,000
THEY OFFERED A WHOPPING 79 MILLION BERRIES FOR HER CAPTURE!
BUT SHE DISAPPEARED AND NO ONE'S SEEN HER SINCE!

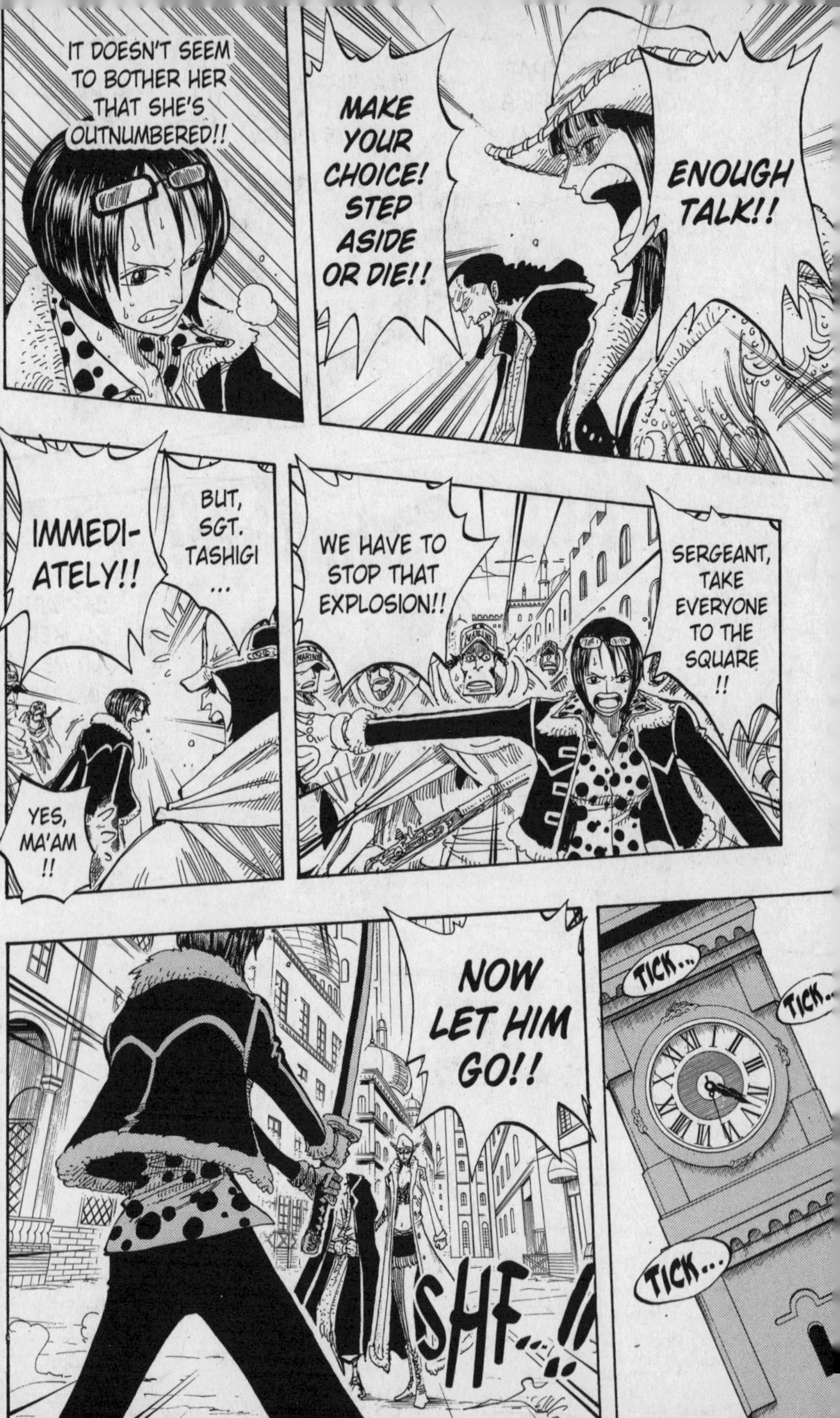
ENOUGH TALK!!
MAKE YOUR CHOICE! STEP ASIDE OR DIE!!
IT DOESN'T SEEM TO BOTHER HER THAT SHE'S OUTNUMBERED!!
SERGEANT, TAKE EVERYONE TO THE SQUARE!!
WE HAVE TO STOP THAT EXPLOSION!!
BUT, SGT. TASHIGI...
IMMEDIATELY!!
YES, MA'AM!!
TICK...
TICK...
TICK...
NOW LET HIM GO!!
SHF...!!

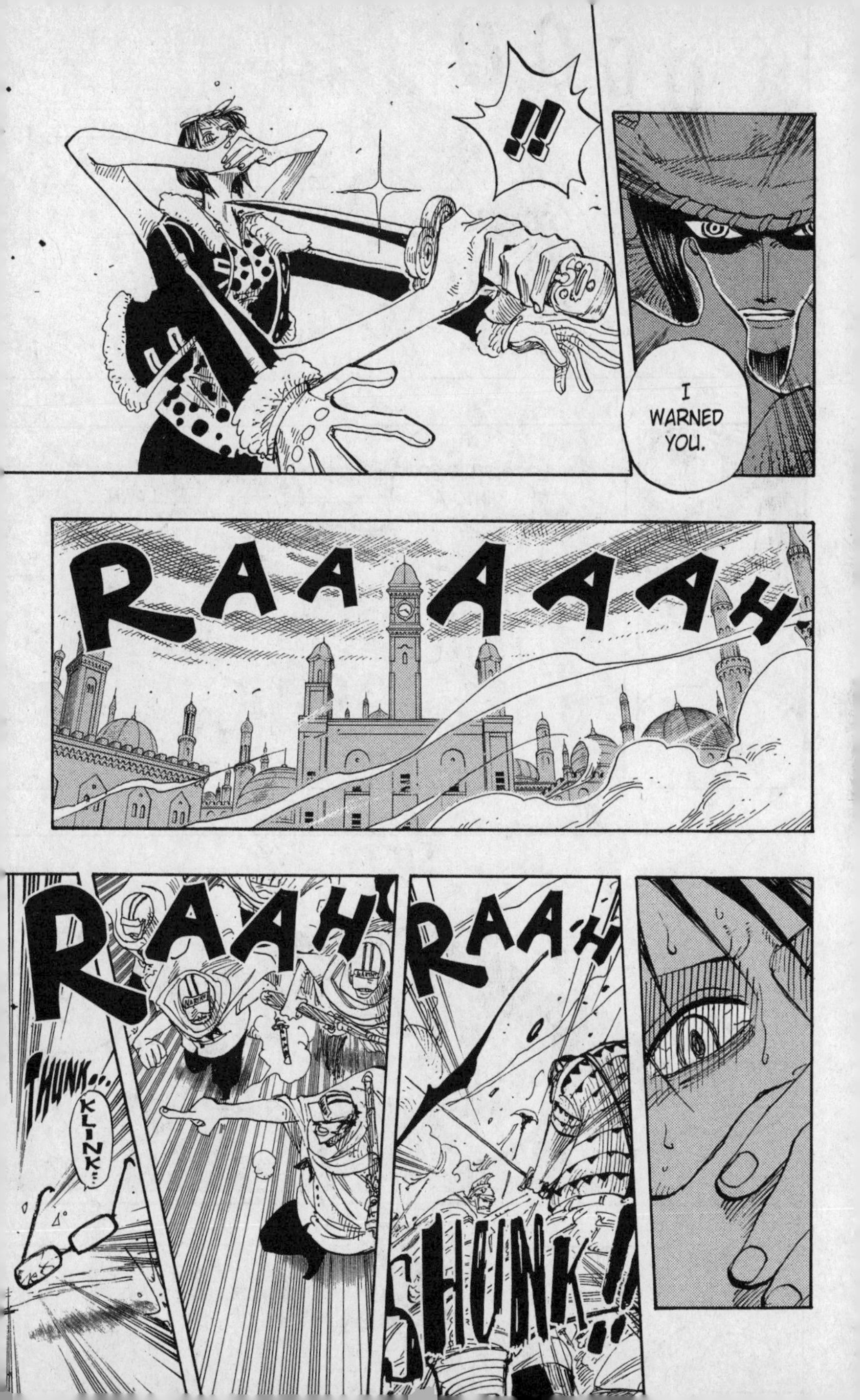
I WARNED YOU.
!!
RAAAAAH
RAAH
SHUNK!!
KLINK...
THUNK...
RAAH

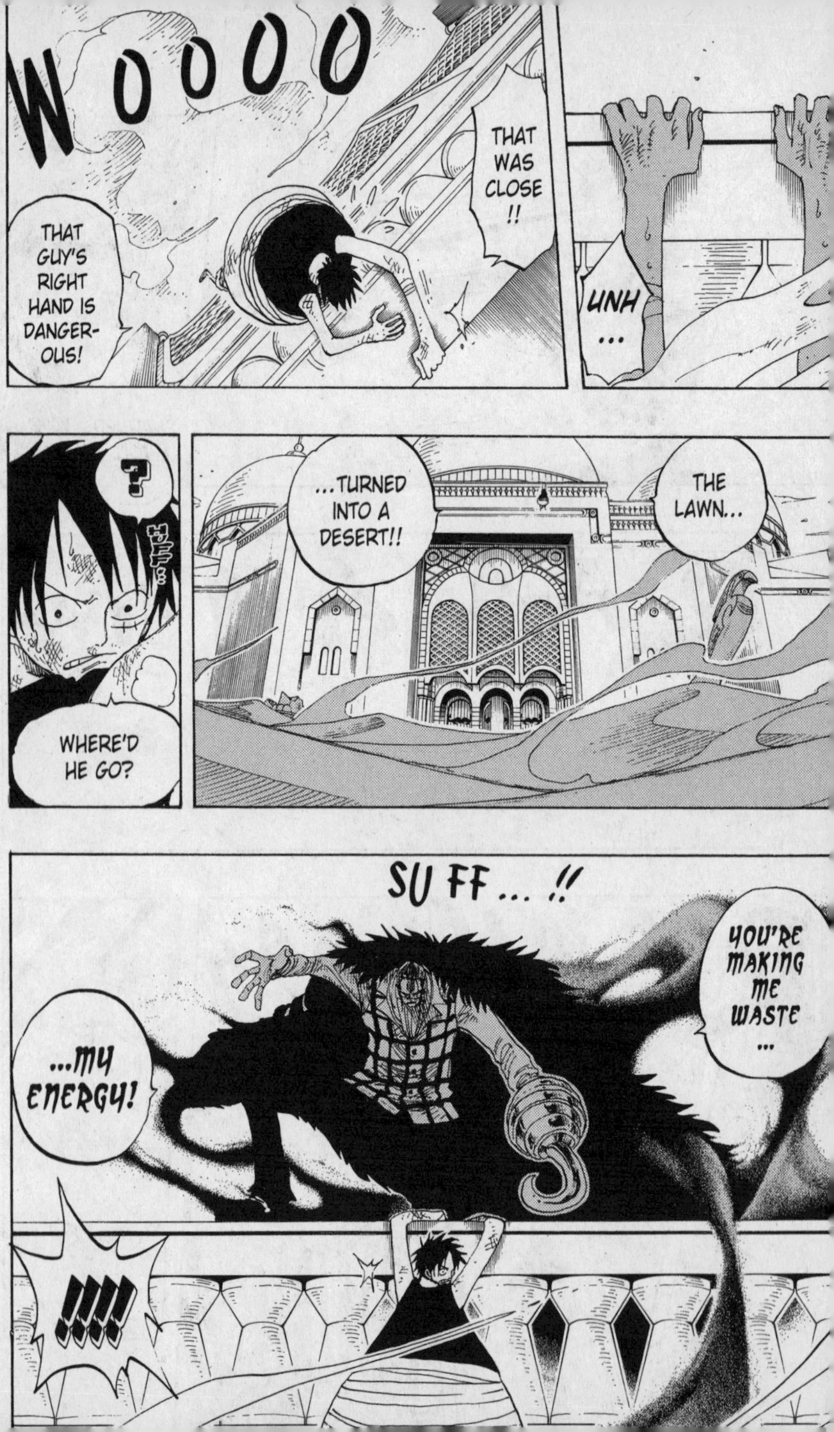
UNH ...
THAT WAS CLOSE !!
WOOOO
THAT GUY'S RIGHT HAND IS DANGER-OUS!
THE LAWN...
...TURNED INTO A DESERT!!
?
HUFF!!
WHERE'D HE GO?
SU FF ... !!
YOU'RE MAKING ME WASTE ...
...MY ENERGY!
!!!!!

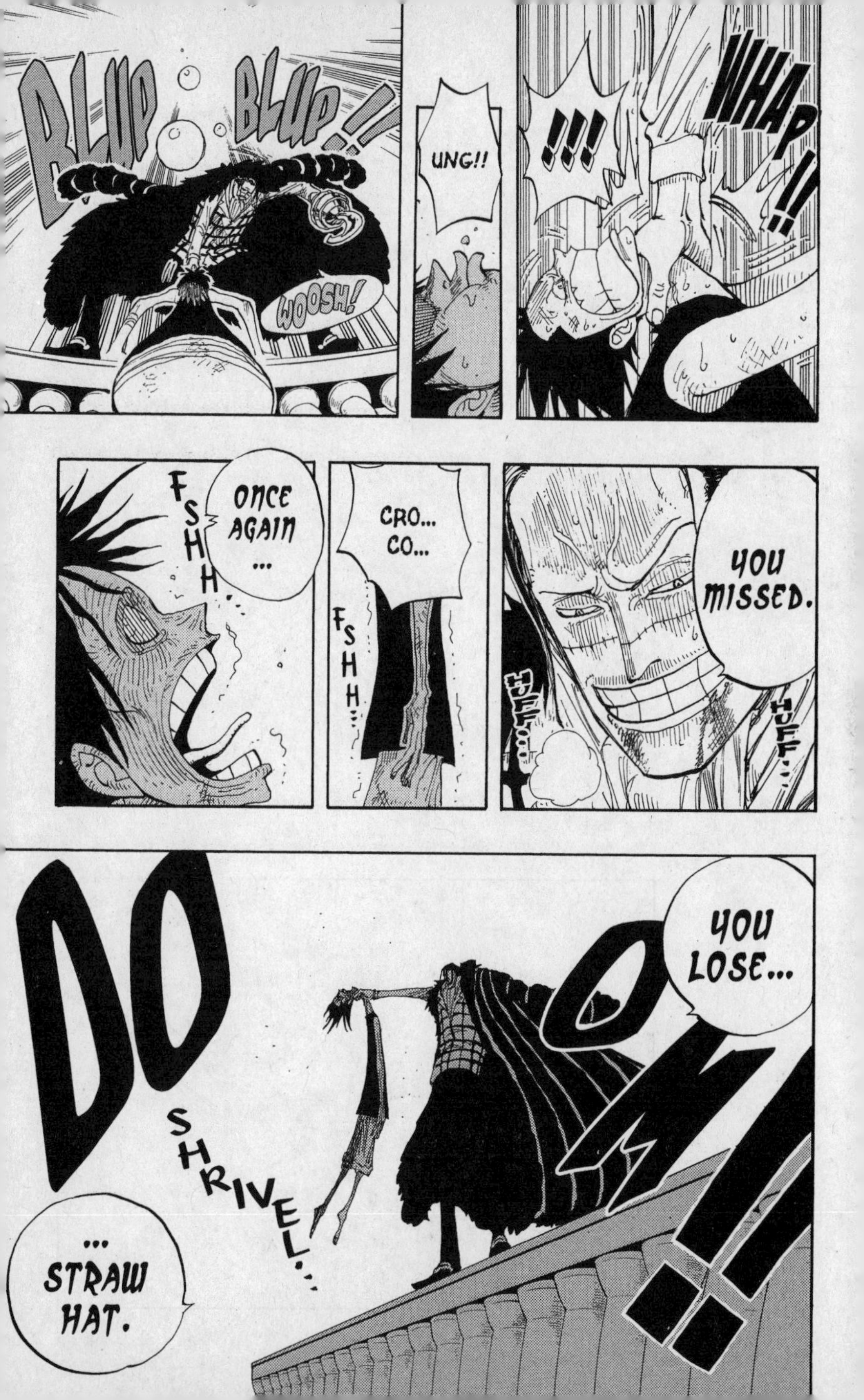
WHAP!!
!!!
UNG!!
BLUP BLUP!!
WOOSH!
YOU MISSED.
HUFF...
HUFF...
CRO... CO...
FSHH...
ONCE AGAIN...
FSHH...
YOU LOSE...
DOOM!!
SHRIVEL...
...STRAW HAT.

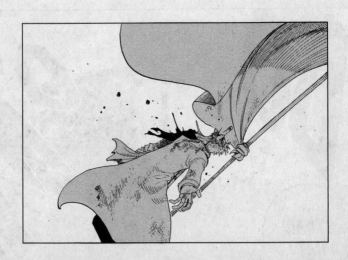

Chapter 202:
THE ROYAL MAUSOLEUM

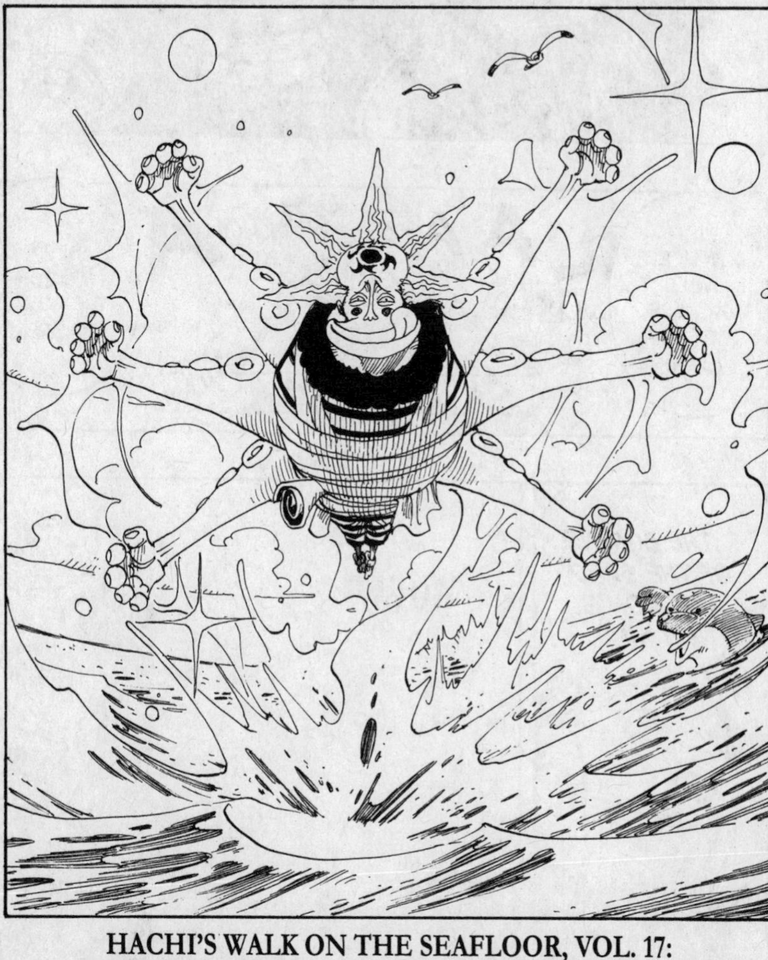

HACHI'S WALK ON THE SEAFLOOR, VOL. 17:
"IN SEARCH OF THE LEGENDARY SUPER-YUMMY OCTOPUS FRITTER RECIPE"

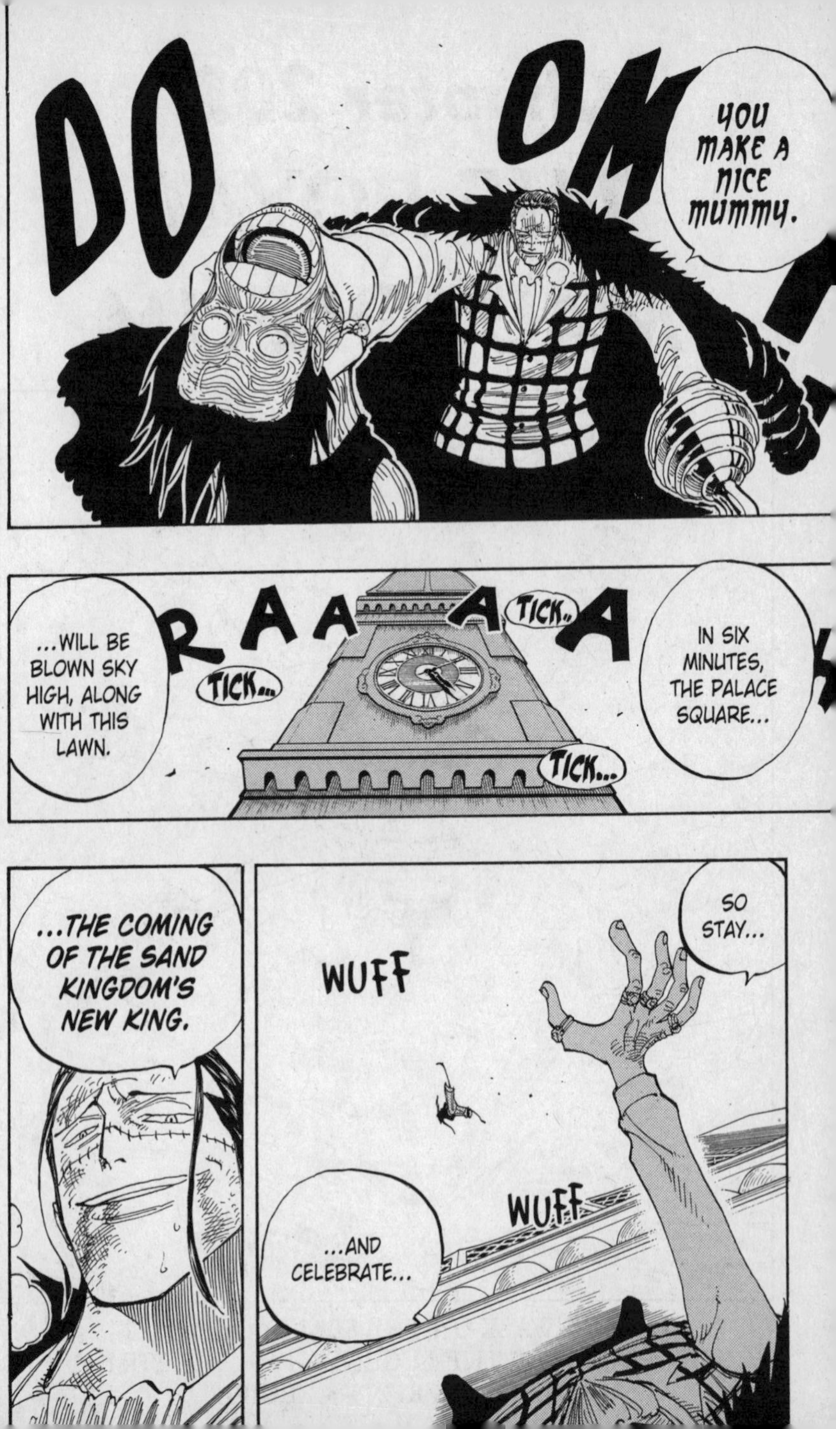
DO OM
YOU MAKE A NICE MUMMY.
IN SIX MINUTES, THE PALACE SQUARE...
TICK..
RAAAA
TICK...
TICK...
...WILL BE BLOWN SKY HIGH, ALONG WITH THIS LAWN.
SO STAY...
WUFF
WUFF
...AND CELEBRATE...
...THE COMING OF THE SAND KINGDOM'S NEW KING.

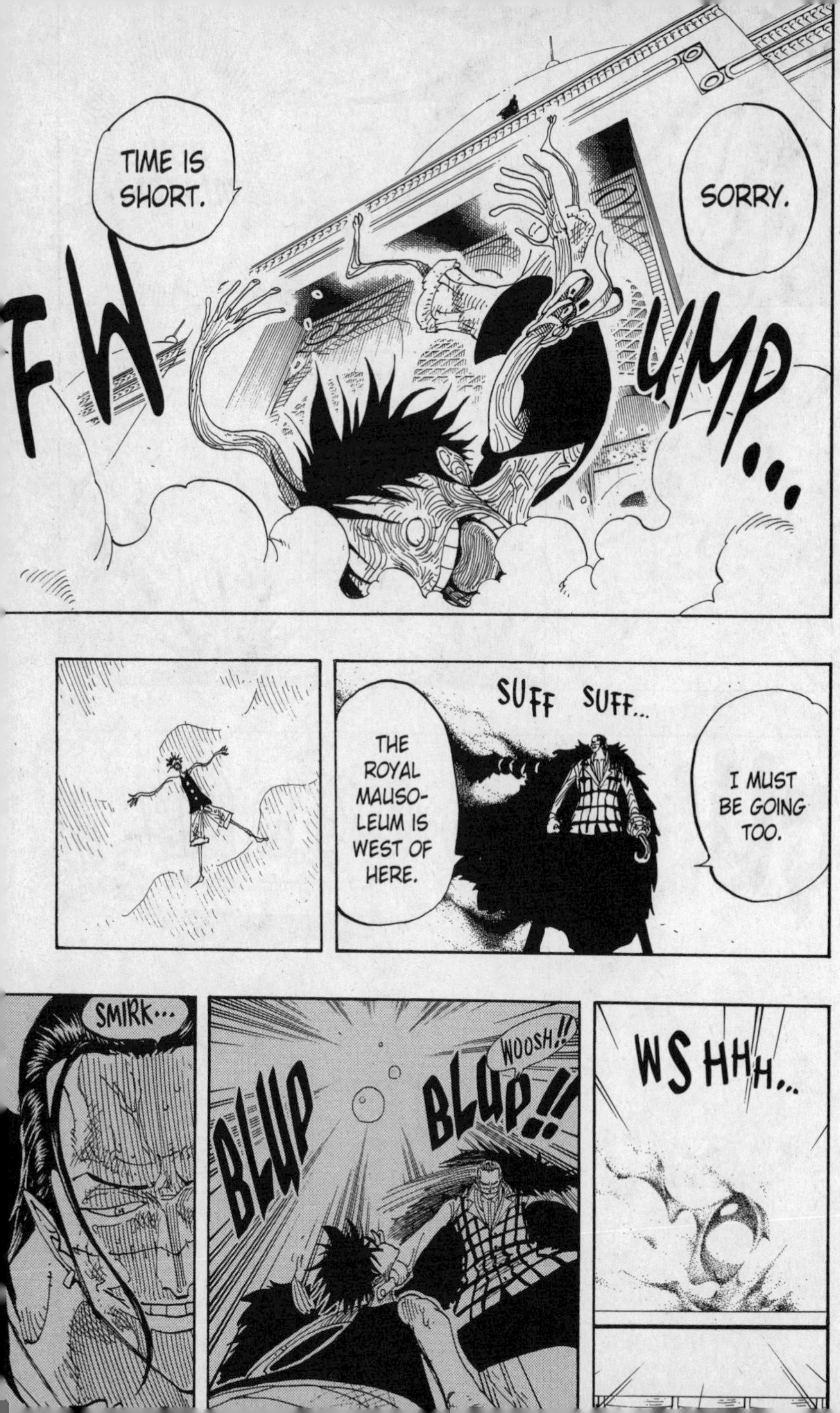
SORRY.
TIME IS SHORT.
FWUMP...
I MUST BE GOING TOO.
SUFF SUFF...
THE ROYAL MAUSO-LEUM IS WEST OF HERE.
WSHHH...
WOOSH!!
BLUP!!
BLUP
SMIRK...

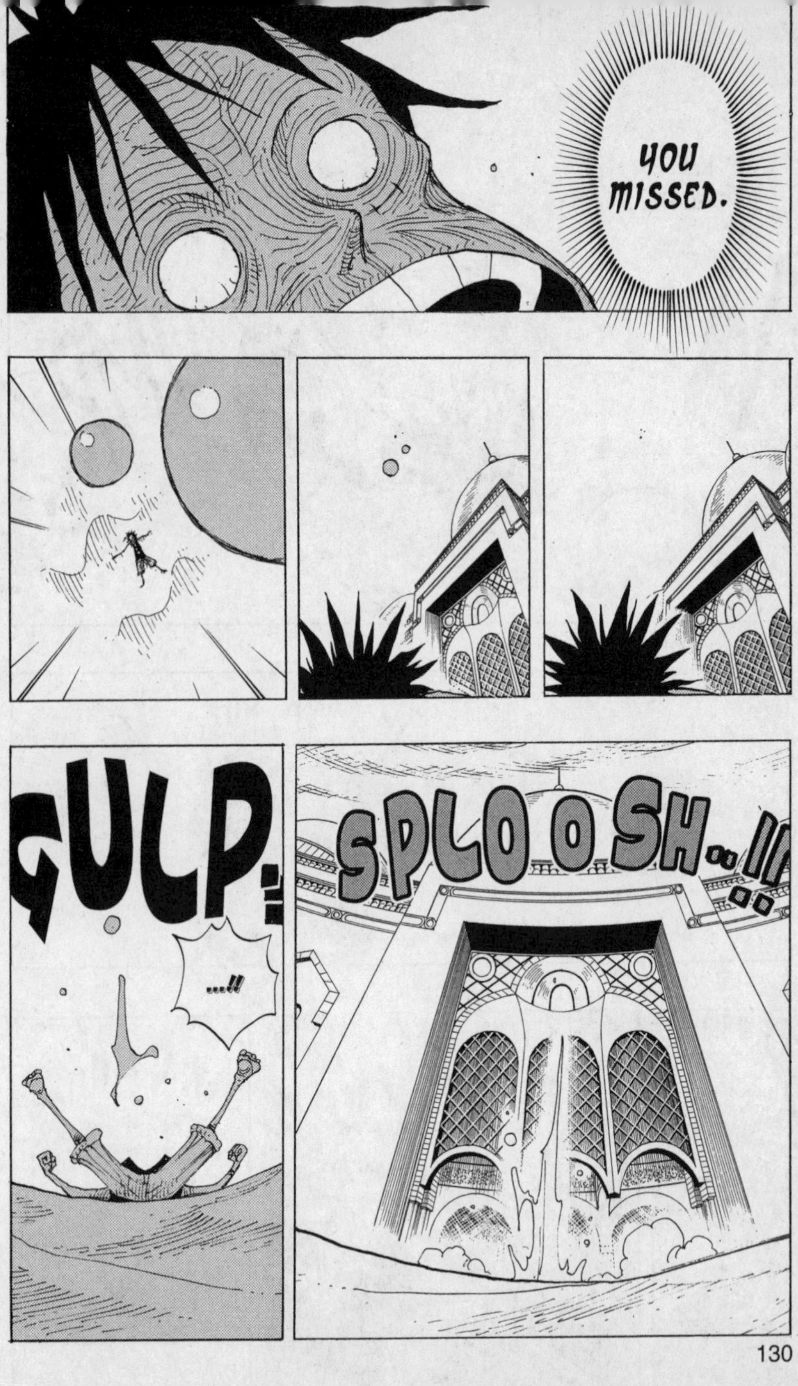
YOU MISSED.
SPLOOSH..!!
GULP
...!!

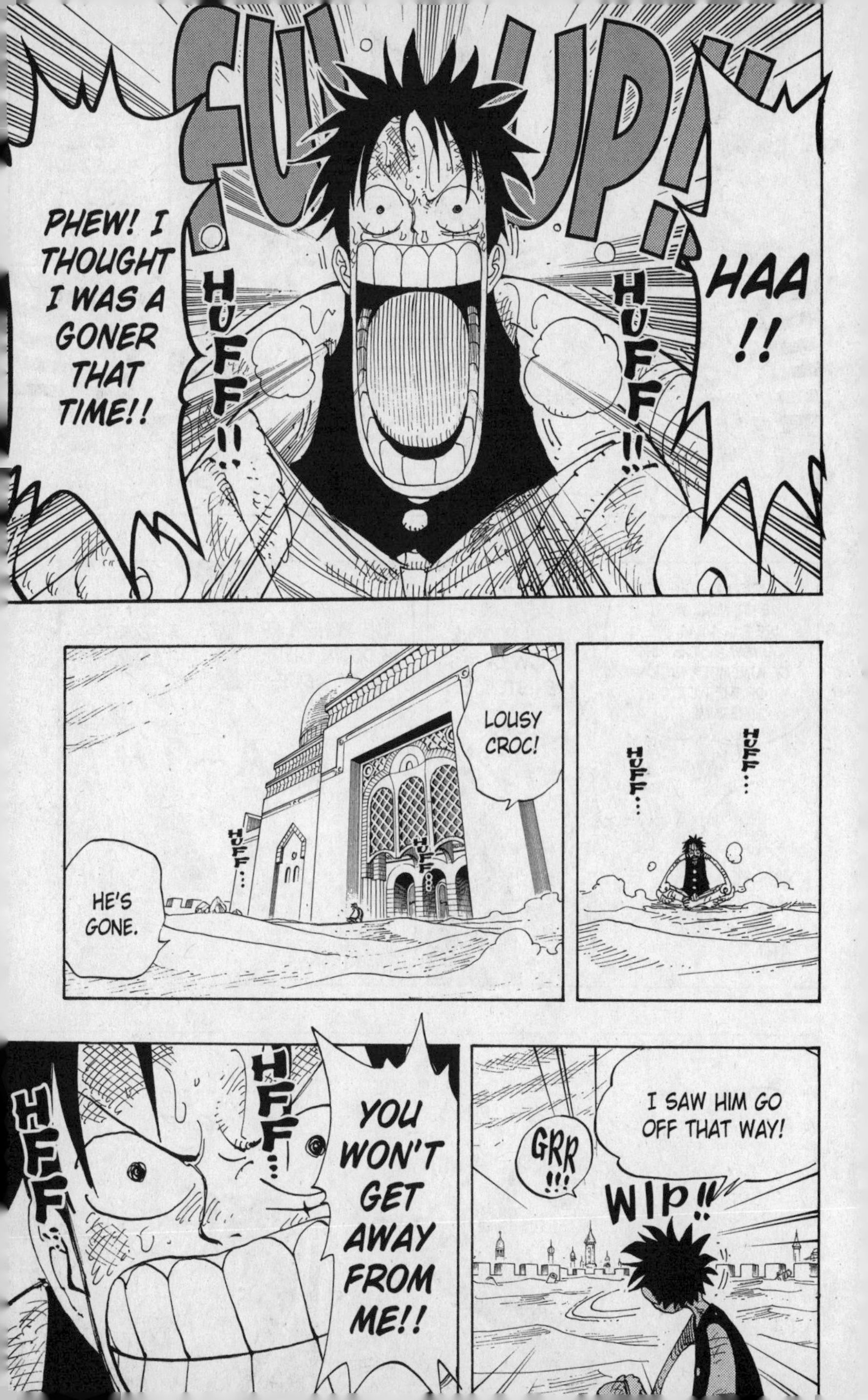
HAA!!
HUFF!!
HUFF!!
PHEW! I THOUGHT I WAS A GONER THAT TIME!!
HUFF...
HUFF...
LOUSY CROC!
HUFF...
HUFF...
HE'S GONE.
I SAW HIM GO OFF THAT WAY!
GRR!!!
WIP!!
YOU WON'T GET AWAY FROM ME!!
HFF...
HFF...

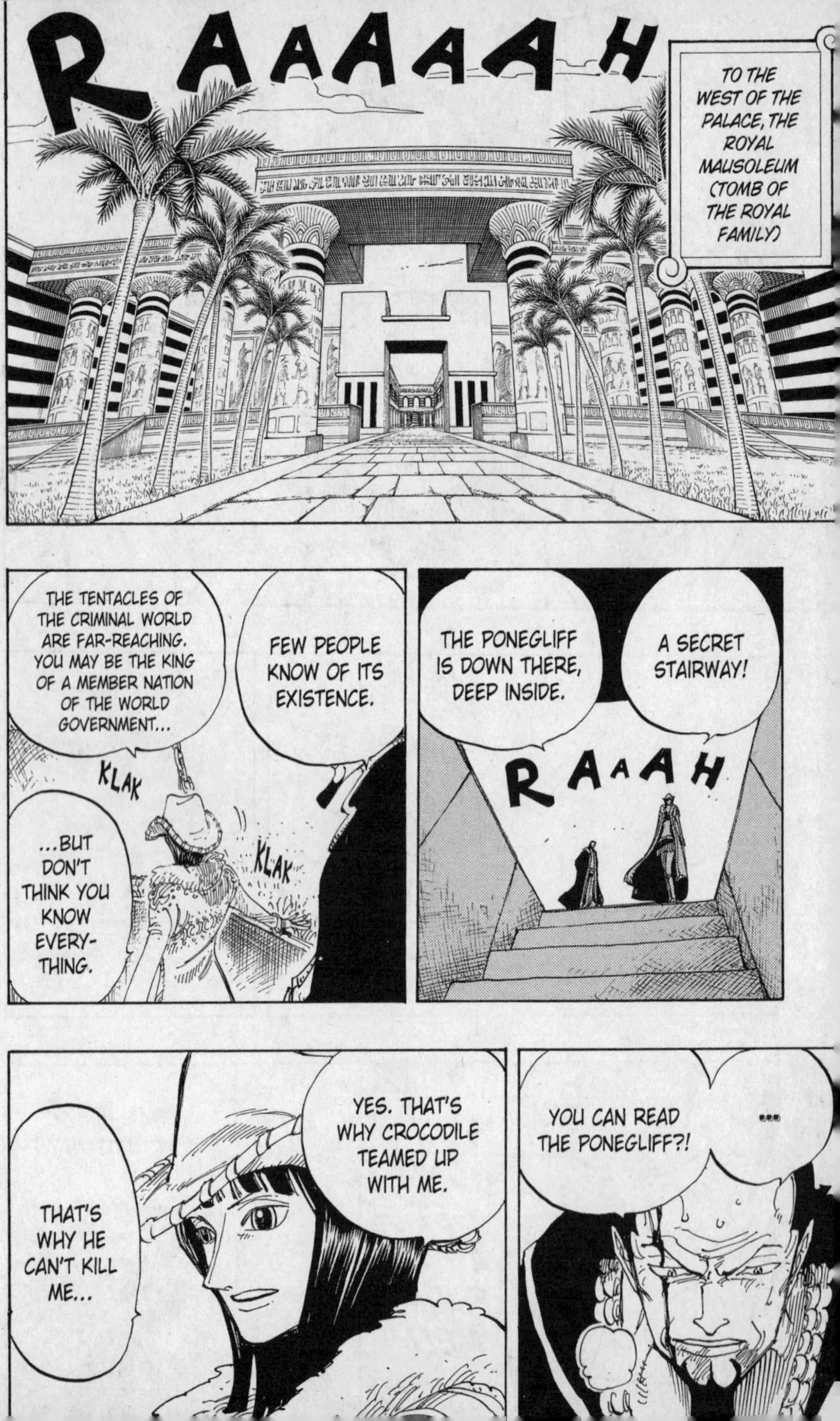
TO THE WEST OF THE PALACE, THE ROYAL MAUSOLEUM (TOMB OF THE ROYAL FAMILY)
RAAAAAH
A SECRET STAIRWAY!
THE PONEGLIFF IS DOWN THERE, DEEP INSIDE.
RAAAH
FEW PEOPLE KNOW OF ITS EXISTENCE.
THE TENTACLES OF THE CRIMINAL WORLD ARE FAR-REACHING. YOU MAY BE THE KING OF A MEMBER NATION OF THE WORLD GOVERNMENT...
KLAK
...BUT DON'T THINK YOU KNOW EVERY-THING.
KLAK
...
YOU CAN READ THE PONEGLIFF?!
YES. THAT'S WHY CROCODILE TEAMED UP WITH ME.
THAT'S WHY HE CAN'T KILL ME...

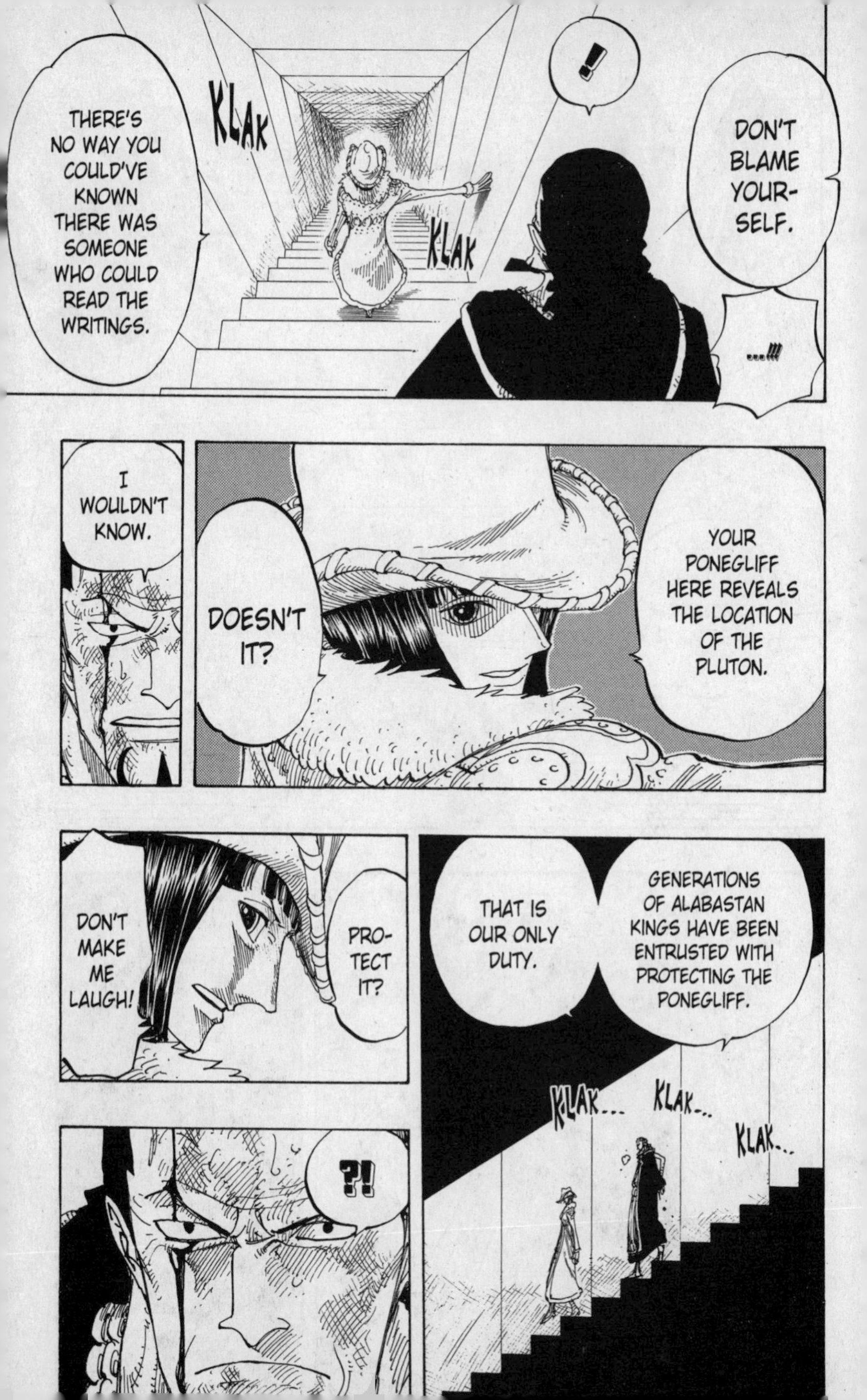

!
DON'T BLAME YOURSELF.
THERE'S NO WAY YOU COULD'VE KNOWN THERE WAS SOMEONE WHO COULD READ THE WRITINGS.
KLAK
KLAK
...!!!
YOUR PONEGLIFF HERE REVEALS THE LOCATION OF THE PLUTON.
DOESN'T IT?
I WOULDN'T KNOW.
GENERATIONS OF ALABASTAN KINGS HAVE BEEN ENTRUSTED WITH PROTECTING THE PONEGLIFF.
THAT IS OUR ONLY DUTY.
KLAK...
KLAK...
KLAK...
PRO-TECT IT?
DON'T MAKE ME LAUGH!
?!

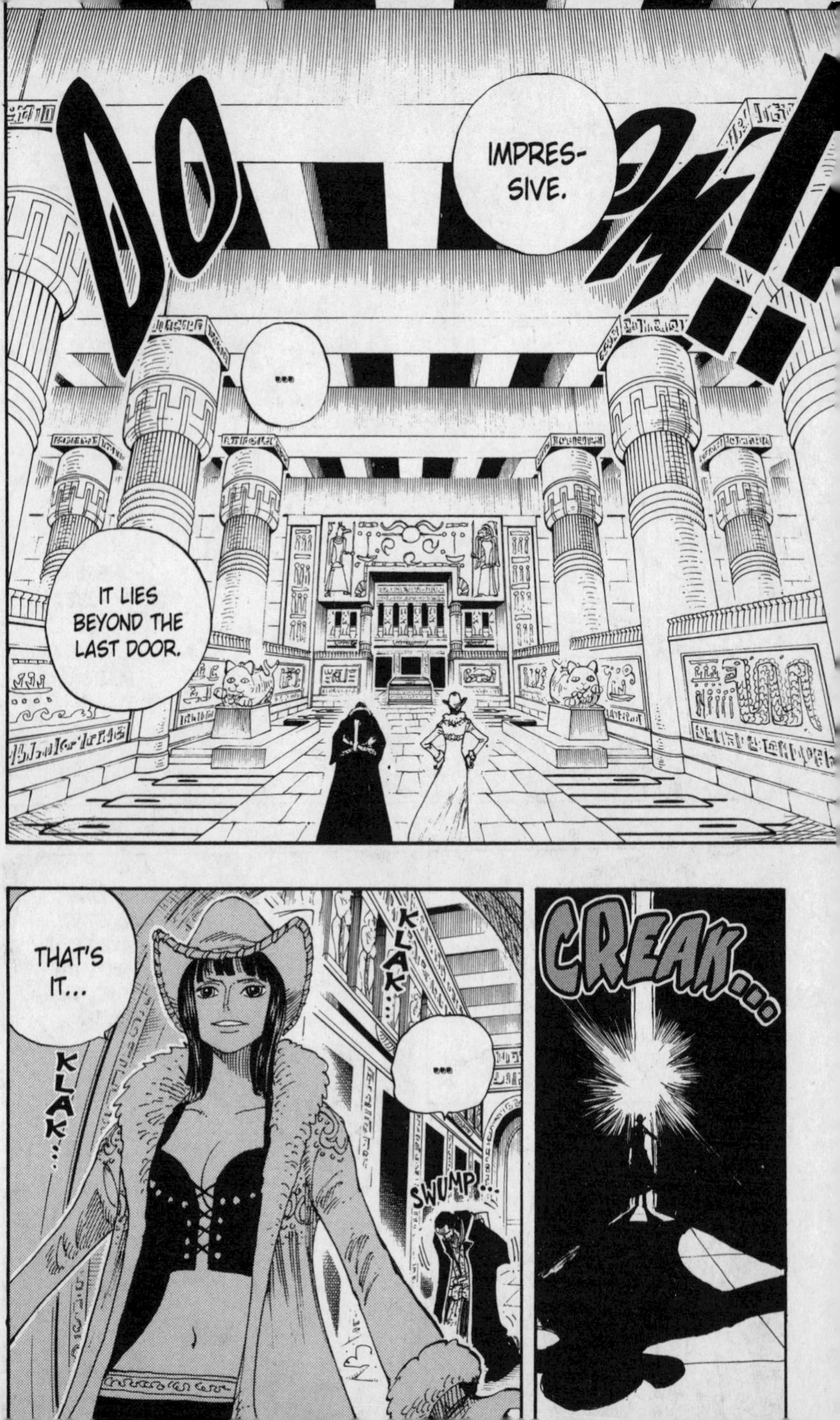
DO-ON!!
IMPRES-SIVE.
...
IT LIES BEYOND THE LAST DOOR.
CREAK...
KLAK...
THAT'S IT...
...
SWUMP...
KLAK...

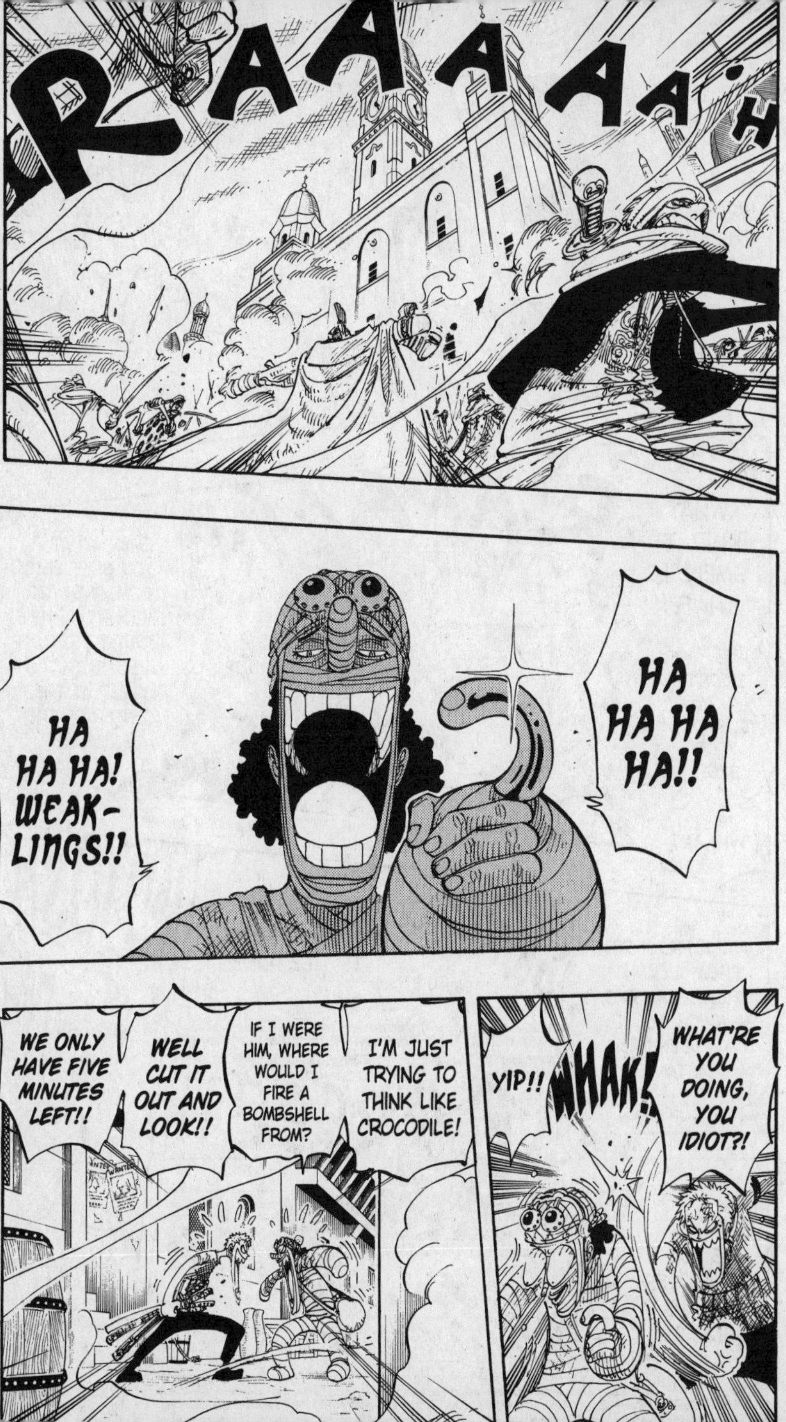
RAAAAAAH
HA HA HA HA!!
HA HA HA! WEAK-LINGS!!
WHAT'RE YOU DOING, YOU IDIOT?!
WHAK!
YIP!!
I'M JUST TRYING TO THINK LIKE CROCODILE!
IF I WERE HIM, WHERE WOULD I FIRE A BOMBSHELL FROM?
WELL CUT IT OUT AND LOOK!!
WE ONLY HAVE FIVE MINUTES LEFT!!

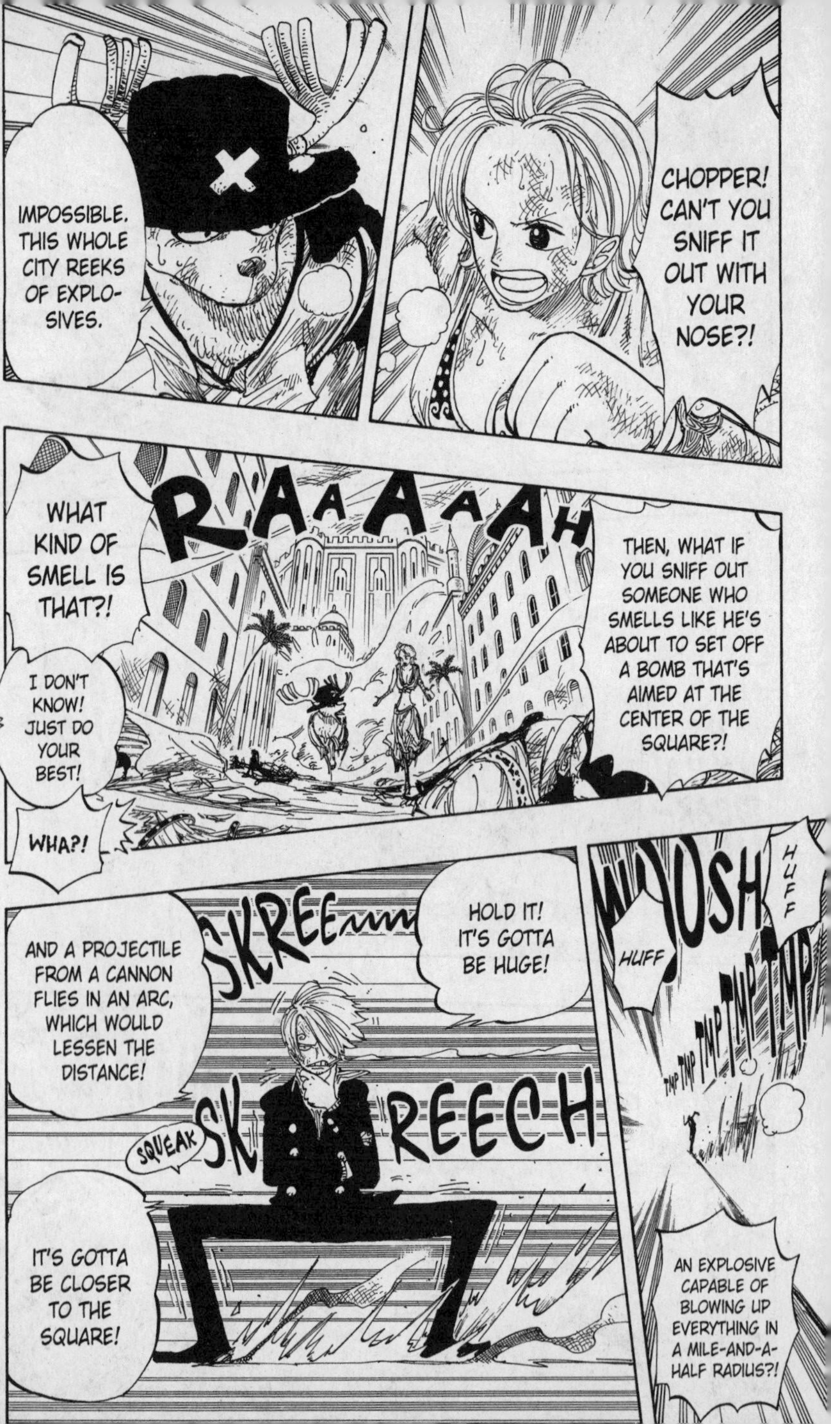

CHOPPER! CAN'T YOU SNIFF IT OUT WITH YOUR NOSE?!
IMPOSSIBLE. THIS WHOLE CITY REEKS OF EXPLOSIVES.
THEN, WHAT IF YOU SNIFF OUT SOMEONE WHO SMELLS LIKE HE'S ABOUT TO SET OFF A BOMB THAT'S AIMED AT THE CENTER OF THE SQUARE?!
RAAAAAH
WHAT KIND OF SMELL IS THAT?!
I DON'T KNOW! JUST DO YOUR BEST!
WHA?!
HUFF
HUFF
TMP TMP TMP TMP TMP TMP TMP
AN EXPLOSIVE CAPABLE OF BLOWING UP EVERYTHING IN A MILE-AND-A-HALF RADIUS?!
HOLD IT! IT'S GOTTA BE HUGE!
SKREE
AND A PROJECTILE FROM A CANNON FLIES IN AN ARC, WHICH WOULD LESSEN THE DISTANCE!
SKREECH
SQUEAK
IT'S GOTTA BE CLOSER TO THE SQUARE!

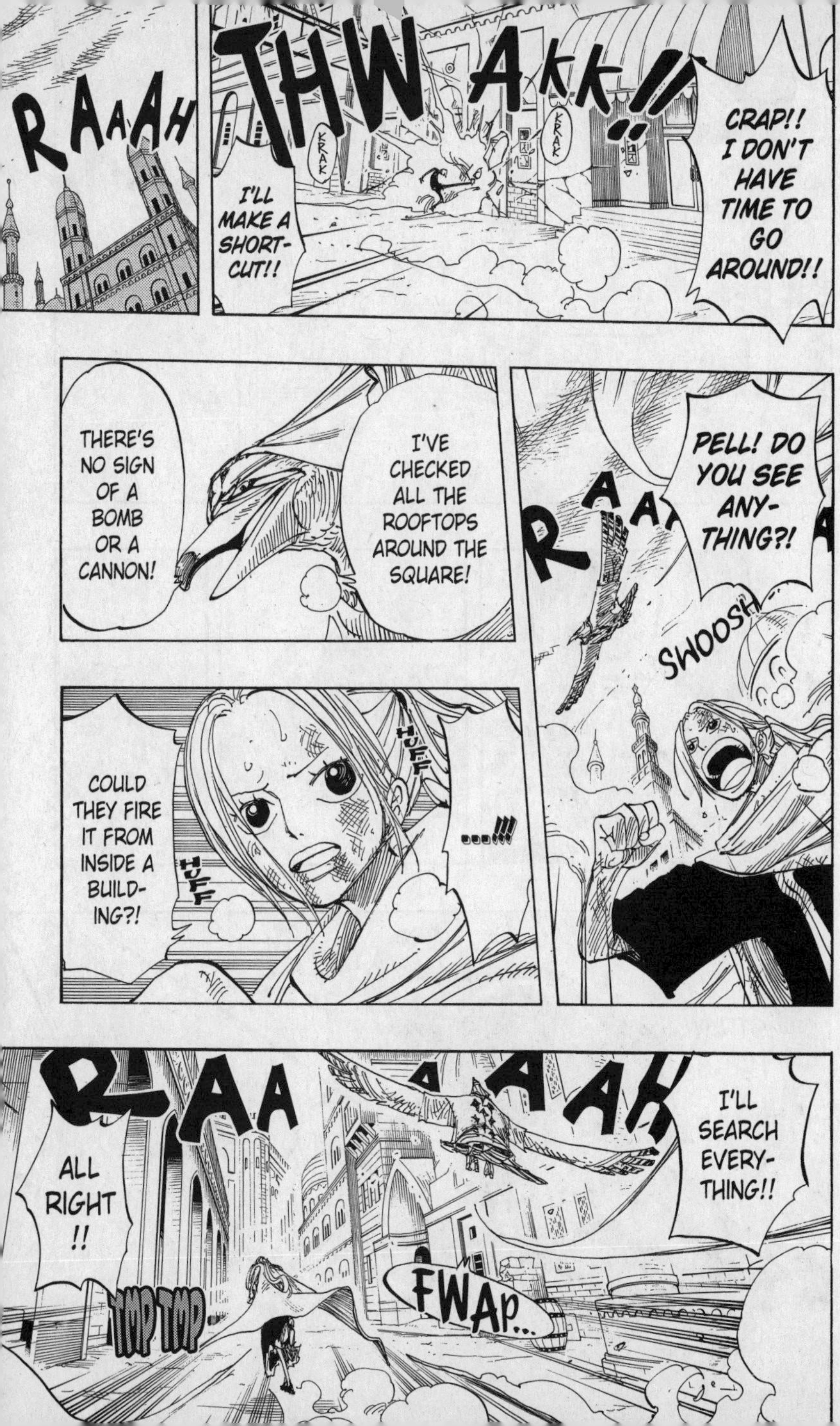
CRAP!! I DON'T HAVE TIME TO GO AROUND!!
THWAKK!!
KRAK
KRAK
I'LL MAKE A SHORT-CUT!!
RAAAH
PELL! DO YOU SEE ANY-THING?!
SWOOSH
I'VE CHECKED ALL THE ROOFTOPS AROUND THE SQUARE!
THERE'S NO SIGN OF A BOMB OR A CANNON!
...!!!
HUFF
COULD THEY FIRE IT FROM INSIDE A BUILD-ING?!
HUFF
I'LL SEARCH EVERY-THING!!
RAAAAAK
FWAP...
ALL RIGHT!!
TMP TMP

RAAAAH... RAAH

HUFF...
HUFF...
!

HUFF...
HUFF...

KLAK...

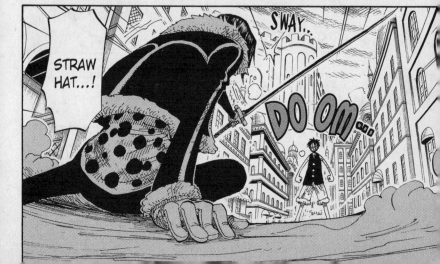

STRAW HAT...!

SWAY...

DOOM...

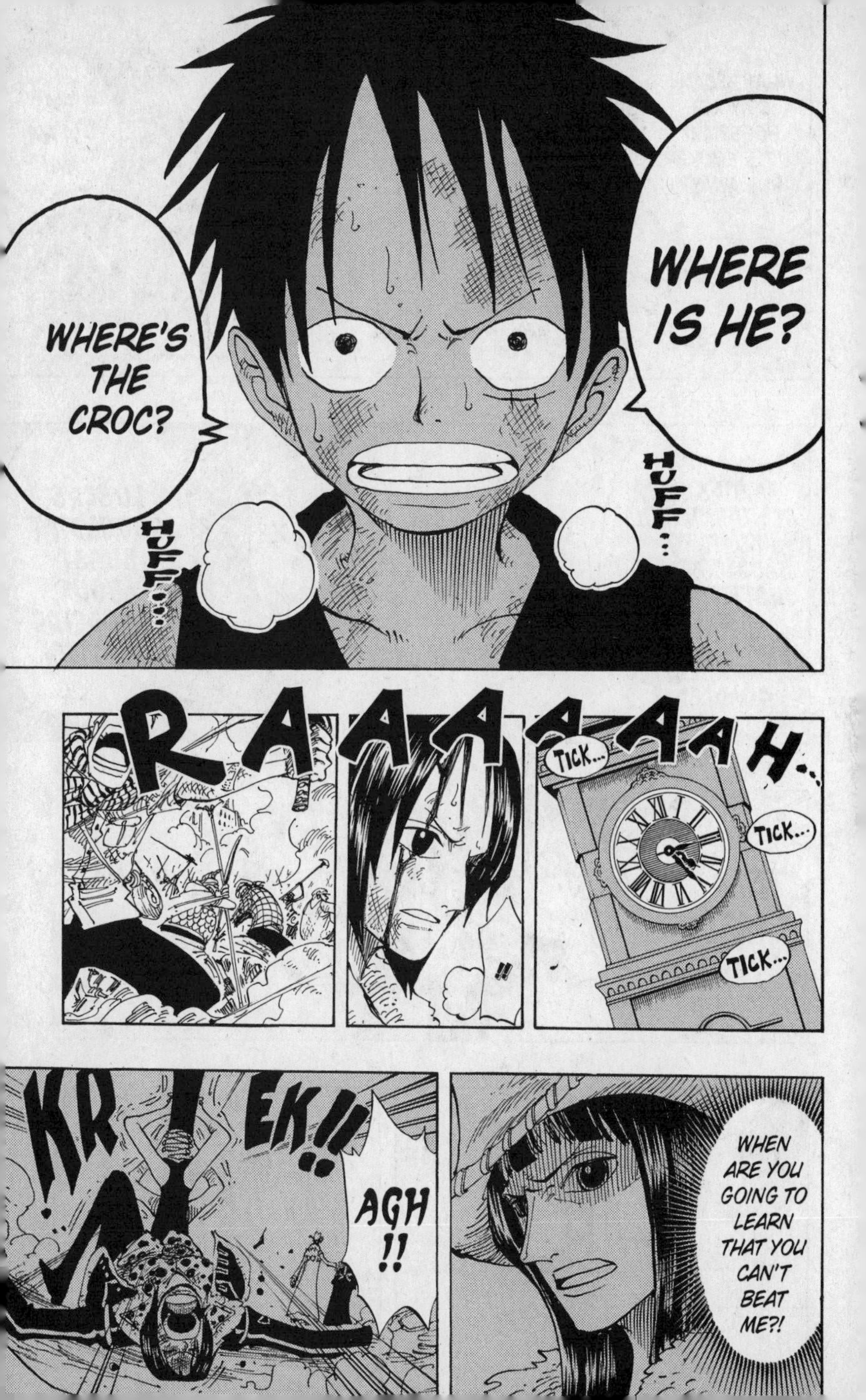
WHERE IS HE?
HUFF...
WHERE'S THE CROC?
HUFF...
RAAAAAAH...
TICK...
TICK...
TICK...
!!
WHEN ARE YOU GOING TO LEARN THAT YOU CAN'T BEAT ME?!
KR EK!!
AGH !!

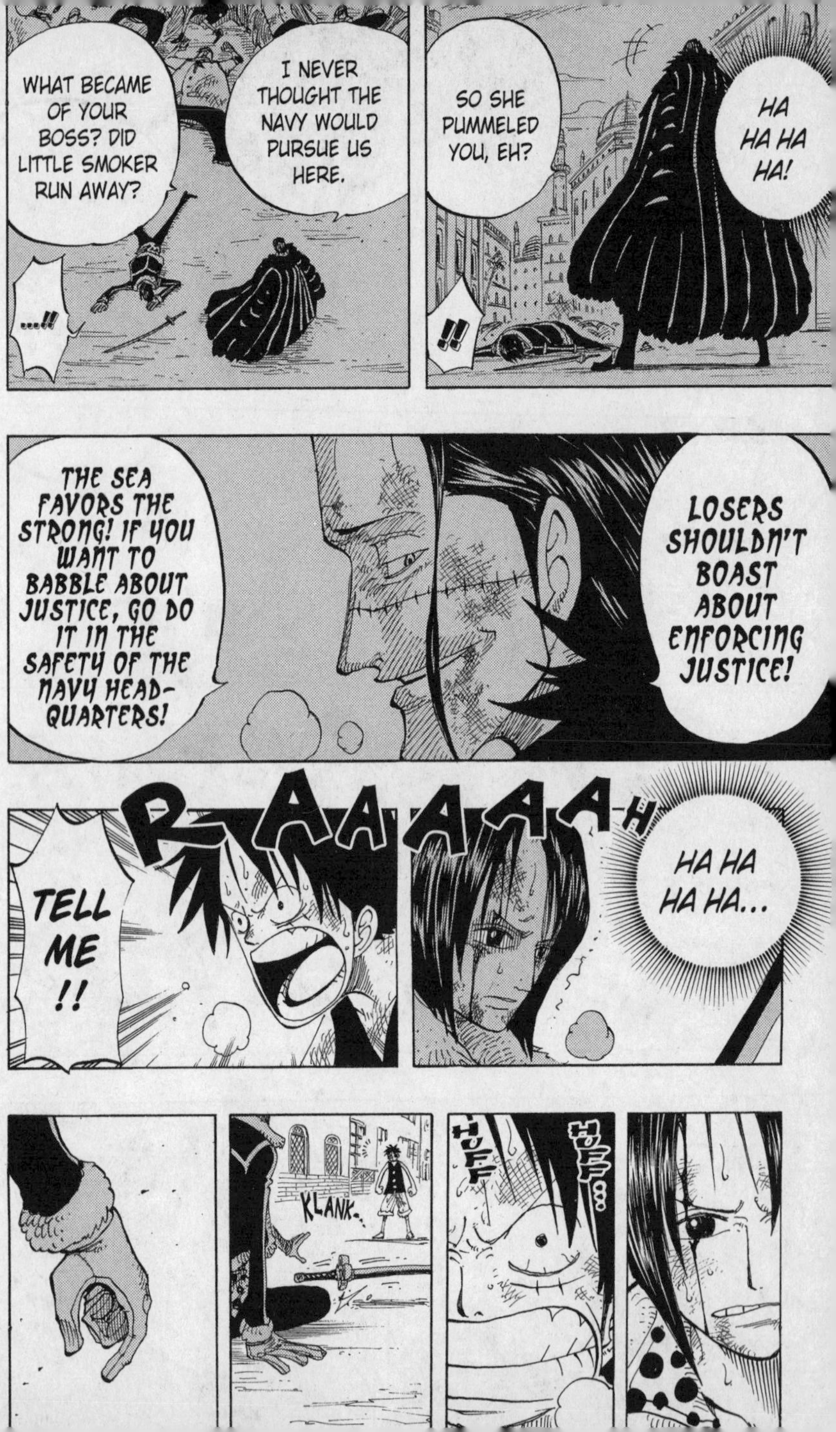
HA HA HA HA!
SO SHE PUMMELED YOU, EH?
!!
I NEVER THOUGHT THE NAVY WOULD PURSUE US HERE.
WHAT BECAME OF YOUR BOSS? DID LITTLE SMOKER RUN AWAY?
...!!
LOSERS SHOULDN'T BOAST ABOUT ENFORCING JUSTICE!
THE SEA FAVORS THE STRONG! IF YOU WANT TO BABBLE ABOUT JUSTICE, GO DO IT IN THE SAFETY OF THE NAVY HEAD-QUARTERS!
RAAAAAH
HA HA HA HA...
TELL ME !!
HUFF
HUFF...
KLANK

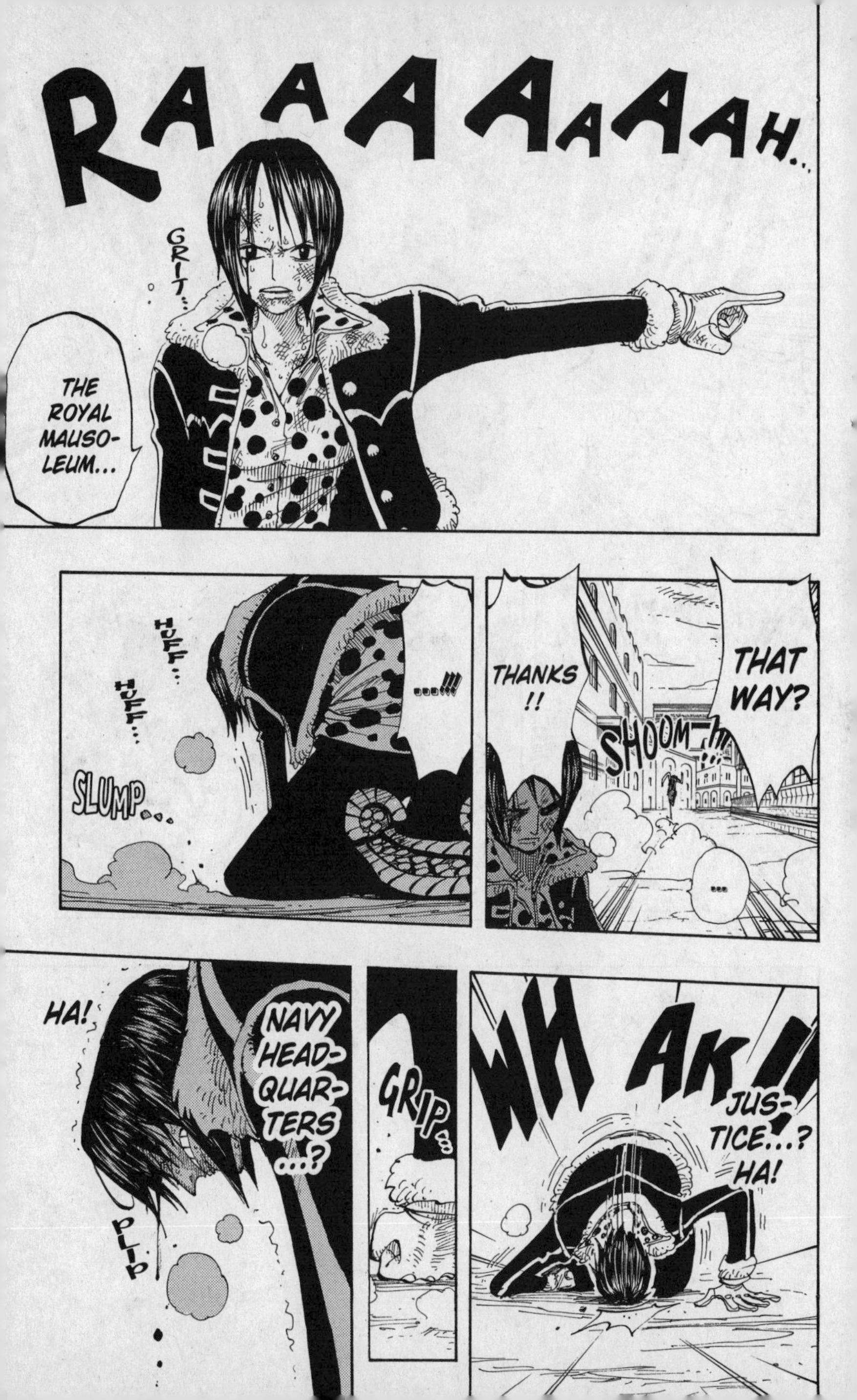
RAAAAAAAH...
GRIT...
THE ROYAL MAUSOLEUM...
THAT WAY?
THANKS!!
SHOOM...!!!
...
...!!!
HUFF...
HUFF...
SLUMP...
WHAK!!
JUSTICE...? HA!
GRIP...
NAVY HEADQUARTERS...?
HA!
PLIP

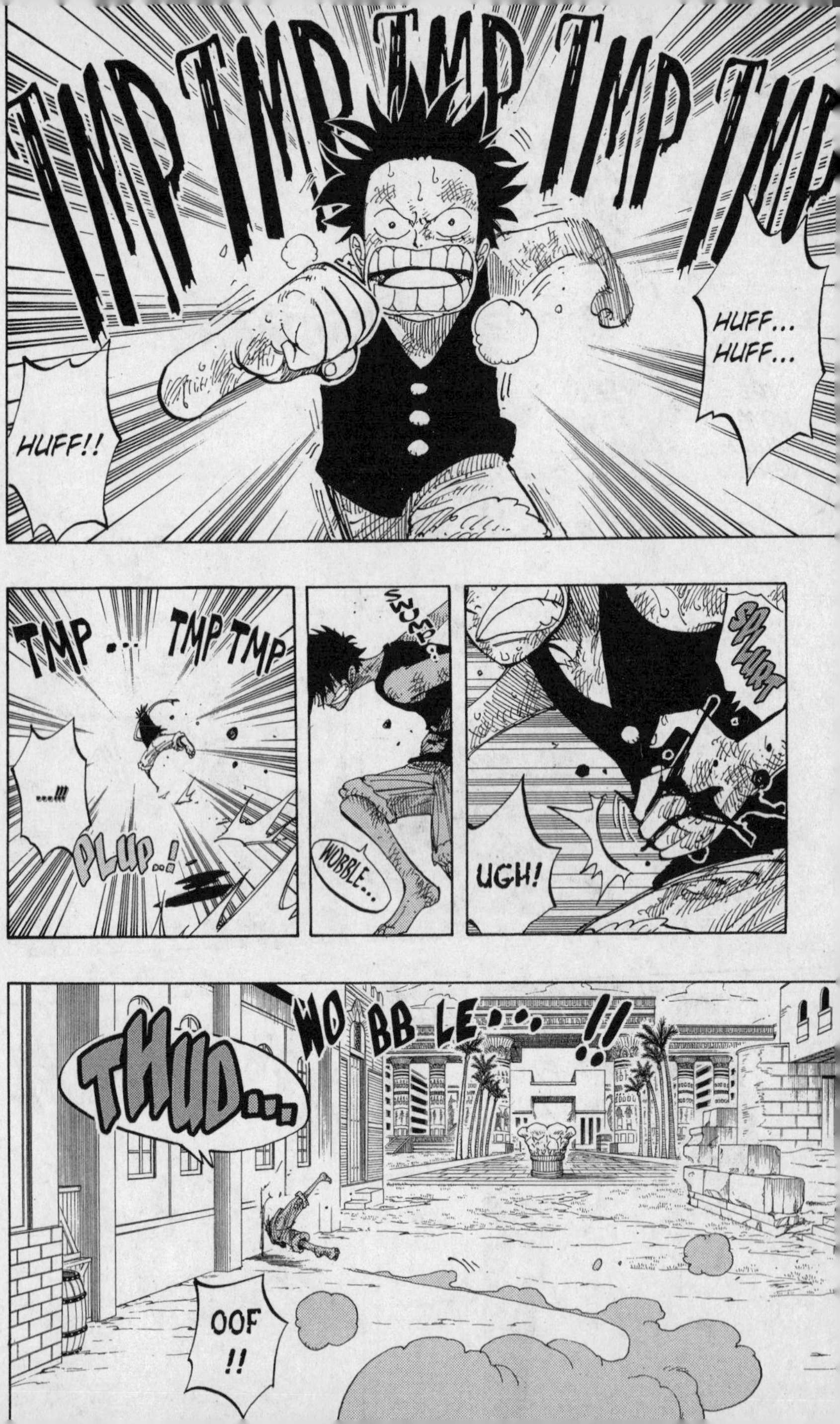
HUFF... HUFF...
TMP TMP TMP TMP TMP TMP
HUFF!!
SPLURT
UGH!
SWUMP..
WOBBLE...
TMP ... TMP TMP
...!!!
PLUP..!
WOBBLE..!!
THUD...
OOF !!

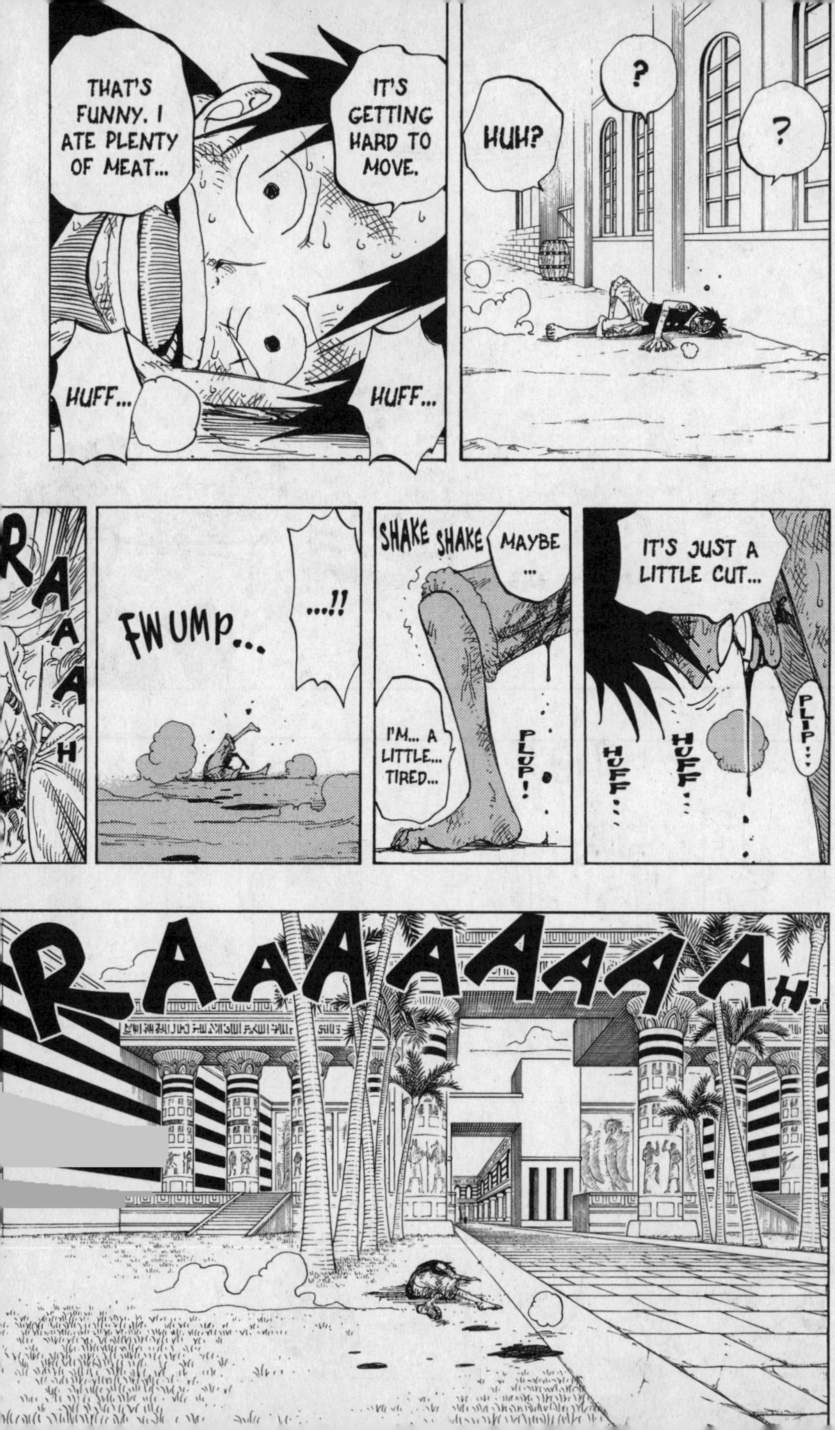
HUH?
?
?
IT'S GETTING HARD TO MOVE.
THAT'S FUNNY. I ATE PLENTY OF MEAT...
HUFF...
HUFF...
IT'S JUST A LITTLE CUT...
PLIP...
HUFF...
HUFF...
MAYBE ...
SHAKE SHAKE
I'M... A LITTLE... TIRED...
PLUP!
...!!
FWUMP...
RAAAH
RAAAAAAAAH

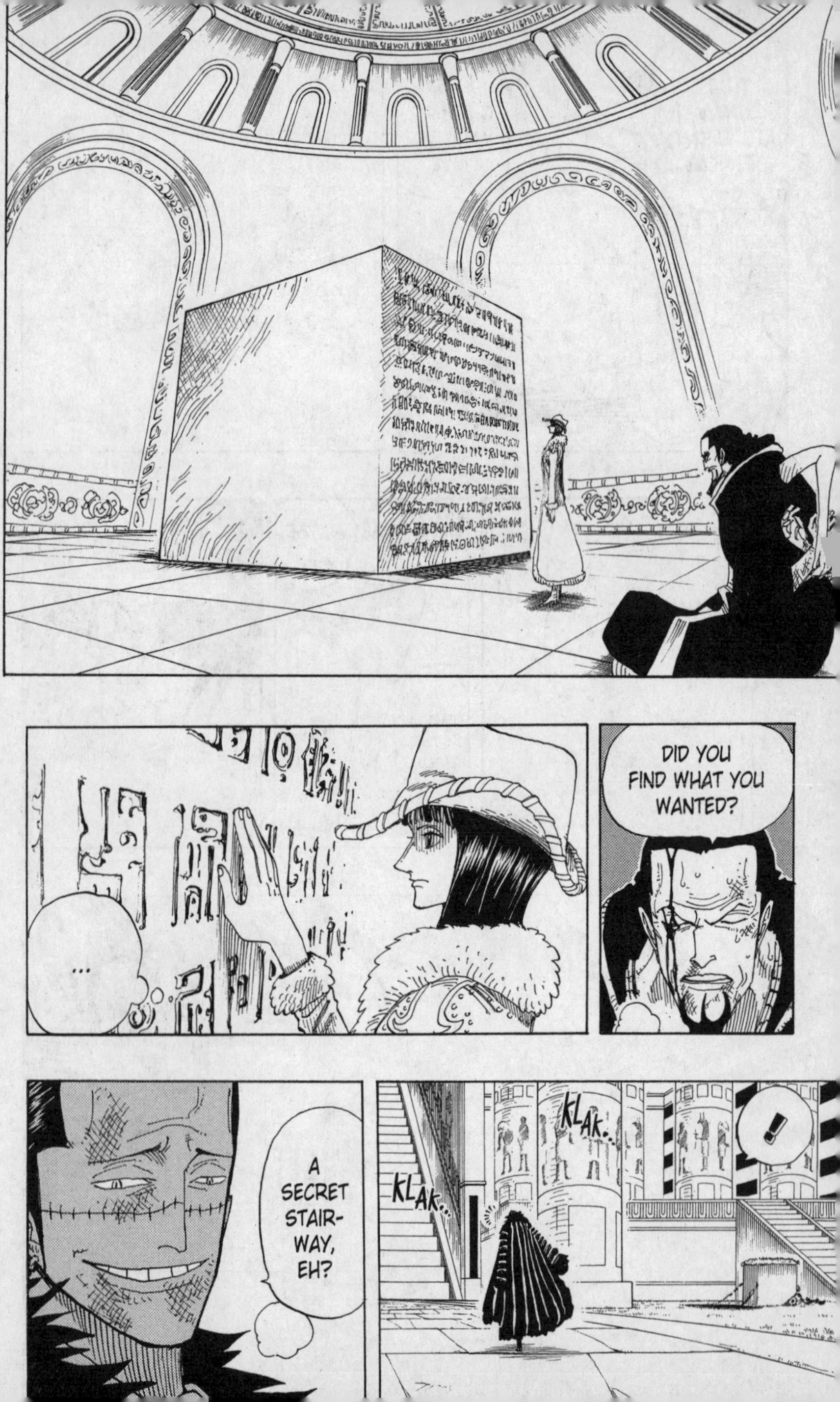
DID YOU FIND WHAT YOU WANTED?
...
!
KLAK...
KLAK...
A SECRET STAIR-WAY, EH?

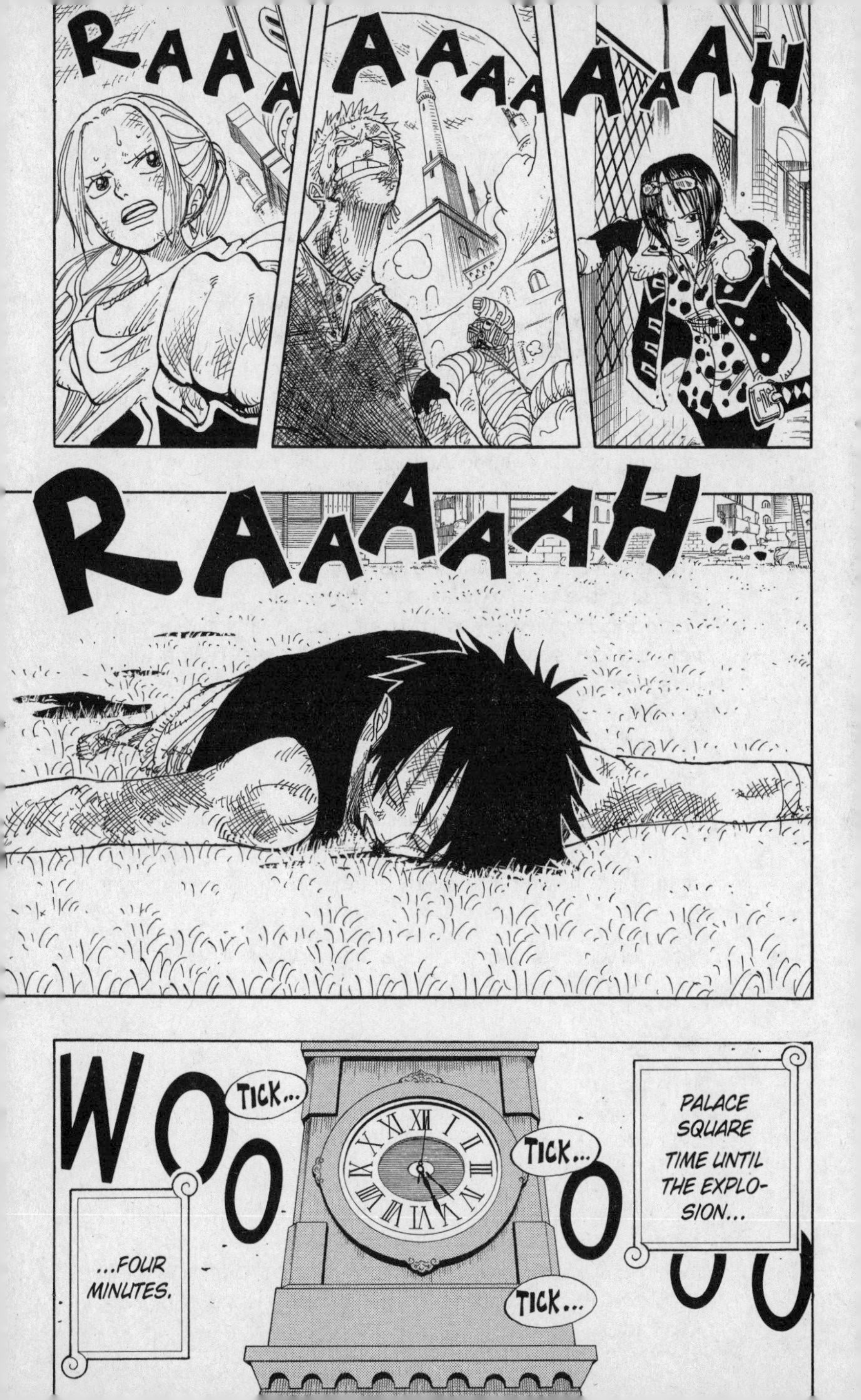
RAAAAAAAAAAH
RAAAAAH
PALACE SQUARE TIME UNTIL THE EXPLOSION...
WOOOOOO
TICK...
TICK...
TICK...
...FOUR MINUTES.

Reader: Found him! Fo!! Pa!! Pa!! Sa!! Also, Que!! Whe!! Do!! …Ack! (Translation) Panda Man!! It's Panda Man!! I saw Panda Man running away!! (Volume 20, page 60, first panel) Also, I have a question. Where does Panda Man live? Does Panda Man like to travel?

Oda: The last part was a little hard to make out. Are you all right there? Anyway, about Panda Man's residence—rumor has it that he's a very important person (on some islands anyway). Maybe that's why he's being pursued, and therefore needs to be on the run... Sorry, but if I say any more, I'll put myself in danger...
Oh no! It's them!! (Runs away)

Reader: Hello, Oda Sensei. I have a question for you! Because Chopper ate the Rumble Ball, he's able to perform seven transformations, right? But Chopper has already done more than seven. Why is that?

Oda: You're wrong there. There are only seven.

Animal form		Man-Beast form				Human form
(Limb Boost)	(Horn Boost)	(Guard Boost)	(Brain Boost)	(Jumping Boost)	(Arm Boost)	(Weight Boost)

↑ And there are the seven. His usual Animal form is "Limb Boost." His usual Man-Beast form is "Brain Boost," and his Human form is "Weight Boost." So the Rumble Ball allows him to do four transformations in addition to these three. I hope this clears that up.

Chapter 203:
CROCODILE-ISH

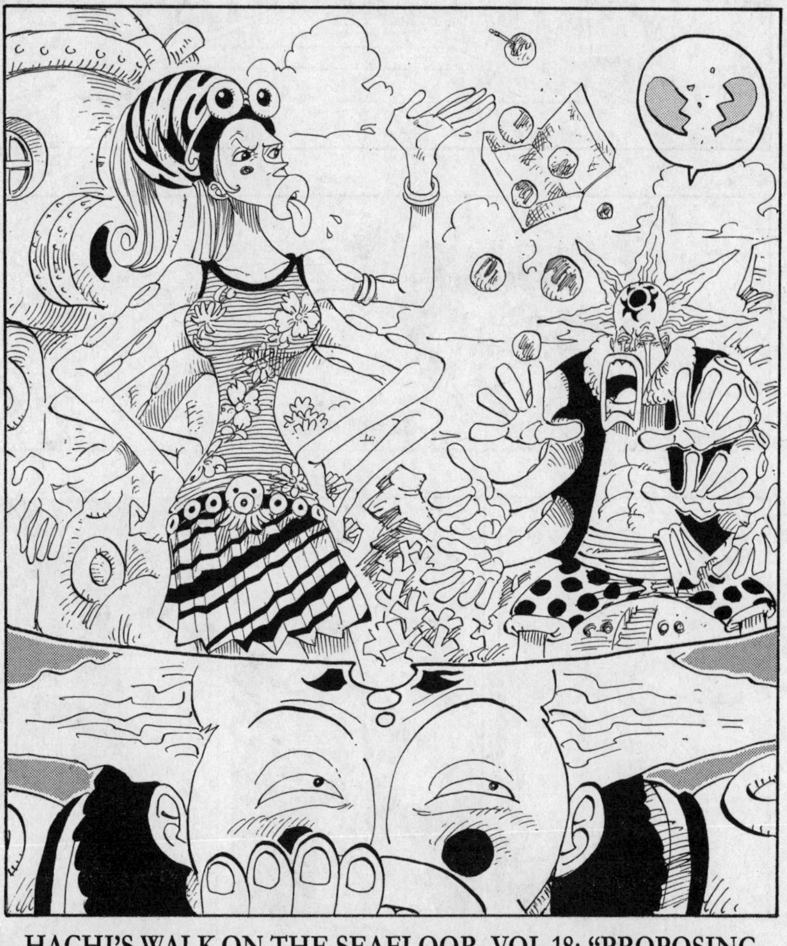

HACHI'S WALK ON THE SEAFLOOR, VOL.18: "PROPOSING TO MY BELOVED OCTOPAKO ONE MORE TIME ♡"

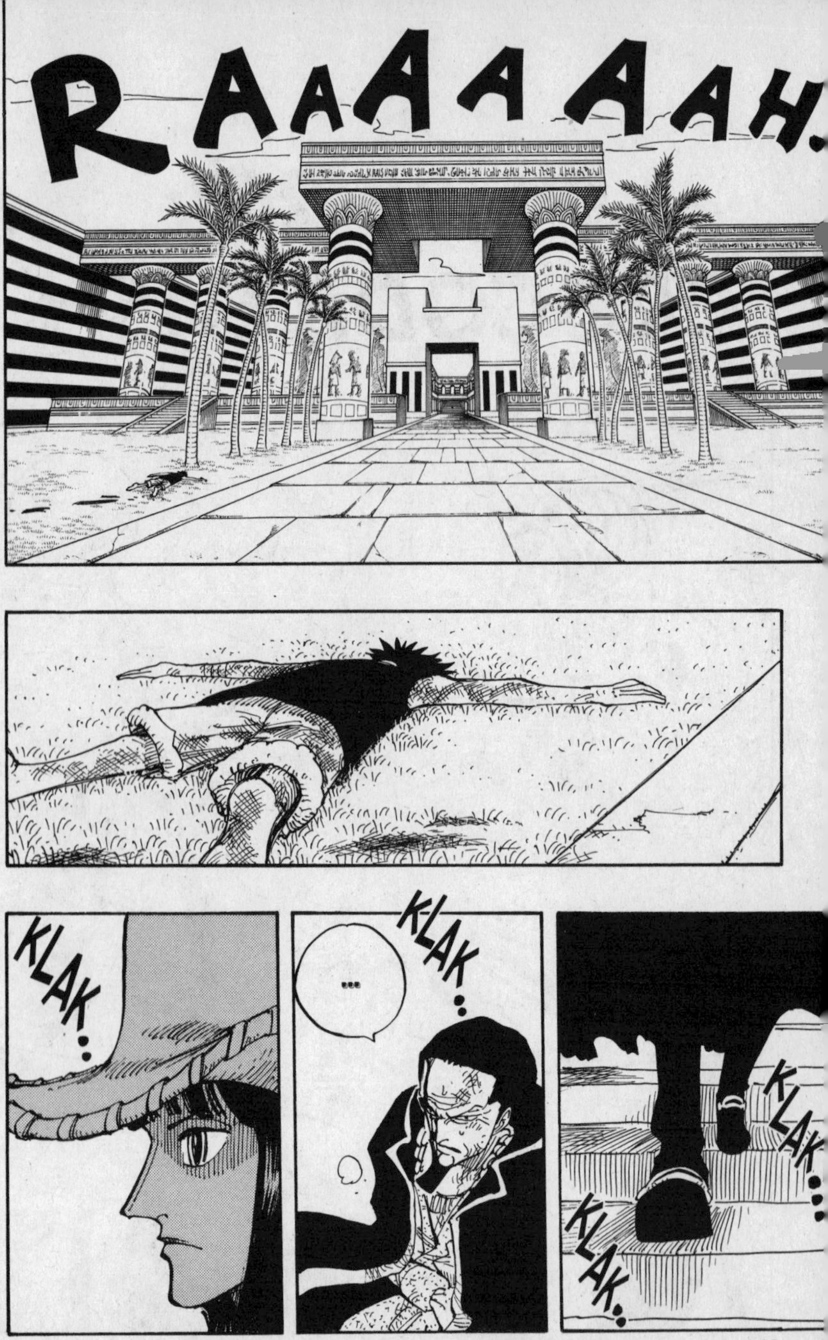
RAAAAAH.
KLAK...
KLAK..
K-LAK...
...
KLAK...

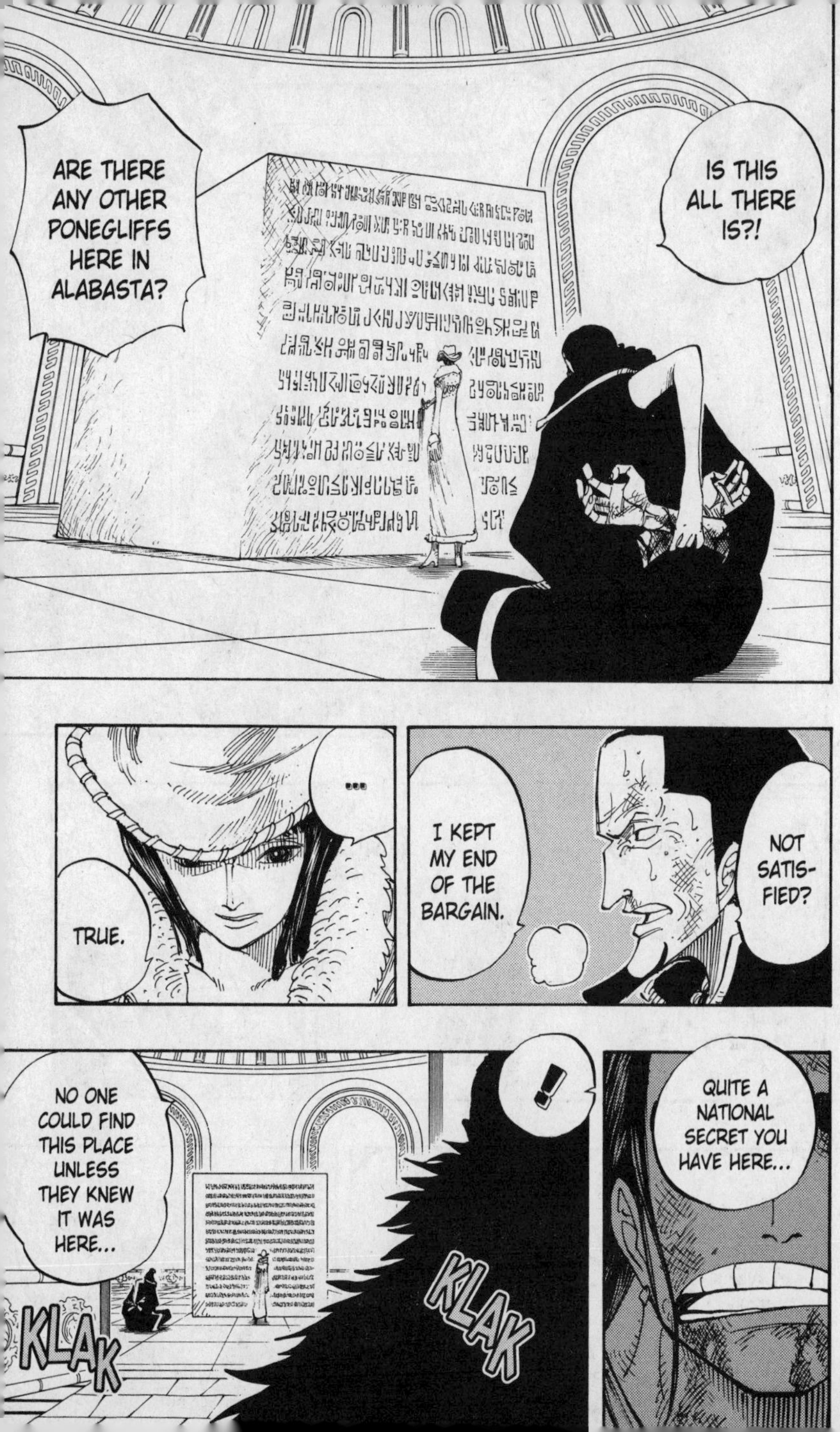
IS THIS ALL THERE IS?!
ARE THERE ANY OTHER PONEGLIFFS HERE IN ALABASTA?
NOT SATIS-FIED?
I KEPT MY END OF THE BARGAIN.
...
TRUE.
QUITE A NATIONAL SECRET YOU HAVE HERE...
!
KLAK
NO ONE COULD FIND THIS PLACE UNLESS THEY KNEW IT WAS HERE...
KLAK

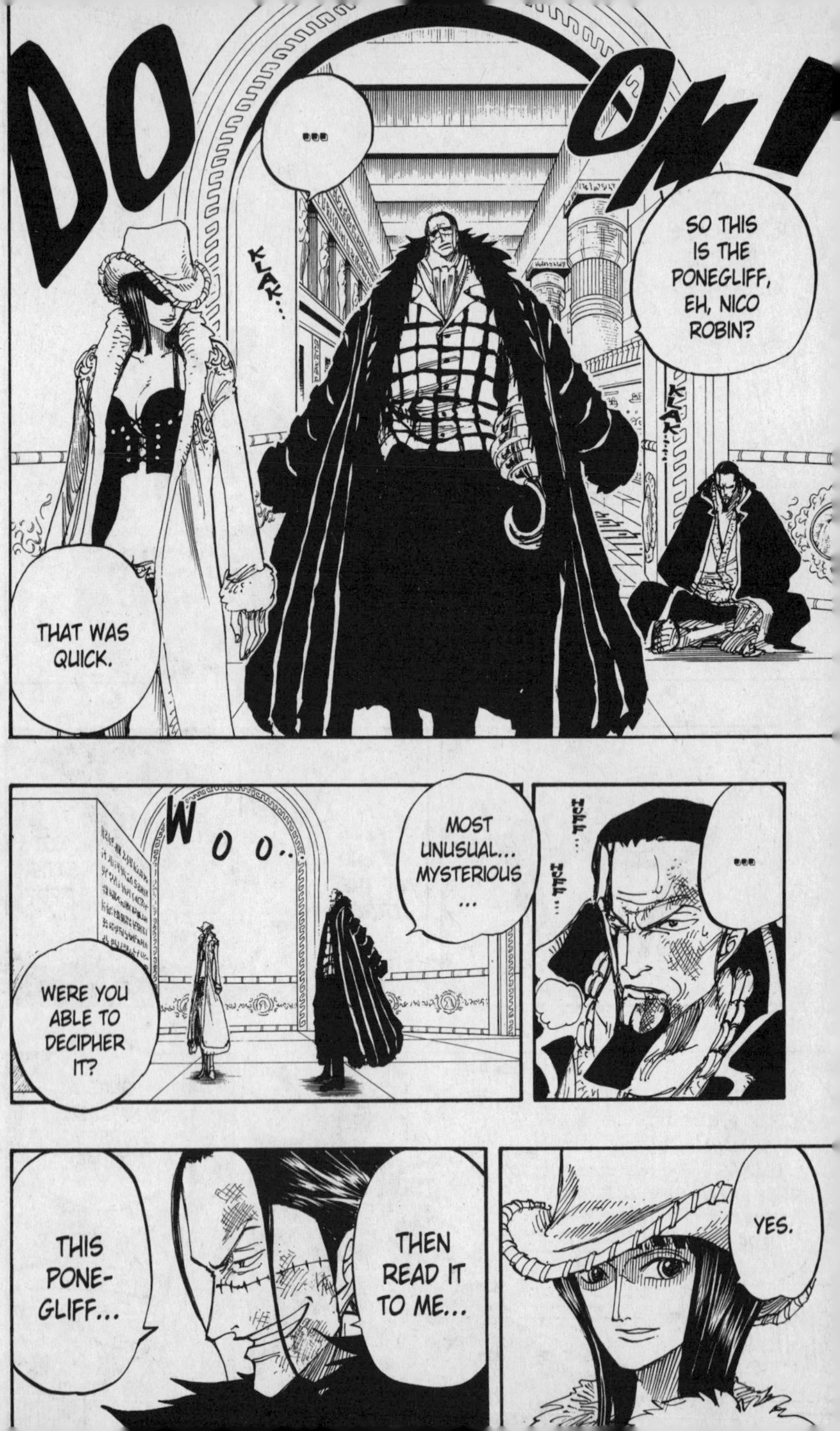
DO-OM!
SO THIS IS THE PONEGLIFF, EH, NICO ROBIN?
...
KLAK...
KLAK...
THAT WAS QUICK.
HUFF...
HUFF...
...
MOST UNUSUAL... MYSTERIOUS ...
WOO..
WERE YOU ABLE TO DECIPHER IT?
YES.
THEN READ IT TO ME...
THIS PONE-GLIFF...

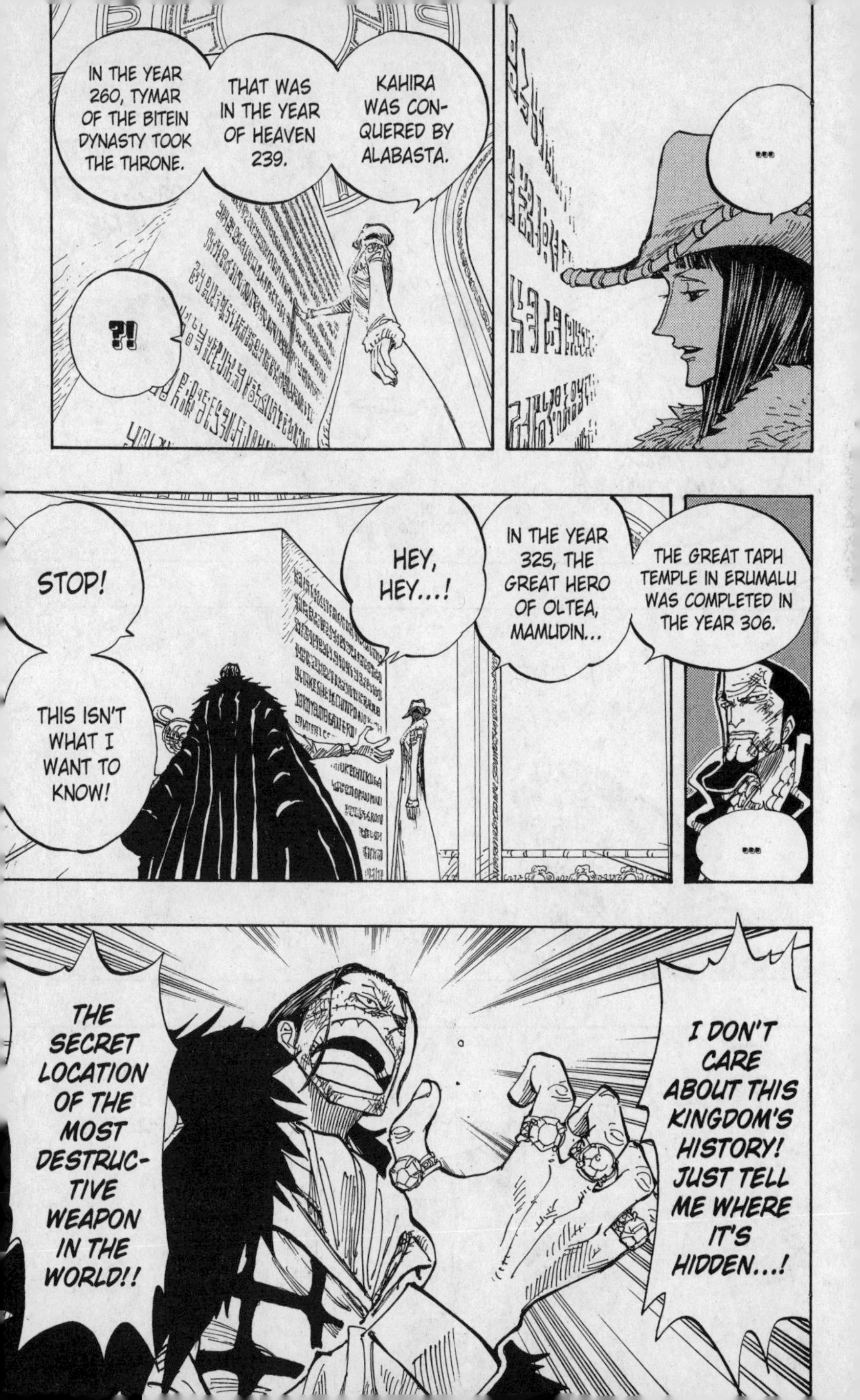
...
KAHIRA WAS CONQUERED BY ALABASTA.
THAT WAS IN THE YEAR OF HEAVEN 239.
IN THE YEAR 260, TYMAR OF THE BITEIN DYNASTY TOOK THE THRONE.
?!
...
THE GREAT TAPH TEMPLE IN ERUMALU WAS COMPLETED IN THE YEAR 306.
IN THE YEAR 325, THE GREAT HERO OF OLTEA, MAMUDIN...
HEY, HEY...!
STOP!
THIS ISN'T WHAT I WANT TO KNOW!
I DON'T CARE ABOUT THIS KINGDOM'S HISTORY! JUST TELL ME WHERE IT'S HIDDEN...!
THE SECRET LOCATION OF THE MOST DESTRUCTIVE WEAPON IN THE WORLD!!

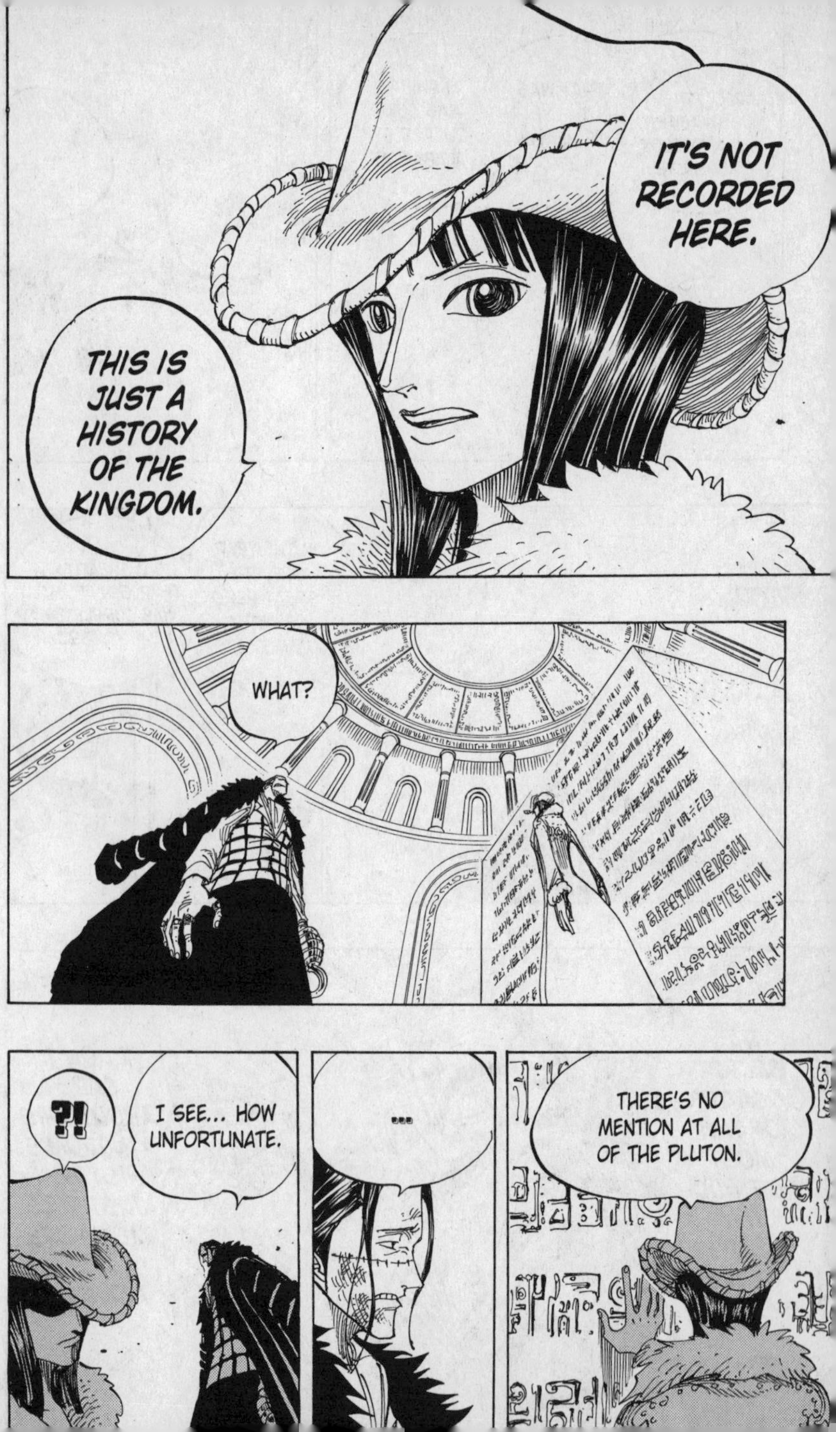
IT'S NOT RECORDED HERE.
THIS IS JUST A HISTORY OF THE KINGDOM.
WHAT?
THERE'S NO MENTION AT ALL OF THE PLUTON.
...
I SEE... HOW UNFORTUNATE.
?!

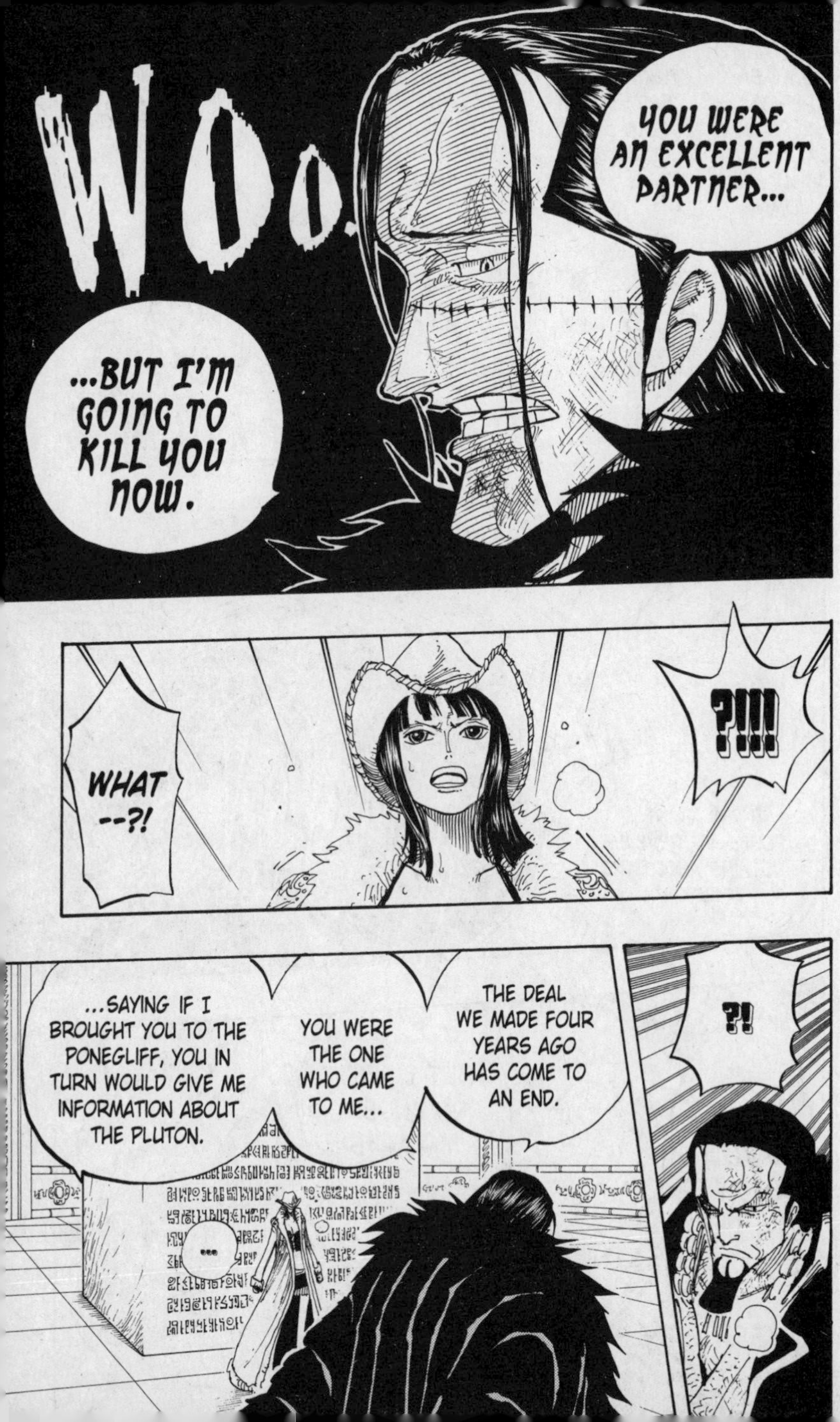
YOU WERE AN EXCELLENT PARTNER...
WOO...
...BUT I'M GOING TO KILL YOU NOW.
?!!!
WHAT --?!
?!
THE DEAL WE MADE FOUR YEARS AGO HAS COME TO AN END.
YOU WERE THE ONE WHO CAME TO ME...
...SAYING IF I BROUGHT YOU TO THE PONEGLIFF, YOU IN TURN WOULD GIVE ME INFORMATION ABOUT THE PLUTON.
...

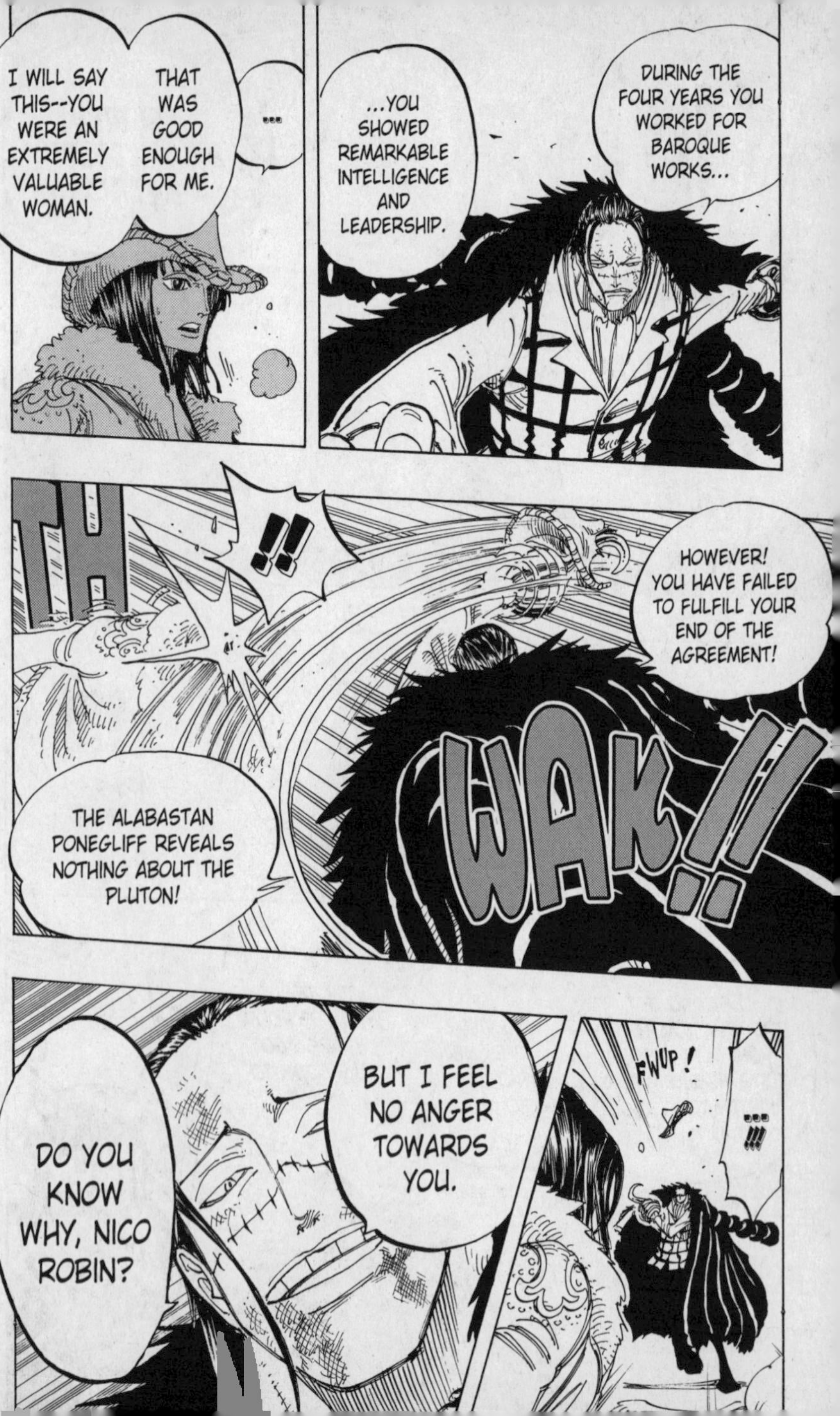
DURING THE FOUR YEARS YOU WORKED FOR BAROQUE WORKS...
...YOU SHOWED REMARKABLE INTELLIGENCE AND LEADERSHIP.
...
THAT WAS GOOD ENOUGH FOR ME.
I WILL SAY THIS--YOU WERE AN EXTREMELY VALUABLE WOMAN.
HOWEVER! YOU HAVE FAILED TO FULFILL YOUR END OF THE AGREEMENT!
!!
WAK!!
THE ALABASTAN PONEGLIFF REVEALS NOTHING ABOUT THE PLUTON!
FWUP!
...!!!
BUT I FEEL NO ANGER TOWARDS YOU.
DO YOU KNOW WHY, NICO ROBIN?

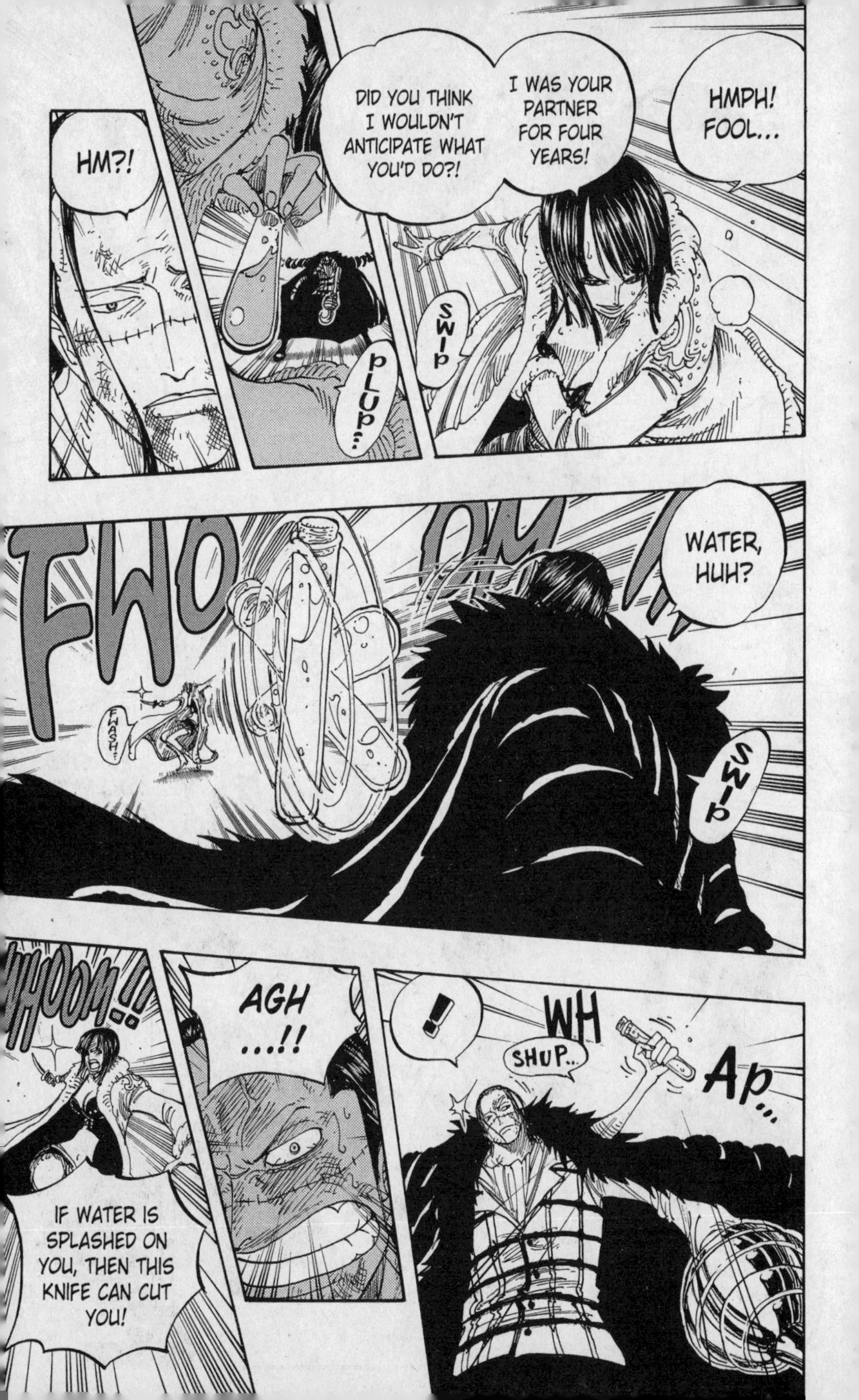
HMPH! FOOL...
I WAS YOUR PARTNER FOR FOUR YEARS!
DID YOU THINK I WOULDN'T ANTICIPATE WHAT YOU'D DO?!
SWIP
PLUP..
HM?!
WATER, HUH?
FWO OM
SWIP
FWASH
!
WH AP...
SHUP..
AGH ...!!
WHOOM!!
IF WATER IS SPLASHED ON YOU, THEN THIS KNIFE CAN CUT YOU!

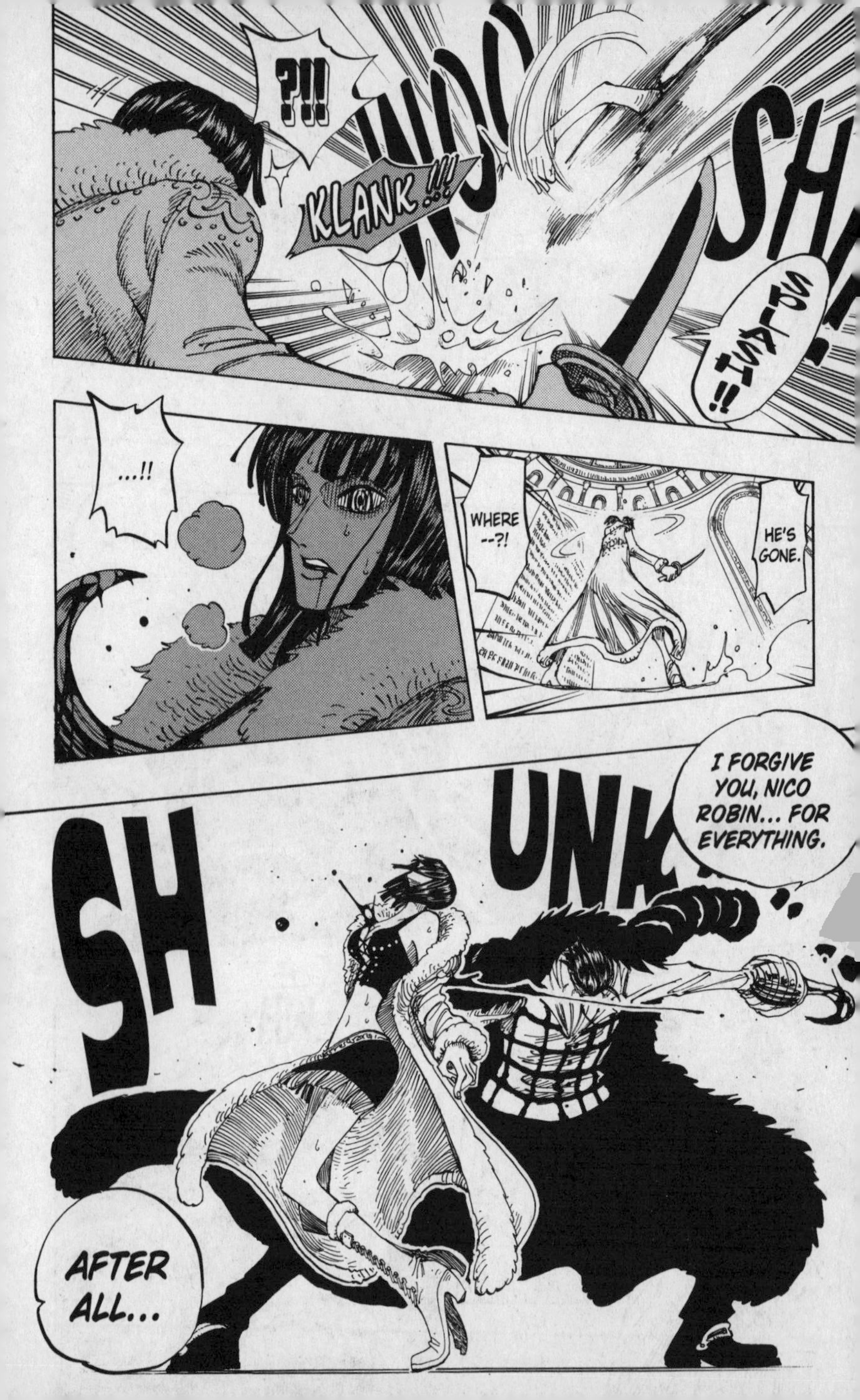
SPLASH!!
KLANK!!!
?!!
HE'S GONE.
WHERE --?!
...!!
I FORGIVE YOU, NICO ROBIN... FOR EVERYTHING.
AFTER ALL...

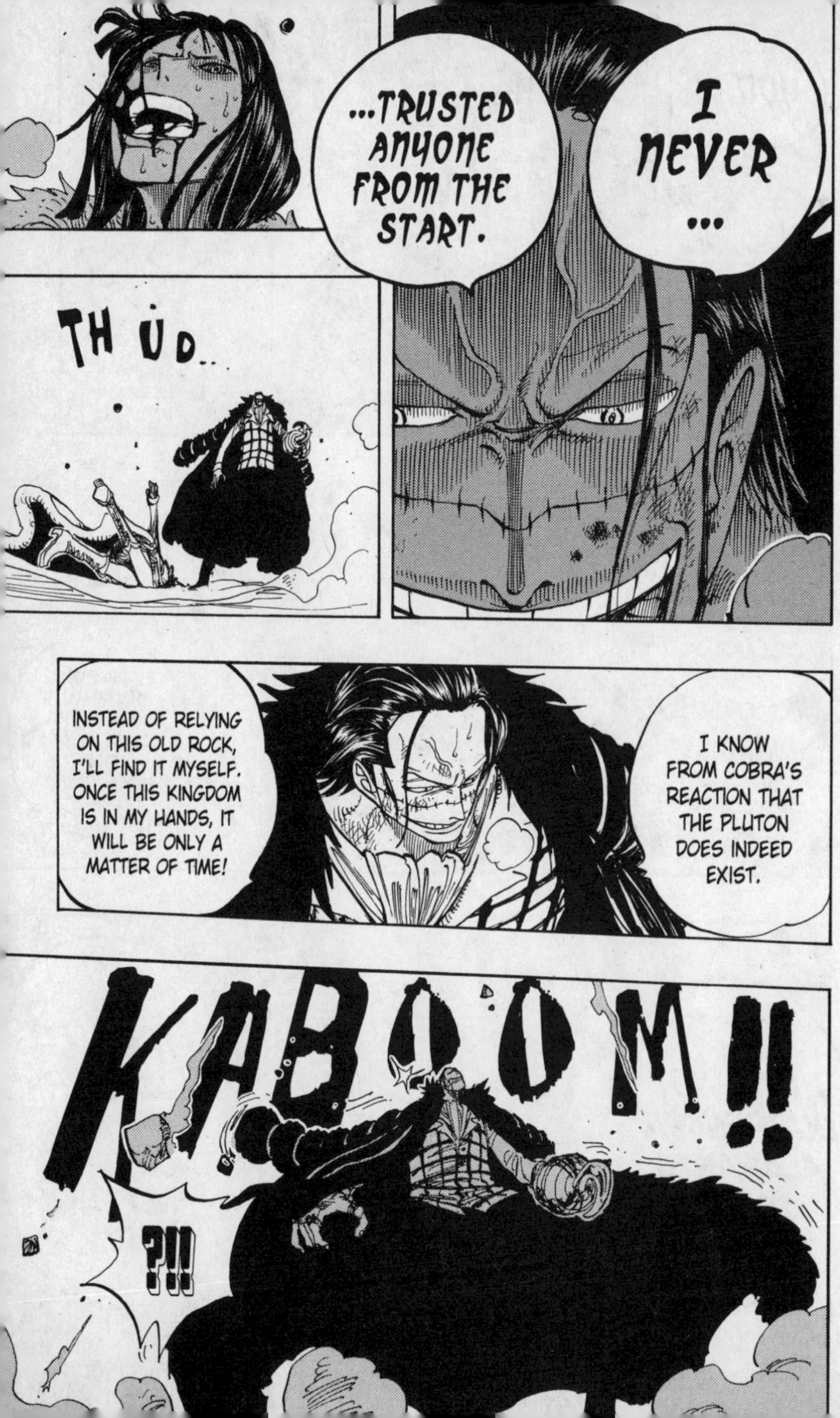
I NEVER...
...TRUSTED ANYONE FROM THE START.
THUD...
I KNOW FROM COBRA'S REACTION THAT THE PLUTON DOES INDEED EXIST.
INSTEAD OF RELYING ON THIS OLD ROCK, I'LL FIND IT MYSELF. ONCE THIS KINGDOM IS IN MY HANDS, IT WILL BE ONLY A MATTER OF TIME!
KABOOM!!
?!!

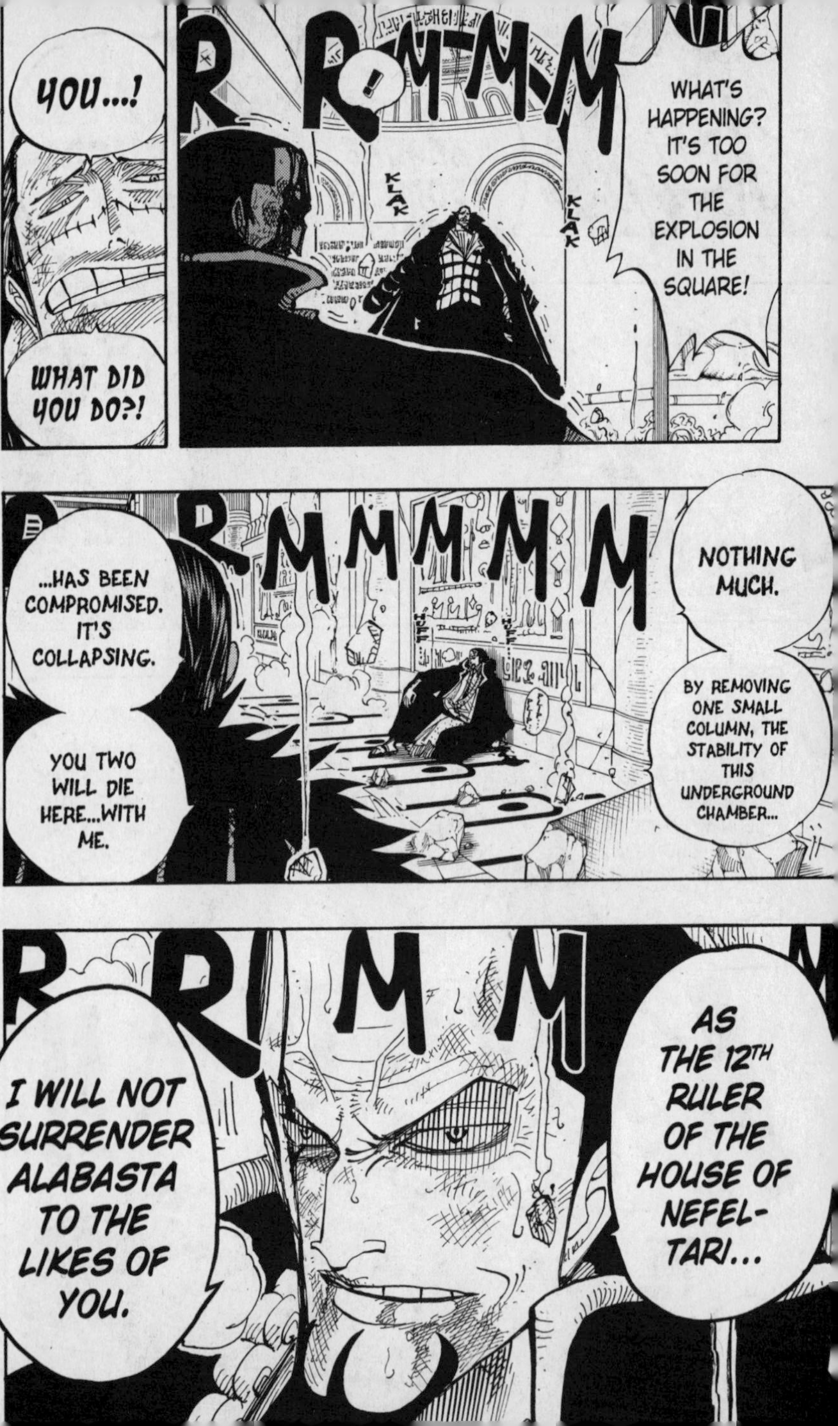
RRMM-M-M
!
KLAK
KLAK
WHAT'S HAPPENING? IT'S TOO SOON FOR THE EXPLOSION IN THE SQUARE!
YOU...!
WHAT DID YOU DO?!
RRMMMMMM
HUFF
HUFF
NOTHING MUCH.
BY REMOVING ONE SMALL COLUMN, THE STABILITY OF THIS UNDERGROUND CHAMBER...
...HAS BEEN COMPROMISED. IT'S COLLAPSING.
YOU TWO WILL DIE HERE...WITH ME.
RRMM
AS THE 12TH RULER OF THE HOUSE OF NEFEL-TARI...
I WILL NOT SURRENDER ALABASTA TO THE LIKES OF YOU.

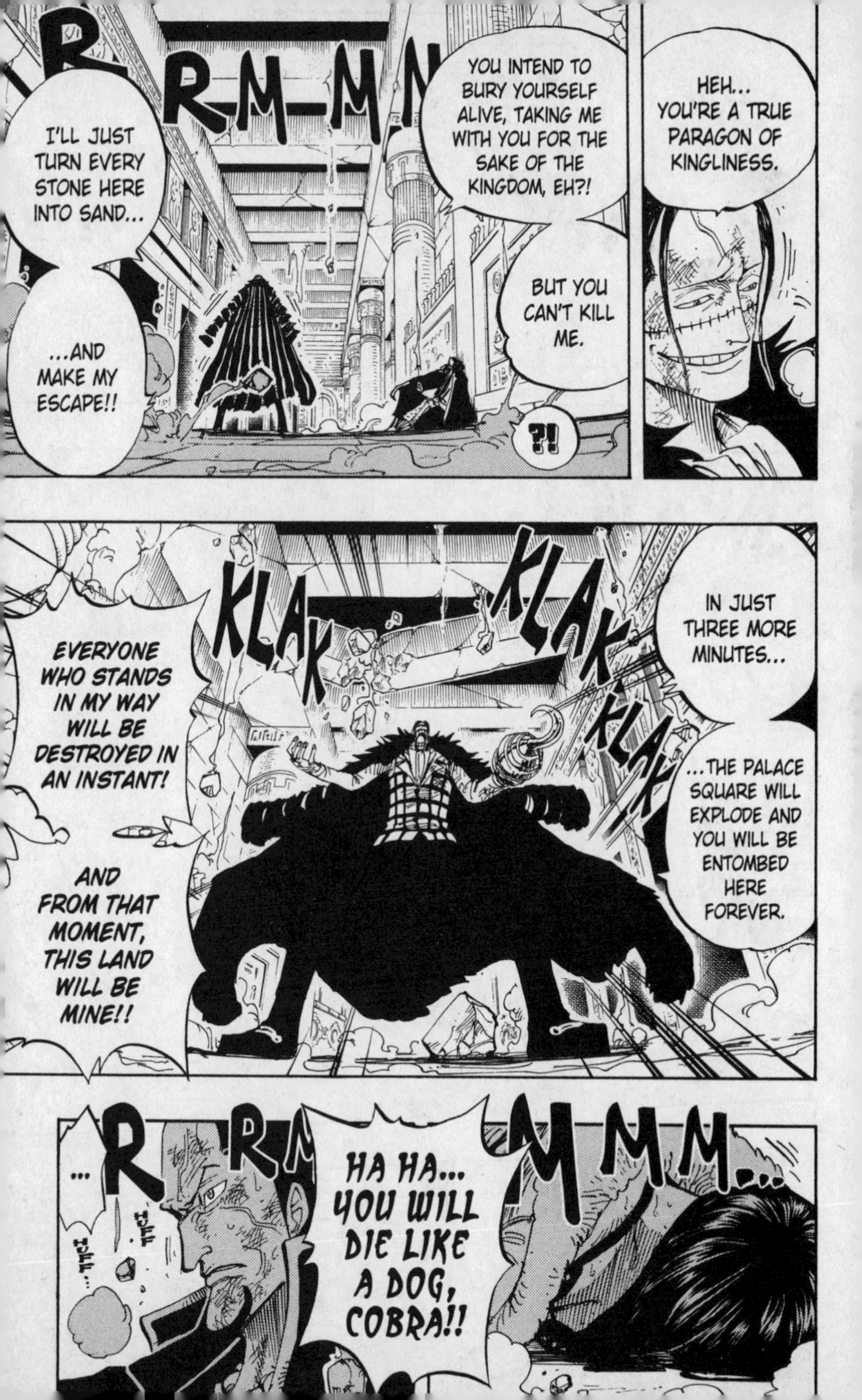
HEH... YOU'RE A TRUE PARAGON OF KINGLINESS.
RRMMMN
YOU INTEND TO BURY YOURSELF ALIVE, TAKING ME WITH YOU FOR THE SAKE OF THE KINGDOM, EH?!
BUT YOU CAN'T KILL ME.
?!
I'LL JUST TURN EVERY STONE HERE INTO SAND...
...AND MAKE MY ESCAPE!!
IN JUST THREE MORE MINUTES...
...THE PALACE SQUARE WILL EXPLODE AND YOU WILL BE ENTOMBED HERE FOREVER.
KLAK KLAK KLAK
KLAK
EVERYONE WHO STANDS IN MY WAY WILL BE DESTROYED IN AN INSTANT!
AND FROM THAT MOMENT, THIS LAND WILL BE MINE!!
RRRMMMM...
HA HA... YOU WILL DIE LIKE A DOG, COBRA!!
HUFF
HUFF...
...

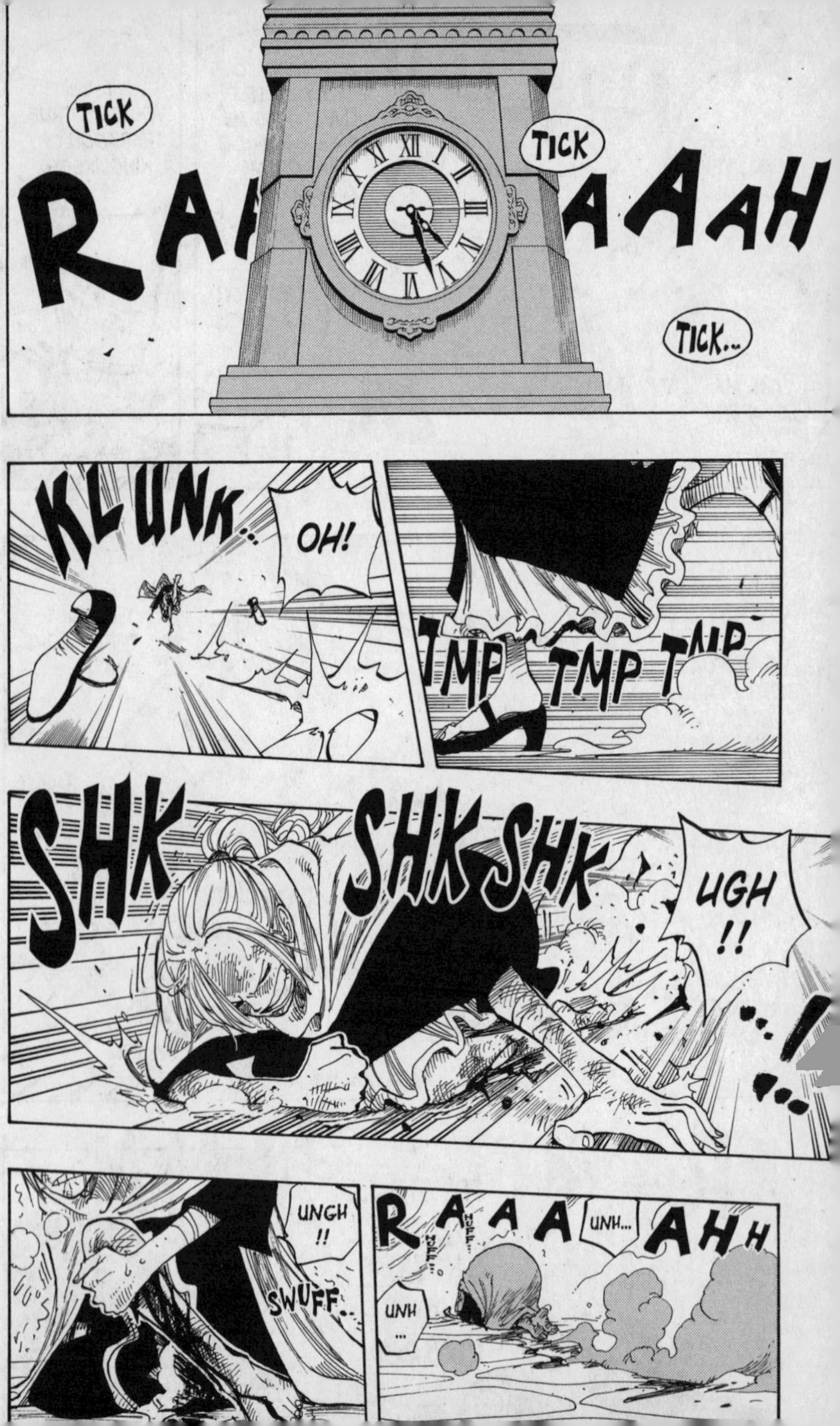
TICK
TICK
TICK...
RA
AAAH
TMP TMP
KLUNK
OH!
UGH !!
...!...
SHK SHK SHK
RAAA
UNH...
AHH
HUFF HUFF
UNH ...
UNGH !!
SWUFF...

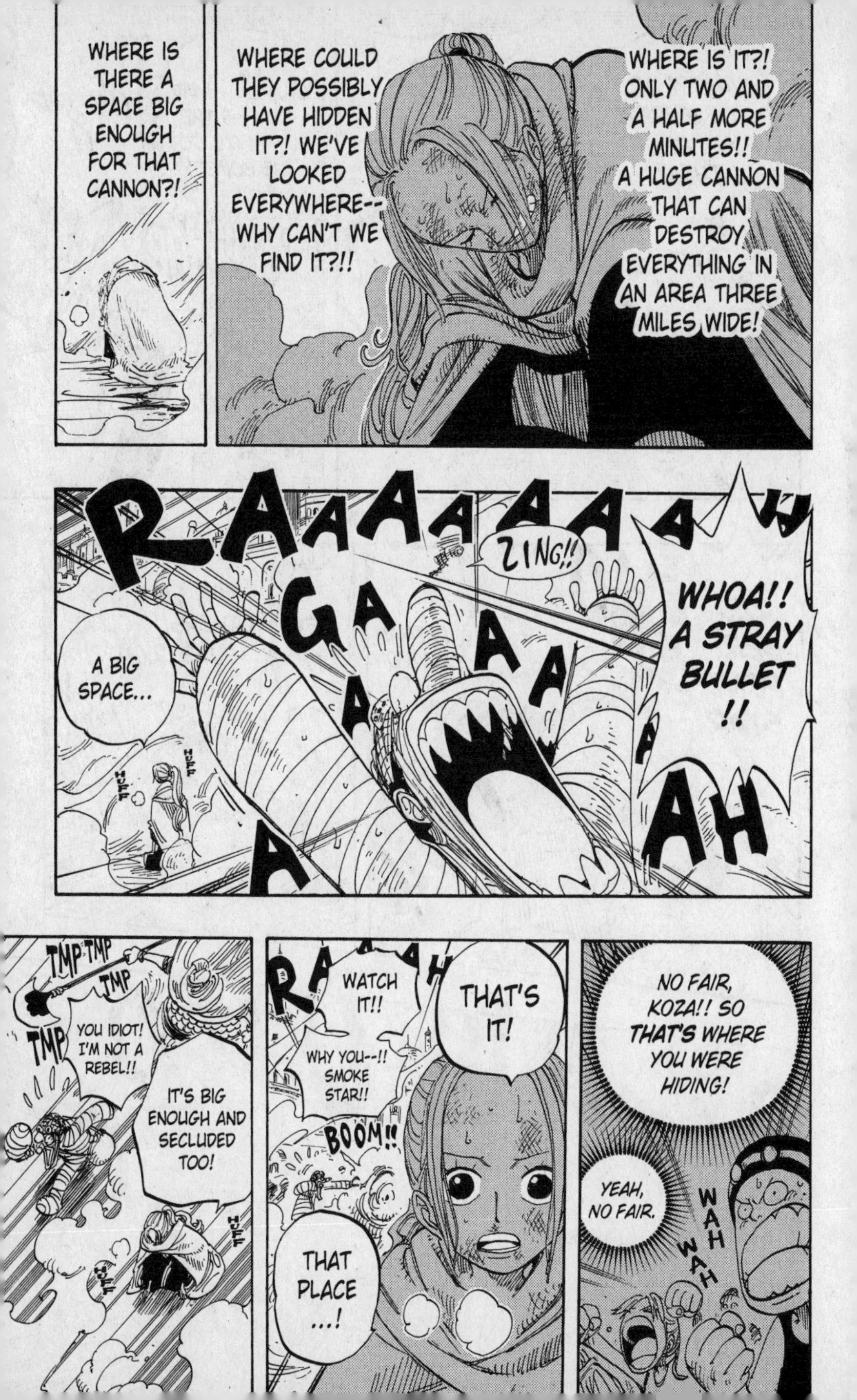
WHERE IS IT?! ONLY TWO AND A HALF MORE MINUTES!! A HUGE CANNON THAT CAN DESTROY EVERYTHING IN AN AREA THREE MILES WIDE!
WHERE COULD THEY POSSIBLY HAVE HIDDEN IT?! WE'VE LOOKED EVERYWHERE-- WHY CAN'T WE FIND IT?!!
WHERE IS THERE A SPACE BIG ENOUGH FOR THAT CANNON?!
WHOA!! A STRAY BULLET!!
RAAAAAAAW
ZING!!
GAAAAAAAH
A BIG SPACE...
HUFF
HUFF
NO FAIR, KOZA!! SO THAT'S WHERE YOU WERE HIDING!
YEAH, NO FAIR.
WAH
WAH
THAT'S IT!
WATCH IT!!
WHY YOU--!! SMOKE STAR!!
BOOM!!
THAT PLACE ...!
TMP TMP
TMP
TMP
YOU IDIOT! I'M NOT A REBEL!!
IT'S BIG ENOUGH AND SECLUDED TOO!
HUFF
HUFF

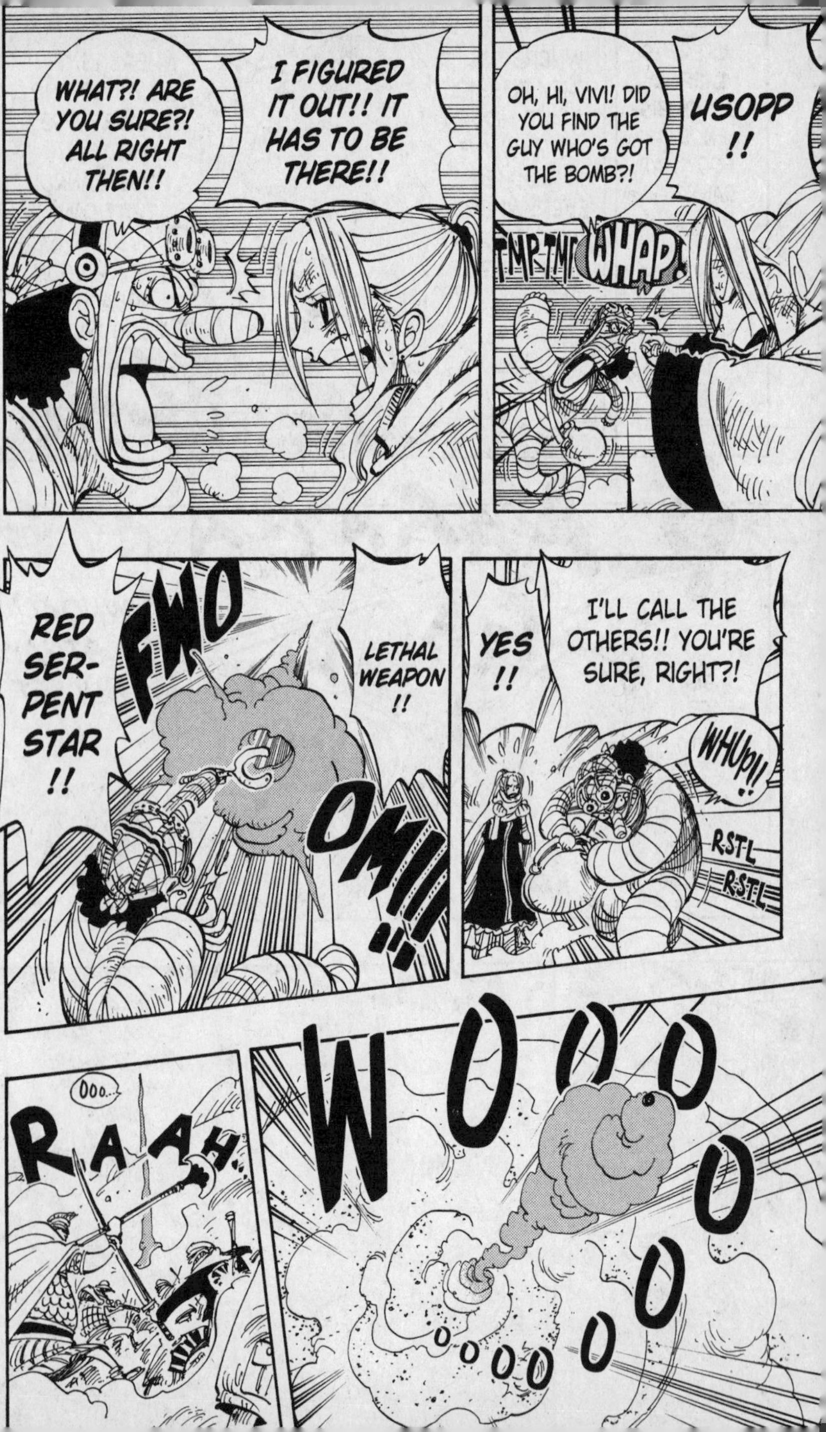
USOPP!!
OH, HI, VIVI! DID YOU FIND THE GUY WHO'S GOT THE BOMB?!
TMP TMP
WHAP
I FIGURED IT OUT!! IT HAS TO BE THERE!!
WHAT?! ARE YOU SURE?! ALL RIGHT THEN!!
I'LL CALL THE OTHERS!! YOU'RE SURE, RIGHT?!
YES!!
WHUP!!
R-ST-L
R-ST-L
LETHAL WEAPON!!
FWOOM!!
RED SER-PENT STAR!!
WOOOOOOOOOOO
OOO...
RAAH

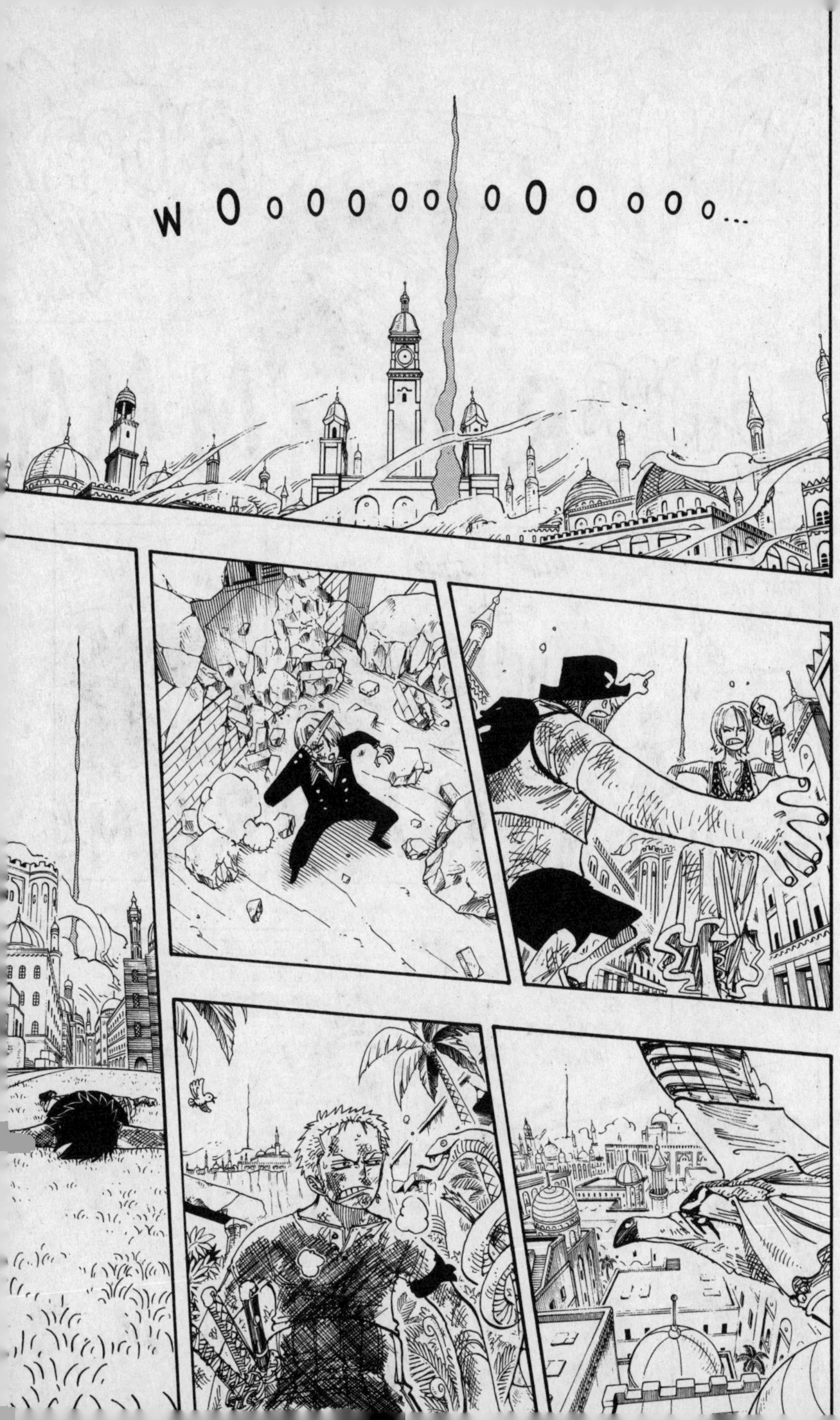
WOoOOOoo oOOooo...

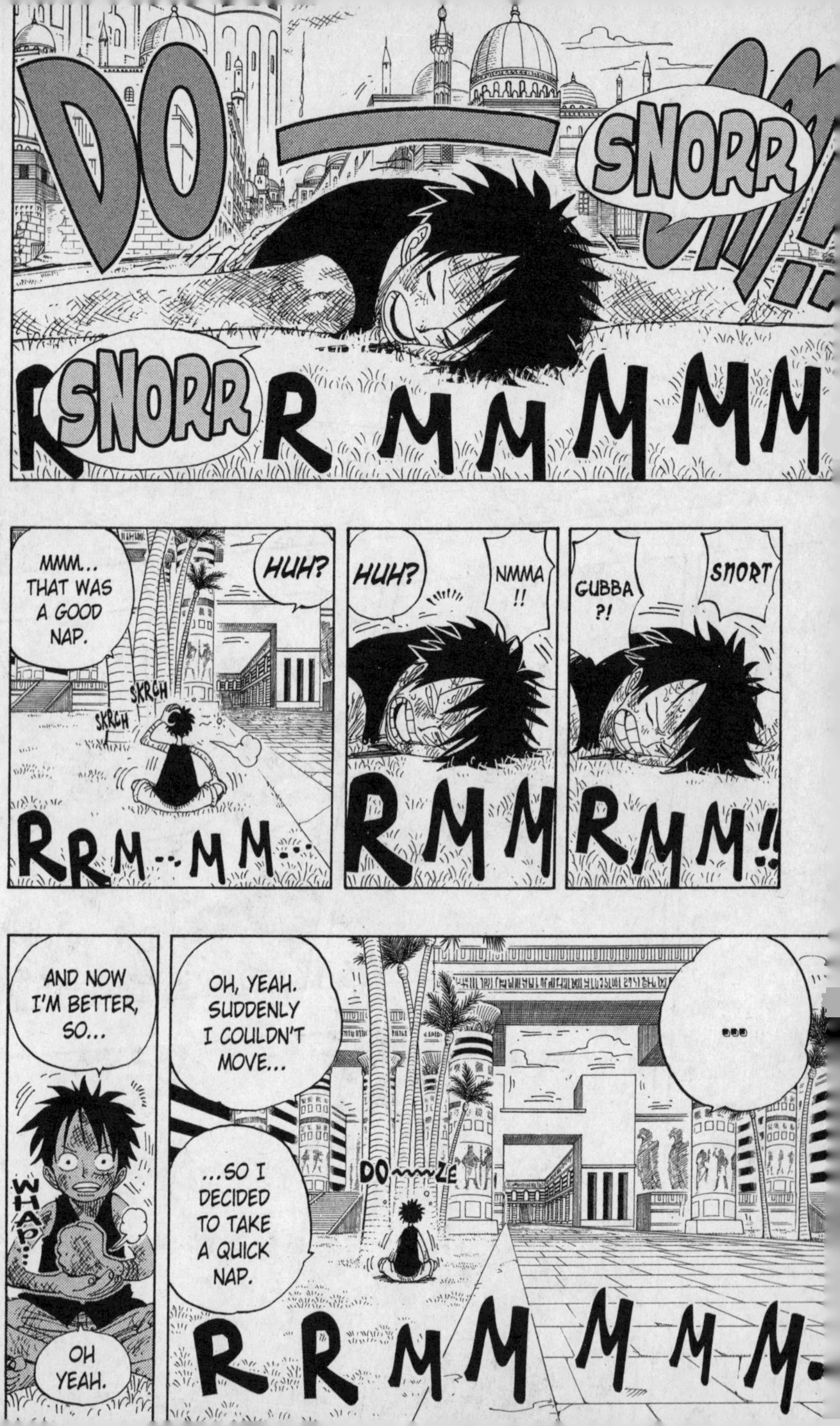
DO——OM!!
SNORR
SNORR
RRMMMMM
SNORT
GUBBA ?!
RMM!!
NMMA !!
HUH?
RMM
HUH?
MMM... THAT WAS A GOOD NAP.
SKRCH
SKRCH
RRM... MM...
...
OH, YEAH. SUDDENLY I COULDN'T MOVE...
...SO I DECIDED TO TAKE A QUICK NAP.
DO~~ZE
RRMMMMM.
AND NOW I'M BETTER, SO...
WHAP!!
OH YEAH.

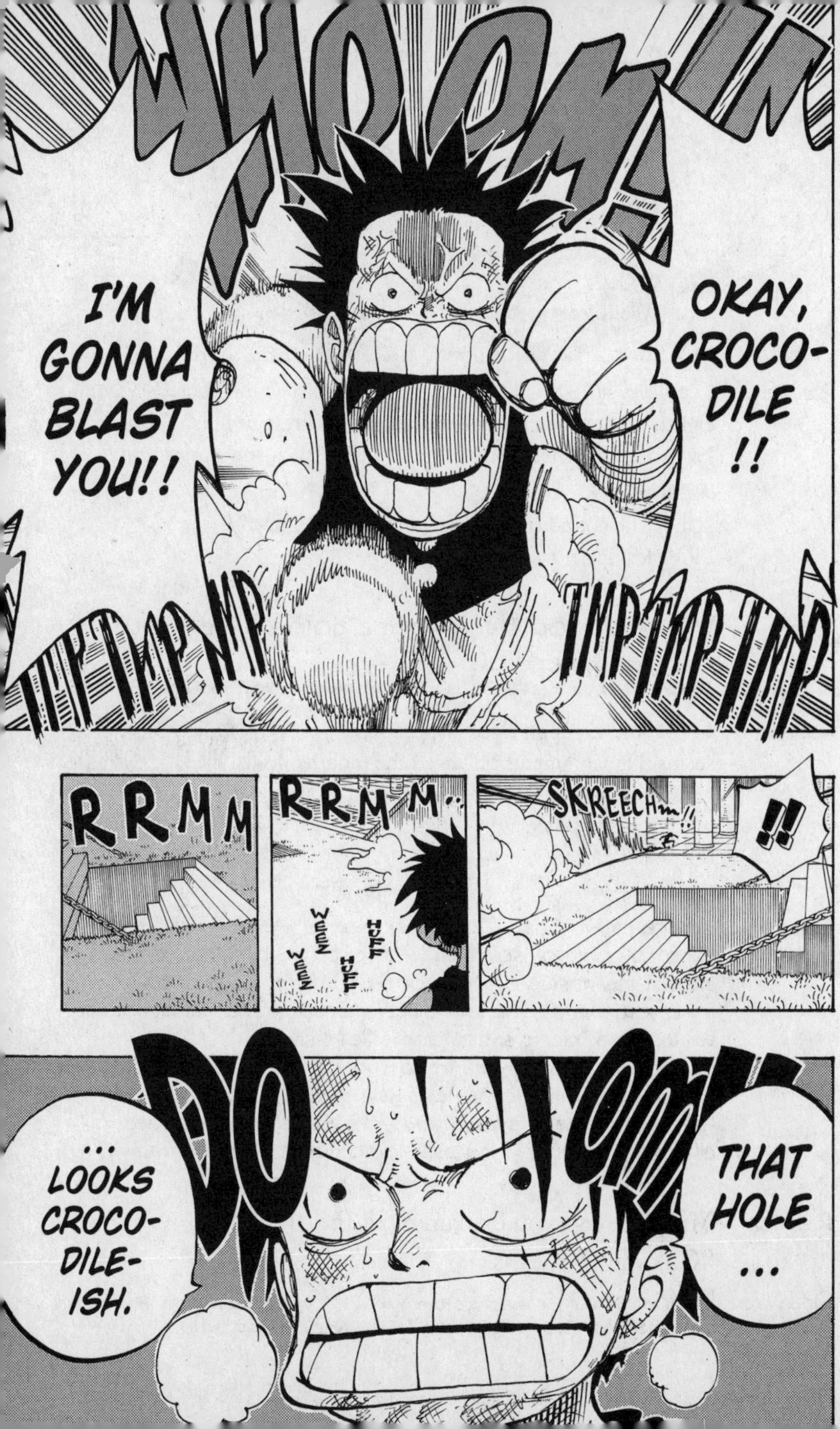

OKAY, CROCO-DILE!!
I'M GONNA BLAST YOU!!
TMP TMP TMP
TMP TMP TMP
SKREECH
!!
RRMM..
HUFF HUFF
WEEZ WEEZ
RRMM
THAT HOLE...
...LOOKS CROCO-DILE-ISH.

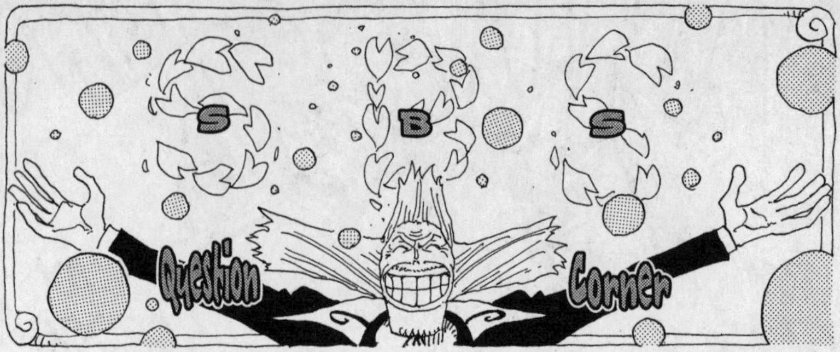
S B S
Question Corner

Reader: *Ding-dong.* Hi, Oda Sensei! You always seem awfully busy, so today, eighth-grader Meg is going to help you with your illustrations.♡ Eighth-grader Meg got an A in Art class, plus she's an aspiring manga artist!

splat (the sound of ink dropping) Oops. Sorry.♡
I'll be leaving now…♡♡

--Eighth-grader Meg

Oda: What do you think you're doing?! Hey, you!! Get back here!!
C'mon... You could at least... white out that inkblot. (pathetic)

Reader: In Volume 19, upon close inspection, it seems that Chopper is pulling at the mouth of the mysterious Crab Mover in order to make it move faster. Why is that? Please tell meeee!!

--Moomin

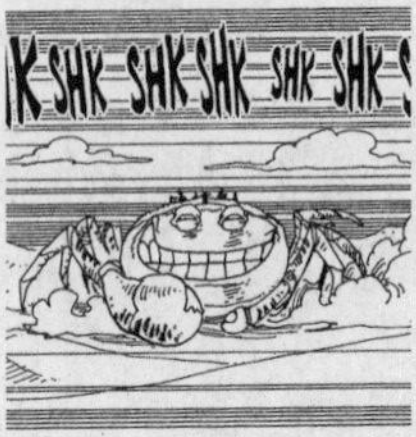
SHK SHK SHK SHK SHK

Oda: You're right. Crab Movers are very hard to control, so if you want it to go right, you tug at the right side of its mouth, and if you want to go left, you tug at the left side. In Crab Mover language, it would be a "right smirk" and a "left smirk." If you want to go slow, you give a little tug on both sides--doing a "right half-smirk" or a "left half-smirk." And if the rider happens to make a lame joke, the Crab Mover's face will cramp up making it impossible to control. So you have to be careful.

Reader: Mr. Oda, can you explain what the "ran" in "Gakuran"* means?

Oda: I dunno. Huh... Maybe it's the "ran" in "RANou" (egg yolk). Hmm... I know! It's "ran" as in "RANpaku" (egg white)! How's that?

*"Gakuran" is a boy's school uniform. "Gaku" means school and "ran(da)" means clothing. --Editor

Chapter 204: RED

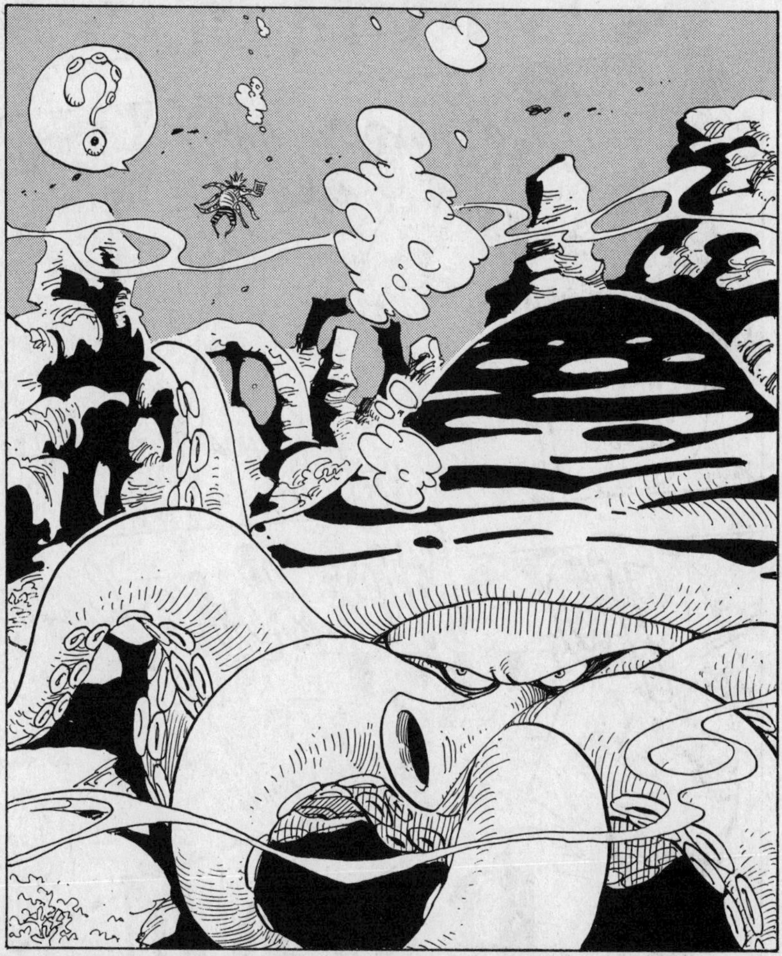

HACHI'S WALK ON THE SEAFLOOR, VOL.19: "X MARKS THE SPOT WHERE THE GREAT OCTOMASH LIVES"

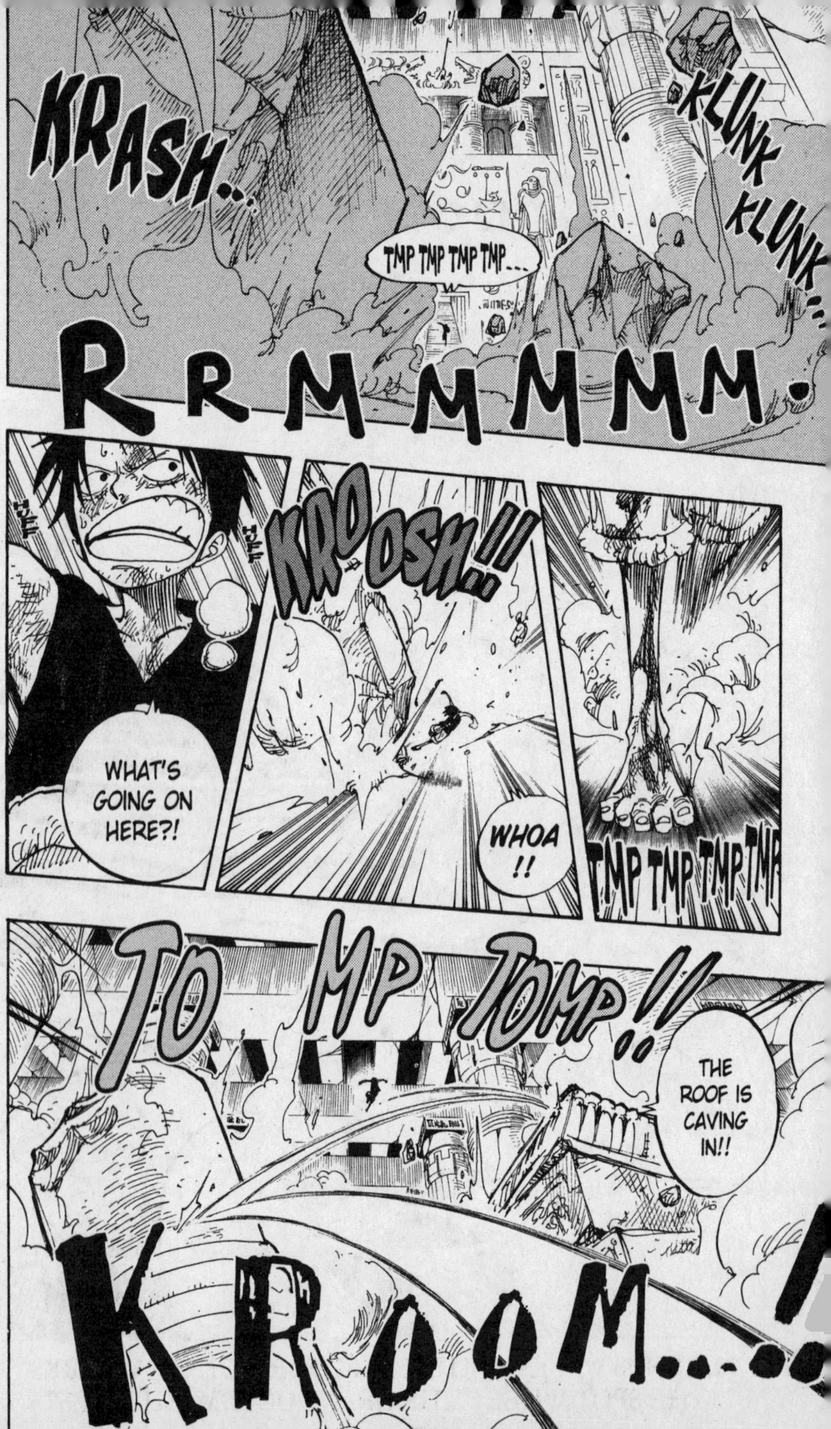
KLUNK KLUNK...
TMP TMP TMP TMP...
KRASH...
RRMMMMMM.
TMP TMP TMP TMP
KROOSH!!
WHOA!!
HUFF HUFF
WHAT'S GOING ON HERE?!
THE ROOF IS CAVING IN!!
TOMP TOMP!!
KROOM...!

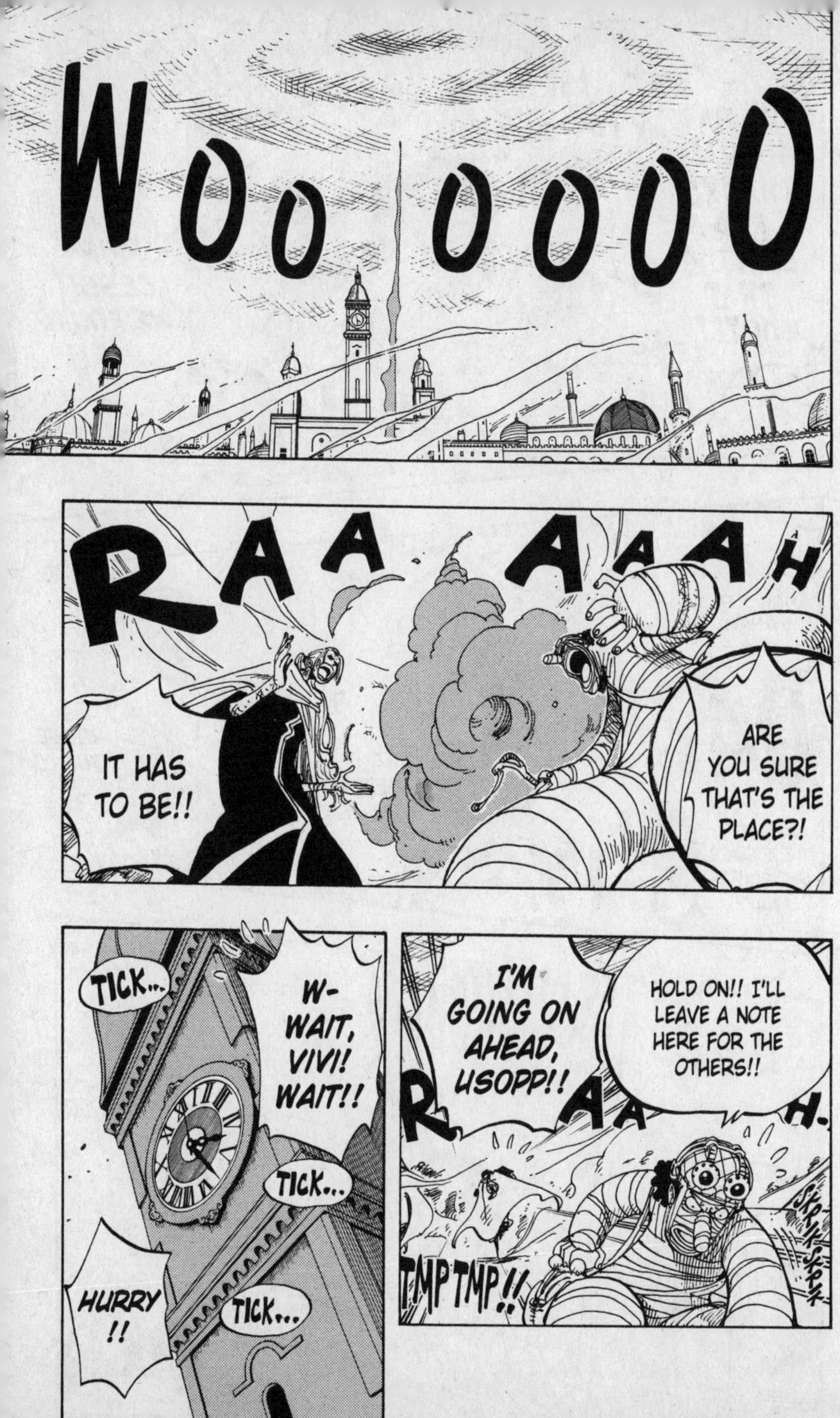
WOOOOOOO
RAAAAAH
ARE YOU SURE THAT'S THE PLACE?!
IT HAS TO BE!!
HOLD ON!! I'LL LEAVE A NOTE HERE FOR THE OTHERS!!
I'M GOING ON AHEAD, USOPP!!
RAAAH-
SKRIK SKRIK
TMP TMP!!
W- WAIT, VIVI! WAIT!!
TICK...
TICK...
HURRY!!
TICK...

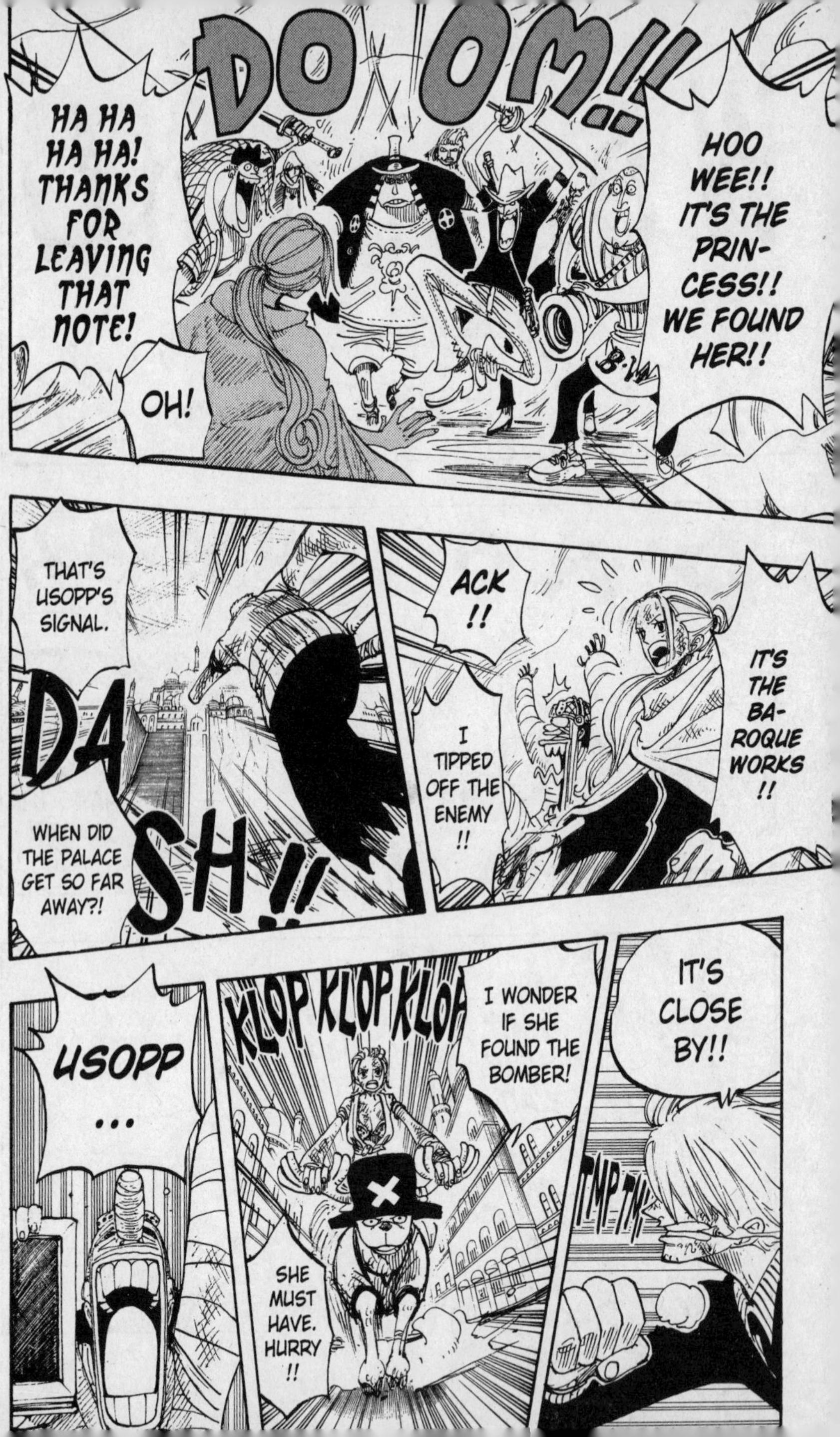
DOOM!!
HOO WEE!! IT'S THE PRIN-CESS!! WE FOUND HER!!
HA HA HA HA! THANKS FOR LEAVING THAT NOTE!
OH!
IT'S THE BA-ROQUE WORKS!!
ACK!!
I TIPPED OFF THE ENEMY!!
THAT'S USOPP'S SIGNAL.
DASH!!
WHEN DID THE PALACE GET SO FAR AWAY?!
IT'S CLOSE BY!!
TMP TM
I WONDER IF SHE FOUND THE BOMBER!
KLOP KLOP KLO
SHE MUST HAVE. HURRY!!
USOPP...

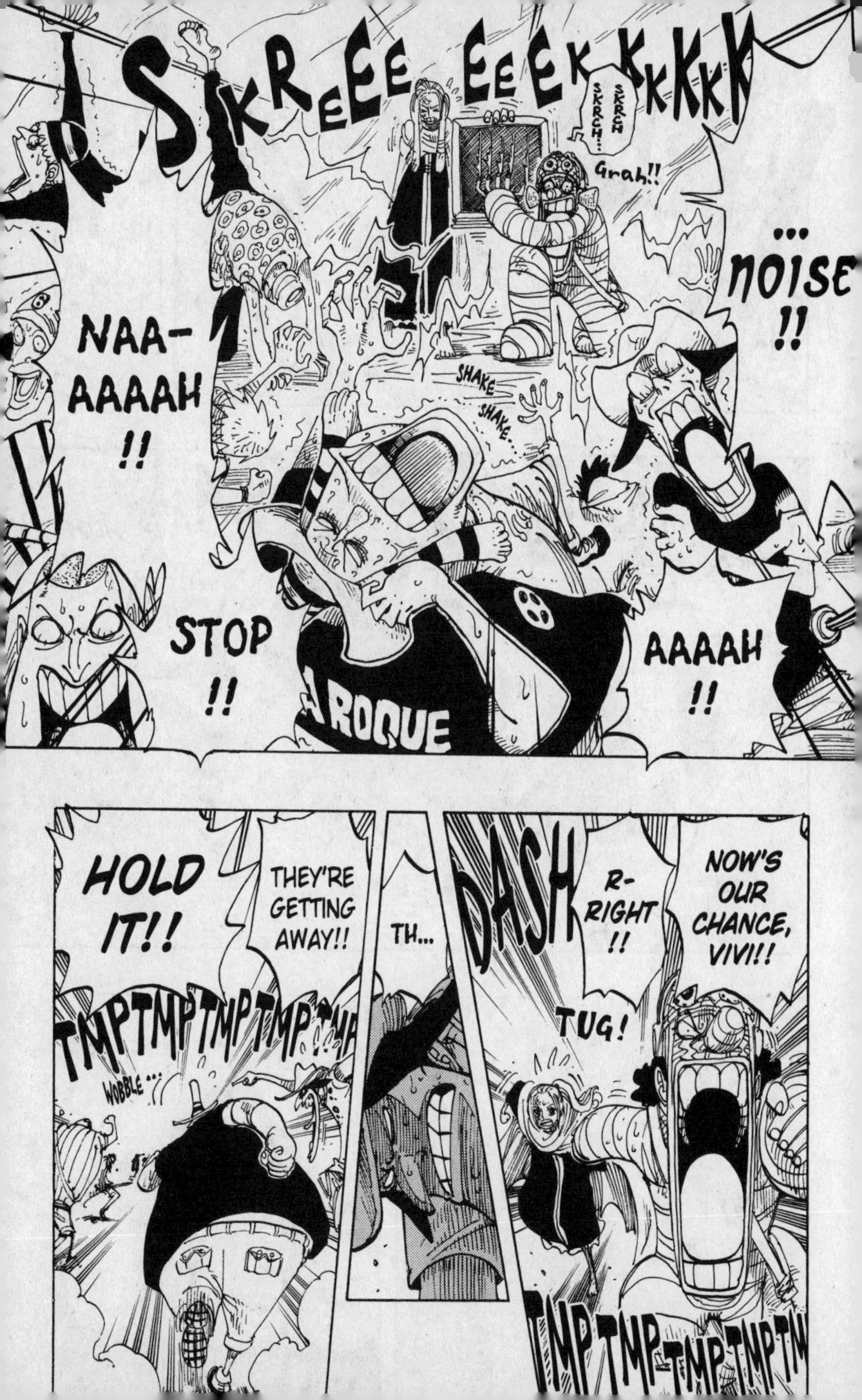
SKREEEEEEEKKKKK
SKRCH SKRCH!...
Grah!!
...NOISE!!
SHAKE SHAKE...
AAAAH!!
STOP!!
NAA-AAAAH!!
NOW'S OUR CHANCE, VIVI!!
R-RIGHT!!
DASH
TUG!
TMP TMP TMP TMPTM
TH...
THEY'RE GETTING AWAY!!
HOLD IT!!
TMPTMPTMPTMPTMP
WOBBLE...

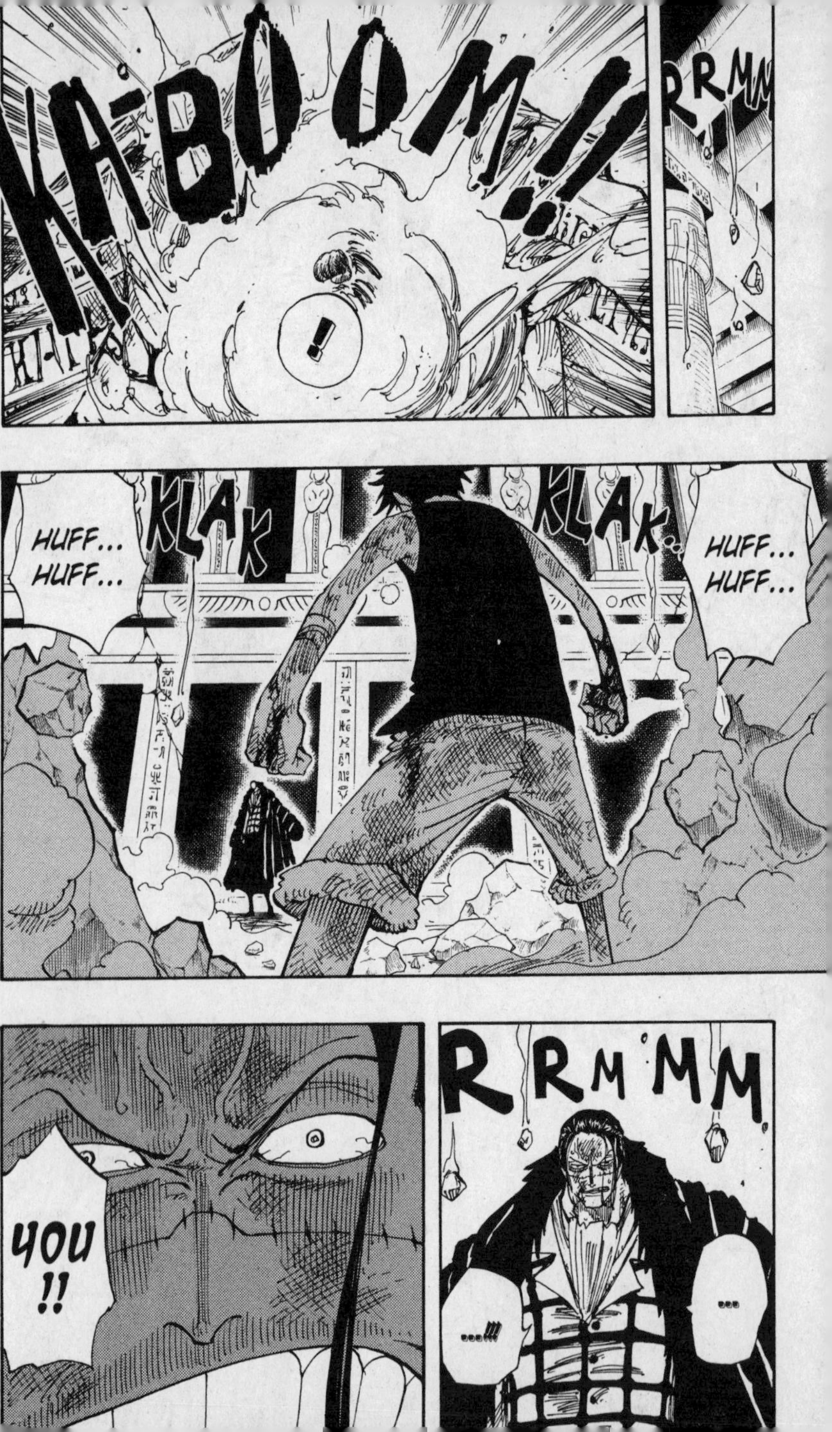
RRMM
KA-BOOM!!
!
HUFF... HUFF...
KLAK...
KLAK
HUFF... HUFF...
RRMMM
...
...!!!
YOU !!

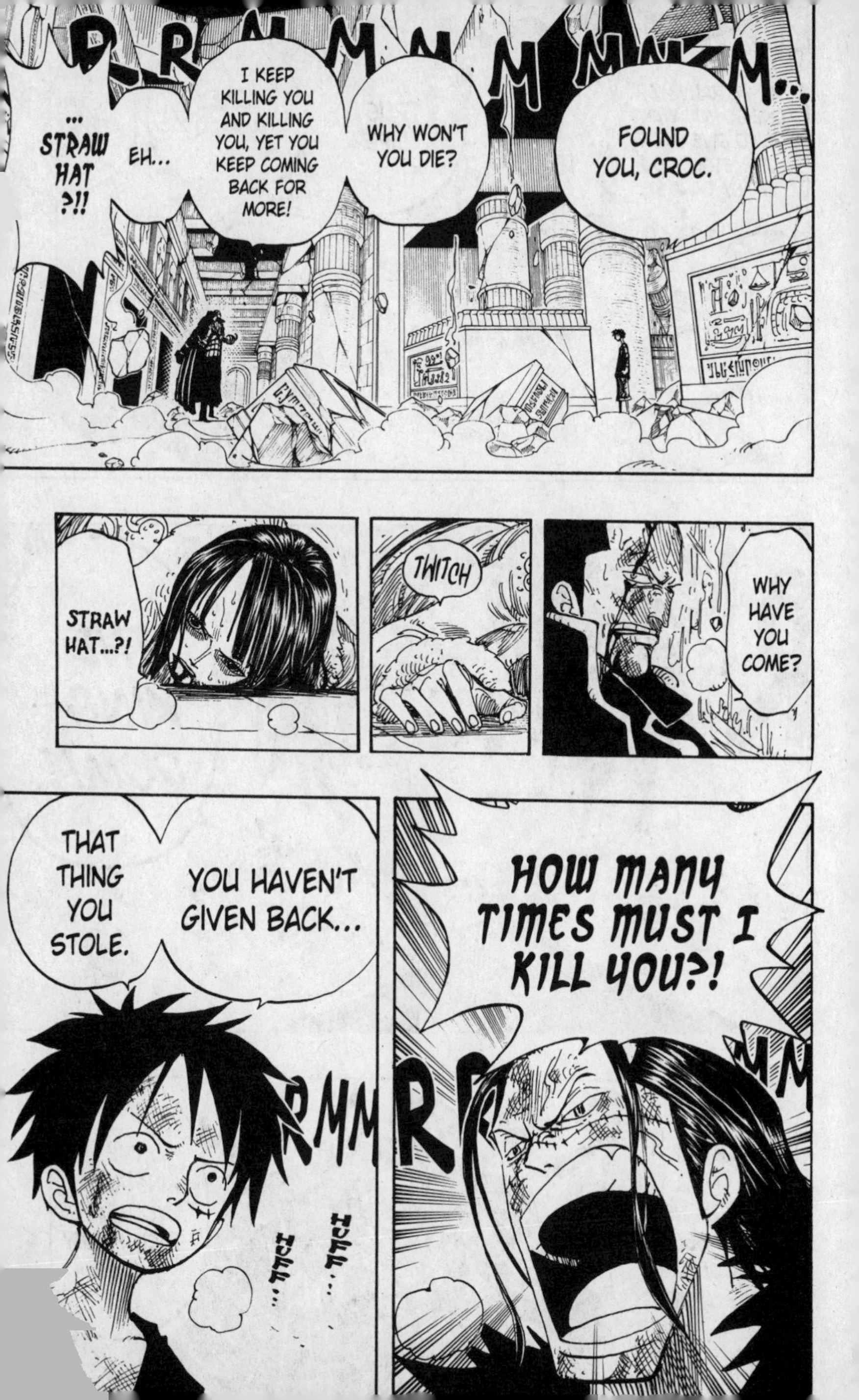
FOUND YOU, CROC.
WHY WON'T YOU DIE?
I KEEP KILLING YOU AND KILLING YOU, YET YOU KEEP COMING BACK FOR MORE!
EH...
... STRAW HAT ?!!
WHY HAVE YOU COME?
TWITCH
STRAW HAT...?!
HOW MANY TIMES MUST I KILL YOU?!
YOU HAVEN'T GIVEN BACK...
THAT THING YOU STOLE.
HUFF...
HUFF...

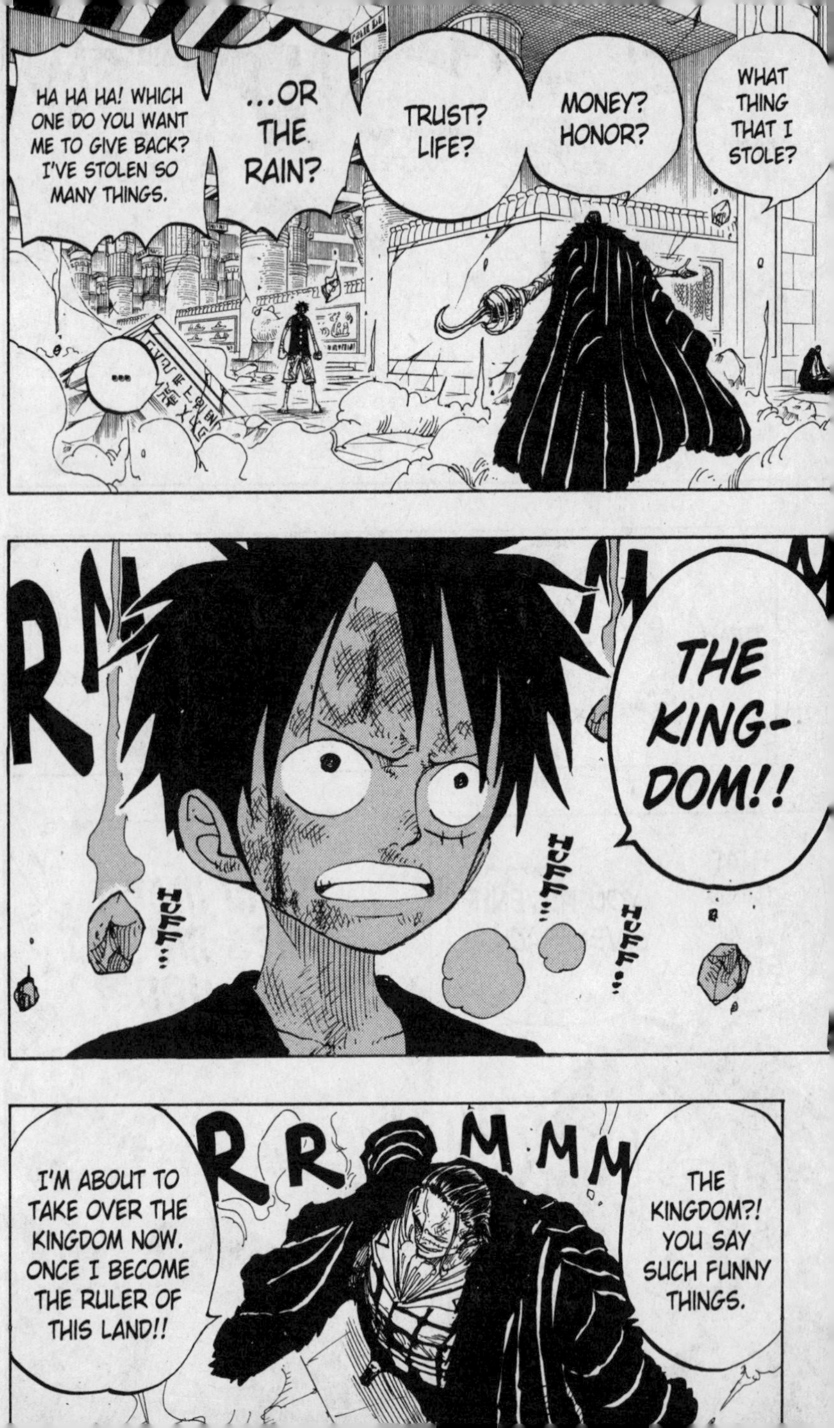
WHAT THING THAT I STOLE?
MONEY? HONOR?
TRUST? LIFE?
...OR THE RAIN?
HA HA HA! WHICH ONE DO YOU WANT ME TO GIVE BACK? I'VE STOLEN SO MANY THINGS.
...
RRMMM
THE KING-DOM!!
HUFF...
HUFF...
HUFF...
THE KINGDOM?! YOU SAY SUCH FUNNY THINGS.
RRRMMM
I'M ABOUT TO TAKE OVER THE KINGDOM NOW. ONCE I BECOME THE RULER OF THIS LAND!!

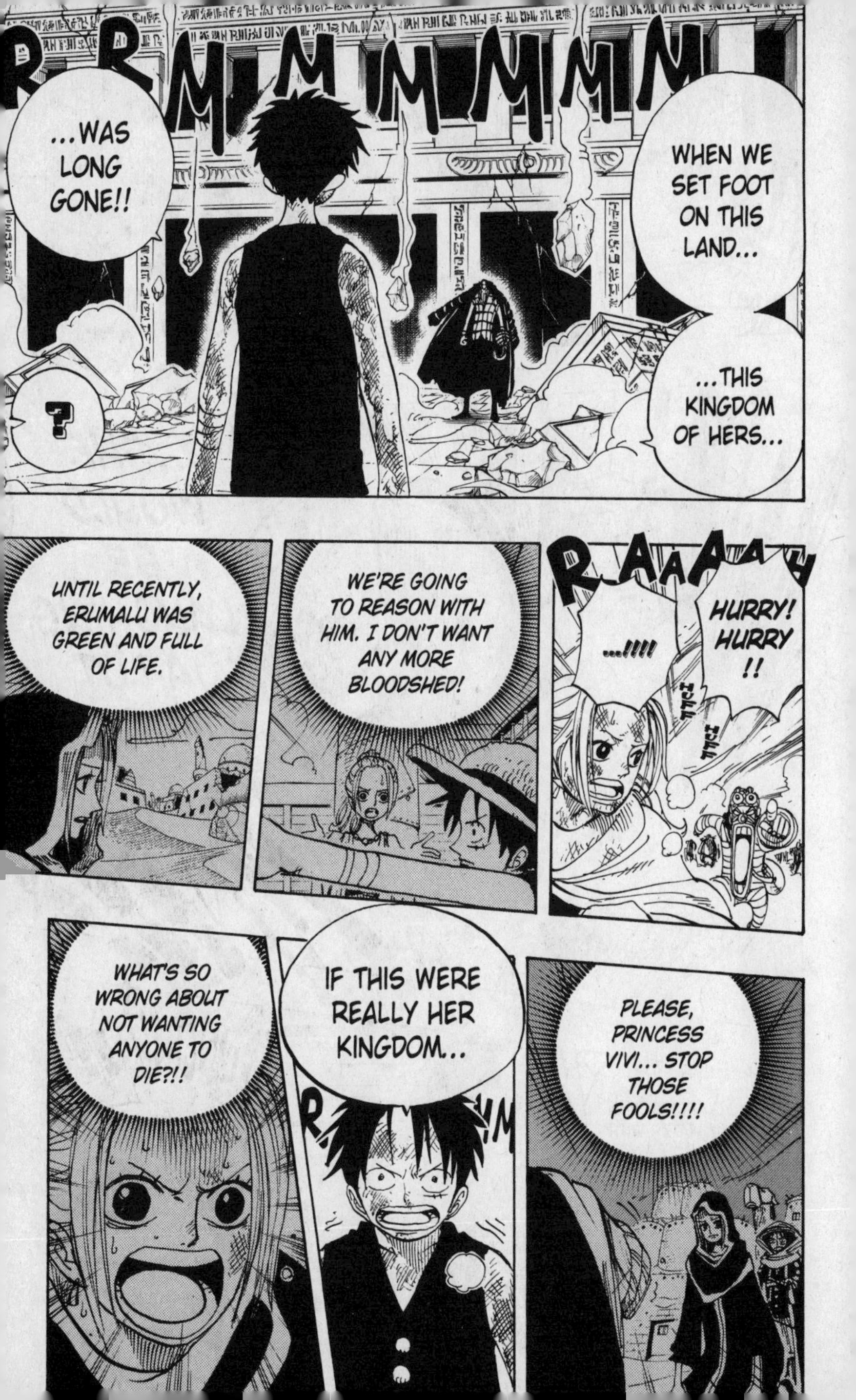
RRMMMMMMM
WHEN WE SET FOOT ON THIS LAND...
...THIS KINGDOM OF HERS...
...WAS LONG GONE!!
?
RAAAAH
HURRY! HURRY!!
...!!!!
HUFF
HUFF
WE'RE GOING TO REASON WITH HIM. I DON'T WANT ANY MORE BLOODSHED!
UNTIL RECENTLY, ERUMALU WAS GREEN AND FULL OF LIFE.
PLEASE, PRINCESS VIVI... STOP THOSE FOOLS!!!!
IF THIS WERE REALLY HER KINGDOM...
WHAT'S SO WRONG ABOUT NOT WANTING ANYONE TO DIE?!!

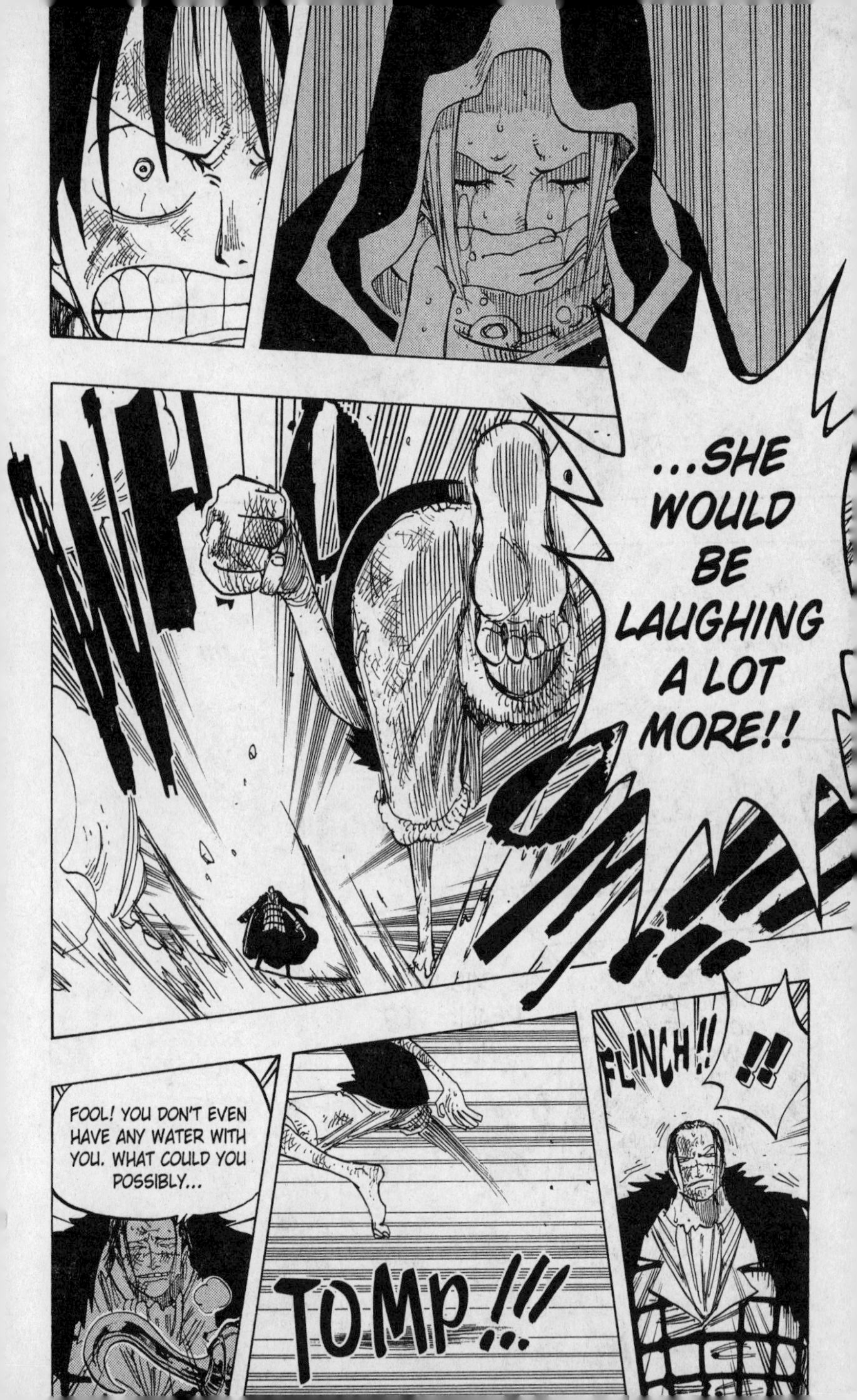

...SHE WOULD BE LAUGHING A LOT MORE!!
FLINCH!!
!!
TOMP!!!
FOOL! YOU DON'T EVEN HAVE ANY WATER WITH YOU. WHAT COULD YOU POSSIBLY...

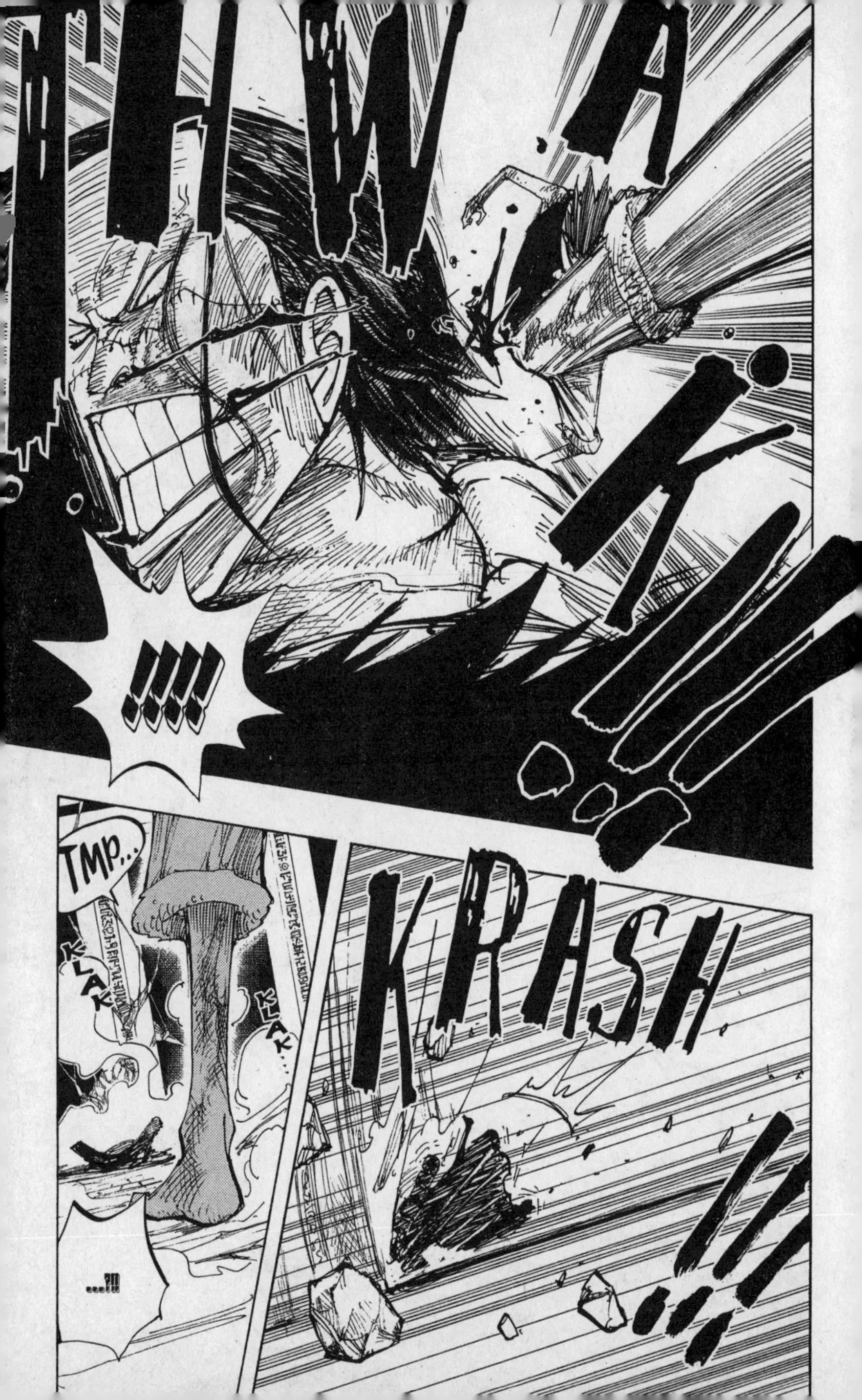
THWAK!!!
!!!!!
KRASH!!!
TMP...
KLAK
KLAK...
...?!!

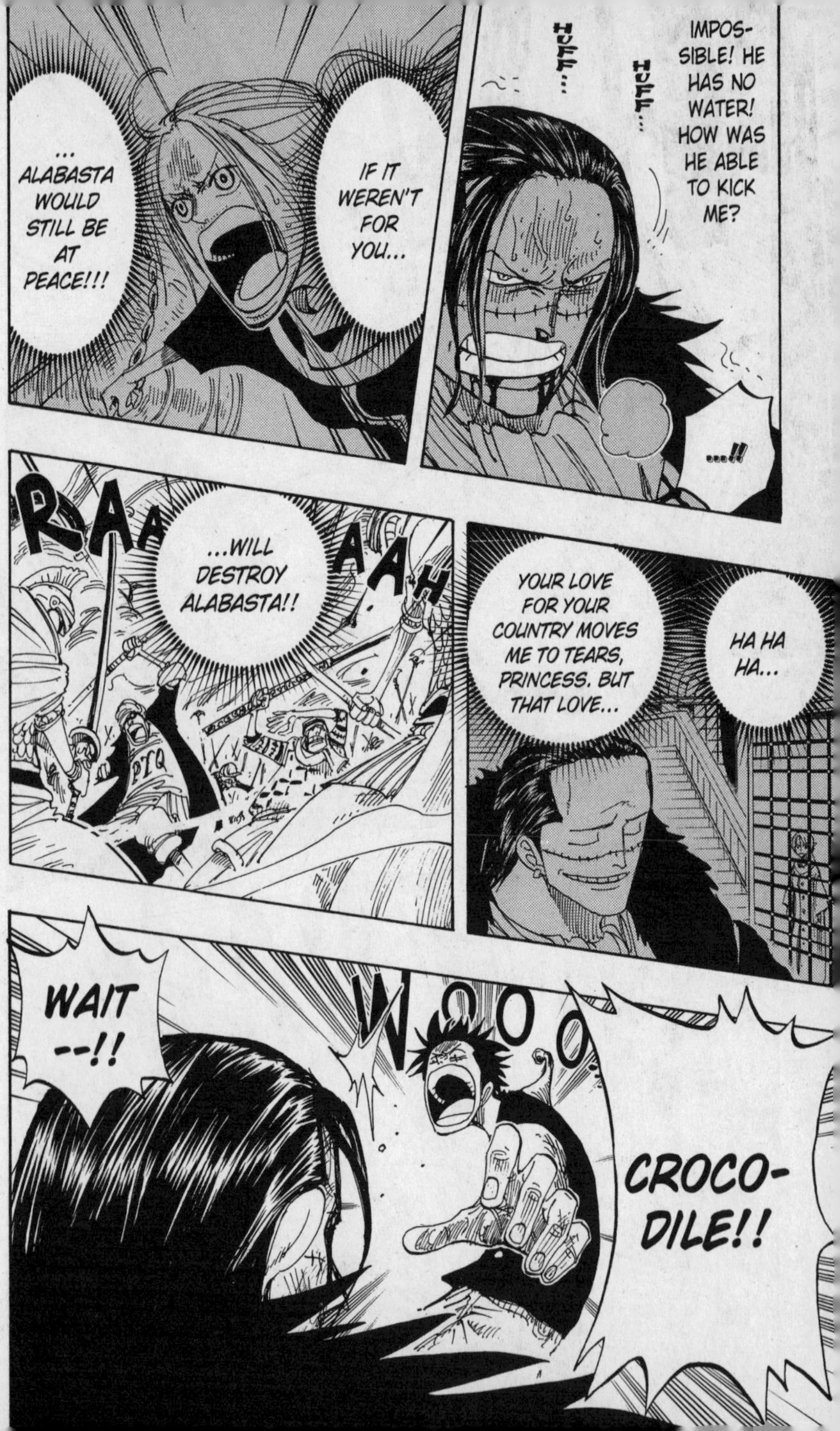
HUFF... HUFF...
IMPOSSIBLE! HE HAS NO WATER! HOW WAS HE ABLE TO KICK ME?
...!!
IF IT WEREN'T FOR YOU...
...ALABASTA WOULD STILL BE AT PEACE!!!
HA HA HA...
YOUR LOVE FOR YOUR COUNTRY MOVES ME TO TEARS, PRINCESS. BUT THAT LOVE...
...WILL DESTROY ALABASTA!!
RAAAAH
WOOO
WAIT --!!
CROCODILE!!

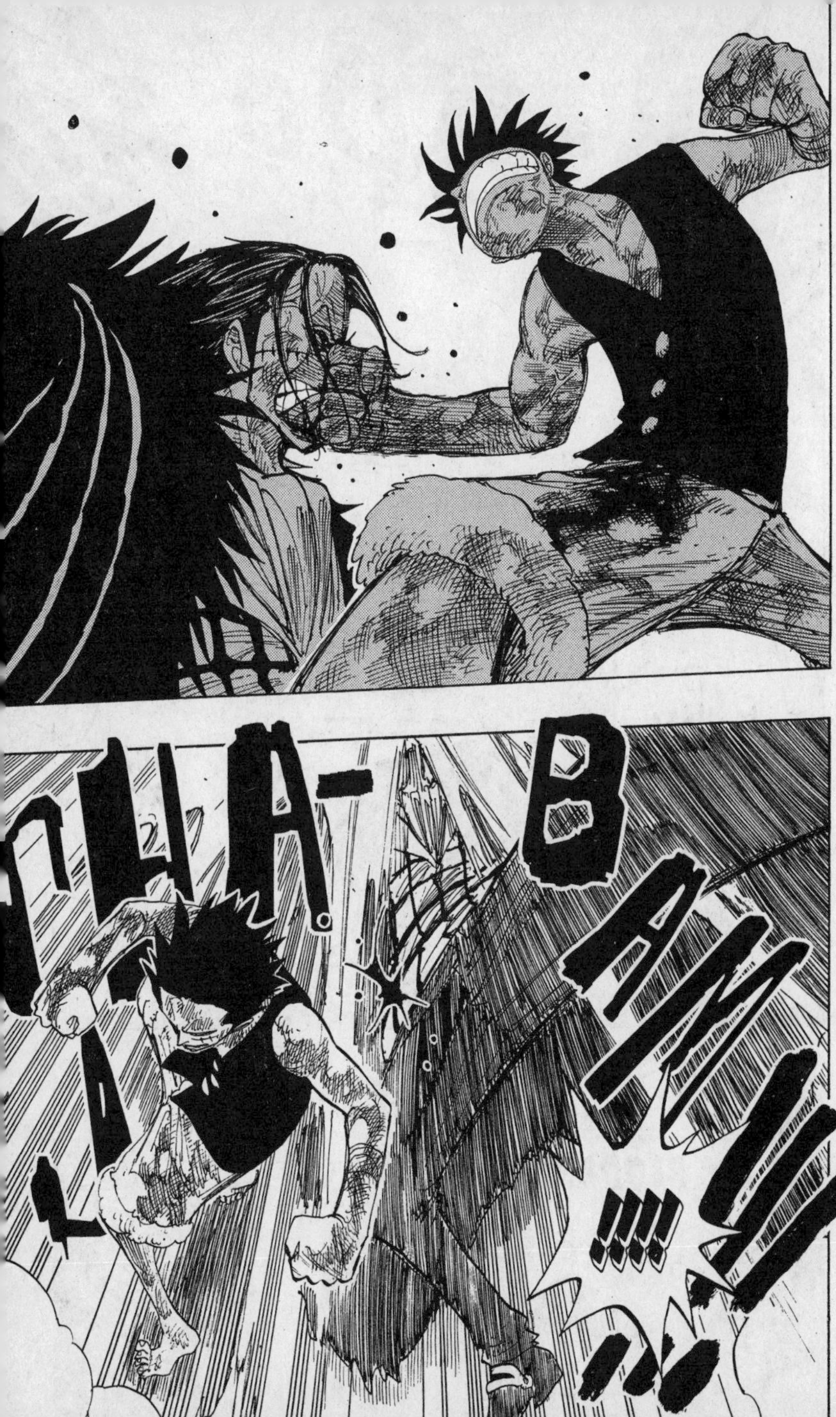
CHA-BAMM!!!!

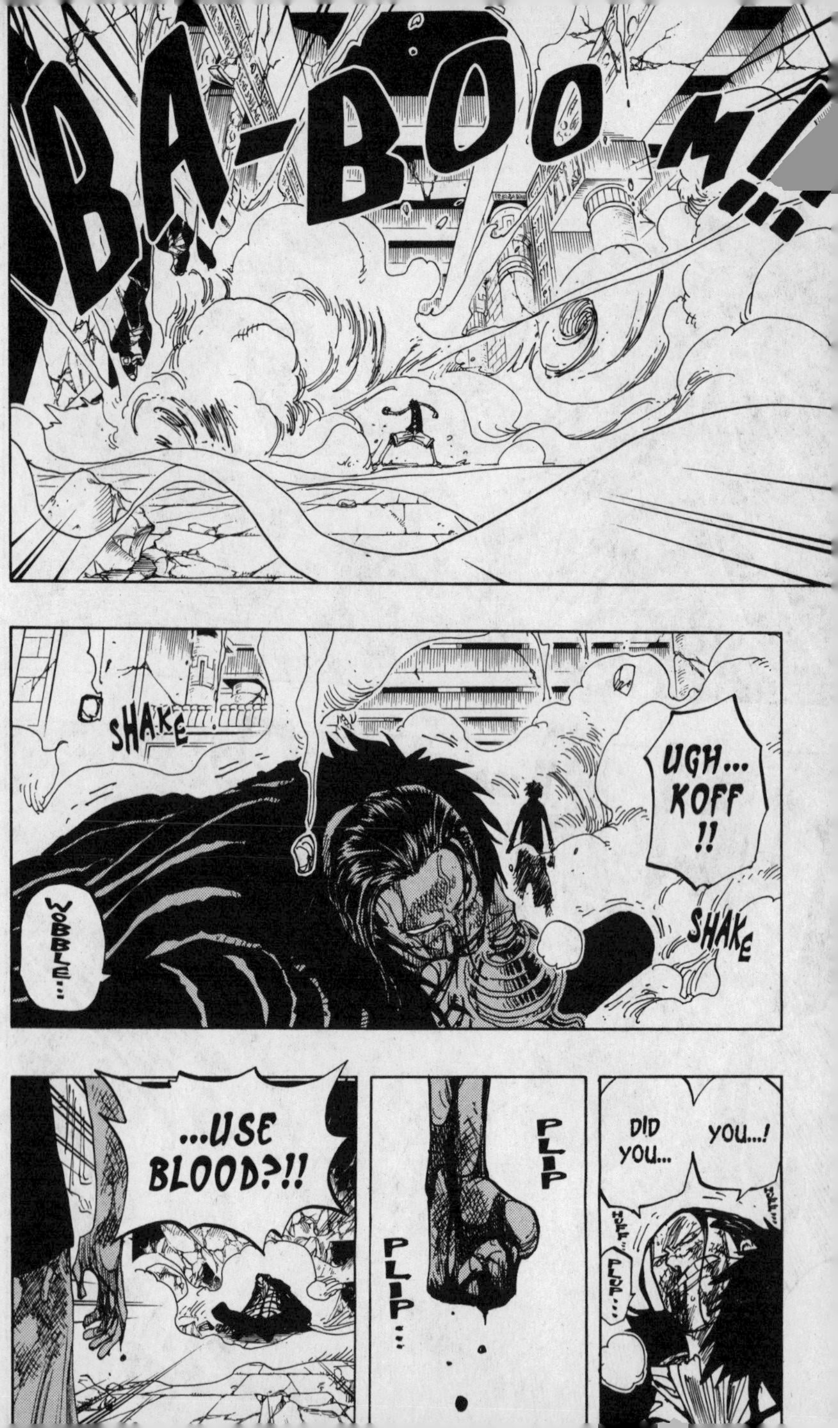
BA-BOOM!!
UGH... KOFF !!
SHAKE
SHAKE
WOBBLE...
YOU...!
DID YOU...
HUFF...
PLUP...
PLIP
PLIP...
...USE BLOOD?!!

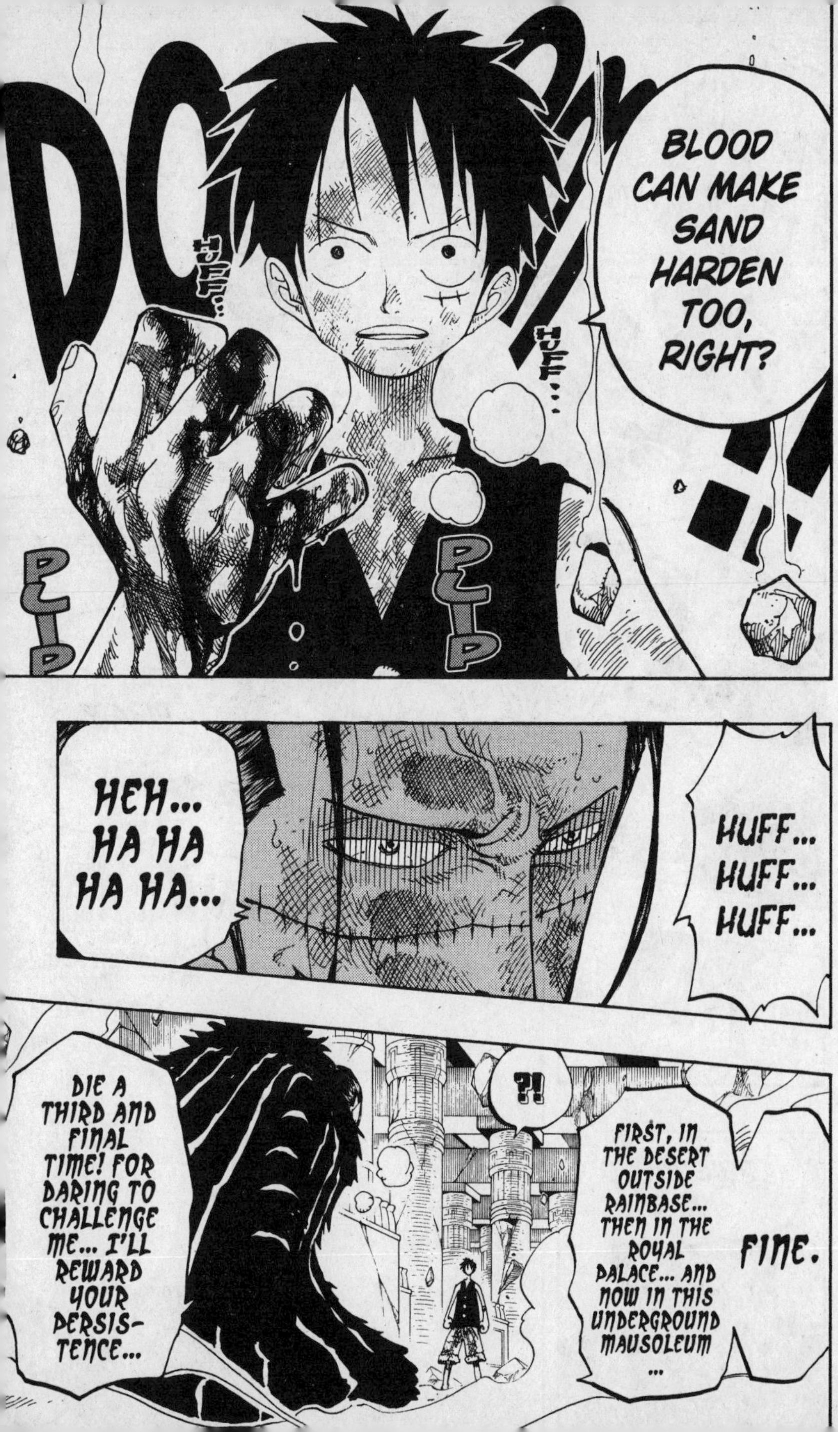
BLOOD CAN MAKE SAND HARDEN TOO, RIGHT?
HUFF...
HUFF...
PLIP
PLIP
HUFF... HUFF... HUFF...
HEH... HA HA HA HA...
FINE.
FIRST, IN THE DESERT OUTSIDE RAINBASE... THEN IN THE ROYAL PALACE... AND NOW IN THIS UNDERGROUND MAUSOLEUM ...
?!
DIE A THIRD AND FINAL TIME! FOR DARING TO CHALLENGE ME... I'LL REWARD YOUR PERSIS-TENCE...

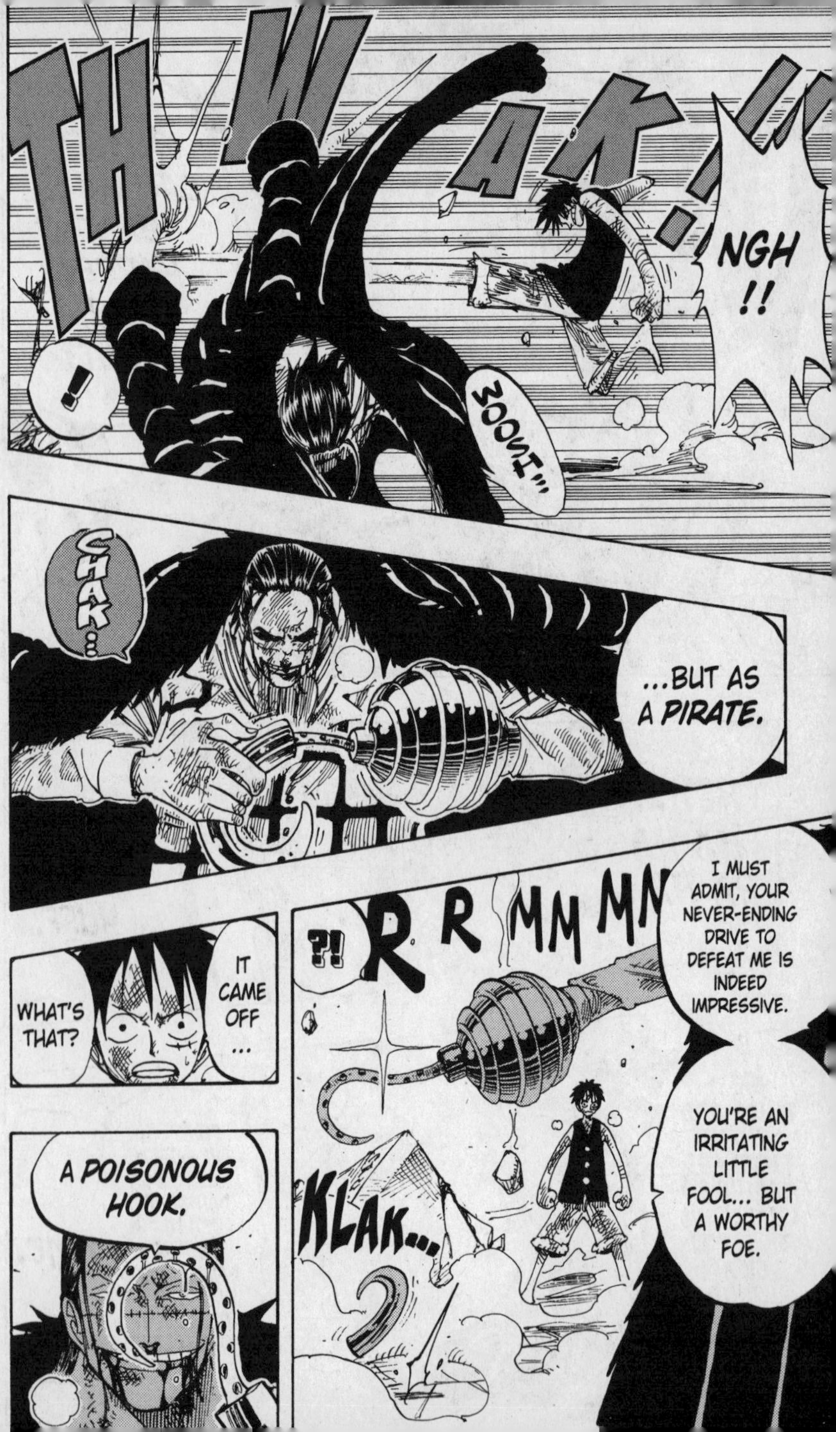
THWAK!!
NGH!!
WOOSH...
!
...BUT AS A PIRATE.
CHAK...
I MUST ADMIT, YOUR NEVER-ENDING DRIVE TO DEFEAT ME IS INDEED IMPRESSIVE.
RRMMMMN
?!
YOU'RE AN IRRITATING LITTLE FOOL... BUT A WORTHY FOE.
KLAK...
IT CAME OFF...
WHAT'S THAT?
A POISONOUS HOOK.

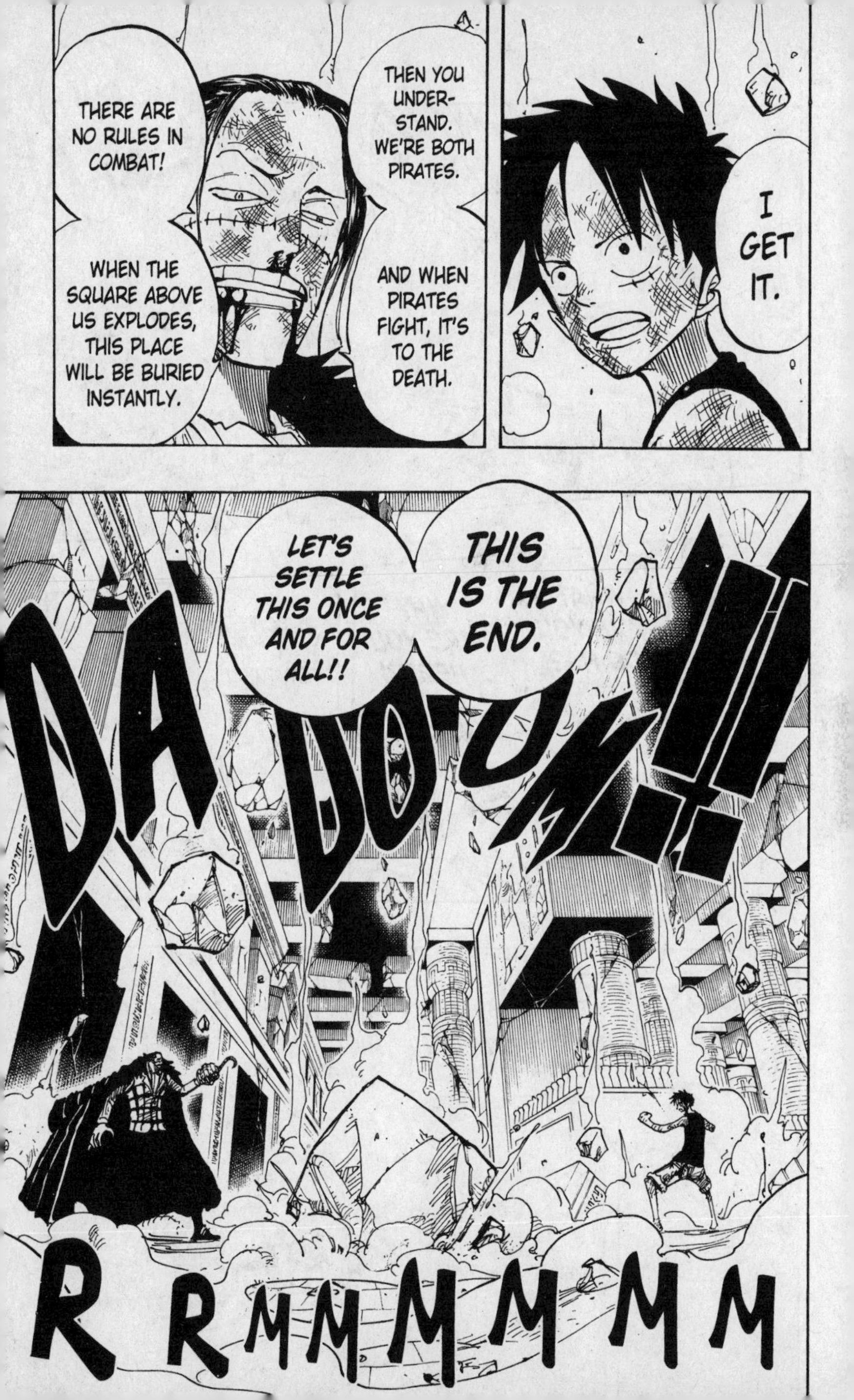
I GET IT.
THEN YOU UNDERSTAND. WE'RE BOTH PIRATES.
AND WHEN PIRATES FIGHT, IT'S TO THE DEATH.
THERE ARE NO RULES IN COMBAT!
WHEN THE SQUARE ABOVE US EXPLODES, THIS PLACE WILL BE BURIED INSTANTLY.
THIS IS THE END.
LET'S SETTLE THIS ONCE AND FOR ALL!!
DA DOM!!
RRMMMMMMM

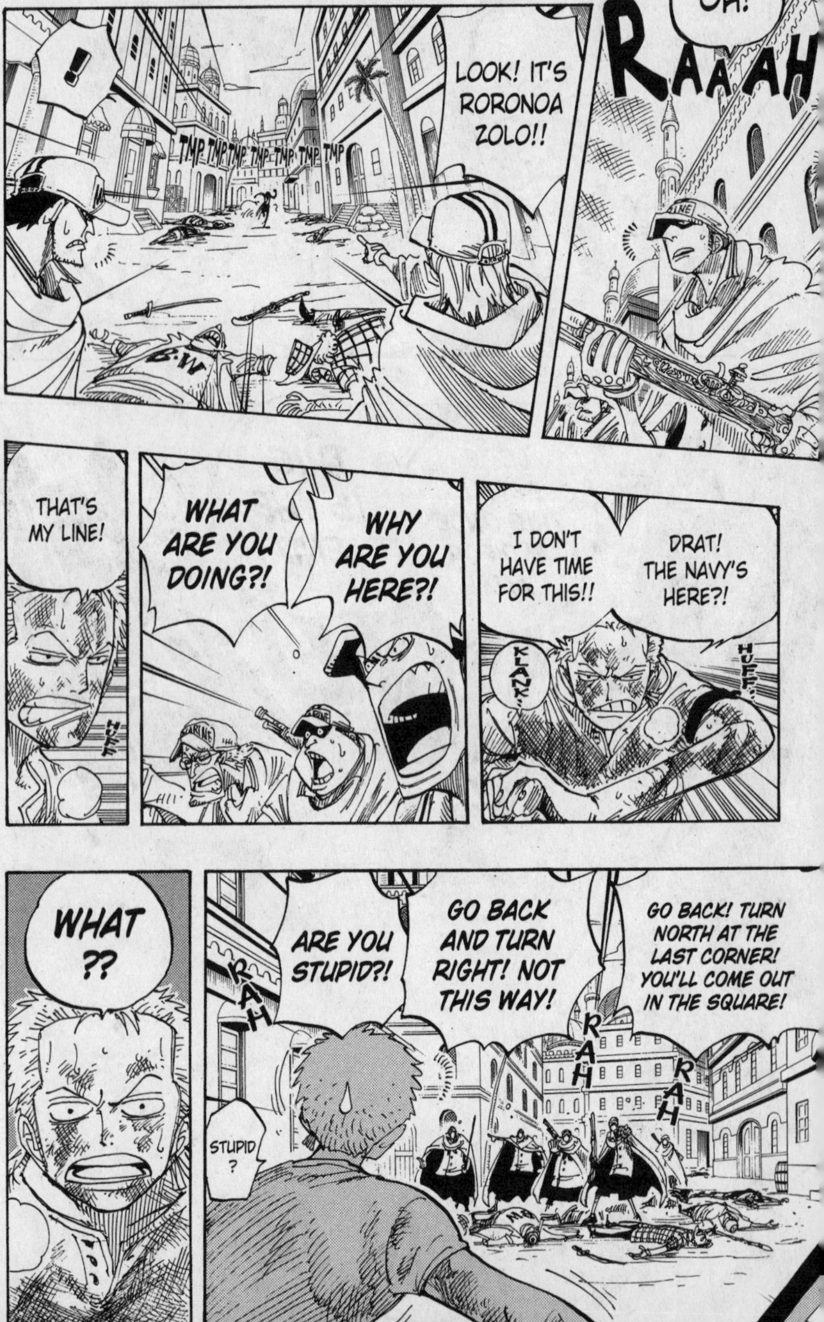
OH!
RAAAH
LOOK! IT'S RORONOA ZOLO!!
!
TMP TMP TMP TMP TMP TMP TMP
DRAT! THE NAVY'S HERE?!
I DON'T HAVE TIME FOR THIS!!
KLANK
HUFF
WHY ARE YOU HERE?!
WHAT ARE YOU DOING?!
THAT'S MY LINE!
HUFF
GO BACK! TURN NORTH AT THE LAST CORNER! YOU'LL COME OUT IN THE SQUARE!
GO BACK AND TURN RIGHT! NOT THIS WAY!
ARE YOU STUPID?!
RAH
RAH
RAH
STUPID ?
WHAT ??

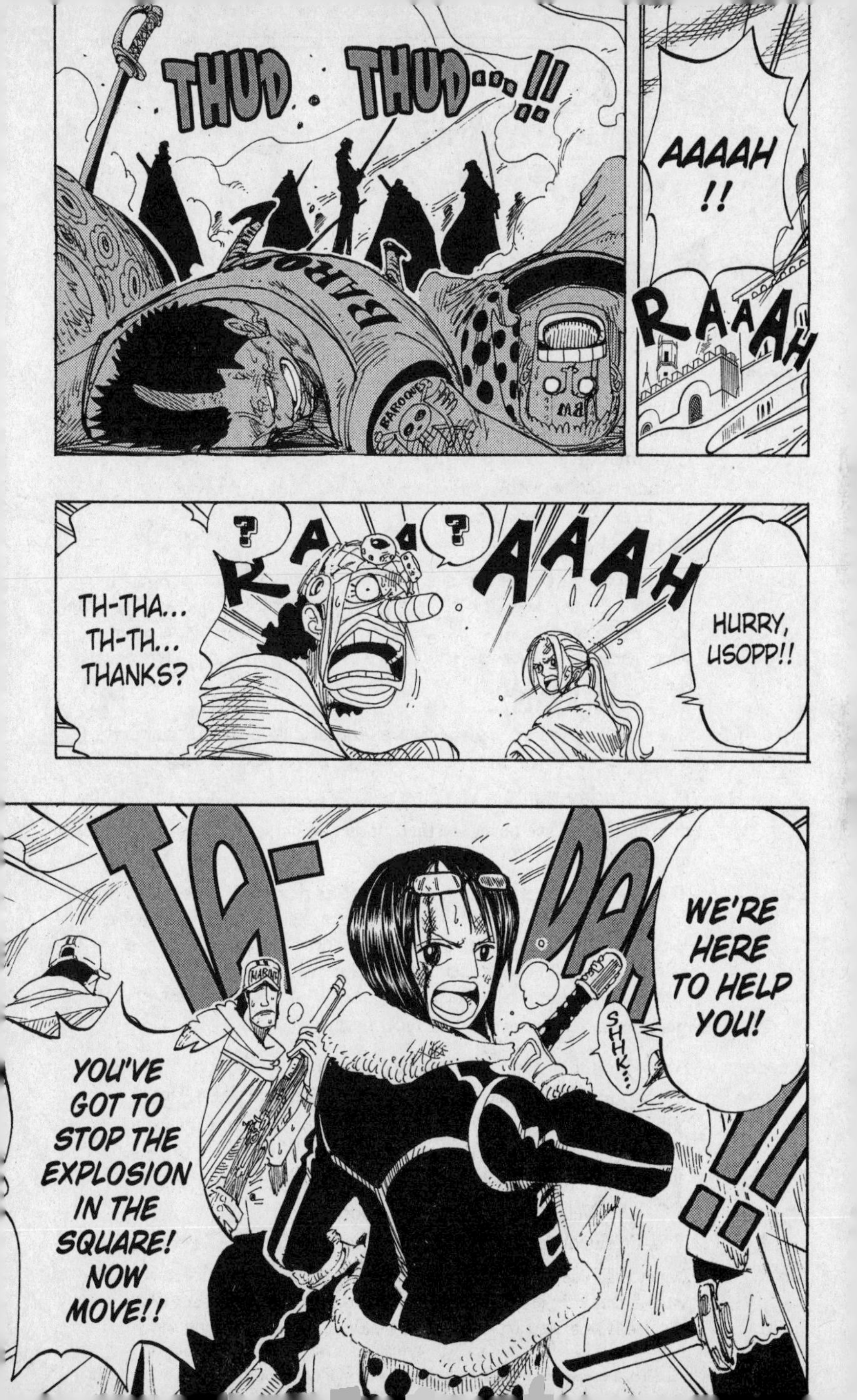
AAAAH !!
RAAAAH
THUD THUD...!!
HURRY, USOPP!!
?
?
RAAAAAH
TH-THA... TH-TH... THANKS?
WE'RE HERE TO HELP YOU!
SHHK...
!!
TA-DA
YOU'VE GOT TO STOP THE EXPLOSION IN THE SQUARE! NOW MOVE!!

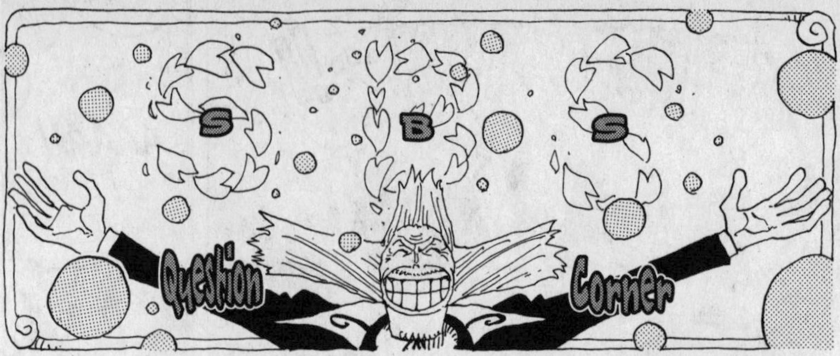
SBS
Question Corner

Reader: Umm, I have a question for Mr. Oda. In Volume 20, page 174, panel one, where Ms. Merry Christmas dives in a hole, the sound effect "woosh" (→) has a fish in it. Why did you do that? I have to know!

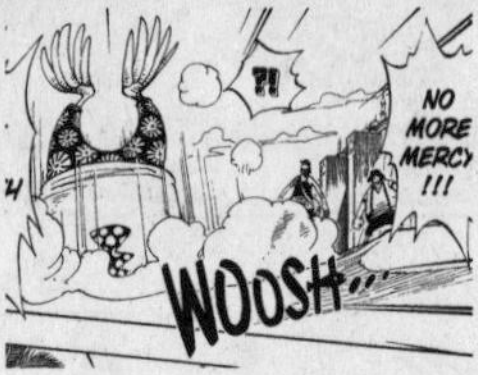
?!
NO MORE MERCY !!!
WOOSH...

Oda: Oh, it was just because she was doing her Mole Swimming Stealth Style. Why don't we try it? How to say "woosh." 1) Arch your eyebrows as high as you can. 2) Without moving your face, look up as high as you can. 3) Push out your lower teeth. Ready? **WOOSH...**

Were you able to do it? Go ahead and show your parents and friends. (But they're going to think you're a goofball!)

Reader: Even though Nami and Ms. All Sunday were wearing short skirts when they're fighting, we never see their undies. What color are they? Please tell me.

Oda: That's rather personal. What a question... And yet you seem so casual about it, as though you'd be surprised if anyone thought that was weird. You shouldn't be asking these things. But if I were to take a guess... Back in volume 14, Nami was wearing a black bra, so... Uh, we'd better end it right there. I value my life, you know.

Reader: Hello, Mr. Oda. What's next week's Question Corner gonna be about? How about "Usopp Lies," "Luffy Finds a Treasure Chest," and "Chopper's Nose Turns Red"? Okay? ♪ I'll be looking forward to it!

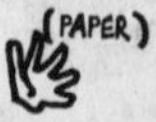
(PAPER)

Rock-paper-scissors!
Hee hee hee... ☆
Well, that's it for the Question Corner!
--President All-Brand Kiri, The Question Corner Conclusion Club

Oda: Darn it!! I was going to do scissors!! I overthought it too much!! Darn it!! I knew I should've gone with scissors!! Oh well, see you in the next volume. Darn it...

Sazae-san, a popular and long-running anime, always ends each episode with a game of rock-paper-scissors. --Editor

Chapter 205:
THE SAND-SAND BAND'S SECRET FORT

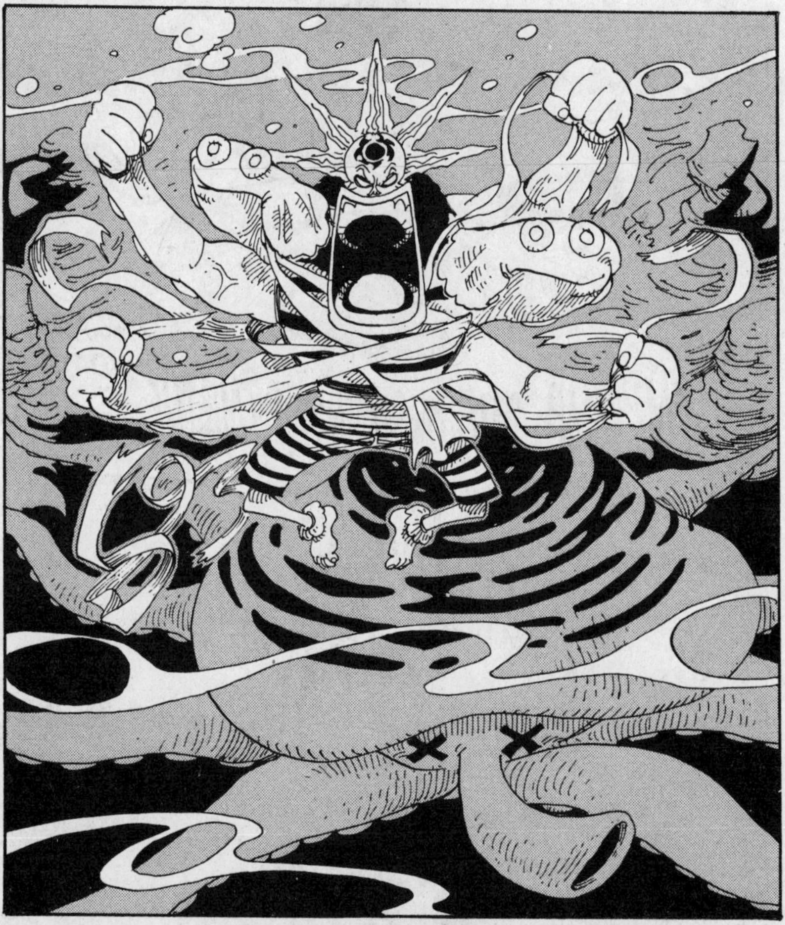

HACHI'S WALK ON THE SEAFLOOR, VOL.20:
"HACHI'S RAGE AT BEING FOOLED"

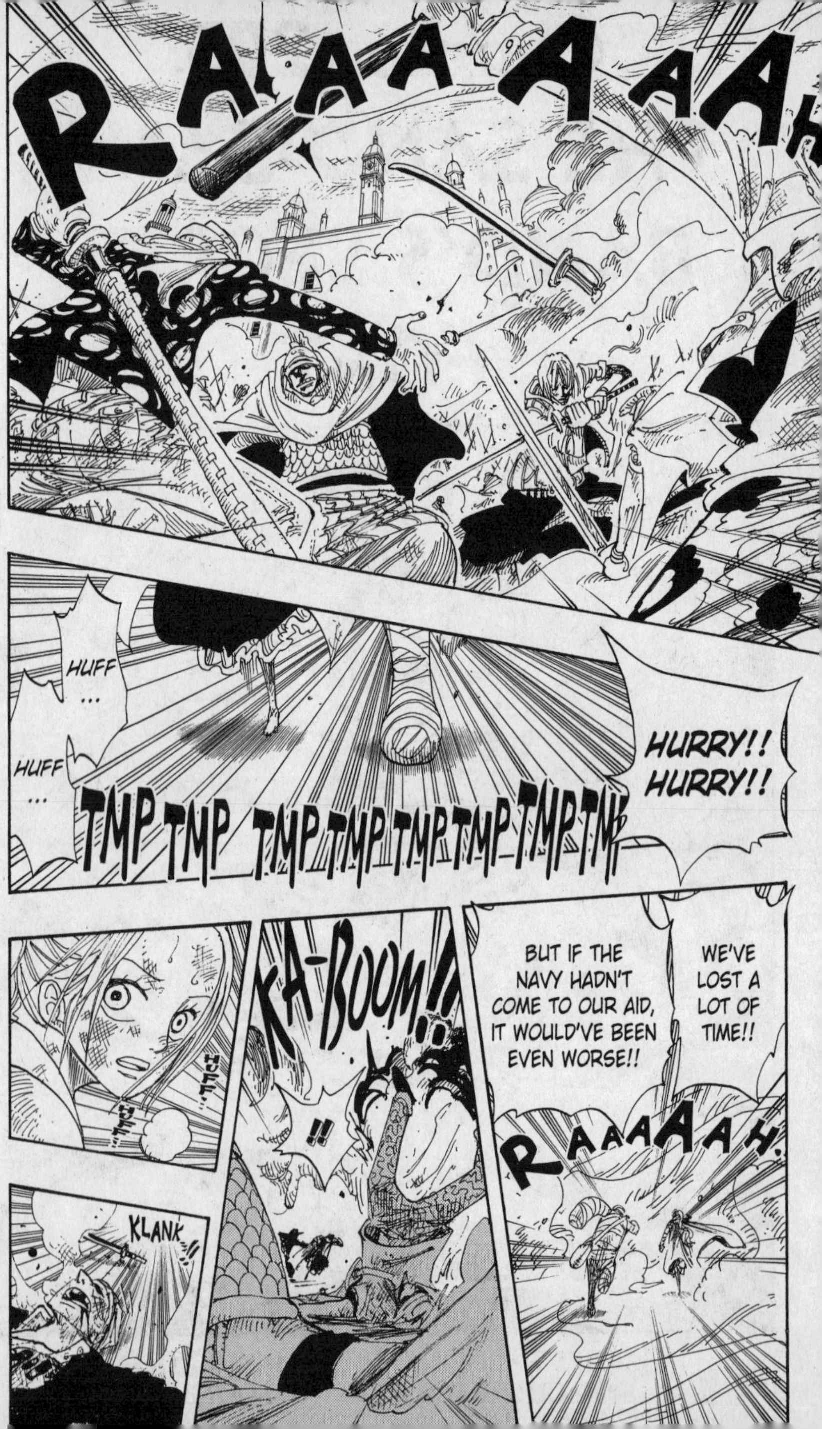
RAAAAAAH
HURRY!! HURRY!!
HUFF...
HUFF...
TMP TMP TMP TMP TMP TMP TMP TMP
WE'VE LOST A LOT OF TIME!!
BUT IF THE NAVY HADN'T COME TO OUR AID, IT WOULD'VE BEEN EVEN WORSE!!
RAAAAAH
KA-BOOM!!
!!
HUFF...
HUFF...
KLANK!!

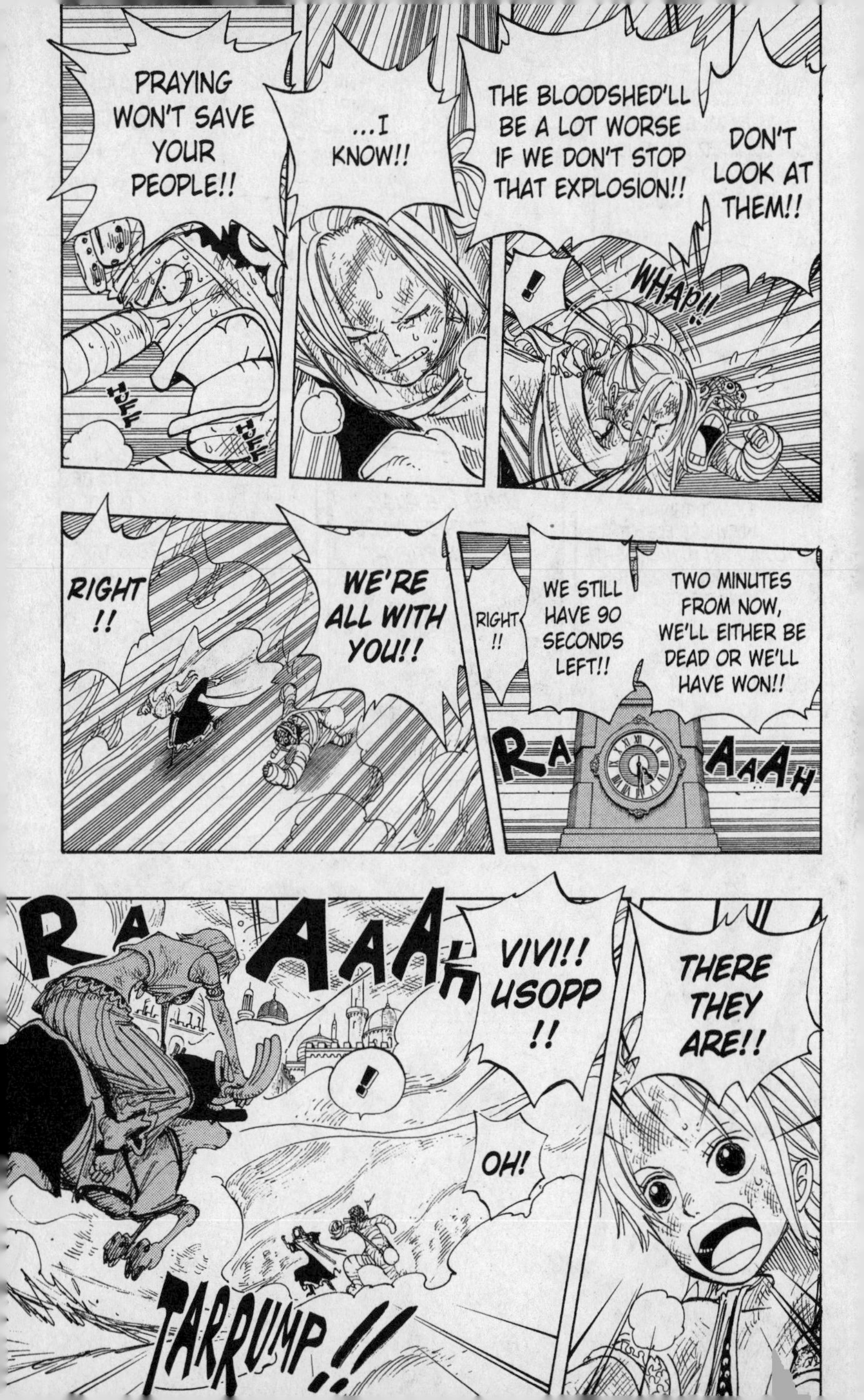
DON'T LOOK AT THEM!!
THE BLOODSHED'LL BE A LOT WORSE IF WE DON'T STOP THAT EXPLOSION!!
!
WHAP!!
...I KNOW!!
PRAYING WON'T SAVE YOUR PEOPLE!!
HUFF
HUFF
TWO MINUTES FROM NOW, WE'LL EITHER BE DEAD OR WE'LL HAVE WON!!
WE STILL HAVE 90 SECONDS LEFT!!
RIGHT!!
RAAAAH
WE'RE ALL WITH YOU!!
RIGHT!!
THERE THEY ARE!!
VIVI!! USOPP!!
RAAAAH
!
OH!
TARRUMP!!

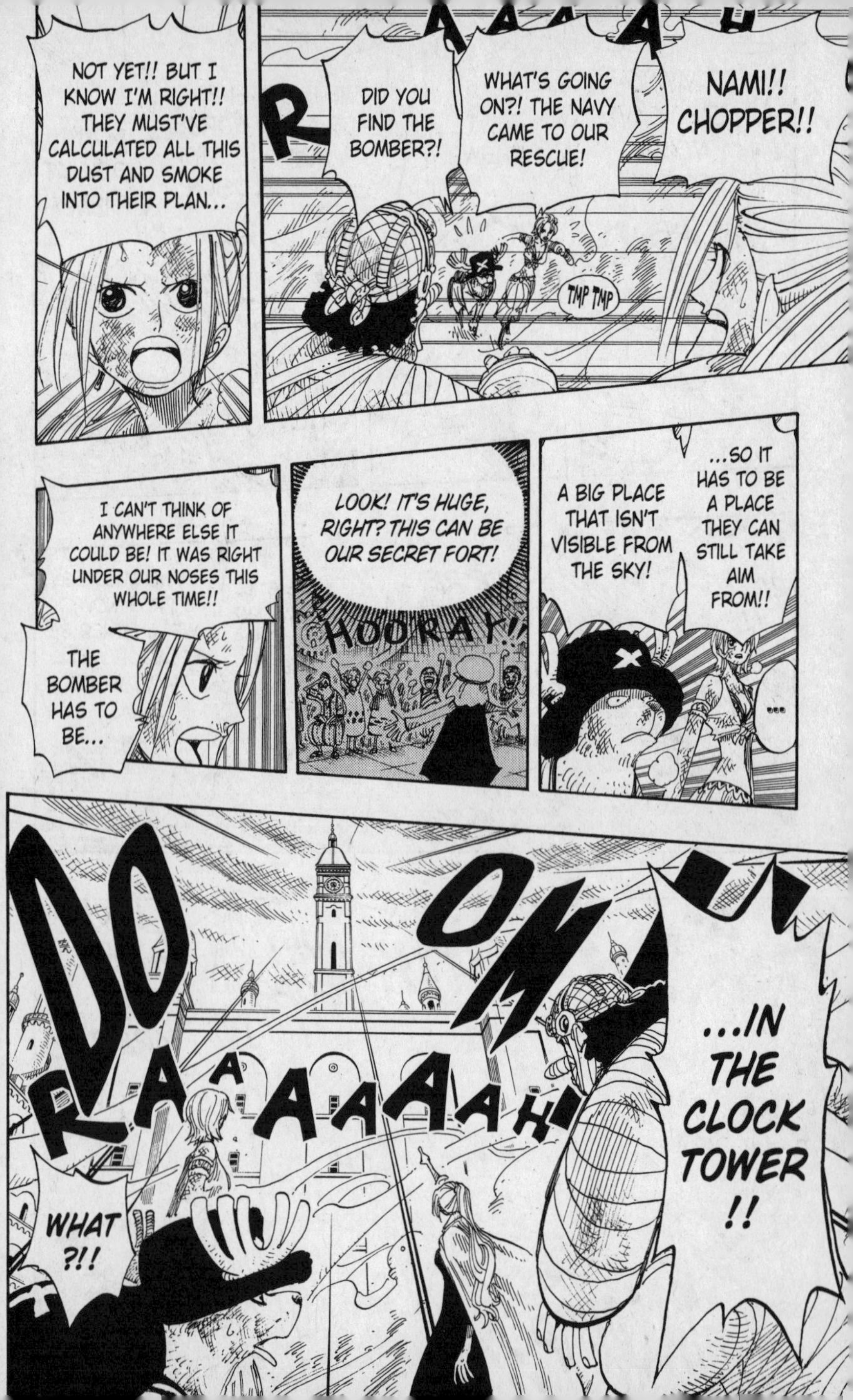
RAAAAAH
NAMI!! CHOPPER!!
WHAT'S GOING ON?! THE NAVY CAME TO OUR RESCUE!
DID YOU FIND THE BOMBER?!
TMP TMP
NOT YET!! BUT I KNOW I'M RIGHT!! THEY MUST'VE CALCULATED ALL THIS DUST AND SMOKE INTO THEIR PLAN...
...SO IT HAS TO BE A PLACE THEY CAN STILL TAKE AIM FROM!!
A BIG PLACE THAT ISN'T VISIBLE FROM THE SKY!
...
LOOK! IT'S HUGE, RIGHT? THIS CAN BE OUR SECRET FORT!
HOORAY!!
I CAN'T THINK OF ANYWHERE ELSE IT COULD BE! IT WAS RIGHT UNDER OUR NOSES THIS WHOLE TIME!!
THE BOMBER HAS TO BE...
...IN THE CLOCK TOWER!!
DOOM
RAAAAAH
WHAT?!!

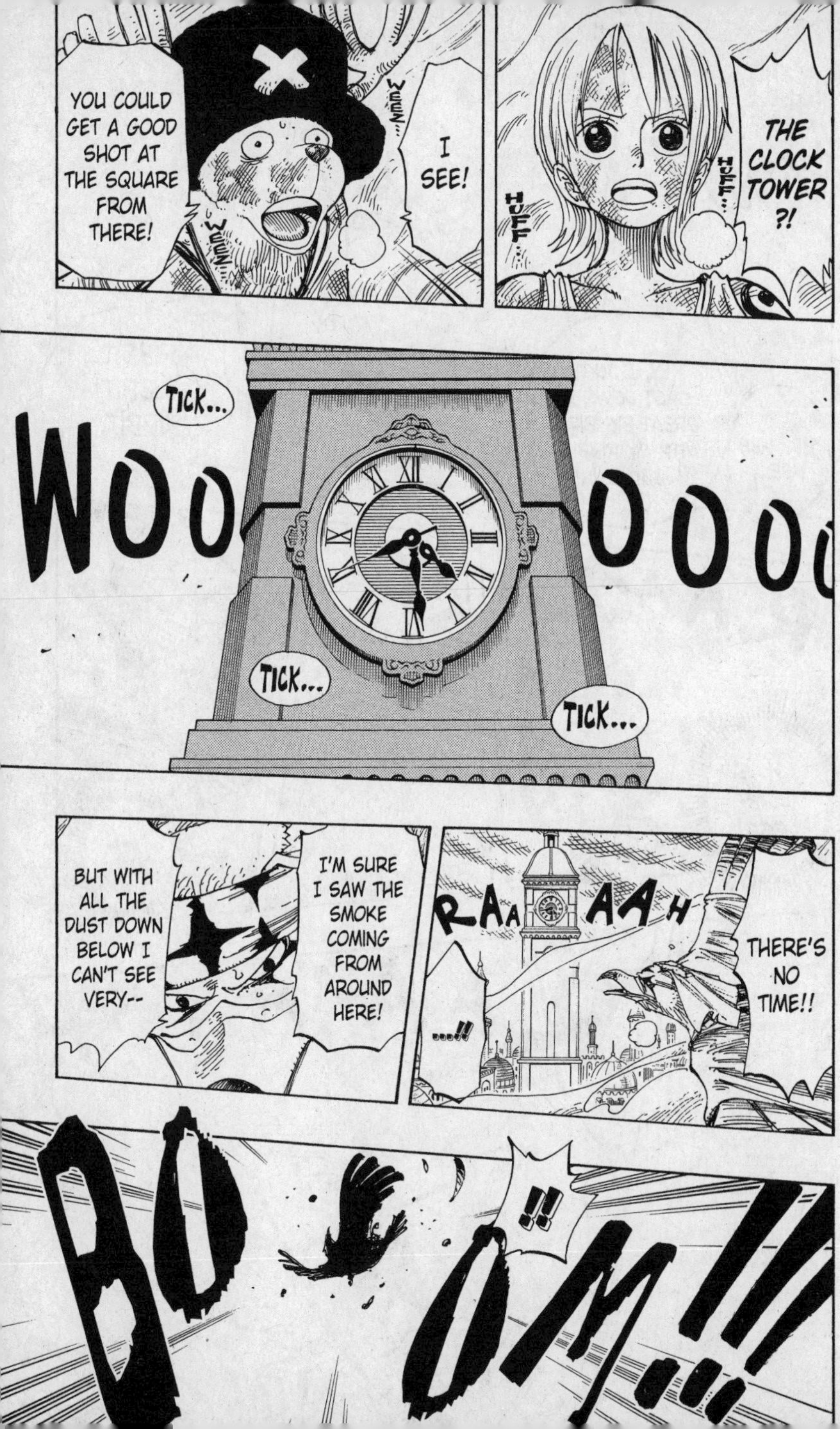
HUFF... HUFF...
THE CLOCK TOWER?!
WEEN...
I SEE!
YOU COULD GET A GOOD SHOT AT THE SQUARE FROM THERE!
WEEN...
TICK...
WOOOOOOO
TICK...
TICK...
THERE'S NO TIME!!
RAAAAH
...!!
I'M SURE I SAW THE SMOKE COMING FROM AROUND HERE!
BUT WITH ALL THE DUST DOWN BELOW I CAN'T SEE VERY--
!!
BOOM!!

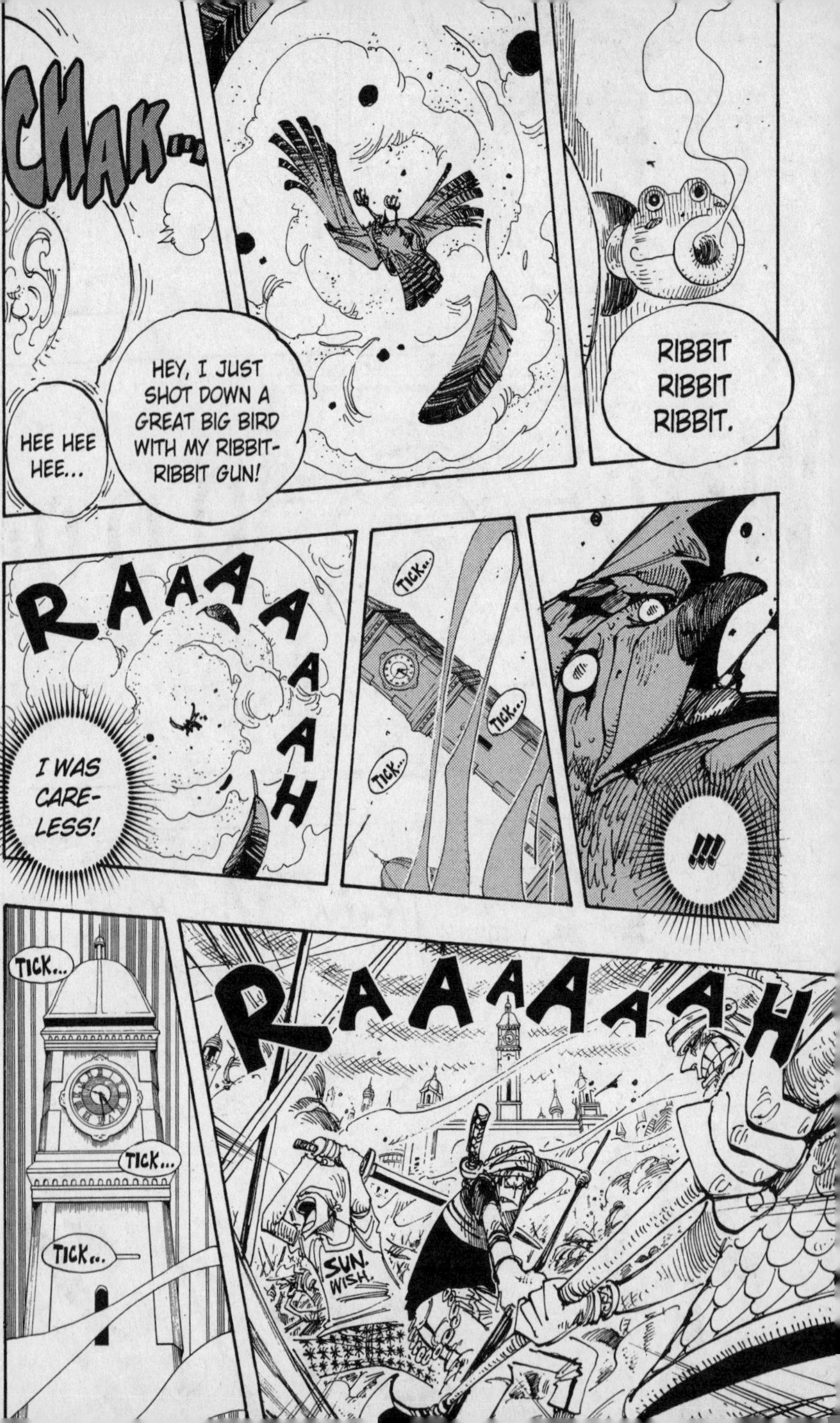
RIBBIT RIBBIT RIBBIT.
CHAK...
HEY, I JUST SHOT DOWN A GREAT BIG BIRD WITH MY RIBBIT-RIBBIT GUN!
HEE HEE HEE...
!!!
TICK...
TICK...
TICK...
RAAAAAAH
I WAS CARE-LESS!
RAAAAAAH
SUN. WISH.
TICK...
TICK...
TICK...

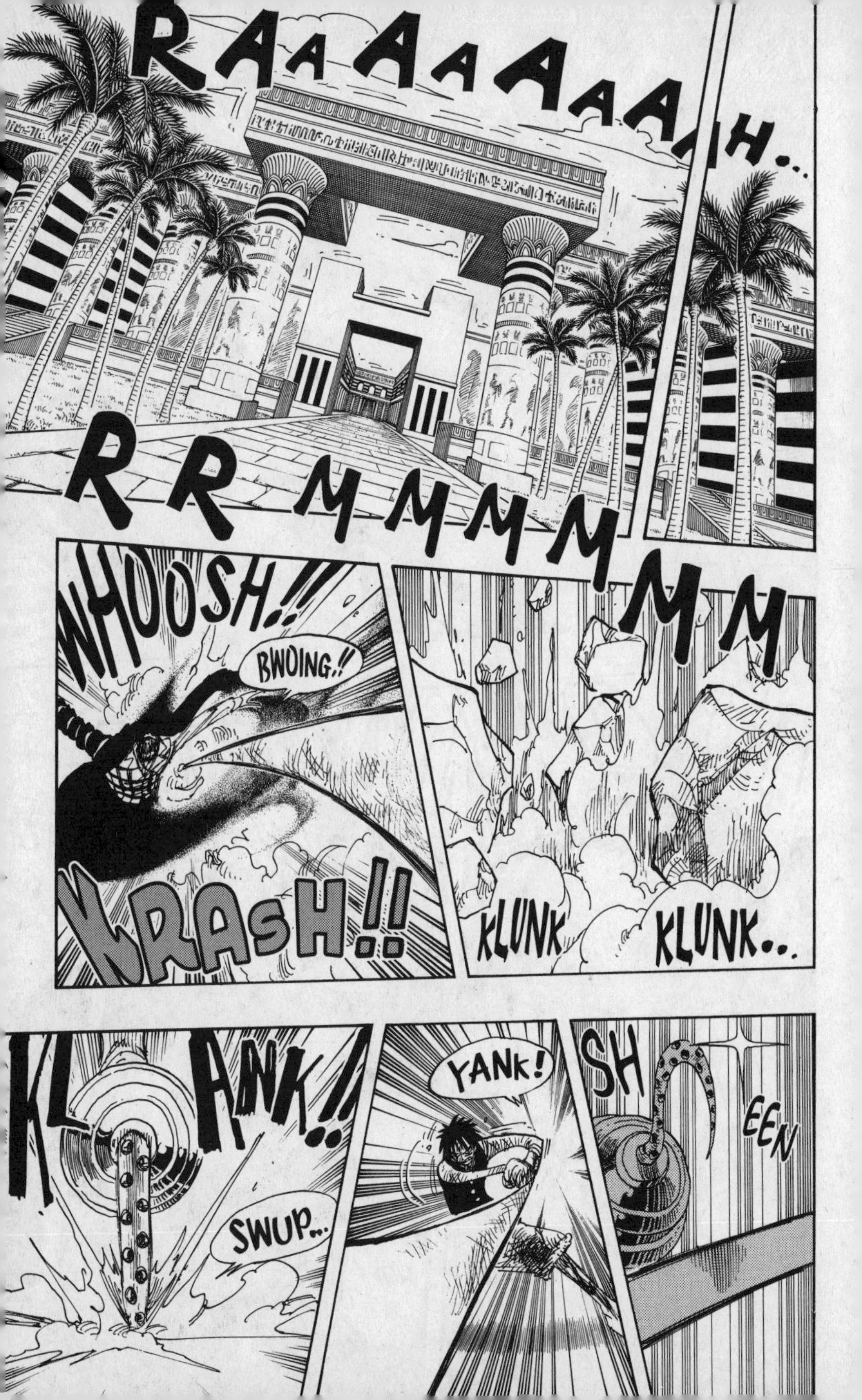
RAAAAAAAAH...
RRMMMMMMMMM
KLUNK
KLUNK...
WHOOSH!!
BWOING!!
KRASH!!
SHEEN
YANK!
KLANK!!
SWUP...

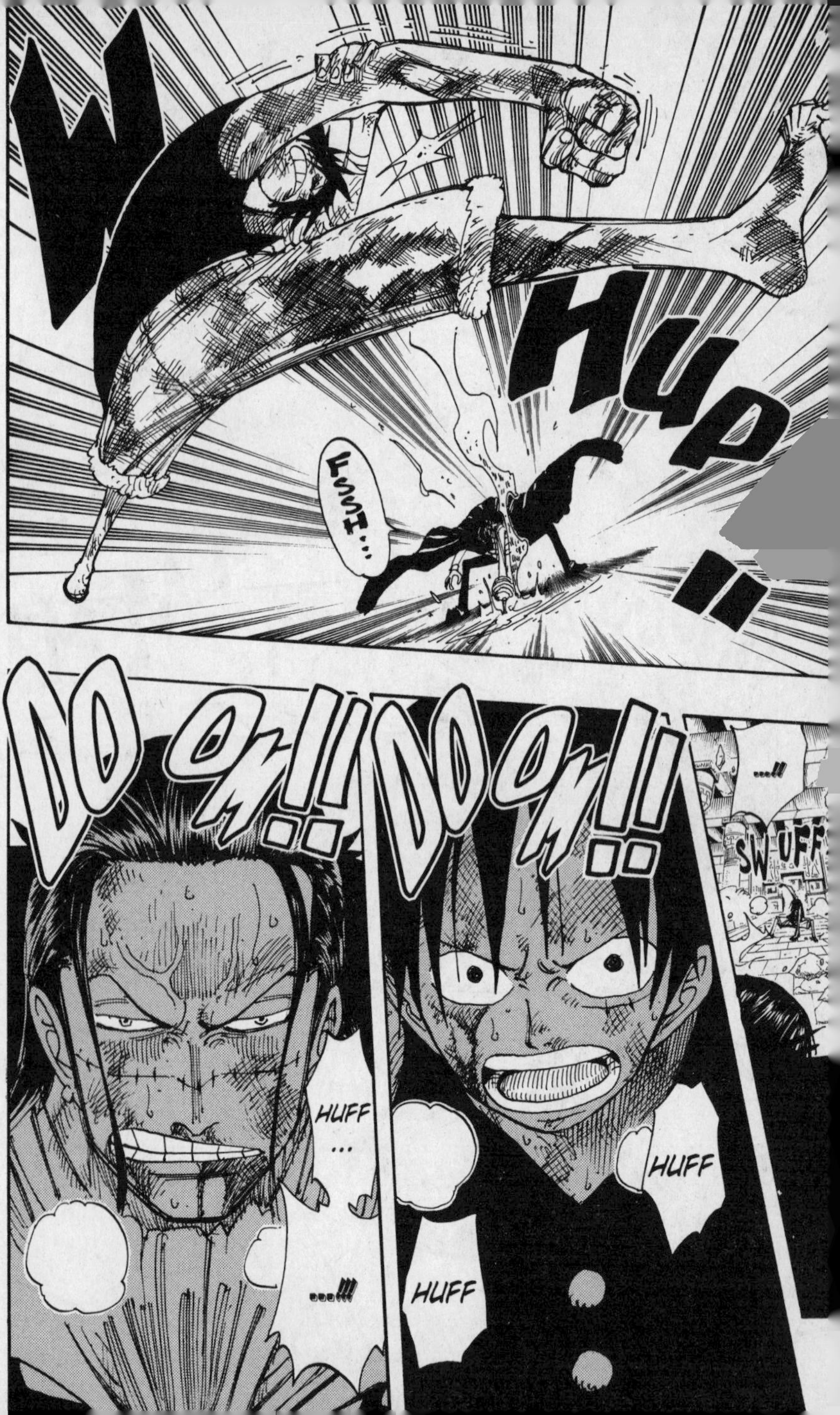
HUP!!
FSSH...
...!!
SWUFF
DOON!!
HUFF
HUFF
DOON!!
HUFF...
...!!!

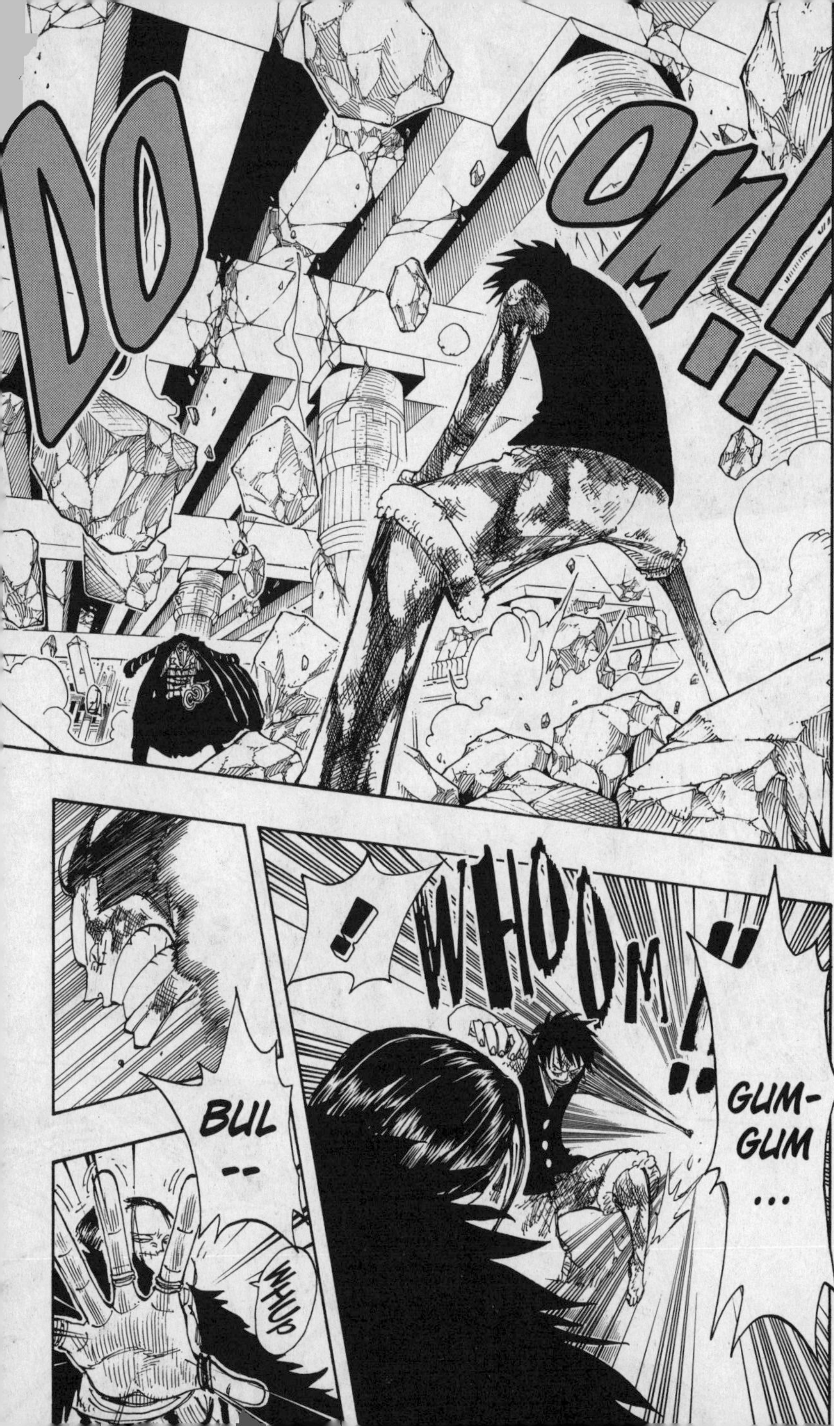
DOOON!!
!
WHOOM!!
GUM-GUM...
BUL--
WHUP

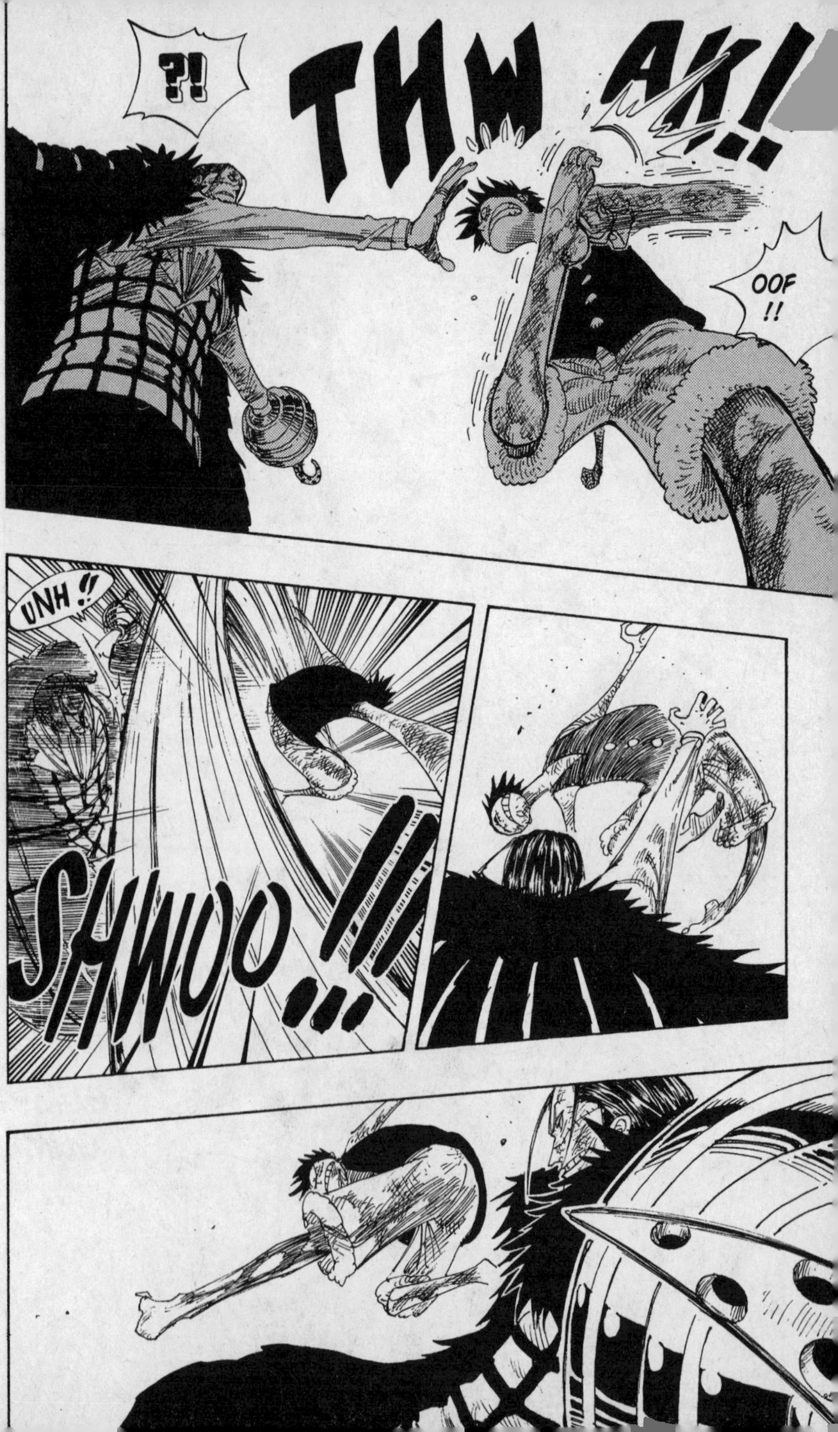

THWAK!!
OOF !!
?!
SHWOO...!!
UNH !!

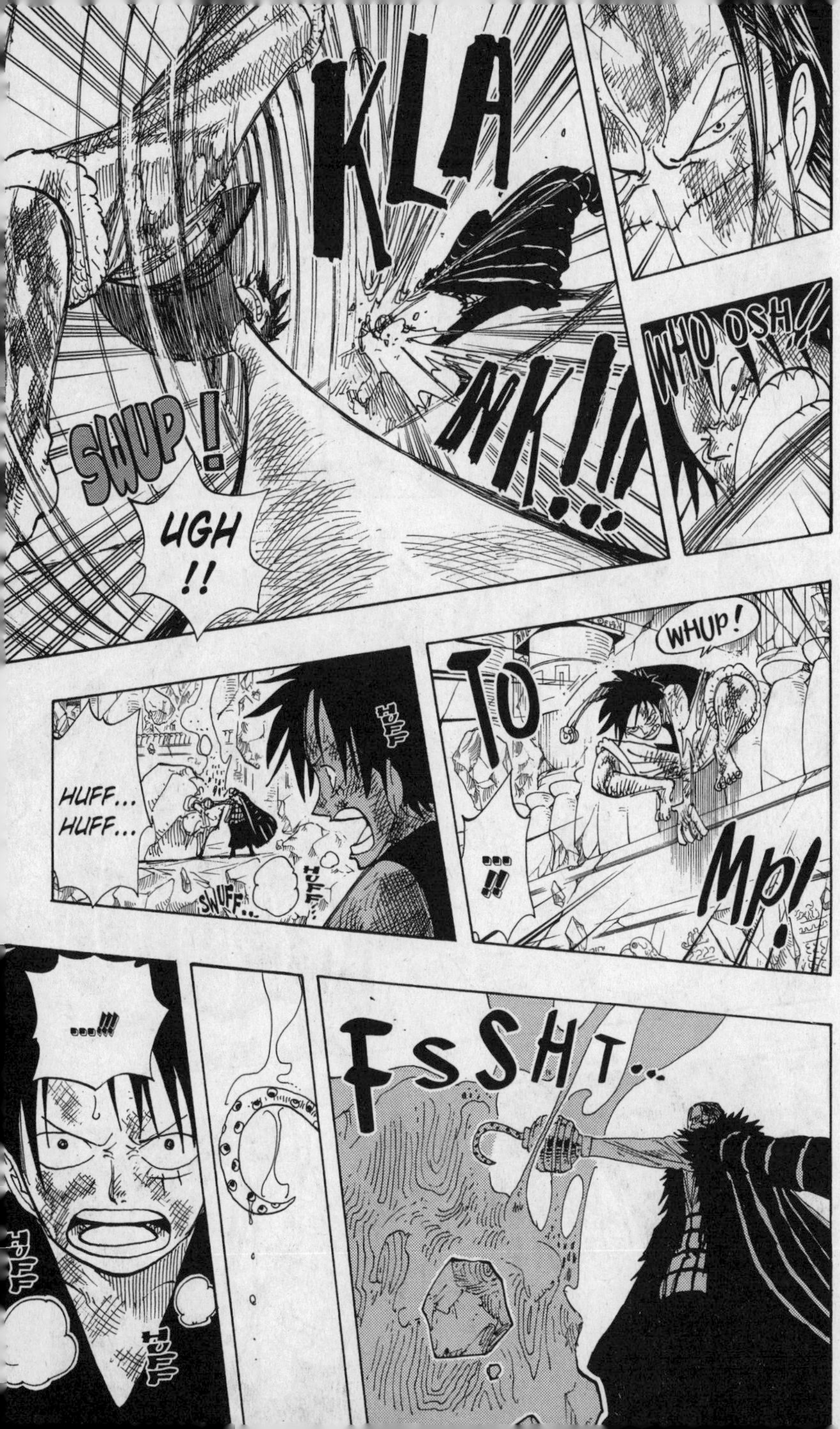
WHOOSH!!
KLANK!!!...
SWUP!
UGH !!
WHUP!
TOMP!
...!!
HUFF
HUFF... HUFF...
SNUFF...
HUFF...
FSSHT...
...!!!
HUFF
HUFF

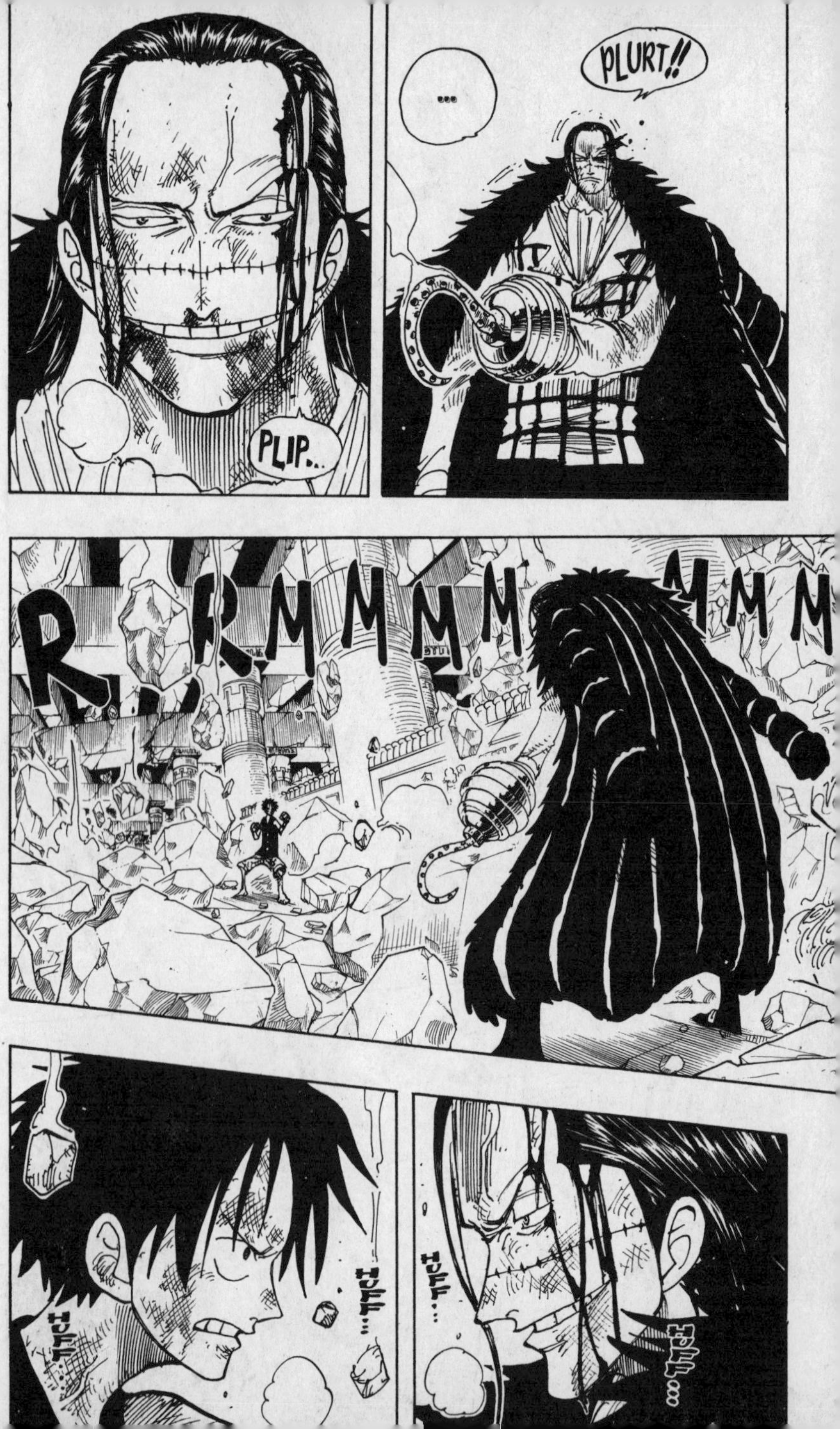
PLURT!!
...
PLIP...
RRMMMMMMM
HUFF...
HUFF...
HUFF...
HUFF...

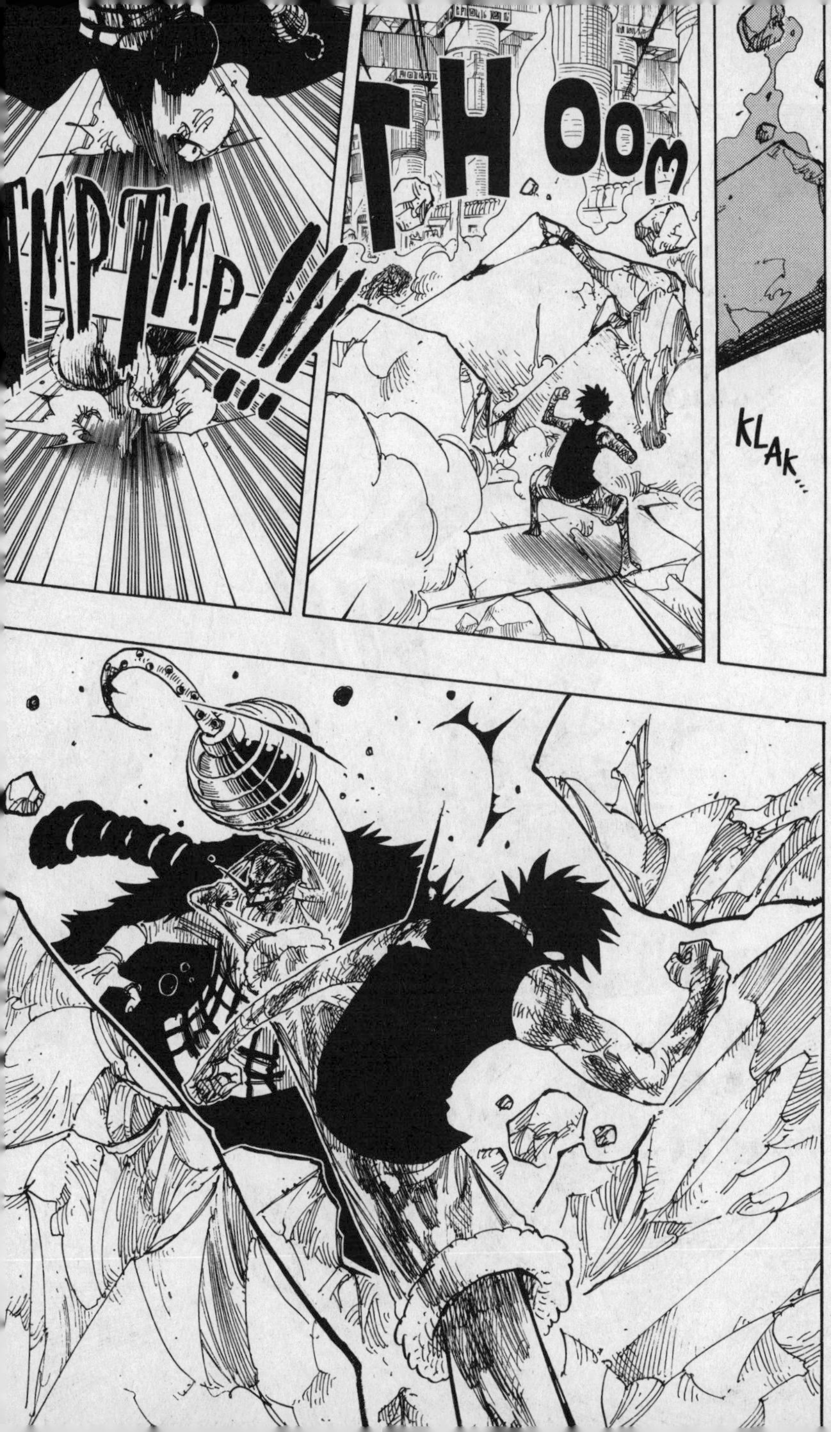
KLAK...
THOOM
TMP TMP!!!...

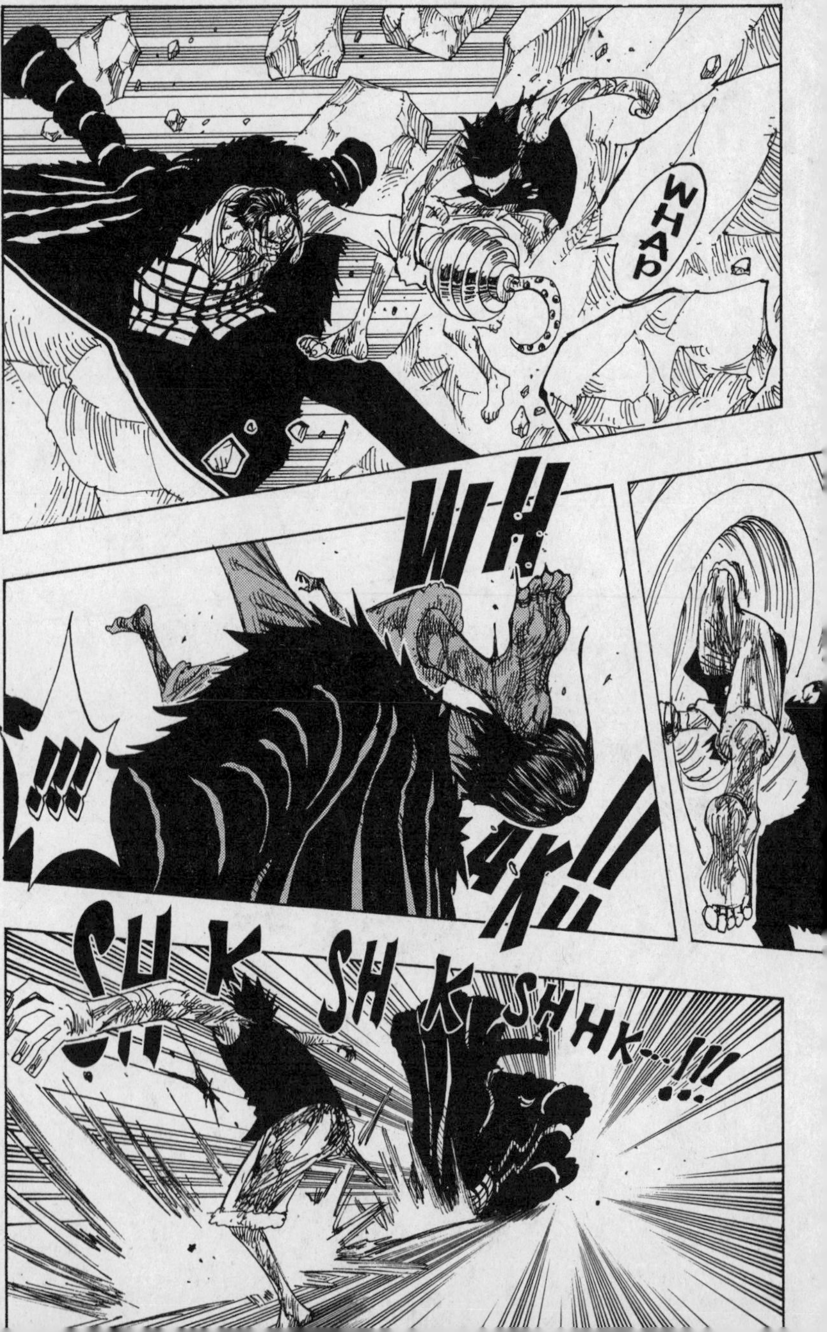

WHAP
WH
K!!
!!!
SUK
SH
K
SHHK...!!!

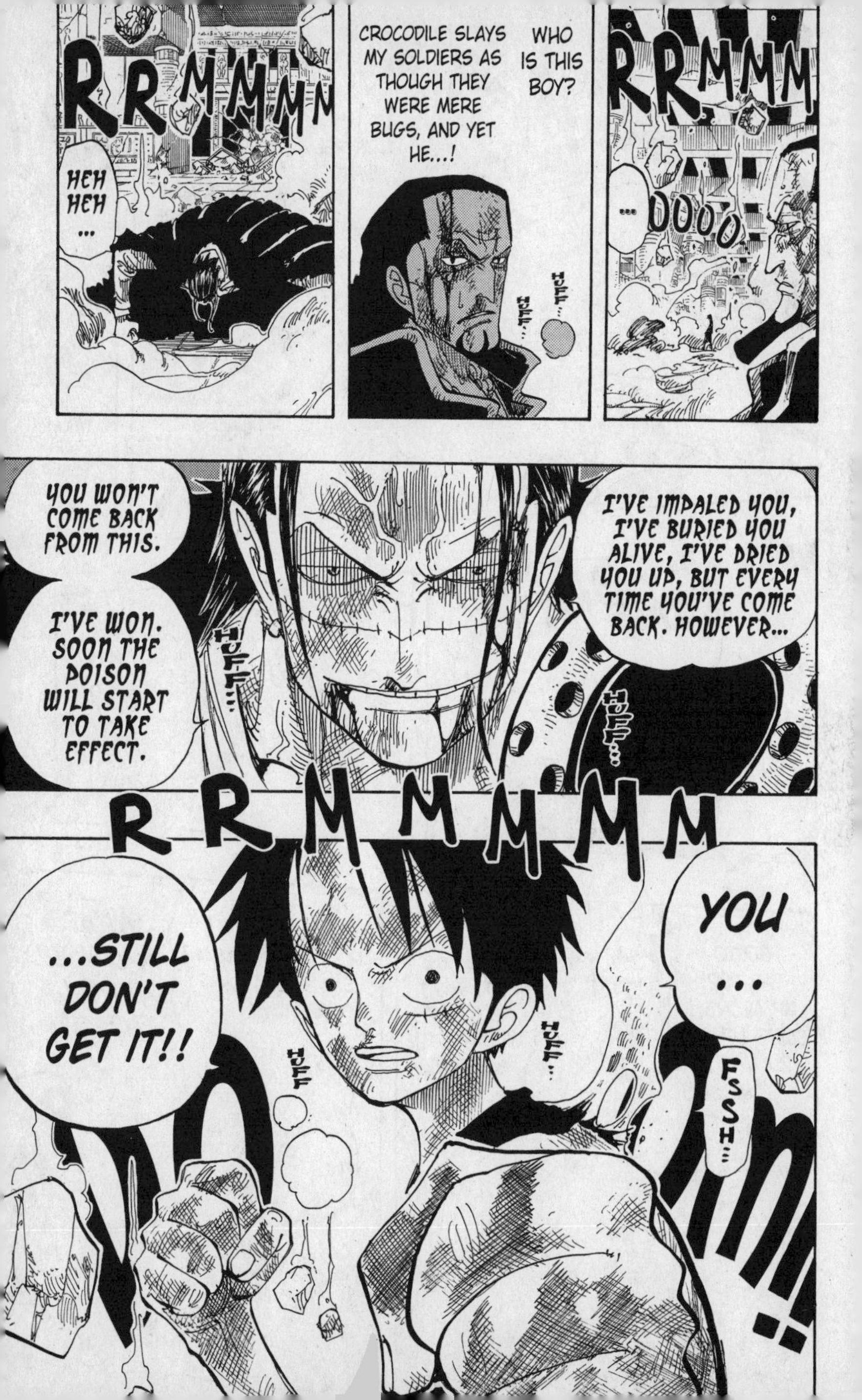
RRMMMM
...OOOO
WHO IS THIS BOY?
CROCODILE SLAYS MY SOLDIERS AS THOUGH THEY WERE MERE BUGS, AND YET HE...!
HUFF...
HUFF...
RRMMMMN
HEH HEH...
I'VE IMPALED YOU, I'VE BURIED YOU ALIVE, I'VE DRIED YOU UP, BUT EVERY TIME YOU'VE COME BACK. HOWEVER...
HUFF...
YOU WON'T COME BACK FROM THIS.
I'VE WON. SOON THE POISON WILL START TO TAKE EFFECT.
HUFF...
RRMMMMMM
YOU...
FSSH!!
HUFF...
...STILL DON'T GET IT!!
HUFF
!!

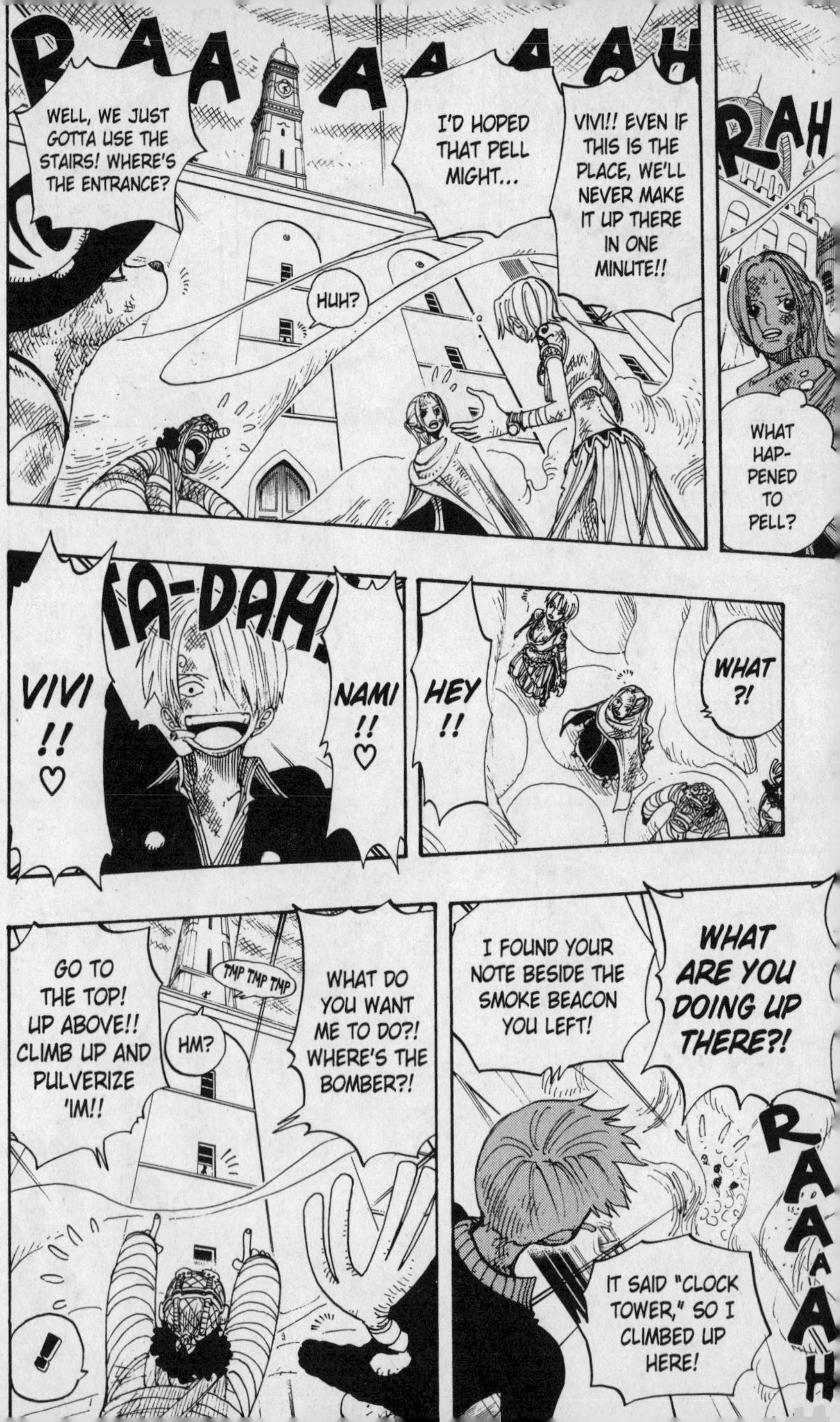
RAH
WHAT HAPPENED TO PELL?
RAAAAAAH
VIVI!! EVEN IF THIS IS THE PLACE, WE'LL NEVER MAKE IT UP THERE IN ONE MINUTE!!
I'D HOPED THAT PELL MIGHT...
HUH?
WELL, WE JUST GOTTA USE THE STAIRS! WHERE'S THE ENTRANCE?
WHAT ?!
HEY !!
NAMI !! ♡
TA-DAH!
VIVI !! ♡
WHAT ARE YOU DOING UP THERE?!
I FOUND YOUR NOTE BESIDE THE SMOKE BEACON YOU LEFT!
RAAAAH
IT SAID "CLOCK TOWER," SO I CLIMBED UP HERE!
WHAT DO YOU WANT ME TO DO?! WHERE'S THE BOMBER?!
TMP TMP TMP
HM?
GO TO THE TOP! UP ABOVE!! CLIMB UP AND PULVERIZE 'IM!!
!

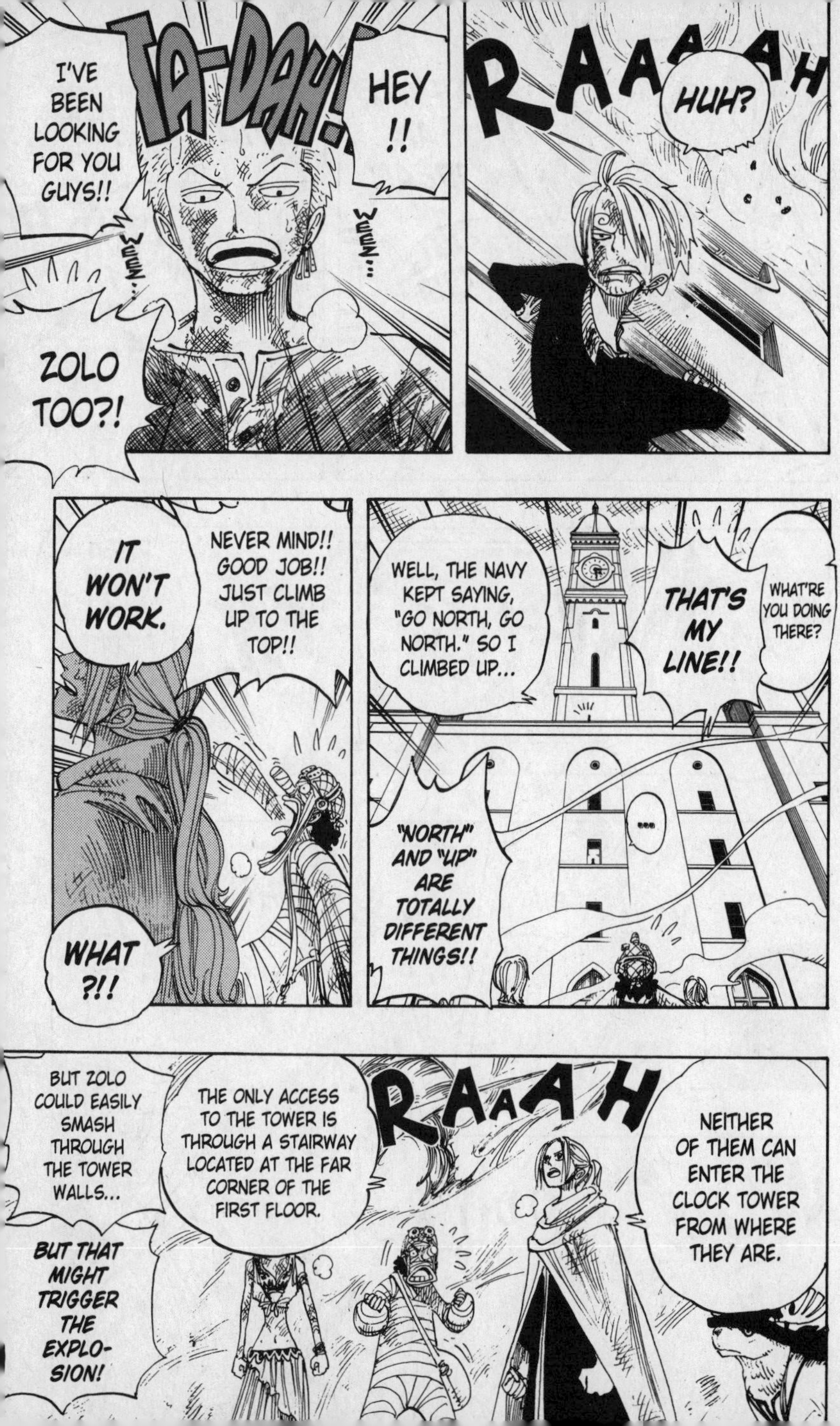
RAAAAAH
HUH?
HEY!!
WEEN...
TA-DAH!!
WEEN...
I'VE BEEN LOOKING FOR YOU GUYS!!
ZOLO TOO?!
WHAT'RE YOU DOING THERE?
THAT'S MY LINE!!
WELL, THE NAVY KEPT SAYING, "GO NORTH, GO NORTH." SO I CLIMBED UP...
...
"NORTH" AND "UP" ARE TOTALLY DIFFERENT THINGS!!
NEVER MIND!! GOOD JOB!! JUST CLIMB UP TO THE TOP!!
IT WON'T WORK.
WHAT?!!
NEITHER OF THEM CAN ENTER THE CLOCK TOWER FROM WHERE THEY ARE.
RAAAH
THE ONLY ACCESS TO THE TOWER IS THROUGH A STAIRWAY LOCATED AT THE FAR CORNER OF THE FIRST FLOOR.
BUT ZOLO COULD EASILY SMASH THROUGH THE TOWER WALLS...
BUT THAT MIGHT TRIGGER THE EXPLOSION!

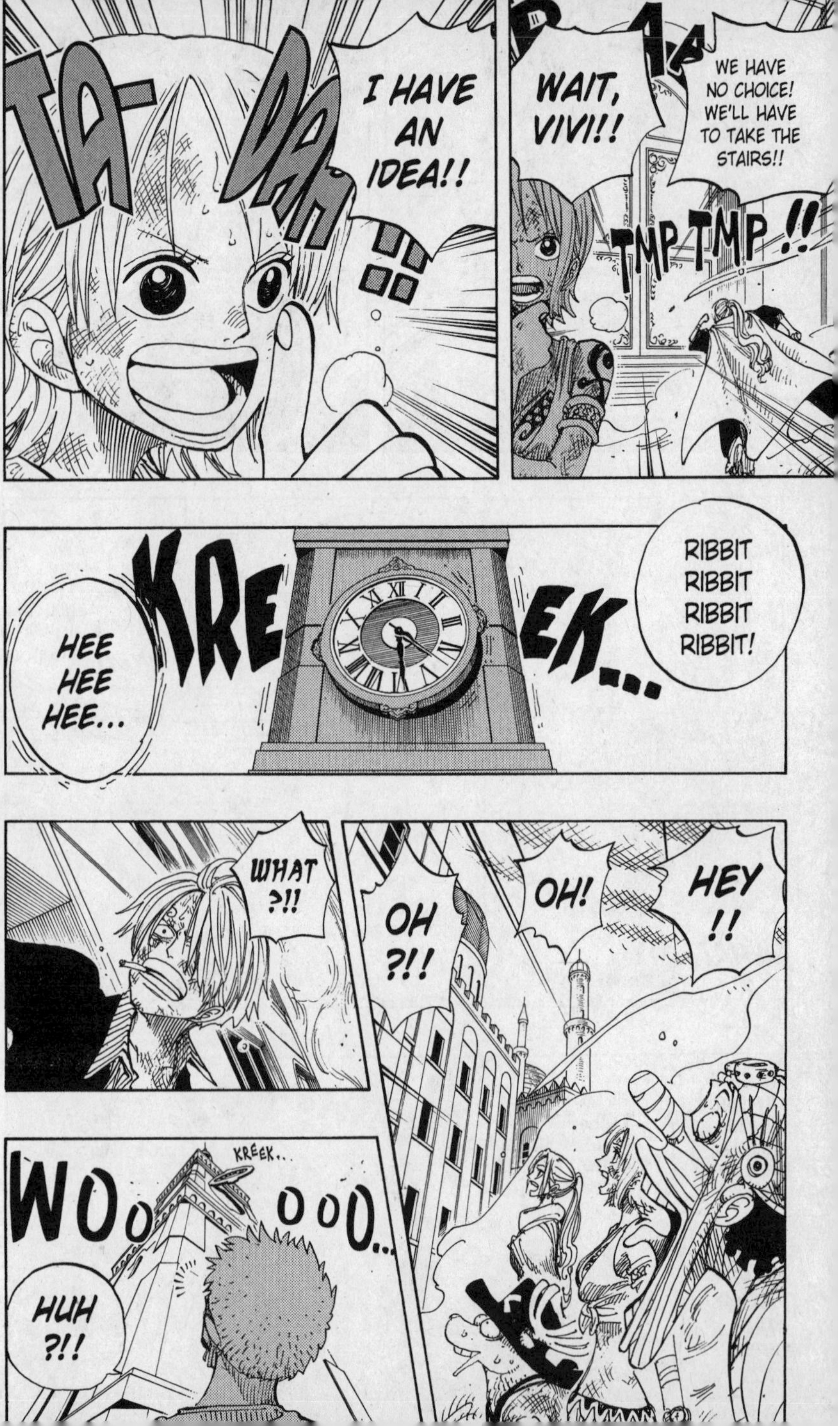
WAIT, VIVI!!
WE HAVE NO CHOICE! WE'LL HAVE TO TAKE THE STAIRS!!
TMP TMP!!
TA-DA!!
I HAVE AN IDEA!!
RIBBIT RIBBIT RIBBIT RIBBIT!
KREEK...
HEE HEE HEE...
HEY!!
OH!
OH?!!
WHAT?!!
KREEK...
WOOOOO...
HUH?!!

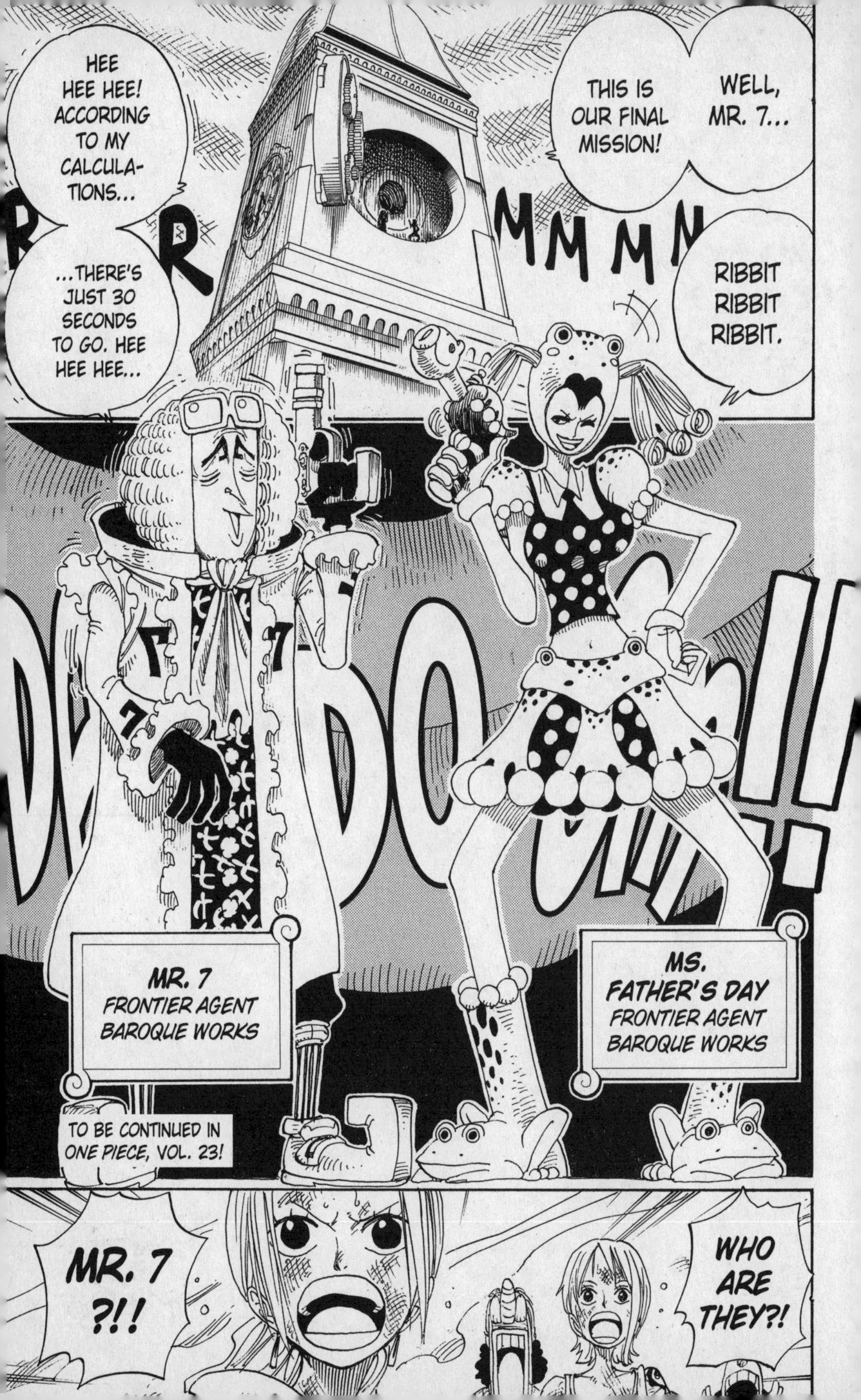
WELL, MR. 7...
THIS IS OUR FINAL MISSION!
RIBBIT RIBBIT RIBBIT.
HEE HEE HEE! ACCORDING TO MY CALCULATIONS...
...THERE'S JUST 30 SECONDS TO GO. HEE HEE HEE...
MS. FATHER'S DAY FRONTIER AGENT BAROQUE WORKS
MR. 7 FRONTIER AGENT BAROQUE WORKS
TO BE CONTINUED IN ONE PIECE, VOL. 23!
WHO ARE THEY?!
MR. 7 ?!!

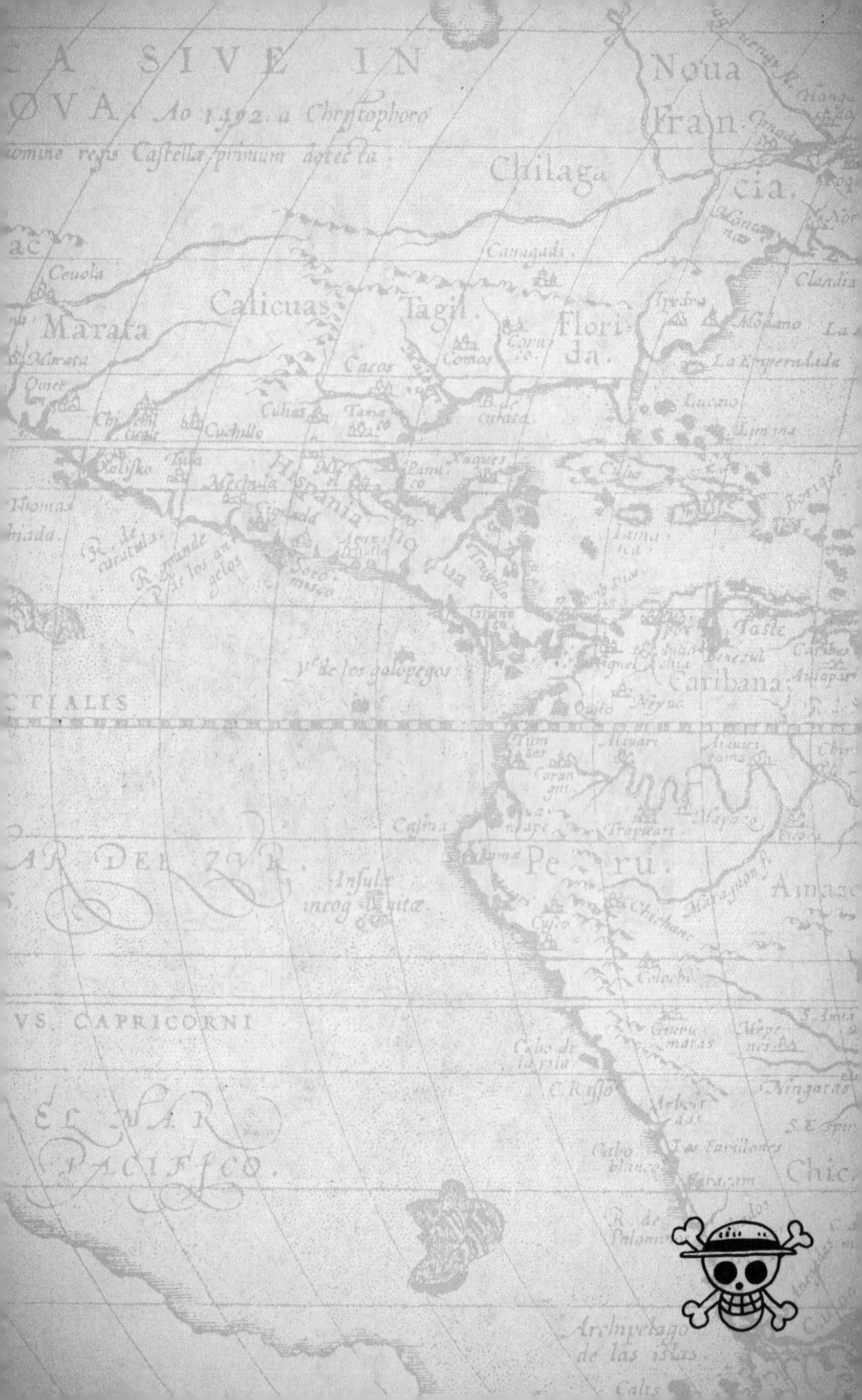

A SIVE IN
OVA. Ao 1492. a Chrystophoro
Noua
Fran
cia.
Chilaga
Calicuas
Tagil
Flori
da.
Marata
Hispania
Caribana
CTIALIS
Pe ru.
AR DEL ZVR.
Insulæ
incog nitæ
VS. CAPRICORNI
EL MAR
PACIFICO.
Archipelago
de las islas

NISHIMURA

Nowadays, every book I read says that the mermaids that sailors of yore saw might actually have been dugongs*. But there's something I'd like to say to those scholars. Imagine a sailor back in the old days. (Let's call him Mr. Nishimura.) He says, "I saw a mermaid," and that's how the mermaid legend gets started. Then you come along and say, "Maybe what you saw was a dugong." Great. And now the whole world believes you. Can you imagine how disappointed Mr. Nishimura is? He's probably crying himself to sleep in the other world right now. **"I saw a mermaid! Really!"** But cheer up, Mr. Nishimura. **Dugongs are pretty cute too.**

– *Eiichiro Oda, 2002*

*Check out all their kung fu action in vol. 18! — Editor

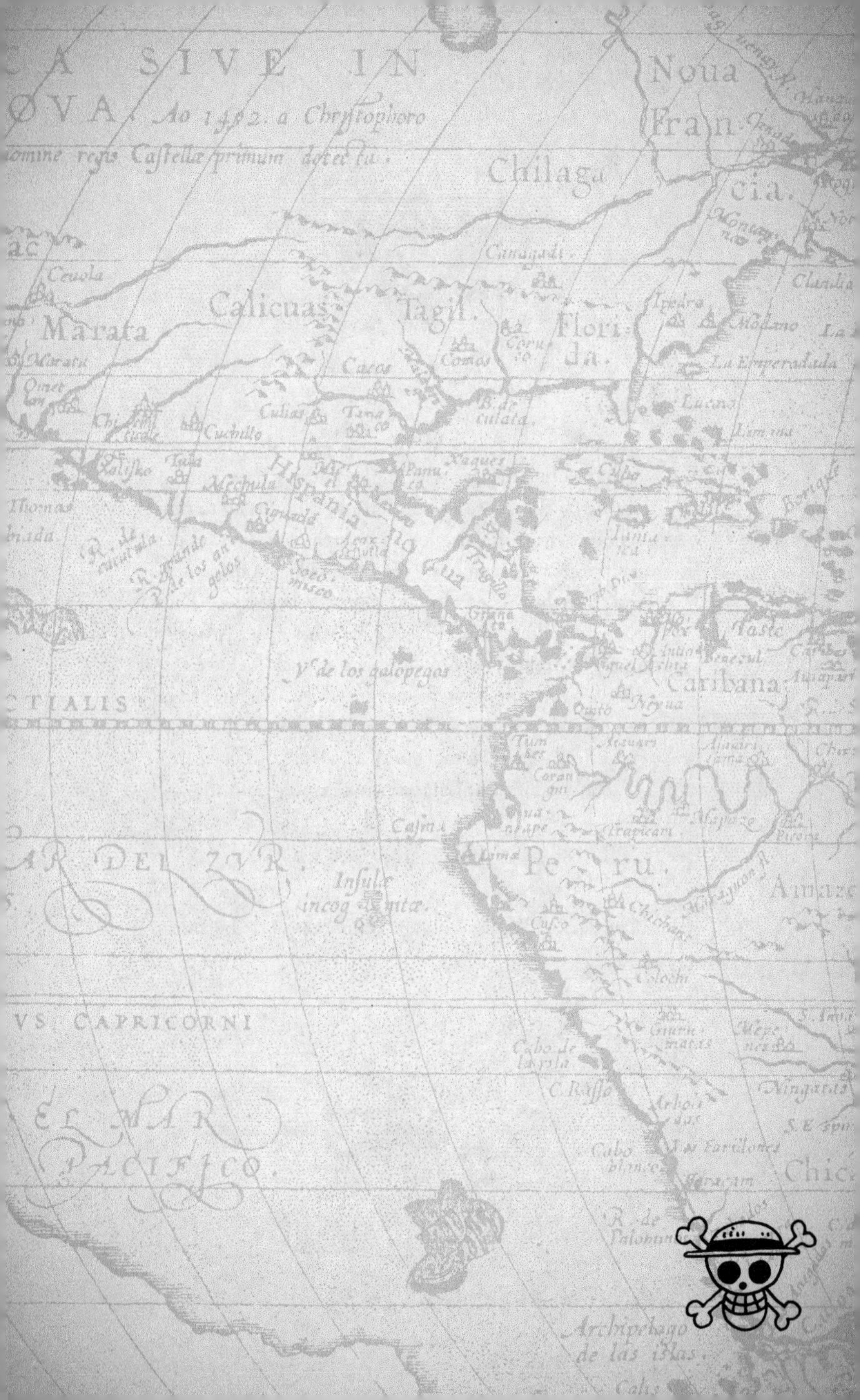
A SIVE IN
OVA. Ao 1492. a Christophoro
Noua
Fran
cia.
Chilaga
Cevola
Marata
Calicuas
Tagil.
Flori
da.
La Emperadada
Cuchillo
Xalisco
Hispania
Noua
Cuba
Iamaica
Ys de los galopegos
CTIALIS
Caribana
Quito
Tumbes
Pe ru.
AR DEL ZVR.
Insulæ
incognitæ.
Cusco
VS. CAPRICORNI
Cabo blanco
EL MAR
PACIFICO.
Archipelago
de las islas

SHONEN JUMP MANGA

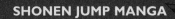

ONE PIECE

Vol. 23
VIVI'S ADVENTURE

STORY AND ART BY
EIICHIRO ODA

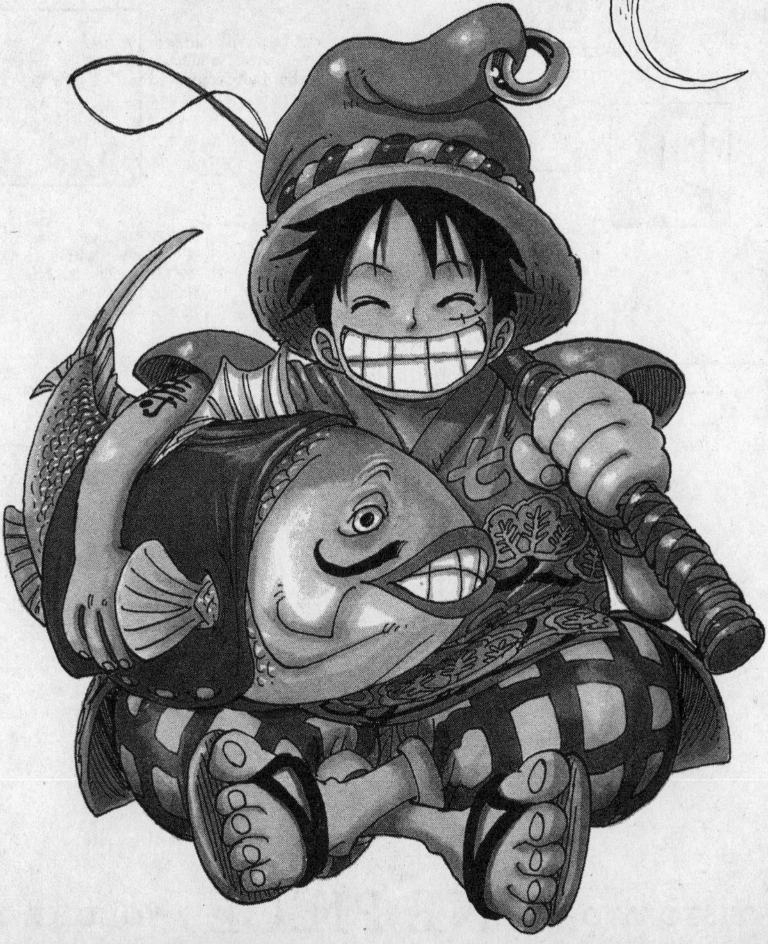

Vivi

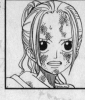

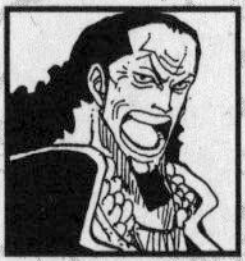

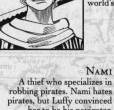

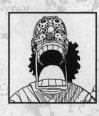

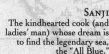

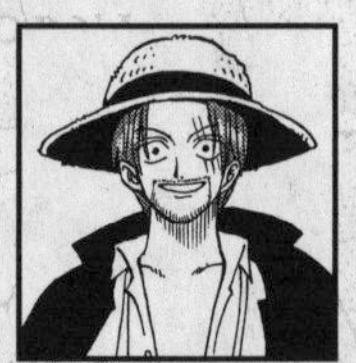

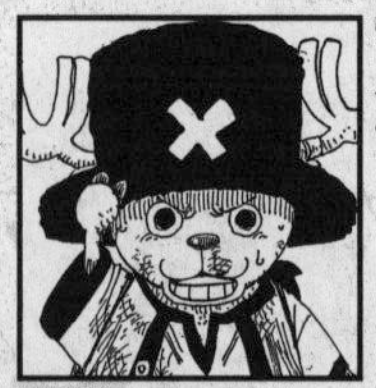

Monkey D. Luffy
Boundlessly optimistic and able to stretch like rubber, he is determined to become King of the Pirates.

Karoo

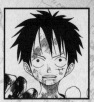

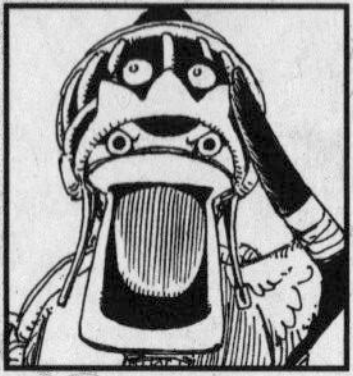

Roronoa Zolo
A former bounty hunter and master of the "three-sword" style. He aspires to be the world's greatest swordsman.

— Royal Forces —

Nefeltari Cobra
(King of Alabasta)

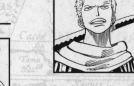

Nami
A thief who specializes in robbing pirates. Nami hates pirates, but Luffy convinced her to be his navigator.

Chaka

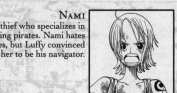

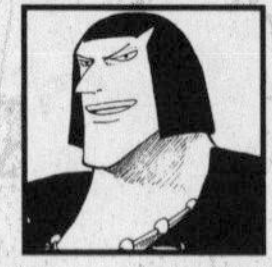

Usopp
A village boy with a talent for telling tall tales. His father, Yasopp, is a member of Shanks's crew.

Pell

— Rebel Forces —

Koza

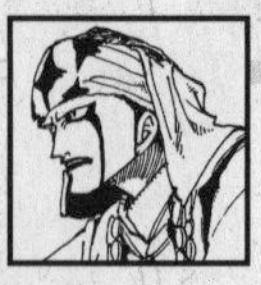

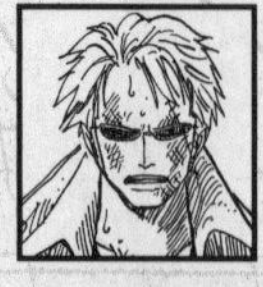

Sanji
The kindhearted cook (and ladies' man) whose dream is to find the legendary sea, the "All Blue."

"Red-Haired" Shanks
A pirate that Luffy idolizes. Shanks gave Luffy his trademark straw hat.

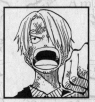

Tony Tony Chopper
A blue-nosed man-reindeer and the ship's doctor.

THE STORY OF ONE PIECE · VOLUME 23 ·

Baroque Works

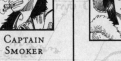

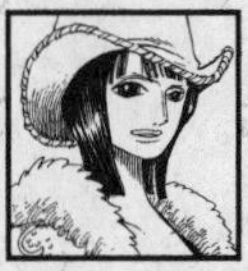
Ms. All Sunday (Nico Robin)

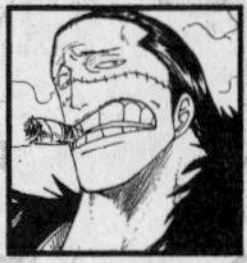
Mr. Zero (Sir Crocodile)

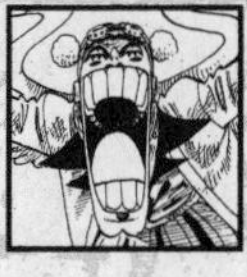
Mr. 2 Bon Clay

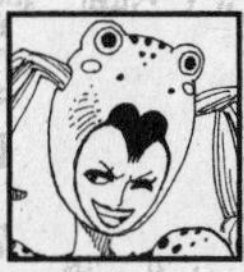
Ms. Father's Day

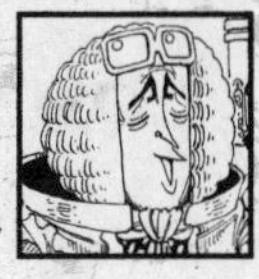
Mr. 7

Navy

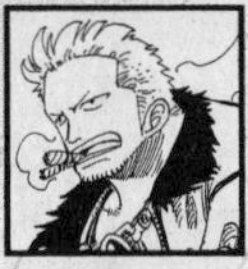
Captain Smoker

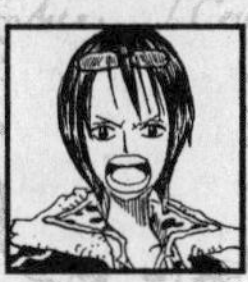
Tashigi

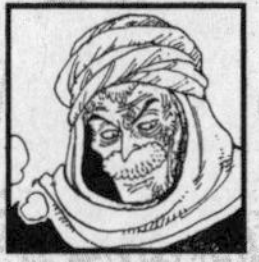
Toh-Toh

Monkey D. Luffy started out as just a kid with a dream—to become the greatest pirate in history! Stirred by the tales of pirate "Red-Haired" Shanks, Luffy vowed to become a pirate himself. That was before the enchanted Devil Fruit gave Luffy the power to stretch like rubber, at the cost of being unable to swim—a serious handicap for an aspiring sea dog. Undeterred, Luffy set out to sea and recruited some crewmates—master swordsman Zolo, treasure-hunting thief Nami, lying sharpshooter Usopp, the high-kicking chef Sanji, and the latest addition, Chopper—the walkin' talkin' reindeer doctor.

Luffy and crew fight to help Princess Vivi save her war-torn and drought-ravaged kingdom from the evil Sir Crocodile and his secret criminal organization, the Baroque Works. Having finally reached the royal palace in Alubarna, Vivi devises a plan to end the civil war, only to be thwarted by the sudden arrival of Crocodile, who reveals his true objective—to get his hands on the most destructive weapon of the ancient world, the Pluton! Now, with just a minute to go before Crocodile's henchmen blast the city of Alubarna into a three-mile wide crater, Luffy battles it out with the evil mastermind down in the Royal Mausoleum. Meanwhile, the Straw Hats, after having defeated Baroque Works' deadly Officer Agents in fierce combat, join Vivi in scouring the city to find the city-destroying bomb. Vivi has her suspicions about where it might be, but with the seconds ticking away, can they possibly reach it in time?

BAROQUE WORKS

Vol. 23
Vivi's Adventure

CONTENTS

Chapter 206:
IGNITION

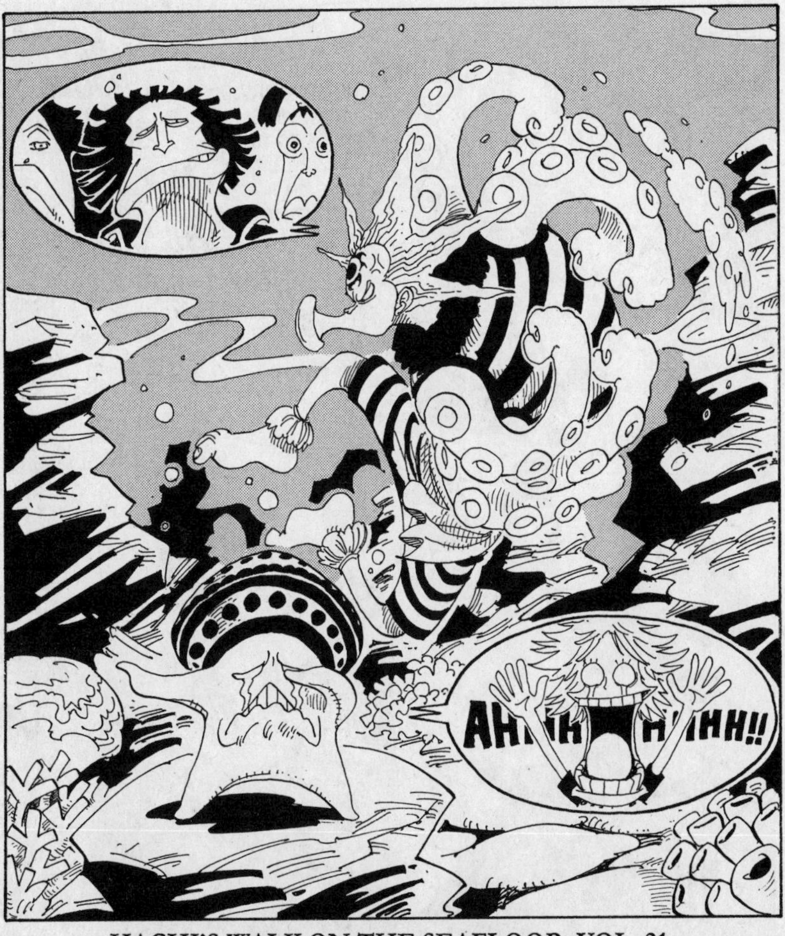
AHHHH HHHHH!!

HACHI'S WALK ON THE SEAFLOOR, VOL. 21:
"THEY WENT THATTAWAY"

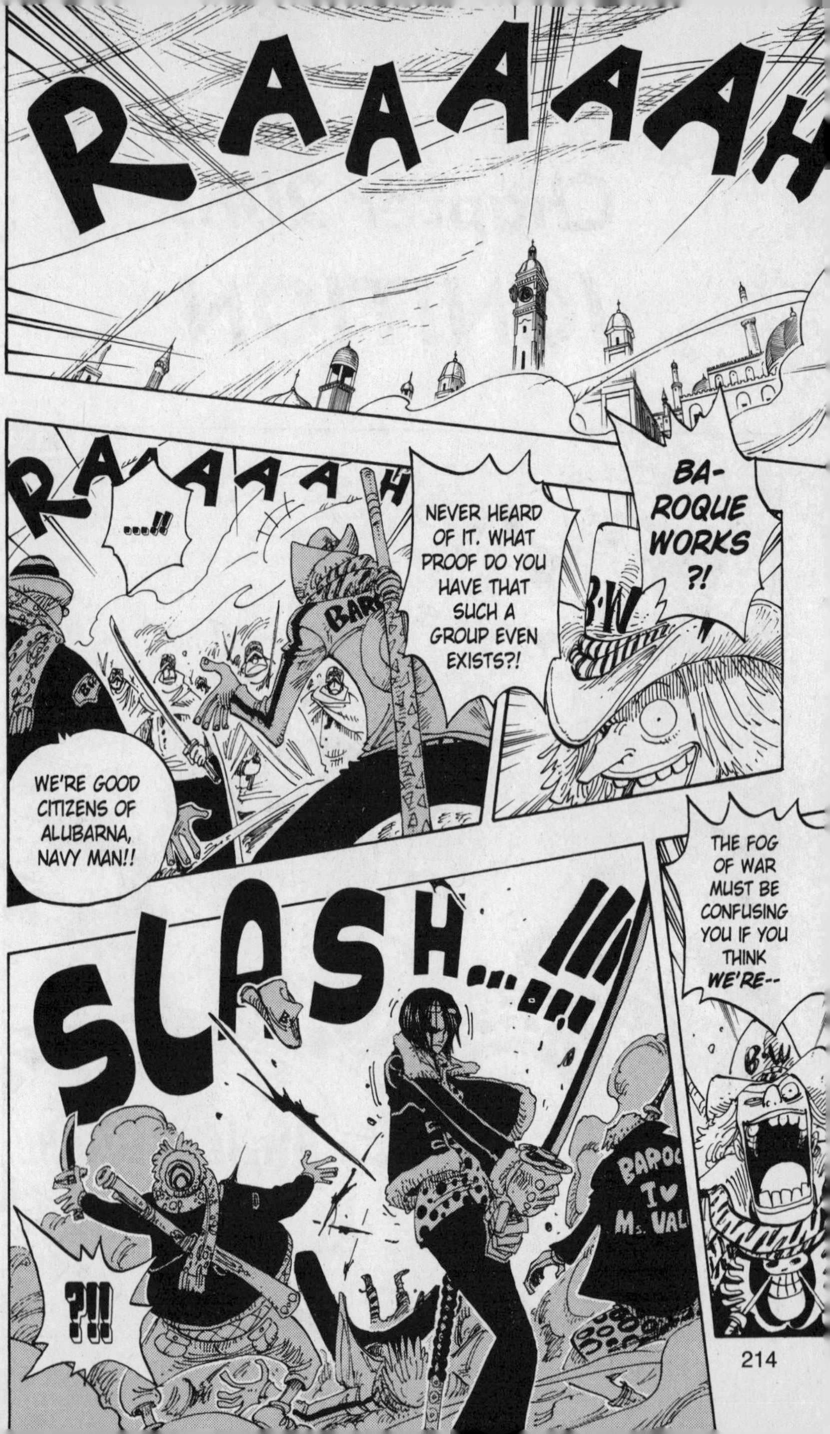
RAAAAAH
BA-ROQUE WORKS?!
NEVER HEARD OF IT. WHAT PROOF DO YOU HAVE THAT SUCH A GROUP EVEN EXISTS?!
RAAAAAH
...!!
WE'RE GOOD CITIZENS OF ALUBARNA, NAVY MAN!!
THE FOG OF WAR MUST BE CONFUSING YOU IF YOU THINK WE'RE--
SLASH...!!
?!!

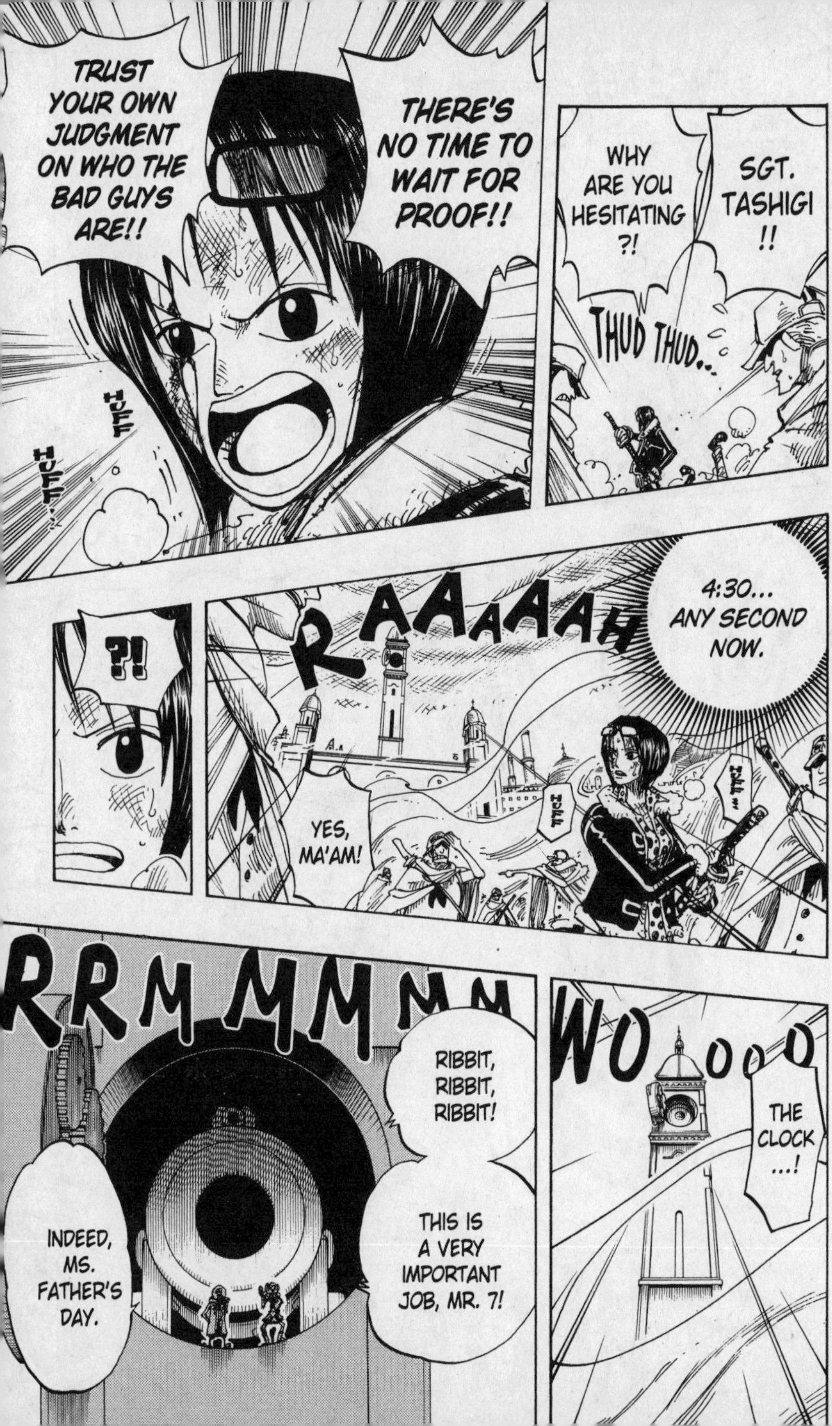
SGT. TASHIGI!!
WHY ARE YOU HESITATING?!
THUD THUD...
THERE'S NO TIME TO WAIT FOR PROOF!!
TRUST YOUR OWN JUDGMENT ON WHO THE BAD GUYS ARE!!
HUFF
HUFF...
4:30... ANY SECOND NOW.
RAAAAAH
HUFF...
HUFF
YES, MA'AM!
?!
RRMMMMMNWOooo
THE CLOCK...!
RIBBIT, RIBBIT, RIBBIT!
THIS IS A VERY IMPORTANT JOB, MR. 7!
INDEED, MS. FATHER'S DAY.

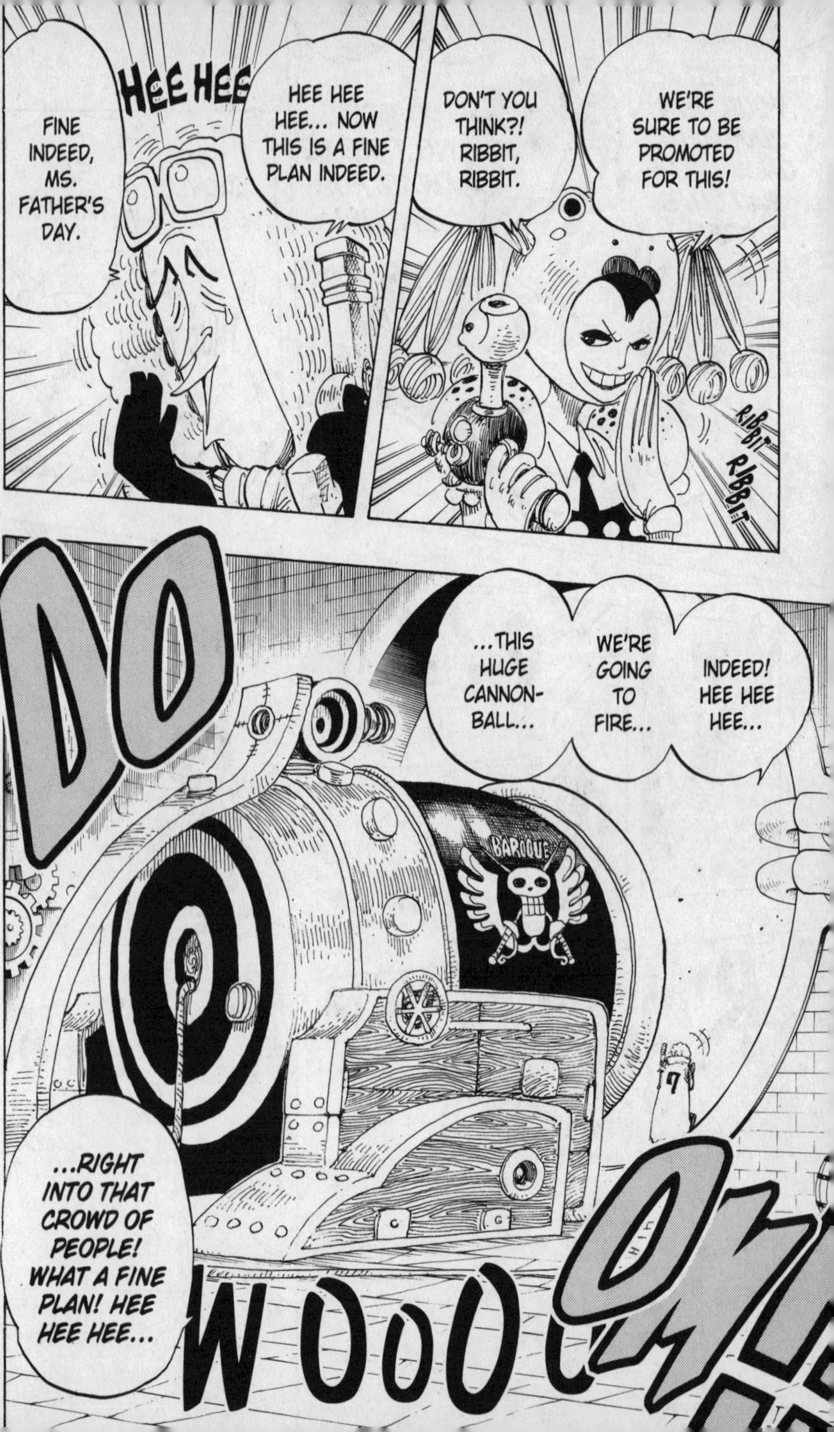
WE'RE SURE TO BE PROMOTED FOR THIS!
DON'T YOU THINK?! RIBBIT, RIBBIT.
RIBBIT RIBBIT
HEE HEE HEE... NOW THIS IS A FINE PLAN INDEED.
HEE HEE
FINE INDEED, MS. FATHER'S DAY.
DO
...THIS HUGE CANNON-BALL... WE'RE GOING TO FIRE... INDEED! HEE HEE HEE...
BAROQUE
...RIGHT INTO THAT CROWD OF PEOPLE! WHAT A FINE PLAN! HEE HEE HEE...
WOOO

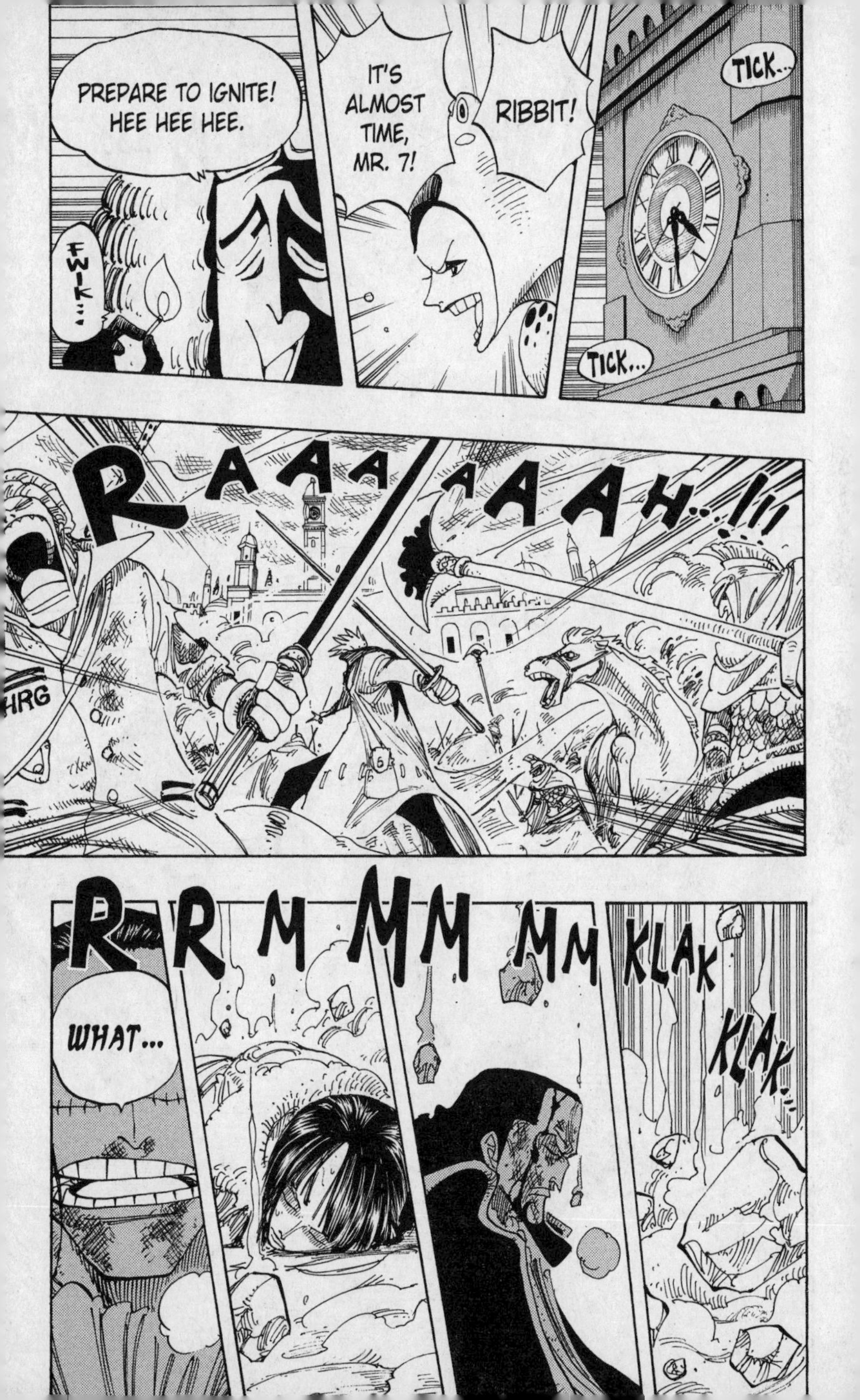
TICK...
TICK...
RIBBIT!
IT'S ALMOST TIME, MR. 7!
PREPARE TO IGNITE! HEE HEE HEE.
FWIK...
RAAAAAAAH...!!!
HRG
KLAK
KLAK
RRMMMMMM
WHAT...

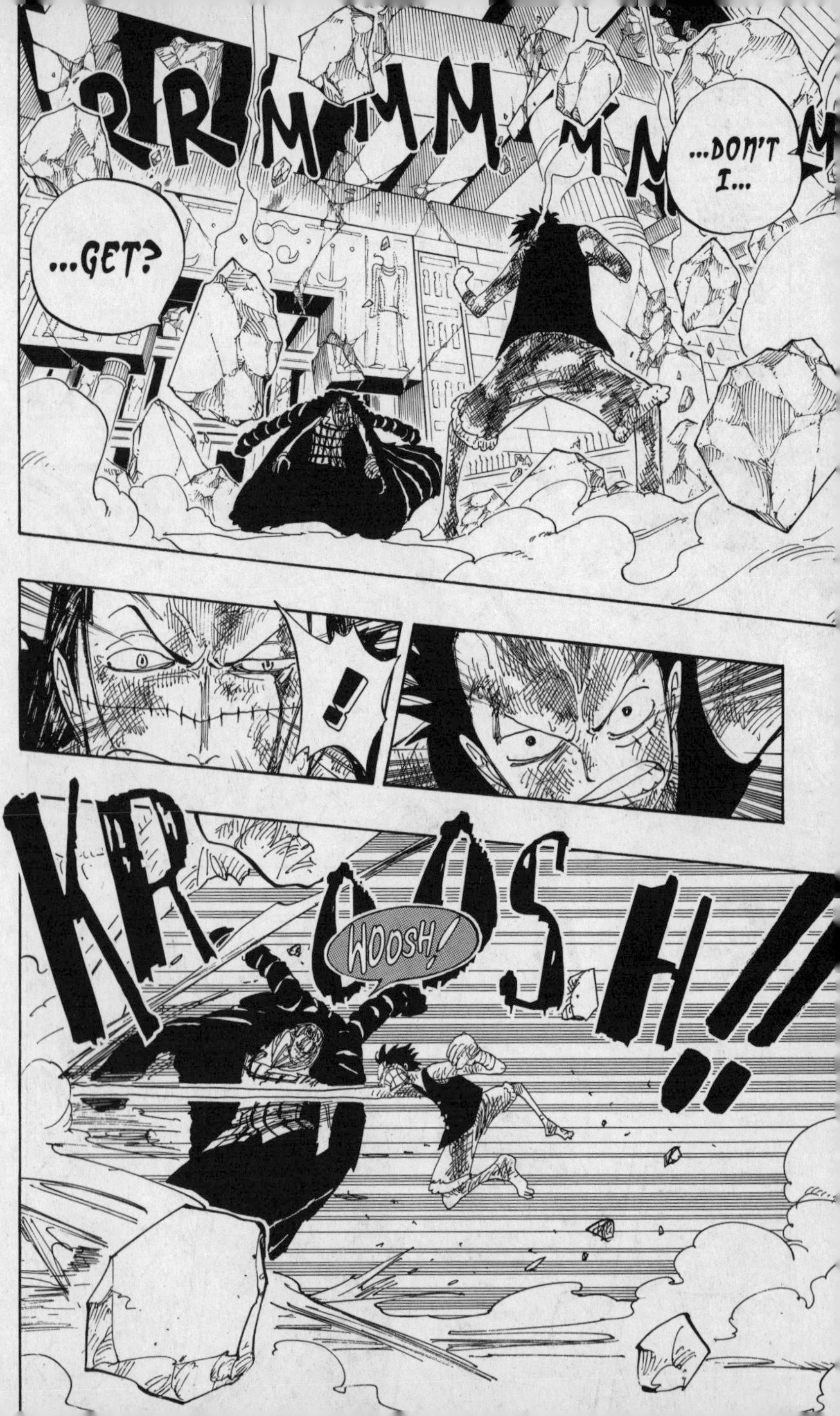
RRMMMMMMM
...DON'T I...
...GET?
!
KRASH!!
WOOSH!

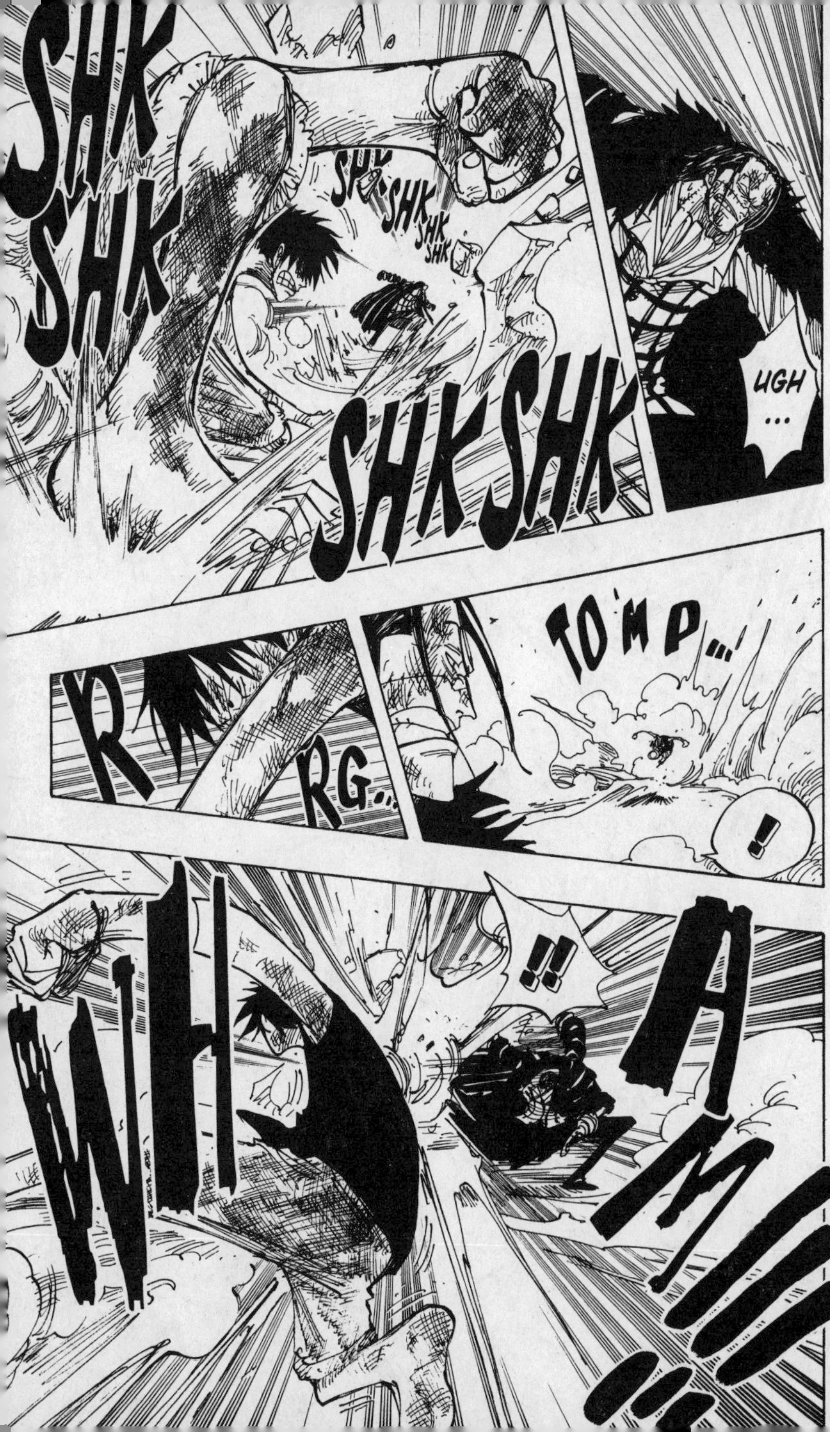
UGH ...
SHK-SHK SHK SHK
SHK SHK
SHK SHK
TOMP...
!
RRG...
!!
WHAM!!

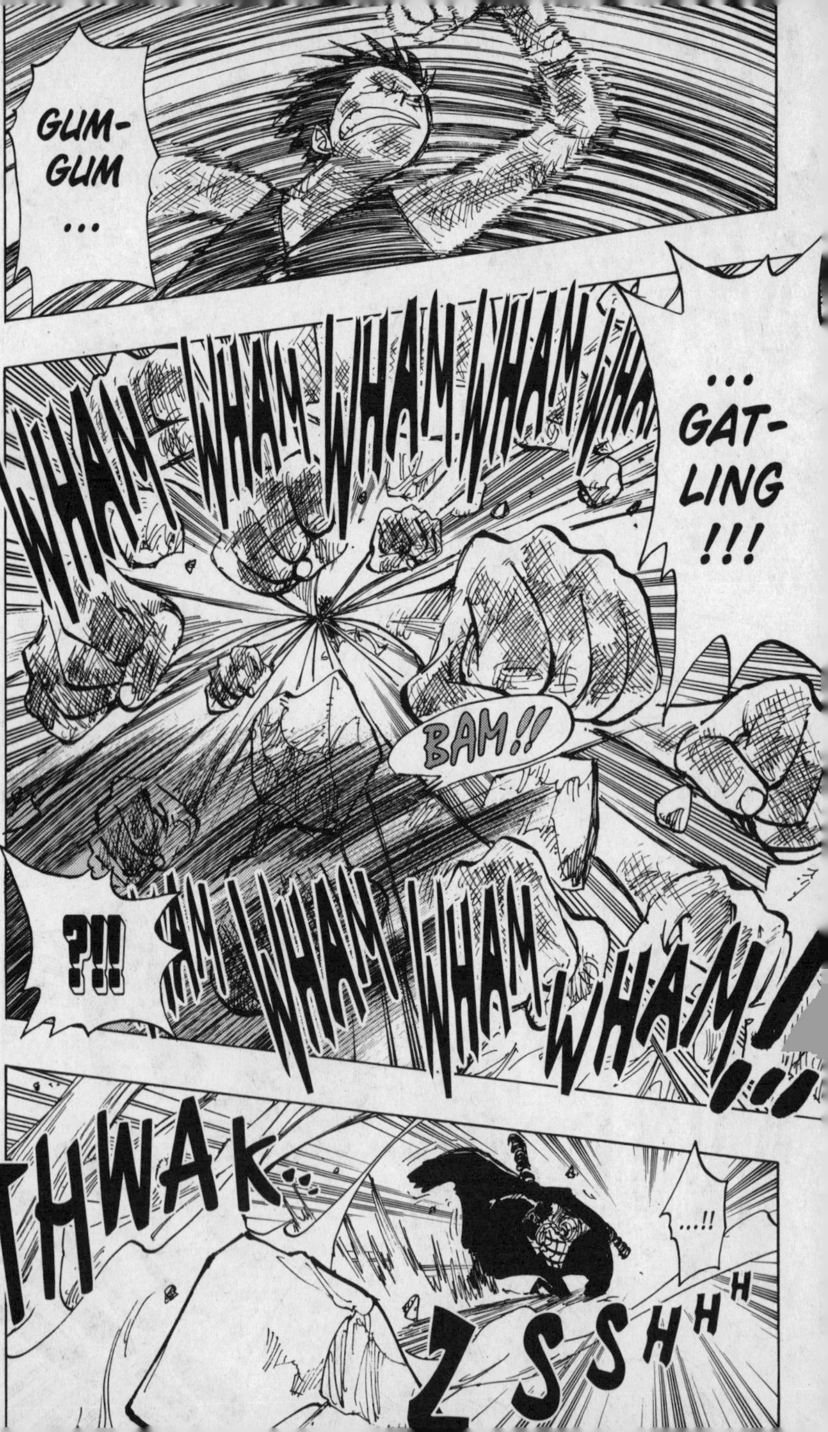
GUM-GUM...
...GATLING!!!
WHAM WHAM WHAM WHAM WHAM
BAM!!
?!!
WHAM WHAM WHAM WHAM!!
...!!
ZSSHHH
THWAK

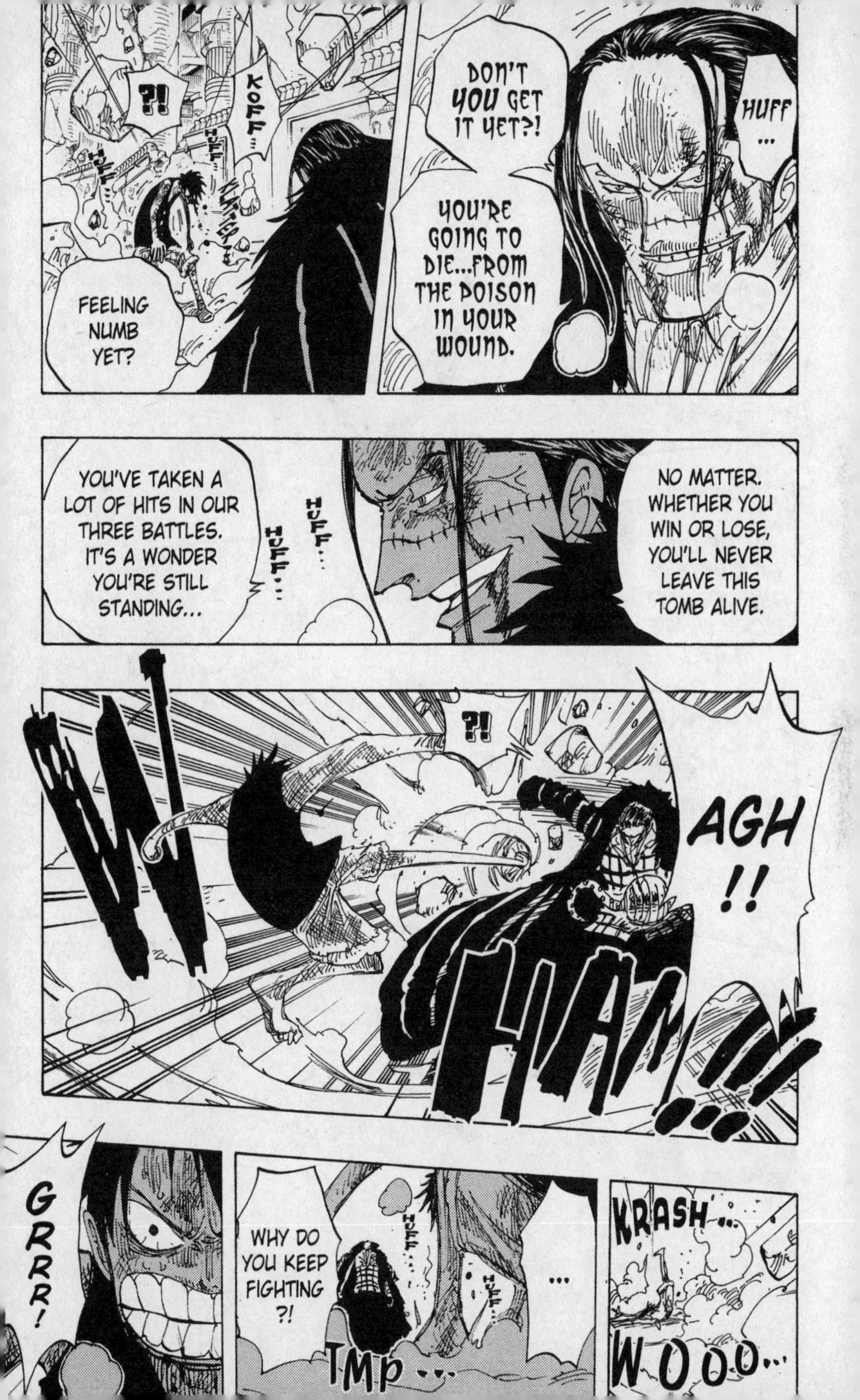

DON'T YOU GET IT YET?!
HUFF...
YOU'RE GOING TO DIE...FROM THE POISON IN YOUR WOUND.
?!
KOFF...
HUFF...
HUFF...
KLATTER
FEELING NUMB YET?
NO MATTER. WHETHER YOU WIN OR LOSE, YOU'LL NEVER LEAVE THIS TOMB ALIVE.
HUFF...
HUFF...
YOU'VE TAKEN A LOT OF HITS IN OUR THREE BATTLES. IT'S A WONDER YOU'RE STILL STANDING...
?!
AGH!!
WHAM!!!
KRASH...
WOOO...
...
HUFF...
HUFF...
WHY DO YOU KEEP FIGHTING?!
TMP...
GRRR!

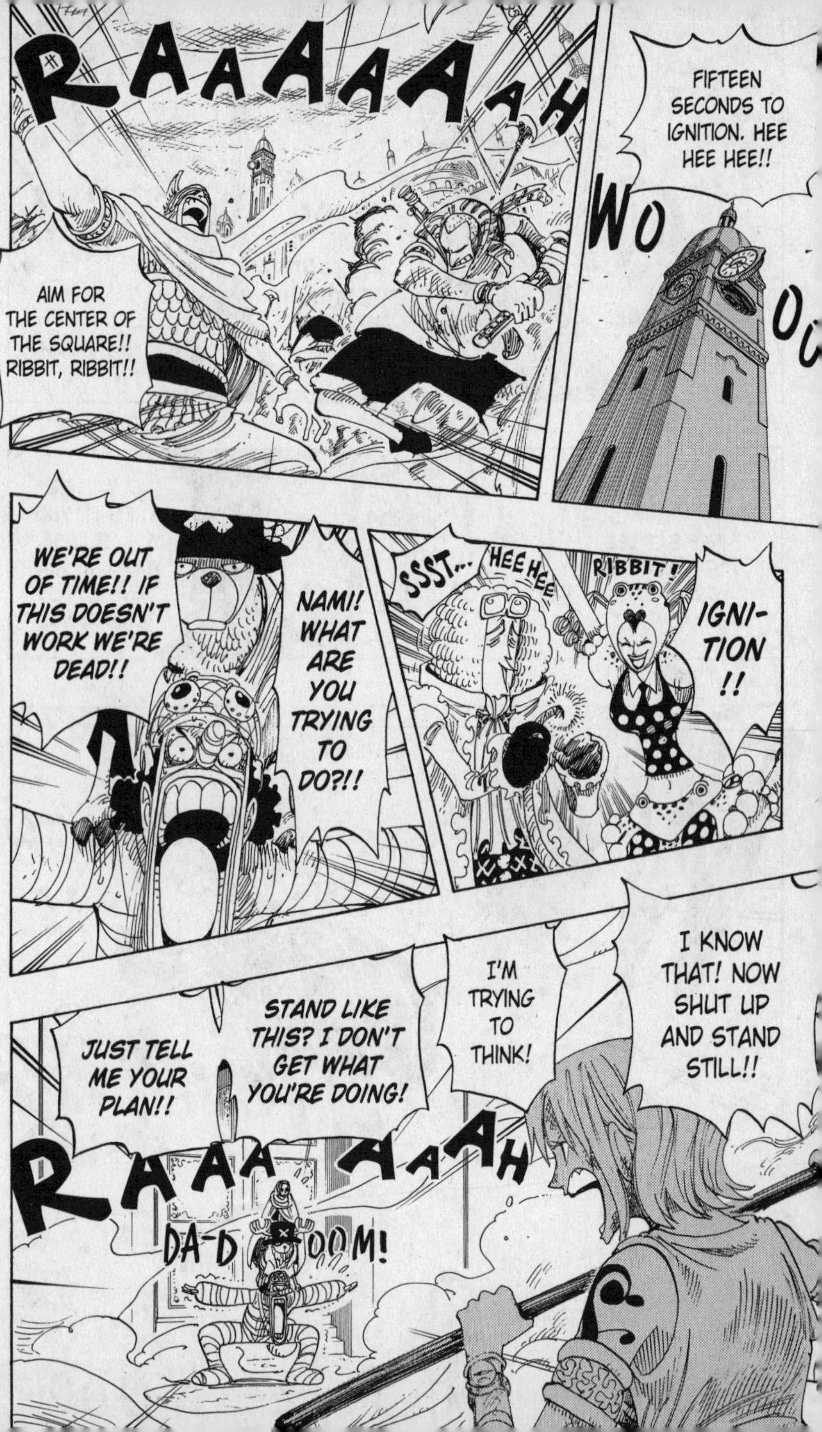
FIFTEEN SECONDS TO IGNITION. HEE HEE HEE!!
WO OU
RAAAAAAH
AIM FOR THE CENTER OF THE SQUARE!! RIBBIT, RIBBIT!!
RIBBIT!
IGNITION!!
HEE HEE
SSST...
NAMI! WHAT ARE YOU TRYING TO DO?!!
WE'RE OUT OF TIME!! IF THIS DOESN'T WORK WE'RE DEAD!!
I KNOW THAT! NOW SHUT UP AND STAND STILL!!
I'M TRYING TO THINK!
STAND LIKE THIS? I DON'T GET WHAT YOU'RE DOING!
JUST TELL ME YOUR PLAN!!
RAAAAAAH
DA-DOOM!

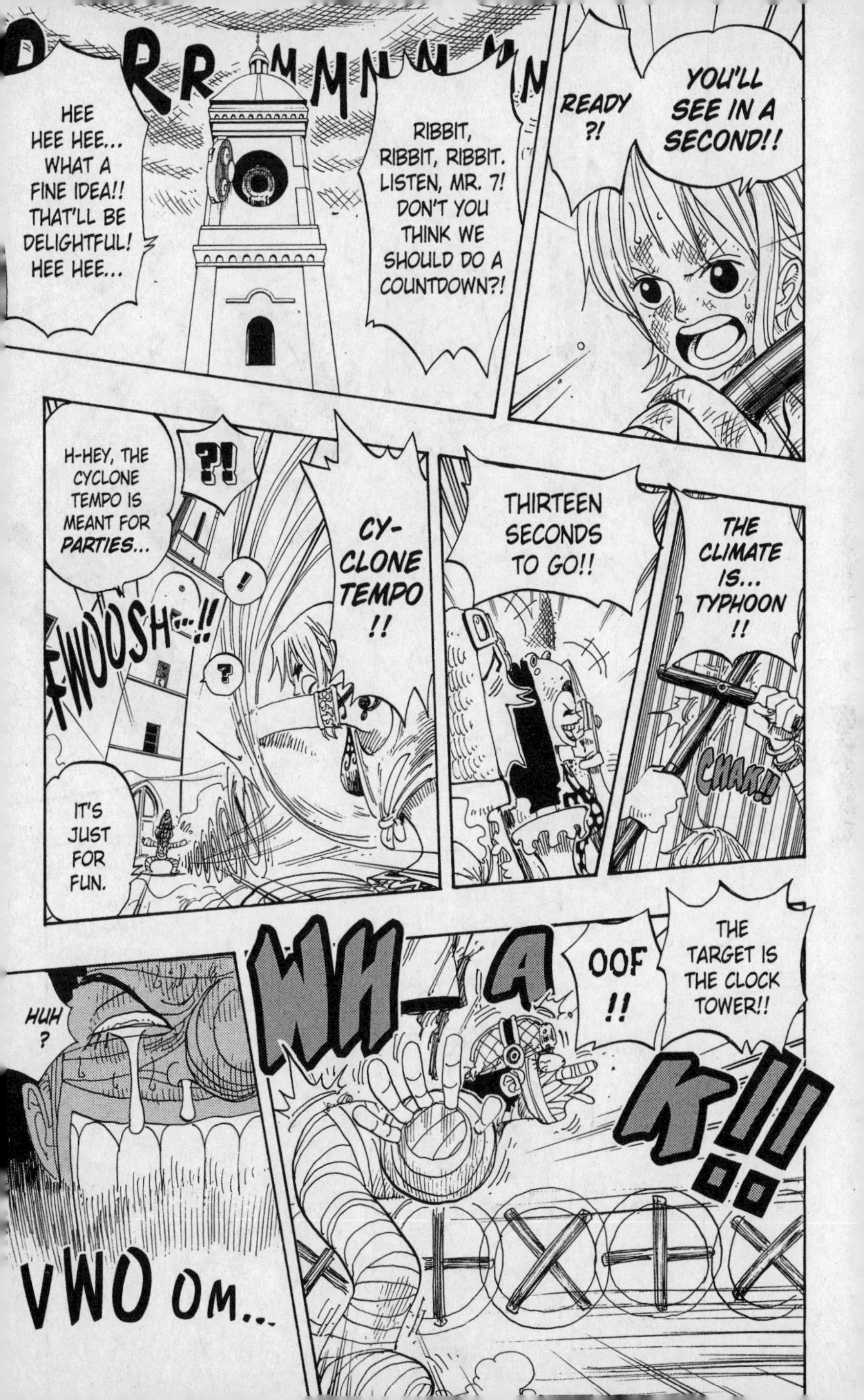
YOU'LL SEE IN A SECOND!!
READY ?!
DRRMMNNNN
RIBBIT, RIBBIT, RIBBIT. LISTEN, MR. 7! DON'T YOU THINK WE SHOULD DO A COUNTDOWN?!
HEE HEE HEE... WHAT A FINE IDEA!! THAT'LL BE DELIGHTFUL! HEE HEE...
THE CLIMATE IS... TYPHOON !!
CHAK!!
THIRTEEN SECONDS TO GO!!
CY-CLONE TEMPO !!
?!
H-HEY, THE CYCLONE TEMPO IS MEANT FOR PARTIES...
!
?
FWOOSH!!
IT'S JUST FOR FUN.
THE TARGET IS THE CLOCK TOWER!!
OOF !!
WH-A-K!!
HUH ?
VWOOM...

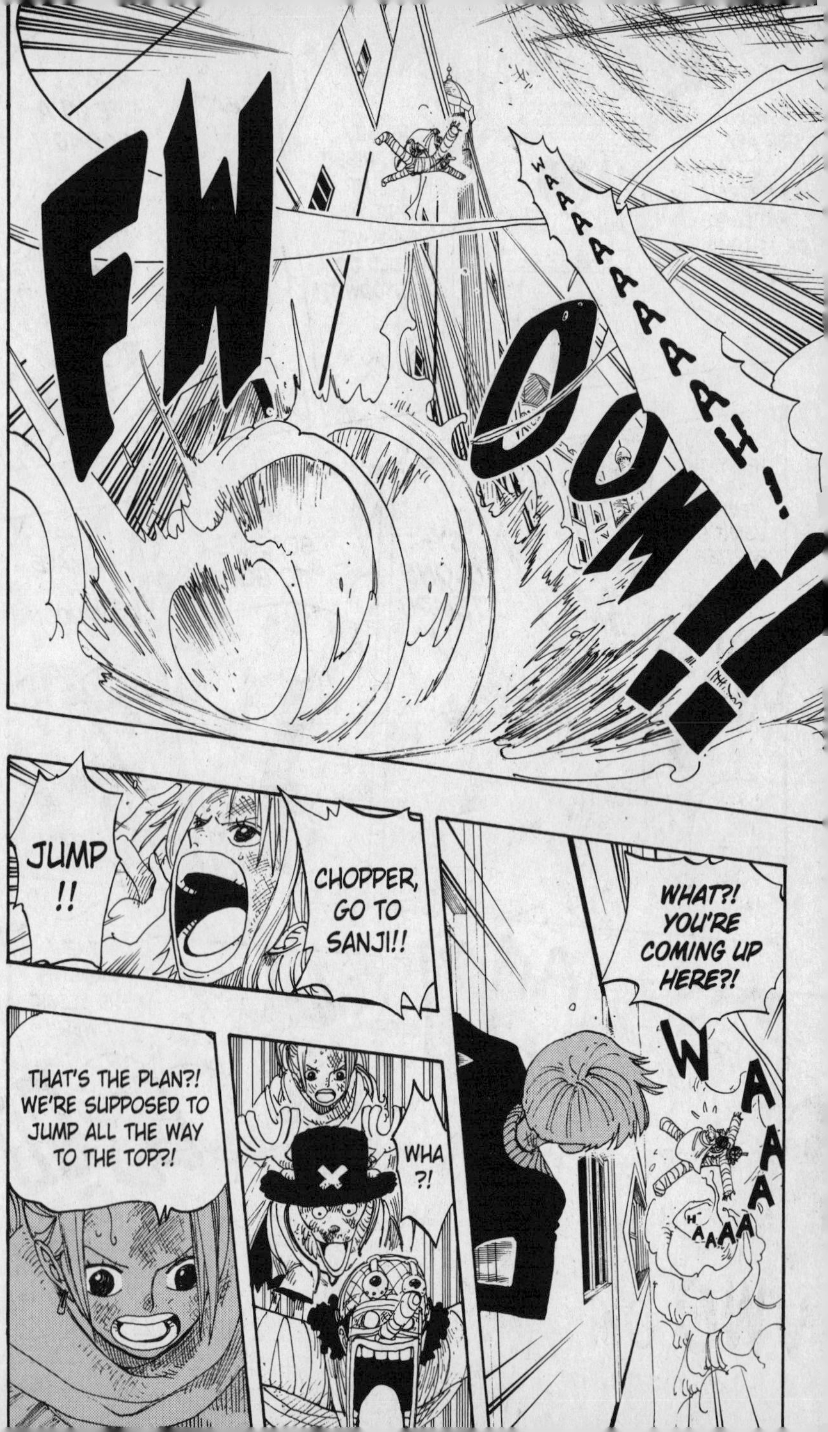
FW...OOM!!!
WAAAAAAAAH!!
WHAT?! YOU'RE COMING UP HERE?!
WAAAAAH AAAA
CHOPPER, GO TO SANJI!!
JUMP !!
WHA ?!
THAT'S THE PLAN?! WE'RE SUPPOSED TO JUMP ALL THE WAY TO THE TOP?!

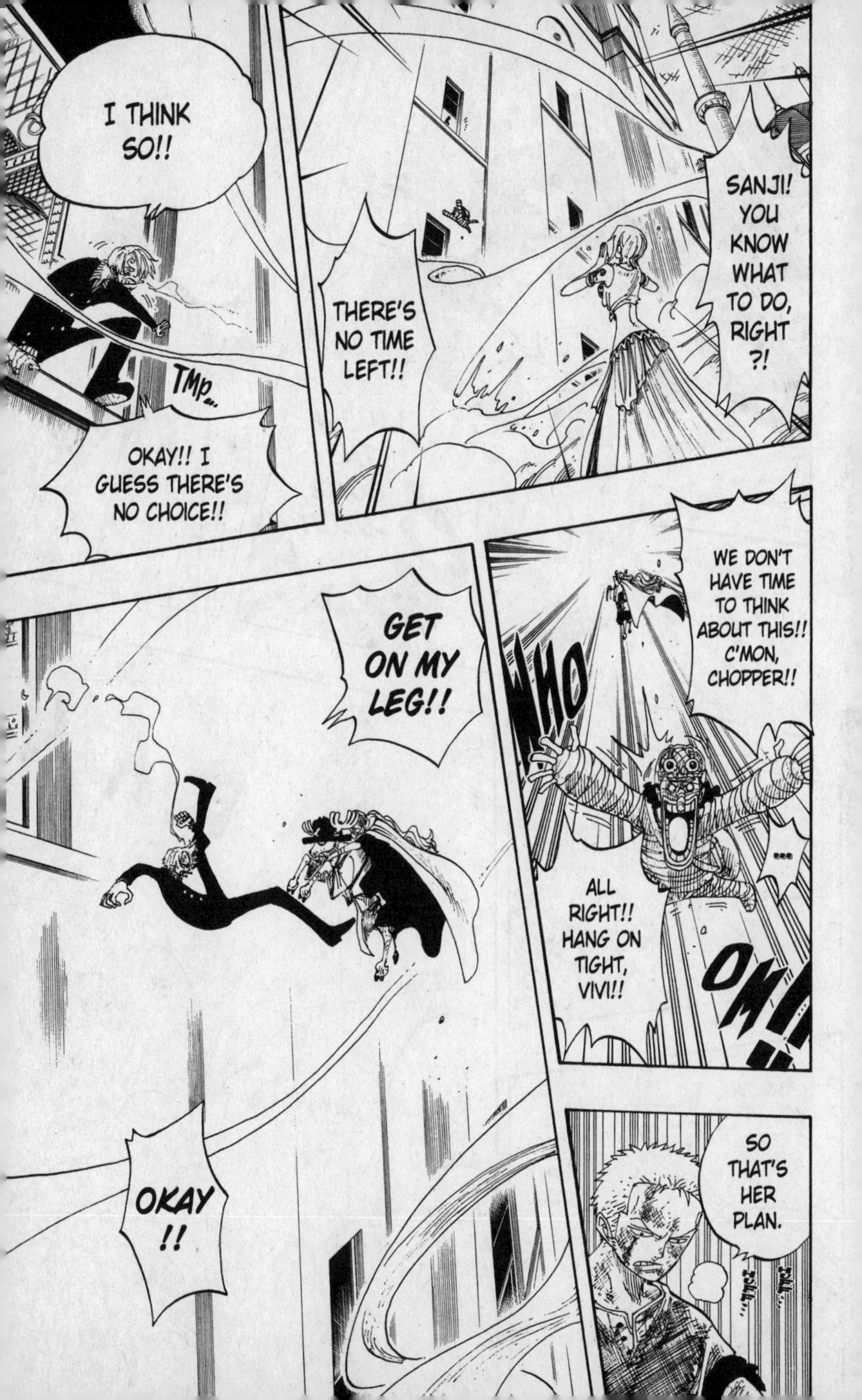
SANJI! YOU KNOW WHAT TO DO, RIGHT?!
THERE'S NO TIME LEFT!!
I THINK SO!!
TMp..
OKAY!! I GUESS THERE'S NO CHOICE!!
WE DON'T HAVE TIME TO THINK ABOUT THIS!! C'MON, CHOPPER!!
WHO
...
ALL RIGHT!! HANG ON TIGHT, VIVI!!
OM!!
SO THAT'S HER PLAN.
GET ON MY LEG!!
OKAY!!

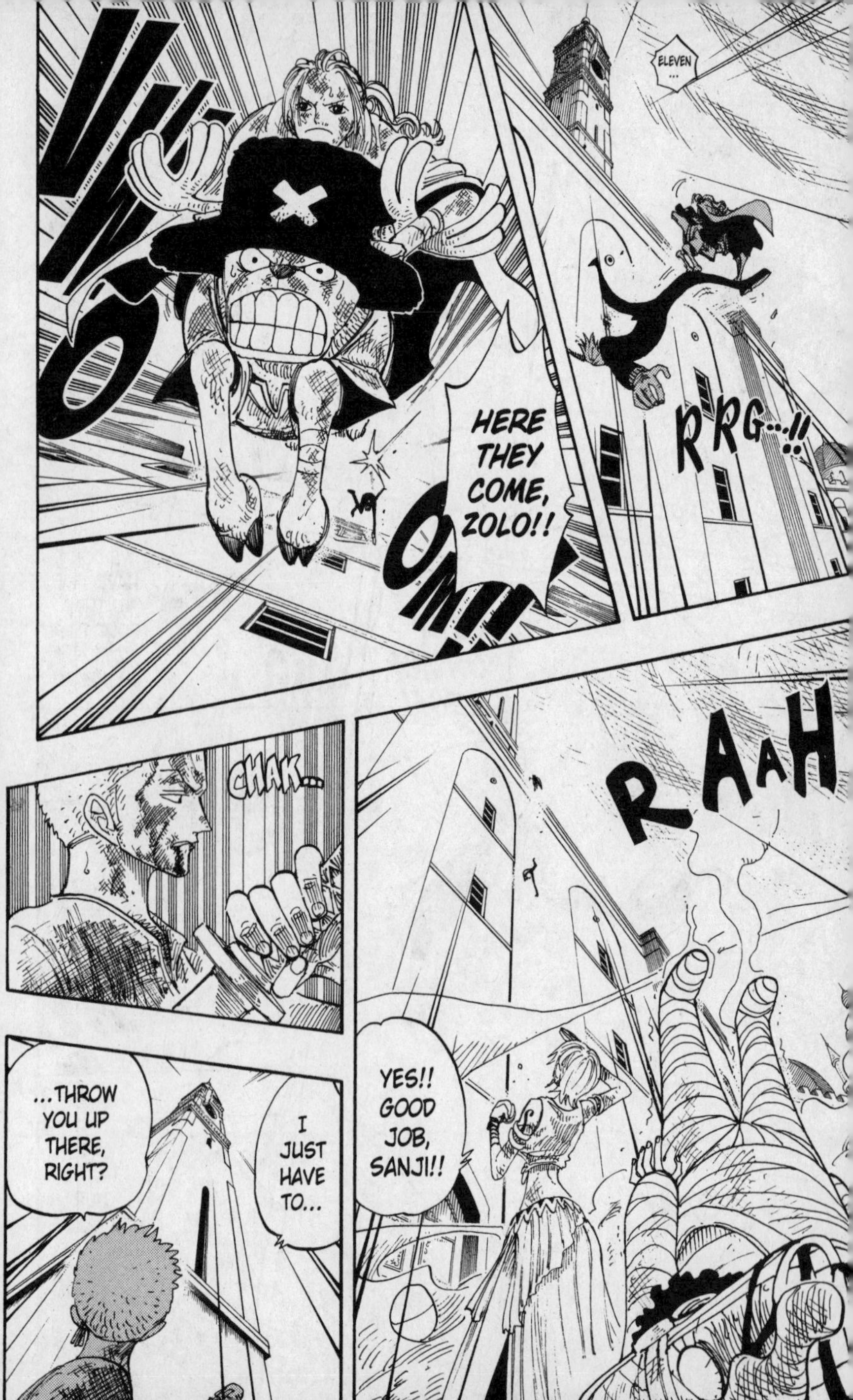
ELEVEN ...
RRG...!!
HERE THEY COME, ZOLO!!
RAAH
YES!! GOOD JOB, SANJI!!
CHAK...
I JUST HAVE TO...
...THROW YOU UP THERE, RIGHT?

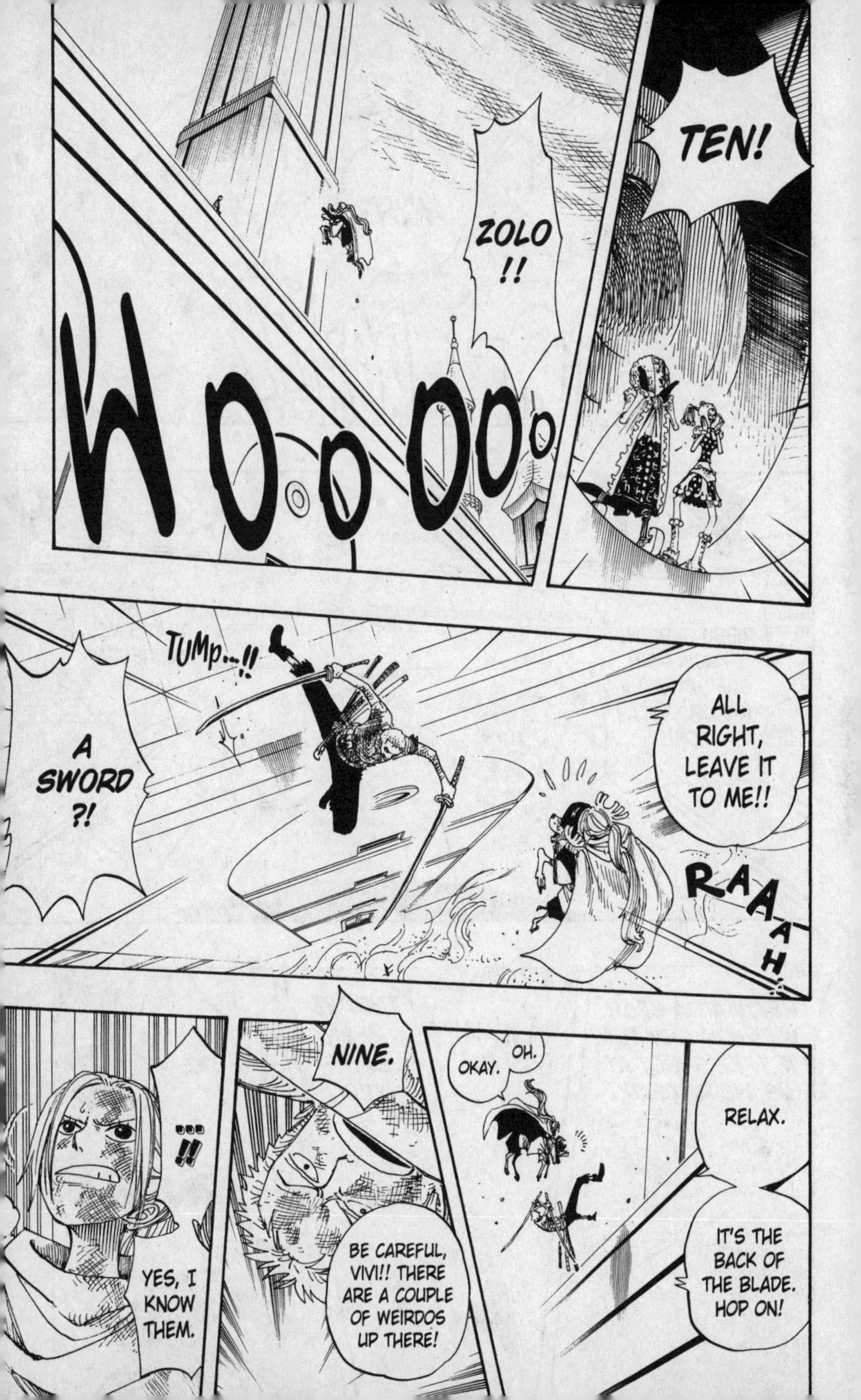

TEN!
ZOLO !!
WHOOOOO
ALL RIGHT, LEAVE IT TO ME!!
RAAAAH!
TUMP...!!
A SWORD ?!
RELAX.
IT'S THE BACK OF THE BLADE. HOP ON!
OH.
OKAY.
NINE.
BE CAREFUL, VIVI!! THERE ARE A COUPLE OF WEIRDOS UP THERE!
...!!
YES, I KNOW THEM.

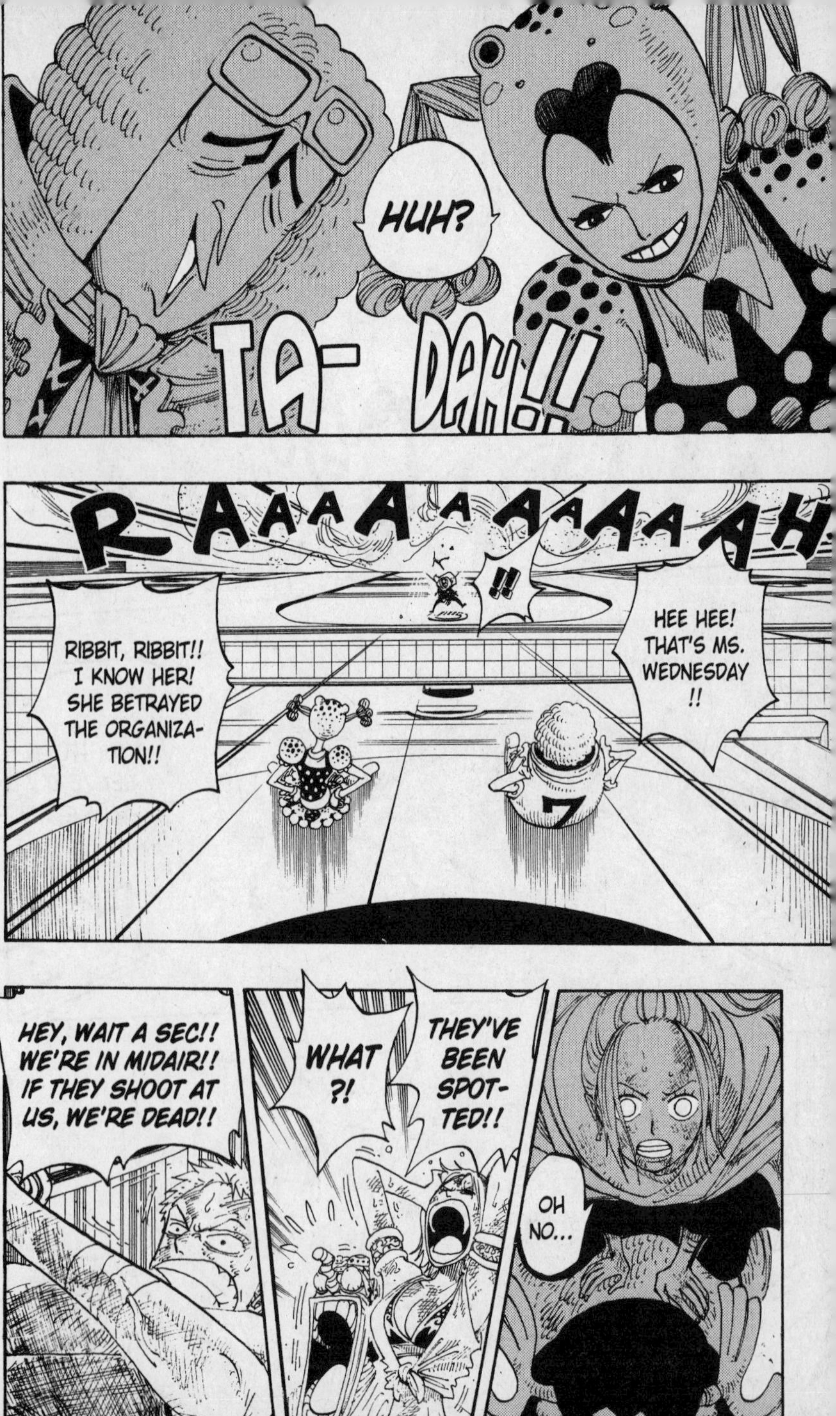
HUH?
TA- DAH!!
RAAAAAAAAAAH
!!
HEE HEE! THAT'S MS. WEDNESDAY!!
RIBBIT, RIBBIT!! I KNOW HER! SHE BETRAYED THE ORGANIZA-TION!!
OH NO...
THEY'VE BEEN SPOT-TED!!
WHAT?!
HEY, WAIT A SEC!! WE'RE IN MIDAIR!! IF THEY SHOOT AT US, WE'RE DEAD!!

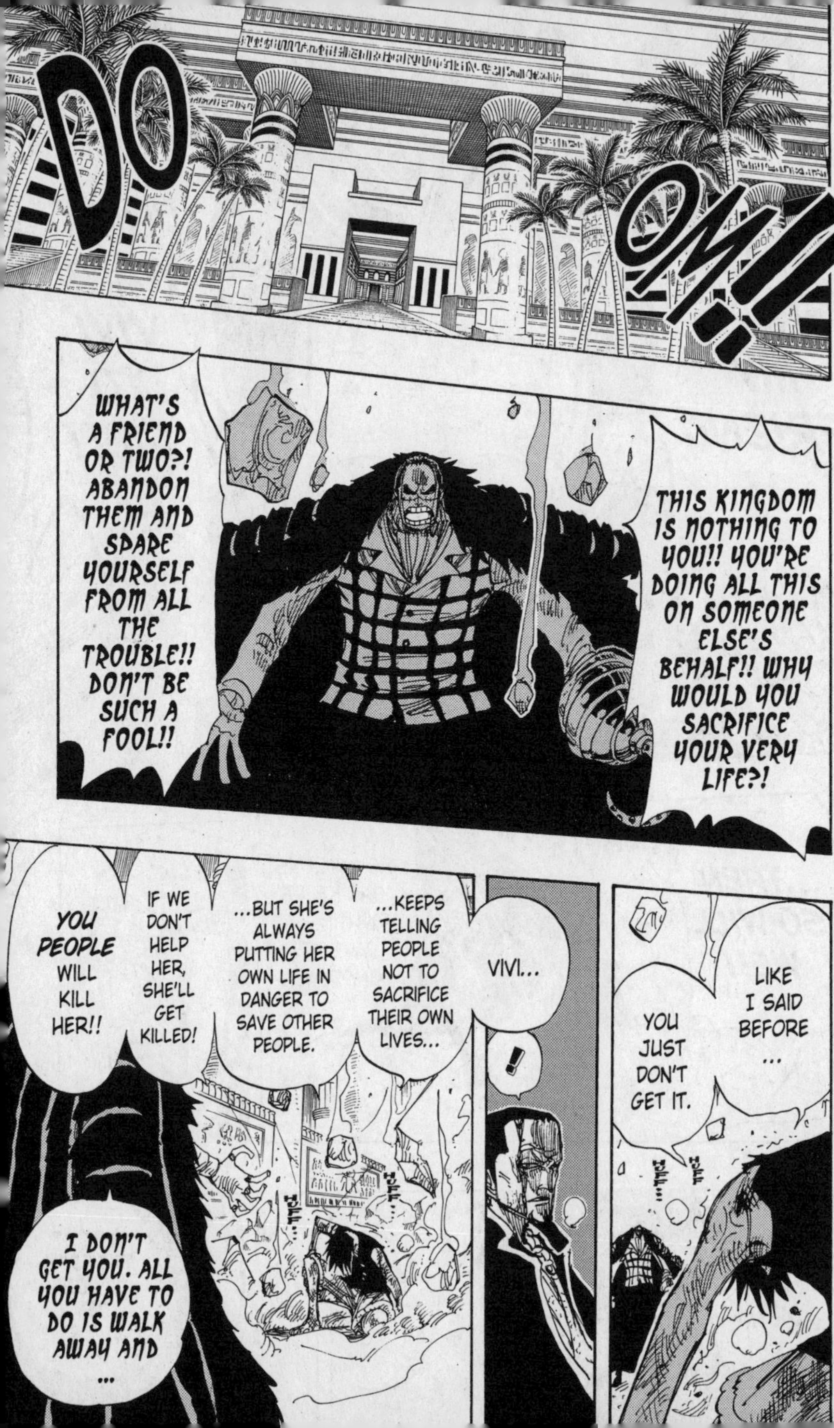
DO
OM!!
THIS KINGDOM IS NOTHING TO YOU!! YOU'RE DOING ALL THIS ON SOMEONE ELSE'S BEHALF!! WHY WOULD YOU SACRIFICE YOUR VERY LIFE?!
WHAT'S A FRIEND OR TWO?! ABANDON THEM AND SPARE YOURSELF FROM ALL THE TROUBLE!! DON'T BE SUCH A FOOL!!
LIKE I SAID BEFORE ...
YOU JUST DON'T GET IT.
HUFF
HUFF...
VIVI...
!
...KEEPS TELLING PEOPLE NOT TO SACRIFICE THEIR OWN LIVES...
...BUT SHE'S ALWAYS PUTTING HER OWN LIFE IN DANGER TO SAVE OTHER PEOPLE.
IF WE DON'T HELP HER, SHE'LL GET KILLED!
YOU PEOPLE WILL KILL HER!!
HUFF...
HUFF...
I DON'T GET YOU. ALL YOU HAVE TO DO IS WALK AWAY AND ...

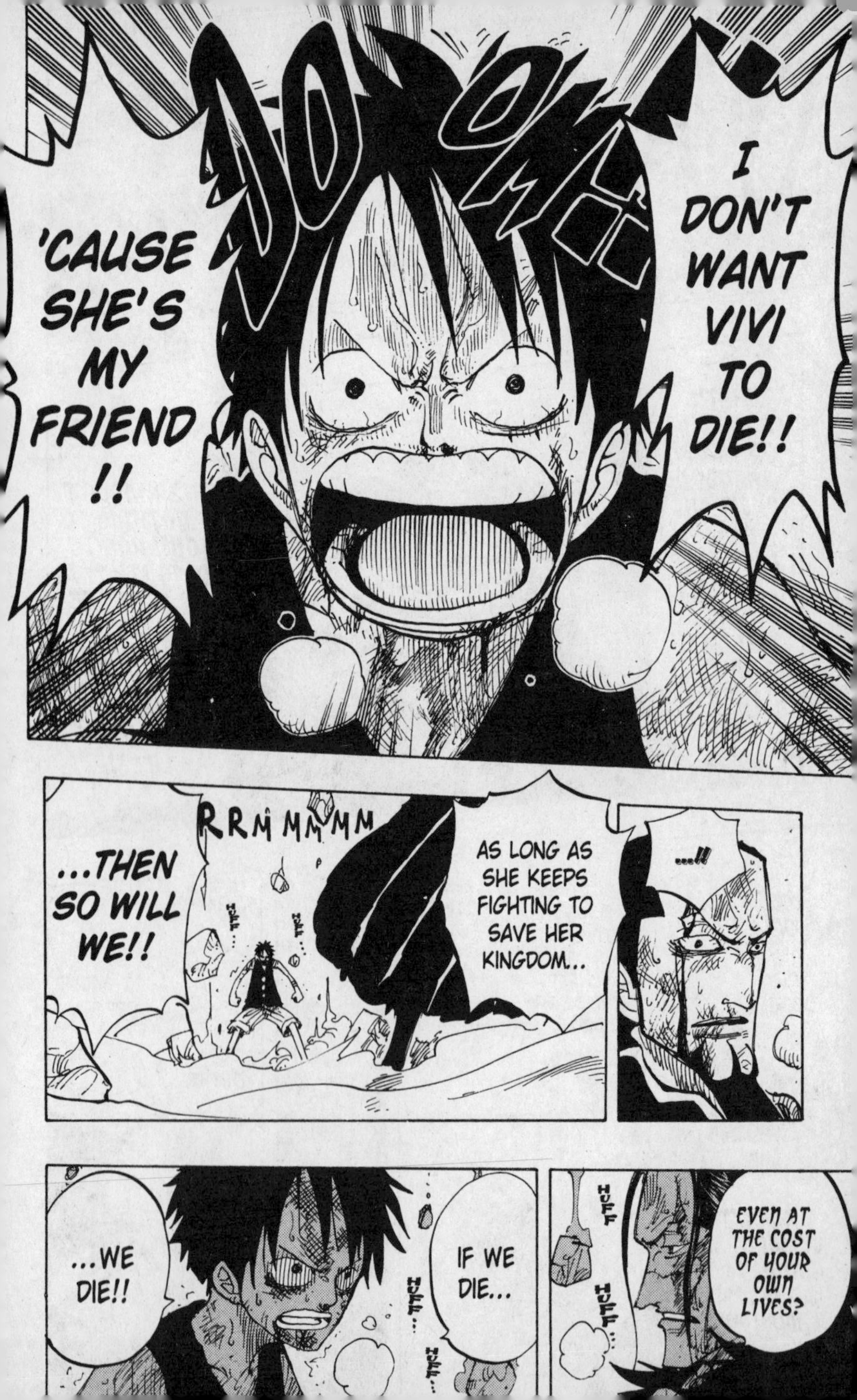
I DON'T WANT VIVI TO DIE!!
'CAUSE SHE'S MY FRIEND!!
...!!
AS LONG AS SHE KEEPS FIGHTING TO SAVE HER KINGDOM...
RRMMMMMM
HUFF...
HUFF...
...THEN SO WILL WE!!
HUFF
HUFF...
EVEN AT THE COST OF YOUR OWN LIVES?
HUFF...
HUFF...
IF WE DIE...
...WE DIE!!

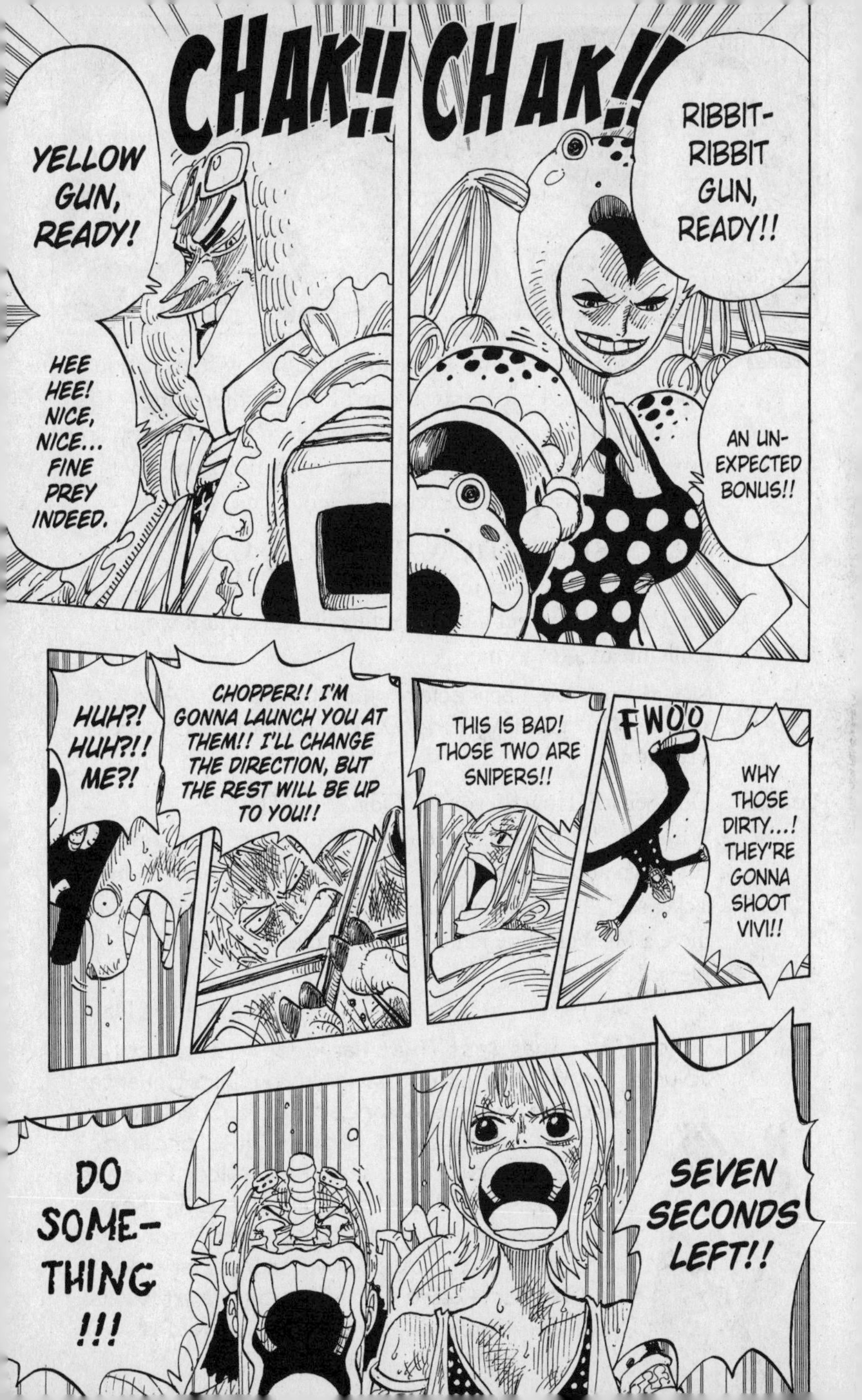
CHAK!!
RIBBIT-RIBBIT GUN, READY!!
AN UN-EXPECTED BONUS!!
CHAK!!
YELLOW GUN, READY!
HEE HEE! NICE, NICE... FINE PREY INDEED.
FWOO
WHY THOSE DIRTY...! THEY'RE GONNA SHOOT VIVI!!
THIS IS BAD! THOSE TWO ARE SNIPERS!!
CHOPPER!! I'M GONNA LAUNCH YOU AT THEM!! I'LL CHANGE THE DIRECTION, BUT THE REST WILL BE UP TO YOU!!
HUH?! HUH?!! ME?!
SEVEN SECONDS LEFT!!
DO SOME-THING!!!

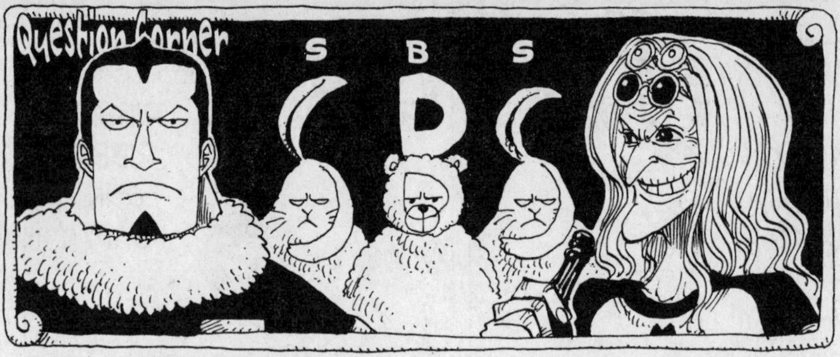
Question Corner
S B S

Reader: Hello, Oda Sensei. This is the first time I've written to you. The thing is… I can't draw, I don't have an interesting question, and there's no way I'll ever get to meet Broggy, so I just have a request. Please allow me to say the words that everyone is dying to say lately. Here goes…

Let's start the Question Corner!

Heh heh heh… That felt so good!

P.S. I'm sure you get a lot of letters like this, but it would really mean a lot to me.

Oda: No, thank you. I appreciate your politeness. And thanks for reading *One Piece*. All right, let's get started.

Reader: Oda Sensei!! How do you do, Oda Sensei?!!!

Who is he?! Who was that Baroque Works agent Sgt. Tashigi cut down at the beginning of this volume?! The back of his jacket said, "I ♡ Ms. Valentine"! Huh?! Do I have a rival?! Is there a Ms. Valentine fan club?! If so, please let me join!! Please!!

--Ms. Letters Day

Oda: Whoa! That was fast. That happened in this very volume, on the very first page of the first chapter.

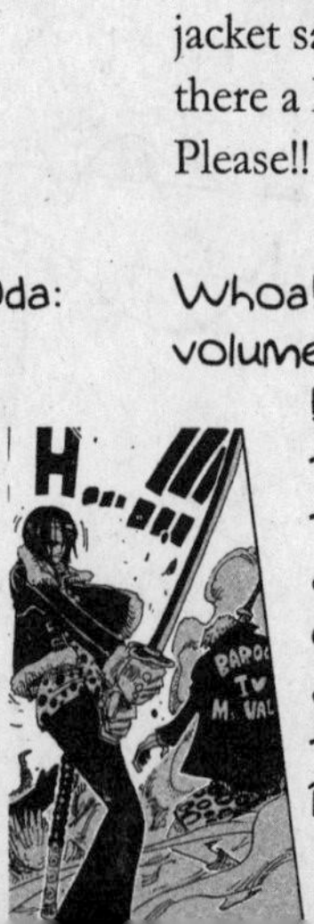

Baroque Works has nearly 2,000 agents, so there are all types of people in the organization. Some of them see the Officer Agents as rivals, but others look up to them. They even have fan clubs. If you're interested, send a postcard with your name, address and age to the Officer Agent Fan Club office at Whisky Peak. Oh, that's right, Zolo destroyed it.

Chapter 207:
NIGHTMARE

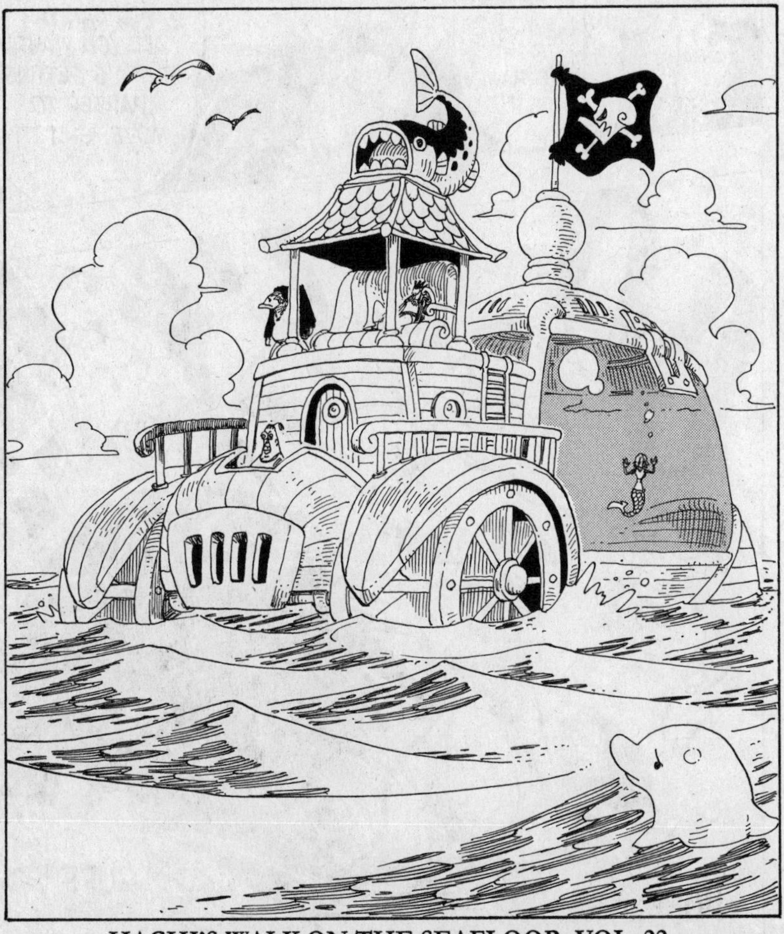

HACHI'S WALK ON THE SEAFLOOR, VOL. 22:
"THE MERMAID-SELLING MACRO"

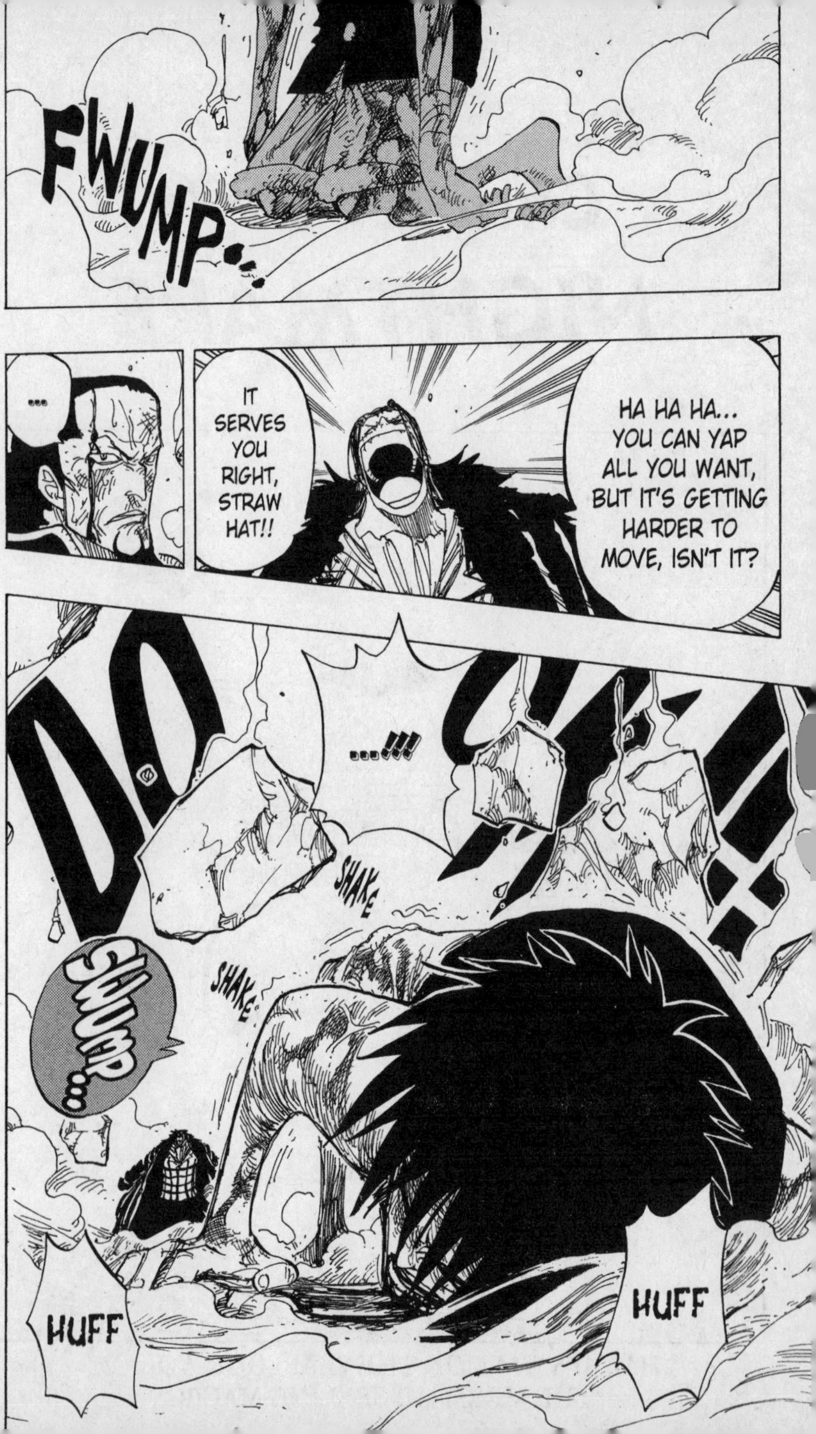
FWUMP...
HA HA HA... YOU CAN YAP ALL YOU WANT, BUT IT'S GETTING HARDER TO MOVE, ISN'T IT?
IT SERVES YOU RIGHT, STRAW HAT!!
...
DO
...!!!
SHAKE
SHAKE
SWUMP...
HUFF
HUFF

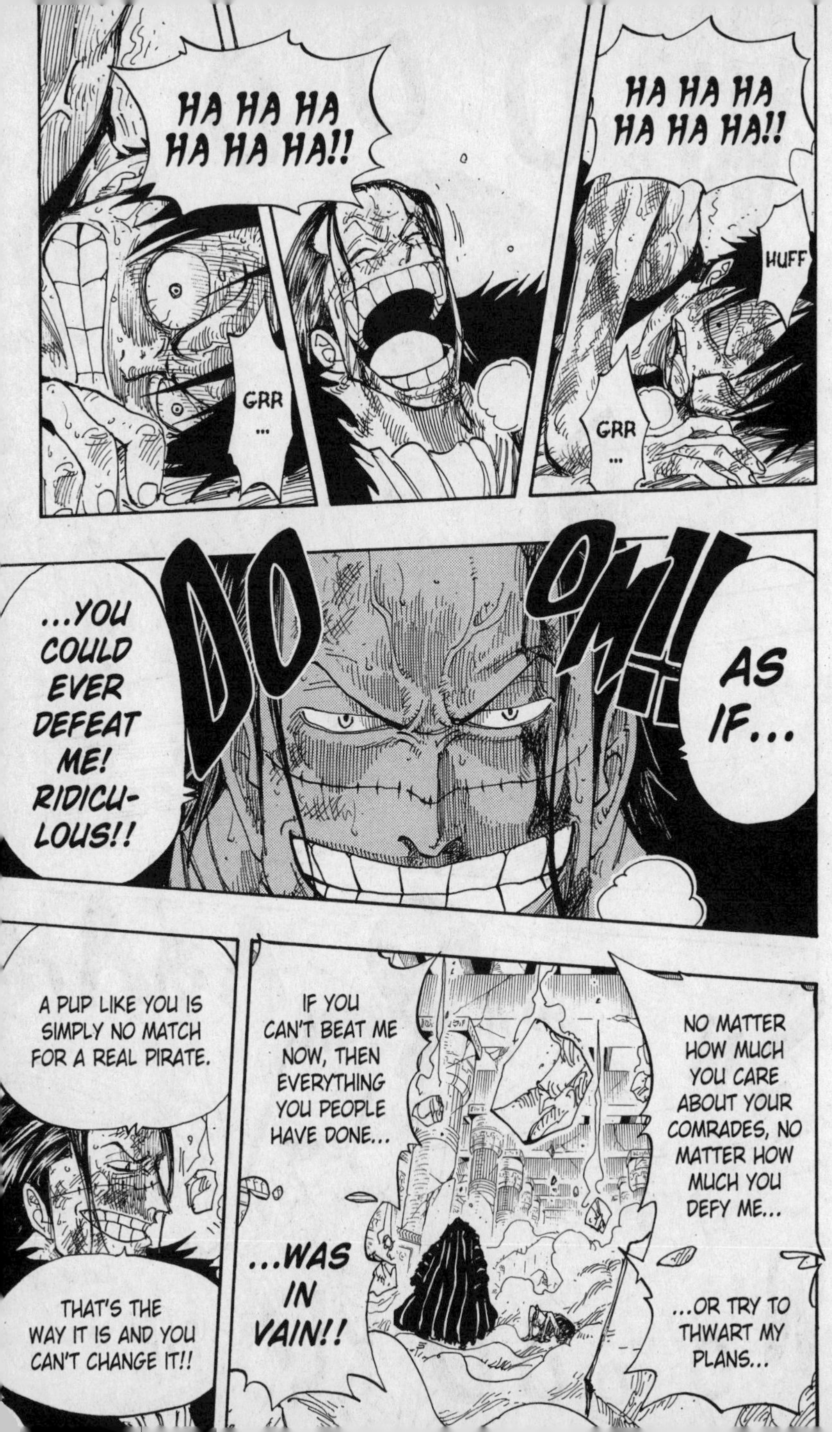
HA HA HA HA HA HA!!
HUFF
GRR...
HA HA HA HA HA HA!!
GRR...
AS IF...
DOON!!
...YOU COULD EVER DEFEAT ME! RIDICULOUS!!
NO MATTER HOW MUCH YOU CARE ABOUT YOUR COMRADES, NO MATTER HOW MUCH YOU DEFY ME...
...OR TRY TO THWART MY PLANS...
IF YOU CAN'T BEAT ME NOW, THEN EVERYTHING YOU PEOPLE HAVE DONE...
...WAS IN VAIN!!
A PUP LIKE YOU IS SIMPLY NO MATCH FOR A REAL PIRATE.
THAT'S THE WAY IT IS AND YOU CAN'T CHANGE IT!!

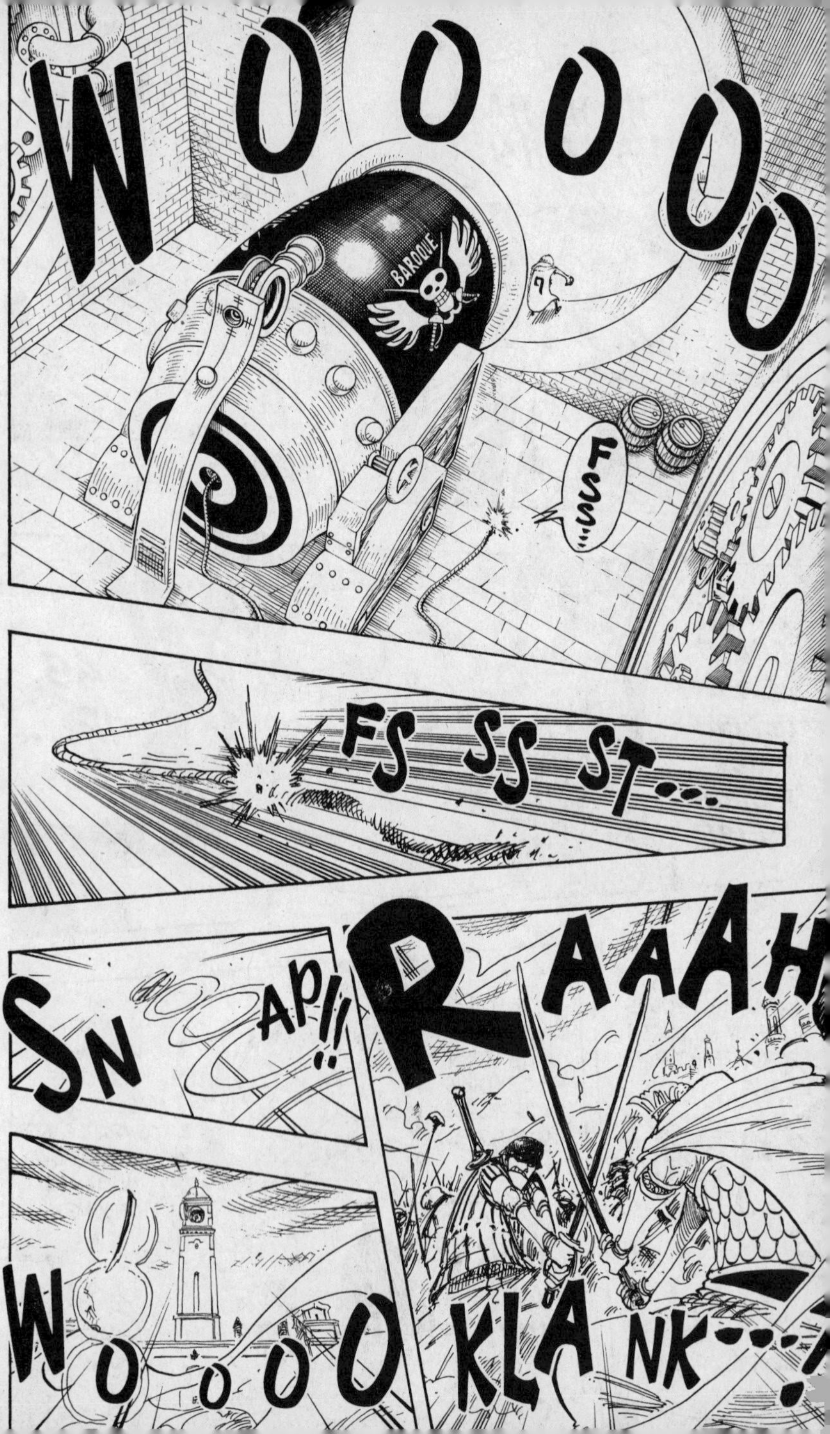

BAROQUE
WOOOOOO
FSS...
FS SS ST...
RAAAH
KLANK...!
SNAP!!
WOOOOO

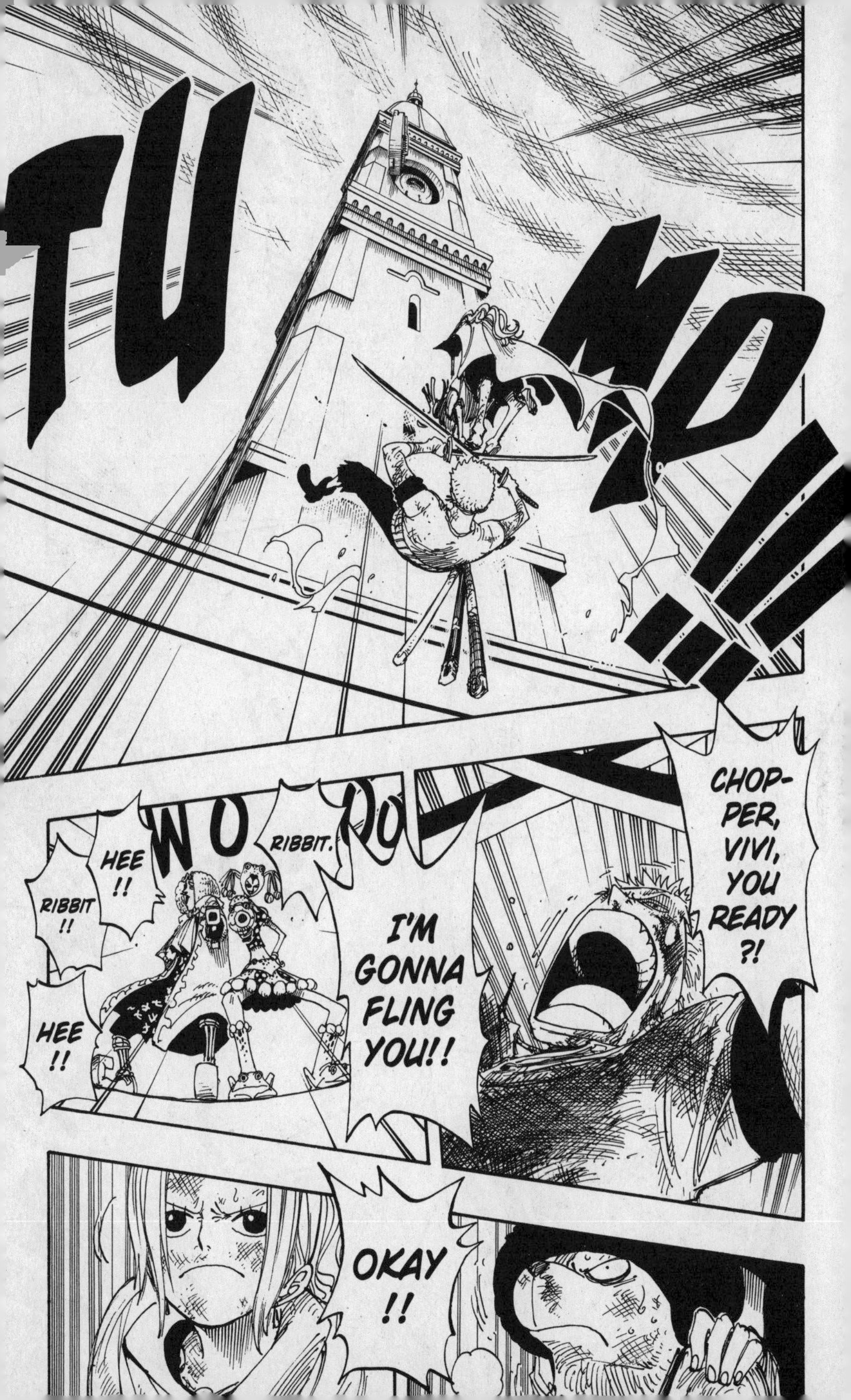

TU
MP!!!
CHOP-PER, VIVI, YOU READY ?!
I'M GONNA FLING YOU!!
RIBBIT.
PO
WO
HEE !!
RIBBIT !!
HEE !!
OKAY !!

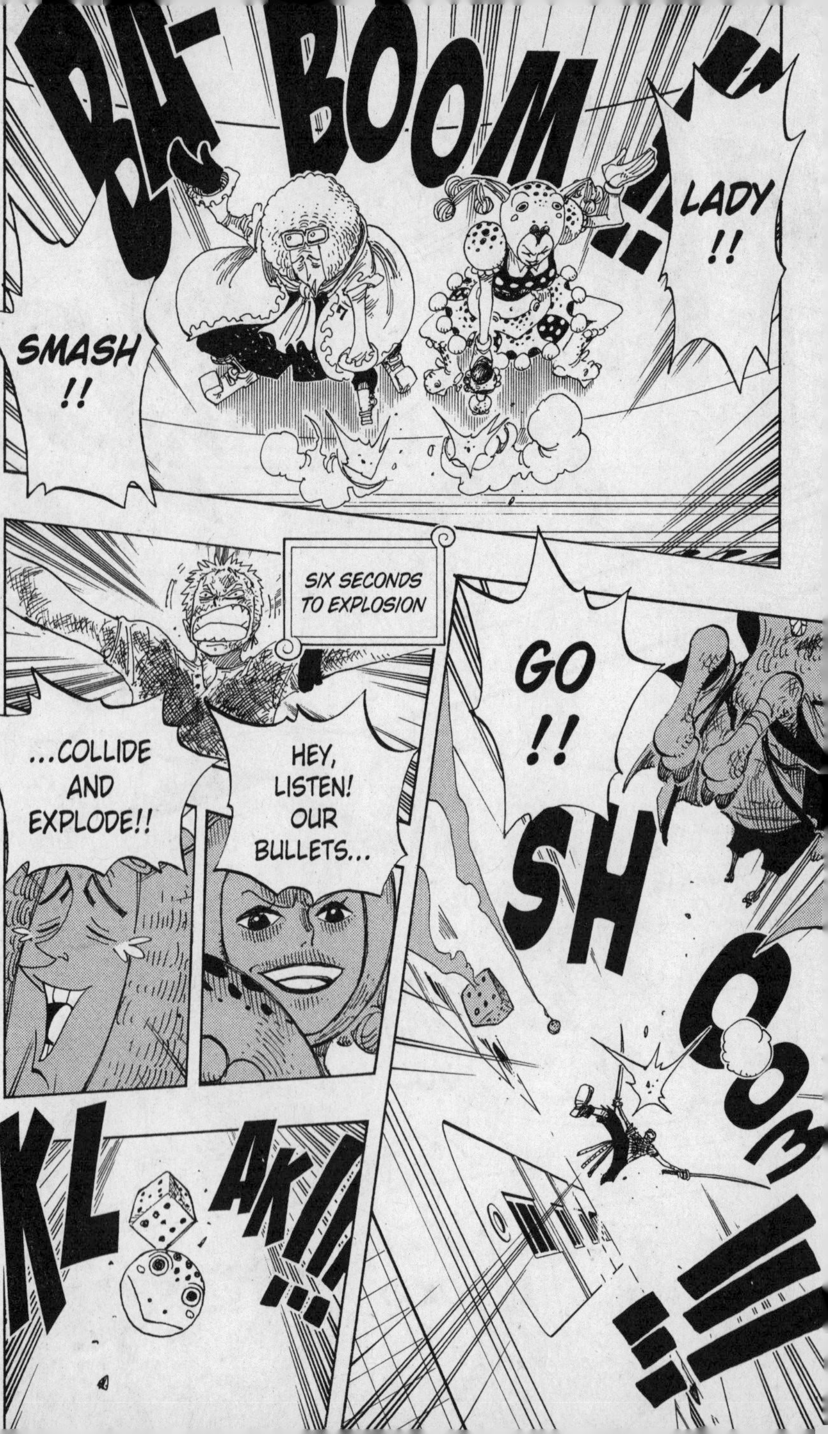
BA-BOOM!!
LADY!!
SMASH!!
GO!!
SHOOM!!
SIX SECONDS TO EXPLOSION
HEY, LISTEN! OUR BULLETS...
...COLLIDE AND EXPLODE!!
KLAK!!

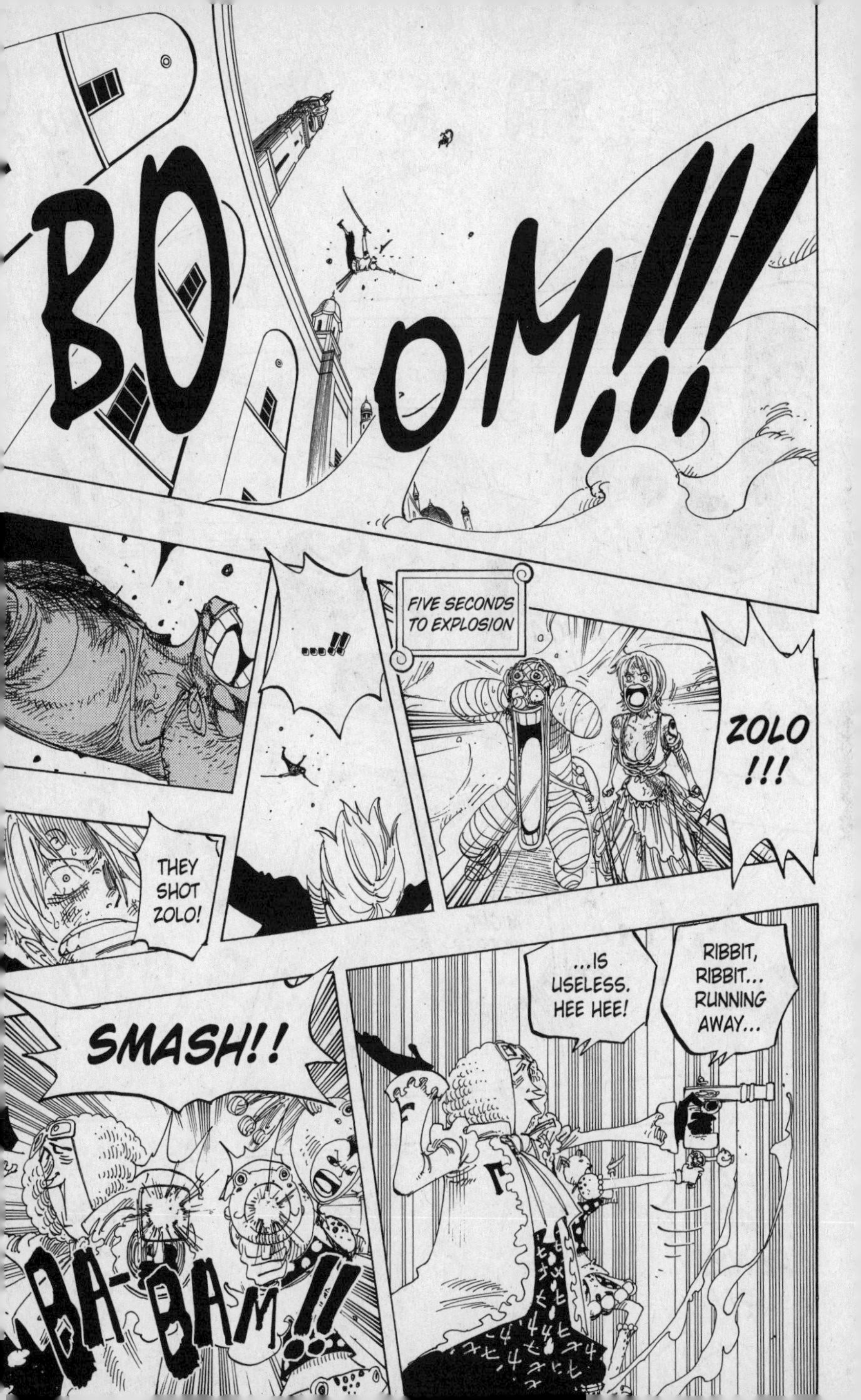
BOOM!!!
FIVE SECONDS TO EXPLOSION
ZOLO !!!
...!!
THEY SHOT ZOLO!
RIBBIT, RIBBIT... RUNNING AWAY...
...IS USELESS. HEE HEE!
SMASH!!
BA-BAM!!

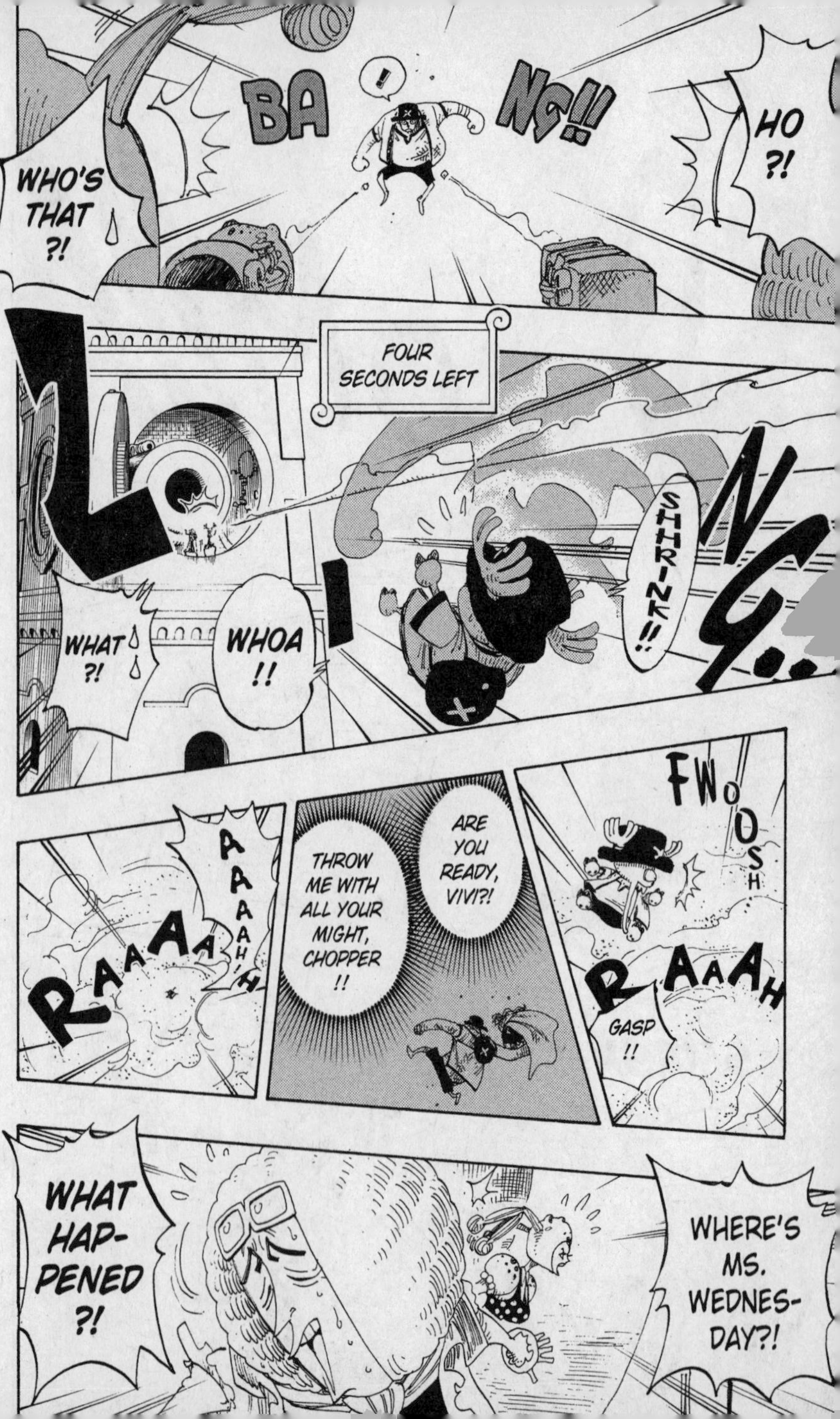
HO ?!
!
BANG!!
WHO'S THAT ?!
FOUR SECONDS LEFT
SHHRINK!!
LING..
WHOA !!
WHAT ?!
FWOOSH
RAAAH
GASP !!
ARE YOU READY, VIVI?!
THROW ME WITH ALL YOUR MIGHT, CHOPPER !!
RAAAAAAAAAH!H
WHERE'S MS. WEDNES-DAY?!
WHAT HAP-PENED ?!

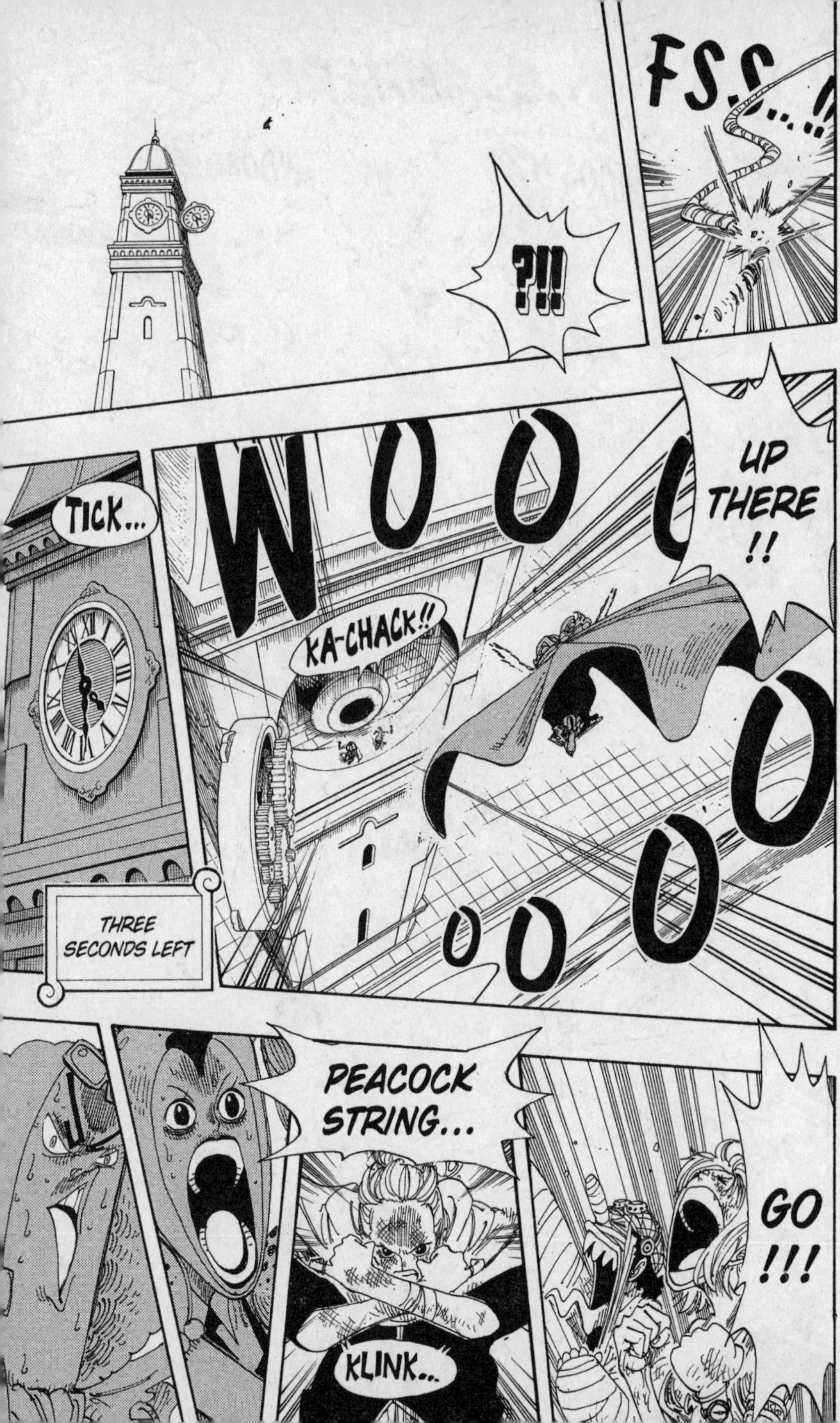
FSS...!!
?!!
UP THERE !!
WOOOOOOOO
KA-CHACK!!
TICK...
THREE SECONDS LEFT
GO !!!
PEACOCK STRING...
KLINK...

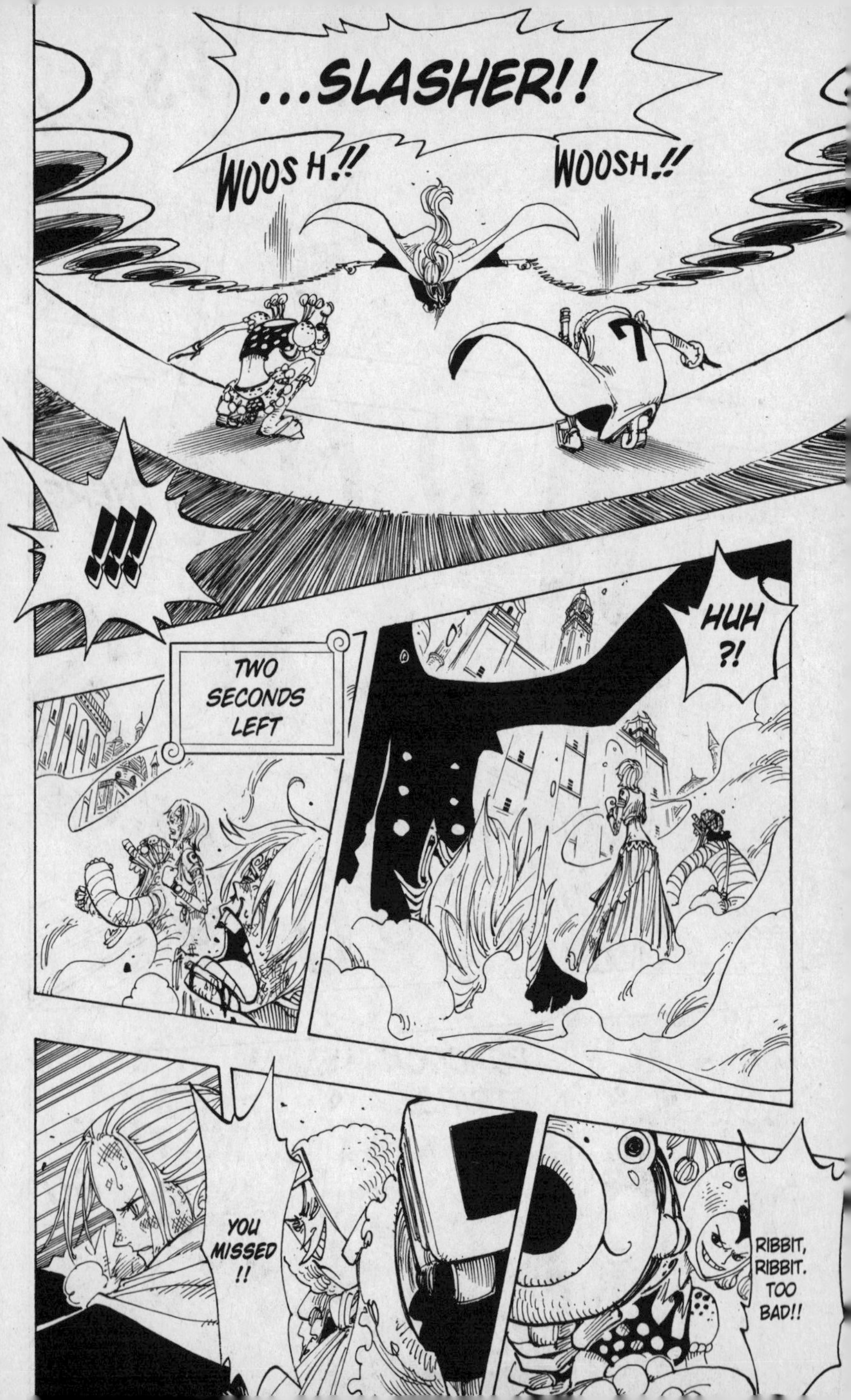
...SLASHER!!
WOOSH.!!
WOOSH.!!
!!!
HUH ?!
TWO SECONDS LEFT
RIBBIT, RIBBIT. TOO BAD!!
YOU MISSED !!

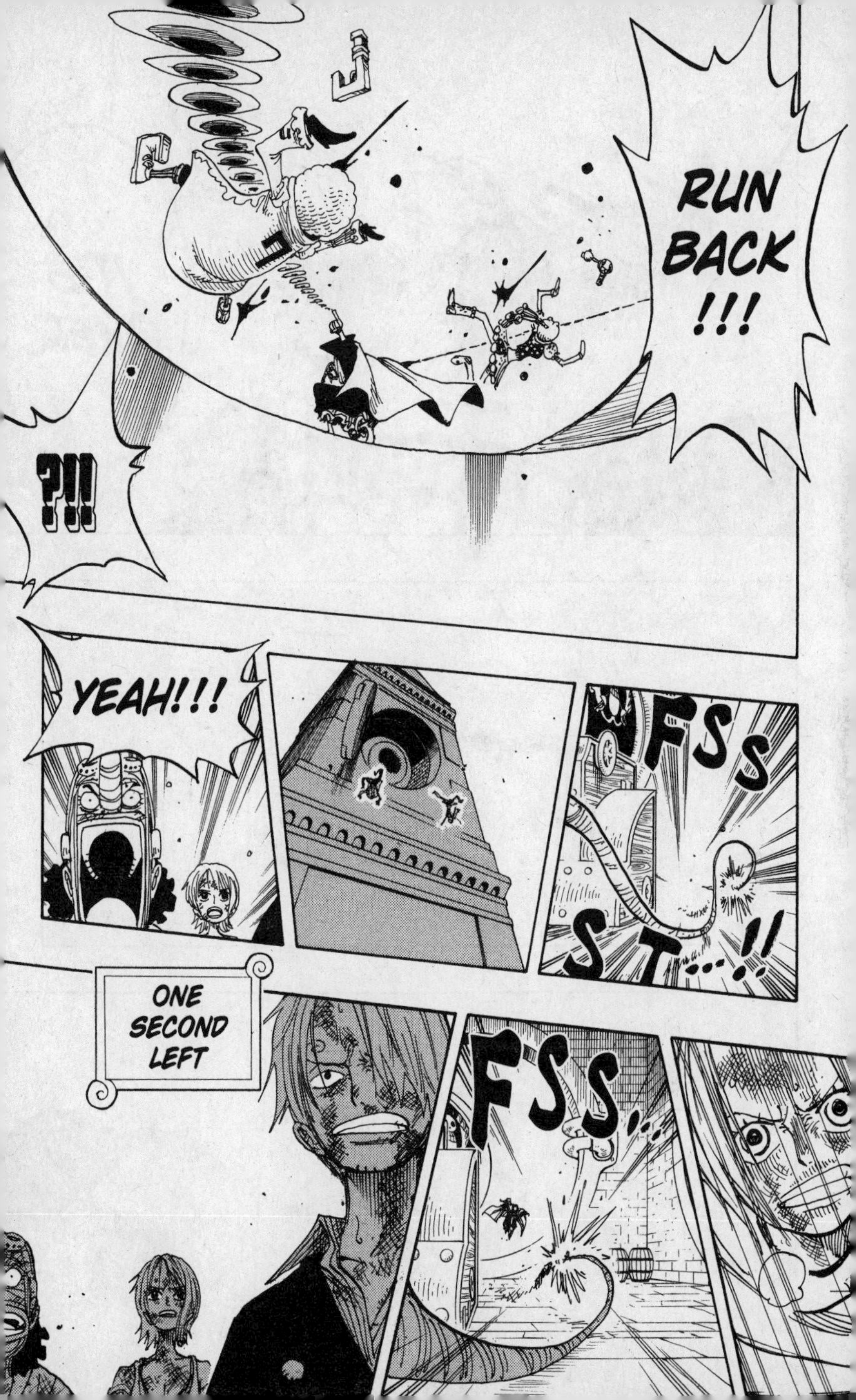
RUN BACK!!!
?!!
YEAH!!!
FSSST...!!
ONE SECOND LEFT
FSS...

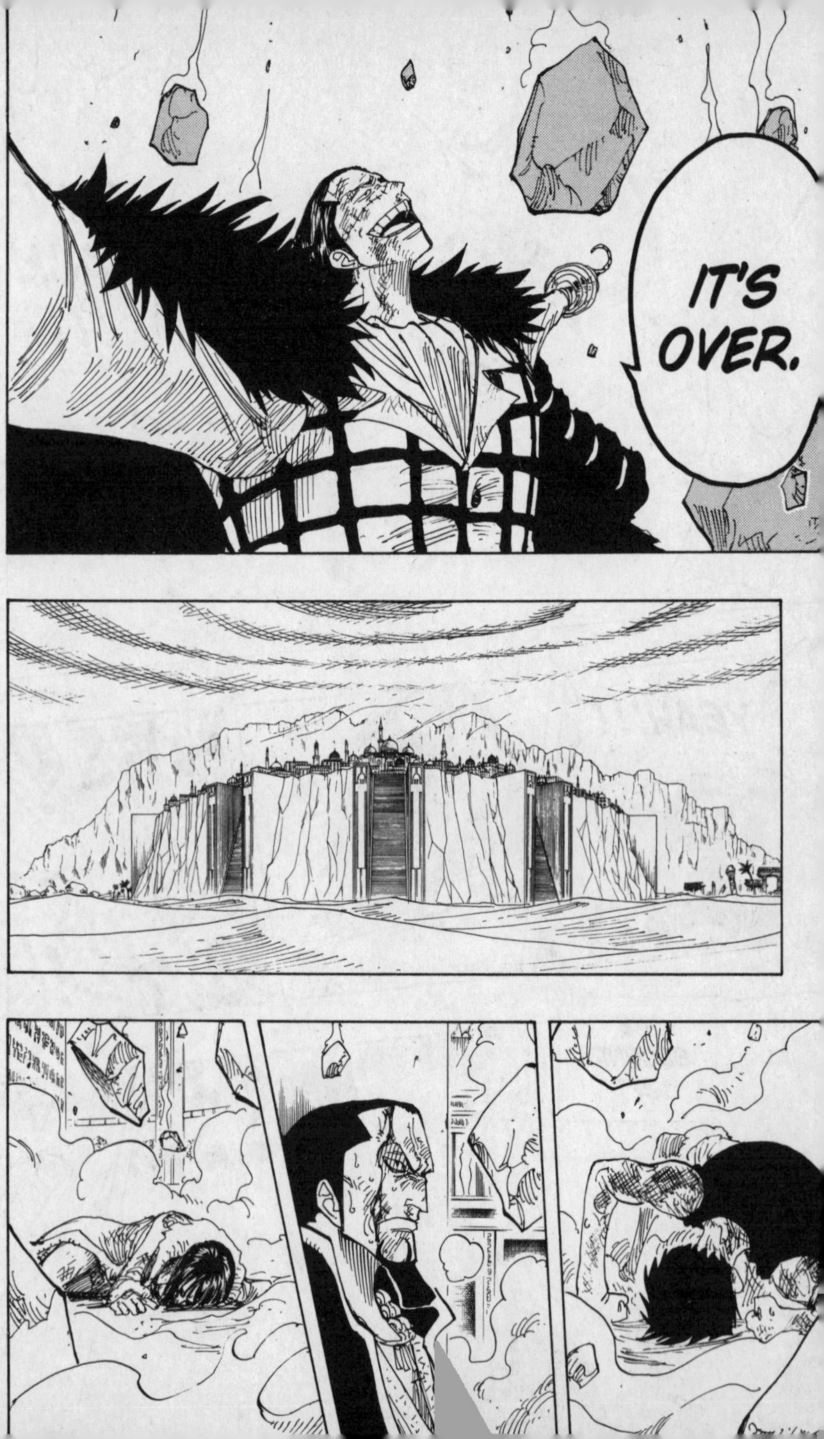
IT'S OVER.

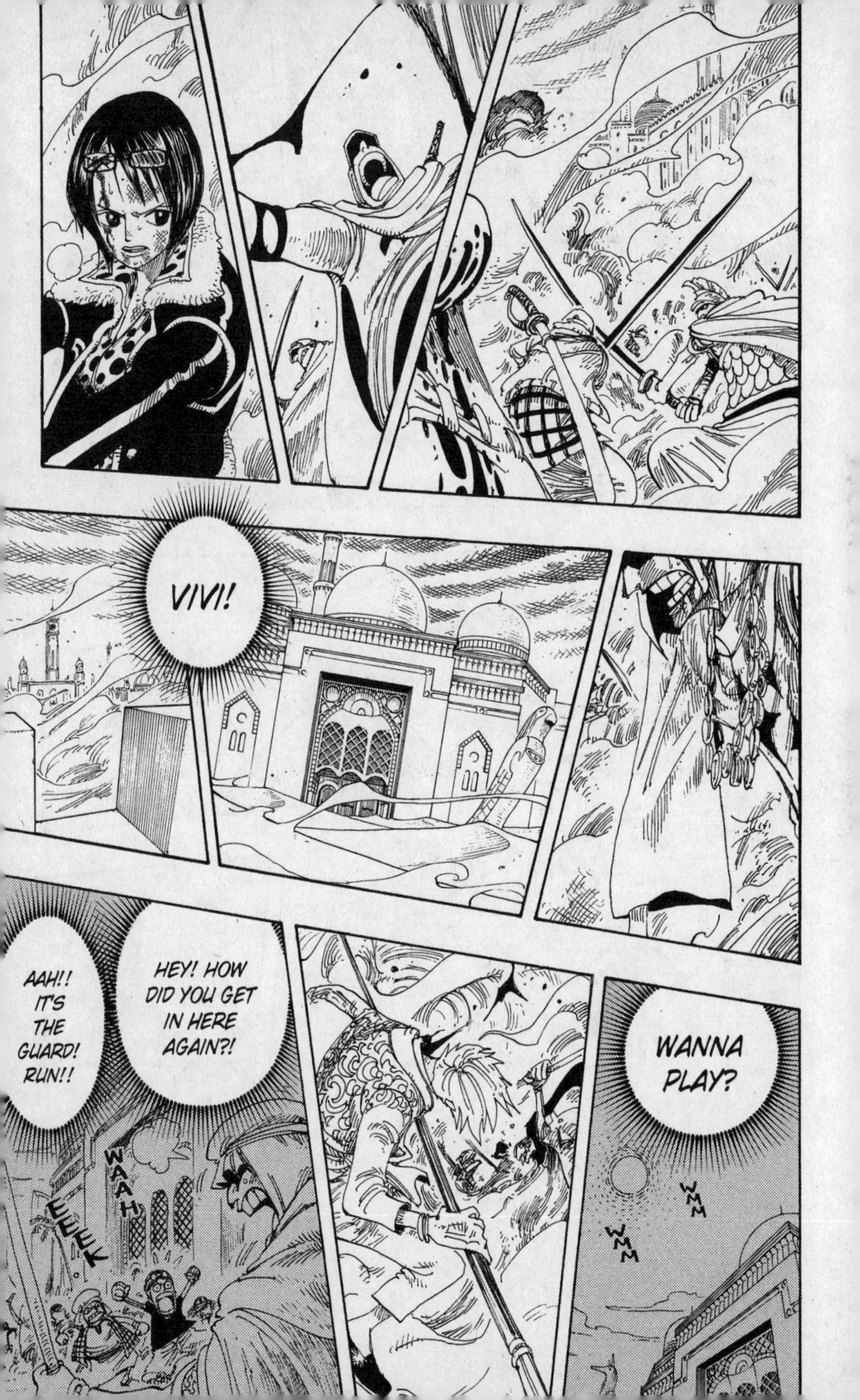
VIVI!
WANNA PLAY?
WMM
WMM
HEY! HOW DID YOU GET IN HERE AGAIN?!
AAH!! IT'S THE GUARD! RUN!!
WAAH
EEEK

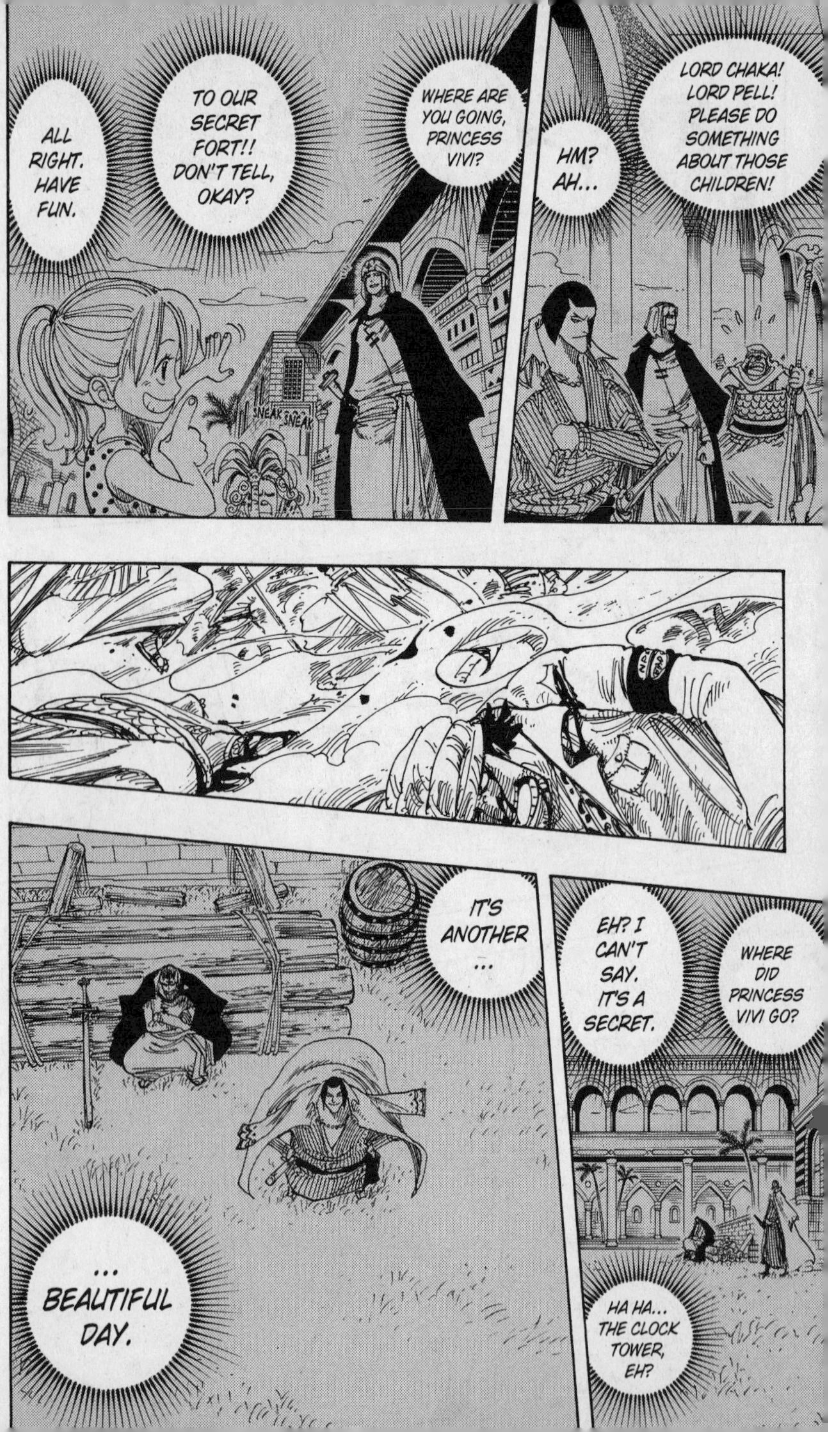
LORD CHAKA! LORD PELL! PLEASE DO SOMETHING ABOUT THOSE CHILDREN!
HM? AH...
WHERE ARE YOU GOING, PRINCESS VIVI?
TO OUR SECRET FORT!! DON'T TELL, OKAY?
SNEAK SNEAK
ALL RIGHT. HAVE FUN.
WHERE DID PRINCESS VIVI GO?
EH? I CAN'T SAY. IT'S A SECRET.
HA HA... THE CLOCK TOWER, EH?
IT'S ANOTHER ...
... BEAUTIFUL DAY.

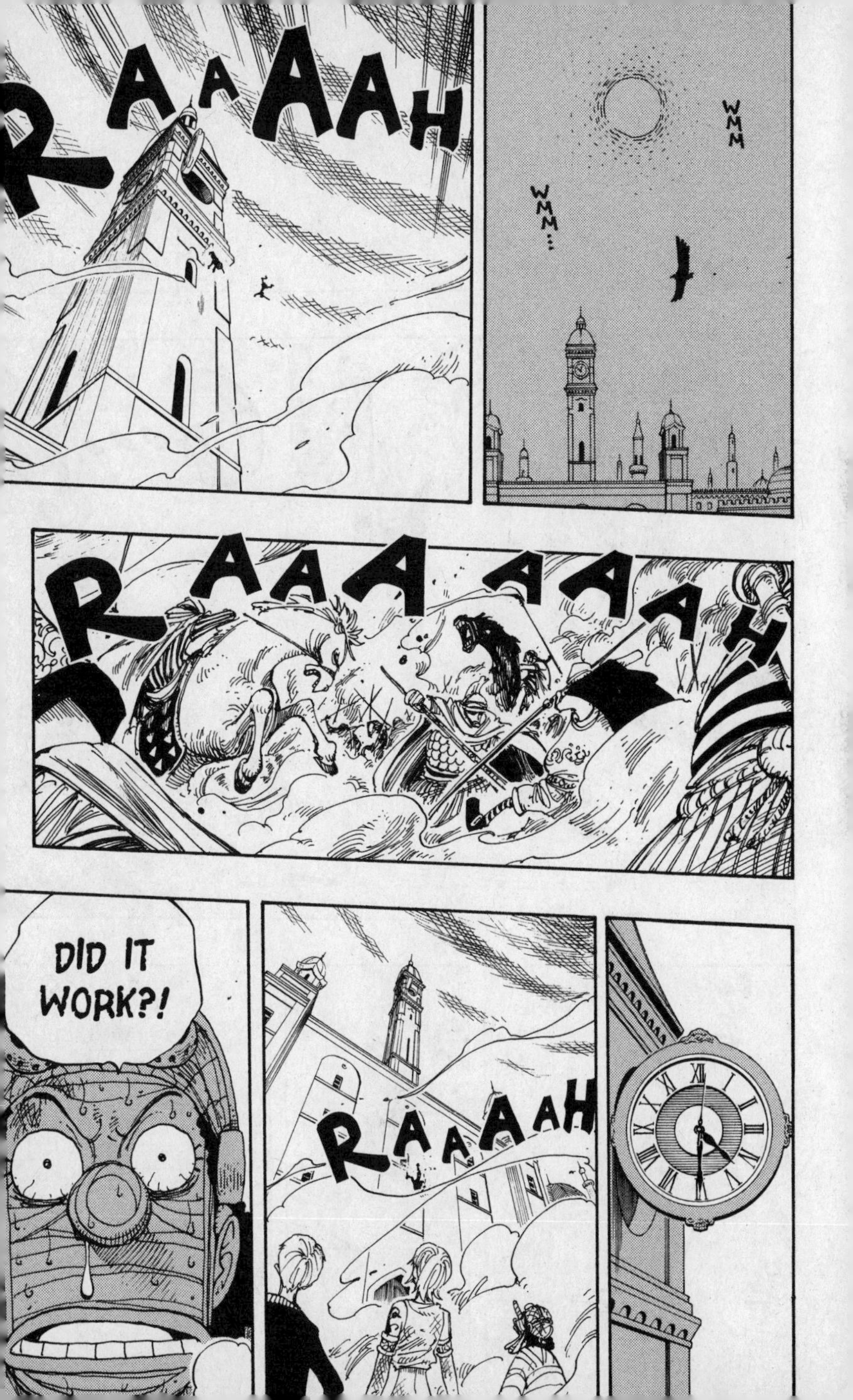
WMM
WMM...
RAAAAH
RAAAAAAH
RAAAAH
DID IT WORK?!

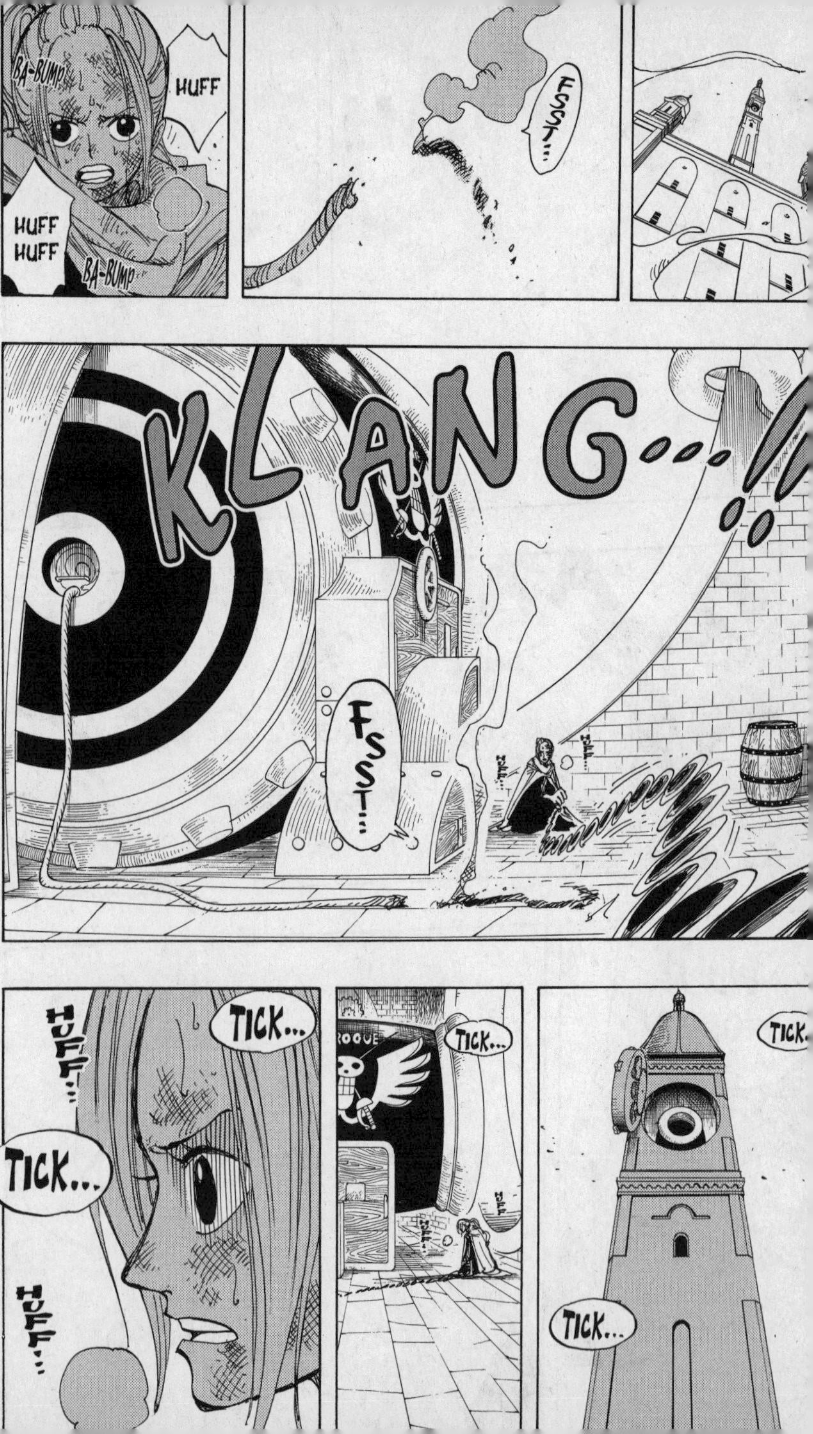

FSSST...
BA-BUMP
HUFF
HUFF HUFF
BA-BUMP
KLANG...!!
FSST...
HUFF...
HUFF...
TICK...
TICK...
TICK...
HUFF
HUFF...
TICK...
HUFF...
TICK...
HUFF...

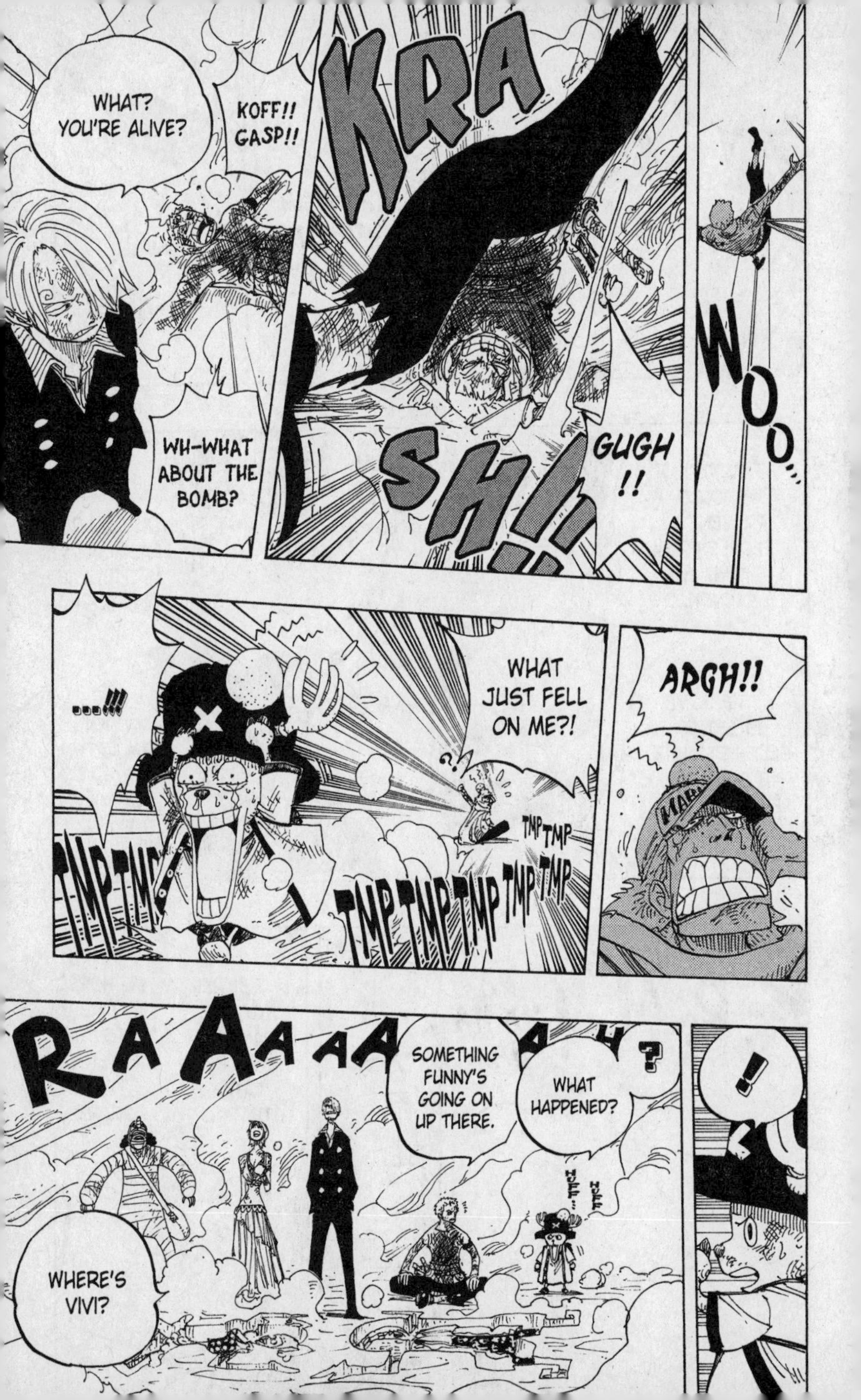
WOO...
KRA
GUGH!!
SH!!
KOFF!! GASP!!
WHAT? YOU'RE ALIVE?
WH-WHAT ABOUT THE BOMB?
ARGH!!
WHAT JUST FELL ON ME?!
TMP TMP TMP TMP
TMP TMP TMP TMP TMP
...!!!
TMP TMP
!
RAAAAAAAH?
WHAT HAPPENED?
SOMETHING FUNNY'S GOING ON UP THERE.
HUFF... HUFF
WHERE'S VIVI?

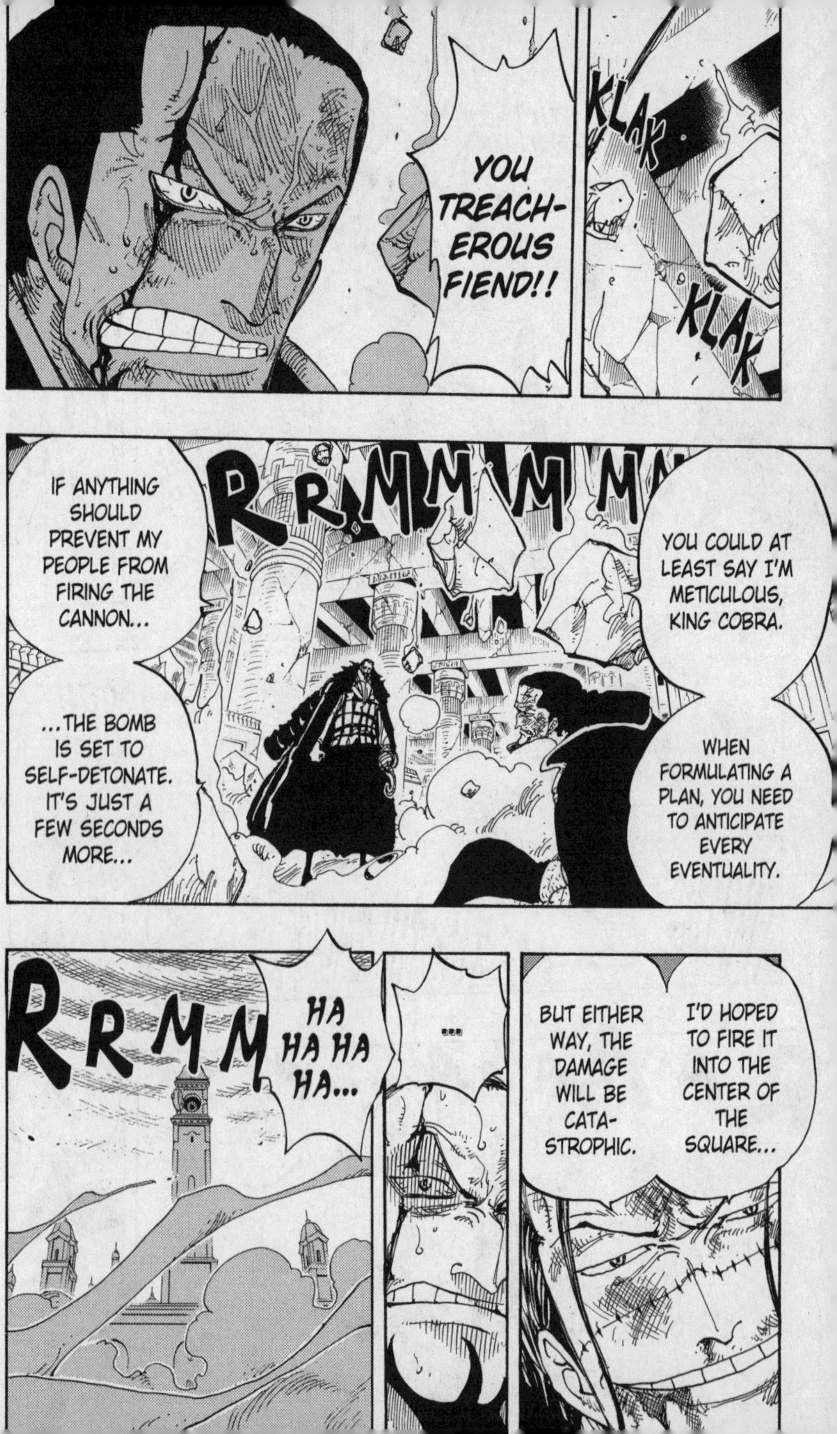
KLAK
KLAK
YOU TREACH-EROUS FIEND!!
RRMMMMMM
YOU COULD AT LEAST SAY I'M METICULOUS, KING COBRA.
WHEN FORMULATING A PLAN, YOU NEED TO ANTICIPATE EVERY EVENTUALITY.
IF ANYTHING SHOULD PREVENT MY PEOPLE FROM FIRING THE CANNON...
...THE BOMB IS SET TO SELF-DETONATE. IT'S JUST A FEW SECONDS MORE...
I'D HOPED TO FIRE IT INTO THE CENTER OF THE SQUARE...
BUT EITHER WAY, THE DAMAGE WILL BE CATA-STROPHIC.
...
HA HA HA HA...
RRMM

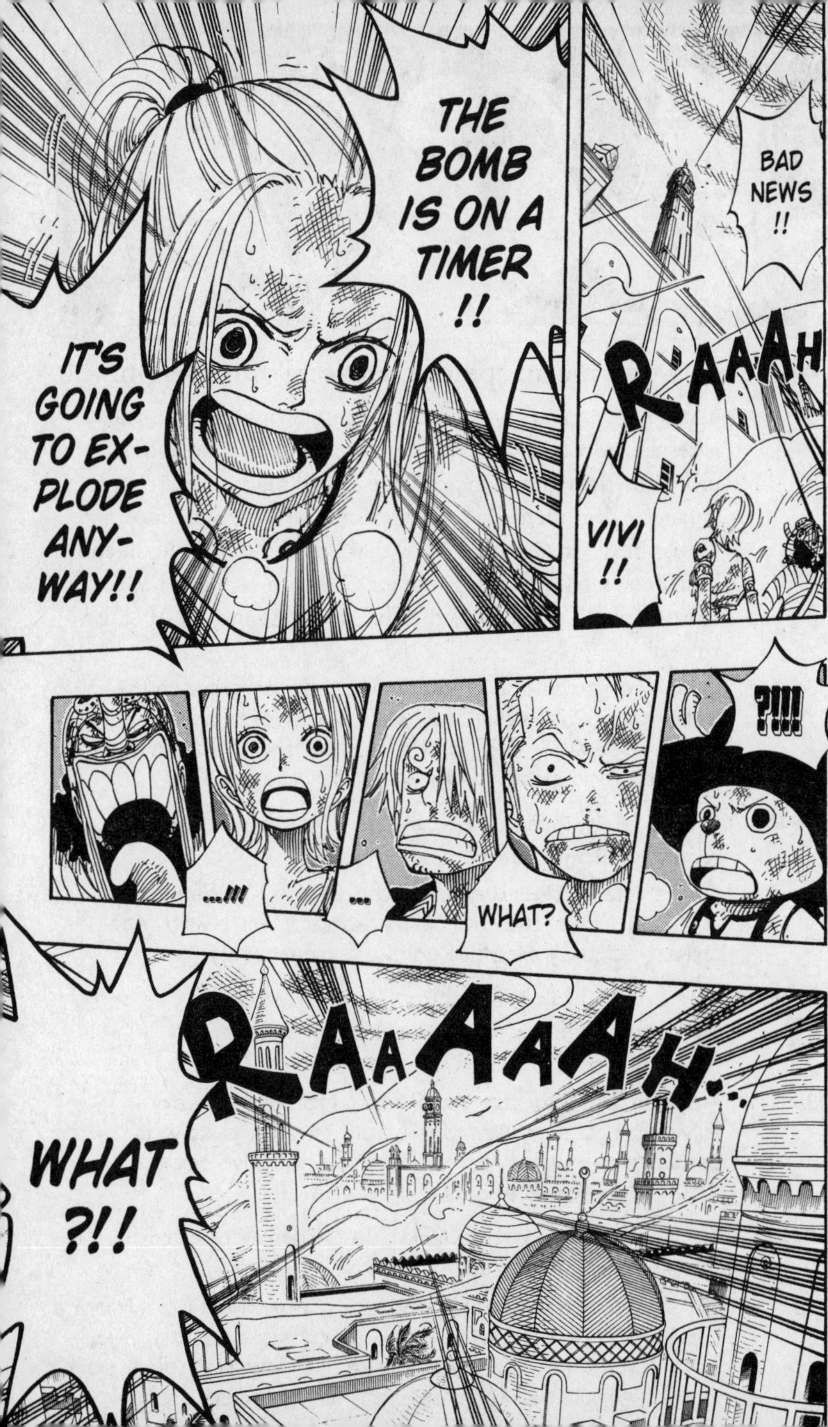
BAD NEWS!!
RAAAH
VIVI!!
THE BOMB IS ON A TIMER!!
IT'S GOING TO EX-PLODE ANY-WAY!!
?!!!
WHAT?
...
...!!!
RAAAAAH
WHAT?!!

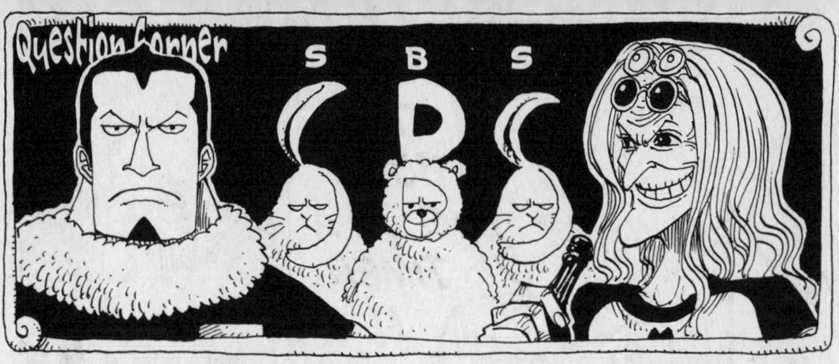
Question Corner
S B S
D

Reader: You owe me an apology, Odacchi! One "big-time" apology… You know all the Marimo terms and Moss head jokes you're using? (anger) Well, my name is Mariko and my nickname since the sixth grade has been "Marimo" (or "moss" in Japanese). But then you had to go and use "Kuromarimo" and "Moss head" in *One Piece*!! Now that I'm in middle school (and ever since the Drum Kingdom arc), kids are saying "Hey, fluffy Kuromarimo" to me (anger). What're you gonna do? My life is ruined!!

Oda: What're you saying? You're probably enjoying all the attention. Right?! If they say that to you again, just hit them back with this. **"Eat this!! Marimo's Static Cling!!"** Now go and show them how cool you are!!

Reader: Where did the members of Baroque Works go on their most recent company vacation?

Oda: I understand they went to the Snow Festival in Hokkaido. But they don't like hanging out with each other, so they all traveled there separately.

Reader: *Ring…ring…* Hello? Odacchi?
Stick your thumb in your mouth and turn around.
Made you do a sexy pose!♡ Hee hee, got you!

Oda: Hey hey. Did you see that? Man, I looked so sexy. Almost too sexy for this book! Whew, that was dangerous--we almost had to change the rating to a T+ (ages 16 and up).

Reader: No greeting, just a question. Has Ms. Golden Week eaten any Devil Fruit?

Oda: No, Ms. Golden Week's powers are derived not from a Devil Fruit but from the power of suggestion. She uses colors to make people feel nervous or weak so that they will be vulnerable to her attacks.

Chapter 208: GUARDIAN SPIRIT

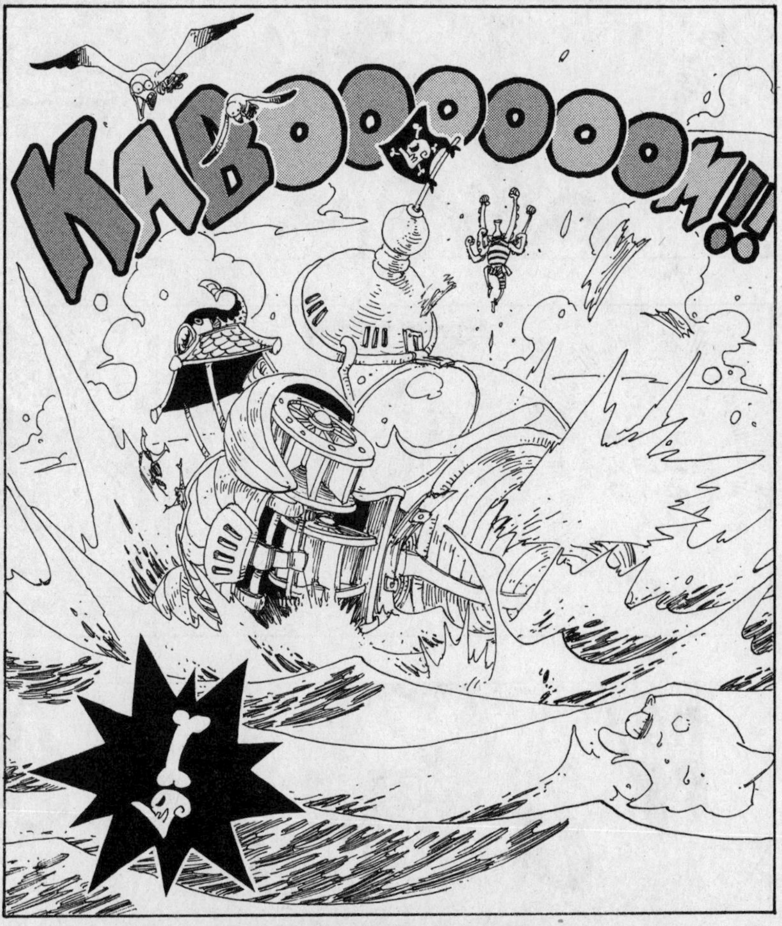
KABOOOOOOOM!!

HACHI'S WALK ON THE SEAFLOOR, VOL. 23:
"OCTOPUS FRITTER PUNCH!!"

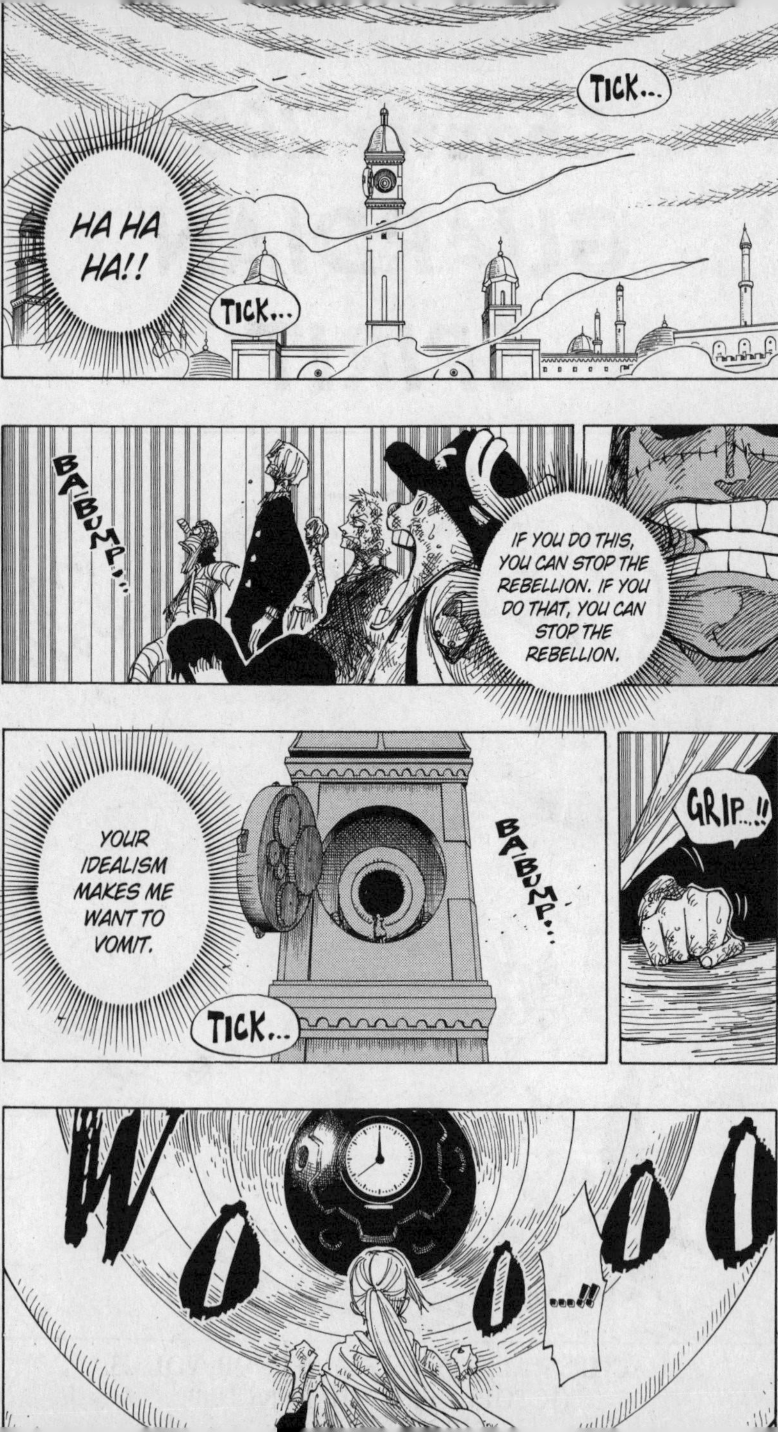
TICK...
HA HA HA!!
TICK...
IF YOU DO THIS, YOU CAN STOP THE REBELLION. IF YOU DO THAT, YOU CAN STOP THE REBELLION.
BA-BUMP...
GRIP...!!
BA-BUMP...
YOUR IDEALISM MAKES ME WANT TO VOMIT.
TICK...
WOOOOO...!!

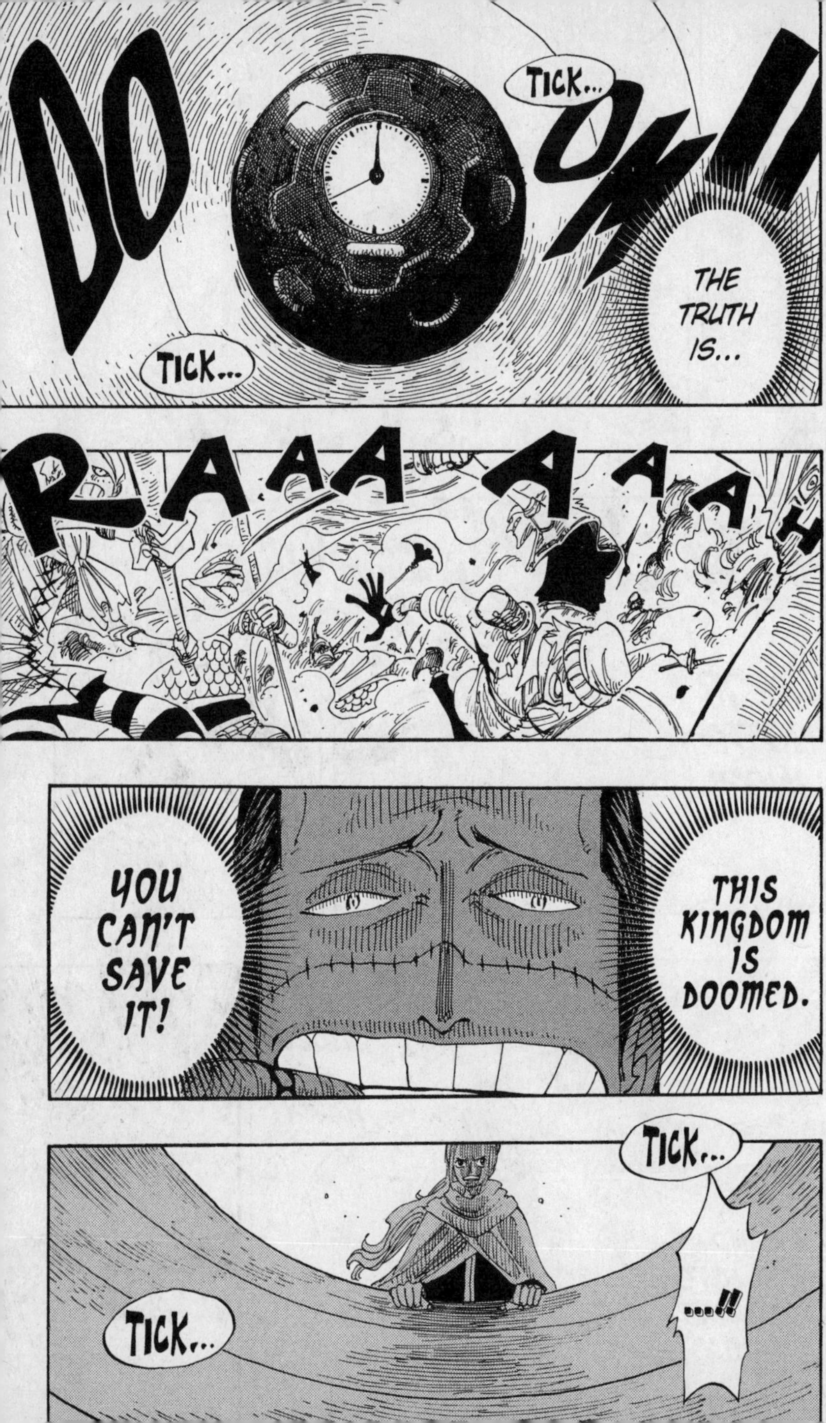
TICK...
DOOM!!
THE TRUTH IS...
TICK...
RAAAAAAAH
THIS KINGDOM IS DOOMED.
YOU CAN'T SAVE IT!
TICK...
...!!
TICK...

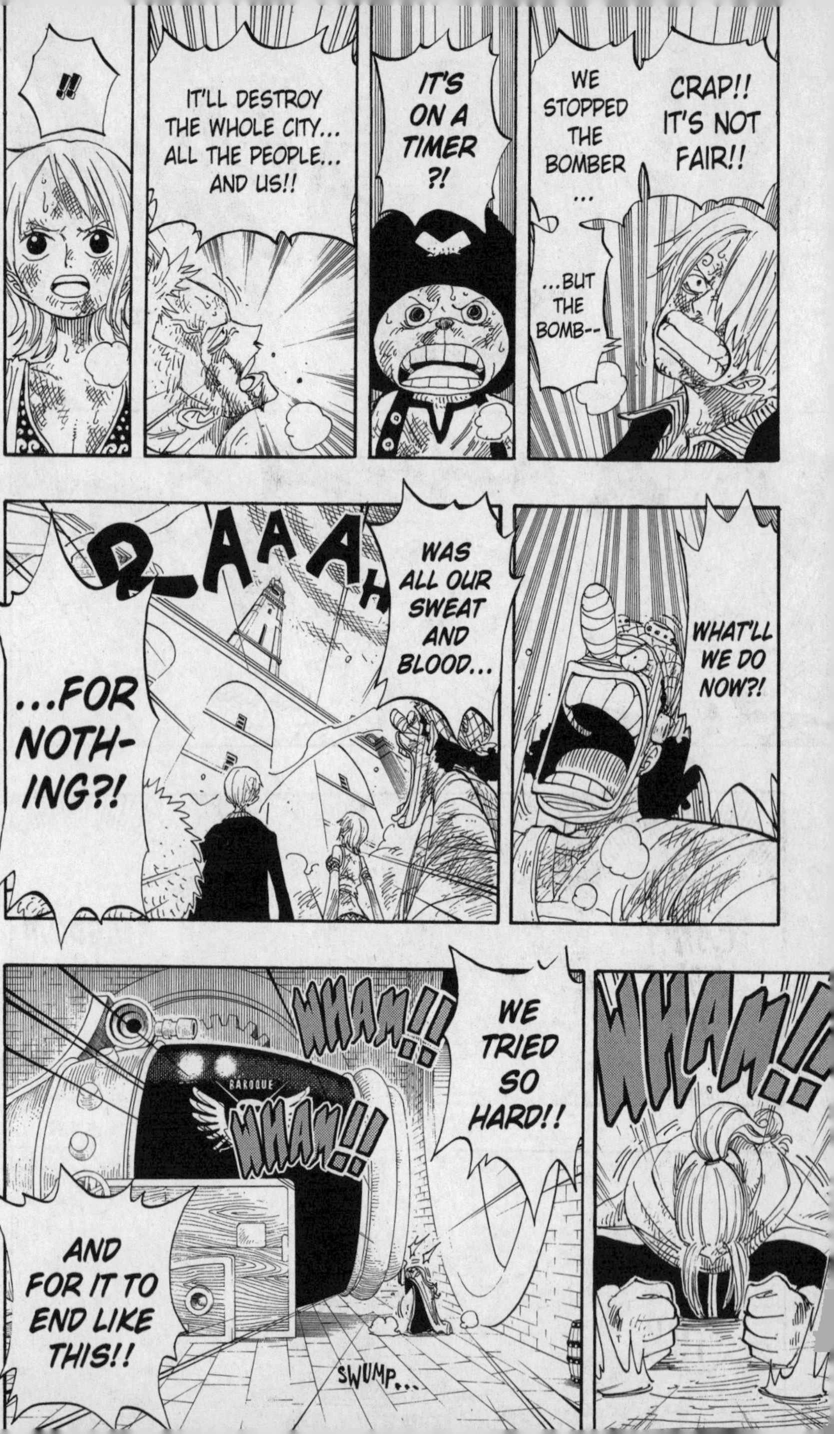
CRAP!! IT'S NOT FAIR!!
WE STOPPED THE BOMBER...
...BUT THE BOMB--
IT'S ON A TIMER?!
IT'LL DESTROY THE WHOLE CITY... ALL THE PEOPLE... AND US!!
!!
WHAT'LL WE DO NOW?!
WAS ALL OUR SWEAT AND BLOOD...
QAAAH
...FOR NOTHING?!
WHAM!!
WE TRIED SO HARD!!
WHAM!!
BAROQUE
WHAM!!
AND FOR IT TO END LIKE THIS!!
SWUMP...

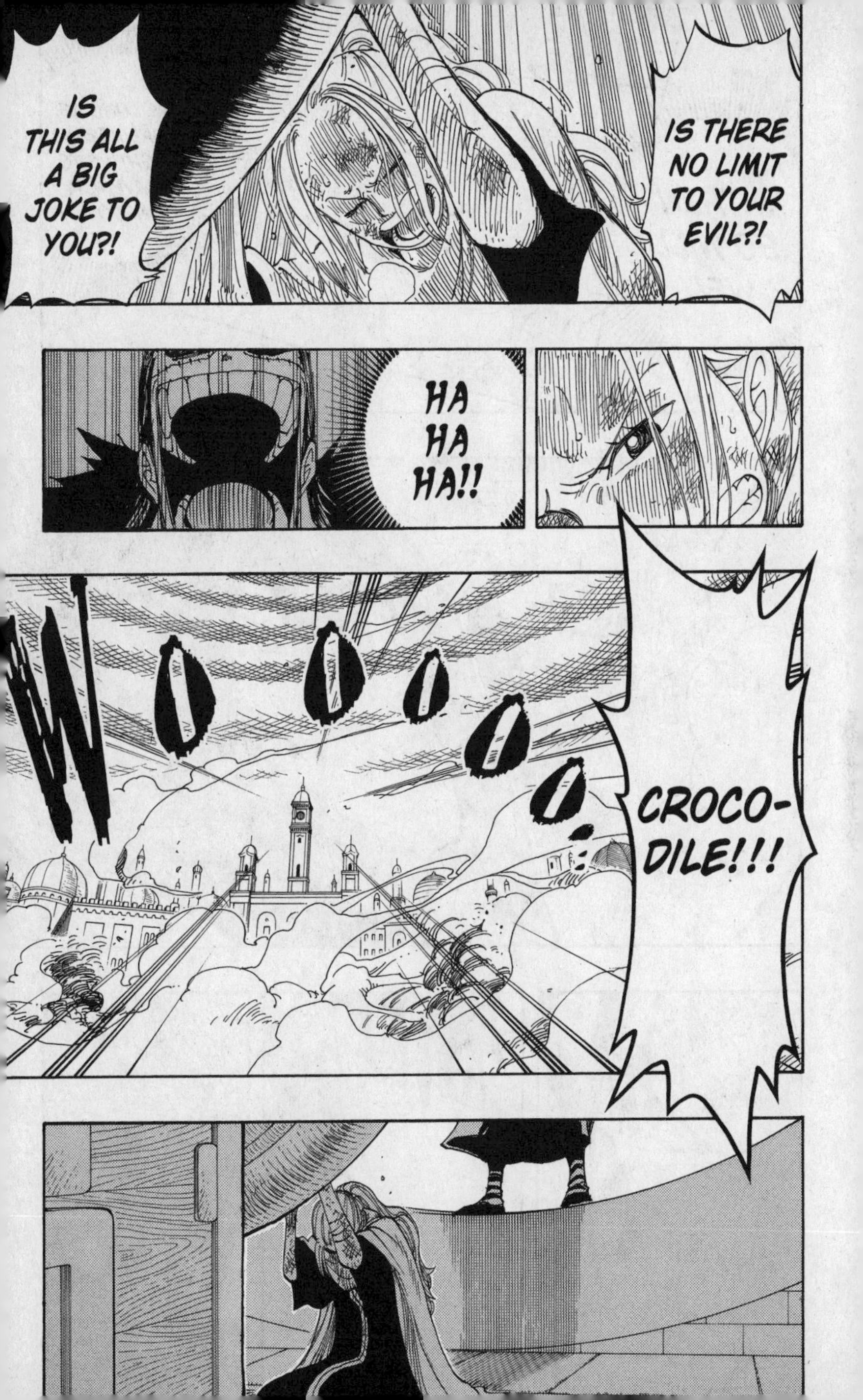
IS THERE NO LIMIT TO YOUR EVIL?!
IS THIS ALL A BIG JOKE TO YOU?!
HA HA HA!!
CROCO-DILE!!!

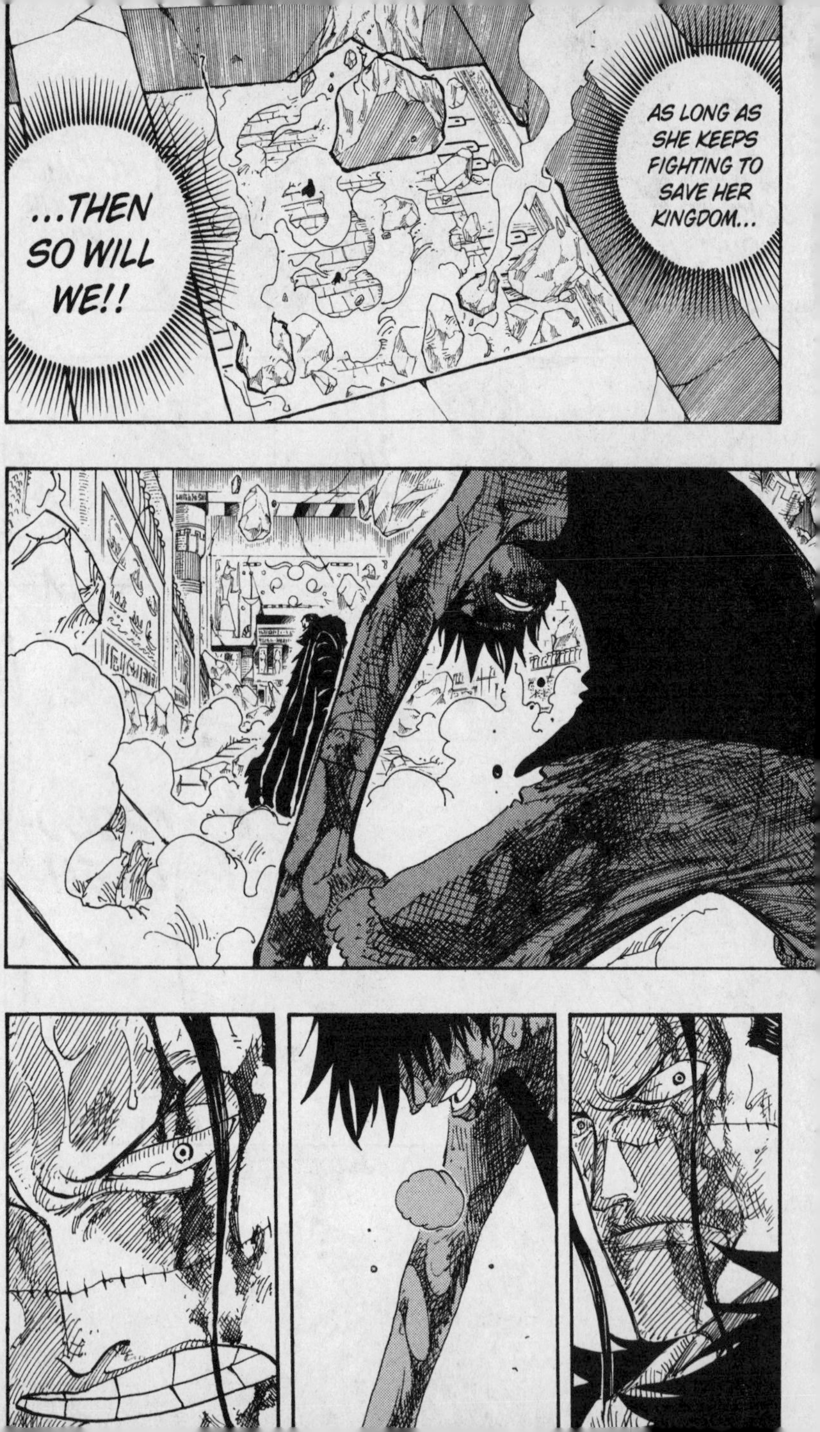
AS LONG AS SHE KEEPS FIGHTING TO SAVE HER KINGDOM...
...THEN SO WILL WE!!

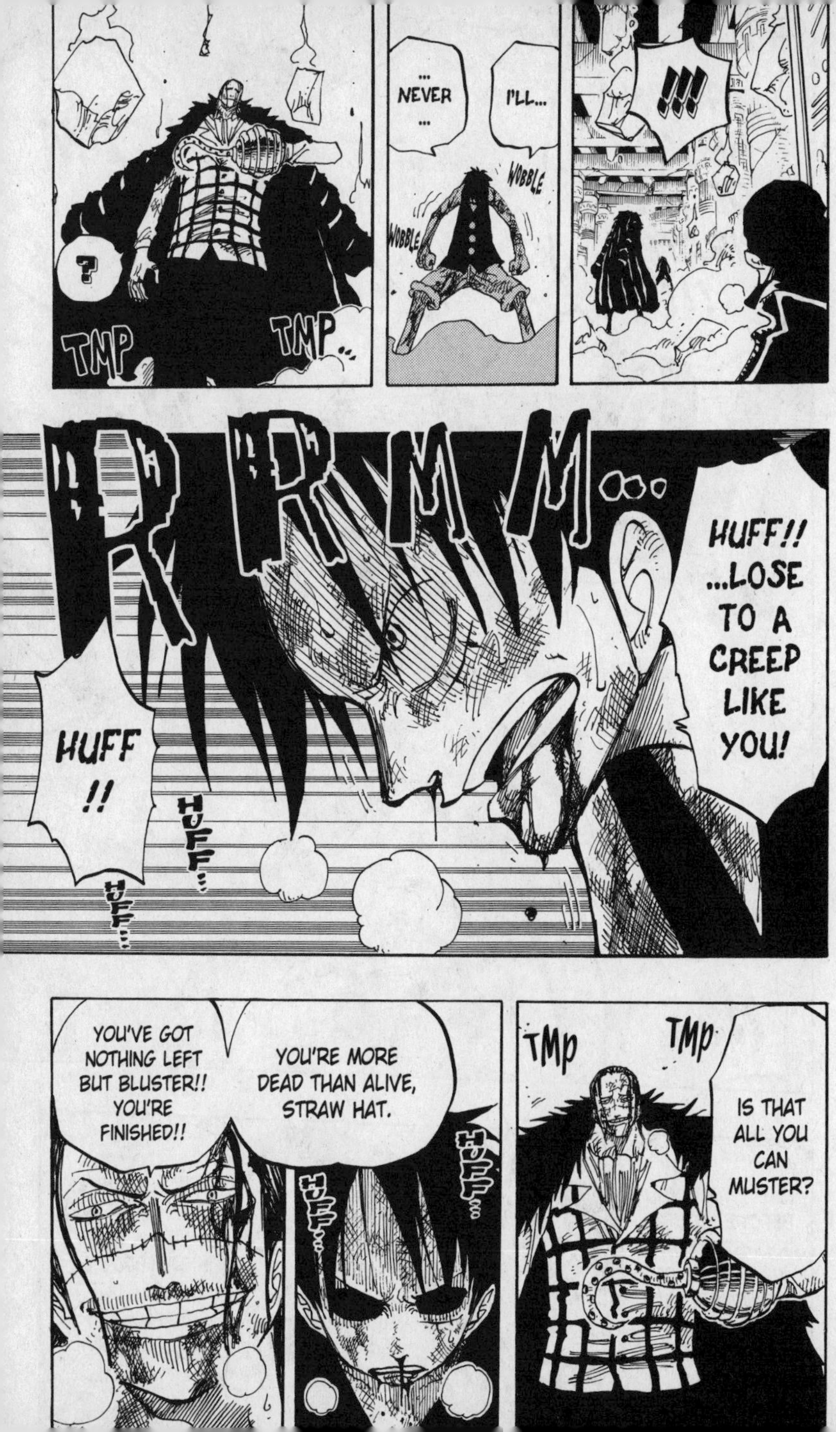
!!!
I'LL...
...NEVER...
WOBBLE
WOBBLE
?
TMP
TMP...
RMMM..
HUFF!! ...LOSE TO A CREEP LIKE YOU!
HUFF!!
HUFF...
HUFF...
TMP
TMP
IS THAT ALL YOU CAN MUSTER?
YOU'RE MORE DEAD THAN ALIVE, STRAW HAT.
YOU'VE GOT NOTHING LEFT BUT BLUSTER!! YOU'RE FINISHED!!
HUFF...
HUFF...

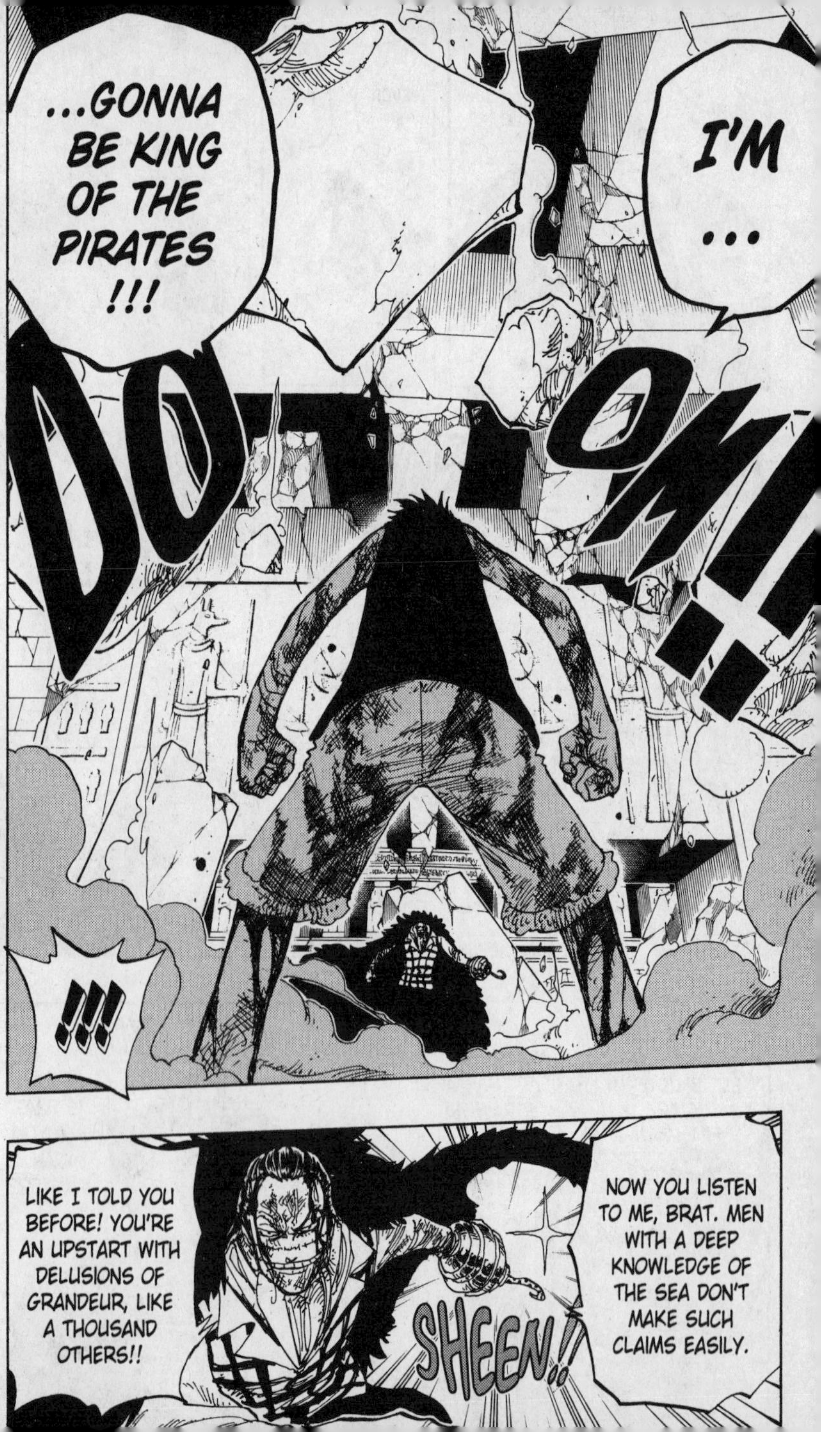
I'M ...
...GONNA BE KING OF THE PIRATES!!!
DOOM!!
!!!
NOW YOU LISTEN TO ME, BRAT. MEN WITH A DEEP KNOWLEDGE OF THE SEA DON'T MAKE SUCH CLAIMS EASILY.
SHEEN!!
LIKE I TOLD YOU BEFORE! YOU'RE AN UPSTART WITH DELUSIONS OF GRANDEUR, LIKE A THOUSAND OTHERS!!

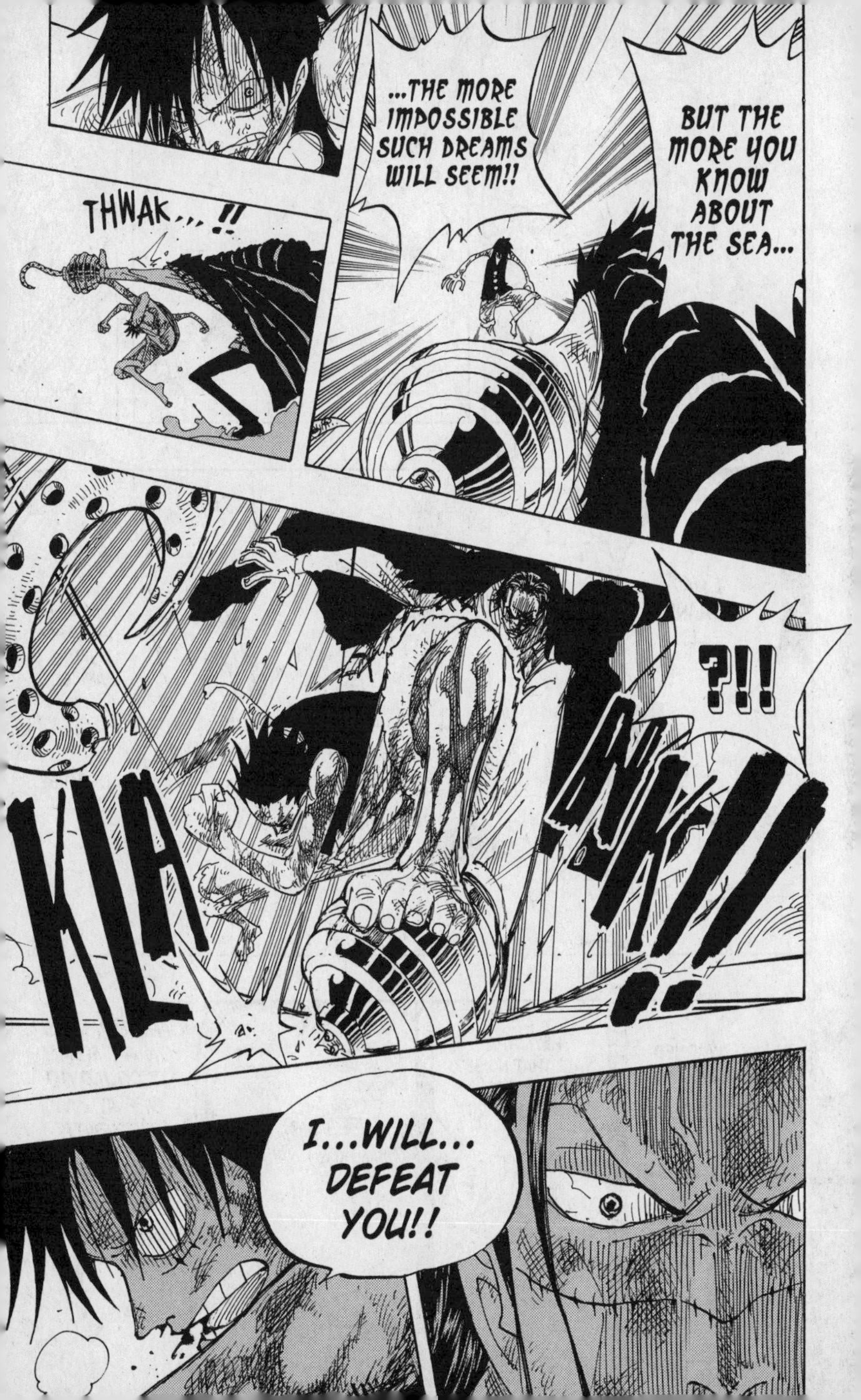
BUT THE MORE YOU KNOW ABOUT THE SEA...
...THE MORE IMPOSSIBLE SUCH DREAMS WILL SEEM!!
THWAK...!!
?!!
KLA
I...WILL... DEFEAT YOU!!

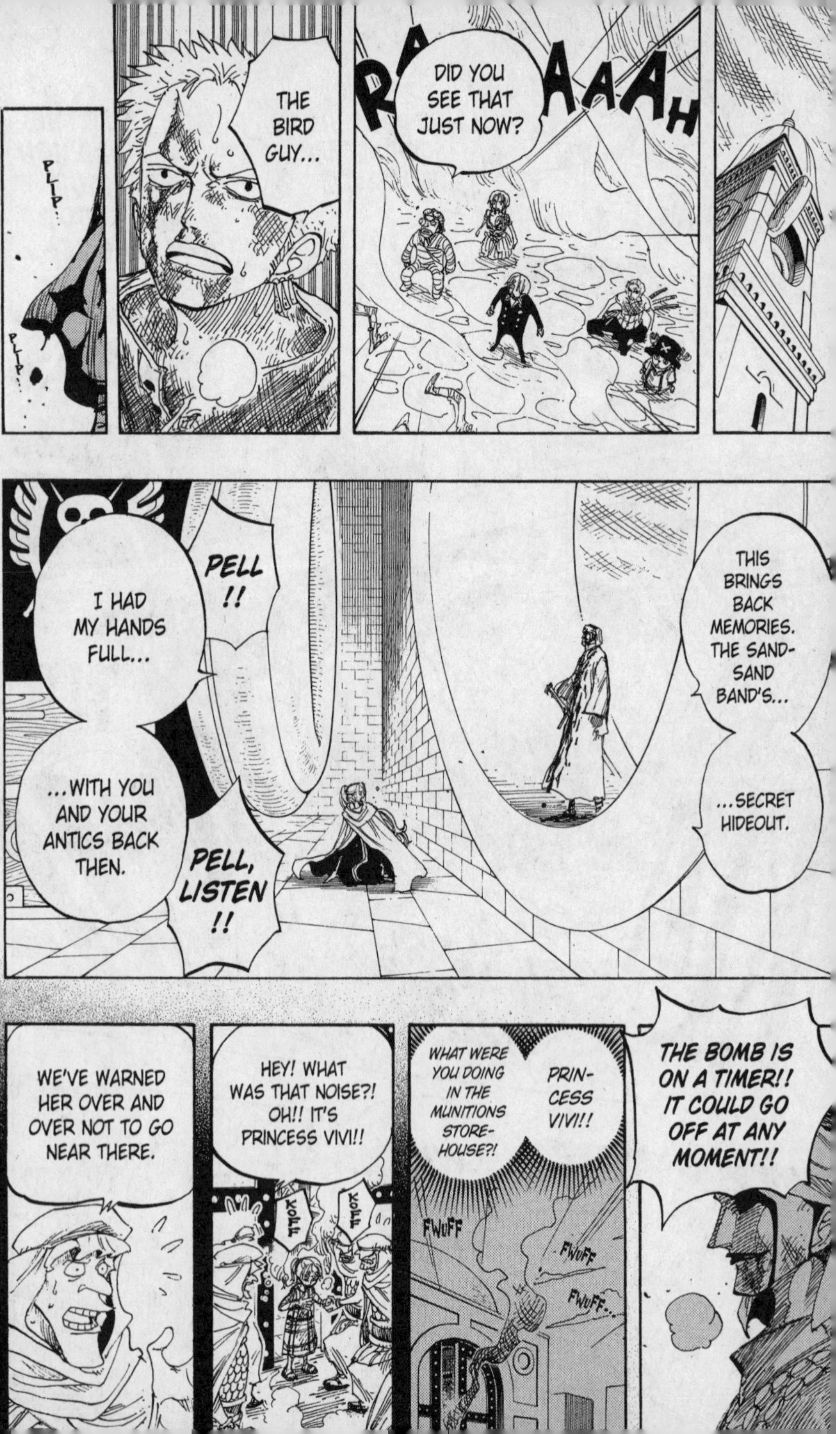
RAAAAH
DID YOU SEE THAT JUST NOW?
THE BIRD GUY...
PLIP...
PLIP...
THIS BRINGS BACK MEMORIES. THE SAND-SAND BAND'S...
...SECRET HIDEOUT.
PELL!!
I HAD MY HANDS FULL...
...WITH YOU AND YOUR ANTICS BACK THEN.
PELL, LISTEN!!
THE BOMB IS ON A TIMER!! IT COULD GO OFF AT ANY MOMENT!!
PRIN-CESS VIVI!!
WHAT WERE YOU DOING IN THE MUNITIONS STORE-HOUSE?!
FWUFF
FWUFF
FWUFF...
HEY! WHAT WAS THAT NOISE?! OH!! IT'S PRINCESS VIVI!!
KOFF
KOFF
WE'VE WARNED HER OVER AND OVER NOT TO GO NEAR THERE.

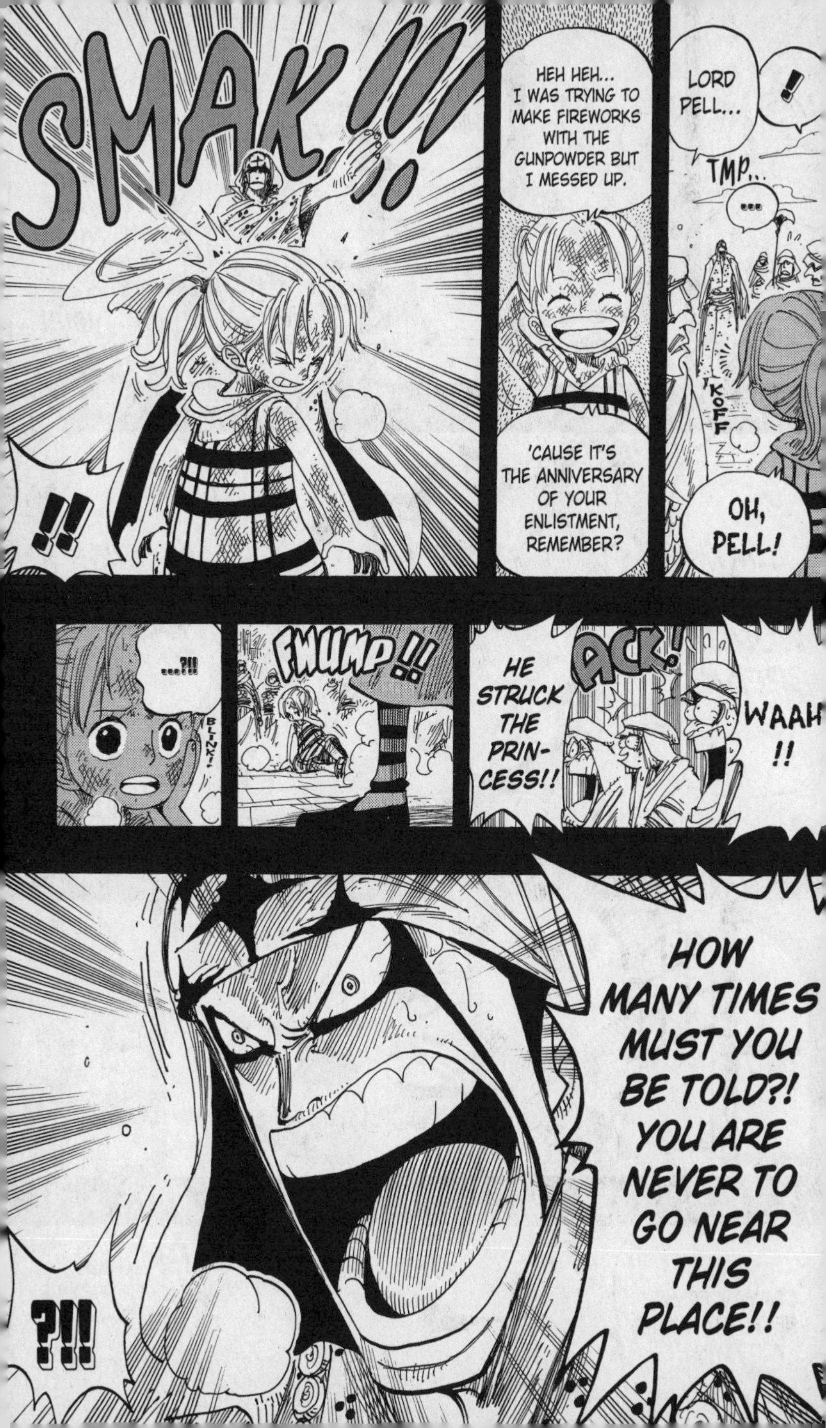
!
LORD PELL...
TMP...
...
KOFF
OH, PELL!
HEH HEH... I WAS TRYING TO MAKE FIREWORKS WITH THE GUNPOWDER BUT I MESSED UP.
'CAUSE IT'S THE ANNIVERSARY OF YOUR ENLISTMENT, REMEMBER?
SMAK!!!
!!
WAAH!!
ACK!
HE STRUCK THE PRIN-CESS!!
FWUMP!!
...?!!
BLINK!
HOW MANY TIMES MUST YOU BE TOLD?! YOU ARE NEVER TO GO NEAR THIS PLACE!!
?!!

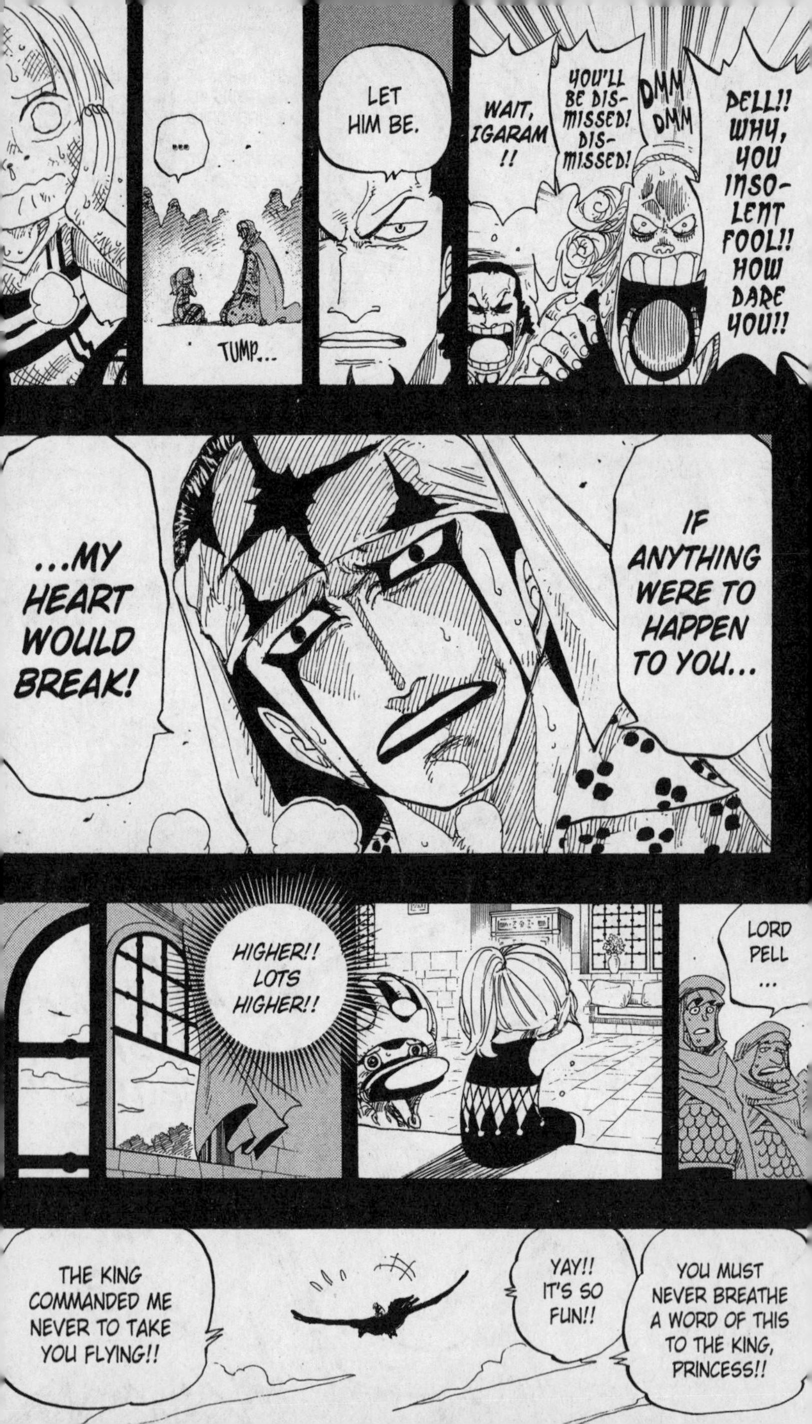
PELL!! WHY, YOU INSOLENT FOOL!! HOW DARE YOU!!
DMM DMM
YOU'LL BE DISMISSED! DISMISSED!
WAIT, IGARAM!!
LET HIM BE.
...
TUMP...
IF ANYTHING WERE TO HAPPEN TO YOU...
...MY HEART WOULD BREAK!
LORD PELL...
HIGHER!! LOTS HIGHER!!
YOU MUST NEVER BREATHE A WORD OF THIS TO THE KING, PRINCESS!!
YAY!! IT'S SO FUN!!
THE KING COMMANDED ME NEVER TO TAKE YOU FLYING!!

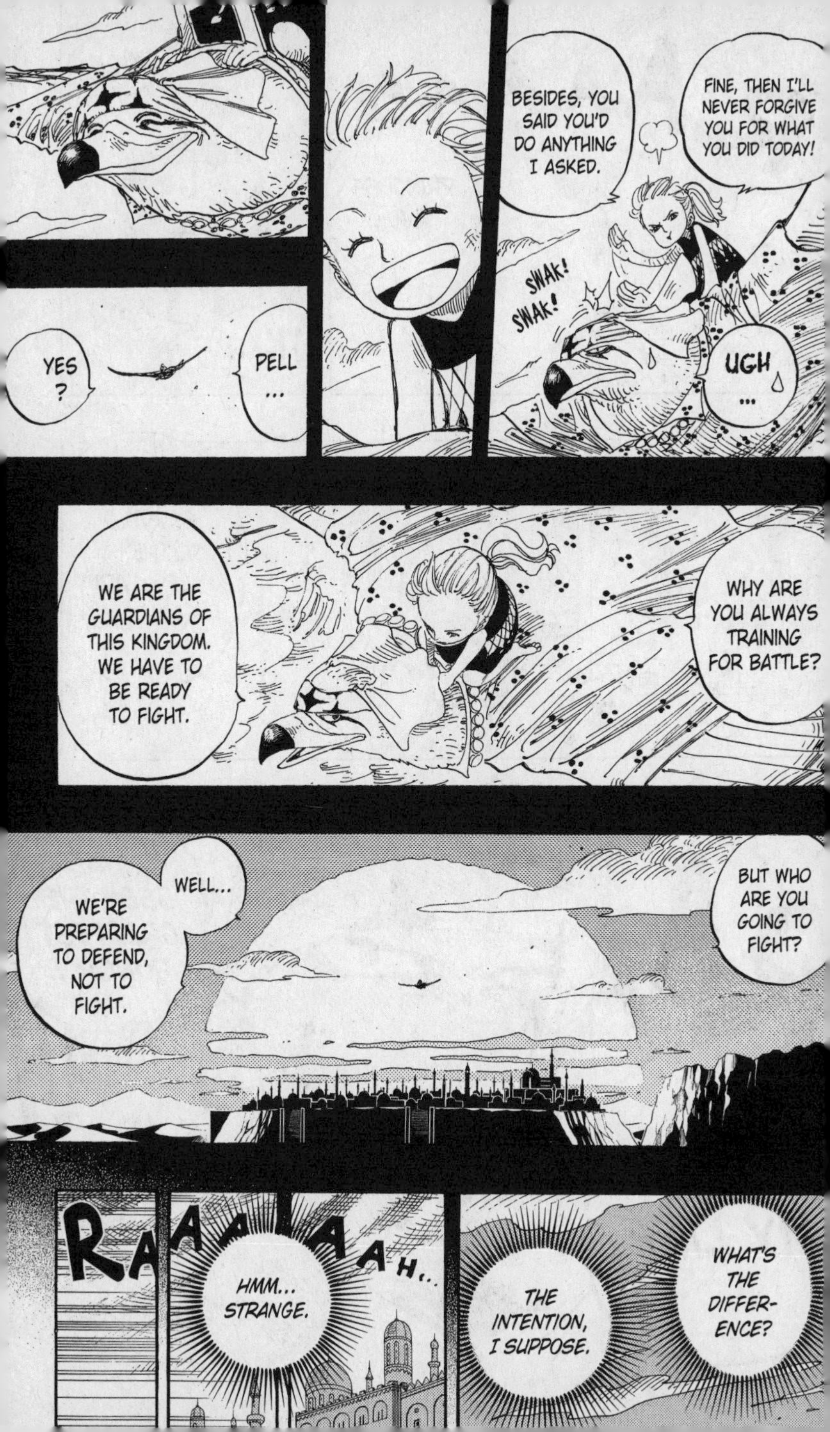
FINE, THEN I'LL NEVER FORGIVE YOU FOR WHAT YOU DID TODAY!
SWAK! SWAK!
UGH...
BESIDES, YOU SAID YOU'D DO ANYTHING I ASKED.
PELL...
YES?
WHY ARE YOU ALWAYS TRAINING FOR BATTLE?
WE ARE THE GUARDIANS OF THIS KINGDOM. WE HAVE TO BE READY TO FIGHT.
BUT WHO ARE YOU GOING TO FIGHT?
WELL...
WE'RE PREPARING TO DEFEND, NOT TO FIGHT.
WHAT'S THE DIFFER-ENCE?
THE INTENTION, I SUPPOSE.
HMM... STRANGE.
RAAAAAH...

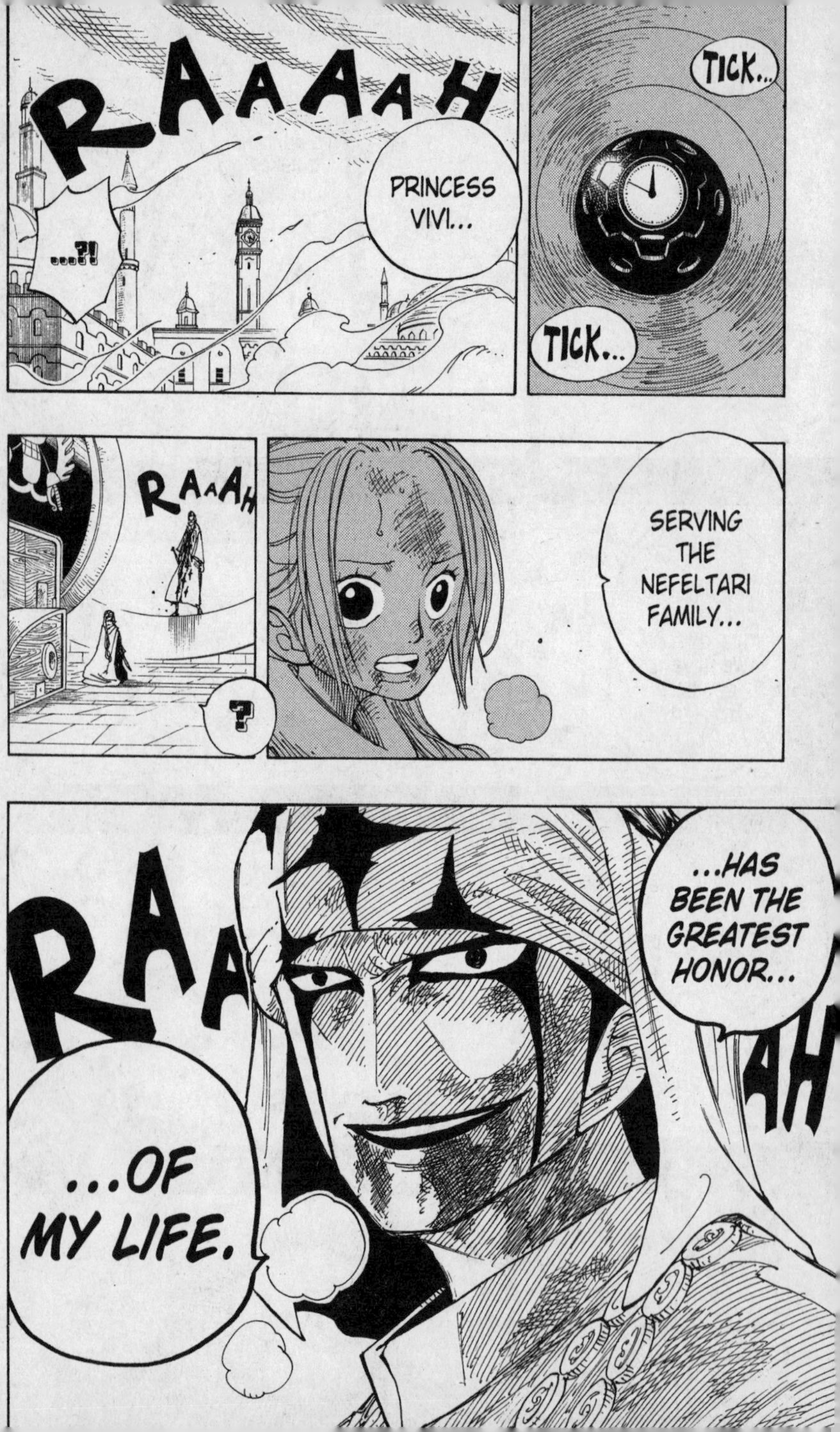
TICK...
TICK...
RAAAAH
PRINCESS VIVI...
...?!
SERVING THE NEFELTARI FAMILY...
RAAAH
?
...HAS BEEN THE GREATEST HONOR...
RAA
AH
...OF MY LIFE.

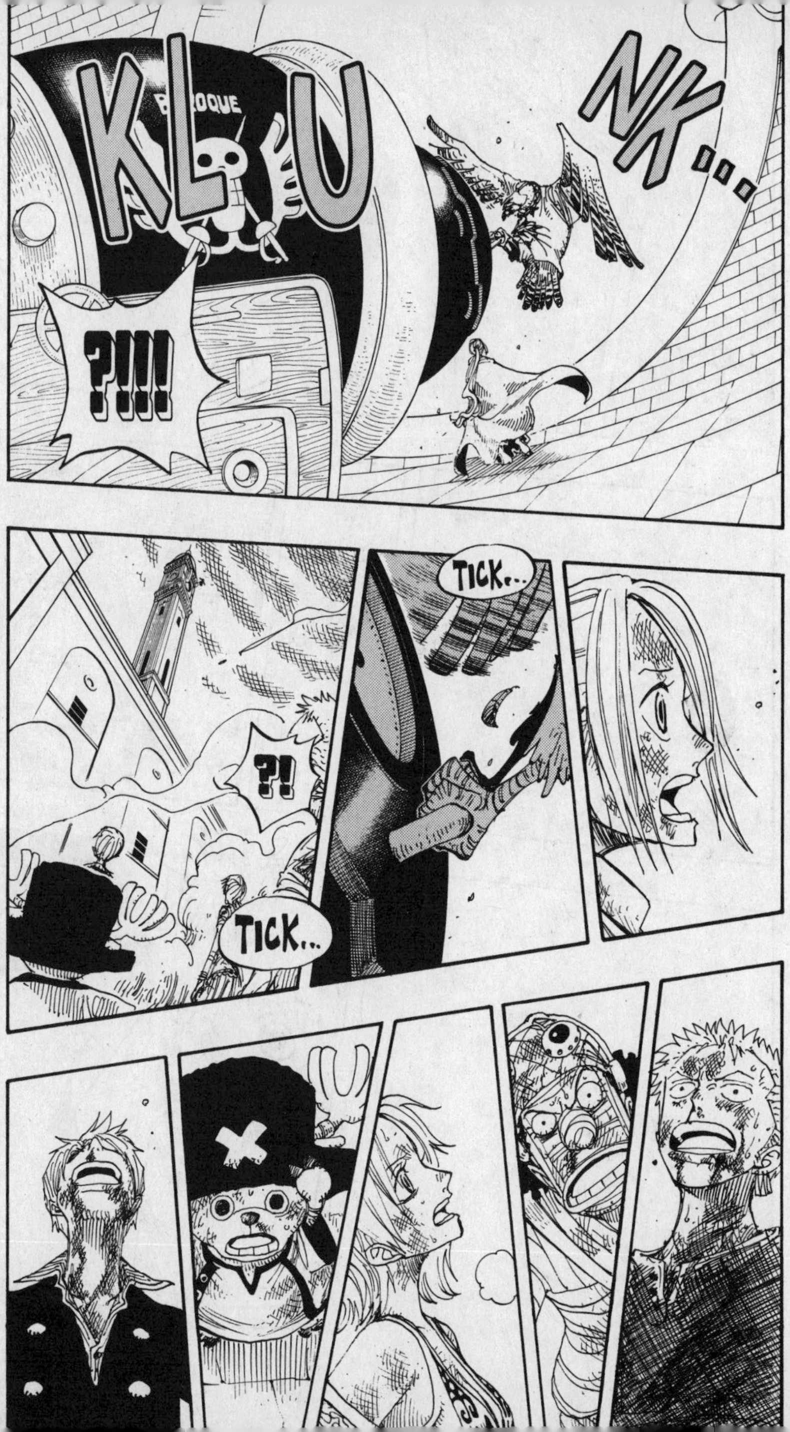
KLUNK...
?!!!
TICK...
?!
TICK...

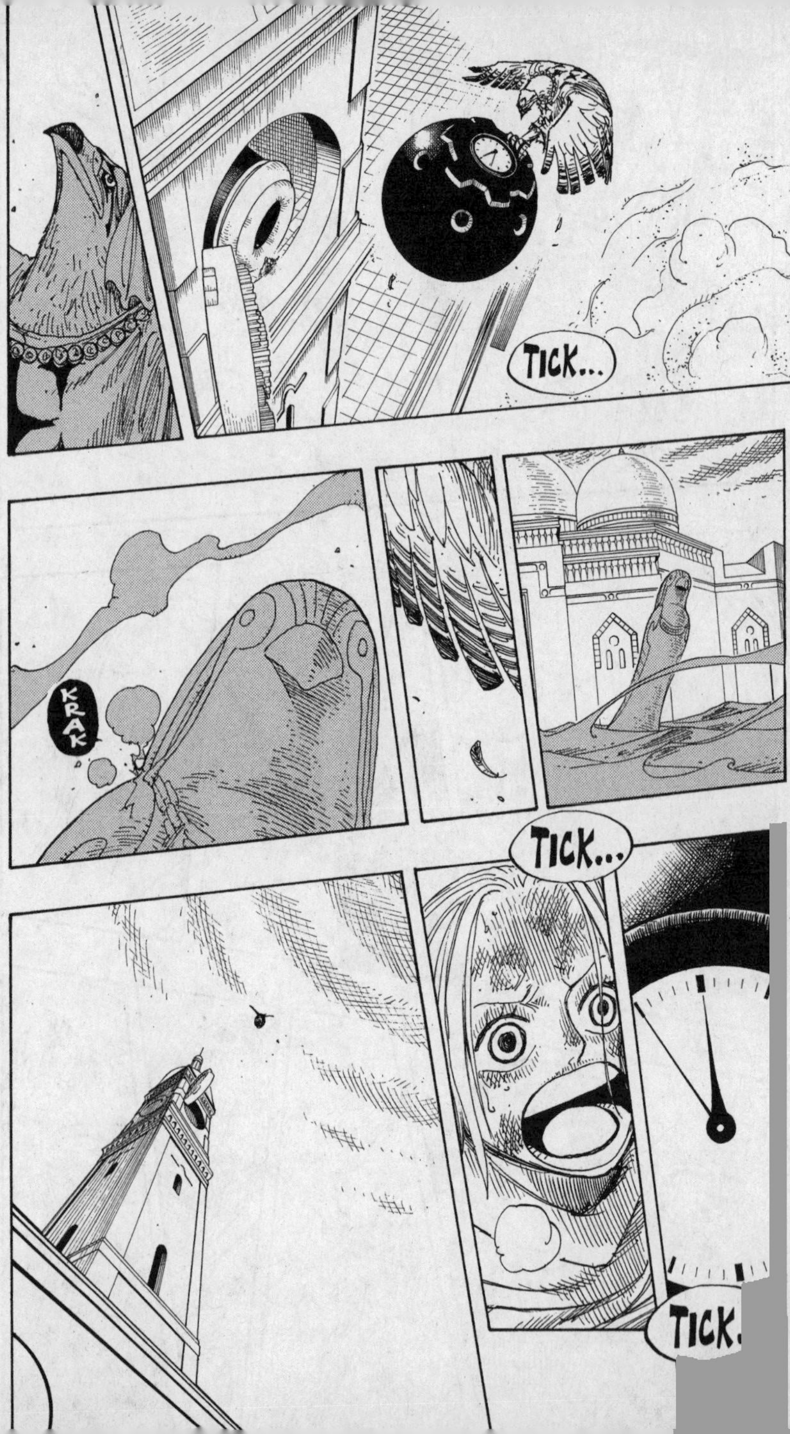
TICK...
KRAK
TICK...
TICK.

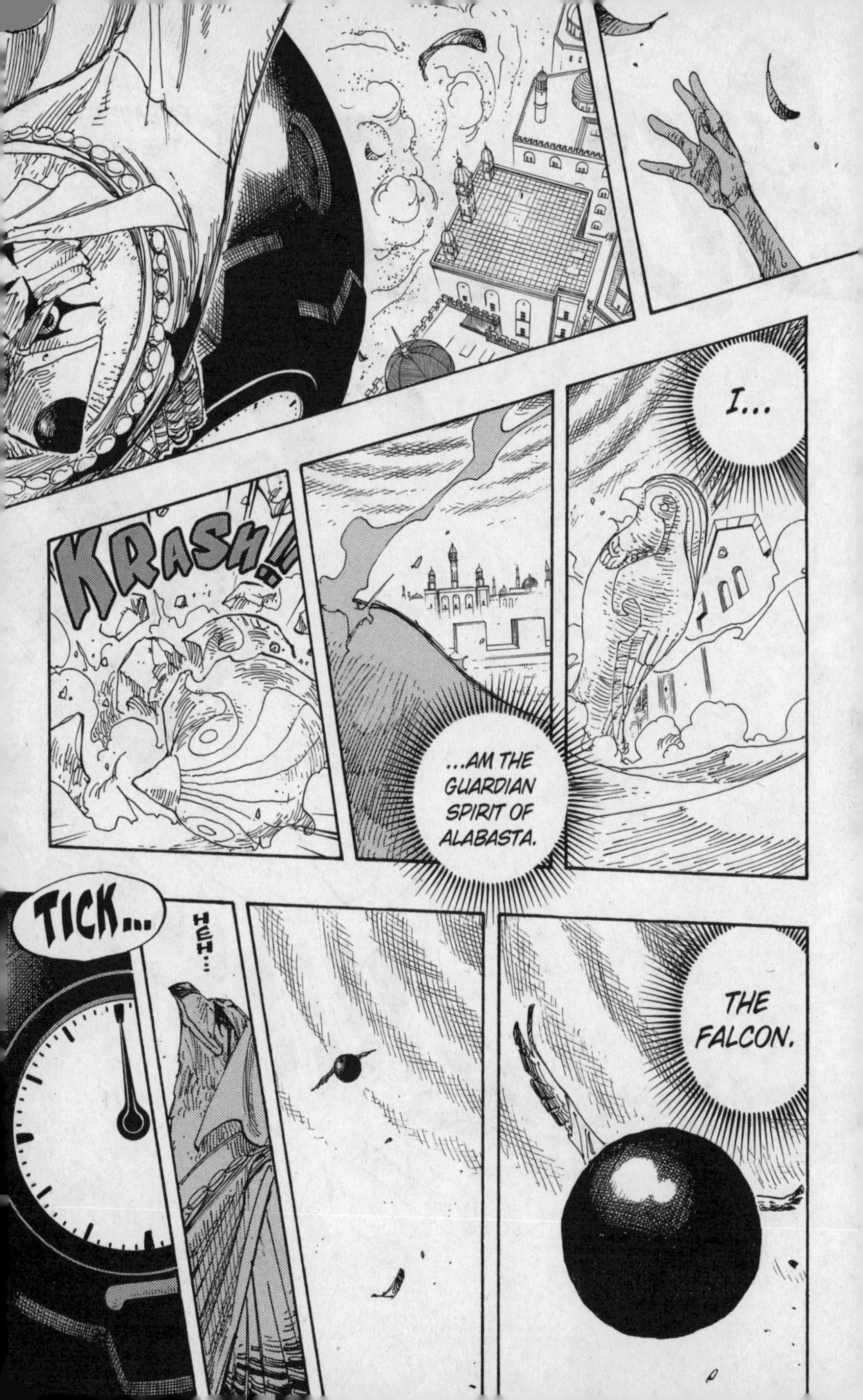
I...
...AM THE GUARDIAN SPIRIT OF ALABASTA.
KRASH!!
THE FALCON.
HEH...
TICK...

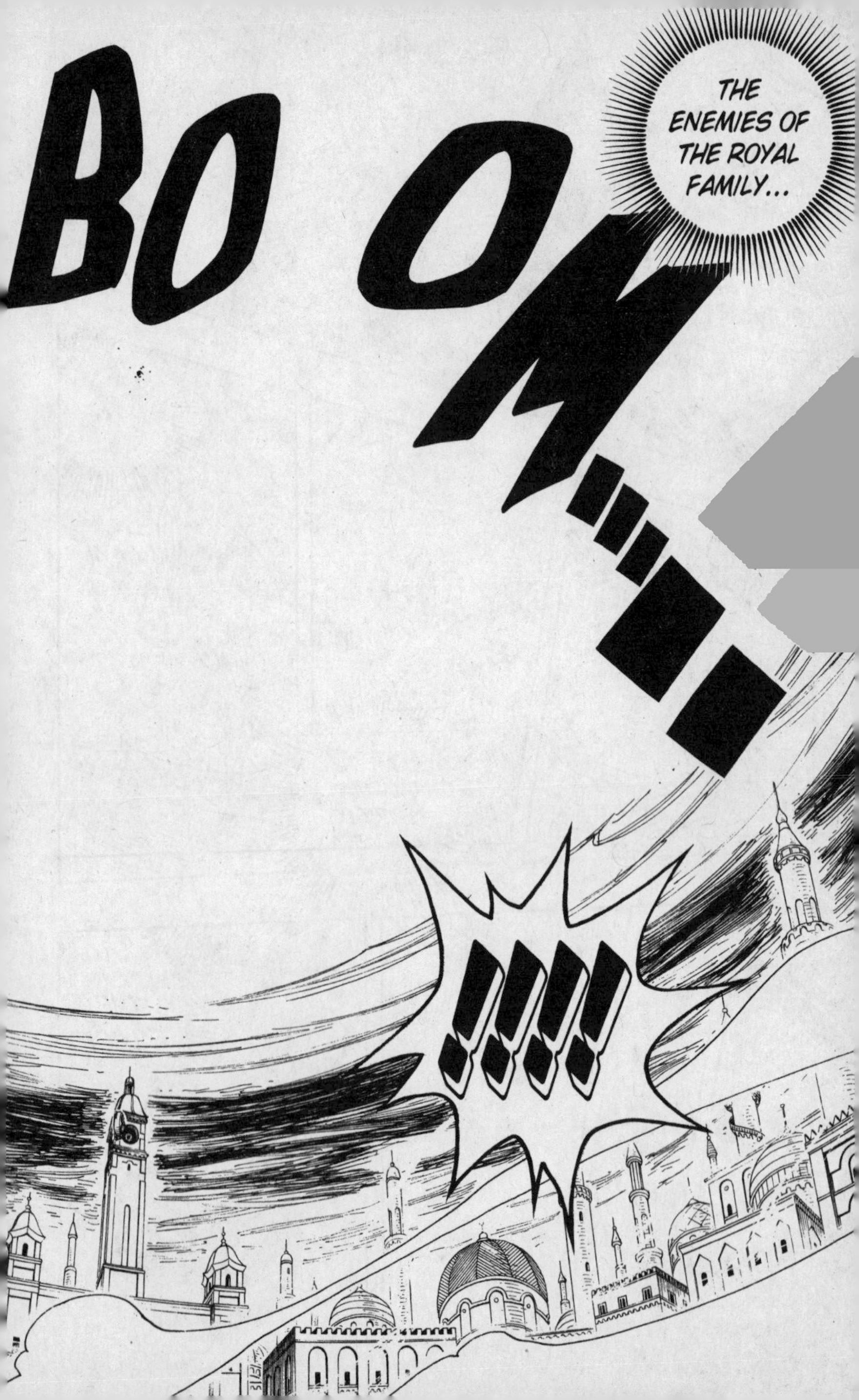
THE ENEMIES OF THE ROYAL FAMILY...
BOOM!!!!

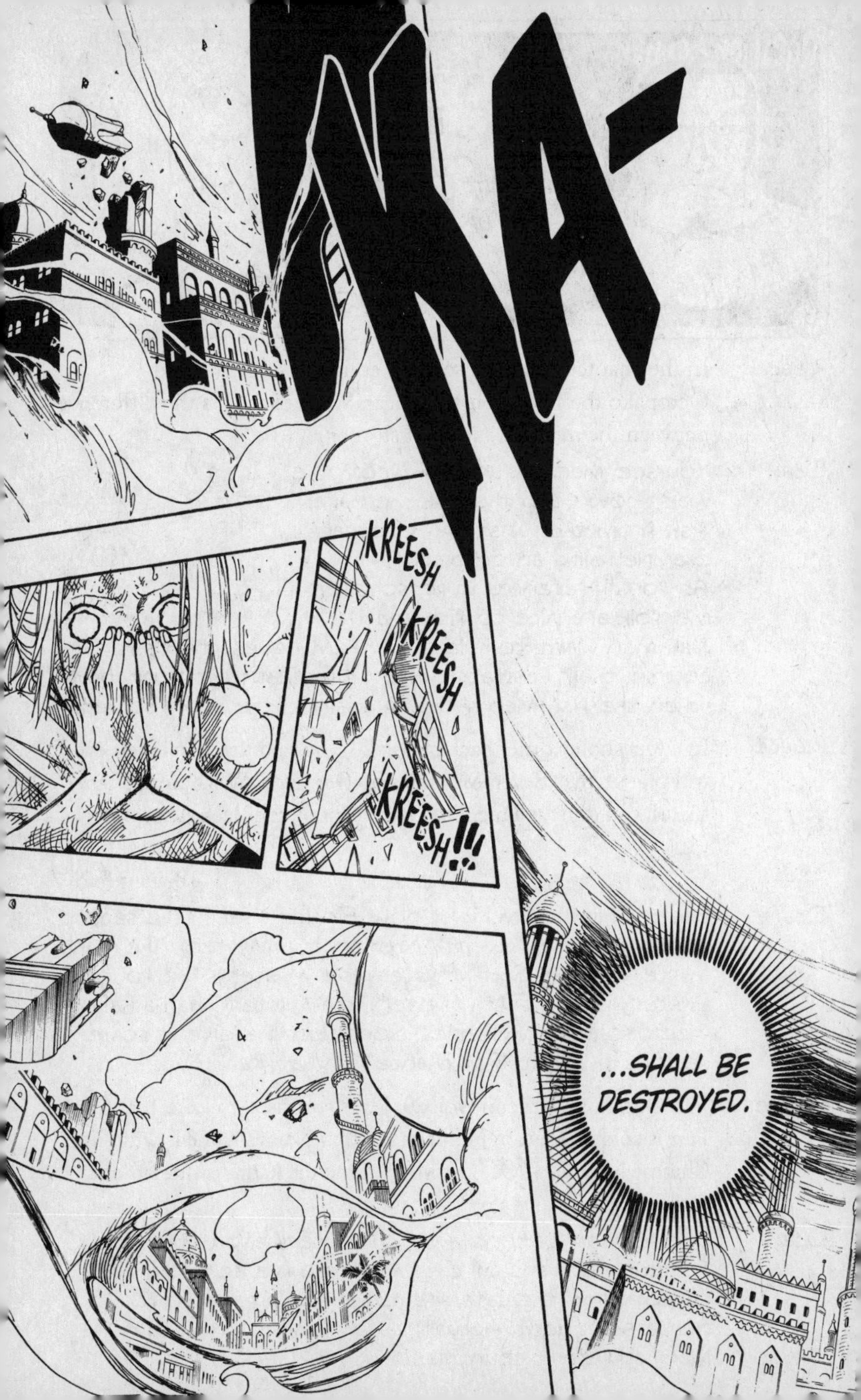
KREESH
KREESH
KREESH!!!
...SHALL BE DESTROYED.

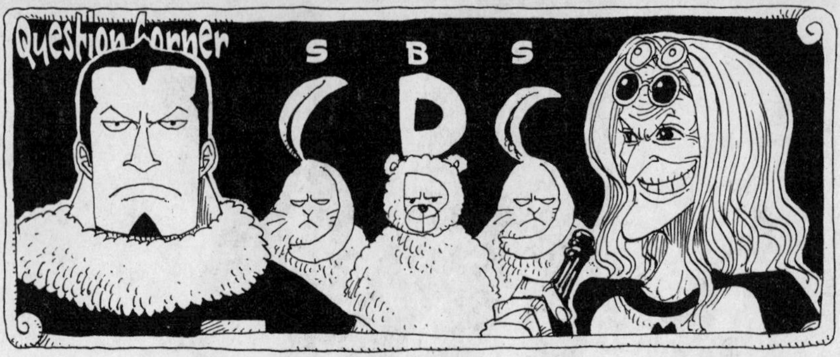
Question Corner
S B S

Reader: In the chapter title page series, Camie the Mermaid and Octopako the Fish-woman appear. What exactly is the difference between the merfolk and the fish-men?

Oda: You see, merfolk are fish from the waist down, and the fish-men are fish from the waist up. Here's an example using an octopus. (→)

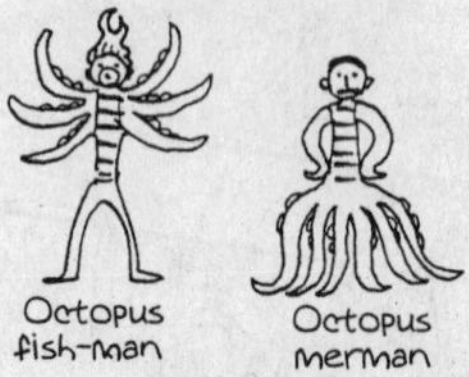
Octopus fish-man
Octopus merman

As for differences in personality, merfolk are nice to fish and the fish-men want to rule over them. I guess that's it. Of course, their habitats differ as well, but more on that when the fish-men show up again in the story someday.

Reader: In a Question Corner back in vol. 20, you said that Sanji's left eye was one of the "Seven Mysteries of *One Piece*." What are the other six? If you don't tell me, I'll do an "Out of the Back Attack" on you!

--Blatant Fool

Oda: Right, I'll list them right now. Er, let's see... The second mystery is...the Seventh Mystery is a Mystery! The third mystery is...the Sixth Mystery is a Mystery! The fourth mystery is...the Fifth Mystery is a Mystery! Ha ha ha! Geez, so many mysteries! Sorry. Let me give it some serious thought. (Fat chance.) (What, really?)

Reader: In a Question Corner in vol. 20, I was surprised to learn that *One Piece* is sold in Taiwan. I understand that Nami's name is written in Chinese like this: 娜実. Can you tell me the kanji for the other main characters and Vivi?

Oda: We've been getting a lot of letters about the foreign versions of *One Piece,* so I've been thinking of compiling the data and dedicating a page to it. So please be patient. Actually, *One Piece* is published in many different countries.

Chapter 209:
I WILL DEFEAT YOU

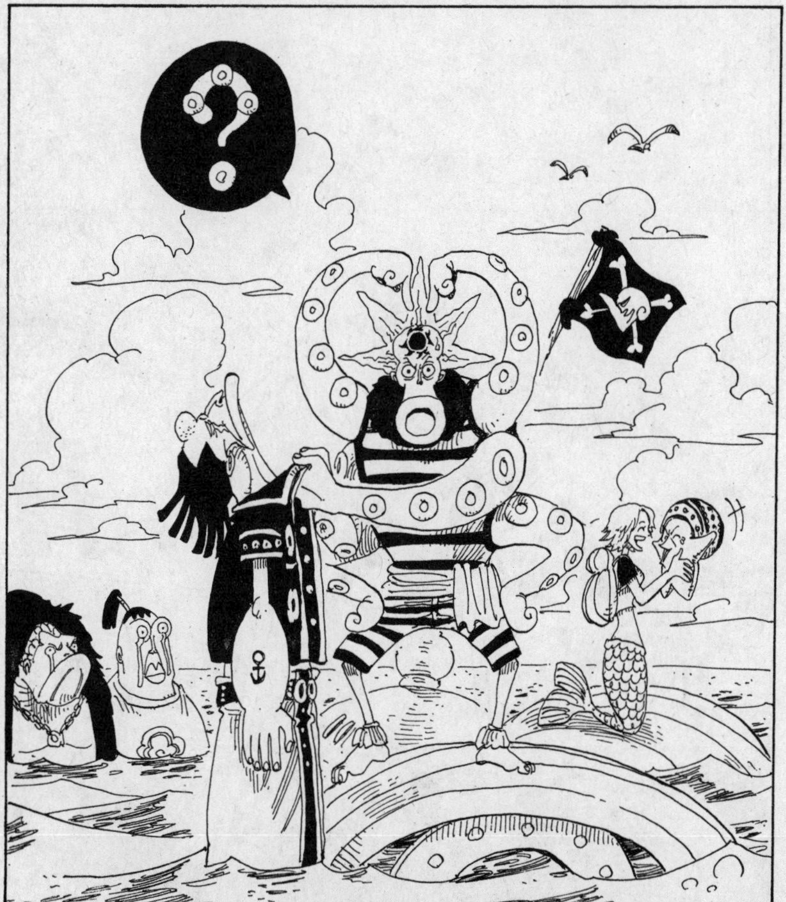
?

HACHI'S WALK ON THE SEAFLOOR, VOL. 24:
"BUT WE DIDN'T TRICK YOU"

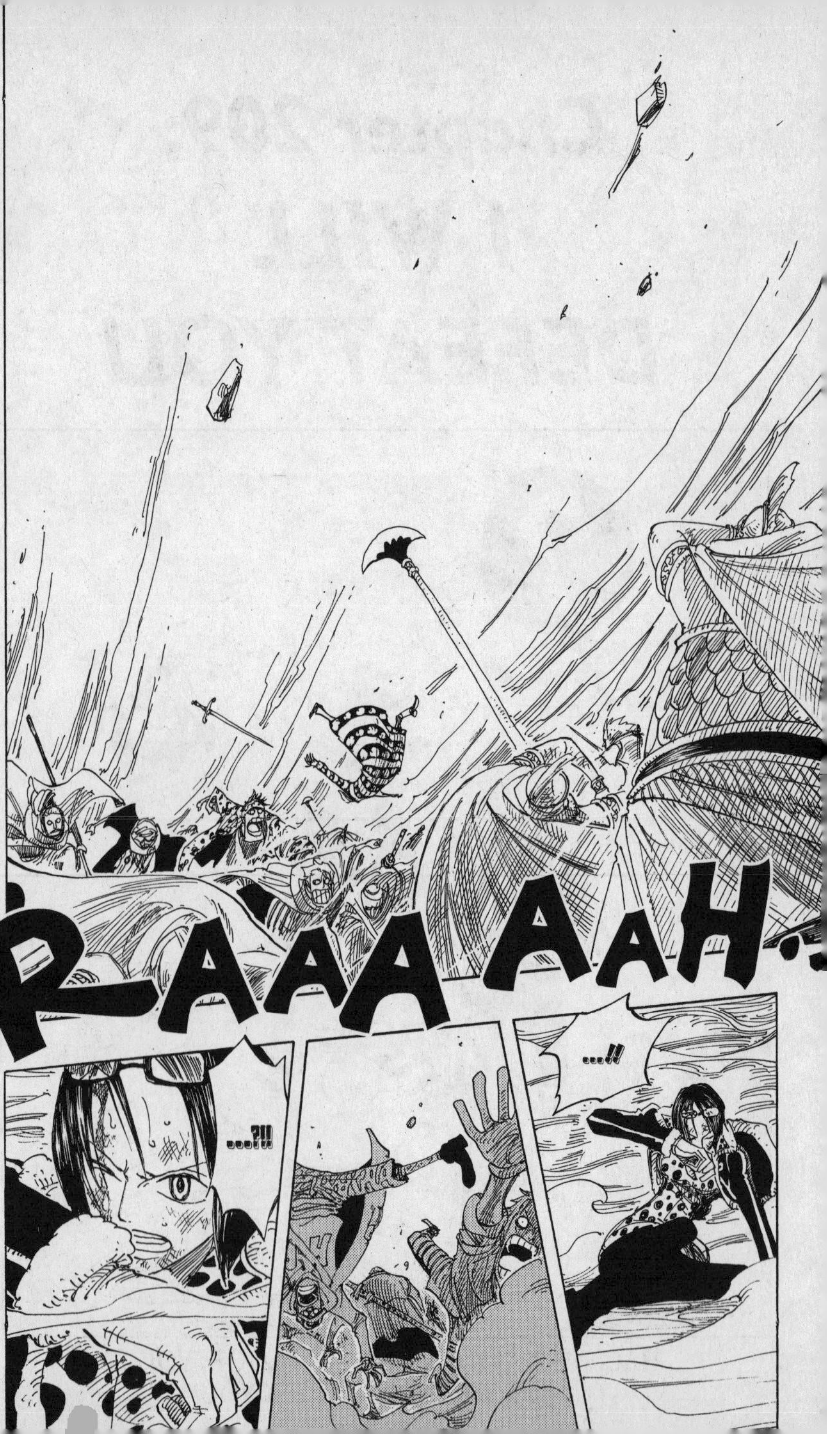
RAAAAAH..
...!!
...?!!

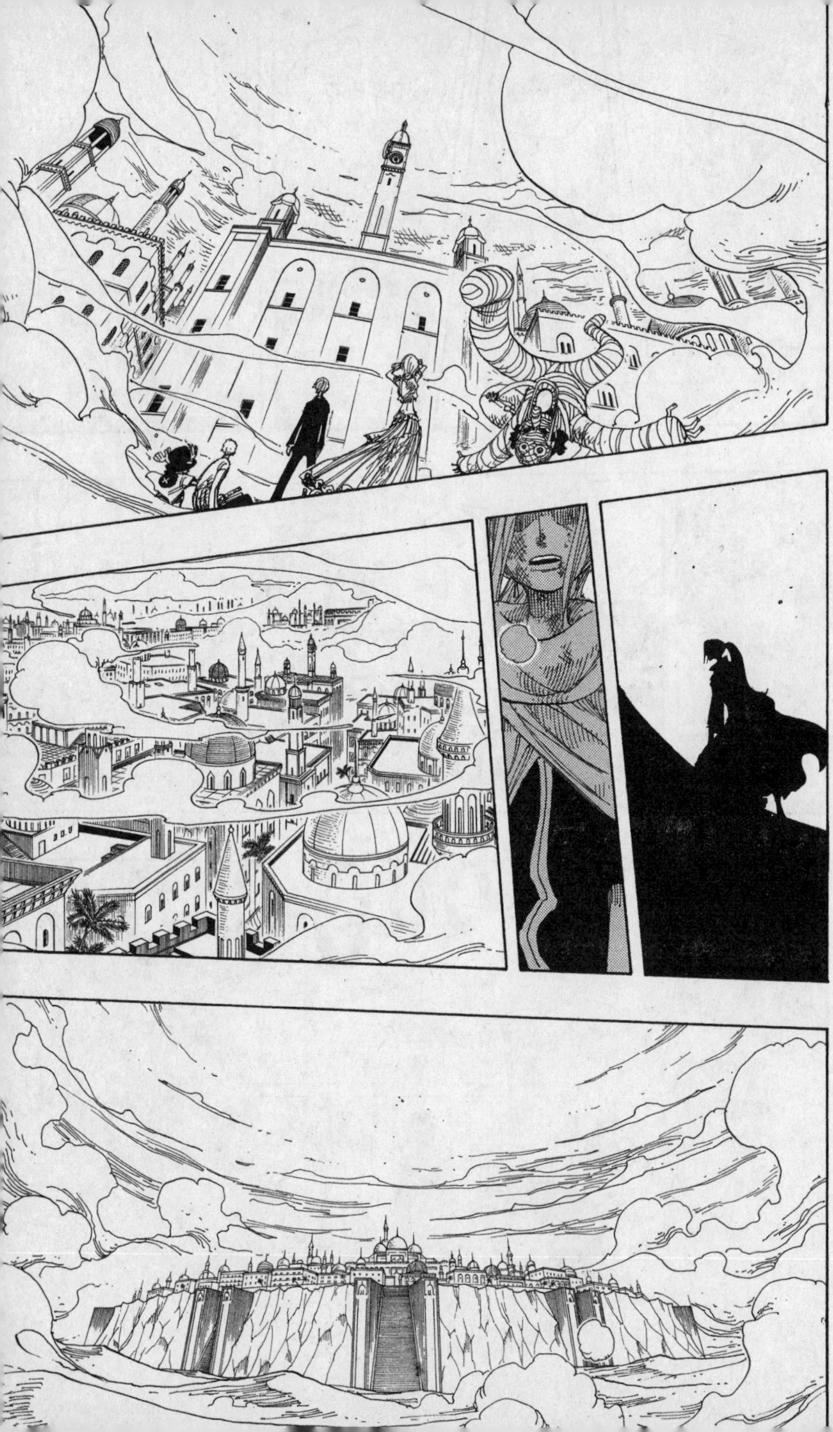

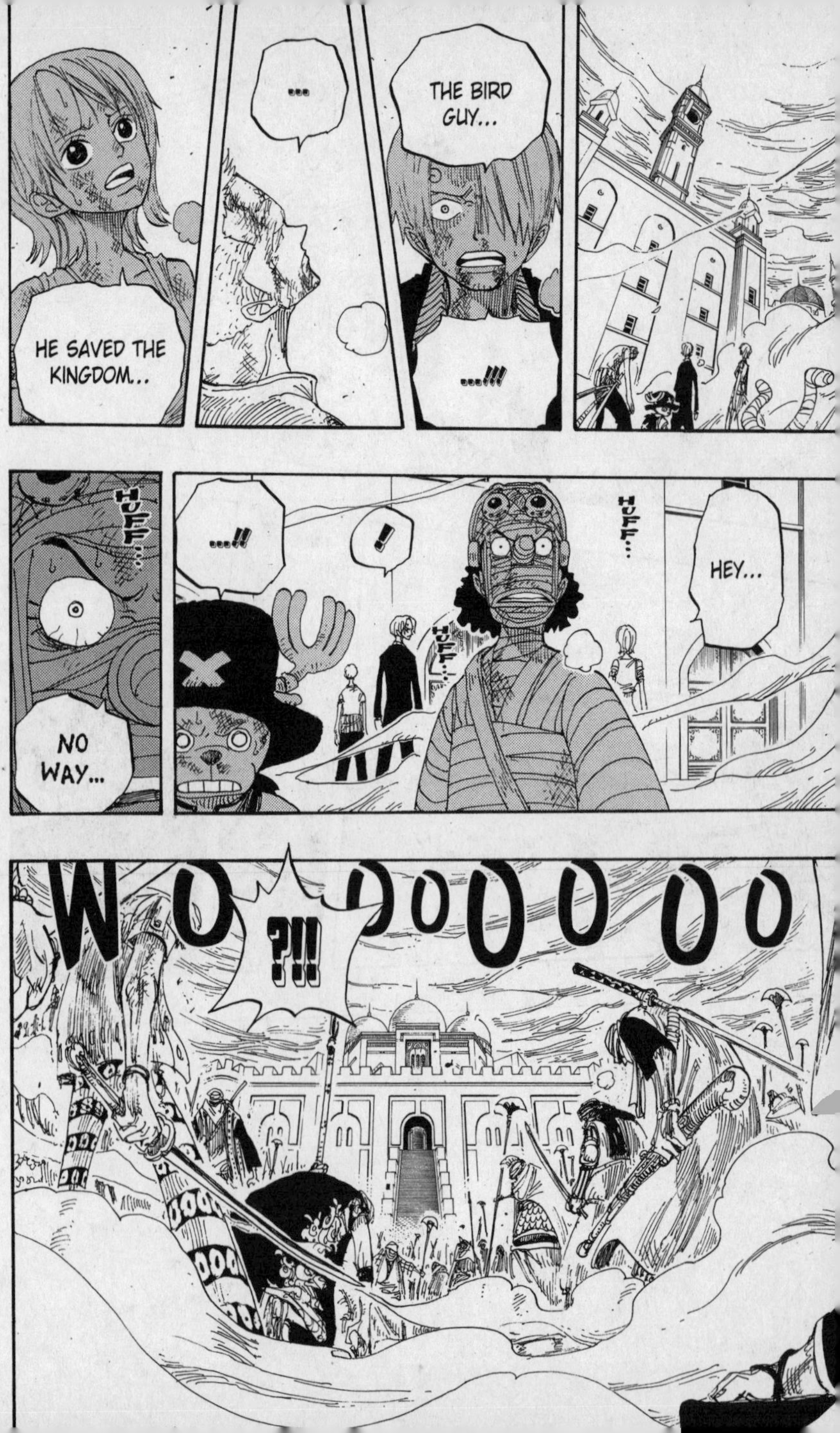
THE BIRD GUY...
...!!!
...
HE SAVED THE KINGDOM...
HEY...
HUFF...
!
...!!
HUFF...
HUFF...
NO WAY...
WOOOOOOOO
?!!

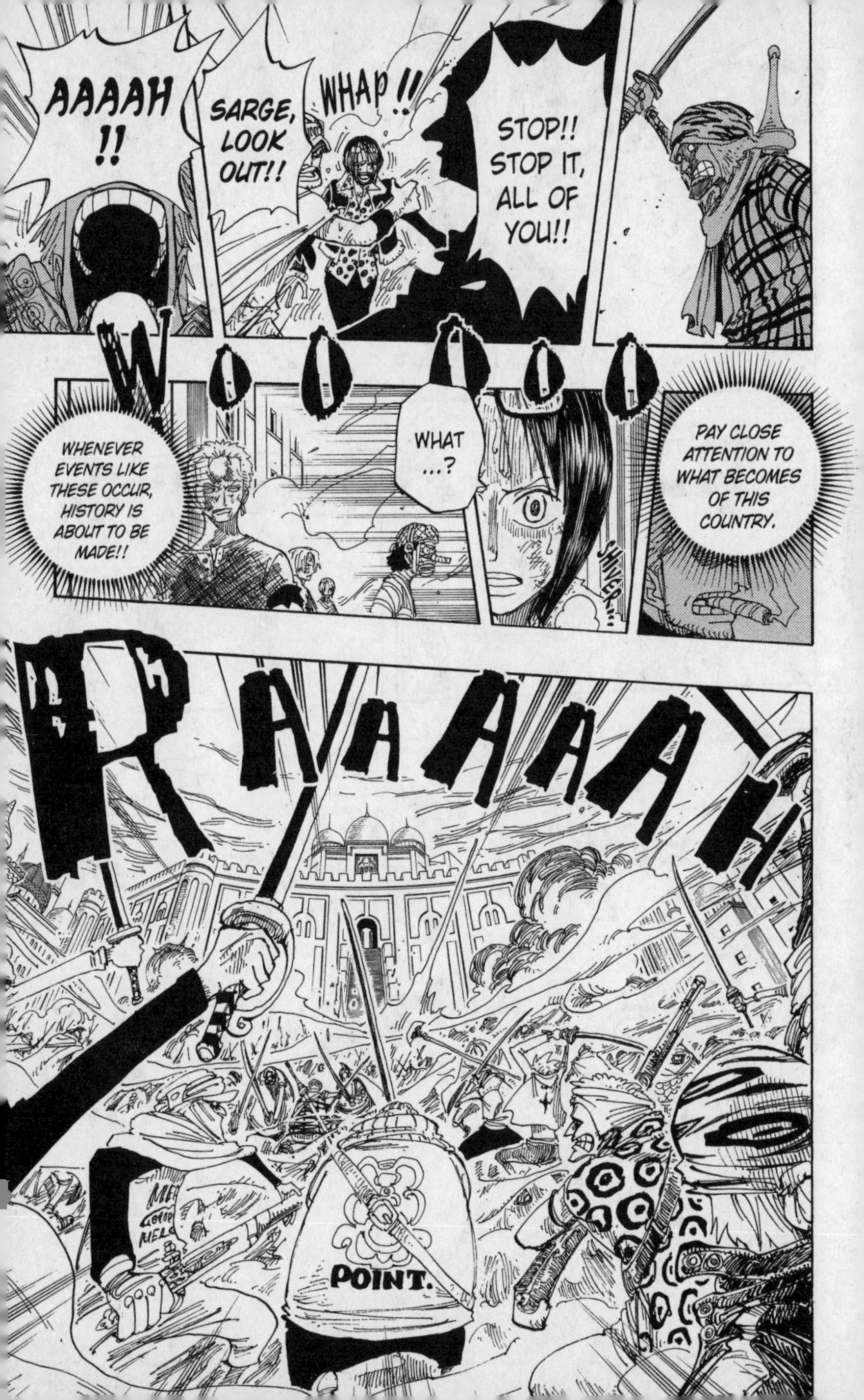
STOP!! STOP IT, ALL OF YOU!!
WHAP!!
SARGE, LOOK OUT!!
AAAAH!!
WOOOOO
PAY CLOSE ATTENTION TO WHAT BECOMES OF THIS COUNTRY.
WHAT ...?
SHIVER...
WHENEVER EVENTS LIKE THESE OCCUR, HISTORY IS ABOUT TO BE MADE!!
RAAAAAH
POINT.

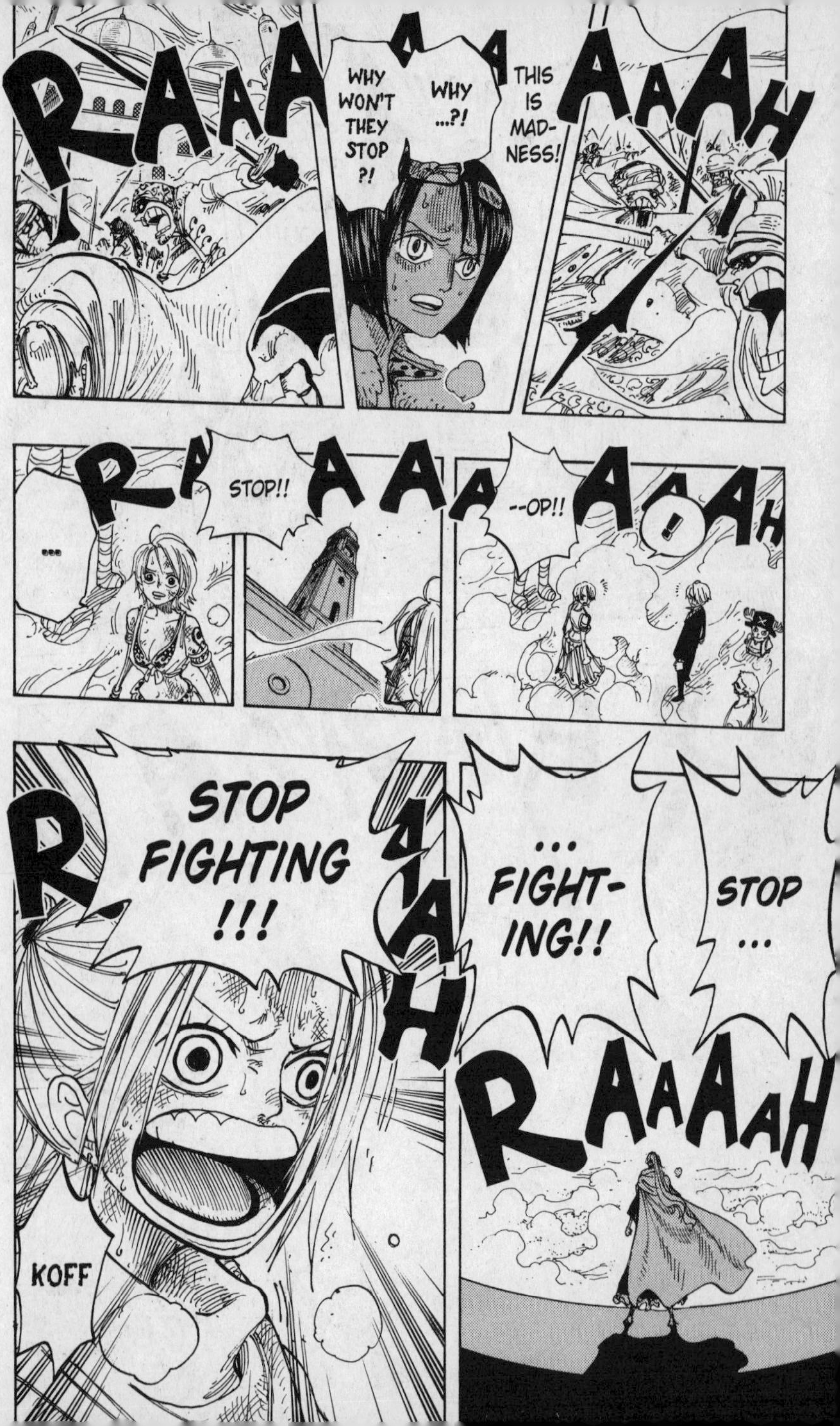
RAAAAAAAAAAH
THIS IS MADNESS!
WHY ...?!
WHY WON'T THEY STOP ?!
RAAAAAAAH
!
--OP!!
STOP!!
...
STOP ...
... FIGHT-ING!!
RAAAAH
STOP FIGHTING !!!
RAAAAH
KOFF

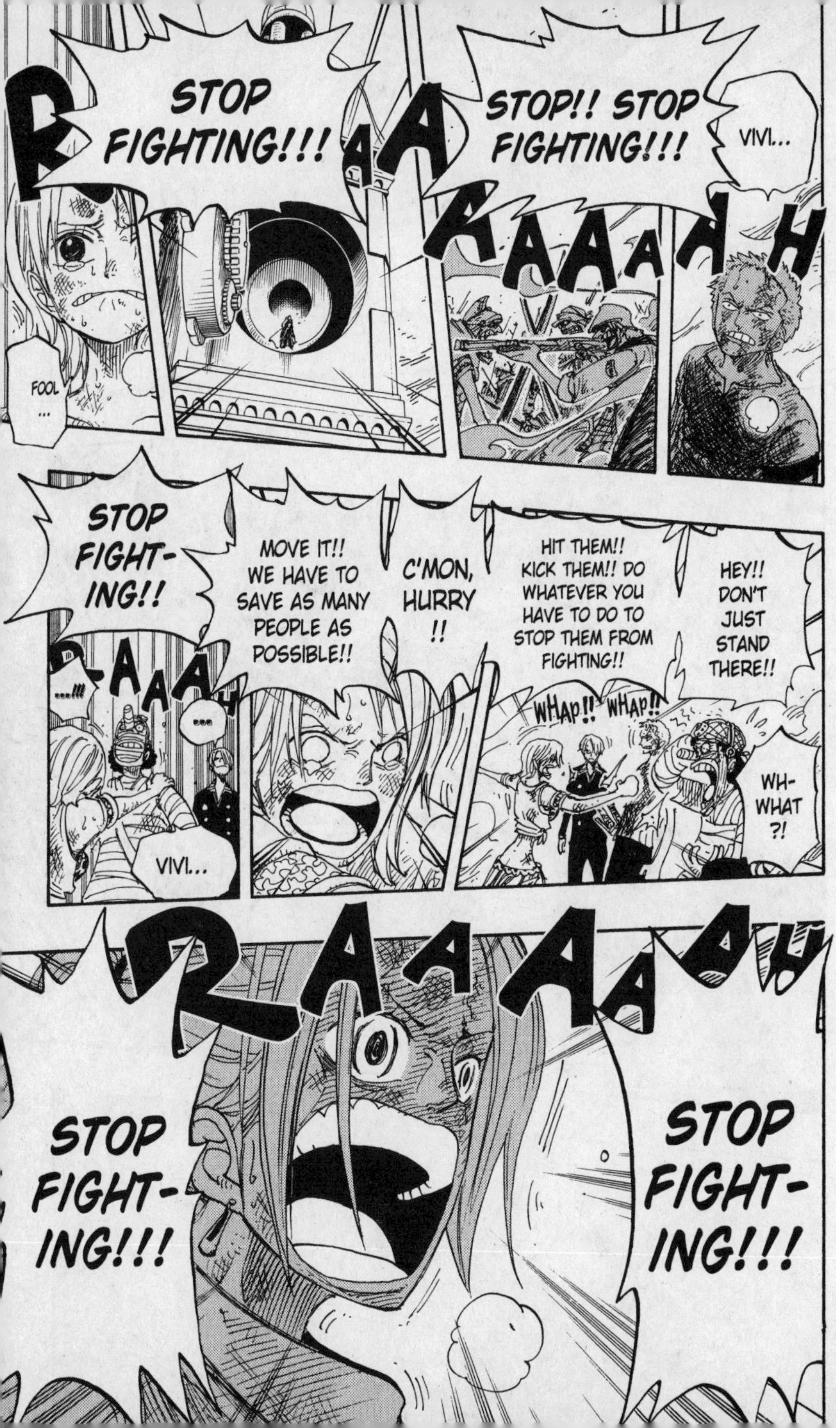

VIVI...
STOP!! STOP FIGHTING!!!
STOP FIGHTING!!!
RAAAAAAAH
FOOL ...
HEY!! DON'T JUST STAND THERE!!
HIT THEM!! KICK THEM!! DO WHATEVER YOU HAVE TO DO TO STOP THEM FROM FIGHTING!!
WHAP!! WHAP!!
WH-WHAT ?!
C'MON, HURRY !!
MOVE IT!! WE HAVE TO SAVE AS MANY PEOPLE AS POSSIBLE!!
STOP FIGHT-ING!!
RAAAAH
...!!
...
VIVI...
RAAAAAAH
STOP FIGHT-ING!!!
STOP FIGHT-ING!!!

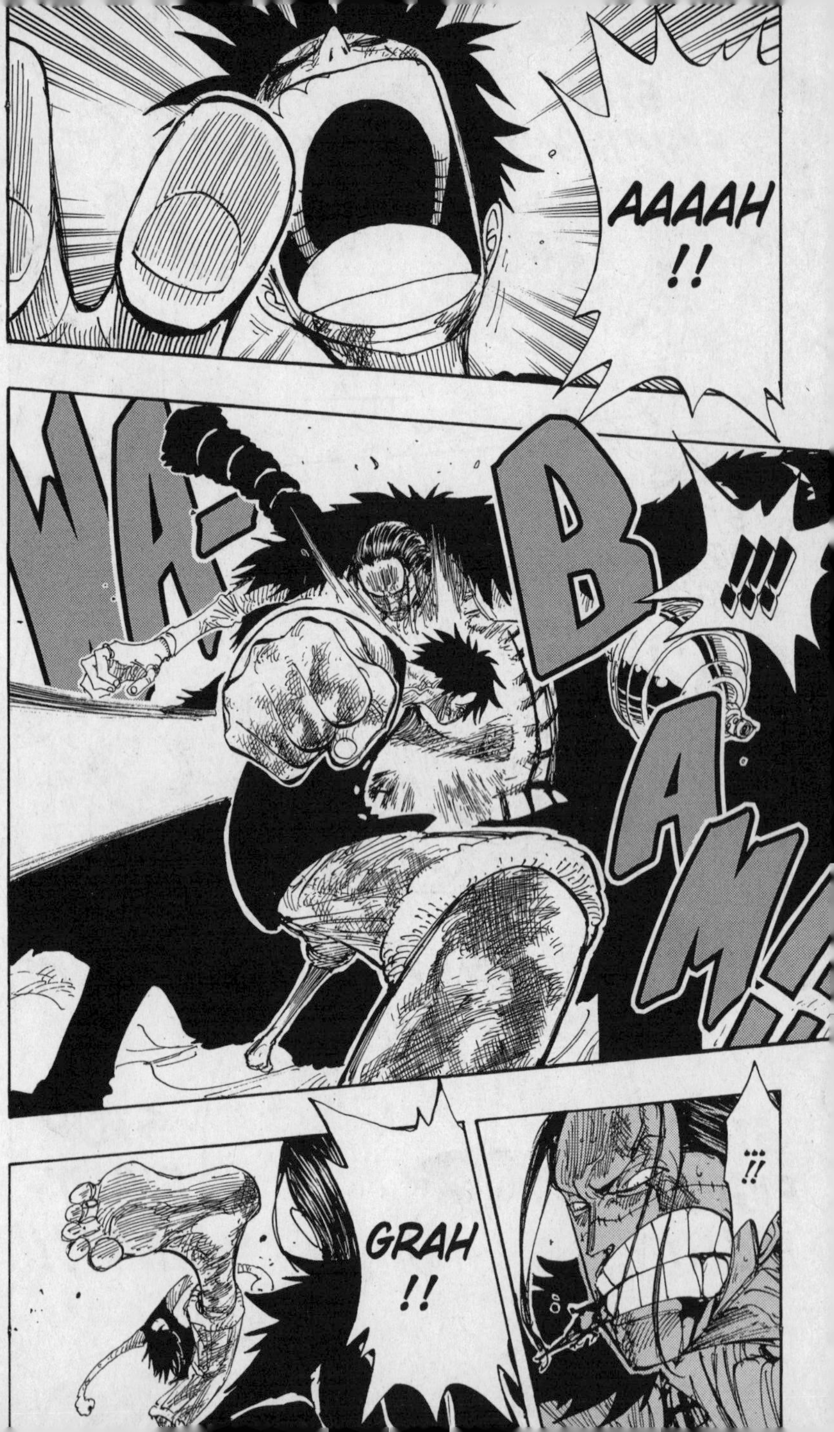
AAAAH
!!
B!!!
WA-
BAM
...!!
GRAH
!!

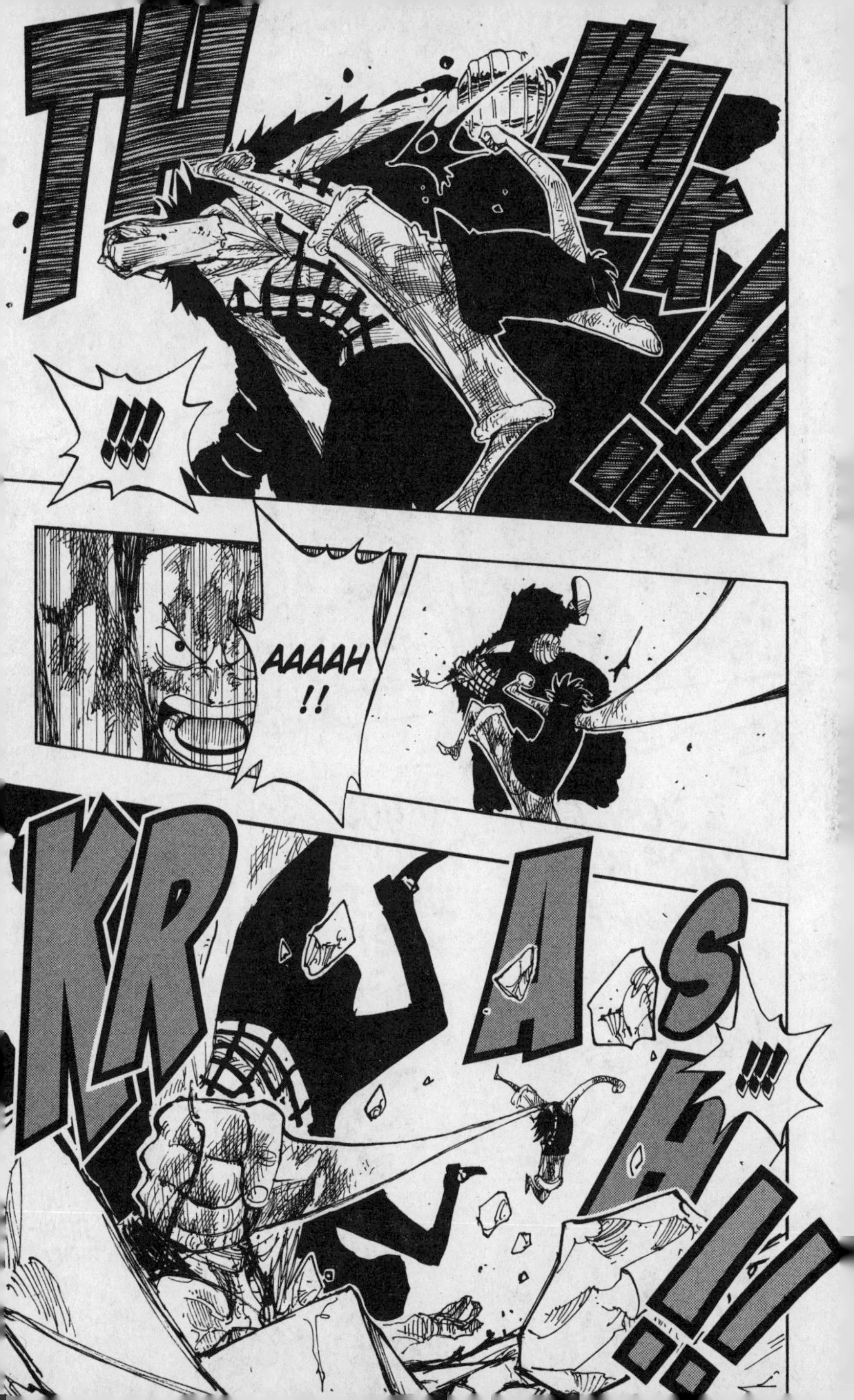
THUNK!!
!!!
AAAAH !!
KRASH!!!
!!!

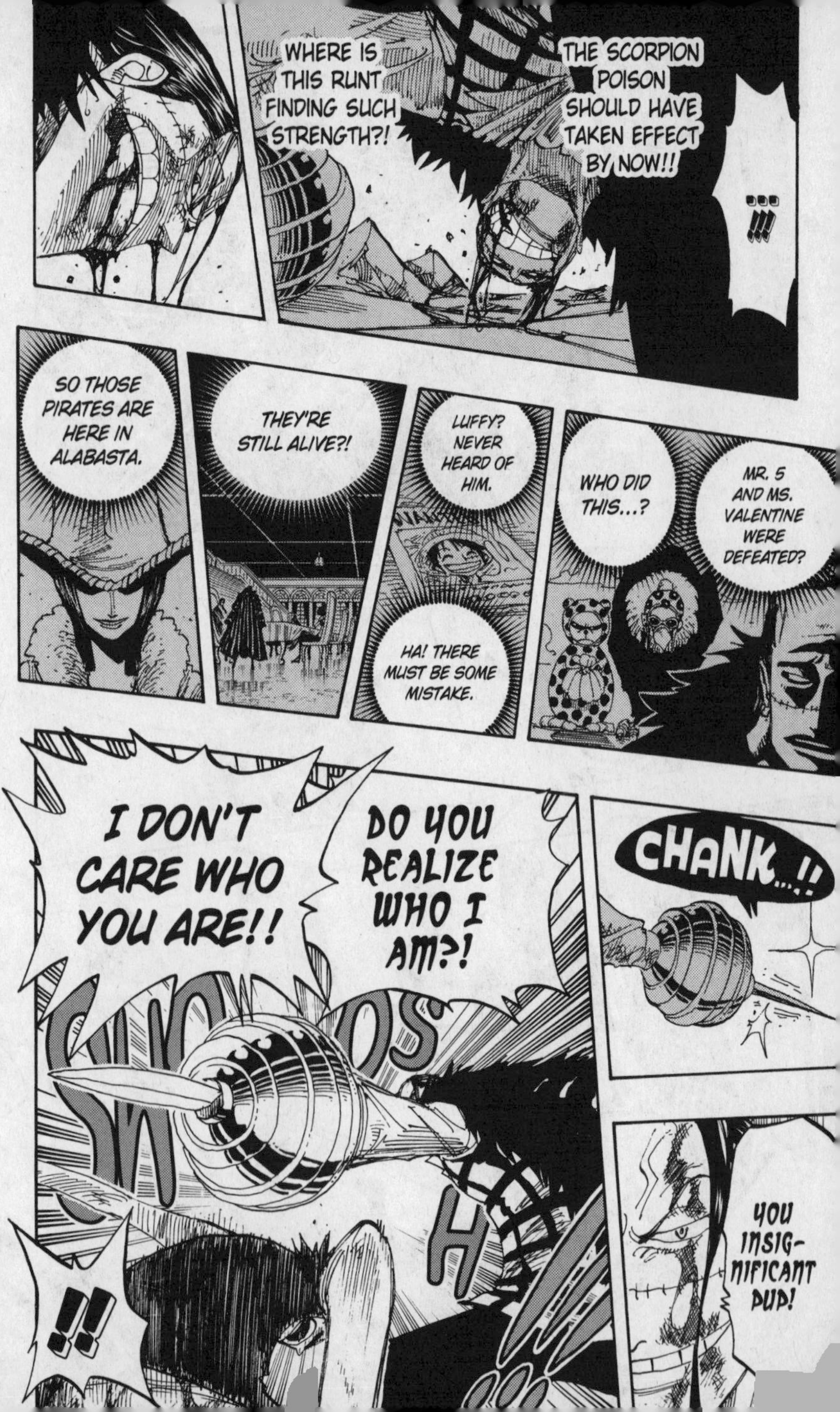
...!!!
THE SCORPION POISON SHOULD HAVE TAKEN EFFECT BY NOW!!
WHERE IS THIS RUNT FINDING SUCH STRENGTH?!
MR. 5 AND MS. VALENTINE WERE DEFEATED?
WHO DID THIS...?
LUFFY? NEVER HEARD OF HIM.
HA! THERE MUST BE SOME MISTAKE.
THEY'RE STILL ALIVE?!
SO THOSE PIRATES ARE HERE IN ALABASTA.
CHANK...!!
YOU INSIGNIFICANT PUP!
DO YOU REALIZE WHO I AM?!
I DON'T CARE WHO YOU ARE!!
SWOOSH
!!

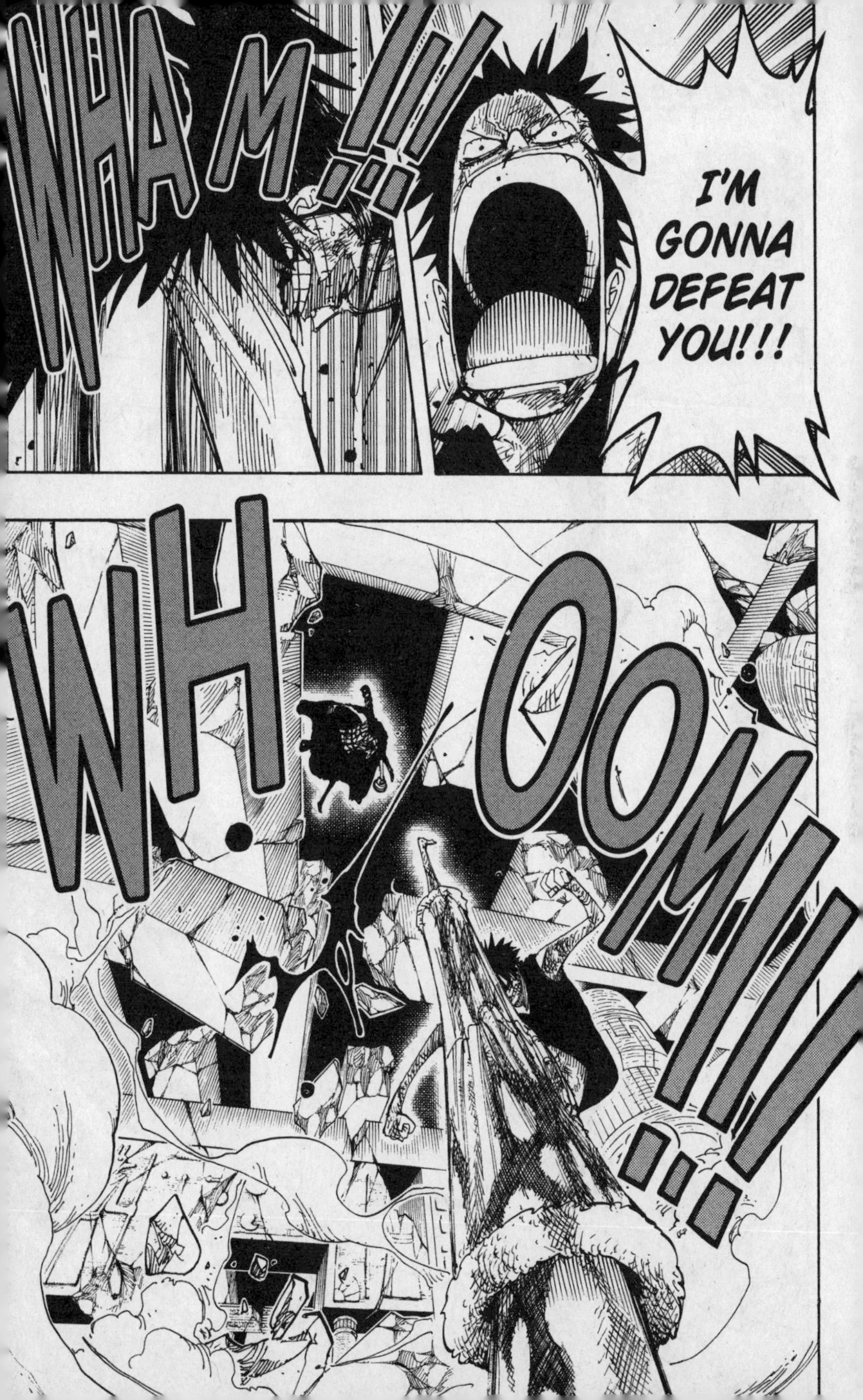
I'M GONNA DEFEAT YOU!!!
WHAM!!!
WHOOM!!!

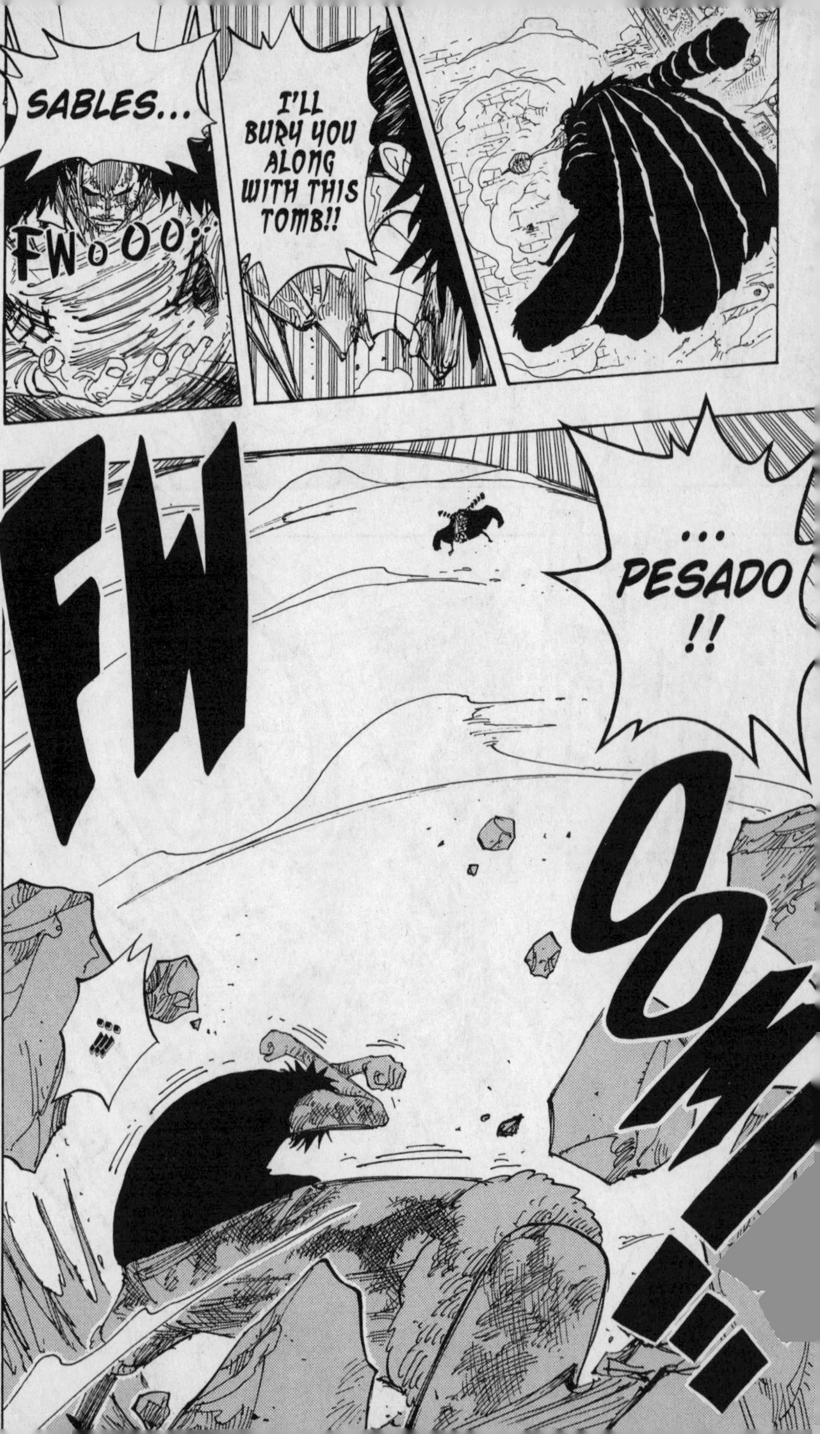
I'LL BURY YOU ALONG WITH THIS TOMB!!
SABLES...
FWOOO..
... PESADO !!
FW
OOM!!
...!!!

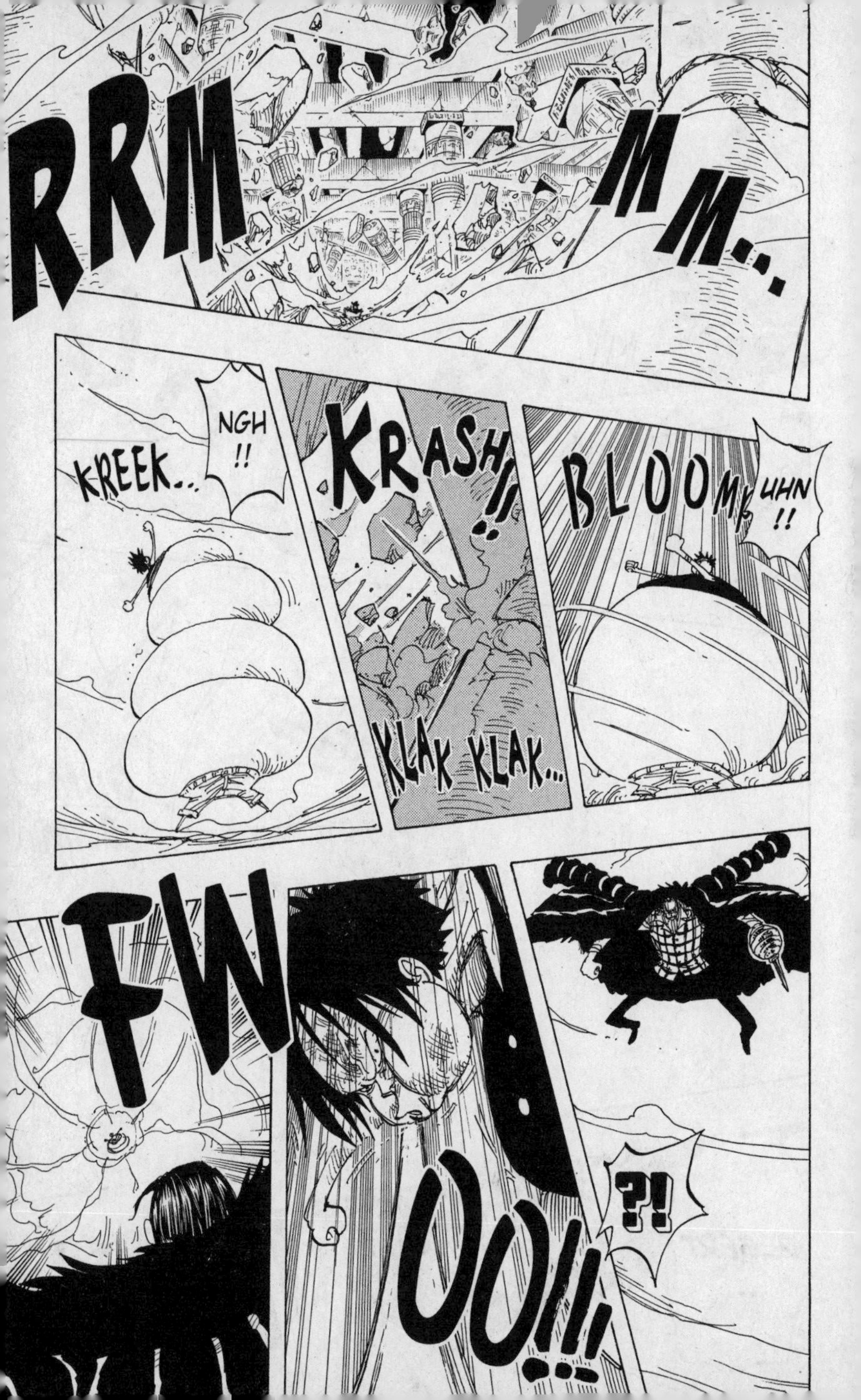
RRM MM..
BLOOM
UHN !!
KRASH!!
KLAK KLAK...
KREEK...
NGH !!
?!
FW OO!!!

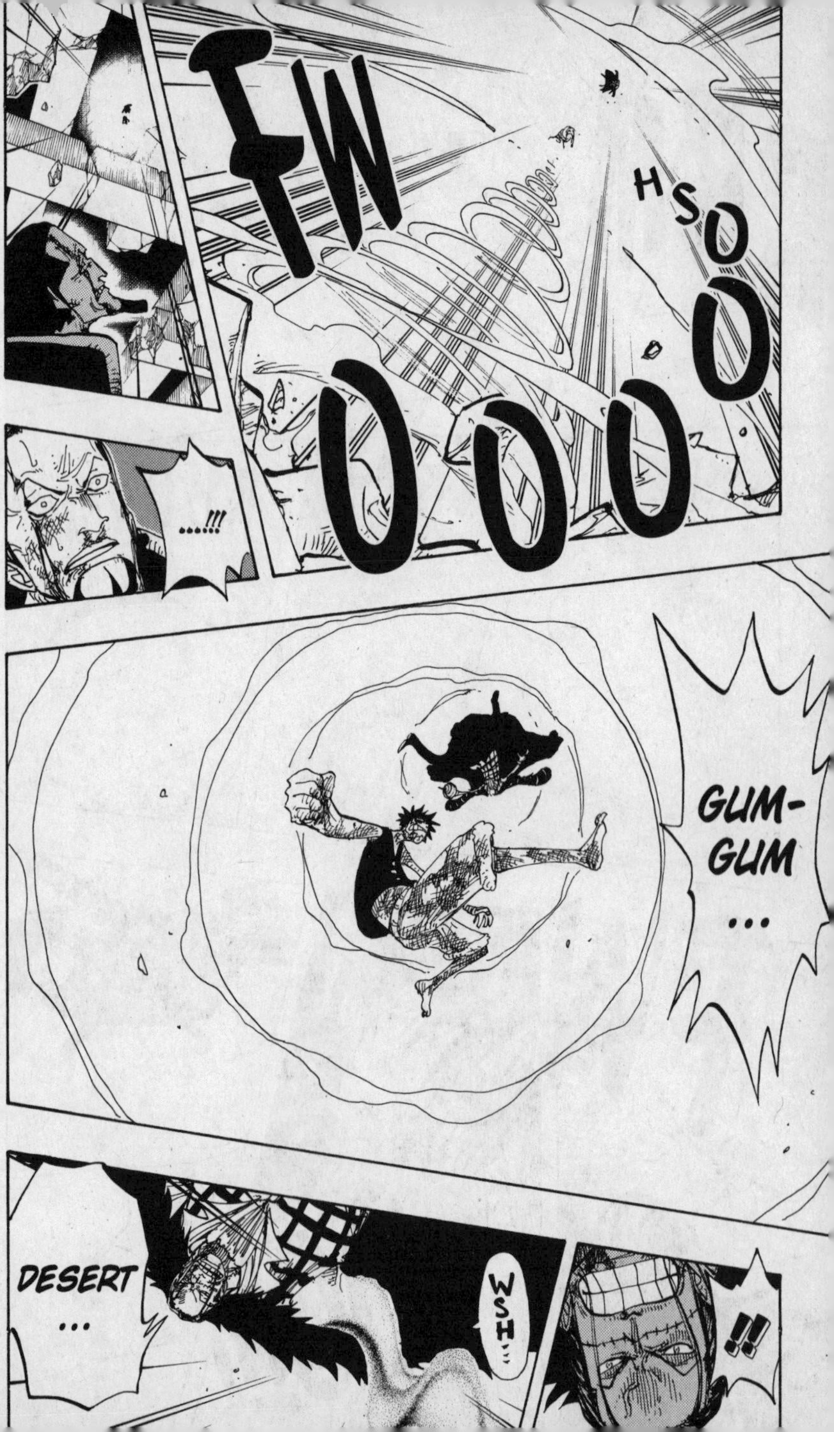
FWOOOOOOSH
....!!!
GUM-GUM ...
!!
WSH...
DESERT ...

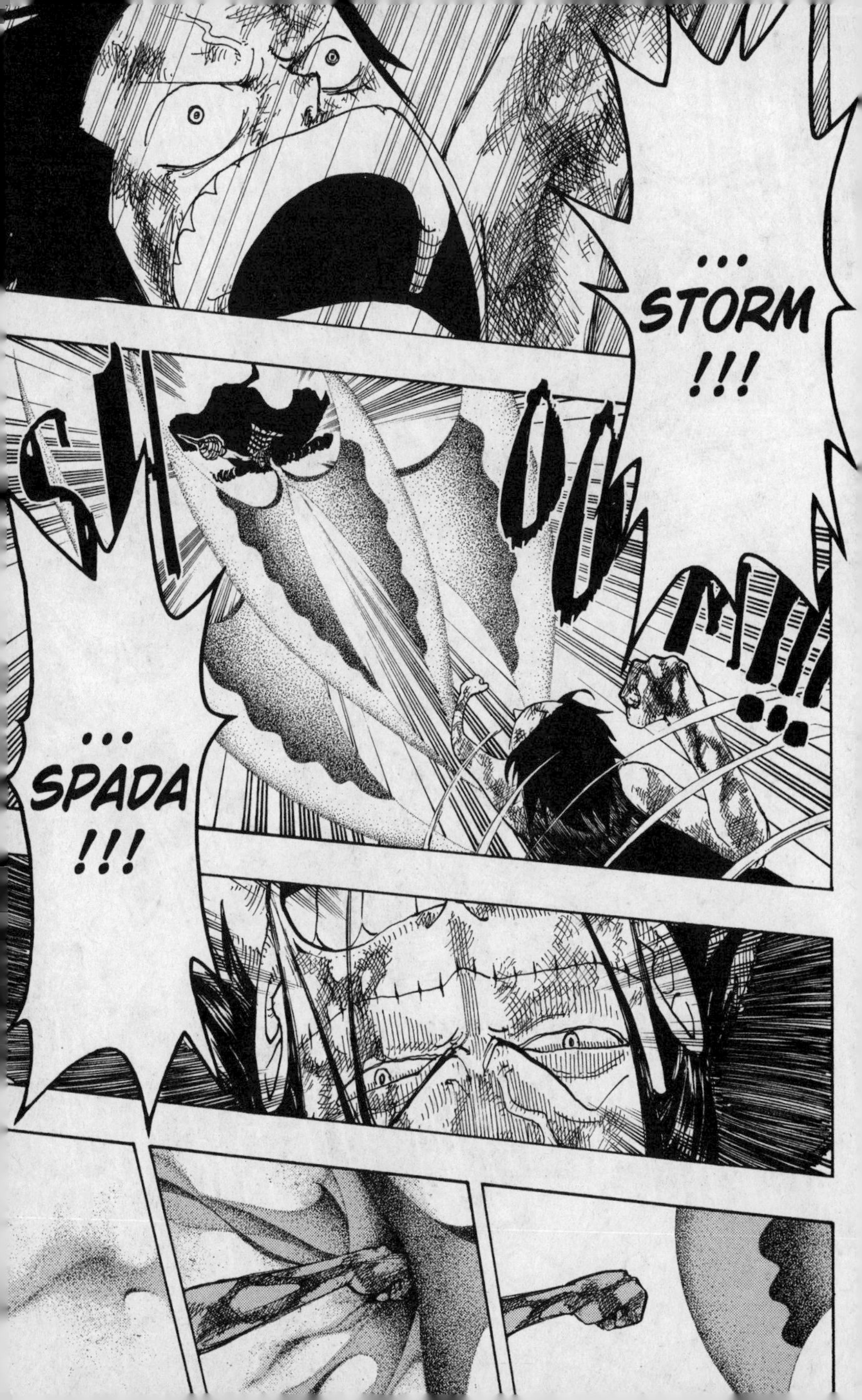
...STORM!!!
...SPADA!!!

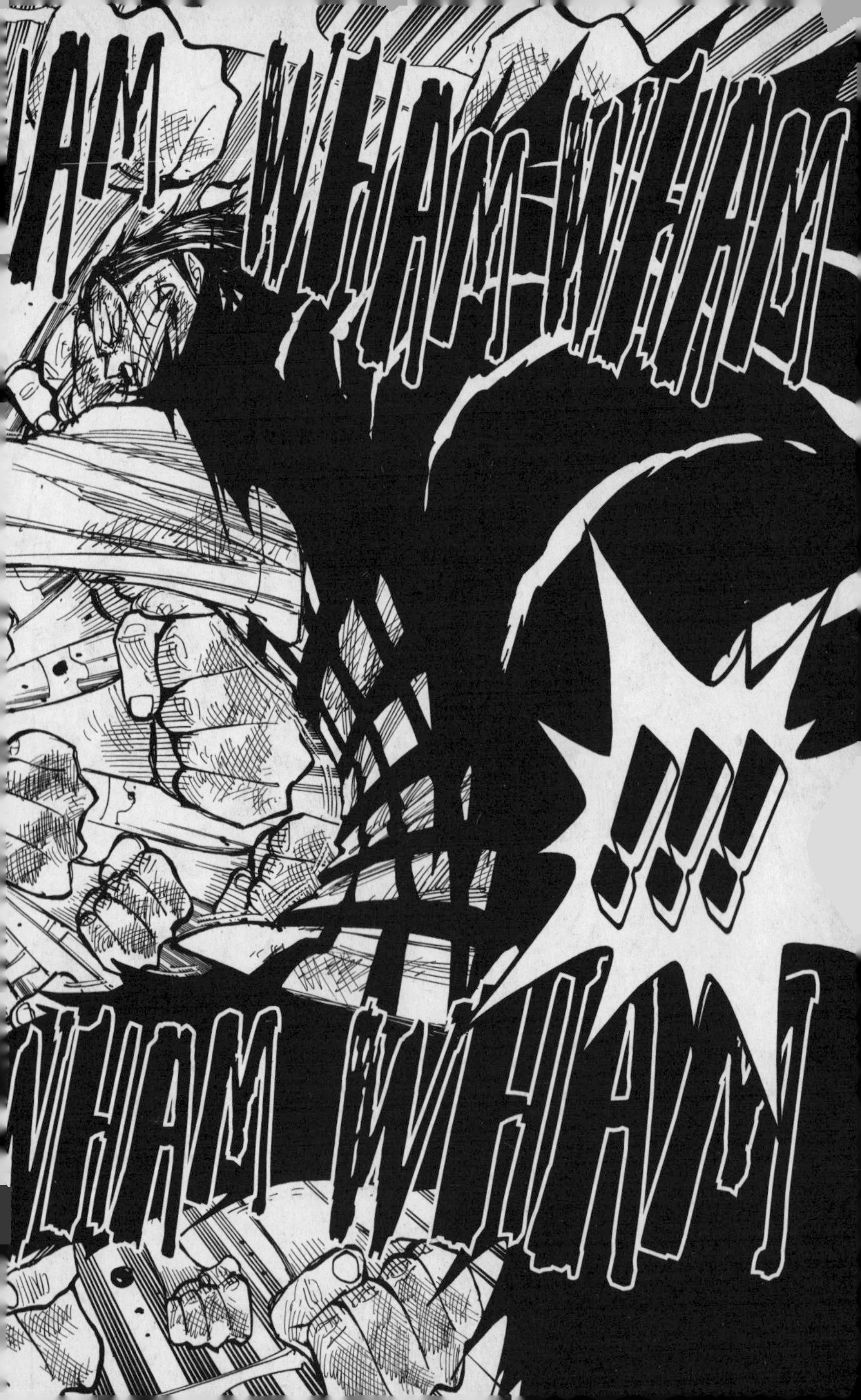
HAM WHAM WHAM WHAM
!!!
WHAM WHAM

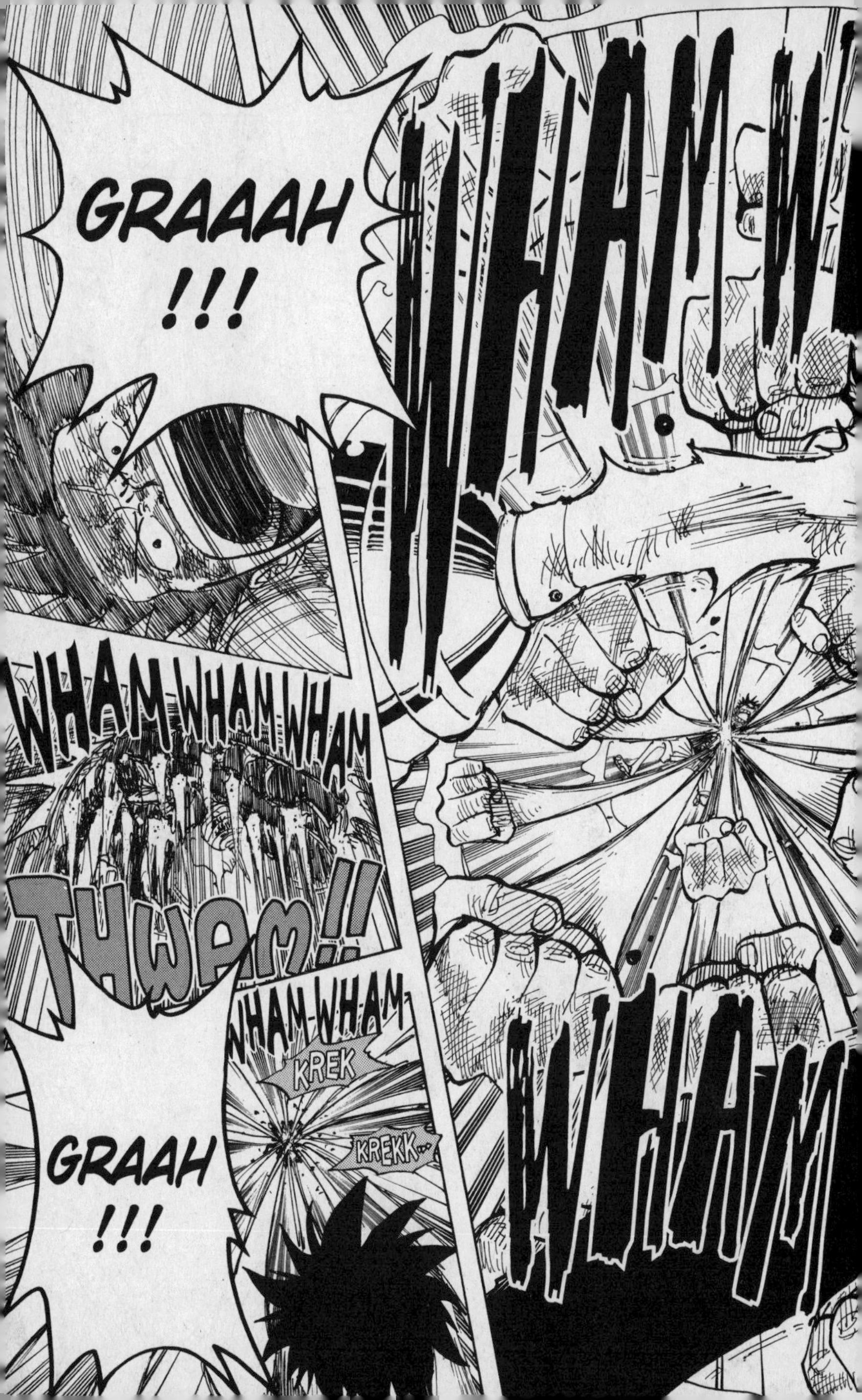
WHAM
WHAM
GRAAAH!!!
WHAM WHAM WHAM
THWAM!!
WHAM WHAM
KREK
KREKK...
GRAAH!!!

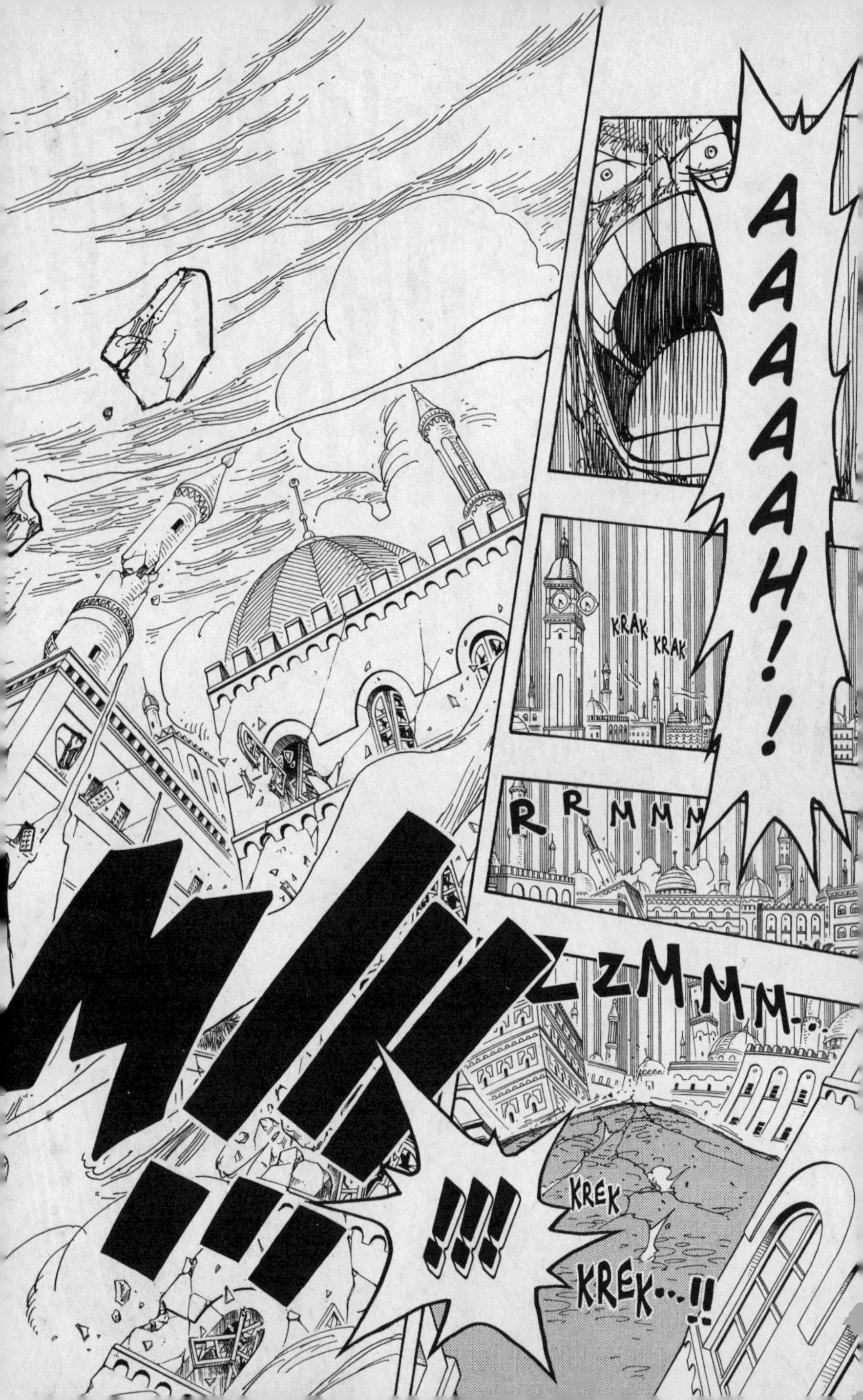

AAAAAH!!
KRAK KRAK
RRMMN
ZMMM...
!!!
KREK
KREK...!!

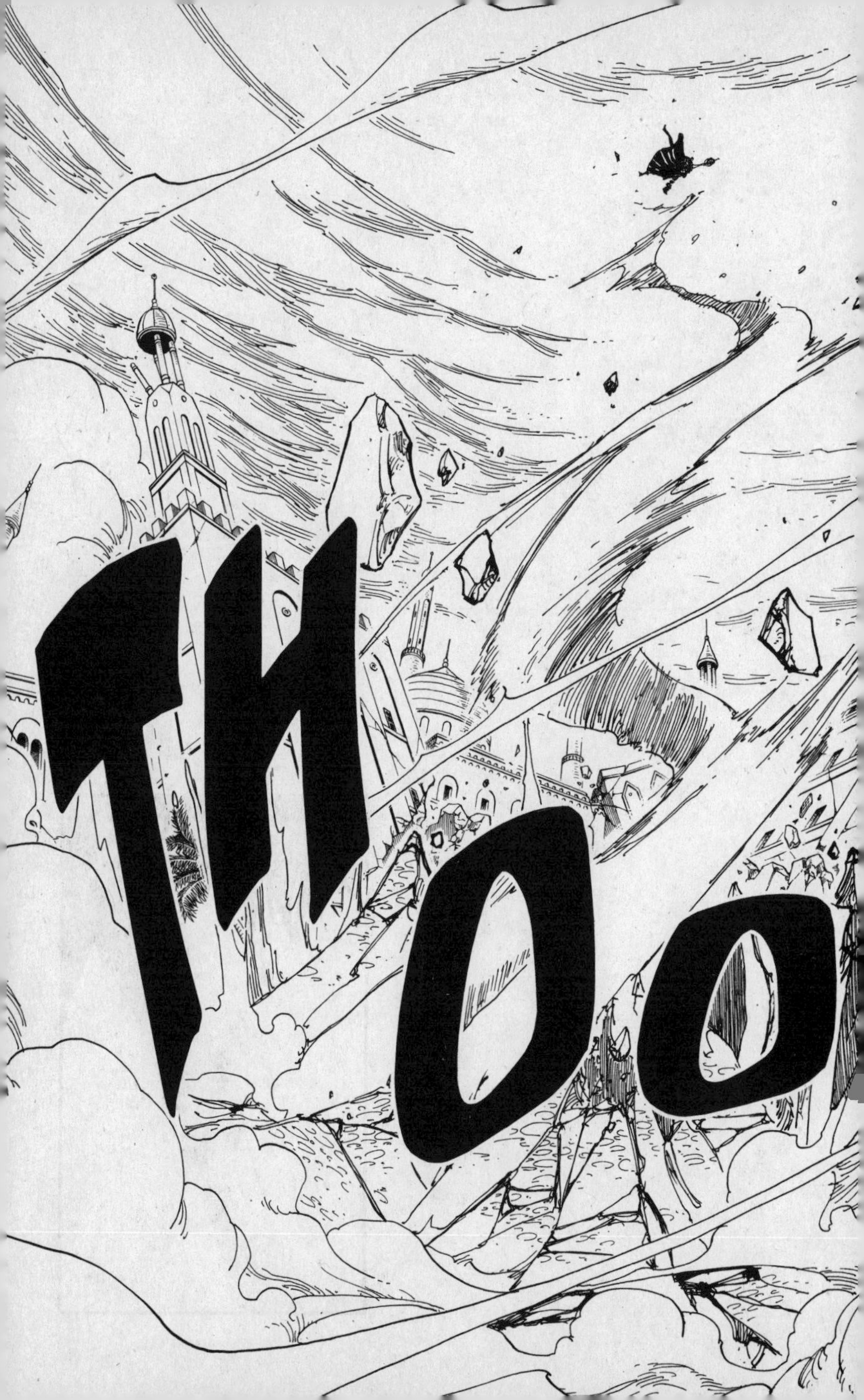
THOO

Chapter 210:
ZERO

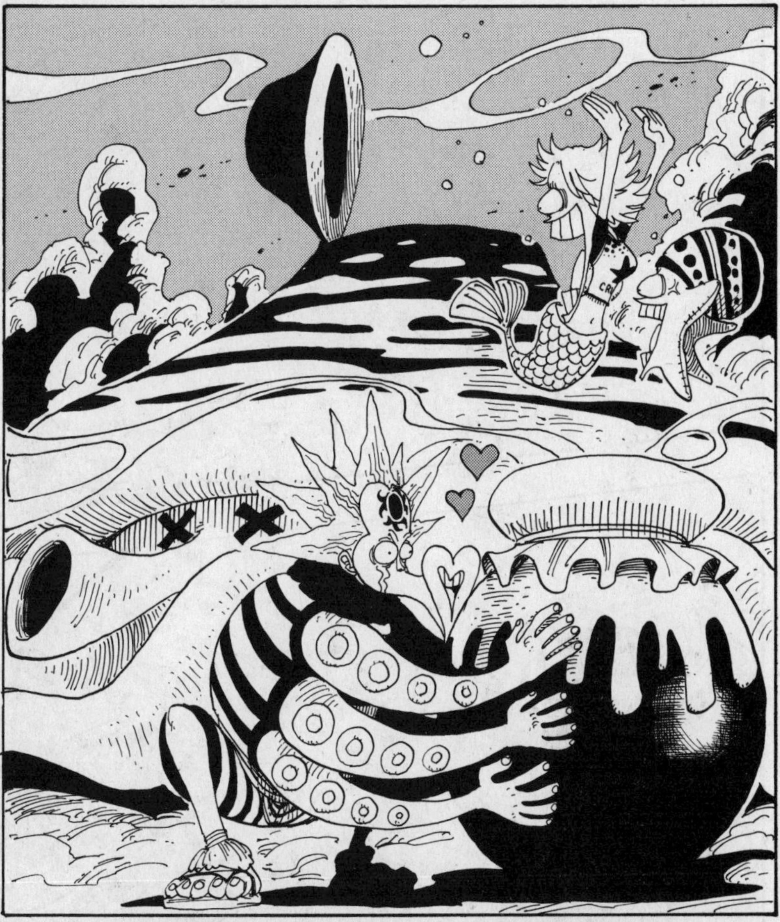

HACHI'S WALK ON THE SEAFLOOR, VOL. 25:
"THE LEGENDARY SAUCE IS FOUND INSIDE THE TOP OF A GRADE-A INGREDIENT"

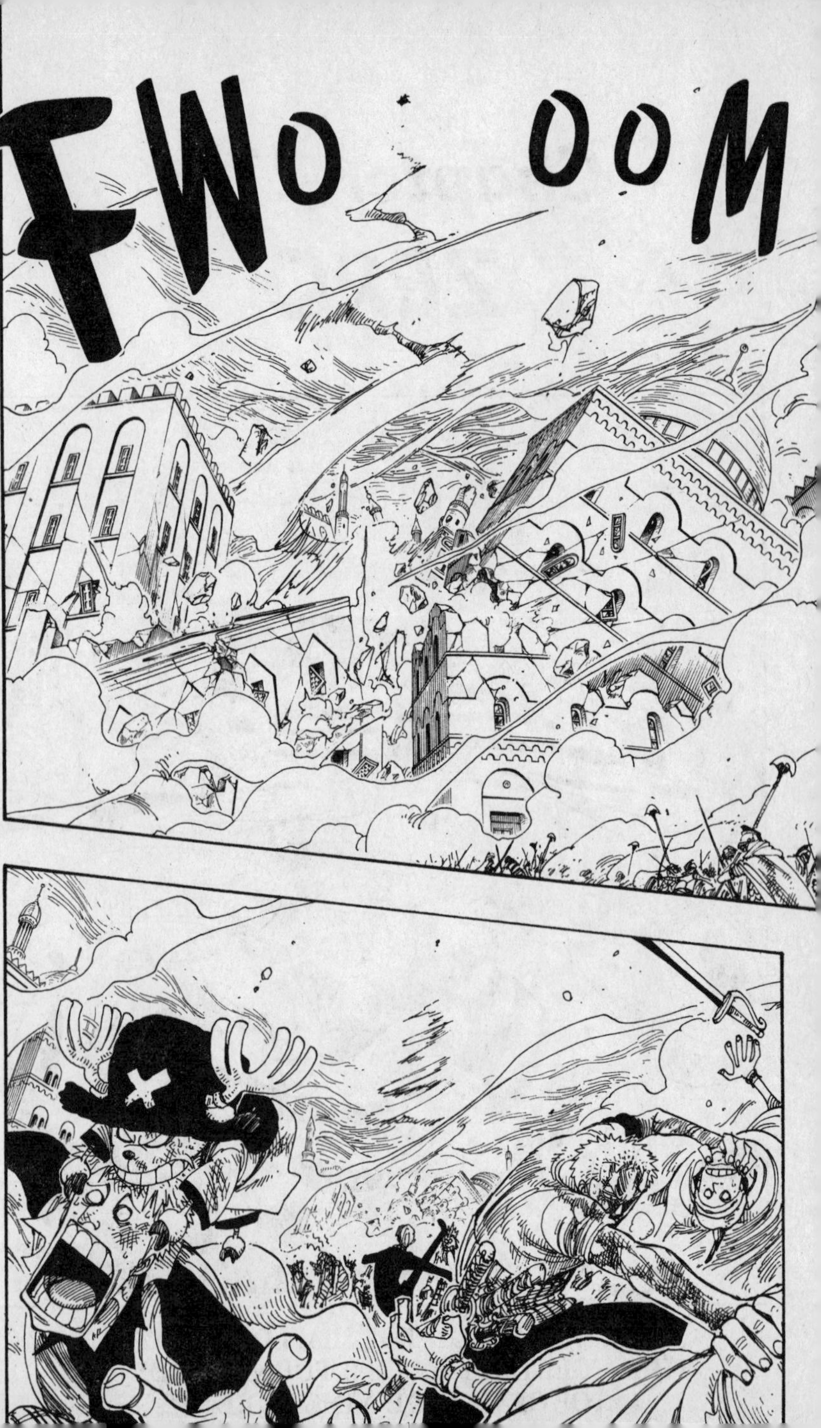
FWOOOM

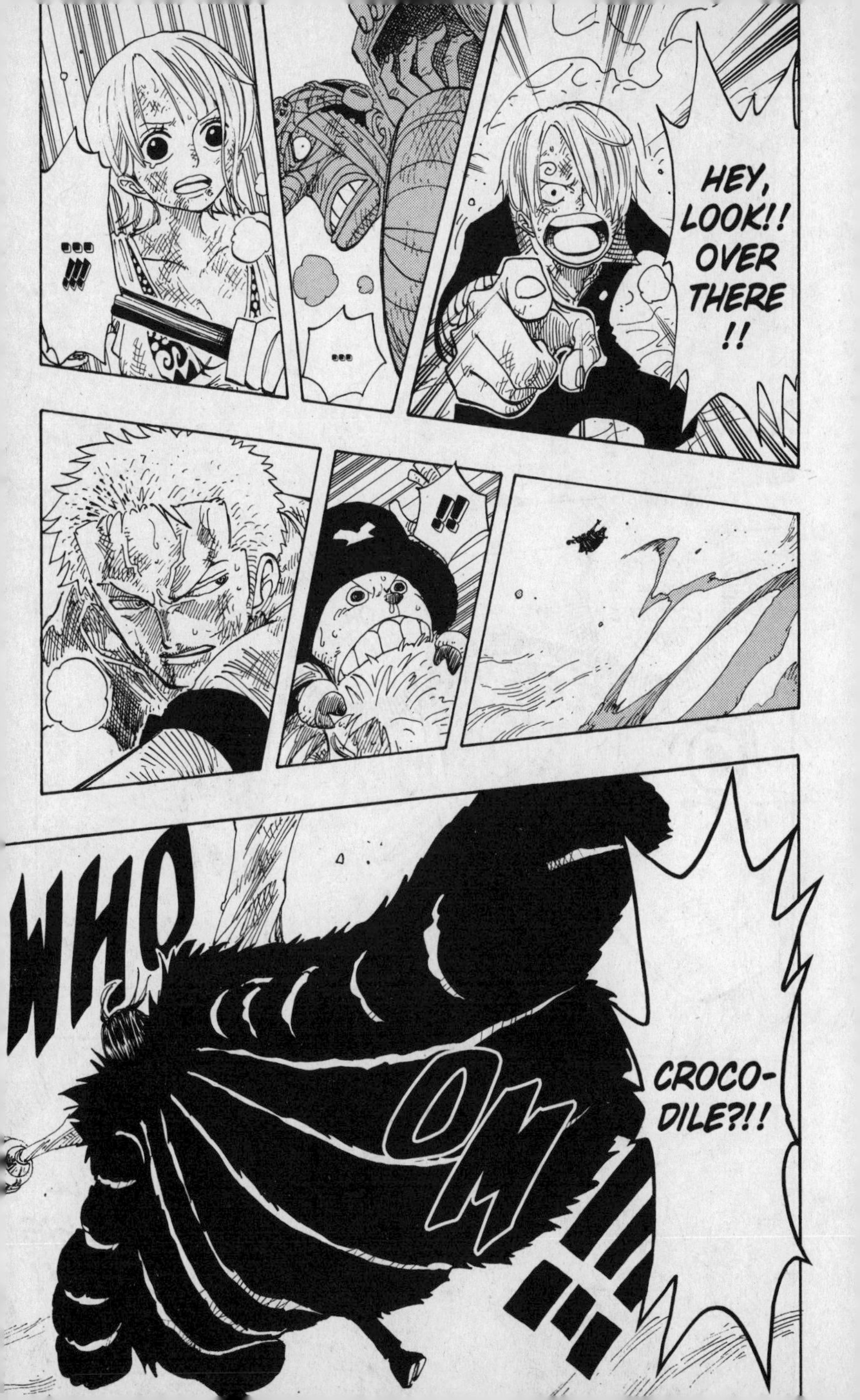
HEY, LOOK!! OVER THERE !!
...
...!!!
!!
CROCO-DILE?!!
WHOOM!!!

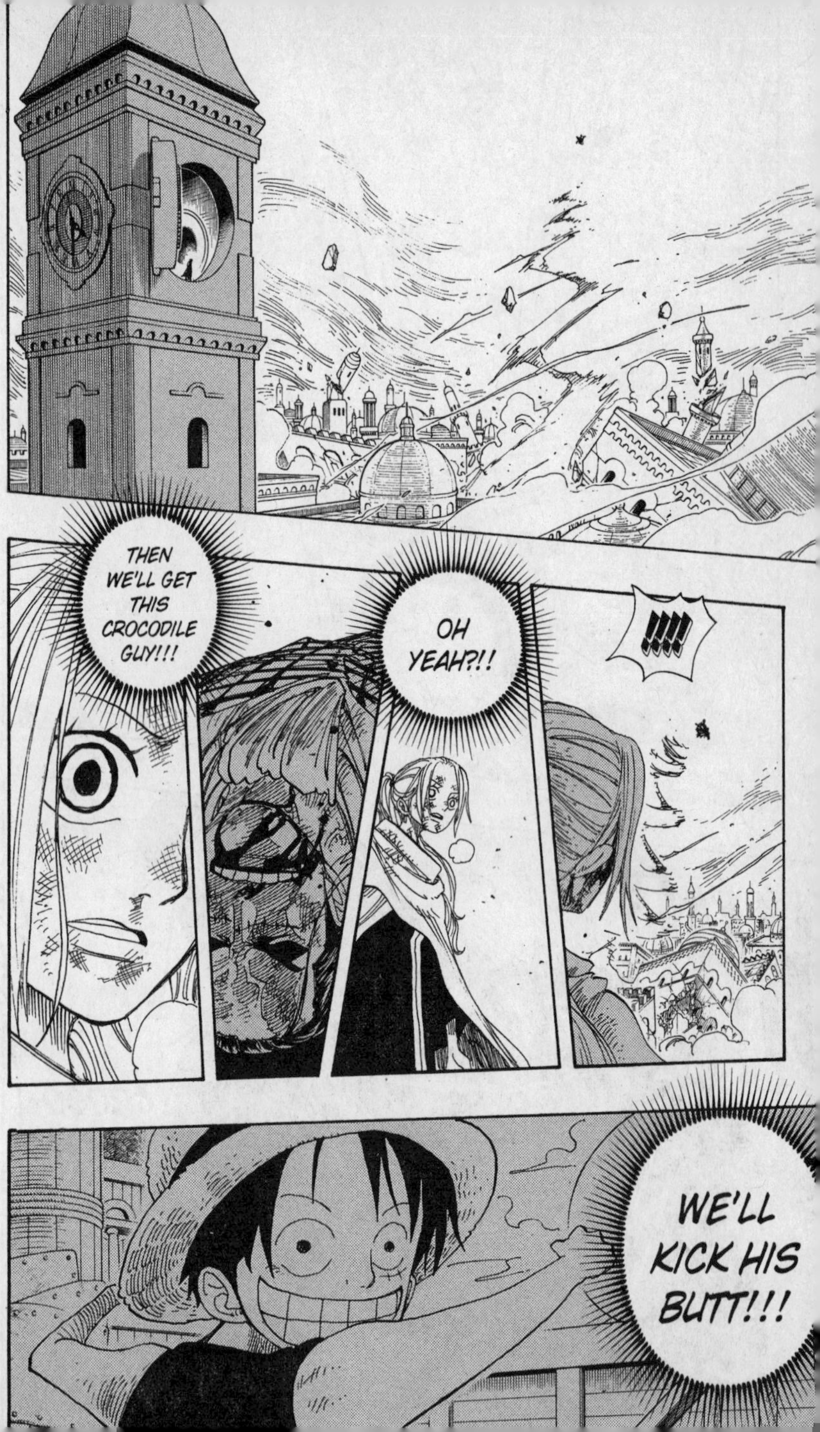
!!!!
OH YEAH?!!
THEN WE'LL GET THIS CROCODILE GUY!!!
WE'LL KICK HIS BUTT!!!

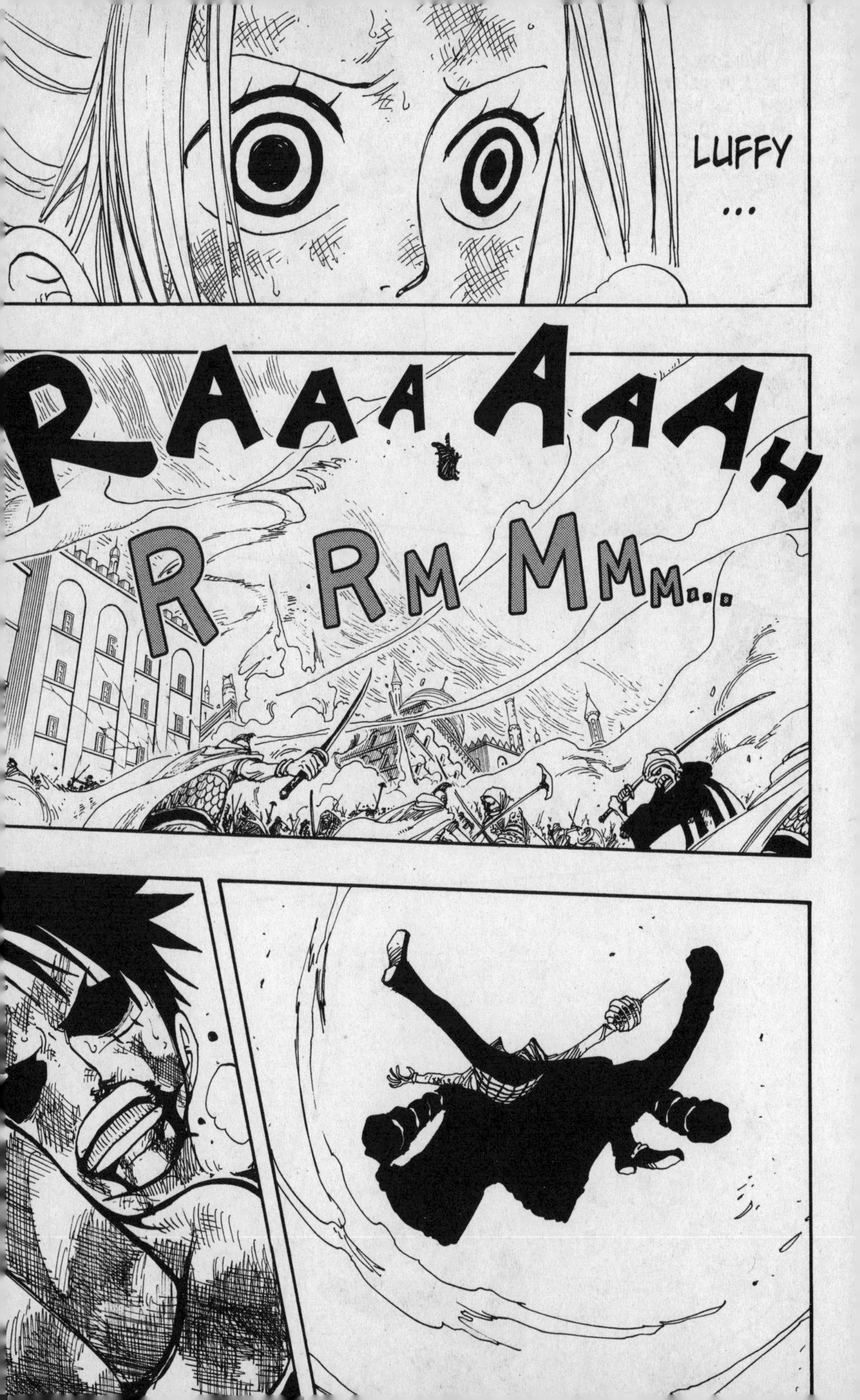
LUFFY
...
RAAAAAAAH
RRMMMMM...

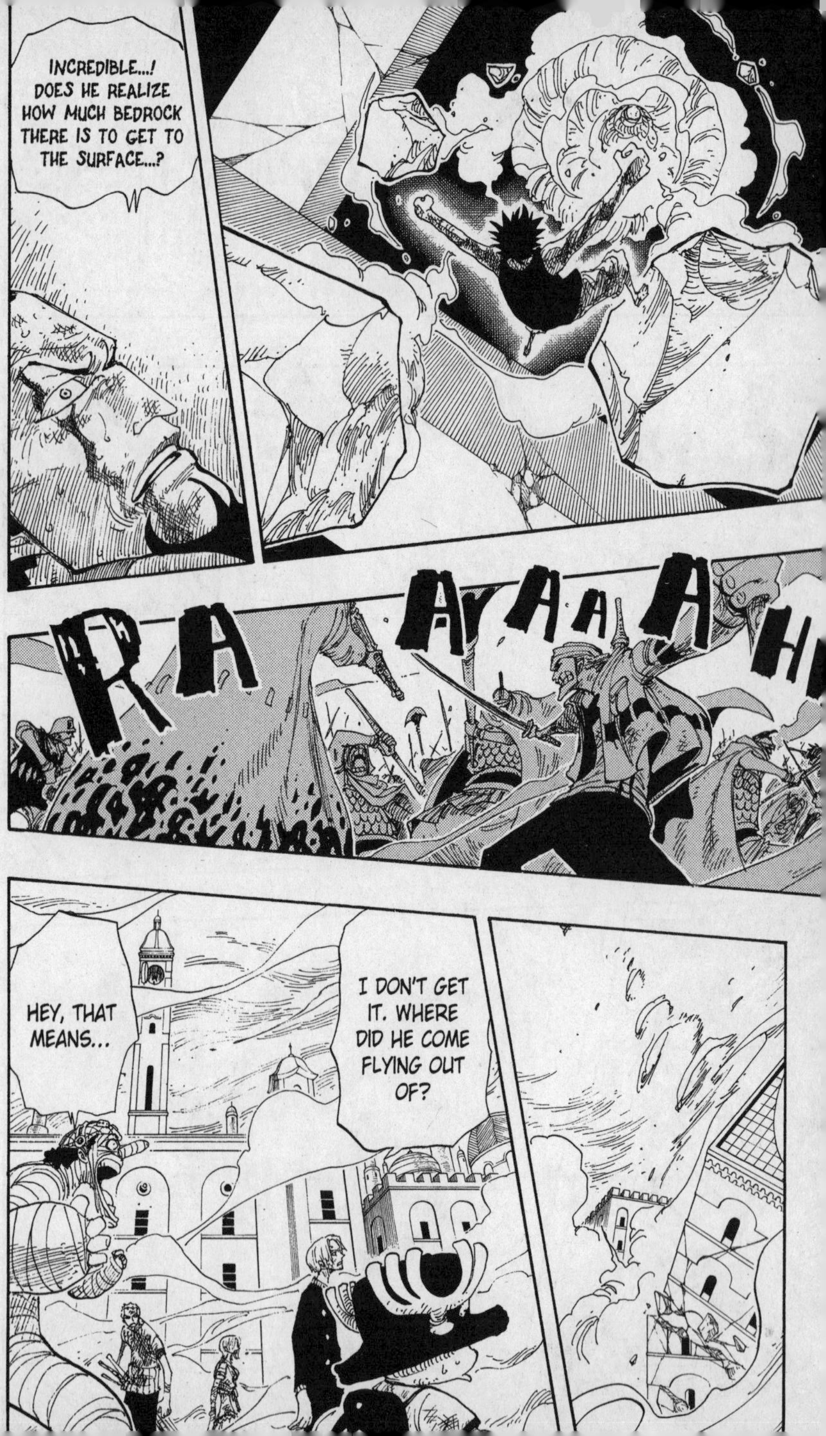
INCREDIBLE...! DOES HE REALIZE HOW MUCH BEDROCK THERE IS TO GET TO THE SURFACE...?
RAAAAAH
I DON'T GET IT. WHERE DID HE COME FLYING OUT OF?
HEY, THAT MEANS...

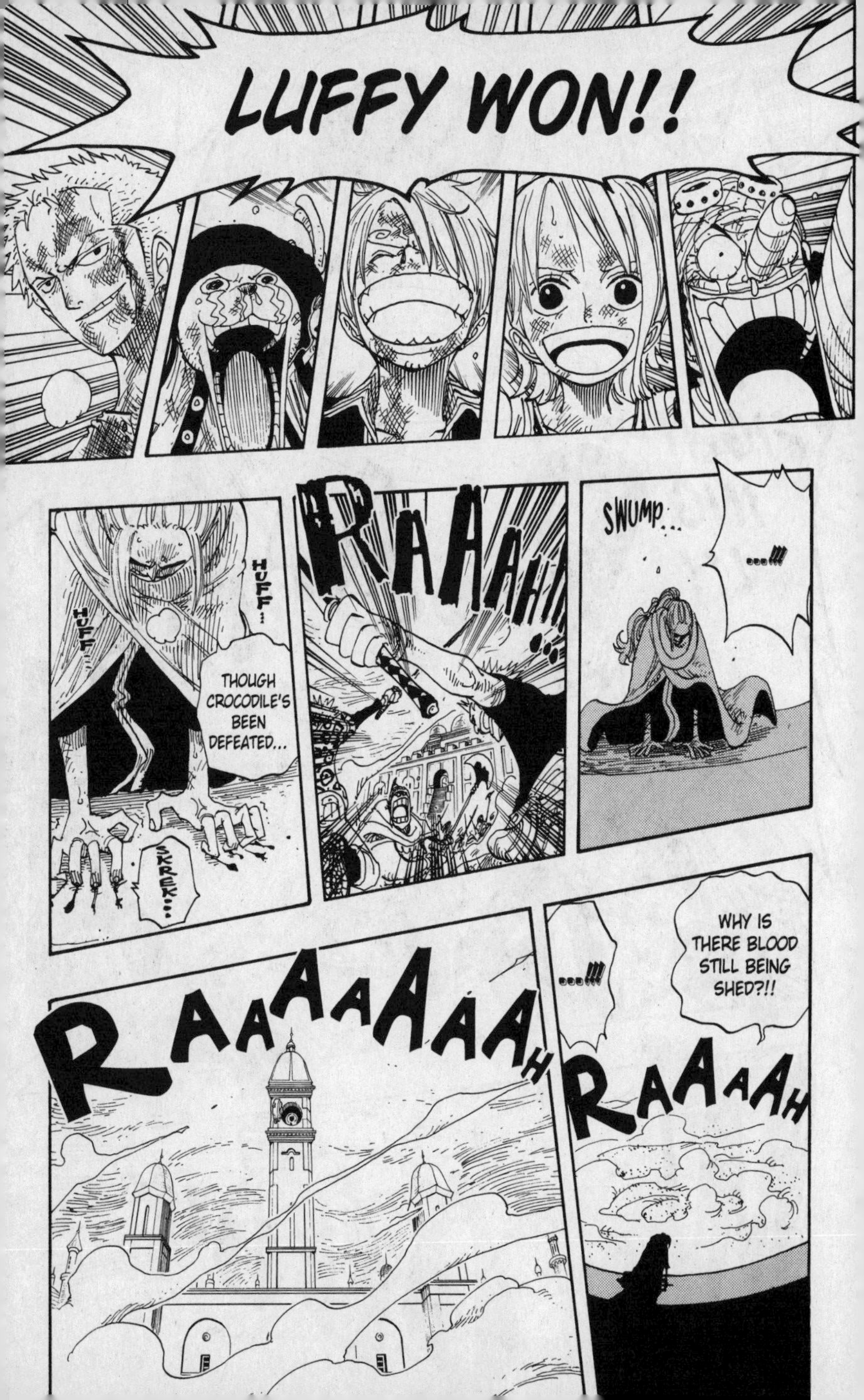
LUFFY WON!!
SWUMP...
...!!!
RAAAHH!!
HUFF...
HUFF...
THOUGH CROCODILE'S BEEN DEFEATED...
SKREK...
WHY IS THERE BLOOD STILL BEING SHED?!!
...!!!
RAAAAAH
RAAAAAAAAH

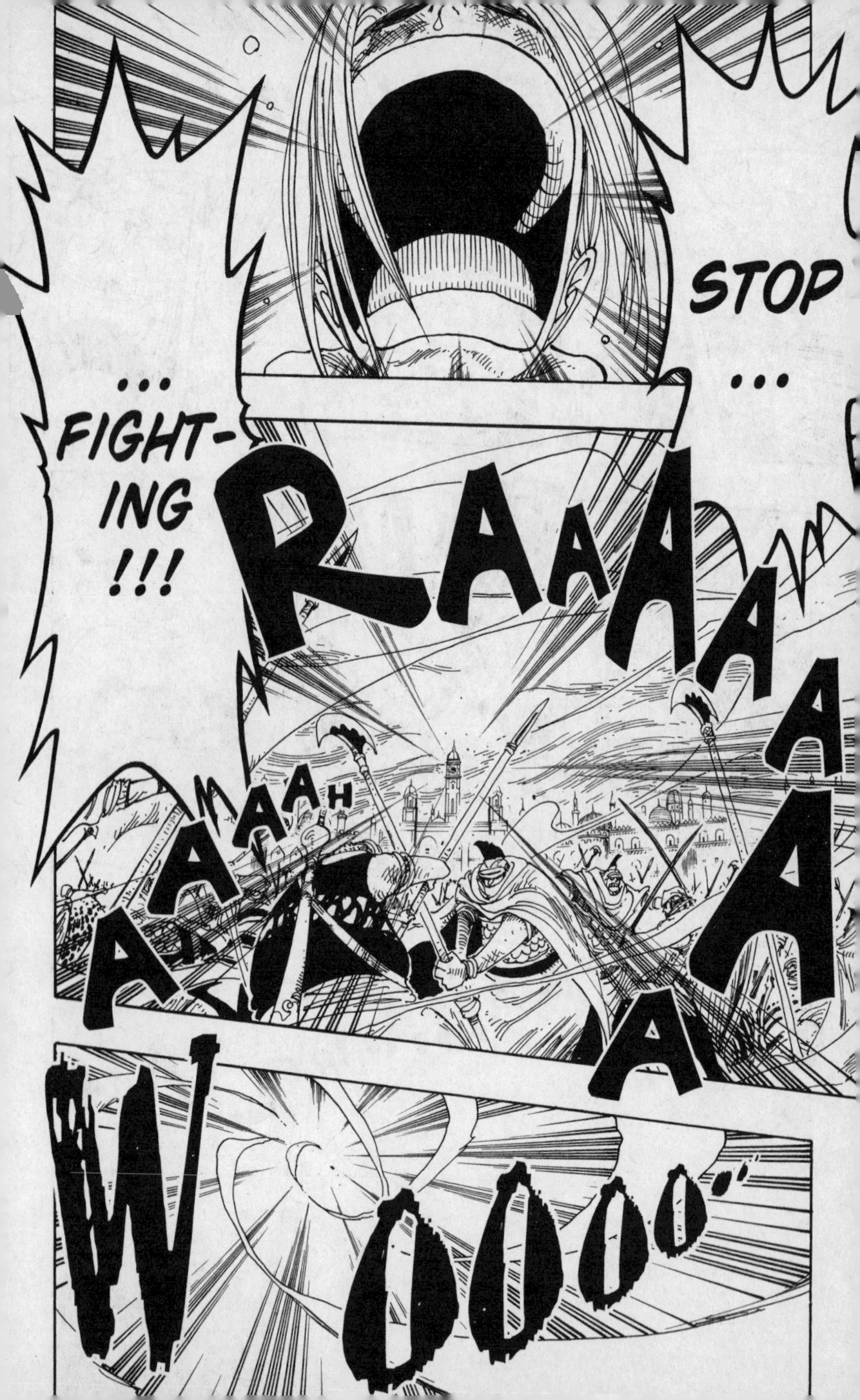
STOP ... ... FIGHT- ING !!!
RAAAAAAAAAAAAAAH
WOOOO

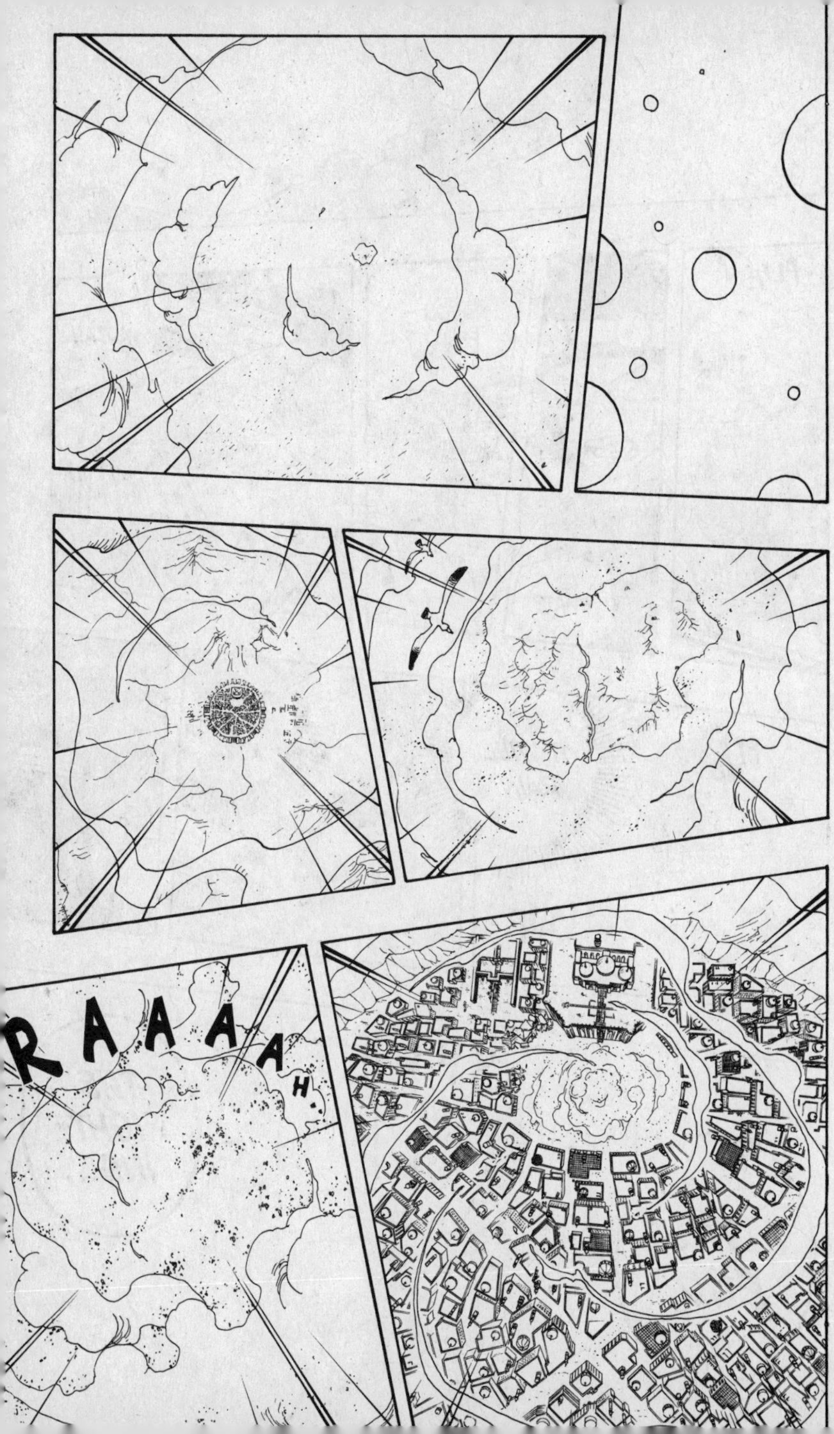
RAAAAH

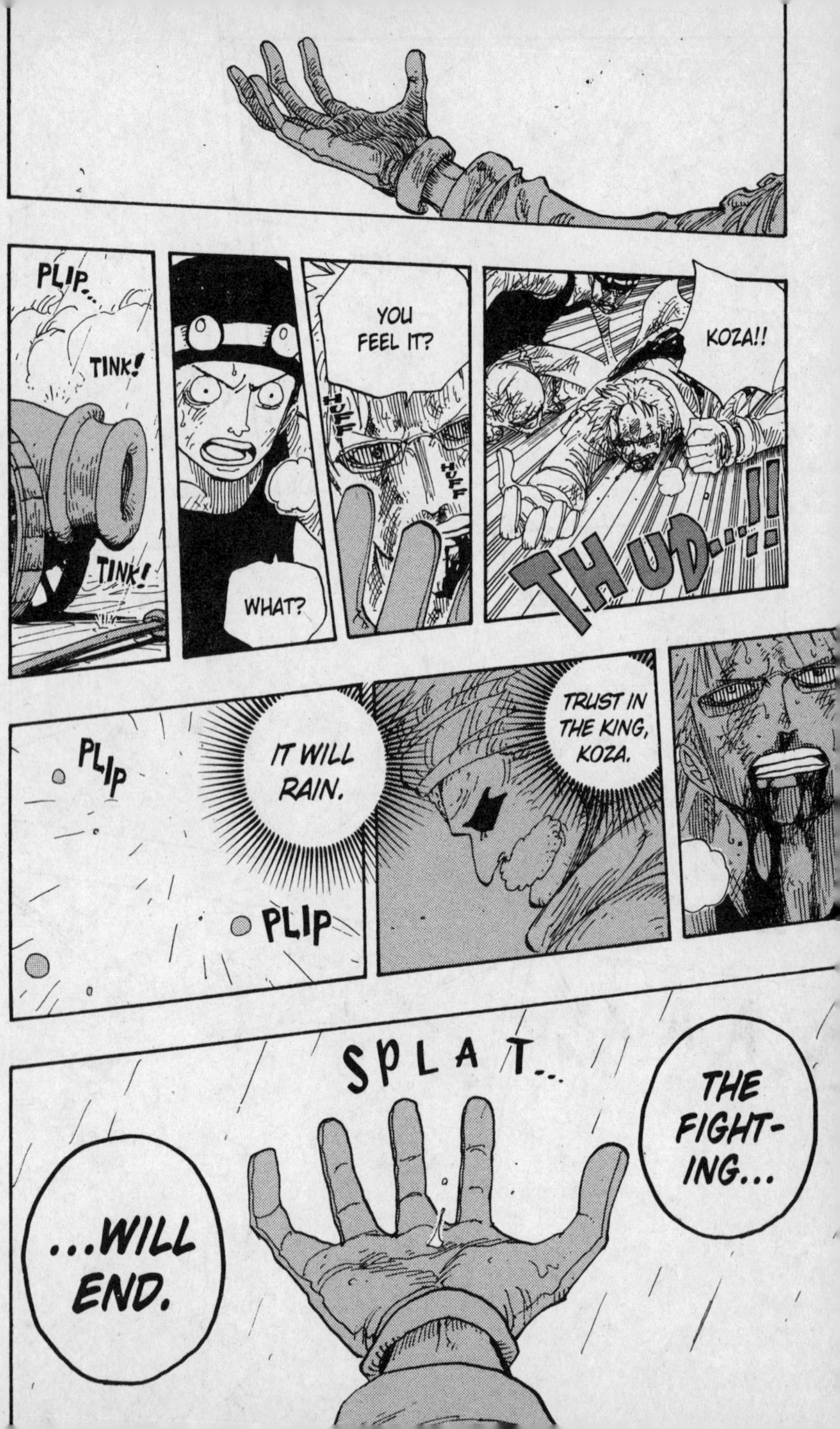
KOZA!!
THUD...!!
YOU FEEL IT?
HUFF
HUFF
WHAT?
PLIP...
TINK!
TINK!
TRUST IN THE KING, KOZA.
IT WILL RAIN.
PLIP
PLIP
SPLAT...
THE FIGHTING...
...WILL END.

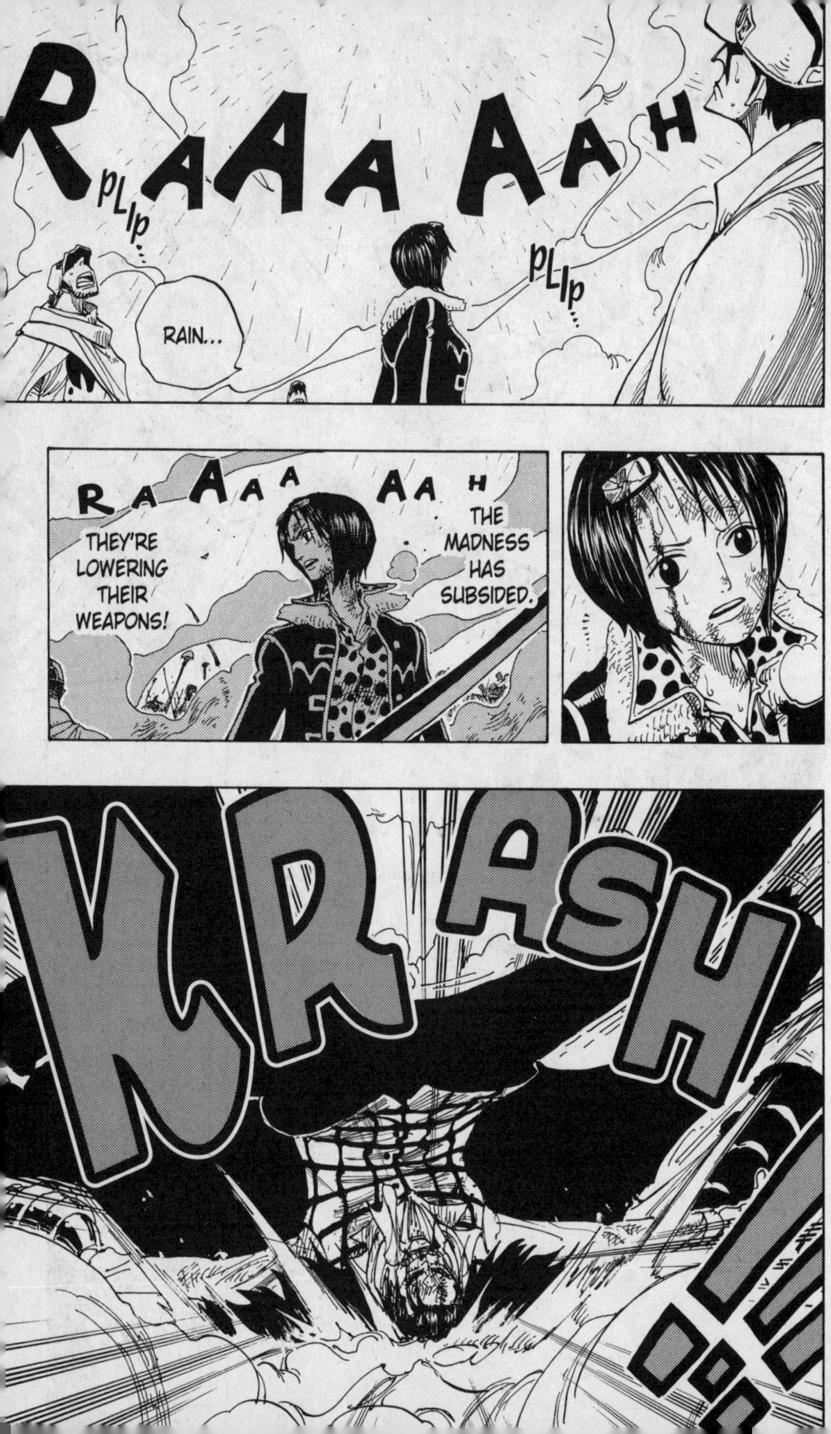
RAAAAAH
PLIP...
PLIP...
RAIN...
RAAAAAH
THE MADNESS HAS SUBSIDED.
THEY'RE LOWERING THEIR WEAPONS!
KRASH

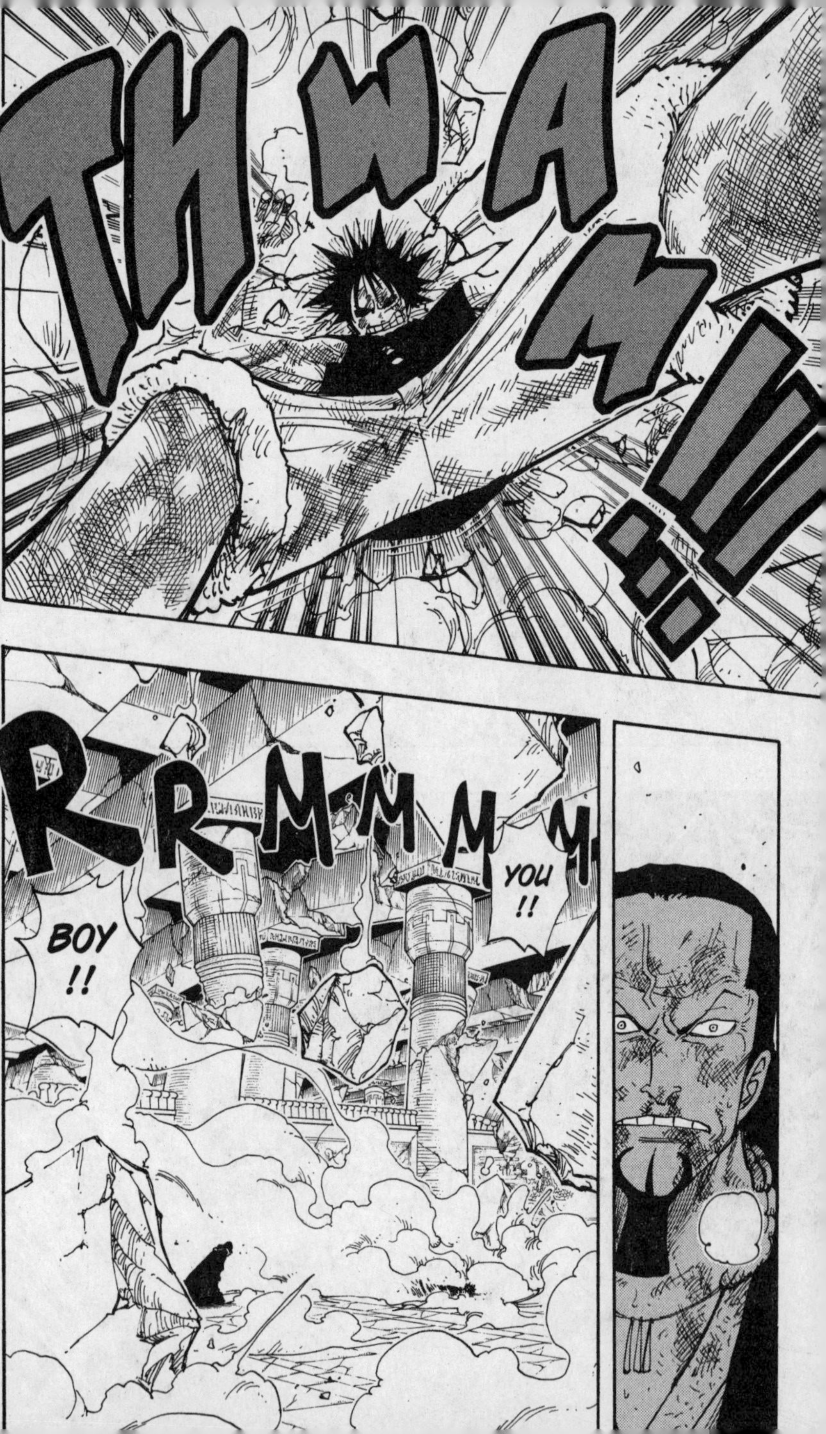
THWAMM!!
RRMMMM
YOU!!
BOY!!

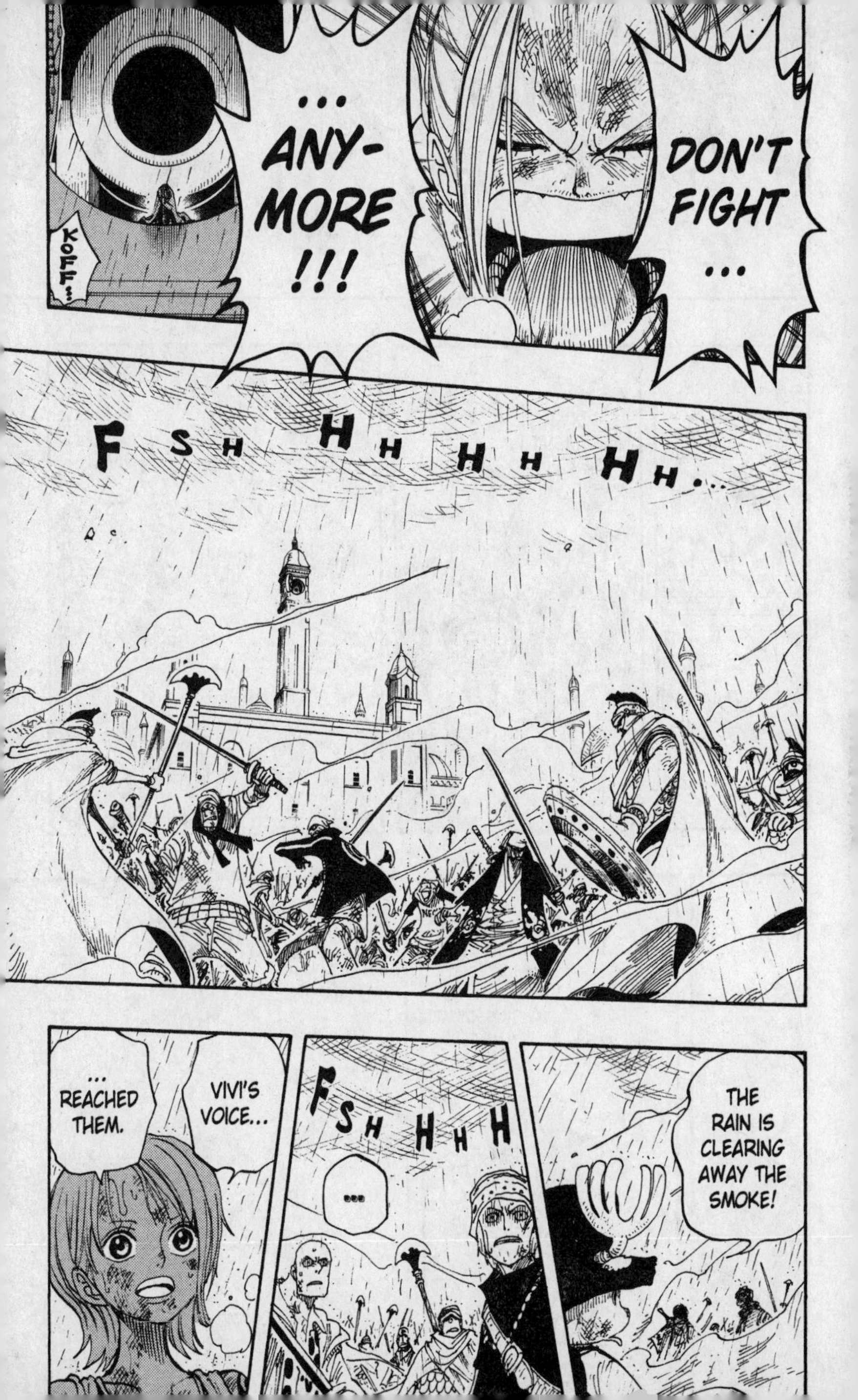
DON'T FIGHT ...
... ANY-MORE !!!
KOFF...
FSHHHHHHH...
THE RAIN IS CLEARING AWAY THE SMOKE!
FSHHHH
...
VIVI'S VOICE...
... REACHED THEM.

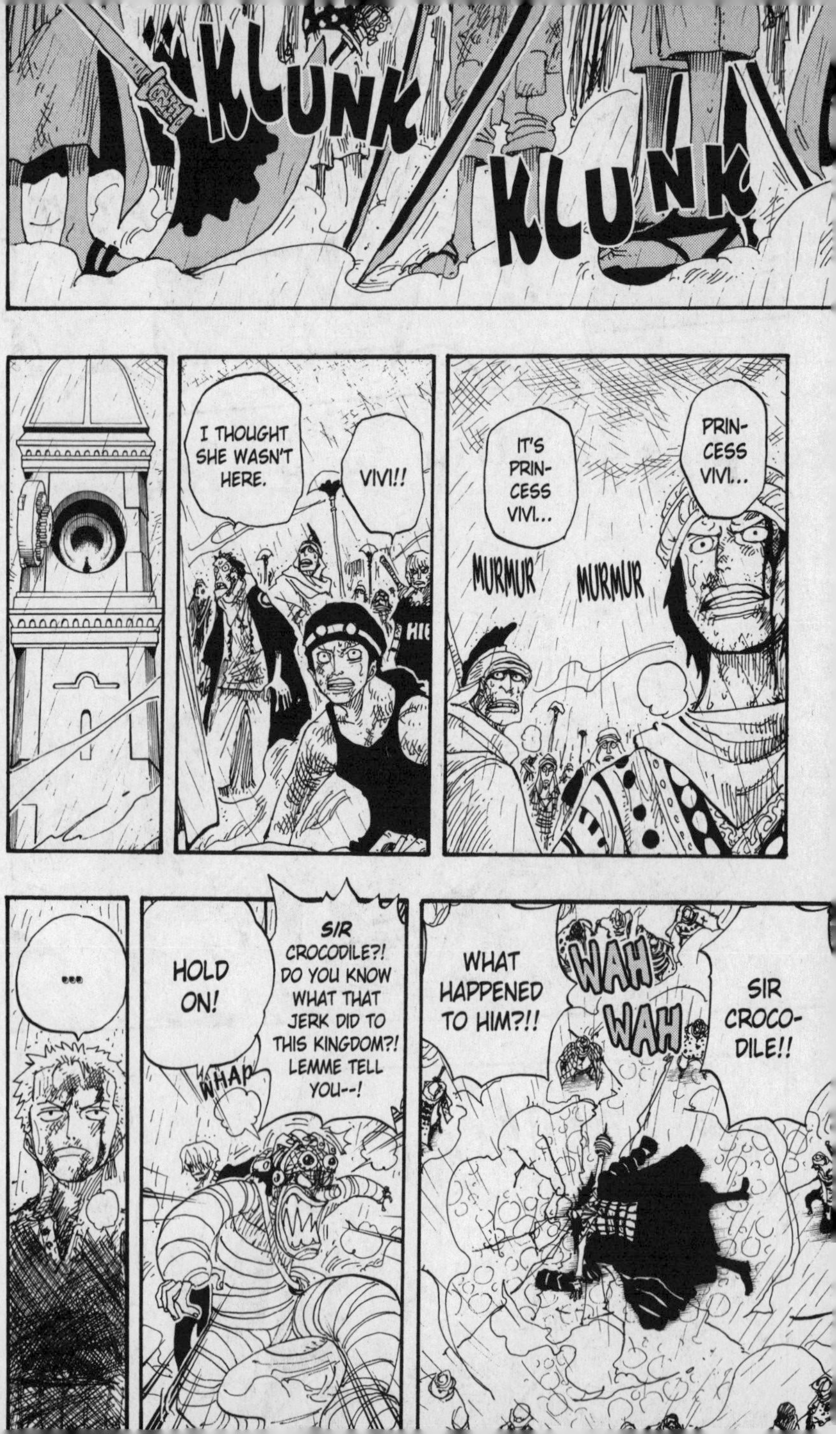
KLUNK
KLUNK
PRINCESS VIVI...
IT'S PRINCESS VIVI...
MURMUR
MURMUR
VIVI!!
I THOUGHT SHE WASN'T HERE.
SIR CROCODILE!!
WAH WAH
WHAT HAPPENED TO HIM?!!
SIR CROCODILE?! DO YOU KNOW WHAT THAT JERK DID TO THIS KINGDOM?! LEMME TELL YOU--!
HOLD ON!
WHAP
...

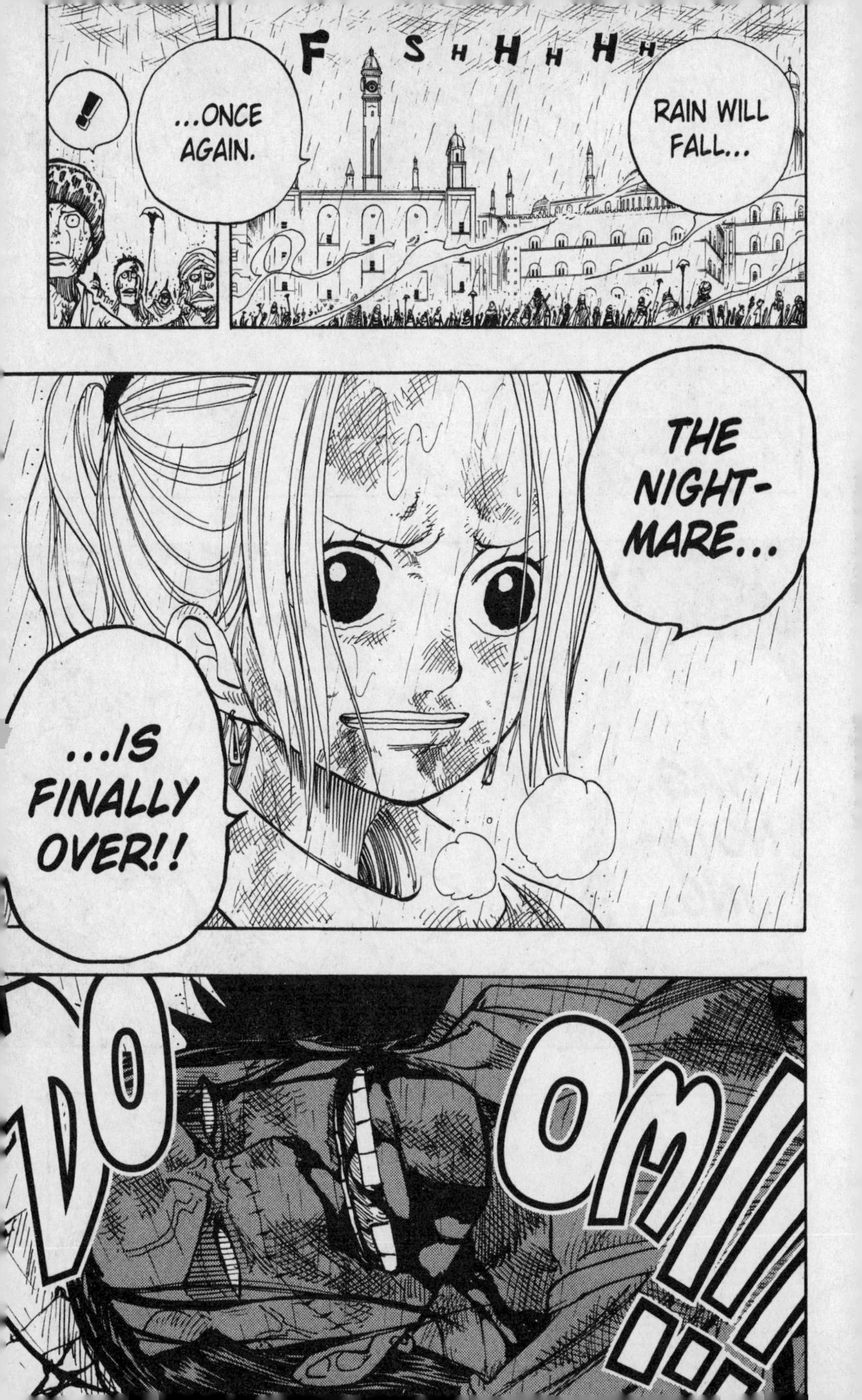
FSHHHHH
RAIN WILL FALL...
...ONCE AGAIN.
!
THE NIGHT-MARE...
...IS FINALLY OVER!!
DOOM!!

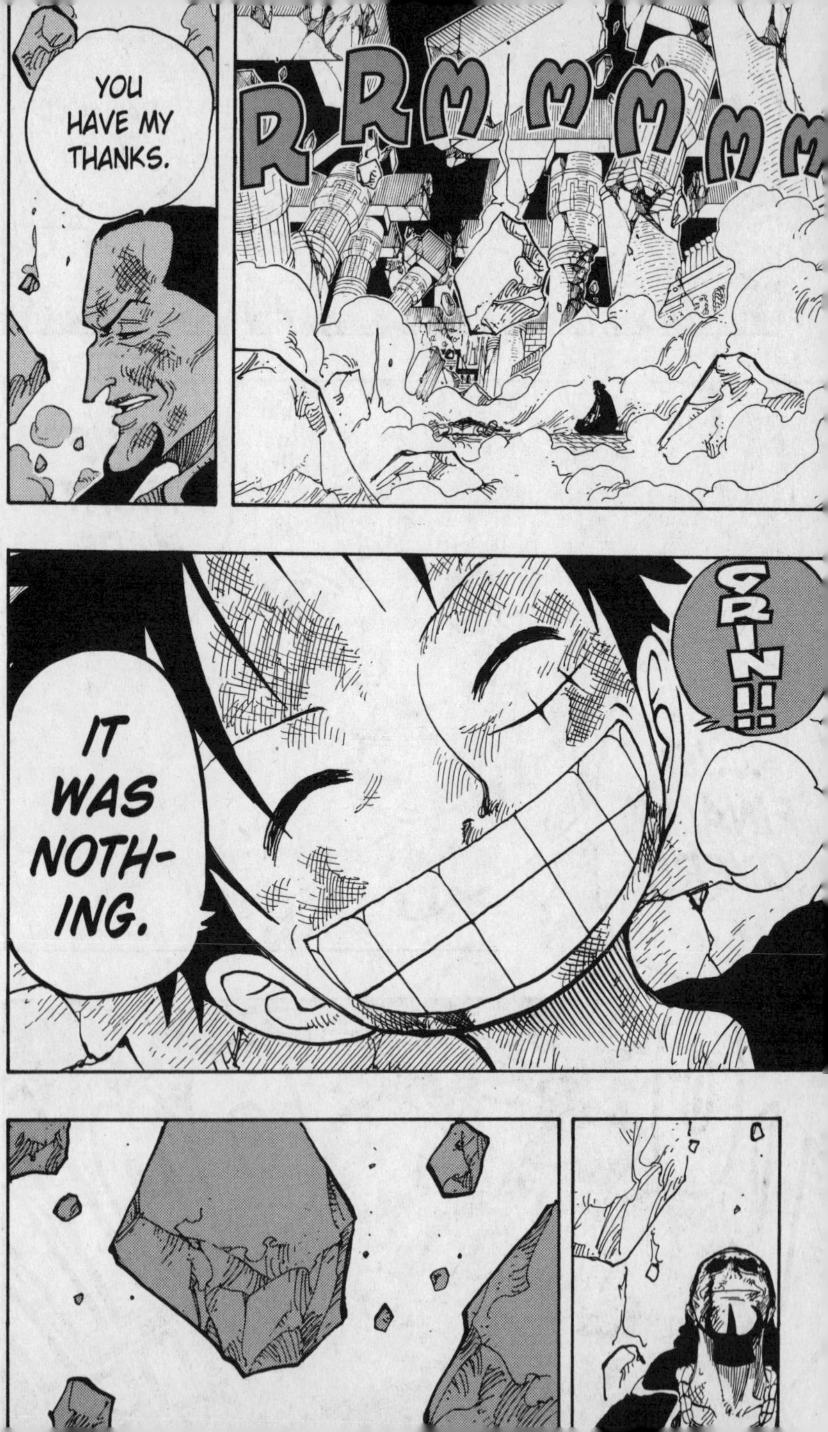
RRMMMMMM
YOU HAVE MY THANKS.
GRIN!!
IT WAS NOTHING.

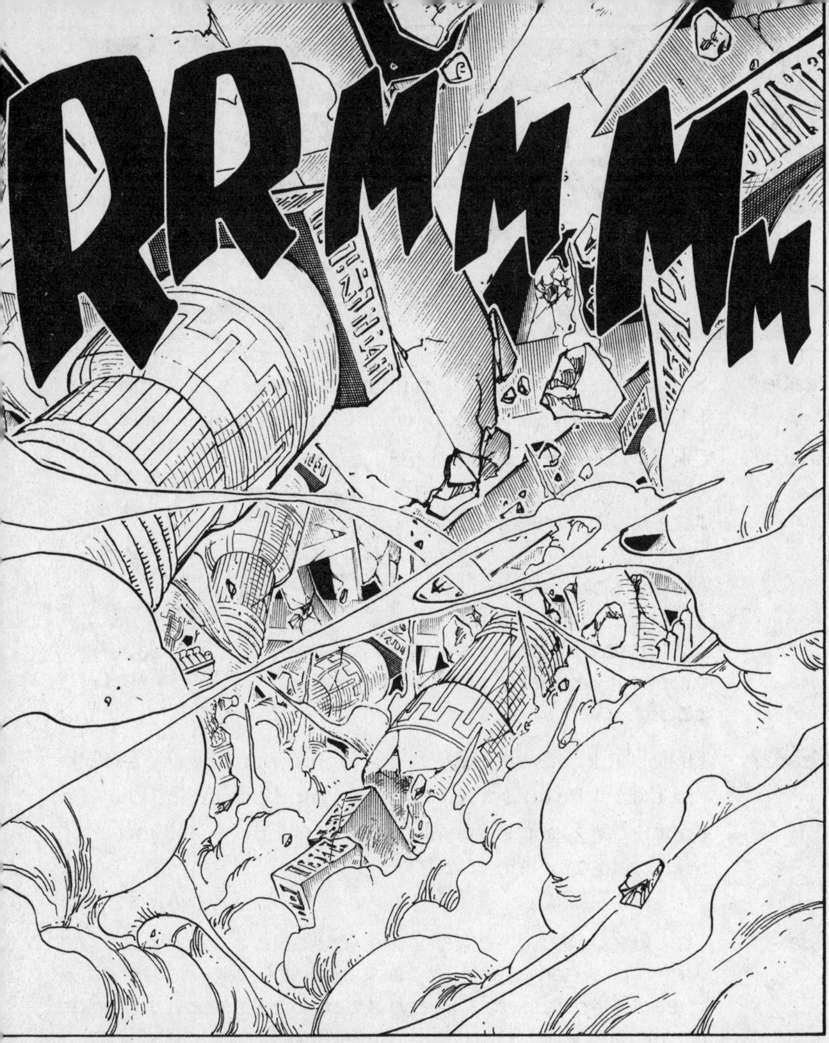
RRMMMM

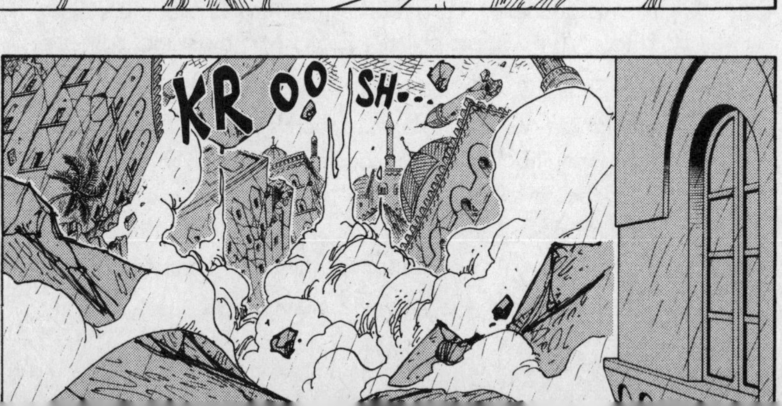
KROOSH...

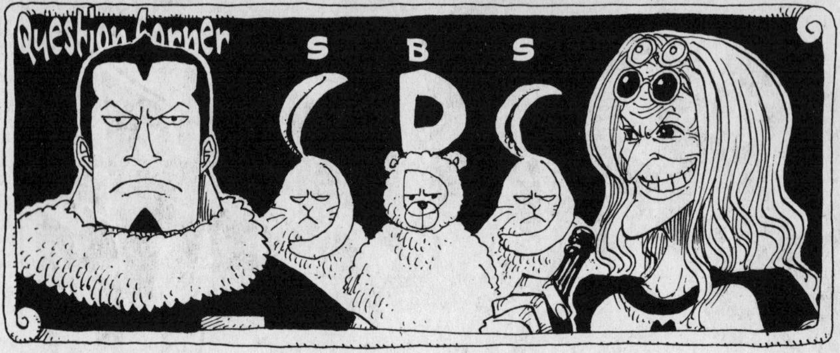
Question Corner
S B S

Reader: Shwennseeei, shwaaiiit a minnatt… (Sensei, wait a minute.) I-I-If Mr. 7 became Mr. 6, what would he look like?

Oda: Oh, if he were promoted, you mean? Well, Mr. 7 does have a face that shows he's "Mr. 7." (→) Maybe something like this. He looks so different! That might work if he were Mr. 9 too.

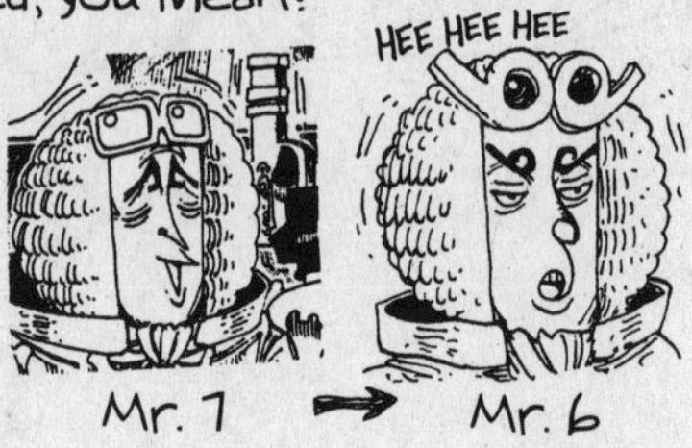
HEE HEE HEE
Mr. 7
Mr. 6

Reader: Hello, Oda Sensei!! I have a question about Vivi and Zolo!! (Ta-dah) Why does Vivi call Zolo "Mr. Bushido"?! (Da doom) I'm super, super, super curious!!! Please tell me. Bye! See you in a million years!

--Mr. Potato

Oda: You know how sometimes you give a friend a weird nickname and it sticks so you can never take it back? I guess it's like that. It would seem strange if she suddenly started calling him Zolo, right? I think Vivi will be calling Zolo Mr. Bushido forever.

Reader: Oda Sensei ♡, I enjoy both the manga and anime for *One Piece*. (^V^) V By the way, there's something I've been wondering about. What is the liquor that Dr. Kureha drinks? The label says "Ume" ("Plum" in English), but what kind of drink is it?

--Chopper's picture is on my cell phone ♡

Oda: It's plum wine. Homemade plum wine.

Chapter 211:
KING

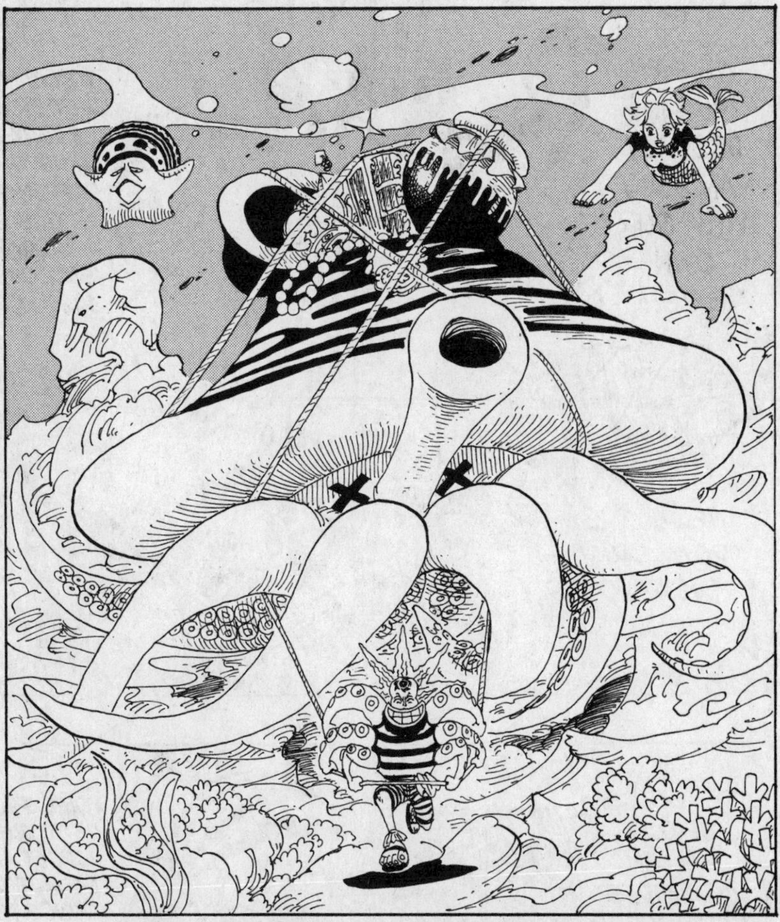

HACHI'S WALK ON THE SEA FLOOR, VOL. 26:
"NOW THAT I'VE GOT MACRO'S TREASURE TOO,
THERE'S NO WAY SHE'LL TURN ME DOWN"

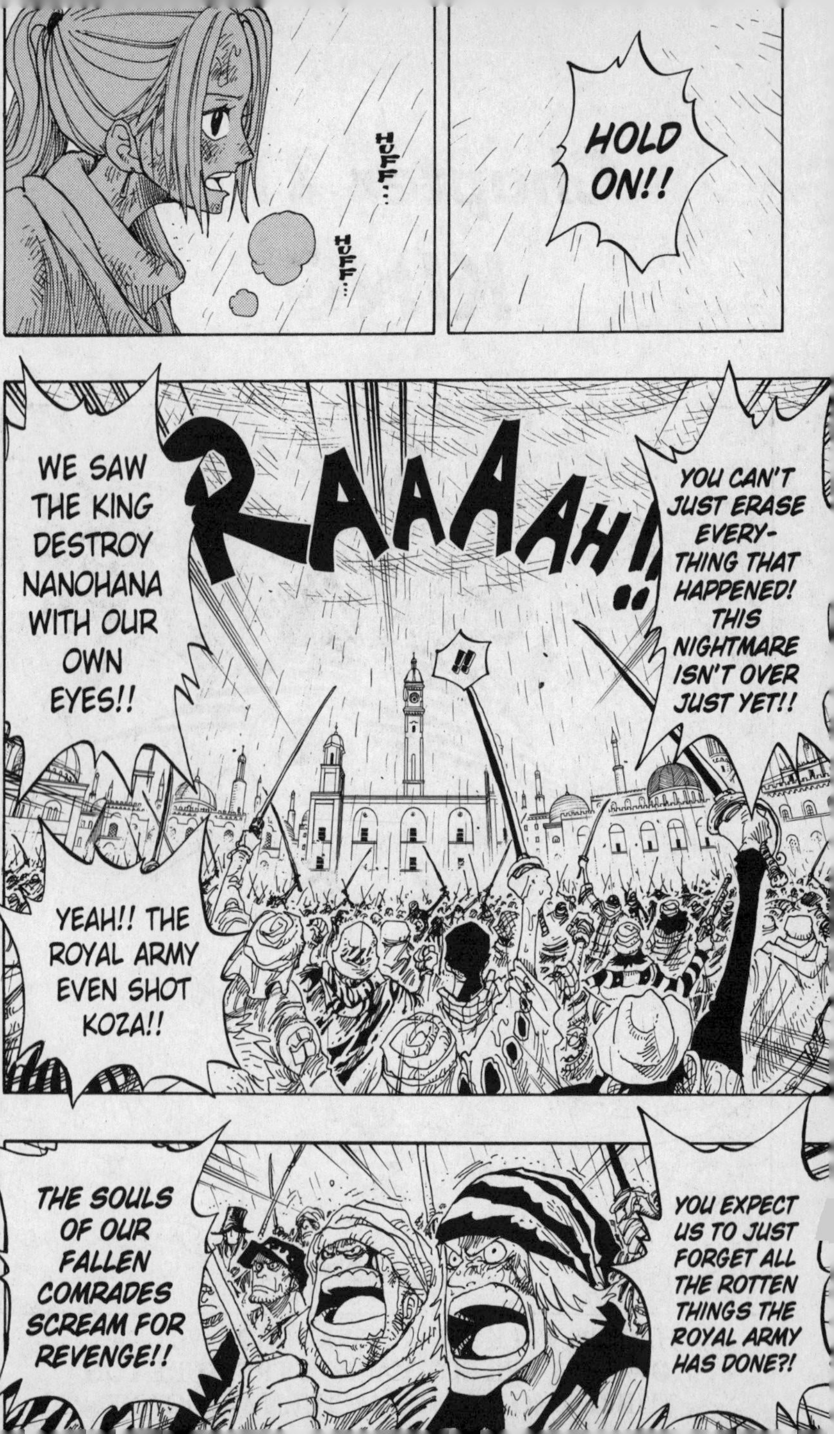
HOLD ON!!
HUFF...
HUFF...
YOU CAN'T JUST ERASE EVERY-THING THAT HAPPENED! THIS NIGHTMARE ISN'T OVER JUST YET!!
RAAAAH!!
!!
WE SAW THE KING DESTROY NANOHANA WITH OUR OWN EYES!!
YEAH!! THE ROYAL ARMY EVEN SHOT KOZA!!
YOU EXPECT US TO JUST FORGET ALL THE ROTTEN THINGS THE ROYAL ARMY HAS DONE?!
THE SOULS OF OUR FALLEN COMRADES SCREAM FOR REVENGE!!

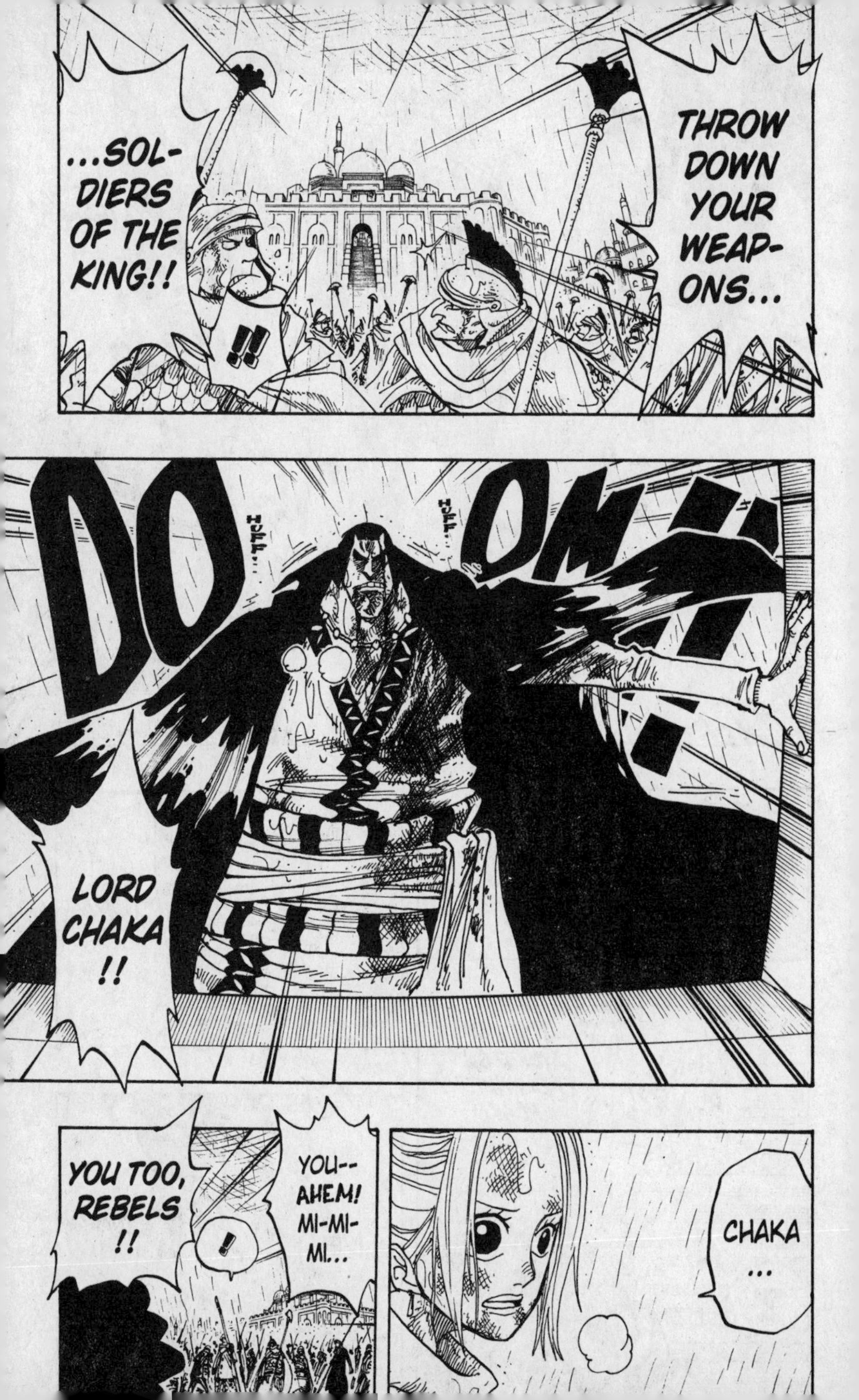
THROW DOWN YOUR WEAP-ONS...
...SOL-DIERS OF THE KING!!
!!
DO
OM!!
HUFF...
HUFF...
LORD CHAKA!!
CHAKA...
YOU-- AHEM! MI-MI-MI...
YOU TOO, REBELS!!
!

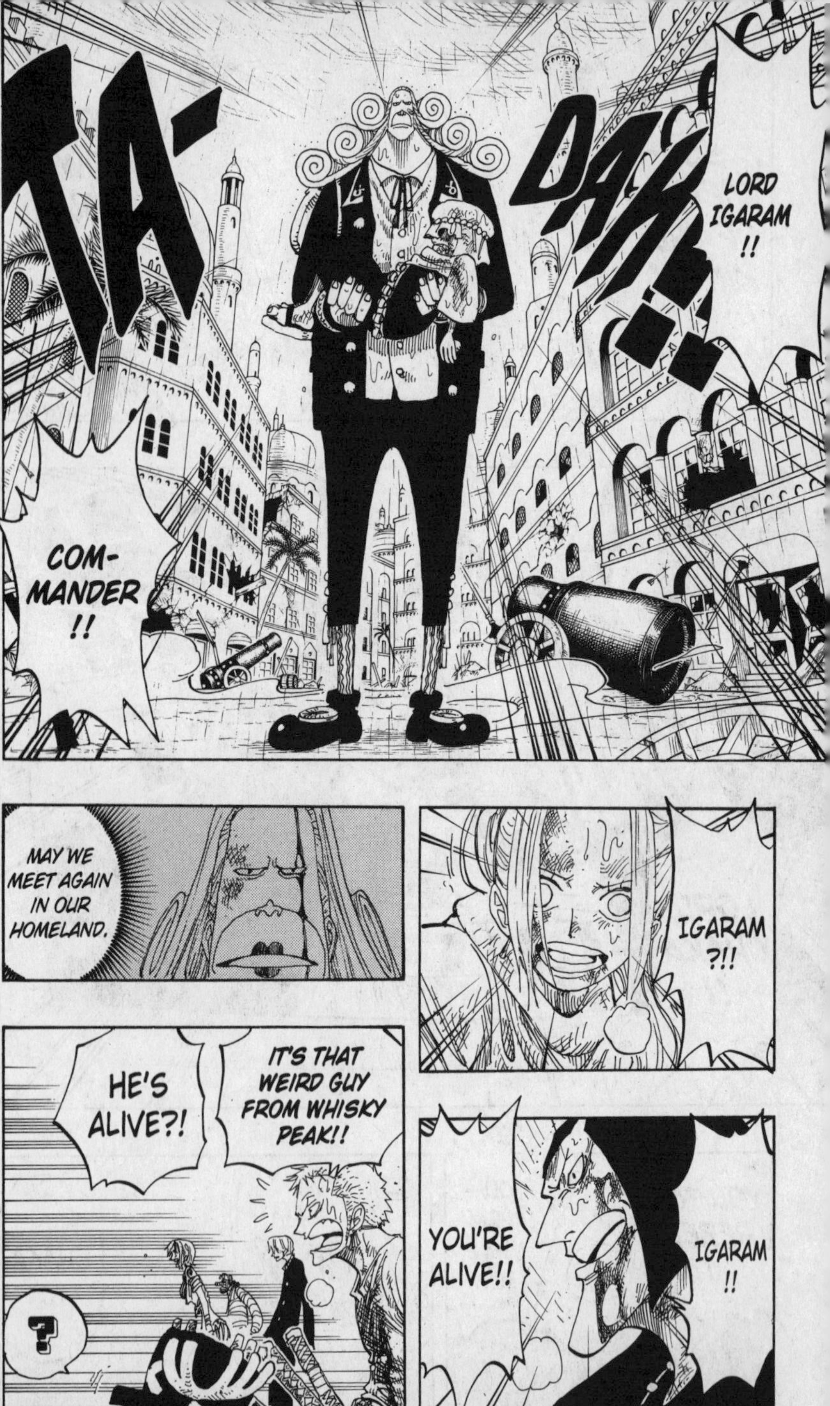
TA-
DAH
LORD IGARAM!!
COMMANDER!!
IGARAM?!!
MAY WE MEET AGAIN IN OUR HOMELAND.
IGARAM!!
YOU'RE ALIVE!!
IT'S THAT WEIRD GUY FROM WHISKY PEAK!!
HE'S ALIVE?!
?

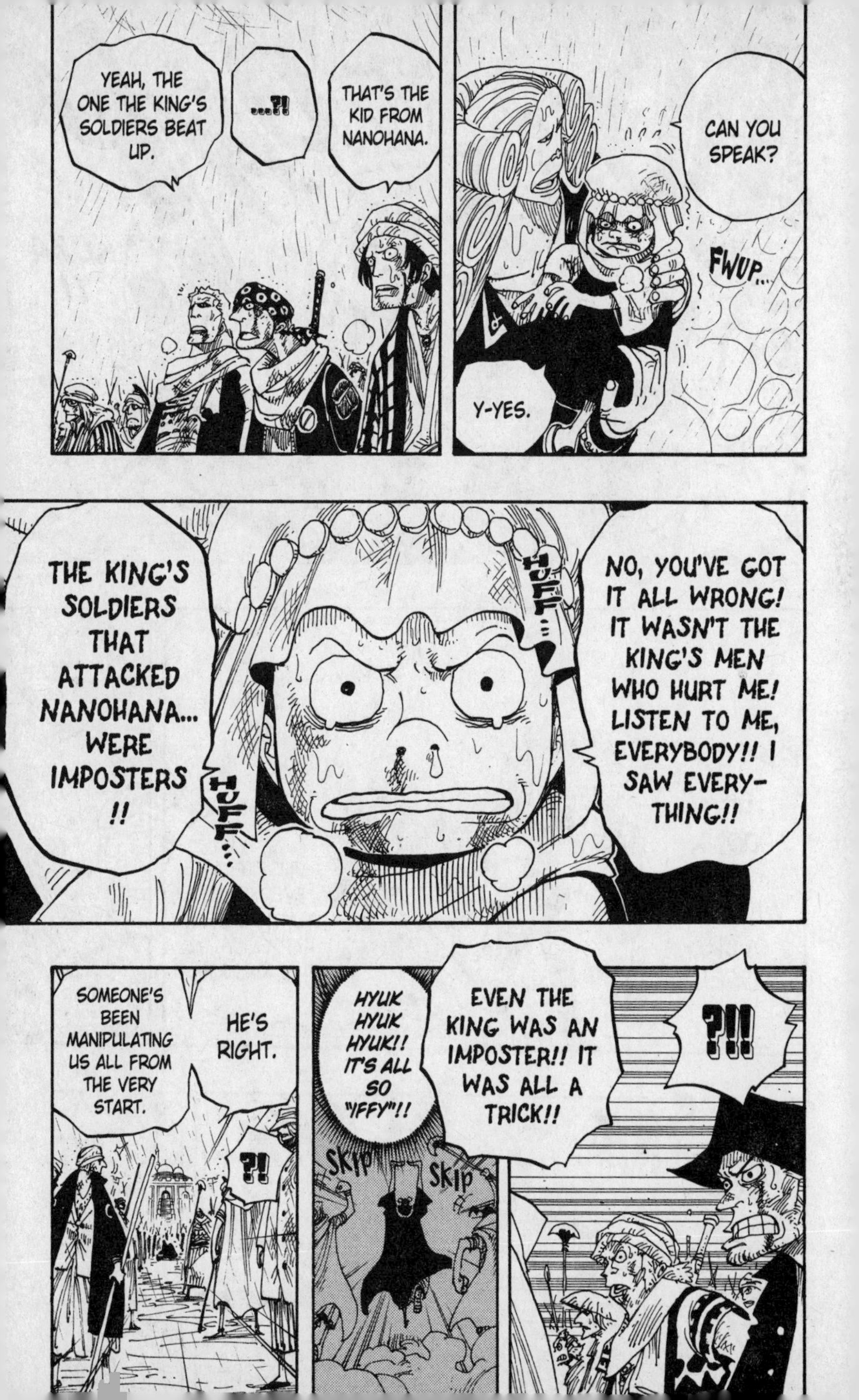
CAN YOU SPEAK?
FWUP...
Y-YES.
THAT'S THE KID FROM NANOHANA.
...?!
YEAH, THE ONE THE KING'S SOLDIERS BEAT UP.
NO, YOU'VE GOT IT ALL WRONG! IT WASN'T THE KING'S MEN WHO HURT ME! LISTEN TO ME, EVERYBODY!! I SAW EVERY-THING!!
HUFF...
THE KING'S SOLDIERS THAT ATTACKED NANOHANA... WERE IMPOSTERS!!
HUFF...
?!!
EVEN THE KING WAS AN IMPOSTER!! IT WAS ALL A TRICK!!
HYUK HYUK HYUK!! IT'S ALL SO "IFFY"!!
SKIP
SKIP
HE'S RIGHT.
SOMEONE'S BEEN MANIPULATING US ALL FROM THE VERY START.
?!

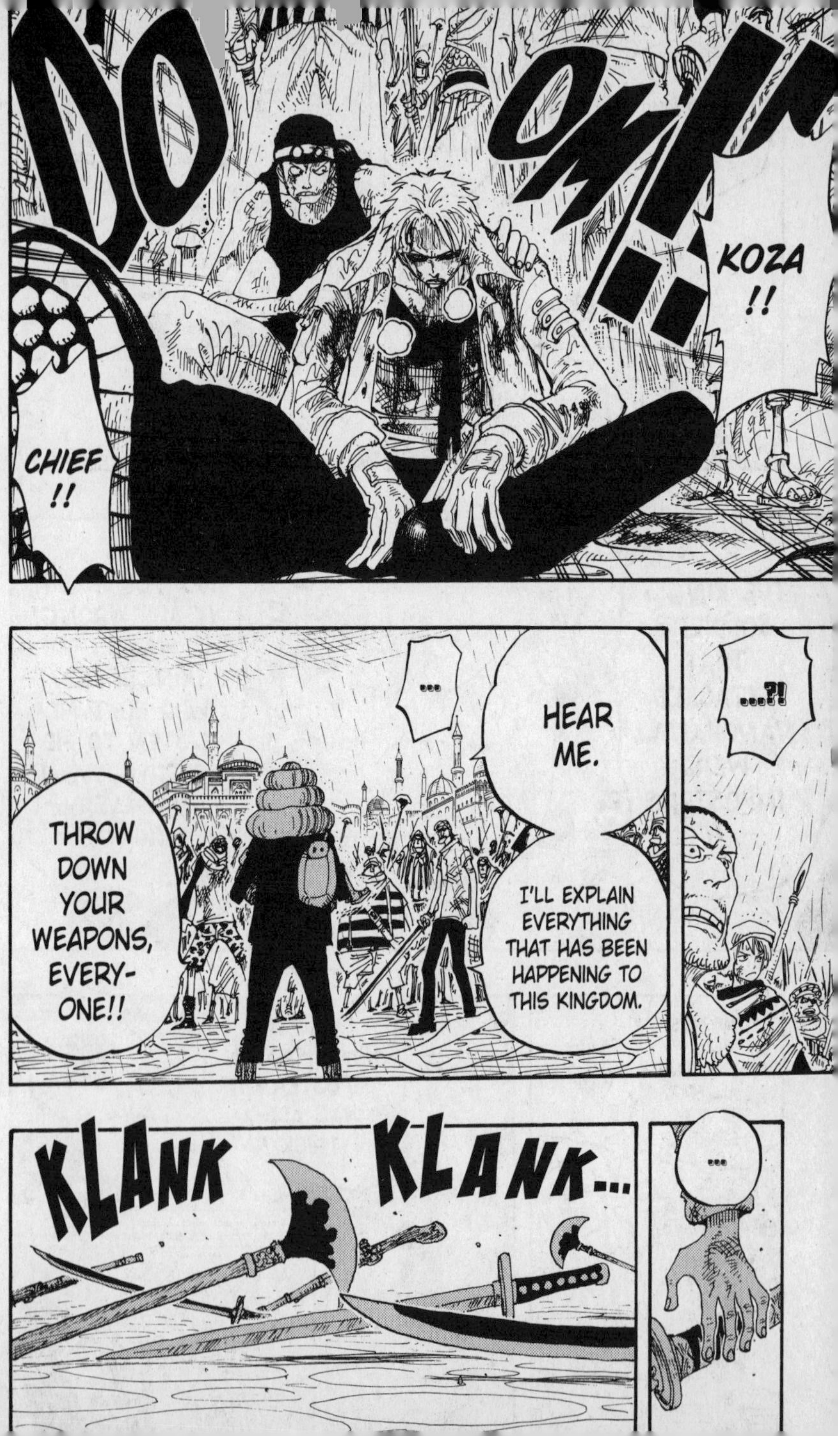
DOOM!!
KOZA !!
CHIEF !!
...?!
HEAR ME.
...
I'LL EXPLAIN EVERYTHING THAT HAS BEEN HAPPENING TO THIS KINGDOM.
THROW DOWN YOUR WEAPONS, EVERY-ONE!!
...
KLANK KLANK...

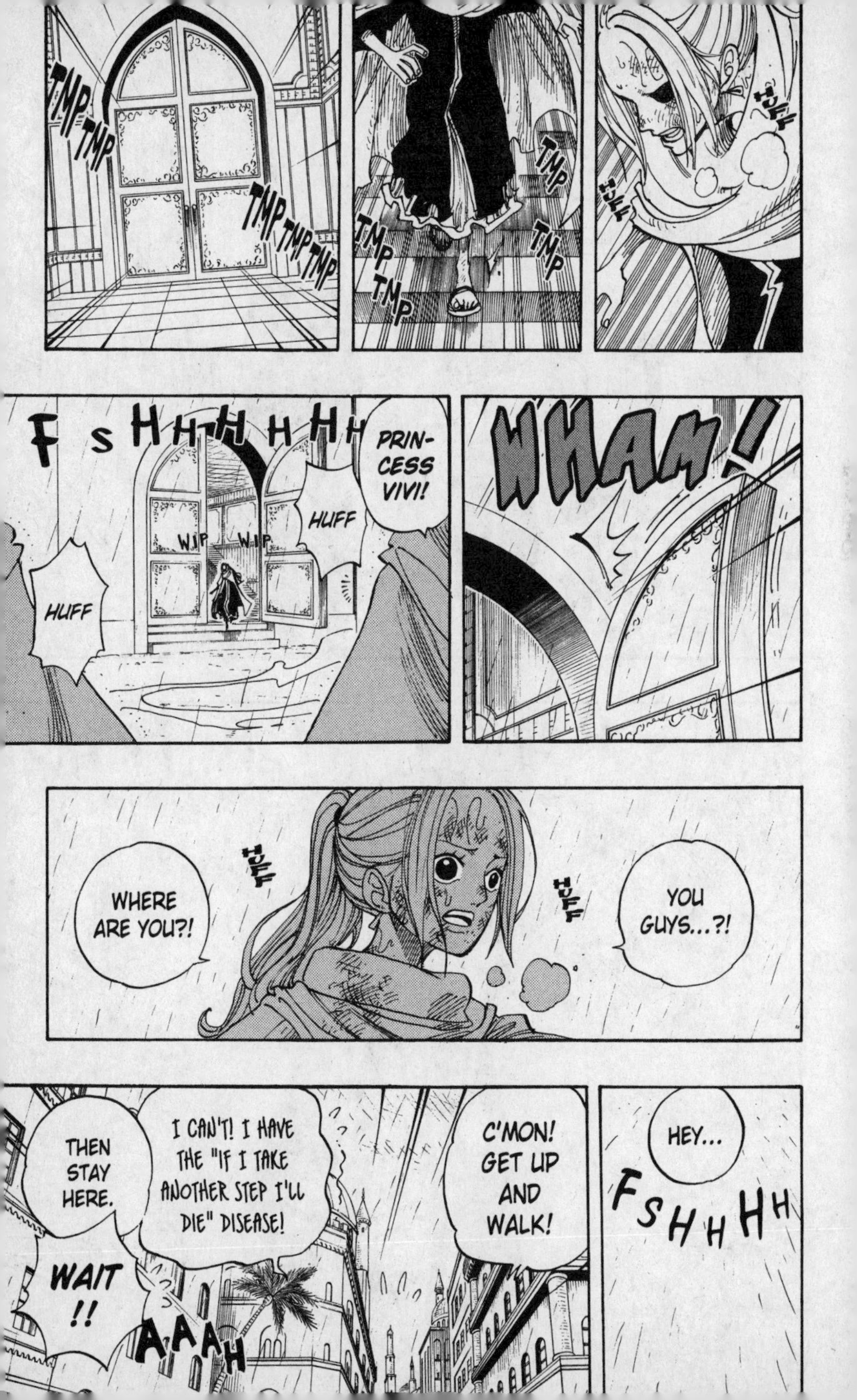
HUFF
HUFF
TMP
TMP
TMP
TMP
TMP TMP
TMP TMP TMP
WHAM!
PRIN-CESS VIVI!
HUFF
WIP WIP
FSHHHHHH
HUFF
YOU GUYS...?!
HUFF
HUFF
WHERE ARE YOU?!
HEY...
FSHHHH
C'MON! GET UP AND WALK!
I CAN'T! I HAVE THE "IF I TAKE ANOTHER STEP I'LL DIE" DISEASE!
THEN STAY HERE.
WAIT!!
AAAH

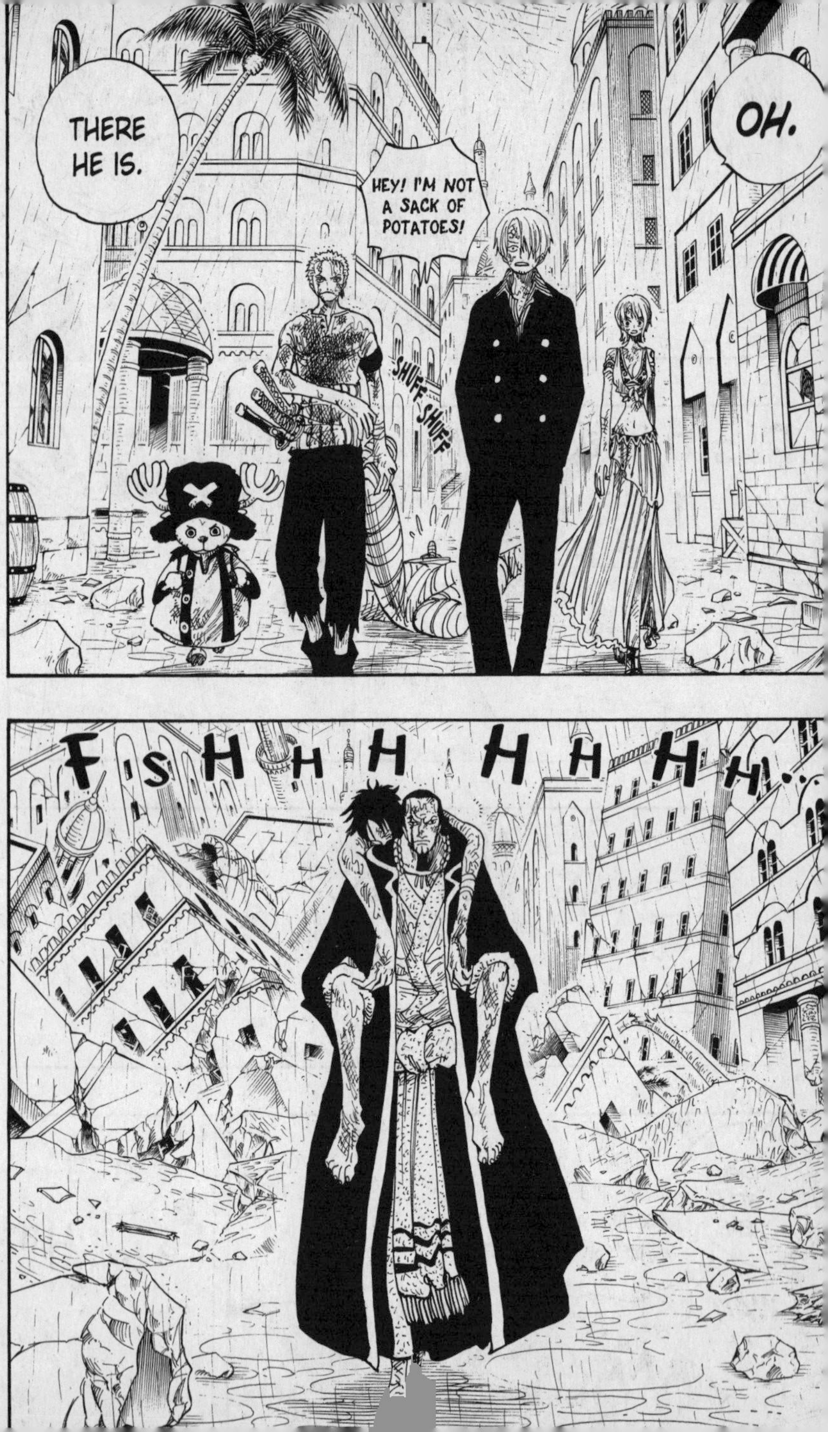
OH.
HEY! I'M NOT A SACK OF POTATOES!
SHUFF SHUFF
THERE HE IS.
FSHHHHHHH...

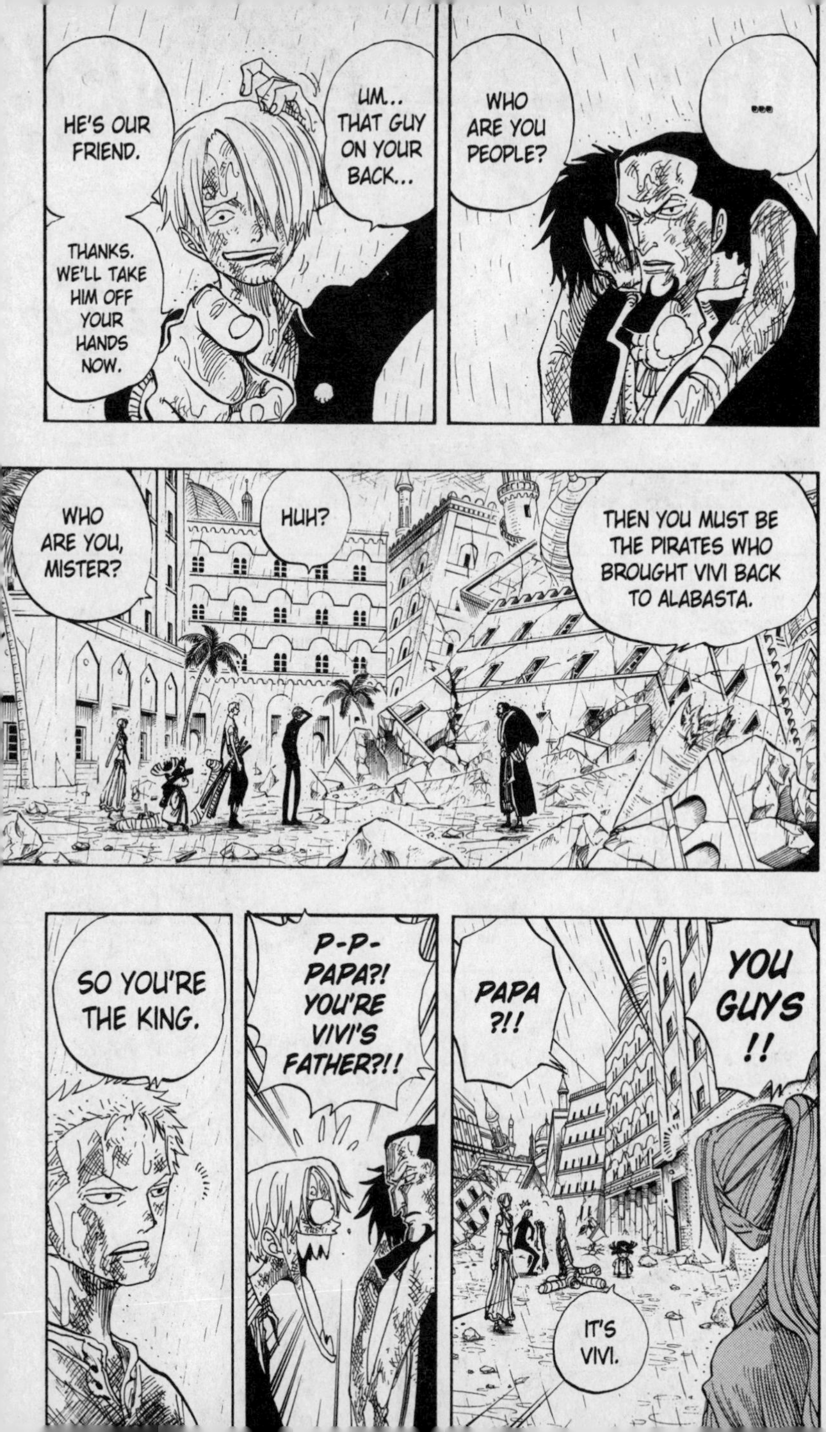
...
WHO ARE YOU PEOPLE?
UM... THAT GUY ON YOUR BACK...
HE'S OUR FRIEND.
THANKS. WE'LL TAKE HIM OFF YOUR HANDS NOW.
THEN YOU MUST BE THE PIRATES WHO BROUGHT VIVI BACK TO ALABASTA.
HUH?
WHO ARE YOU, MISTER?
YOU GUYS !!
PAPA ?!!
IT'S VIVI.
P-P-PAPA?! YOU'RE VIVI'S FATHER?!!
SO YOU'RE THE KING.

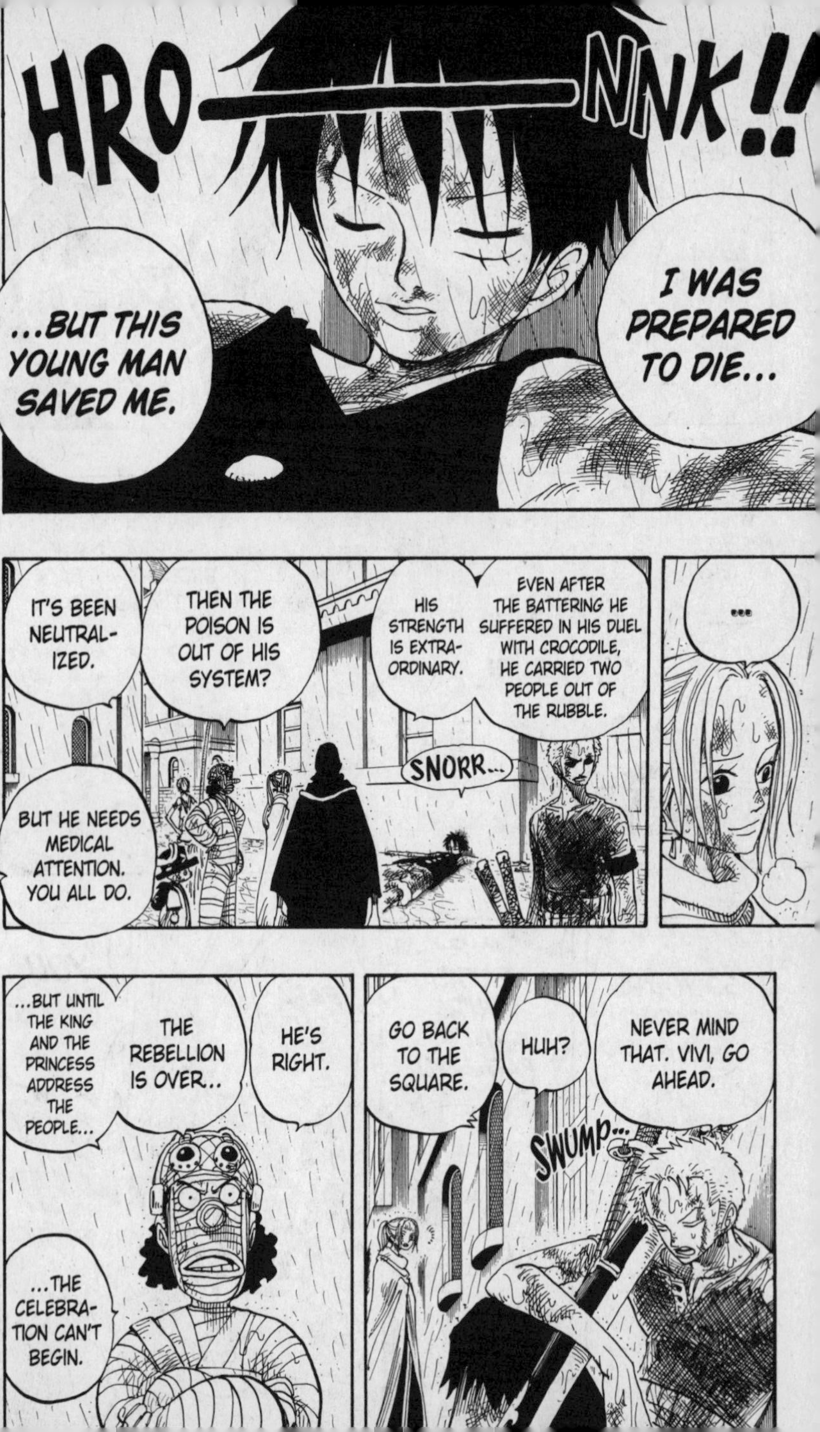
HRO—NNK!!
I WAS PREPARED TO DIE...
...BUT THIS YOUNG MAN SAVED ME.
...
EVEN AFTER THE BATTERING HE SUFFERED IN HIS DUEL WITH CROCODILE, HE CARRIED TWO PEOPLE OUT OF THE RUBBLE.
HIS STRENGTH IS EXTRAORDINARY.
THEN THE POISON IS OUT OF HIS SYSTEM?
IT'S BEEN NEUTRALIZED.
SNORR...
BUT HE NEEDS MEDICAL ATTENTION. YOU ALL DO.
NEVER MIND THAT. VIVI, GO AHEAD.
HUH?
GO BACK TO THE SQUARE.
SWUMP...
HE'S RIGHT.
THE REBELLION IS OVER...
...BUT UNTIL THE KING AND THE PRINCESS ADDRESS THE PEOPLE...
...THE CELEBRATION CAN'T BEGIN.

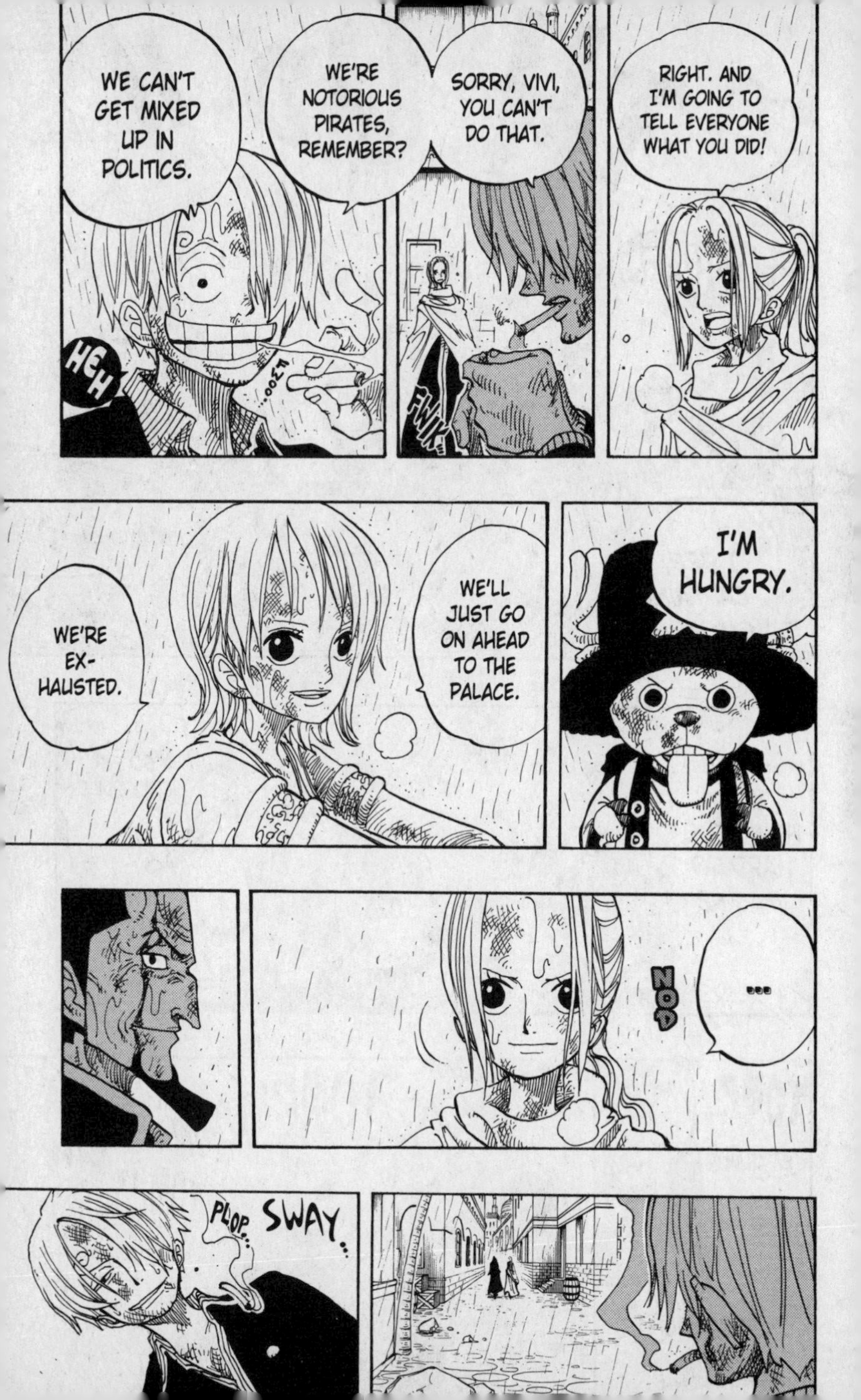
RIGHT. AND I'M GOING TO TELL EVERYONE WHAT YOU DID!
SORRY, VIVI, YOU CAN'T DO THAT.
FWIP
WE'RE NOTORIOUS PIRATES, REMEMBER?
WE CAN'T GET MIXED UP IN POLITICS.
HEH
I'M HUNGRY.
WE'LL JUST GO ON AHEAD TO THE PALACE.
WE'RE EX-HAUSTED.
...
NOD
PLOP
SWAY...

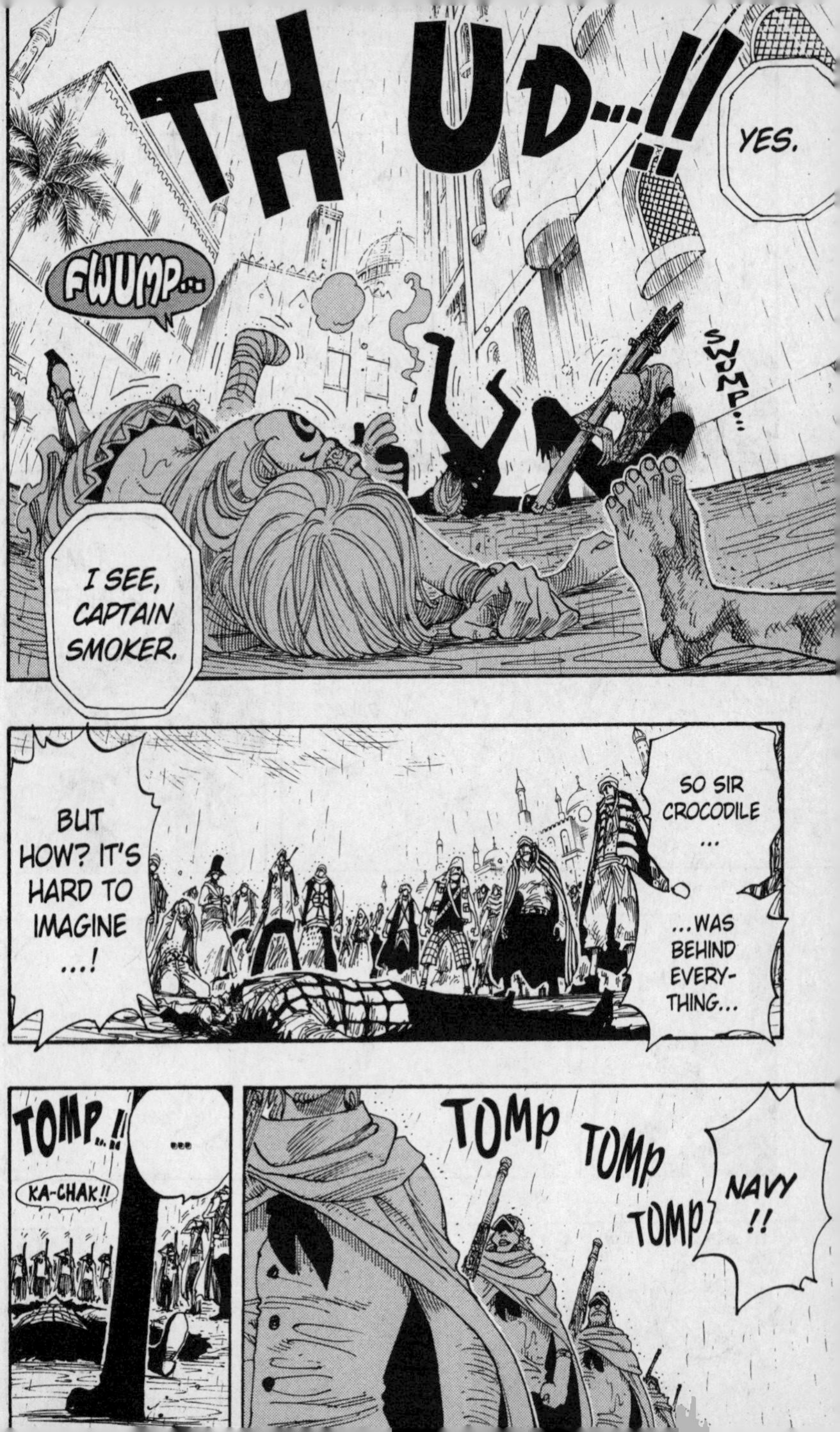
YES.
THUD...!!
SWUMP...
FWUMP...
I SEE, CAPTAIN SMOKER.
SO SIR CROCODILE...
...WAS BEHIND EVERYTHING...
BUT HOW? IT'S HARD TO IMAGINE...!
NAVY!!
TOMP TOMP TOMP TOMP
TOMP..!!
...
KA-CHAK!!

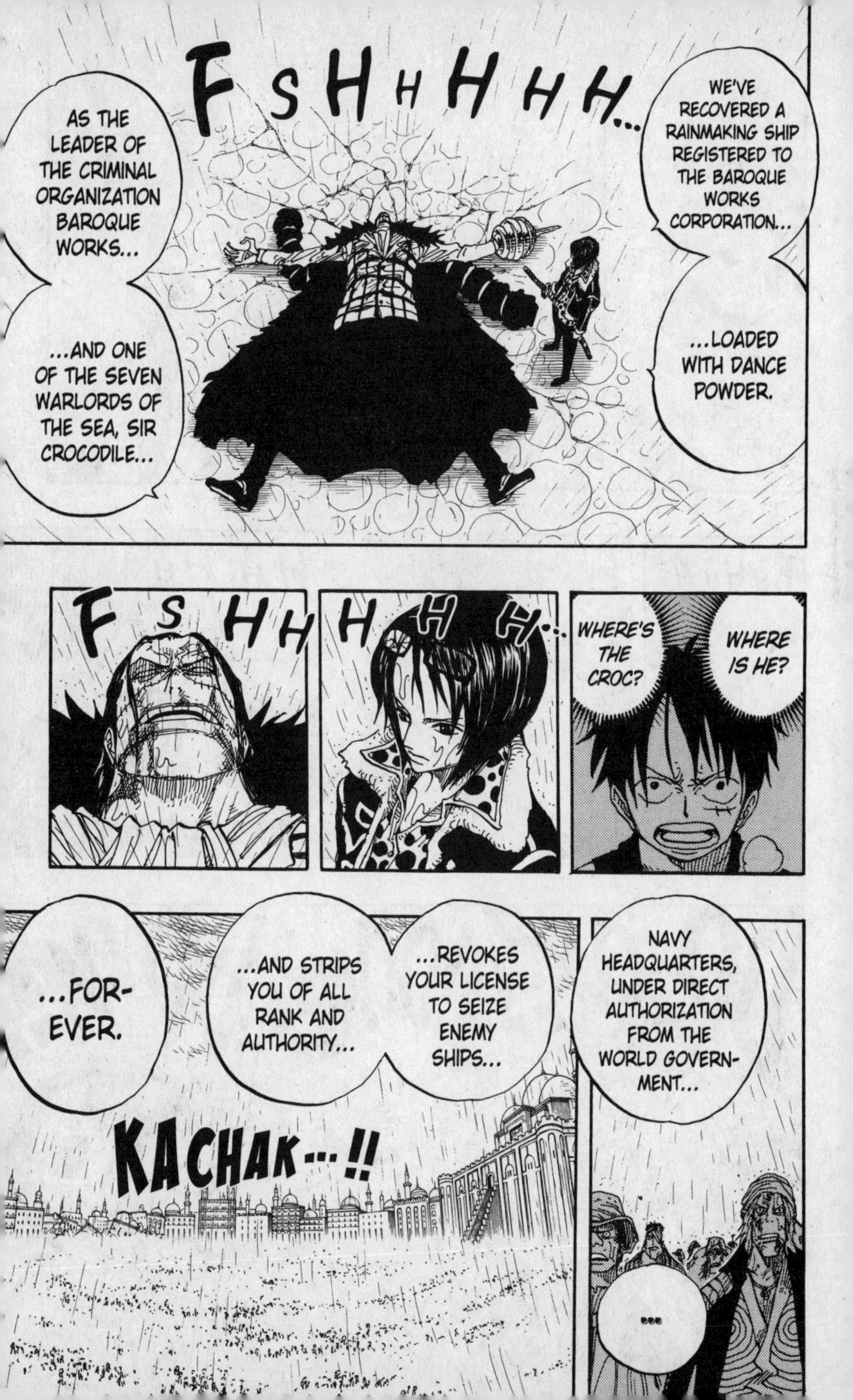
FSHHHHH...
WE'VE RECOVERED A RAINMAKING SHIP REGISTERED TO THE BAROQUE WORKS CORPORATION...
...LOADED WITH DANCE POWDER.
AS THE LEADER OF THE CRIMINAL ORGANIZATION BAROQUE WORKS...
...AND ONE OF THE SEVEN WARLORDS OF THE SEA, SIR CROCODILE...
FSHHHHH...
WHERE IS HE?
WHERE'S THE CROC?
NAVY HEADQUARTERS, UNDER DIRECT AUTHORIZATION FROM THE WORLD GOVERN-MENT...
...
...REVOKES YOUR LICENSE TO SEIZE ENEMY SHIPS...
...AND STRIPS YOU OF ALL RANK AND AUTHORITY...
...FOR-EVER.
KACHAK...!!

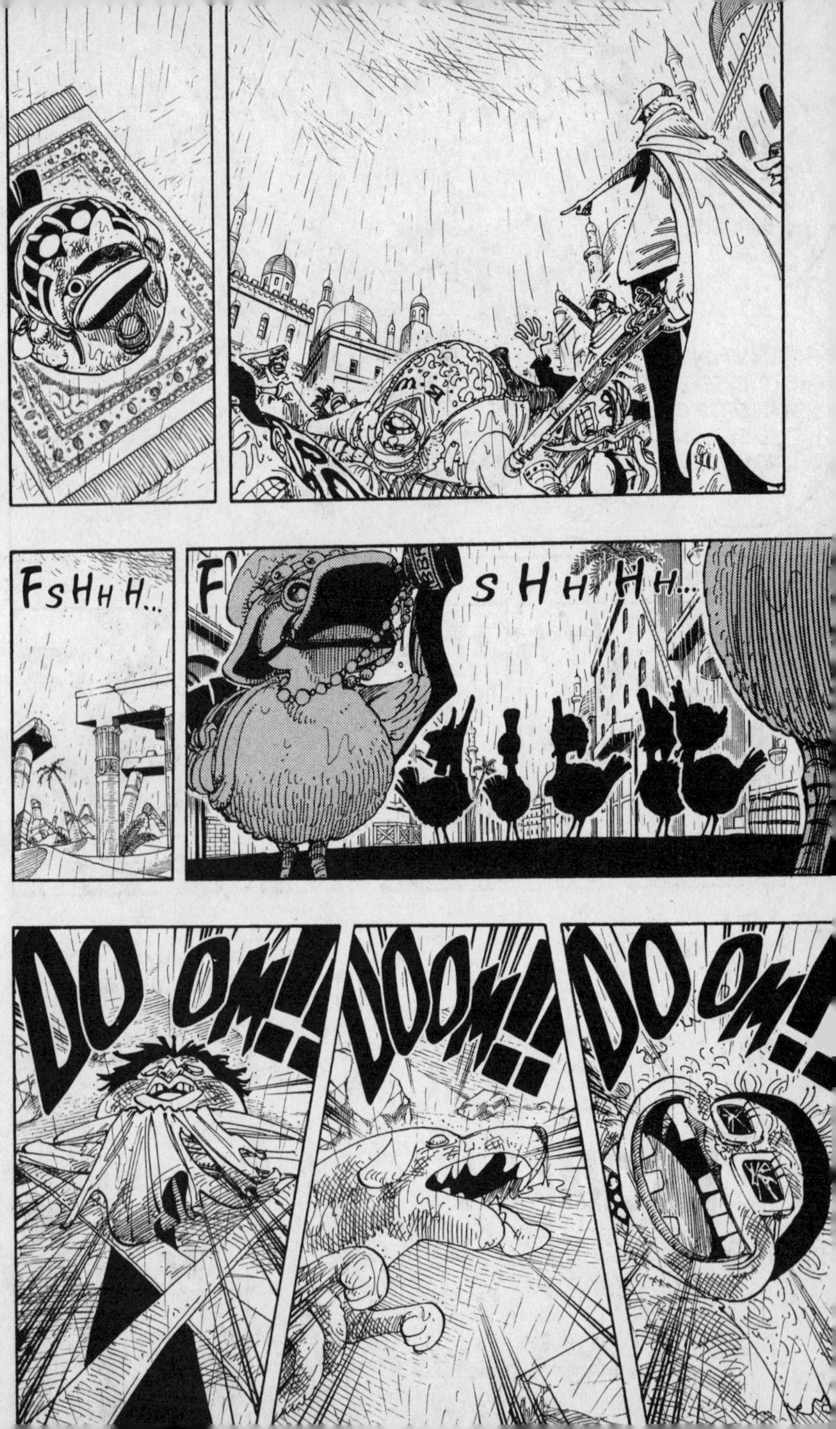
FSHHHH...
FSHHH...
DOOM!!
DOOM!!
DOOM!!

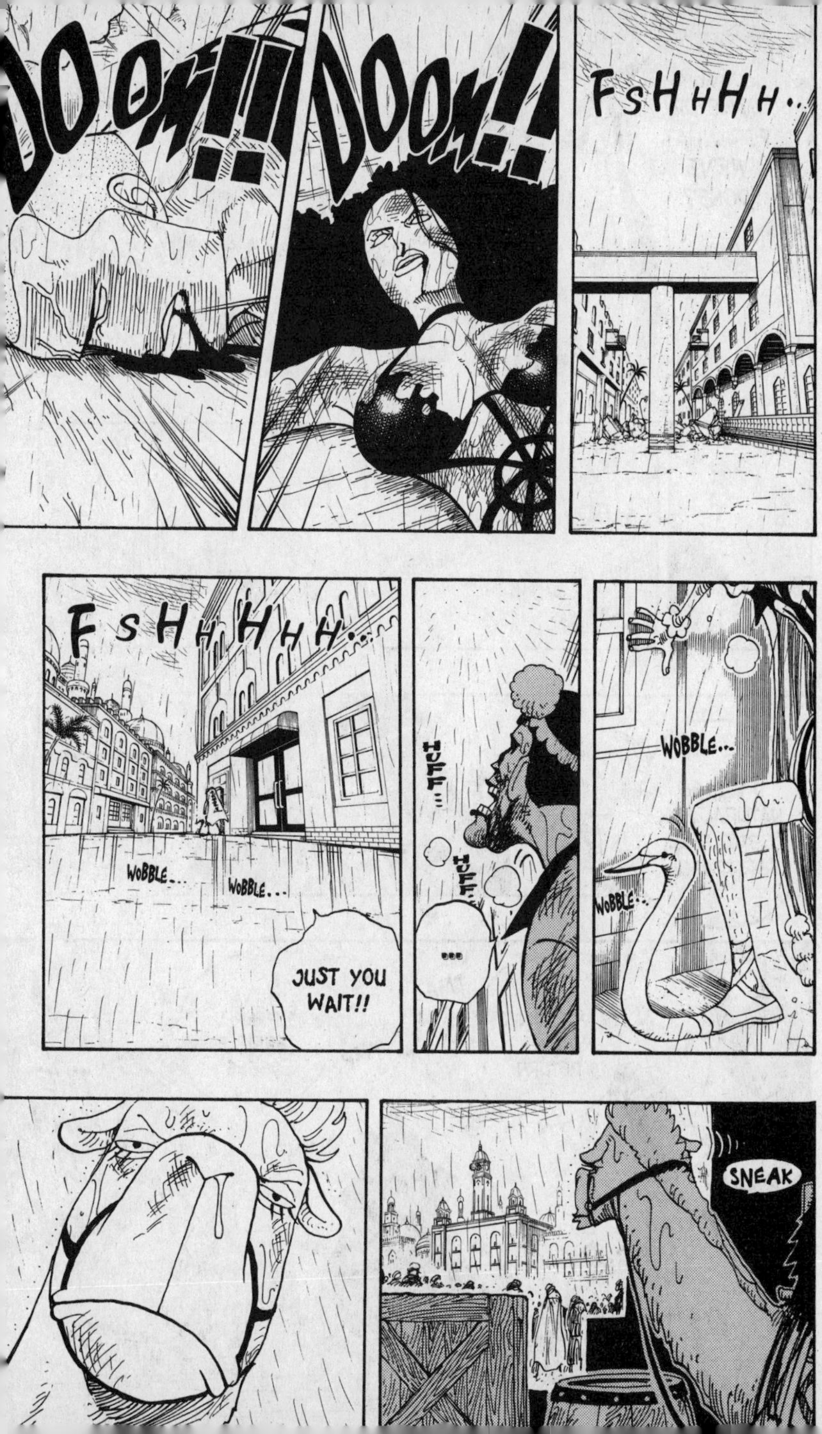
FSHHHH..
DOOM!!
DOOM!!
WOBBLE...
WOBBLE..
HUFF...
HUFF...
...
FSHHHHH...
WOBBLE...
WOBBLE...
JUST YOU WAIT!!
SNEAK

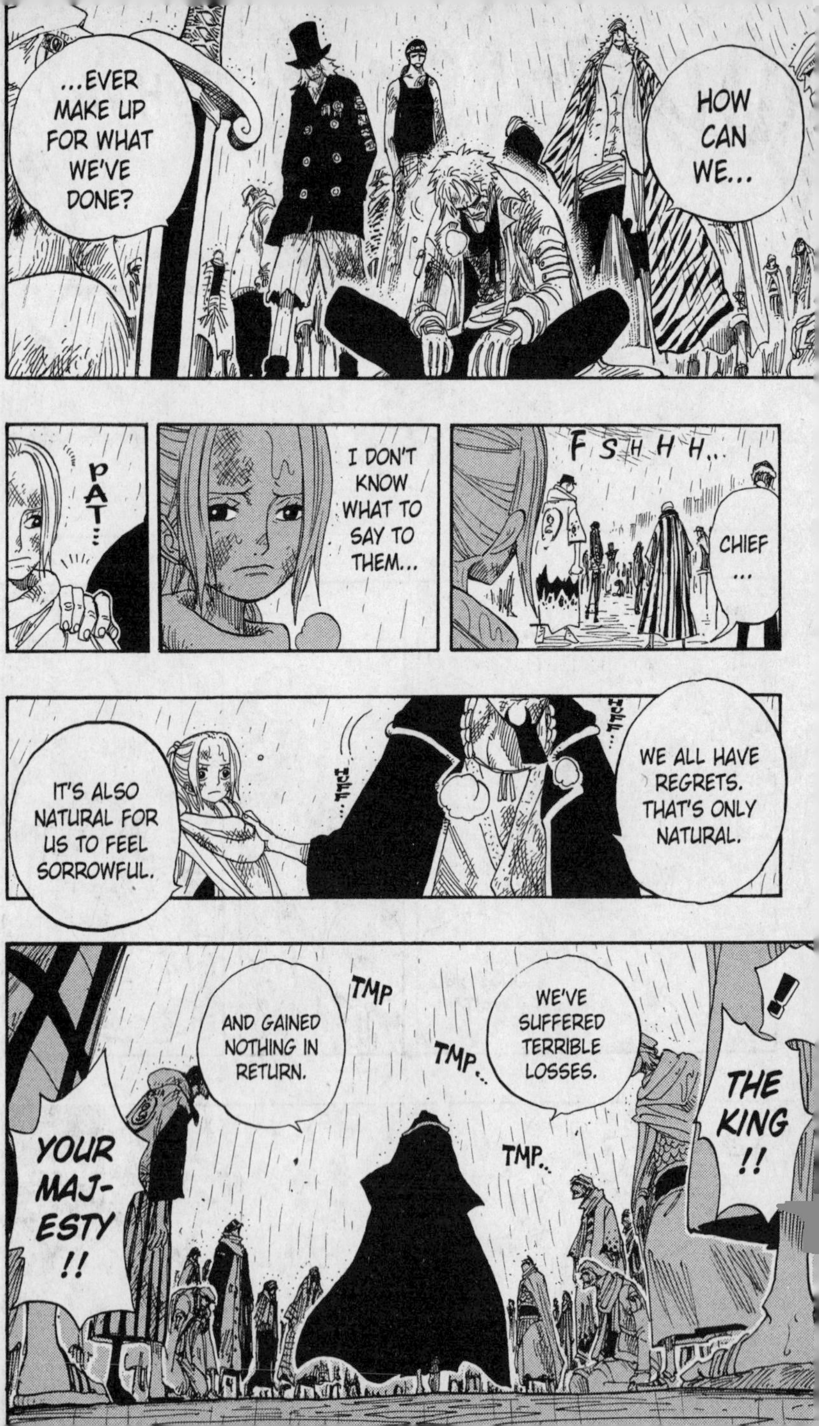
HOW CAN WE...
...EVER MAKE UP FOR WHAT WE'VE DONE?
FSHHH...
CHIEF...
I DON'T KNOW WHAT TO SAY TO THEM...
PAT...
HUFF...
WE ALL HAVE REGRETS. THAT'S ONLY NATURAL.
HUFF...
IT'S ALSO NATURAL FOR US TO FEEL SORROWFUL.
!
THE KING!!
WE'VE SUFFERED TERRIBLE LOSSES.
TMP...
TMP...
TMP
AND GAINED NOTHING IN RETURN.
YOUR MAJ-ESTY!!

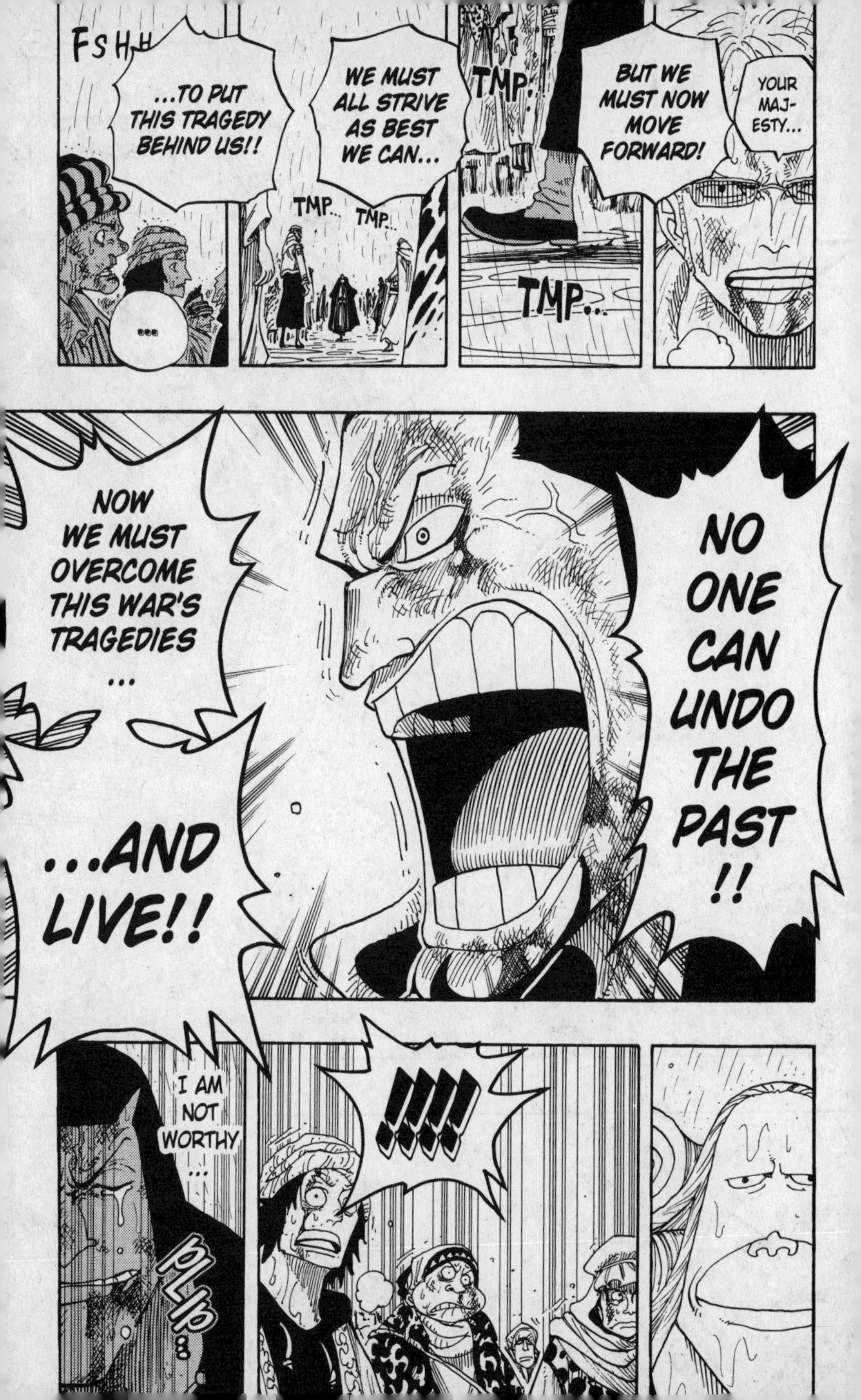
YOUR MAJESTY...
BUT WE MUST NOW MOVE FORWARD!
TMP...
TMP...
WE MUST ALL STRIVE AS BEST WE CAN...
TMP...
TMP...
FSHH
...TO PUT THIS TRAGEDY BEHIND US!!
...
NO ONE CAN UNDO THE PAST!!
NOW WE MUST OVERCOME THIS WAR'S TRAGEDIES...
...AND LIVE!!
!!!!!
I AM NOT WORTHY...
PLIP...

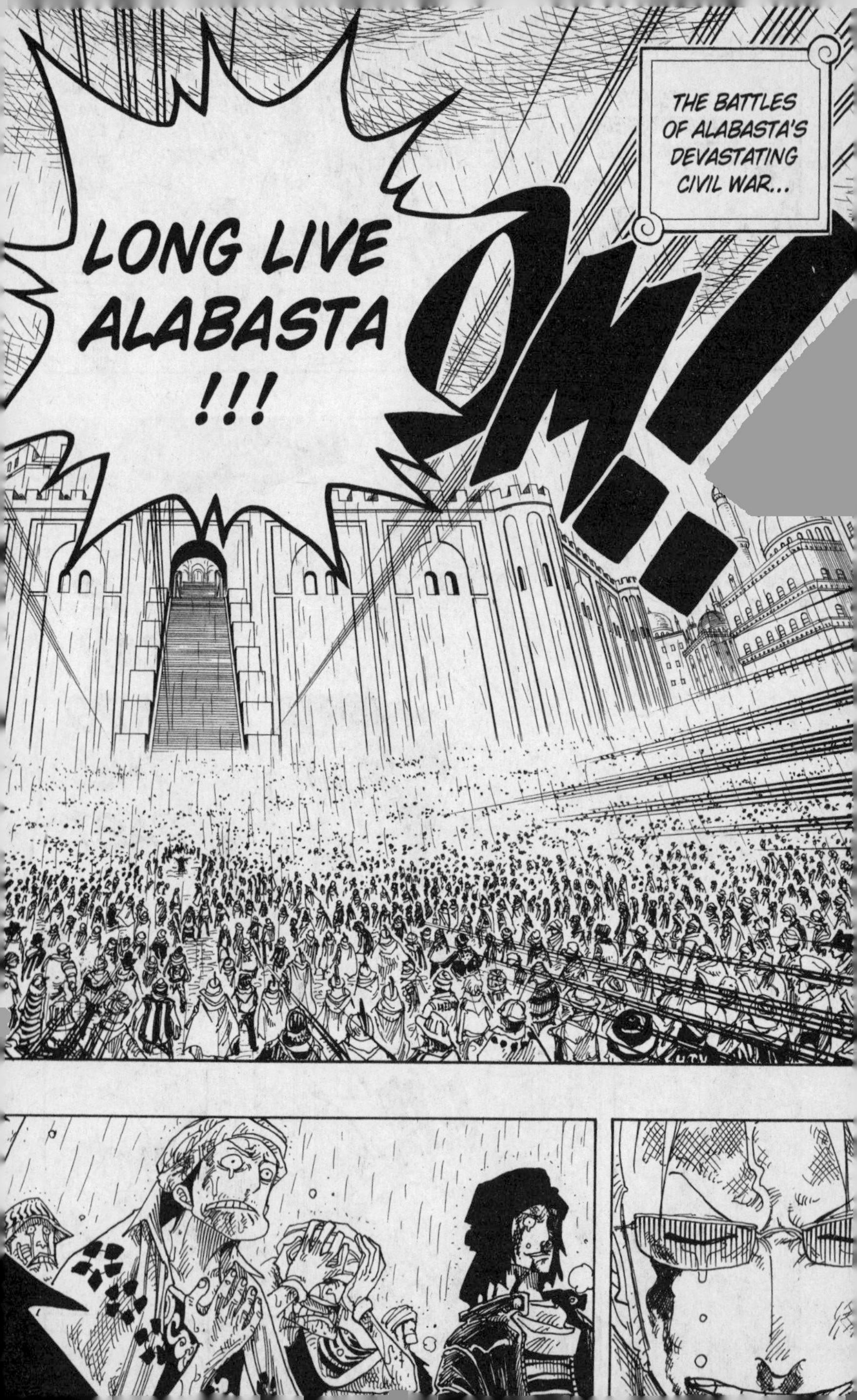
THE BATTLES OF ALABASTA'S DEVASTATING CIVIL WAR...
LONG LIVE ALABASTA !!!

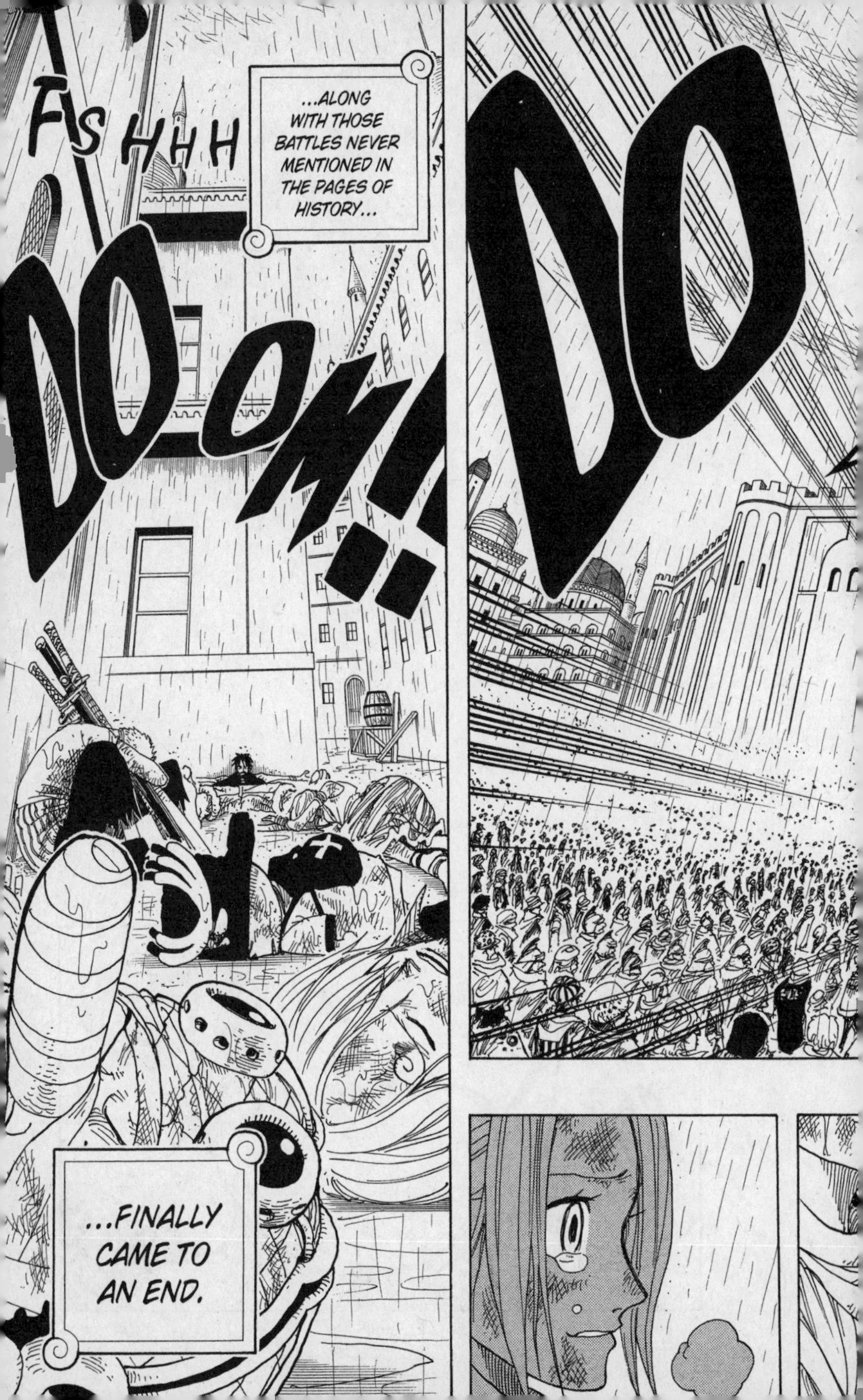
DO
FSHHH
...ALONG WITH THOSE BATTLES NEVER MENTIONED IN THE PAGES OF HISTORY...
DO-OM!!
...FINALLY CAME TO AN END.

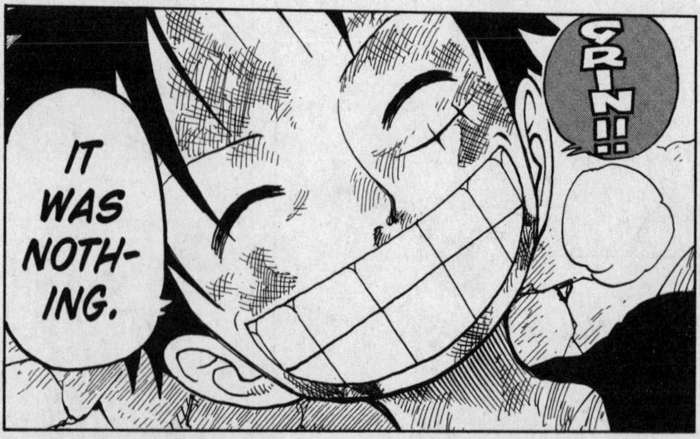
GRIN!!
IT WAS NOTH-ING.

Chapter 212:
SOME JUSTICE

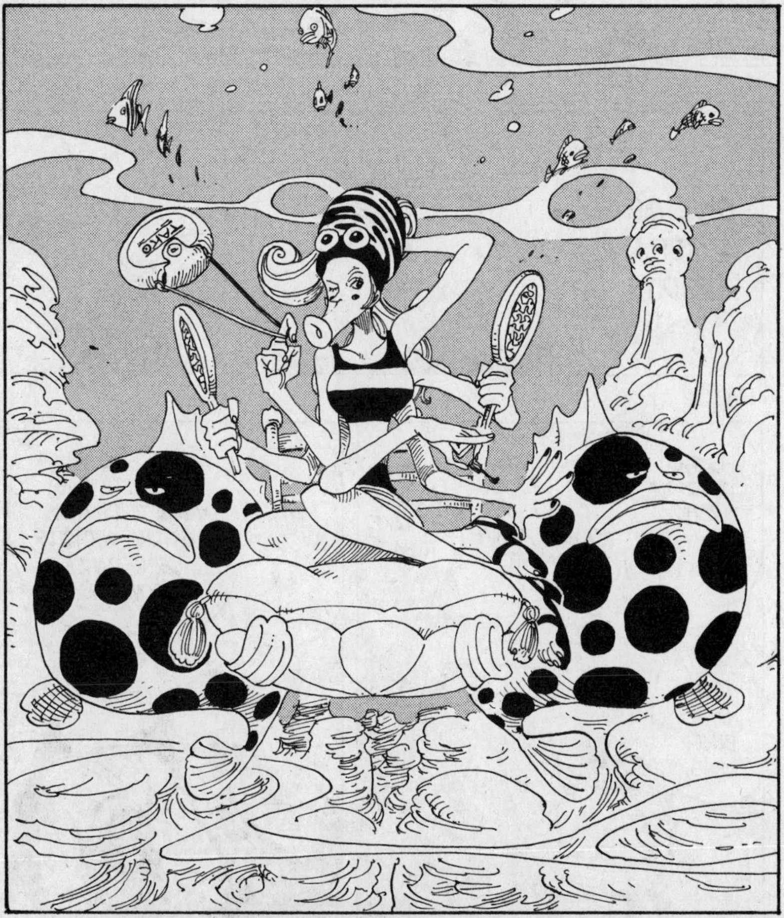

HACHI'S WALK ON THE SEA FLOOR, VOL. 27:
"MEANWHILE, OCTOPAKO IS ON THE MOVE"

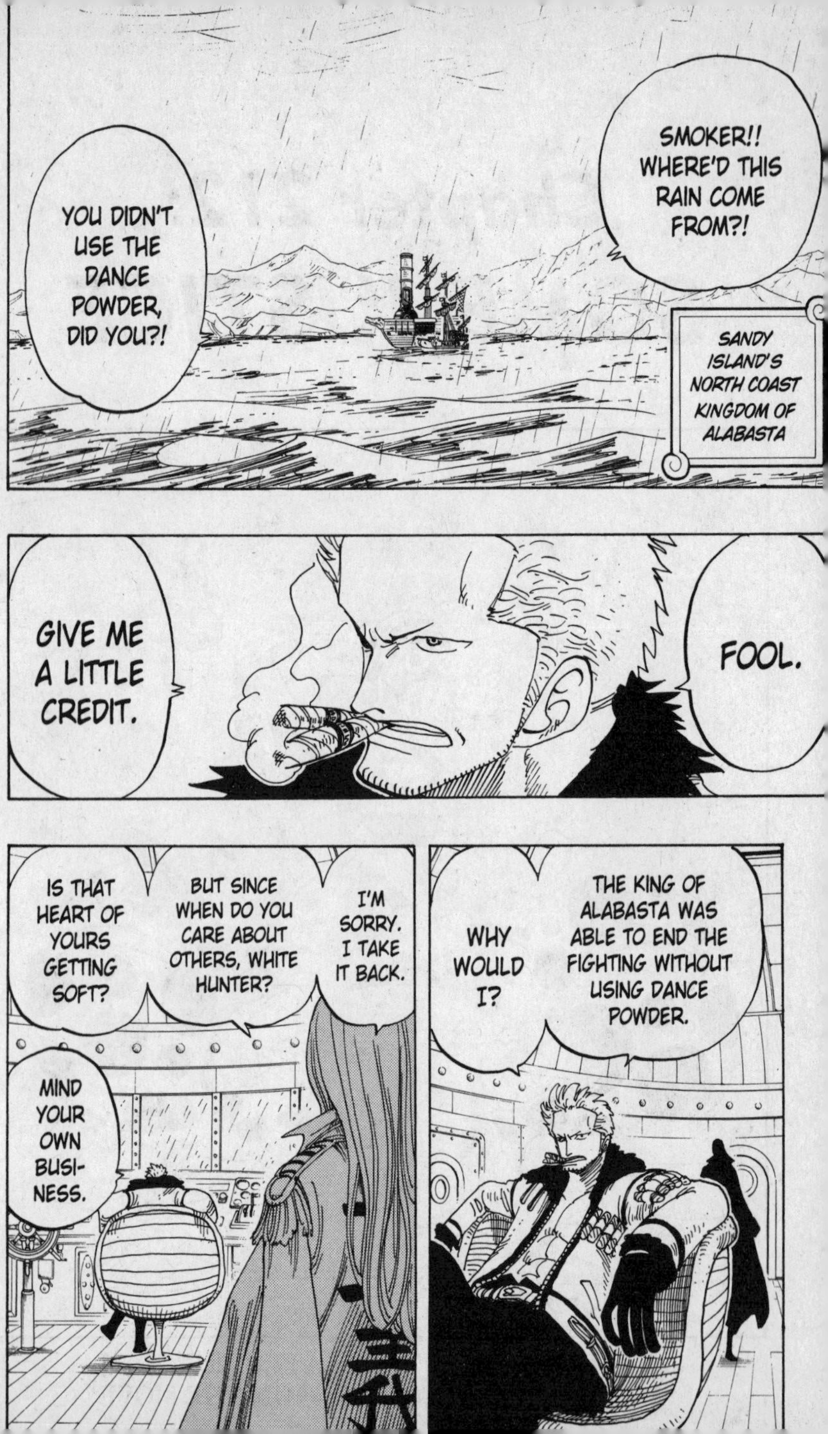
SMOKER!! WHERE'D THIS RAIN COME FROM?!
SANDY ISLAND'S NORTH COAST KINGDOM OF ALABASTA
YOU DIDN'T USE THE DANCE POWDER, DID YOU?!
FOOL.
GIVE ME A LITTLE CREDIT.
THE KING OF ALABASTA WAS ABLE TO END THE FIGHTING WITHOUT USING DANCE POWDER.
WHY WOULD I?
I'M SORRY. I TAKE IT BACK.
BUT SINCE WHEN DO YOU CARE ABOUT OTHERS, WHITE HUNTER?
IS THAT HEART OF YOURS GETTING SOFT?
MIND YOUR OWN BUSI-NESS.

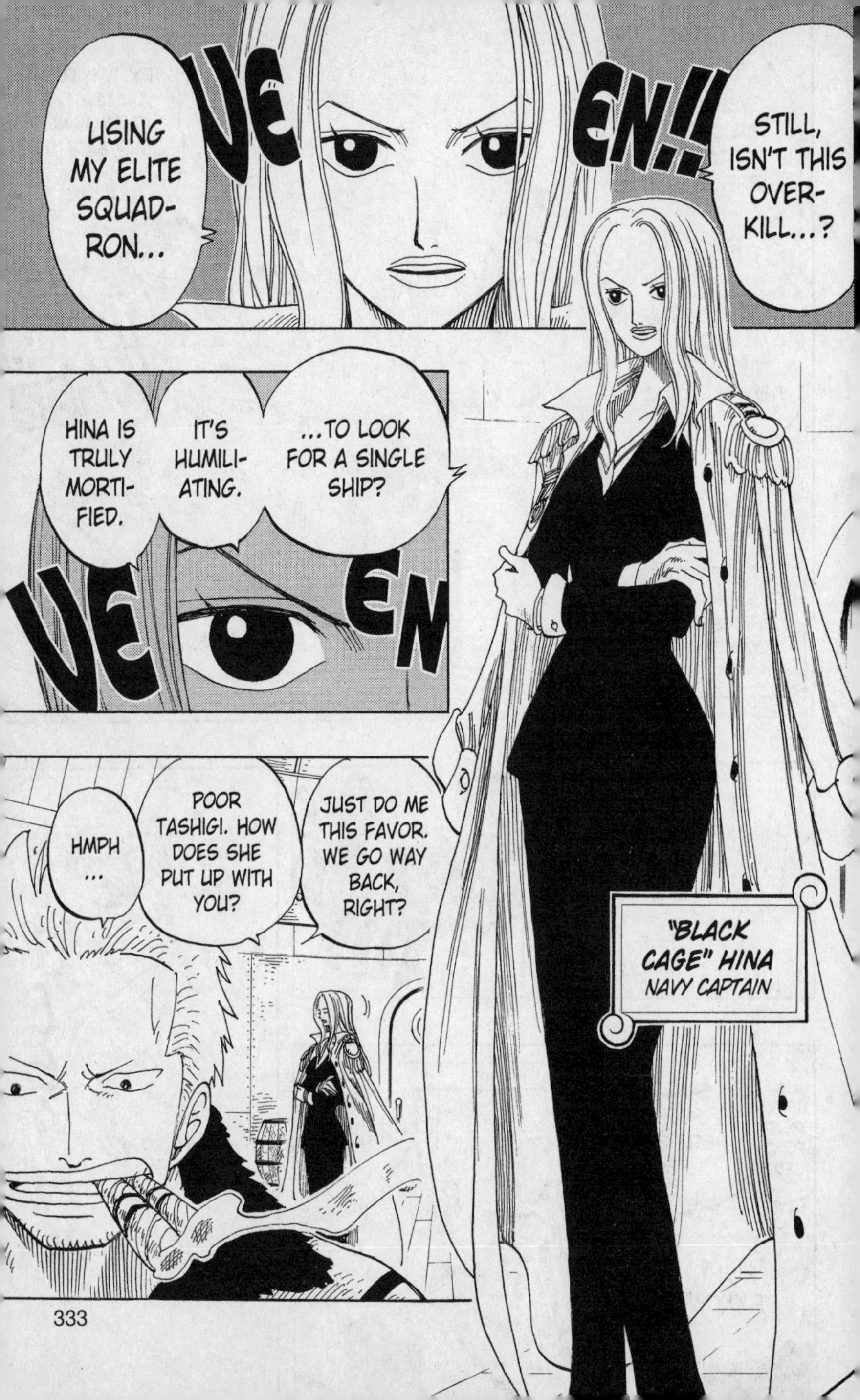
STILL, ISN'T THIS OVER-KILL...?
VE EN!!
USING MY ELITE SQUAD-RON...
"BLACK CAGE" HINA
NAVY CAPTAIN
...TO LOOK FOR A SINGLE SHIP?
IT'S HUMILI-ATING.
HINA IS TRULY MORTI-FIED.
VE EN
JUST DO ME THIS FAVOR. WE GO WAY BACK, RIGHT?
POOR TASHIGI. HOW DOES SHE PUT UP WITH YOU?
HMPH ...

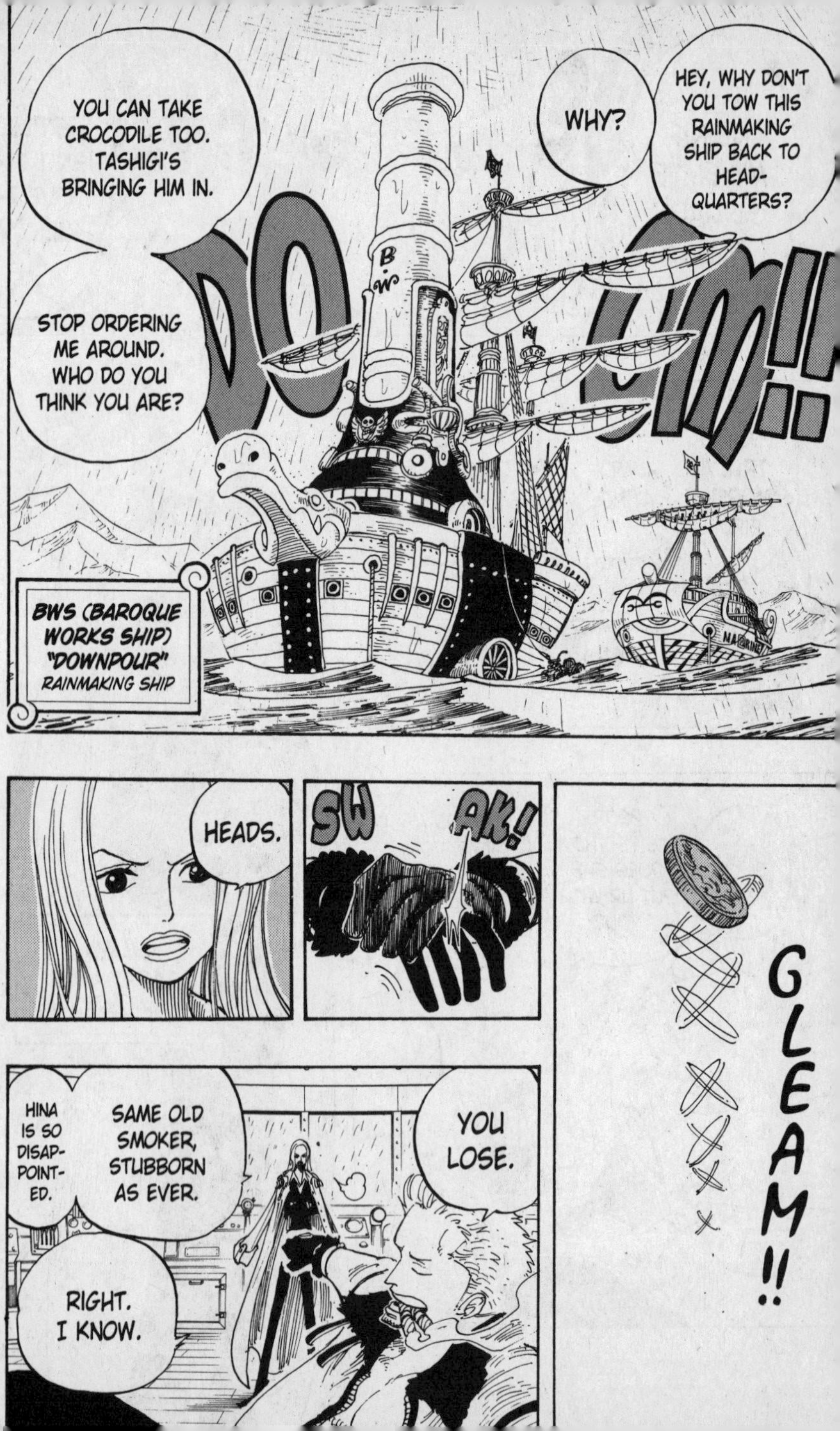
HEY, WHY DON'T YOU TOW THIS RAINMAKING SHIP BACK TO HEAD-QUARTERS?
WHY?
YOU CAN TAKE CROCODILE TOO. TASHIGI'S BRINGING HIM IN.
STOP ORDERING ME AROUND. WHO DO YOU THINK YOU ARE?
DOOM!!
BWS (BAROQUE WORKS SHIP) "DOWNPOUR" RAINMAKING SHIP
GLEAM!!
SWAK!
HEADS.
YOU LOSE.
SAME OLD SMOKER, STUBBORN AS EVER.
HINA IS SO DISAP-POINT-ED.
RIGHT. I KNOW.

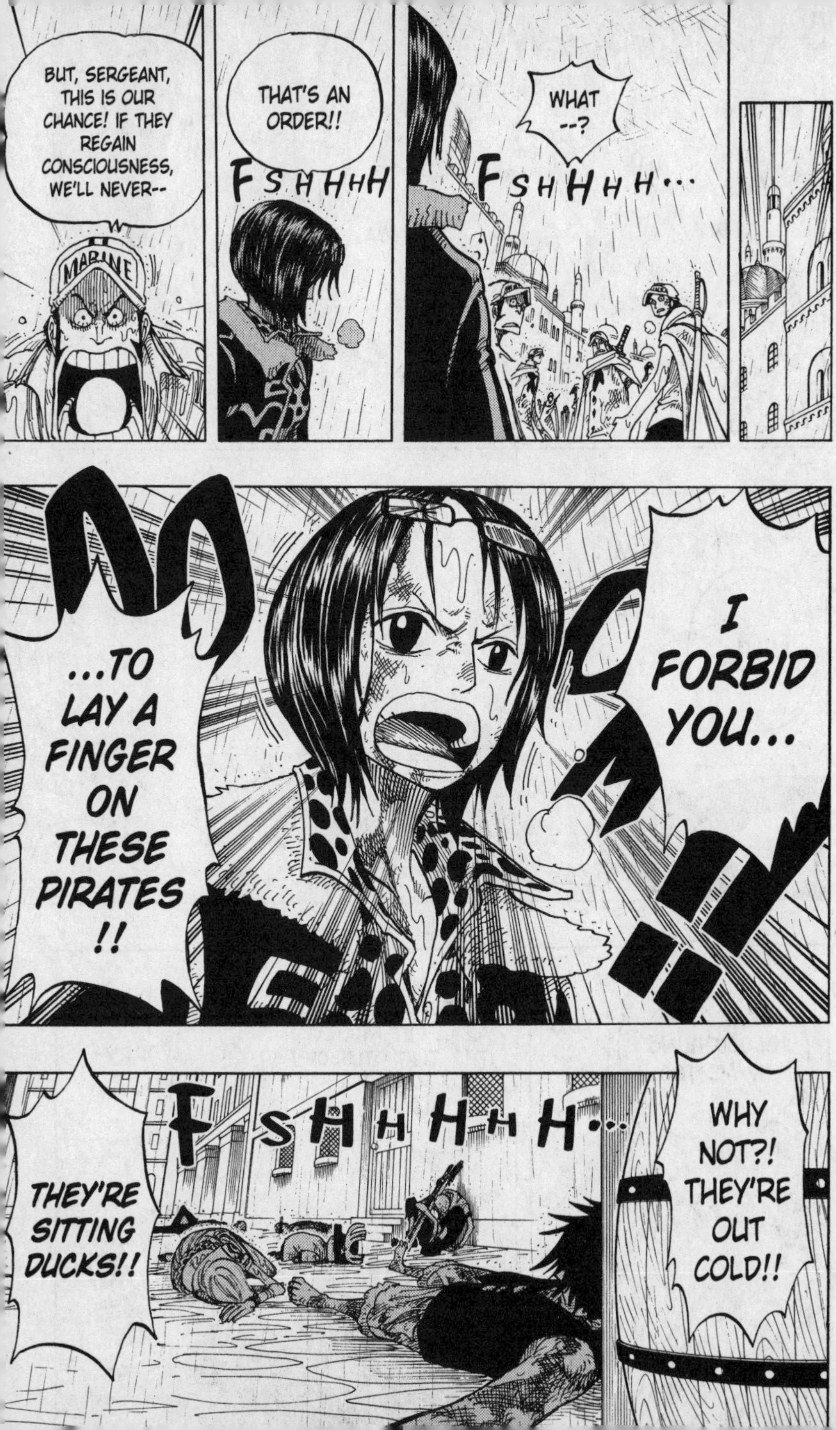
WHAT --?
FSHHHHH...
THAT'S AN ORDER!!
FSHHHHH
BUT, SERGEANT, THIS IS OUR CHANCE! IF THEY REGAIN CONSCIOUSNESS, WE'LL NEVER--
I FORBID YOU...
...TO LAY A FINGER ON THESE PIRATES!!
WHY NOT?! THEY'RE OUT COLD!!
FSHHHHHH...
THEY'RE SITTING DUCKS!!

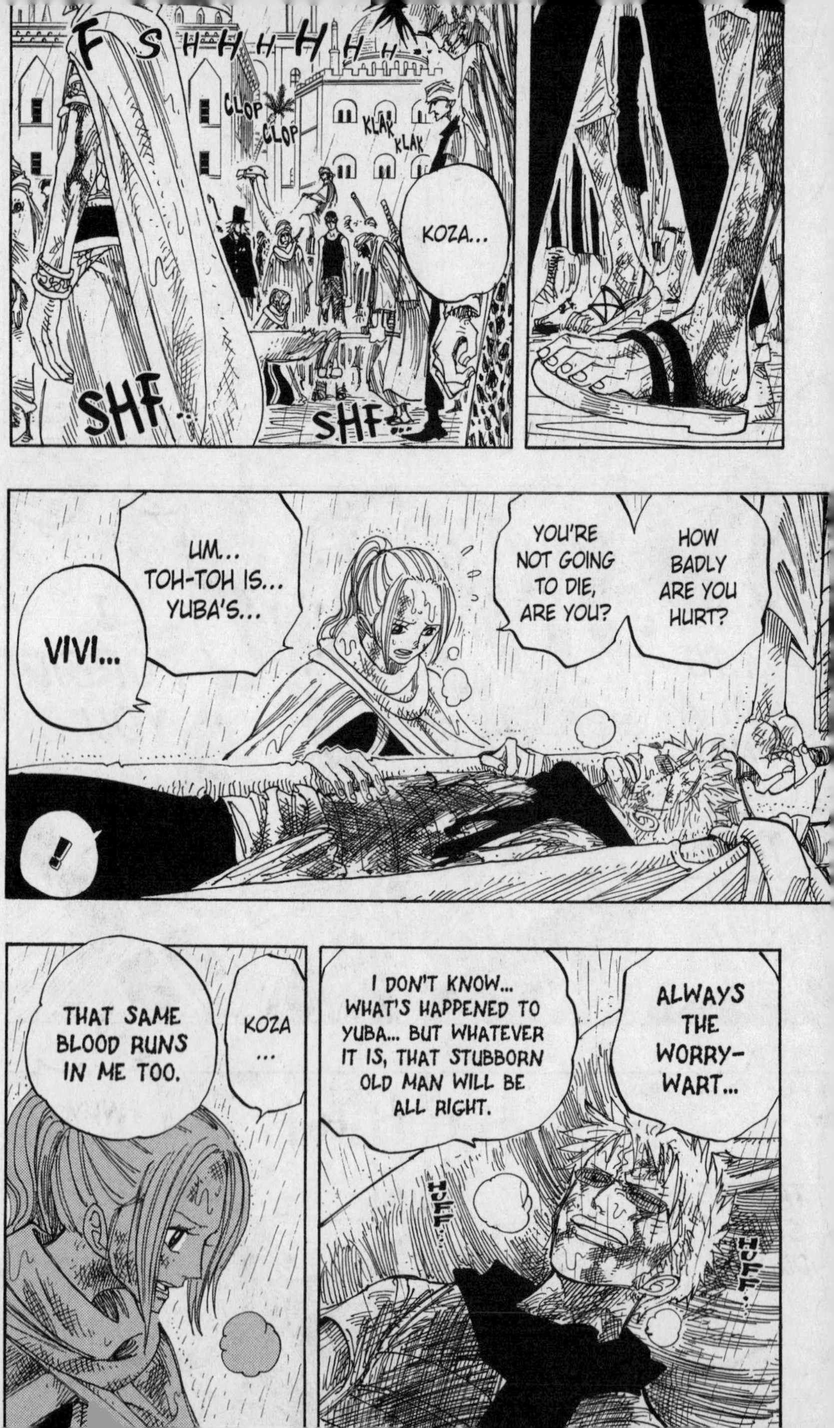
FSHHHHH...
CLOP
CLOP
KLAK
KLAK
KOZA...
SHF...
SHF...
HOW BADLY ARE YOU HURT?
YOU'RE NOT GOING TO DIE, ARE YOU?
UM... TOH-TOH IS... YUBA'S...
VIVI...
!
ALWAYS THE WORRY-WART...
I DON'T KNOW... WHAT'S HAPPENED TO YUBA... BUT WHATEVER IT IS, THAT STUBBORN OLD MAN WILL BE ALL RIGHT.
HUFF...
HUFF...
KOZA ...
THAT SAME BLOOD RUNS IN ME TOO.

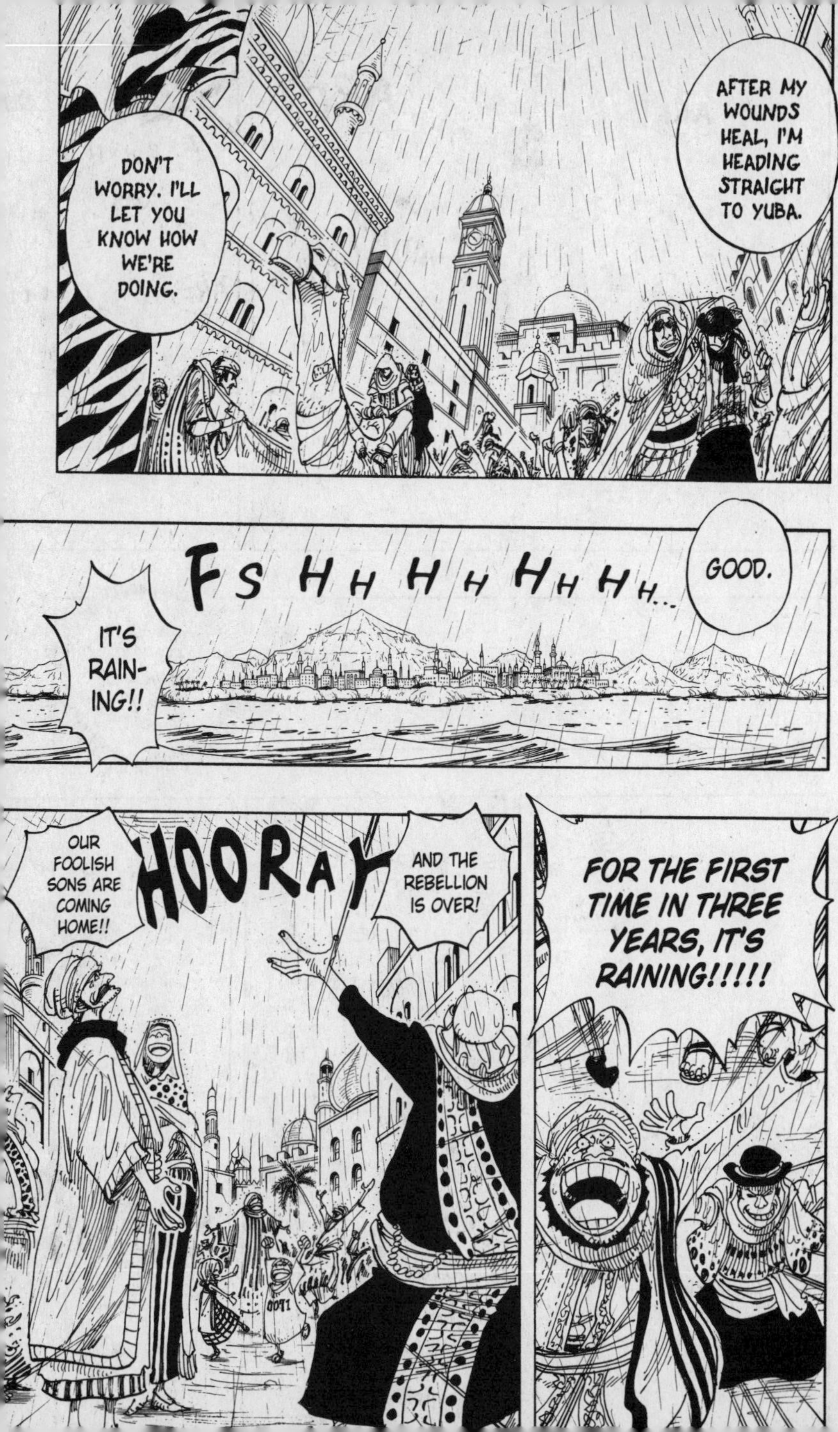
AFTER MY WOUNDS HEAL, I'M HEADING STRAIGHT TO YUBA.
DON'T WORRY. I'LL LET YOU KNOW HOW WE'RE DOING.
GOOD.
FSHHHHHHHH...
IT'S RAINING!!
FOR THE FIRST TIME IN THREE YEARS, IT'S RAINING!!!!!
AND THE REBELLION IS OVER!
HOORAY
OUR FOOLISH SONS ARE COMING HOME!!

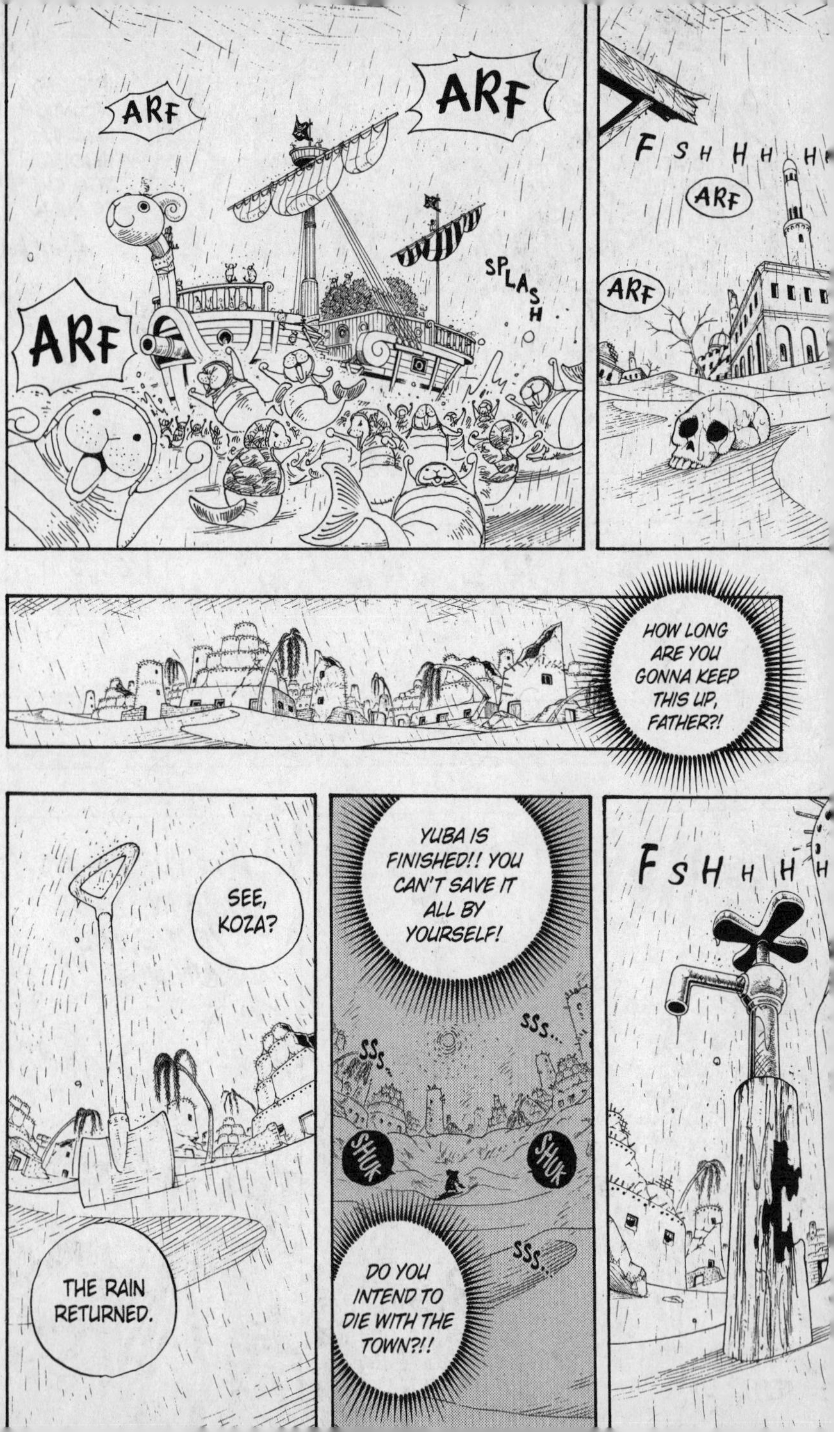
FSHHHH
ARF
ARF
ARF
ARF
SPLASH
ARF
HOW LONG ARE YOU GONNA KEEP THIS UP, FATHER?!
FSHHHH
YUBA IS FINISHED!! YOU CAN'T SAVE IT ALL BY YOURSELF!
SSS...
SSS...
SHUK
SHUK
SSS...
DO YOU INTEND TO DIE WITH THE TOWN?!!
SEE, KOZA?
THE RAIN RETURNED.

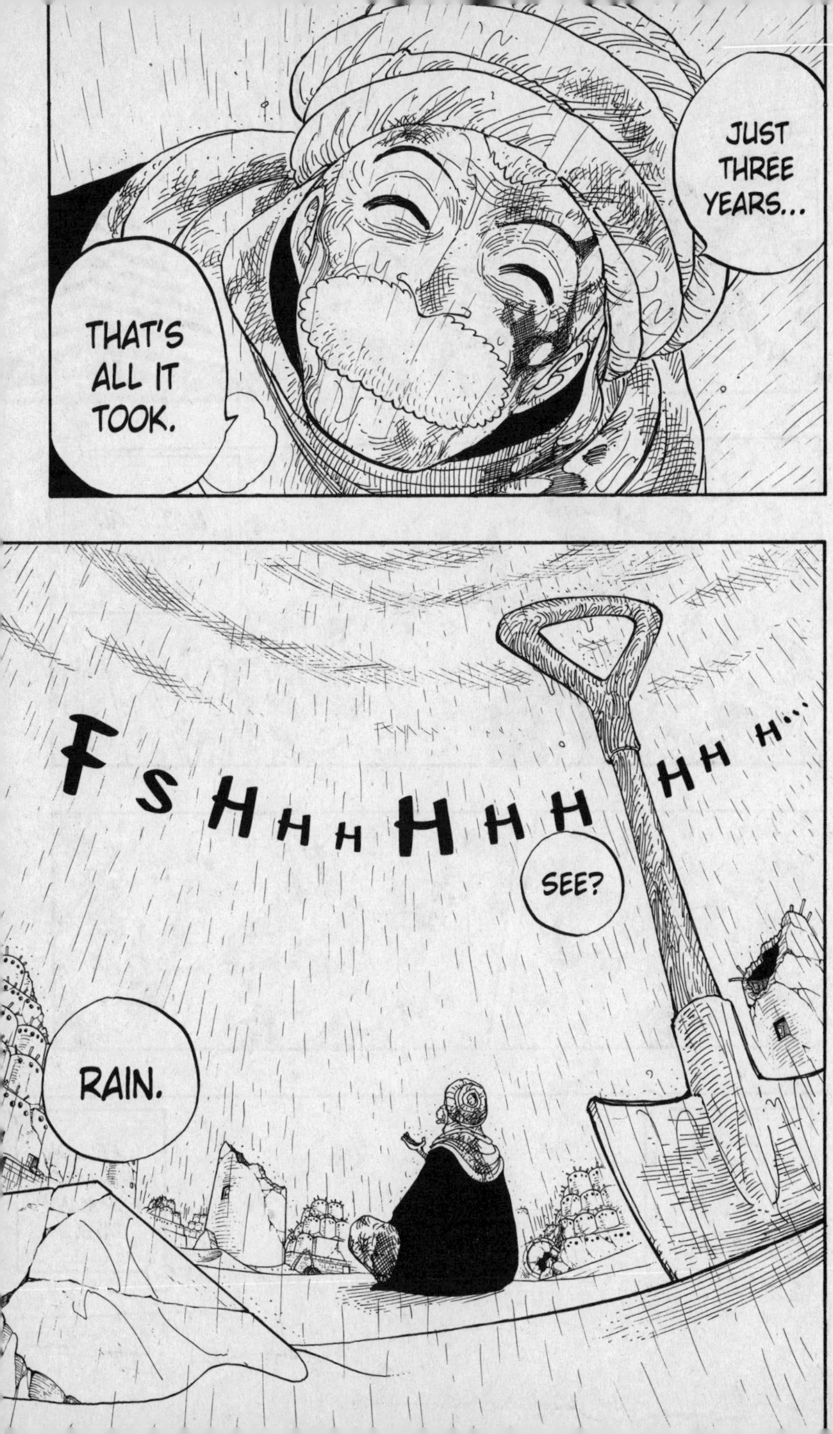
JUST THREE YEARS...
THAT'S ALL IT TOOK.
FSHHHHHHHHHH...
SEE?
RAIN.

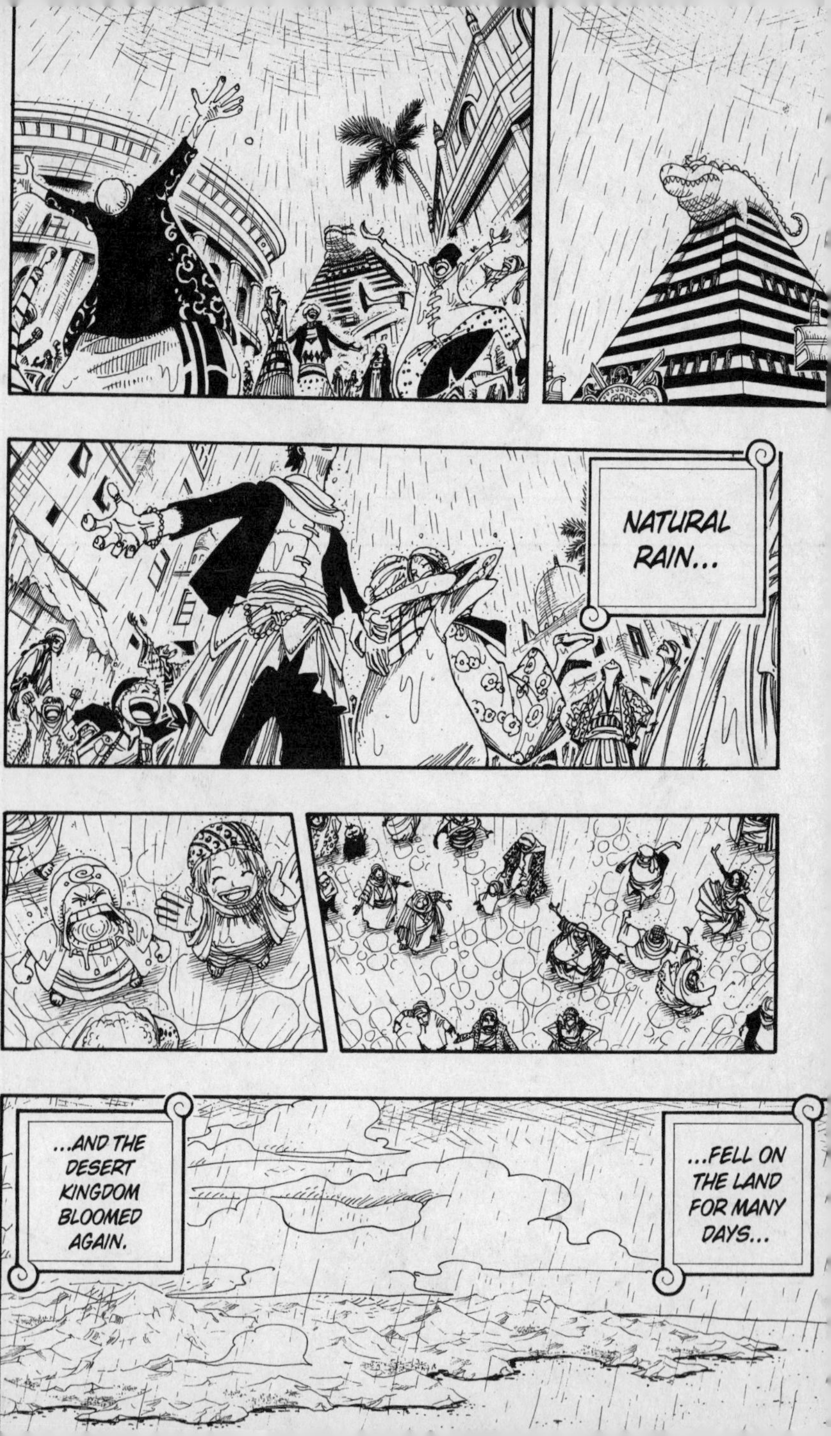
NATURAL RAIN...
...FELL ON THE LAND FOR MANY DAYS...
...AND THE DESERT KINGDOM BLOOMED AGAIN.

FsHHHHHHHH...

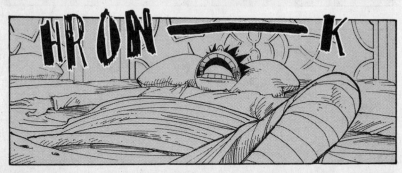

HRON——K

SNNOORRR...

ZZZ

ZZZZZZZZ...

CHAK

SNO

RR

HRON——K FSHHH...

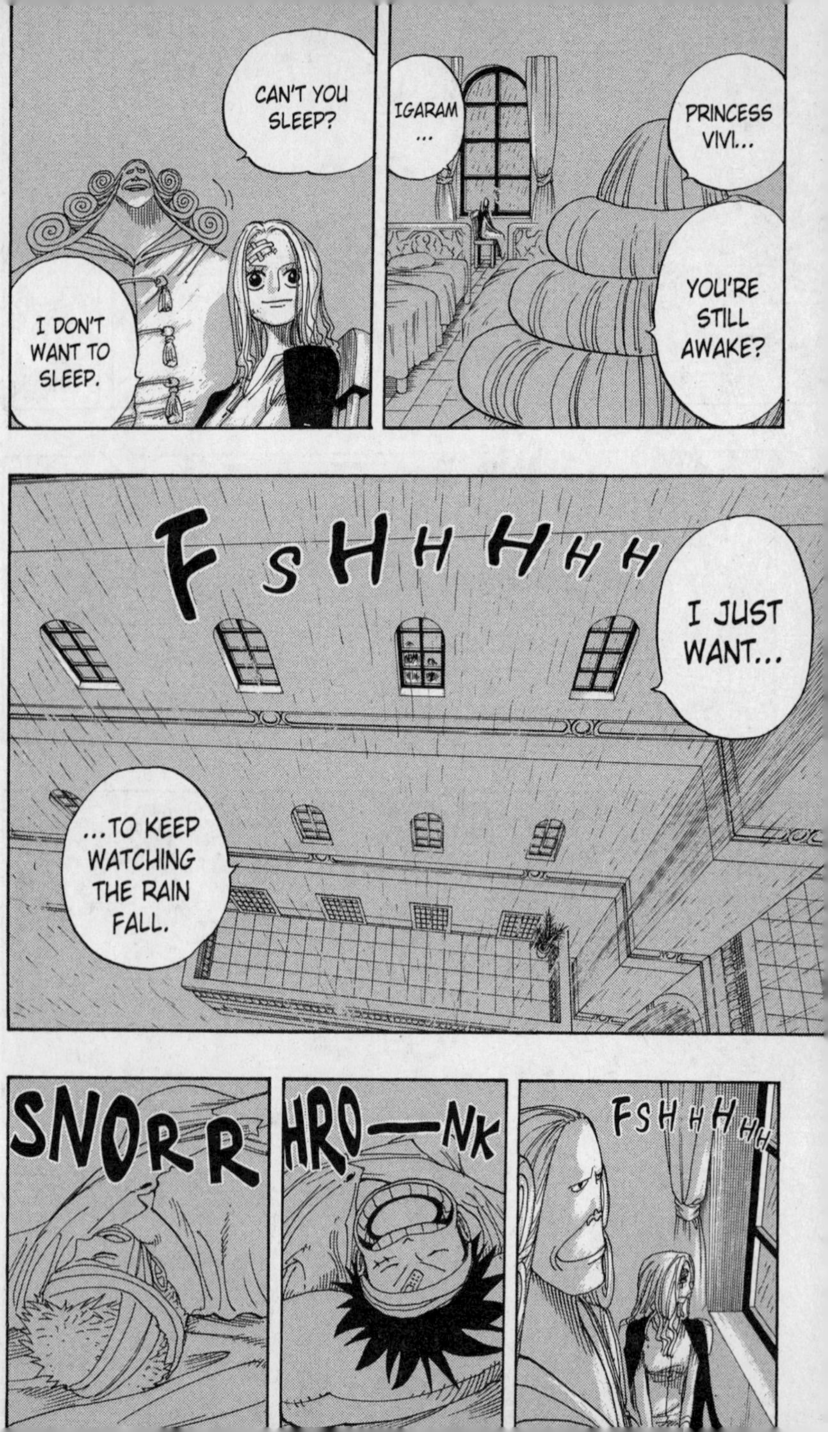
PRINCESS VIVI...
YOU'RE STILL AWAKE?
IGARAM ...
CAN'T YOU SLEEP?
I DON'T WANT TO SLEEP.
FSHHHHHH
I JUST WANT...
...TO KEEP WATCHING THE RAIN FALL.
FSHHHHHH
HRO—NK
SNORR

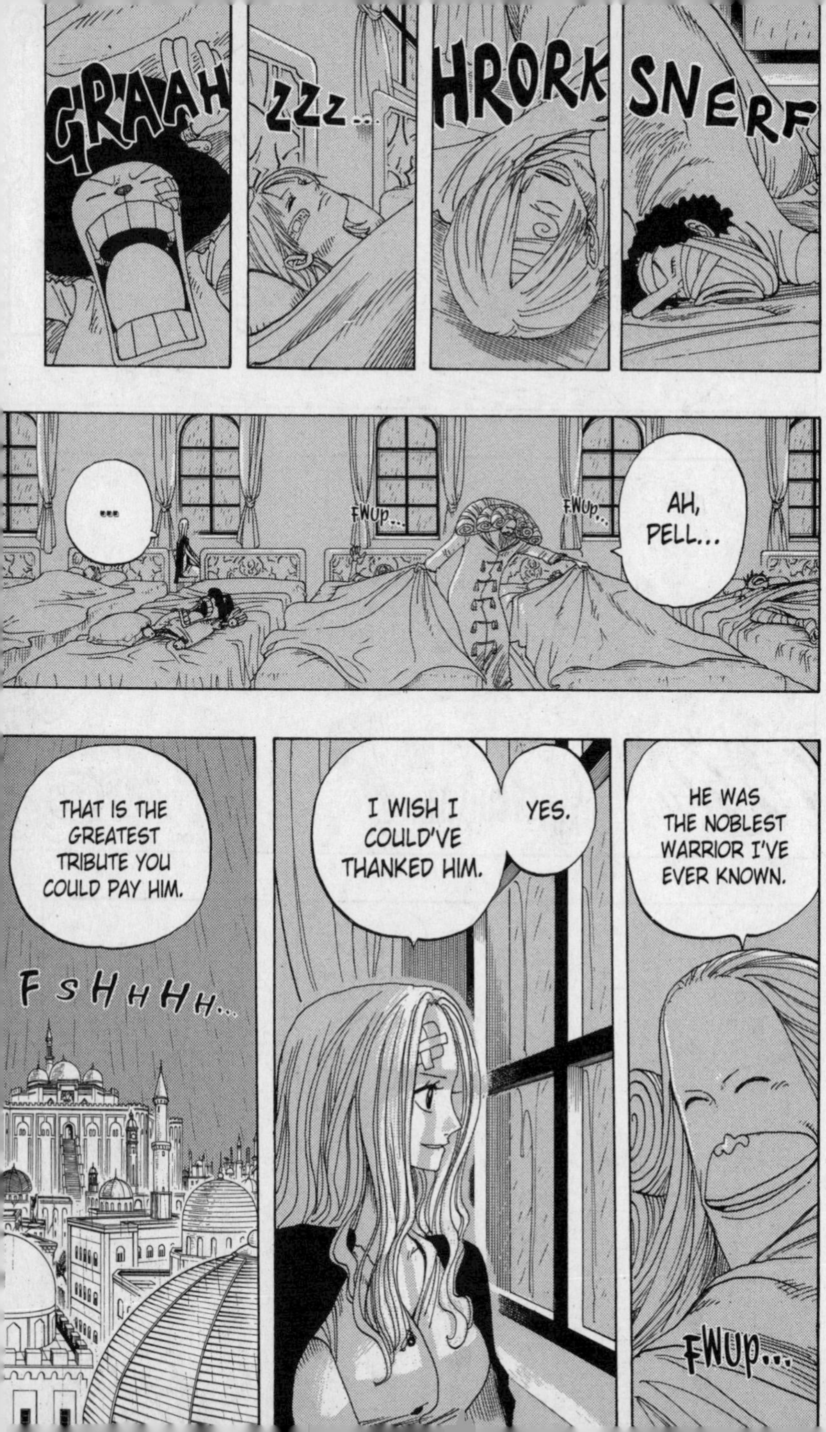
SNERF
HRORK
ZZZ...
GRAAH
AH, PELL...
FWUP...
FWUP...
...
HE WAS THE NOBLEST WARRIOR I'VE EVER KNOWN.
FWUP...
YES.
I WISH I COULD'VE THANKED HIM.
THAT IS THE GREATEST TRIBUTE YOU COULD PAY HIM.
FSHHHH...

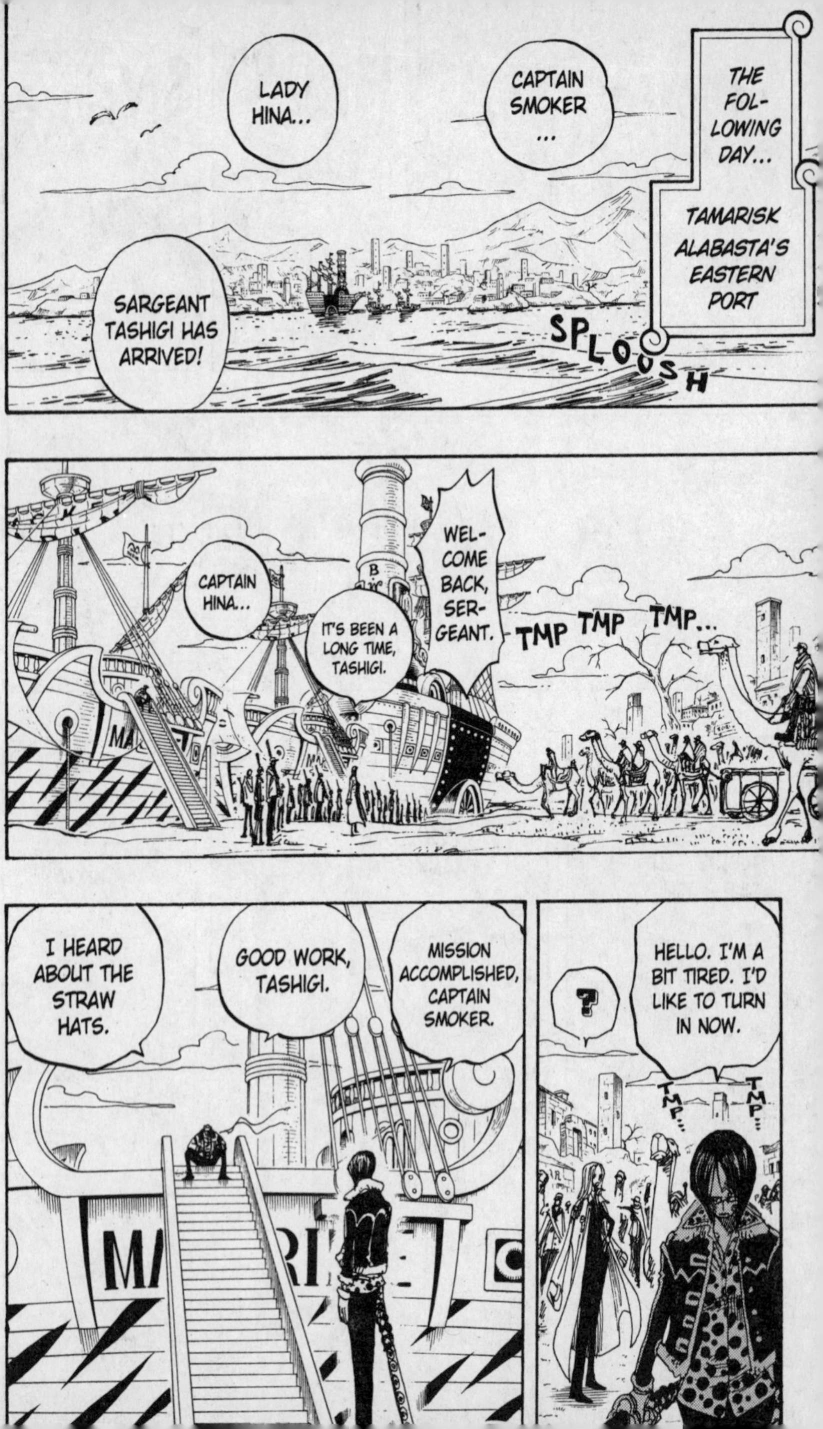
THE FOL-LOWING DAY...
TAMARISK ALABASTA'S EASTERN PORT
CAPTAIN SMOKER ...
LADY HINA...
SPLOOSH
SARGEANT TASHIGI HAS ARRIVED!
TMP TMP TMP...
WEL-COME BACK, SER-GEANT.
IT'S BEEN A LONG TIME, TASHIGI.
CAPTAIN HINA...
HELLO. I'M A BIT TIRED. I'D LIKE TO TURN IN NOW.
TMP... TMP...
?
MISSION ACCOMPLISHED, CAPTAIN SMOKER.
GOOD WORK, TASHIGI.
I HEARD ABOUT THE STRAW HATS.

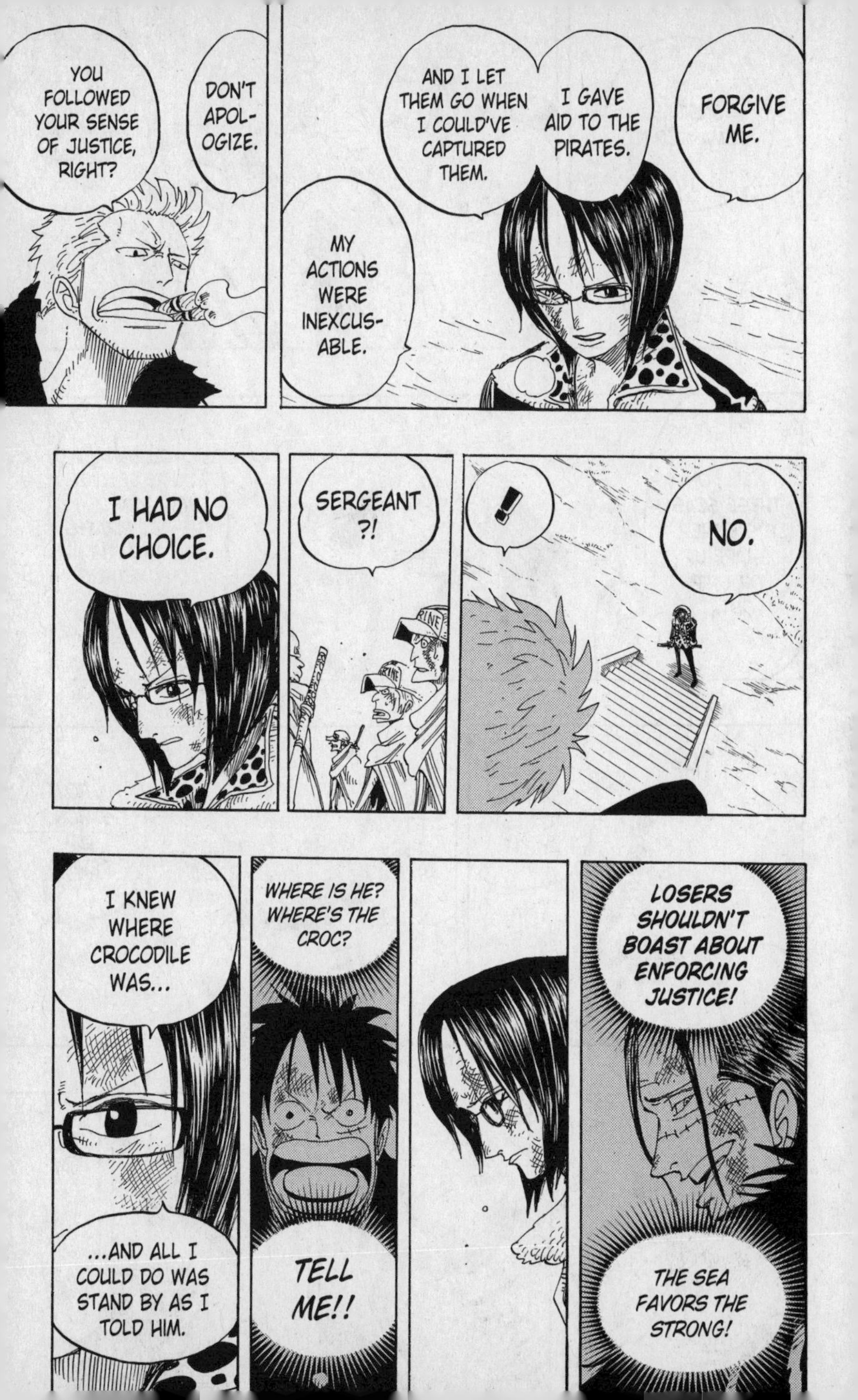
FORGIVE ME.
I GAVE AID TO THE PIRATES.
AND I LET THEM GO WHEN I COULD'VE CAPTURED THEM.
MY ACTIONS WERE INEXCUS-ABLE.
DON'T APOL-OGIZE.
YOU FOLLOWED YOUR SENSE OF JUSTICE, RIGHT?
NO.
!
SERGEANT?!
I HAD NO CHOICE.
LOSERS SHOULDN'T BOAST ABOUT ENFORCING JUSTICE!
THE SEA FAVORS THE STRONG!
WHERE IS HE? WHERE'S THE CROC?
TELL ME!!
I KNEW WHERE CROCODILE WAS...
...AND ALL I COULD DO WAS STAND BY AS I TOLD HIM.

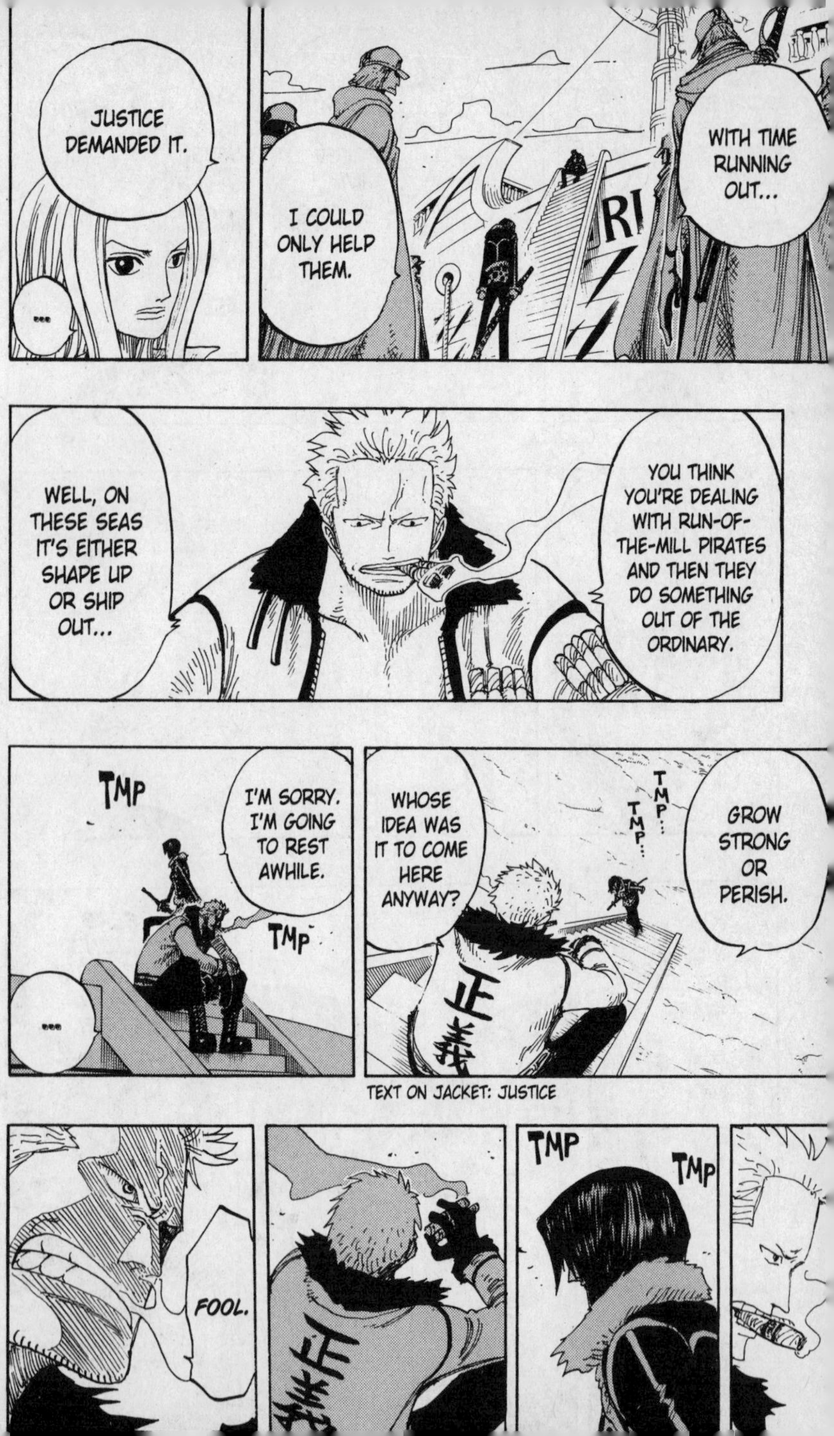
WITH TIME RUNNING OUT...
I COULD ONLY HELP THEM.
JUSTICE DEMANDED IT.
...
YOU THINK YOU'RE DEALING WITH RUN-OF-THE-MILL PIRATES AND THEN THEY DO SOMETHING OUT OF THE ORDINARY.
WELL, ON THESE SEAS IT'S EITHER SHAPE UP OR SHIP OUT...
GROW STRONG OR PERISH.
TMP...
TMP...
WHOSE IDEA WAS IT TO COME HERE ANYWAY?
I'M SORRY. I'M GOING TO REST AWHILE.
TMP
TMP
...
TEXT ON JACKET: JUSTICE
TMP
TMP
FOOL.

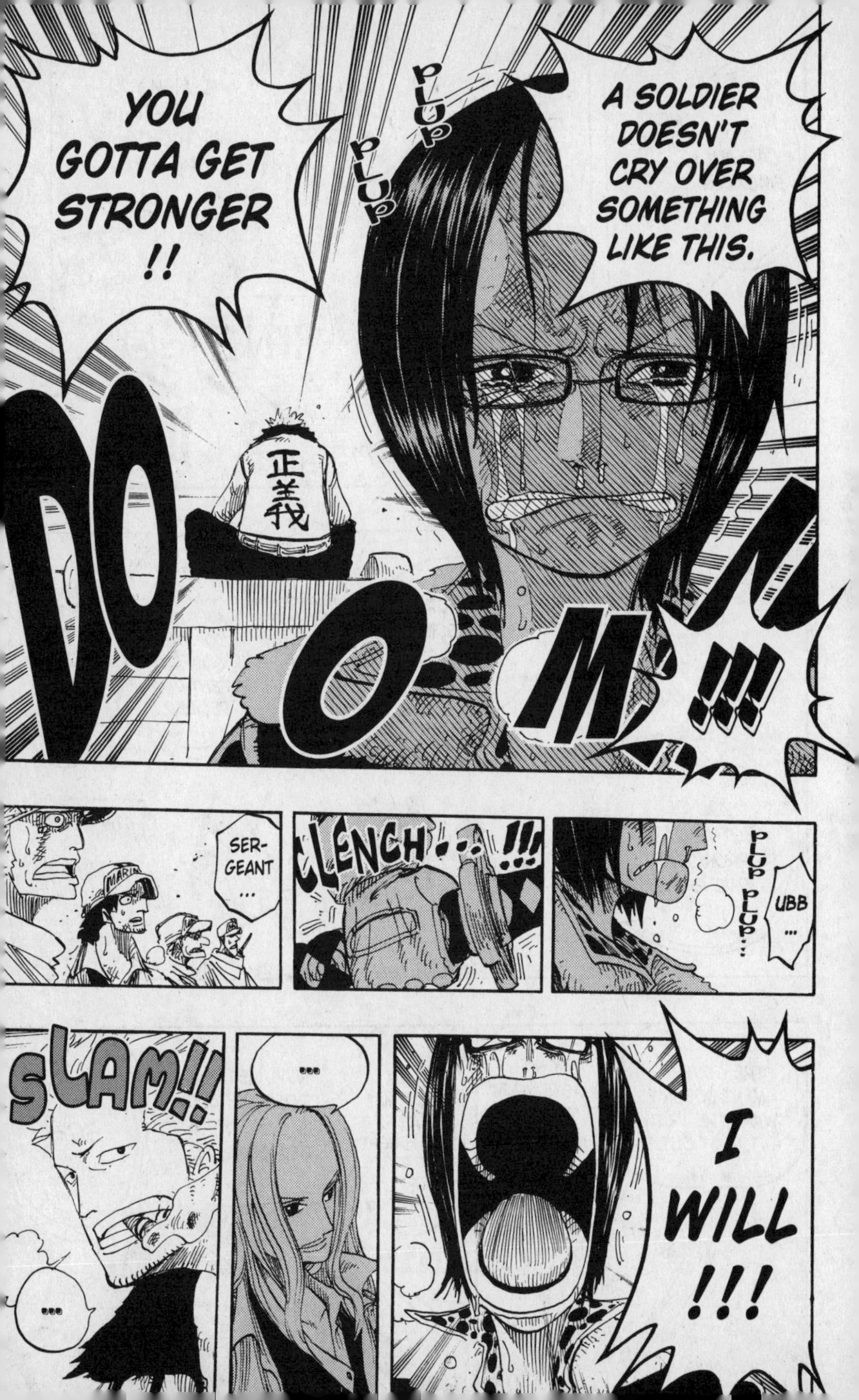
A SOLDIER DOESN'T CRY OVER SOMETHING LIKE THIS.
PLUP
PLUP
YOU GOTTA GET STRONGER !!
DOOM!!!
PLUP PLUP...
UBB ...
CLENCH...!!!
SER- GEANT ...
I WILL !!!
...
SLAM!!
...

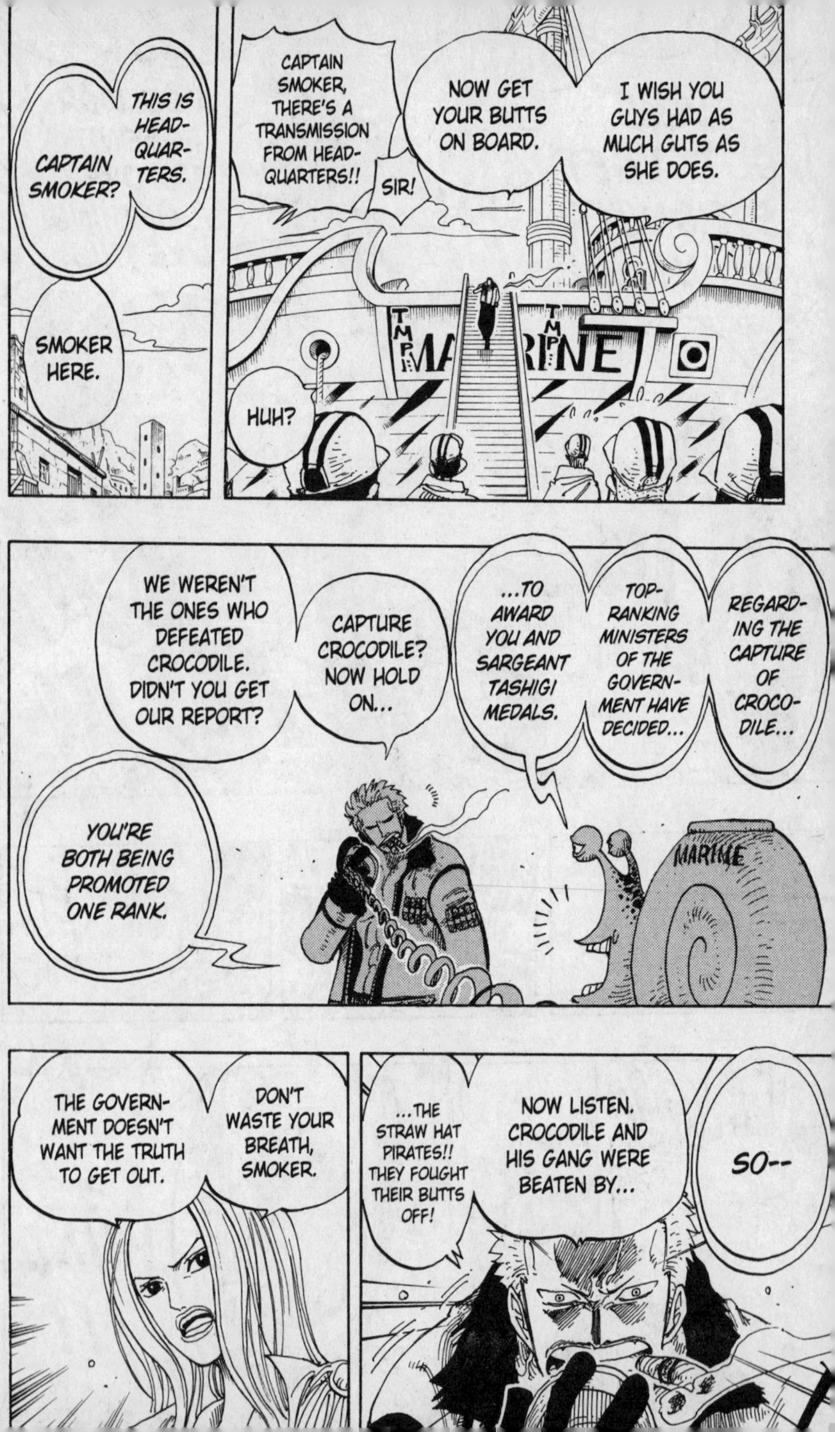
I WISH YOU GUYS HAD AS MUCH GUTS AS SHE DOES.
NOW GET YOUR BUTTS ON BOARD.
SIR!
CAPTAIN SMOKER, THERE'S A TRANSMISSION FROM HEADQUARTERS!!
HUH?
THIS IS HEADQUARTERS.
CAPTAIN SMOKER?
SMOKER HERE.
MARINE
REGARDING THE CAPTURE OF CROCODILE...
TOP-RANKING MINISTERS OF THE GOVERNMENT HAVE DECIDED...
...TO AWARD YOU AND SARGEANT TASHIGI MEDALS.
CAPTURE CROCODILE? NOW HOLD ON...
WE WEREN'T THE ONES WHO DEFEATED CROCODILE. DIDN'T YOU GET OUR REPORT?
YOU'RE BOTH BEING PROMOTED ONE RANK.
MARINE
SO--
NOW LISTEN. CROCODILE AND HIS GANG WERE BEATEN BY...
...THE STRAW HAT PIRATES!! THEY FOUGHT THEIR BUTTS OFF!
DON'T WASTE YOUR BREATH, SMOKER.
THE GOVERNMENT DOESN'T WANT THE TRUTH TO GET OUT.

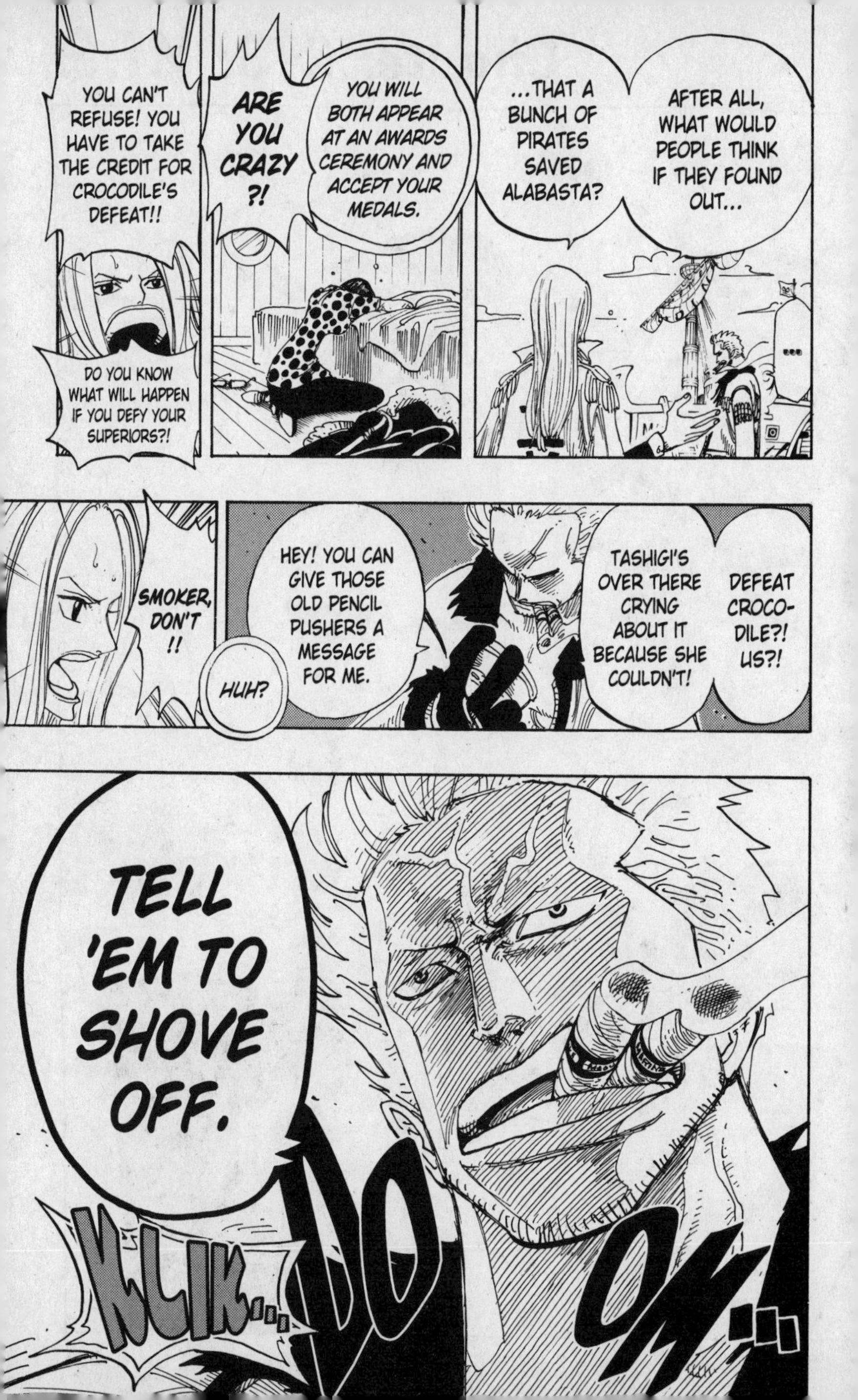

AFTER ALL, WHAT WOULD PEOPLE THINK IF THEY FOUND OUT...
...THAT A BUNCH OF PIRATES SAVED ALABASTA?
YOU WILL BOTH APPEAR AT AN AWARDS CEREMONY AND ACCEPT YOUR MEDALS.
ARE YOU CRAZY?!
YOU CAN'T REFUSE! YOU HAVE TO TAKE THE CREDIT FOR CROCODILE'S DEFEAT!!
DO YOU KNOW WHAT WILL HAPPEN IF YOU DEFY YOUR SUPERIORS?!
DEFEAT CROCO-DILE?! US?!
TASHIGI'S OVER THERE CRYING ABOUT IT BECAUSE SHE COULDN'T!
HEY! YOU CAN GIVE THOSE OLD PENCIL PUSHERS A MESSAGE FOR ME.
HUH?
SMOKER, DON'T!!
TELL 'EM TO SHOVE OFF.
DO
OM...
KLIK...

Chapter 213: V.I.P.

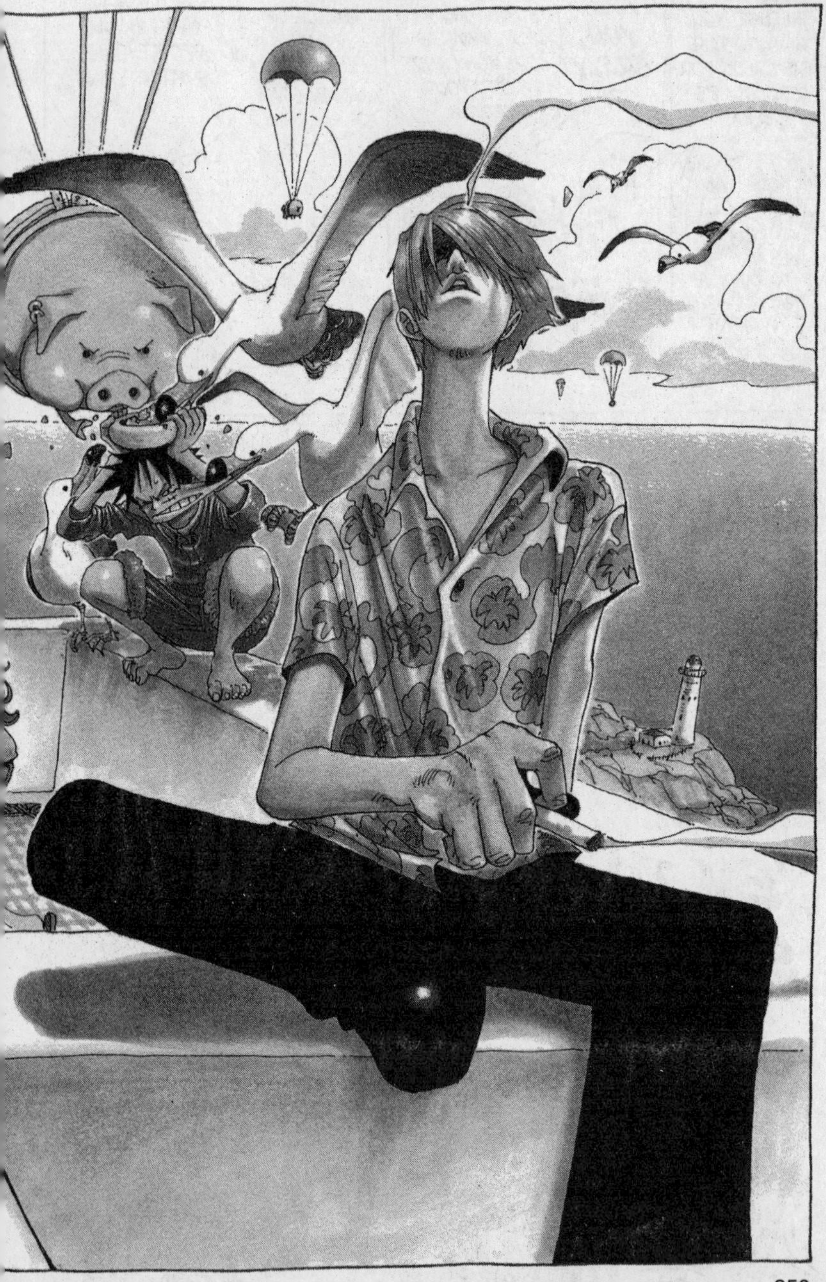

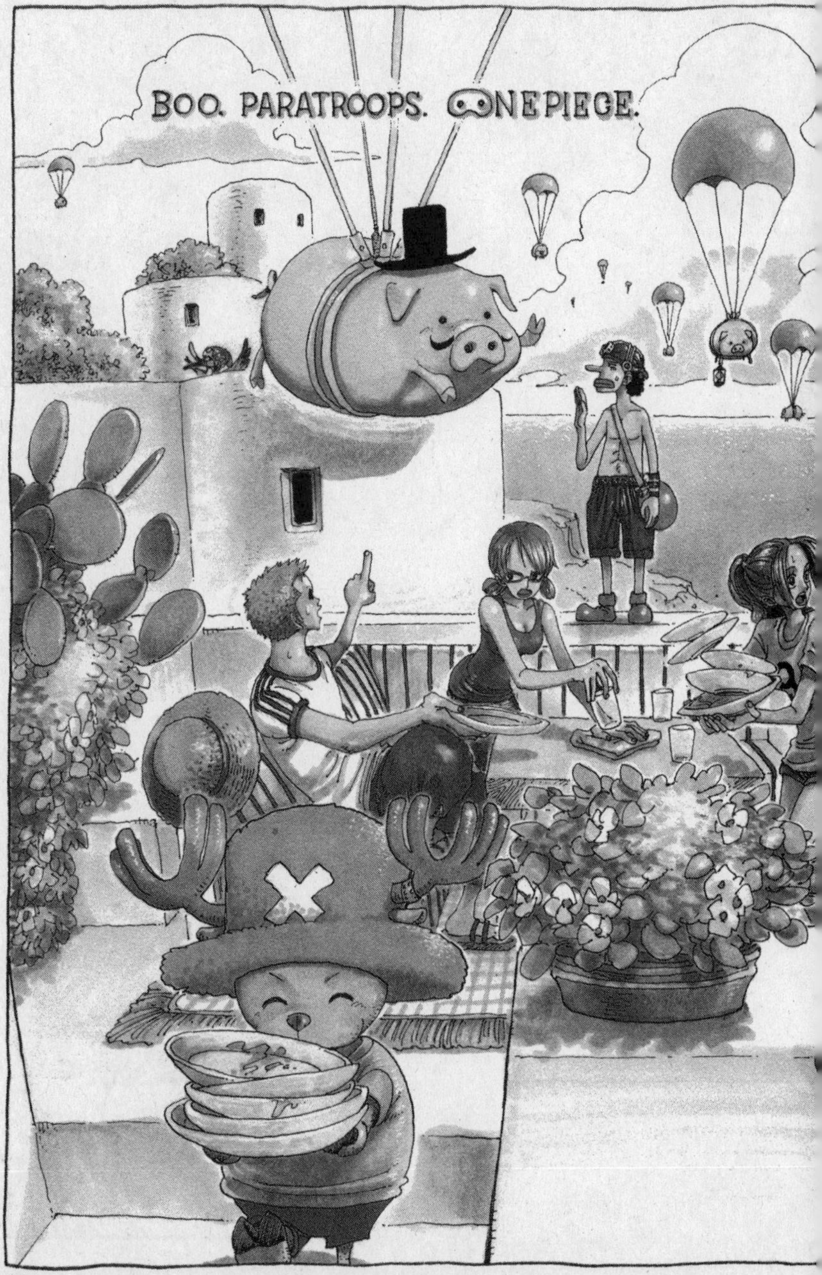
BOO. PARATROOPS. ONE PIECE.

READ THIS WAY

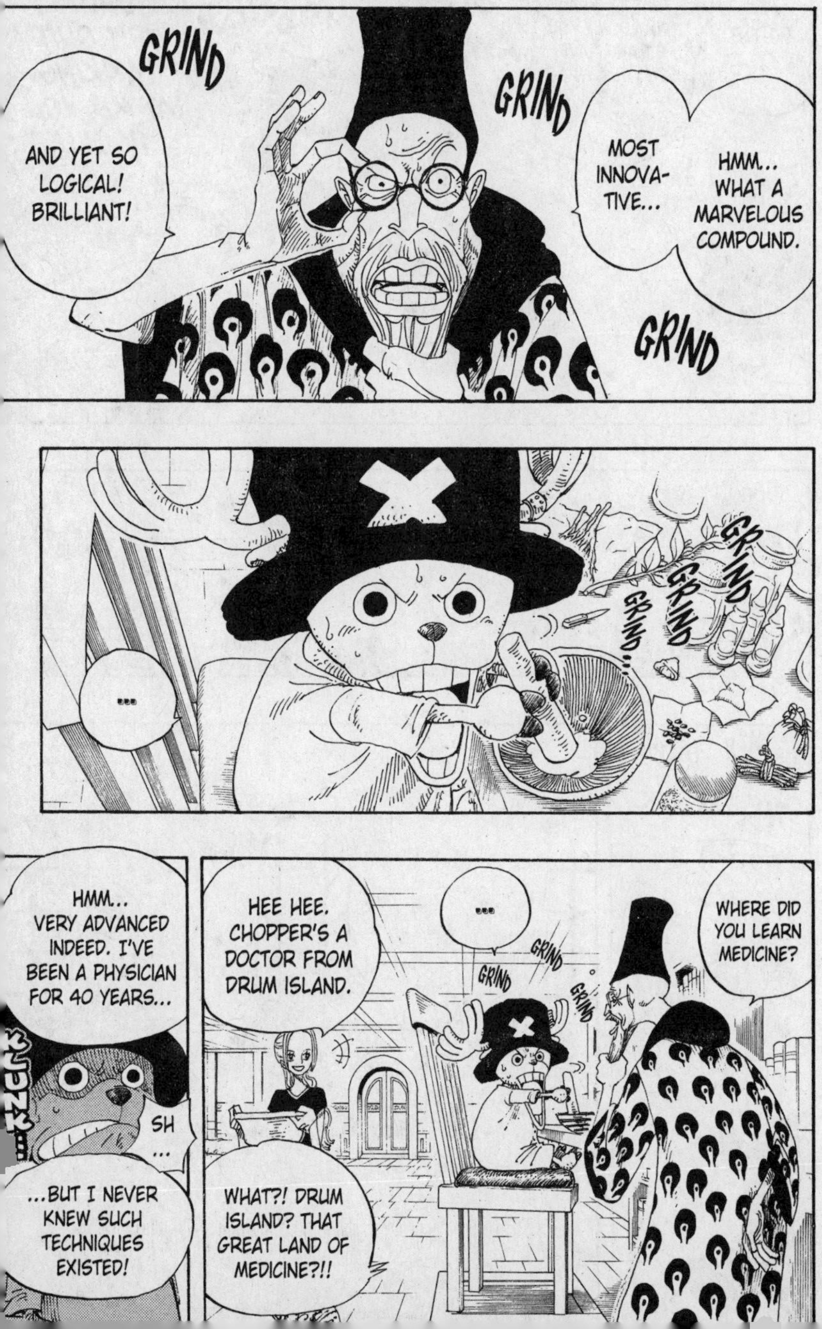
GRIND
HMM... WHAT A MARVELOUS COMPOUND.
MOST INNOVATIVE...
GRIND
AND YET SO LOGICAL! BRILLIANT!
GRIND
GRIND
GRIND
GRIND..!!
...
WHERE DID YOU LEARN MEDICINE?
GRIND
GRIND
...
GRIND
HEE HEE. CHOPPER'S A DOCTOR FROM DRUM ISLAND.
WHAT?! DRUM ISLAND? THAT GREAT LAND OF MEDICINE?!!
HMM... VERY ADVANCED INDEED. I'VE BEEN A PHYSICIAN FOR 40 YEARS...
SH...
...BUT I NEVER KNEW SUCH TECHNIQUES EXISTED!

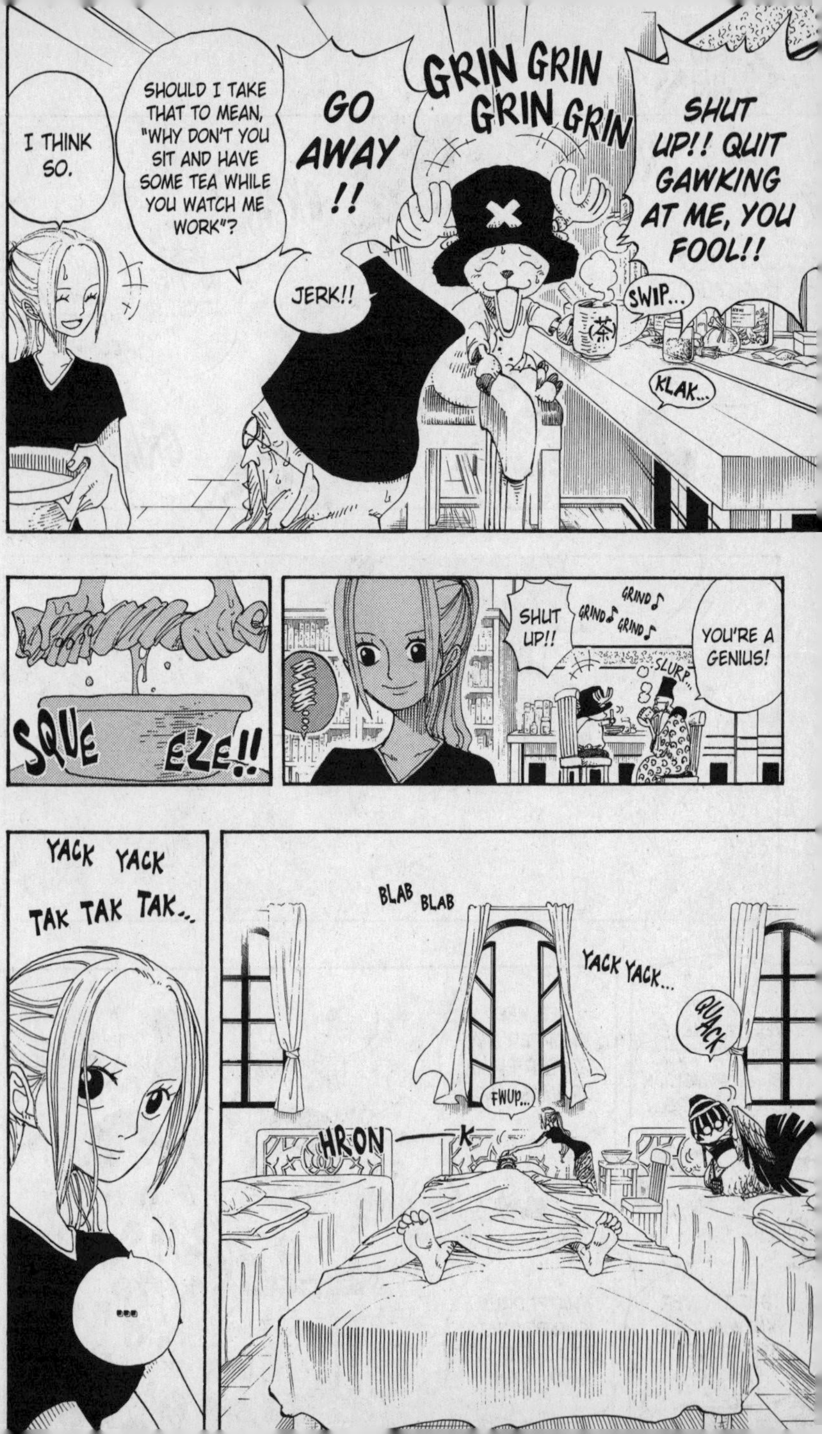
SHUT UP!! QUIT GAWKING AT ME, YOU FOOL!!
GRIN GRIN GRIN GRIN
SWIP...
KLAK...
GO AWAY!!
JERK!!
SHOULD I TAKE THAT TO MEAN, "WHY DON'T YOU SIT AND HAVE SOME TEA WHILE YOU WATCH ME WORK"?
I THINK SO.
YOU'RE A GENIUS!
GRIND GRIND GRIND
SHUT UP!!
SLURP...
SQUEEZE!!
QUACK
YACK YACK...
BLAB BLAB
FWUP...
HRON—K
YACK YACK
TAK TAK TAK...
...

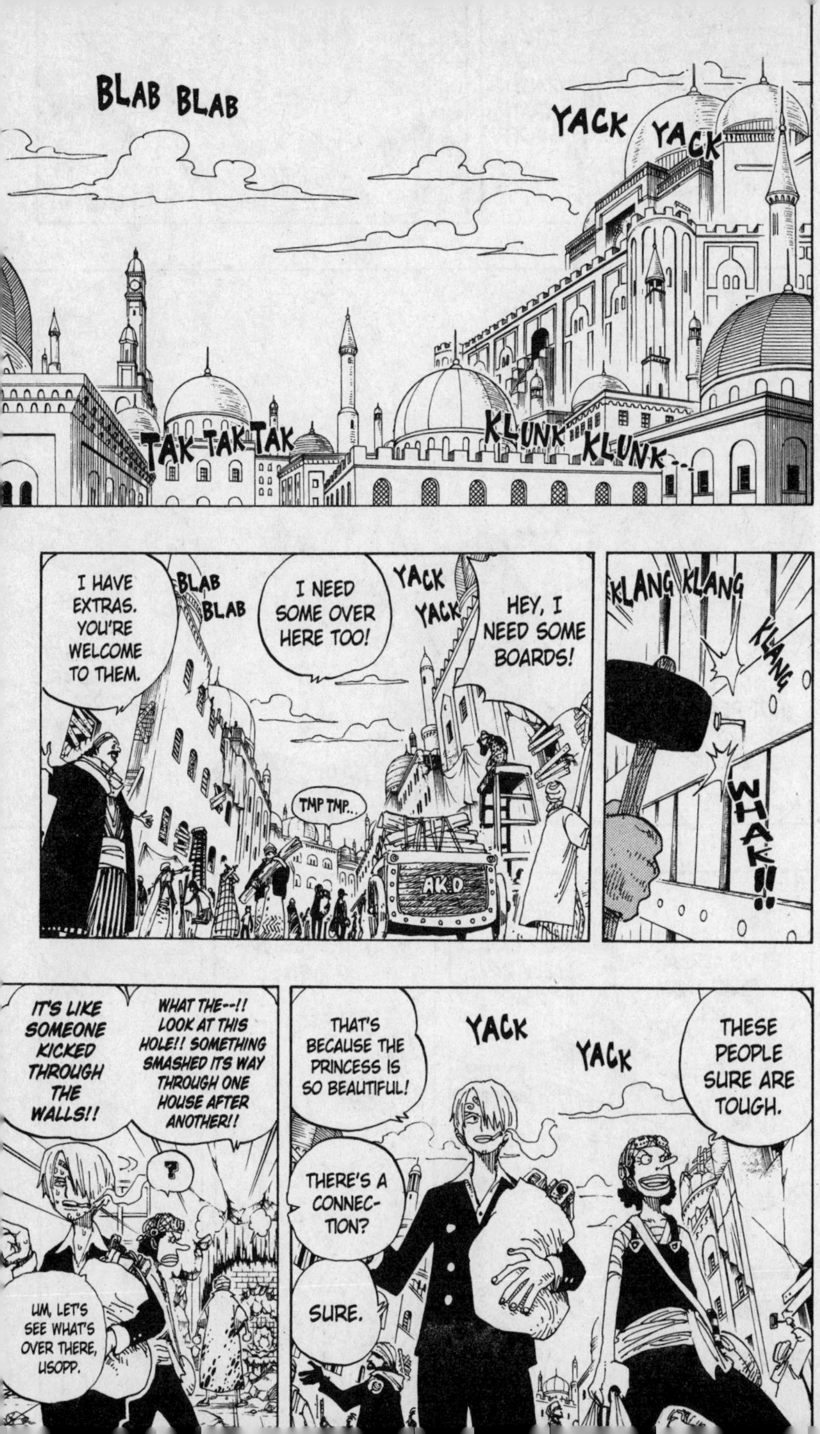
YACK YACK
BLAB BLAB
KLUNK KLUNK...
TAK TAK TAK
KLANG KLANG
KLANG
WHAK!!
HEY, I NEED SOME BOARDS!
YACK YACK
I NEED SOME OVER HERE TOO!
BLAB BLAB
I HAVE EXTRAS. YOU'RE WELCOME TO THEM.
TMP TMP...
AKD
THESE PEOPLE SURE ARE TOUGH.
YACK YACK
THAT'S BECAUSE THE PRINCESS IS SO BEAUTIFUL!
THERE'S A CONNEC-TION?
SURE.
WHAT THE--!! LOOK AT THIS HOLE!! SOMETHING SMASHED ITS WAY THROUGH ONE HOUSE AFTER ANOTHER!!
IT'S LIKE SOMEONE KICKED THROUGH THE WALLS!!
?
UM, LET'S SEE WHAT'S OVER THERE, USOPP.

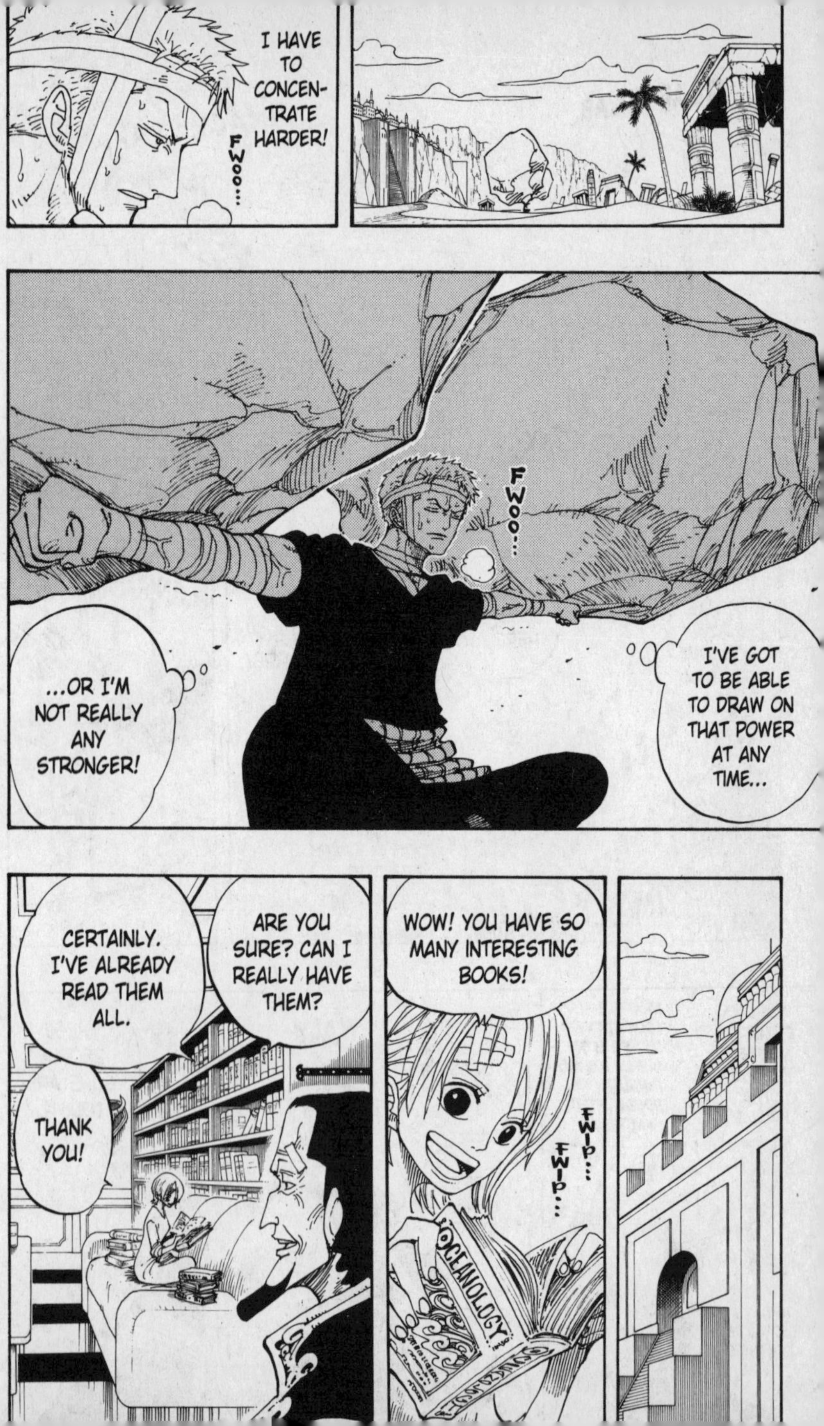
I HAVE TO CONCENTRATE HARDER!
FWOO...
I'VE GOT TO BE ABLE TO DRAW ON THAT POWER AT ANY TIME...
FWOO...
...OR I'M NOT REALLY ANY STRONGER!
WOW! YOU HAVE SO MANY INTERESTING BOOKS!
FWIP...
FWIP...
OCEANOLOGY
ARE YOU SURE? CAN I REALLY HAVE THEM?
CERTAINLY. I'VE ALREADY READ THEM ALL.
THANK YOU!

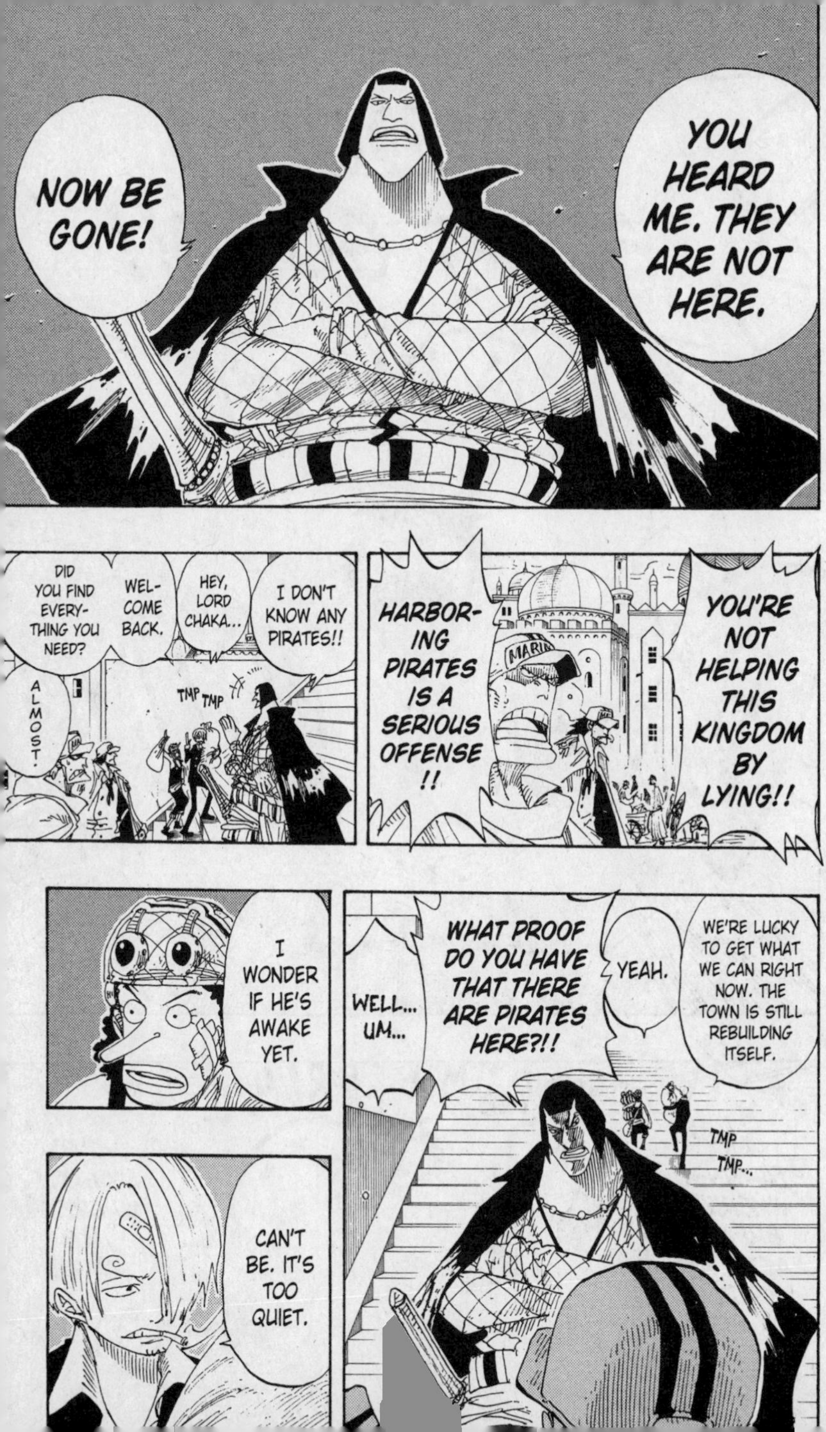
YOU HEARD ME. THEY ARE NOT HERE.
NOW BE GONE!
YOU'RE NOT HELPING THIS KINGDOM BY LYING!!
HARBORING PIRATES IS A SERIOUS OFFENSE!!
I DON'T KNOW ANY PIRATES!!
HEY, LORD CHAKA...
WELCOME BACK.
DID YOU FIND EVERYTHING YOU NEED?
TMP TMP
ALMOST.
WE'RE LUCKY TO GET WHAT WE CAN RIGHT NOW. THE TOWN IS STILL REBUILDING ITSELF.
YEAH.
WHAT PROOF DO YOU HAVE THAT THERE ARE PIRATES HERE?!!
WELL... UM...
TMP TMP...
I WONDER IF HE'S AWAKE YET.
CAN'T BE. IT'S TOO QUIET.

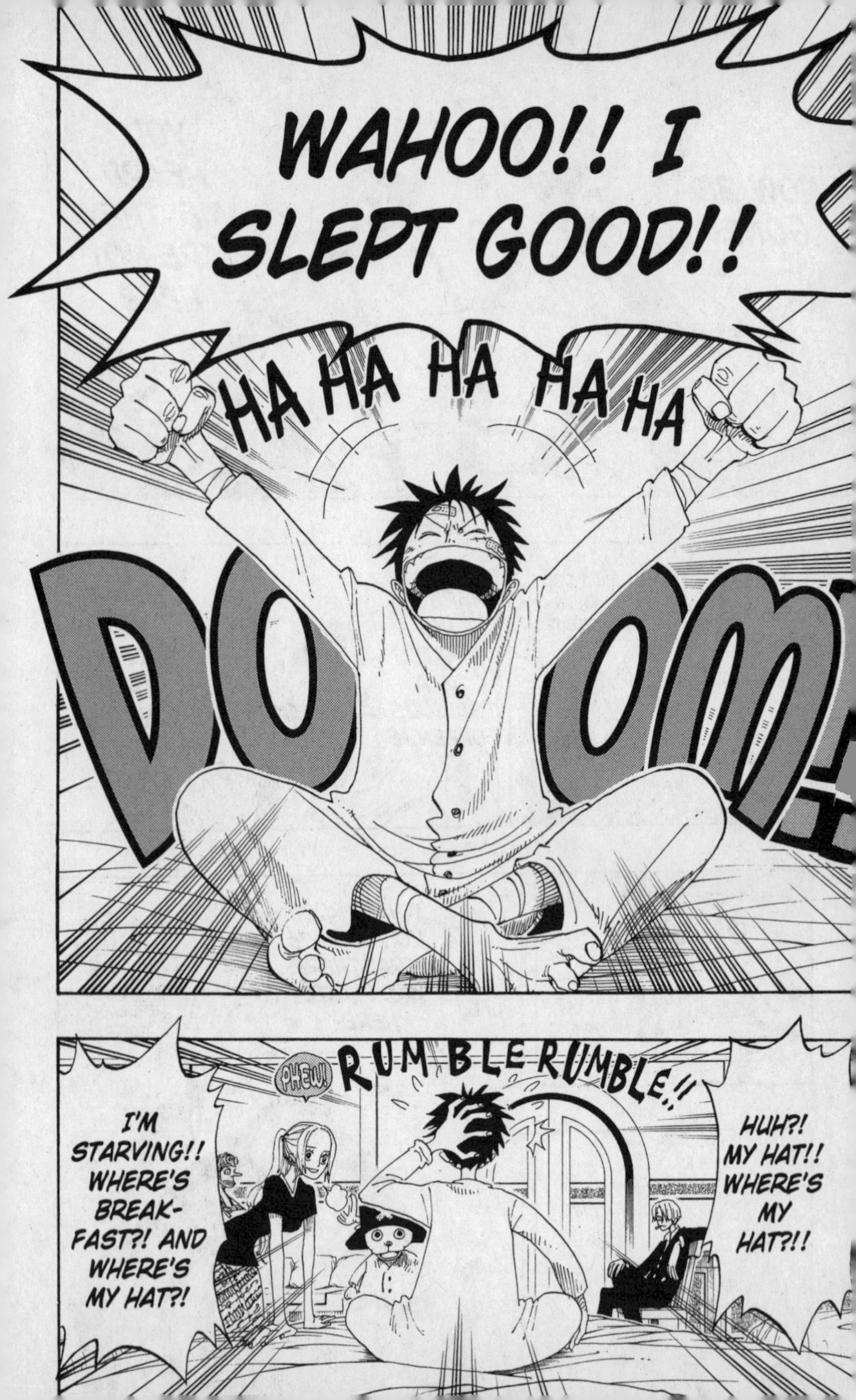
WAHOO!! I SLEPT GOOD!!
HA HA HA HA HA
DOOM
RUMBLE RUMBLE!!
HUH?! MY HAT!! WHERE'S MY HAT?!!
PHEW!
I'M STARVING!! WHERE'S BREAK-FAST?! AND WHERE'S MY HAT?!

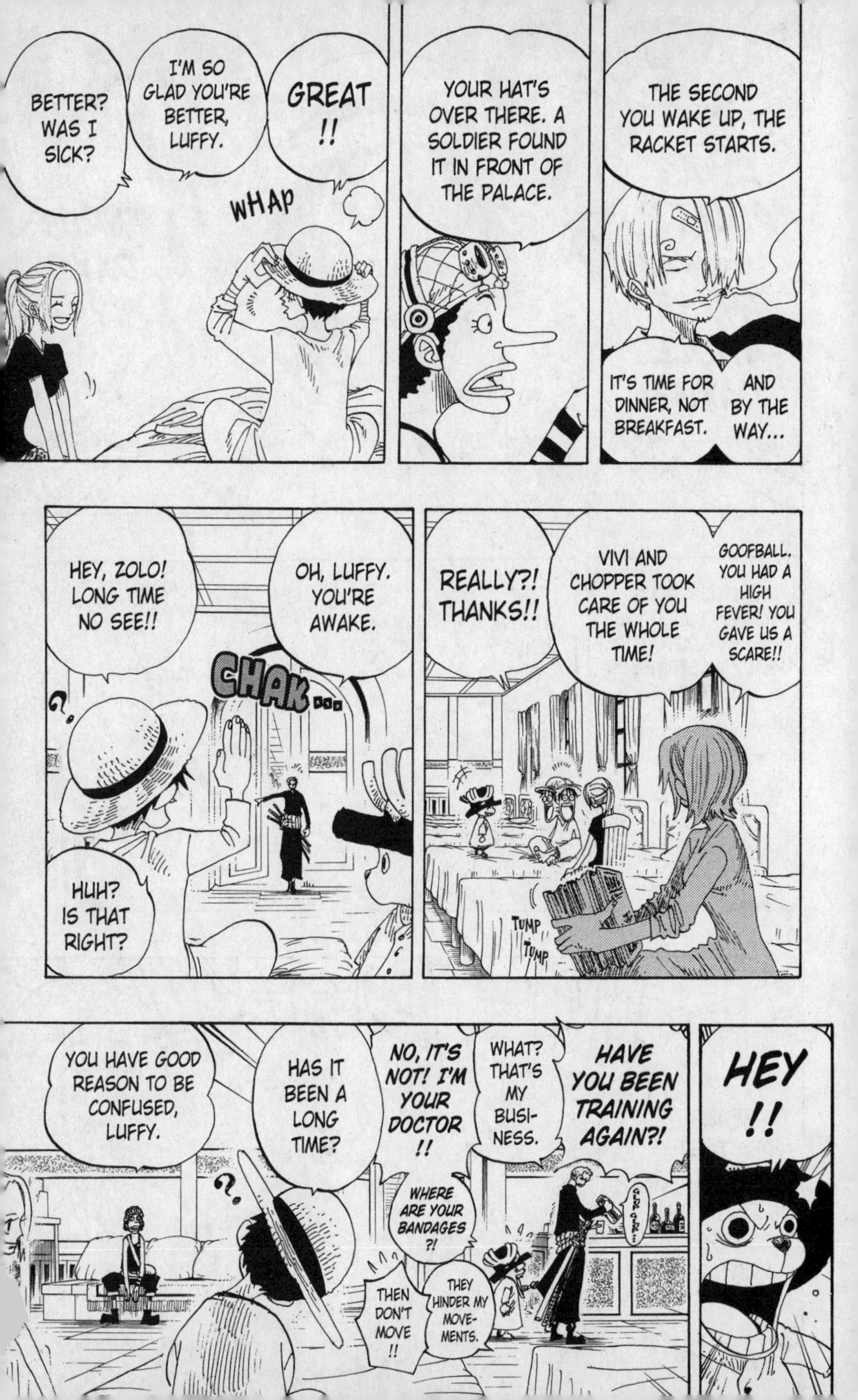
THE SECOND YOU WAKE UP, THE RACKET STARTS.
AND BY THE WAY...
IT'S TIME FOR DINNER, NOT BREAKFAST.
YOUR HAT'S OVER THERE. A SOLDIER FOUND IT IN FRONT OF THE PALACE.
GREAT!!
WHAP
I'M SO GLAD YOU'RE BETTER, LUFFY.
BETTER? WAS I SICK?
GOOFBALL. YOU HAD A HIGH FEVER! YOU GAVE US A SCARE!!
VIVI AND CHOPPER TOOK CARE OF YOU THE WHOLE TIME!
REALLY?! THANKS!!
TUMP
TUMP
OH, LUFFY. YOU'RE AWAKE.
CHAK...
HEY, ZOLO! LONG TIME NO SEE!!
HUH? IS THAT RIGHT?
HEY!!
HAVE YOU BEEN TRAINING AGAIN?!
WHAT? THAT'S MY BUSINESS.
NO, IT'S NOT! I'M YOUR DOCTOR!!
WHERE ARE YOUR BANDAGES?!
THEY HINDER MY MOVEMENTS.
THEN DON'T MOVE!!
HAS IT BEEN A LONG TIME?
YOU HAVE GOOD REASON TO BE CONFUSED, LUFFY.

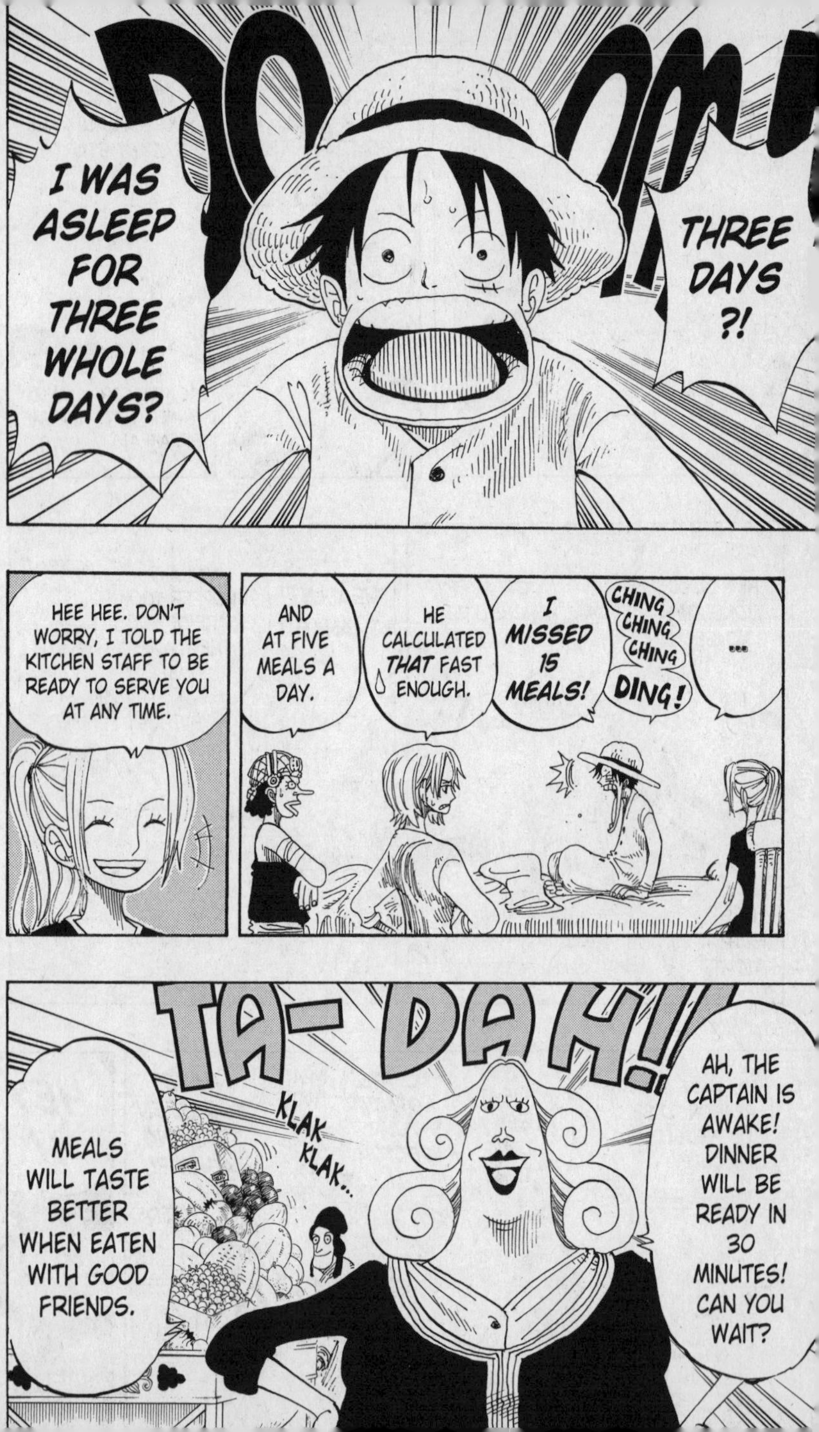
THREE DAYS ?!
I WAS ASLEEP FOR THREE WHOLE DAYS?
...
CHING CHING CHING DING!
I MISSED 15 MEALS!
HE CALCULATED THAT FAST ENOUGH.
AND AT FIVE MEALS A DAY.
HEE HEE. DON'T WORRY, I TOLD THE KITCHEN STAFF TO BE READY TO SERVE YOU AT ANY TIME.
TA-DAH!!
AH, THE CAPTAIN IS AWAKE! DINNER WILL BE READY IN 30 MINUTES! CAN YOU WAIT?
KLAK KLAK...
MEALS WILL TASTE BETTER WHEN EATEN WITH GOOD FRIENDS.

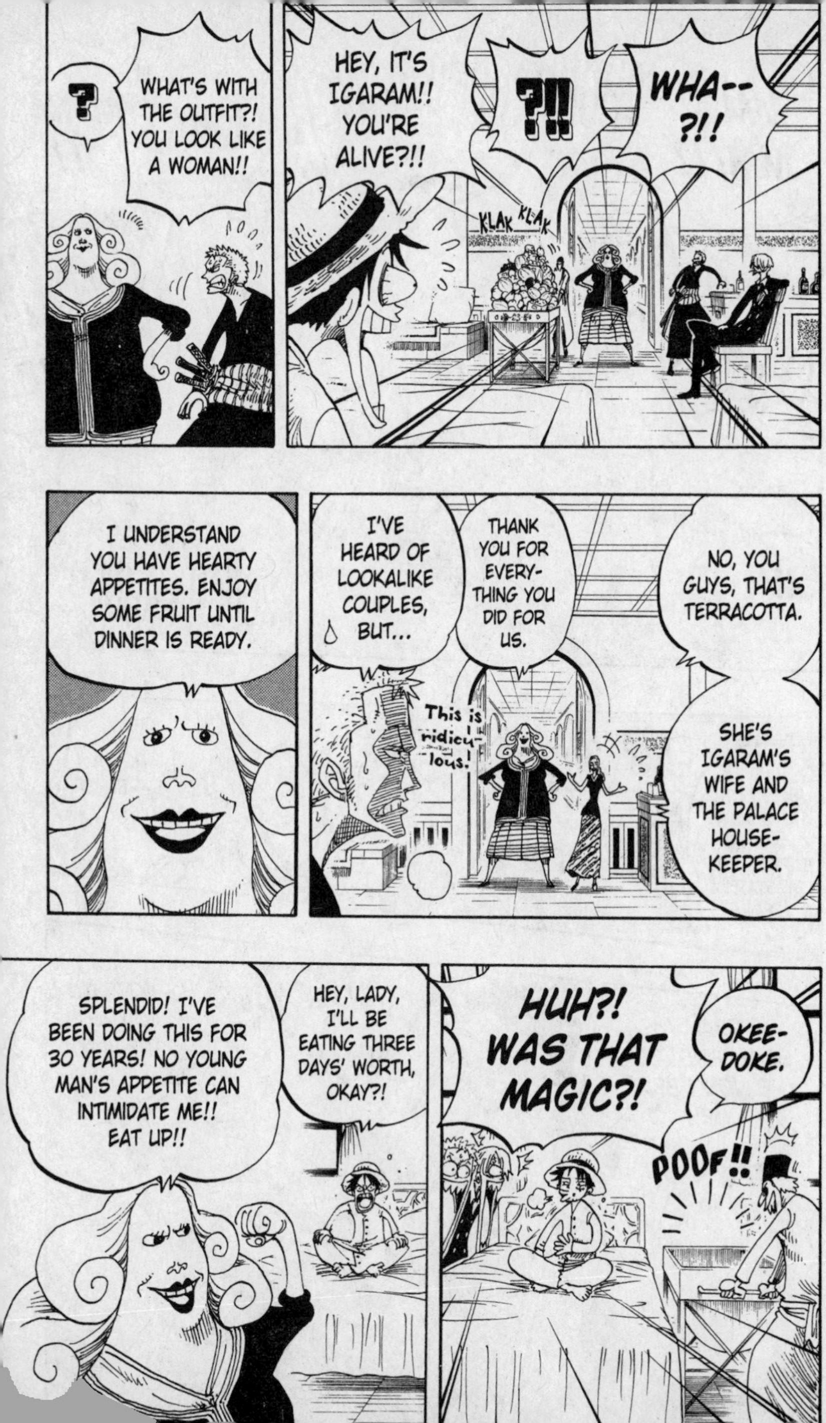
WHA-- ?!!
?!!
HEY, IT'S IGARAM!! YOU'RE ALIVE?!!
KLAK KLAK
WHAT'S WITH THE OUTFIT?! YOU LOOK LIKE A WOMAN!!
?
NO, YOU GUYS, THAT'S TERRACOTTA.
SHE'S IGARAM'S WIFE AND THE PALACE HOUSE-KEEPER.
THANK YOU FOR EVERY-THING YOU DID FOR US.
I'VE HEARD OF LOOKALIKE COUPLES, BUT...
This is ridicu-lous!
I UNDERSTAND YOU HAVE HEARTY APPETITES. ENJOY SOME FRUIT UNTIL DINNER IS READY.
OKEE-DOKE.
HUH?! WAS THAT MAGIC?!
POOF!!
HEY, LADY, I'LL BE EATING THREE DAYS' WORTH, OKAY?!
SPLENDID! I'VE BEEN DOING THIS FOR 30 YEARS! NO YOUNG MAN'S APPETITE CAN INTIMIDATE ME!! EAT UP!!

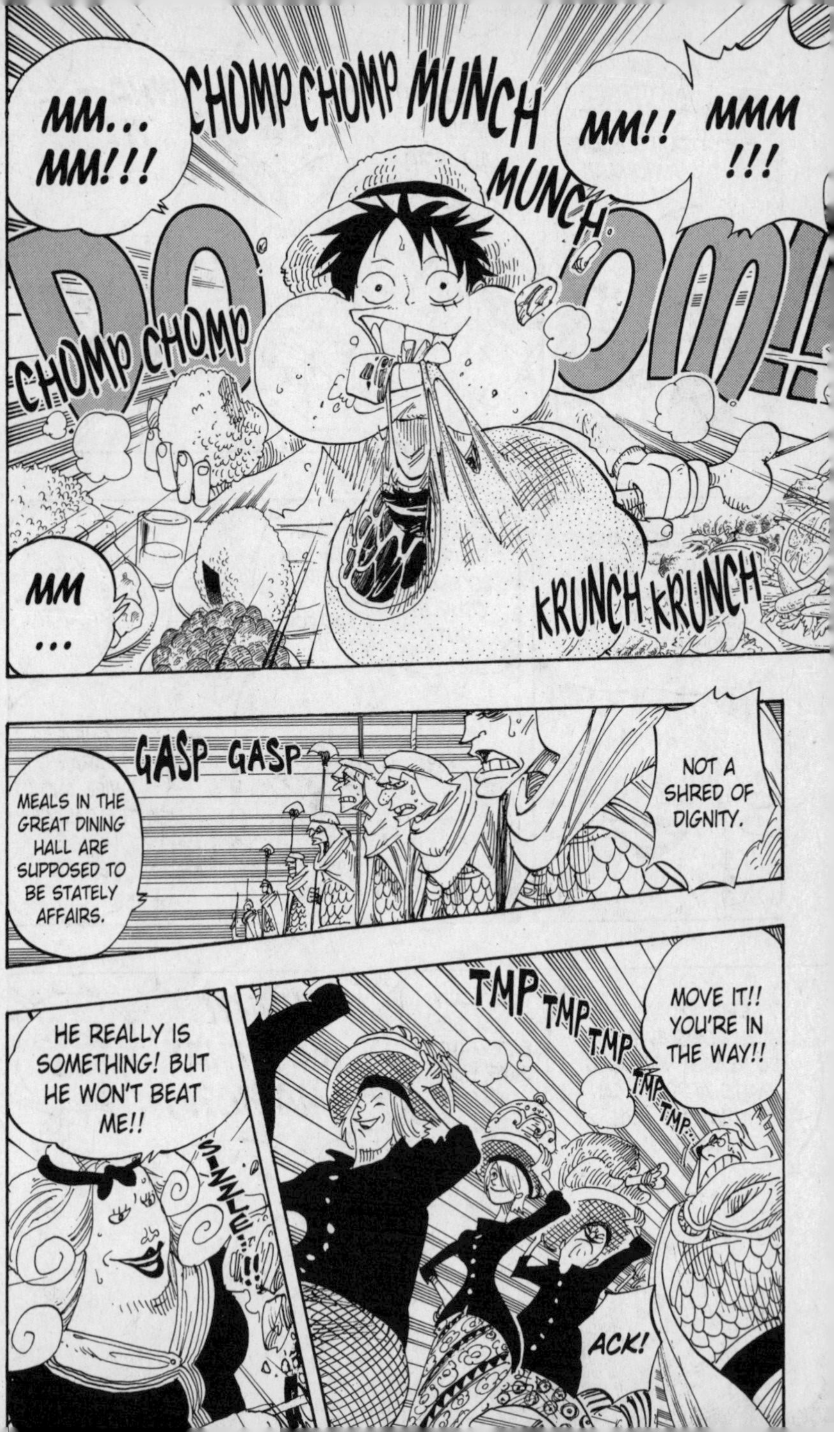
MMM !!!
MM!!
CHOMP CHOMP MUNCH
MUNCH
MM... MM!!!
CHOMP CHOMP
KRUNCH KRUNCH
MM ...
NOT A SHRED OF DIGNITY.
GASP GASP
MEALS IN THE GREAT DINING HALL ARE SUPPOSED TO BE STATELY AFFAIRS.
MOVE IT!! YOU'RE IN THE WAY!!
TMP TMP TMP TMP TMP...
ACK!
HE REALLY IS SOMETHING! BUT HE WON'T BEAT ME!!
SIZZLE...!!

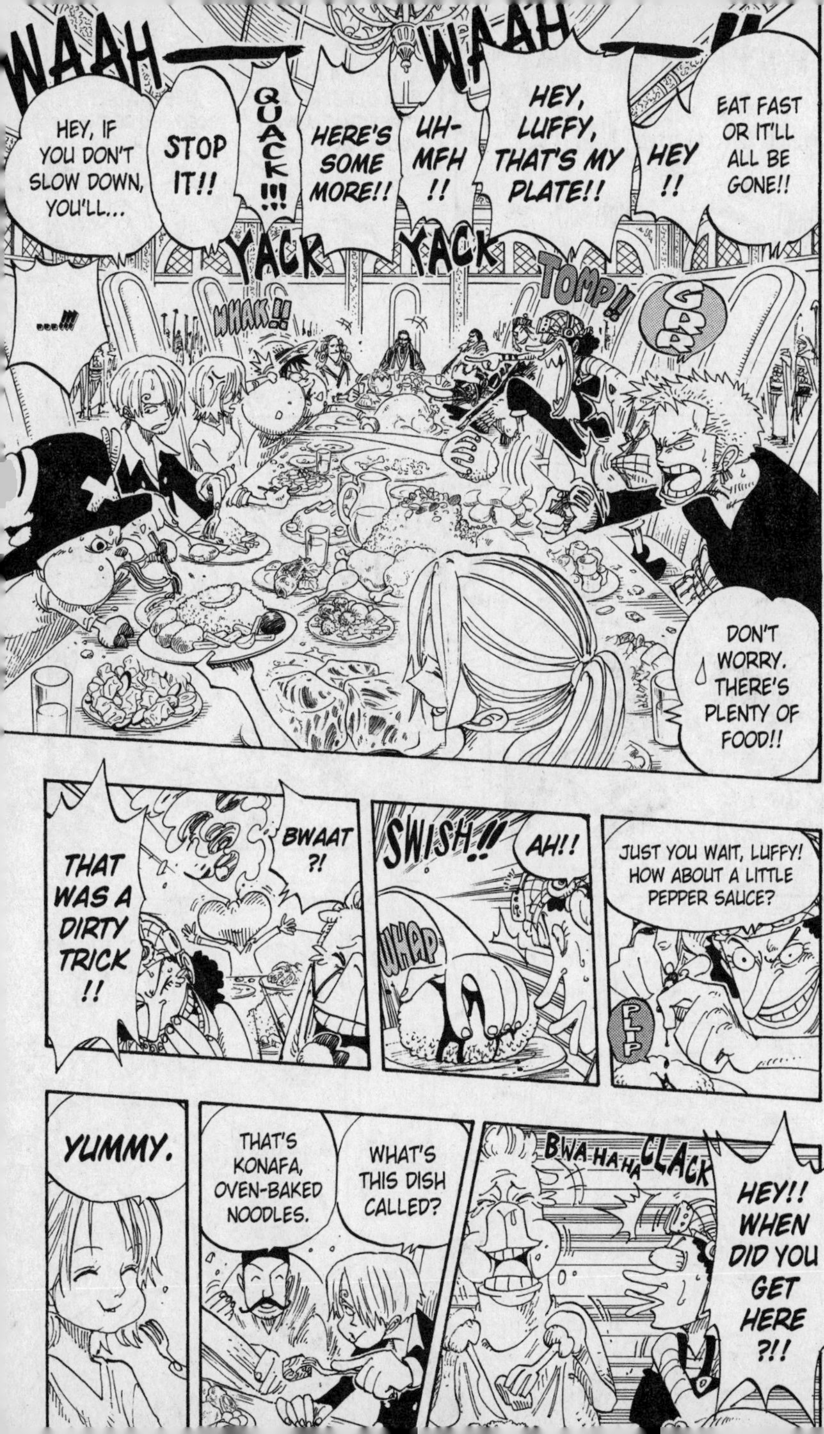
WAAH— WAAH—
EAT FAST OR IT'LL ALL BE GONE!!
HEY !!
HEY, LUFFY, THAT'S MY PLATE!!
UH-MFH !!
HERE'S SOME MORE!!
QUACK!!!
STOP IT!!
HEY, IF YOU DON'T SLOW DOWN, YOU'LL...
YACK YACK
GRR
TOMP!!
WHAK!!
...!!!
DON'T WORRY. THERE'S PLENTY OF FOOD!!
JUST YOU WAIT, LUFFY! HOW ABOUT A LITTLE PEPPER SAUCE?
FLIP
AH!!
SWISH!!
WHAP
BWAAT ?!
THAT WAS A DIRTY TRICK !!
HEY!! WHEN DID YOU GET HERE ?!!
CLACK
BWAHAHA
WHAT'S THIS DISH CALLED?
THAT'S KONAFA, OVEN-BAKED NOODLES.
YUMMY.

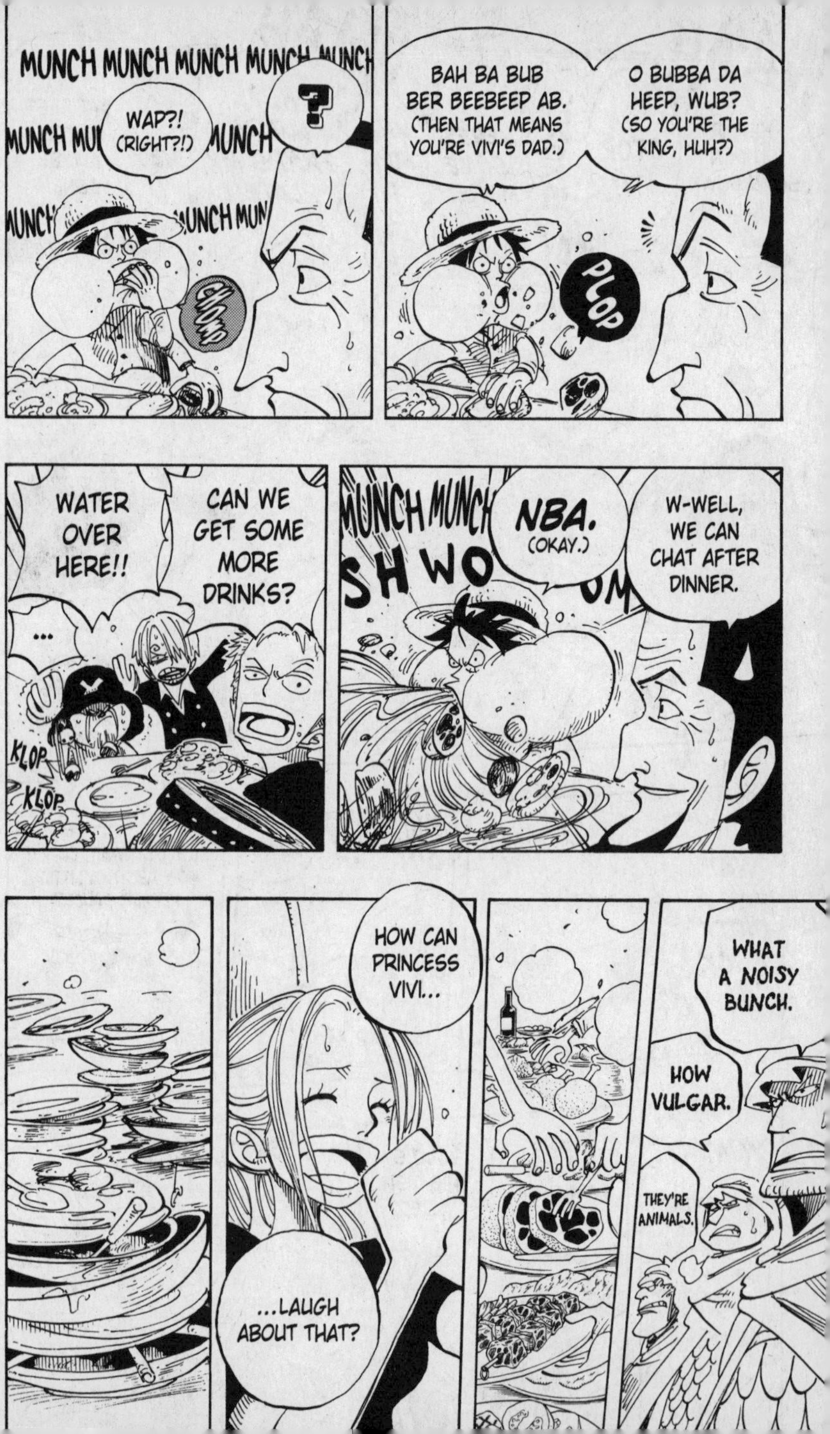
O BUBBA DA HEEP, WUB? (SO YOU'RE THE KING, HUH?)
BAH BA BUB BER BEEBEEP AB. (THEN THAT MEANS YOU'RE VIVI'S DAD.)
PLOP
?
MUNCH MUNCH MUNCH MUNCH MUNCH
MUNCH MU MUNCH
WAP?! (RIGHT?!)
MUNCH MUNCH MUN
CHOMP
W-WELL, WE CAN CHAT AFTER DINNER.
NBA. (OKAY.)
MUNCH MUNCH
SH WO OM
CAN WE GET SOME MORE DRINKS?
WATER OVER HERE!!
...
KLOP KLOP
WHAT A NOISY BUNCH.
HOW VULGAR.
THEY'RE ANIMALS.
HOW CAN PRINCESS VIVI...
...LAUGH ABOUT THAT?

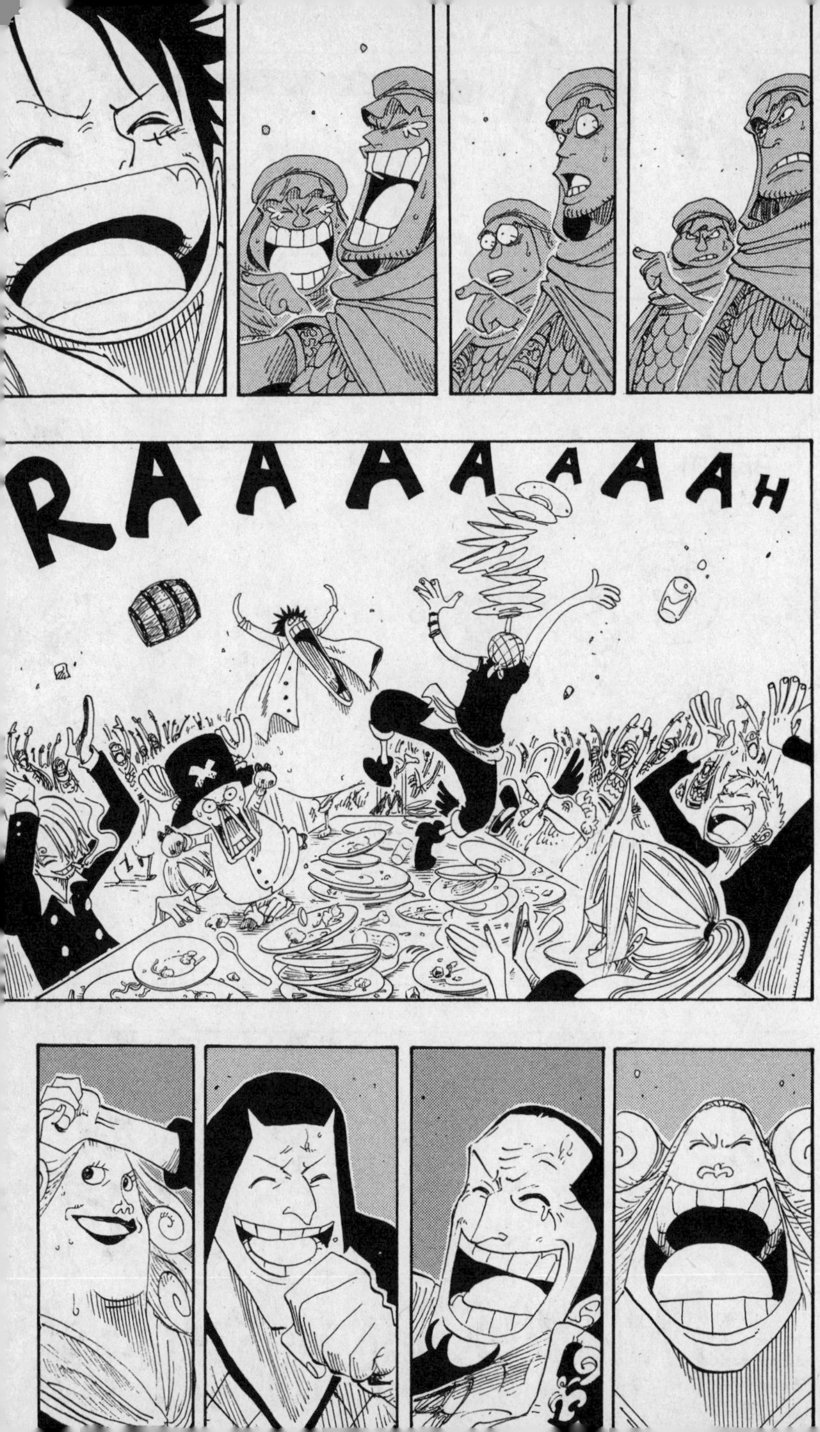
RAAAAAAH

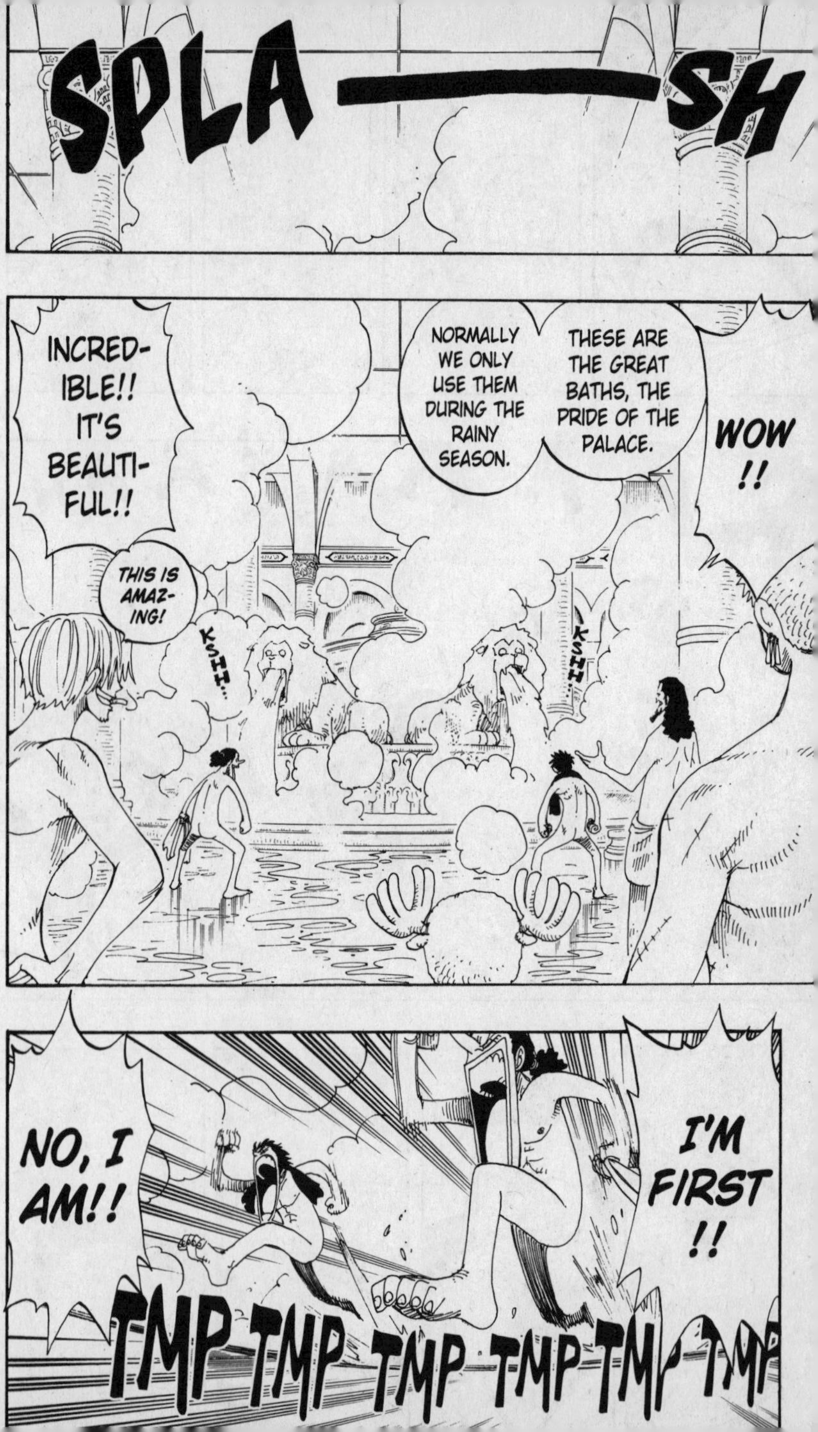
SPLA—SH
WOW!!
THESE ARE THE GREAT BATHS, THE PRIDE OF THE PALACE.
NORMALLY WE ONLY USE THEM DURING THE RAINY SEASON.
INCREDIBLE!! IT'S BEAUTIFUL!!
THIS IS AMAZING!
KSHH...
KSHH...
I'M FIRST!!
NO, I AM!!
TMP TMP TMP TMP TMP TMP

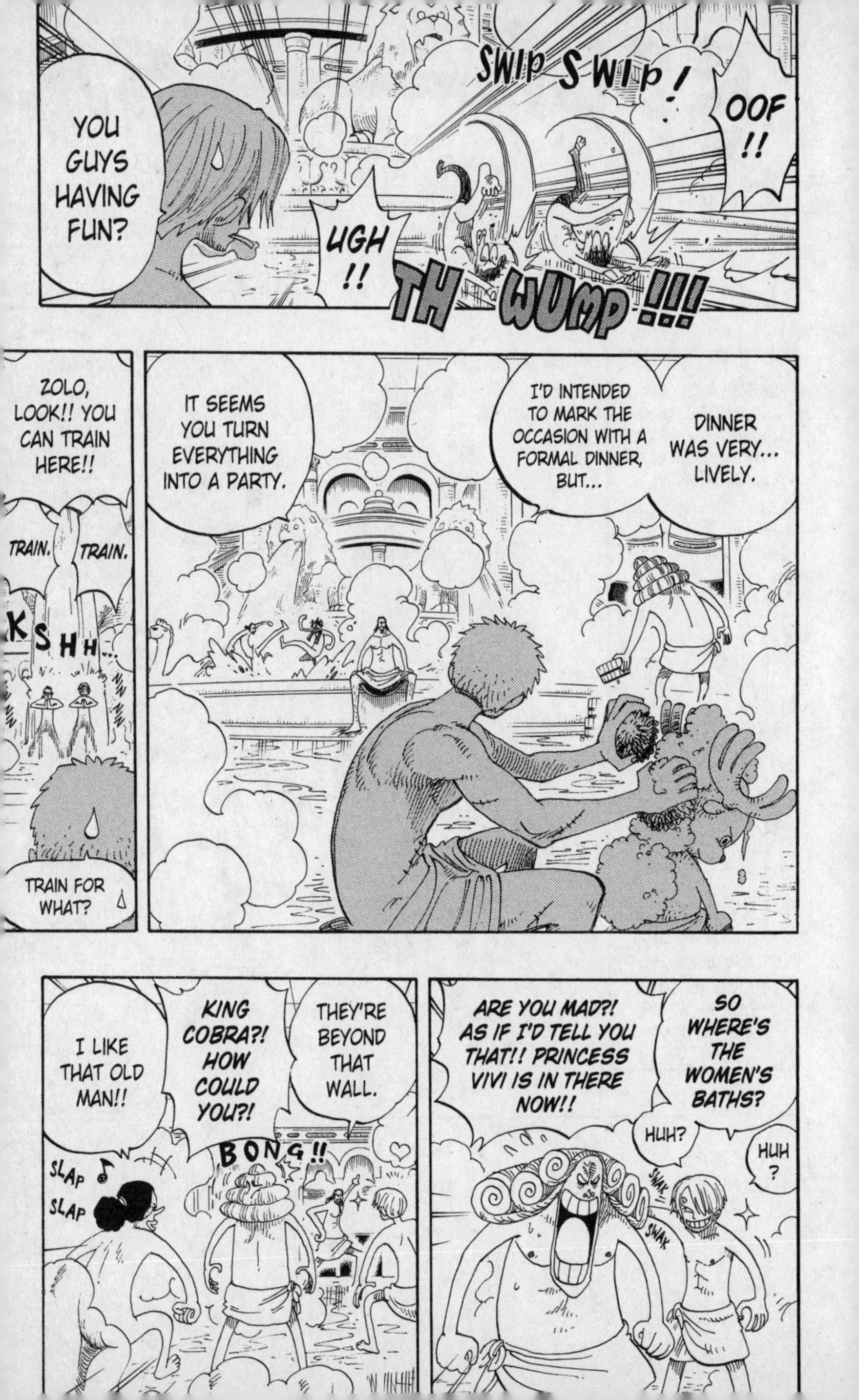
OOF !!
SWIP SWIP!
UGH !!
YOU GUYS HAVING FUN?
THWUMP!!!
DINNER WAS VERY... LIVELY.
I'D INTENDED TO MARK THE OCCASION WITH A FORMAL DINNER, BUT...
IT SEEMS YOU TURN EVERYTHING INTO A PARTY.
ZOLO, LOOK!! YOU CAN TRAIN HERE!!
TRAIN.
TRAIN.
TRAIN FOR WHAT?
SO WHERE'S THE WOMEN'S BATHS?
ARE YOU MAD?! AS IF I'D TELL YOU THAT!! PRINCESS VIVI IS IN THERE NOW!!
HUH?
HUH?
SWAK
SWAK
THEY'RE BEYOND THAT WALL.
KING COBRA?! HOW COULD YOU?!
I LIKE THAT OLD MAN!!
BONG!!
SLAP
SLAP

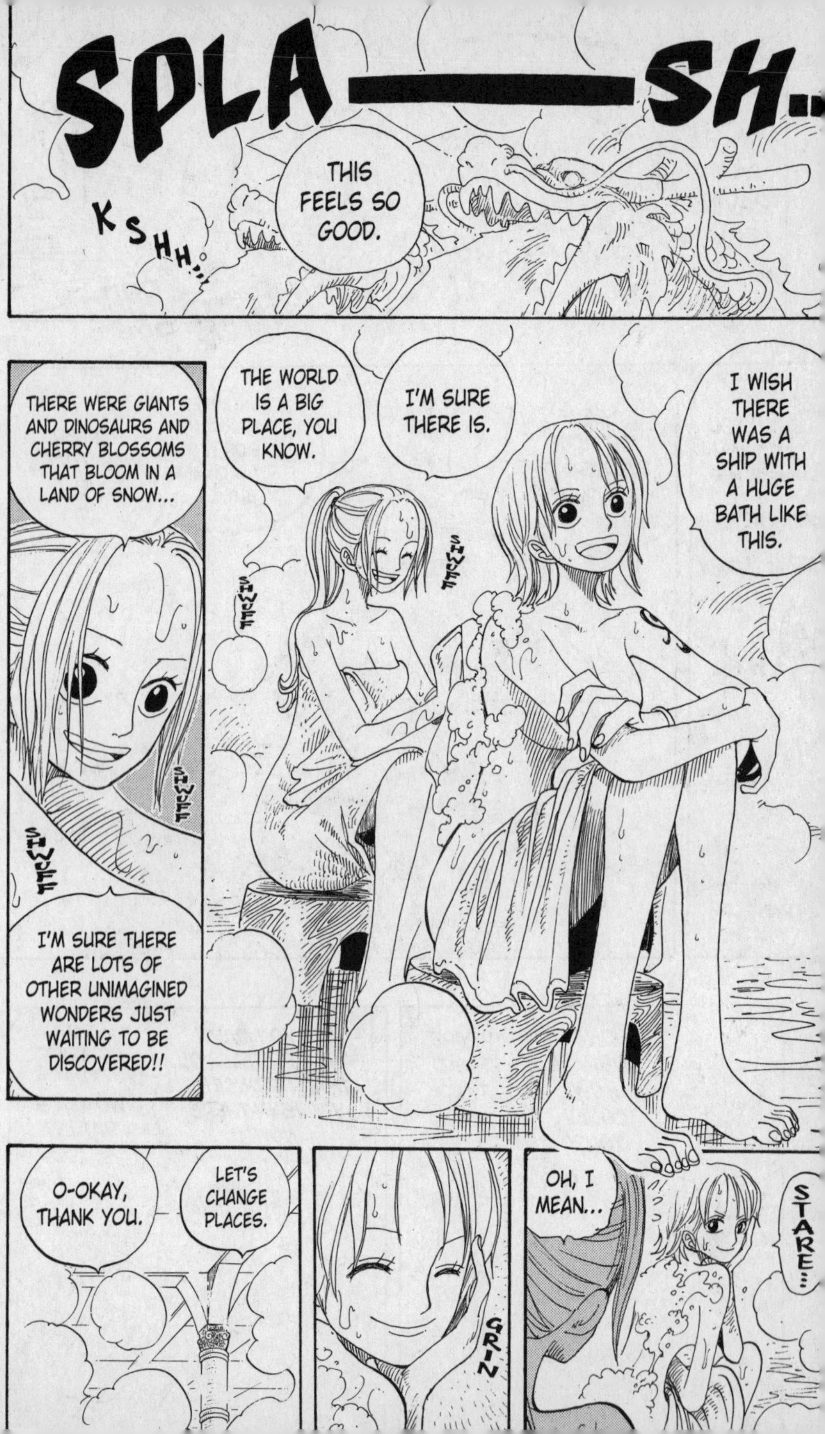
SPLA—SH..
THIS FEELS SO GOOD.
KSHH...
I WISH THERE WAS A SHIP WITH A HUGE BATH LIKE THIS.
I'M SURE THERE IS.
THE WORLD IS A BIG PLACE, YOU KNOW.
SHWUFF
SHWUFF
THERE WERE GIANTS AND DINOSAURS AND CHERRY BLOSSOMS THAT BLOOM IN A LAND OF SNOW...
SHWUFF
SHWUFF
I'M SURE THERE ARE LOTS OF OTHER UNIMAGINED WONDERS JUST WAITING TO BE DISCOVERED!!
STARE...
OH, I MEAN...
GRIN
LET'S CHANGE PLACES.
O-OKAY, THANK YOU.

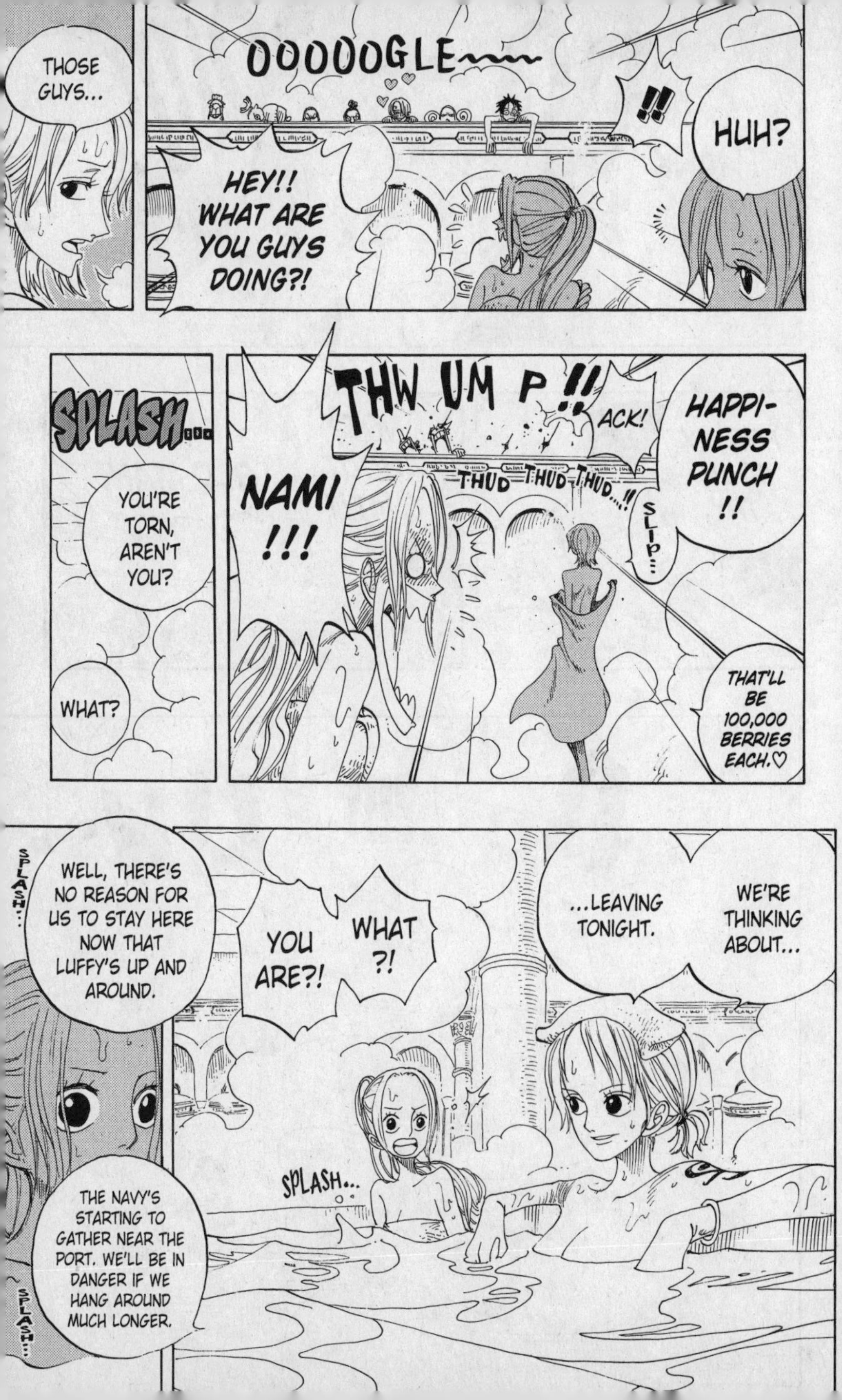

OOOOOGLE~~~
!!
HUH?
HEY!! WHAT ARE YOU GUYS DOING?!
THOSE GUYS...
HAPPI-NESS PUNCH!!
THWUMP!!
ACK!
THUD THUD THUD...!!
SLIP...
NAMI!!!
THAT'LL BE 100,000 BERRIES EACH.♡
SPLASH...
YOU'RE TORN, AREN'T YOU?
WHAT?
WE'RE THINKING ABOUT...
...LEAVING TONIGHT.
WHAT?!
YOU ARE?!
SPLASH...
SPLASH...
WELL, THERE'S NO REASON FOR US TO STAY HERE NOW THAT LUFFY'S UP AND AROUND.
THE NAVY'S STARTING TO GATHER NEAR THE PORT. WE'LL BE IN DANGER IF WE HANG AROUND MUCH LONGER.
SPLASH...

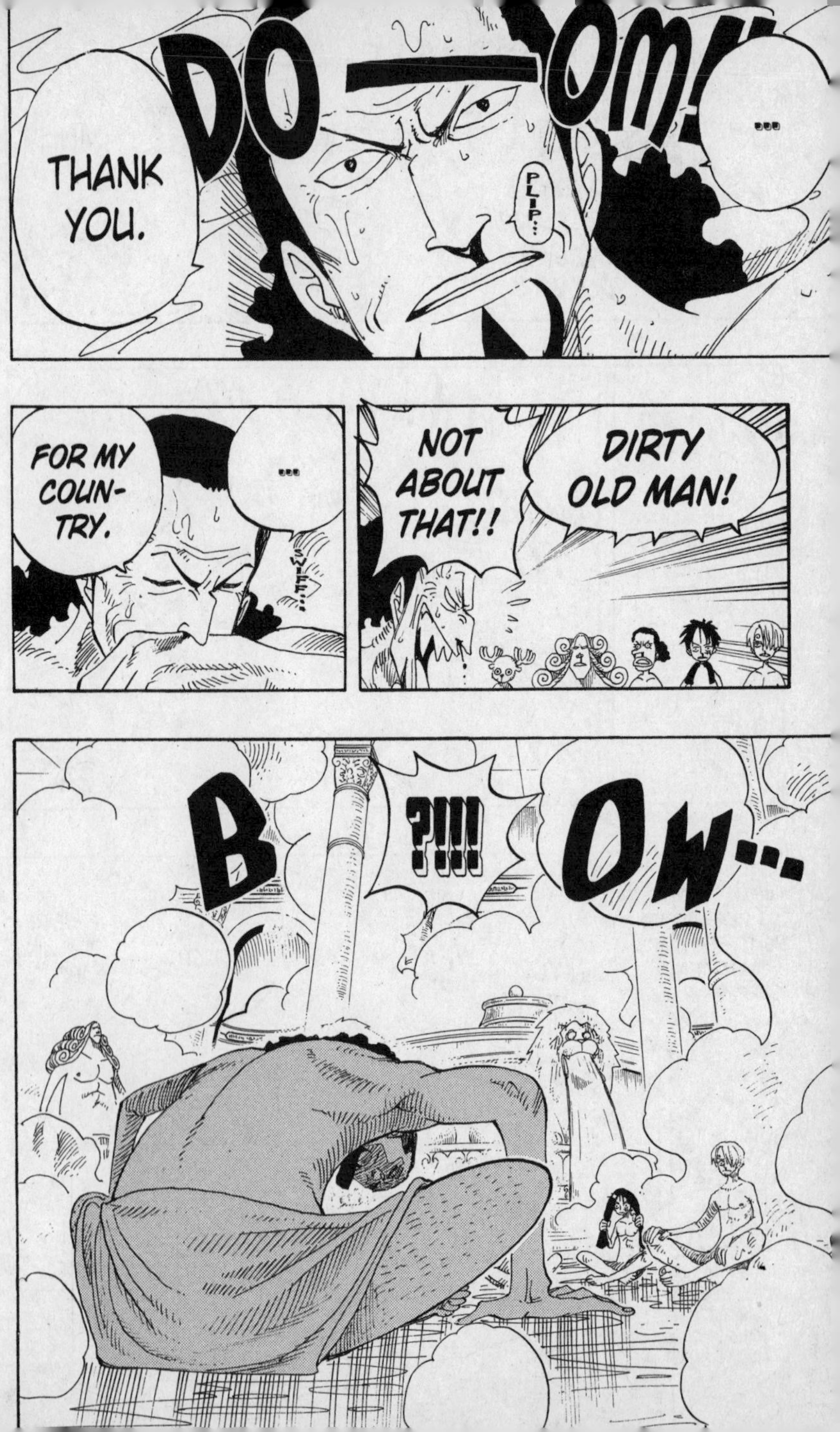
...
DO—OM!
FLIP...
THANK YOU.
DIRTY OLD MAN!
NOT ABOUT THAT!!
...
SWIFF...
FOR MY COUN-TRY.
?!!!
BOW...

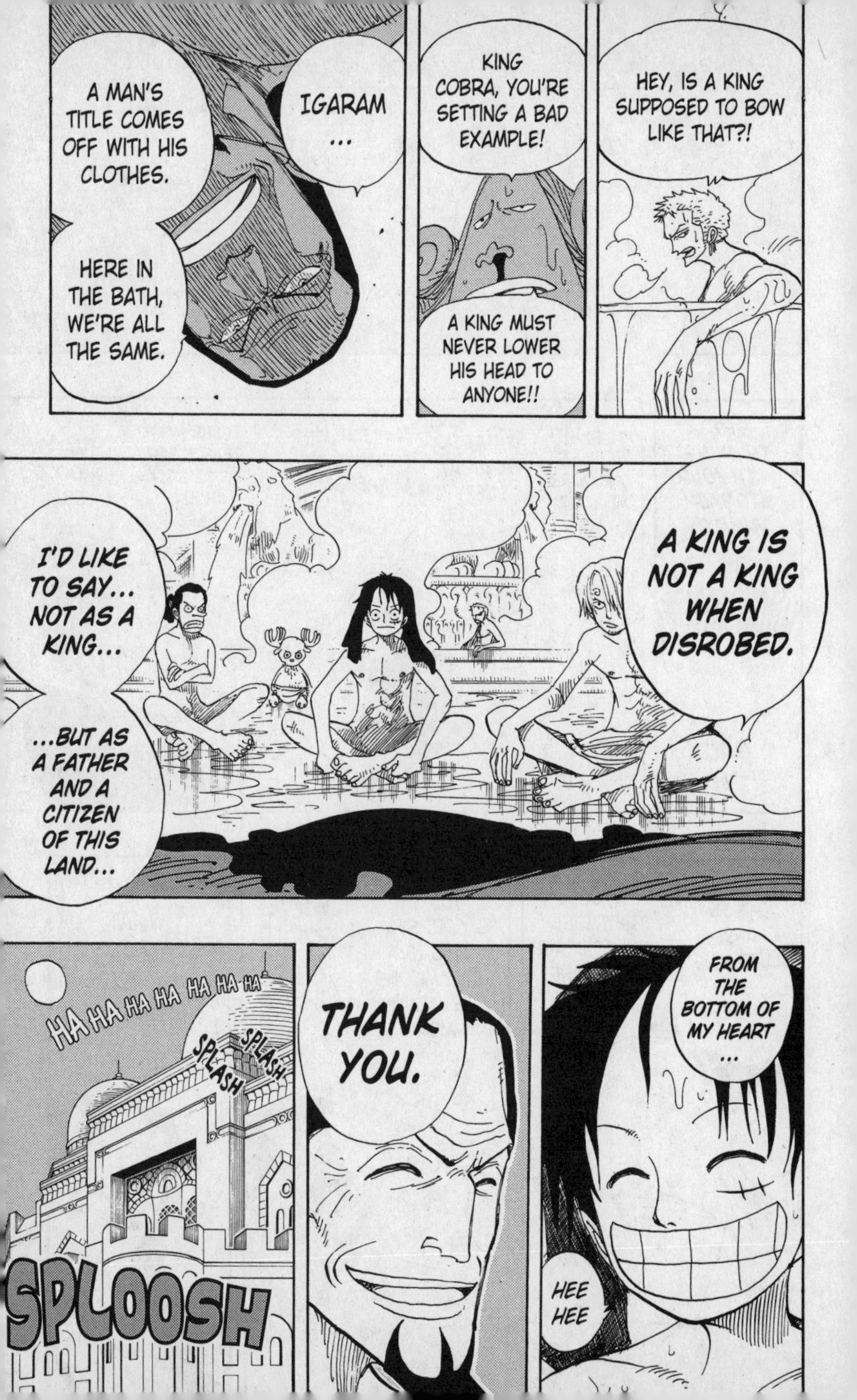
HEY, IS A KING SUPPOSED TO BOW LIKE THAT?!
KING COBRA, YOU'RE SETTING A BAD EXAMPLE!
A KING MUST NEVER LOWER HIS HEAD TO ANYONE!!
IGARAM ...
A MAN'S TITLE COMES OFF WITH HIS CLOTHES.
HERE IN THE BATH, WE'RE ALL THE SAME.
A KING IS NOT A KING WHEN DISROBED.
I'D LIKE TO SAY... NOT AS A KING...
...BUT AS A FATHER AND A CITIZEN OF THIS LAND...
FROM THE BOTTOM OF MY HEART ...
HEE HEE
THANK YOU.
HA HA HA HA HA HA HA
SPLASH
SPLASH
SPLOOSH

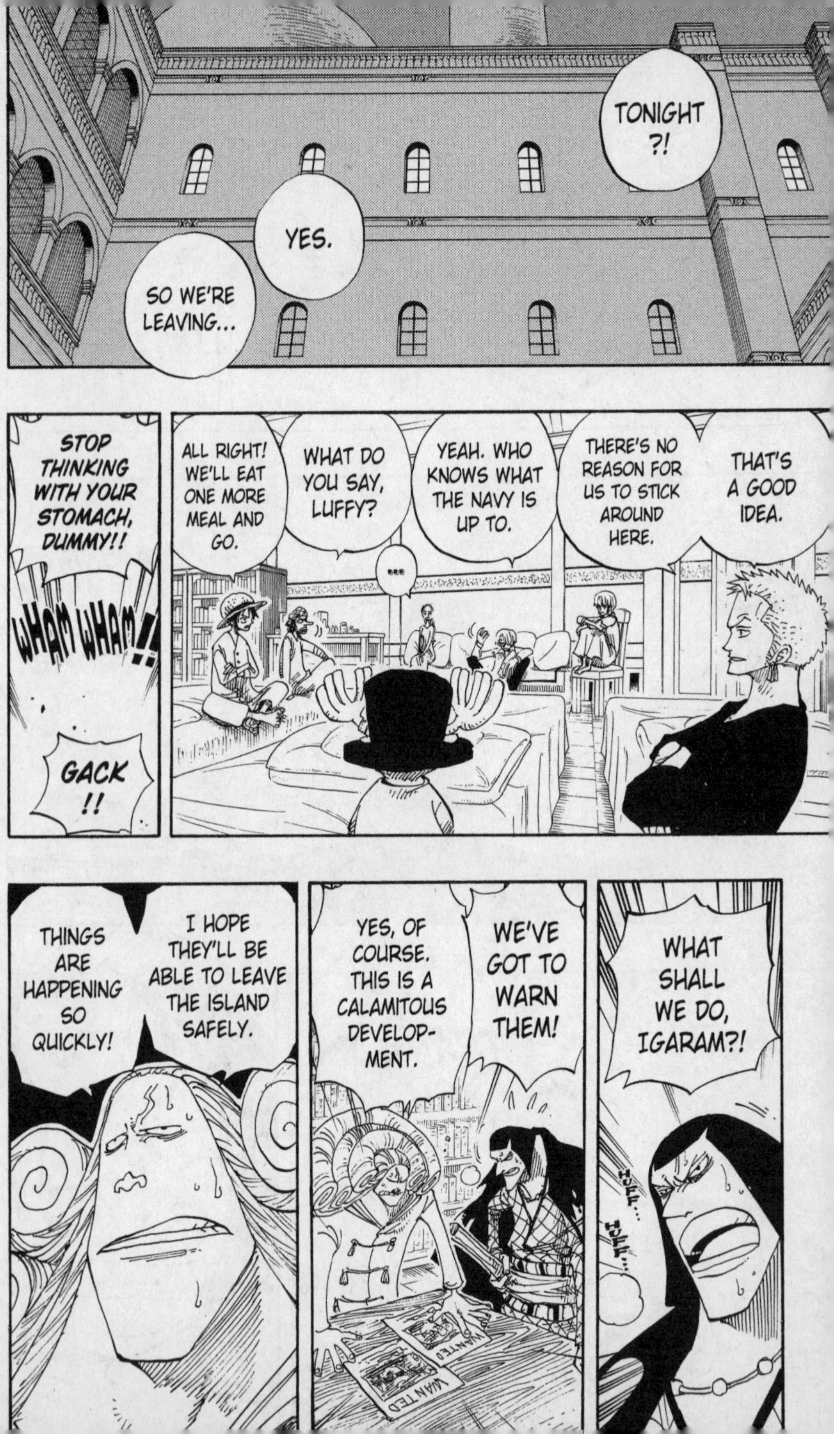
TONIGHT ?!
YES.
SO WE'RE LEAVING...
THAT'S A GOOD IDEA.
THERE'S NO REASON FOR US TO STICK AROUND HERE.
YEAH. WHO KNOWS WHAT THE NAVY IS UP TO.
WHAT DO YOU SAY, LUFFY?
...
ALL RIGHT! WE'LL EAT ONE MORE MEAL AND GO.
STOP THINKING WITH YOUR STOMACH, DUMMY!!
WHAM WHAM!!
GACK !!
WHAT SHALL WE DO, IGARAM?!
HUFF...
HUFF...
WE'VE GOT TO WARN THEM!
YES, OF COURSE. THIS IS A CALAMITOUS DEVELOP-MENT.
WANTED
WANTED
I HOPE THEY'LL BE ABLE TO LEAVE THE ISLAND SAFELY.
THINGS ARE HAPPENING SO QUICKLY!

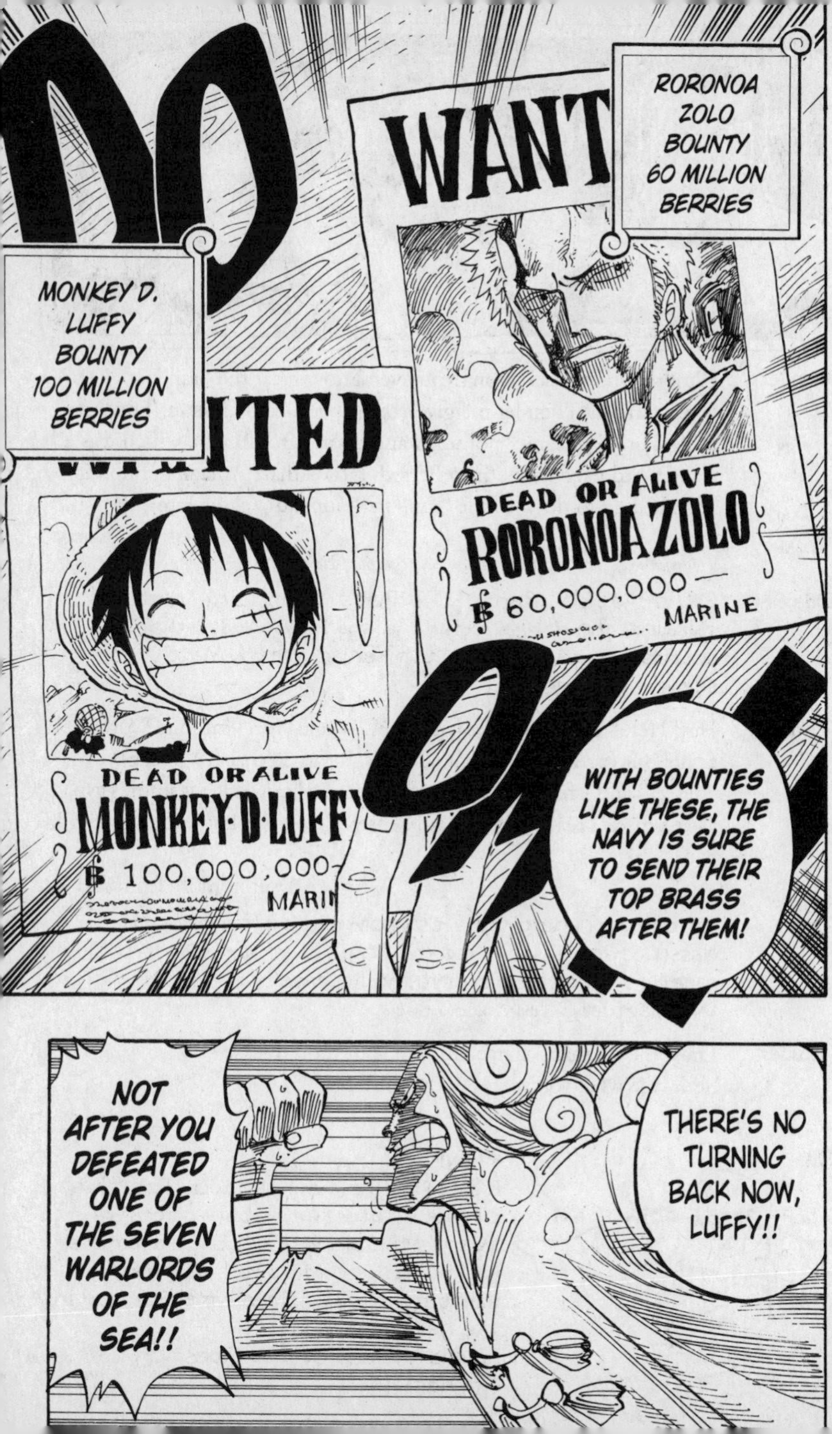
RORONOA ZOLO BOUNTY 60 MILLION BERRIES
WANT
DEAD OR ALIVE
RORONOA ZOLO
฿ 60,000,000—
MARINE
MONKEY D. LUFFY BOUNTY 100 MILLION BERRIES
ITED
DEAD OR ALIVE
MONKEY·D·LUFF
฿ 100,000,000—
MARIN
WITH BOUNTIES LIKE THESE, THE NAVY IS SURE TO SEND THEIR TOP BRASS AFTER THEM!
THERE'S NO TURNING BACK NOW, LUFFY!!
NOT AFTER YOU DEFEATED ONE OF THE SEVEN WARLORDS OF THE SEA!!

Reader: C'mon, Oda Sensei! Don't you even know what the "ran" in "gakuran" is? Then let me give you a special kanji lesson! The "ran" in "gakuran" means "clothing" and comes from *randa,* which was a slang word used in the Edo Period. How's that? Amazing, huh? It has nothing to do with the "ran" in "ranpaku" (egg white).

--Miss Bon Curry

This refers to an SBS question in volume 22, page 166. --Editor

Oda: Oh, is that so? *Randa,* huh? That's the origin? Well, I'd been thinking about it all this time and I'd concluded that it sounds like it was from "Lumberjack Death Match." It seems I was wrong.

Reader: Hey! Here's a question for you. "B.W." stands for "Baroque Works," right? But recently in geography class, I learned that BW means "desert" and I felt a jolt of surprise! You're knowledge is impressive, Oda Sensei! I really admire you! Sensei… You **did** know that, didn't you?

--A sophomore from Akita

Oda: Of course I knew that. It's from the Köppen climate classification system, right? How's that for smart?! I give careful thought to everything I create!! Really!! Well…actually… I didn't know that…

Reader: Draw the six main characters with your foot. (Please.) Show me what you've got, Oda Sensei.

--Ainya

Oda: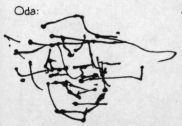

Hey!!
It's Luffy! The man who would be King of the Pirates!! I'm getting a cramp! What's the big idea? All six characters? No thanks! I could do it, I just don't want to!! Oh well! Take care! See you in the next volume!
This is the end of the Question Corner!

Chapter 214: STRATEGY TO ESCAPE THE SAND KINGDOM

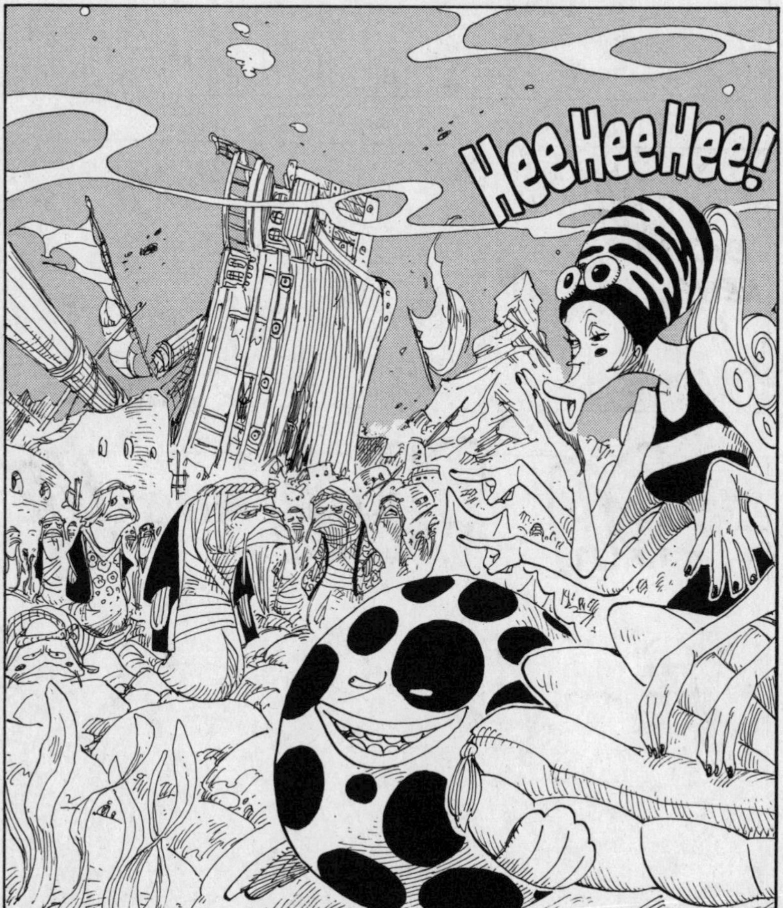
Hee Hee Hee!

HACHI'S WALK ON THE SEA FLOOR, VOL. 28:
"ALAS, THE VILLAGE OF THE HEADBAND-WEARING CATFISH IS CRUSHED BY A SHIPWRECK"

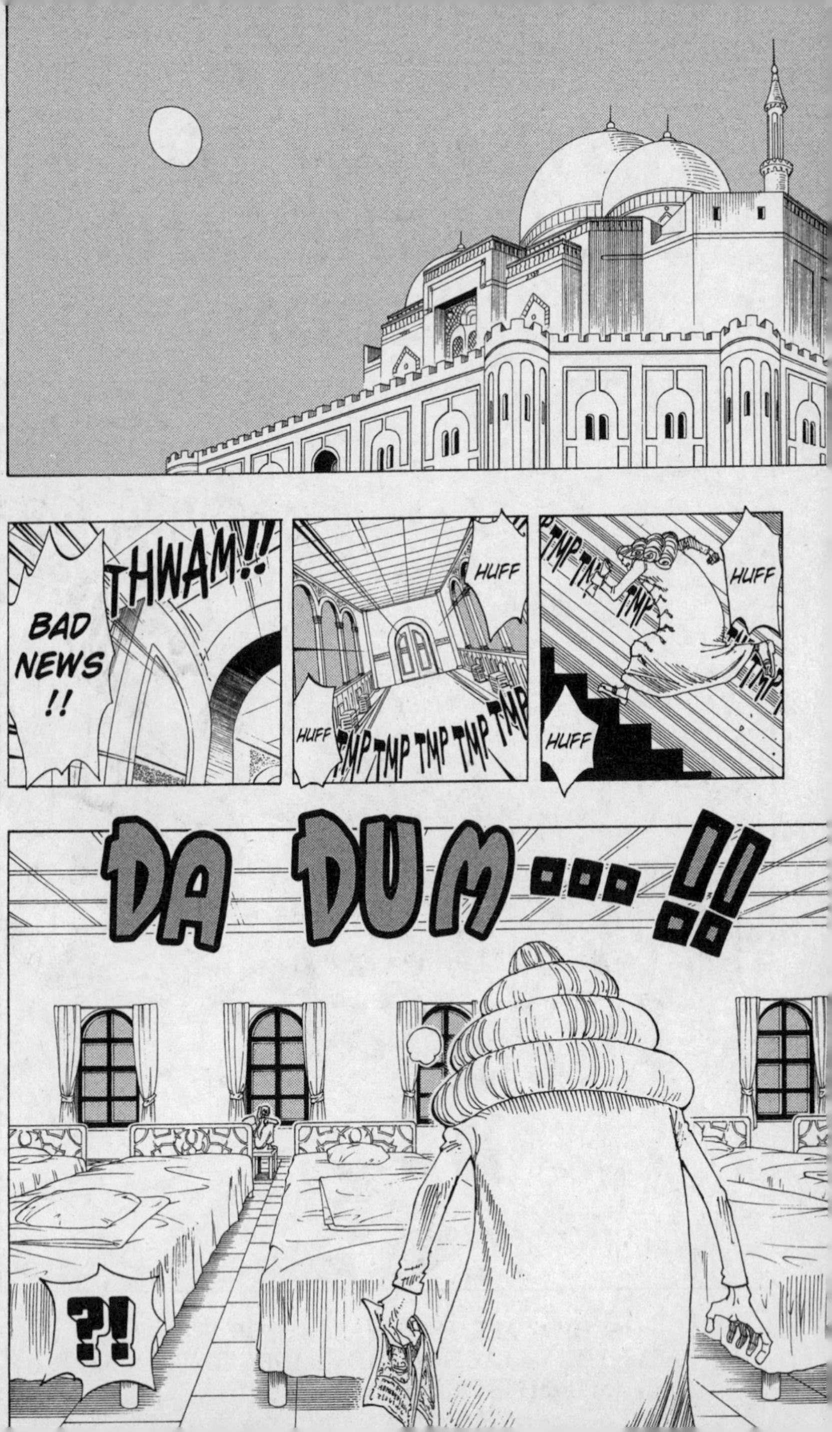
HUFF
TMP TMP TMP TMP
HUFF
HUFF
HUFF
TMP TMP TMP TMP TMB
THWAM!!
BAD NEWS!!
DA DUM...!!
?!

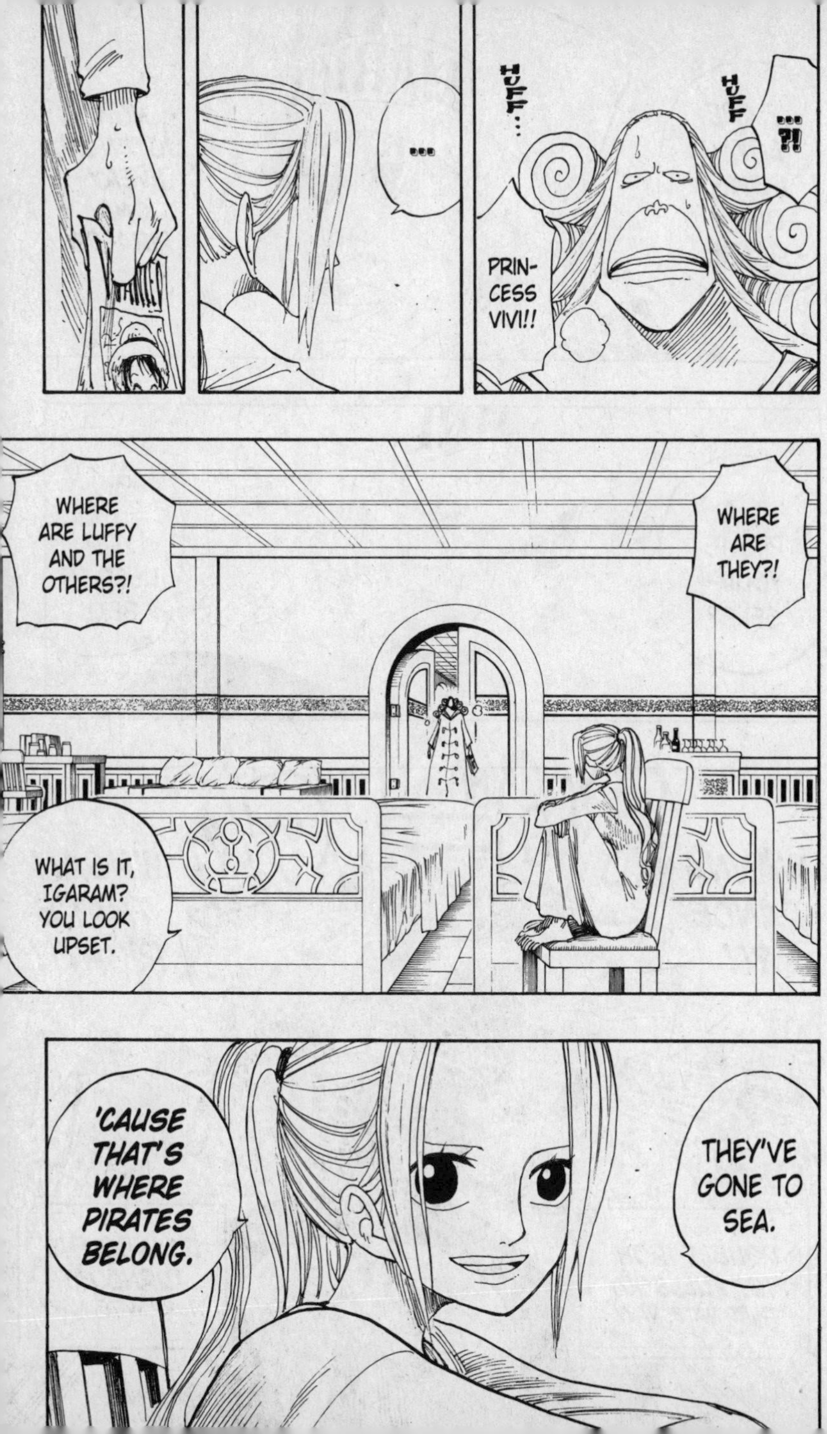
HUFF
...?!
HUFF...
PRIN-CESS VIVI!!
...
WHERE ARE THEY?!
WHERE ARE LUFFY AND THE OTHERS?!
WHAT IS IT, IGARAM? YOU LOOK UPSET.
THEY'VE GONE TO SEA.
'CAUSE THAT'S WHERE PIRATES BELONG.

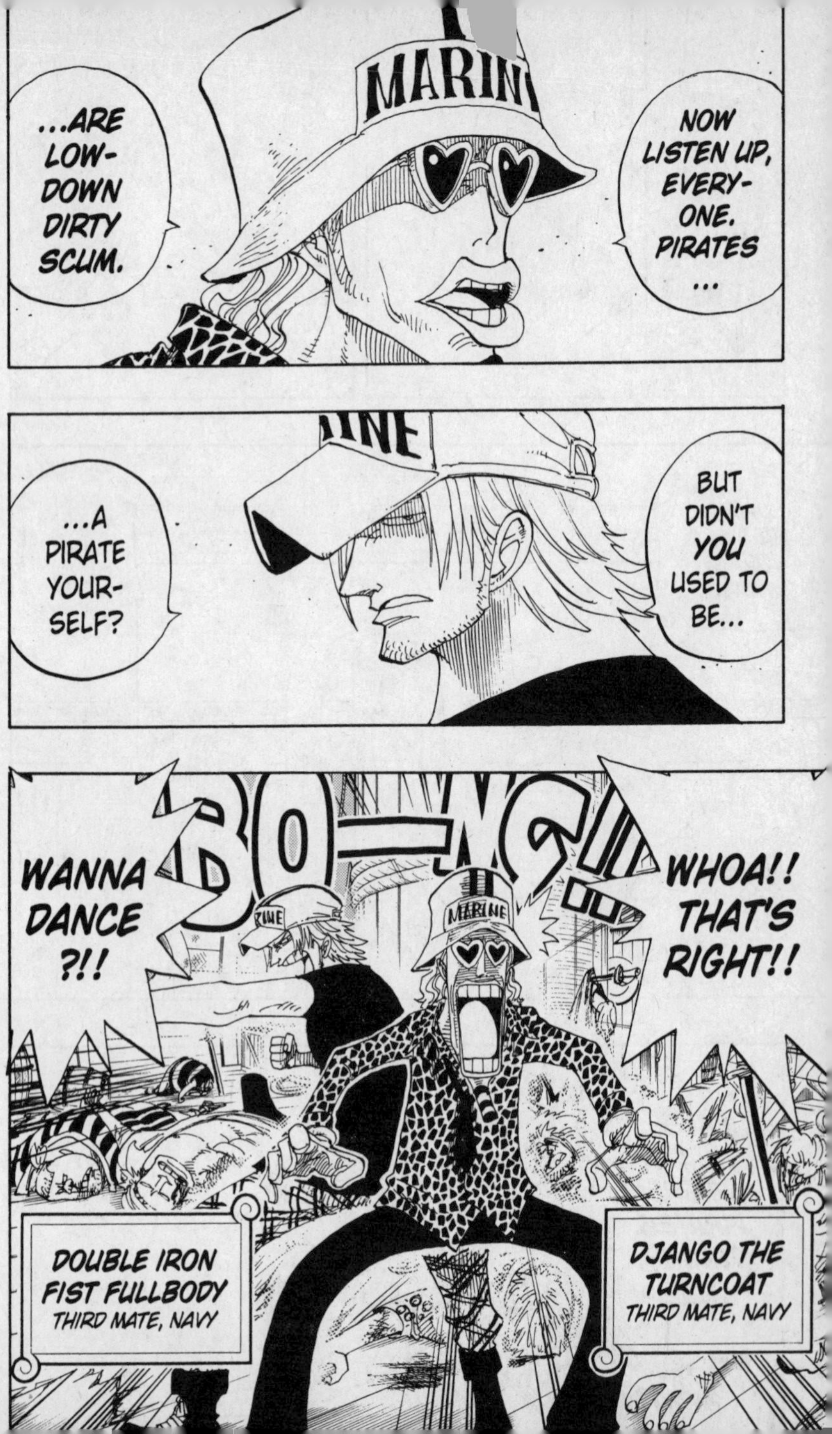
NOW LISTEN UP, EVERY-ONE. PIRATES ...
...ARE LOW-DOWN DIRTY SCUM.
BUT DIDN'T YOU USED TO BE...
...A PIRATE YOUR-SELF?
WHOA!! THAT'S RIGHT!!
WANNA DANCE ?!!
DJANGO THE TURNCOAT
THIRD MATE, NAVY
DOUBLE IRON FIST FULLBODY
THIRD MATE, NAVY

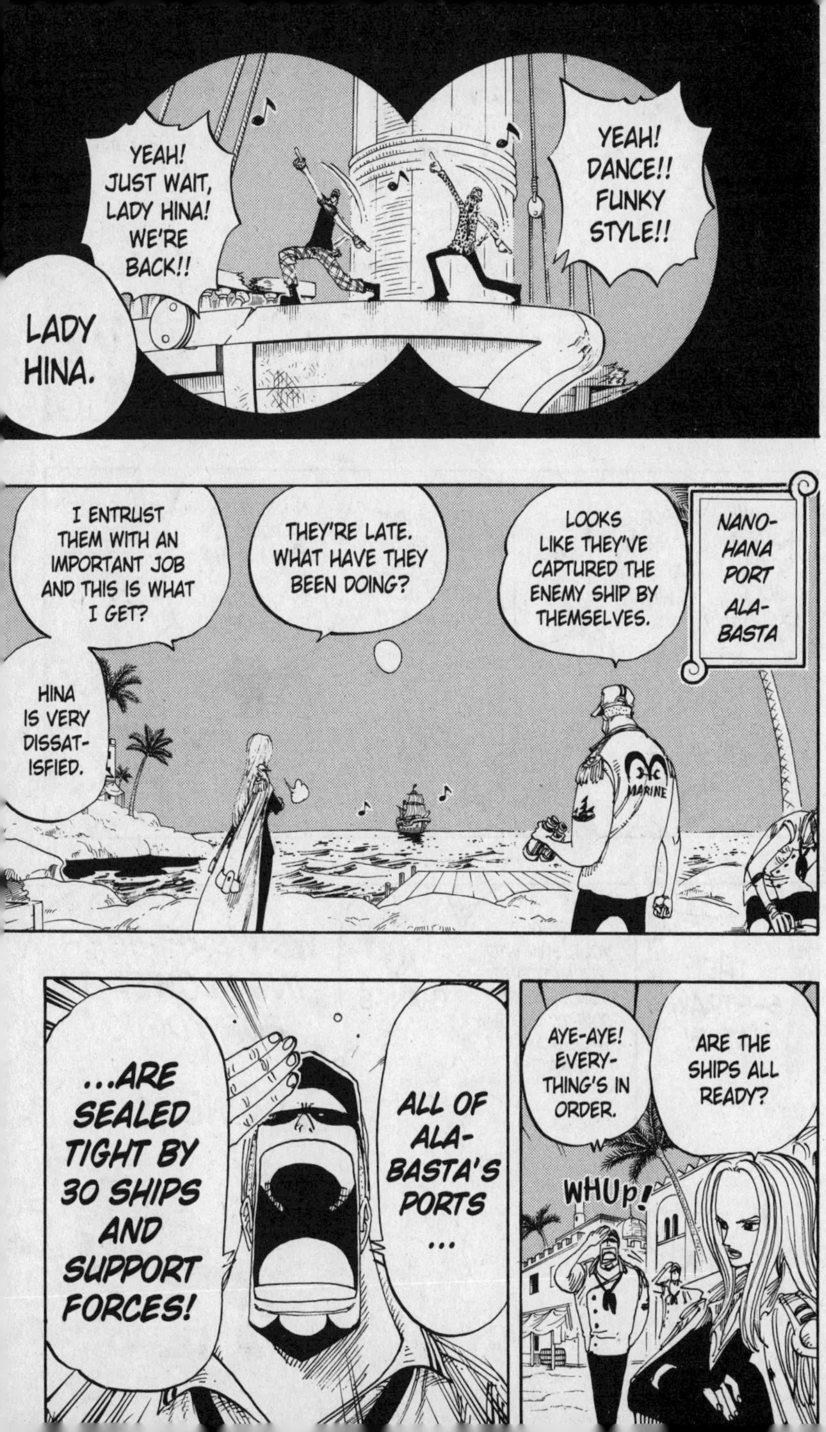
YEAH! DANCE!! FUNKY STYLE!!
YEAH! JUST WAIT, LADY HINA! WE'RE BACK!!
LADY HINA.
NANO-HANA PORT ALA-BASTA
LOOKS LIKE THEY'VE CAPTURED THE ENEMY SHIP BY THEMSELVES.
THEY'RE LATE. WHAT HAVE THEY BEEN DOING?
I ENTRUST THEM WITH AN IMPORTANT JOB AND THIS IS WHAT I GET?
HINA IS VERY DISSAT-ISFIED.
MARINE
ARE THE SHIPS ALL READY?
AYE-AYE! EVERY-THING'S IN ORDER.
WHUp!
ALL OF ALA-BASTA'S PORTS ...
...ARE SEALED TIGHT BY 30 SHIPS AND SUPPORT FORCES!

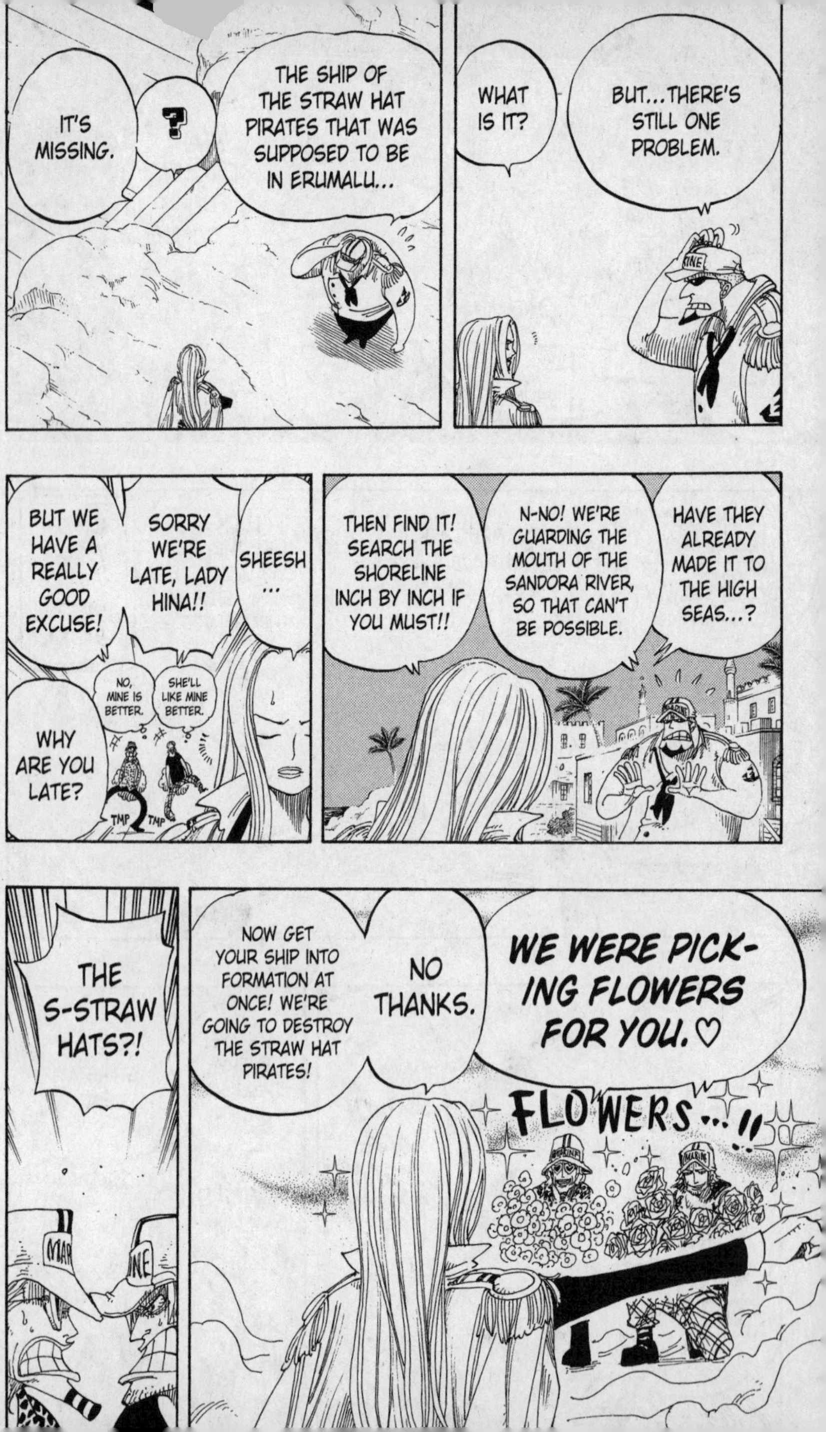
BUT...THERE'S STILL ONE PROBLEM.
WHAT IS IT?
THE SHIP OF THE STRAW HAT PIRATES THAT WAS SUPPOSED TO BE IN ERUMALU...
?
IT'S MISSING.
HAVE THEY ALREADY MADE IT TO THE HIGH SEAS...?
N-NO! WE'RE GUARDING THE MOUTH OF THE SANDORA RIVER, SO THAT CAN'T BE POSSIBLE.
THEN FIND IT! SEARCH THE SHORELINE INCH BY INCH IF YOU MUST!!
SHEESH...
SORRY WE'RE LATE, LADY HINA!!
BUT WE HAVE A REALLY GOOD EXCUSE!
SHE'LL LIKE MINE BETTER.
NO, MINE IS BETTER.
WHY ARE YOU LATE?
TMP TMP
WE WERE PICK-ING FLOWERS FOR YOU.♡
NO THANKS.
NOW GET YOUR SHIP INTO FORMATION AT ONCE! WE'RE GOING TO DESTROY THE STRAW HAT PIRATES!
FLOWERS...!!
THE S-STRAW HATS?!

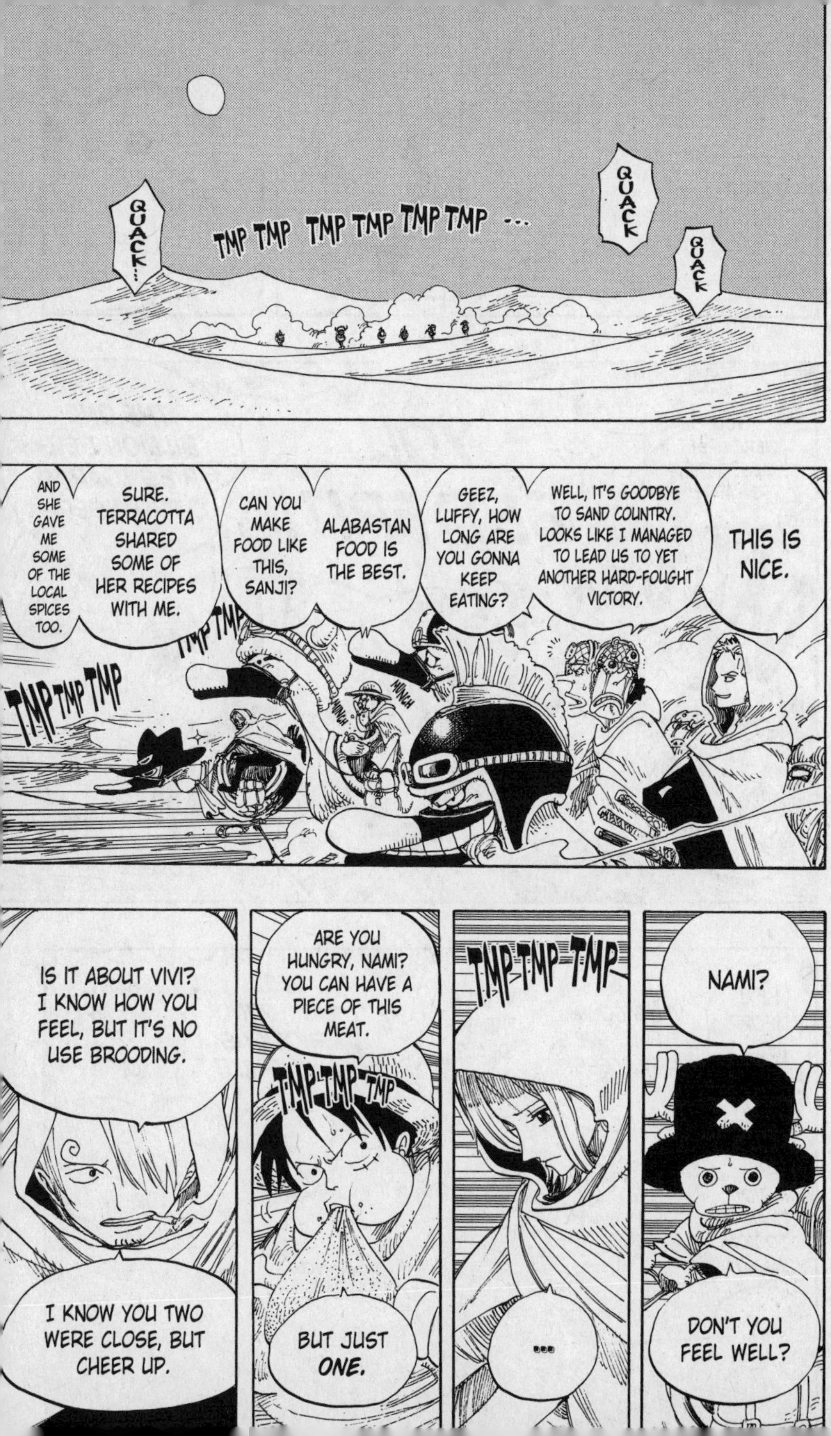
QUACK
QUACK
TMP TMP TMP TMP TMP TMP ...
QUACK...
THIS IS NICE.
WELL, IT'S GOODBYE TO SAND COUNTRY. LOOKS LIKE I MANAGED TO LEAD US TO YET ANOTHER HARD-FOUGHT VICTORY.
GEEZ, LUFFY, HOW LONG ARE YOU GONNA KEEP EATING?
MUNCH
MUNCH
ALABASTAN FOOD IS THE BEST.
CAN YOU MAKE FOOD LIKE THIS, SANJI?
TMP TMP
SURE. TERRACOTTA SHARED SOME OF HER RECIPES WITH ME.
AND SHE GAVE ME SOME OF THE LOCAL SPICES TOO.
TMP TMP TMP
NAMI?
DON'T YOU FEEL WELL?
TMP TMP TMP
...
ARE YOU HUNGRY, NAMI? YOU CAN HAVE A PIECE OF THIS MEAT.
TMP TMP TMP
BUT JUST ONE.
IS IT ABOUT VIVI? I KNOW HOW YOU FEEL, BUT IT'S NO USE BROODING.
I KNOW YOU TWO WERE CLOSE, BUT CHEER UP.

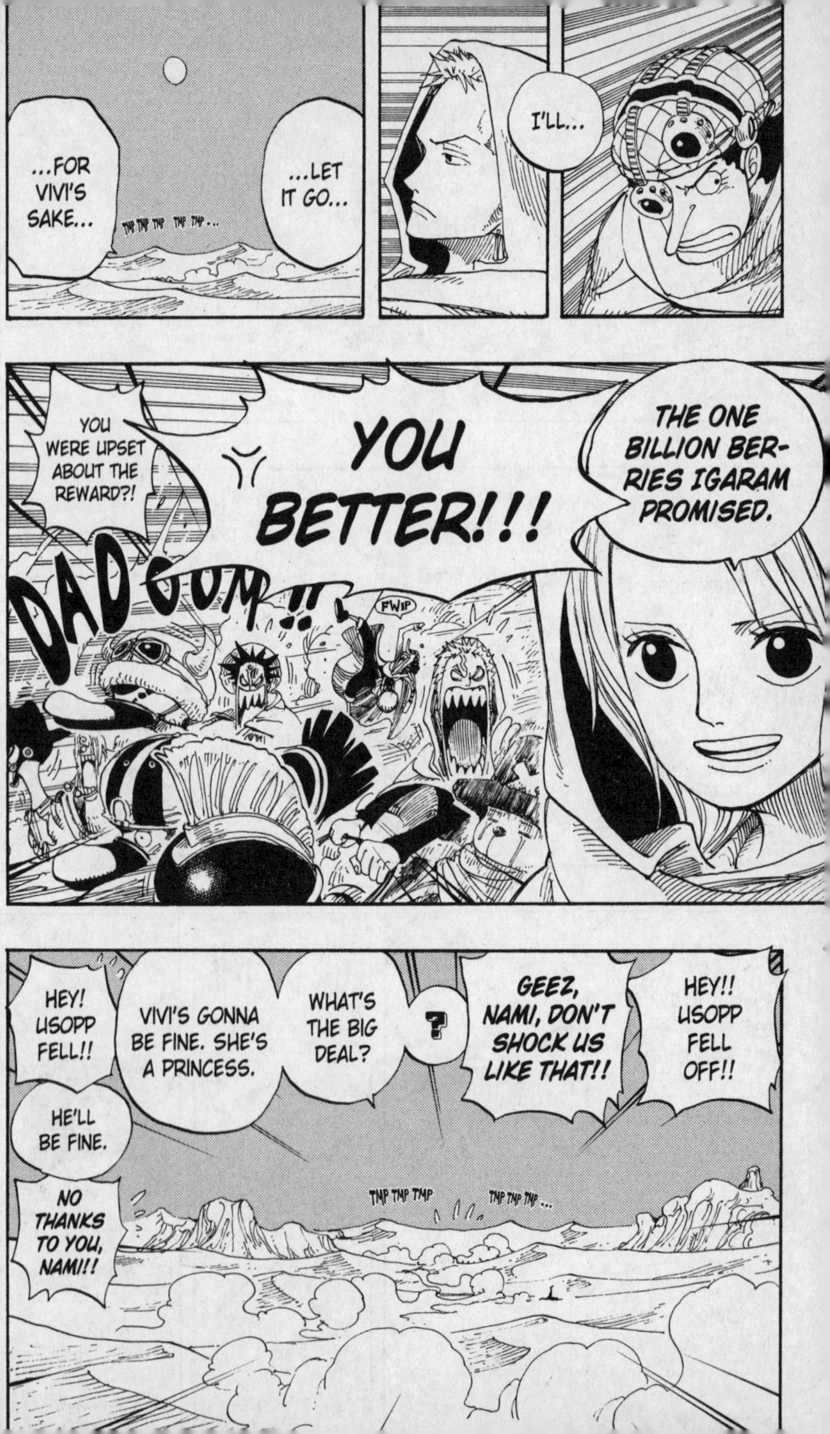
I'LL...
...LET IT GO...
...FOR VIVI'S SAKE...
TMP TMP TMP TMP TMP...
THE ONE BILLION BERRIES IGARAM PROMISED.
YOU BETTER!!!
YOU WERE UPSET ABOUT THE REWARD?!
FWIP
DADOOM!!
HEY!! USOPP FELL OFF!!
GEEZ, NAMI, DON'T SHOCK US LIKE THAT!!
?
WHAT'S THE BIG DEAL?
VIVI'S GONNA BE FINE. SHE'S A PRINCESS.
HEY! USOPP FELL!!
HE'LL BE FINE.
NO THANKS TO YOU, NAMI!!
TMP TMP TMP
TMP TMP TMP...

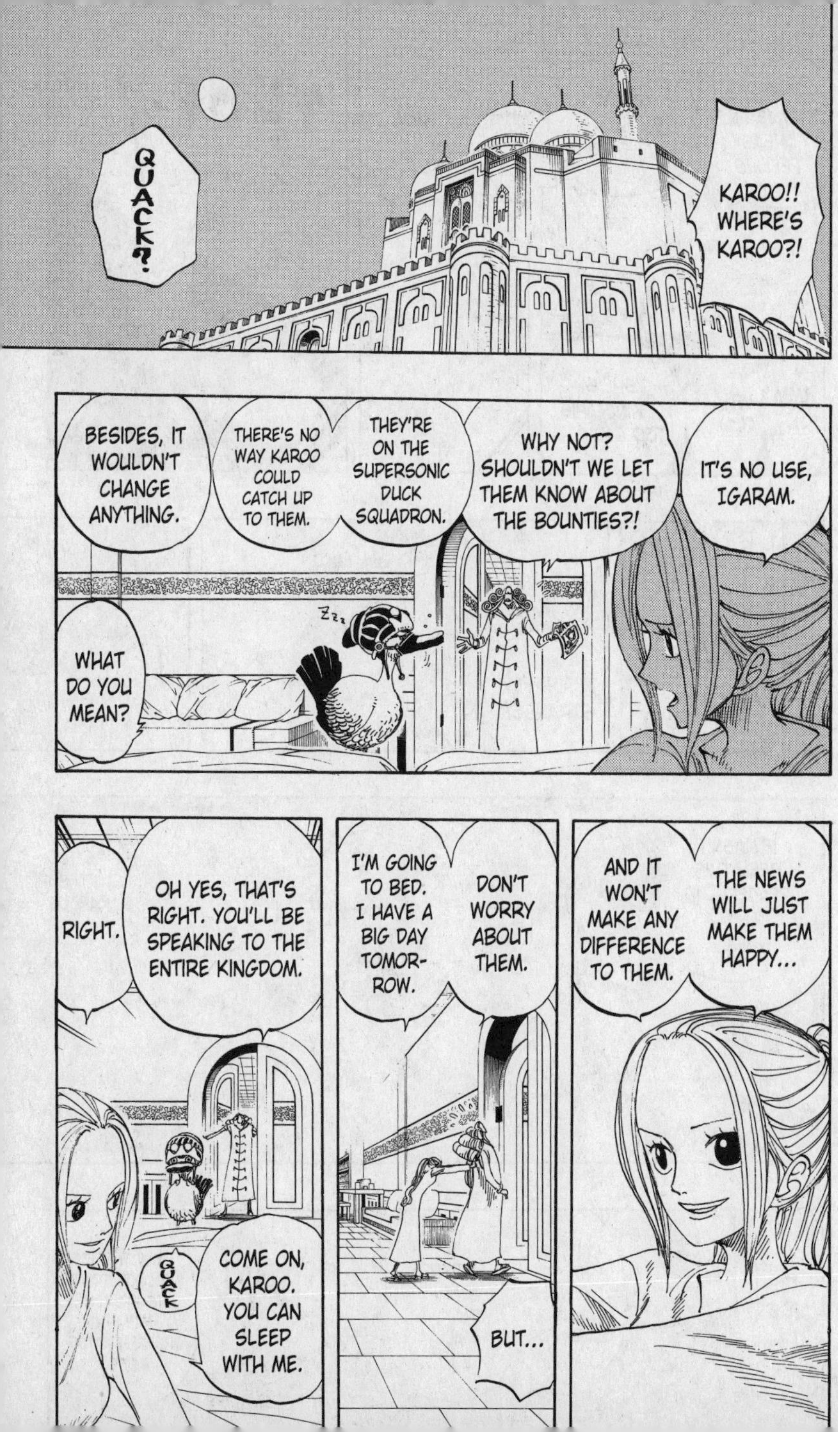
KAROO!! WHERE'S KAROO?!
QUACK?
IT'S NO USE, IGARAM.
WHY NOT? SHOULDN'T WE LET THEM KNOW ABOUT THE BOUNTIES?!
THEY'RE ON THE SUPERSONIC DUCK SQUADRON.
THERE'S NO WAY KAROO COULD CATCH UP TO THEM.
BESIDES, IT WOULDN'T CHANGE ANYTHING.
WHAT DO YOU MEAN?
THE NEWS WILL JUST MAKE THEM HAPPY...
AND IT WON'T MAKE ANY DIFFERENCE TO THEM.
DON'T WORRY ABOUT THEM.
I'M GOING TO BED. I HAVE A BIG DAY TOMORROW.
BUT...
OH YES, THAT'S RIGHT. YOU'LL BE SPEAKING TO THE ENTIRE KINGDOM.
RIGHT.
COME ON, KAROO. YOU CAN SLEEP WITH ME.
QUACK

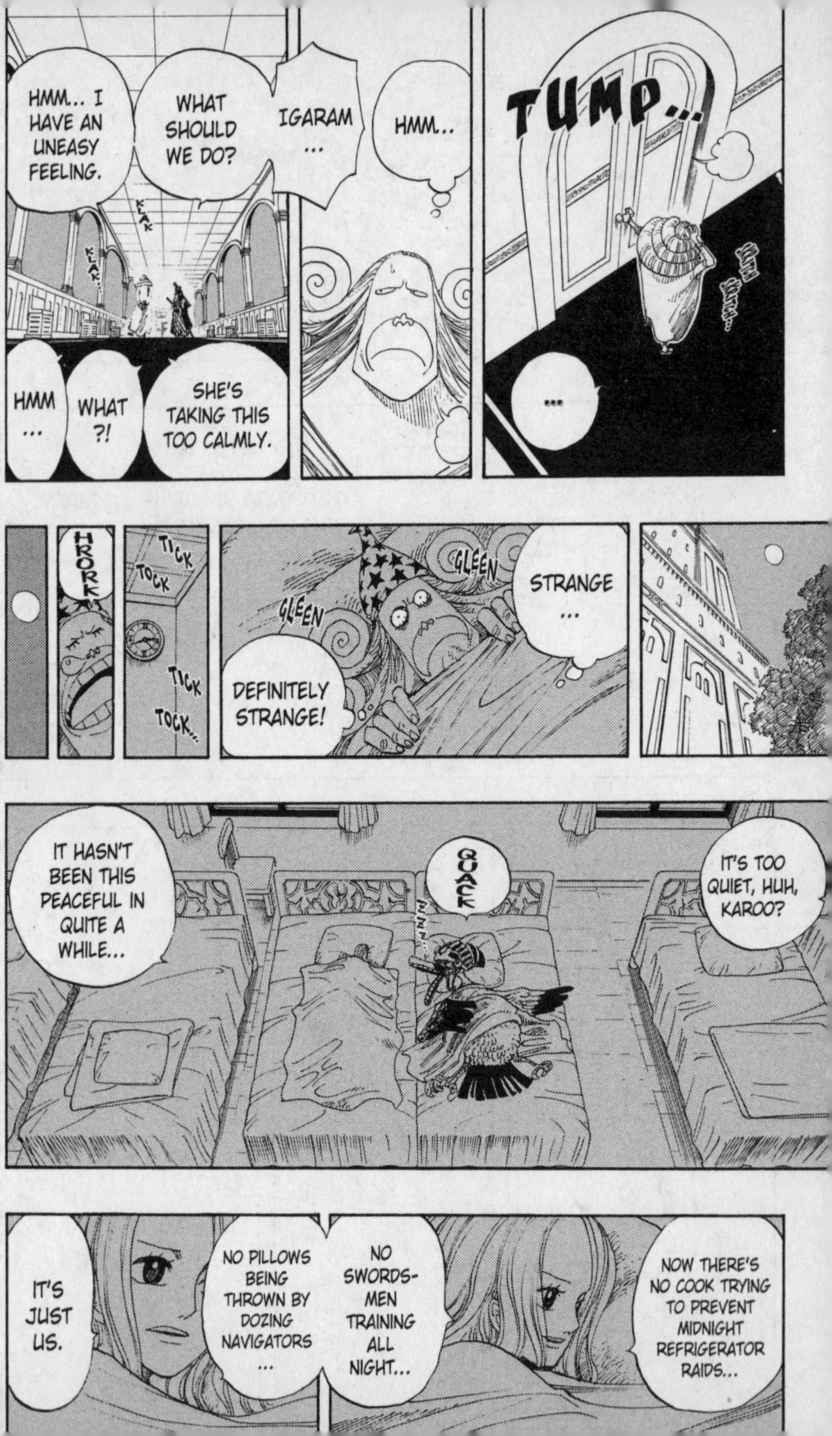
TUMP...
SKITCH SKITCH...
...
HMM...
IGARAM...
WHAT SHOULD WE DO?
HMM... I HAVE AN UNEASY FEELING.
KLAK
KLAK...
SHE'S TAKING THIS TOO CALMLY.
WHAT?!
HMM...
STRANGE...
GLEEN
GLEEN
DEFINITELY STRANGE!
TICK
TOCK
TICK
TOCK...
HRORK
IT'S TOO QUIET, HUH, KAROO?
QUACK
ZZZ...
IT HASN'T BEEN THIS PEACEFUL IN QUITE A WHILE...
NOW THERE'S NO COOK TRYING TO PREVENT MIDNIGHT REFRIGERATOR RAIDS...
NO SWORDS-MEN TRAINING ALL NIGHT...
NO PILLOWS BEING THROWN BY DOZING NAVIGATORS...
IT'S JUST US.

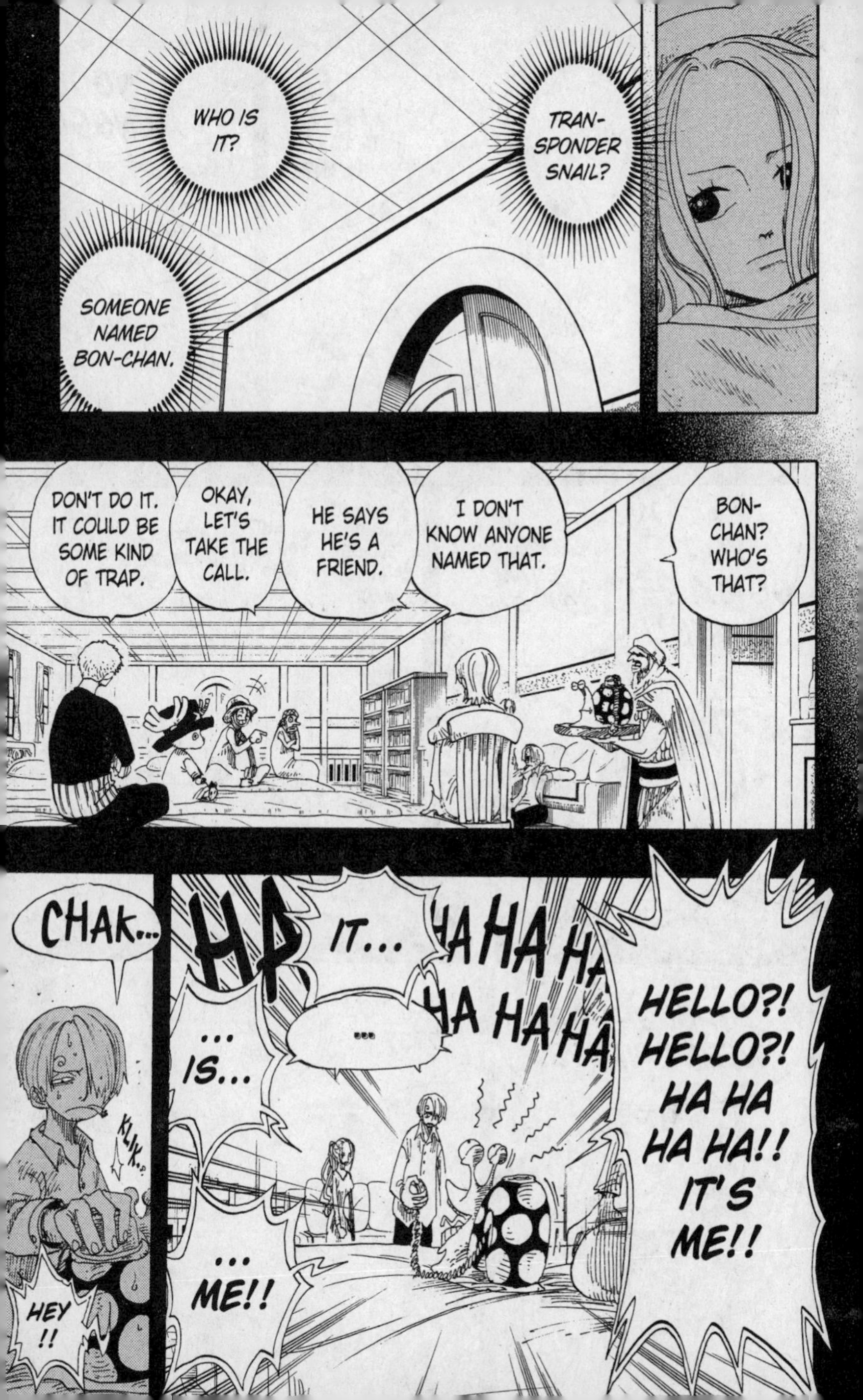
TRAN-SPONDER SNAIL?
WHO IS IT?
SOMEONE NAMED BON-CHAN.
BON-CHAN? WHO'S THAT?
I DON'T KNOW ANYONE NAMED THAT.
HE SAYS HE'S A FRIEND.
OKAY, LET'S TAKE THE CALL.
DON'T DO IT. IT COULD BE SOME KIND OF TRAP.
HELLO?! HELLO?! HA HA HA HA!! IT'S ME!!
HA HA HA HA HA HA HA HA
IT...
...
...IS...
...ME!!
CHAK...
KLIK
HEY!!

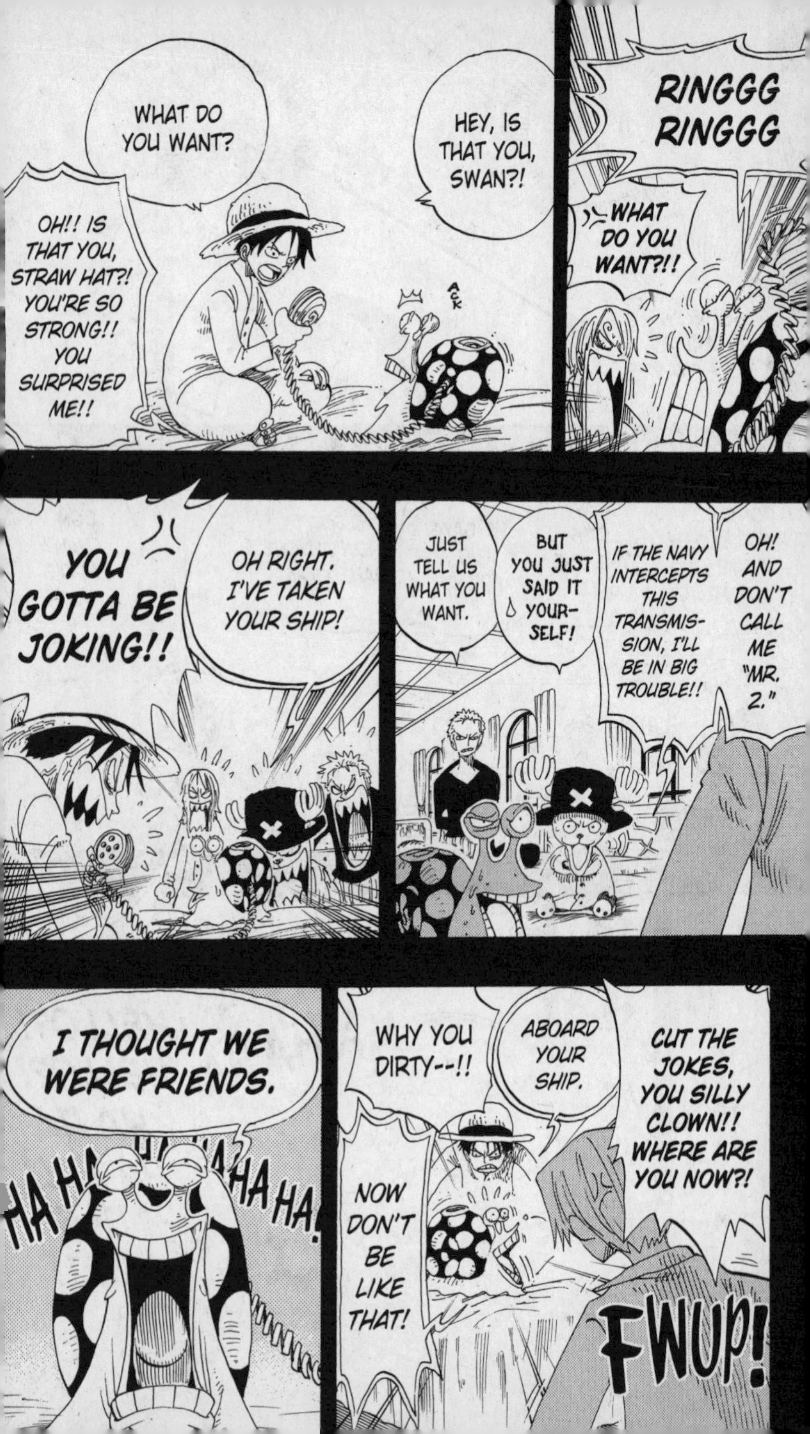
RINGGG RINGGG
WHAT DO YOU WANT?!!
HEY, IS THAT YOU, SWAN?!
ACK
WHAT DO YOU WANT?
OH!! IS THAT YOU, STRAW HAT?! YOU'RE SO STRONG!! YOU SURPRISED ME!!
OH! AND DON'T CALL ME "MR. 2."
IF THE NAVY INTERCEPTS THIS TRANSMISSION, I'LL BE IN BIG TROUBLE!!
BUT YOU JUST SAID IT YOURSELF!
JUST TELL US WHAT YOU WANT.
OH RIGHT. I'VE TAKEN YOUR SHIP!
YOU GOTTA BE JOKING!!
CUT THE JOKES, YOU SILLY CLOWN!! WHERE ARE YOU NOW?!
ABOARD YOUR SHIP.
WHY YOU DIRTY--!!
NOW DON'T BE LIKE THAT!
FWUP!
I THOUGHT WE WERE FRIENDS.
HA HA HAHA HA HA!

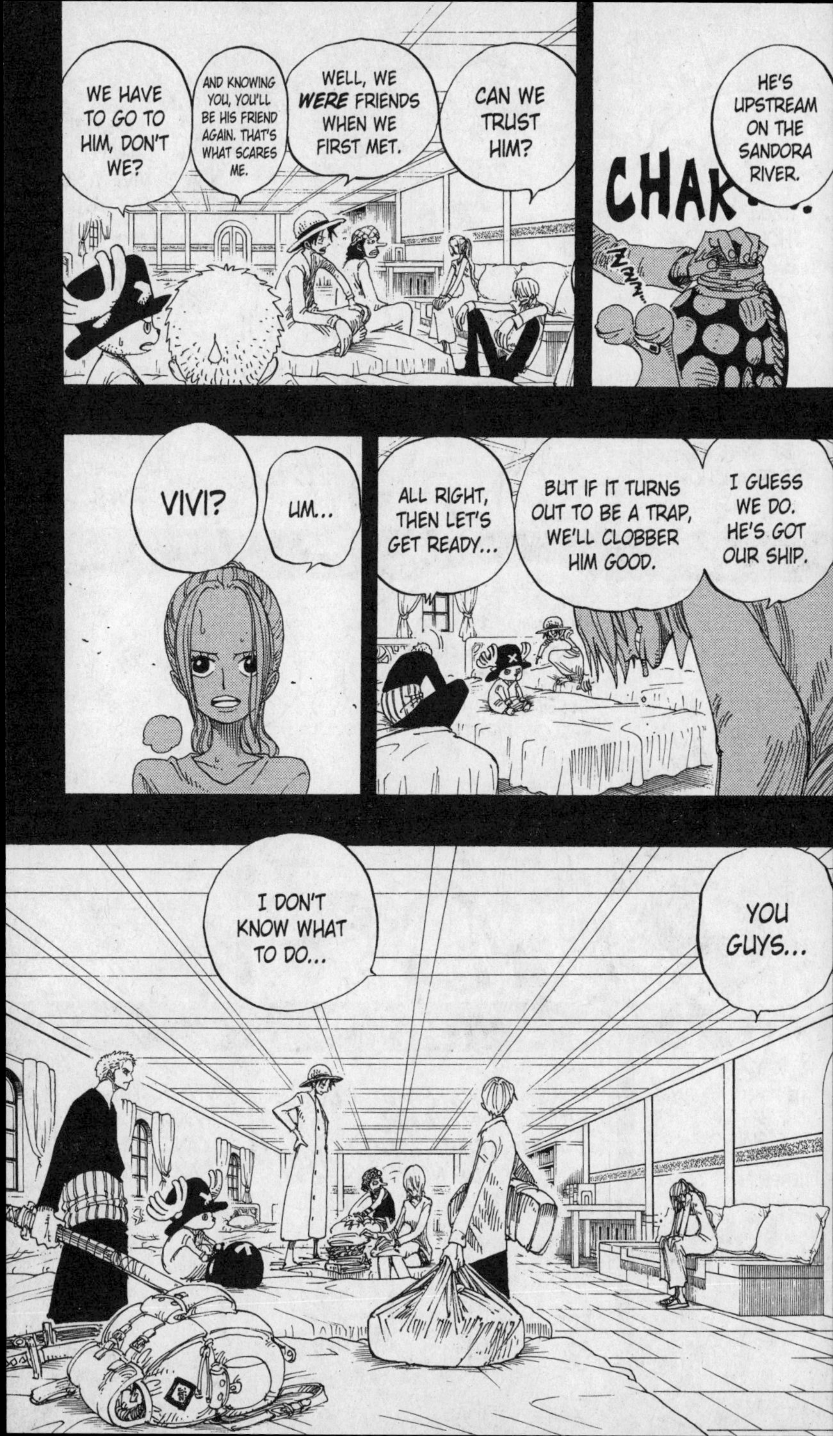

HE'S UPSTREAM ON THE SANDORA RIVER.
CHAK
CAN WE TRUST HIM?
WELL, WE *WERE* FRIENDS WHEN WE FIRST MET.
AND KNOWING YOU, YOU'LL BE HIS FRIEND AGAIN. THAT'S WHAT SCARES ME.
WE HAVE TO GO TO HIM, DON'T WE?
I GUESS WE DO. HE'S GOT OUR SHIP.
BUT IF IT TURNS OUT TO BE A TRAP, WE'LL CLOBBER HIM GOOD.
ALL RIGHT, THEN LET'S GET READY...
UM...
VIVI?
YOU GUYS...
I DON'T KNOW WHAT TO DO...

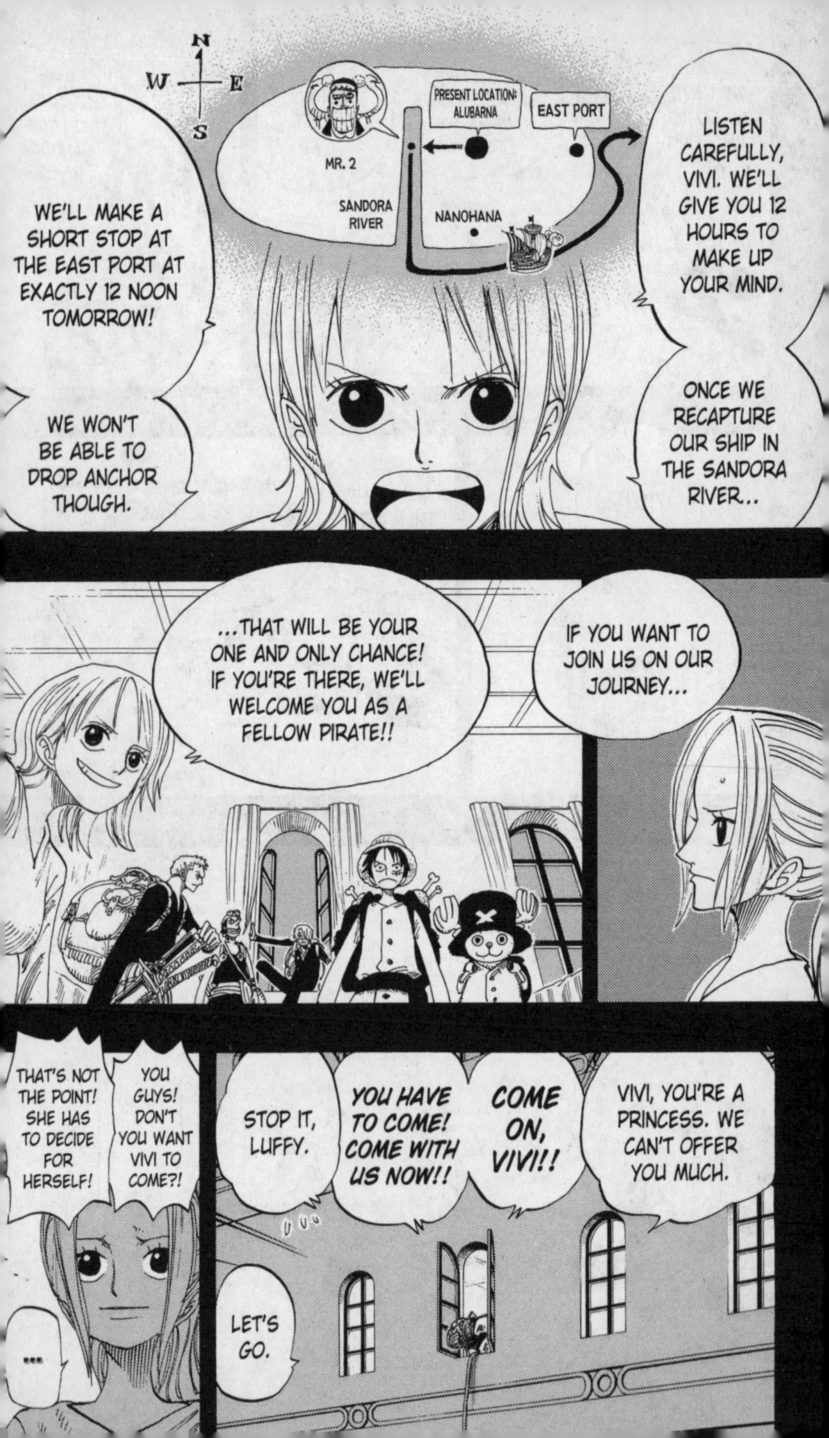
LISTEN CAREFULLY, VIVI. WE'LL GIVE YOU 12 HOURS TO MAKE UP YOUR MIND.
ONCE WE RECAPTURE OUR SHIP IN THE SANDORA RIVER...
N
W
E
S
PRESENT LOCATION: ALUBARNA
EAST PORT
MR. 2
SANDORA RIVER
NANOHANA
WE'LL MAKE A SHORT STOP AT THE EAST PORT AT EXACTLY 12 NOON TOMORROW!
WE WON'T BE ABLE TO DROP ANCHOR THOUGH.
IF YOU WANT TO JOIN US ON OUR JOURNEY...
...THAT WILL BE YOUR ONE AND ONLY CHANCE! IF YOU'RE THERE, WE'LL WELCOME YOU AS A FELLOW PIRATE!!
VIVI, YOU'RE A PRINCESS. WE CAN'T OFFER YOU MUCH.
COME ON, VIVI!!
YOU HAVE TO COME! COME WITH US NOW!!
STOP IT, LUFFY.
LET'S GO.
YOU GUYS! DON'T YOU WANT VIVI TO COME?!
THAT'S NOT THE POINT! SHE HAS TO DECIDE FOR HERSELF!
...

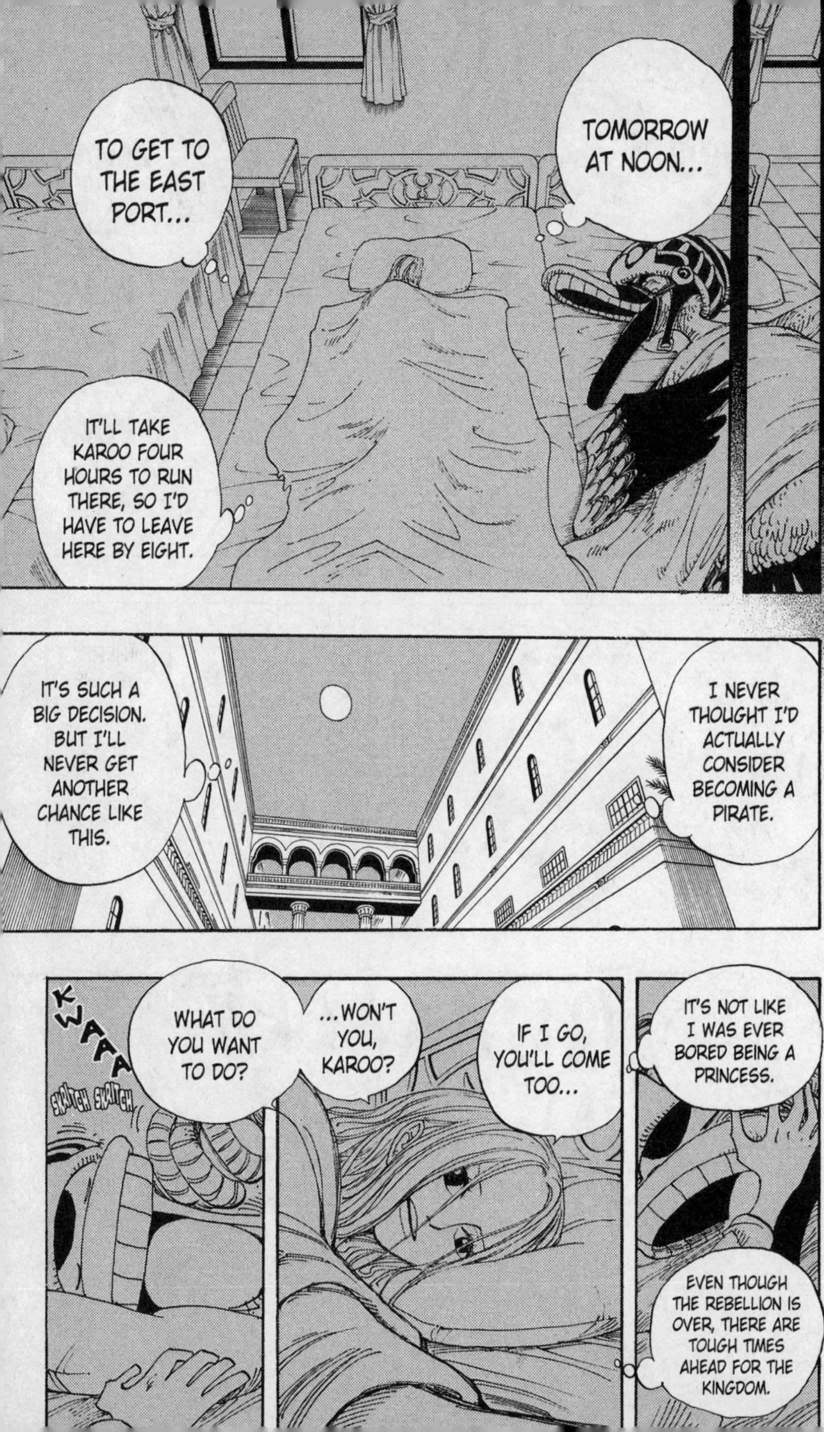
TOMORROW AT NOON...
TO GET TO THE EAST PORT...
IT'LL TAKE KAROO FOUR HOURS TO RUN THERE, SO I'D HAVE TO LEAVE HERE BY EIGHT.
I NEVER THOUGHT I'D ACTUALLY CONSIDER BECOMING A PIRATE.
IT'S SUCH A BIG DECISION. BUT I'LL NEVER GET ANOTHER CHANCE LIKE THIS.
IT'S NOT LIKE I WAS EVER BORED BEING A PRINCESS.
EVEN THOUGH THE REBELLION IS OVER, THERE ARE TOUGH TIMES AHEAD FOR THE KINGDOM.
IF I GO, YOU'LL COME TOO...
...WON'T YOU, KAROO?
WHAT DO YOU WANT TO DO?
KWAAA
SWITCH SWITCH

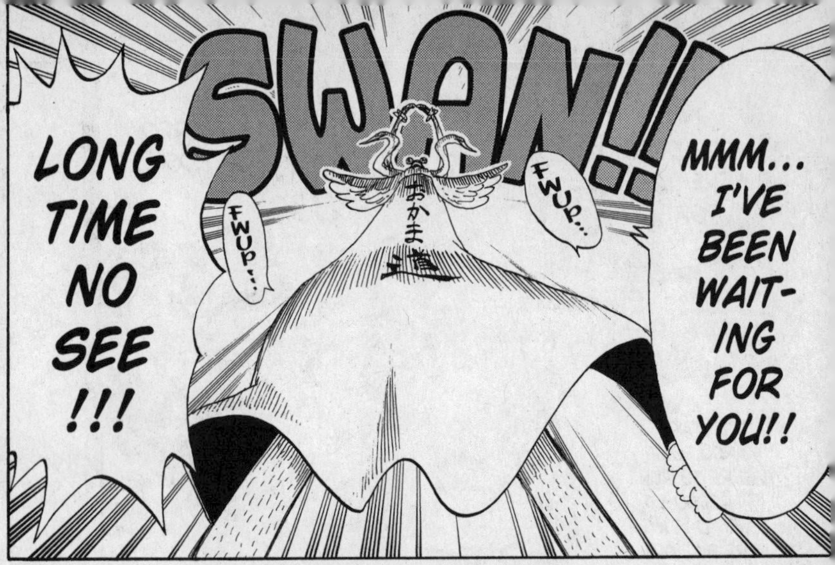
MMM... I'VE BEEN WAIT-ING FOR YOU!!
FWUP...
SWAN!!
おかま道
FWUP...
LONG TIME NO SEE !!!

TEXT ON COAT SAYS "OH COME MY WAY" --ED.

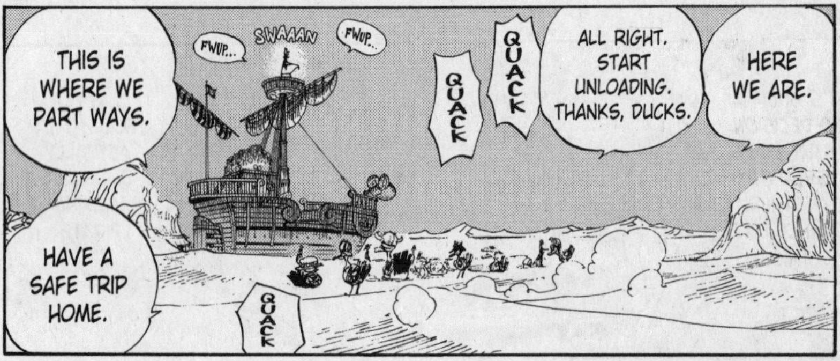
HERE WE ARE.
ALL RIGHT. START UNLOADING. THANKS, DUCKS.
QUACK
QUACK
FWUP...
SWAAAN
FWUP...
THIS IS WHERE WE PART WAYS.
HAVE A SAFE TRIP HOME.
QUACK

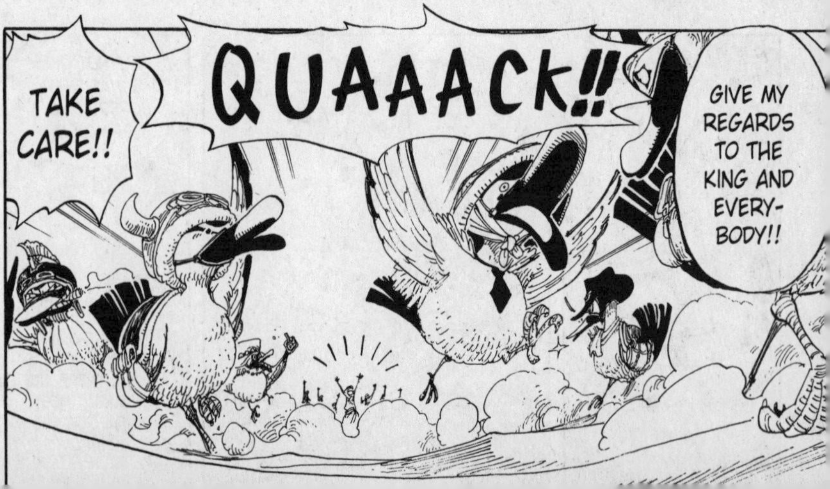
GIVE MY REGARDS TO THE KING AND EVERY-BODY!!
QUAAACK!!
TAKE CARE!!

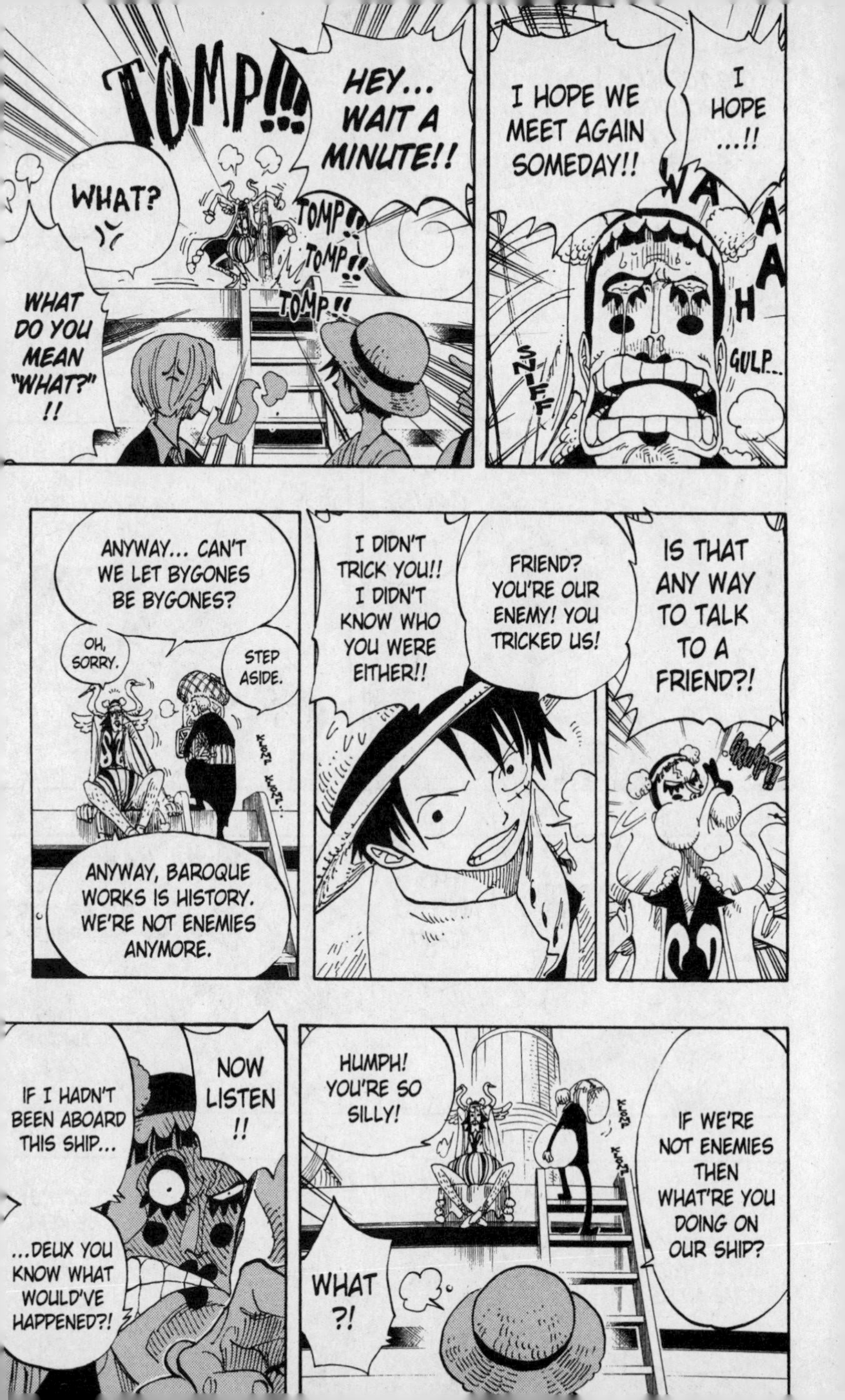
I HOPE ...!!
I HOPE WE MEET AGAIN SOMEDAY!!
WAAAAH
GULP...
SNIFF
HEY... WAIT A MINUTE!!
TOMP!!!
TOMP!!
TOMP!!
TOMP!!
WHAT?
WHAT DO YOU MEAN "WHAT?" !!
IS THAT ANY WAY TO TALK TO A FRIEND?!
GRUMP!!
FRIEND? YOU'RE OUR ENEMY! YOU TRICKED US!
I DIDN'T TRICK YOU!! I DIDN'T KNOW WHO YOU WERE EITHER!!
ANYWAY... CAN'T WE LET BYGONES BE BYGONES?
STEP ASIDE.
OH, SORRY.
ANYWAY, BAROQUE WORKS IS HISTORY. WE'RE NOT ENEMIES ANYMORE.
IF WE'RE NOT ENEMIES THEN WHAT'RE YOU DOING ON OUR SHIP?
HUMPH! YOU'RE SO SILLY!
WHAT ?!
NOW LISTEN !!
IF I HADN'T BEEN ABOARD THIS SHIP...
...DEUX YOU KNOW WHAT WOULD'VE HAPPENED?!

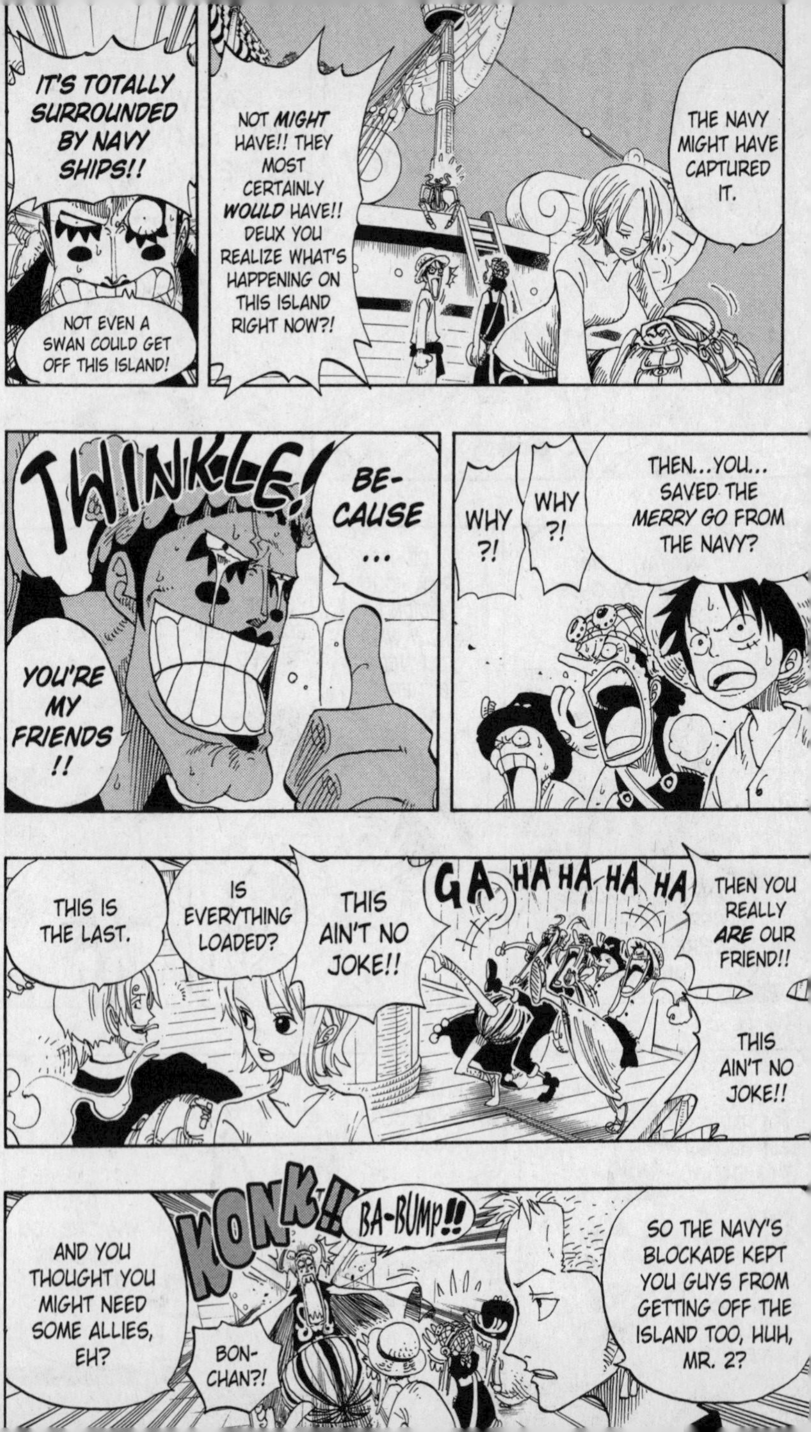
THE NAVY MIGHT HAVE CAPTURED IT.
NOT MIGHT HAVE!! THEY MOST CERTAINLY WOULD HAVE!! DEUX YOU REALIZE WHAT'S HAPPENING ON THIS ISLAND RIGHT NOW?!
IT'S TOTALLY SURROUNDED BY NAVY SHIPS!!
NOT EVEN A SWAN COULD GET OFF THIS ISLAND!
THEN...YOU... SAVED THE MERRY GO FROM THE NAVY?
WHY ?!
WHY ?!
BE-CAUSE ...
TWINKLE!
YOU'RE MY FRIENDS !!
THEN YOU REALLY ARE OUR FRIEND!!
GA HA HA HA HA HA
THIS AIN'T NO JOKE!!
THIS AIN'T NO JOKE!!
IS EVERYTHING LOADED?
THIS IS THE LAST.
SO THE NAVY'S BLOCKADE KEPT YOU GUYS FROM GETTING OFF THE ISLAND TOO, HUH, MR. 2?
BA-BUMP!!
KONK!!
BON-CHAN?!
AND YOU THOUGHT YOU MIGHT NEED SOME ALLIES, EH?

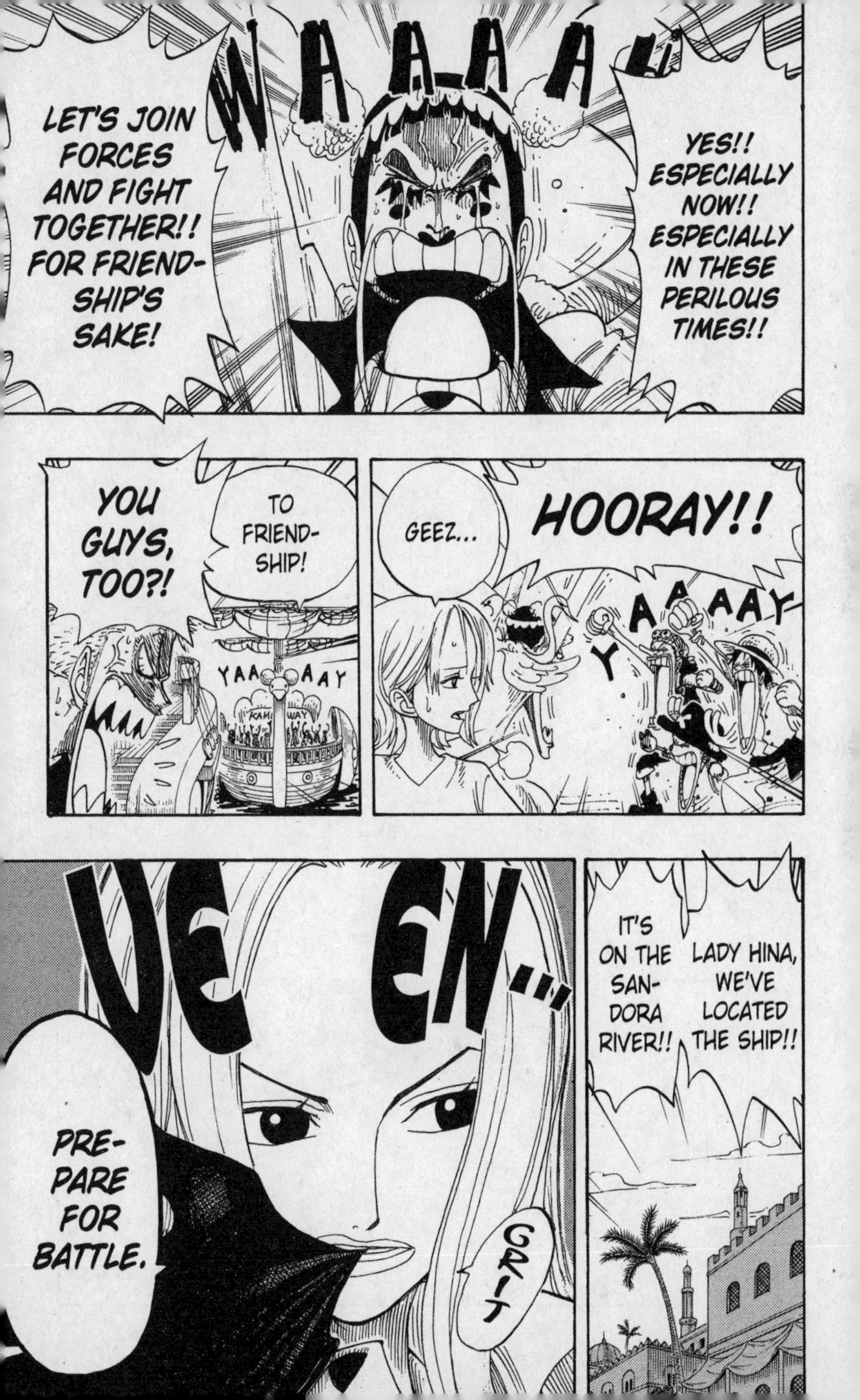
WAAAA
YES!! ESPECIALLY NOW!! ESPECIALLY IN THESE PERILOUS TIMES!!
LET'S JOIN FORCES AND FIGHT TOGETHER!! FOR FRIEND-SHIP'S SAKE!
HOORAY!!
GEEZ...
YAAAAY
TO FRIEND-SHIP!
YOU GUYS, TOO?!
YAA AAY
LADY HINA, WE'VE LOCATED THE SHIP!!
IT'S ON THE SAN-DORA RIVER!!
VE EN...
GRIT
PRE-PARE FOR BATTLE.

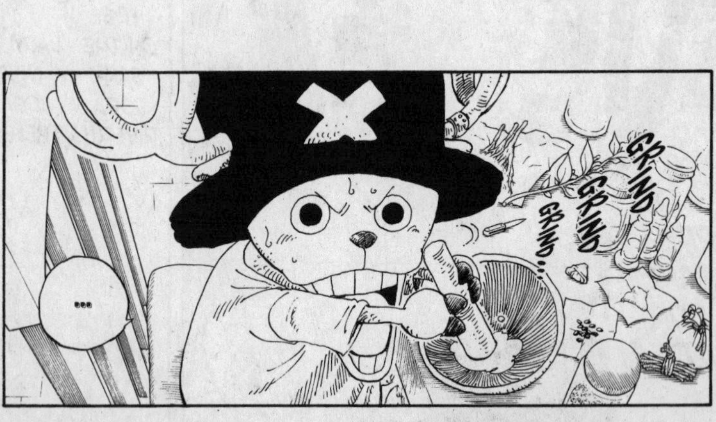
GRIND GRIND GRIND...!!
...

Chapter 215:
LAST WALTZ

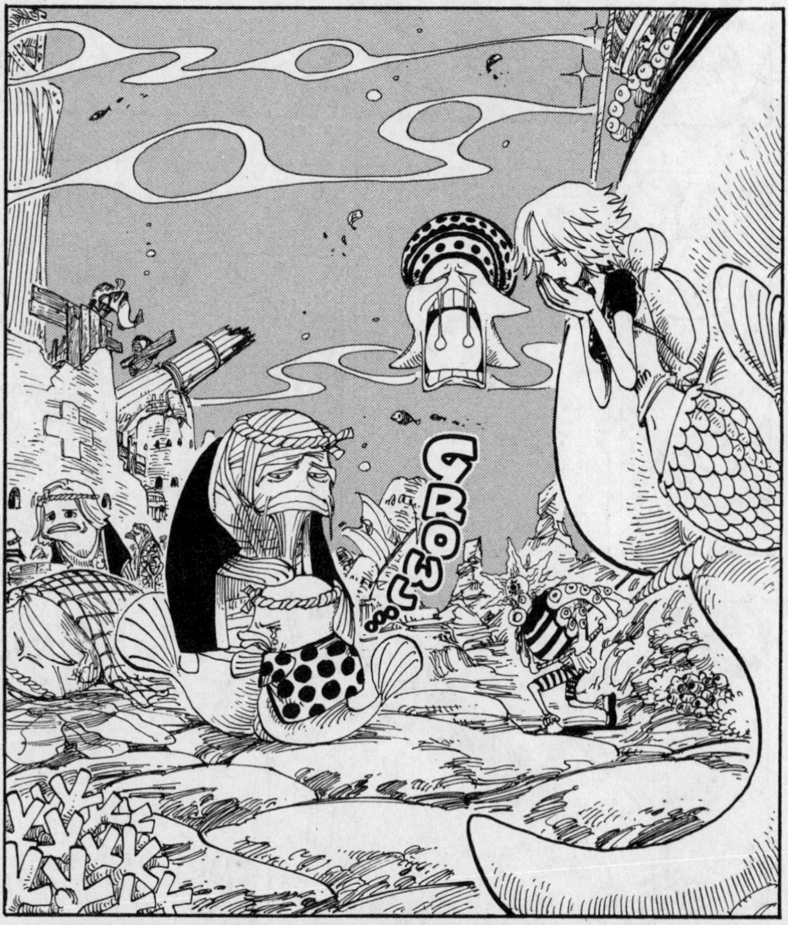
GROWL

HACHI'S WALK ON THE SEA FLOOR, VOL. 29: "HACHI COMES UPON THE VILLAGE OF STARVING CATFISH"

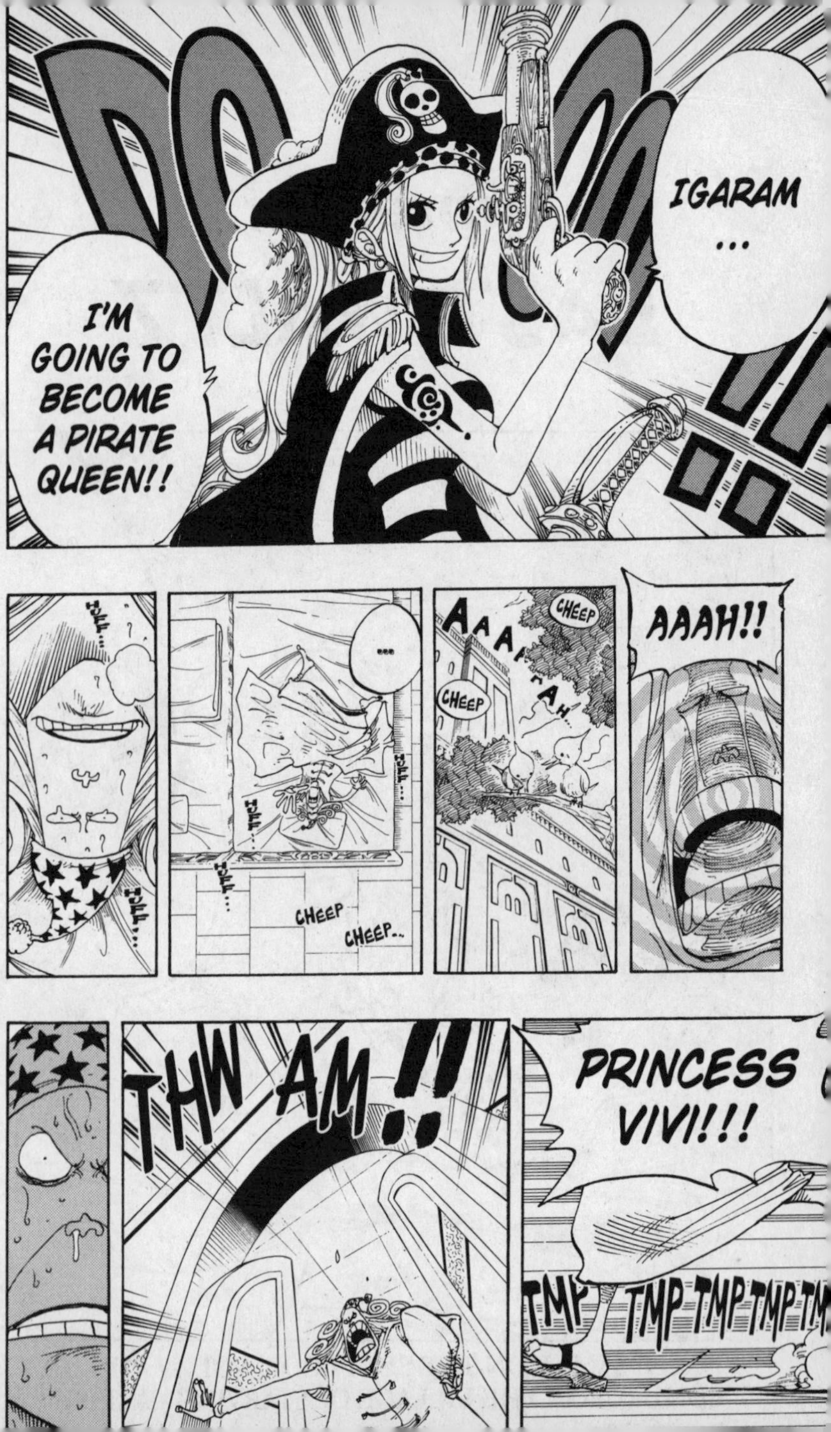
IGARAM ...
I'M GOING TO BECOME A PIRATE QUEEN!!
AAAH!!
AAAAAAH...
CHEEP
CHEEP
...
HUFF...
HUFF...
HUFF...
CHEEP CHEEP...
HUFF...
HUFF...
PRINCESS VIVI!!!
TMP TMP TMP TMP TMP
THWAM!!

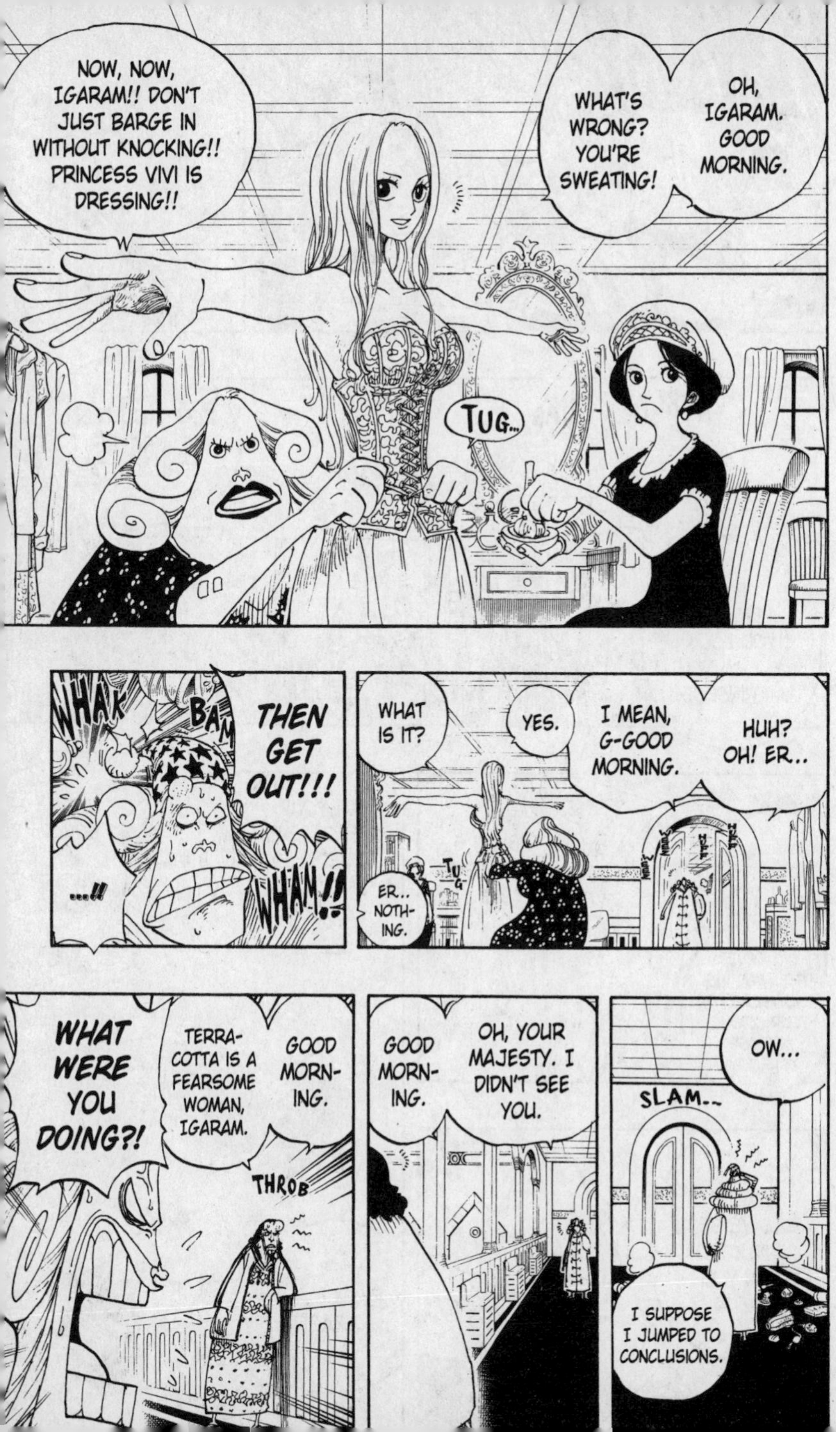
OH, IGARAM. GOOD MORNING.
WHAT'S WRONG? YOU'RE SWEATING!
NOW, NOW, IGARAM!! DON'T JUST BARGE IN WITHOUT KNOCKING!! PRINCESS VIVI IS DRESSING!!
TUG...
HUH? OH! ER..
I MEAN, G-GOOD MORNING.
YES.
WHAT IS IT?
TUG
ER.. NOTH-ING.
THEN GET OUT!!!
BAM
WHAK
WHAM!!
...!!
OW...
SLAM...
I SUPPOSE I JUMPED TO CONCLUSIONS.
OH, YOUR MAJESTY. I DIDN'T SEE YOU.
GOOD MORN-ING.
GOOD MORN-ING.
TERRA-COTTA IS A FEARSOME WOMAN, IGARAM.
WHAT WERE YOU DOING?!
THROB

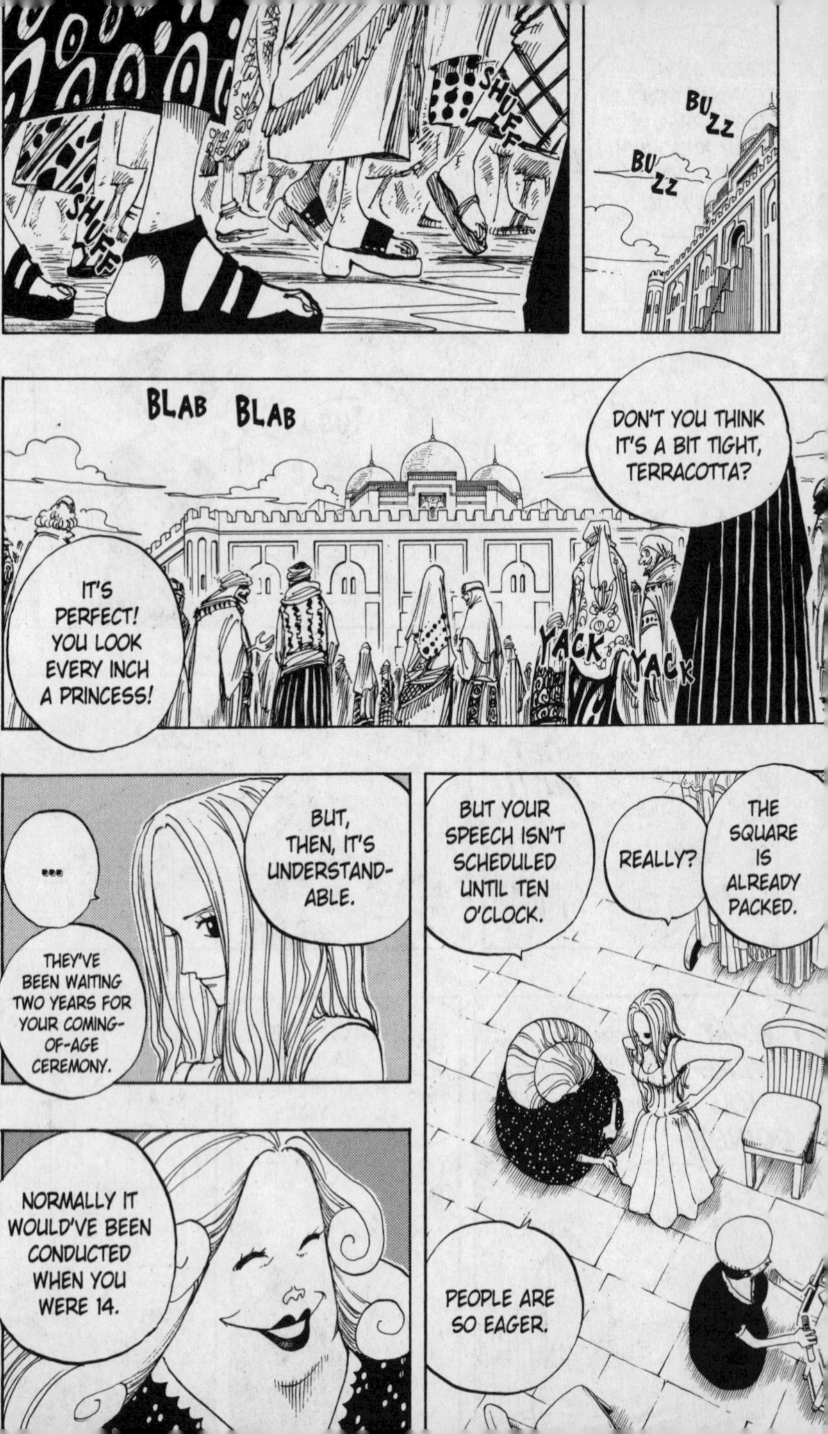
BUZZ
BUZZ
SHUFF
SHUFF
DON'T YOU THINK IT'S A BIT TIGHT, TERRACOTTA?
BLAB BLAB
YACK YACK
IT'S PERFECT! YOU LOOK EVERY INCH A PRINCESS!
THE SQUARE IS ALREADY PACKED.
REALLY?
BUT YOUR SPEECH ISN'T SCHEDULED UNTIL TEN O'CLOCK.
PEOPLE ARE SO EAGER.
BUT, THEN, IT'S UNDERSTANDABLE.
...
THEY'VE BEEN WAITING TWO YEARS FOR YOUR COMING-OF-AGE CEREMONY.
NORMALLY IT WOULD'VE BEEN CONDUCTED WHEN YOU WERE 14.

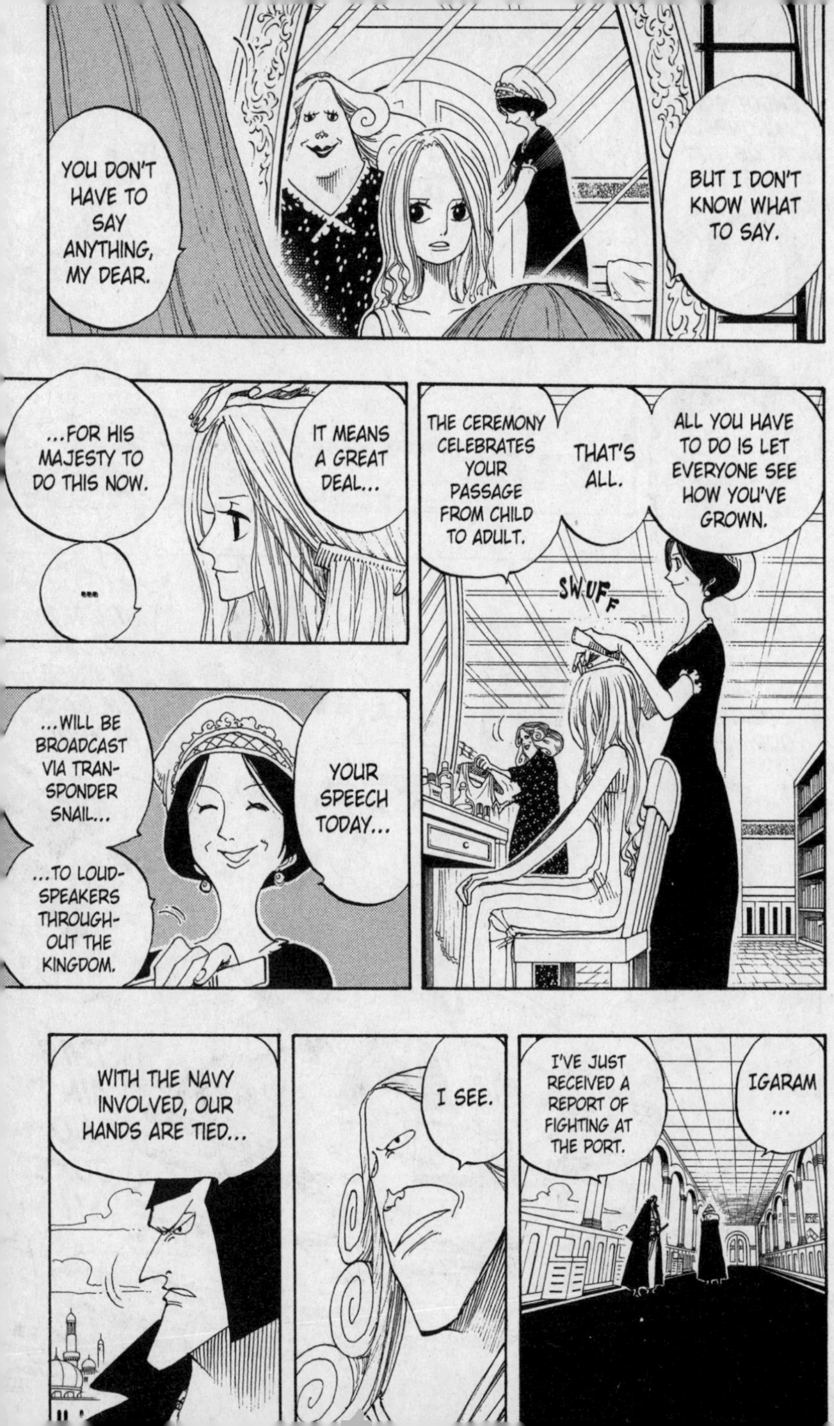
BUT I DON'T KNOW WHAT TO SAY.
YOU DON'T HAVE TO SAY ANYTHING, MY DEAR.
ALL YOU HAVE TO DO IS LET EVERYONE SEE HOW YOU'VE GROWN.
THAT'S ALL.
THE CEREMONY CELEBRATES YOUR PASSAGE FROM CHILD TO ADULT.
SWUFF
IT MEANS A GREAT DEAL...
...FOR HIS MAJESTY TO DO THIS NOW.
...
YOUR SPEECH TODAY...
...WILL BE BROADCAST VIA TRANS-SPONDER SNAIL...
...TO LOUD-SPEAKERS THROUGH-OUT THE KINGDOM.
IGARAM...
I'VE JUST RECEIVED A REPORT OF FIGHTING AT THE PORT.
I SEE.
WITH THE NAVY INVOLVED, OUR HANDS ARE TIED...

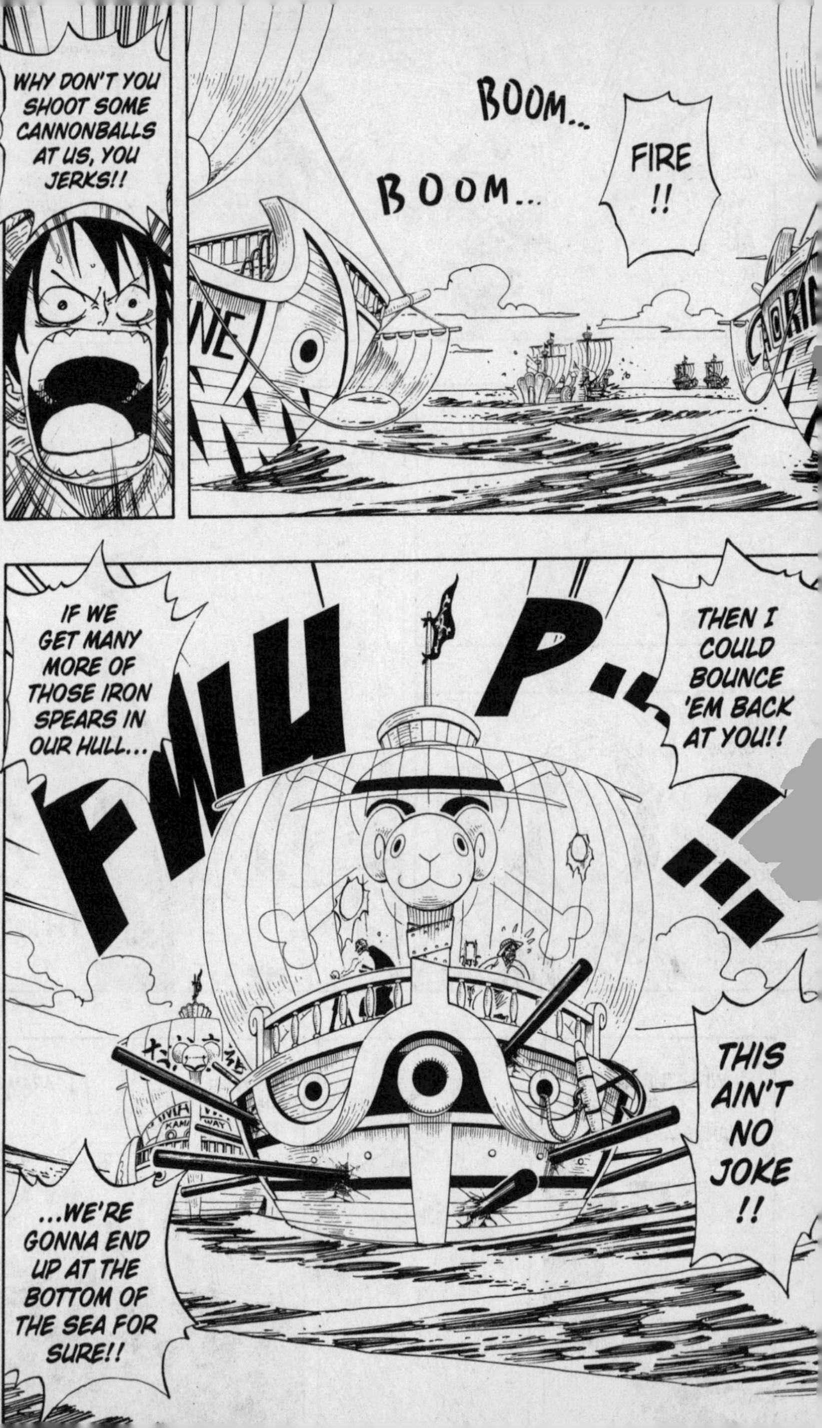
BOOM...
BOOM...
FIRE!!
WHY DON'T YOU SHOOT SOME CANNONBALLS AT US, YOU JERKS!!
THEN I COULD BOUNCE 'EM BACK AT YOU!!
FWUP..!!
IF WE GET MANY MORE OF THOSE IRON SPEARS IN OUR HULL...
THIS AIN'T NO JOKE!!
...WE'RE GONNA END UP AT THE BOTTOM OF THE SEA FOR SURE!!

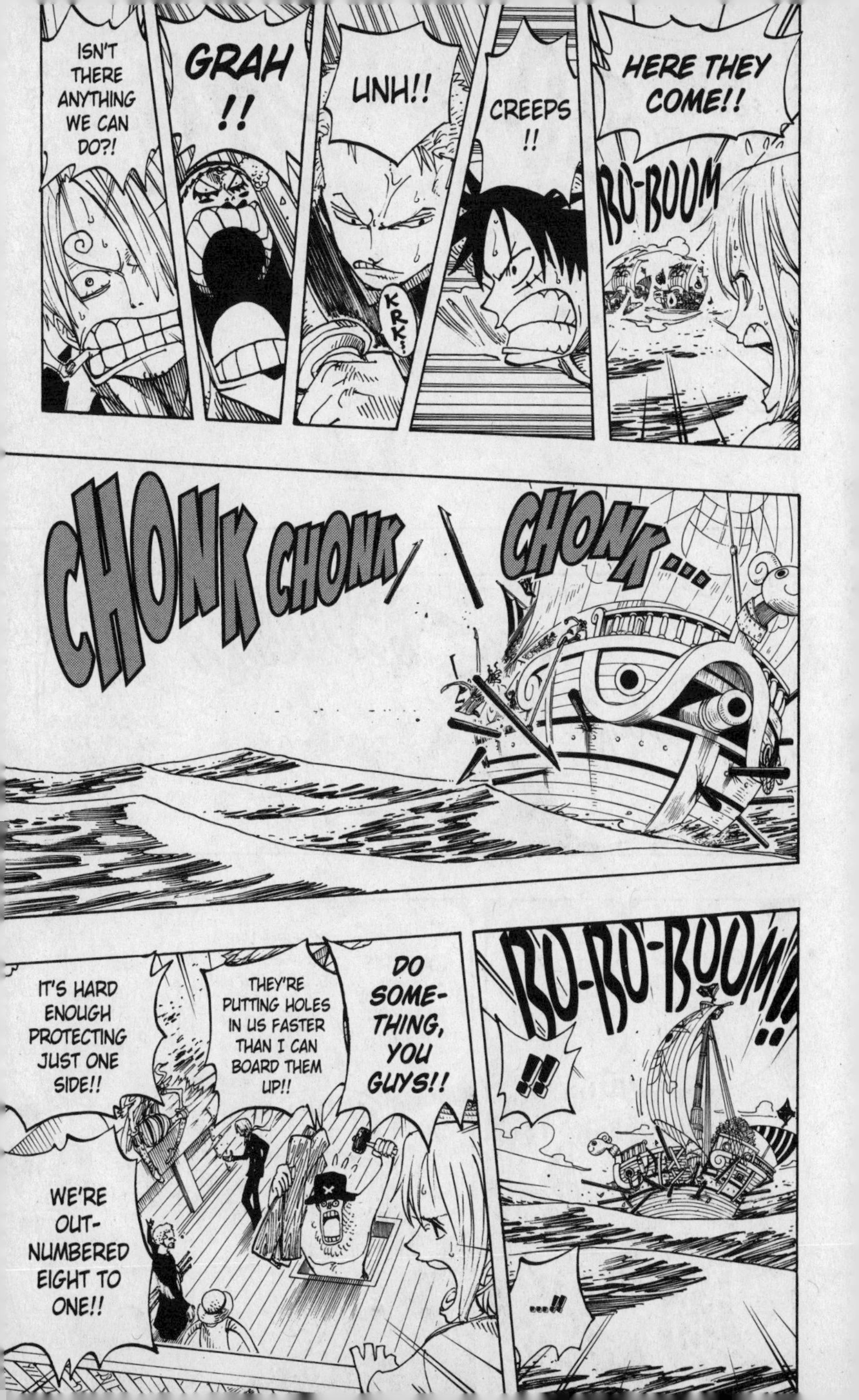
HERE THEY COME!!
BO-BOOM
CREEPS!!
UNH!!
KRK
GRAH!!
ISN'T THERE ANYTHING WE CAN DO?!
CHONK CHONK
CHONK...
BO-BO-BOOM!!
!!
...!!
DO SOME-THING, YOU GUYS!!
THEY'RE PUTTING HOLES IN US FASTER THAN I CAN BOARD THEM UP!!
IT'S HARD ENOUGH PROTECTING JUST ONE SIDE!!
WE'RE OUT-NUMBERED EIGHT TO ONE!!

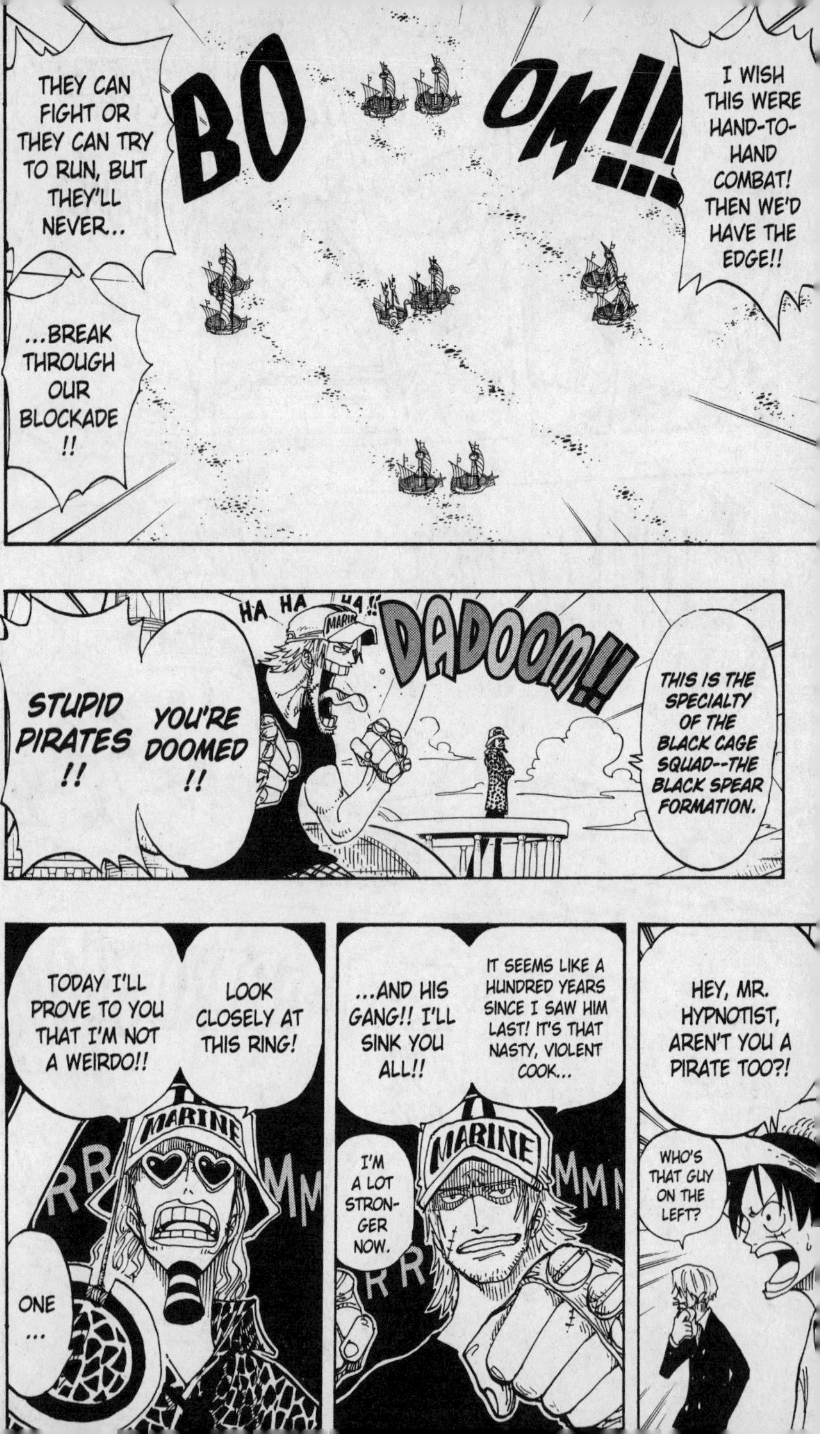
I WISH THIS WERE HAND-TO-HAND COMBAT! THEN WE'D HAVE THE EDGE!!
BO OM!!!
THEY CAN FIGHT OR THEY CAN TRY TO RUN, BUT THEY'LL NEVER...
...BREAK THROUGH OUR BLOCKADE !!
THIS IS THE SPECIALTY OF THE BLACK CAGE SQUAD--THE BLACK SPEAR FORMATION.
DADOOM!!
HA HA HA!!
YOU'RE DOOMED !!
STUPID PIRATES !!
HEY, MR. HYPNOTIST, AREN'T YOU A PIRATE TOO?!
WHO'S THAT GUY ON THE LEFT?
IT SEEMS LIKE A HUNDRED YEARS SINCE I SAW HIM LAST! IT'S THAT NASTY, VIOLENT COOK...
...AND HIS GANG!! I'LL SINK YOU ALL!!
MARINE
MMM
I'M A LOT STRONGER NOW.
RR
LOOK CLOSELY AT THIS RING!
TODAY I'LL PROVE TO YOU THAT I'M NOT A WEIRDO!!
MARINE
MM
RR
ONE ...

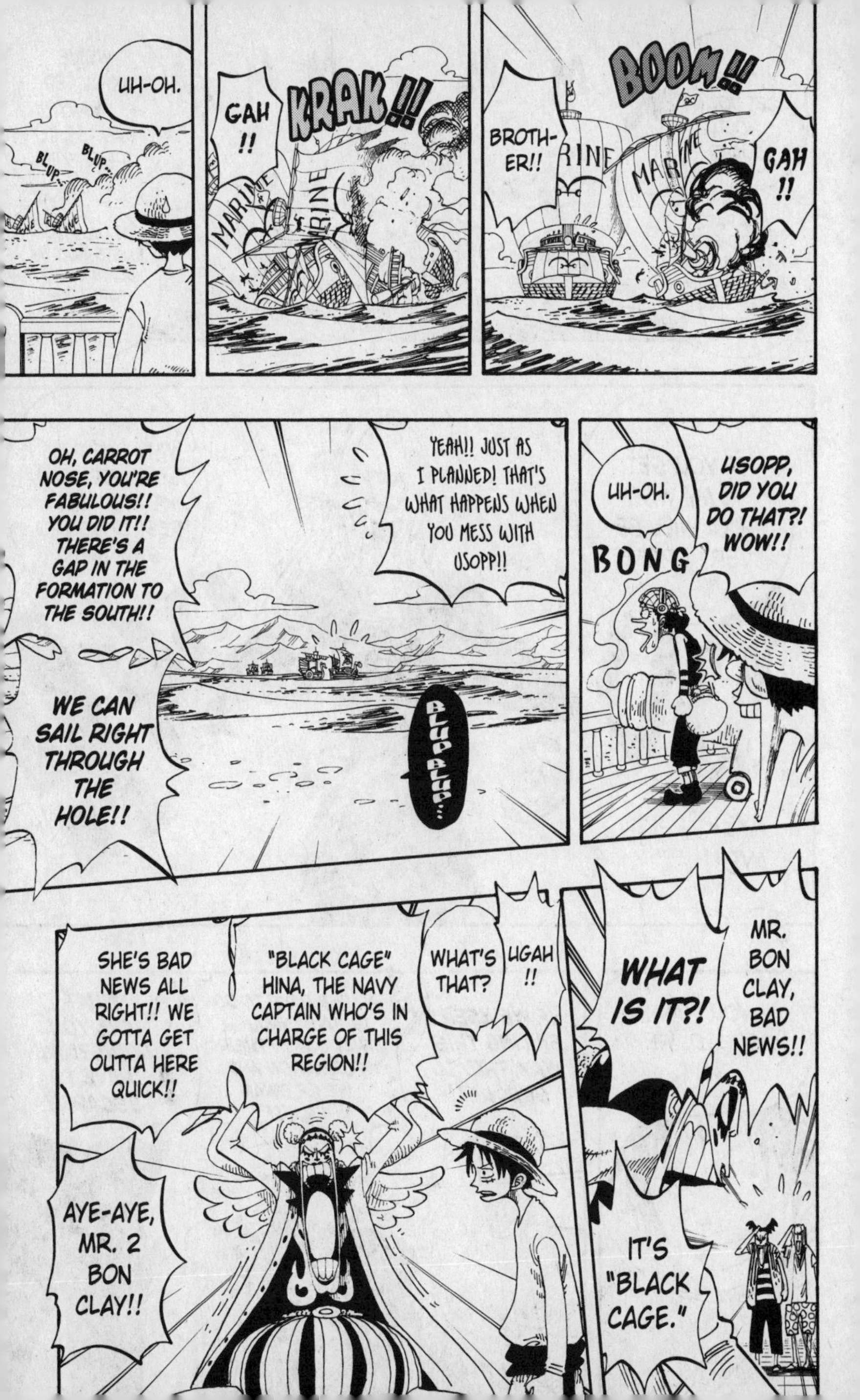
BOOM!!
GAH!!
BROTHER!!
KRAK!!
GAH!!
UH-OH.
BLUP...
BLUP...
USOPP, DID YOU DO THAT?! WOW!!
UH-OH.
BONG
YEAH!! JUST AS I PLANNED! THAT'S WHAT HAPPENS WHEN YOU MESS WITH USOPP!!
OH, CARROT NOSE, YOU'RE FABULOUS!! YOU DID IT!! THERE'S A GAP IN THE FORMATION TO THE SOUTH!!
WE CAN SAIL RIGHT THROUGH THE HOLE!!
BLUP BLUP...
MR. BON CLAY, BAD NEWS!!
WHAT IS IT?!
IT'S "BLACK CAGE."
UGAH!!
WHAT'S THAT?
"BLACK CAGE" HINA, THE NAVY CAPTAIN WHO'S IN CHARGE OF THIS REGION!!
SHE'S BAD NEWS ALL RIGHT!! WE GOTTA GET OUTTA HERE QUICK!!
AYE-AYE, MR. 2 BON CLAY!!

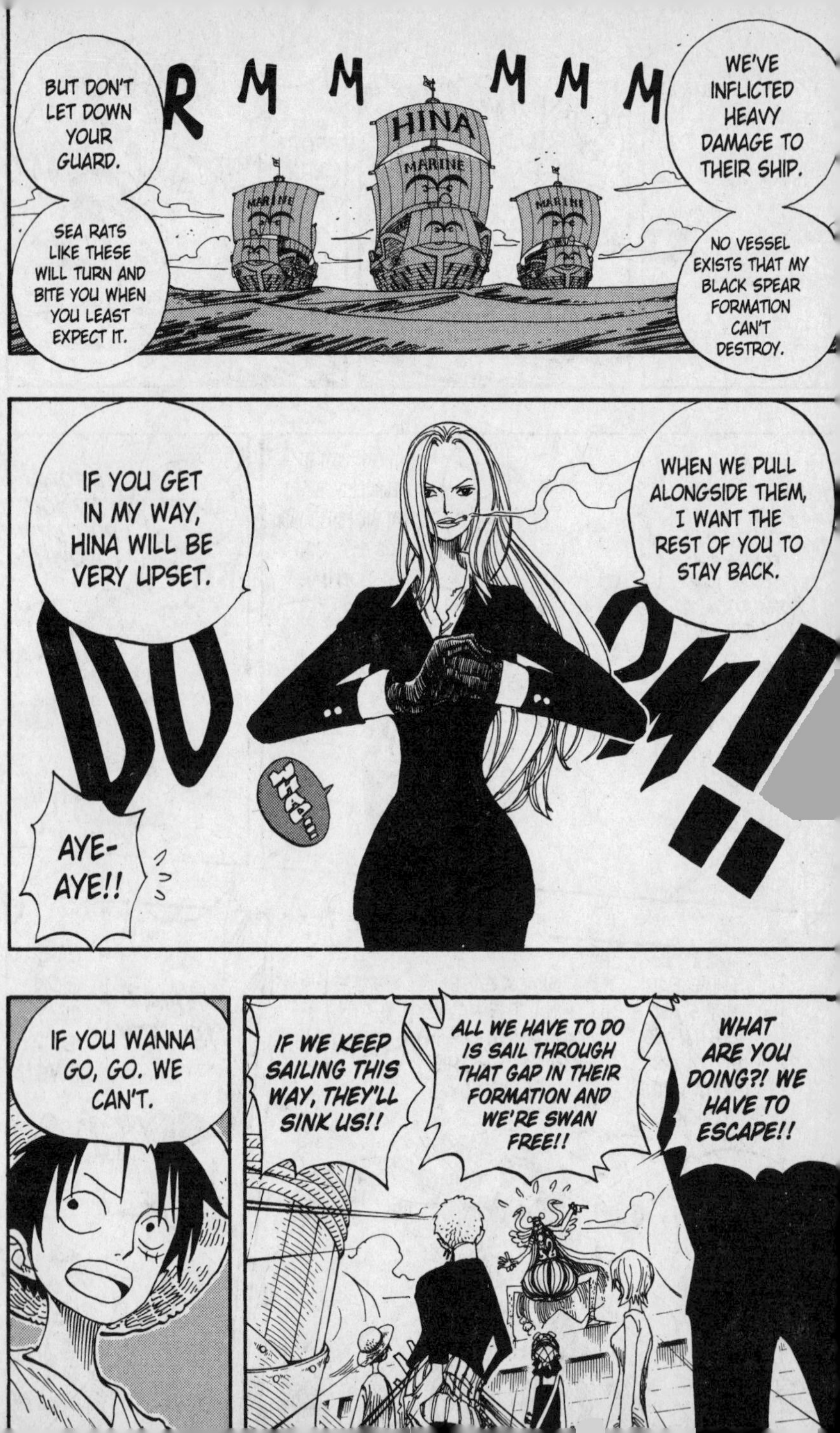
RMM MMM
WE'VE INFLICTED HEAVY DAMAGE TO THEIR SHIP.
NO VESSEL EXISTS THAT MY BLACK SPEAR FORMATION CAN'T DESTROY.
BUT DON'T LET DOWN YOUR GUARD.
SEA RATS LIKE THESE WILL TURN AND BITE YOU WHEN YOU LEAST EXPECT IT.
WHEN WE PULL ALONGSIDE THEM, I WANT THE REST OF YOU TO STAY BACK.
IF YOU GET IN MY WAY, HINA WILL BE VERY UPSET.
DOOM!!
AYE-AYE!!
WHAT ARE YOU DOING?! WE HAVE TO ESCAPE!!
ALL WE HAVE TO DO IS SAIL THROUGH THAT GAP IN THEIR FORMATION AND WE'RE SWAN FREE!!
IF WE KEEP SAILING THIS WAY, THEY'LL SINK US!!
IF YOU WANNA GO, GO. WE CAN'T.

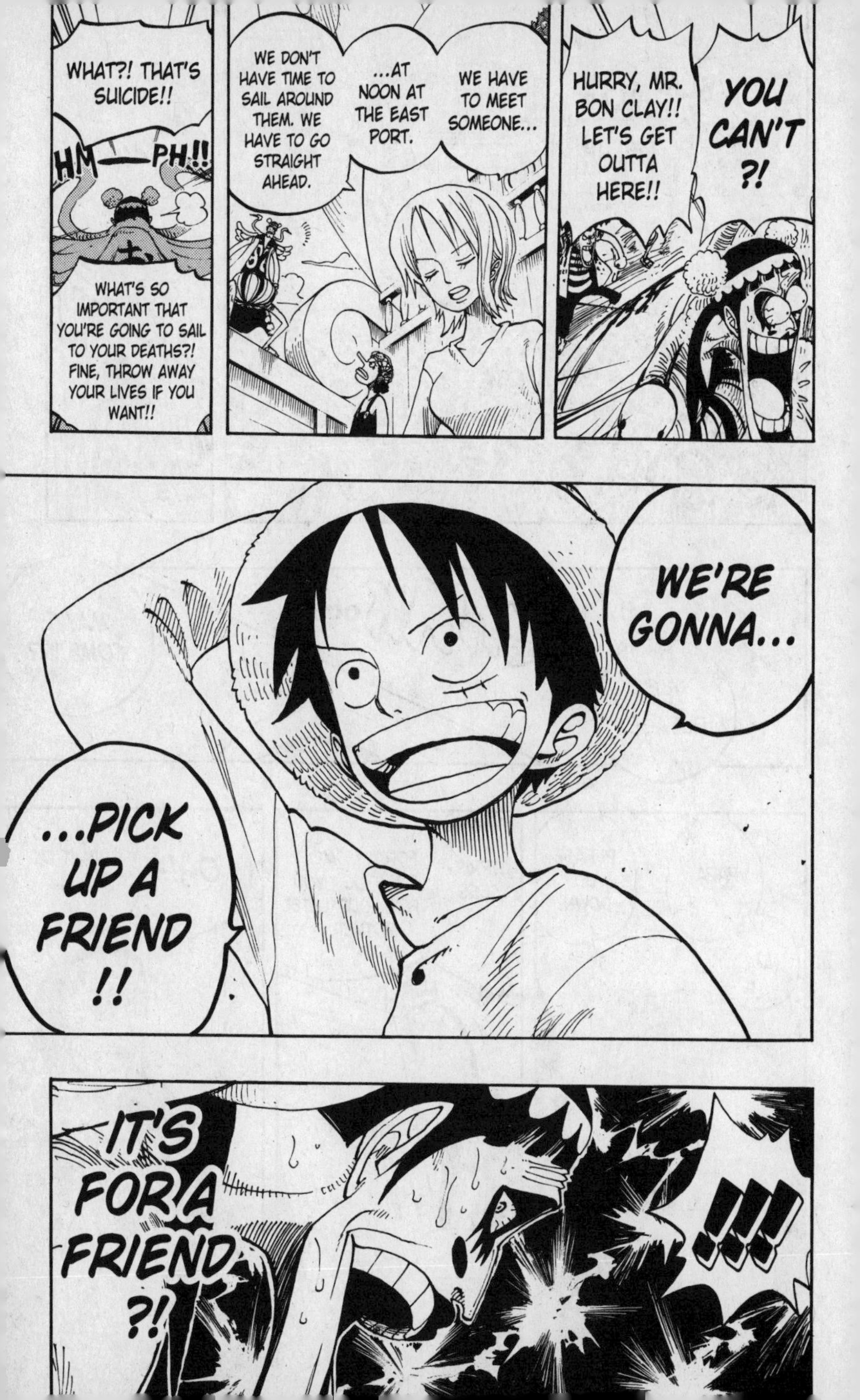

YOU CAN'T ?!
HURRY, MR. BON CLAY!! LET'S GET OUTTA HERE!!
WE HAVE TO MEET SOMEONE...
...AT NOON AT THE EAST PORT.
WE DON'T HAVE TIME TO SAIL AROUND THEM. WE HAVE TO GO STRAIGHT AHEAD.
WHAT?! THAT'S SUICIDE!!
HM—PH!!!
WHAT'S SO IMPORTANT THAT YOU'RE GOING TO SAIL TO YOUR DEATHS?! FINE, THROW AWAY YOUR LIVES IF YOU WANT!!
WE'RE GONNA...
...PICK UP A FRIEND !!
IT'S FOR A FRIEND ?!
!!!

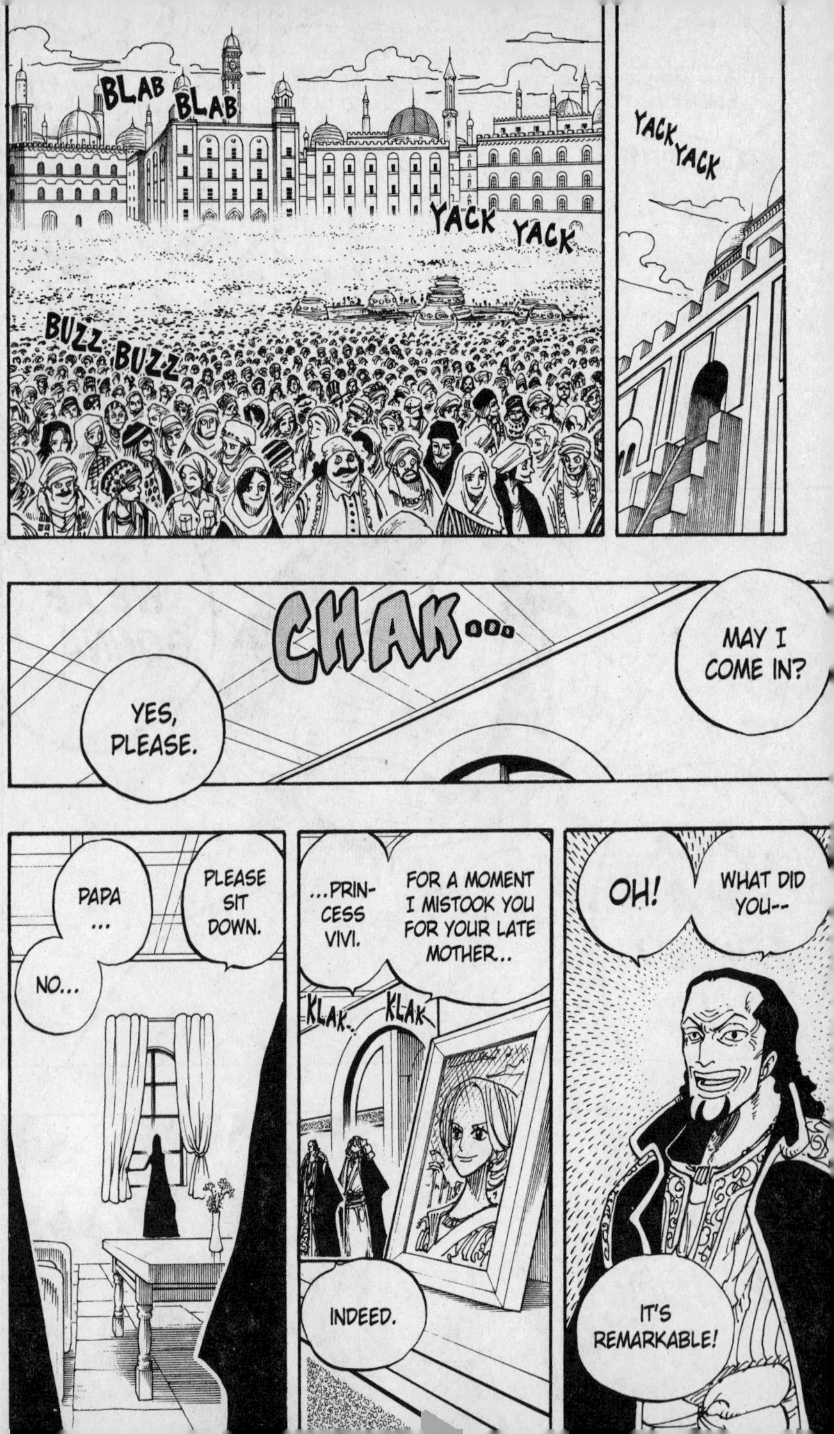
YACK YACK
BLAB BLAB
YACK YACK
BUZZ BUZZ
MAY I COME IN?
CHAK...
YES, PLEASE.
WHAT DID YOU--
OH!
IT'S REMARKABLE!
FOR A MOMENT I MISTOOK YOU FOR YOUR LATE MOTHER...
...PRIN-CESS VIVI.
KLAK KLAK
INDEED.
PLEASE SIT DOWN.
PAPA ...
NO...

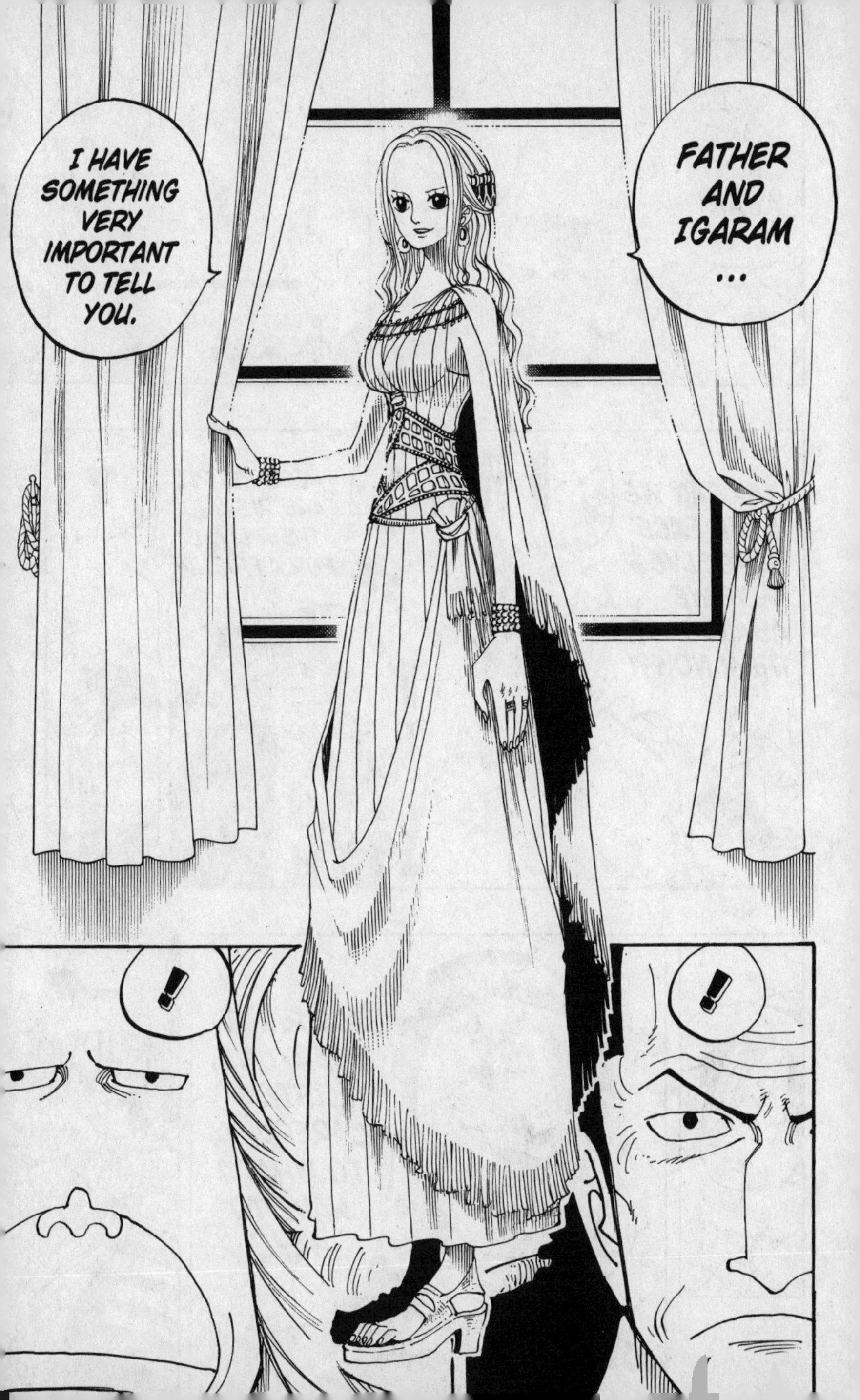
FATHER AND IGARAM...
I HAVE SOMETHING VERY IMPORTANT TO TELL YOU.
!
!

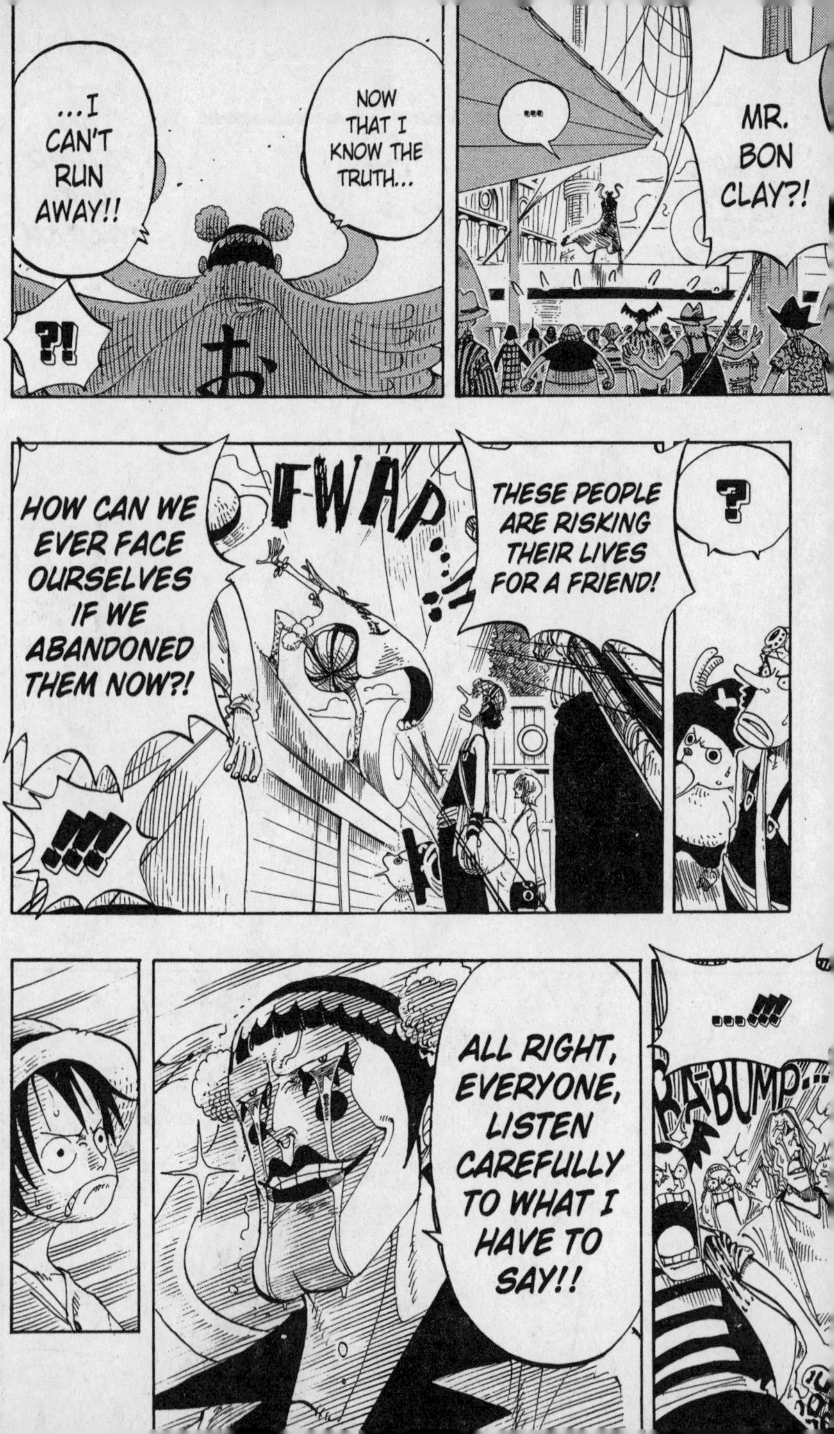
MR. BON CLAY?!
...
NOW THAT I KNOW THE TRUTH...
...I CAN'T RUN AWAY!!
?!
お
?
THESE PEOPLE ARE RISKING THEIR LIVES FOR A FRIEND!
FWAP
HOW CAN WE EVER FACE OURSELVES IF WE ABANDONED THEM NOW?!
!!!
...!!!
BA-BUMP...
ALL RIGHT, EVERYONE, LISTEN CAREFULLY TO WHAT I HAVE TO SAY!!

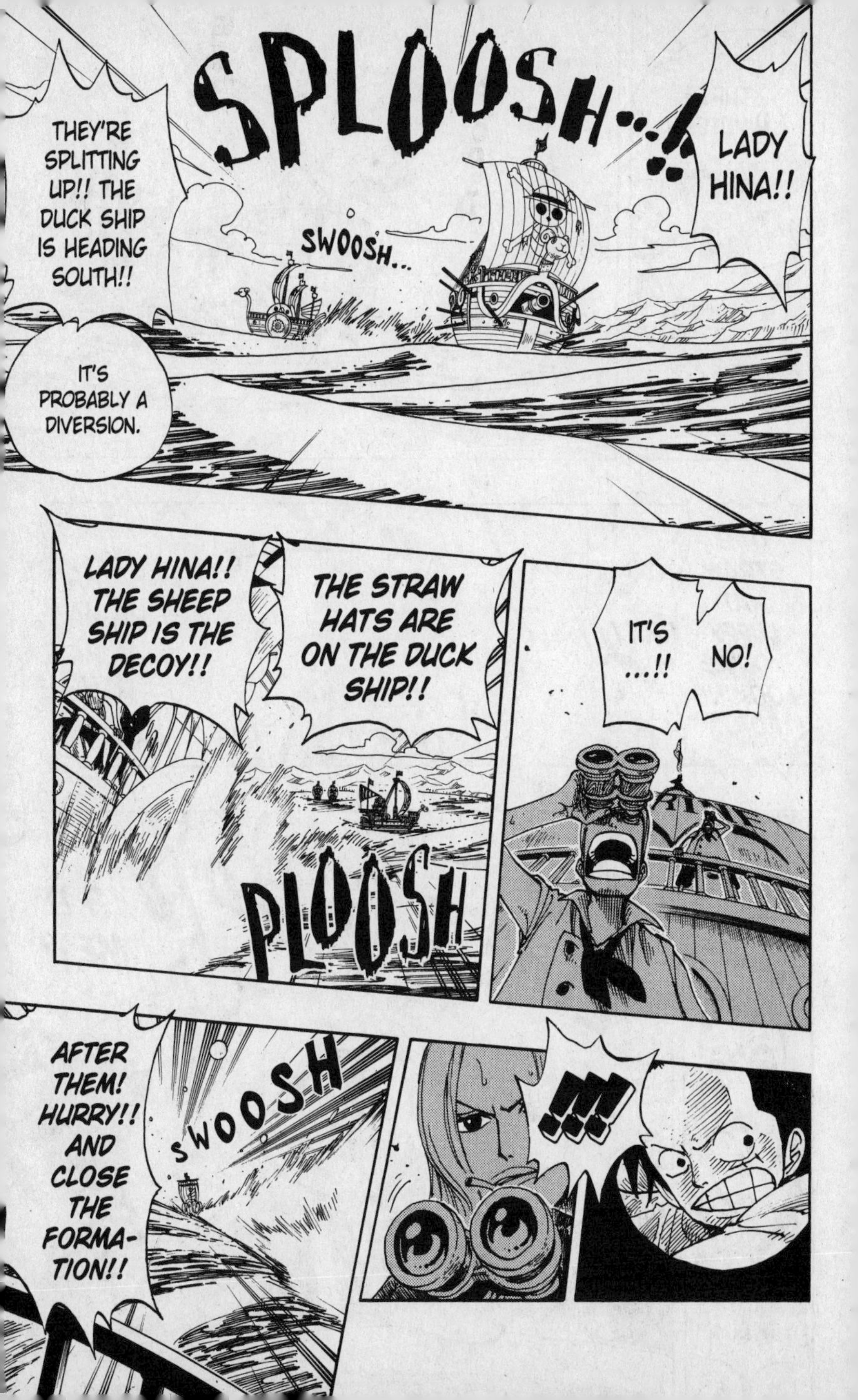
SPLOOSH...!
LADY HINA!!
THEY'RE SPLITTING UP!! THE DUCK SHIP IS HEADING SOUTH!!
SWOOSH...
IT'S PROBABLY A DIVERSION.
NO!
IT'S ...!!
THE STRAW HATS ARE ON THE DUCK SHIP!!
LADY HINA!! THE SHEEP SHIP IS THE DECOY!!
PLOOSH
!!!
AFTER THEM! HURRY!! AND CLOSE THE FORMATION!!
SWOOSH

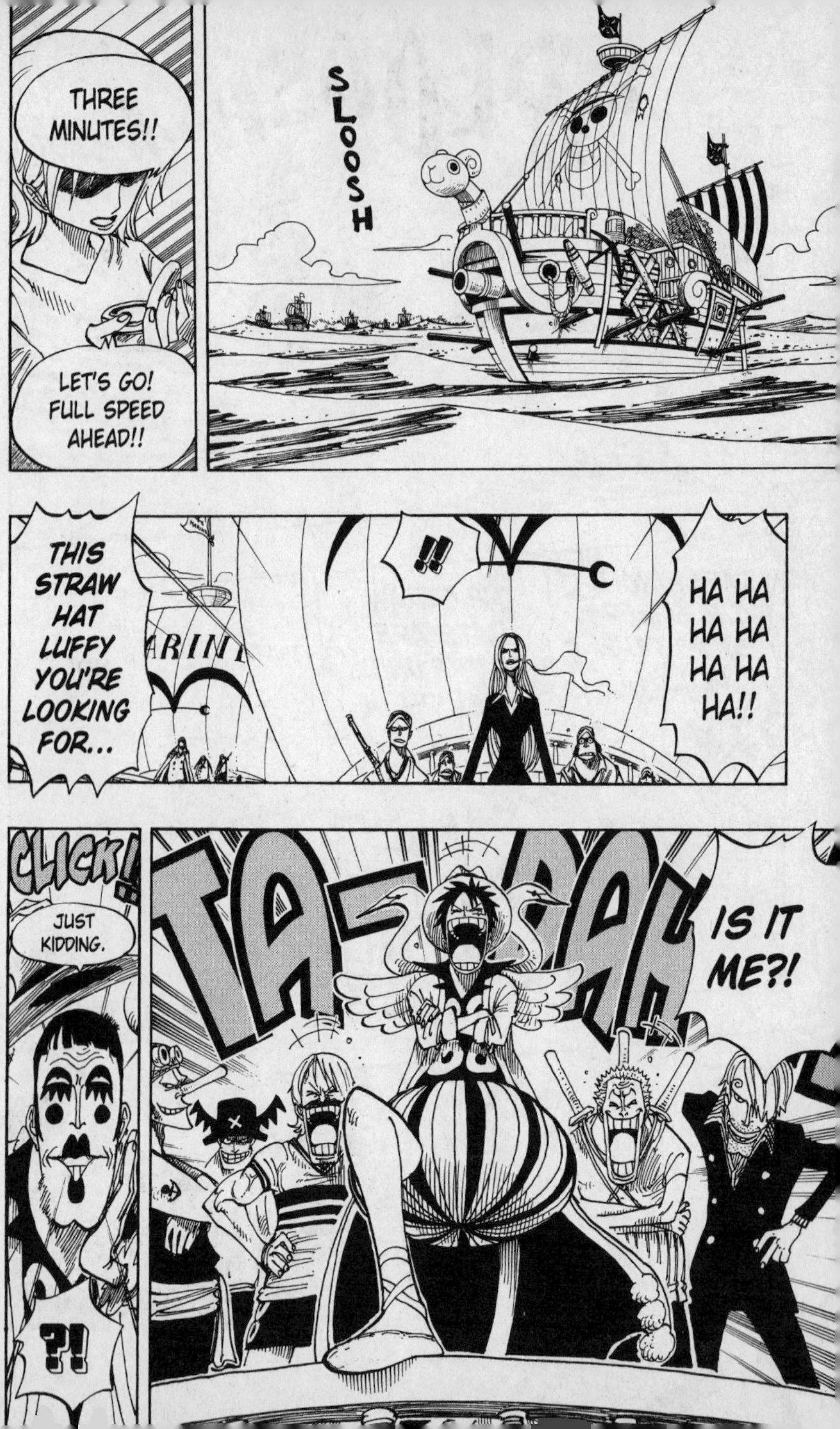
SLOOSH
THREE MINUTES!!
LET'S GO! FULL SPEED AHEAD!!
HA HA HA HA HA HA HA!!
!!
THIS STRAW HAT LUFFY YOU'RE LOOKING FOR...
IS IT ME?!
TA-DAH
CLICK!
JUST KIDDING.
?!

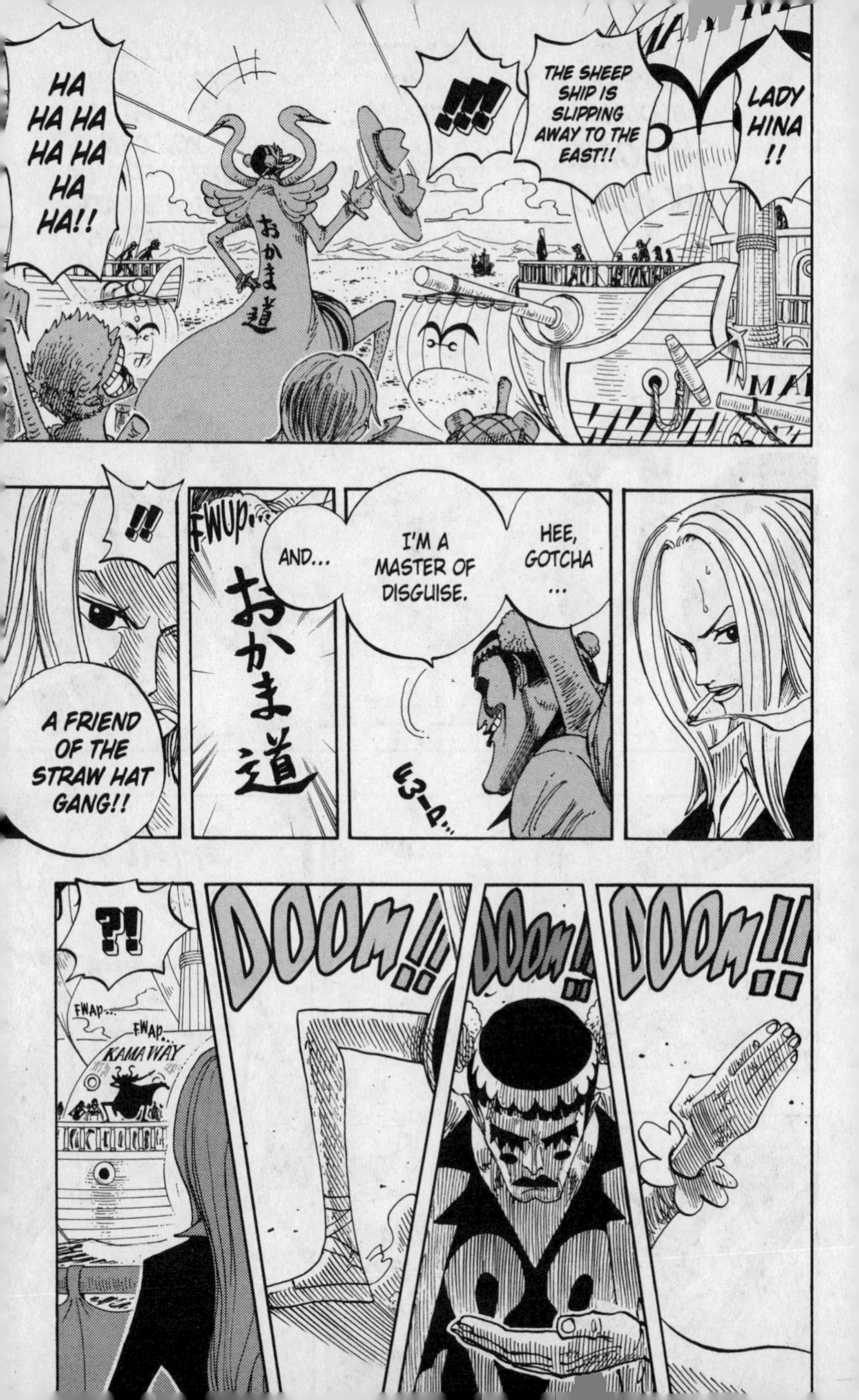
LADY HINA!!
THE SHEEP SHIP IS SLIPPING AWAY TO THE EAST!!
!!!
HA HA HA HA HA HA HA HA!!
おかま道
HEE, GOTCHA ...
I'M A MASTER OF DISGUISE.
AND...
FWUP...
おかま道
!!
A FRIEND OF THE STRAW HAT GANG!!
DOOM!!
DOOM!!
DOOM!!
?!
FWAP...
FWAP...
KAMA WAY

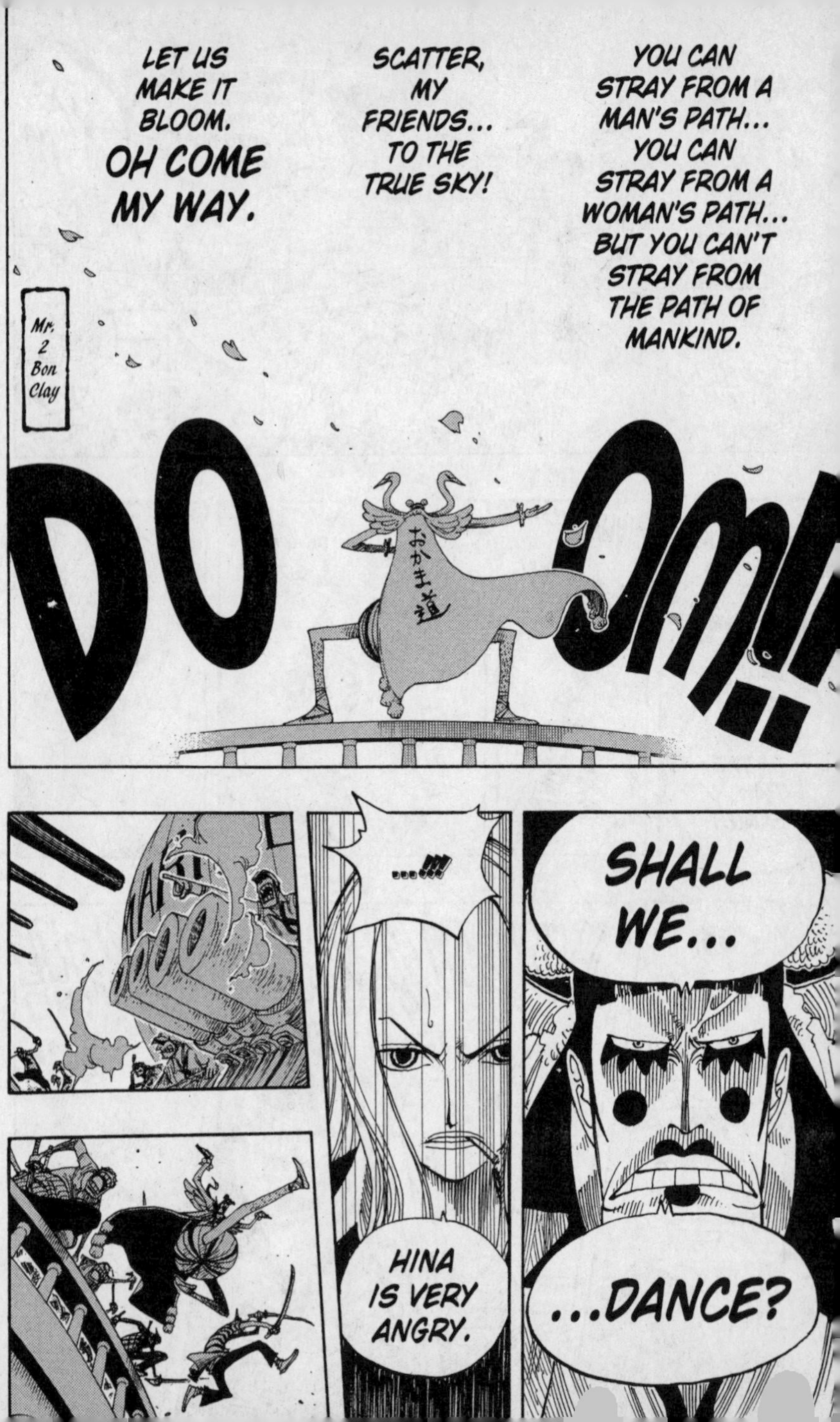
YOU CAN STRAY FROM A MAN'S PATH... YOU CAN STRAY FROM A WOMAN'S PATH... BUT YOU CAN'T STRAY FROM THE PATH OF MANKIND.
SCATTER, MY FRIENDS... TO THE TRUE SKY!
LET US MAKE IT BLOOM. OH COME MY WAY.
Mr. 2 Bon Clay
おかま道
DOOM!!
SHALL WE...
...DANCE?
...!!!
HINA IS VERY ANGRY.

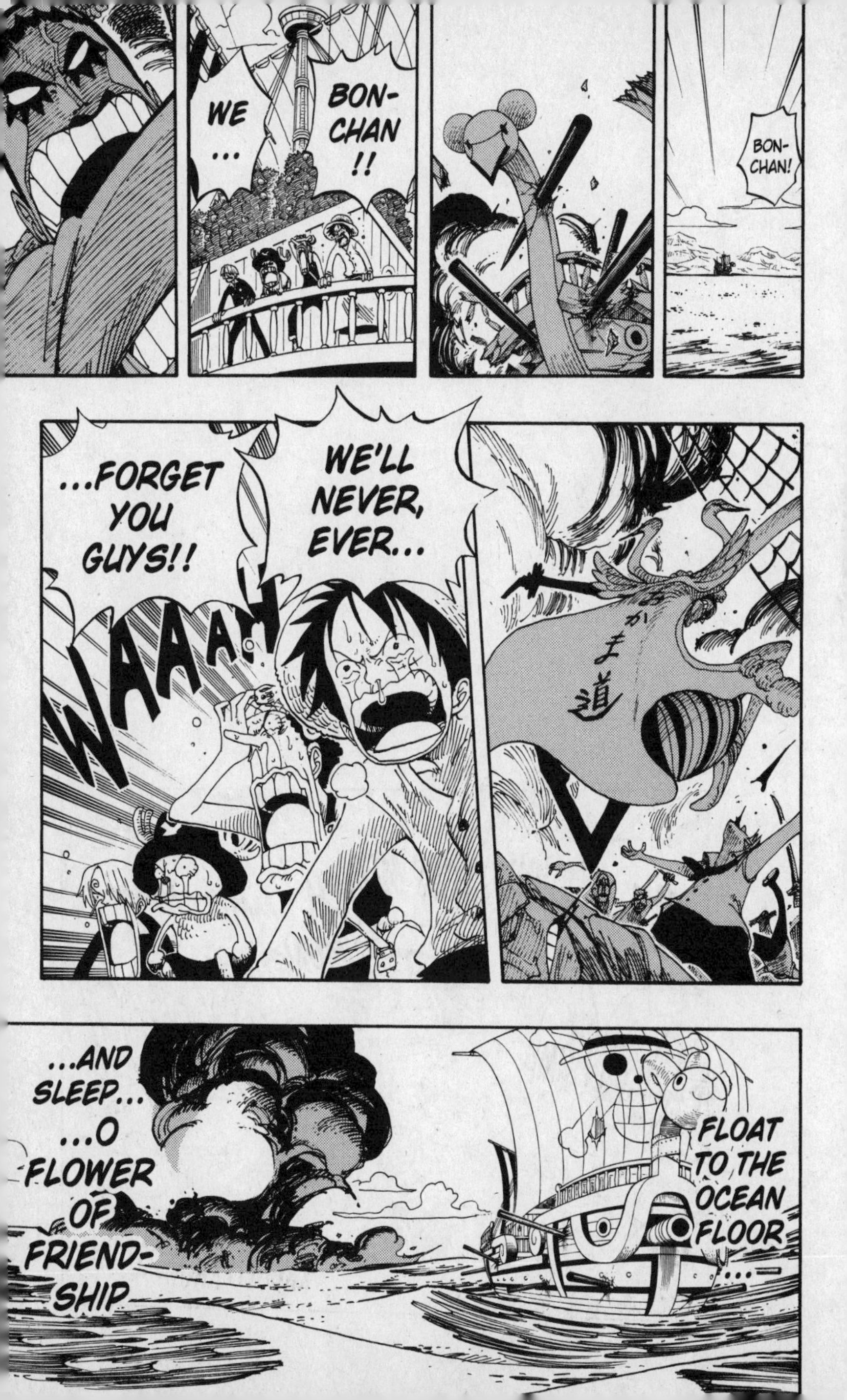
BON-CHAN!
BON-CHAN!!
WE ...
おかま道
WE'LL NEVER, EVER...
...FORGET YOU GUYS!!
WAAAH
FLOAT TO THE OCEAN FLOOR...
...AND SLEEP...
...O FLOWER OF FRIEND-SHIP

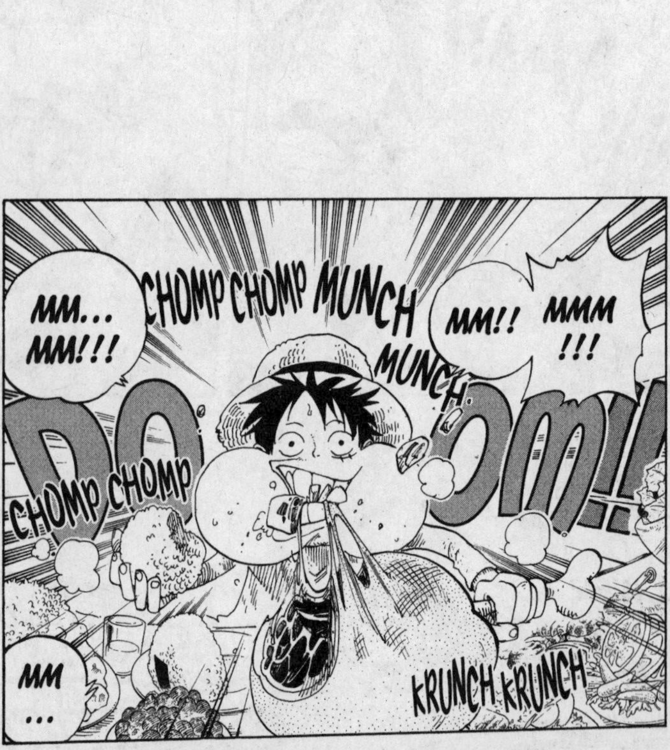
MMM !!!
MM!!
CHOMP CHOMP MUNCH
MUNCH
MM... MM!!!
CHOMP CHOMP
KRUNCH KRUNCH
MM ...

Chapter 21

VIVI'S ADVENTURE

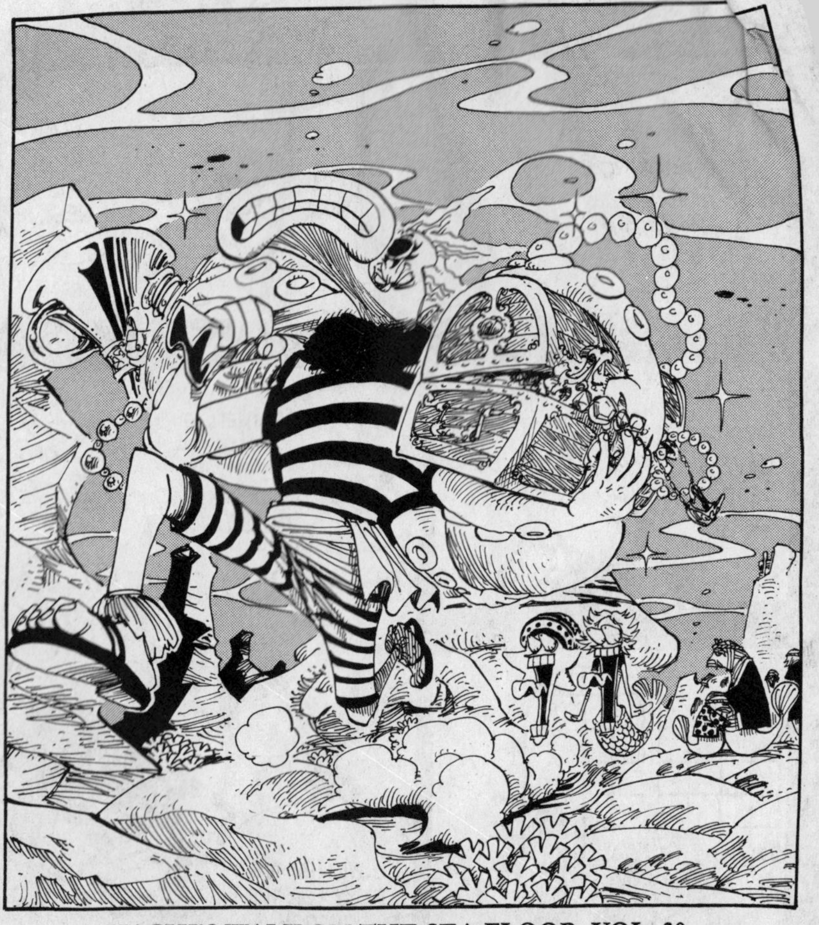

HACHI'S WALK ON THE SEA FLOOR, VOL. 30:
"HACHI RUNS FOR IT!!"

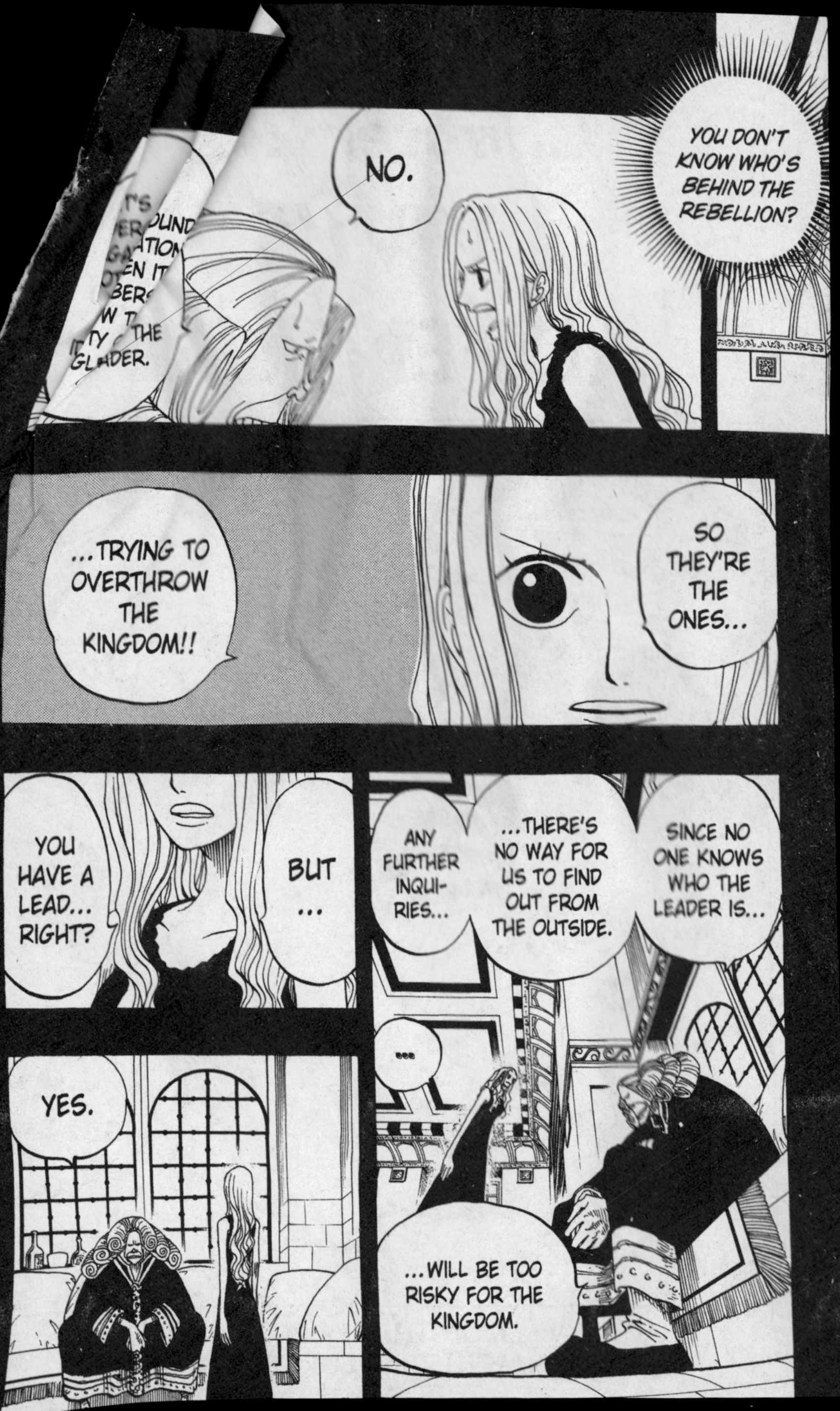
YOU DON'T KNOW WHO'S BEHIND THE REBELLION?
NO.
SO THEY'RE THE ONES...
...TRYING TO OVERTHROW THE KINGDOM!!
SINCE NO ONE KNOWS WHO THE LEADER IS...
...THERE'S NO WAY FOR US TO FIND OUT FROM THE OUTSIDE.
ANY FURTHER INQUIRIES...
...
...WILL BE TOO RISKY FOR THE KINGDOM.
BUT ...
YOU HAVE A LEAD... RIGHT?
YES.

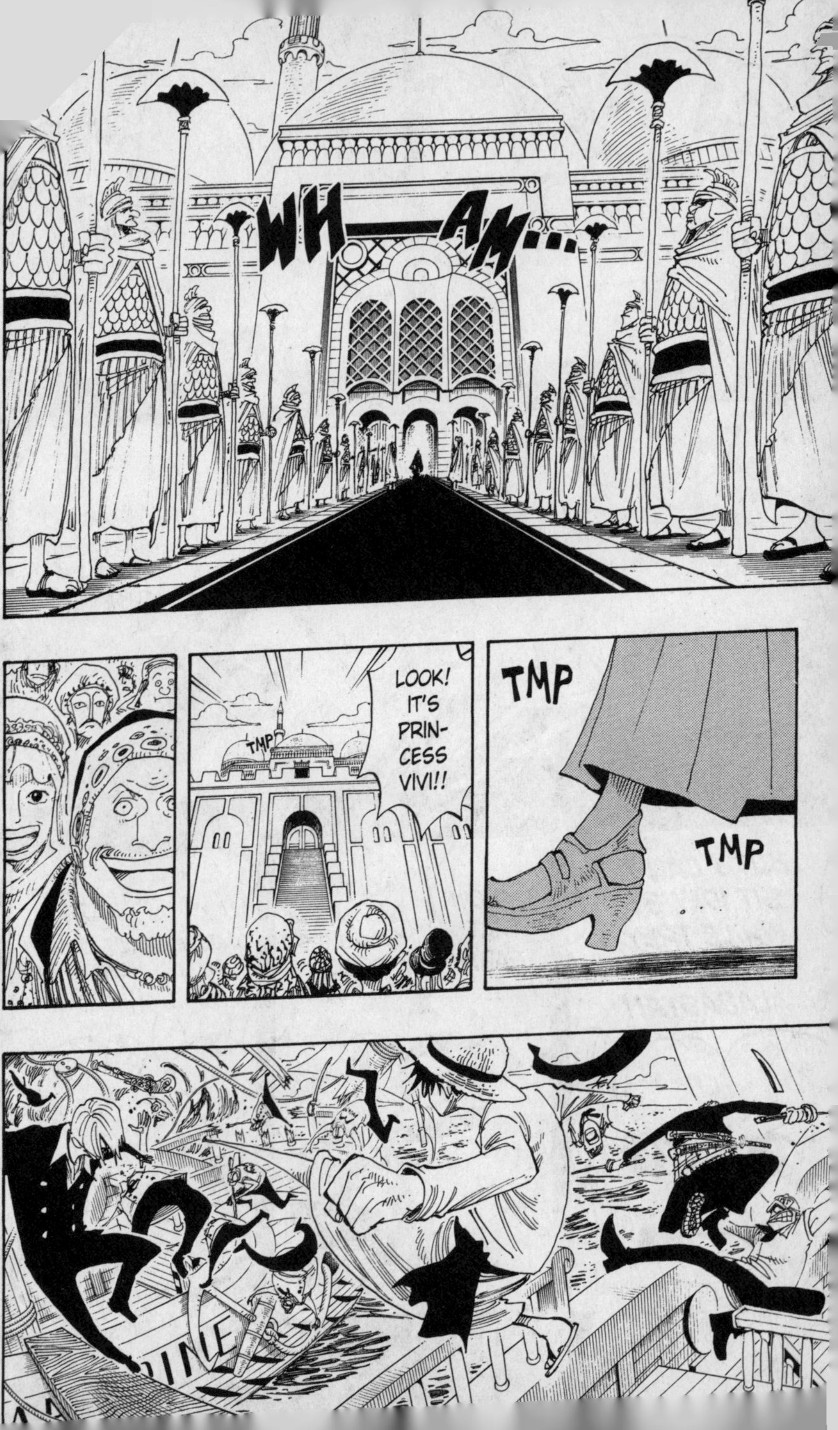
WH—AM...
TMP
TMP
LOOK! IT'S PRIN-CESS VIVI!!
TMP

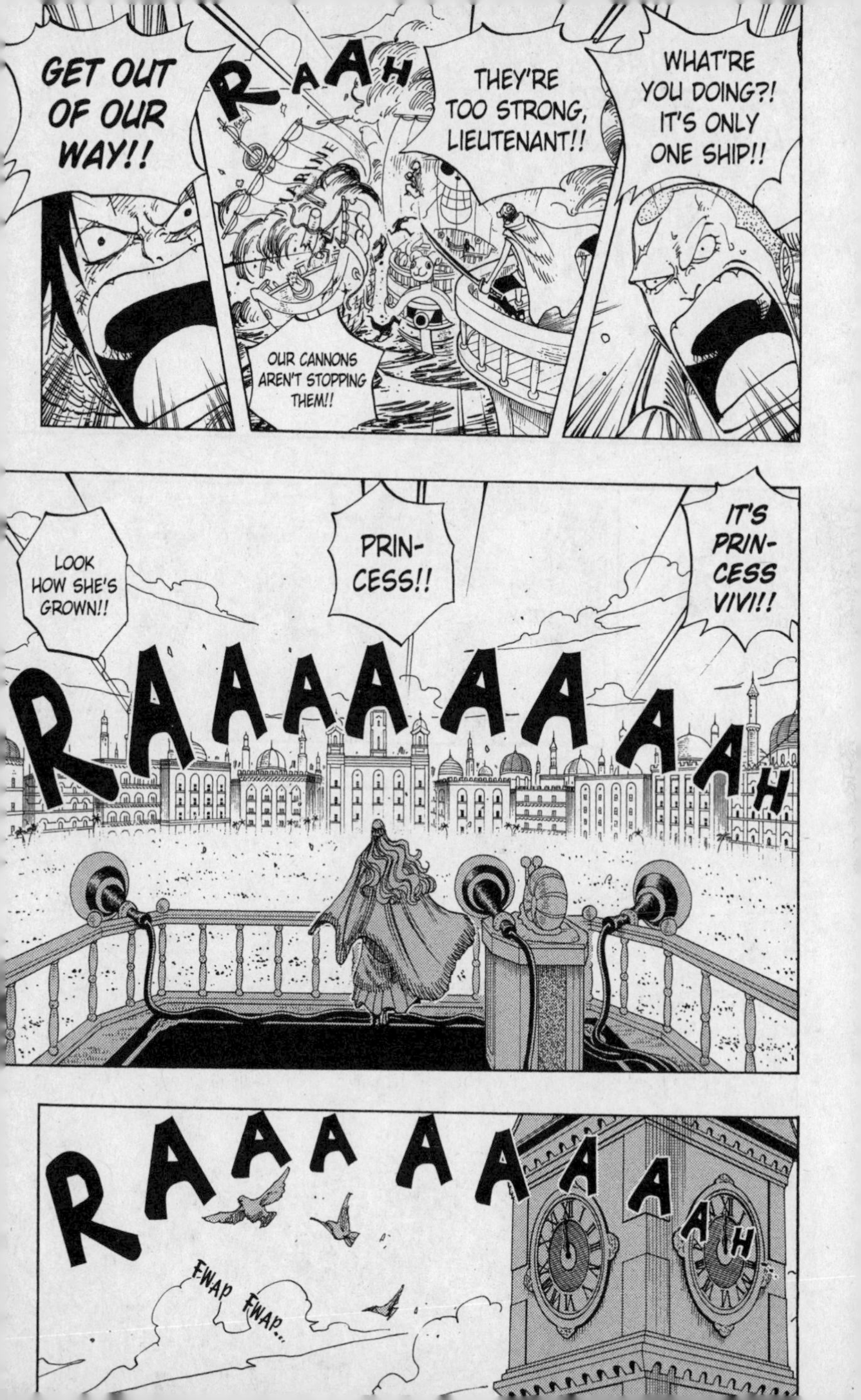
WHAT'RE YOU DOING?! IT'S ONLY ONE SHIP!!
THEY'RE TOO STRONG, LIEUTENANT!!
RAAH
OUR CANNONS AREN'T STOPPING THEM!!
GET OUT OF OUR WAY!!
IT'S PRINCESS VIVI!!
PRINCESS!!
LOOK HOW SHE'S GROWN!!
RAAAAAAAAH
RAAAAAAAAH
FWAP FWAP...

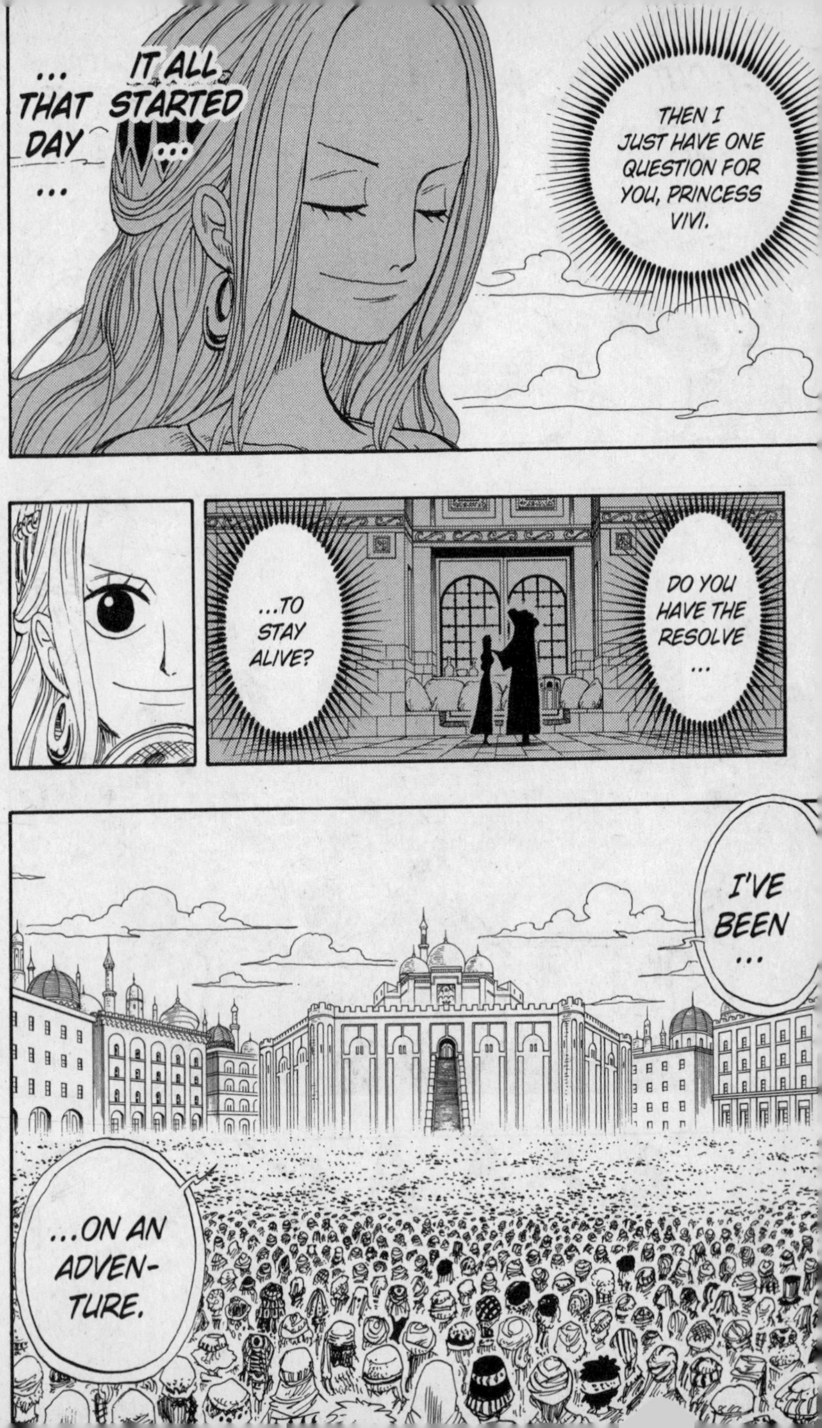
THEN I JUST HAVE ONE QUESTION FOR YOU, PRINCESS VIVI.
IT ALL STARTED...
...THAT DAY...
DO YOU HAVE THE RESOLVE...
...TO STAY ALIVE?
I'VE BEEN...
...ON AN ADVEN-TURE.

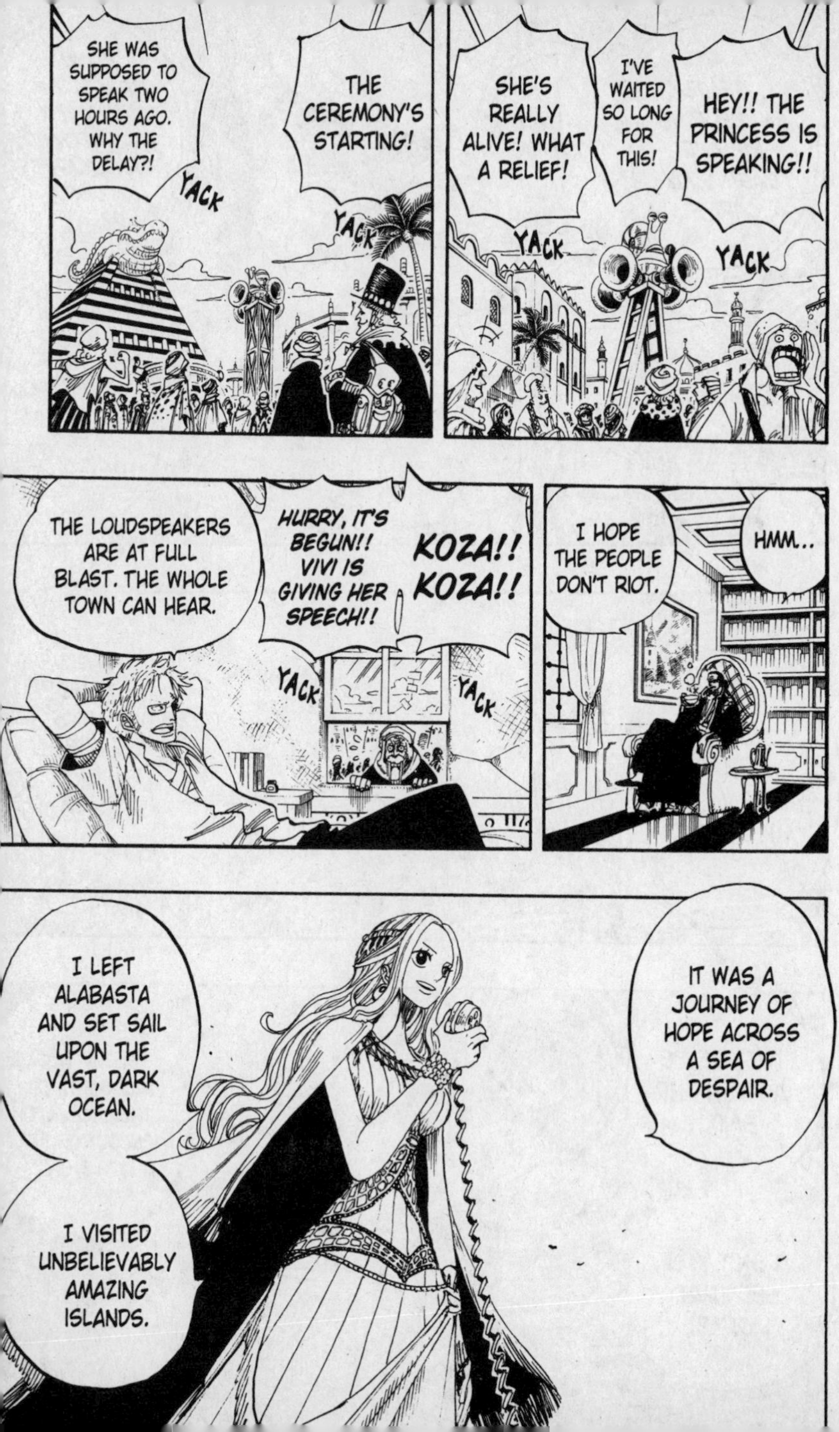
HEY!! THE PRINCESS IS SPEAKING!!
I'VE WAITED SO LONG FOR THIS!
SHE'S REALLY ALIVE! WHAT A RELIEF!
YACK
YACK
THE CEREMONY'S STARTING!
SHE WAS SUPPOSED TO SPEAK TWO HOURS AGO. WHY THE DELAY?!
YACK
YACK
HMM...
I HOPE THE PEOPLE DON'T RIOT.
KOZA!! KOZA!!
HURRY, IT'S BEGUN!! VIVI IS GIVING HER SPEECH!!
THE LOUDSPEAKERS ARE AT FULL BLAST. THE WHOLE TOWN CAN HEAR.
YACK
YACK
IT WAS A JOURNEY OF HOPE ACROSS A SEA OF DESPAIR.
I LEFT ALABASTA AND SET SAIL UPON THE VAST, DARK OCEAN.
I VISITED UNBELIEVABLY AMAZING ISLANDS.

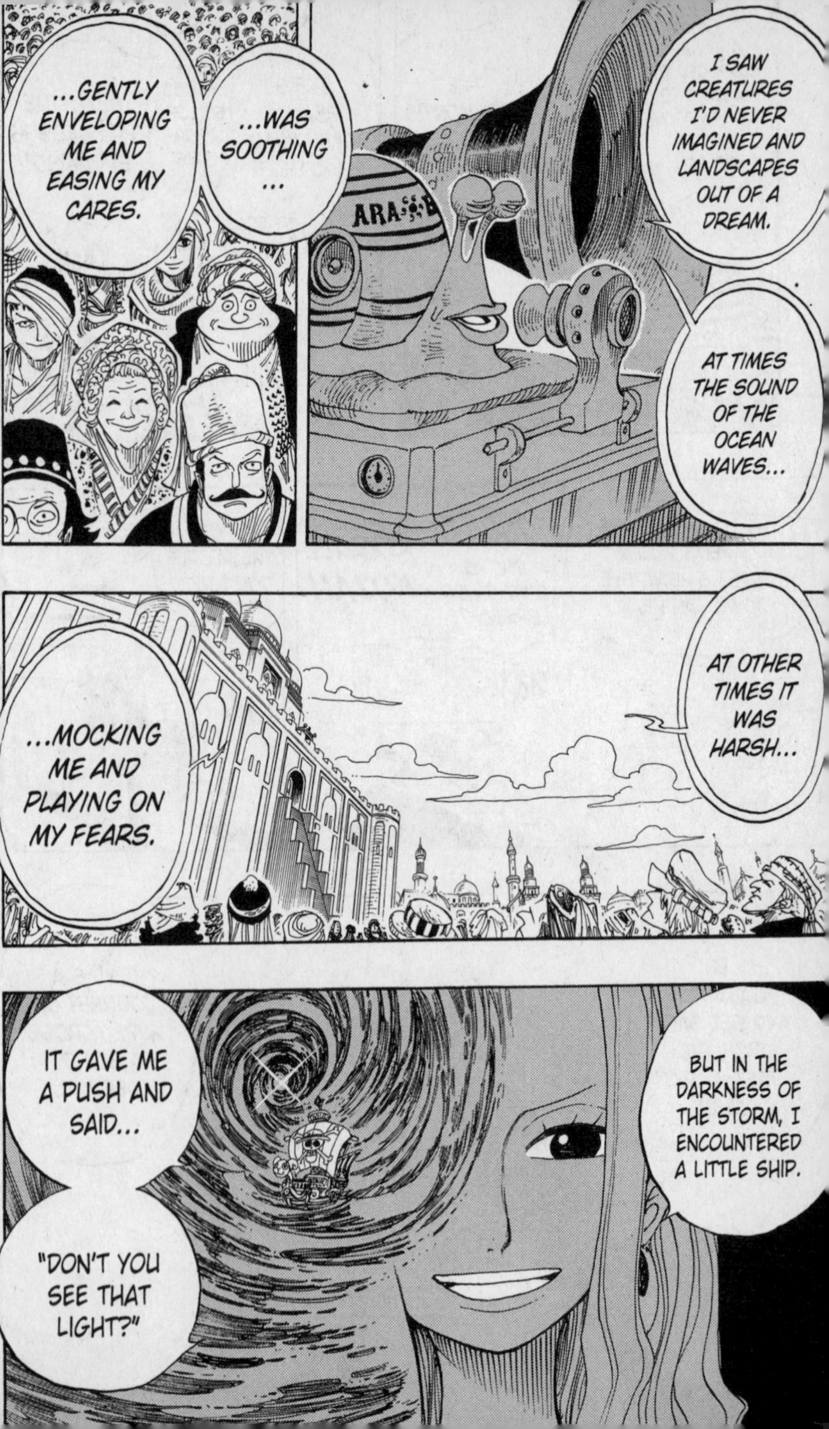
I SAW CREATURES I'D NEVER IMAGINED AND LANDSCAPES OUT OF A DREAM.
AT TIMES THE SOUND OF THE OCEAN WAVES...
...WAS SOOTHING ...
...GENTLY ENVELOPING ME AND EASING MY CARES.
AT OTHER TIMES IT WAS HARSH...
...MOCKING ME AND PLAYING ON MY FEARS.
BUT IN THE DARKNESS OF THE STORM, I ENCOUNTERED A LITTLE SHIP.
IT GAVE ME A PUSH AND SAID...
"DON'T YOU SEE THAT LIGHT?"

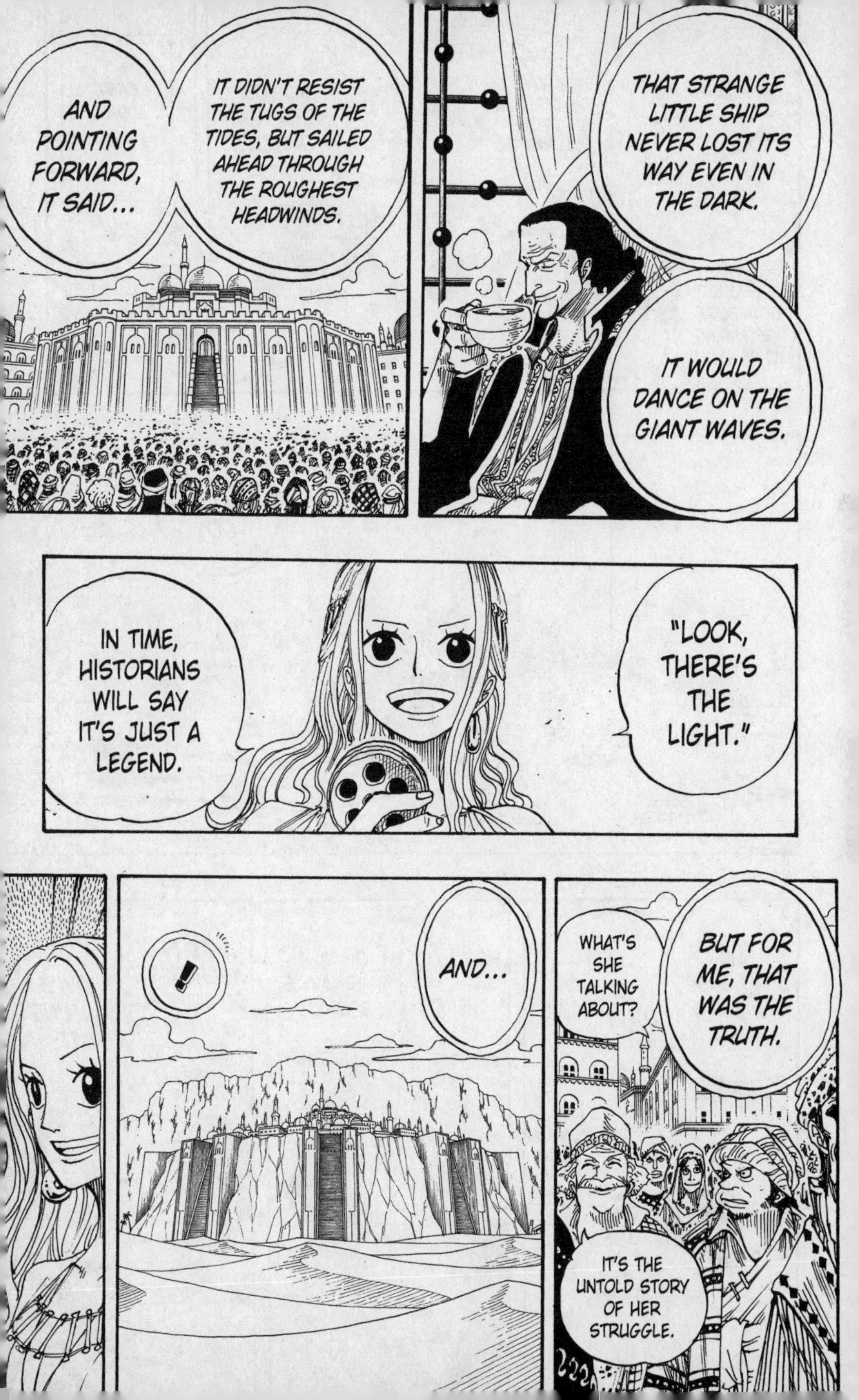
THAT STRANGE LITTLE SHIP NEVER LOST ITS WAY EVEN IN THE DARK.
IT WOULD DANCE ON THE GIANT WAVES.
IT DIDN'T RESIST THE TUGS OF THE TIDES, BUT SAILED AHEAD THROUGH THE ROUGHEST HEADWINDS.
AND POINTING FORWARD, IT SAID...
"LOOK, THERE'S THE LIGHT."
IN TIME, HISTORIANS WILL SAY IT'S JUST A LEGEND.
BUT FOR ME, THAT WAS THE TRUTH.
WHAT'S SHE TALKING ABOUT?
IT'S THE UNTOLD STORY OF HER STRUGGLE.
AND...
!

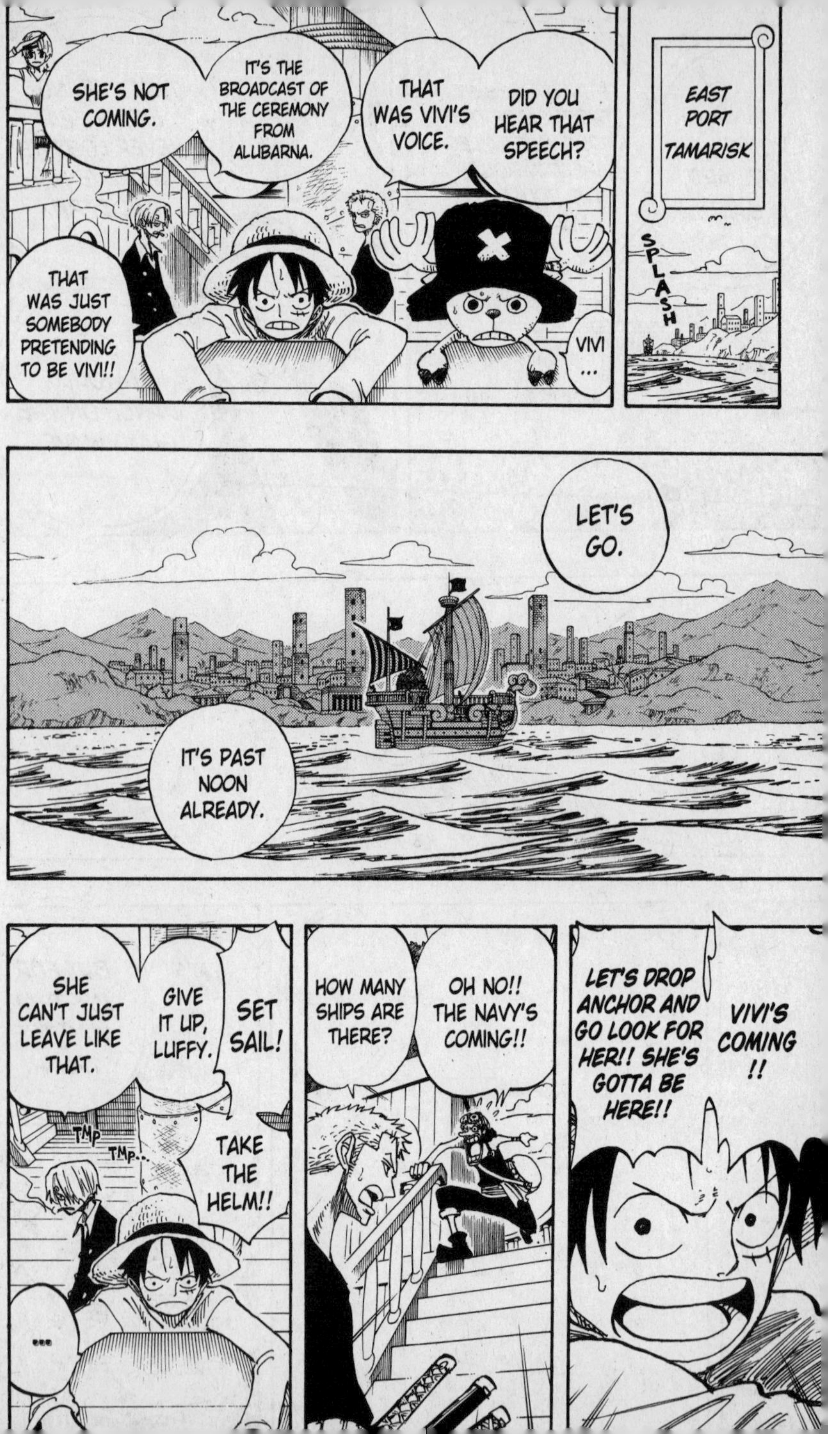
EAST PORT TAMARISK
SPLASH
DID YOU HEAR THAT SPEECH?
THAT WAS VIVI'S VOICE.
IT'S THE BROADCAST OF THE CEREMONY FROM ALUBARNA.
SHE'S NOT COMING.
VIVI ...
THAT WAS JUST SOMEBODY PRETENDING TO BE VIVI!!
LET'S GO.
IT'S PAST NOON ALREADY.
VIVI'S COMING !!
LET'S DROP ANCHOR AND GO LOOK FOR HER!! SHE'S GOTTA BE HERE!!
OH NO!! THE NAVY'S COMING!!
HOW MANY SHIPS ARE THERE?
SET SAIL!
GIVE IT UP, LUFFY.
SHE CAN'T JUST LEAVE LIKE THAT.
TAKE THE HELM!!
TMP
TMP...
...

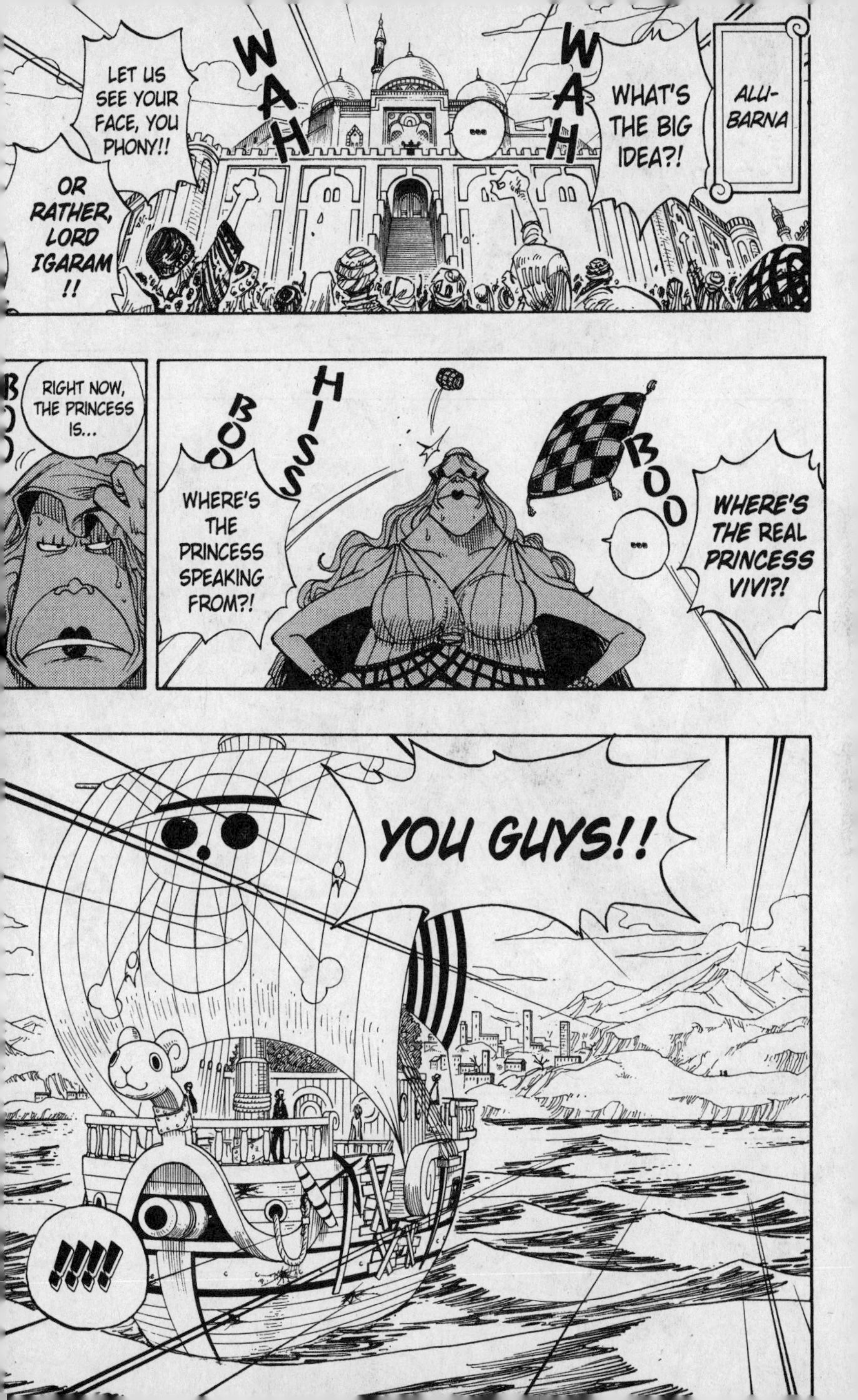
ALU-BARNA
WAH
WHAT'S THE BIG IDEA?!
...
WAH
LET US SEE YOUR FACE, YOU PHONY!!
OR RATHER, LORD IGARAM!!
WHERE'S THE REAL PRINCESS VIVI?!
BOO
...
HISS
BOO
WHERE'S THE PRINCESS SPEAKING FROM?!
RIGHT NOW, THE PRINCESS IS...
YOU GUYS!!
!!!!

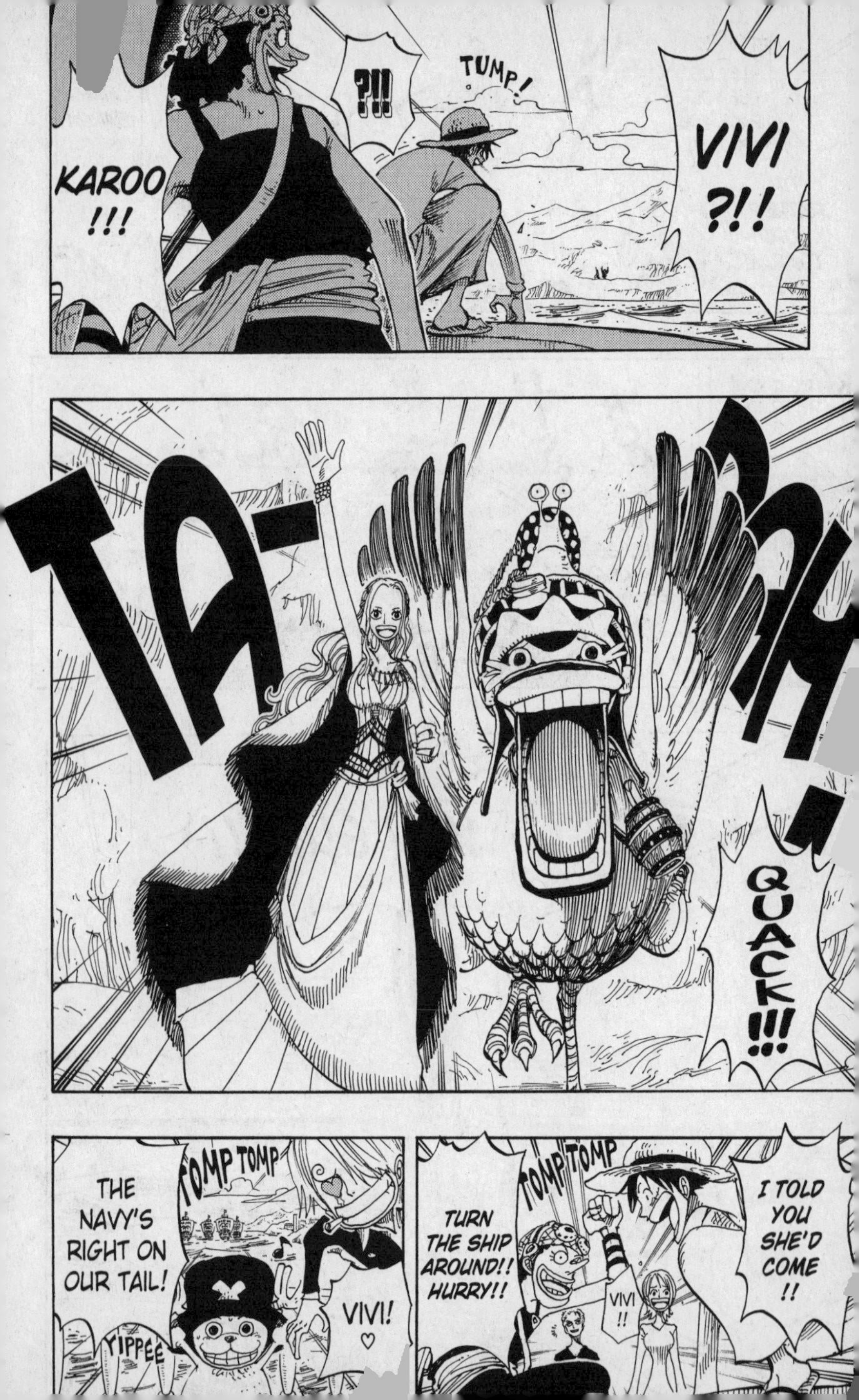
VIVI ?!!
TUMP!
?!!
KAROO !!!
TA-DAH!
QUACK!!!
I TOLD YOU SHE'D COME !!
TOMP TOMP
TURN THE SHIP AROUND!! HURRY!!
VIVI !!
TOMP TOMP
THE NAVY'S RIGHT ON OUR TAIL!
VIVI! ♥
YIPPEE

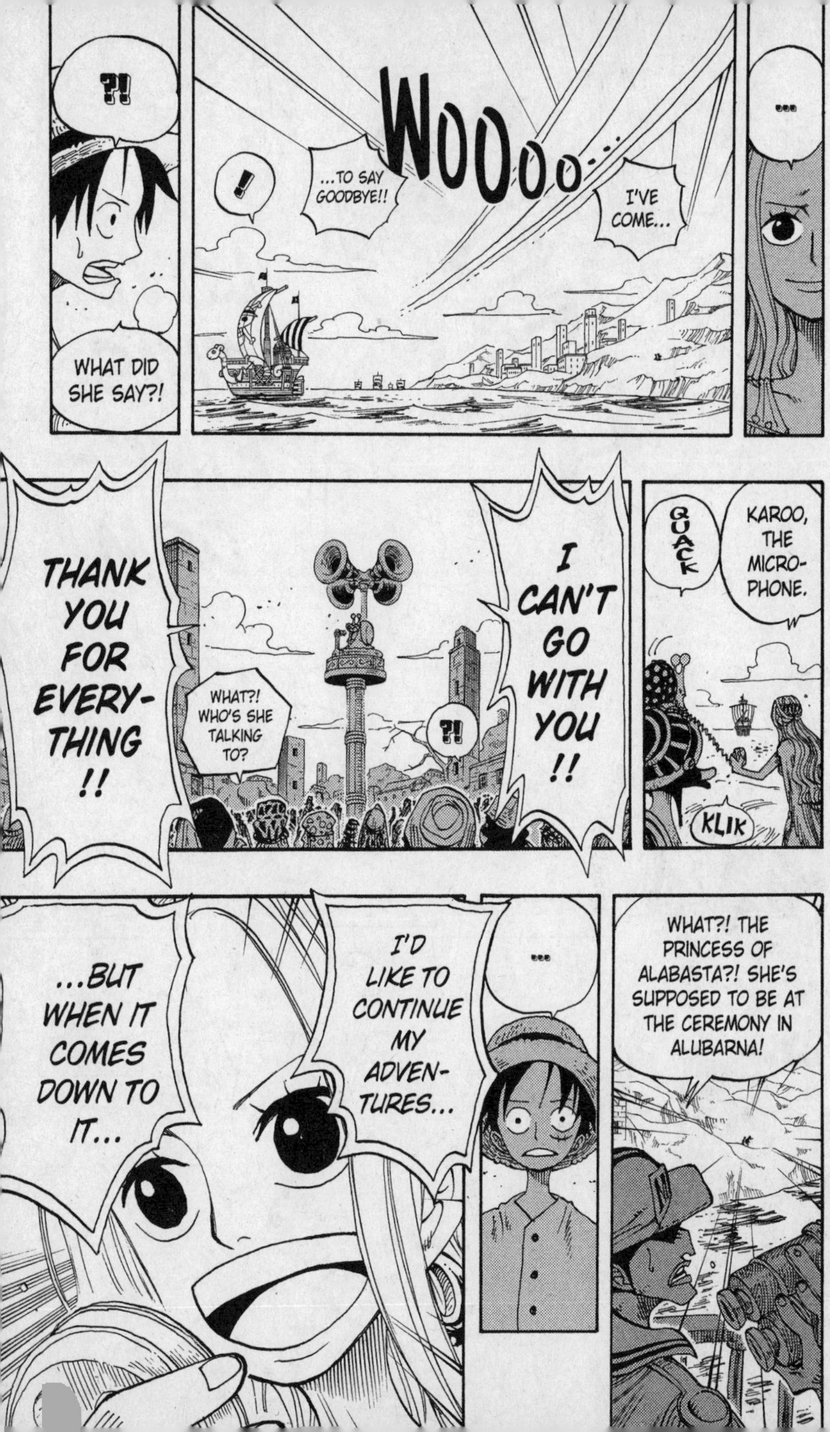
...
I'VE COME...
WOOOoo...
...TO SAY GOODBYE!!
!
?!
WHAT DID SHE SAY?!
KAROO, THE MICROPHONE.
QUACK
KLIK
I CAN'T GO WITH YOU!!
?!
WHAT?! WHO'S SHE TALKING TO?
THANK YOU FOR EVERYTHING!!
WHAT?! THE PRINCESS OF ALABASTA?! SHE'S SUPPOSED TO BE AT THE CEREMONY IN ALUBARNA!
...
I'D LIKE TO CONTINUE MY ADVENTURES...
...BUT WHEN IT COMES DOWN TO IT...

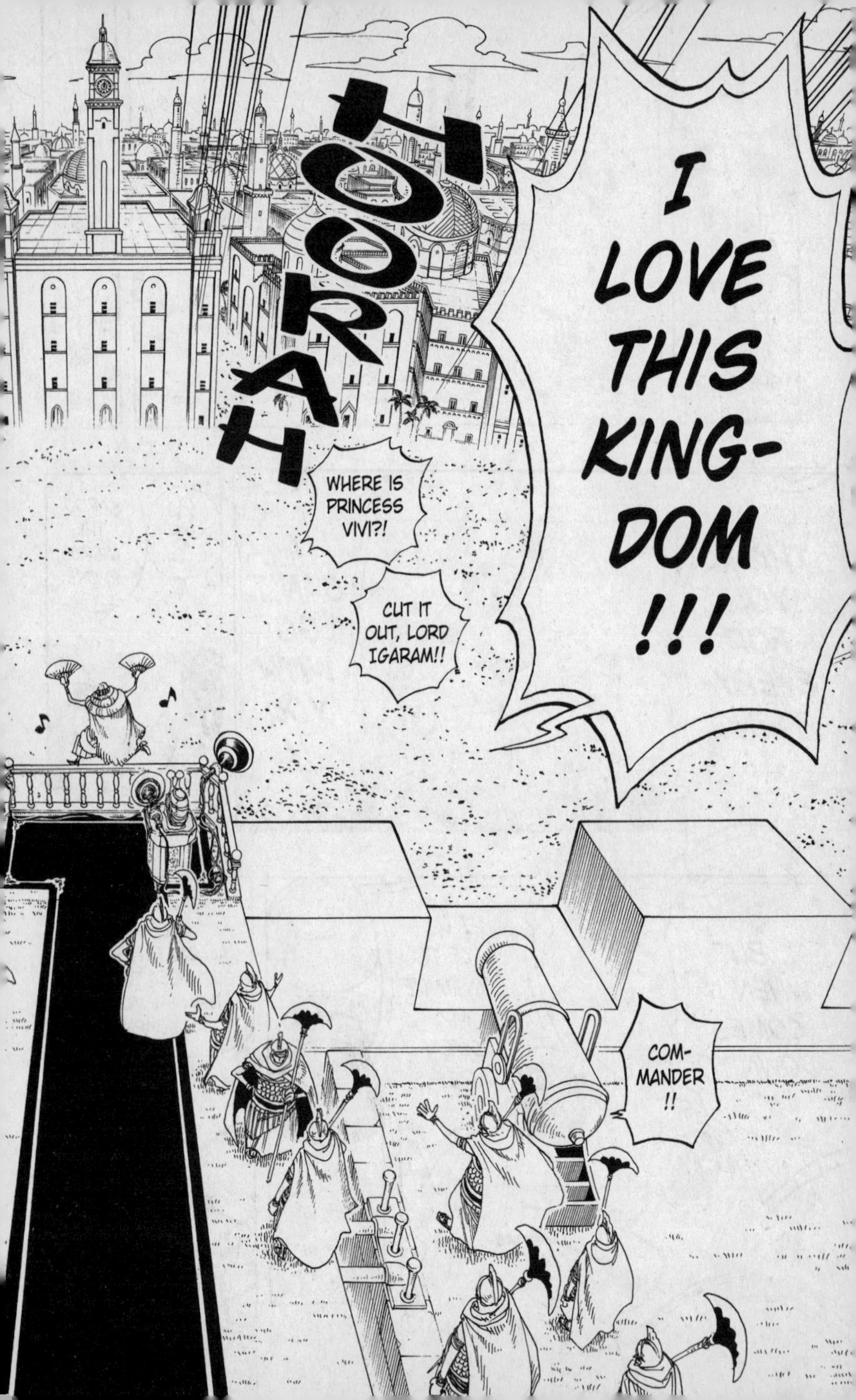
I LOVE THIS KING-DOM!!!
HOORAH
WHERE IS PRINCESS VIVI?!
CUT IT OUT, LORD IGARAM!!
COM-MANDER!!

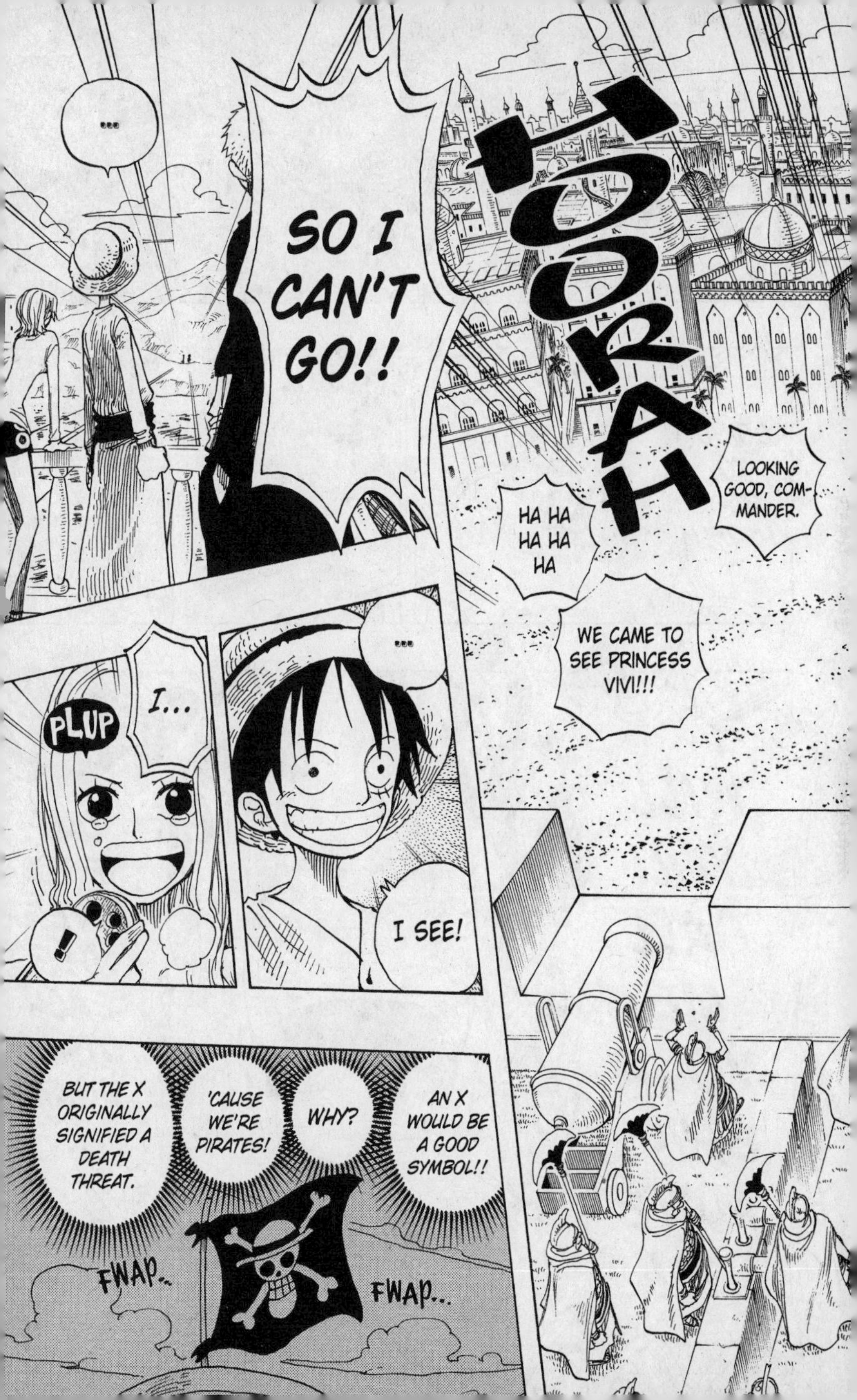
HOORAH
LOOKING GOOD, COMMANDER.
HA HA HA HA HA
WE CAME TO SEE PRINCESS VIVI!!!
...
SO I CAN'T GO!!
...
I SEE!
I...
PLUP
!
AN X WOULD BE A GOOD SYMBOL!!
WHY?
'CAUSE WE'RE PIRATES!
BUT THE X ORIGINALLY SIGNIFIED A DEATH THREAT.
FWAP...
FWAP..

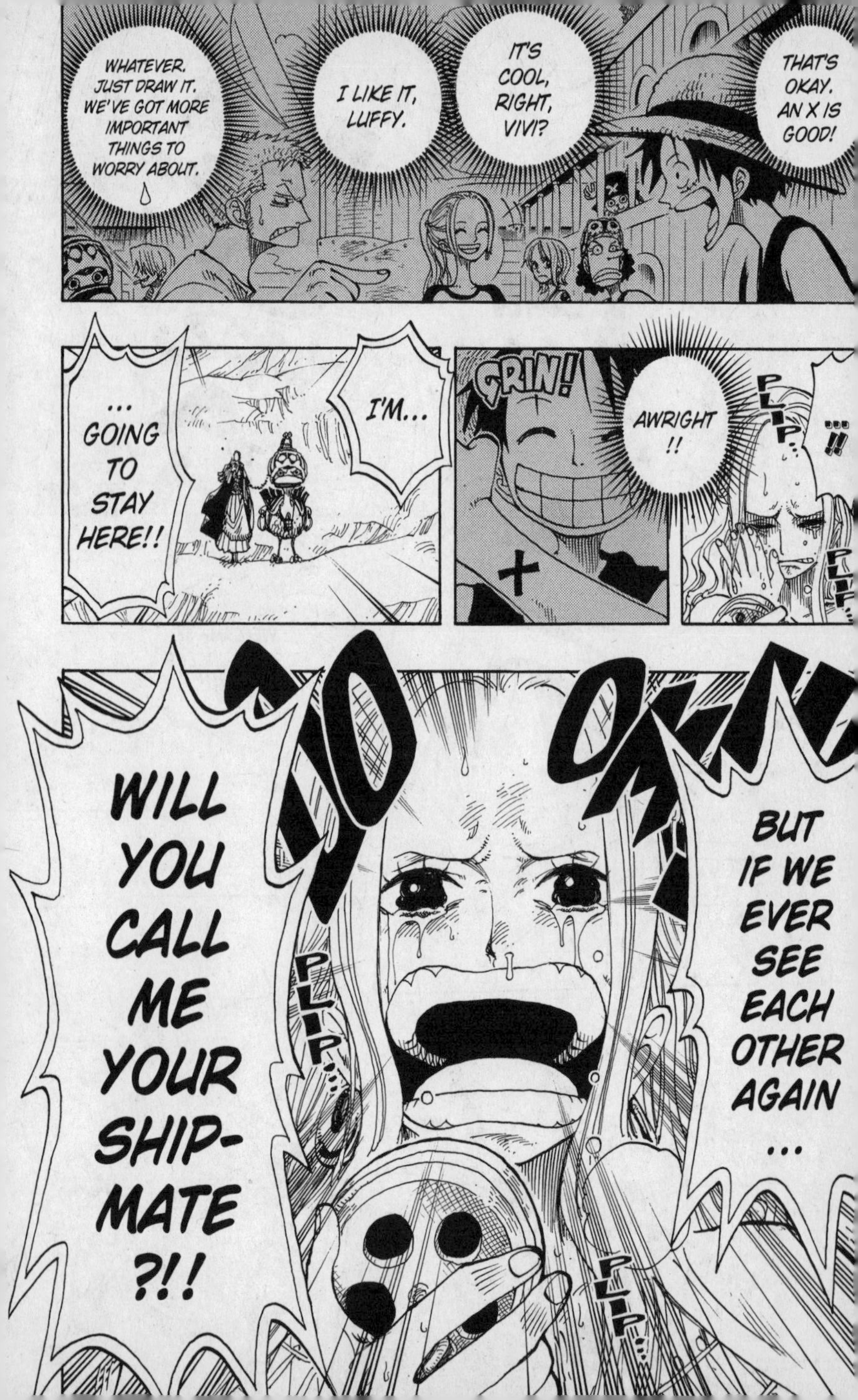

THAT'S OKAY. AN X IS GOOD!
IT'S COOL, RIGHT, VIVI?
I LIKE IT, LUFFY.
WHATEVER. JUST DRAW IT. WE'VE GOT MORE IMPORTANT THINGS TO WORRY ABOUT.
PLIP...
...!!
PLIP...
GRIN!
AWRIGHT!!
I'M...
...GOING TO STAY HERE!!
BUT IF WE EVER SEE EACH OTHER AGAIN...
WILL YOU CALL ME YOUR SHIP-MATE?!!
PLIP...
PLIP...

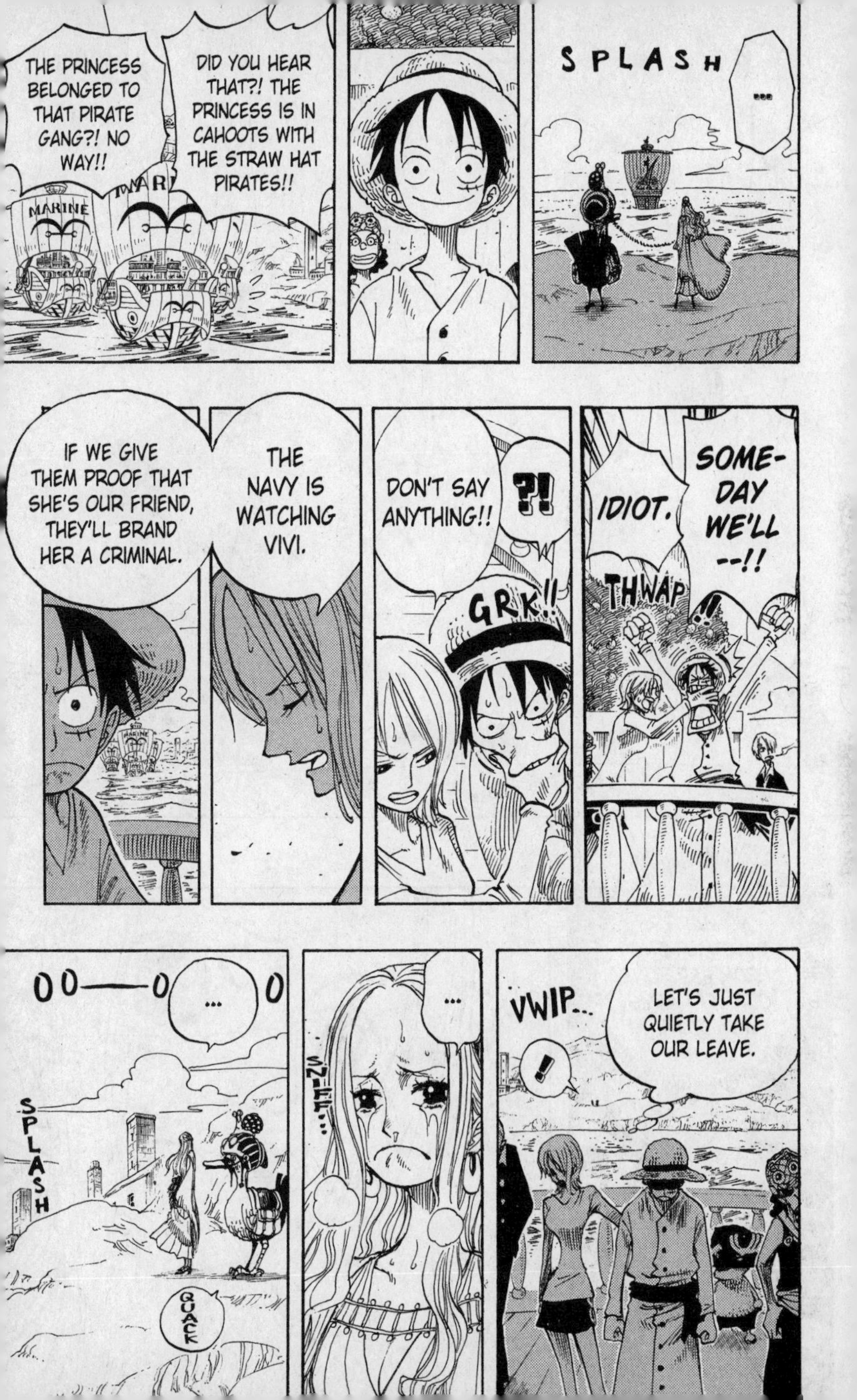
SPLASH
...
DID YOU HEAR THAT?! THE PRINCESS IS IN CAHOOTS WITH THE STRAW HAT PIRATES!!
THE PRINCESS BELONGED TO THAT PIRATE GANG?! NO WAY!!
MARINE
SOME-DAY WE'LL --!!
IDIOT.
THWAP
!
?!
DON'T SAY ANYTHING!!
GRK!!
THE NAVY IS WATCHING VIVI.
IF WE GIVE THEM PROOF THAT SHE'S OUR FRIEND, THEY'LL BRAND HER A CRIMINAL.
LET'S JUST QUIETLY TAKE OUR LEAVE.
VWIP...
!
...
SNIFF...
OO——O
...
O
SPLASH
QUACK

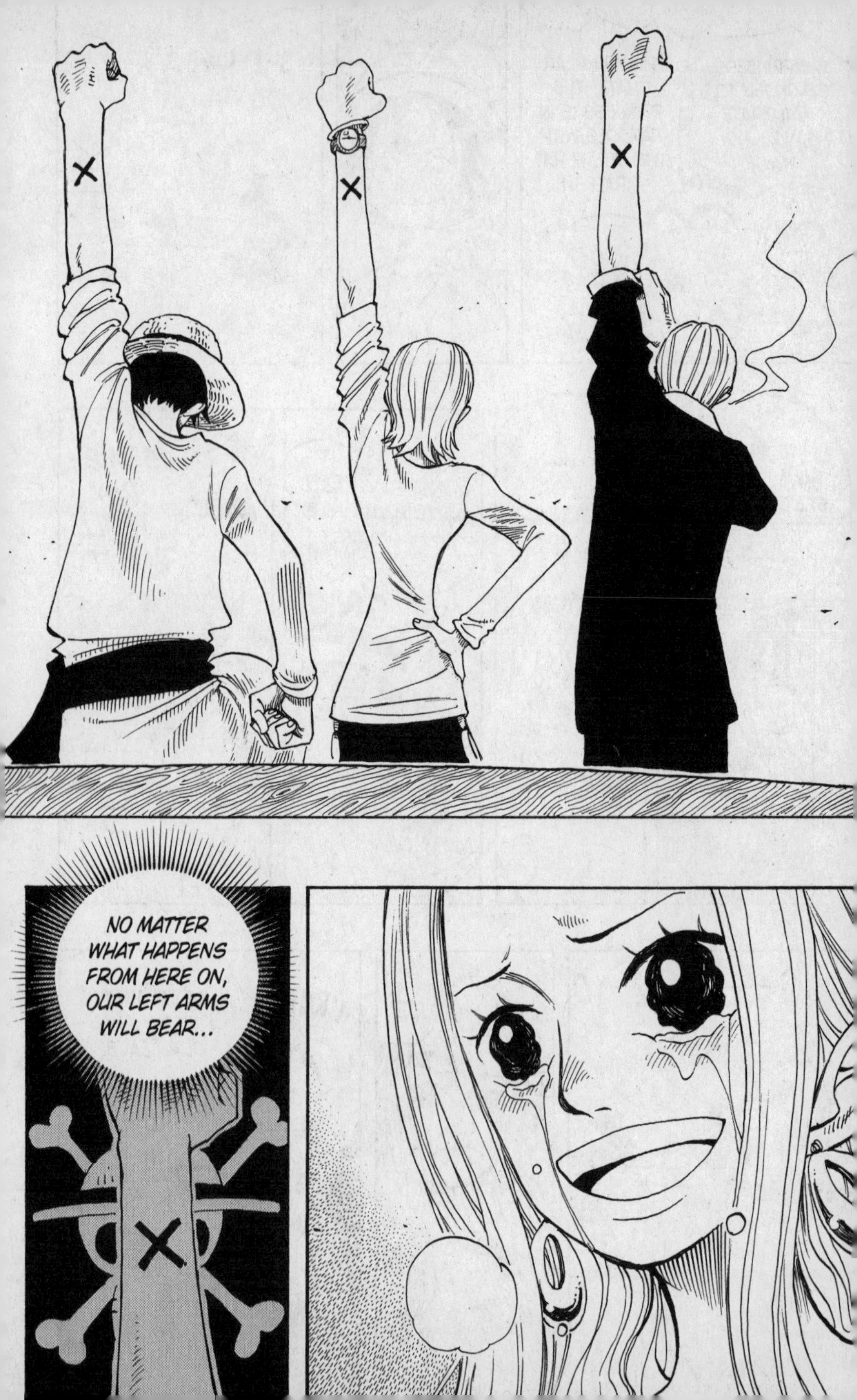
NO MATTER WHAT HAPPENS FROM HERE ON, OUR LEFT ARMS WILL BEAR...

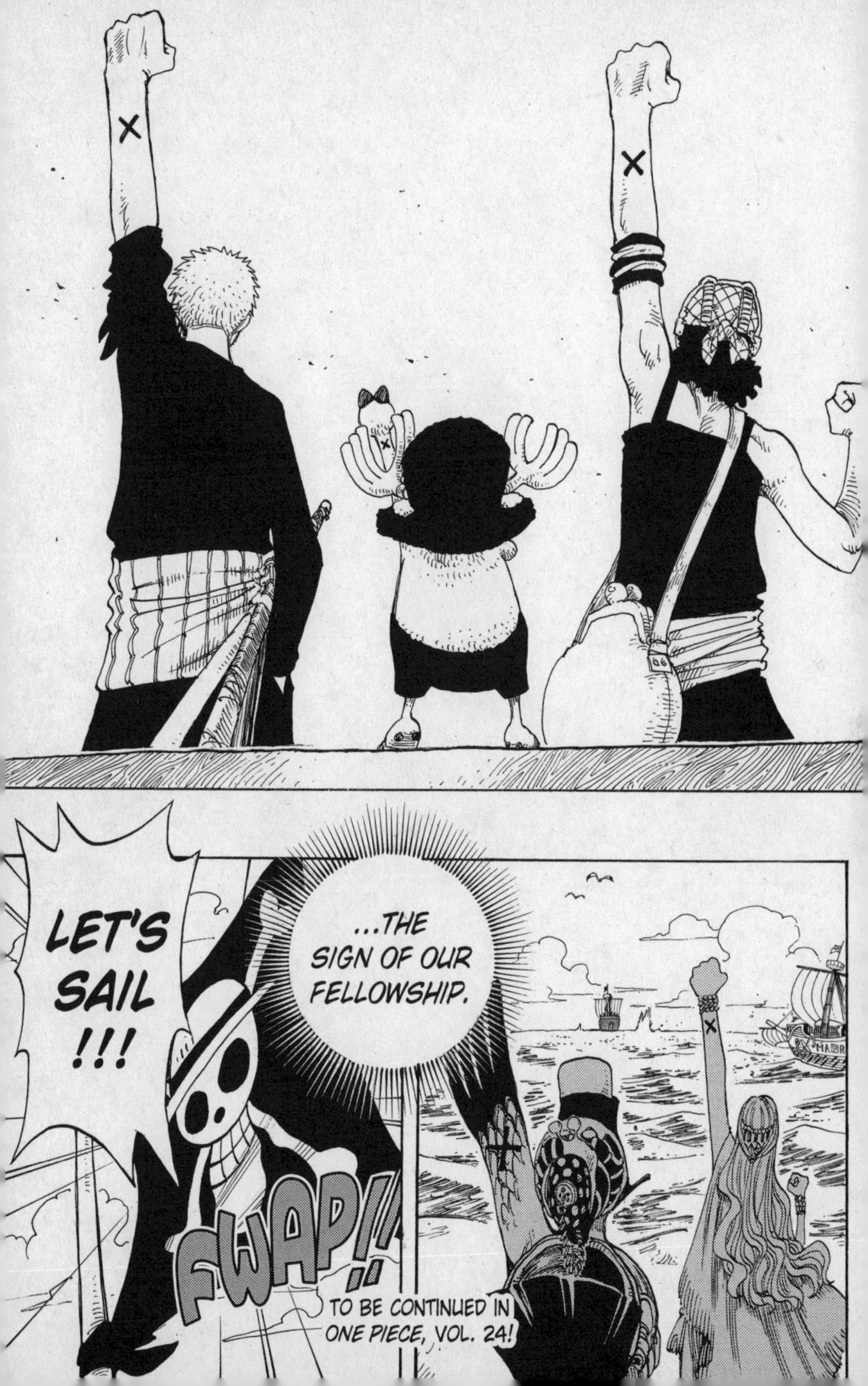
...THE SIGN OF OUR FELLOWSHIP.
LET'S SAIL!!!
FWAP!!
MARINE
TO BE CONTINUED IN ONE PIECE, VOL. 24!

A SIVE IN   Noua
OVA. Ao 1492. a Christophoro   Fran
nomine regis Castella primum detecta.   cia.

Chilaga

ac
Ceuola   Clandia
Marata   Calicuas   Tagil.   Florida.   Michano   La
Marata   Corito   La Emperulada
Quire   Cacos
Chi   Cuchillo   Tama   B. de   Lucino   Limua
culiad

Polisko   Mechula   Hispania   Panu   Caia
Thomas   Siguald   Noua   Borqui
Triada   R. de   R. grande   Sancta
cuchibula   de los an   Noua   Trugillo
gelos   Speci   Grana   Sancta
misco   ica

Yle de los galopegos   Panu   Caribana
Quito   Negua

TIALES

Tum   Azuani   Aquiri   Chi
bes   tama
Coran
qua
Casraa   Trapicari   Asapa

AR DEL ZVR   Lima   Peru   Amaze
Insule   Archipelago Morauon
incognita   Custo   Chichan

Colochi

VS CAPRICORNI   Guana   Nepe
maras   merida
Cabo de   Ningatals
la Isla
C. Rasso   Arboli   S.E.spi
das
EL MAR   Cabo.   Jas Farillones
PACIFICO.   blanco   Saragan   Chic

R. de
Palomin

Archipelago
de las islas.
Calis

When I visited my family recently, my parents expressed
an opinion about *ONE PIECE* for the very first time.
"That story about the deer was really good."
...Deer?

– *Eiichiro Oda, 2002*

CA SIVE IN
NOVA. Ao 1492. a Chryſtophoro
nomine regis Caſtellæ primum detecta.

Noua
Fran
cia.

Chilaga

Canagadi

ac
Ceuola
Marata
Calicuas
Tagil
Flori
da.

Quiui
ra
Cacos
Comos
Coru
co

Chi
tuale
Cuchillo
Culiaſ
Tana
B. de
culiata.

Calisko
Tula
Mechula
Ciguada
Pamu
co
Xaques

Thomas
biada
R. de
cuiuiula
Punte
de los an
gelos
Soco
misco
Hispania
Noua
Gua
Trugillo

Aguſtin
Grana
da

CTIALIS
Y de los galopegos

Caribana

Tun
bes
Atuari

Coraſ
gua
Maja

Caſira
Paſſa
Trapucan

AR DEL ZVR.
Inſulæ
incognitæ
Pe ru.
Amazo

Cuſco

Colochi

VS CAPRICORNI
Cabo de
Tayla
C. Raſſo
Arboli
das

Ningatas

EL MAR
PACIFICO.
Cabo
blanco
Las Barillones
Chic

R. de
Palomini

Archipelago
de las islas.

Calts

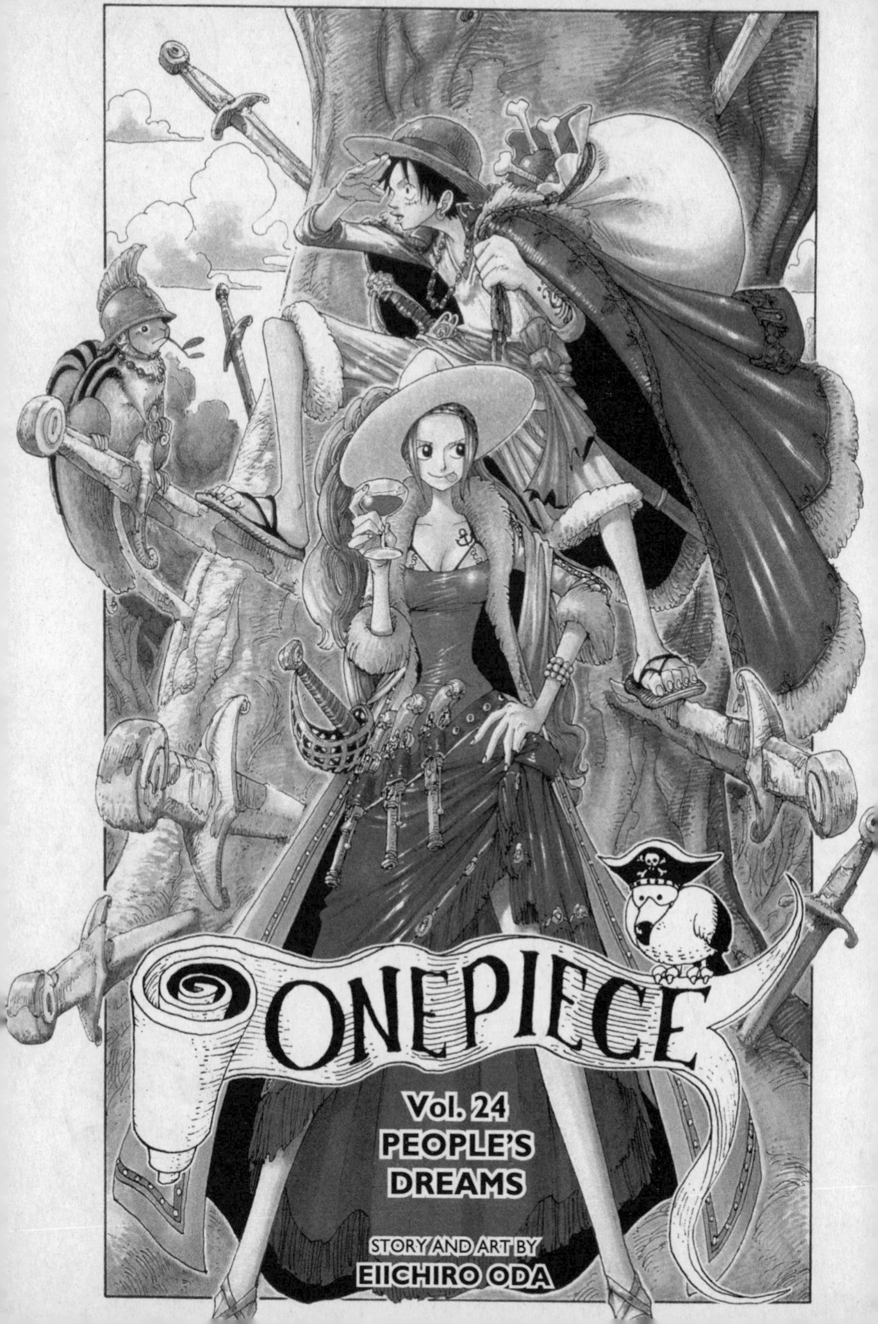
ONE PIECE
Vol. 24
PEOPLE'S DREAMS
STORY AND ART BY
EIICHIRO ODA

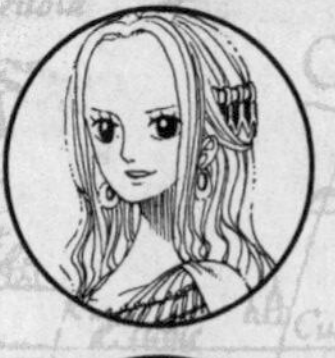

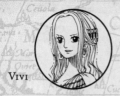

Vivi

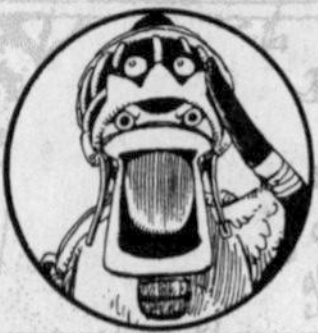

Karoo

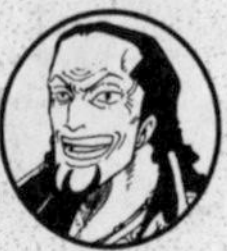

Nefeltari Cobra (King of Alabasta)

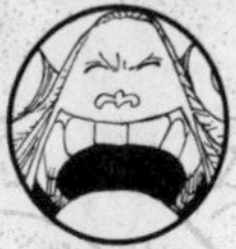

Igaram

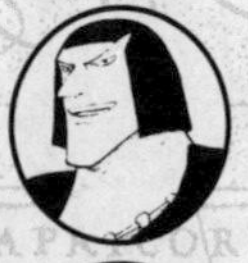

Chaka

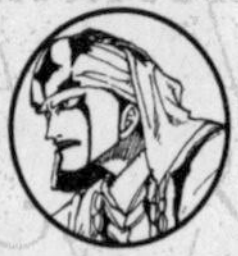

Pell

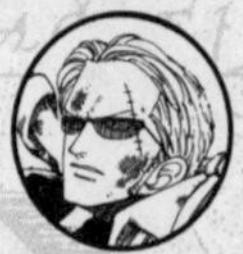

Koza

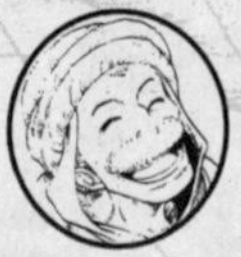

Toh-Toh

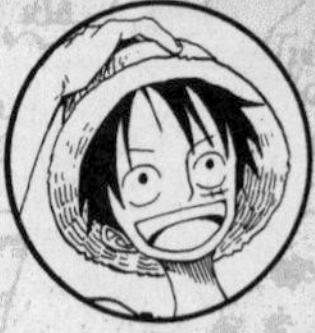

Boundlessly optimistic and able to stretch like rubber, he is determined to become King of the Pirates.

Monkey D. Luffy

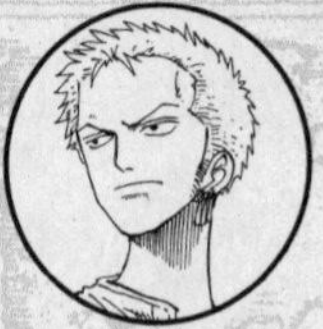

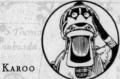

A former bounty hunter and master of the "three-sword" style. He aspires to be the world's greatest swordsman.

Roronoa Zolo

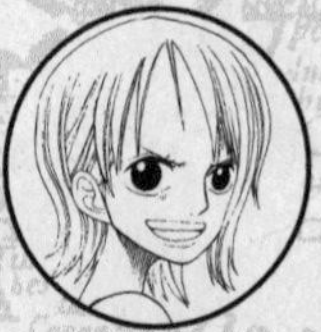

A thief who specializes in robbing pirates. Nami hates pirates, but Luffy convinced her to be his navigator.

Nami

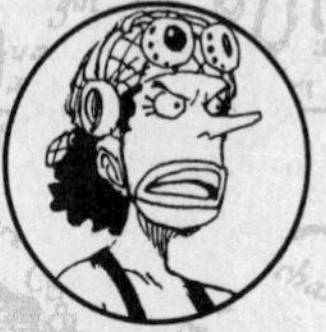

A village boy with a talent for telling tall tales. His father, Yasopp, is a member of Shanks's crew.

Usopp

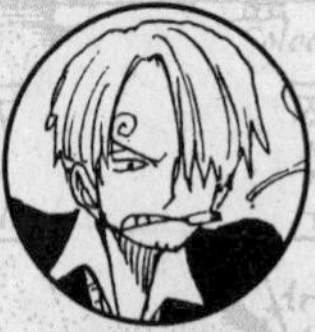

The kindhearted cook (and ladies' man) whose dream is to find the legendary sea, the "All Blue."

Sanji

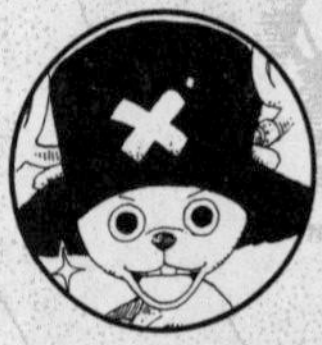

A blue-nosed man-reindeer and the ship's doctor.

Tony Tony Chopper

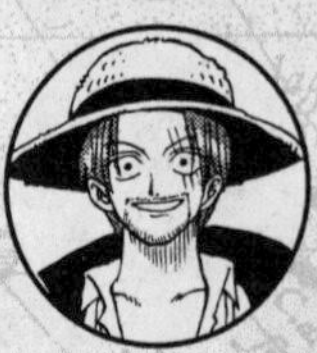

A pirate that Luffy idolizes. Shanks gave Luffy his trademark straw hat.

"Red-Haired" Shanks

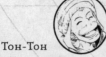

THE STORY OF ONE PIECE • VOLUME 24 •

Monkey D. Luffy started out as just a kid with a dream—to become the greatest pirate in history! Stirred by the tales of pirate "Red-Haired" Shanks, Luffy vowed to become a pirate himself. That was before the enchanted Devil Fruit gave Luffy the power to stretch like rubber, at the cost of being unable to swim—a serious handicap for an aspiring sea dog. Undeterred, Luffy set out to sea and recruited some crewmates: master swordsman Zolo, treasure-hunting thief Nami, lying sharpshooter Usopp, the high-kicking chef Sanji, and the latest addition, Chopper—the walkin' talkin' reindeer doctor.

Luffy and crew fight to help Princess Vivi save her war-torn and drought-ravaged kingdom from the evil Sir Crocodile and his secret criminal organization, the Baroque Works. But Crocodile's true objective was to get his hands on the most destructive weapon of the ancient world, the Pluton! With such a weapon, world domination would be his! After numerous hair-raising battles, Crocodile and Baroque Works are defeated and the kingdom is saved. The people rejoice and Luffy and the others recover from their wounds. But there is little time to rest as the Navy is hot on their trail! So Luffy and crew bid farewell to Vivi and set sail once more. Their hearts are heavy, but they all find solace in the friendship that remains forever in their hearts.

NAVY

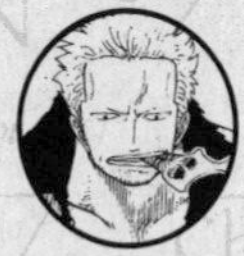

CAPTAIN SMOKER

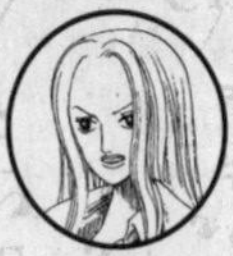

HINA

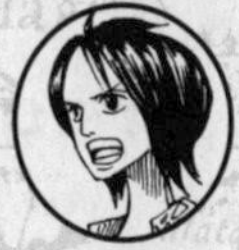

TASHIGI

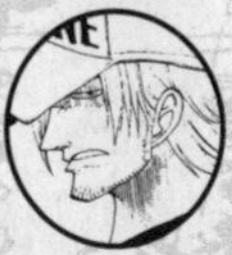
NE

FULLBODY

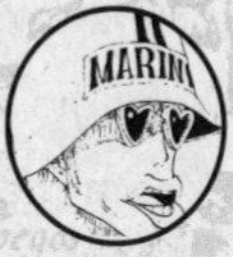
MARIN

DJANGO

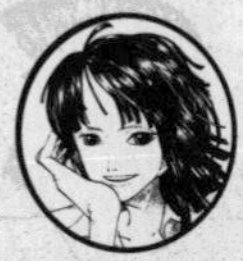

NICO ROBIN

Vol. 24
People's Dreams

CONTENTS

Chapter 217:
STOWAWAY

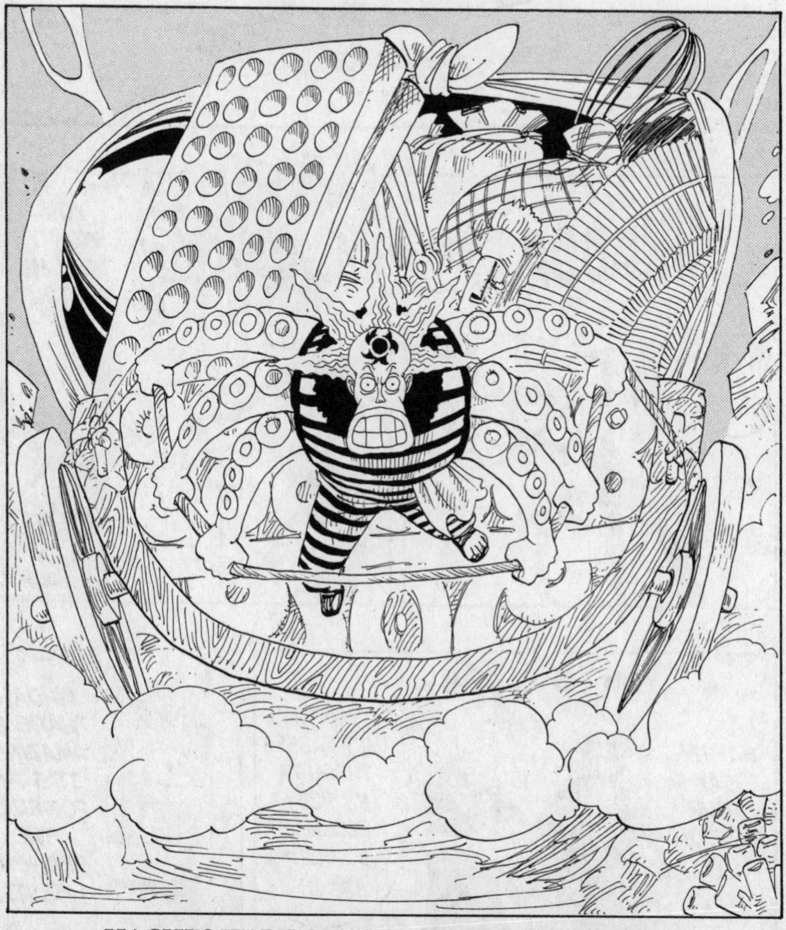

HACHI'S WALK ON THE SEAFLOOR, VOL. 31:
"SAVE THE CATFISH VILLAGE!! EXCHANGE THE TREASURE FOR COOKING EQUIPMENT"

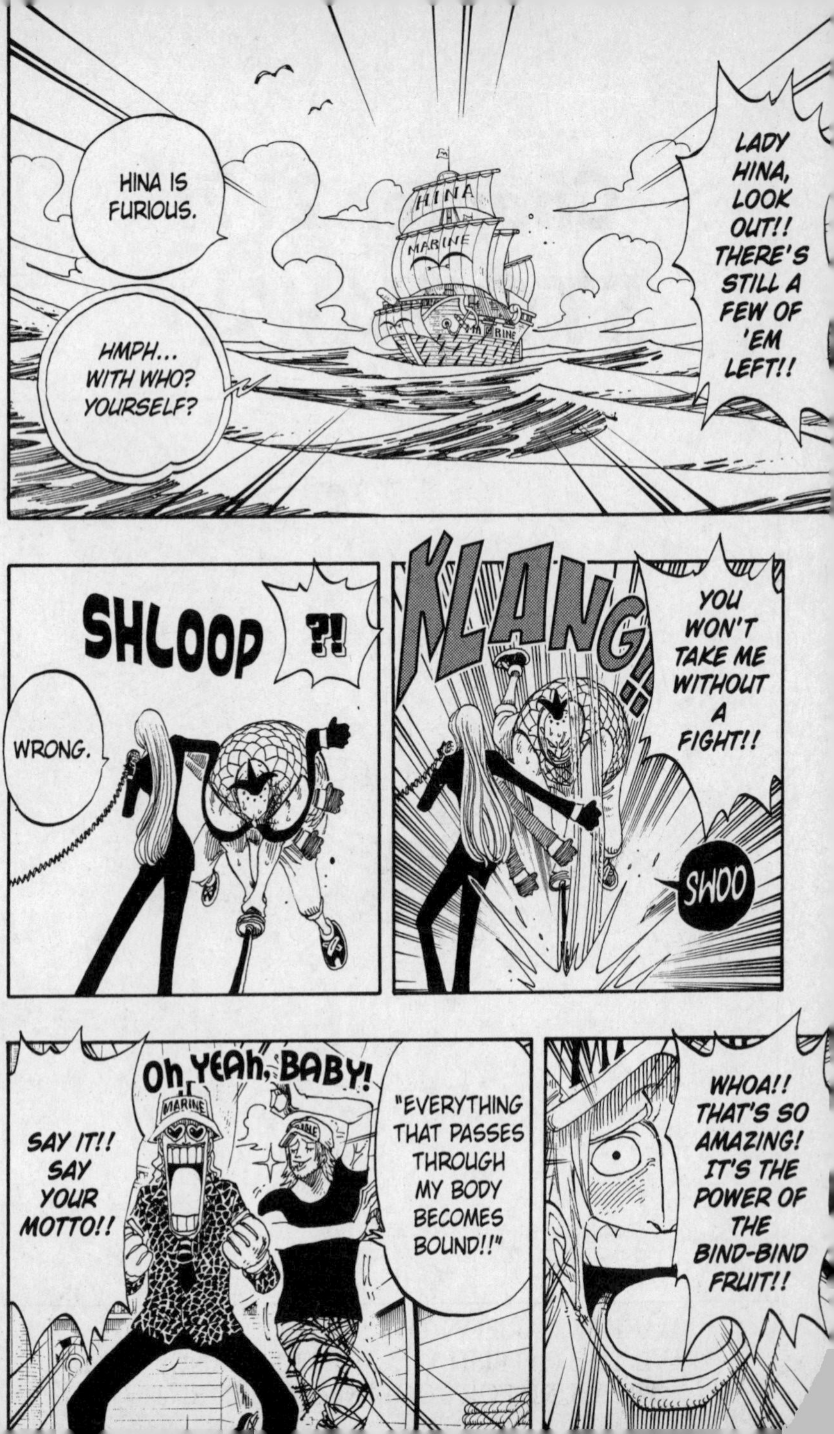
LADY HINA, LOOK OUT!! THERE'S STILL A FEW OF 'EM LEFT!!
HINA
MARINE
HINA IS FURIOUS.
HMPH... WITH WHO? YOURSELF?
KLANG!!
YOU WON'T TAKE ME WITHOUT A FIGHT!!
SWOO
?!
SHLOOP
WRONG.
WHOA!! THAT'S SO AMAZING! IT'S THE POWER OF THE BIND-BIND FRUIT!!
"EVERYTHING THAT PASSES THROUGH MY BODY BECOMES BOUND!!"
Oh YEAh, BABY!
MARINE
SAY IT!! SAY YOUR MOTTO!!

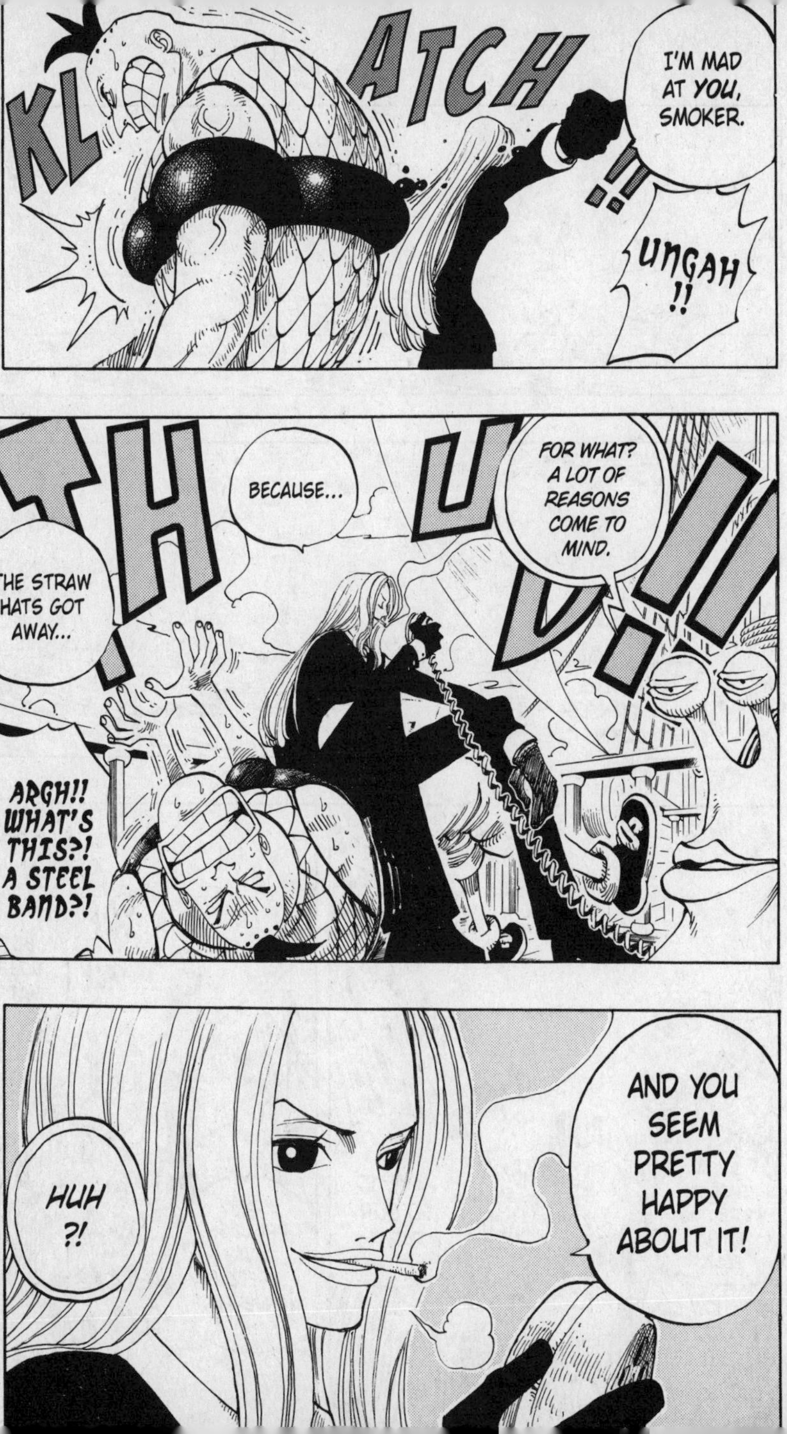
I'M MAD AT YOU, SMOKER.
KLATCH!!
UNGAH !!
FOR WHAT? A LOT OF REASONS COME TO MIND.
THUD!!
BECAUSE...
THE STRAW HATS GOT AWAY...
ARGH!! WHAT'S THIS?! A STEEL BAND?!
AND YOU SEEM PRETTY HAPPY ABOUT IT!
HUH ?!

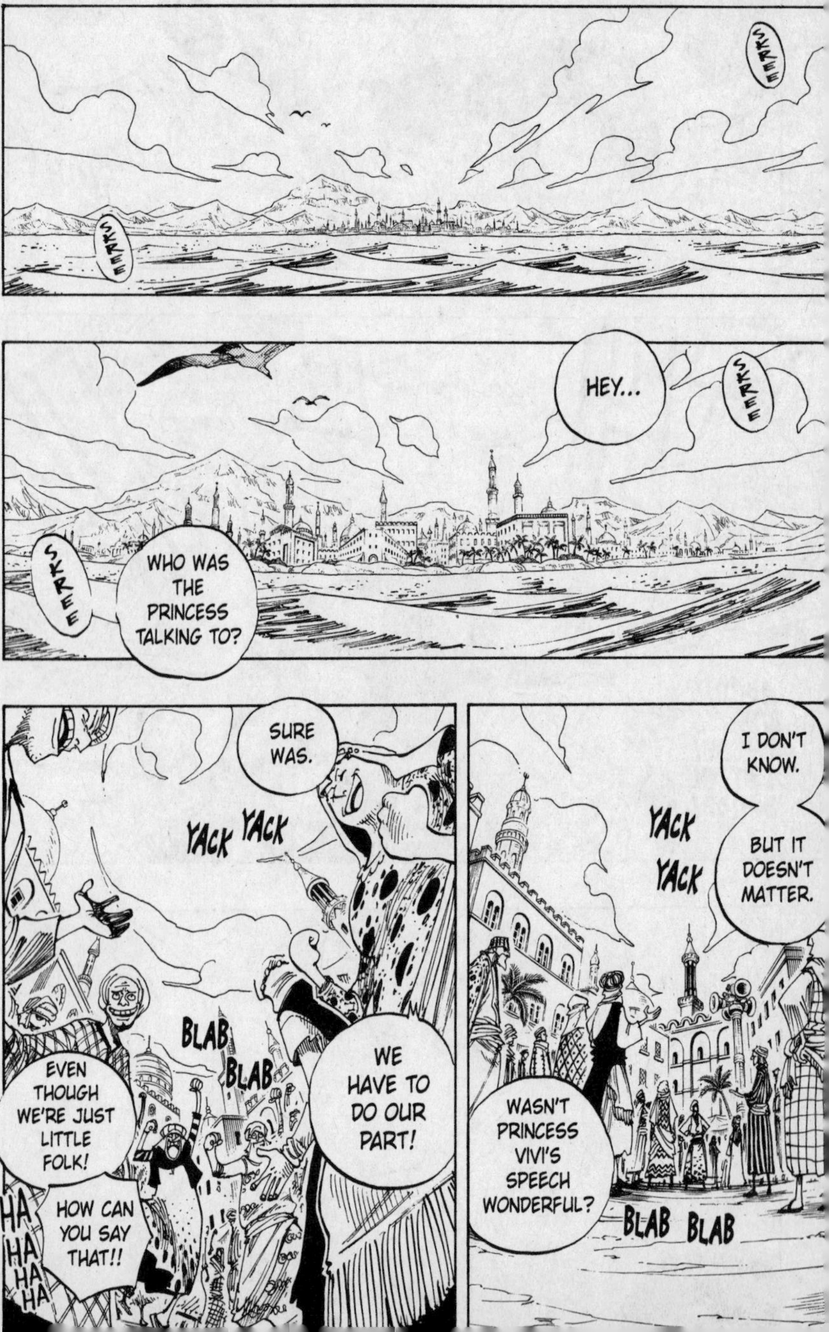
SKREE
SKREE
SKREE
HEY...
SKREE
WHO WAS THE PRINCESS TALKING TO?
I DON'T KNOW.
BUT IT DOESN'T MATTER.
YACK YACK
WASN'T PRINCESS VIVI'S SPEECH WONDERFUL?
BLAB BLAB
SURE WAS.
YACK YACK
BLAB BLAB
WE HAVE TO DO OUR PART!
EVEN THOUGH WE'RE JUST LITTLE FOLK!
HOW CAN YOU SAY THAT!!
HA HA HA HA

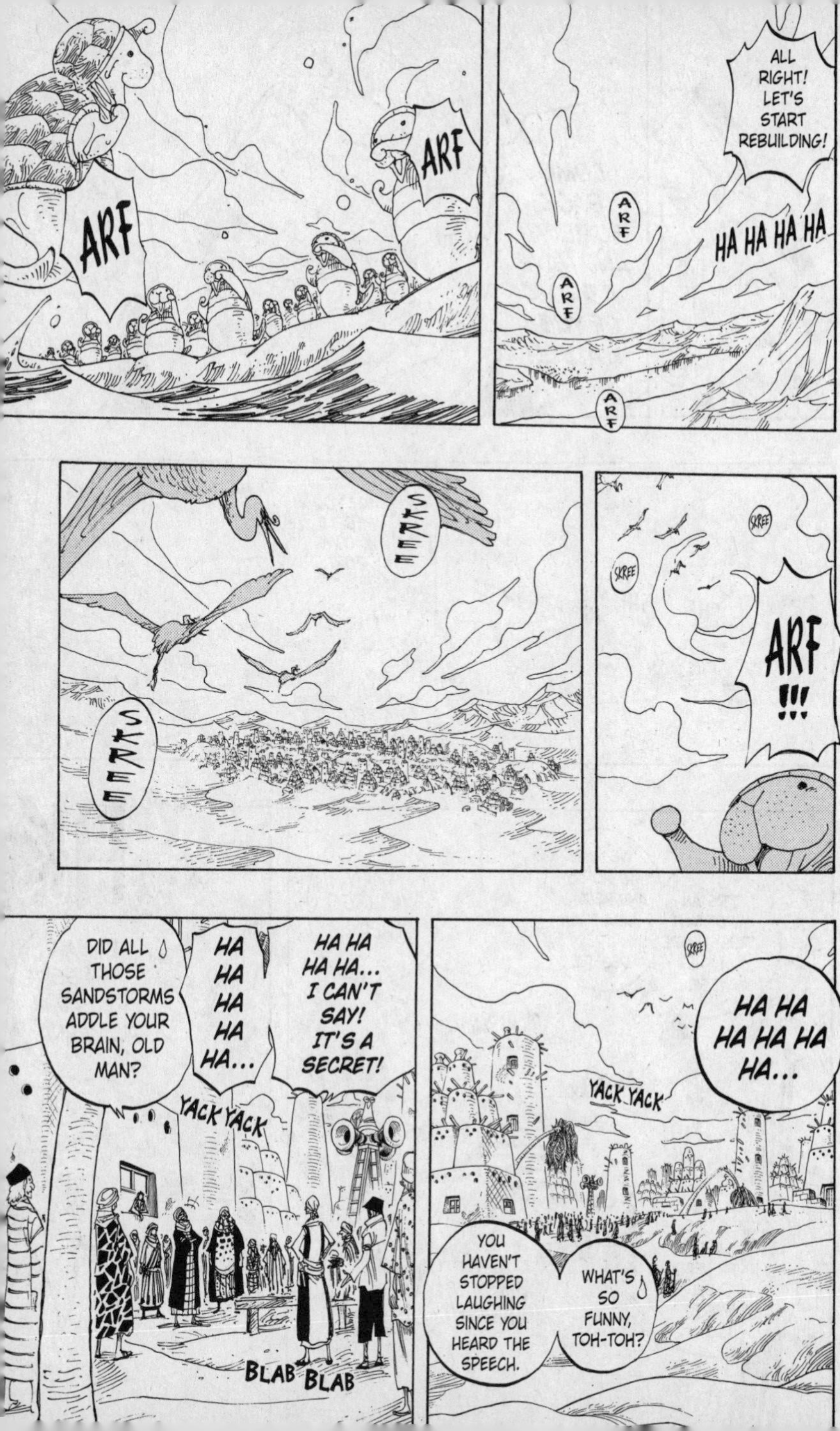
ALL RIGHT! LET'S START REBUILDING!
ARF
HA HA HA HA
ARF
ARF
ARF
ARF
SKREE
SKREE
ARF!!!
SKREE
SKREE
SKREE
HA HA HA HA HA HA...
YACK YACK
WHAT'S SO FUNNY, TOH-TOH?
YOU HAVEN'T STOPPED LAUGHING SINCE YOU HEARD THE SPEECH.
HA HA HA HA... I CAN'T SAY! IT'S A SECRET!
HA HA HA HA HA...
DID ALL THOSE SANDSTORMS ADDLE YOUR BRAIN, OLD MAN?
YACK YACK
BLAB BLAB

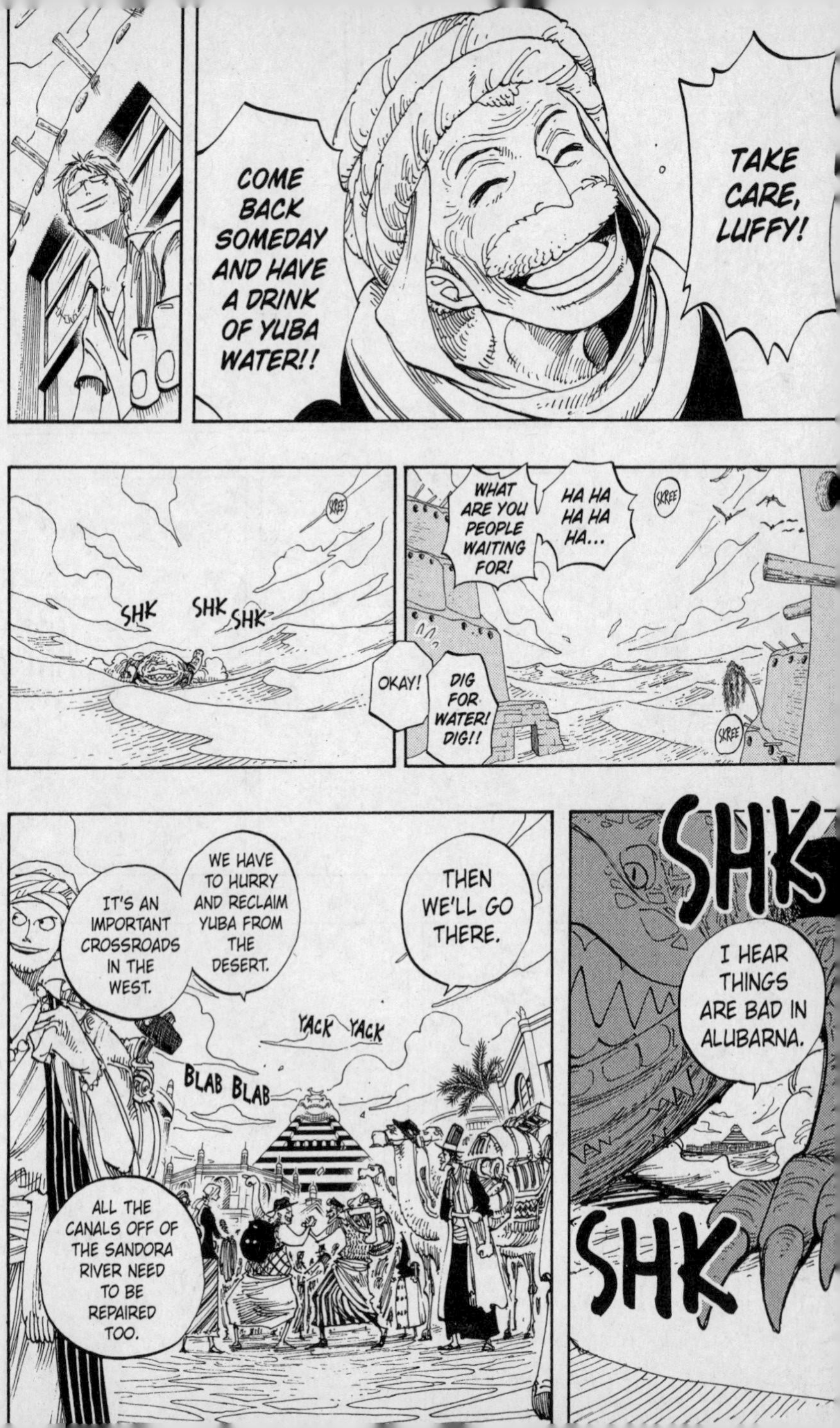
TAKE CARE, LUFFY!
COME BACK SOMEDAY AND HAVE A DRINK OF YUBA WATER!!
HA HA HA HA HA...
WHAT ARE YOU PEOPLE WAITING FOR!
SKREE
DIG FOR WATER! DIG!!
OKAY!
SKREE
SKREE
SHK SHK SHK
SHK
I HEAR THINGS ARE BAD IN ALUBARNA.
SHK
THEN WE'LL GO THERE.
WE HAVE TO HURRY AND RECLAIM YUBA FROM THE DESERT.
IT'S AN IMPORTANT CROSSROADS IN THE WEST.
YACK YACK
BLAB BLAB
ALL THE CANALS OFF OF THE SANDORA RIVER NEED TO BE REPAIRED TOO.

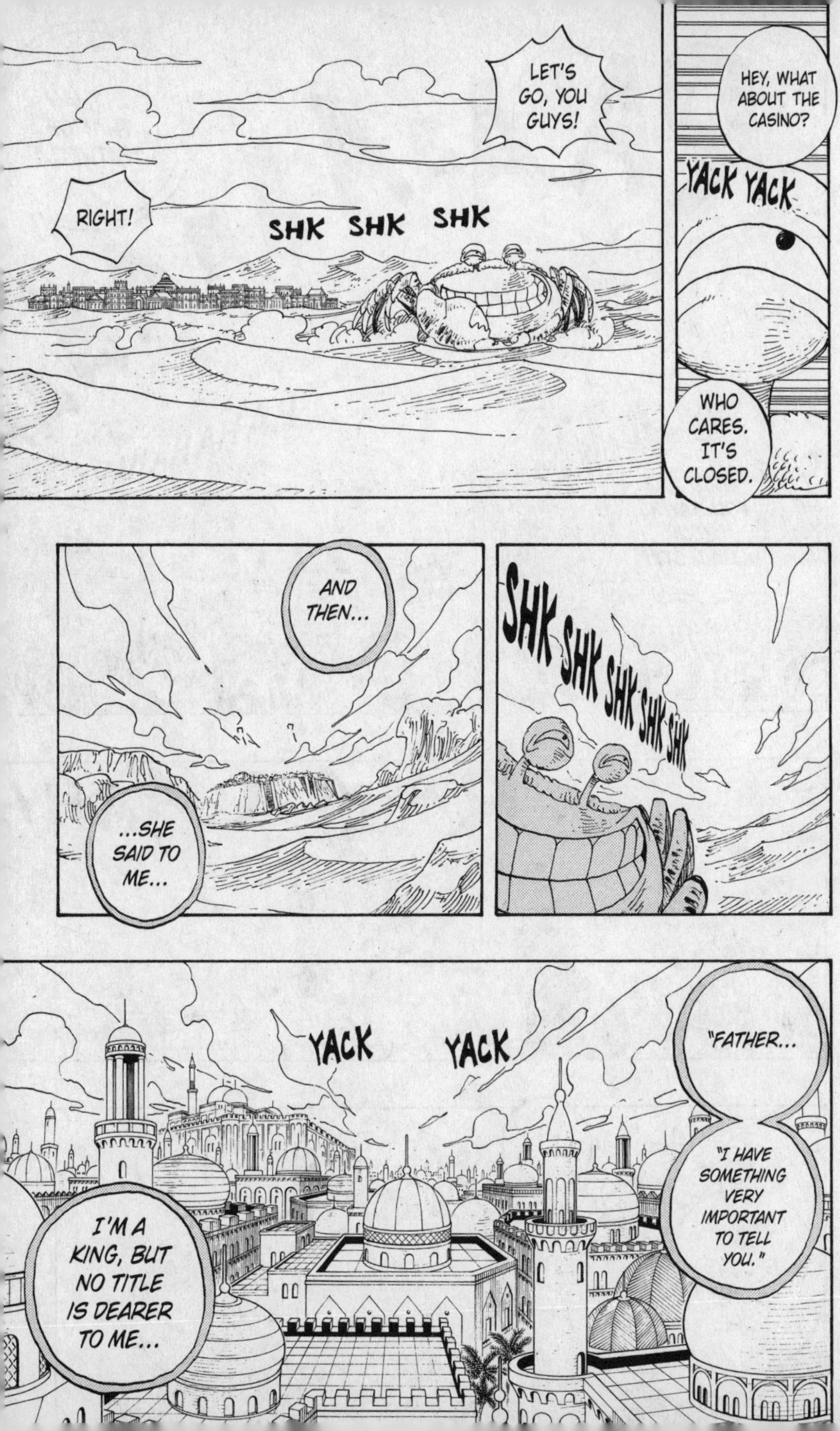
HEY, WHAT ABOUT THE CASINO?
YACK YACK
WHO CARES. IT'S CLOSED.
LET'S GO, YOU GUYS!
RIGHT!
SHK SHK SHK
SHK SHK SHK SHK SHK
AND THEN...
...SHE SAID TO ME...
"FATHER...
"I HAVE SOMETHING VERY IMPORTANT TO TELL YOU."
YACK YACK
I'M A KING, BUT NO TITLE IS DEARER TO ME...

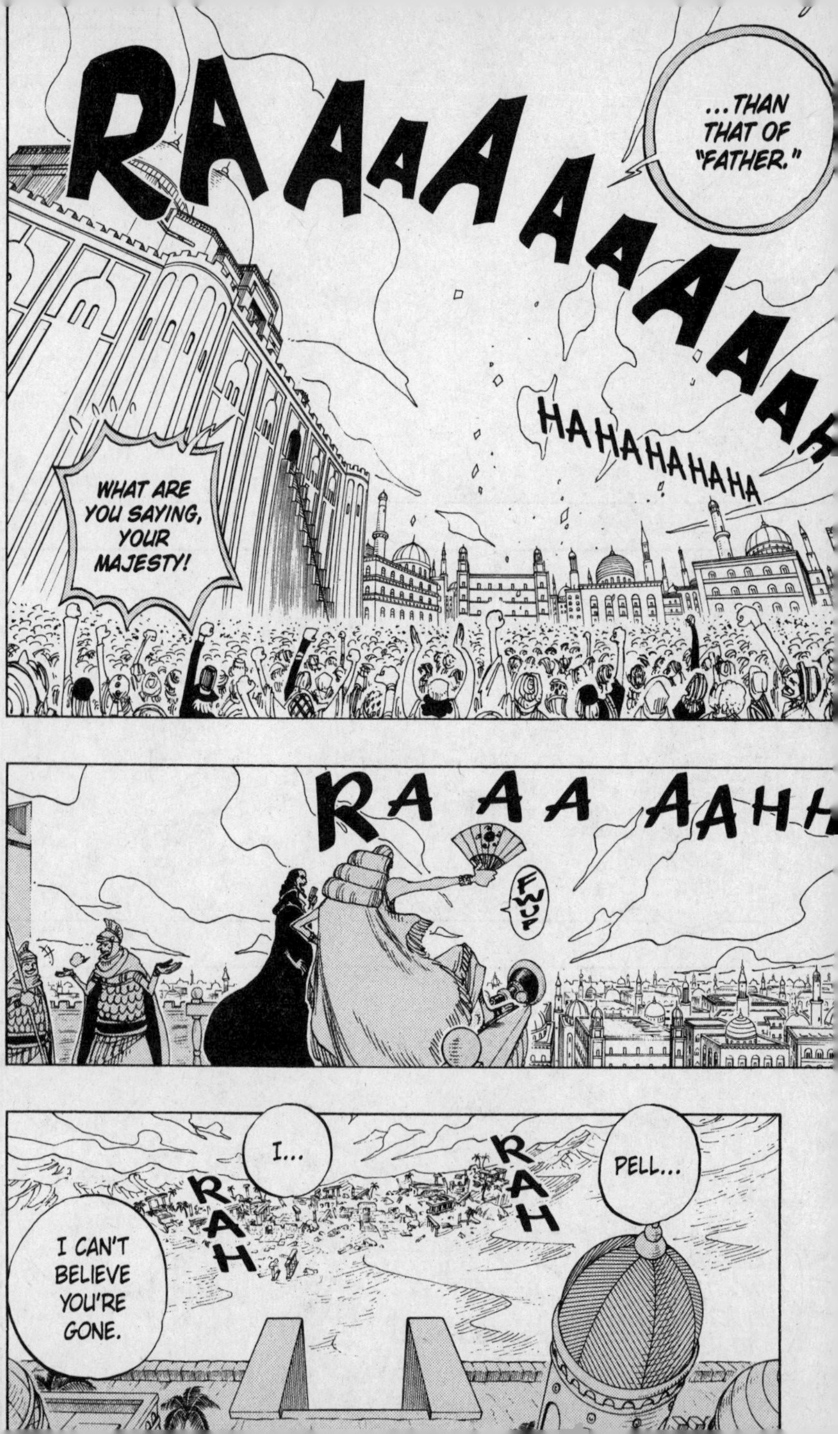
...THAN THAT OF "FATHER."
RAAAAAAAAAAH
HAHAHAHAHA
WHAT ARE YOU SAYING, YOUR MAJESTY!
RA A A AAHH
FWUP
PELL...
RAH
I...
RAH
I CAN'T BELIEVE YOU'RE GONE.

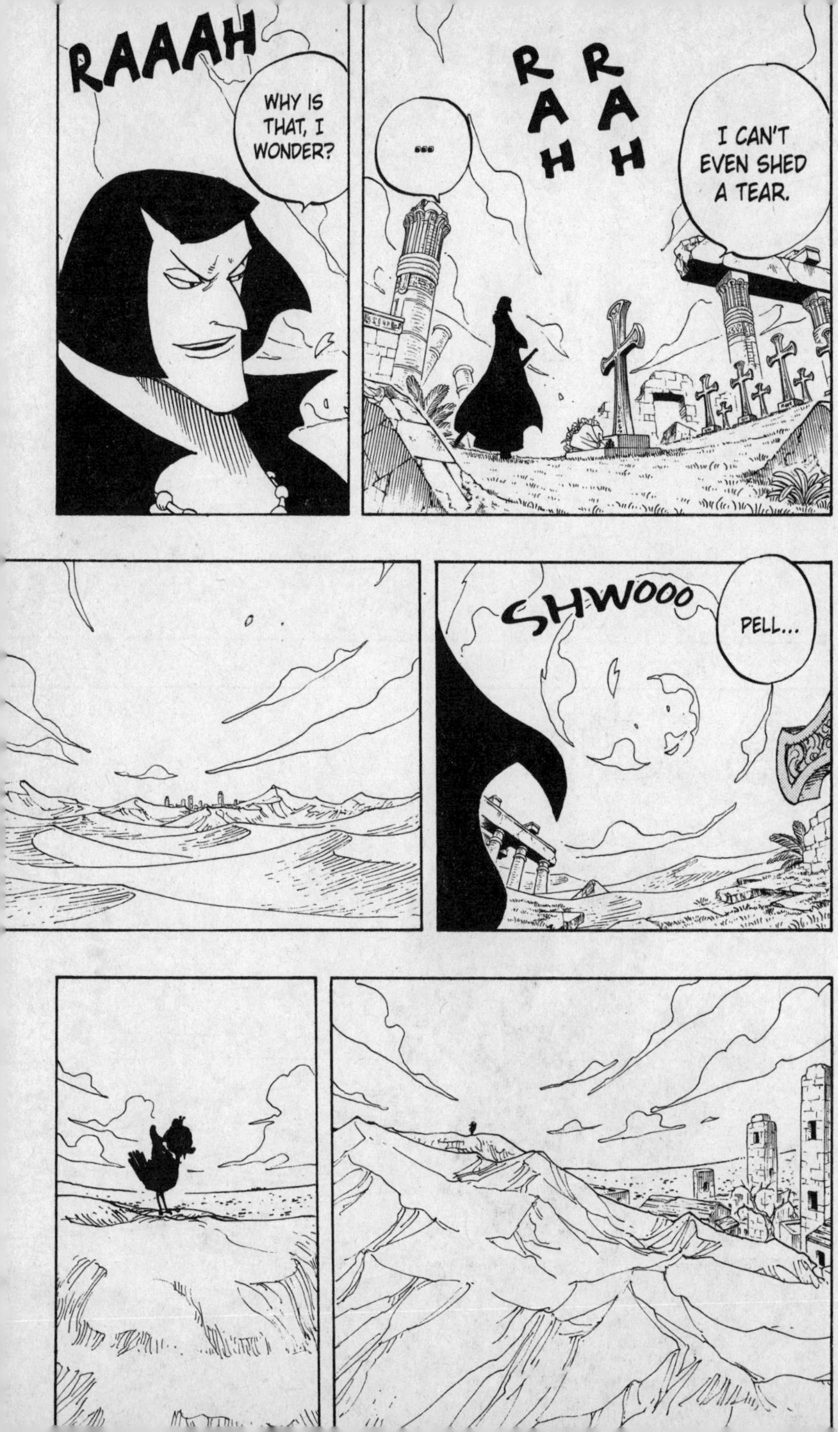
I CAN'T EVEN SHED A TEAR.
RAH
RAH
...
RAAAH
WHY IS THAT, I WONDER?
PELL...
SHWOOO

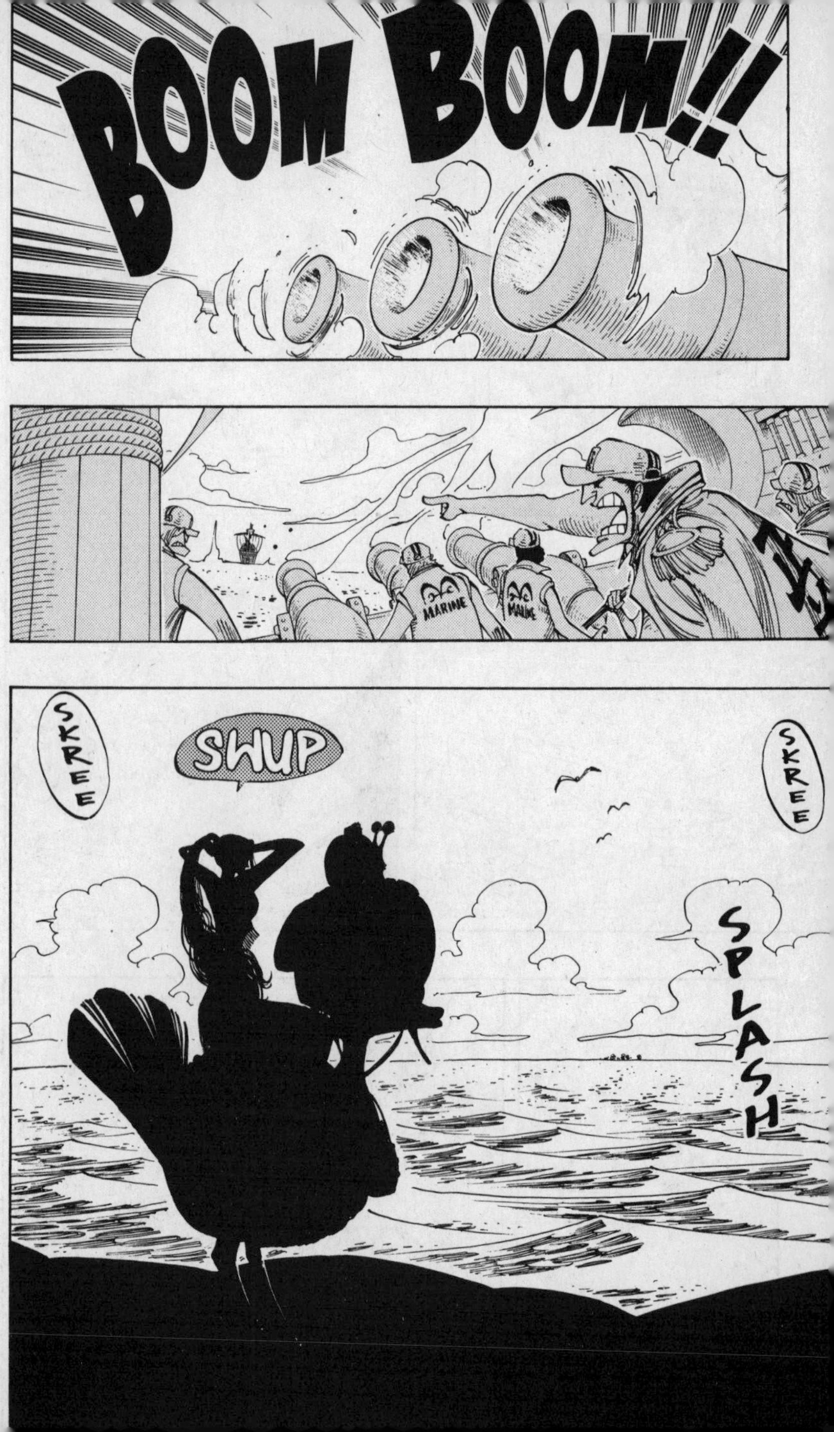
BOOM BOOM!!
SKREE
SKREE
SWUP
SPLASH

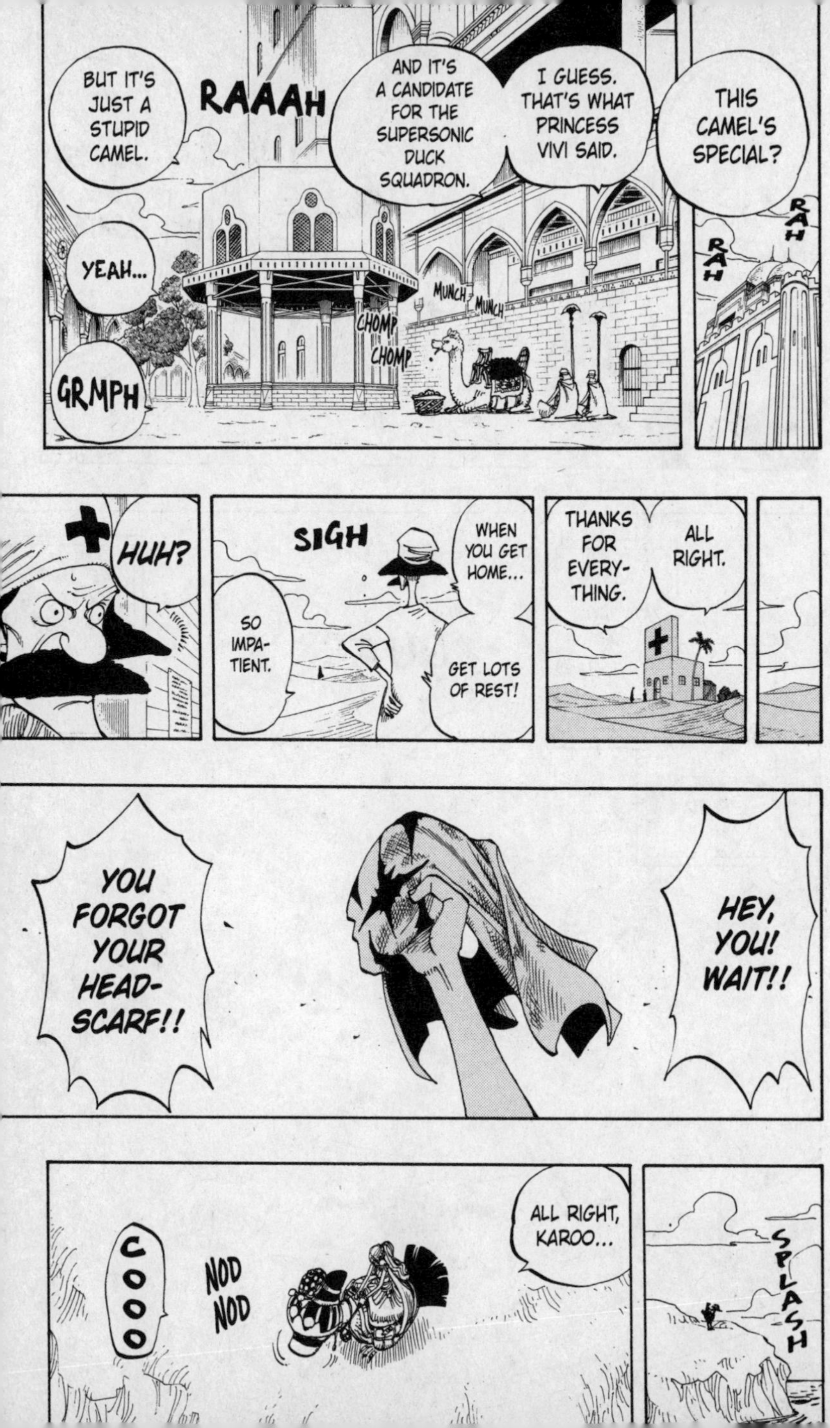
RAH
RAH
THIS CAMEL'S SPECIAL?
I GUESS. THAT'S WHAT PRINCESS VIVI SAID.
AND IT'S A CANDIDATE FOR THE SUPERSONIC DUCK SQUADRON.
RAAAH
BUT IT'S JUST A STUPID CAMEL.
MUNCH MUNCH
CHOMP CHOMP
YEAH...
GRMPH
ALL RIGHT.
THANKS FOR EVERY-THING.
WHEN YOU GET HOME...
GET LOTS OF REST!
SIGH
SO IMPA-TIENT.
HUH?
HEY, YOU! WAIT!!
YOU FORGOT YOUR HEAD-SCARF!!
SPLASH
ALL RIGHT, KAROO...
NOD NOD
COOO

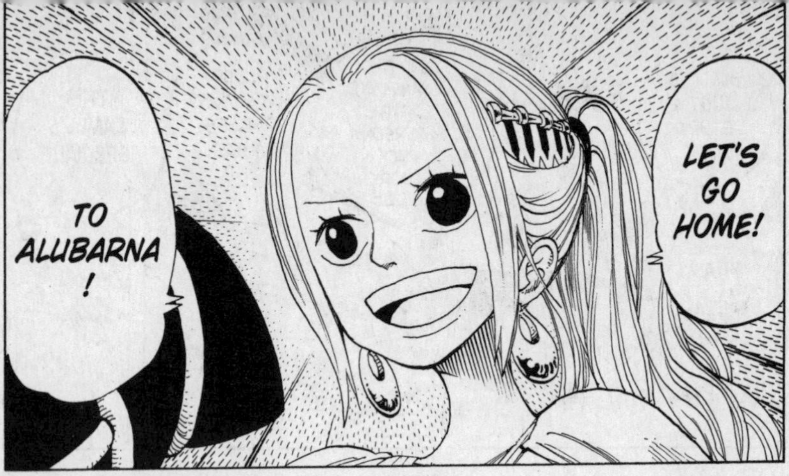
LET'S GO HOME!
TO ALUBARNA!

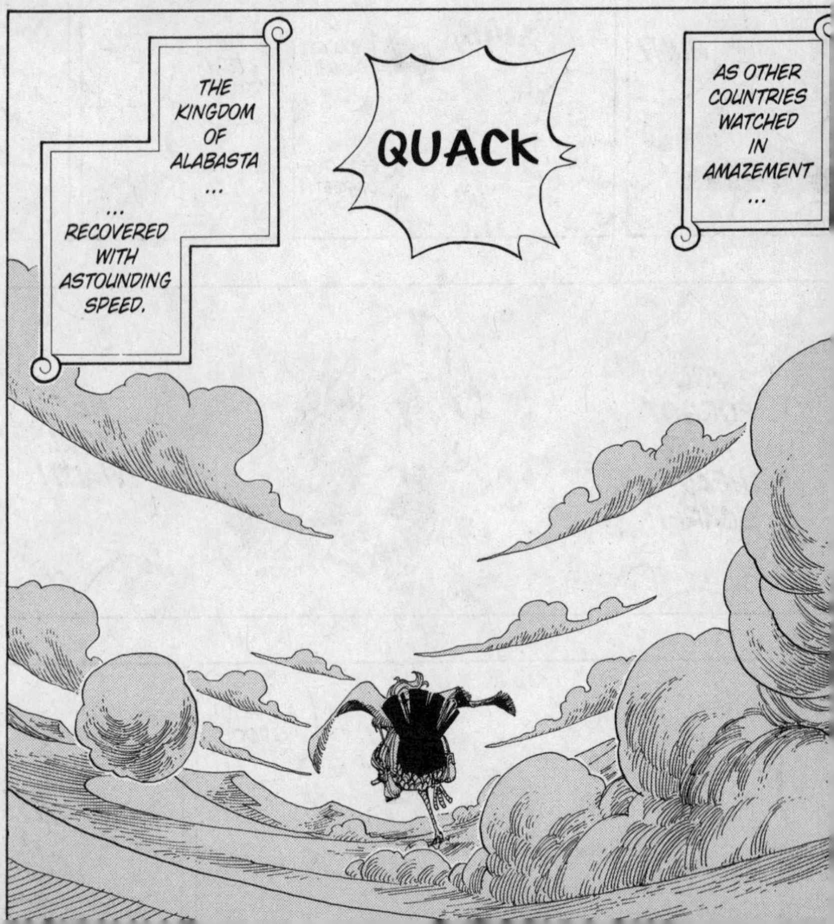
AS OTHER COUNTRIES WATCHED IN AMAZEMENT...
QUACK
THE KINGDOM OF ALABASTA... ...RECOVERED WITH ASTOUNDING SPEED.

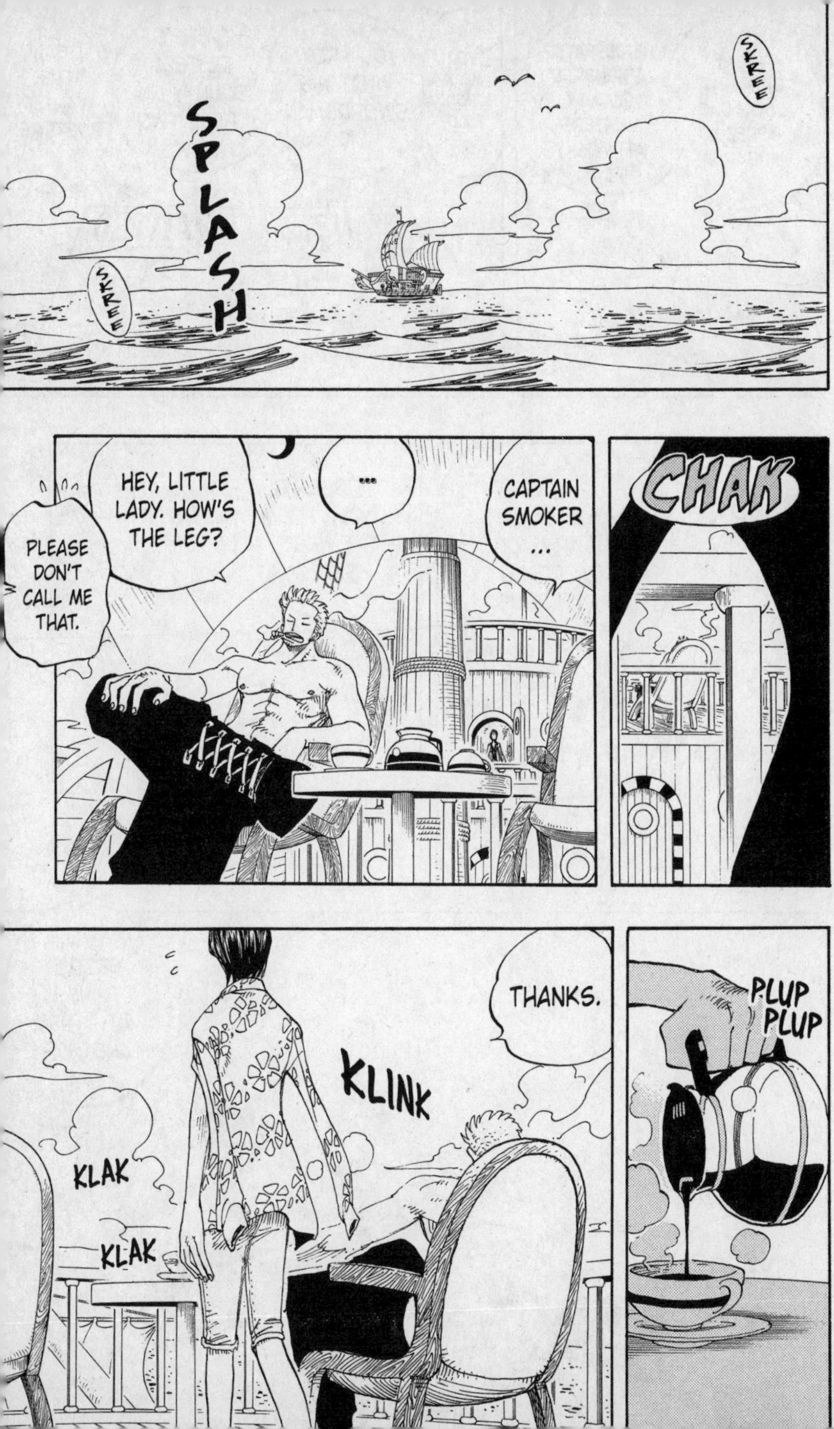
SKREE
SPLASH
SKREE
CHAK
CAPTAIN SMOKER ...
...
HEY, LITTLE LADY. HOW'S THE LEG?
PLEASE DON'T CALL ME THAT.
PLUP PLUP
THANKS.
KLINK
KLAK
KLAK

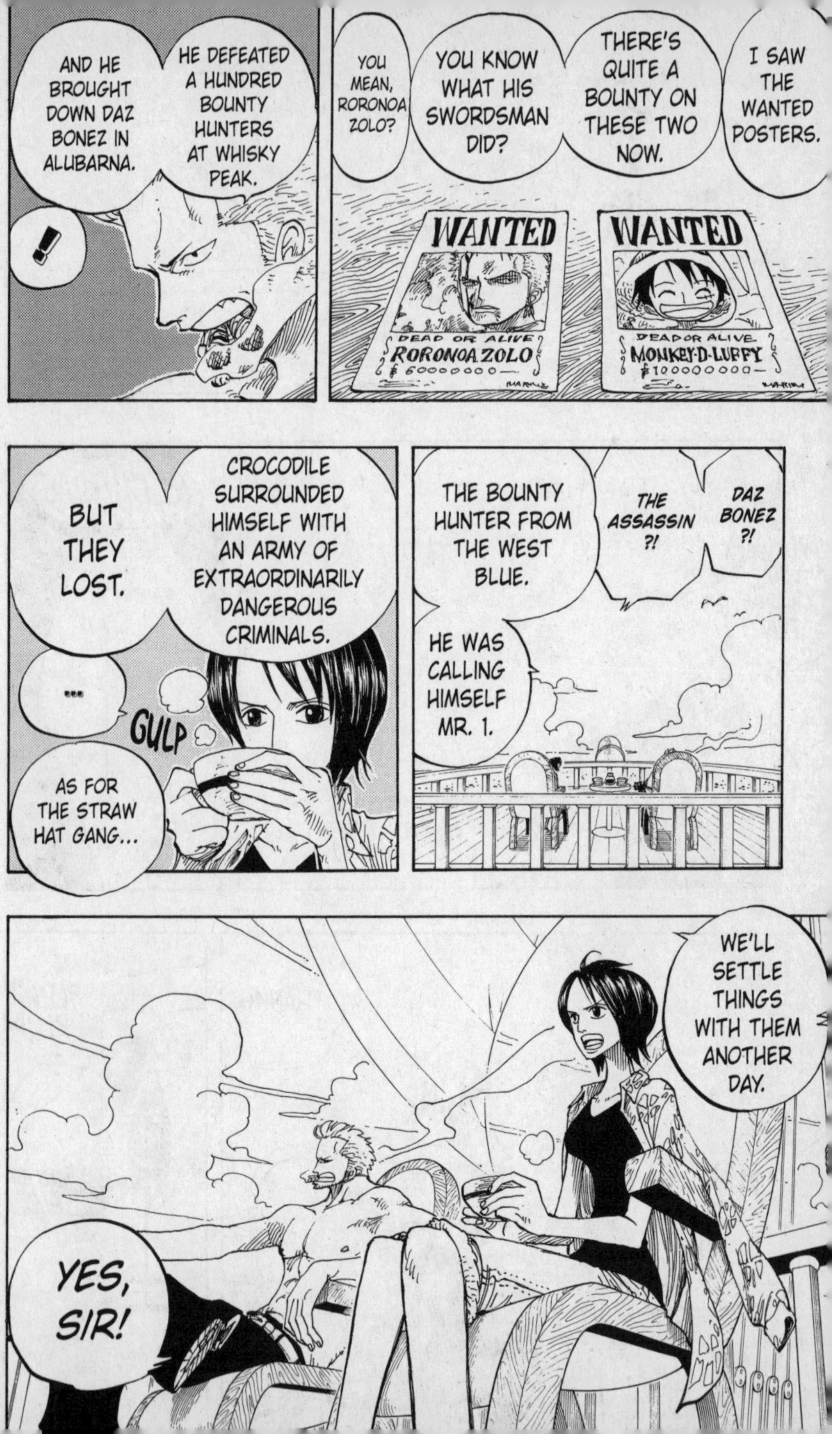
I SAW THE WANTED POSTERS.
THERE'S QUITE A BOUNTY ON THESE TWO NOW.
YOU KNOW WHAT HIS SWORDSMAN DID?
YOU MEAN, RORONOA ZOLO?
WANTED
DEAD OR ALIVE
MONKEY·D·LUFFY
฿100000000—
MARINE
WANTED
DEAD OR ALIVE
RORONOA ZOLO
฿60000000—
MARINE
HE DEFEATED A HUNDRED BOUNTY HUNTERS AT WHISKY PEAK.
AND HE BROUGHT DOWN DAZ BONEZ IN ALUBARNA.
!
DAZ BONEZ ?!
THE ASSASSIN ?!
THE BOUNTY HUNTER FROM THE WEST BLUE.
HE WAS CALLING HIMSELF MR. 1.
CROCODILE SURROUNDED HIMSELF WITH AN ARMY OF EXTRAORDINARILY DANGEROUS CRIMINALS.
BUT THEY LOST.
...
GULP
AS FOR THE STRAW HAT GANG...
WE'LL SETTLE THINGS WITH THEM ANOTHER DAY.
YES, SIR!

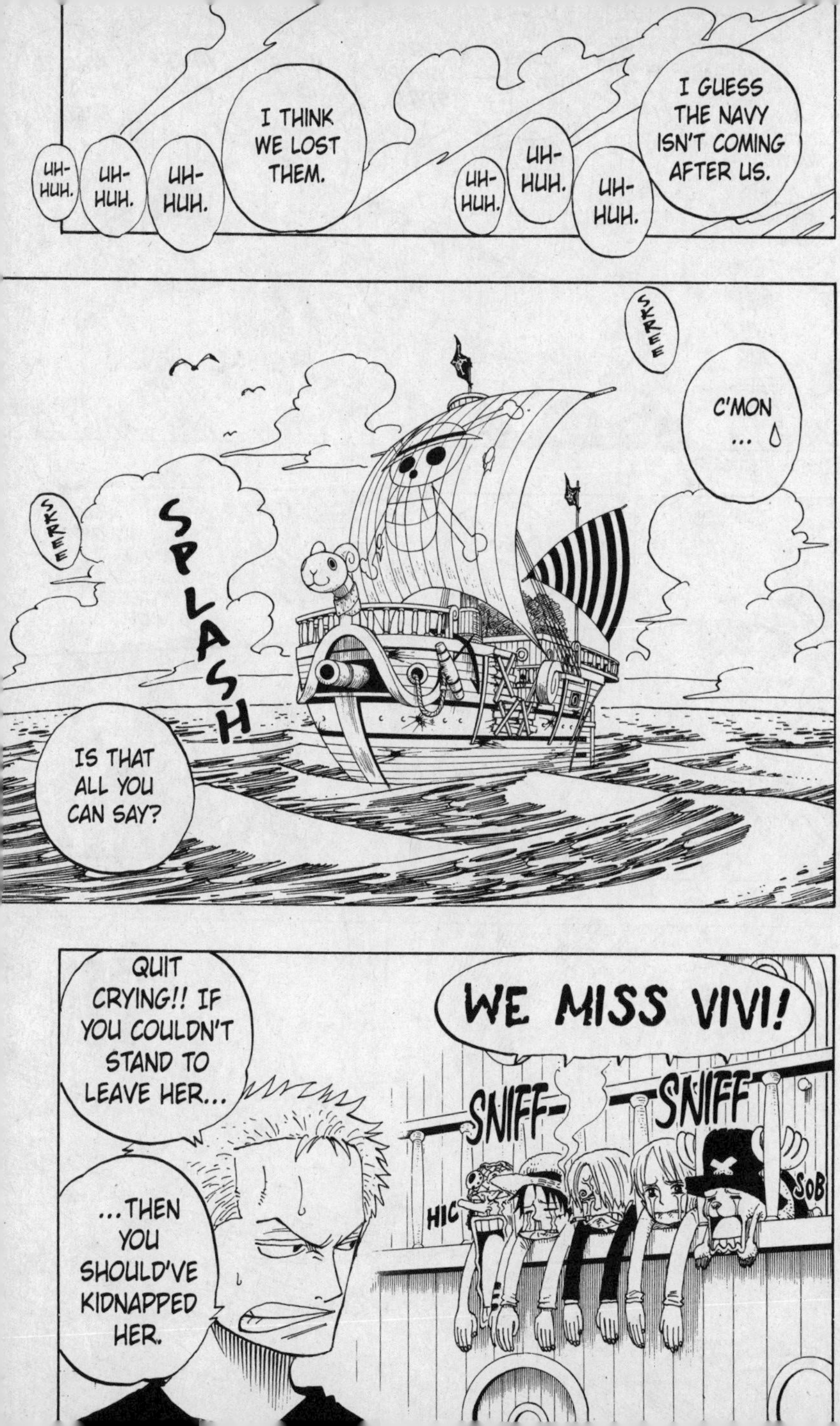
I GUESS THE NAVY ISN'T COMING AFTER US.
UH-HUH.
UH-HUH.
UH-HUH.
I THINK WE LOST THEM.
UH-HUH.
UH-HUH.
UH-HUH.
SKREE
C'MON ...
SPLASH
SKREE
IS THAT ALL YOU CAN SAY?
WE MISS VIVI!
SNIFF-SNIFF
SOB
HIC
QUIT CRYING!! IF YOU COULDN'T STAND TO LEAVE HER...
...THEN YOU SHOULD'VE KIDNAPPED HER.

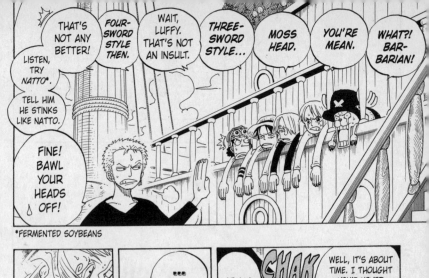

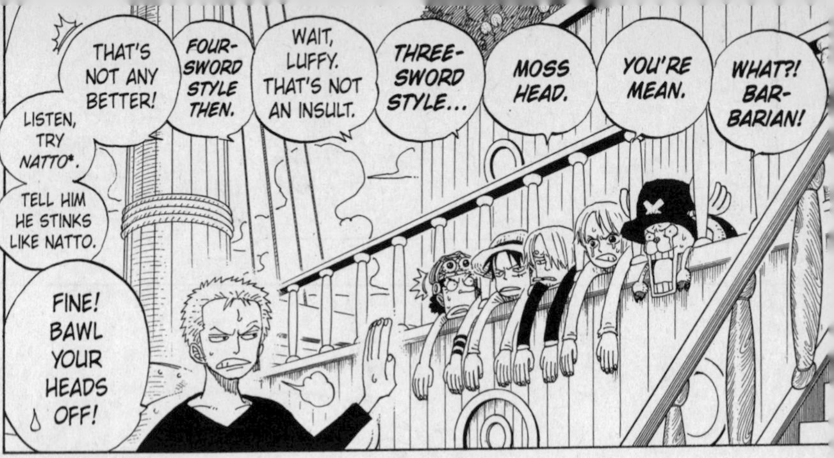
WHAT?! BAR-BARIAN!
YOU'RE MEAN.
MOSS HEAD.
THREE-SWORD STYLE...
WAIT, LUFFY. THAT'S NOT AN INSULT.
FOUR-SWORD STYLE THEN.
THAT'S NOT ANY BETTER!
LISTEN, TRY NATTO*.
TELL HIM HE STINKS LIKE NATTO.
FINE! BAWL YOUR HEADS OFF!

*FERMENTED SOYBEANS

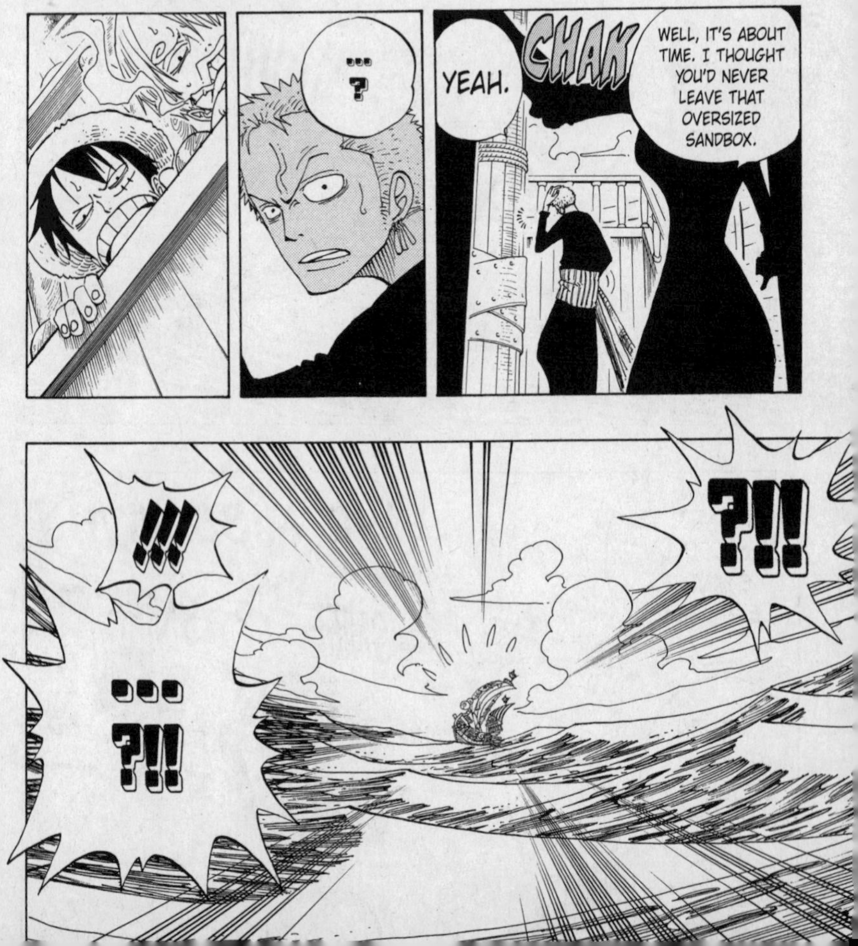
WELL, IT'S ABOUT TIME. I THOUGHT YOU'D NEVER LEAVE THAT OVERSIZED SANDBOX.
CHAK
YEAH.
...?
?!!
!!!!
...?!!

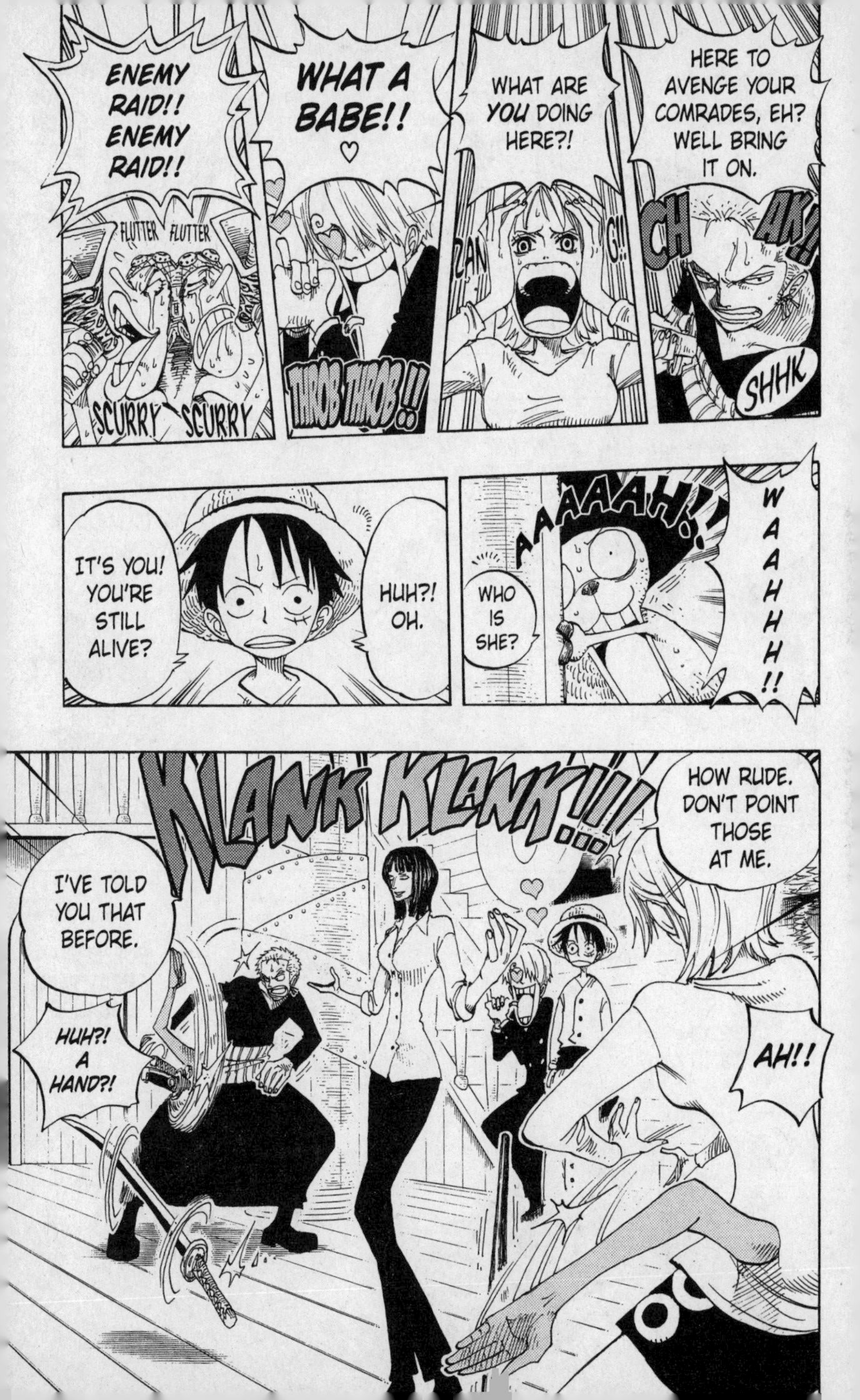
HERE TO AVENGE YOUR COMRADES, EH? WELL BRING IT ON.
CHAK!!
SHHK
WHAT ARE YOU DOING HERE?!
WHAT A BABE!! ♡
THROB THROB!!
ENEMY RAID!! ENEMY RAID!!
FLUTTER FLUTTER
SCURRY SCURRY
WAAAHHH!!
AAAAAH!!
WHO IS SHE?
HUH?! OH.
IT'S YOU! YOU'RE STILL ALIVE?
HOW RUDE. DON'T POINT THOSE AT ME.
KLANK KLANK!!!
I'VE TOLD YOU THAT BEFORE.
AH!!
HUH?! A HAND?!

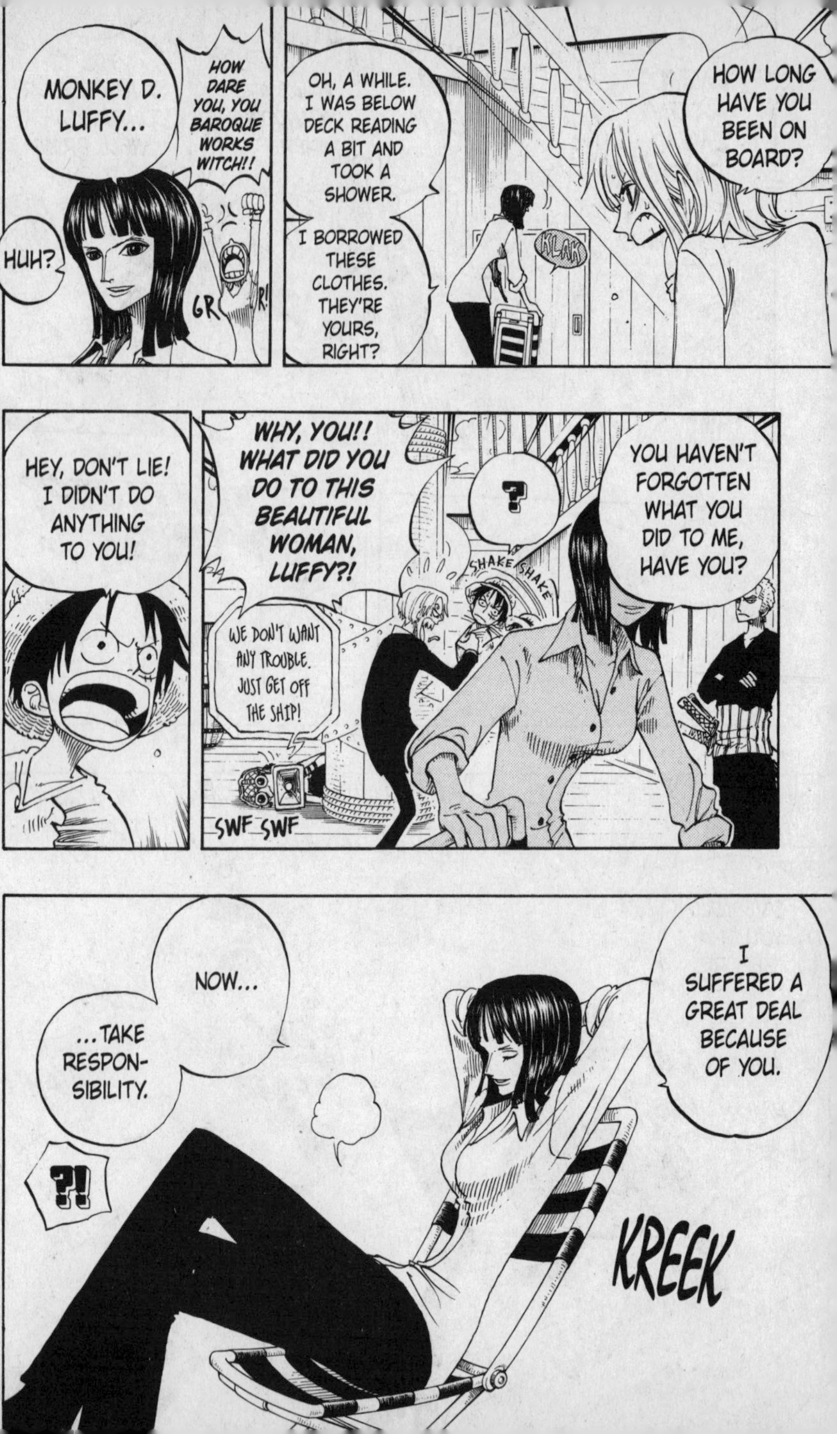

HOW LONG HAVE YOU BEEN ON BOARD?
KLAK
OH, A WHILE. I WAS BELOW DECK READING A BIT AND TOOK A SHOWER.
I BORROWED THESE CLOTHES. THEY'RE YOURS, RIGHT?
HOW DARE YOU, YOU BAROQUE WORKS WITCH!!
GR R!
MONKEY D. LUFFY...
HUH?
YOU HAVEN'T FORGOTTEN WHAT YOU DID TO ME, HAVE YOU?
?
SHAKE SHAKE
WHY, YOU!! WHAT DID YOU DO TO THIS BEAUTIFUL WOMAN, LUFFY?!
WE DON'T WANT ANY TROUBLE. JUST GET OFF THE SHIP!
SWF SWF
HEY, DON'T LIE! I DIDN'T DO ANYTHING TO YOU!
I SUFFERED A GREAT DEAL BECAUSE OF YOU.
KREEK
NOW...
...TAKE RESPONSIBILITY.
?!

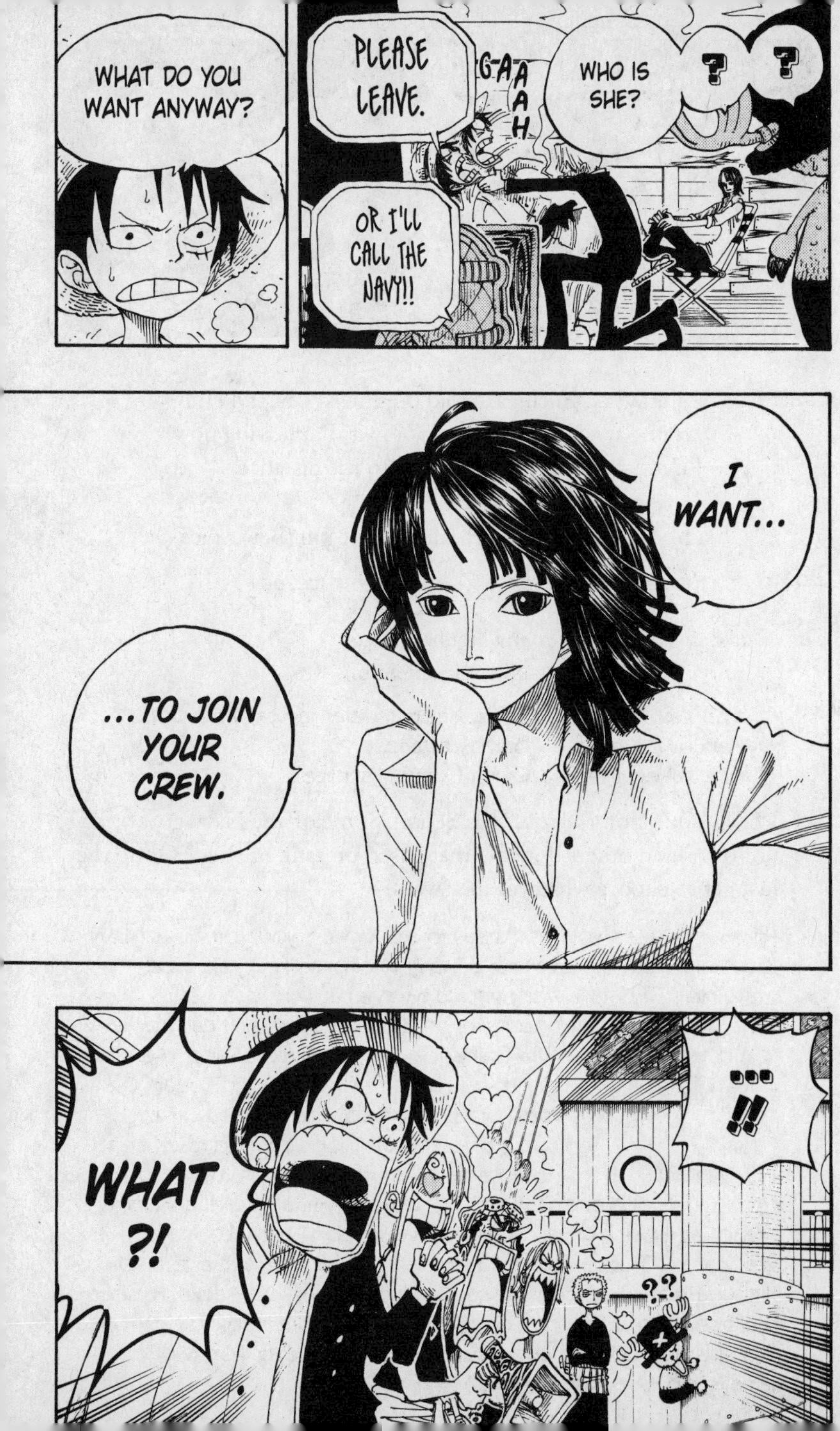
? ?
WHO IS SHE?
GAAAH
PLEASE LEAVE.
OR I'LL CALL THE NAVY!!
WHAT DO YOU WANT ANYWAY?
I WANT...
...TO JOIN YOUR CREW.
...!!
??
WHAT ?!

Question Corner
SBS

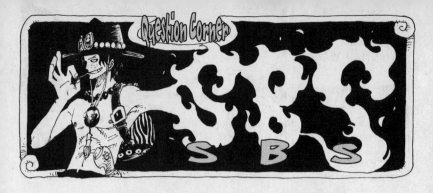

Reader: Huh? What, Eiichiro? Hold on! I'm in a hurry! Huh? Say it? Say what?! No, I won't say it! I'm leaving now! I'm outta here! (running off into the distance)

The Question Corner will now begin! (Being nice)

Oda: You said it after all?! ...Have a nice day.

Q: Oda Sensei, just how many liters are you?

--Nori (liquid glue)

A: That's right. It must have been in elementary school... When I was in the fourth grade... That's when I saw a kappa (water sprite).

Q: I have a question for you, Oda Sensei. Some of the Navy guys wear uniforms and others don't. Is that based on rank or what? Or do they just get to choose whatever they want?

A: Hmm... I guess you could say that. When you join the Navy, you're issued the standard Navy uniform and cap. (see drawing) This is a very proud moment for the new

MARINE

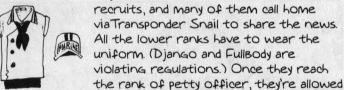

recruits, and many of them call home viaTransponder Snail to share the news. All the lower ranks have to wear the uniform. (Django and Fullbody are violating regulations.) Once they reach the rank of petty officer, they're allowed to choose different types of uniforms, and civilian clothes are okay too. But all clothing must conform to Navy standards. Those above the rank of lieutenant are also allowed to wear the word "Justice" on their backs. It seems the preferred attire for those above the rank of captain is a Justice coat over a suit. (See volume 8 for more details on the Navy ranks.)

Chapter 218:
WHY THE LOG POSE IS DOME-SHAPED

SIGN SAYS "TAKOYAKI (OCTOPUS FRITTERS)" --ED.

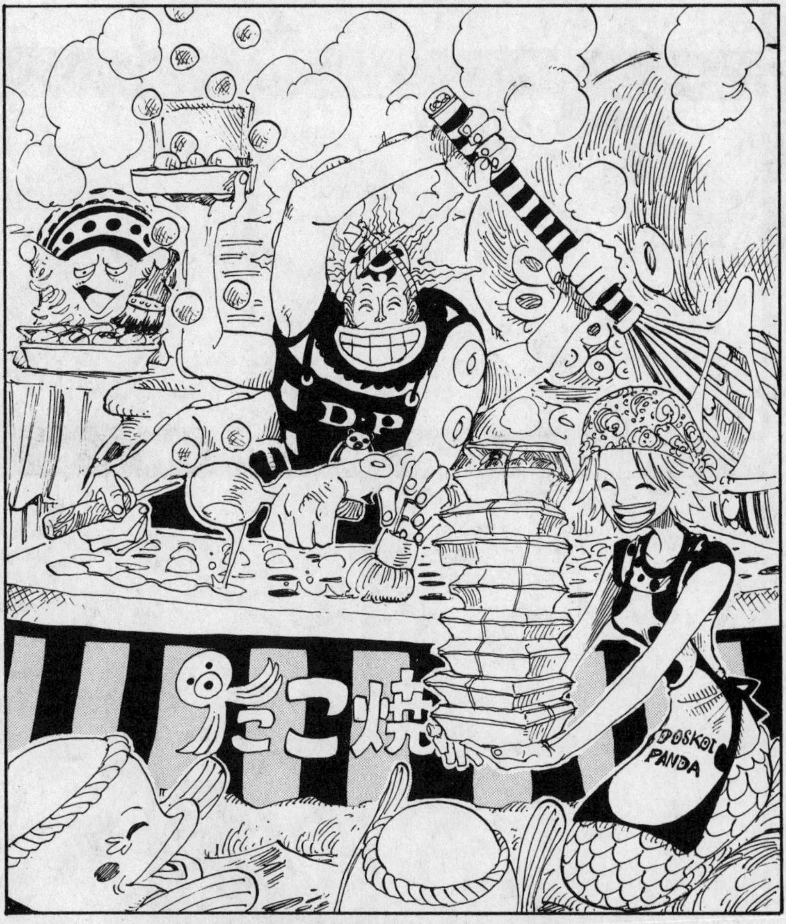

D.P
たこ焼
DOSKOI PANDA

HACHI'S WALK ON THE SEAFLOOR, VOL. 32:
"THE SUDDEN GRAND OPENING OF THE LEGENDARY OCTOPUS FRITTER SHOP"

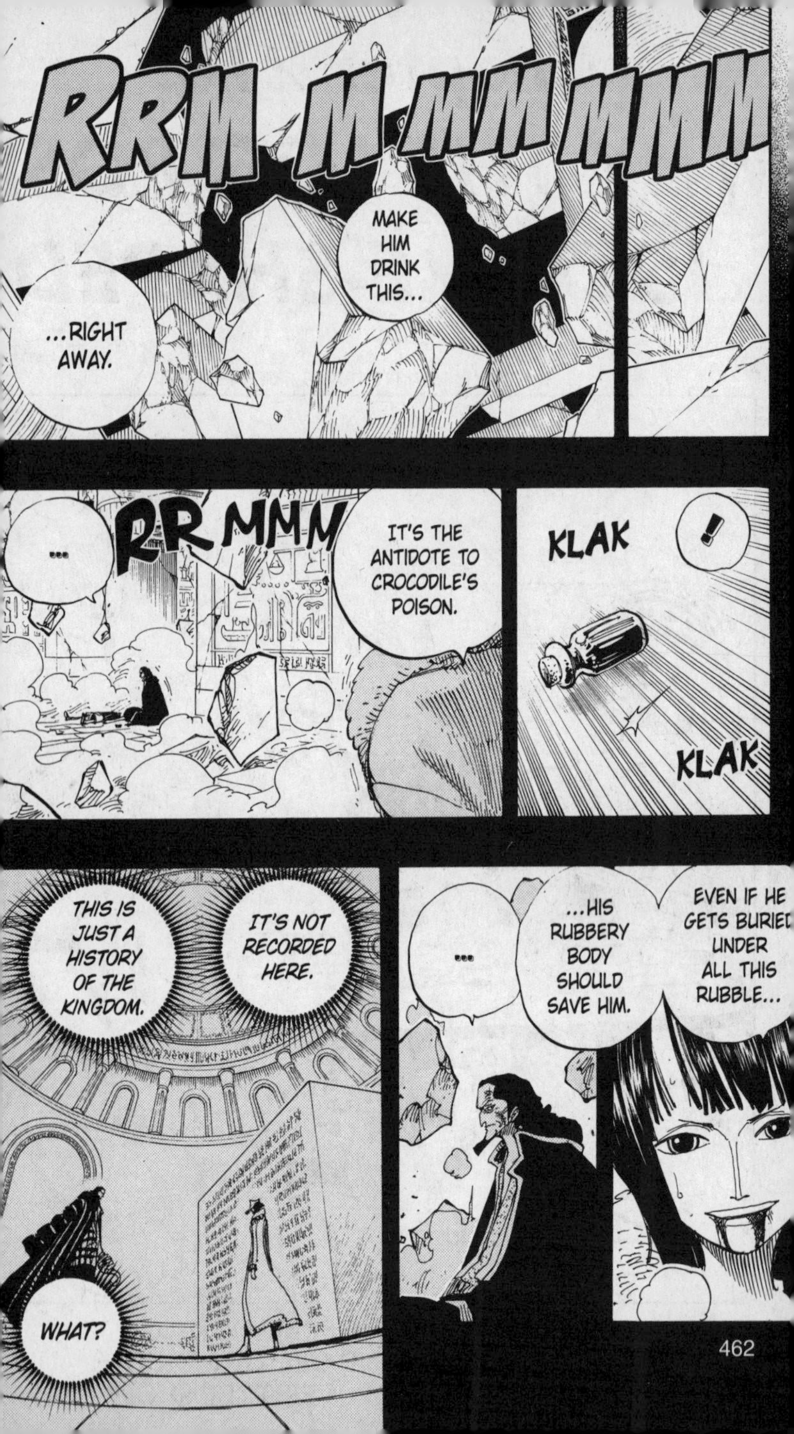
RRM M MM MMMM
MAKE HIM DRINK THIS...
...RIGHT AWAY.
KLAK
!
KLAK
IT'S THE ANTIDOTE TO CROCODILE'S POISON.
RRMMM
...
EVEN IF HE GETS BURIED UNDER ALL THIS RUBBLE...
...HIS RUBBERY BODY SHOULD SAVE HIM.
...
IT'S NOT RECORDED HERE.
THIS IS JUST A HISTORY OF THE KINGDOM.
WHAT?

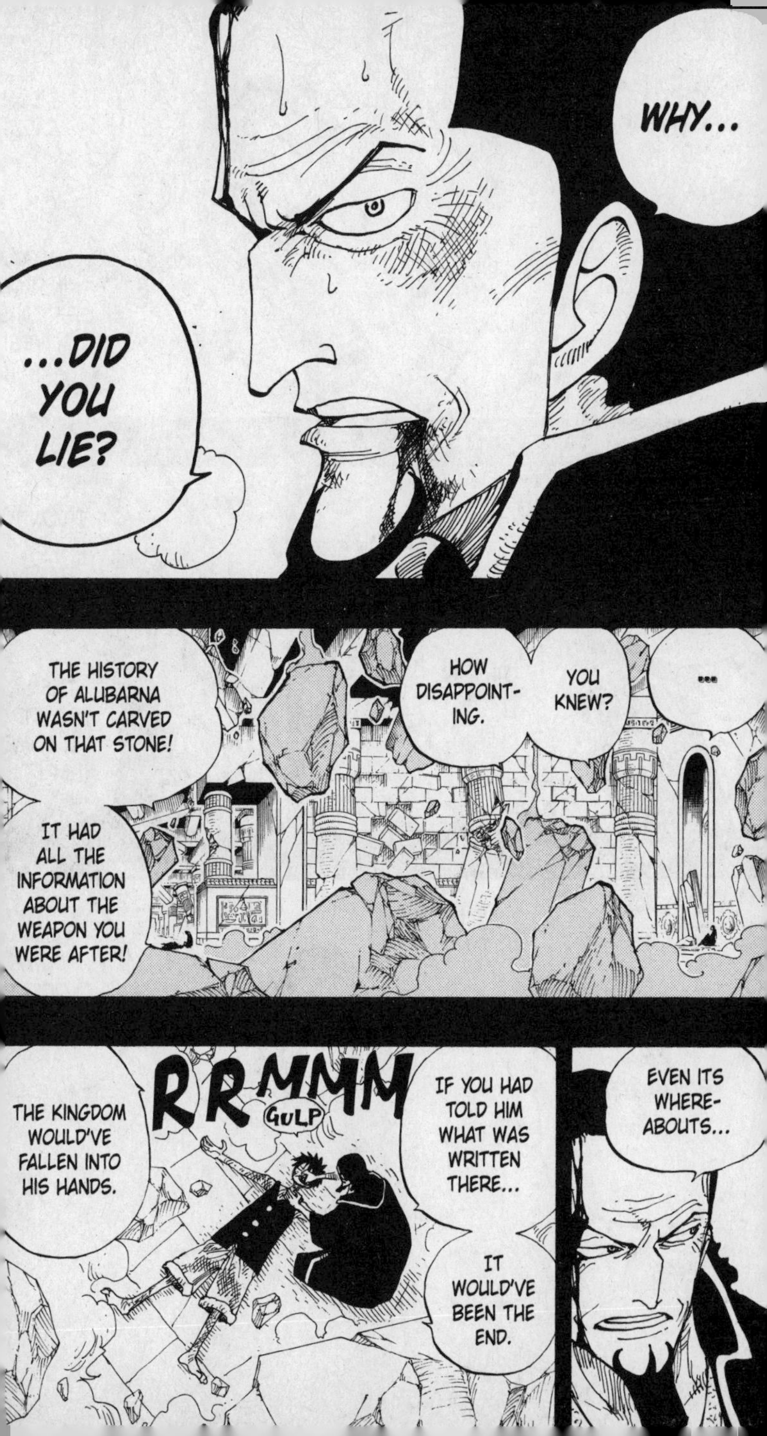
WHY...
...DID YOU LIE?
...
YOU KNEW?
HOW DISAPPOINTING.
THE HISTORY OF ALUBARNA WASN'T CARVED ON THAT STONE!
IT HAD ALL THE INFORMATION ABOUT THE WEAPON YOU WERE AFTER!
EVEN ITS WHEREABOUTS...
IF YOU HAD TOLD HIM WHAT WAS WRITTEN THERE...
IT WOULD'VE BEEN THE END.
RRMMM
GULP
THE KINGDOM WOULD'VE FALLEN INTO HIS HANDS.

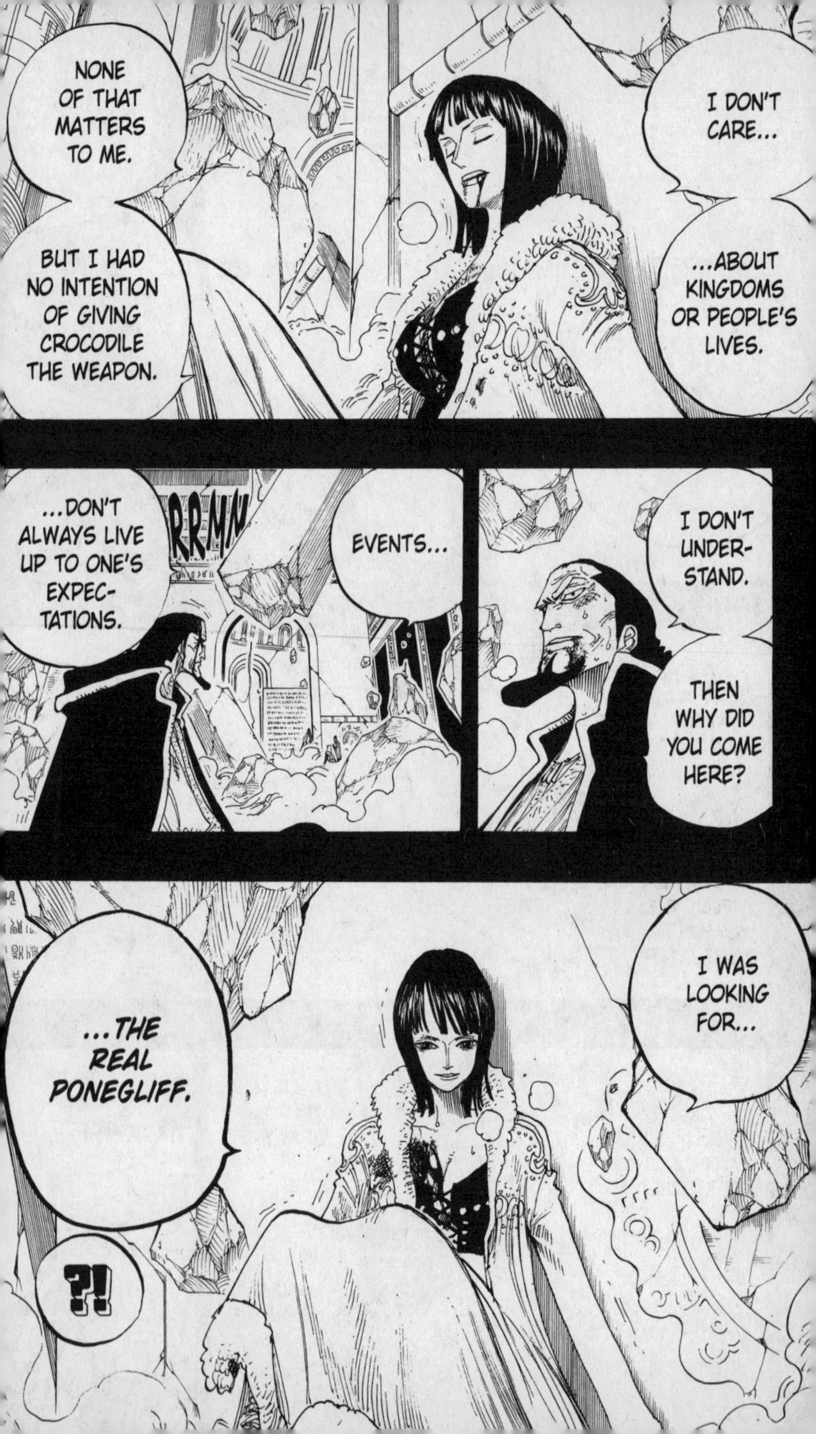
I DON'T CARE...
...ABOUT KINGDOMS OR PEOPLE'S LIVES.
NONE OF THAT MATTERS TO ME.
BUT I HAD NO INTENTION OF GIVING CROCODILE THE WEAPON.
I DON'T UNDER-STAND.
THEN WHY DID YOU COME HERE?
EVENTS...
RRMN
...DON'T ALWAYS LIVE UP TO ONE'S EXPEC-TATIONS.
I WAS LOOKING FOR...
...THE REAL PONEGLIFF.
?!

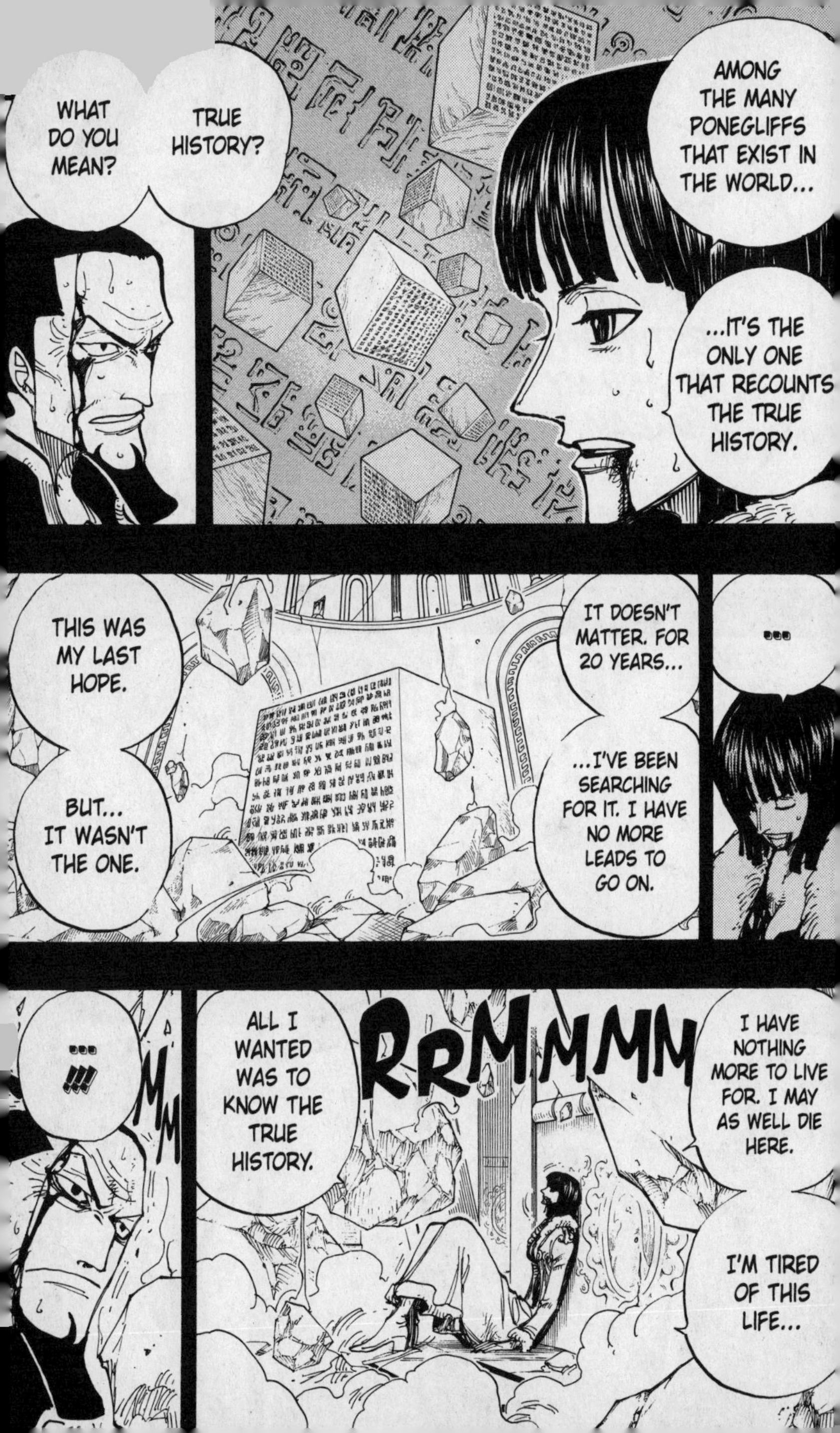
AMONG THE MANY PONEGLIFFS THAT EXIST IN THE WORLD...
...IT'S THE ONLY ONE THAT RECOUNTS THE TRUE HISTORY.
TRUE HISTORY?
WHAT DO YOU MEAN?
...
IT DOESN'T MATTER. FOR 20 YEARS...
...I'VE BEEN SEARCHING FOR IT. I HAVE NO MORE LEADS TO GO ON.
THIS WAS MY LAST HOPE.
BUT... IT WASN'T THE ONE.
I HAVE NOTHING MORE TO LIVE FOR. I MAY AS WELL DIE HERE.
I'M TIRED OF THIS LIFE...
RRMMMM
ALL I WANTED WAS TO KNOW THE TRUE HISTORY.
MM
...!!!

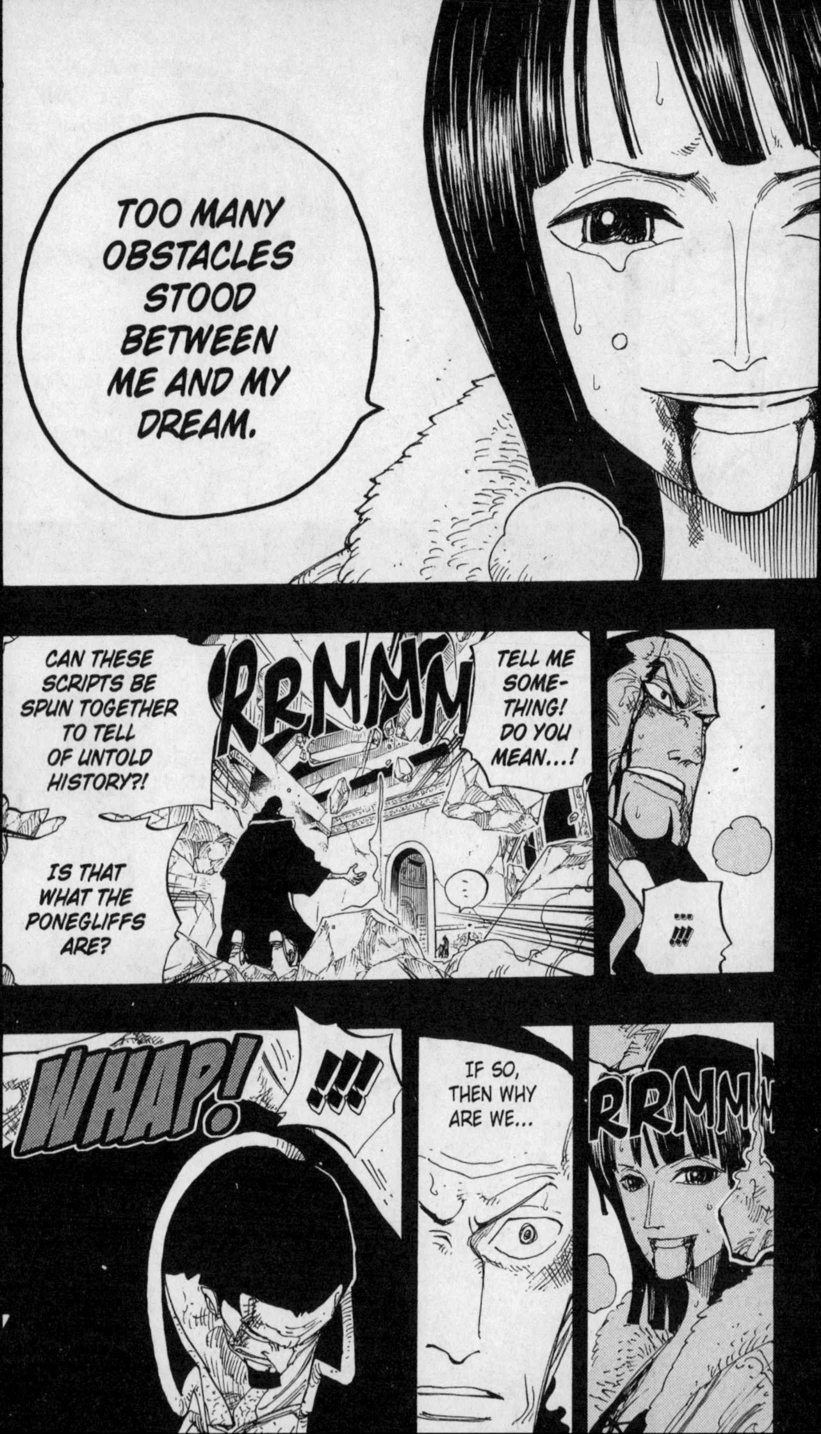
TOO MANY OBSTACLES STOOD BETWEEN ME AND MY DREAM.
...!!!
TELL ME SOMETHING! DO YOU MEAN...!
RRMMM
CAN THESE SCRIPTS BE SPUN TOGETHER TO TELL OF UNTOLD HISTORY?!
IS THAT WHAT THE PONEGLIFFS ARE?
RRMM
IF SO, THEN WHY ARE WE...
!!!
WHAP!

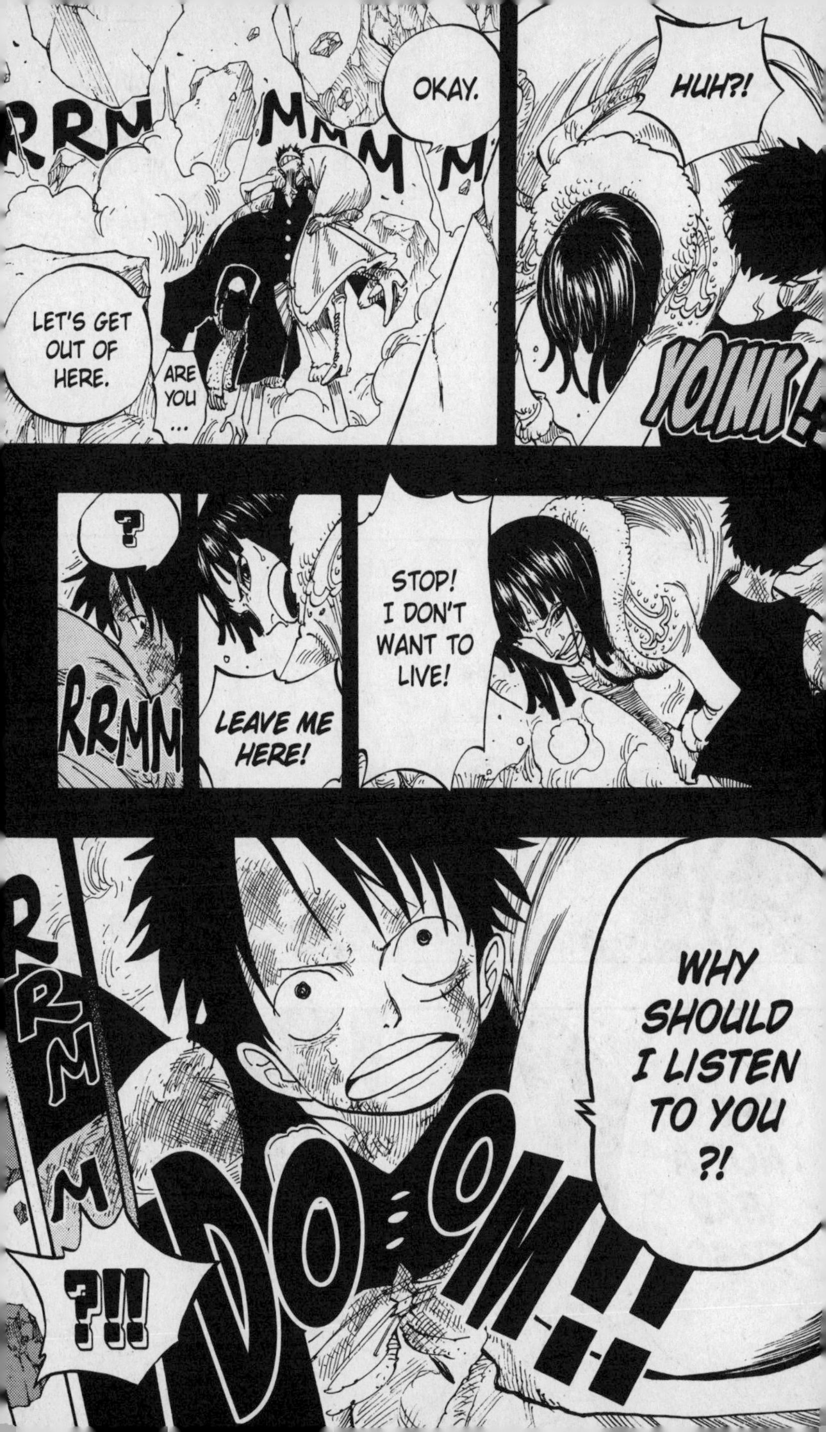
HUH?!
YOINK!!
OKAY.
RRMMMMMM
LET'S GET OUT OF HERE.
ARE YOU ...
STOP! I DON'T WANT TO LIVE!
LEAVE ME HERE!
?
RRMM
WHY SHOULD I LISTEN TO YOU ?!
DOOOM!!
RRMM
?!!

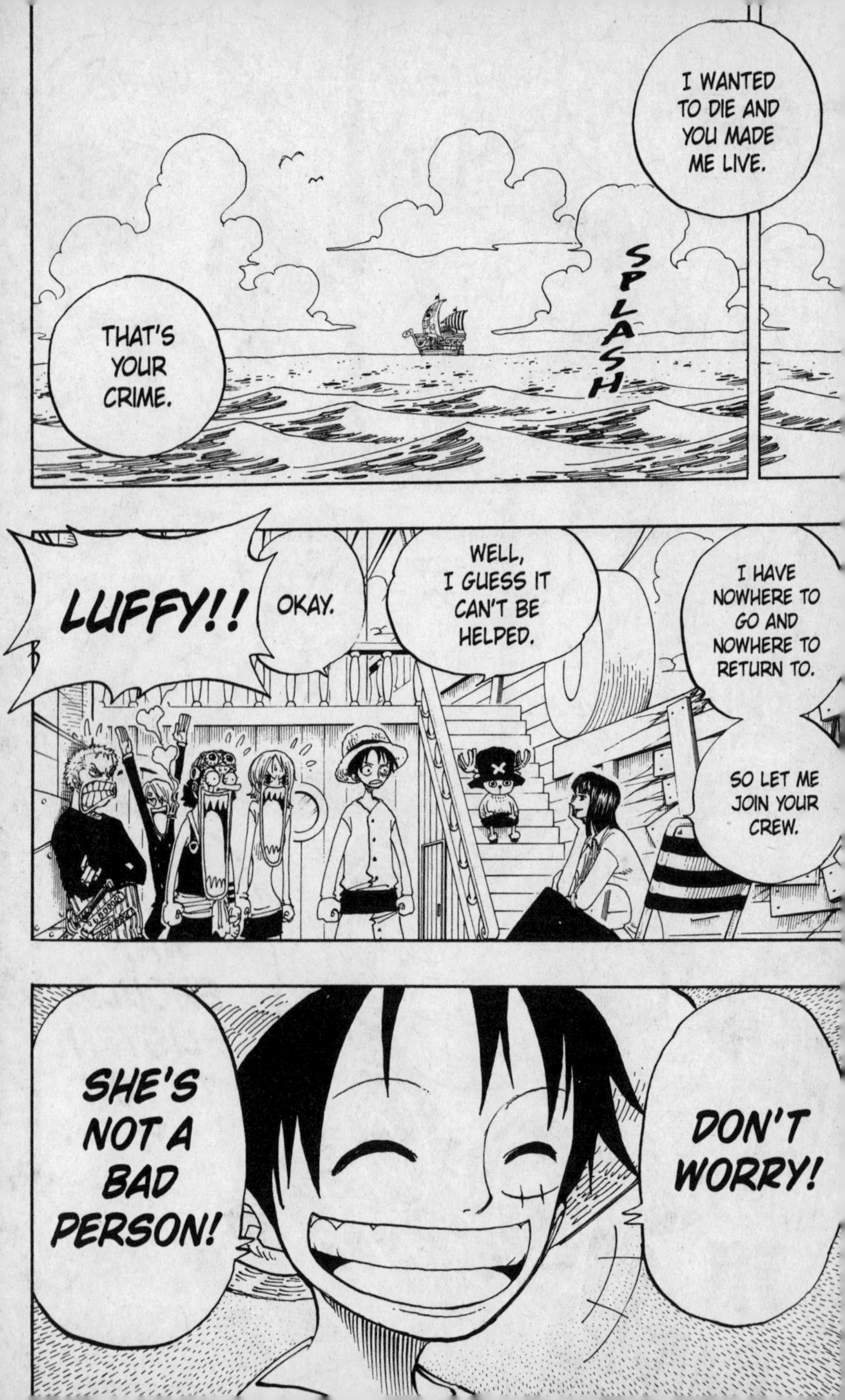
I WANTED TO DIE AND YOU MADE ME LIVE.
SPLASH
THAT'S YOUR CRIME.
I HAVE NOWHERE TO GO AND NOWHERE TO RETURN TO.
SO LET ME JOIN YOUR CREW.
WELL, I GUESS IT CAN'T BE HELPED.
OKAY.
LUFFY!!
DON'T WORRY!
SHE'S NOT A BAD PERSON!

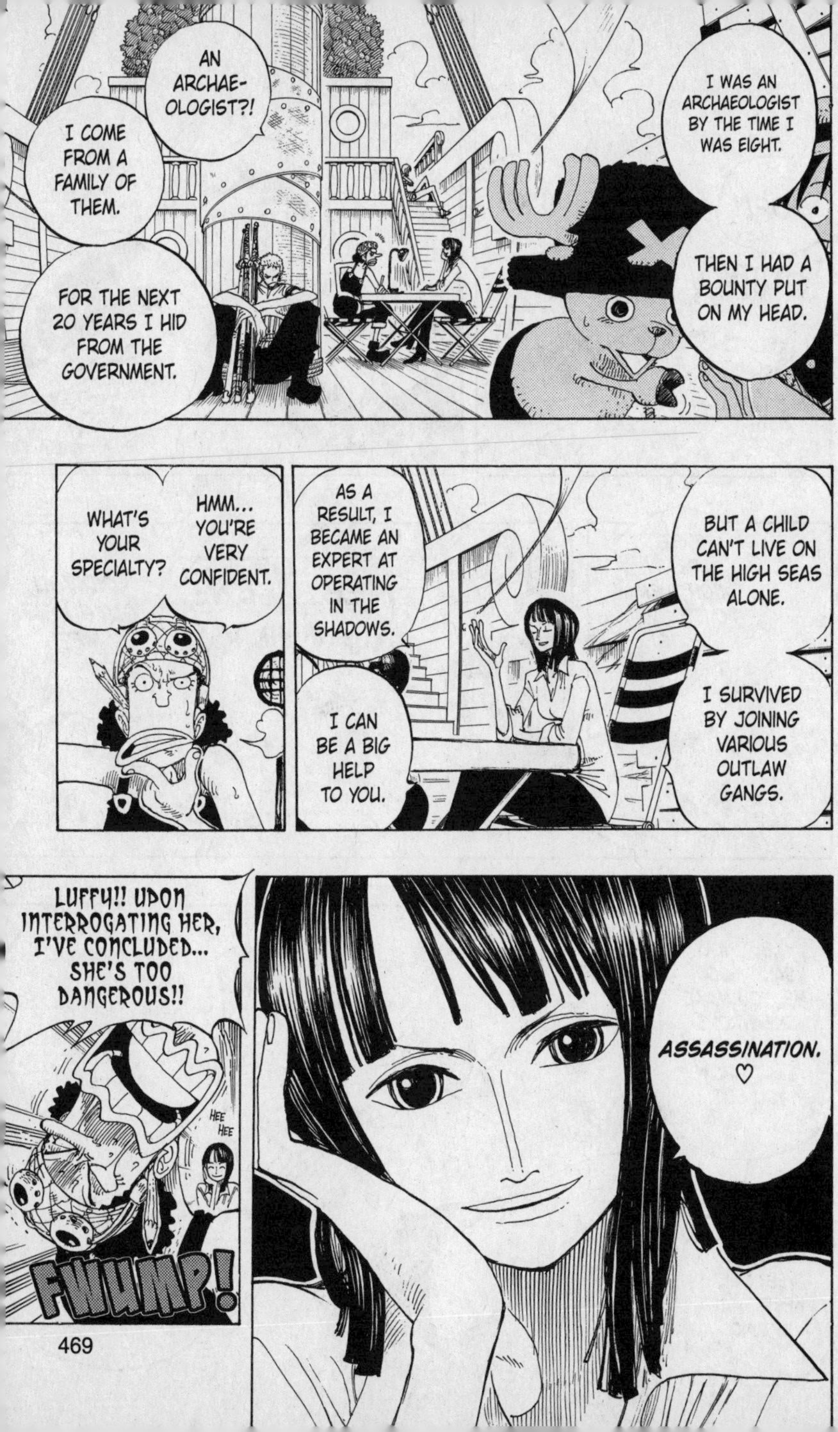
I WAS AN ARCHAEOLOGIST BY THE TIME I WAS EIGHT.
THEN I HAD A BOUNTY PUT ON MY HEAD.
AN ARCHAE-OLOGIST?!
I COME FROM A FAMILY OF THEM.
FOR THE NEXT 20 YEARS I HID FROM THE GOVERNMENT.
BUT A CHILD CAN'T LIVE ON THE HIGH SEAS ALONE.
I SURVIVED BY JOINING VARIOUS OUTLAW GANGS.
AS A RESULT, I BECAME AN EXPERT AT OPERATING IN THE SHADOWS.
I CAN BE A BIG HELP TO YOU.
HMM... YOU'RE VERY CONFIDENT.
WHAT'S YOUR SPECIALTY?
ASSASSINATION. ♡
LUFFY!! UPON INTERROGATING HER, I'VE CONCLUDED... SHE'S TOO DANGEROUS!!
HEE HEE
FWUMP!

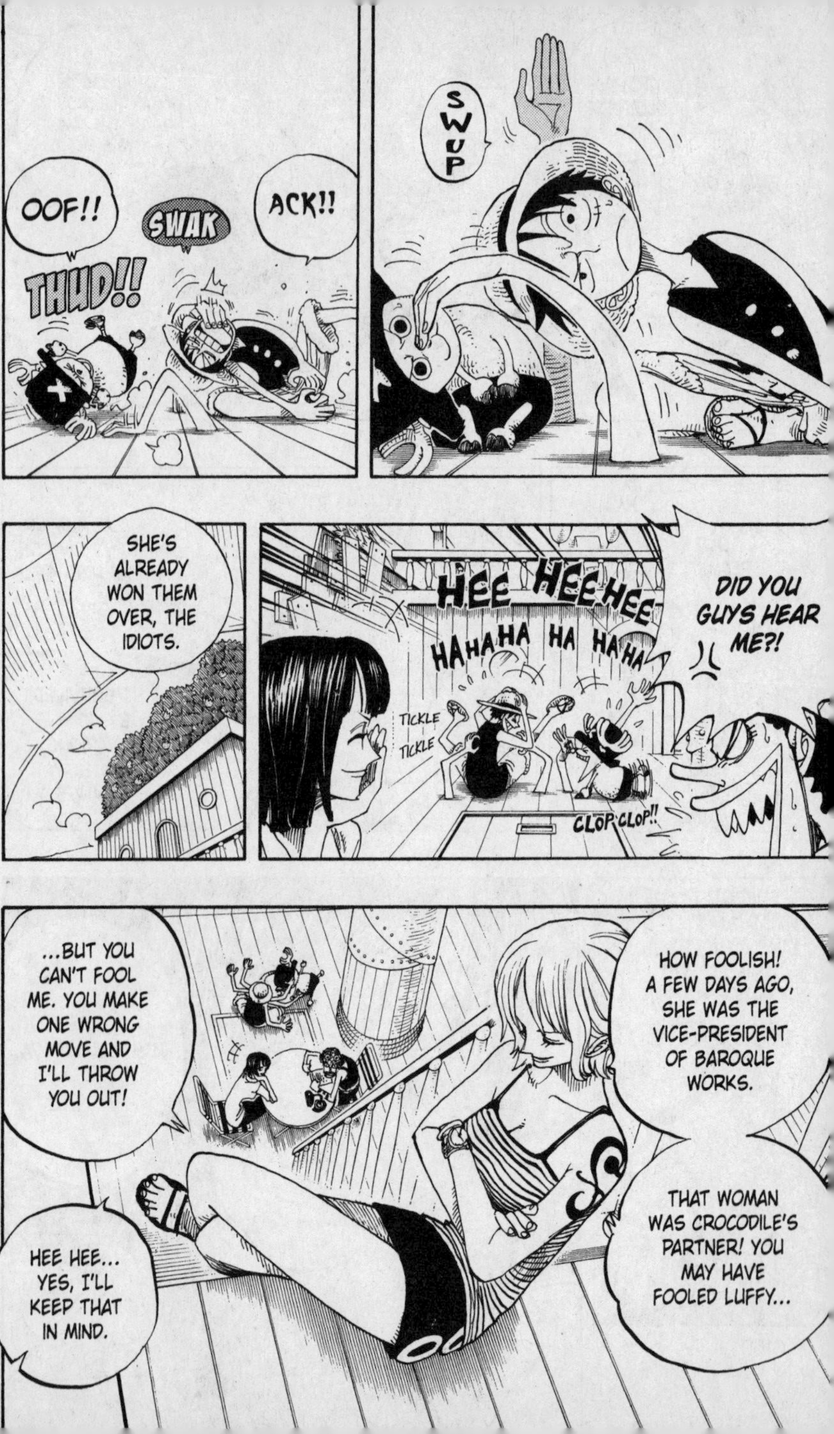
SWUP
ACK!!
SWAK
OOF!!
THUD!!
DID YOU GUYS HEAR ME?!
HEE HEE HEE
HA HA HA HA HA HA HA
TICKLE TICKLE
CLOP CLOP!!
SHE'S ALREADY WON THEM OVER, THE IDIOTS.
HOW FOOLISH! A FEW DAYS AGO, SHE WAS THE VICE-PRESIDENT OF BAROQUE WORKS.
THAT WOMAN WAS CROCODILE'S PARTNER! YOU MAY HAVE FOOLED LUFFY...
...BUT YOU CAN'T FOOL ME. YOU MAKE ONE WRONG MOVE AND I'LL THROW YOU OUT!
HEE HEE... YES, I'LL KEEP THAT IN MIND.

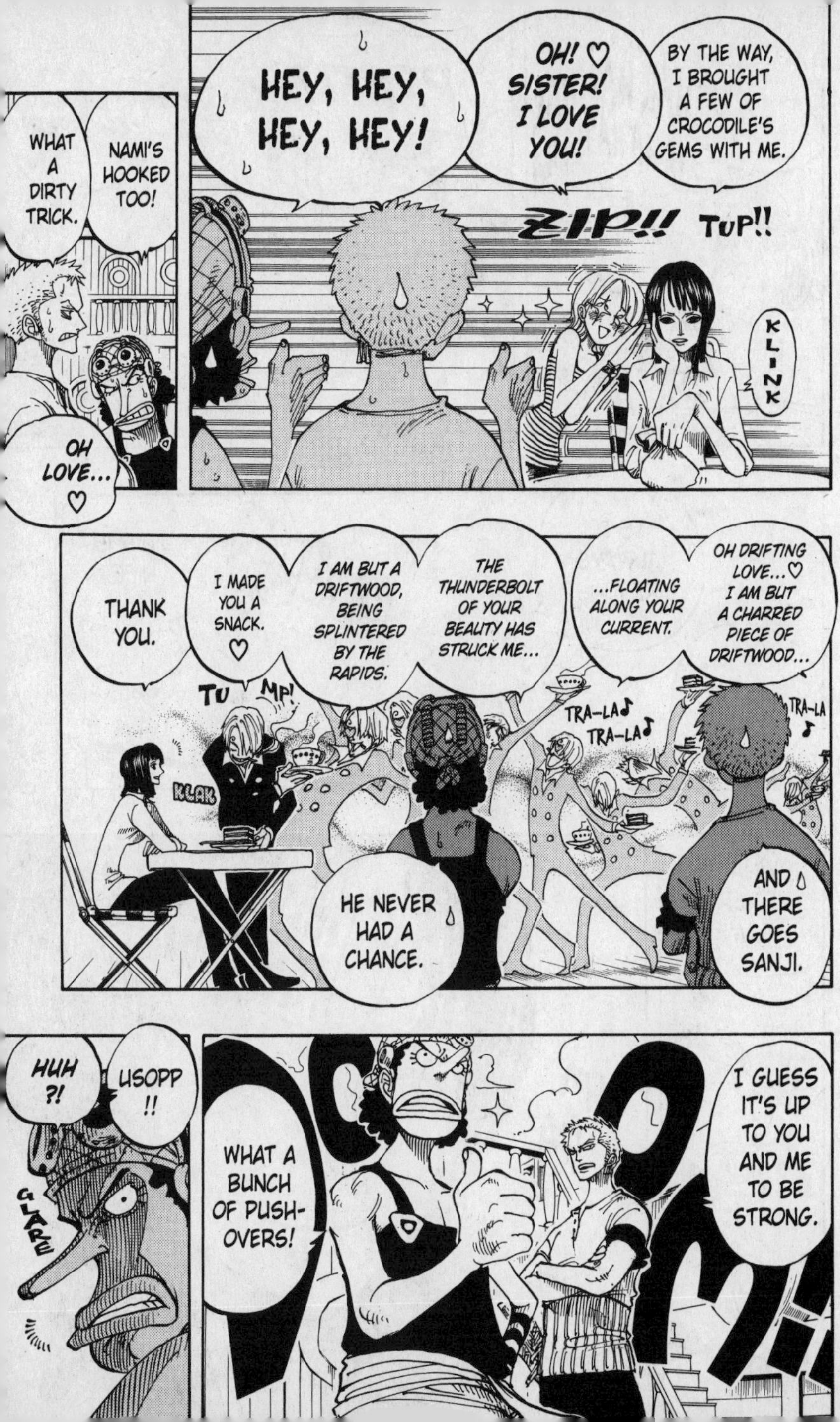

BY THE WAY, I BROUGHT A FEW OF CROCODILE'S GEMS WITH ME.
OH! ♡ SISTER! I LOVE YOU!
HEY, HEY, HEY, HEY!
TUP!!
ZIP!!
KLINK
NAMI'S HOOKED TOO!
WHAT A DIRTY TRICK.
OH LOVE... ♡
OH DRIFTING LOVE... ♡ I AM BUT A CHARRED PIECE OF DRIFTWOOD...
...FLOATING ALONG YOUR CURRENT.
THE THUNDERBOLT OF YOUR BEAUTY HAS STRUCK ME...
I AM BUT A DRIFTWOOD, BEING SPLINTERED BY THE RAPIDS.
I MADE YOU A SNACK. ♡
THANK YOU.
TRA-LA♪
TRA-LA♪ TRA-LA♪
TUMP!
KLAK
AND THERE GOES SANJI.
HE NEVER HAD A CHANCE.
I GUESS IT'S UP TO YOU AND ME TO BE STRONG.
WHAT A BUNCH OF PUSH-OVERS!
USOPP!!
HUH?!
GLARE

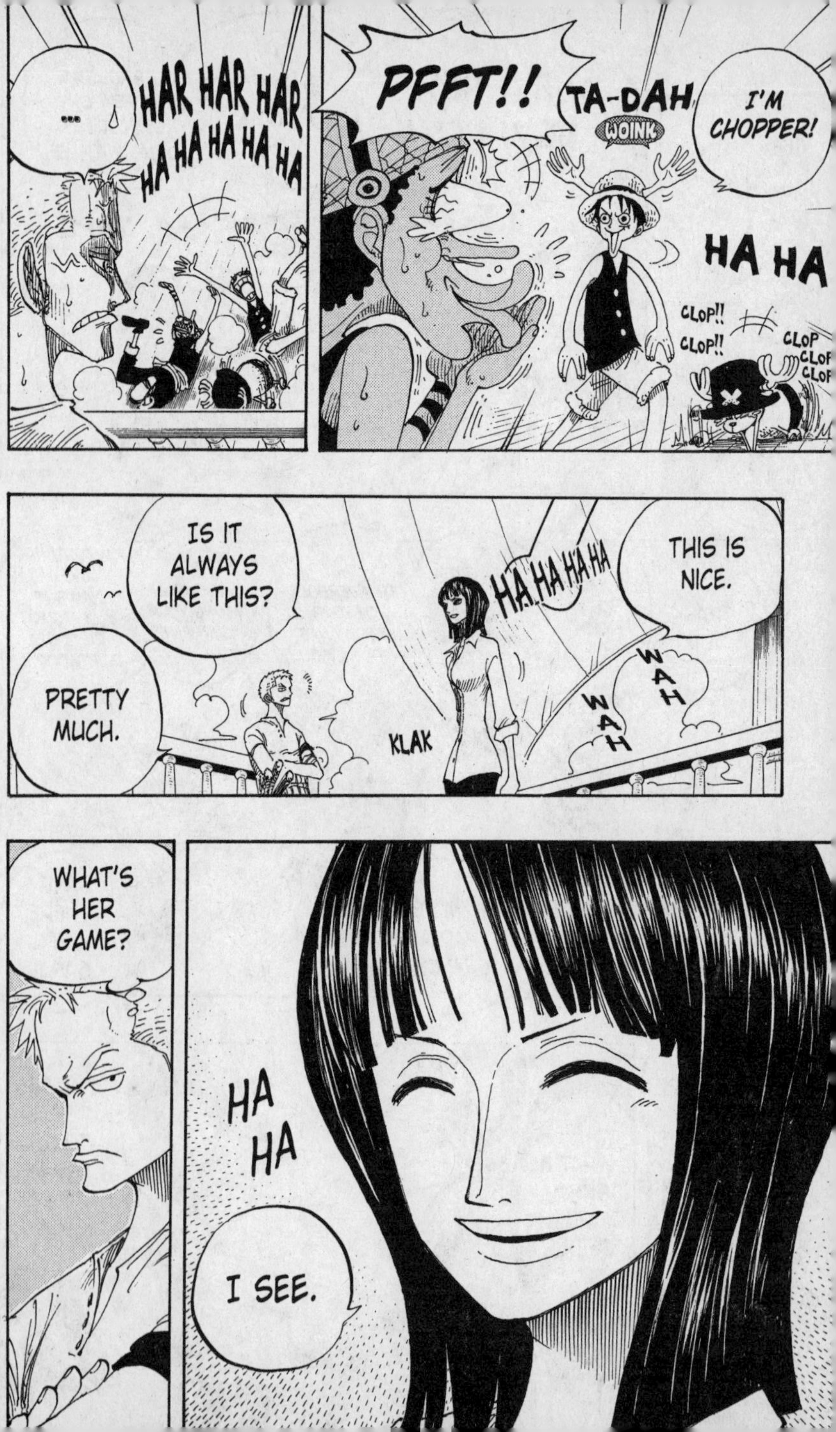
I'M CHOPPER!
TA-DAH
WOINK
PFFT!!
HA HA
CLOP CLOP CLOP
CLOP!! CLOP!!
HAR HAR HAR HA HA HA HA HA
...
THIS IS NICE.
HA HA HA HA
IS IT ALWAYS LIKE THIS?
WAH WAH
WAH WAH
PRETTY MUCH.
KLAK
HA HA
I SEE.
WHAT'S HER GAME?

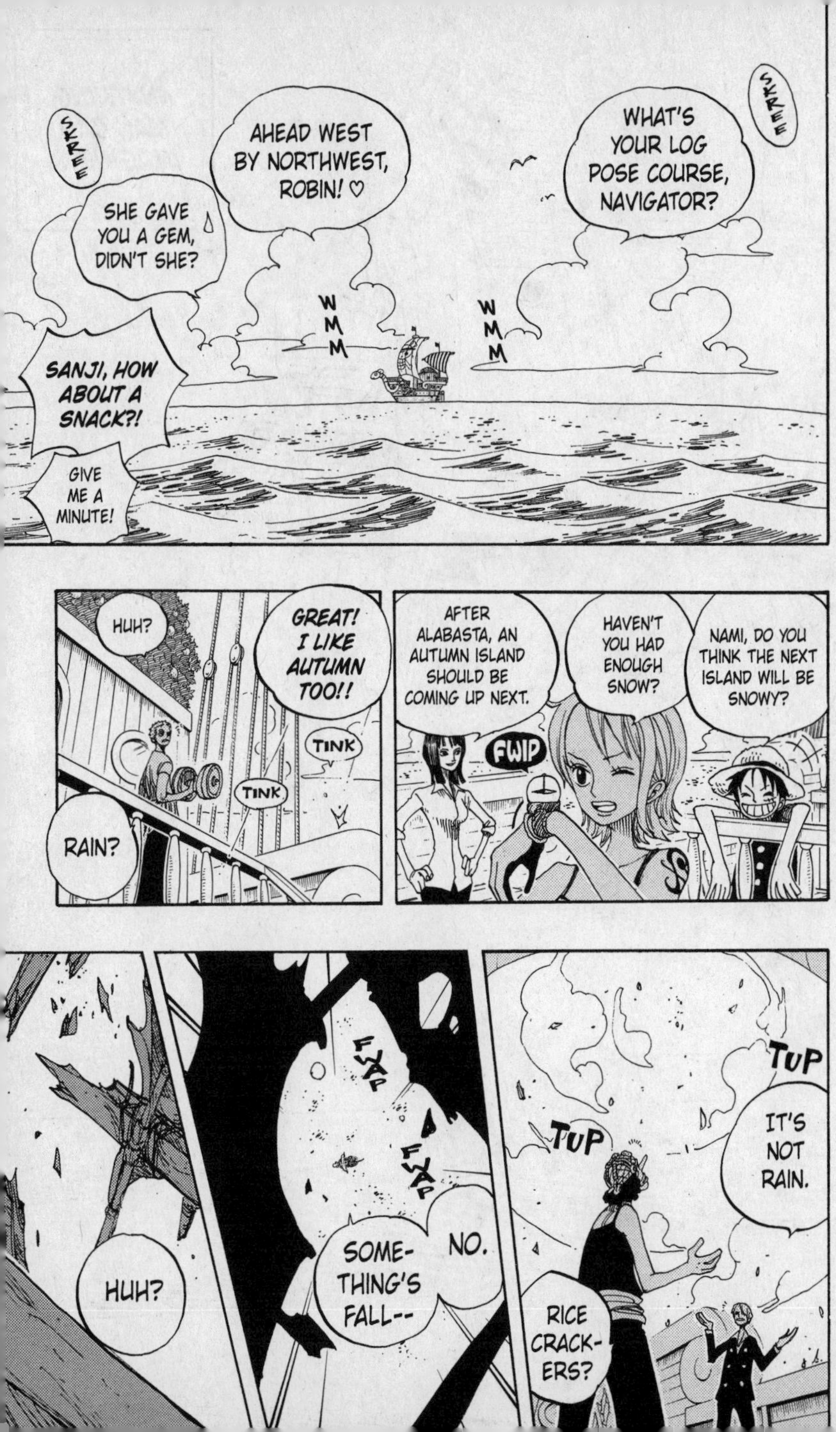
SKREE
WHAT'S YOUR LOG POSE COURSE, NAVIGATOR?
AHEAD WEST BY NORTHWEST, ROBIN! ♡
SKREE
SHE GAVE YOU A GEM, DIDN'T SHE?
WMM
WMM
SANJI, HOW ABOUT A SNACK?!
GIVE ME A MINUTE!
NAMI, DO YOU THINK THE NEXT ISLAND WILL BE SNOWY?
HAVEN'T YOU HAD ENOUGH SNOW?
AFTER ALABASTA, AN AUTUMN ISLAND SHOULD BE COMING UP NEXT.
FWIP
GREAT! I LIKE AUTUMN TOO!!
HUH?
TINK
TINK
RAIN?
TUP
IT'S NOT RAIN.
TUP
RICE CRACK-ERS?
FWAP
FWAP
NO.
SOME-THING'S FALL--
HUH?

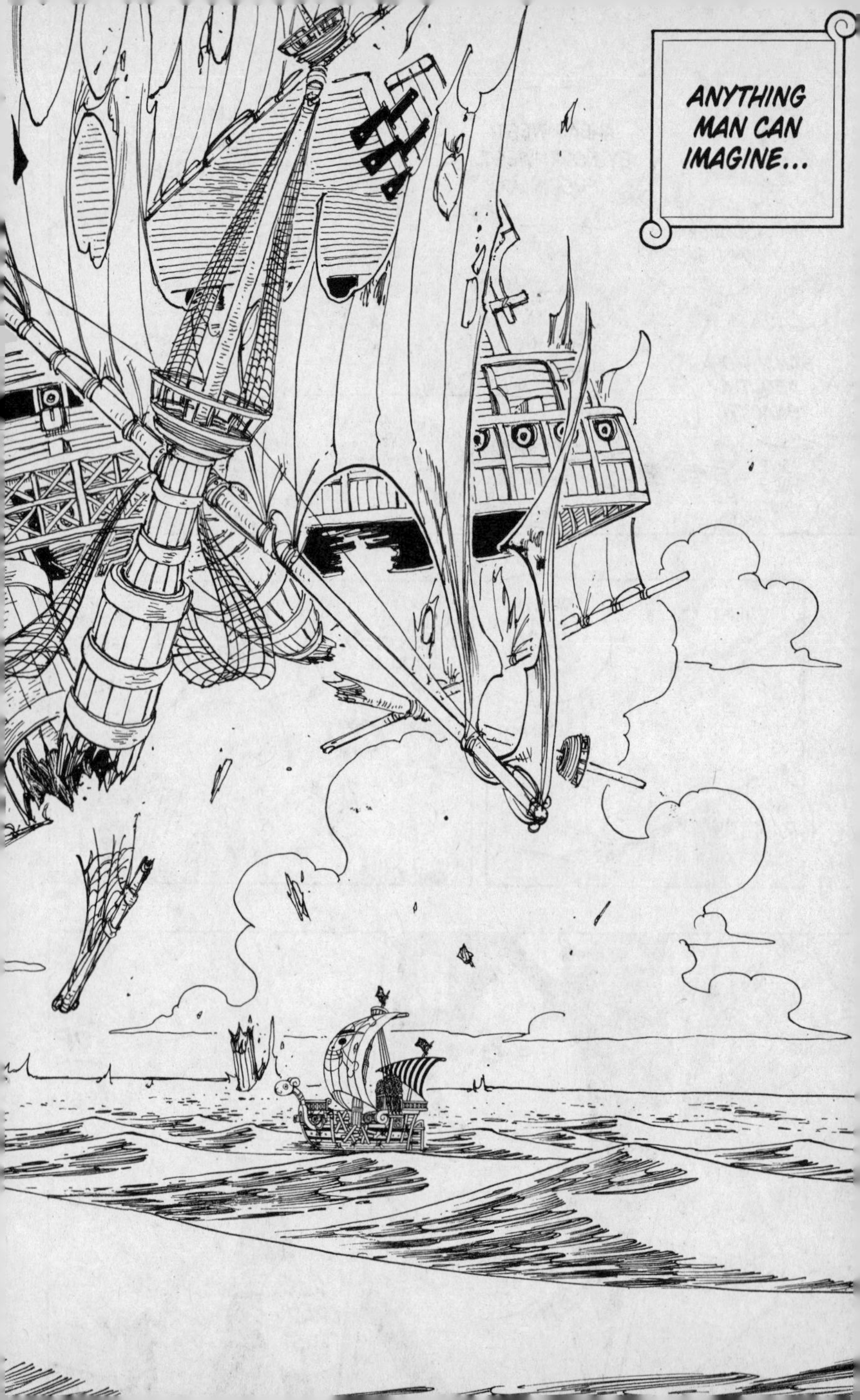
ANYTHING MAN CAN IMAGINE...

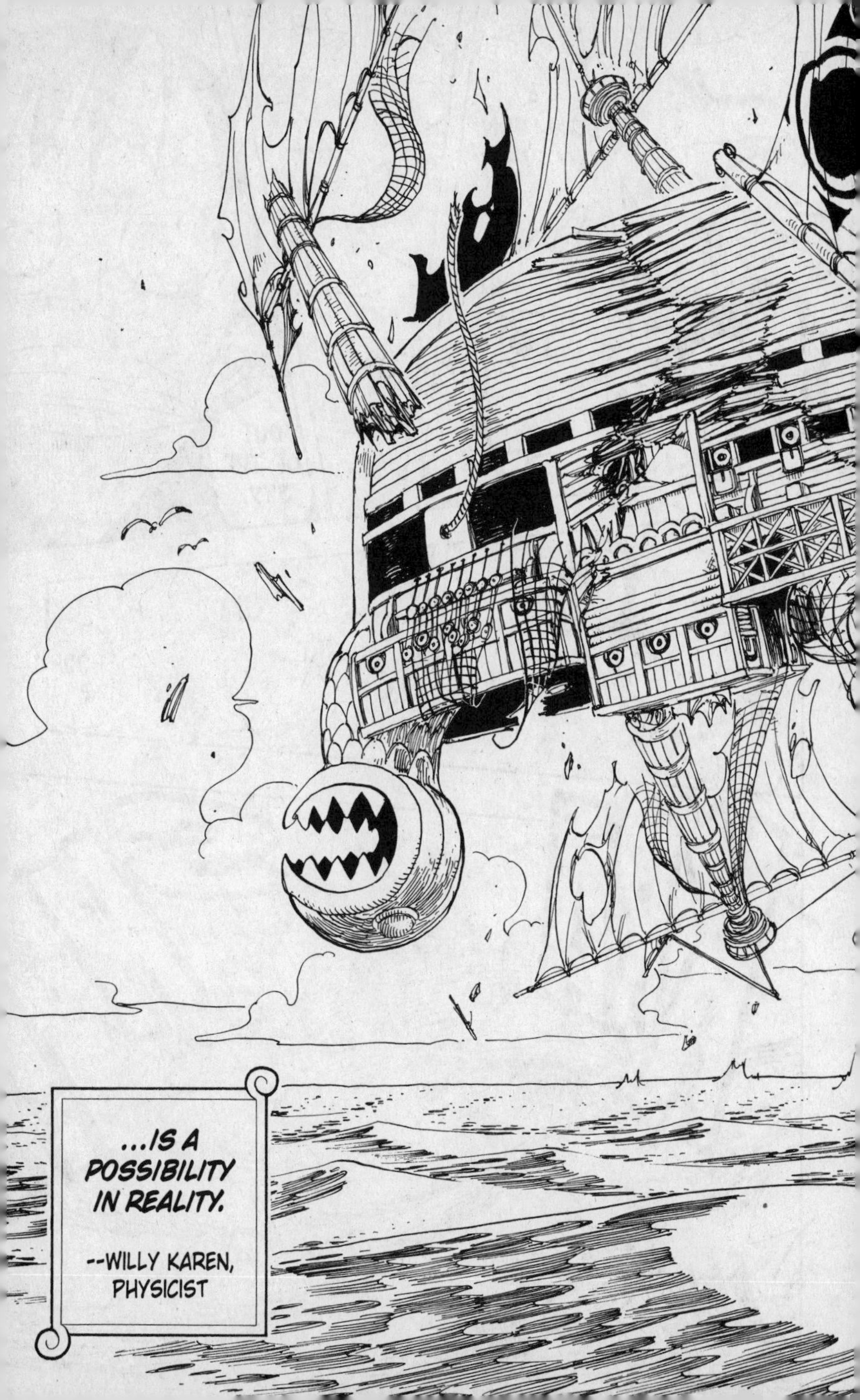
...IS A POSSIBILITY IN REALITY.
--WILLY KAREN, PHYSICIST

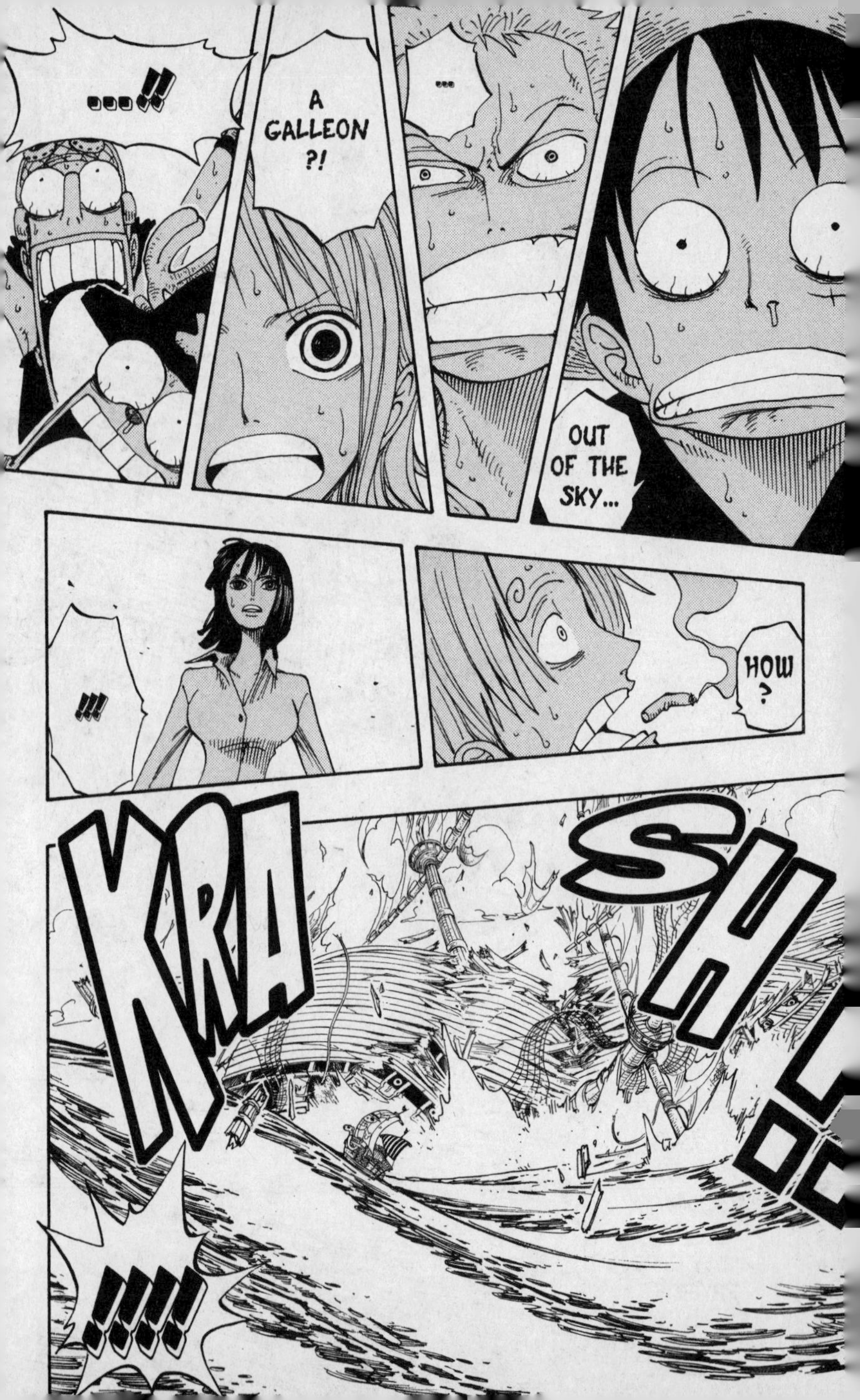

OUT OF THE SKY...
...
A GALLEON ?!
...!!
HOW ?
!!!
KRA
SHH
!!!!!

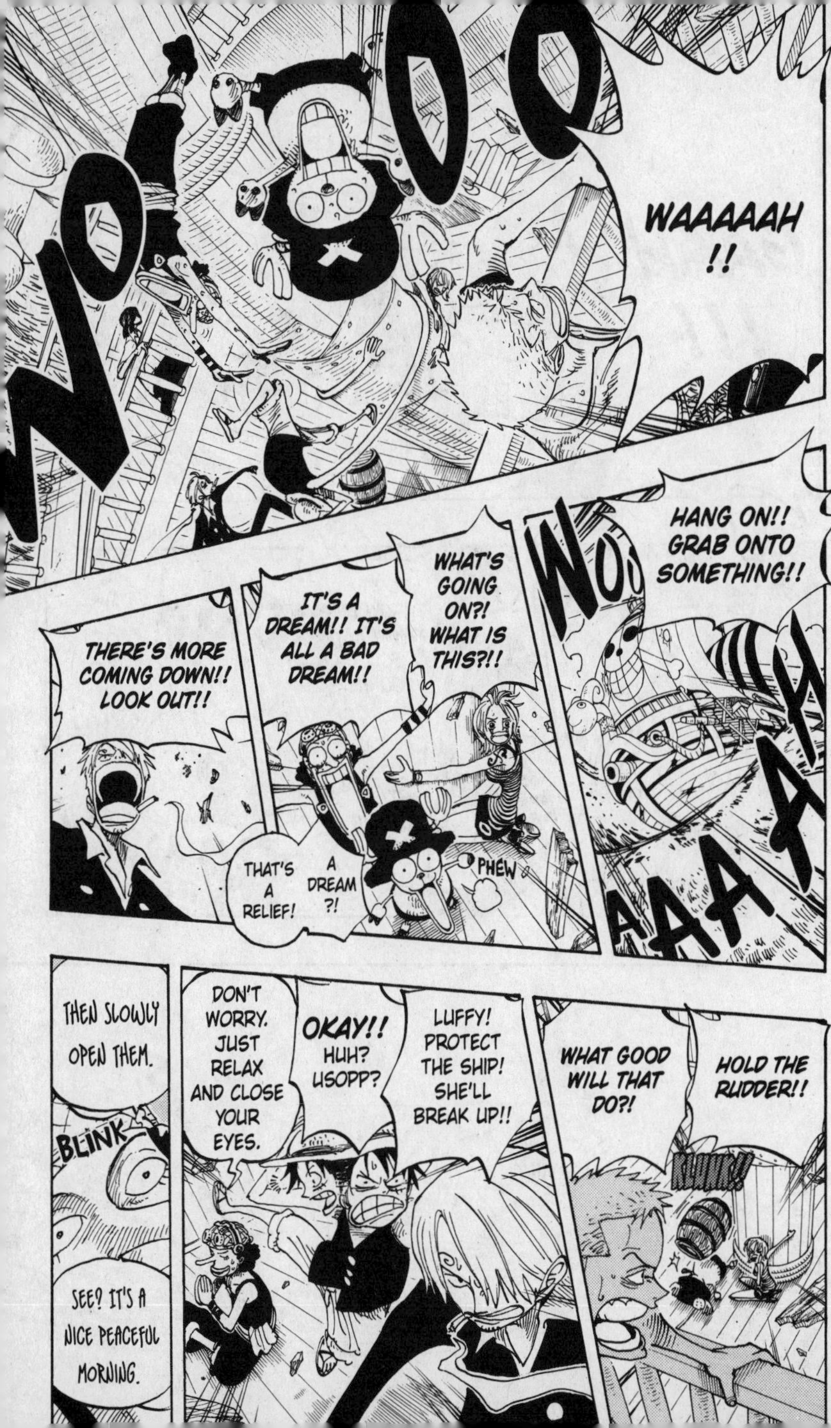
WAAAAAH !!
HANG ON!! GRAB ONTO SOMETHING!!
WHAT'S GOING ON?! WHAT IS THIS?!!
IT'S A DREAM!! IT'S ALL A BAD DREAM!!
A DREAM ?!
THAT'S A RELIEF!
PHEW
THERE'S MORE COMING DOWN!! LOOK OUT!!
HOLD THE RUDDER!!
WHAT GOOD WILL THAT DO?!
LUFFY! PROTECT THE SHIP! SHE'LL BREAK UP!!
OKAY!!
HUH? USOPP?
DON'T WORRY. JUST RELAX AND CLOSE YOUR EYES.
THEN SLOWLY OPEN THEM.
BLINK
SEE? IT'S A NICE PEACEFUL MORNING.

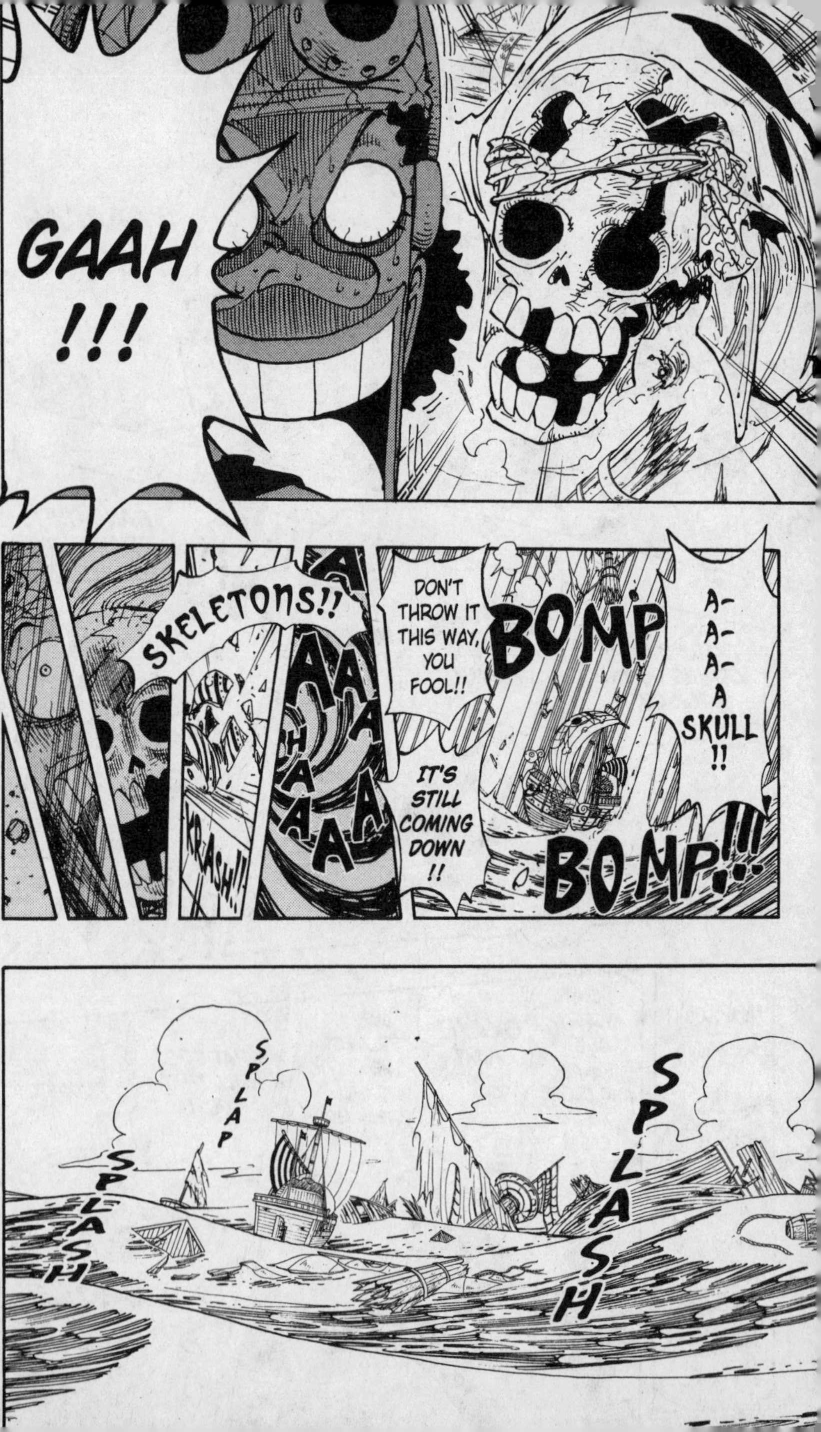
GAAH!!!
A-A-A-A SKULL!!
BOMP
BOMP!!!
IT'S STILL COMING DOWN!!
DON'T THROW IT THIS WAY, YOU FOOL!!
KRASH!!
SKELETONS!!
SPLASH
SPLAP
SPLASH

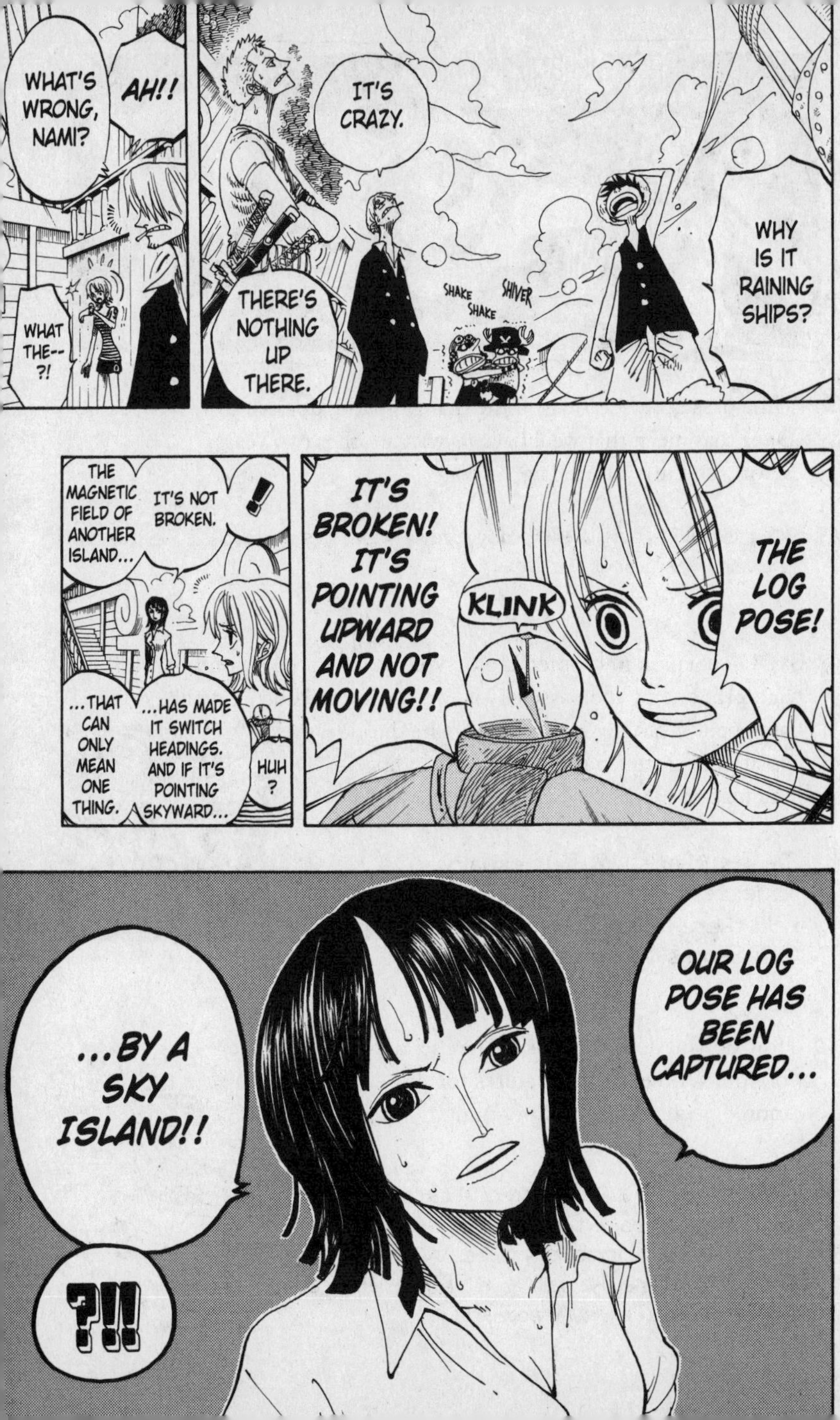
WHY IS IT RAINING SHIPS?
IT'S CRAZY.
SHIVER
SHAKE SHAKE
THERE'S NOTHING UP THERE.
AH!!
WHAT'S WRONG, NAMI?
WHAT THE--?!
THE LOG POSE!
IT'S BROKEN! IT'S POINTING UPWARD AND NOT MOVING!!
KLINK
!
IT'S NOT BROKEN.
THE MAGNETIC FIELD OF ANOTHER ISLAND...
HUH?
...HAS MADE IT SWITCH HEADINGS. AND IF IT'S POINTING SKYWARD...
...THAT CAN ONLY MEAN ONE THING.
OUR LOG POSE HAS BEEN CAPTURED...
...BY A SKY ISLAND!!
?!!

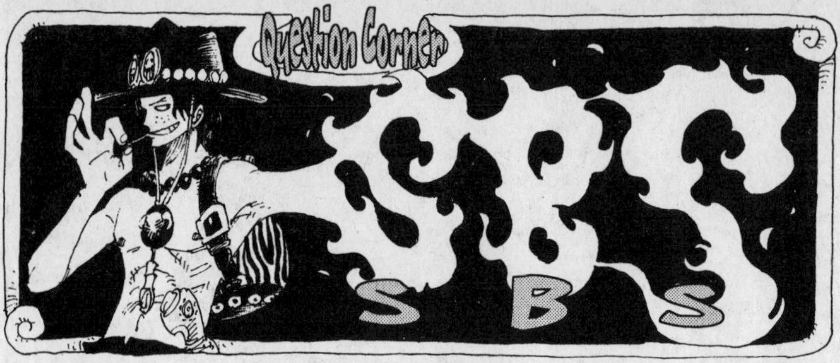
Question Corner
SBS

Q: Time passes more slowly in the manga world, doesn't it? Does that mean that we'll have to wait another two years before it's Luffy's birthday?

A: No, no, Luffy has a birthday every year. It's just that he turns 17 every year. Isn't he lucky?

Q: Say, Oda Sensei, in chapter 216 of volume 23 in the second panel of page 215, one of the passersby is Mr. 3. He's walking along like nothing happened! What's going on? Didn't he die? Please explain in exactly 75 letters! (Not including punctuation marks.)

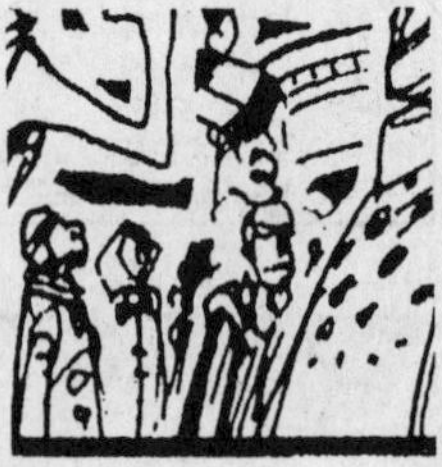

A: Oh yes, that's him. But explaining it in 75 letters won't be easy. The reason he's there? Easy. I felt like it.
Oh!! Shucks, I was too long.

Q: How do you do, Oda Sensei. Here's a question for you. Who takes the pictures for those wanted posters the Navy put out?

A: That's him (→). Real name: Atatchi. Also known as: Atacchan. He's very agile and can sneak into any place. When he snaps a picture, he yells out: "Fire!!" Hence, his nickname "Fire Atacchan."

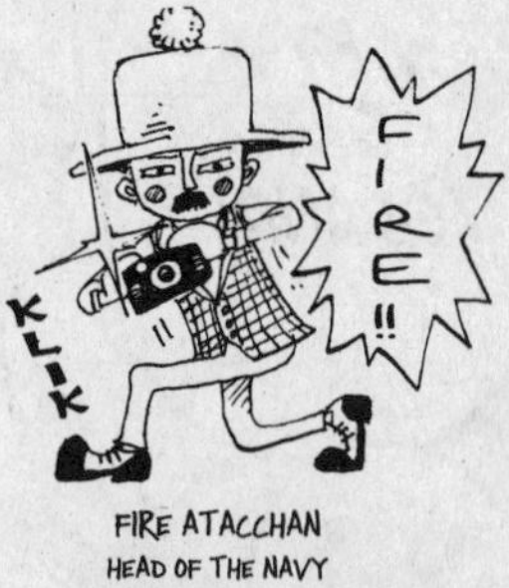
FIRE!!
KLIK

FIRE ATACCHAN
HEAD OF THE NAVY
PHOTOGRAPHY DEPARTMENT

Chapter 219:
MASIRA THE SALVAGE KING

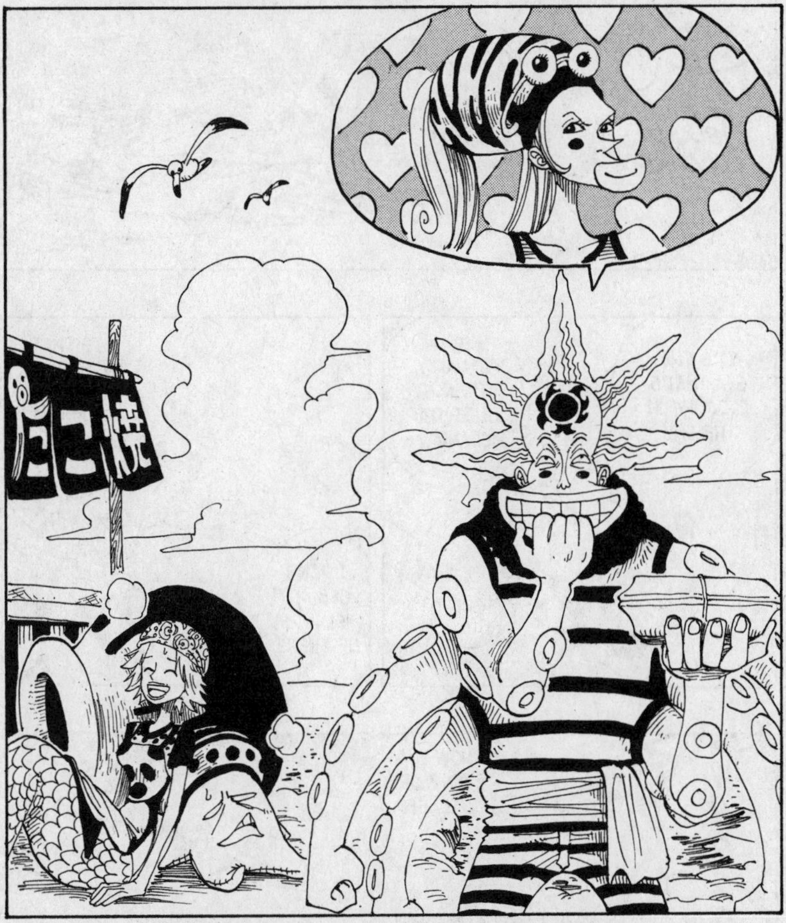
たこ焼

HACHI'S WALK ON THE SEAFLOOR, VOL. 33:
"THE CATFISH VILLAGE IS SAVED;
PROPOSING WITH THE LAST BOX ♡ "

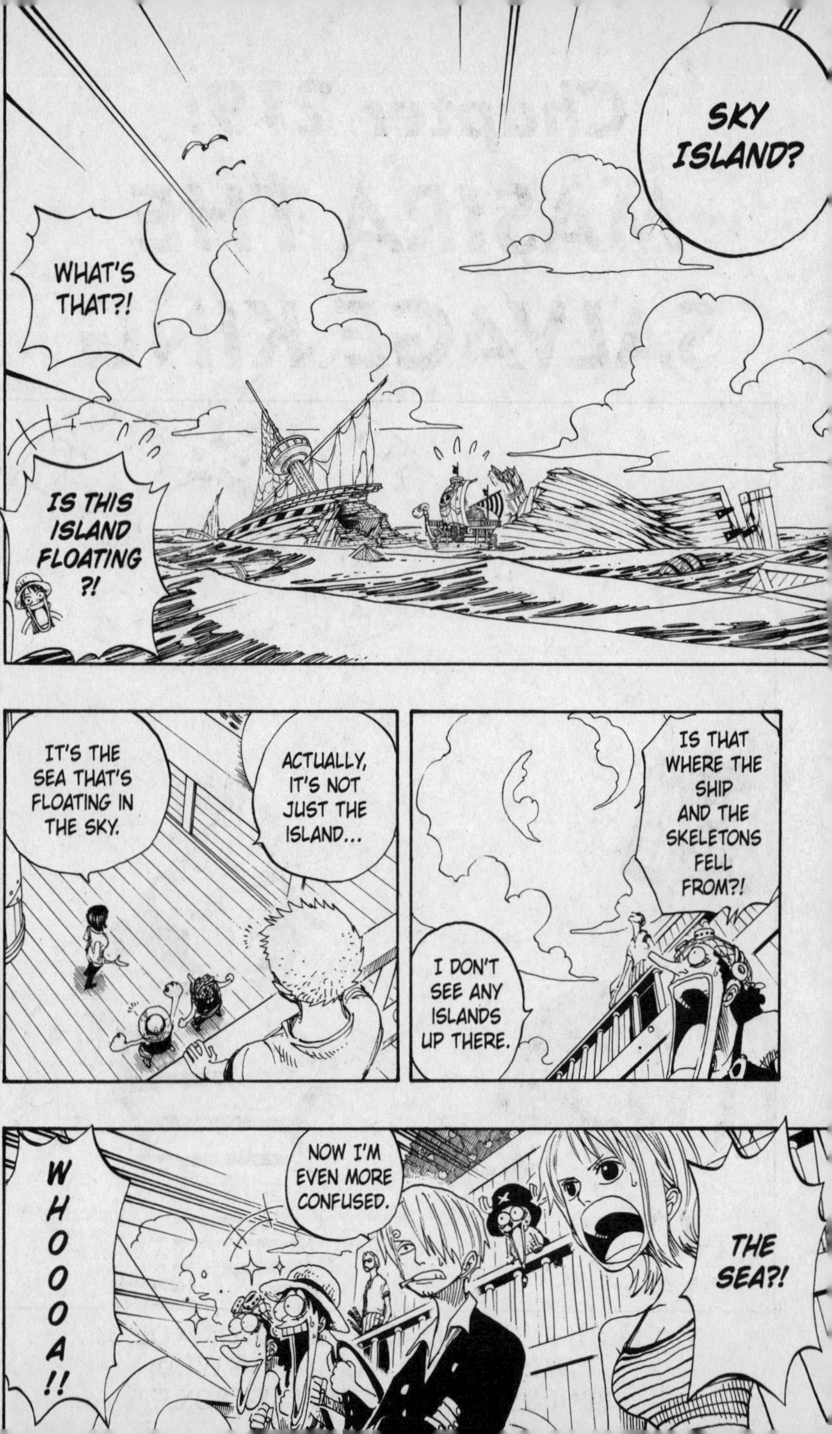
SKY ISLAND?
WHAT'S THAT?!
IS THIS ISLAND FLOATING?!
IS THAT WHERE THE SHIP AND THE SKELETONS FELL FROM?!
I DON'T SEE ANY ISLANDS UP THERE.
ACTUALLY, IT'S NOT JUST THE ISLAND...
IT'S THE SEA THAT'S FLOATING IN THE SKY.
THE SEA?!
NOW I'M EVEN MORE CONFUSED.
WHOOOOA!!

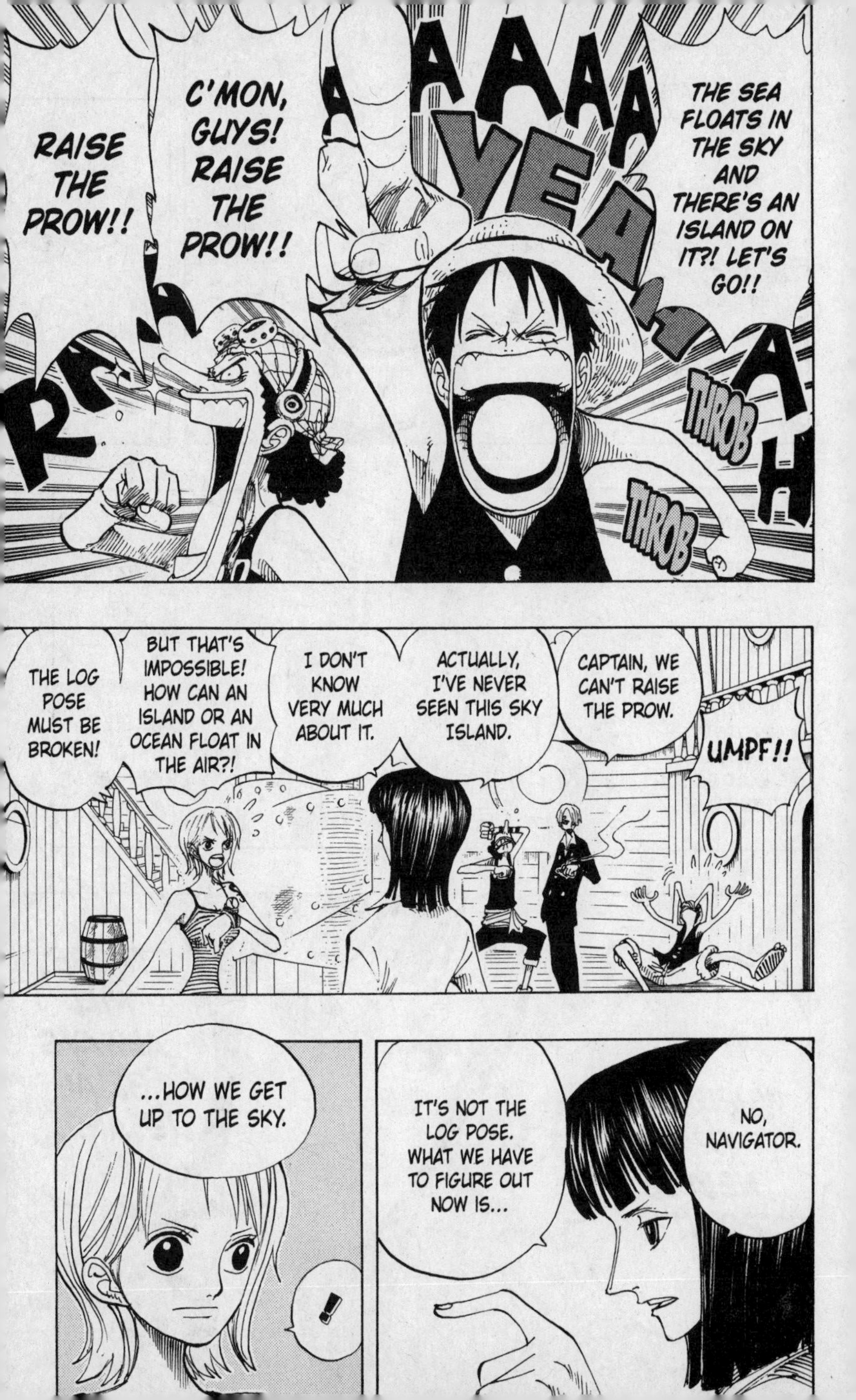
THE SEA FLOATS IN THE SKY AND THERE'S AN ISLAND ON IT?! LET'S GO!!
YEA
THROB
THROB
C'MON, GUYS! RAISE THE PROW!!
RAISE THE PROW!!
CAPTAIN, WE CAN'T RAISE THE PROW.
UMPF!!
ACTUALLY, I'VE NEVER SEEN THIS SKY ISLAND.
I DON'T KNOW VERY MUCH ABOUT IT.
BUT THAT'S IMPOSSIBLE! HOW CAN AN ISLAND OR AN OCEAN FLOAT IN THE AIR?!
THE LOG POSE MUST BE BROKEN!
NO, NAVIGATOR.
IT'S NOT THE LOG POSE. WHAT WE HAVE TO FIGURE OUT NOW IS...
...HOW WE GET UP TO THE SKY.
!

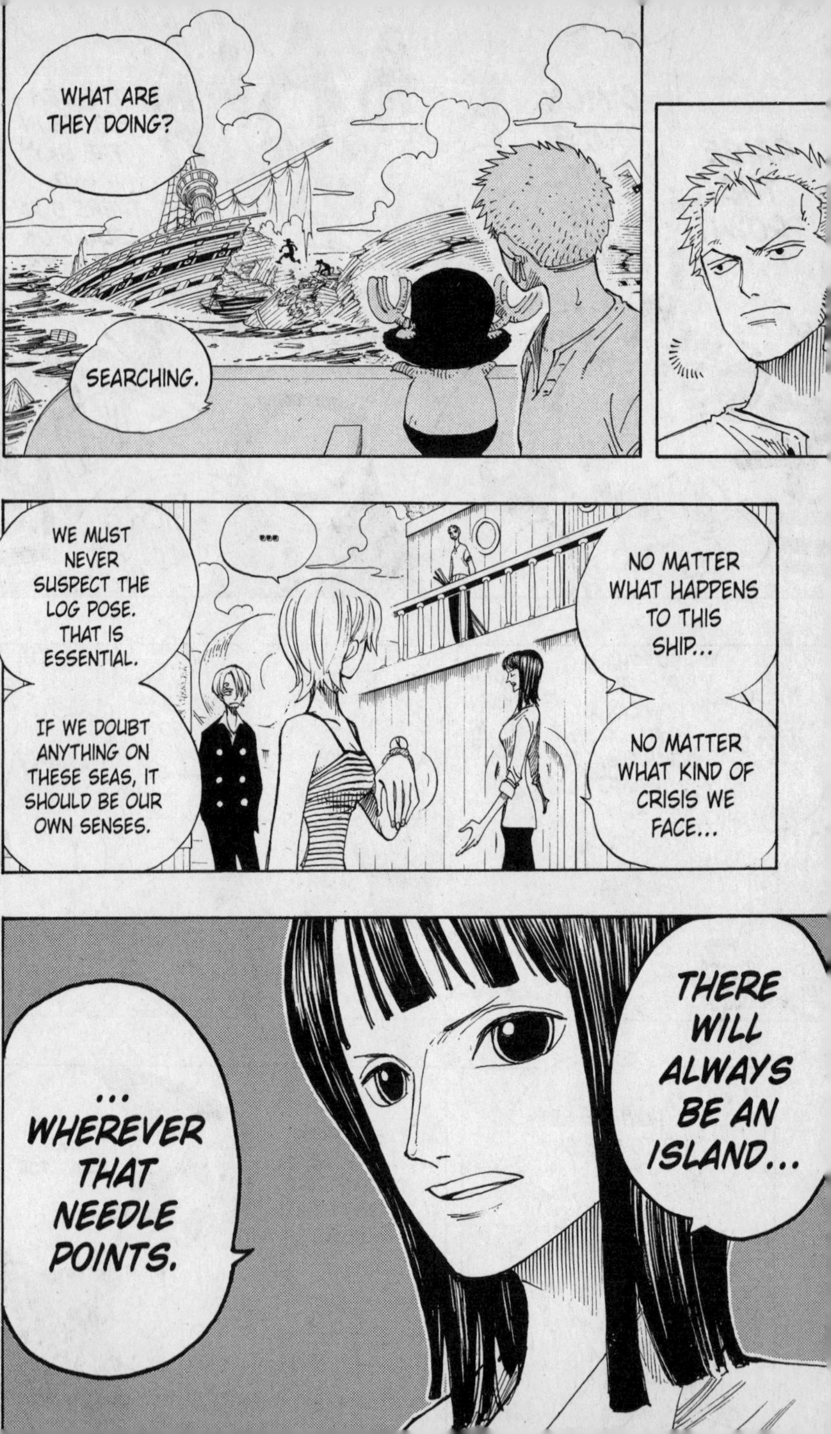
WHAT ARE THEY DOING?
SEARCHING.
NO MATTER WHAT HAPPENS TO THIS SHIP...
NO MATTER WHAT KIND OF CRISIS WE FACE...
...
WE MUST NEVER SUSPECT THE LOG POSE. THAT IS ESSENTIAL.
IF WE DOUBT ANYTHING ON THESE SEAS, IT SHOULD BE OUR OWN SENSES.
THERE WILL ALWAYS BE AN ISLAND...
...WHEREVER THAT NEEDLE POINTS.

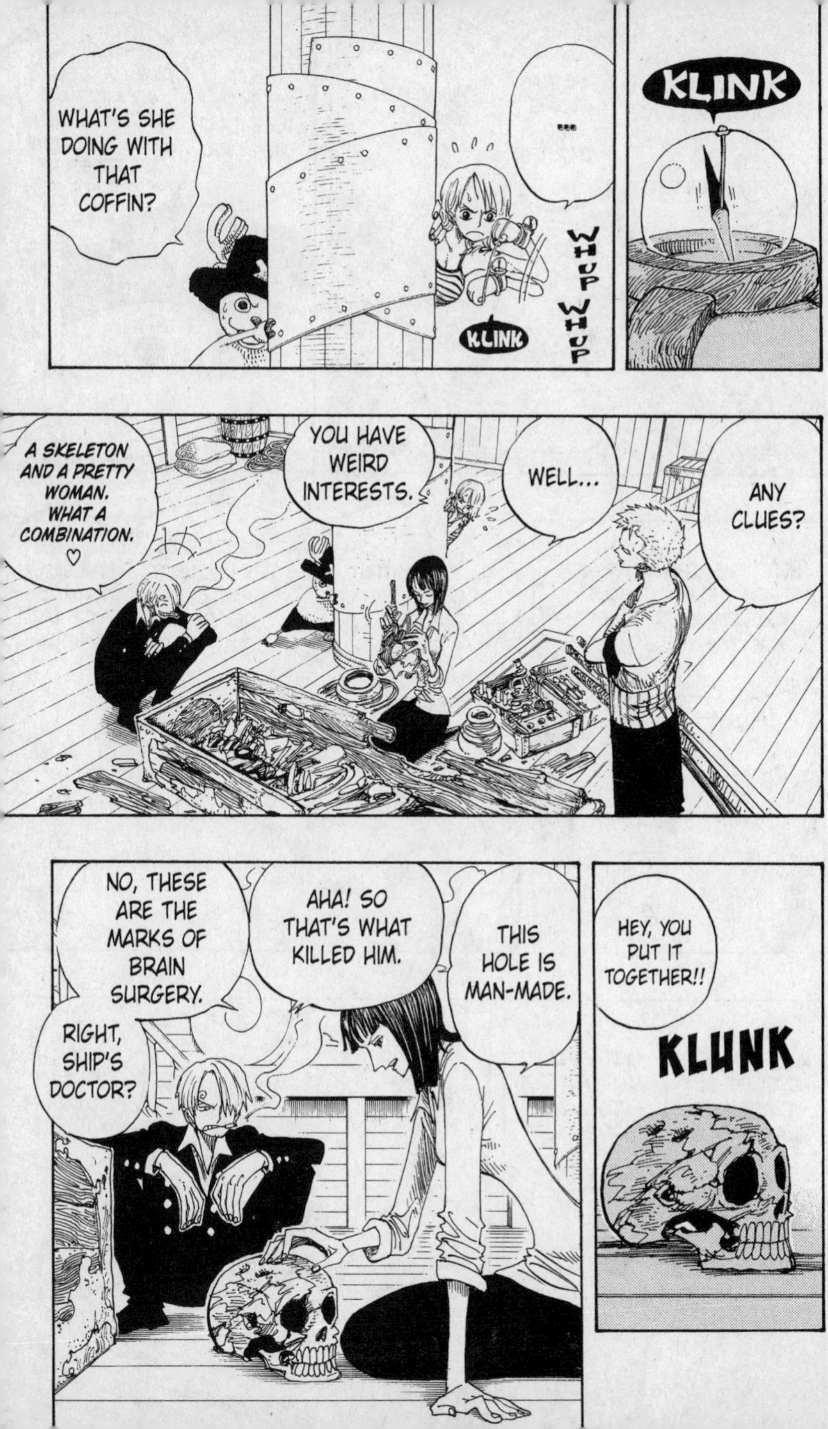
KLINK
...
WHAT'S SHE DOING WITH THAT COFFIN?
WHUP WHUP
KLINK
ANY CLUES?
WELL...
YOU HAVE WEIRD INTERESTS.
A SKELETON AND A PRETTY WOMAN. WHAT A COMBINATION. ♡
HEY, YOU PUT IT TOGETHER!!
KLUNK
THIS HOLE IS MAN-MADE.
AHA! SO THAT'S WHAT KILLED HIM.
NO, THESE ARE THE MARKS OF BRAIN SURGERY.
RIGHT, SHIP'S DOCTOR?

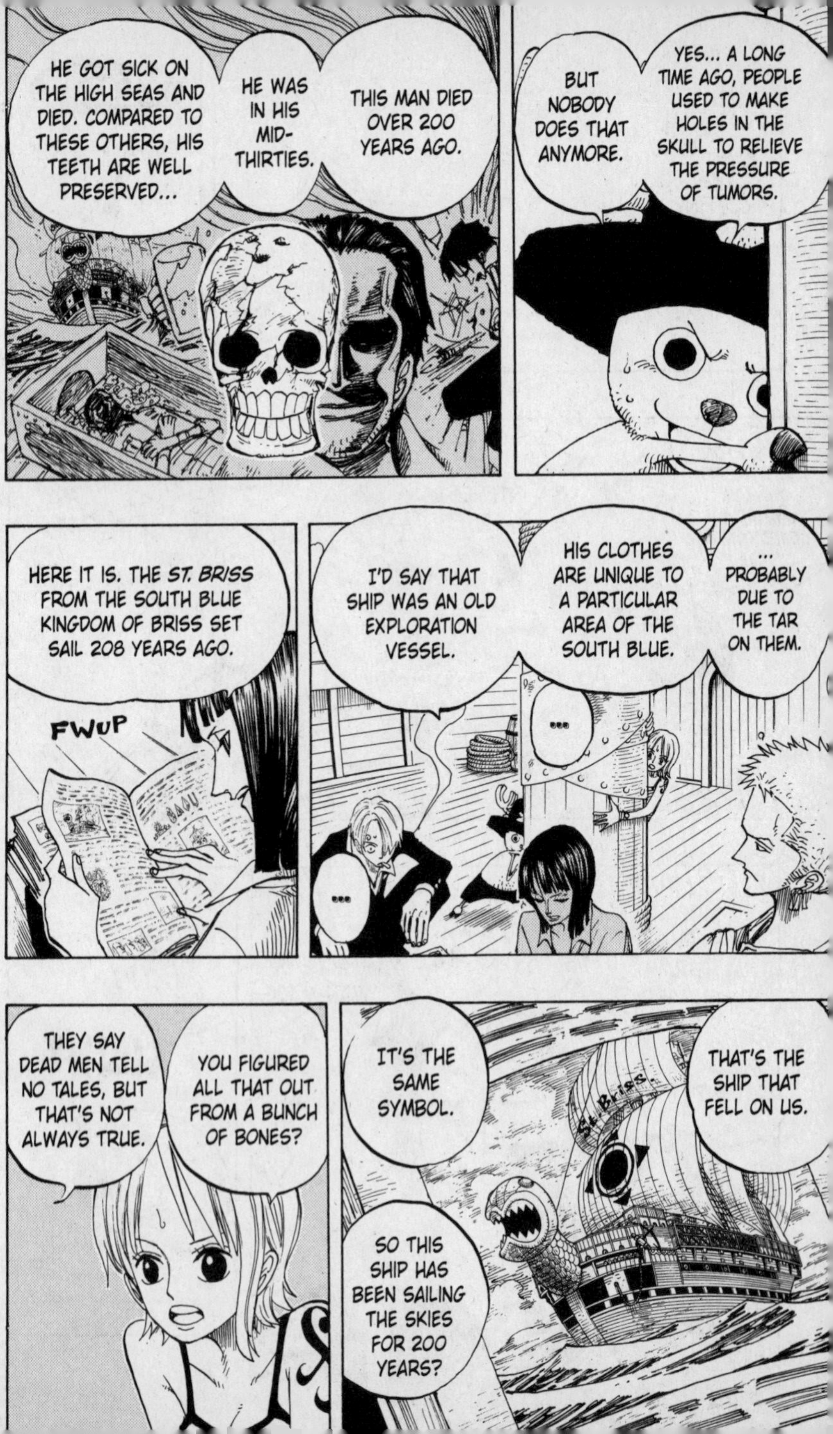
YES... A LONG TIME AGO, PEOPLE USED TO MAKE HOLES IN THE SKULL TO RELIEVE THE PRESSURE OF TUMORS.
BUT NOBODY DOES THAT ANYMORE.
THIS MAN DIED OVER 200 YEARS AGO.
HE WAS IN HIS MID-THIRTIES.
HE GOT SICK ON THE HIGH SEAS AND DIED. COMPARED TO THESE OTHERS, HIS TEETH ARE WELL PRESERVED...
...PROBABLY DUE TO THE TAR ON THEM.
HIS CLOTHES ARE UNIQUE TO A PARTICULAR AREA OF THE SOUTH BLUE.
I'D SAY THAT SHIP WAS AN OLD EXPLORATION VESSEL.
...
...
HERE IT IS. THE *ST. BRISS* FROM THE SOUTH BLUE KINGDOM OF BRISS SET SAIL 208 YEARS AGO.
FWUP
THAT'S THE SHIP THAT FELL ON US.
IT'S THE SAME SYMBOL.
St. Briss
SO THIS SHIP HAS BEEN SAILING THE SKIES FOR 200 YEARS?
YOU FIGURED ALL THAT OUT FROM A BUNCH OF BONES?
THEY SAY DEAD MEN TELL NO TALES, BUT THAT'S NOT ALWAYS TRUE.

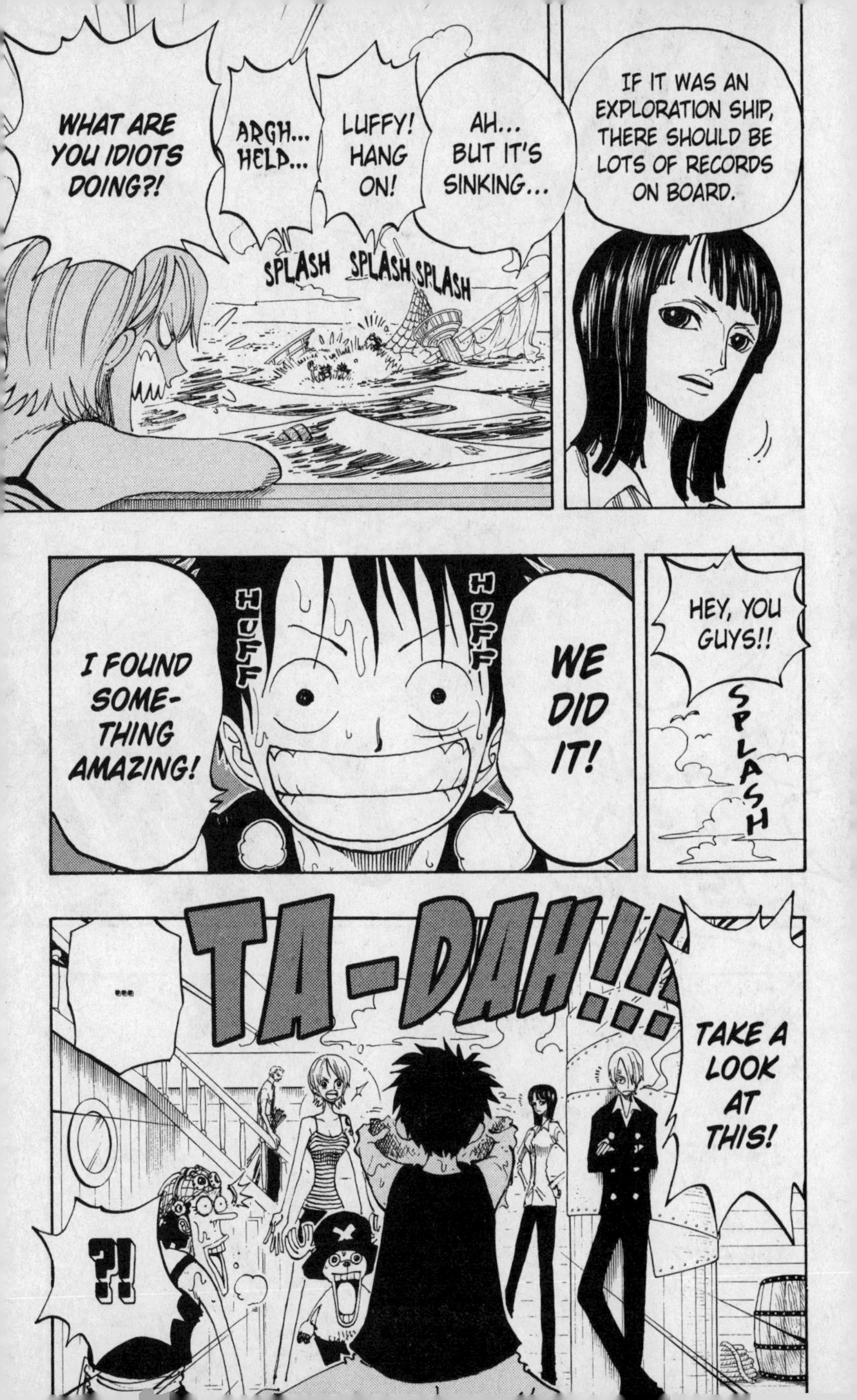
IF IT WAS AN EXPLORATION SHIP, THERE SHOULD BE LOTS OF RECORDS ON BOARD.
AH... BUT IT'S SINKING...
LUFFY! HANG ON!
ARGH... HELP...
WHAT ARE YOU IDIOTS DOING?!
SPLASH SPLASH SPLASH
HEY, YOU GUYS!!
SPLASH
WE DID IT!
HUFF
HUFF
I FOUND SOME-THING AMAZING!
TAKE A LOOK AT THIS!
TA-DAH!!
...
?!

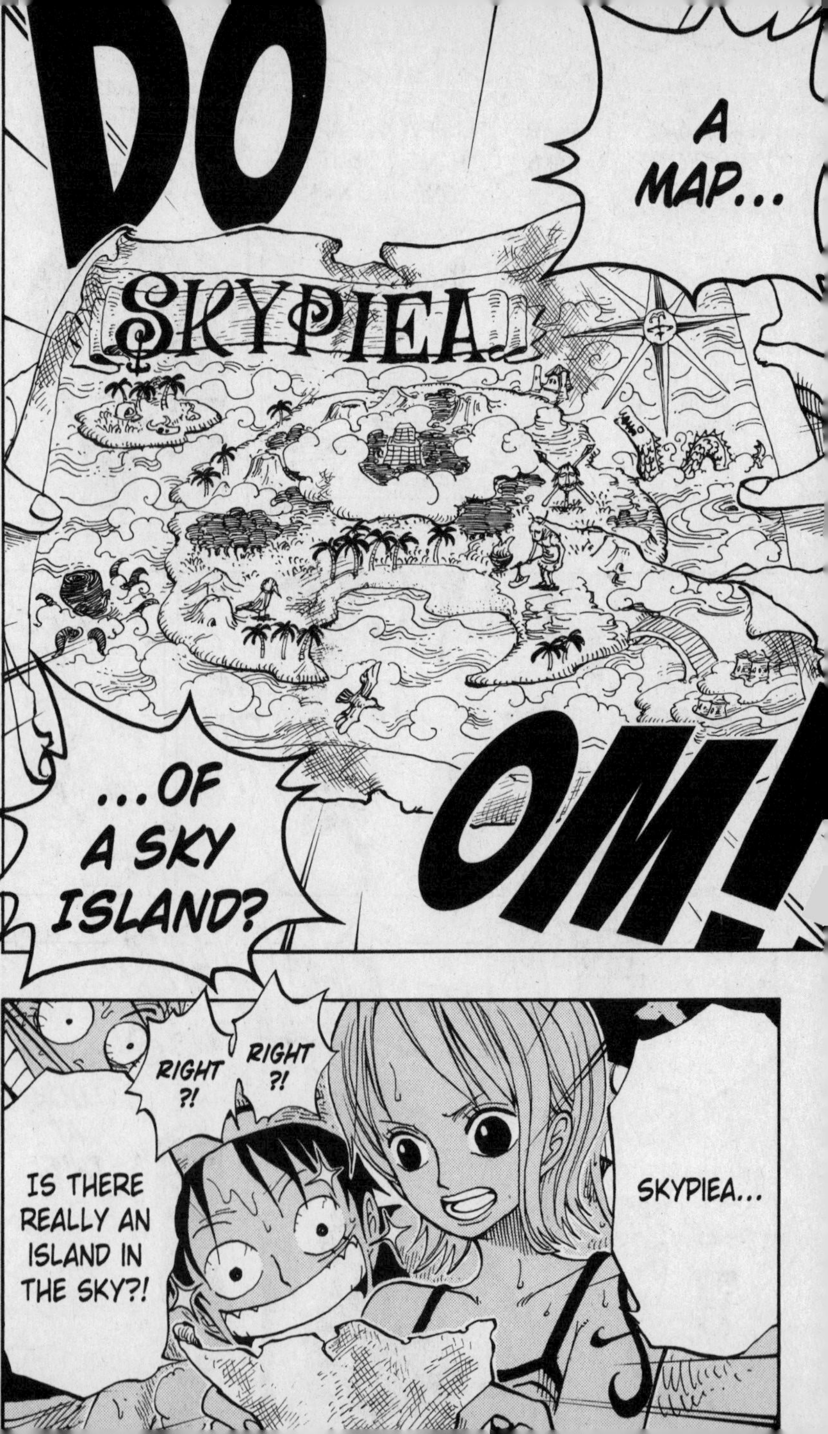
A MAP...
DO
SKYPIEA
OM!!
...OF A SKY ISLAND?
SKYPIEA...
RIGHT ?!
RIGHT ?!
IS THERE REALLY AN ISLAND IN THE SKY?!

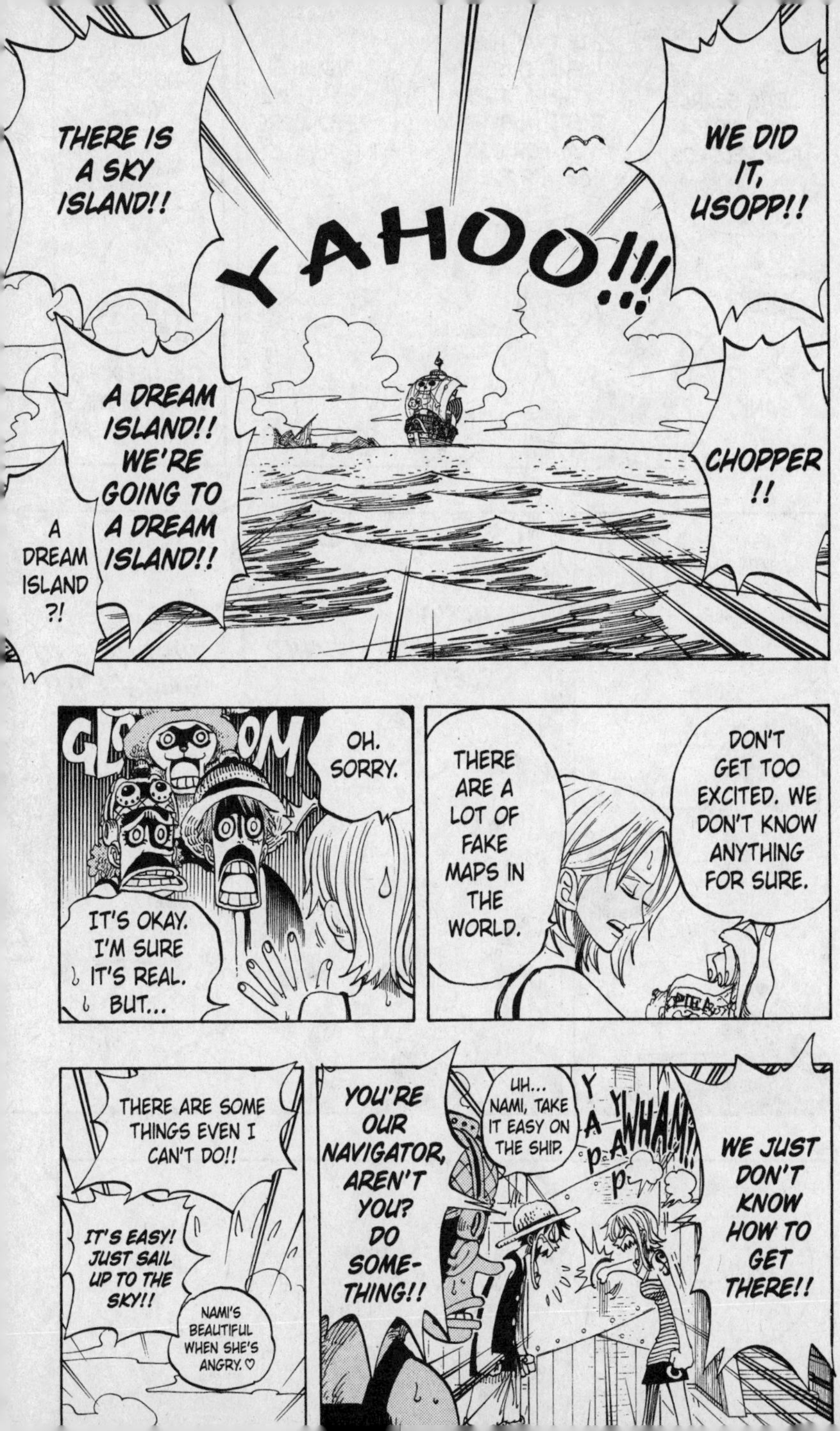
WE DID IT, USOPP!!
YAHOO!!!
THERE IS A SKY ISLAND!!
CHOPPER!!
A DREAM ISLAND!! WE'RE GOING TO A DREAM ISLAND!!
A DREAM ISLAND ?!
DON'T GET TOO EXCITED. WE DON'T KNOW ANYTHING FOR SURE.
THERE ARE A LOT OF FAKE MAPS IN THE WORLD.
GL OM
OH. SORRY.
IT'S OKAY. I'M SURE IT'S REAL. BUT...
WE JUST DON'T KNOW HOW TO GET THERE!!
WHAM!!
YAP YAP
UH... NAMI, TAKE IT EASY ON THE SHIP.
YOU'RE OUR NAVIGATOR, AREN'T YOU? DO SOME-THING!!
THERE ARE SOME THINGS EVEN I CAN'T DO!!
IT'S EASY! JUST SAIL UP TO THE SKY!!
NAMI'S BEAUTIFUL WHEN SHE'S ANGRY.♡

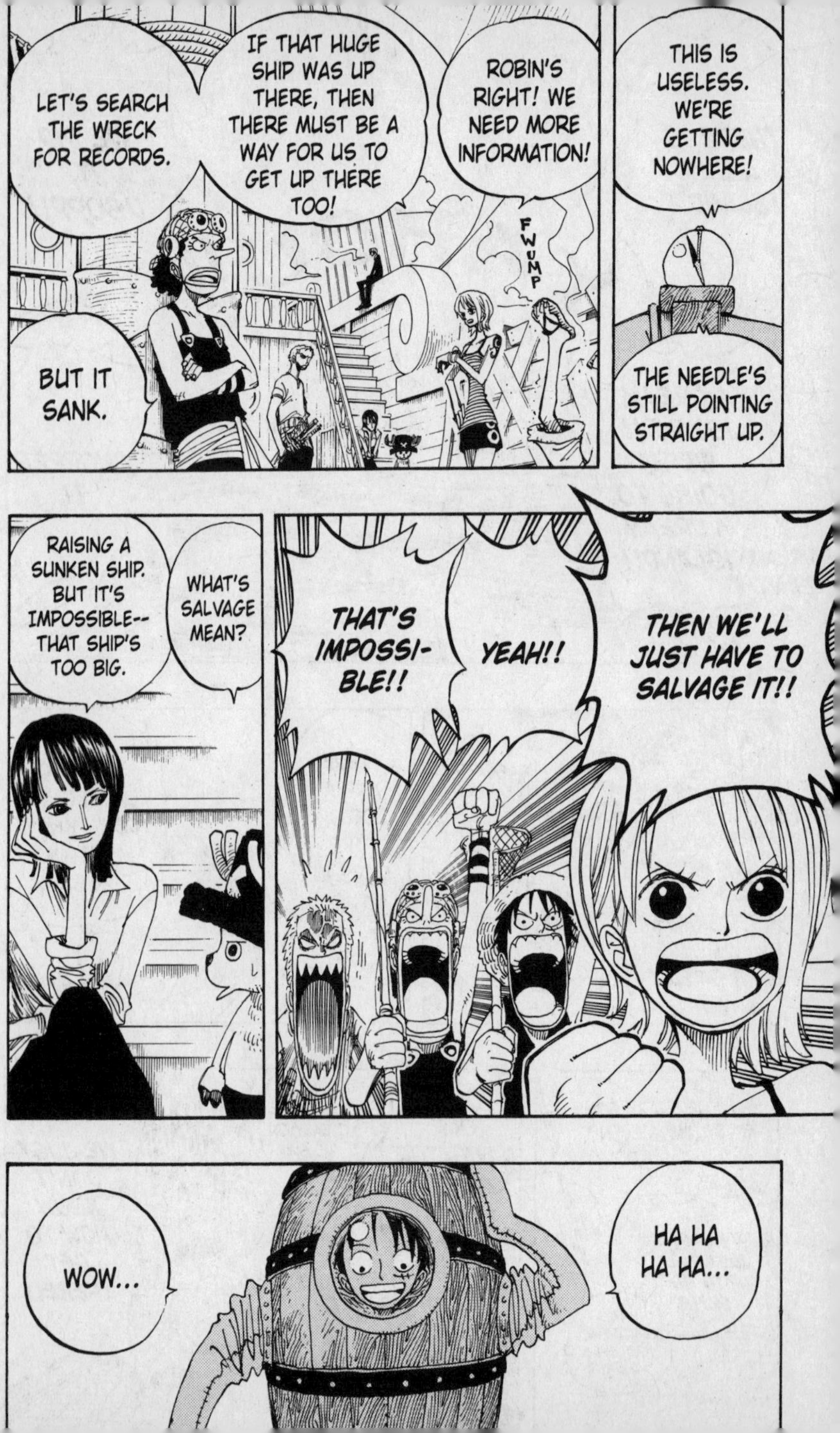
THIS IS USELESS. WE'RE GETTING NOWHERE!
THE NEEDLE'S STILL POINTING STRAIGHT UP.
ROBIN'S RIGHT! WE NEED MORE INFORMATION!
FWUMP
IF THAT HUGE SHIP WAS UP THERE, THEN THERE MUST BE A WAY FOR US TO GET UP THERE TOO!
LET'S SEARCH THE WRECK FOR RECORDS.
BUT IT SANK.
THEN WE'LL JUST HAVE TO SALVAGE IT!!
YEAH!!
THAT'S IMPOSSI-BLE!!
WHAT'S SALVAGE MEAN?
RAISING A SUNKEN SHIP. BUT IT'S IMPOSSIBLE--THAT SHIP'S TOO BIG.
HA HA HA HA...
WOW...

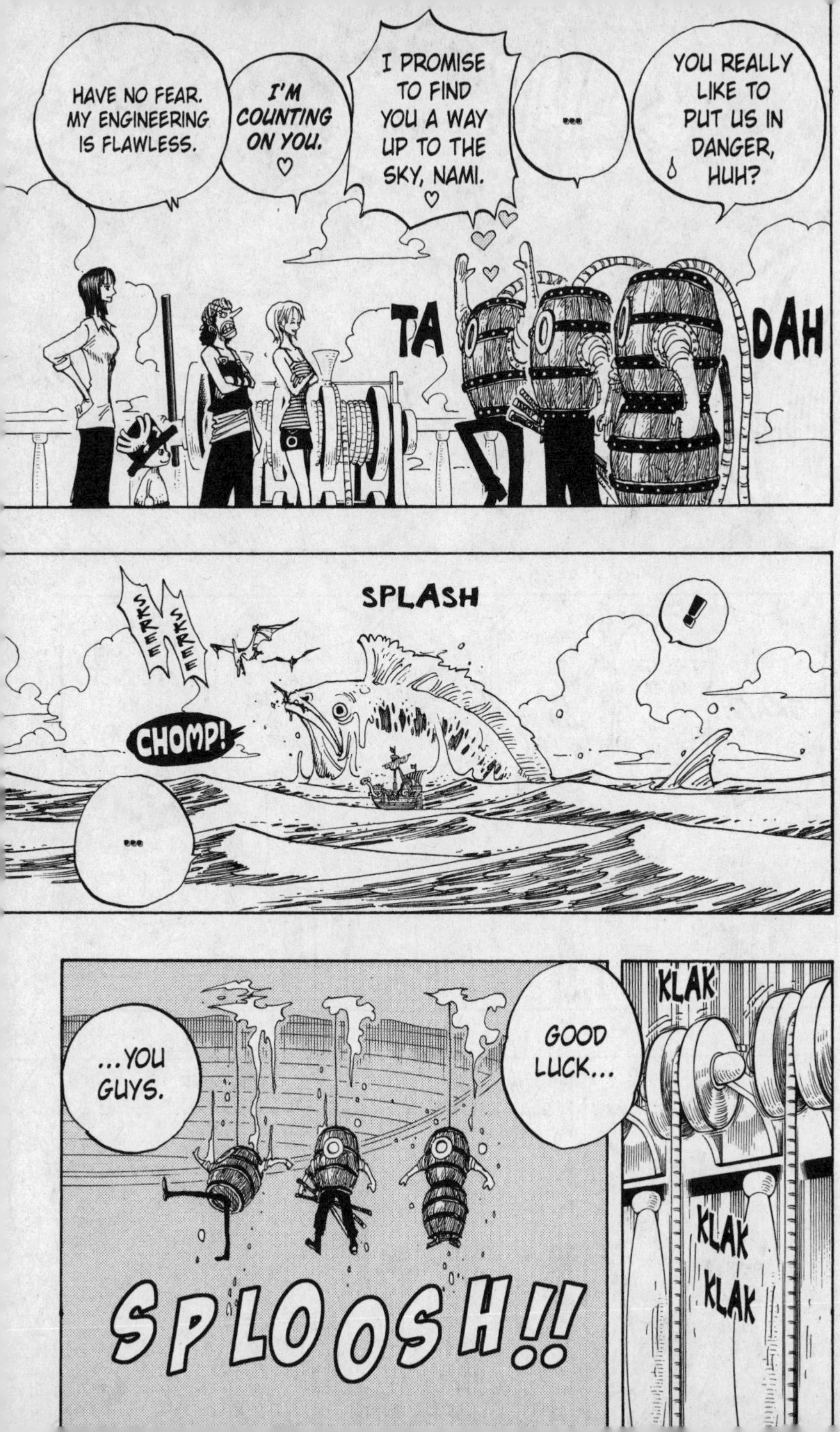
YOU REALLY LIKE TO PUT US IN DANGER, HUH?
...
I PROMISE TO FIND YOU A WAY UP TO THE SKY, NAMI.
I'M COUNTING ON YOU.
HAVE NO FEAR. MY ENGINEERING IS FLAWLESS.
TA DAH
!
SPLASH
SKREE SKREE
CHOMP!
...
KLAK
KLAK KLAK
GOOD LUCK...
...YOU GUYS.
SPLOOSH!!

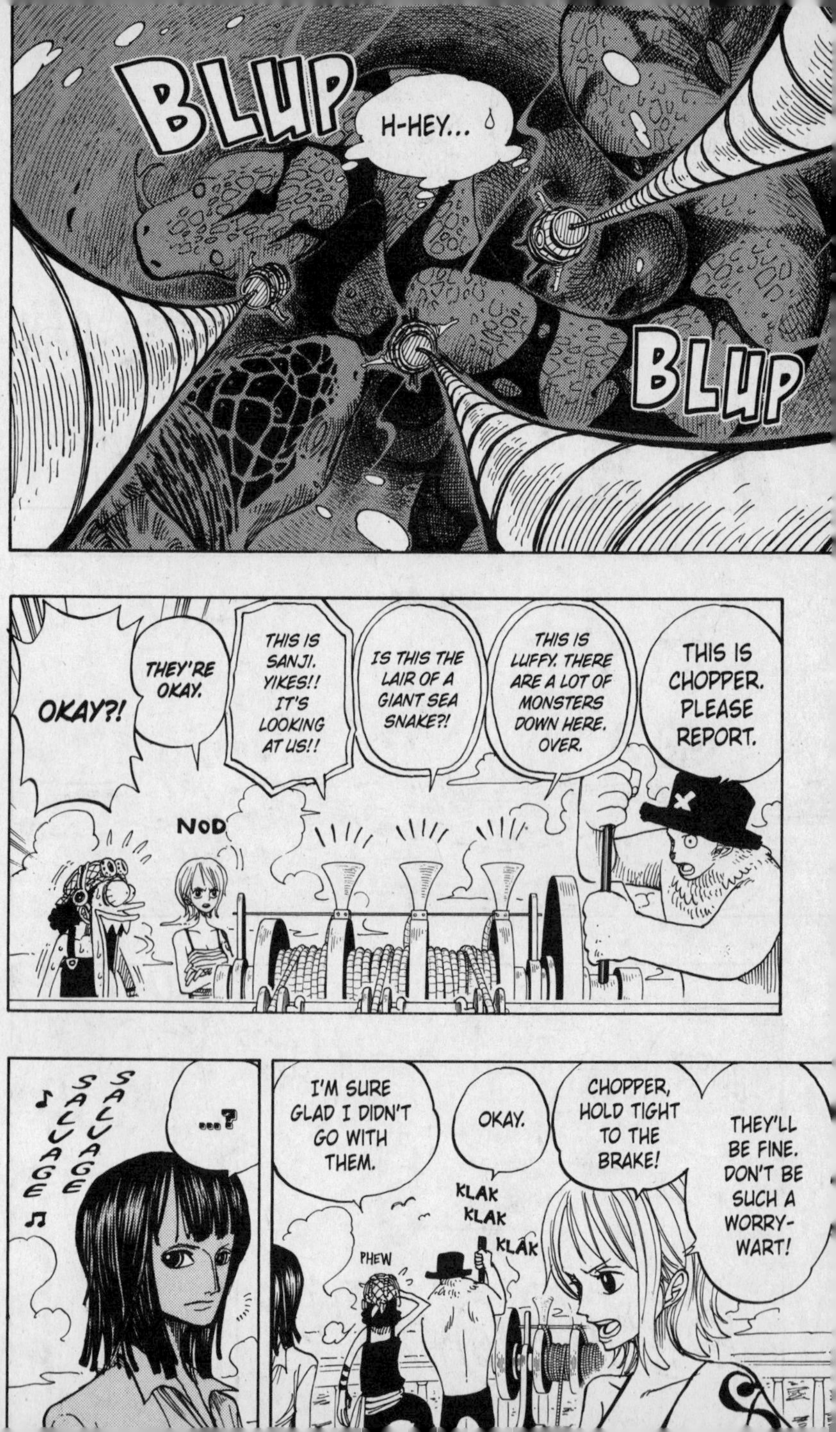
H-HEY...
BLUP
BLUP
THIS IS CHOPPER. PLEASE REPORT.
THIS IS LUFFY. THERE ARE A LOT OF MONSTERS DOWN HERE. OVER.
IS THIS THE LAIR OF A GIANT SEA SNAKE?!
THIS IS SANJI. YIKES!! IT'S LOOKING AT US!!
THEY'RE OKAY.
NOD
OKAY?!
THEY'LL BE FINE. DON'T BE SUCH A WORRY-WART!
CHOPPER, HOLD TIGHT TO THE BRAKE!
OKAY.
KLAK
KLAK
KLAK
I'M SURE GLAD I DIDN'T GO WITH THEM.
PHEW
...?
♪ SALVAGE SALVAGE ♫

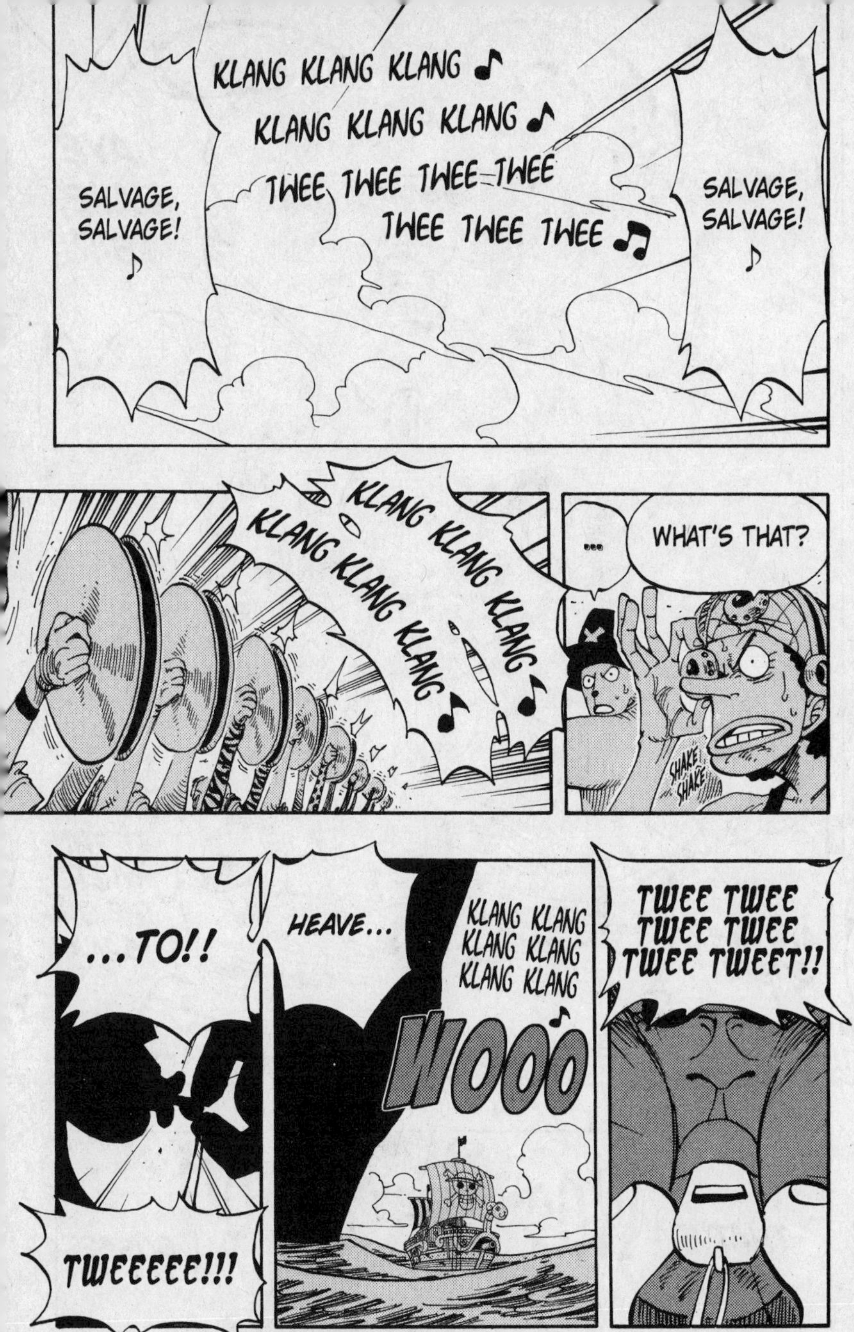
SALVAGE, SALVAGE! ♪
KLANG KLANG KLANG ♪
KLANG KLANG KLANG ♪
TWEE TWEE TWEE TWEE
TWEE TWEE TWEE ♫
SALVAGE, SALVAGE! ♪
...
WHAT'S THAT?
SHAKE SHAKE
KLANG KLANG KLANG KLANG ♪
KLANG KLANG KLANG KLANG ♪
TWEE TWEE TWEE TWEE TWEE TWEET!!
KLANG KLANG KLANG KLANG KLANG KLANG ♪
HEAVE...
WOOO
...TO!!
TWEEEEEE!!!

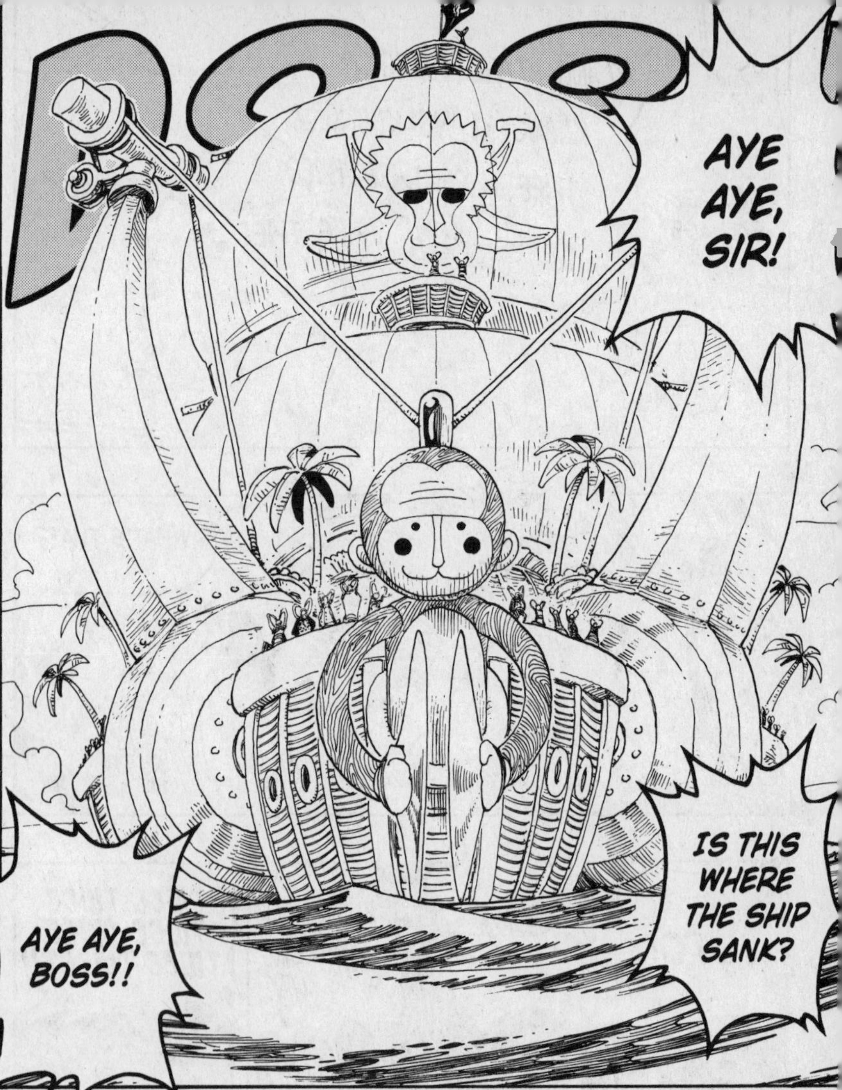
AYE AYE, SIR!
IS THIS WHERE THE SHIP SANK?
AYE AYE, BOSS!!
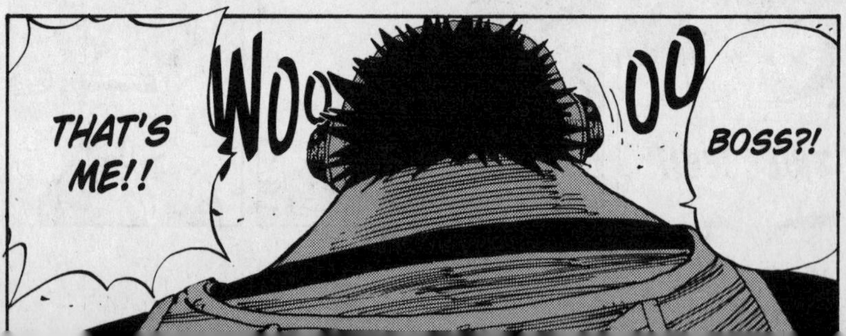
BOSS?!
THAT'S ME!!

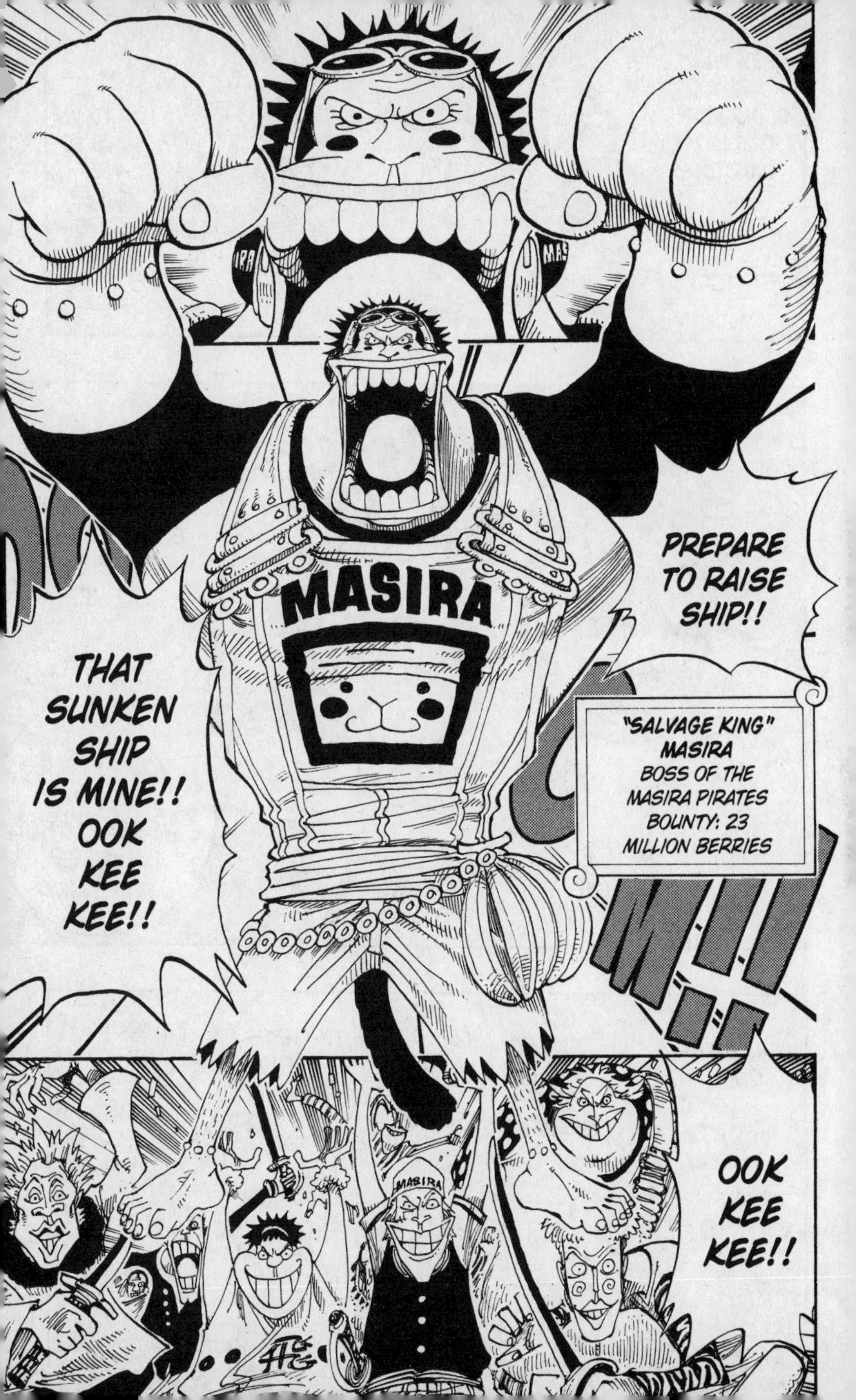
PREPARE TO RAISE SHIP!!
"SALVAGE KING" MASIRA BOSS OF THE MASIRA PIRATES BOUNTY: 23 MILLION BERRIES
THAT SUNKEN SHIP IS MINE!! OOK KEE KEE!!
OOK KEE KEE!!

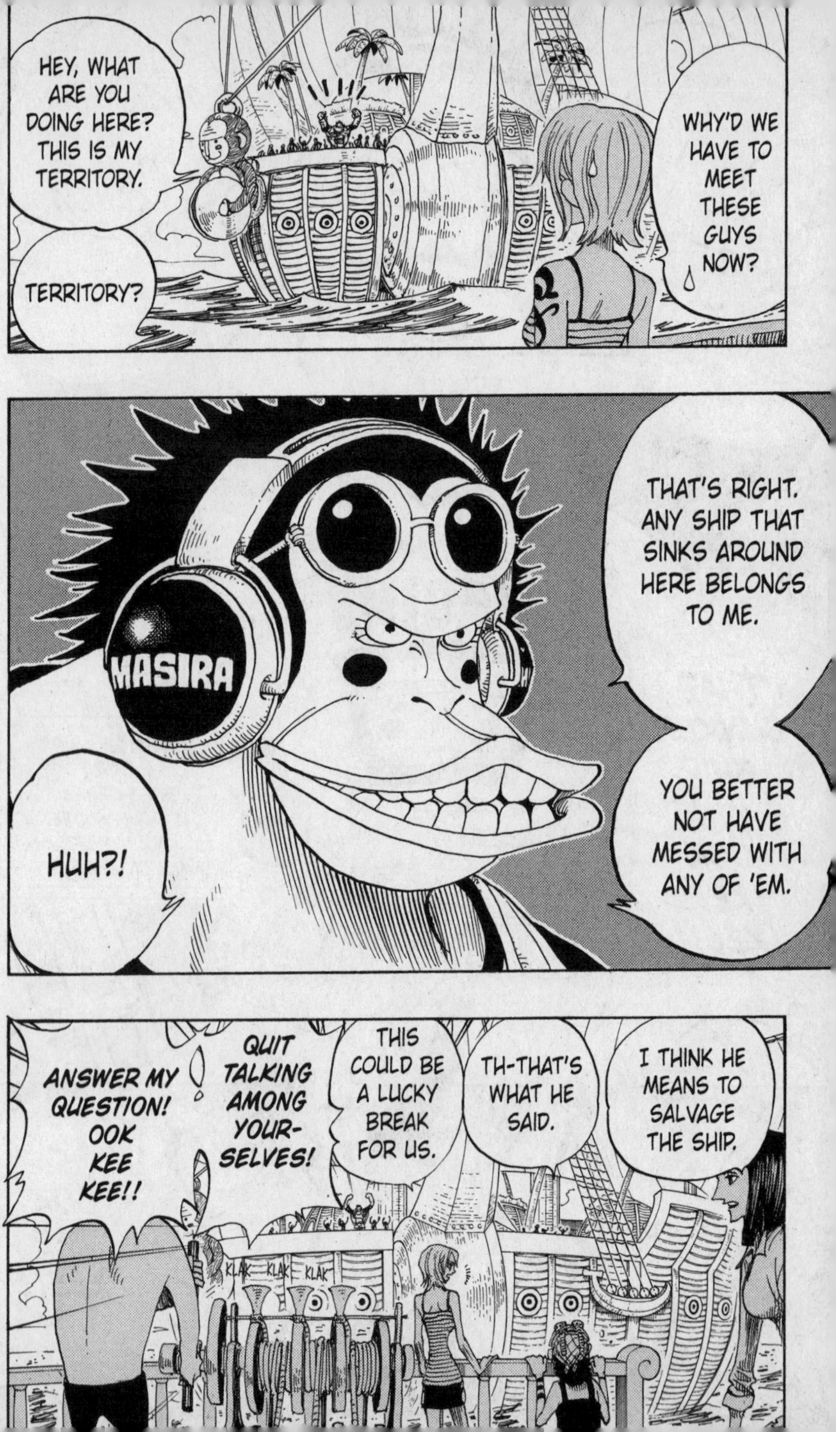
WHY'D WE HAVE TO MEET THESE GUYS NOW?
HEY, WHAT ARE YOU DOING HERE? THIS IS MY TERRITORY.
TERRITORY?
THAT'S RIGHT. ANY SHIP THAT SINKS AROUND HERE BELONGS TO ME.
YOU BETTER NOT HAVE MESSED WITH ANY OF 'EM.
MASIRA
HUH?!
I THINK HE MEANS TO SALVAGE THE SHIP.
TH-THAT'S WHAT HE SAID.
THIS COULD BE A LUCKY BREAK FOR US.
QUIT TALKING AMONG YOUR-SELVES!
ANSWER MY QUESTION! OOK KEE KEE!!
KLAK KLAK KLAK

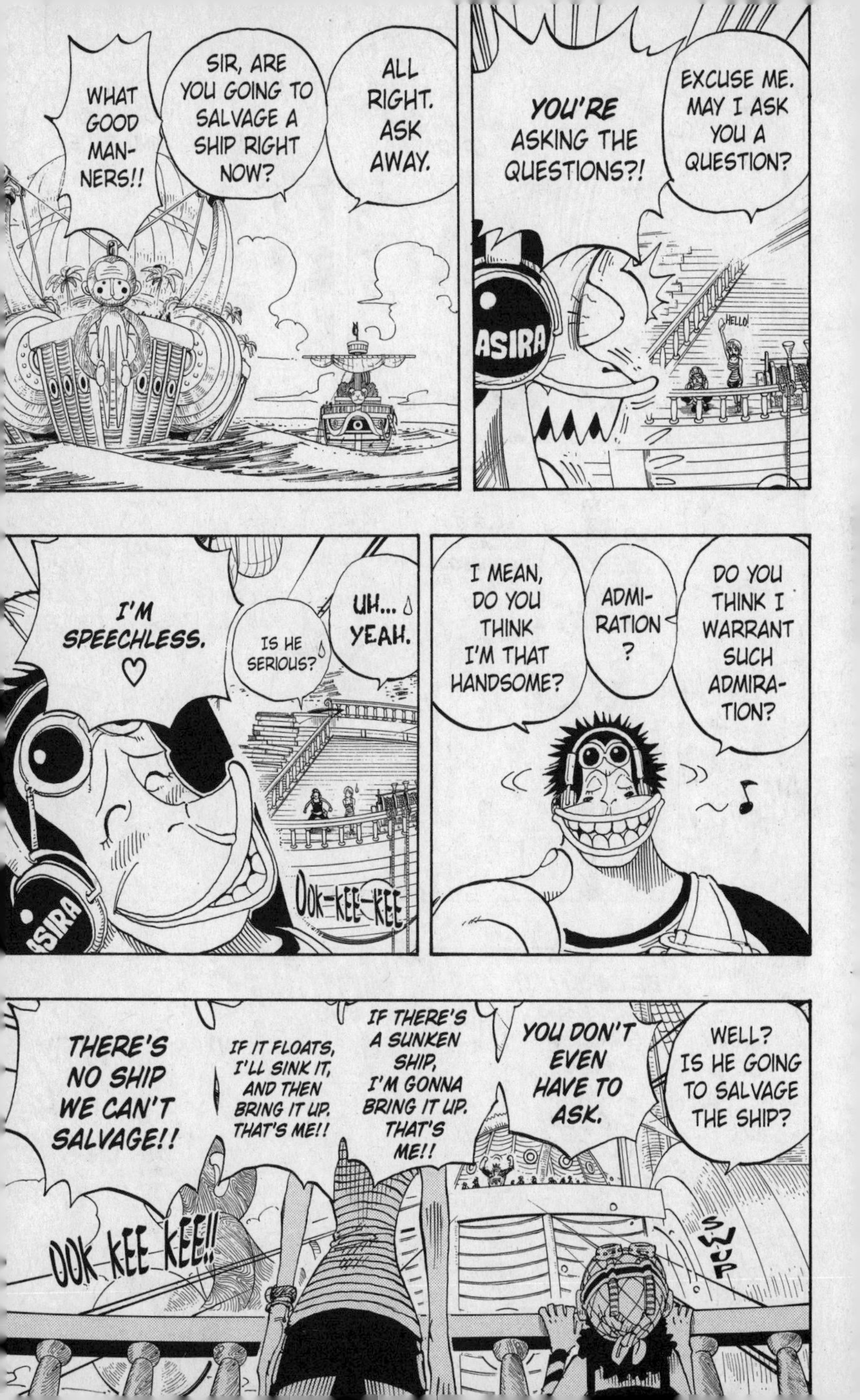
EXCUSE ME. MAY I ASK YOU A QUESTION?
YOU'RE ASKING THE QUESTIONS?!
ASIRA
HELLO!
ALL RIGHT. ASK AWAY.
SIR, ARE YOU GOING TO SALVAGE A SHIP RIGHT NOW?
WHAT GOOD MAN-NERS!!
DO YOU THINK I WARRANT SUCH ADMIRA-TION?
ADMI-RATION?
I MEAN, DO YOU THINK I'M THAT HANDSOME?
UH... YEAH.
IS HE SERIOUS?
I'M SPEECHLESS. ♡
ASIRA
OOK-KEE-KEE
WELL? IS HE GOING TO SALVAGE THE SHIP?
YOU DON'T EVEN HAVE TO ASK.
IF THERE'S A SUNKEN SHIP, I'M GONNA BRING IT UP. THAT'S ME!!
IF IT FLOATS, I'LL SINK IT, AND THEN BRING IT UP. THAT'S ME!!
THERE'S NO SHIP WE CAN'T SALVAGE!!
SWUP
OOK KEE KEE!!

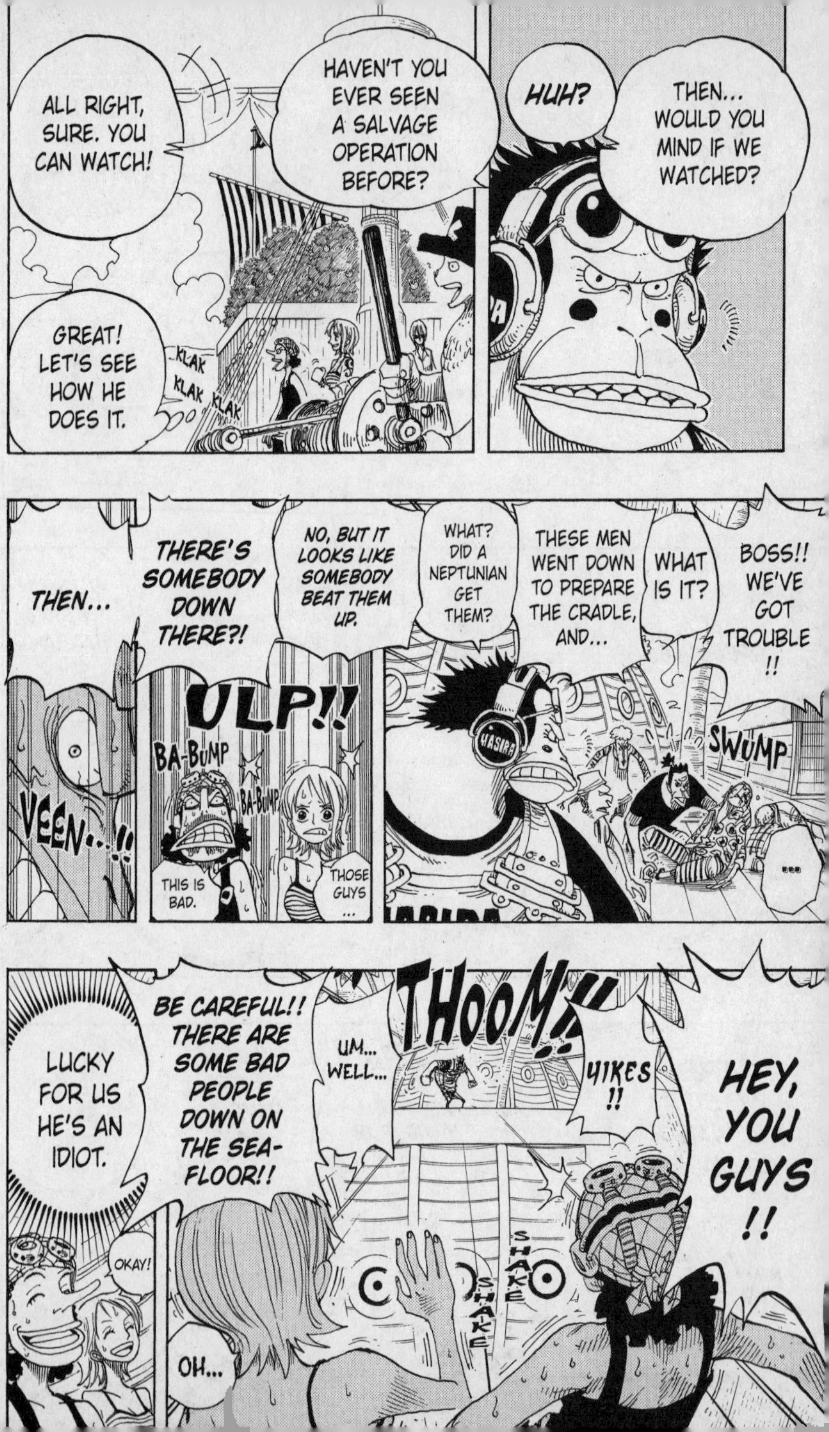
THEN... WOULD YOU MIND IF WE WATCHED?
HUH?
HAVEN'T YOU EVER SEEN A SALVAGE OPERATION BEFORE?
ALL RIGHT, SURE. YOU CAN WATCH!
GREAT! LET'S SEE HOW HE DOES IT.
KLAK KLAK KLAK
BOSS!! WE'VE GOT TROUBLE!!
WHAT IS IT?
THESE MEN WENT DOWN TO PREPARE THE CRADLE, AND...
WHAT? DID A NEPTUNIAN GET THEM?
NO, BUT IT LOOKS LIKE SOMEBODY BEAT THEM UP.
SWUMP
...
ULP!!
BA-BUMP
BA-BUMP
THIS IS BAD.
THOSE GUYS...
THERE'S SOMEBODY DOWN THERE?!
THEN...
VEEN...!!
HEY, YOU GUYS!!
YIKES!!
THOOM!!
UM... WELL...
SHAKE
SHAKE
BE CAREFUL!! THERE ARE SOME BAD PEOPLE DOWN ON THE SEA-FLOOR!!
OH...
OKAY!
LUCKY FOR US HE'S AN IDIOT.

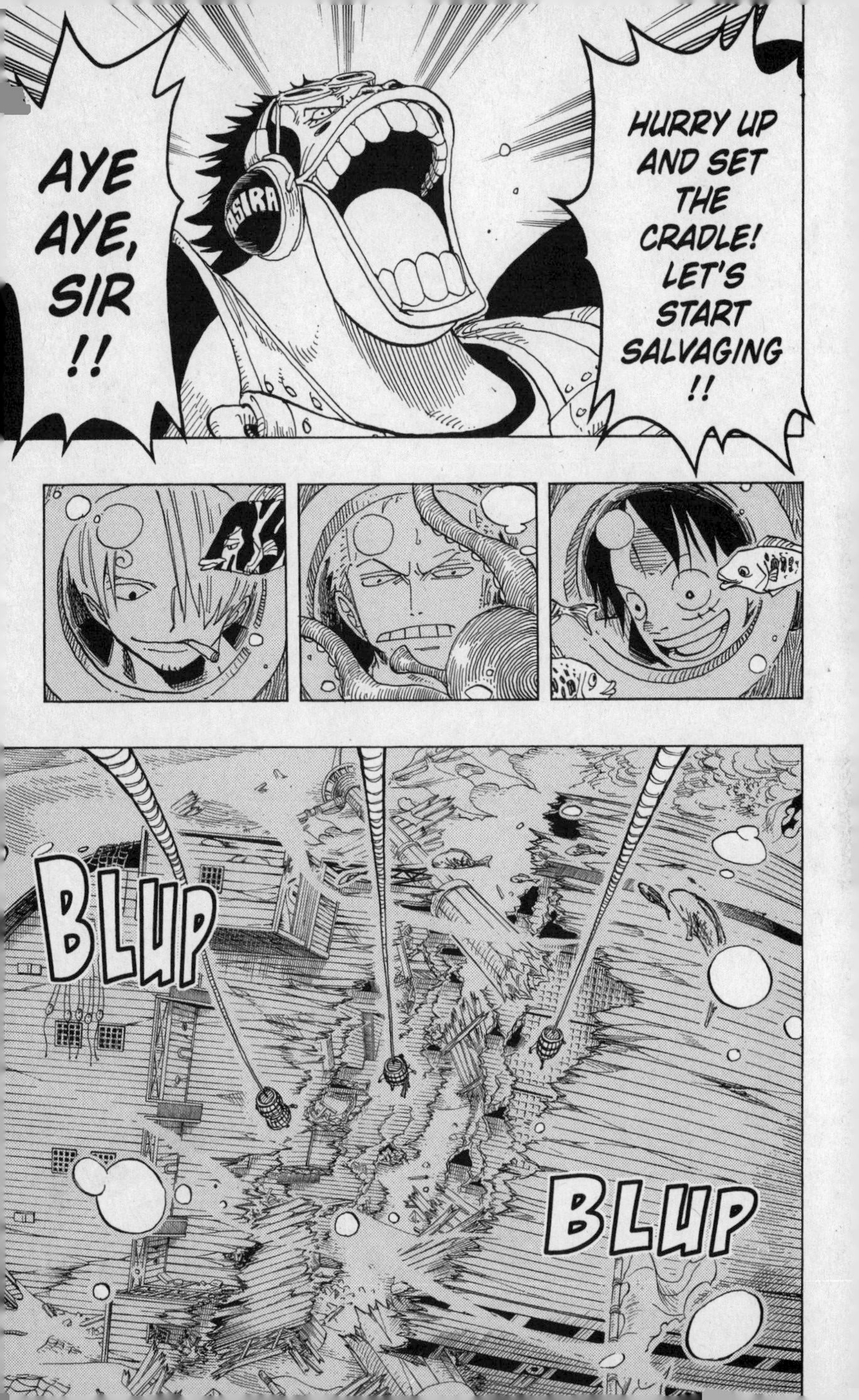
HURRY UP AND SET THE CRADLE! LET'S START SALVAGING!!
AYE AYE, SIR!!
BLUP
BLUP

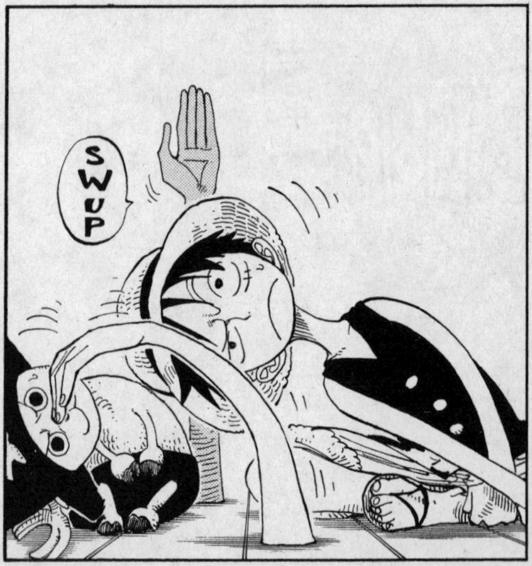
SWUP

Chapter 220:

A WALK ON THE SEAFLOOR

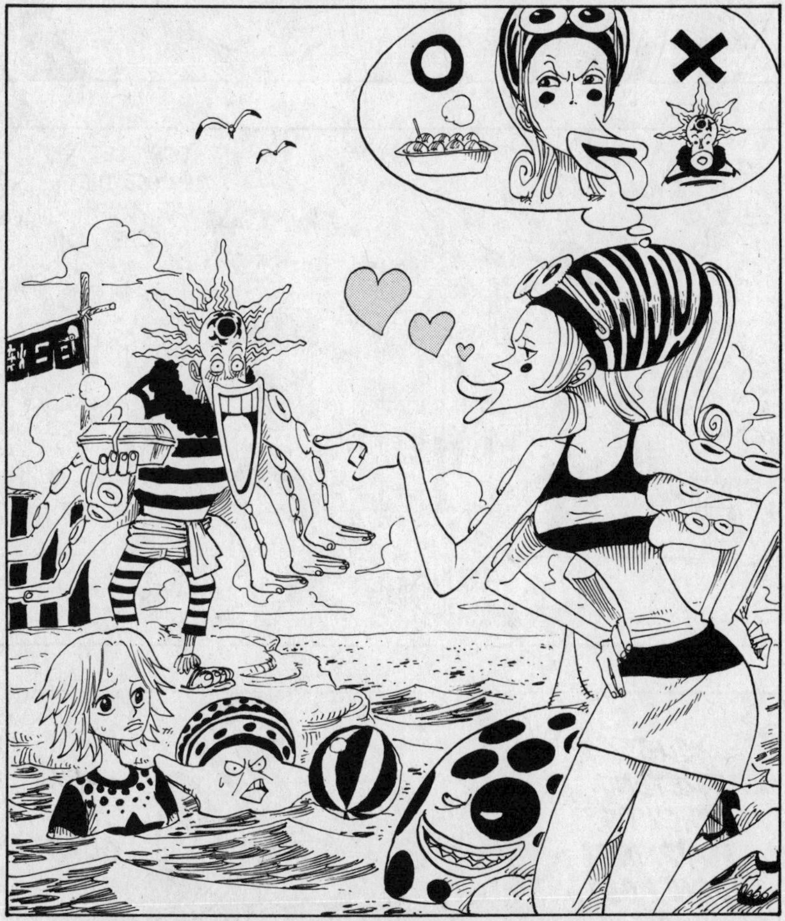

HACHI'S WALK ON THE SEAFLOOR, VOL. 34:
"OCTOPAKO IS DRAWN BY THE AROMA OF THE SAUCE"

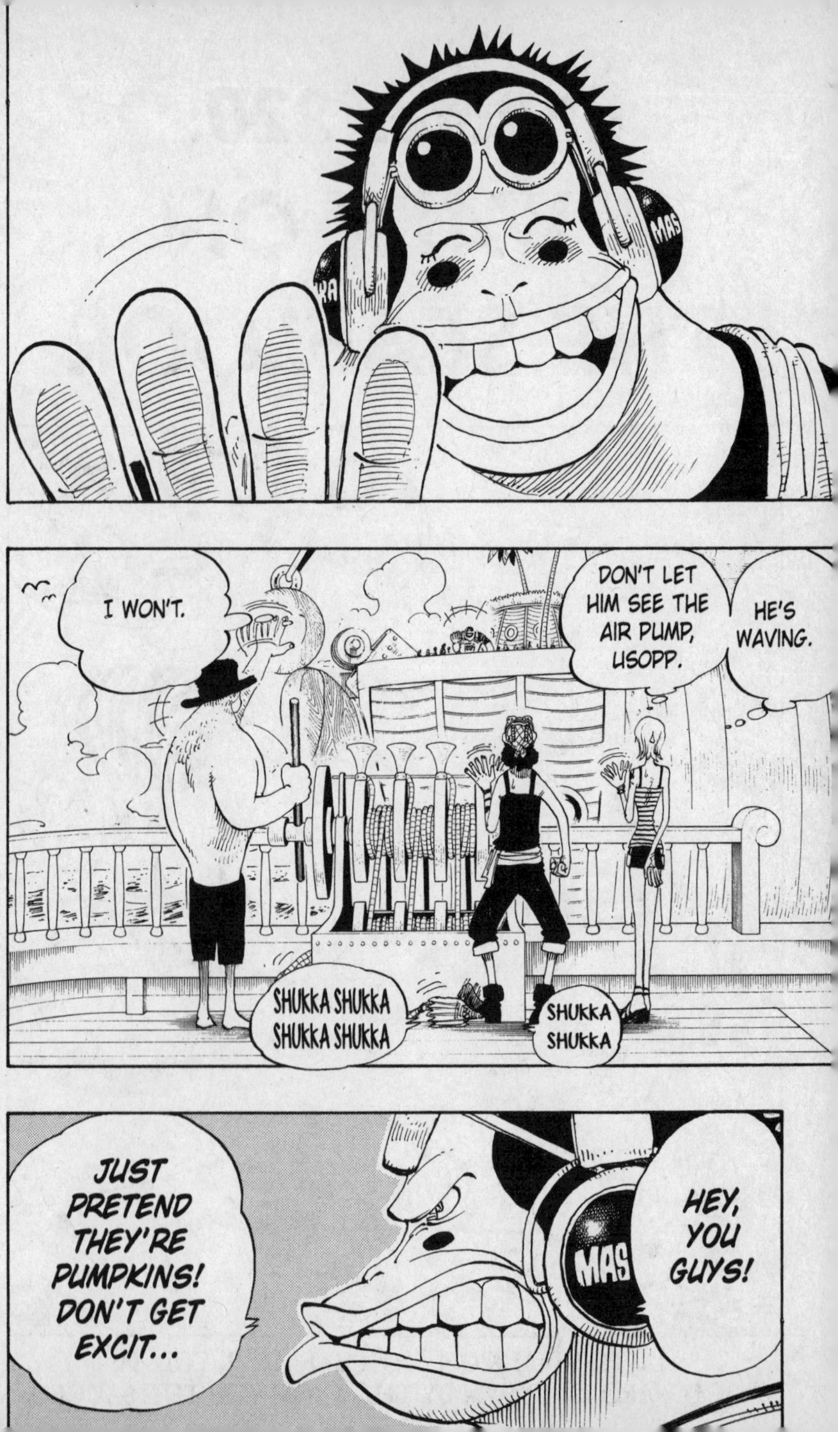
KA
MAS
HE'S WAVING.
DON'T LET HIM SEE THE AIR PUMP, USOPP.
I WON'T.
SHUKKA SHUKKA
SHUKKA SHUKKA SHUKKA SHUKKA
MAS
HEY, YOU GUYS!
JUST PRETEND THEY'RE PUMPKINS! DON'T GET EXCIT...

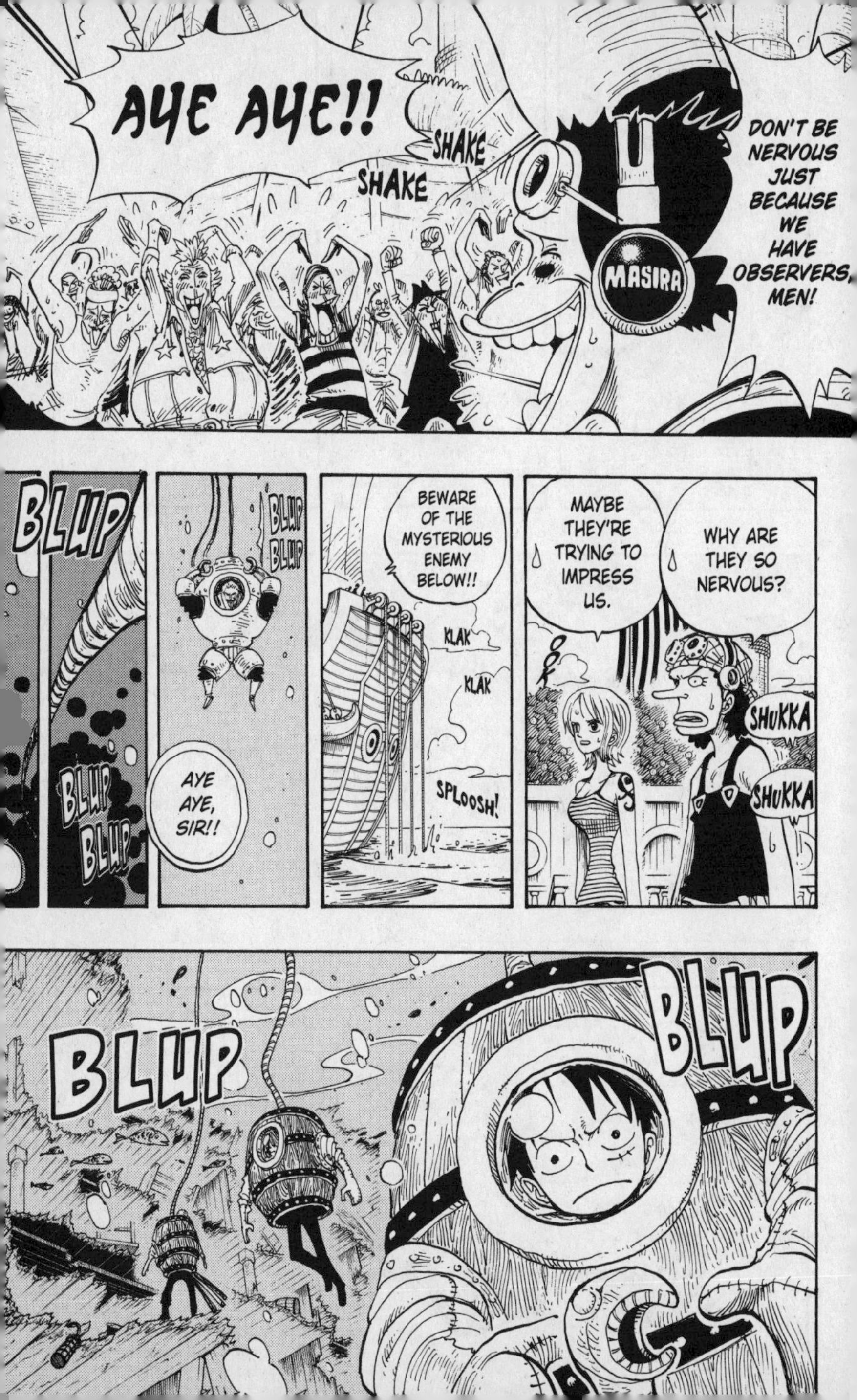
DON'T BE NERVOUS JUST BECAUSE WE HAVE OBSERVERS, MEN!
SHAKE
SHAKE
AYE AYE!!
WHY ARE THEY SO NERVOUS?
MAYBE THEY'RE TRYING TO IMPRESS US.
SHUKKA
SHUKKA
BEWARE OF THE MYSTERIOUS ENEMY BELOW!!
KLAK
KLAK
SPLOOSH!
BLUP BLUP
AYE AYE, SIR!!
BLUP
BLUP BLUP
BLUP
BLUP

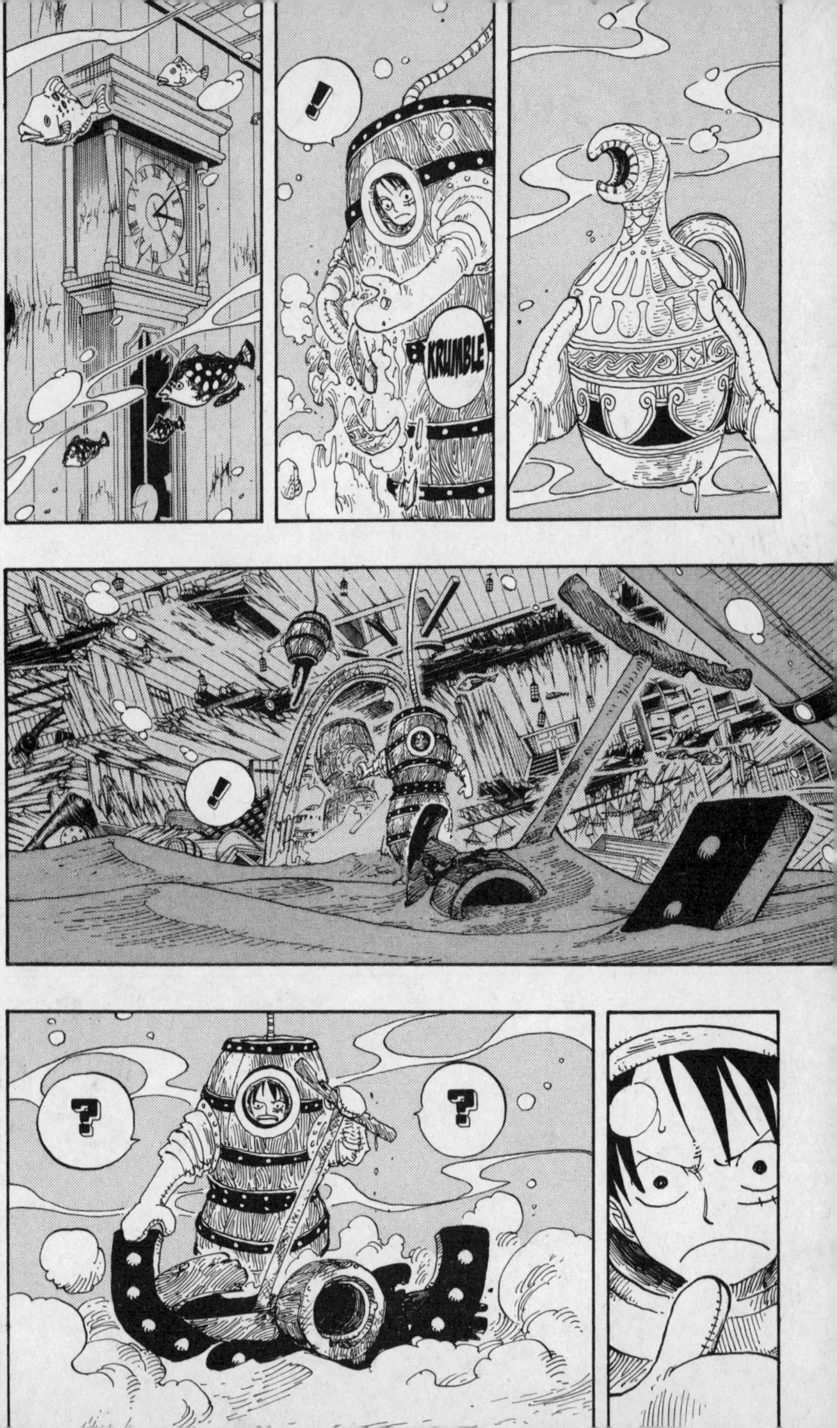
!
KRUMBLE
!
?
?

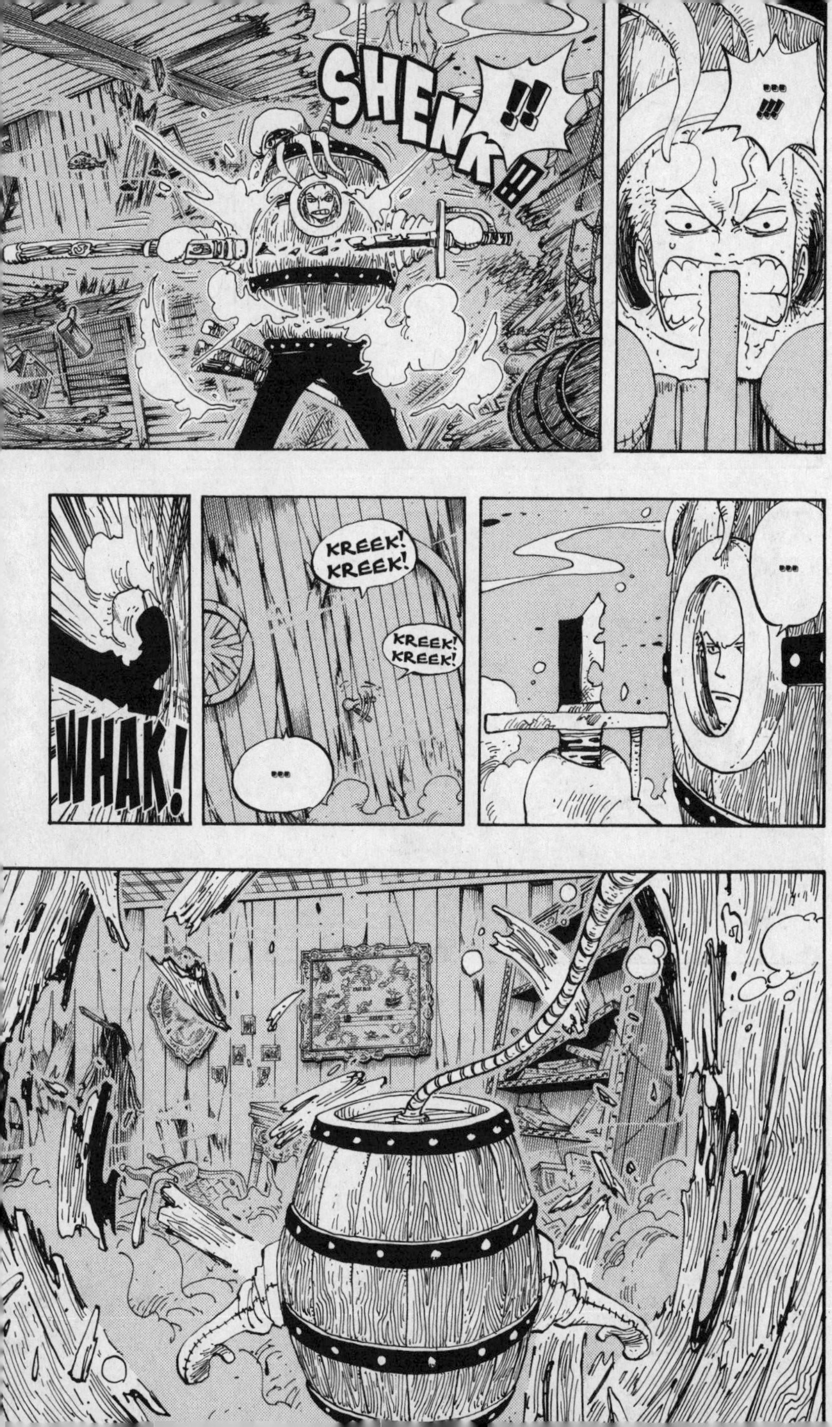

...!!
SHENK!!
SHENK!!
...
KREEK! KREEK!
KREEK! KREEK!
...
WHAK!

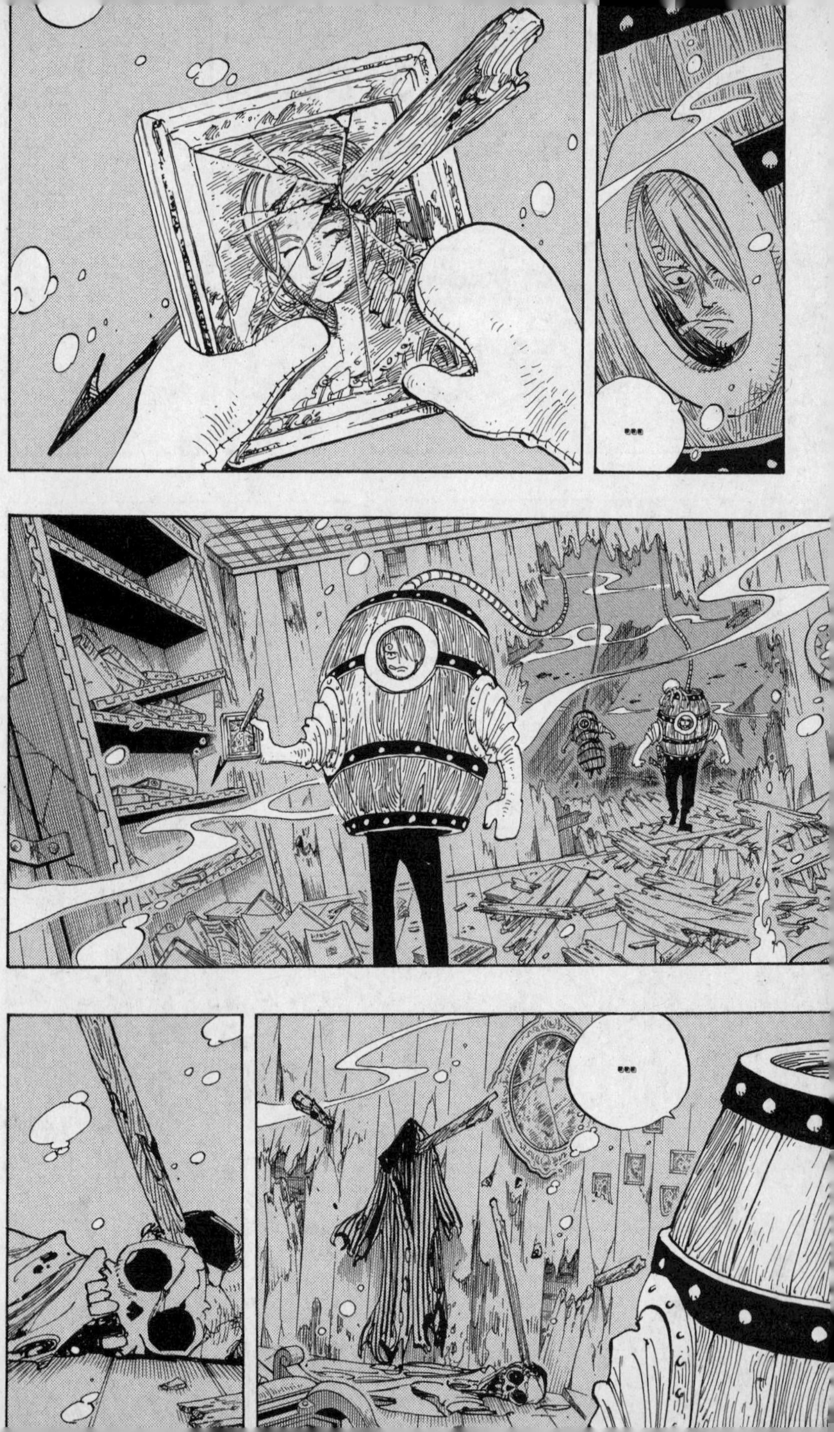
...
...

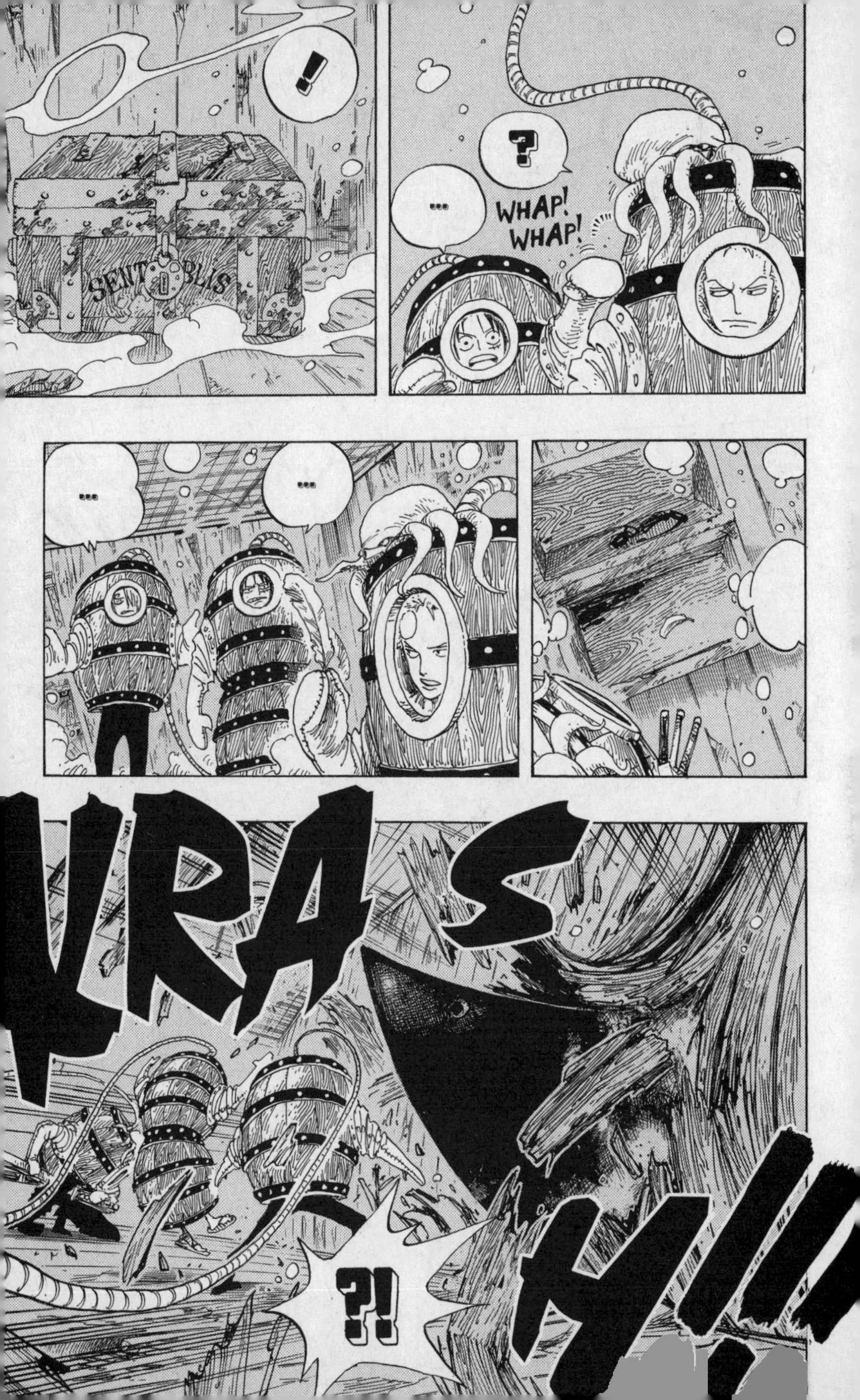

?
...
WHAP! WHAP!
!
...
...
?!

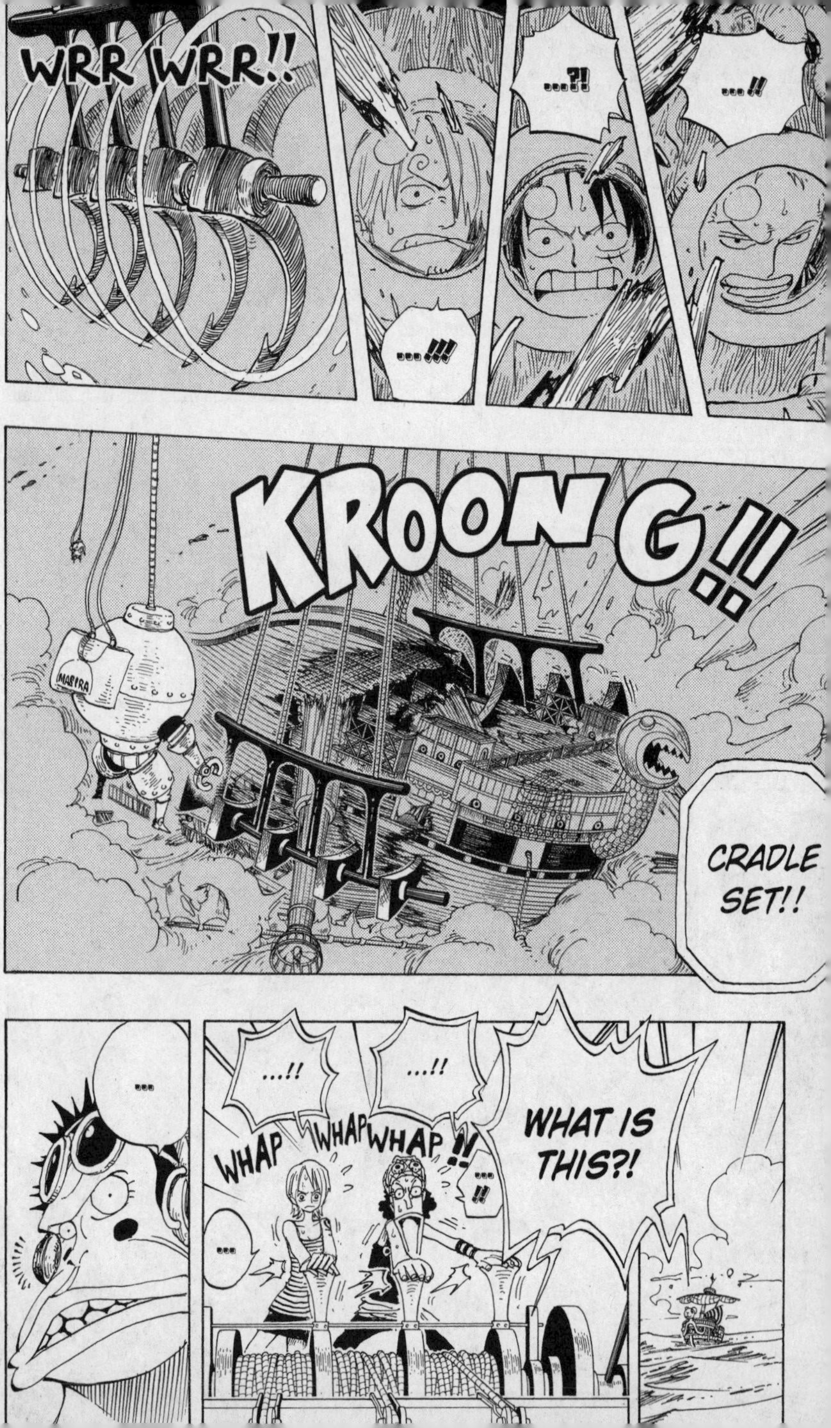
...!!
...?!
...!!!
WRR WRR!!
KROONG!!
CRADLE SET!!
WHAT IS THIS?!
...!!
...!!
WHAP WHAP WHAP!!
...!!
...
...

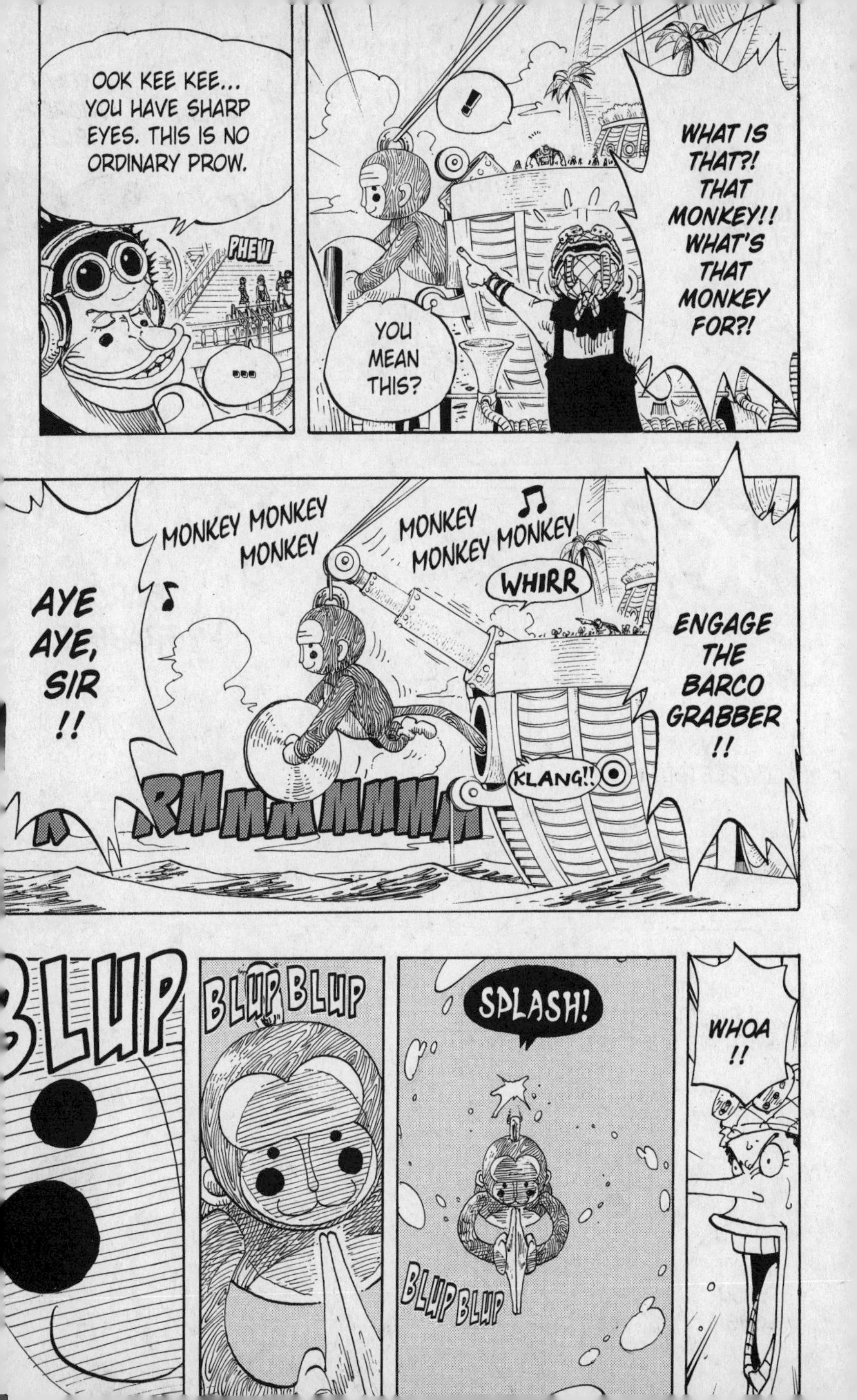
WHAT IS THAT?! THAT MONKEY!! WHAT'S THAT MONKEY FOR?!
!
YOU MEAN THIS?
OOK KEE KEE... YOU HAVE SHARP EYES. THIS IS NO ORDINARY PROW.
PHEW
...
ENGAGE THE BARCO GRABBER!!
WHIRR
MONKEY MONKEY MONKEY
MONKEY MONKEY MONKEY
KLANG!!
AYE AYE, SIR!!
RMMMMMMM
WHOA!!
SPLASH!
BLUP BLUP
BLUP BLUP
BLUP

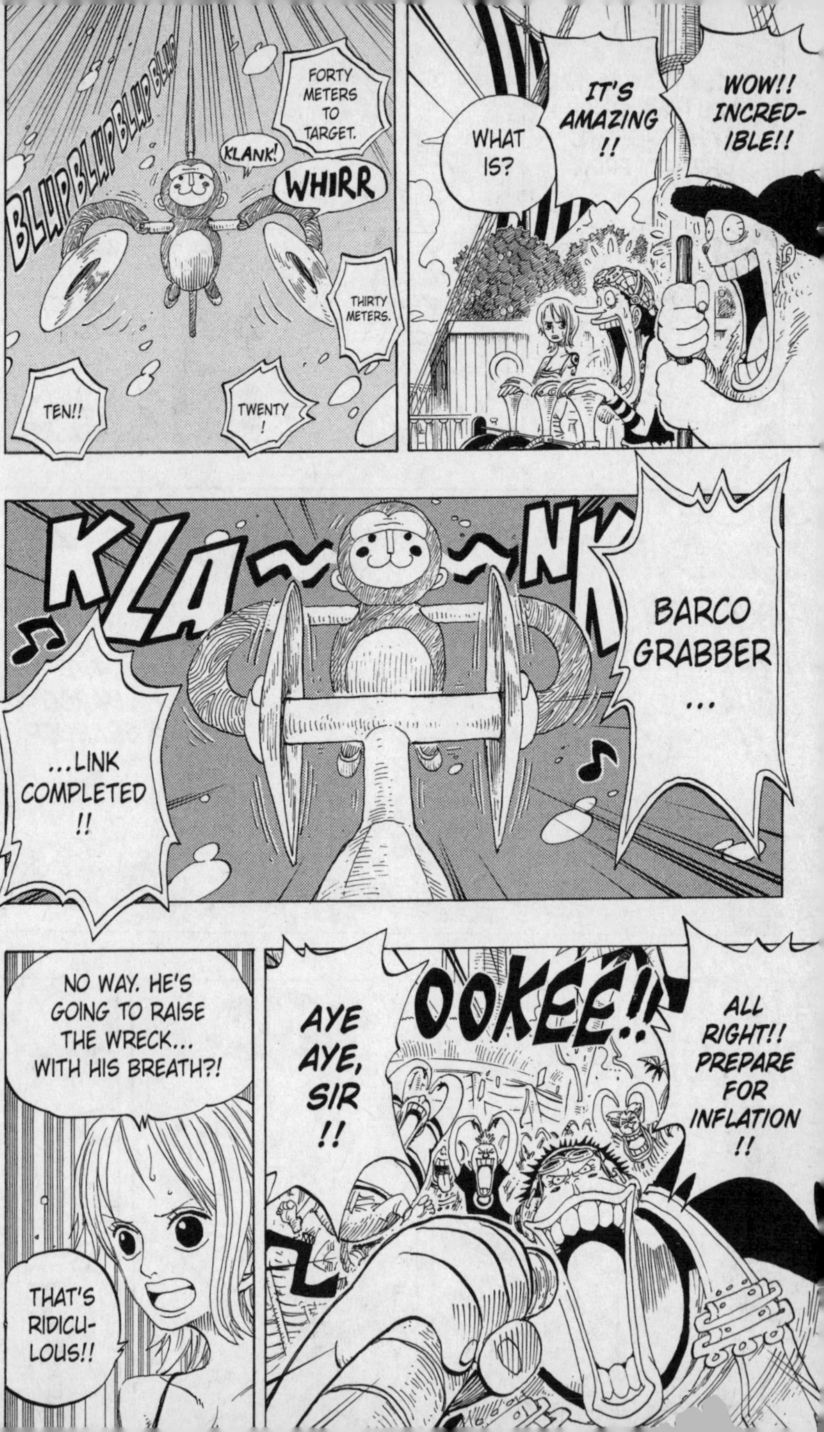
WOW!! INCREDIBLE!!
IT'S AMAZING!!
WHAT IS?
FORTY METERS TO TARGET.
KLANK!
WHIRR
BLUPBLUPBLUPBLUP
THIRTY METERS.
TWENTY!
TEN!!
BARCO GRABBER...
KLA~~~NK
...LINK COMPLETED!!
ALL RIGHT!! PREPARE FOR INFLATION!!
OOKEE!!
AYE AYE, SIR!!
NO WAY. HE'S GOING TO RAISE THE WRECK... WITH HIS BREATH?!
THAT'S RIDICULOUS!!

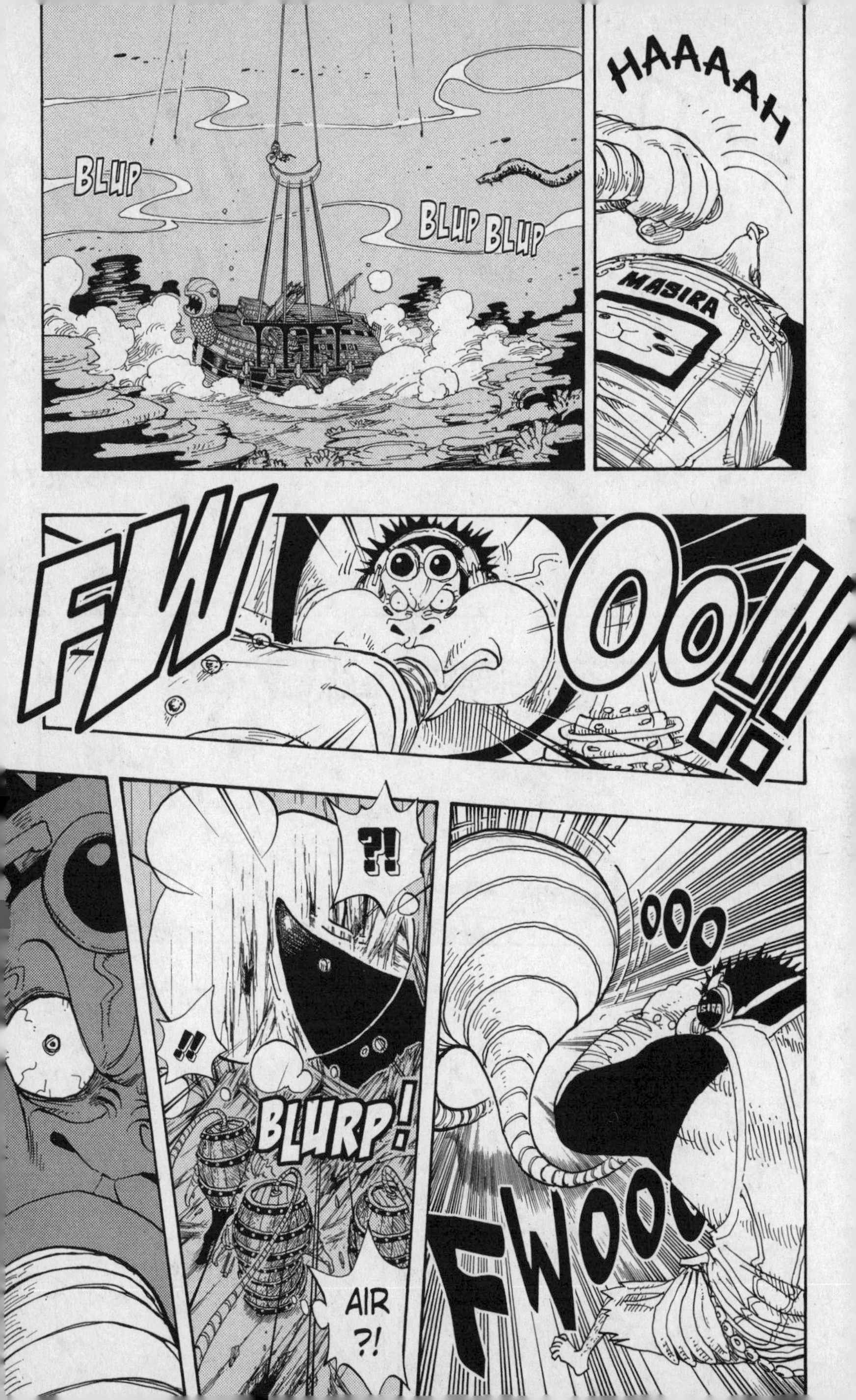
HAAAAH
MASIRA
BLUP
BLUP BLUP
FWOOO!!
OOO
FWOO
?!
!!
BLURP!
AIR ?!

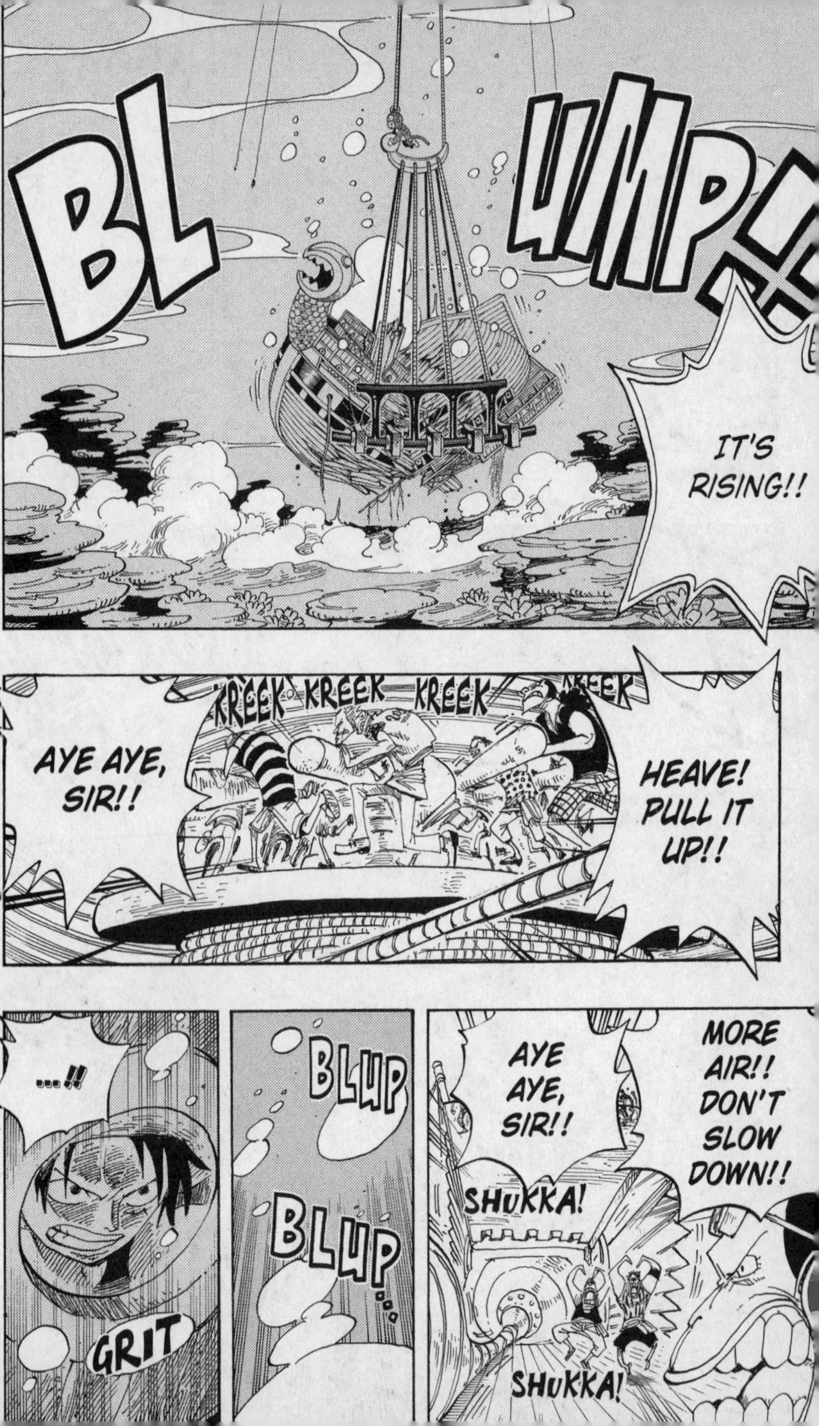
BLUMP!!
IT'S RISING!!
HEAVE! PULL IT UP!!
KREEK KREEK KREEK KREEK
AYE AYE, SIR!!
MORE AIR!! DON'T SLOW DOWN!!
AYE AYE, SIR!!
SHUKKA!
SHUKKA!
BLUP
BLUP...
...!!
GRIT

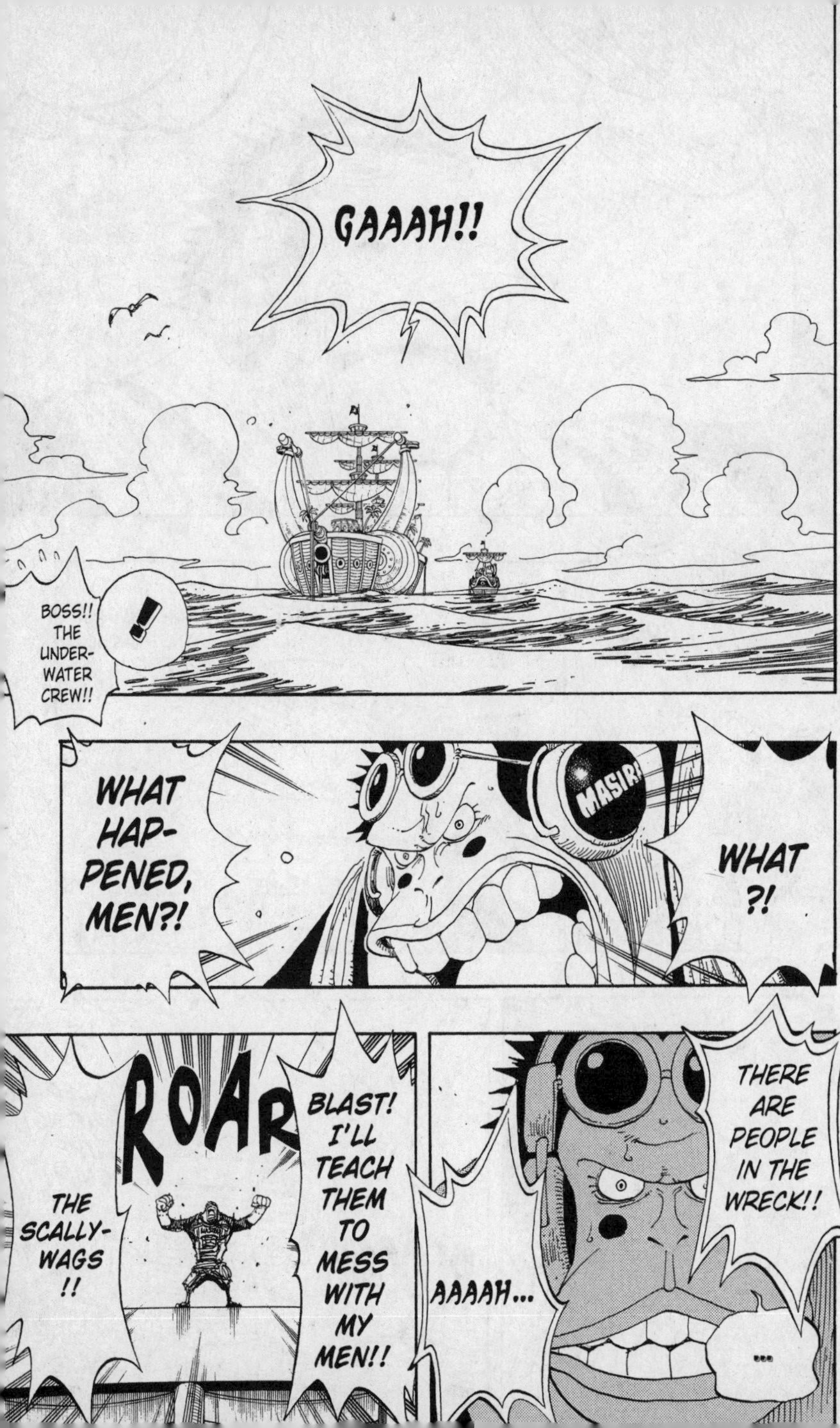
GAAAH!!
!
BOSS!! THE UNDER-WATER CREW!!
WHAT ?!
WHAT HAP-PENED, MEN?!
THERE ARE PEOPLE IN THE WRECK!!
...
AAAAH...
BLAST! I'LL TEACH THEM TO MESS WITH MY MEN!!
ROAR
THE SCALLY-WAGS !!

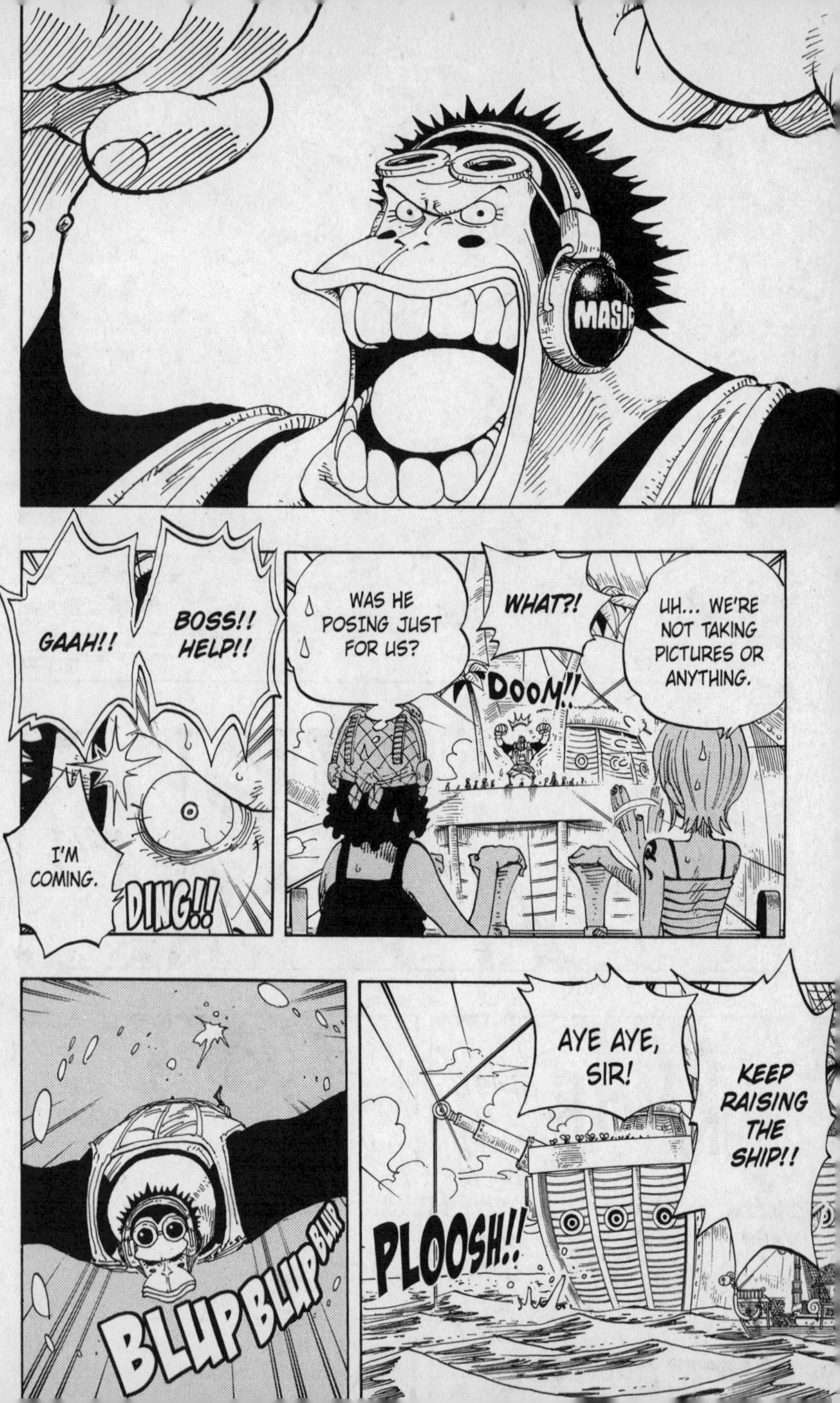
MASIC
UH... WE'RE NOT TAKING PICTURES OR ANYTHING.
WHAT?!
WAS HE POSING JUST FOR US?
DOOM!!
BOSS!! HELP!!
GAAH!!
I'M COMING.
DING!!
KEEP RAISING THE SHIP!!
AYE AYE, SIR!
PLOOSH!!
BLUP BLUP BLUP

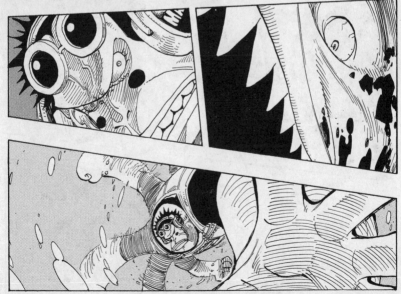

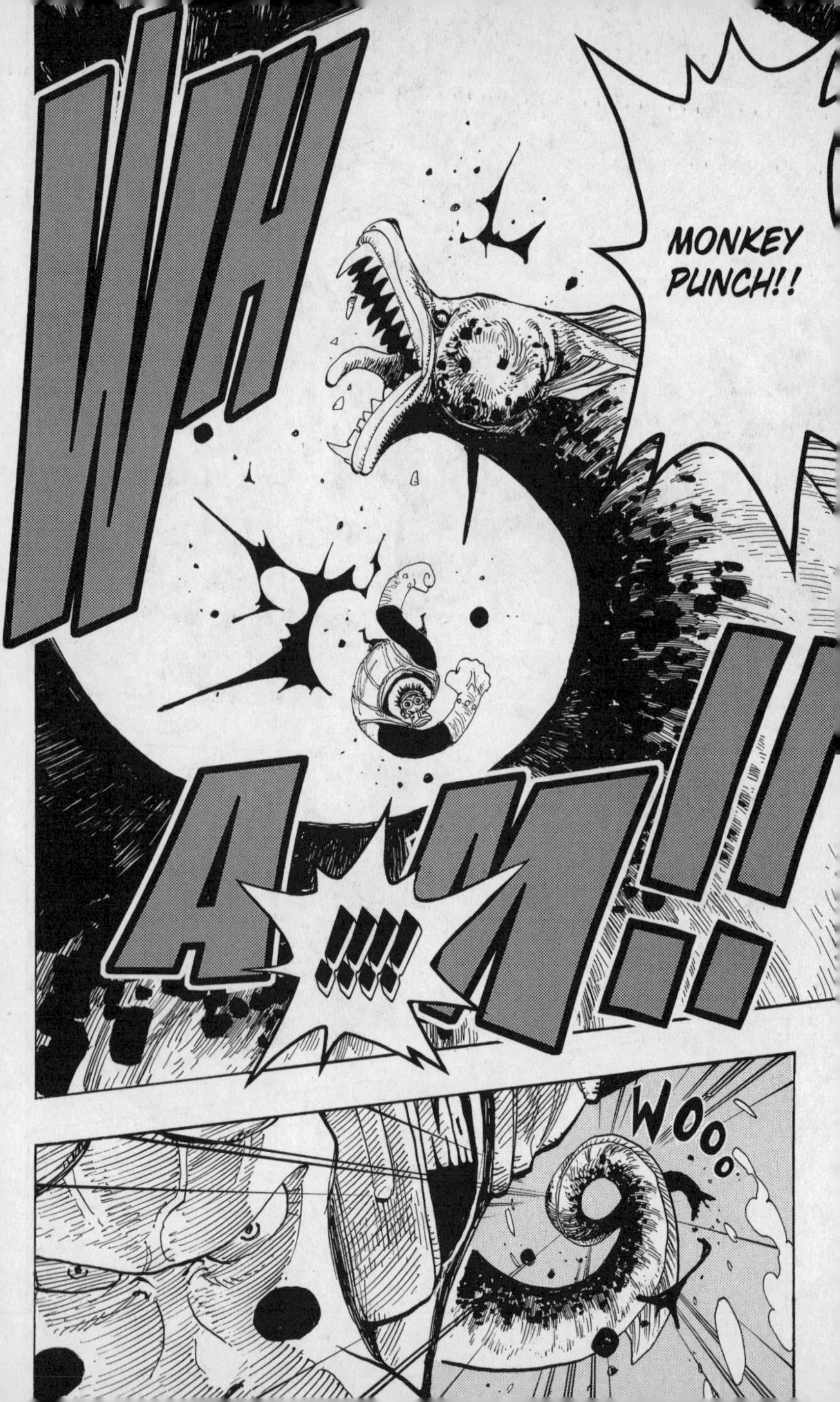
MONKEY PUNCH!!
WOOO...

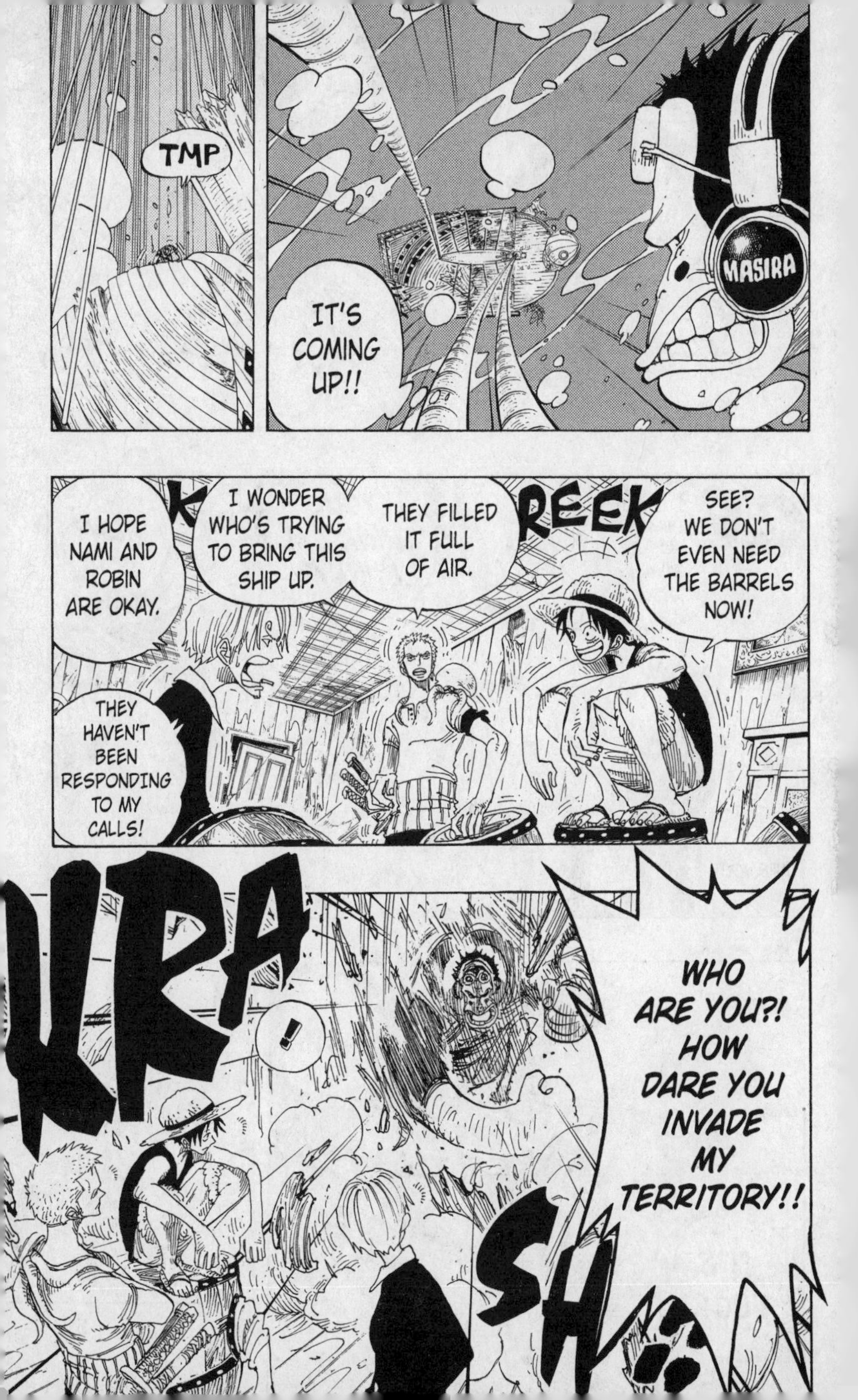
IT'S COMING UP!!
TMP
SEE? WE DON'T EVEN NEED THE BARRELS NOW!
REEK
THEY FILLED IT FULL OF AIR.
I WONDER WHO'S TRYING TO BRING THIS SHIP UP.
K
I HOPE NAMI AND ROBIN ARE OKAY.
THEY HAVEN'T BEEN RESPONDING TO MY CALLS!
WHO ARE YOU?! HOW DARE YOU INVADE MY TERRITORY!!
SH
!

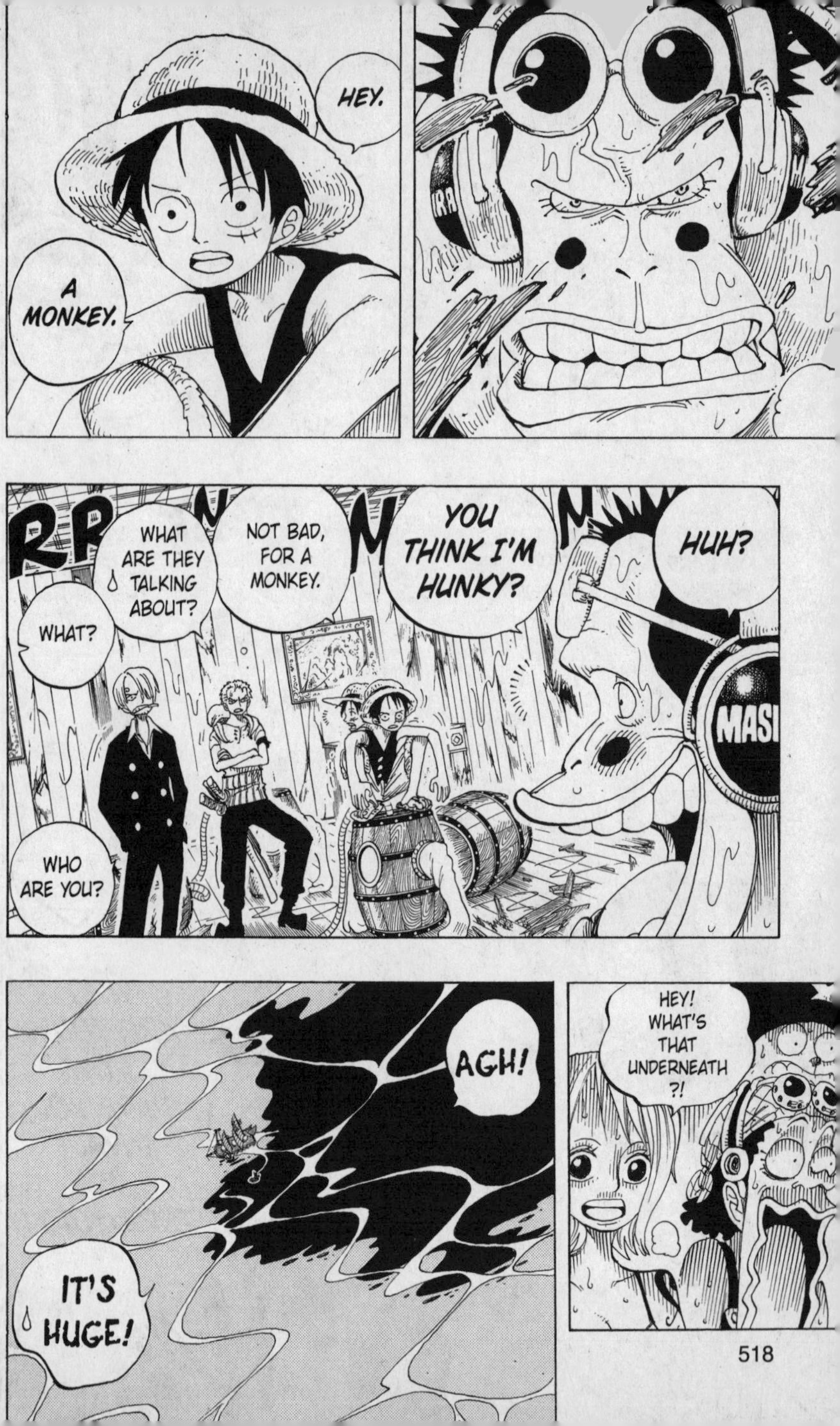
HEY.
A MONKEY.
HUH?
YOU THINK I'M HUNKY?
NOT BAD, FOR A MONKEY.
WHAT ARE THEY TALKING ABOUT?
WHAT?
WHO ARE YOU?
HEY! WHAT'S THAT UNDERNEATH?!
AGH!
IT'S HUGE!

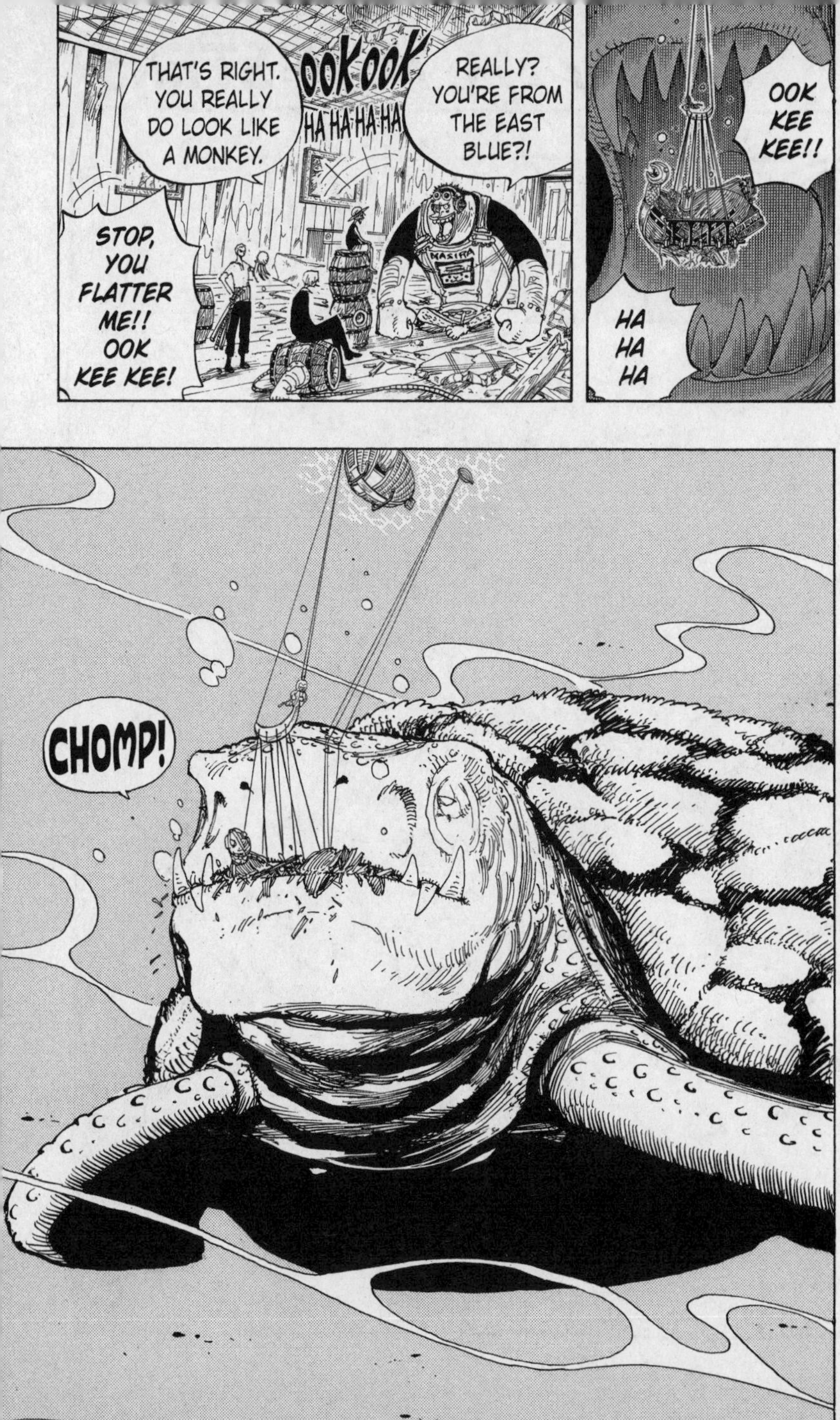
OOK KEE KEE!!
HA HA HA
REALLY? YOU'RE FROM THE EAST BLUE?!
OOKOOK
HA HA HA HA
THAT'S RIGHT. YOU REALLY DO LOOK LIKE A MONKEY.
STOP, YOU FLATTER ME!! OOK KEE KEE!
CHOMP!

Chapter 221: MONSTERS

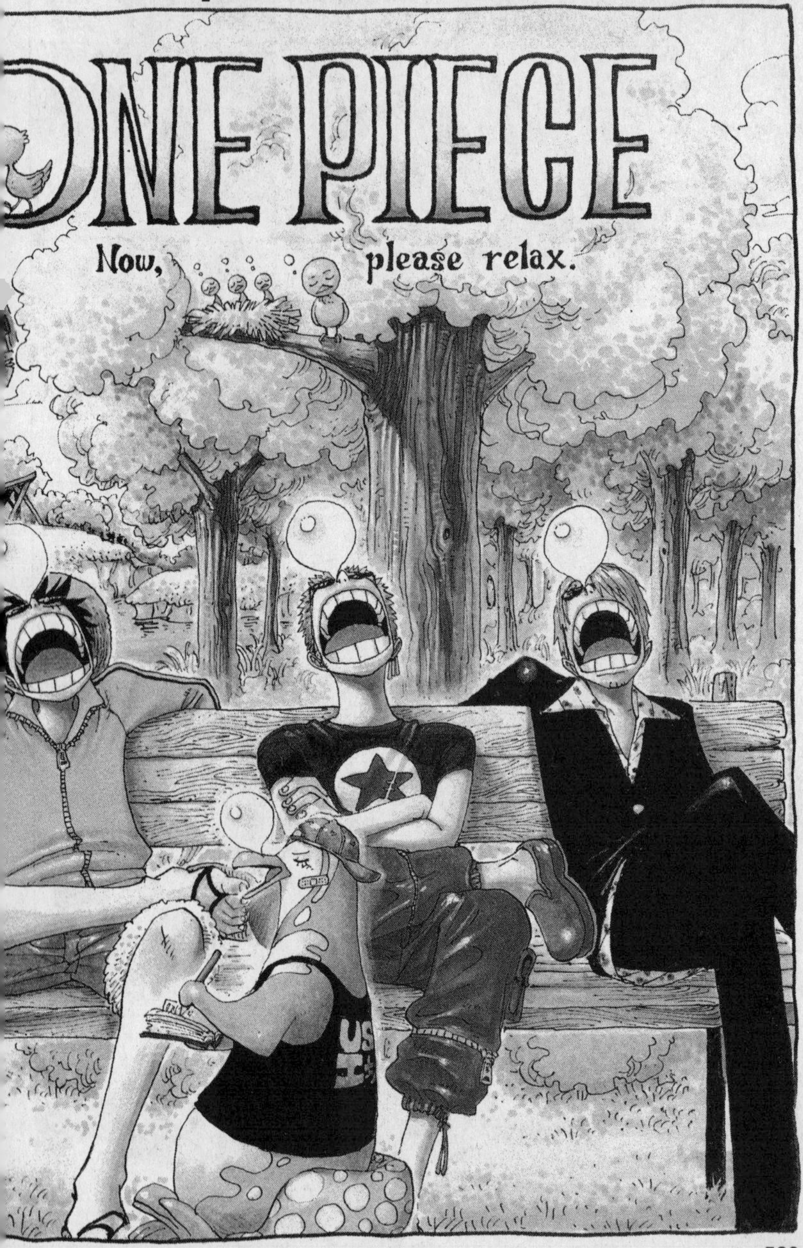
ONE PIECE
Now, please relax.

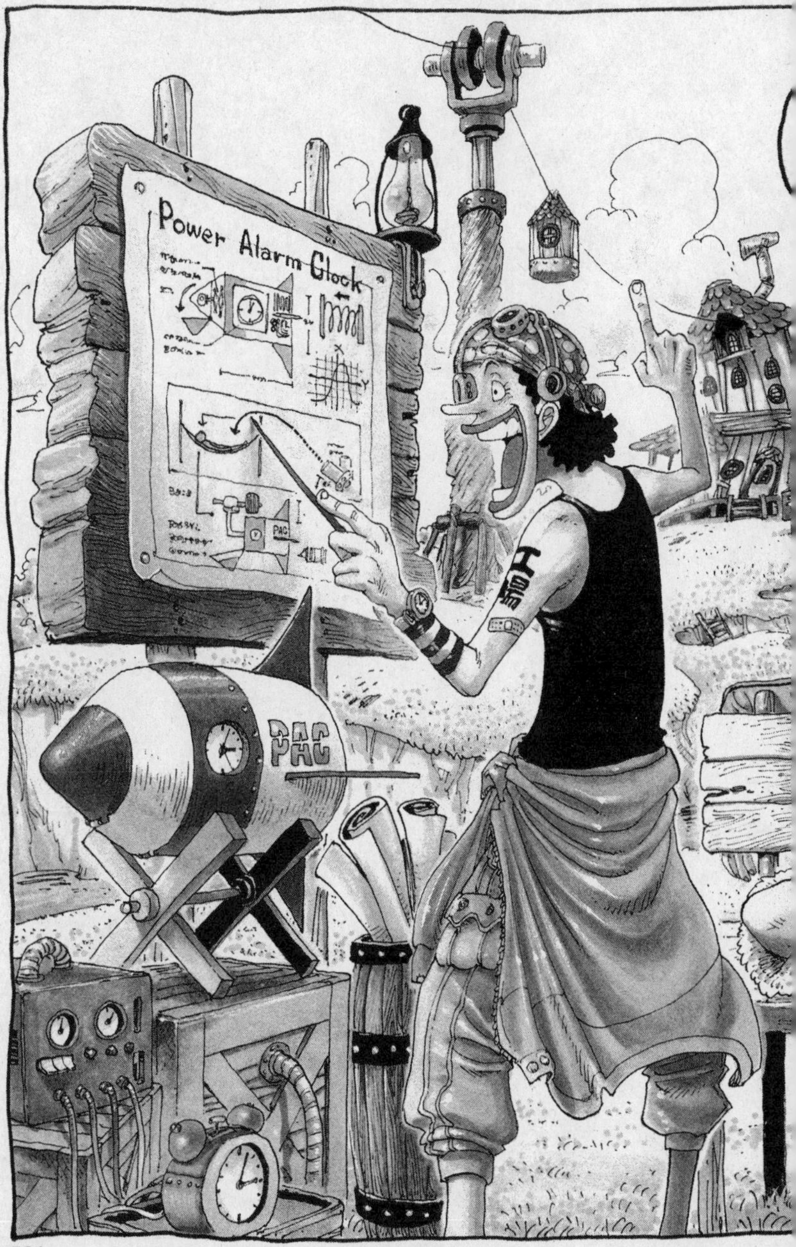
Power Alarm Clock
PAC
PAC

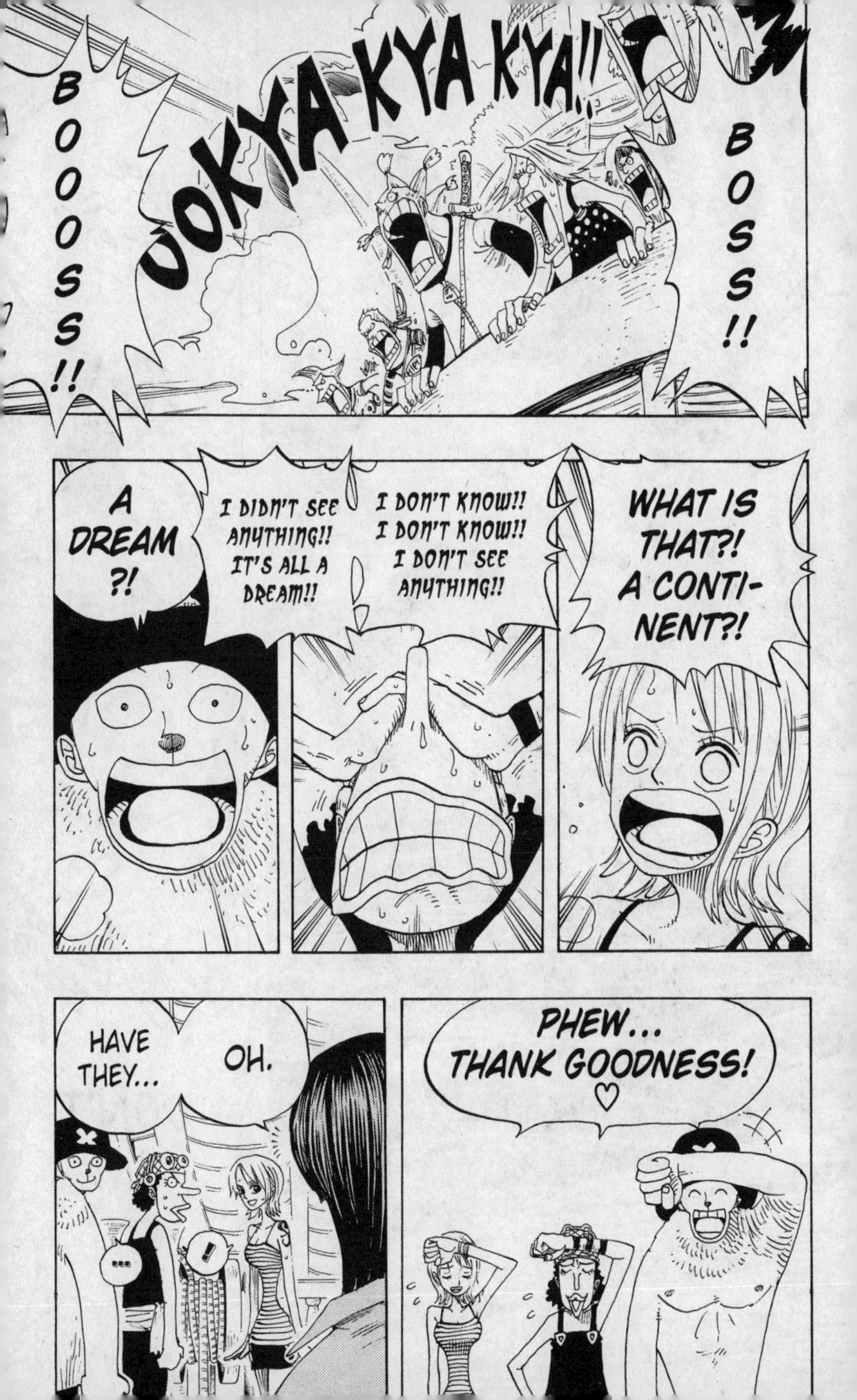
BOSS!!
UOKYA KYA KYA!!
BOOOSS!!
WHAT IS THAT?! A CONTI-NENT?!
I DON'T KNOW!! I DON'T KNOW!! I DON'T SEE ANYTHING!!
I DIDN'T SEE ANYTHING!! IT'S ALL A DREAM!!
A DREAM ?!
PHEW... THANK GOODNESS! ♡
OH.
HAVE THEY...
!
...

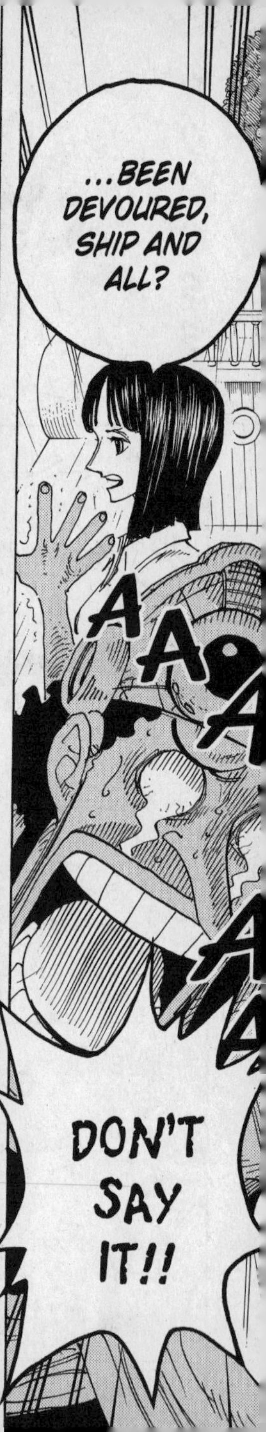
...BEEN DEVOURED, SHIP AND ALL?
AAAAAAA
DON'T SAY IT!!
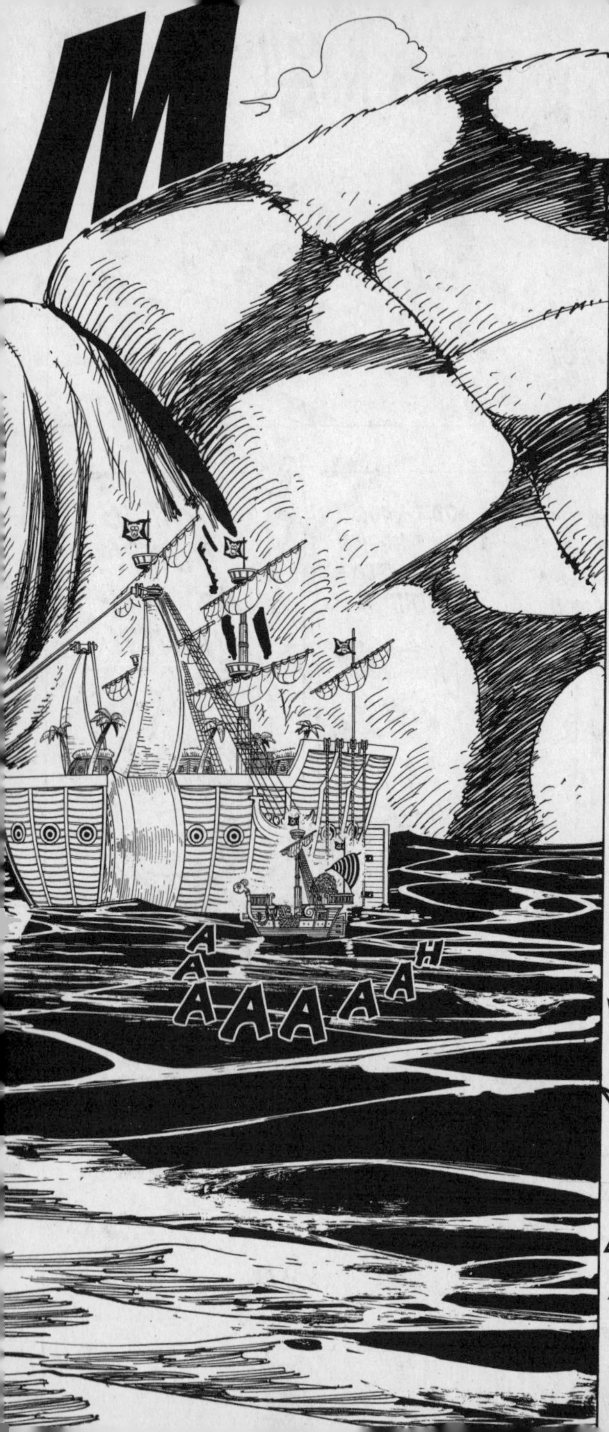
M
AAAAAAAAH

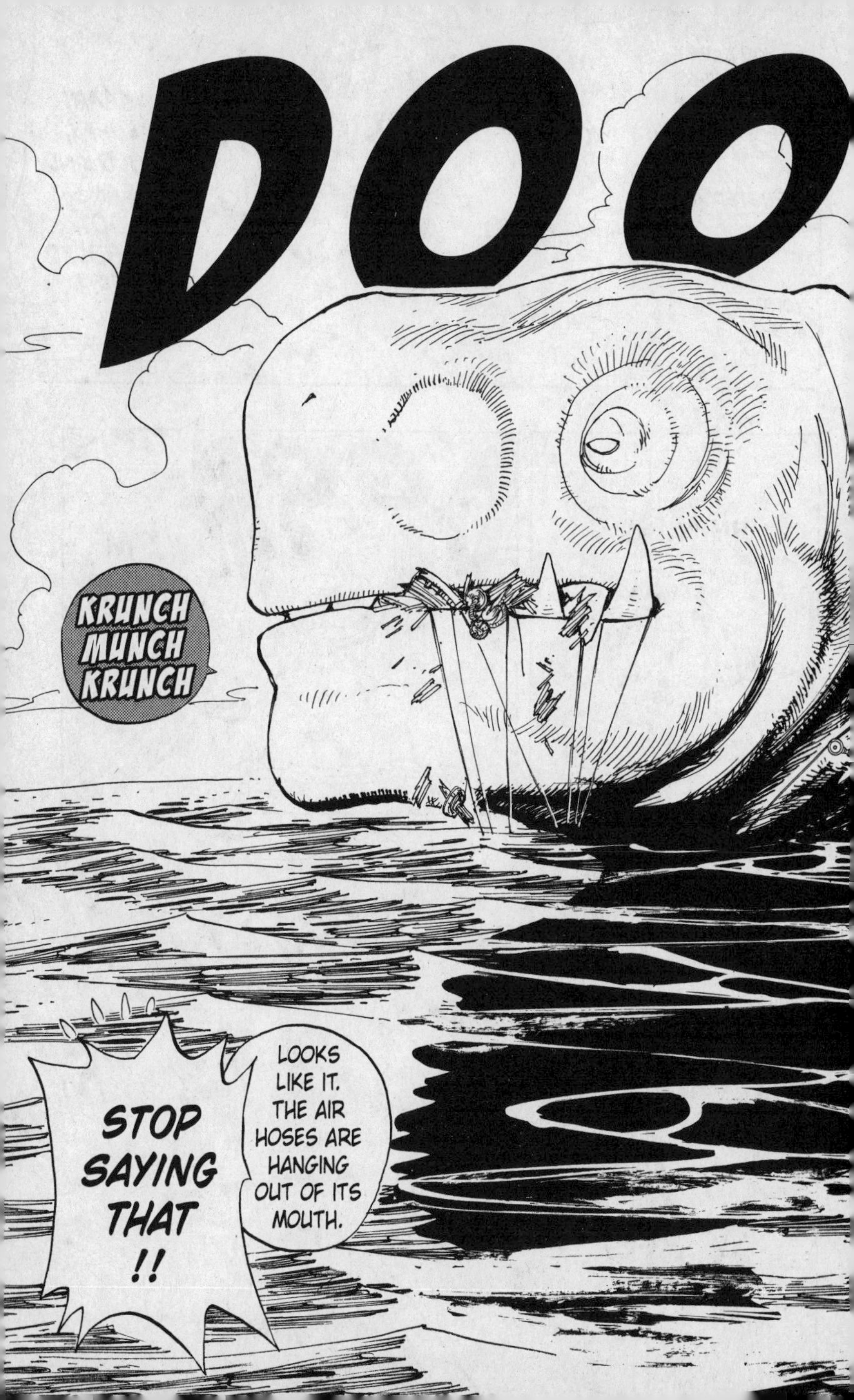
DOO
KRUNCH MUNCH KRUNCH
LOOKS LIKE IT. THE AIR HOSES ARE HANGING OUT OF ITS MOUTH.
STOP SAYING THAT!!

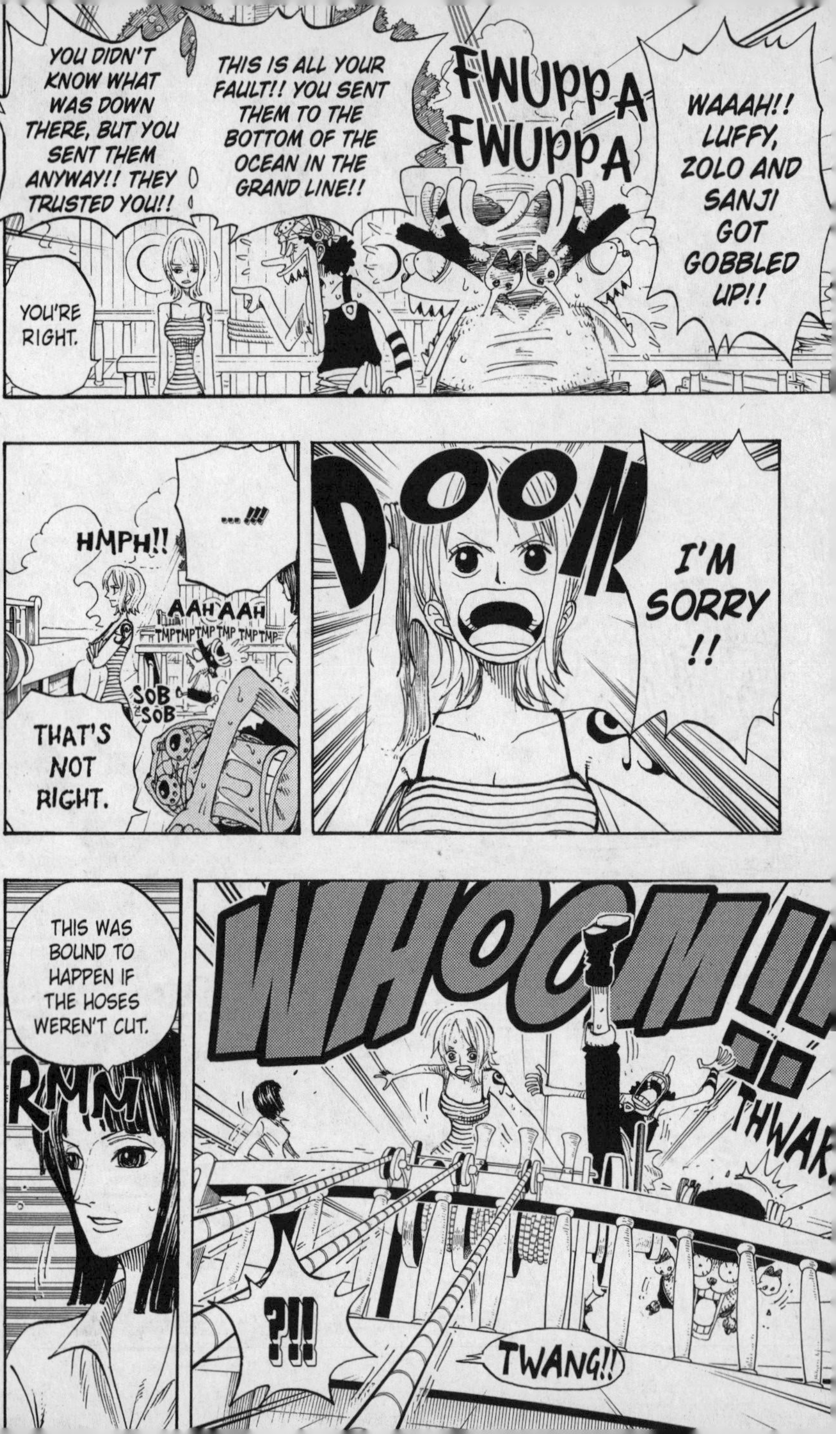
WAAAH!! LUFFY, ZOLO AND SANJI GOT GOBBLED UP!!
FWUPPA FWUPPA
THIS IS ALL YOUR FAULT!! YOU SENT THEM TO THE BOTTOM OF THE OCEAN IN THE GRAND LINE!!
YOU DIDN'T KNOW WHAT WAS DOWN THERE, BUT YOU SENT THEM ANYWAY!! THEY TRUSTED YOU!!
YOU'RE RIGHT.
DOOM
I'M SORRY!!
...!!!
HMPH!!
AAH AAH
TMP TMP TMP TMP TMP TMP
SOB SOB
THAT'S NOT RIGHT.
WHOOM!!
THWAK
?!!
TWANG!!
THIS WAS BOUND TO HAPPEN IF THE HOSES WEREN'T CUT.
RMM

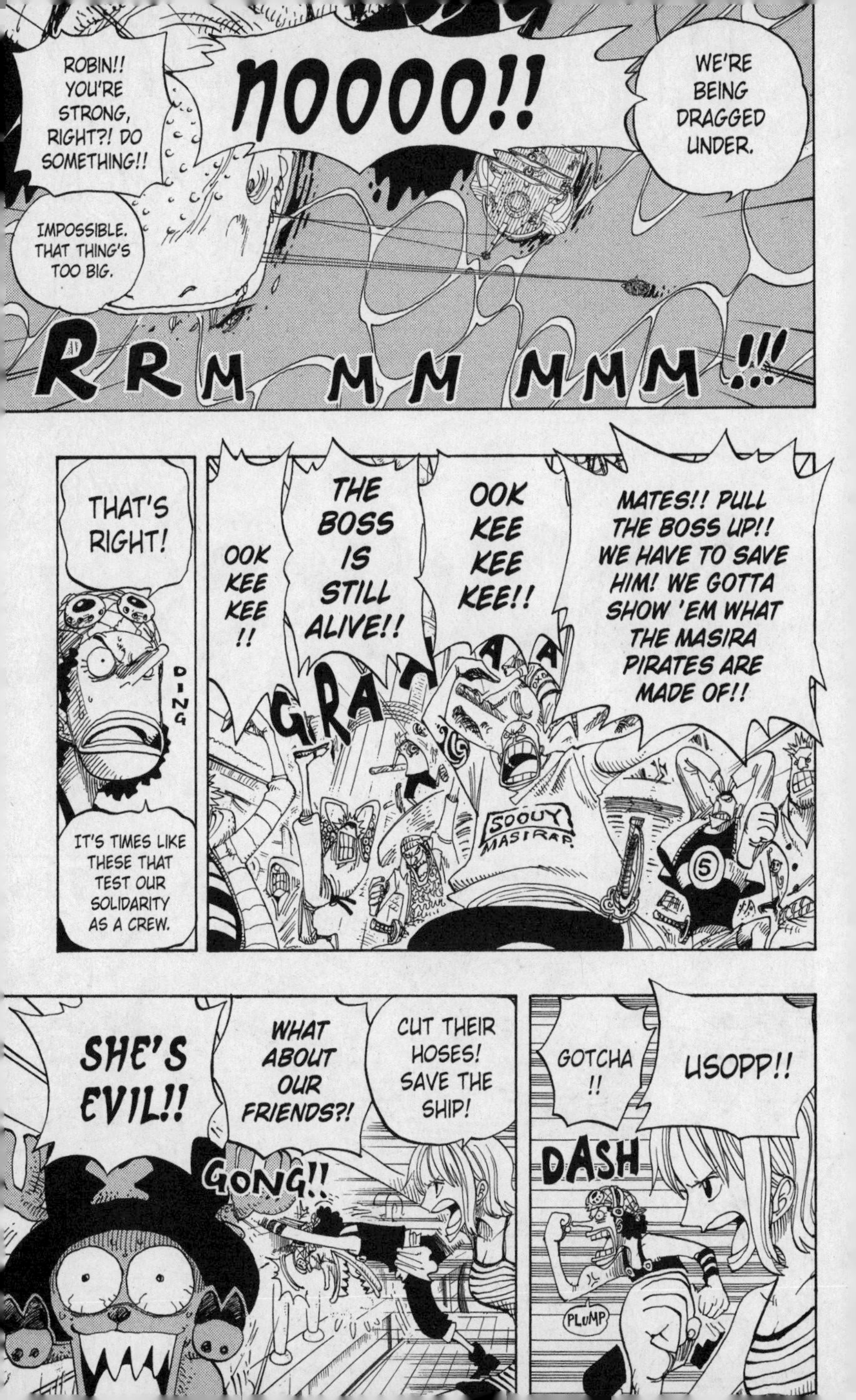
WE'RE BEING DRAGGED UNDER.
NOOOO!!
ROBIN!! YOU'RE STRONG, RIGHT?! DO SOMETHING!!
IMPOSSIBLE. THAT THING'S TOO BIG.
RRMMMMMM!!!
MATES!! PULL THE BOSS UP!! WE HAVE TO SAVE HIM! WE GOTTA SHOW 'EM WHAT THE MASIRA PIRATES ARE MADE OF!!
OOK KEE KEE KEE!!
THE BOSS IS STILL ALIVE!!
OOK KEE KEE !!
THAT'S RIGHT!
DING
IT'S TIMES LIKE THESE THAT TEST OUR SOLIDARITY AS A CREW.
USOPP!!
GOTCHA !!
DASH
PLUMP
CUT THEIR HOSES! SAVE THE SHIP!
WHAT ABOUT OUR FRIENDS?!
SHE'S EVIL!!
GONG!!

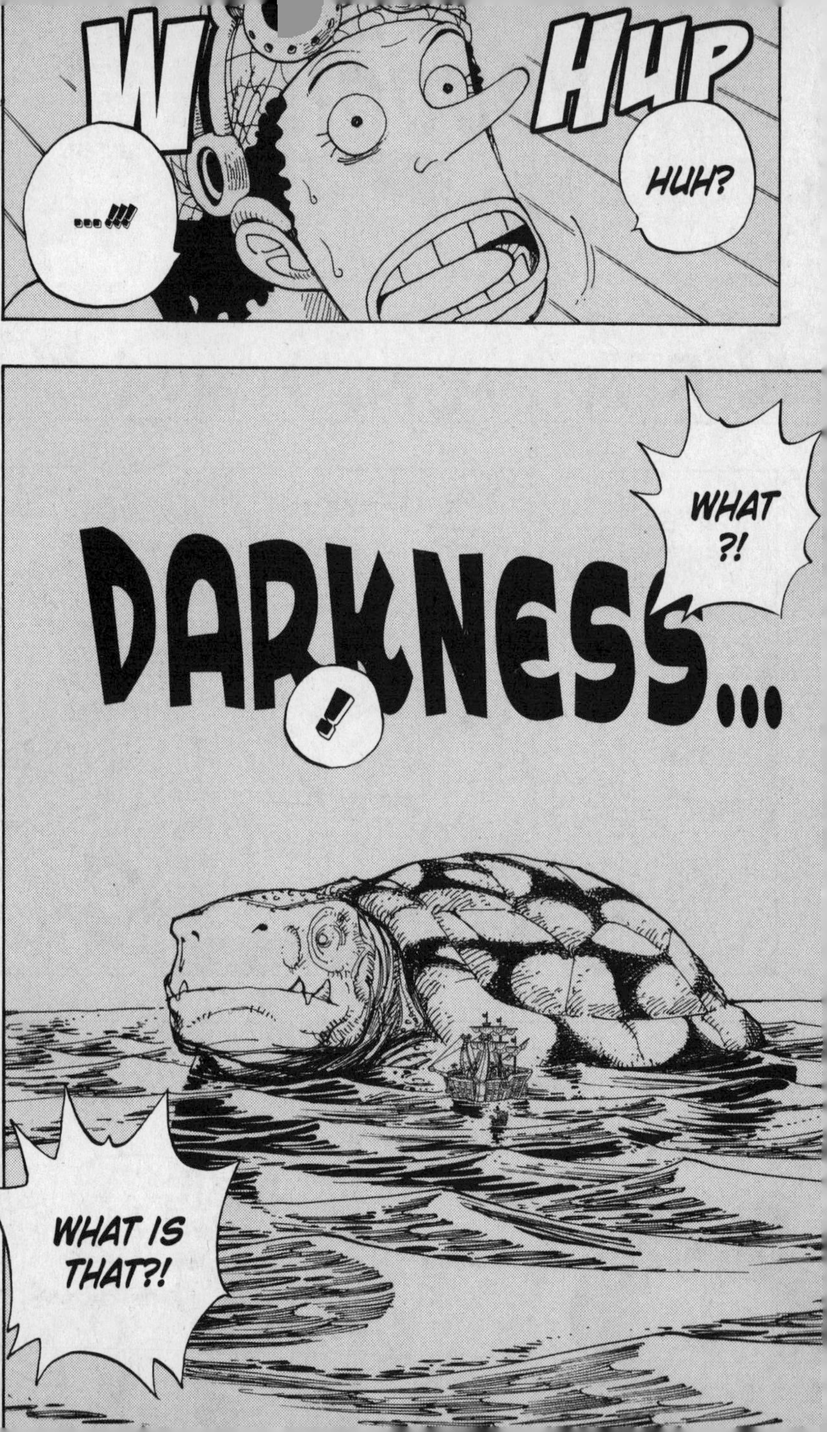
HUH?
WHUP
...!!!
WHAT ?!
DARKNESS...
!
WHAT IS THAT?!

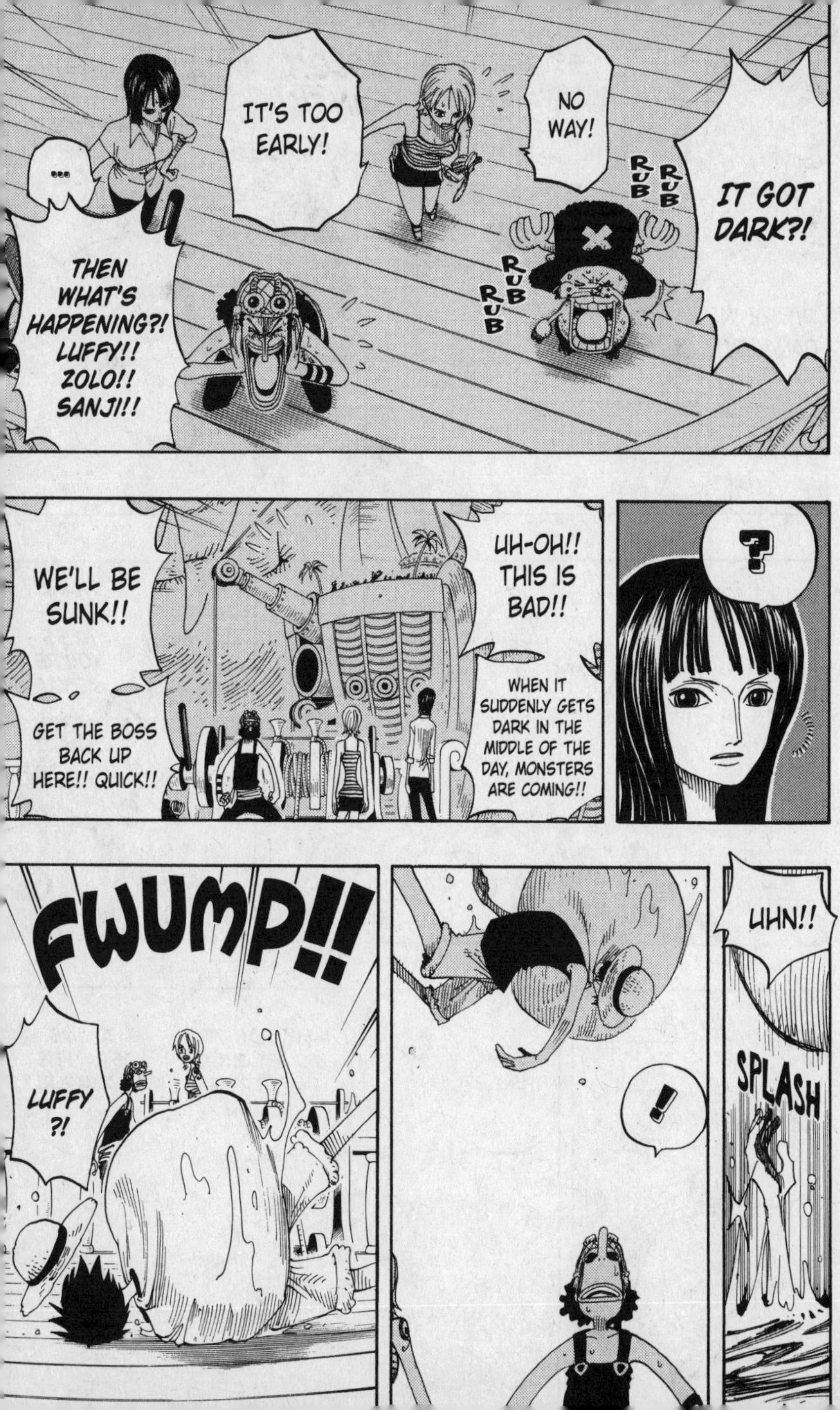
IT GOT DARK?!
NO WAY!
RUB RUB
RUB RUB
IT'S TOO EARLY!
...
THEN WHAT'S HAPPENING?! LUFFY!! ZOLO!! SANJI!!
?
UH-OH!! THIS IS BAD!!
WHEN IT SUDDENLY GETS DARK IN THE MIDDLE OF THE DAY, MONSTERS ARE COMING!!
WE'LL BE SUNK!!
GET THE BOSS BACK UP HERE!! QUICK!!
UHN!!
SPLASH
!
FWUMP!!
LUFFY ?!

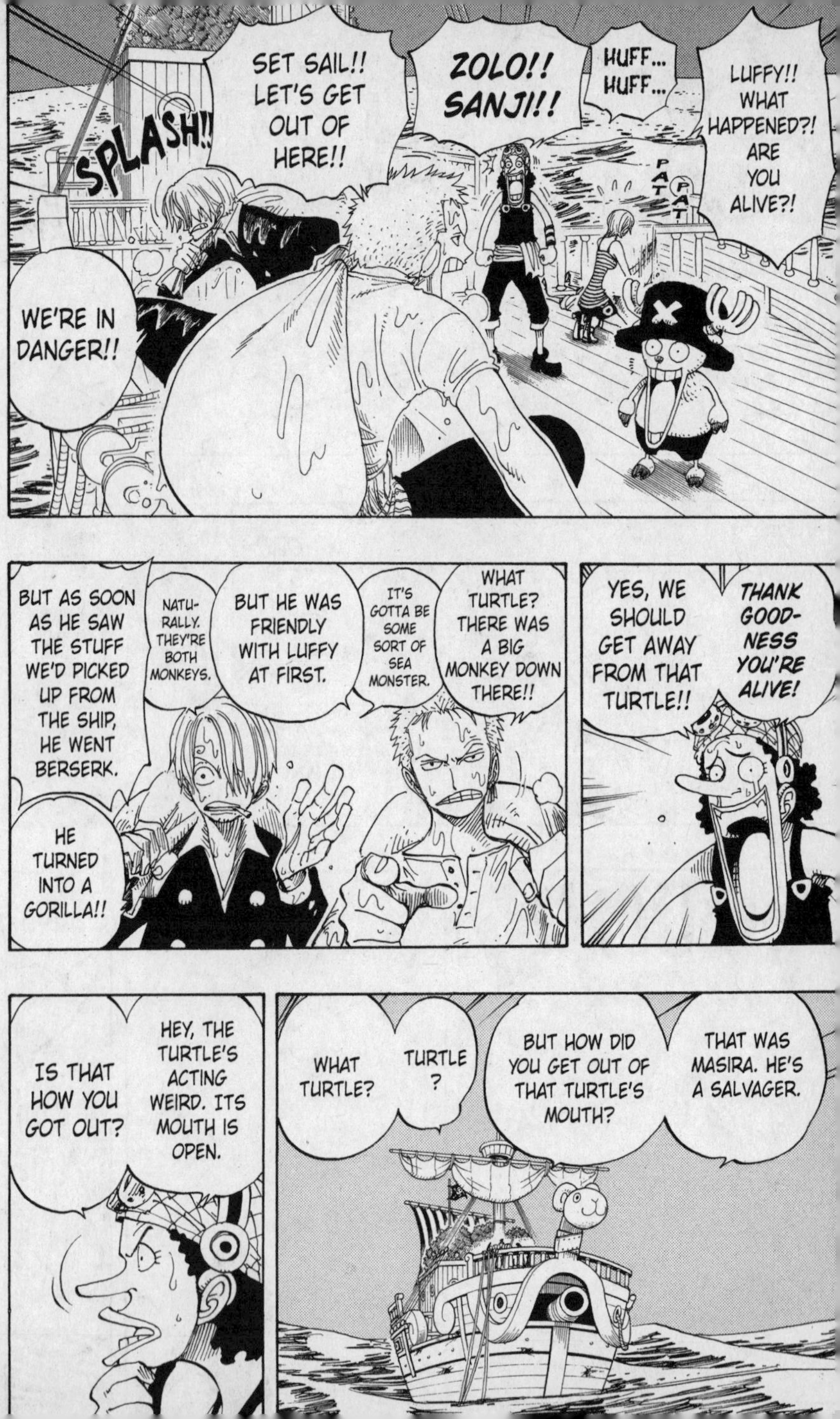
LUFFY!! WHAT HAPPENED?! ARE YOU ALIVE?!
PAT PAT
HUFF... HUFF...
ZOLO!! SANJI!!
SET SAIL!! LET'S GET OUT OF HERE!!
SPLASH!!
WE'RE IN DANGER!!
THANK GOOD-NESS YOU'RE ALIVE!
YES, WE SHOULD GET AWAY FROM THAT TURTLE!!
WHAT TURTLE? THERE WAS A BIG MONKEY DOWN THERE!!
IT'S GOTTA BE SOME SORT OF SEA MONSTER.
BUT HE WAS FRIENDLY WITH LUFFY AT FIRST.
NATU-RALLY. THEY'RE BOTH MONKEYS.
BUT AS SOON AS HE SAW THE STUFF WE'D PICKED UP FROM THE SHIP, HE WENT BERSERK.
HE TURNED INTO A GORILLA!!
THAT WAS MASIRA. HE'S A SALVAGER.
BUT HOW DID YOU GET OUT OF THAT TURTLE'S MOUTH?
TURTLE?
WHAT TURTLE?
HEY, THE TURTLE'S ACTING WEIRD. ITS MOUTH IS OPEN.
IS THAT HOW YOU GOT OUT?

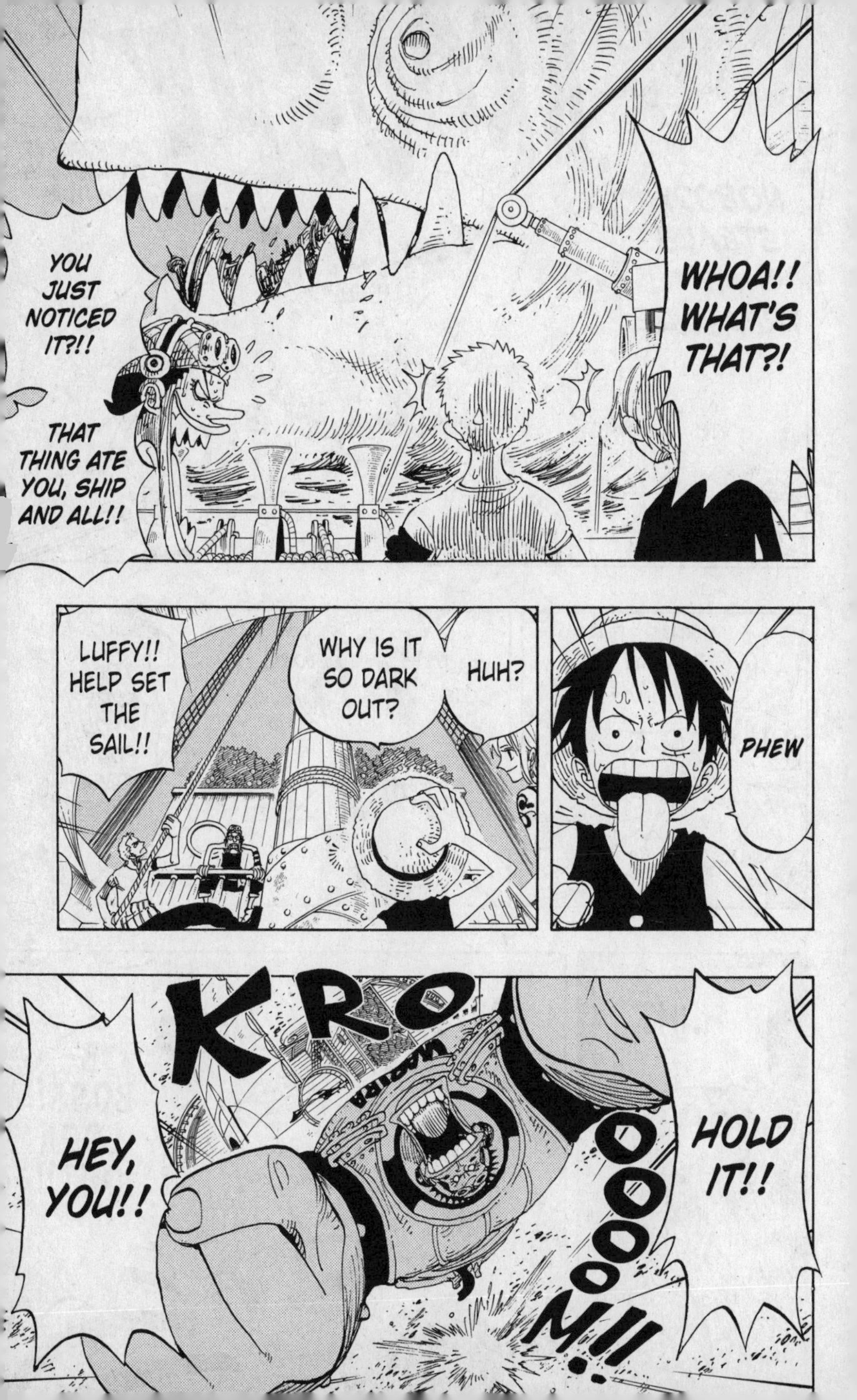
WHOA!! WHAT'S THAT?!
YOU JUST NOTICED IT?!!
THAT THING ATE YOU, SHIP AND ALL!!
PHEW
HUH?
WHY IS IT SO DARK OUT?
LUFFY!! HELP SET THE SAIL!!
HOLD IT!!
KROOOOOOM!!
HEY, YOU!!

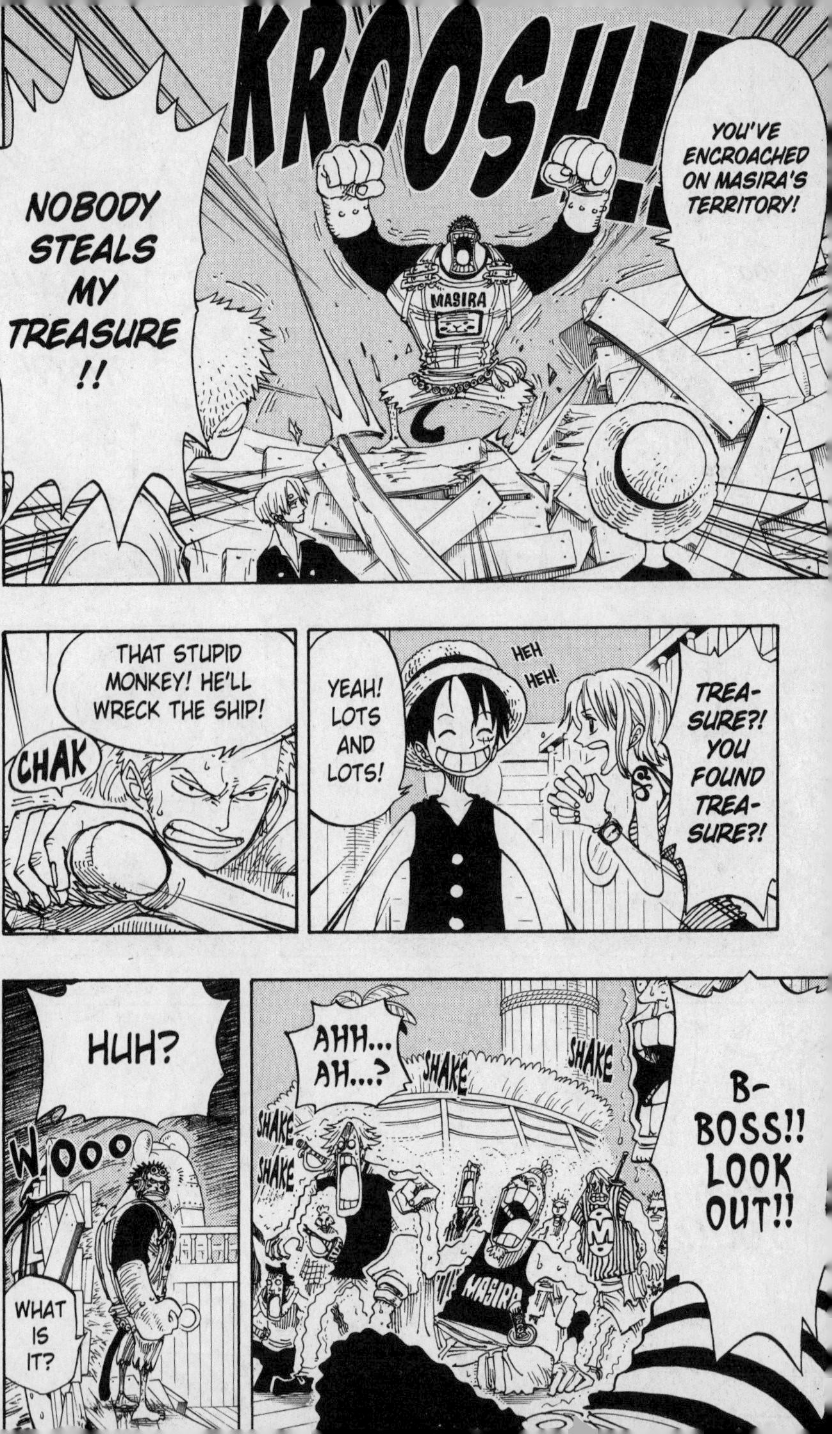
KROOSH!!
YOU'VE ENCROACHED ON MASIRA'S TERRITORY!
NOBODY STEALS MY TREASURE !!
TREA-SURE?! YOU FOUND TREA-SURE?!
HEH HEH!
YEAH! LOTS AND LOTS!
THAT STUPID MONKEY! HE'LL WRECK THE SHIP!
CHAK
B-BOSS!! LOOK OUT!!
SHAKE
SHAKE
AHH... AH...?
SHAKE SHAKE
HUH?
WOOO
WHAT IS IT?

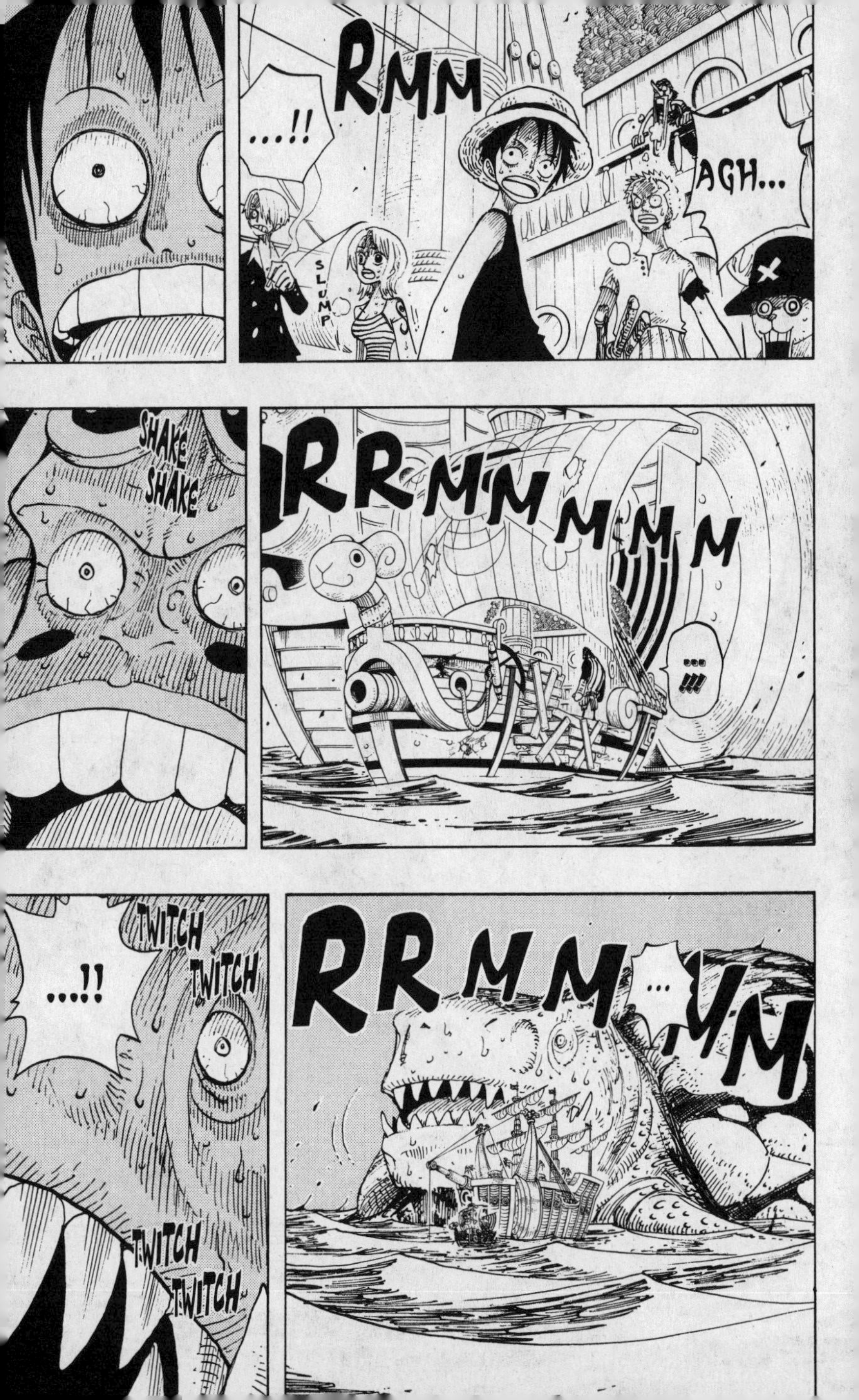
AGH...
RMM
...!!
SLUMP
RRMMMMMMN
...!!!
SHAKE SHAKE
RRMMMMM
...
...!!
TWITCH TWITCH
TWITCH TWITCH

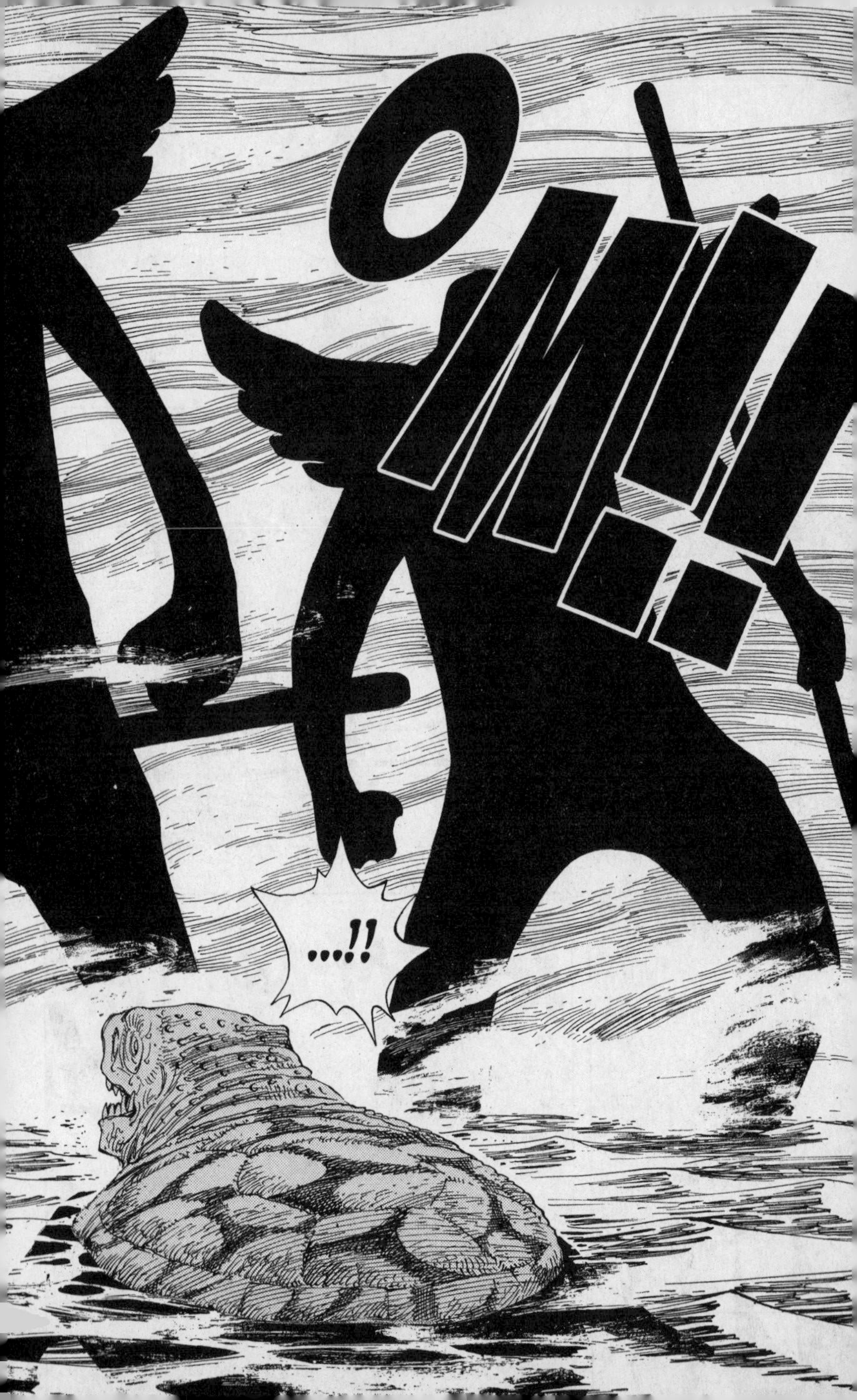

OH!!
...!!

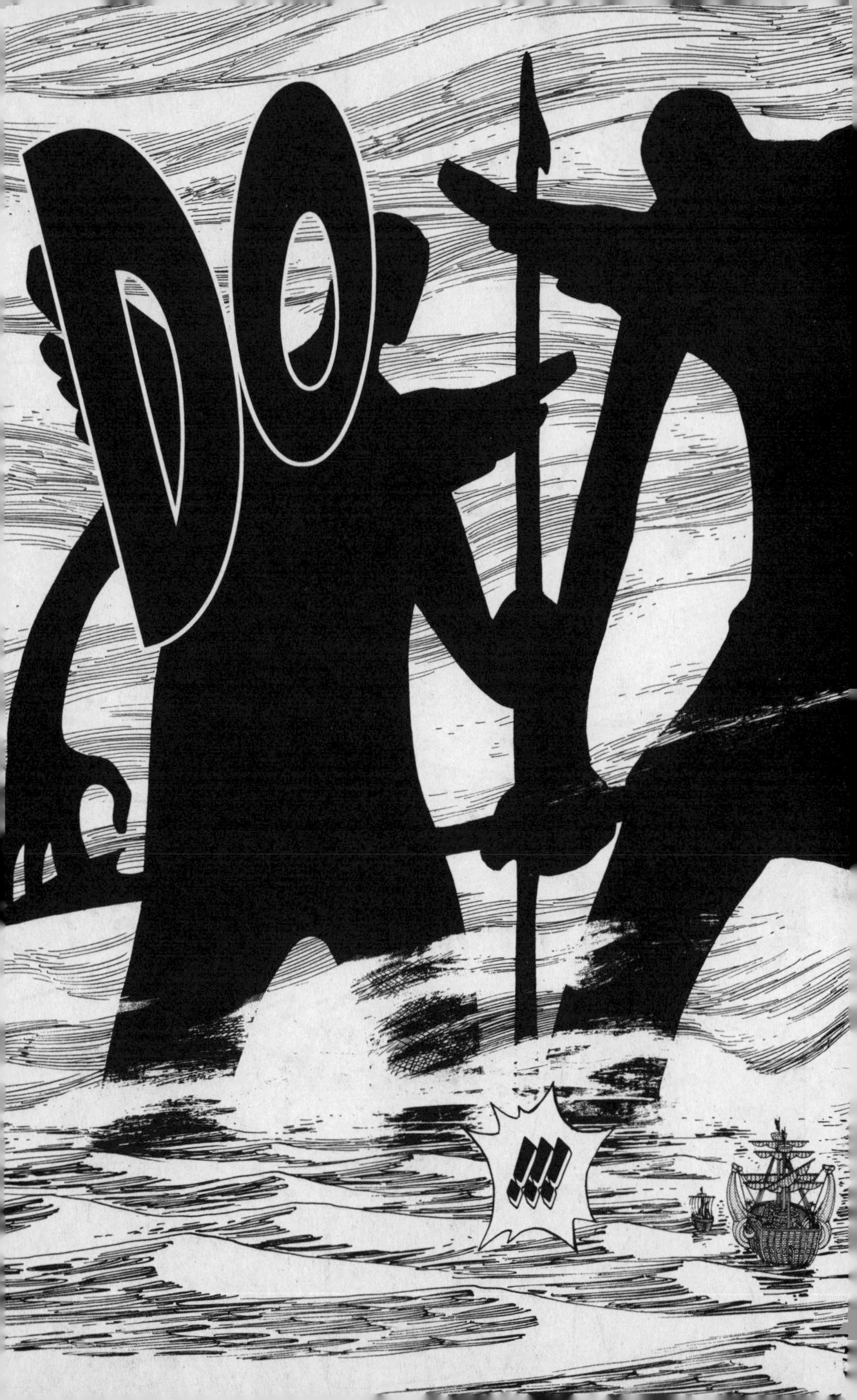
DO
!!!

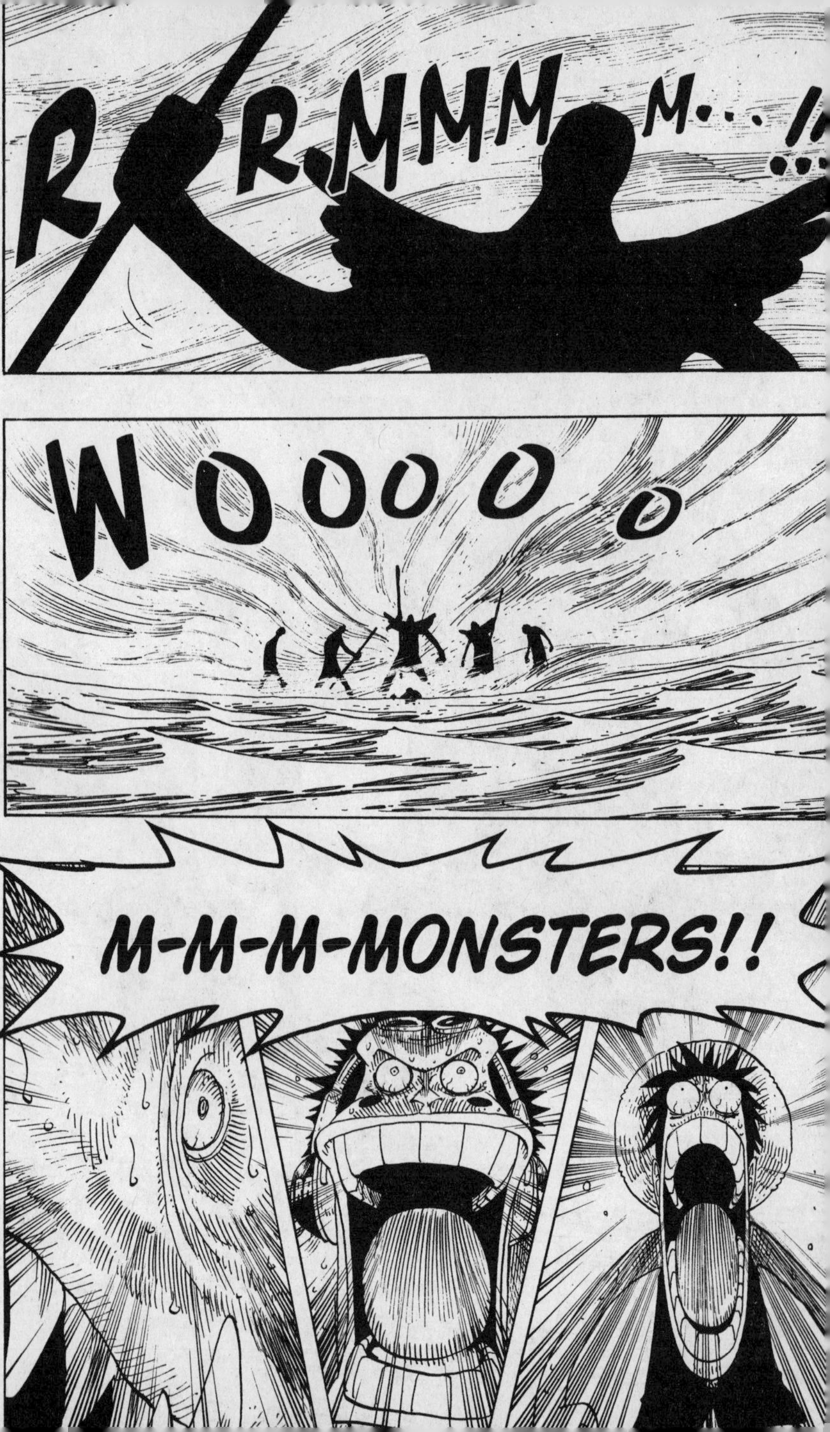
RRRMMMM M...!!
WOOOOO
M-M-M-MONSTERS!!

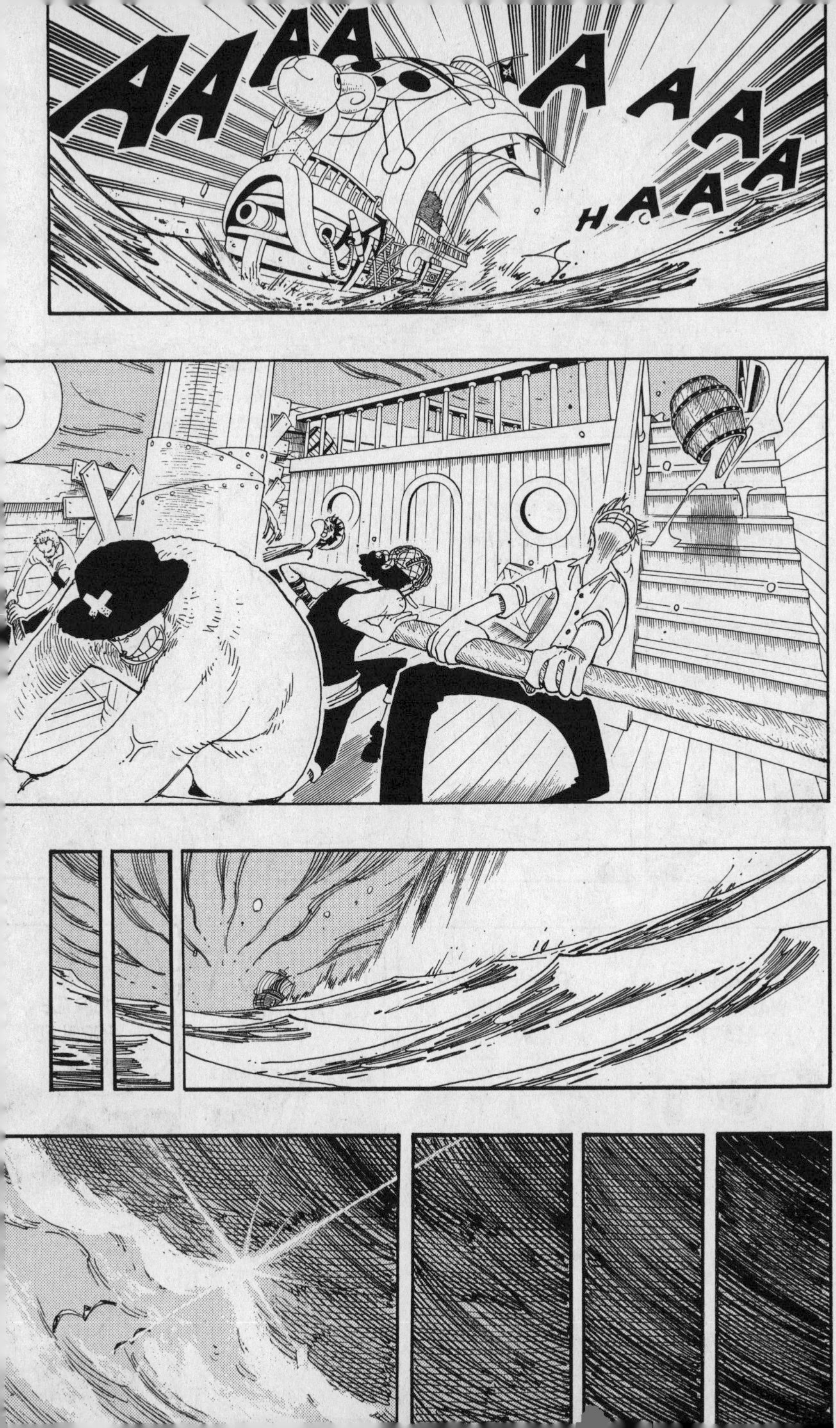
AAAAAAAAA
HAAAA

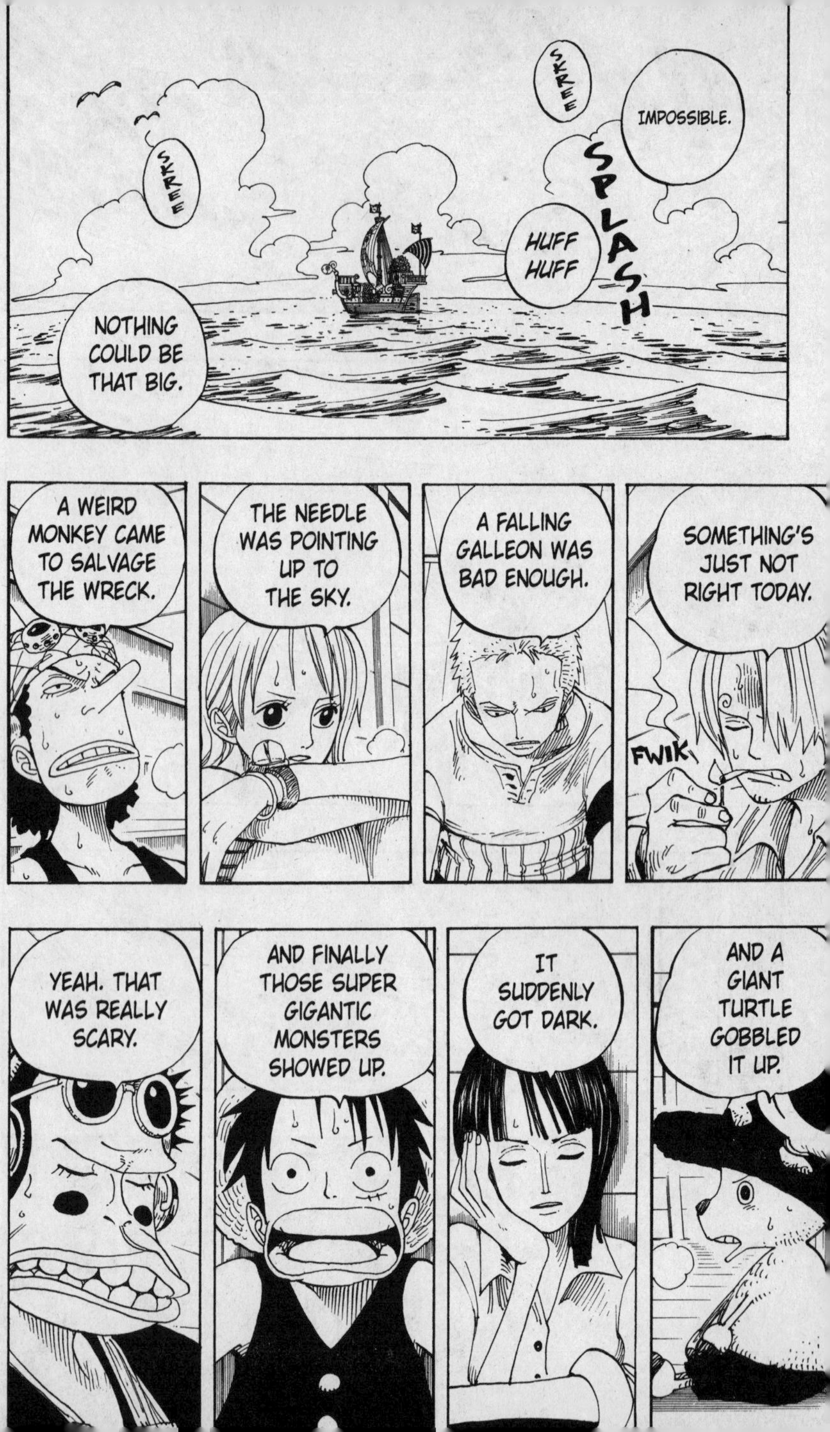
SKREE
IMPOSSIBLE.
SPLASH
HUFF HUFF
SKREE
NOTHING COULD BE THAT BIG.
SOMETHING'S JUST NOT RIGHT TODAY.
FWIK
A FALLING GALLEON WAS BAD ENOUGH.
THE NEEDLE WAS POINTING UP TO THE SKY.
A WEIRD MONKEY CAME TO SALVAGE THE WRECK.
AND A GIANT TURTLE GOBBLED IT UP.
IT SUDDENLY GOT DARK.
AND FINALLY THOSE SUPER GIGANTIC MONSTERS SHOWED UP.
YEAH. THAT WAS REALLY SCARY.

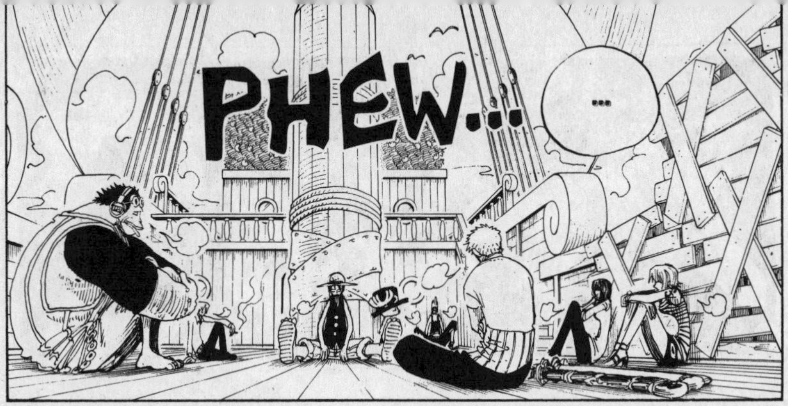
...
PHEW...
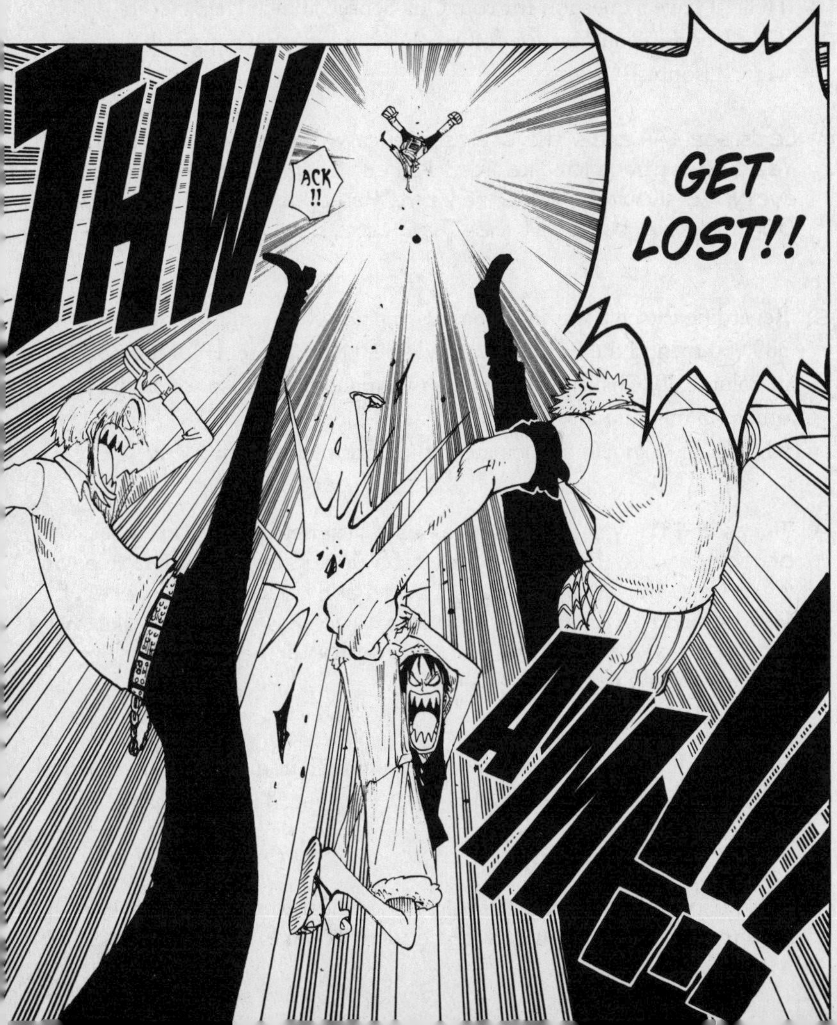
GET LOST!!
ACK !!
THW

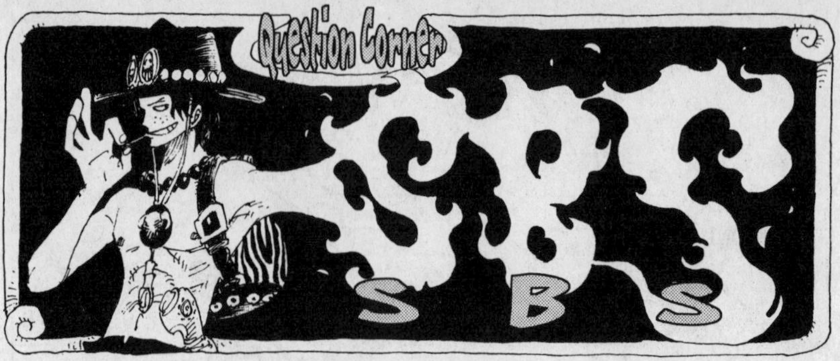
Question Corner
SBS

Q: Hello, I have a question for you, Oda Sensei. Which character in *One Piece* do you most resemble? (I'm thinking you're probably very "Usoppish.")

A: Let's see... There's the brains, the calm demeanor, the clothes... Yes, I guess I'm a lot like "Red-haired" Shanks! Yeah! I can hear everyone shouting in agreement. Ha ha ha... Huh? Ow! Don't throw things at me! That hurts!

Q: Regarding the civil war in Alabasta, originally, you said there were 300,000 men in the Royal Army and 700,000 in the rebel forces. But in volume 20, Chaka says there are two million rebels, so where did the other 1.3 million more come from? (Are they people like Toh-Toh, who didn't originally participate in the uprising but joined later?)

A: That's it. In any case, Alabasta has a population of ten million. In order to make the story easier to understand, I left out a lot of details. Alabasta has many towns and villages that weren't mentioned in the story. So two million may not seem like many compared to ten million, but two million armed people is a lot. This is a really serious uprising.

Q: Hello, Eiichiro Oda Sensei. I recently went on a homestay in England and discovered something I wanted to share with you. The toilet paper there is brown! (But kind of orange)

A: No kidding?! That's bad. Visibility is critical with toilet paper! Is that because England is tea country?! Are they evoking images of tea?!

Chapter 222:
THE GIANT NOVICE

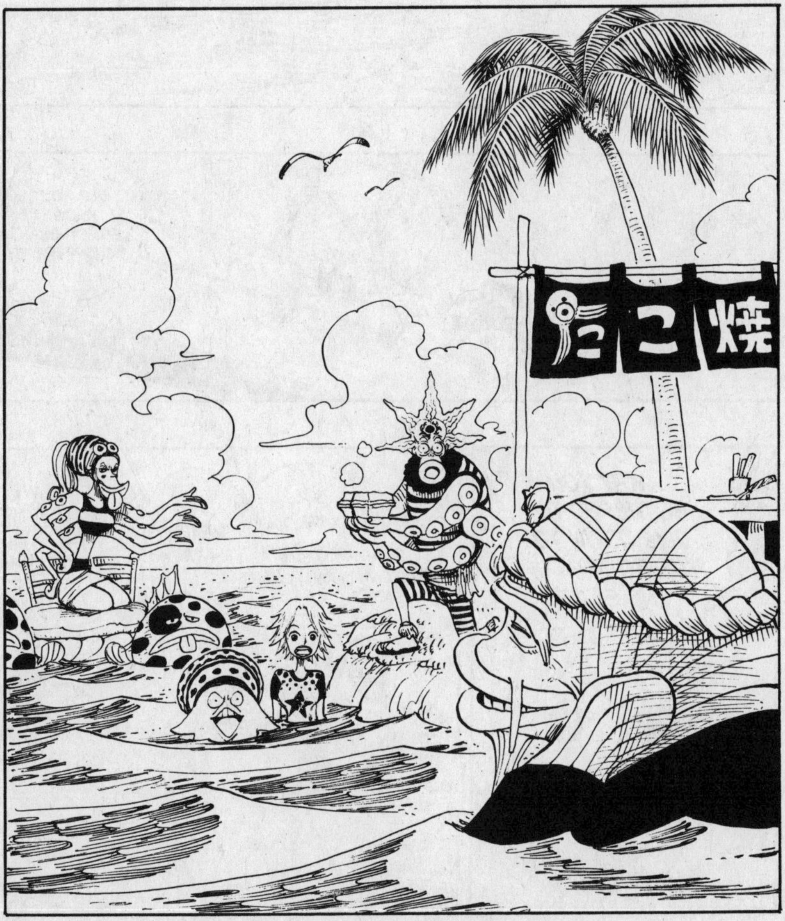
たこ焼

HACHI'S WALK ON THE SEAFLOOR, VOL. 35:
"THE OLD CATFISH WHO CAME LATE"

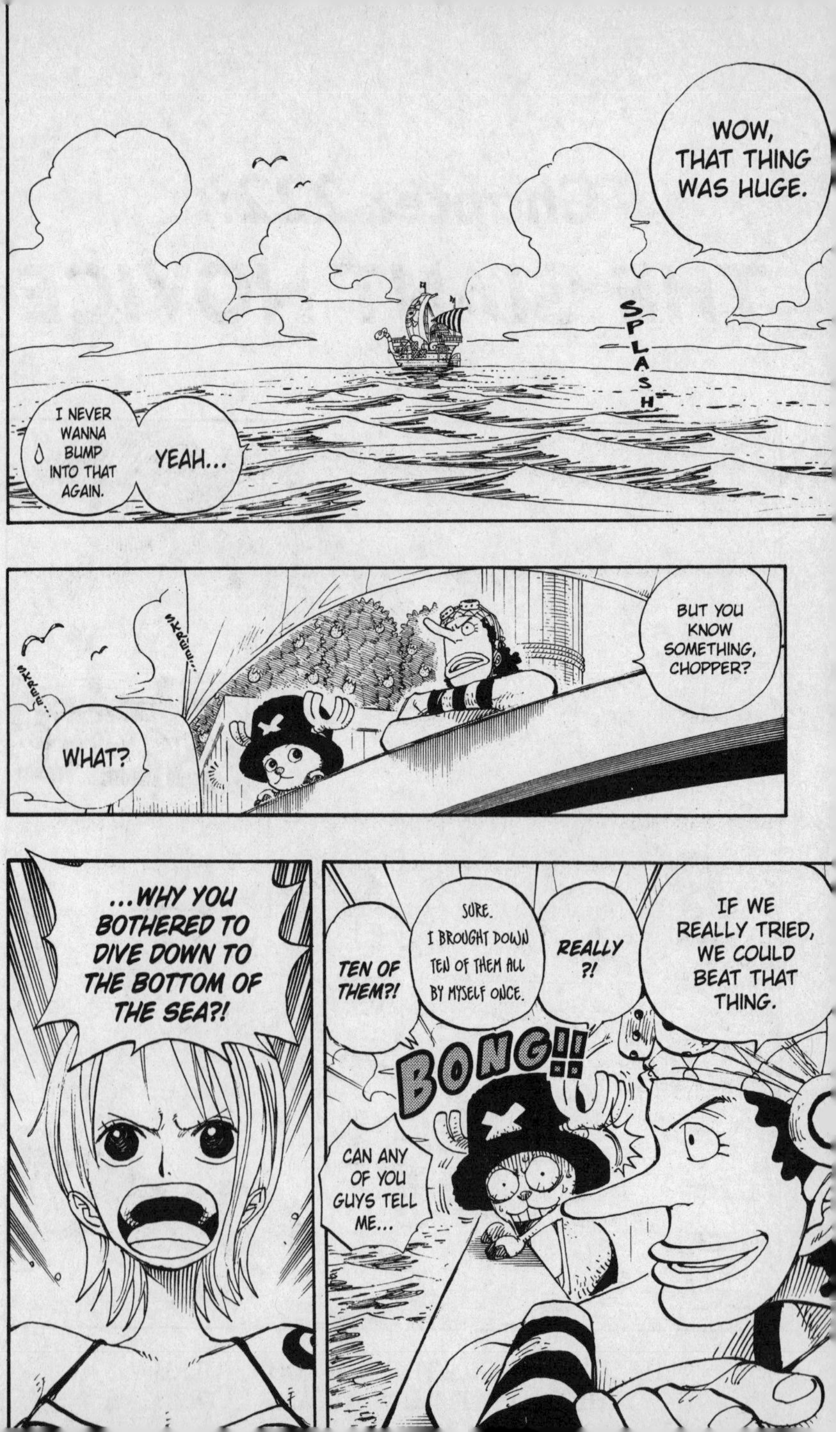
WOW, THAT THING WAS HUGE.
SPLASH
YEAH...
I NEVER WANNA BUMP INTO THAT AGAIN.
BUT YOU KNOW SOMETHING, CHOPPER?
WHAT?
IF WE REALLY TRIED, WE COULD BEAT THAT THING.
REALLY ?!
SURE. I BROUGHT DOWN TEN OF THEM ALL BY MYSELF ONCE.
TEN OF THEM?!
BONG!!
CAN ANY OF YOU GUYS TELL ME...
...WHY YOU BOTHERED TO DIVE DOWN TO THE BOTTOM OF THE SEA?!

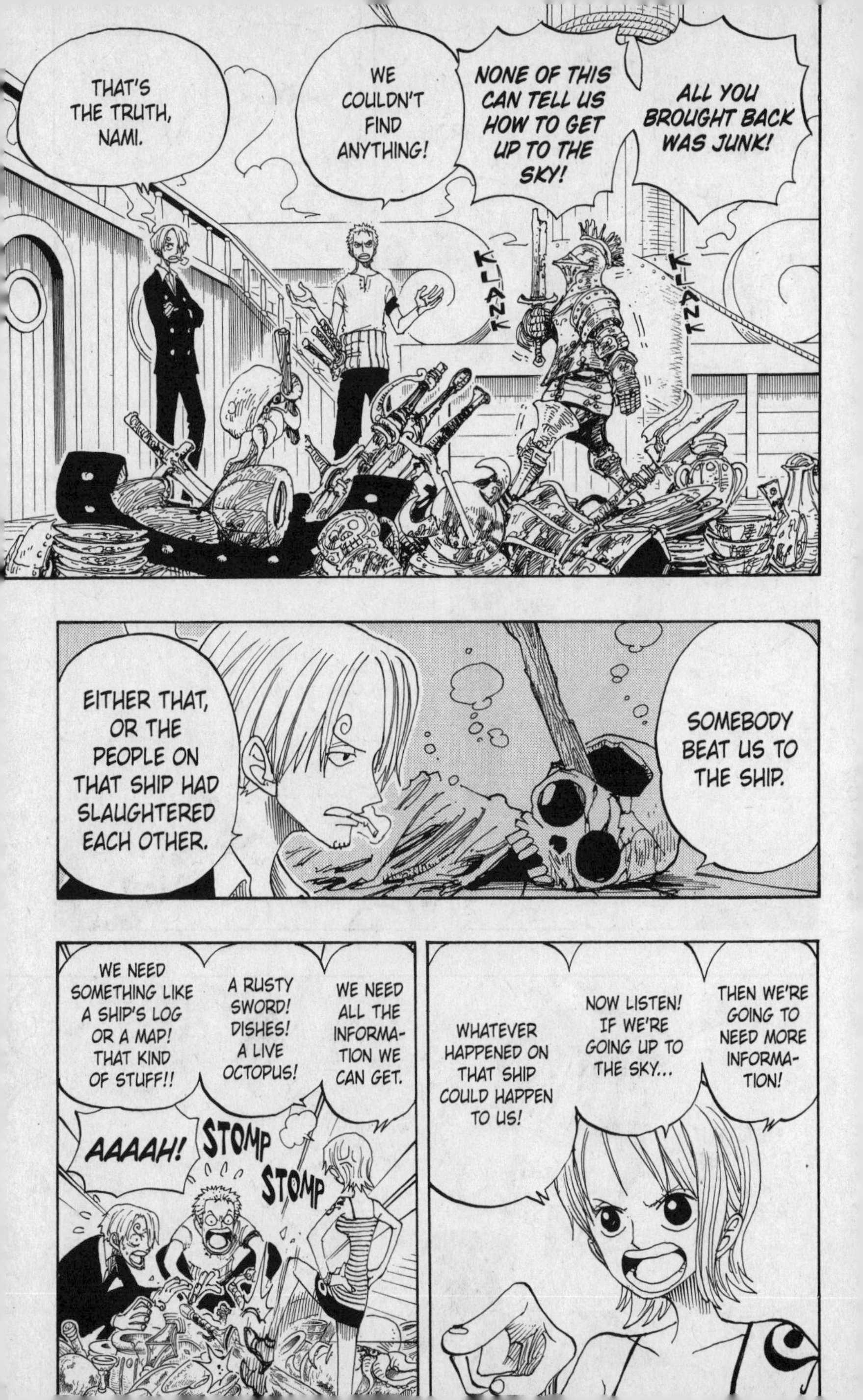
ALL YOU BROUGHT BACK WAS JUNK!
NONE OF THIS CAN TELL US HOW TO GET UP TO THE SKY!
WE COULDN'T FIND ANYTHING!
THAT'S THE TRUTH, NAMI.
KLANK
KLANK
SOMEBODY BEAT US TO THE SHIP.
EITHER THAT, OR THE PEOPLE ON THAT SHIP HAD SLAUGHTERED EACH OTHER.
THEN WE'RE GOING TO NEED MORE INFORMATION!
NOW LISTEN! IF WE'RE GOING UP TO THE SKY...
WHATEVER HAPPENED ON THAT SHIP COULD HAPPEN TO US!
WE NEED ALL THE INFORMATION WE CAN GET.
A RUSTY SWORD! DISHES! A LIVE OCTOPUS!
WE NEED SOMETHING LIKE A SHIP'S LOG OR A MAP! THAT KIND OF STUFF!!
STOMP
STOMP
AAAAH!

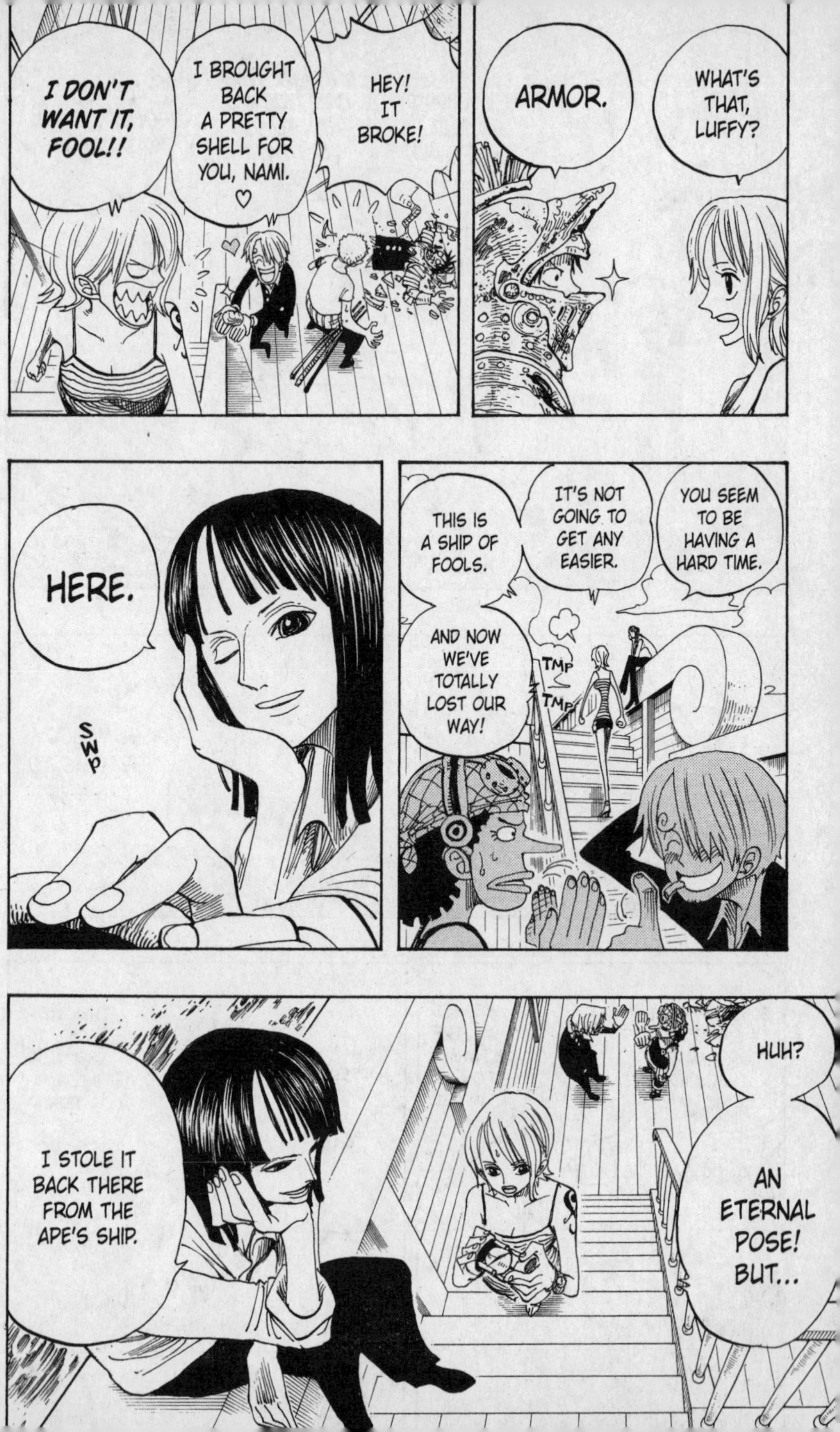
WHAT'S THAT, LUFFY?
ARMOR.
HEY! IT BROKE!
I BROUGHT BACK A PRETTY SHELL FOR YOU, NAMI. ♡
I DON'T WANT IT, FOOL!!
YOU SEEM TO BE HAVING A HARD TIME.
IT'S NOT GOING TO GET ANY EASIER.
THIS IS A SHIP OF FOOLS.
AND NOW WE'VE TOTALLY LOST OUR WAY!
TMP
TMP
HERE.
SWP
HUH?
AN ETERNAL POSE! BUT...
I STOLE IT BACK THERE FROM THE APE'S SHIP.

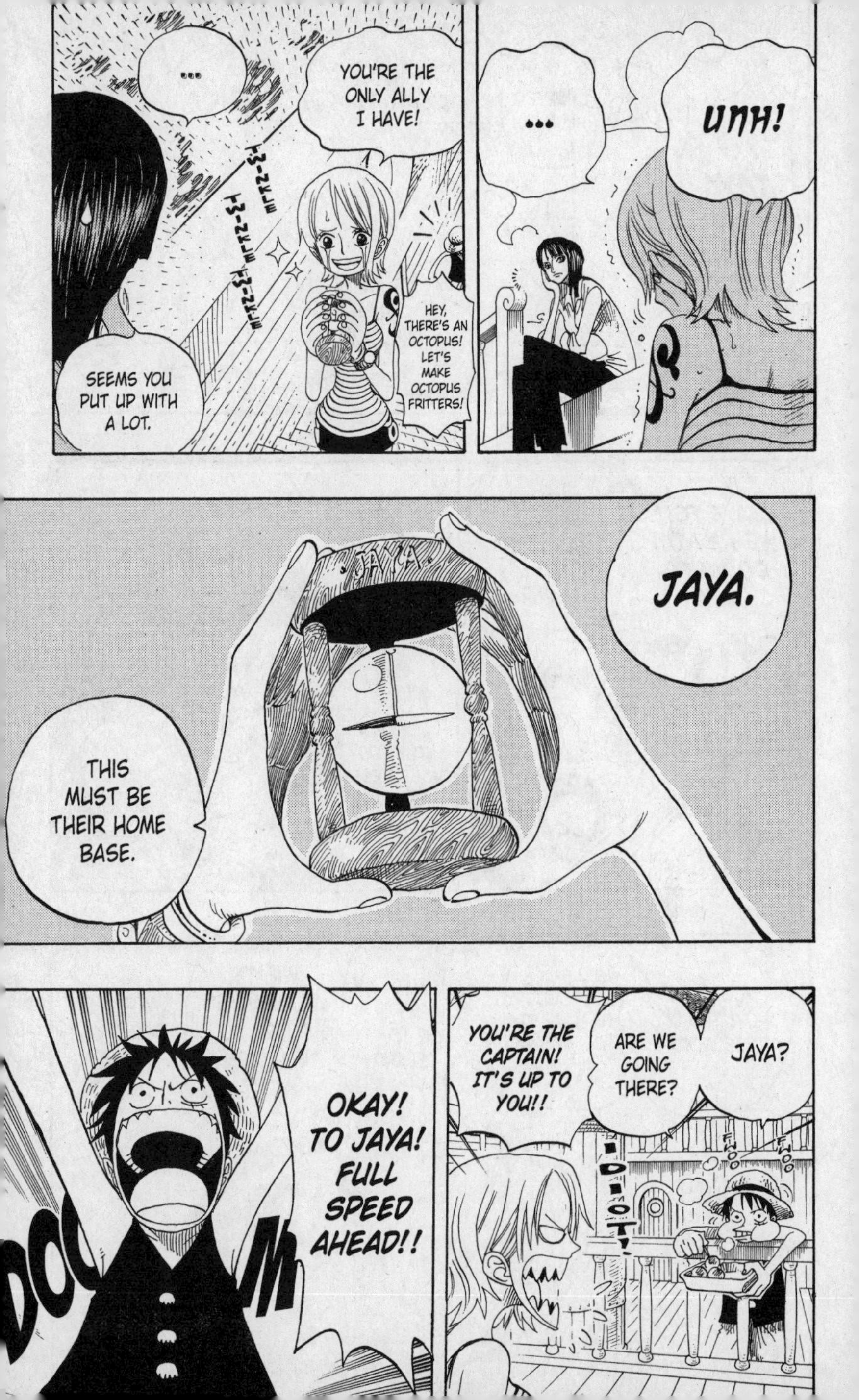
UNH!
...
YOU'RE THE ONLY ALLY I HAVE!
...
TWINKLE TWINKLE
HEY, THERE'S AN OCTOPUS! LET'S MAKE OCTOPUS FRITTERS!
SEEMS YOU PUT UP WITH A LOT.
JAYA.
JAYA
THIS MUST BE THEIR HOME BASE.
JAYA?
ARE WE GOING THERE?
YOU'RE THE CAPTAIN! IT'S UP TO YOU!!
FWOO FWOO
IDIOT!
OKAY! TO JAYA! FULL SPEED AHEAD!!
DOOM

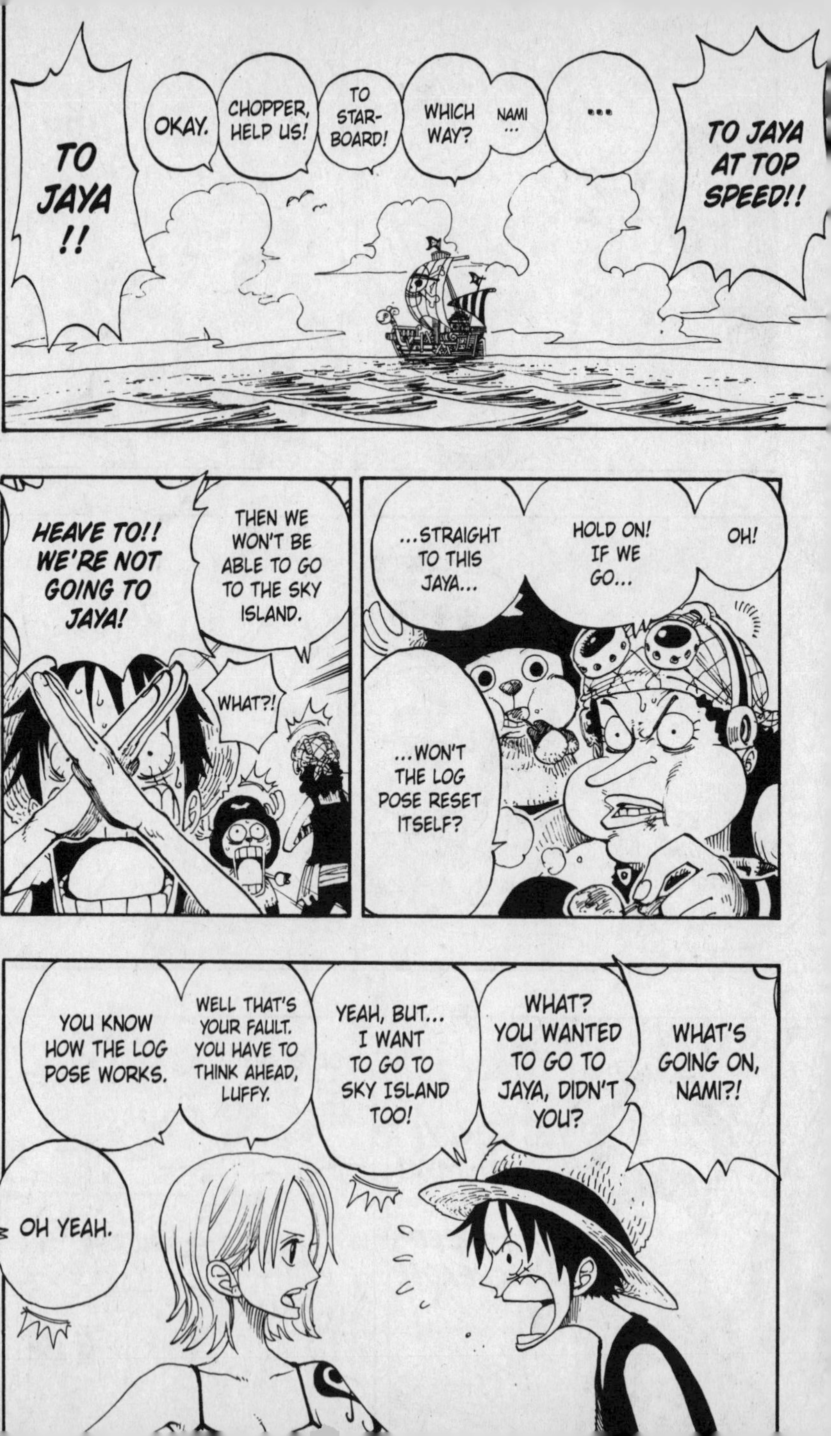
TO JAYA AT TOP SPEED!!
...
NAMI ...
WHICH WAY?
TO STARBOARD!
CHOPPER, HELP US!
OKAY.
TO JAYA!!
OH!
HOLD ON! IF WE GO...
...STRAIGHT TO THIS JAYA...
...WON'T THE LOG POSE RESET ITSELF?
THEN WE WON'T BE ABLE TO GO TO THE SKY ISLAND.
HEAVE TO!! WE'RE NOT GOING TO JAYA!
WHAT?!
WHAT'S GOING ON, NAMI?!
WHAT? YOU WANTED TO GO TO JAYA, DIDN'T YOU?
YEAH, BUT... I WANT TO GO TO SKY ISLAND TOO!
WELL THAT'S YOUR FAULT. YOU HAVE TO THINK AHEAD, LUFFY.
YOU KNOW HOW THE LOG POSE WORKS.
OH YEAH.

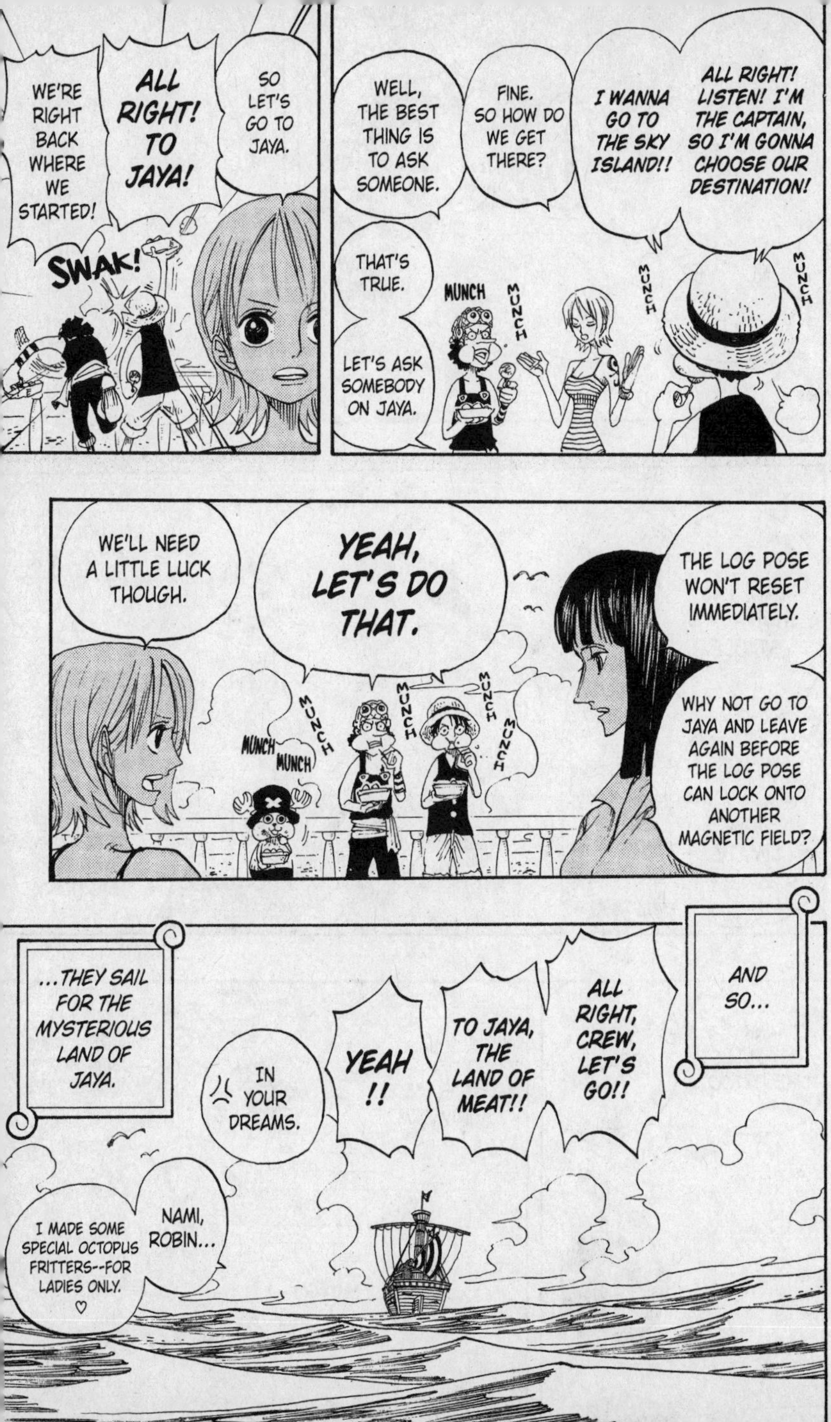
ALL RIGHT! LISTEN! I'M THE CAPTAIN, SO I'M GONNA CHOOSE OUR DESTINATION!
I WANNA GO TO THE SKY ISLAND!!
MUNCH
MUNCH
FINE. SO HOW DO WE GET THERE?
WELL, THE BEST THING IS TO ASK SOMEONE.
MUNCH
MUNCH
THAT'S TRUE.
LET'S ASK SOMEBODY ON JAYA.
SO LET'S GO TO JAYA.
ALL RIGHT! TO JAYA!
WE'RE RIGHT BACK WHERE WE STARTED!
SWAK!
THE LOG POSE WON'T RESET IMMEDIATELY.
WHY NOT GO TO JAYA AND LEAVE AGAIN BEFORE THE LOG POSE CAN LOCK ONTO ANOTHER MAGNETIC FIELD?
MUNCH
MUNCH
YEAH, LET'S DO THAT.
MUNCH
MUNCH
MUNCH
MUNCH
WE'LL NEED A LITTLE LUCK THOUGH.
AND SO...
ALL RIGHT, CREW, LET'S GO!!
TO JAYA, THE LAND OF MEAT!!
YEAH !!
IN YOUR DREAMS.
...THEY SAIL FOR THE MYSTERIOUS LAND OF JAYA.
NAMI, ROBIN...
I MADE SOME SPECIAL OCTOPUS FRITTERS--FOR LADIES ONLY. ♡

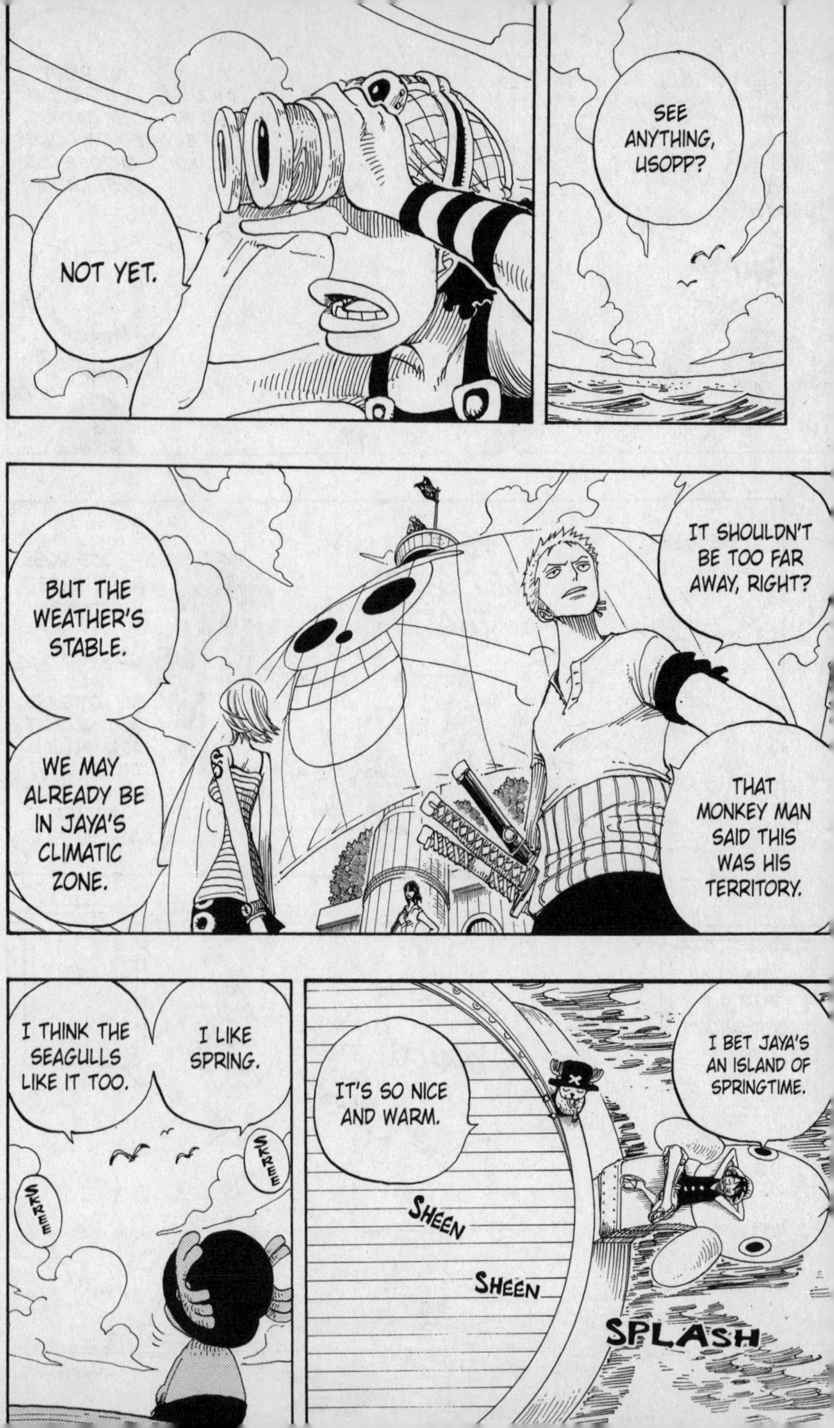
SEE ANYTHING, USOPP?
NOT YET.
IT SHOULDN'T BE TOO FAR AWAY, RIGHT?
THAT MONKEY MAN SAID THIS WAS HIS TERRITORY.
BUT THE WEATHER'S STABLE.
WE MAY ALREADY BE IN JAYA'S CLIMATIC ZONE.
I BET JAYA'S AN ISLAND OF SPRINGTIME.
IT'S SO NICE AND WARM.
SHEEN
SHEEN
SPLASH
I LIKE SPRING.
I THINK THE SEAGULLS LIKE IT TOO.
SKREE
SKREE

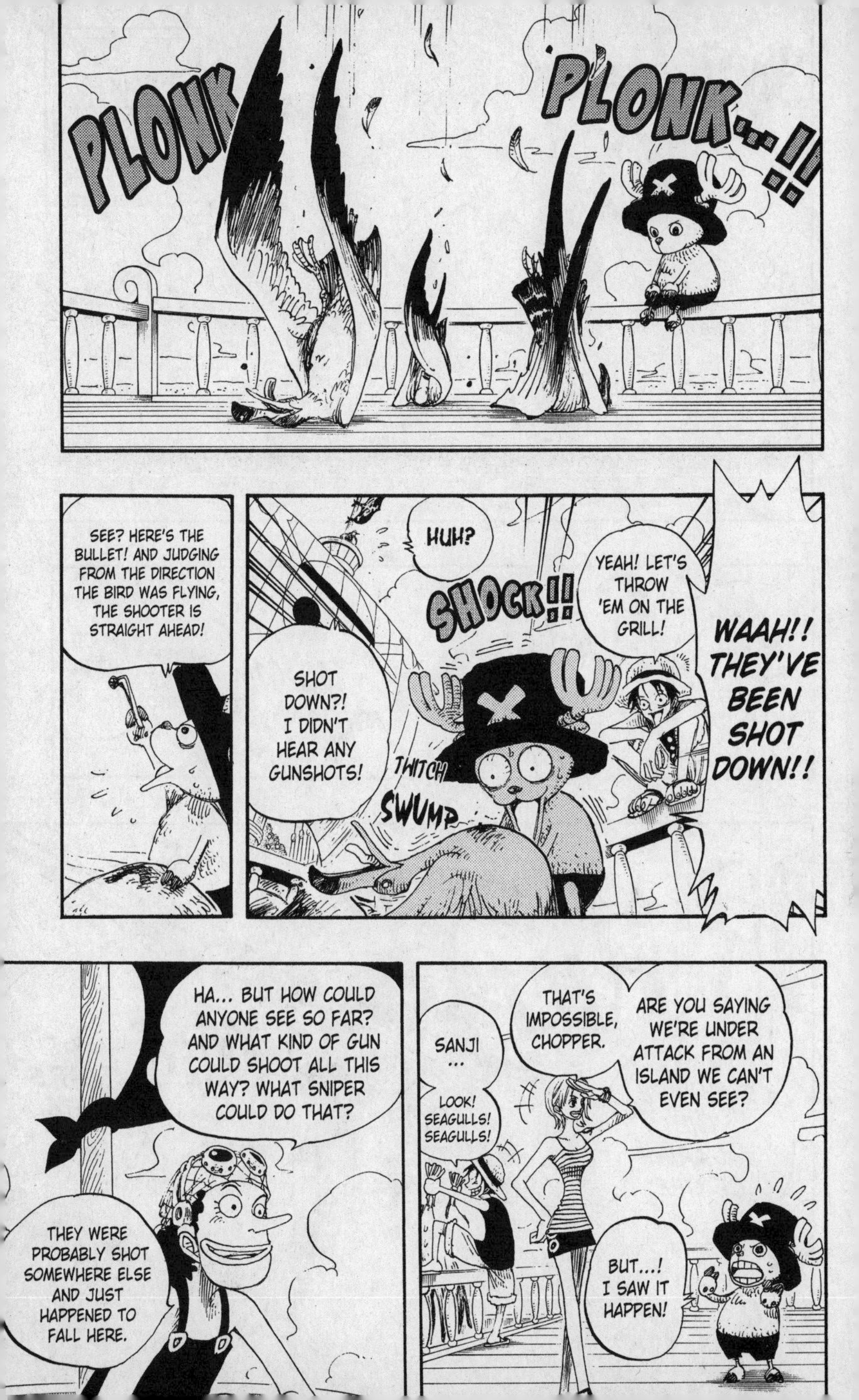
PLONK...!!
PLONK
WAAH!! THEY'VE BEEN SHOT DOWN!!
YEAH! LET'S THROW 'EM ON THE GRILL!
HUH?
SHOCK!!
SHOT DOWN?! I DIDN'T HEAR ANY GUNSHOTS!
TWITCH
SWUMP
SEE? HERE'S THE BULLET! AND JUDGING FROM THE DIRECTION THE BIRD WAS FLYING, THE SHOOTER IS STRAIGHT AHEAD!
ARE YOU SAYING WE'RE UNDER ATTACK FROM AN ISLAND WE CAN'T EVEN SEE?
THAT'S IMPOSSIBLE, CHOPPER.
SANJI ...
LOOK! SEAGULLS! SEAGULLS!
BUT...! I SAW IT HAPPEN!
HA... BUT HOW COULD ANYONE SEE SO FAR? AND WHAT KIND OF GUN COULD SHOOT ALL THIS WAY? WHAT SNIPER COULD DO THAT?
THEY WERE PROBABLY SHOT SOMEWHERE ELSE AND JUST HAPPENED TO FALL HERE.

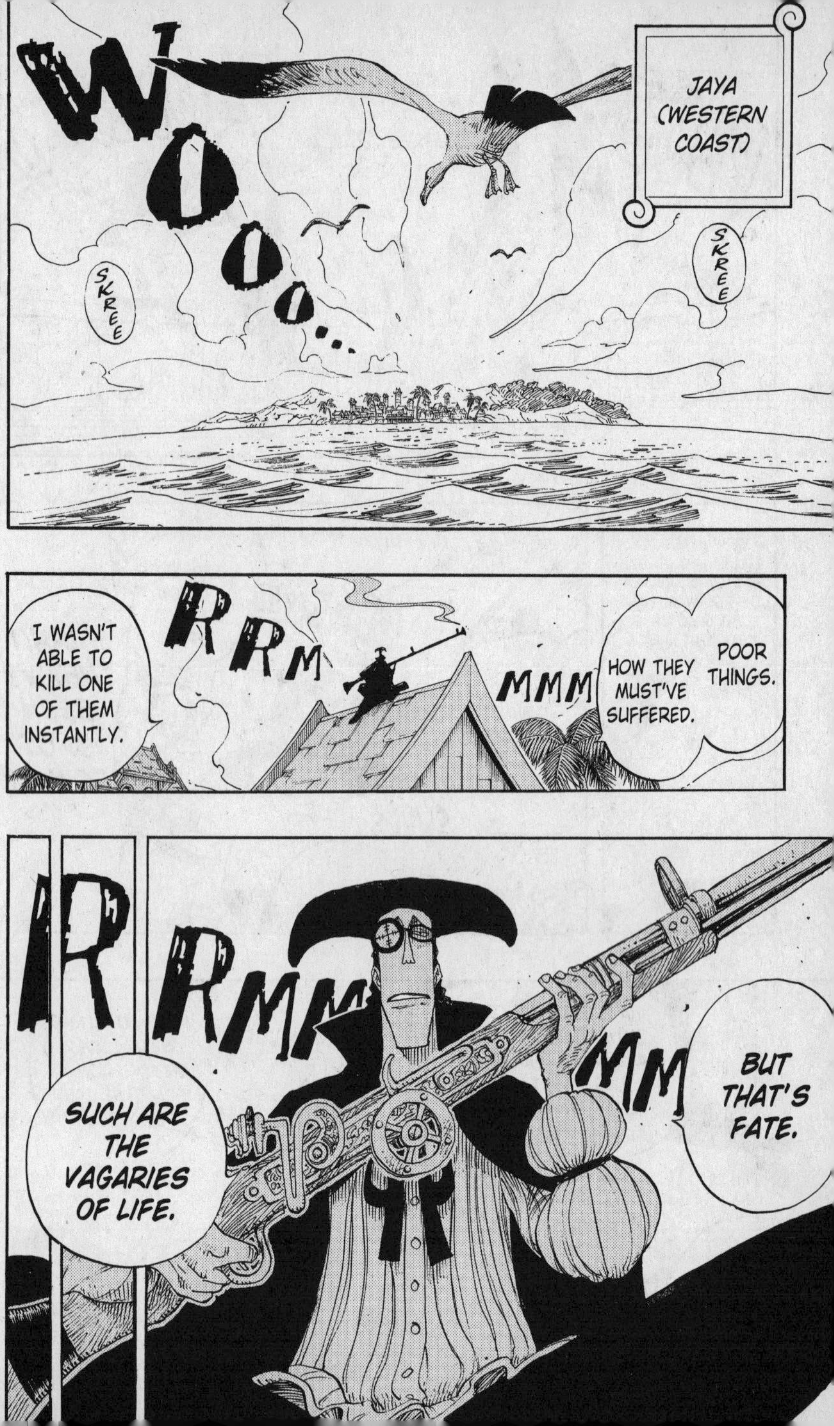
JAYA (WESTERN COAST)
SKREE
WOOOO...
SKREE
POOR THINGS.
HOW THEY MUST'VE SUFFERED.
RRRMMMM
I WASN'T ABLE TO KILL ONE OF THEM INSTANTLY.
BUT THAT'S FATE.
RRRMMMM
SUCH ARE THE VAGARIES OF LIFE.

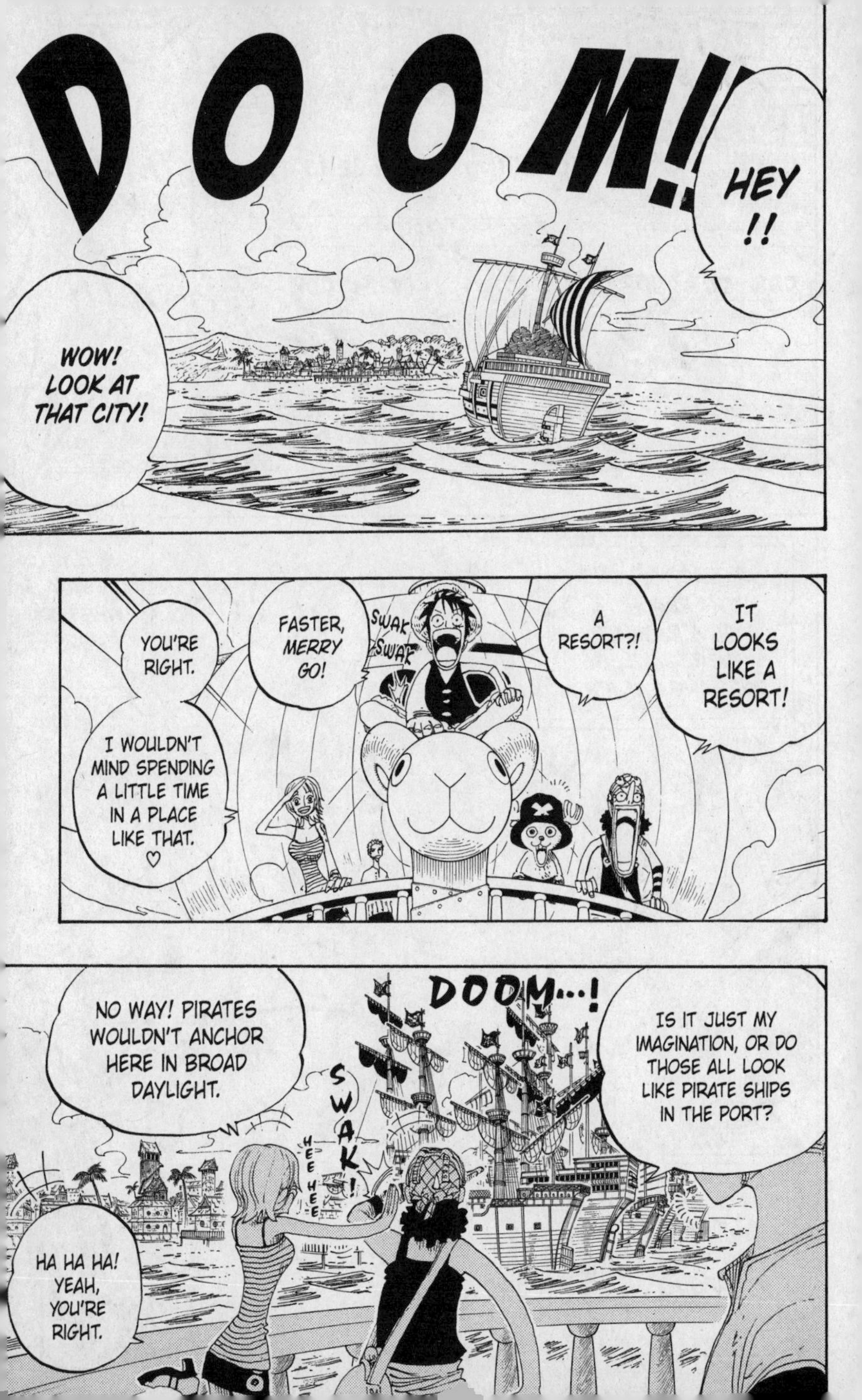
DOOM!!
HEY!!
WOW! LOOK AT THAT CITY!
IT LOOKS LIKE A RESORT!
A RESORT?!
FASTER, MERRY GO!
SWAK SWAK
YOU'RE RIGHT.
I WOULDN'T MIND SPENDING A LITTLE TIME IN A PLACE LIKE THAT. ♡
DOOM...!
IS IT JUST MY IMAGINATION, OR DO THOSE ALL LOOK LIKE PIRATE SHIPS IN THE PORT?
SWAK!
NO WAY! PIRATES WOULDN'T ANCHOR HERE IN BROAD DAYLIGHT.
HEE HEE
HA HA HA! YEAH, YOU'RE RIGHT.

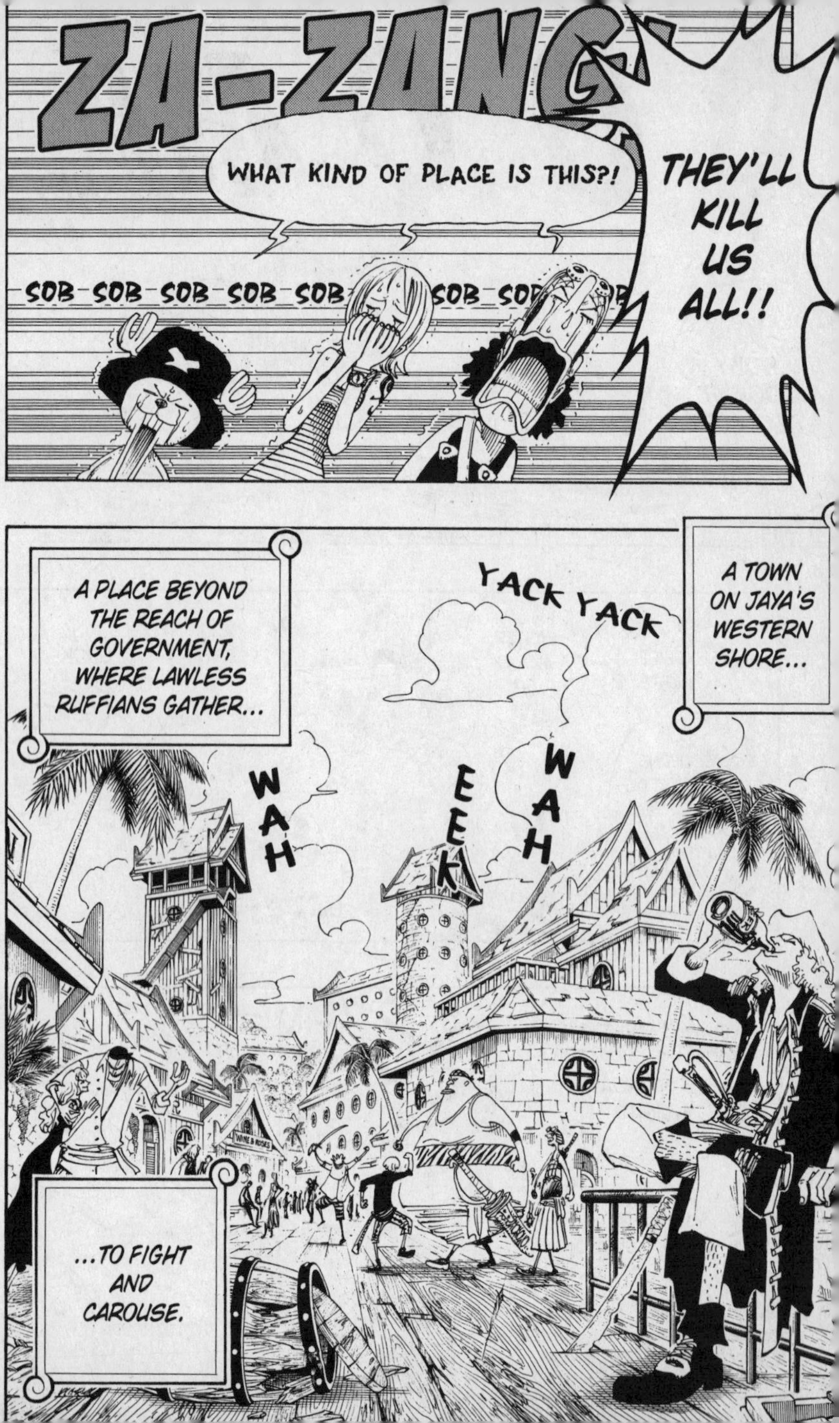
ZA-ZANG
THEY'LL KILL US ALL!!
WHAT KIND OF PLACE IS THIS?!
SOB SOB SOB SOB SOB SOB SOB
A TOWN ON JAYA'S WESTERN SHORE...
YACK YACK
WAH
EEEK
WAH
A PLACE BEYOND THE REACH OF GOVERNMENT, WHERE LAWLESS RUFFIANS GATHER...
...TO FIGHT AND CAROUSE.

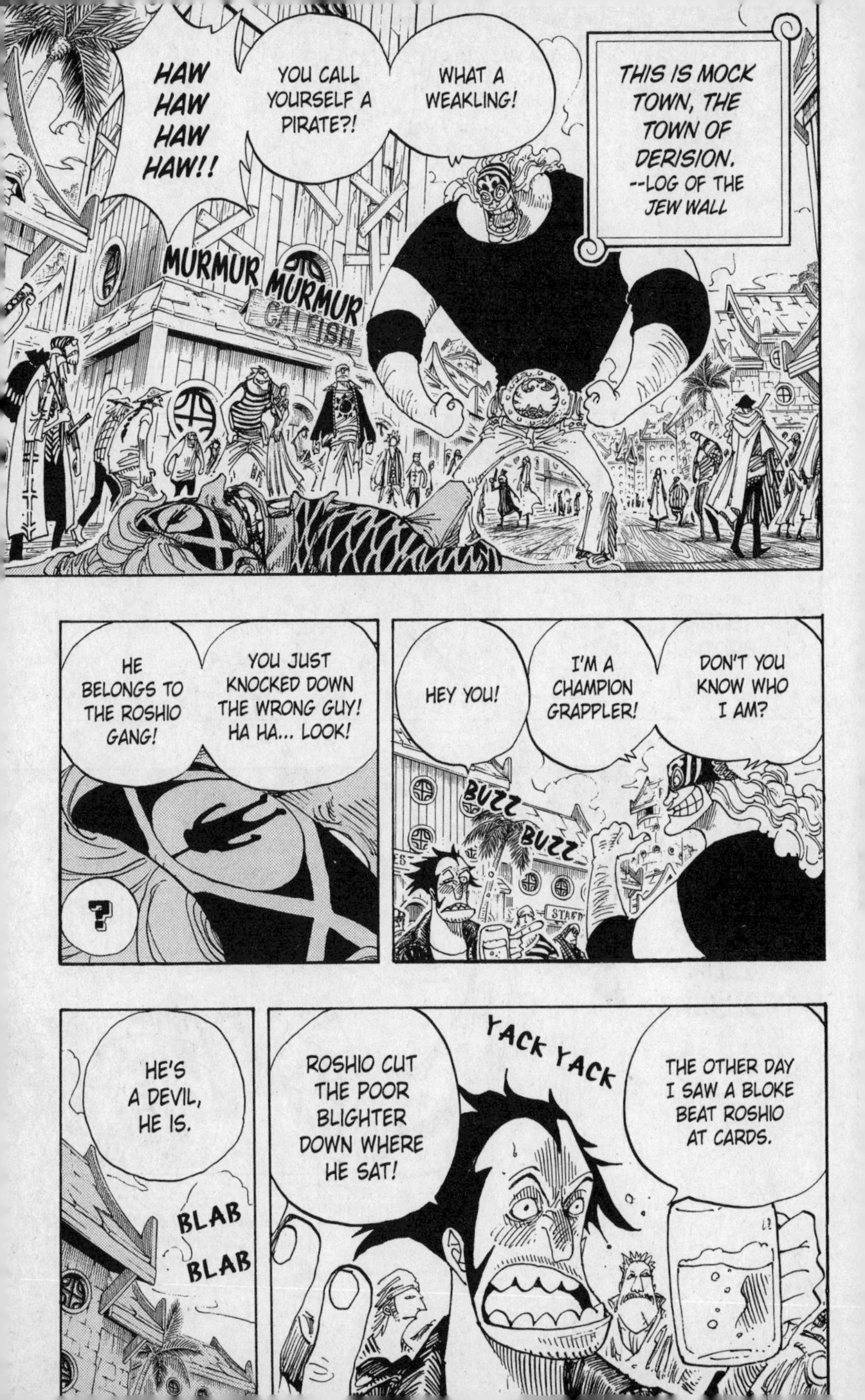
THIS IS MOCK TOWN, THE TOWN OF DERISION.
--LOG OF THE JEW WALL
WHAT A WEAKLING!
YOU CALL YOURSELF A PIRATE?!
HAW HAW HAW HAW!!
MURMUR
MURMUR
DON'T YOU KNOW WHO I AM?
I'M A CHAMPION GRAPPLER!
HEY YOU!
BUZZ
BUZZ
YOU JUST KNOCKED DOWN THE WRONG GUY! HA HA... LOOK!
HE BELONGS TO THE ROSHIO GANG!
?
THE OTHER DAY I SAW A BLOKE BEAT ROSHIO AT CARDS.
YACK YACK
ROSHIO CUT THE POOR BLIGHTER DOWN WHERE HE SAT!
HE'S A DEVIL, HE IS.
BLAB
BLAB

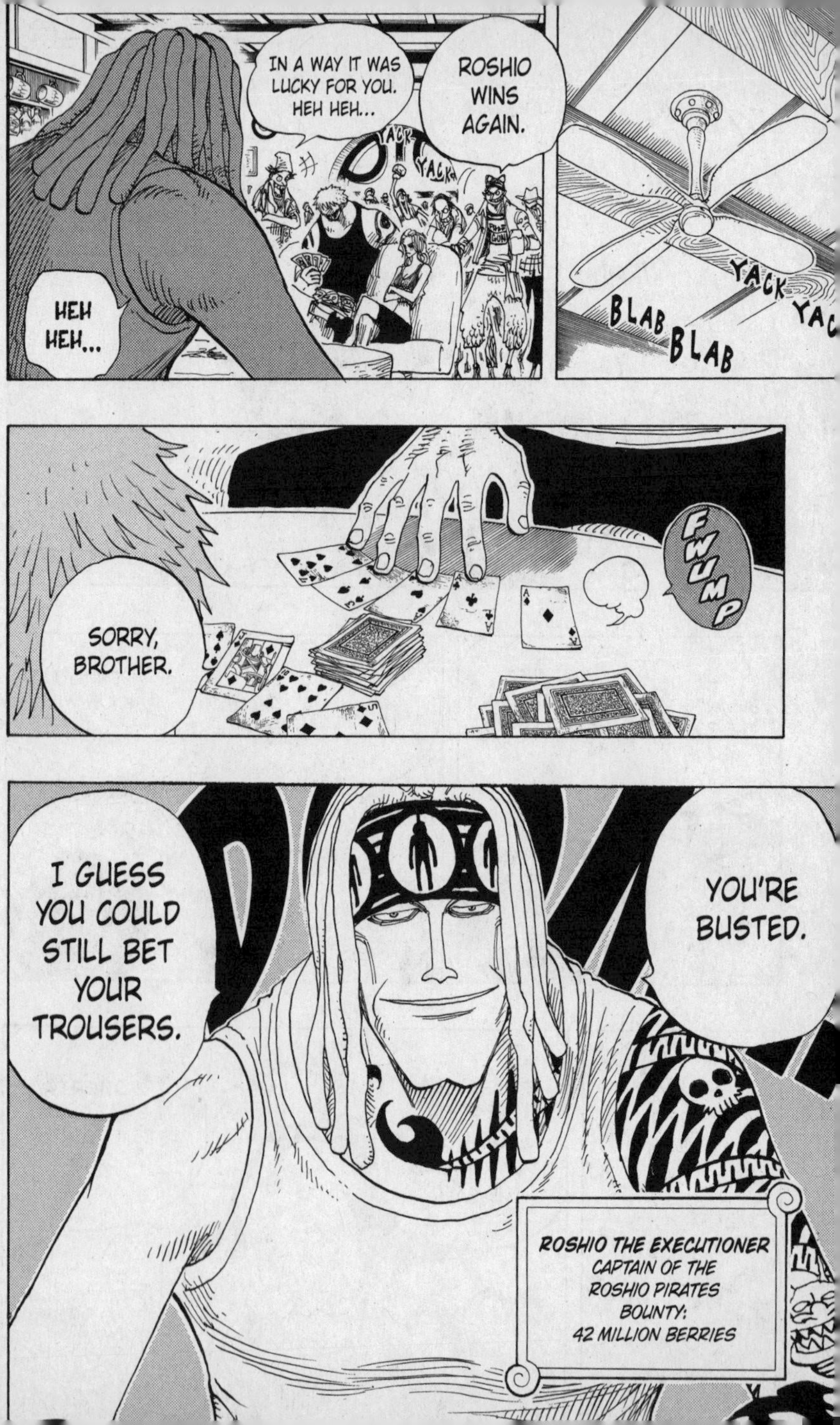
YACK YAC
BLAB BLAB
ROSHIO WINS AGAIN.
IN A WAY IT WAS LUCKY FOR YOU. HEH HEH...
YACK YACK
HEH HEH...
FWUMP
SORRY, BROTHER.
YOU'RE BUSTED.
I GUESS YOU COULD STILL BET YOUR TROUSERS.
ROSHIO THE EXECUTIONER
CAPTAIN OF THE ROSHIO PIRATES
BOUNTY: 42 MILLION BERRIES

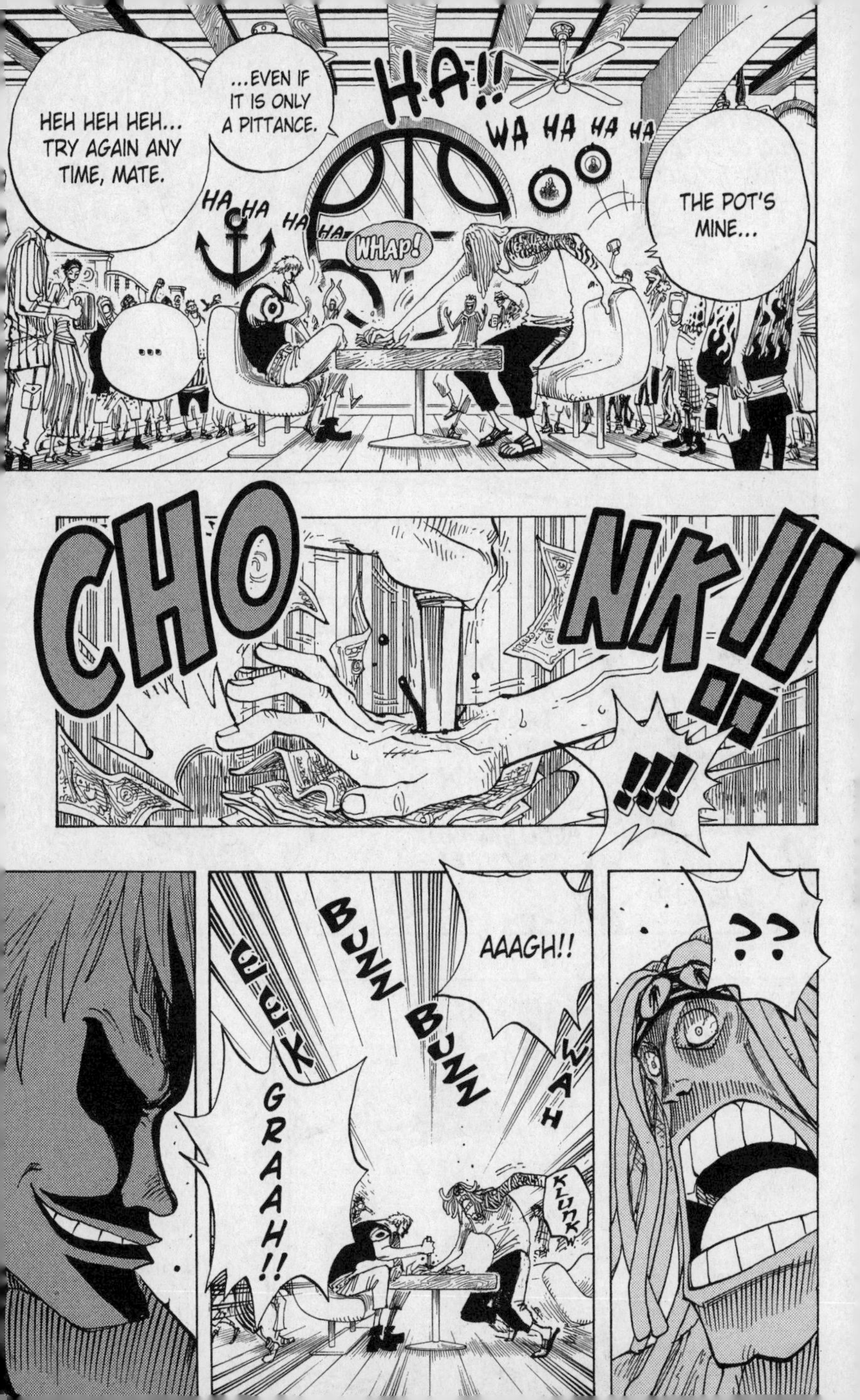
THE POT'S MINE...
WA HA HA HA
HA!!
...EVEN IF IT IS ONLY A PITTANCE.
HEH HEH HEH... TRY AGAIN ANY TIME, MATE.
HA HA HA HA
WHAP!
...
CHONK!!
!!!
??
AAAGH!!
WAH
BUZZ BUZZ
EEEK
GRAAAH!!
KLUNK

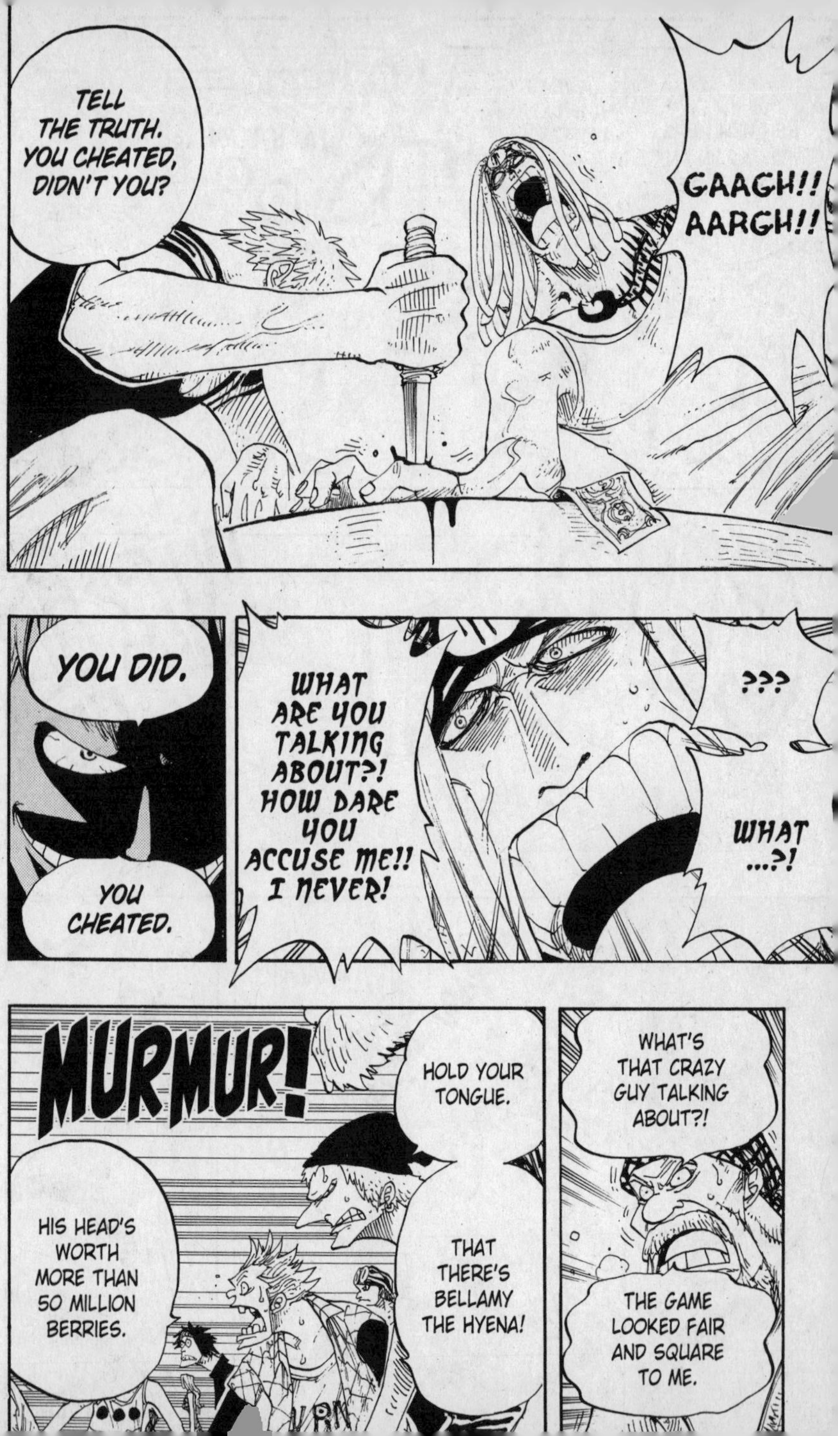
GAAGH!! AARGH!!
TELL THE TRUTH. YOU CHEATED, DIDN'T YOU?
???
WHAT ...?!
WHAT ARE YOU TALKING ABOUT?! HOW DARE YOU ACCUSE ME!! I NEVER!
YOU DID.
YOU CHEATED.
WHAT'S THAT CRAZY GUY TALKING ABOUT?!
THE GAME LOOKED FAIR AND SQUARE TO ME.
HOLD YOUR TONGUE.
MURMUR!
THAT THERE'S BELLAMY THE HYENA!
HIS HEAD'S WORTH MORE THAN 50 MILLION BERRIES.

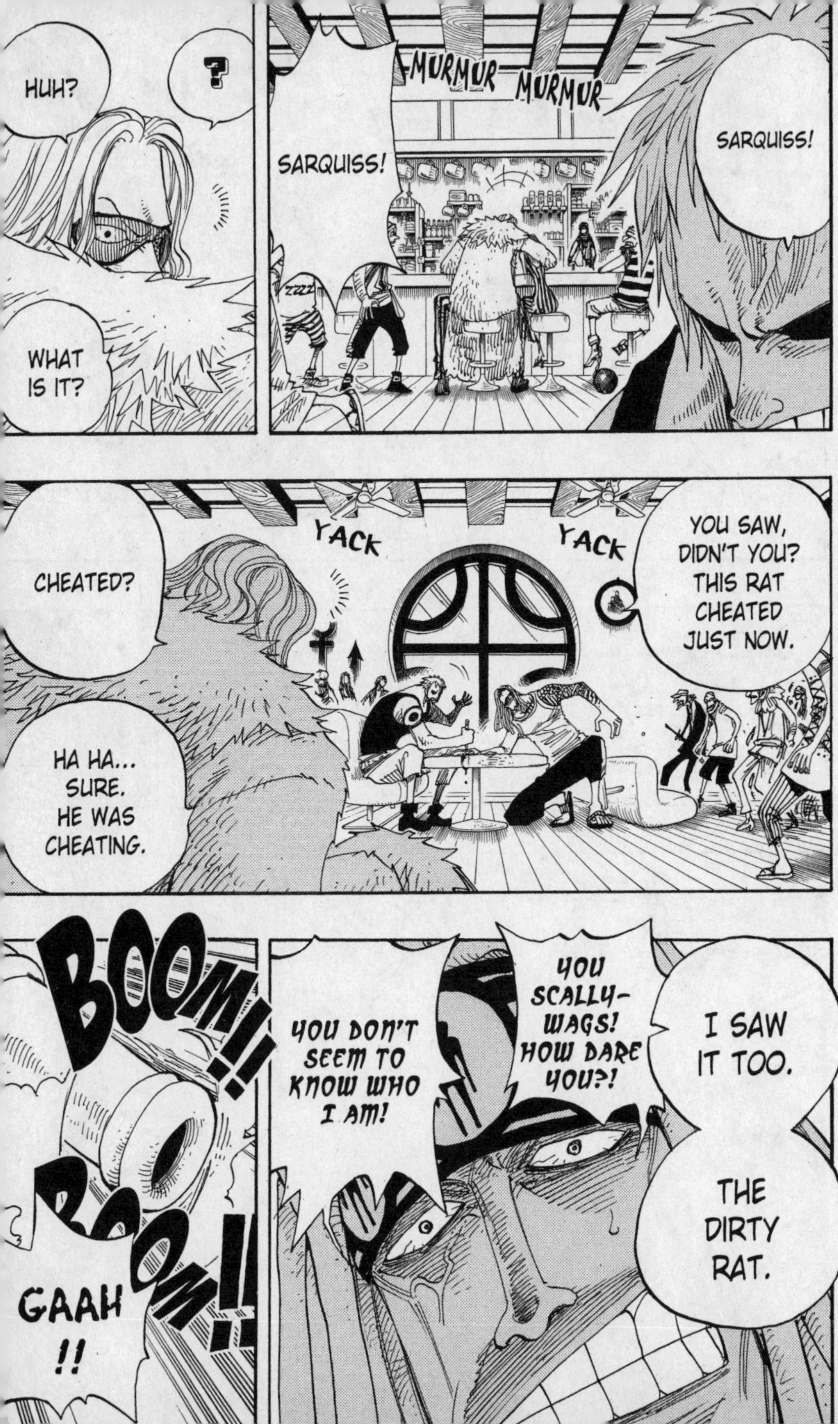
MURMUR
MURMUR
SARQUISS!
SARQUISS!
?
HUH?
WHAT IS IT?
YOU SAW, DIDN'T YOU? THIS RAT CHEATED JUST NOW.
YACK
YACK
CHEATED?
HA HA... SURE. HE WAS CHEATING.
I SAW IT TOO.
THE DIRTY RAT.
YOU SCALLYWAGS! HOW DARE YOU?!
YOU DON'T SEEM TO KNOW WHO I AM!
BOOM!!
BOOM!!
GAAH!!

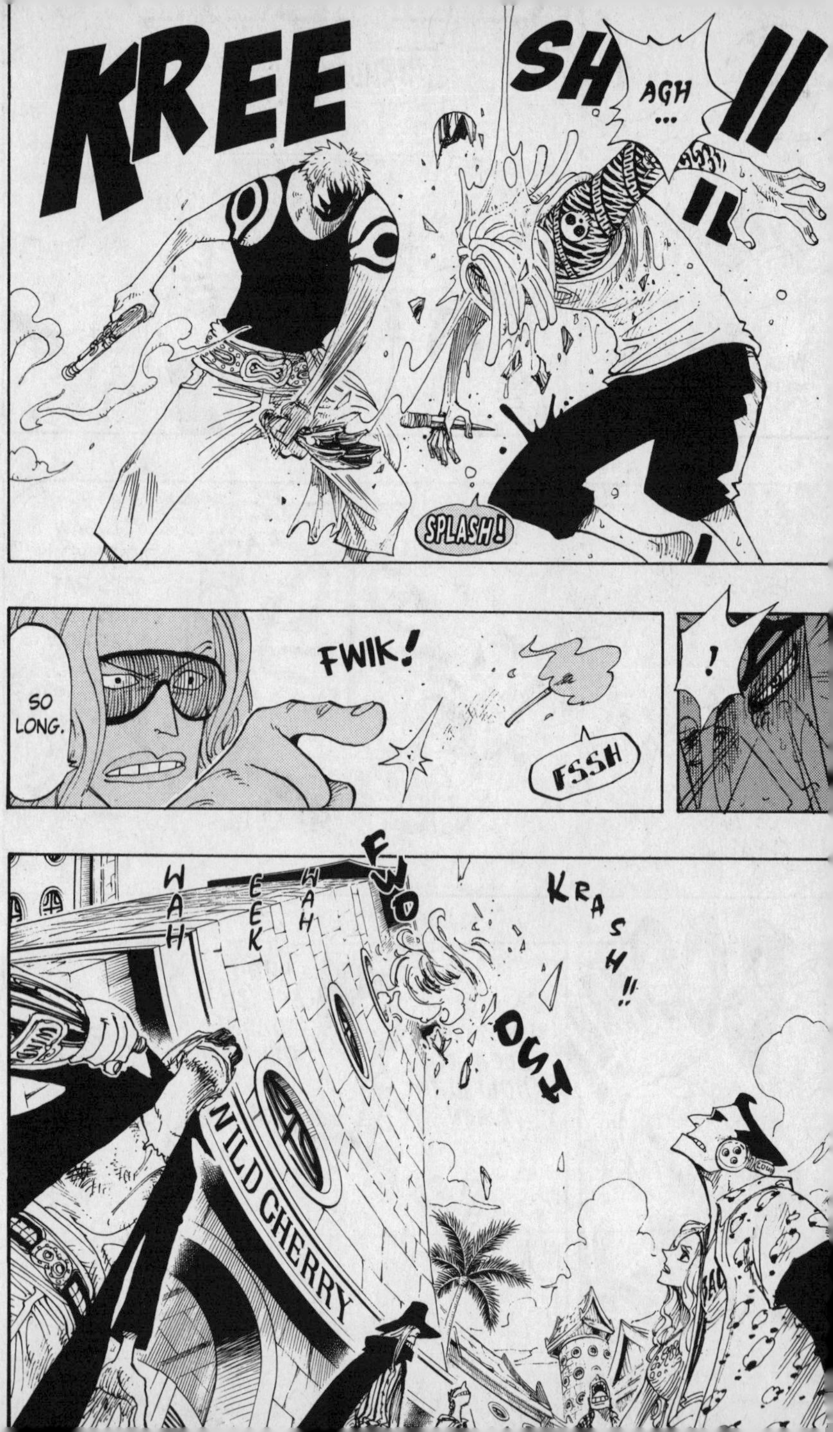
KREE SH!!
AGH ...
SPLASH!
!
FSSH
FWIK!
SO LONG.
KRASH!!
FWOOSH
WAH
EEK
WAH
WILD CHERRY

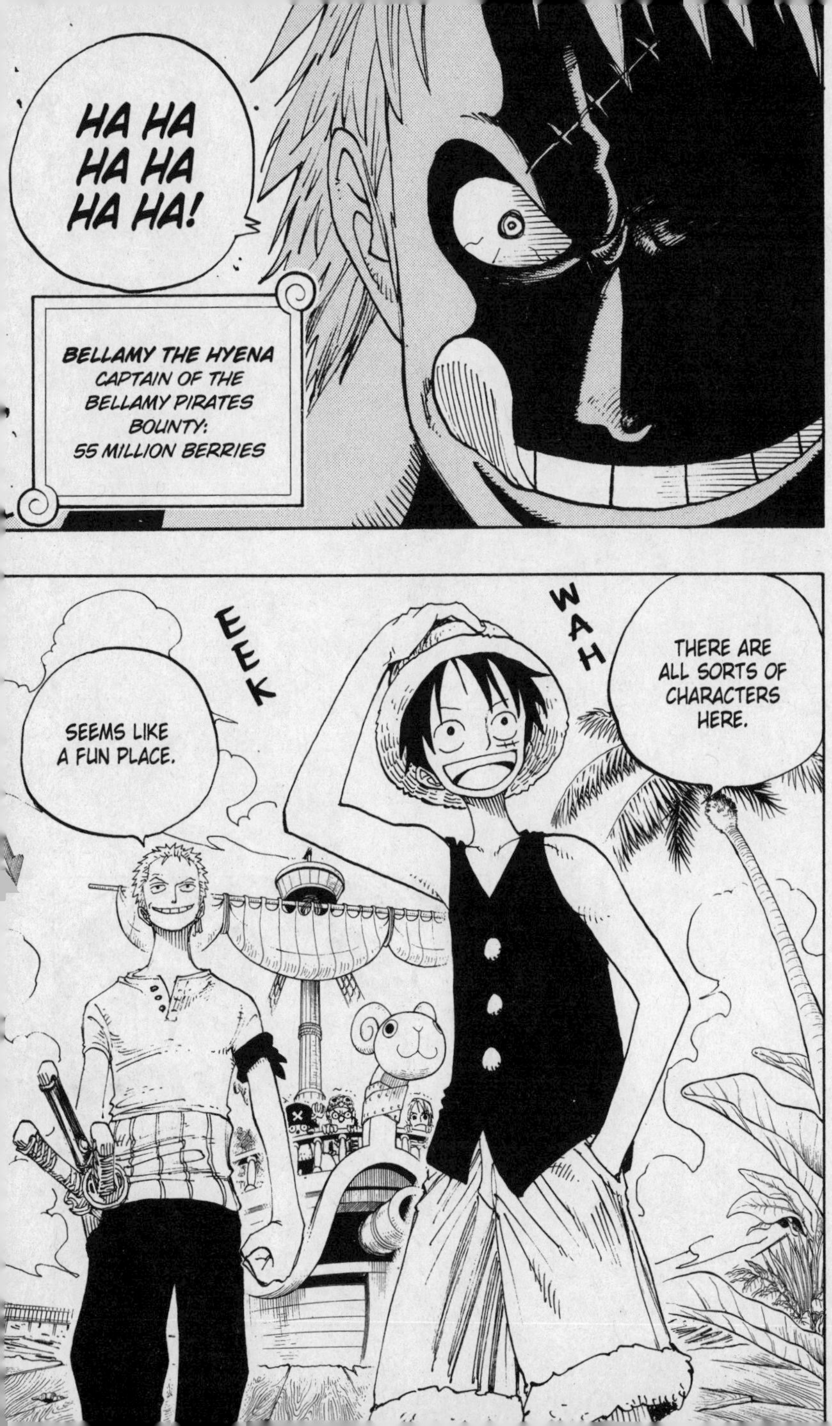
HA HA HA HA HA HA!
BELLAMY THE HYENA CAPTAIN OF THE BELLAMY PIRATES BOUNTY: 55 MILLION BERRIES
THERE ARE ALL SORTS OF CHARACTERS HERE.
WAH
EEK
SEEMS LIKE A FUN PLACE.

Chapter 223:
I PROMISE NEVER TO FIGHT IN THIS TOWN

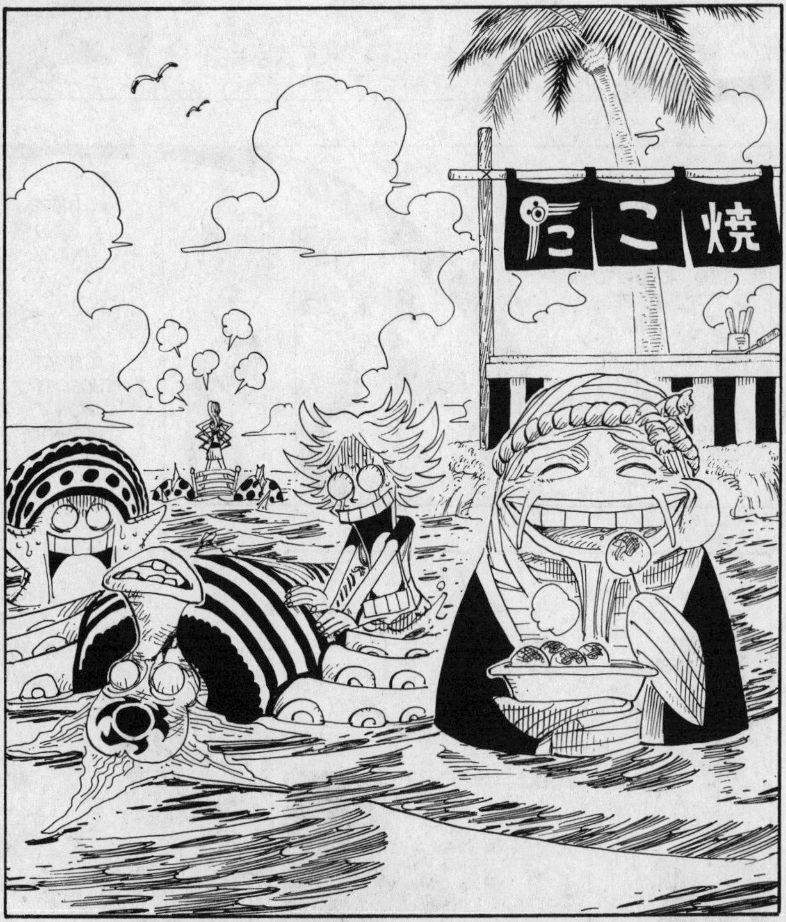
たこ焼

HACHI'S WALK ON THE SEAFLOOR, VOL. 36:
"OCTOPUNCH AND THE SMILING ELDER"

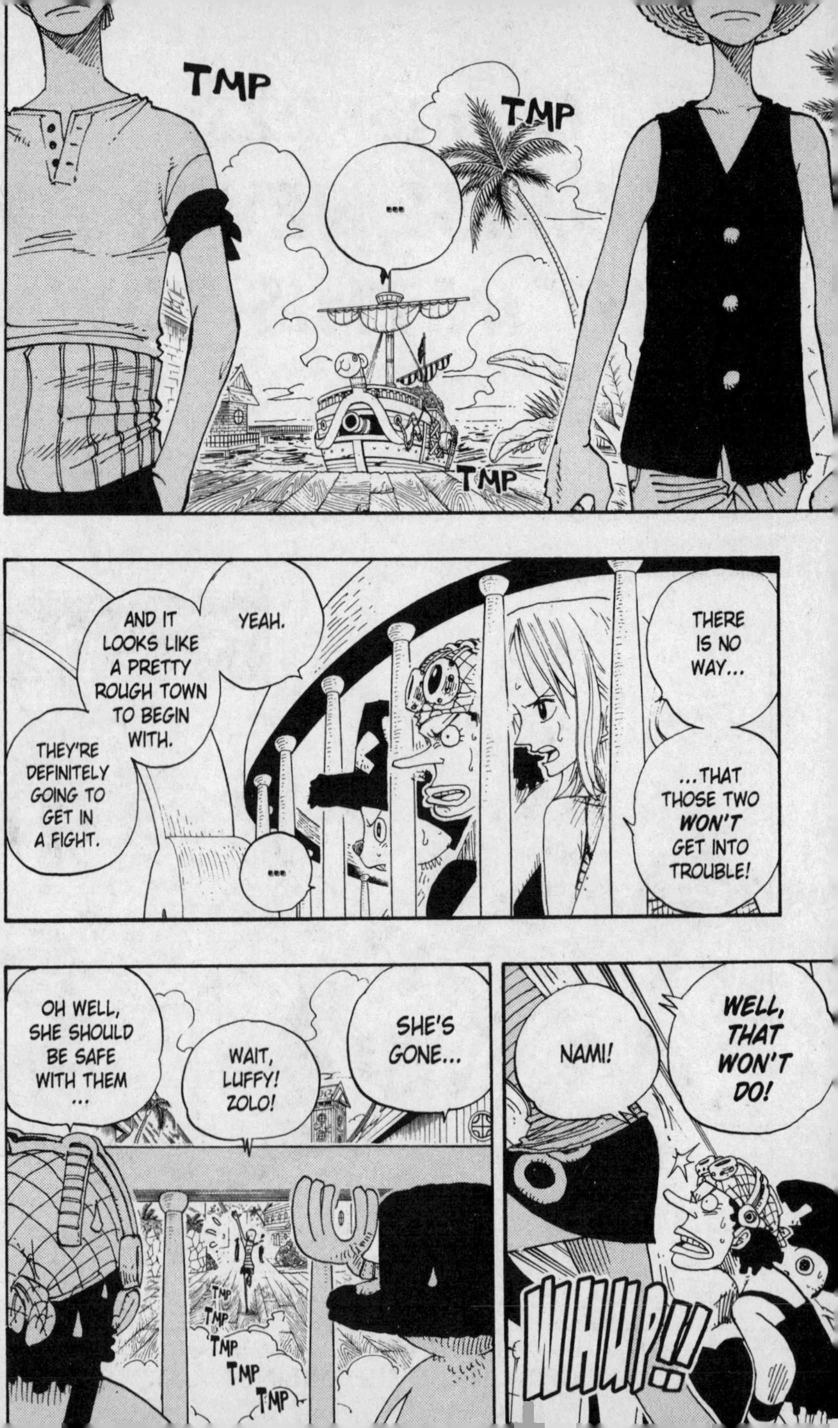
TMP
TMP
...
TMP
THERE IS NO WAY...
...THAT THOSE TWO *WON'T* GET INTO TROUBLE!
YEAH.
AND IT LOOKS LIKE A PRETTY ROUGH TOWN TO BEGIN WITH.
THEY'RE DEFINITELY GOING TO GET IN A FIGHT.
...
WELL, THAT WON'T DO!
NAMI!
WHAP!!
SHE'S GONE...
WAIT, LUFFY! ZOLO!
OH WELL, SHE SHOULD BE SAFE WITH THEM ...
TMP
TMP
TMP
TMP
TMP

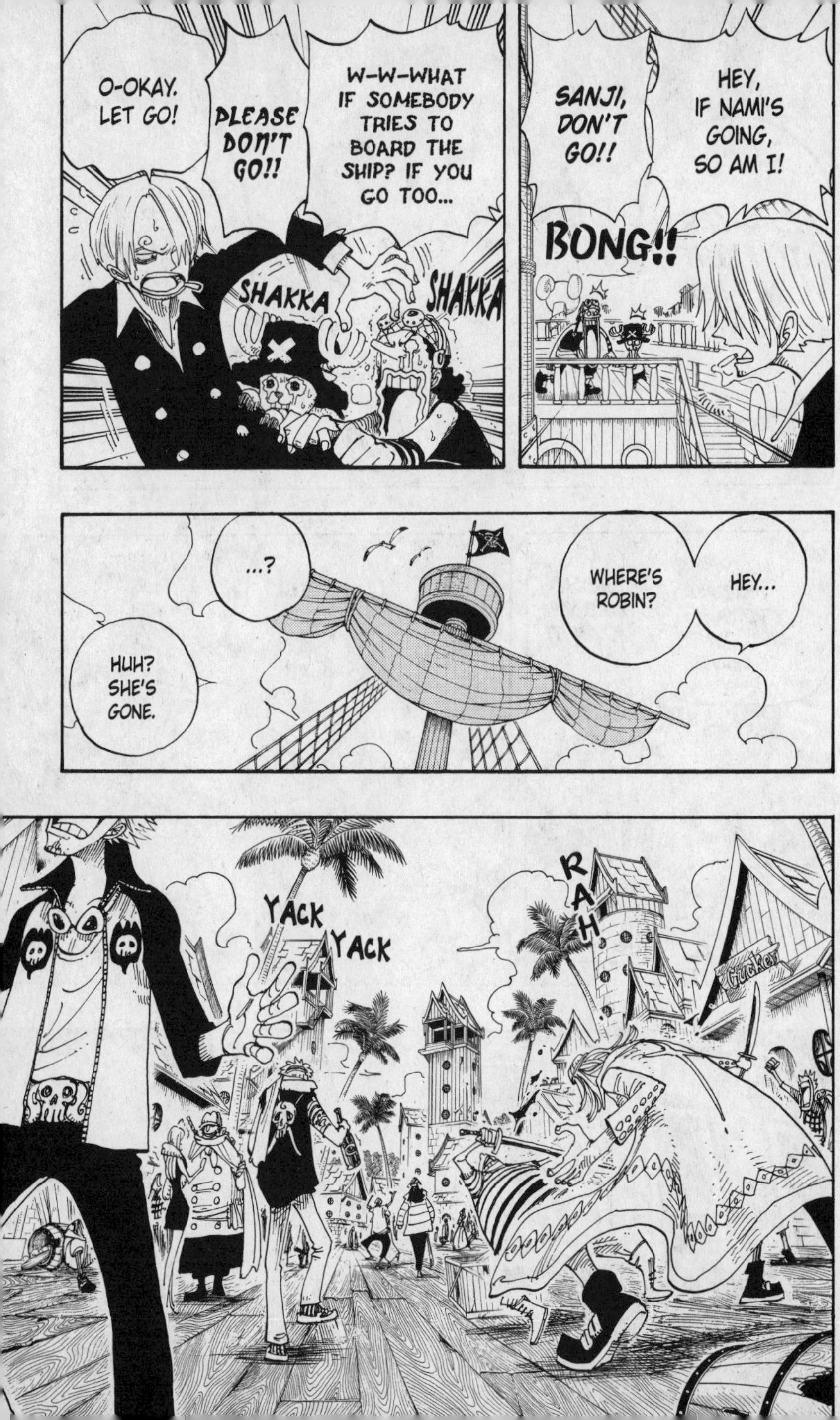
HEY, IF NAMI'S GOING, SO AM I!
SANJI, DON'T GO!!
BONG!!
W-W-WHAT IF SOMEBODY TRIES TO BOARD THE SHIP? IF YOU GO TOO...
SHAKKA
PLEASE DON'T GO!!
SHAKKA
O-OKAY. LET GO!
HEY...
WHERE'S ROBIN?
...?
HUH? SHE'S GONE.
RAH
YACK
YACK

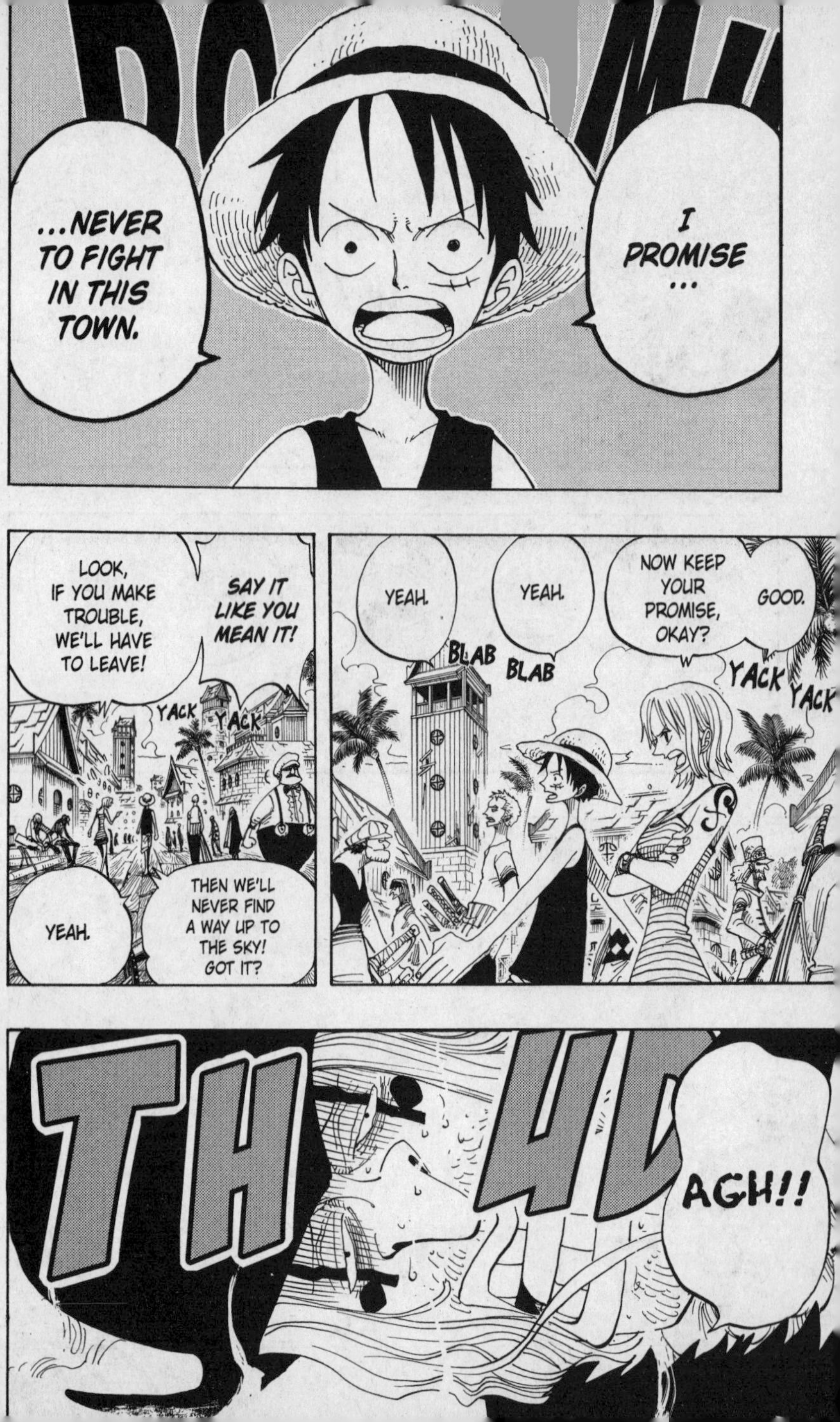
I PROMISE...
...NEVER TO FIGHT IN THIS TOWN.
GOOD.
NOW KEEP YOUR PROMISE, OKAY?
YACK YACK
YEAH.
YEAH.
BLAB BLAB
SAY IT LIKE YOU MEAN IT!
LOOK, IF YOU MAKE TROUBLE, WE'LL HAVE TO LEAVE!
YACK YACK
THEN WE'LL NEVER FIND A WAY UP TO THE SKY! GOT IT?
YEAH.
AGH!!

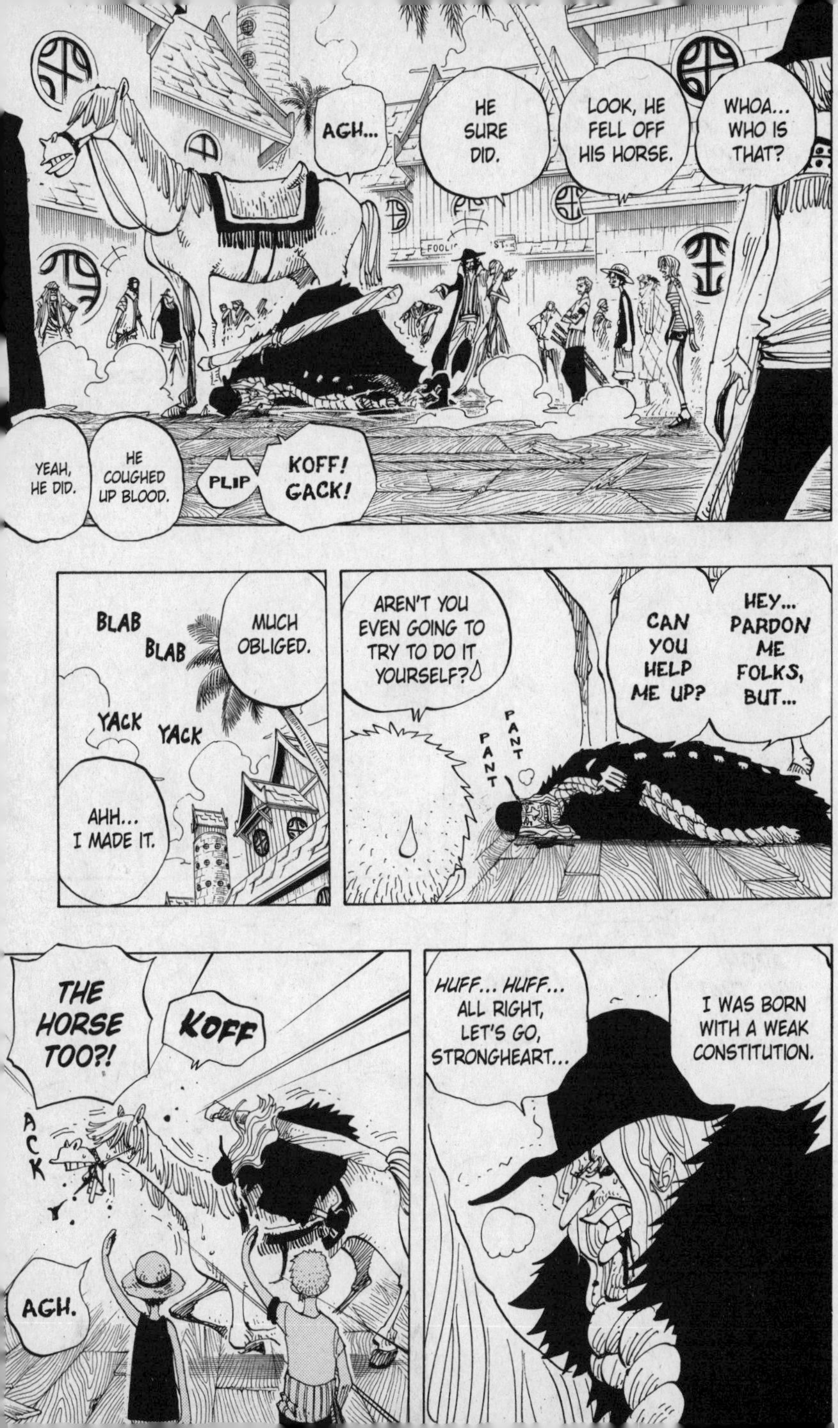
WHOA... WHO IS THAT?
LOOK, HE FELL OFF HIS HORSE.
HE SURE DID.
AGH...
KOFF! GACK!
PLIP
HE COUGHED UP BLOOD.
YEAH, HE DID.
HEY... PARDON ME FOLKS, BUT...
CAN YOU HELP ME UP?
PANT PANT
AREN'T YOU EVEN GOING TO TRY TO DO IT YOURSELF?
MUCH OBLIGED.
BLAB BLAB
YACK YACK
AHH... I MADE IT.
I WAS BORN WITH A WEAK CONSTITUTION.
HUFF... HUFF... ALL RIGHT, LET'S GO, STRONGHEART...
KOFF
THE HORSE TOO?!
ACK
AGH.

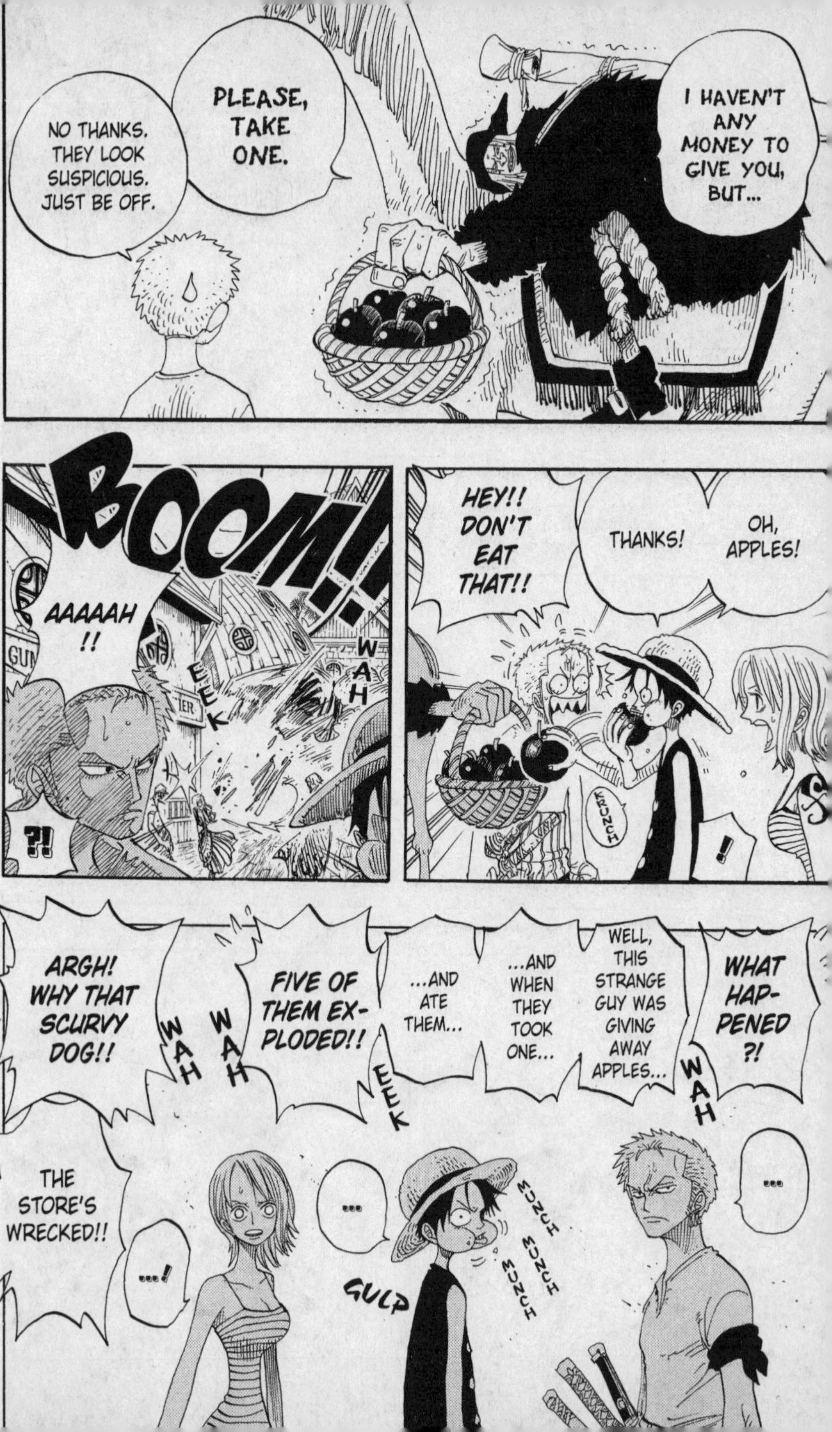
I HAVEN'T ANY MONEY TO GIVE YOU, BUT...
PLEASE, TAKE ONE.
NO THANKS. THEY LOOK SUSPICIOUS. JUST BE OFF.
OH, APPLES!
THANKS!
HEY!! DON'T EAT THAT!!
KRUNCH
!
BOOM!!
WAH
EEK
AAAAAH!!
?!
WHAT HAP-PENED?!
WAH
WELL, THIS STRANGE GUY WAS GIVING AWAY APPLES...
...AND WHEN THEY TOOK ONE...
...AND ATE THEM...
EEEK
FIVE OF THEM EX-PLODED!!
WAH
WAH
ARGH! WHY THAT SCURVY DOG!!
...
MUNCH
MUNCH
MUNCH
GULP
...
...!
THE STORE'S WRECKED!!

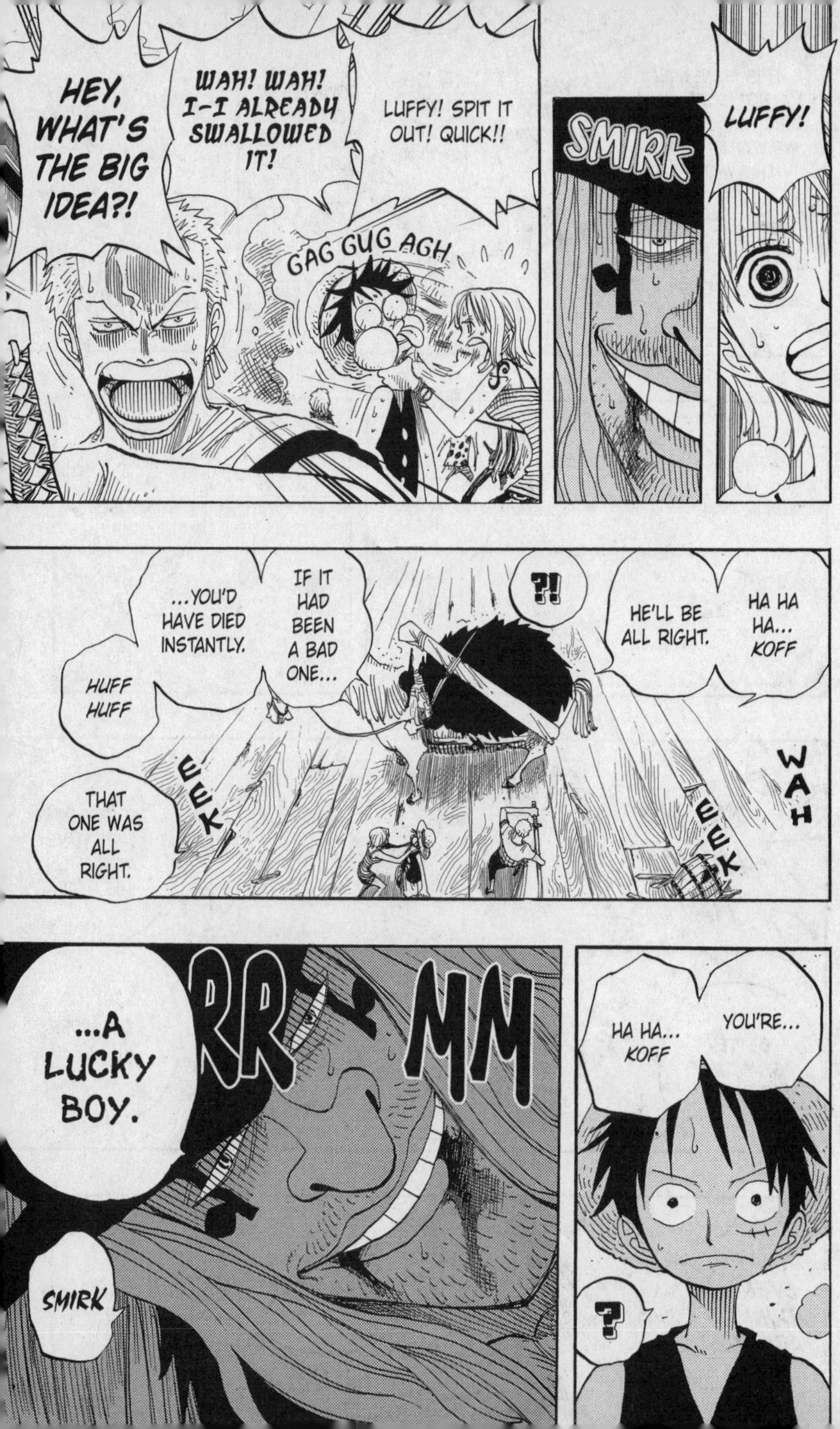
LUFFY!
SMIRK
LUFFY! SPIT IT OUT! QUICK!!
WAH! WAH! I-I ALREADY SWALLOWED IT!
GAG GUG AGH
HEY, WHAT'S THE BIG IDEA?!
WAH
HA HA HA... KOFF
HE'LL BE ALL RIGHT.
?!
EEK
IF IT HAD BEEN A BAD ONE...
...YOU'D HAVE DIED INSTANTLY.
HUFF HUFF
EEK
THAT ONE WAS ALL RIGHT.
YOU'RE...
HA HA... KOFF
?
RR MM
...A LUCKY BOY.
SMIRK

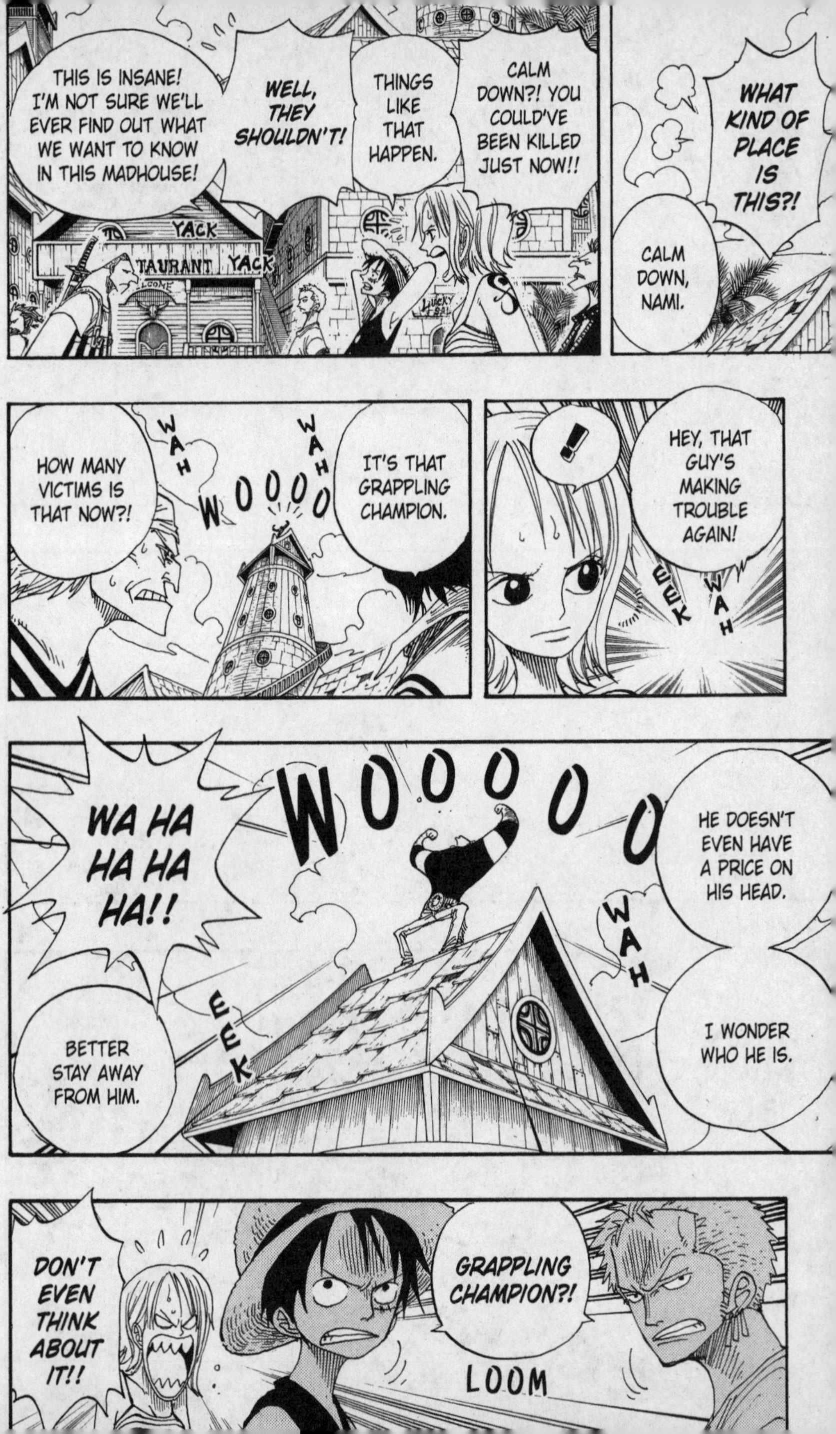
WHAT KIND OF PLACE IS THIS?!
CALM DOWN, NAMI.
CALM DOWN?! YOU COULD'VE BEEN KILLED JUST NOW!!
THINGS LIKE THAT HAPPEN.
WELL, THEY SHOULDN'T!
THIS IS INSANE! I'M NOT SURE WE'LL EVER FIND OUT WHAT WE WANT TO KNOW IN THIS MADHOUSE!
YACK
TAURANT
YACK
!
HEY, THAT GUY'S MAKING TROUBLE AGAIN!
EEK
WAH
IT'S THAT GRAPPLING CHAMPION.
WAH
WOOOOO
WAH
HOW MANY VICTIMS IS THAT NOW?!
HE DOESN'T EVEN HAVE A PRICE ON HIS HEAD.
WOOOOO
WA HA HA HA HA!!
WAH
I WONDER WHO HE IS.
EEK
BETTER STAY AWAY FROM HIM.
GRAPPLING CHAMPION?!
LOOM
DON'T EVEN THINK ABOUT IT!!

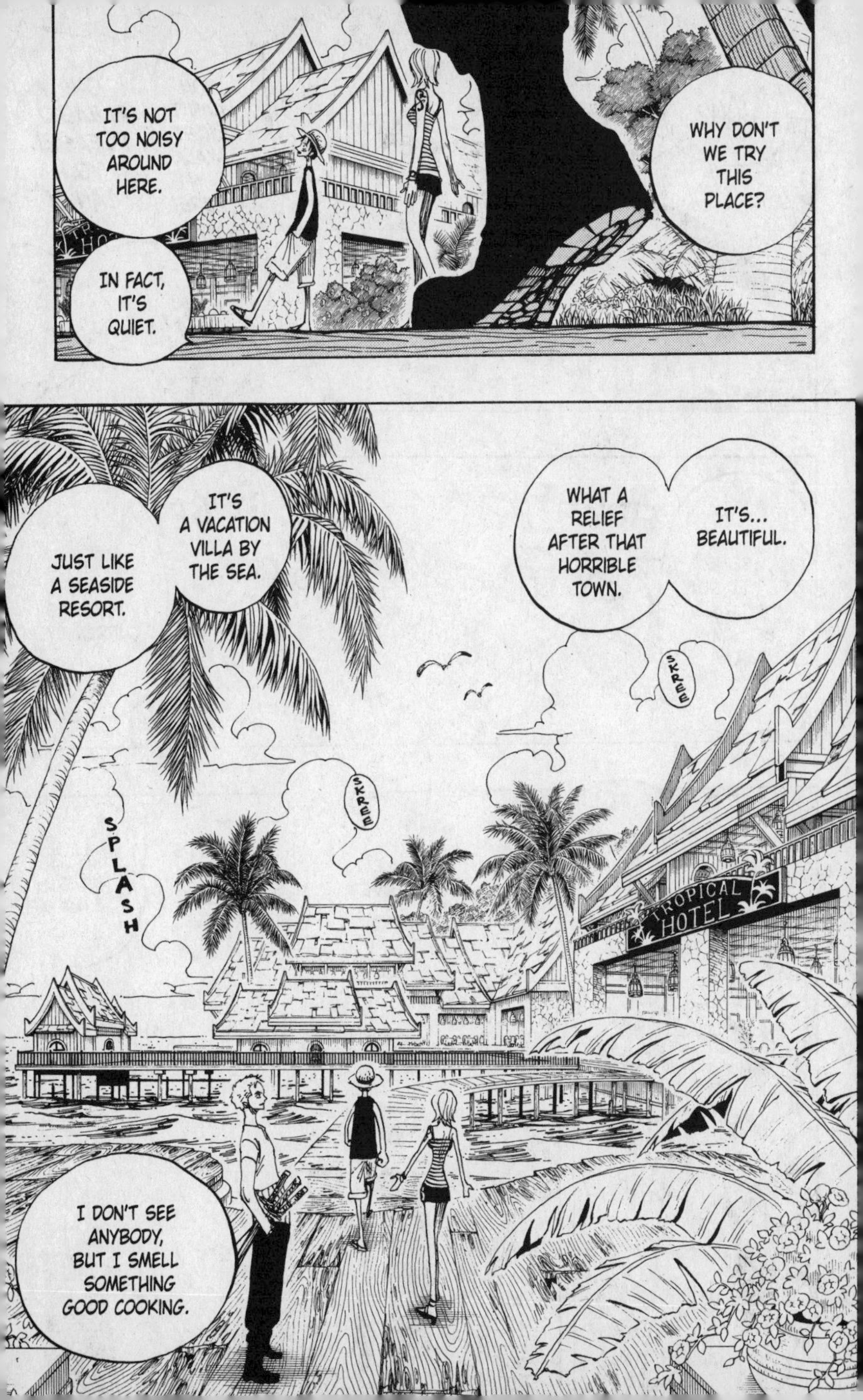
WHY DON'T WE TRY THIS PLACE?
IT'S NOT TOO NOISY AROUND HERE.
IN FACT, IT'S QUIET.
IT'S... BEAUTIFUL.
WHAT A RELIEF AFTER THAT HORRIBLE TOWN.
IT'S A VACATION VILLA BY THE SEA.
JUST LIKE A SEASIDE RESORT.
SKREE
SKREE
SPLASH
TROPICAL HOTEL
I DON'T SEE ANYBODY, BUT I SMELL SOMETHING GOOD COOKING.

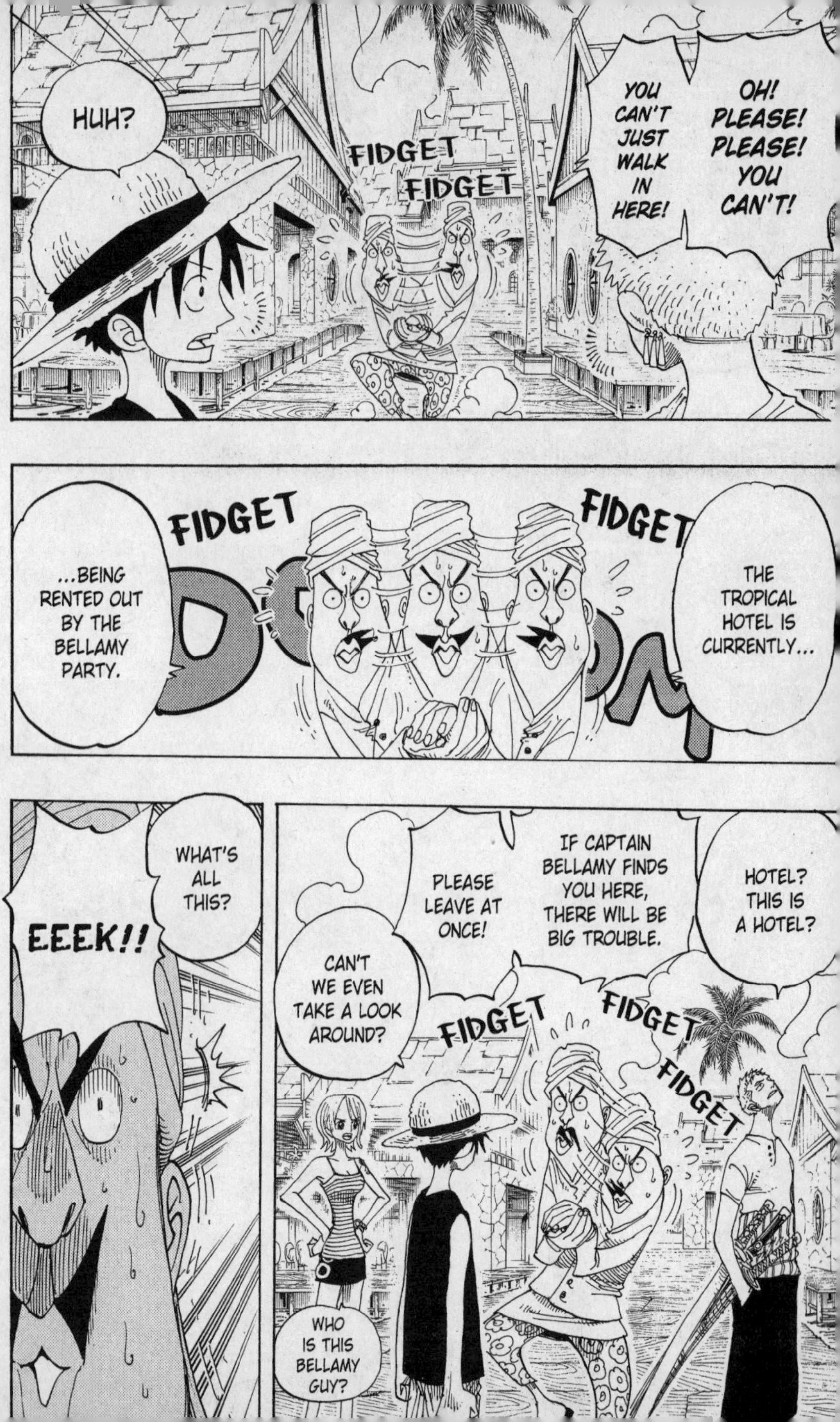

OH! PLEASE! PLEASE! YOU CAN'T!
YOU CAN'T JUST WALK IN HERE!
FIDGET
FIDGET
HUH?
THE TROPICAL HOTEL IS CURRENTLY...
FIDGET
FIDGET
...BEING RENTED OUT BY THE BELLAMY PARTY.
HOTEL? THIS IS A HOTEL?
IF CAPTAIN BELLAMY FINDS YOU HERE, THERE WILL BE BIG TROUBLE.
PLEASE LEAVE AT ONCE!
CAN'T WE EVEN TAKE A LOOK AROUND?
FIDGET
FIDGET
FIDGET
WHO IS THIS BELLAMY GUY?
WHAT'S ALL THIS?
EEEK!!

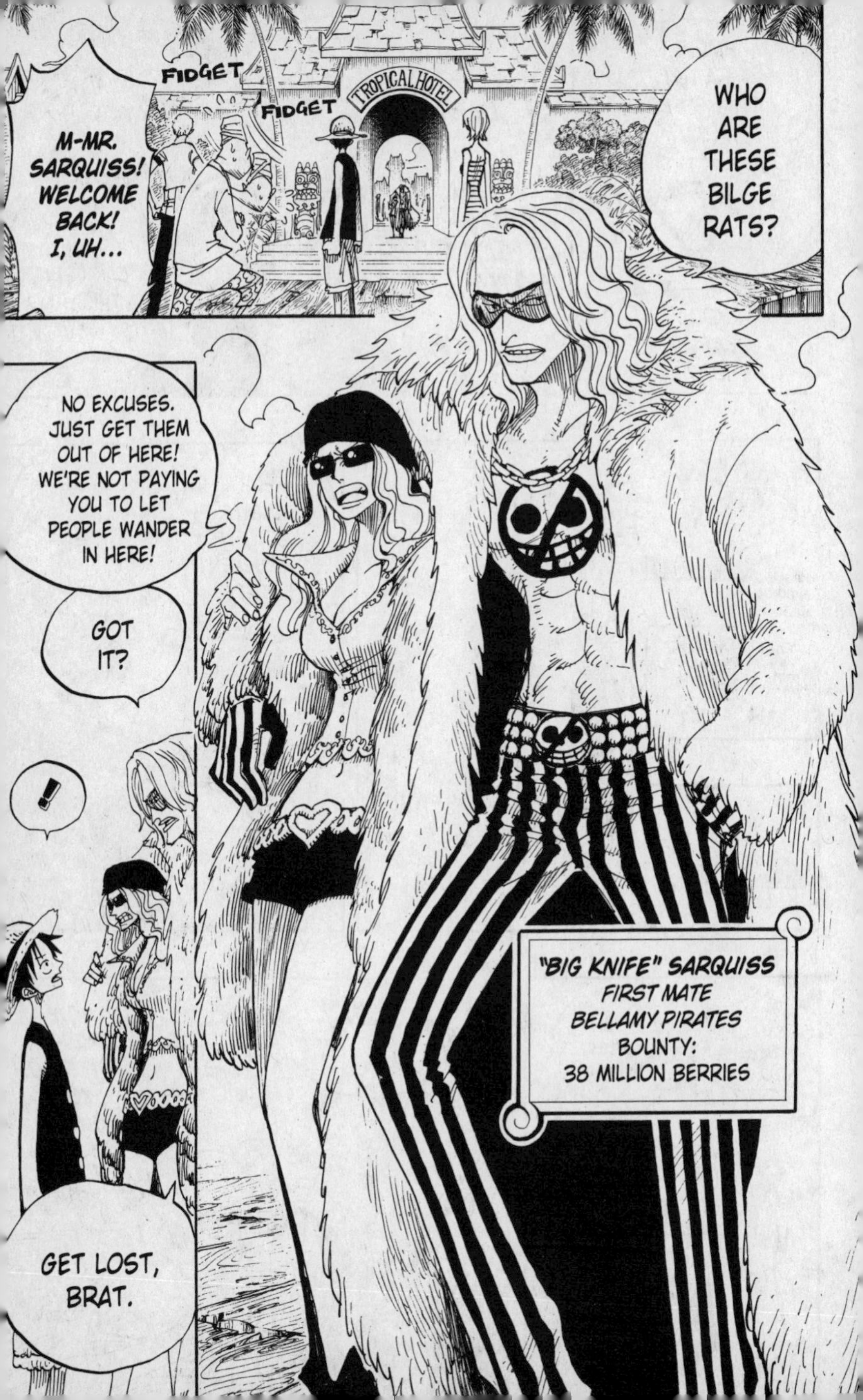
WHO ARE THESE BILGE RATS?
TROPICAL HOTEL
FIDGET
FIDGET
M-MR. SARQUISS! WELCOME BACK! I, UH...
"BIG KNIFE" SARQUISS
FIRST MATE
BELLAMY PIRATES
BOUNTY:
38 MILLION BERRIES
NO EXCUSES. JUST GET THEM OUT OF HERE! WE'RE NOT PAYING YOU TO LET PEOPLE WANDER IN HERE!
GOT IT?
!
GET LOST, BRAT.

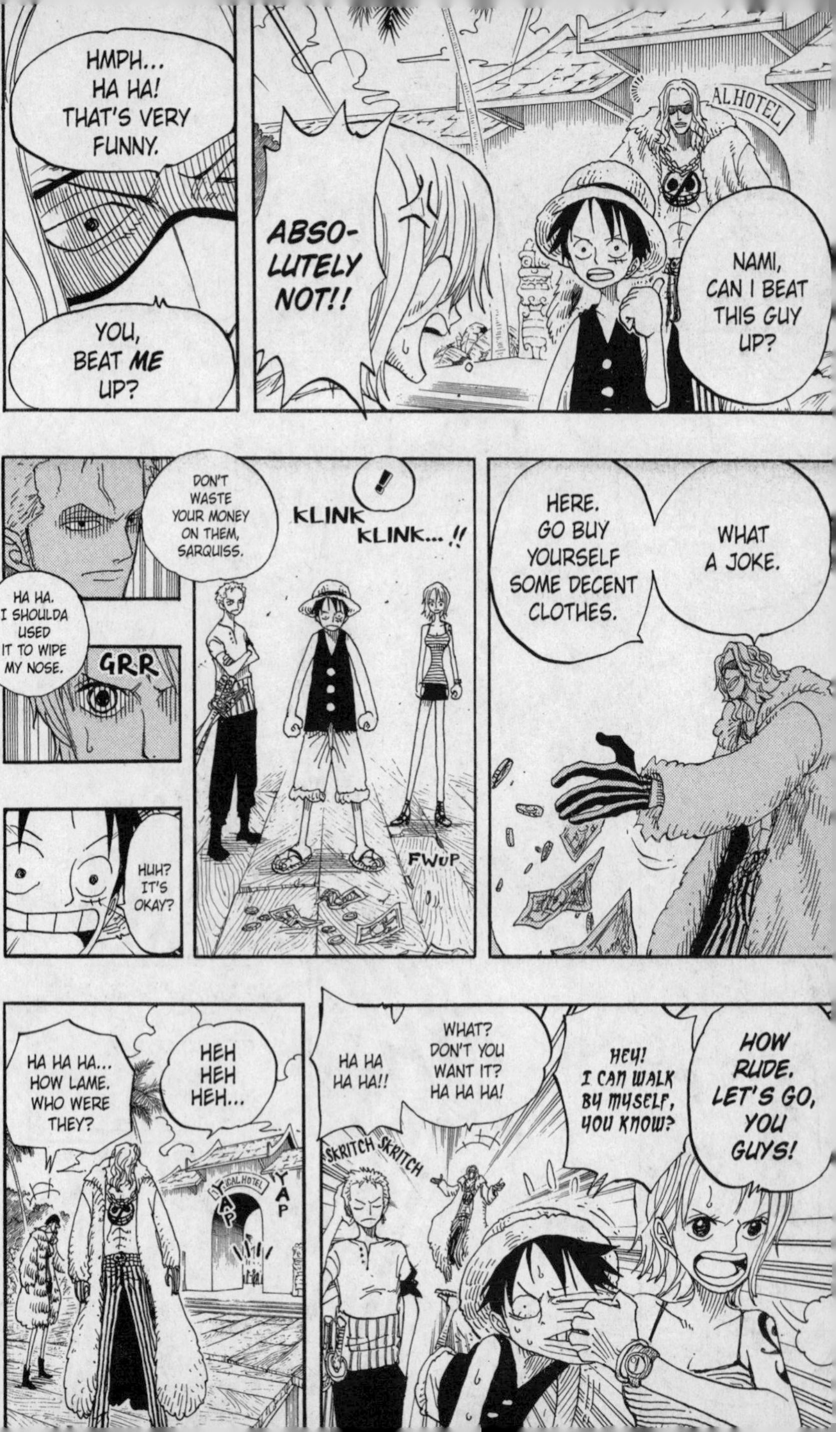
AL HOTEL
NAMI, CAN I BEAT THIS GUY UP?
ABSOLUTELY NOT!!
HMPH... HA HA! THAT'S VERY FUNNY.
YOU, BEAT ME UP?
WHAT A JOKE.
HERE. GO BUY YOURSELF SOME DECENT CLOTHES.
!
KLINK KLINK...!!
FWUP
DON'T WASTE YOUR MONEY ON THEM, SARQUISS.
HA HA. I SHOULDA USED IT TO WIPE MY NOSE.
GRR
HUH? IT'S OKAY?
HOW RUDE. LET'S GO, YOU GUYS!
HEY! I CAN WALK BY MYSELF, YOU KNOW?
WHAT? DON'T YOU WANT IT? HA HA HA!
HA HA HA HA!!
SKRITCH SKRITCH
HEH HEH HEH...
HA HA HA... HOW LAME. WHO WERE THEY?
CAL HOTEL
YAP YAP

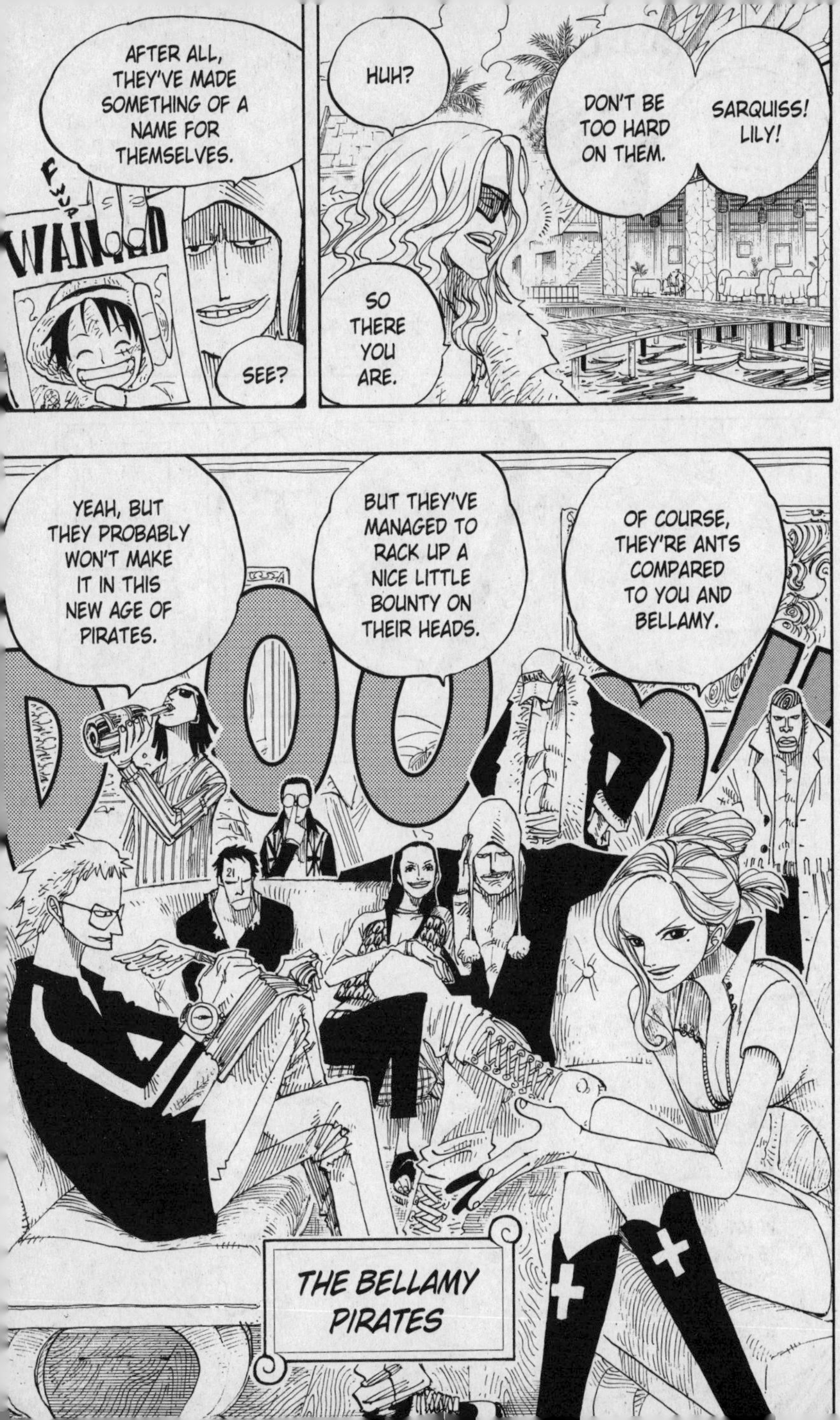
SARQUISS! LILY!
DON'T BE TOO HARD ON THEM.
HUH?
SO THERE YOU ARE.
AFTER ALL, THEY'VE MADE SOMETHING OF A NAME FOR THEMSELVES.
FWUP
SEE?
OF COURSE, THEY'RE ANTS COMPARED TO YOU AND BELLAMY.
BUT THEY'VE MANAGED TO RACK UP A NICE LITTLE BOUNTY ON THEIR HEADS.
YEAH, BUT THEY PROBABLY WON'T MAKE IT IN THIS NEW AGE OF PIRATES.
THE BELLAMY PIRATES

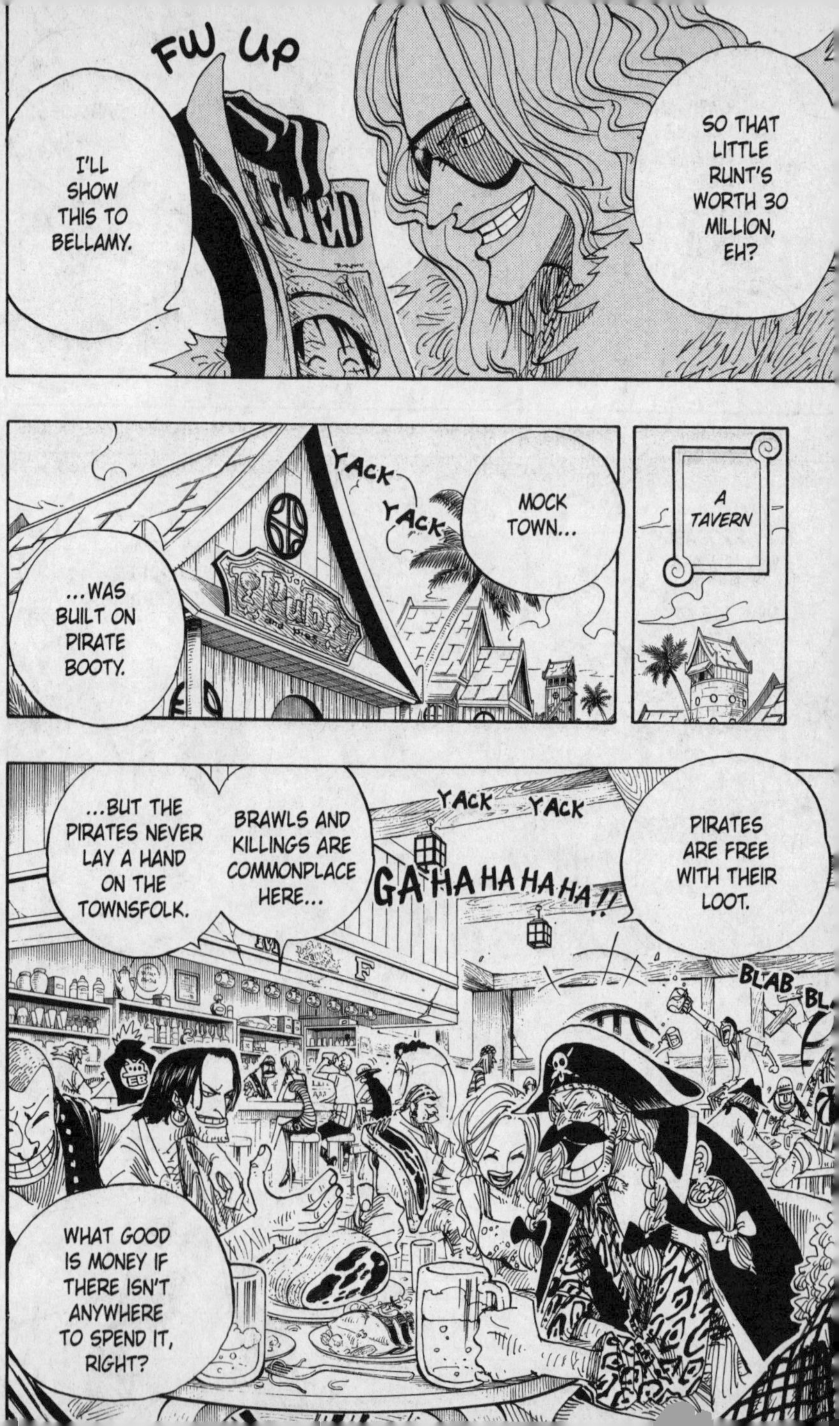
SO THAT LITTLE RUNT'S WORTH 30 MILLION, EH?
FW UP
I'LL SHOW THIS TO BELLAMY.
A TAVERN
MOCK TOWN...
YACK YACK
...WAS BUILT ON PIRATE BOOTY.
PIRATES ARE FREE WITH THEIR LOOT.
YACK YACK
GAHAHAHAHA!!
BRAWLS AND KILLINGS ARE COMMONPLACE HERE...
...BUT THE PIRATES NEVER LAY A HAND ON THE TOWNSFOLK.
BLAB
WHAT GOOD IS MONEY IF THERE ISN'T ANYWHERE TO SPEND IT, RIGHT?

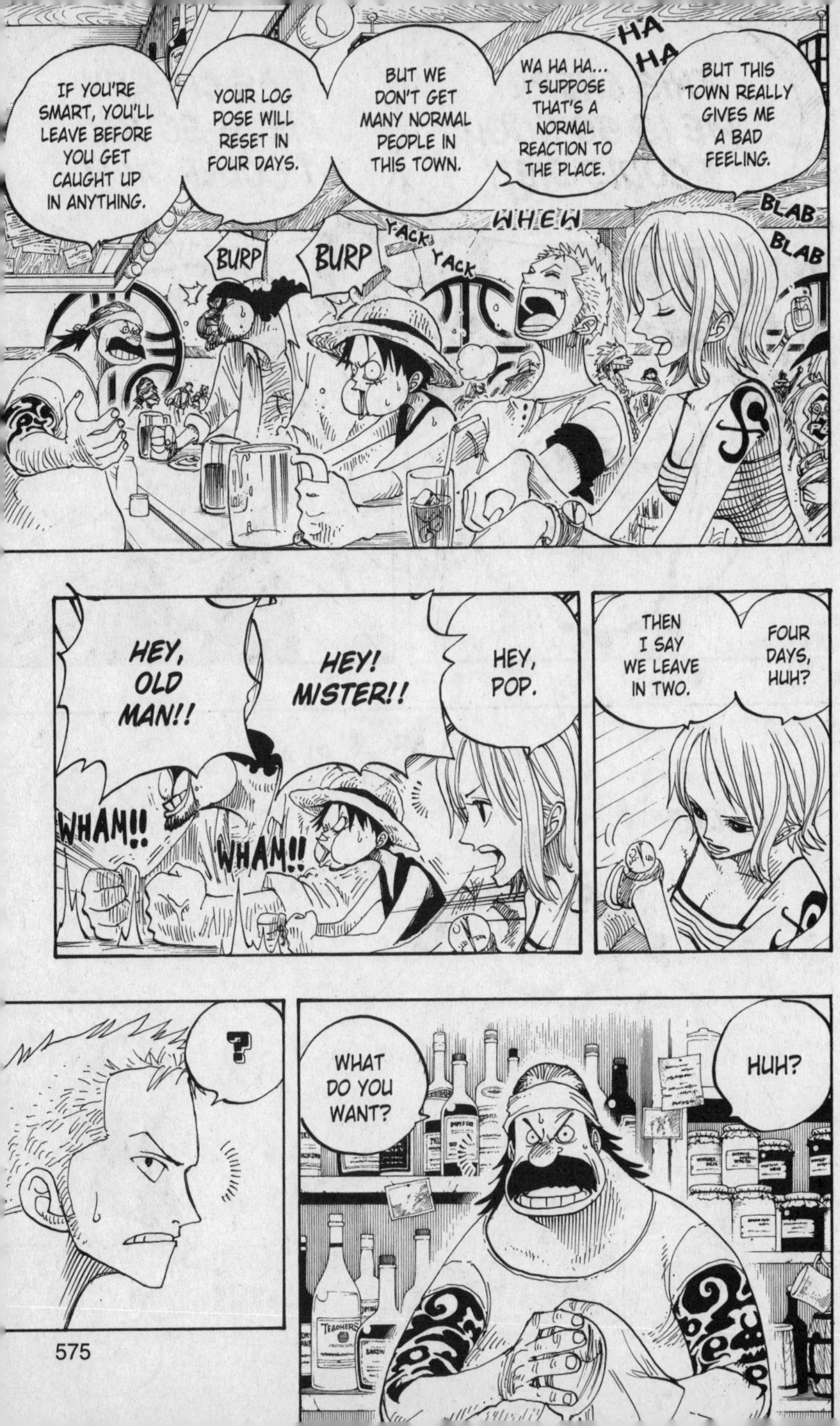
BUT THIS TOWN REALLY GIVES ME A BAD FEELING.
HA HA
WA HA HA... I SUPPOSE THAT'S A NORMAL REACTION TO THE PLACE.
BUT WE DON'T GET MANY NORMAL PEOPLE IN THIS TOWN.
YOUR LOG POSE WILL RESET IN FOUR DAYS.
IF YOU'RE SMART, YOU'LL LEAVE BEFORE YOU GET CAUGHT UP IN ANYTHING.
BLAB BLAB
WHEW
YACK YACK
BURP
BURP
FOUR DAYS, HUH?
THEN I SAY WE LEAVE IN TWO.
HEY, POP.
HEY! MISTER!!
HEY, OLD MAN!!
WHAM!!
WHAM!!
HUH?
WHAT DO YOU WANT?
?

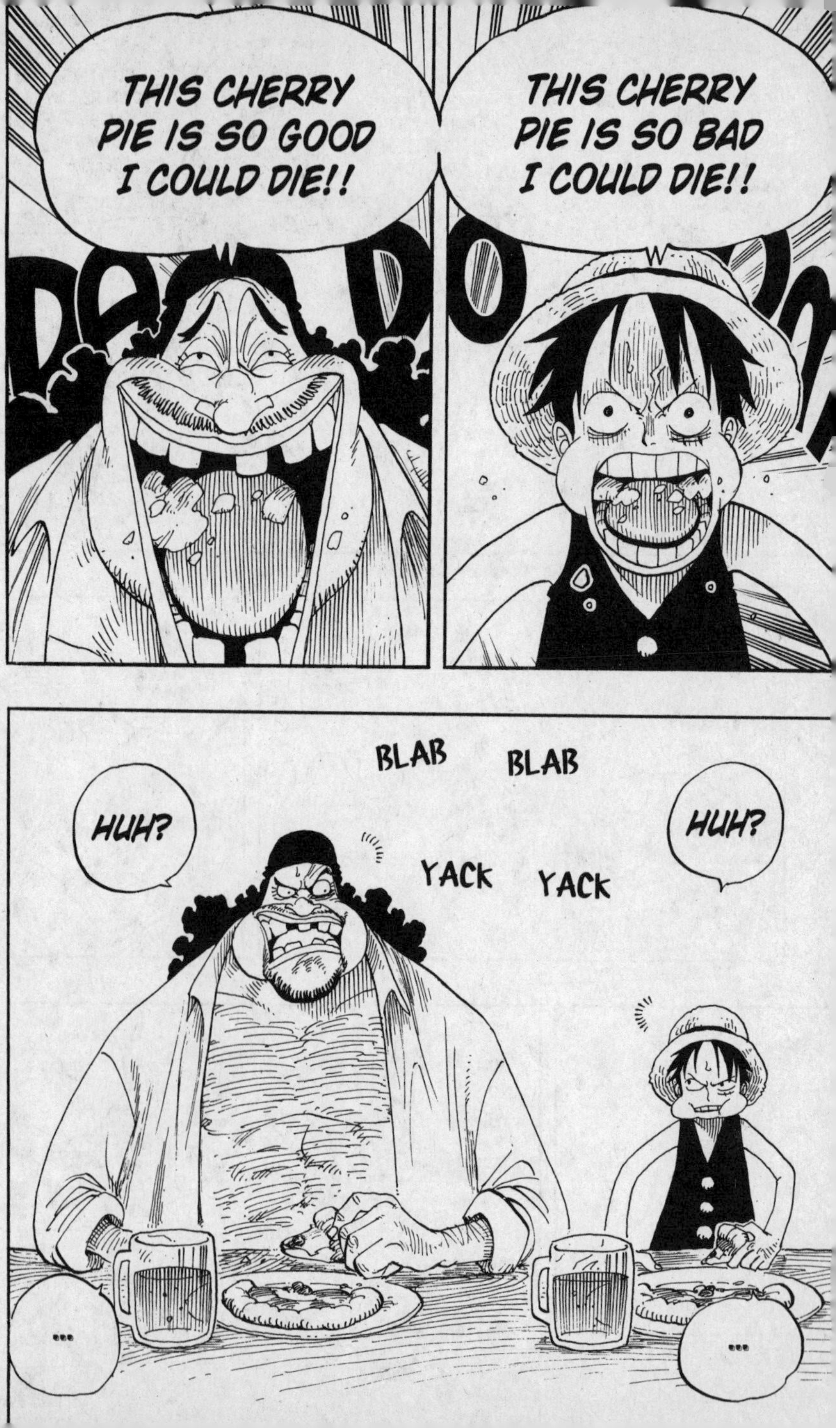
THIS CHERRY PIE IS SO BAD I COULD DIE!!
THIS CHERRY PIE IS SO GOOD I COULD DIE!!
HUH?
BLAB BLAB
YACK YACK
HUH?
...
...

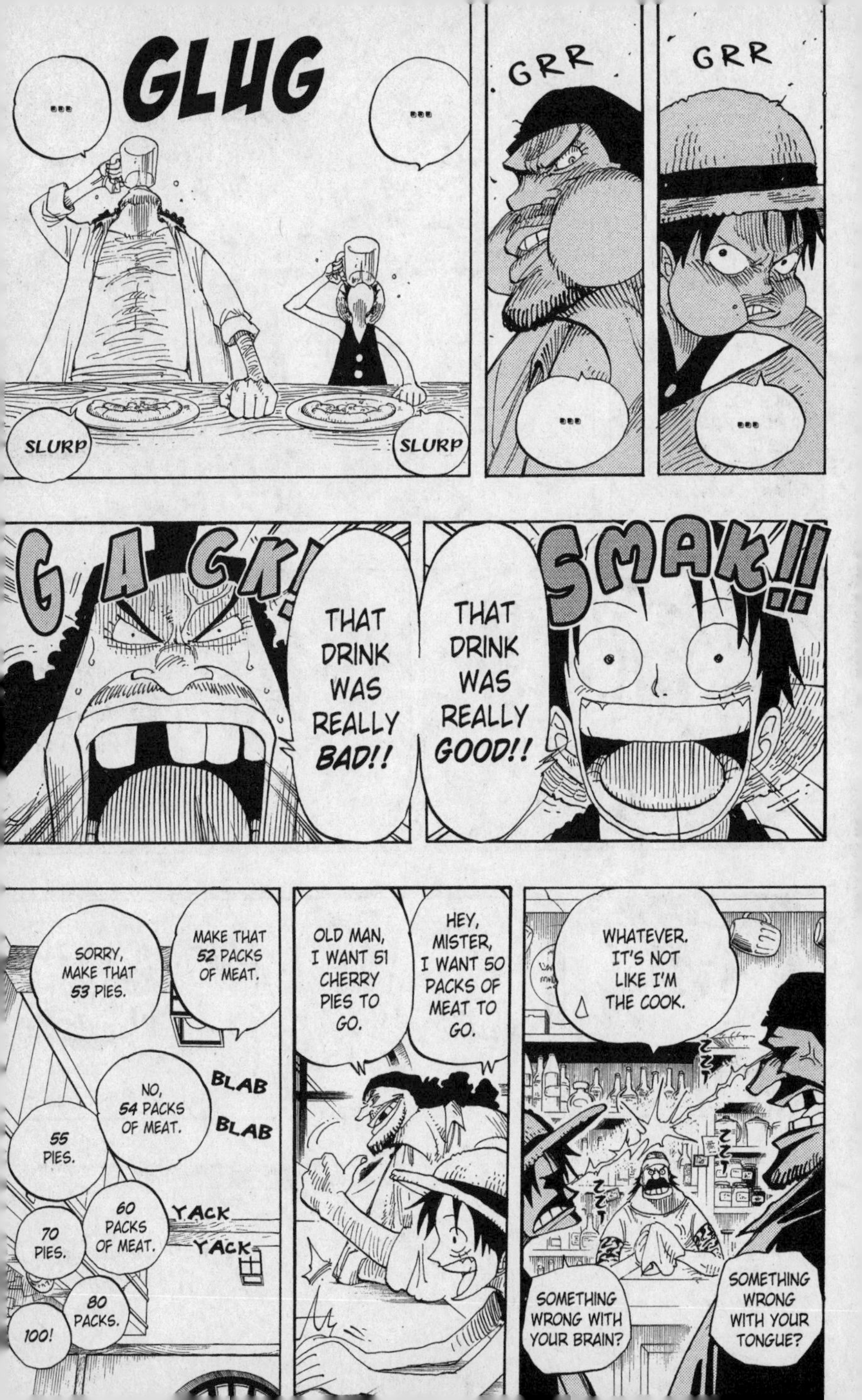
GRR
...
GRR
...
...
GLUG
...
SLURP
SLURP
SMAK!!
THAT DRINK WAS REALLY GOOD!!
GACK!
THAT DRINK WAS REALLY BAD!!
WHATEVER. IT'S NOT LIKE I'M THE COOK.
SOMETHING WRONG WITH YOUR TONGUE?
SOMETHING WRONG WITH YOUR BRAIN?
HEY, MISTER, I WANT 50 PACKS OF MEAT TO GO.
OLD MAN, I WANT 51 CHERRY PIES TO GO.
MAKE THAT 52 PACKS OF MEAT.
SORRY, MAKE THAT 53 PIES.
BLAB
BLAB
NO, 54 PACKS OF MEAT.
55 PIES.
YACK
YACK
60 PACKS OF MEAT.
70 PIES.
80 PACKS.
100!

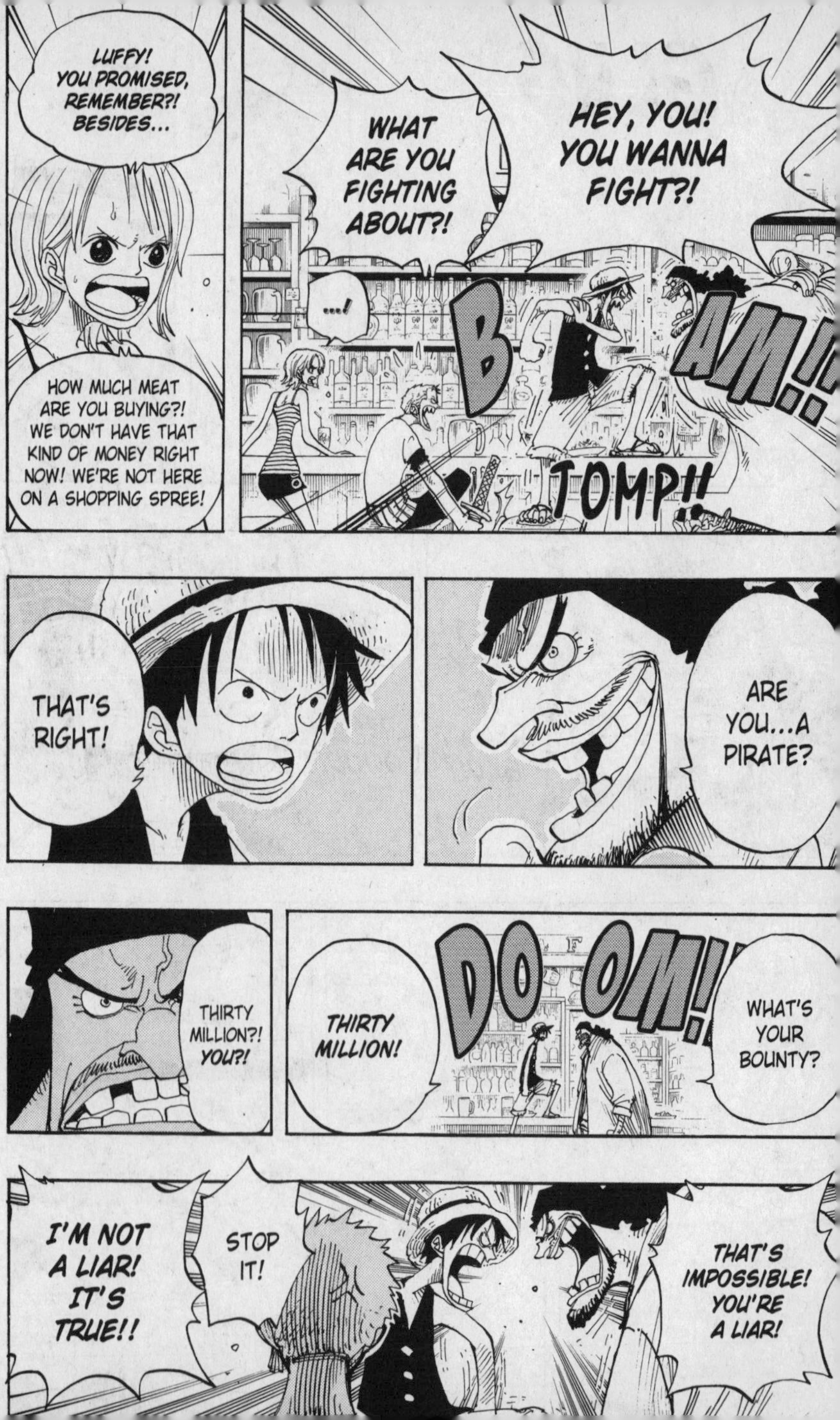
HEY, YOU! YOU WANNA FIGHT?!
WHAT ARE YOU FIGHTING ABOUT?!
...!
BAM!!
TOMP!!
LUFFY! YOU PROMISED, REMEMBER?! BESIDES...
HOW MUCH MEAT ARE YOU BUYING?! WE DON'T HAVE THAT KIND OF MONEY RIGHT NOW! WE'RE NOT HERE ON A SHOPPING SPREE!
ARE YOU...A PIRATE?
THAT'S RIGHT!
WHAT'S YOUR BOUNTY?
DOOM!!
THIRTY MILLION!
THIRTY MILLION?! YOU?!
THAT'S IMPOSSIBLE! YOU'RE A LIAR!
STOP IT!
I'M NOT A LIAR! IT'S TRUE!!

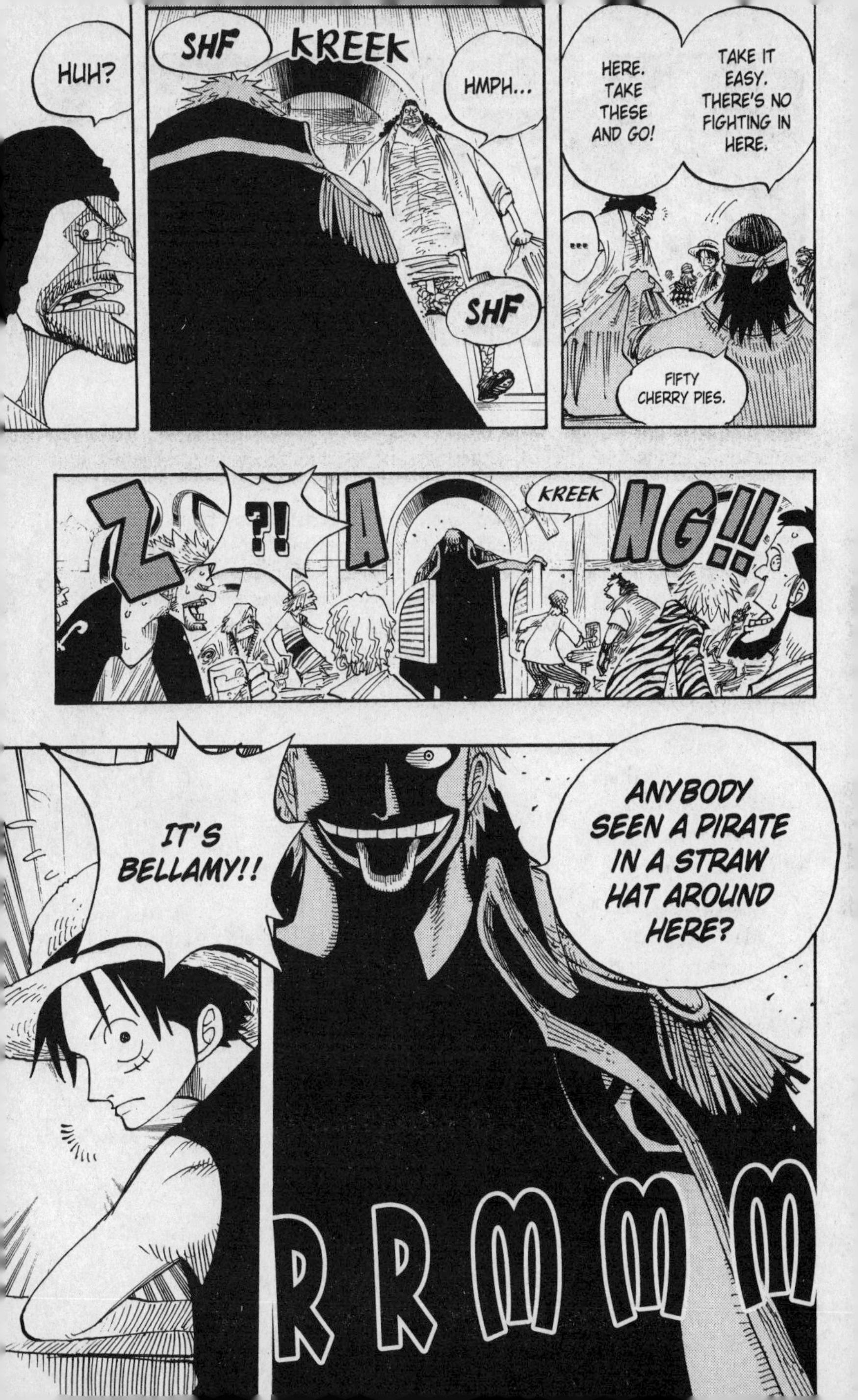
TAKE IT EASY. THERE'S NO FIGHTING IN HERE.
HERE. TAKE THESE AND GO!
...
FIFTY CHERRY PIES.
HMPH...
KREEK
SHF
SHF
HUH?
KREEK
ZANG!!
?!
ANYBODY SEEN A PIRATE IN A STRAW HAT AROUND HERE?
IT'S BELLAMY!!
RRMMMM

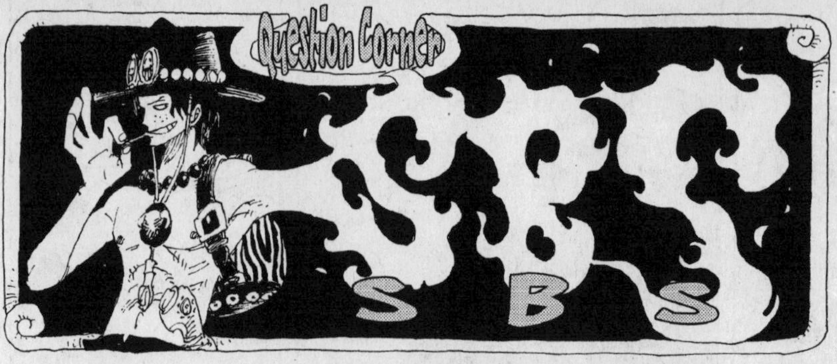
Question Corner
SBS

Q. Oda-chan! How are you? I have a question. ♡ In *One Piece* volume 18 (chapter 157) Luffy and the crew are hungry and crying for food. But just behind them is a tree full of tangerines. So why didn't they just eat them? ◯

A. Tangerines... Yes, there are tangerines, but if they took a bite, it would mean instant death. Definitely certain death. A man can live without food for a week. He can be strong and live with hope for the future, or he can eat the tangerine and battle with the navigator. But that would be taking a big risk with his life... I'm sure if it were a life-or-death situation, she wouldn't be so mean as to let them die. (Shiver shiver)

Q. Oda Sensei!
Your phone is ringing.

--Souda ☆

A. Oh, let it ring. It's just my editor.

Q. Oda Sensei, may I ask you something? I want to send a letter to you personally, but I don't know your address. Can you give it to me?

A. My address? For a letter?
Oh, I do get letters...! (BONG!!)
Uh... I have two addresses. You can send your letter to the editorial department of Jump magazine, or you can send it to the special Question Corner mailbox Either way, I'll get it, rest assured.

FOR NON-JAPANESE READERS, YOU CAN SEND YOUR LETTERS TO THE *ONE PIECE* EDITOR AT VIZ MEDIA.

Chapter 224:
DO NOT DREAM

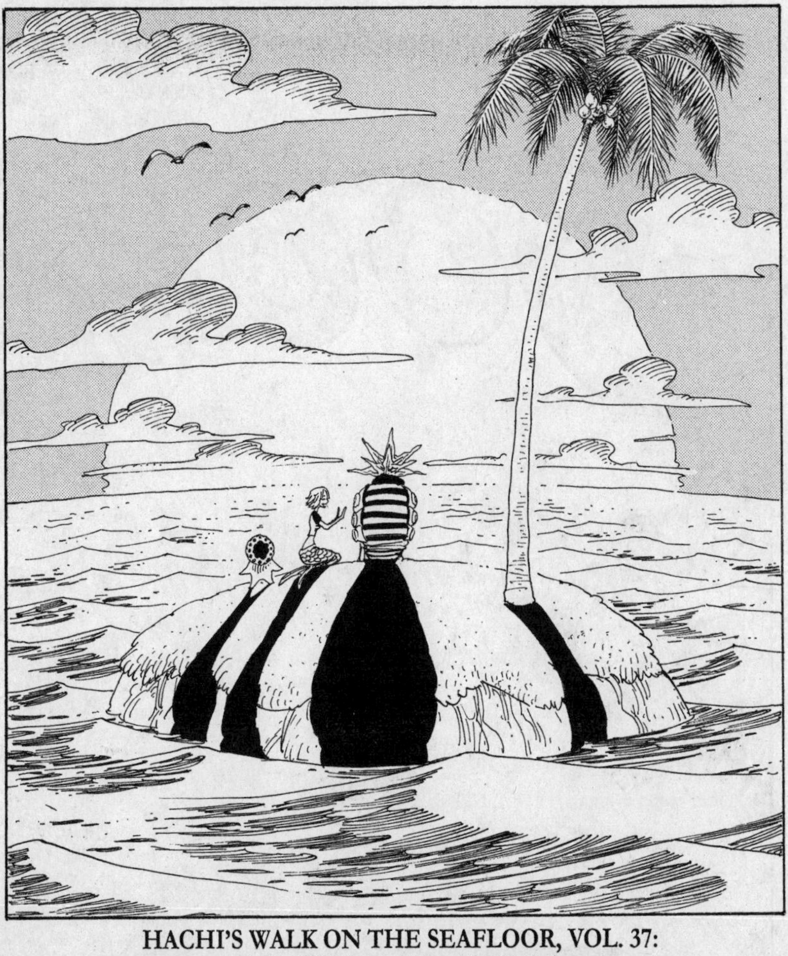

HACHI'S WALK ON THE SEAFLOOR, VOL. 37:
"HACHI AND THE SUNSET"

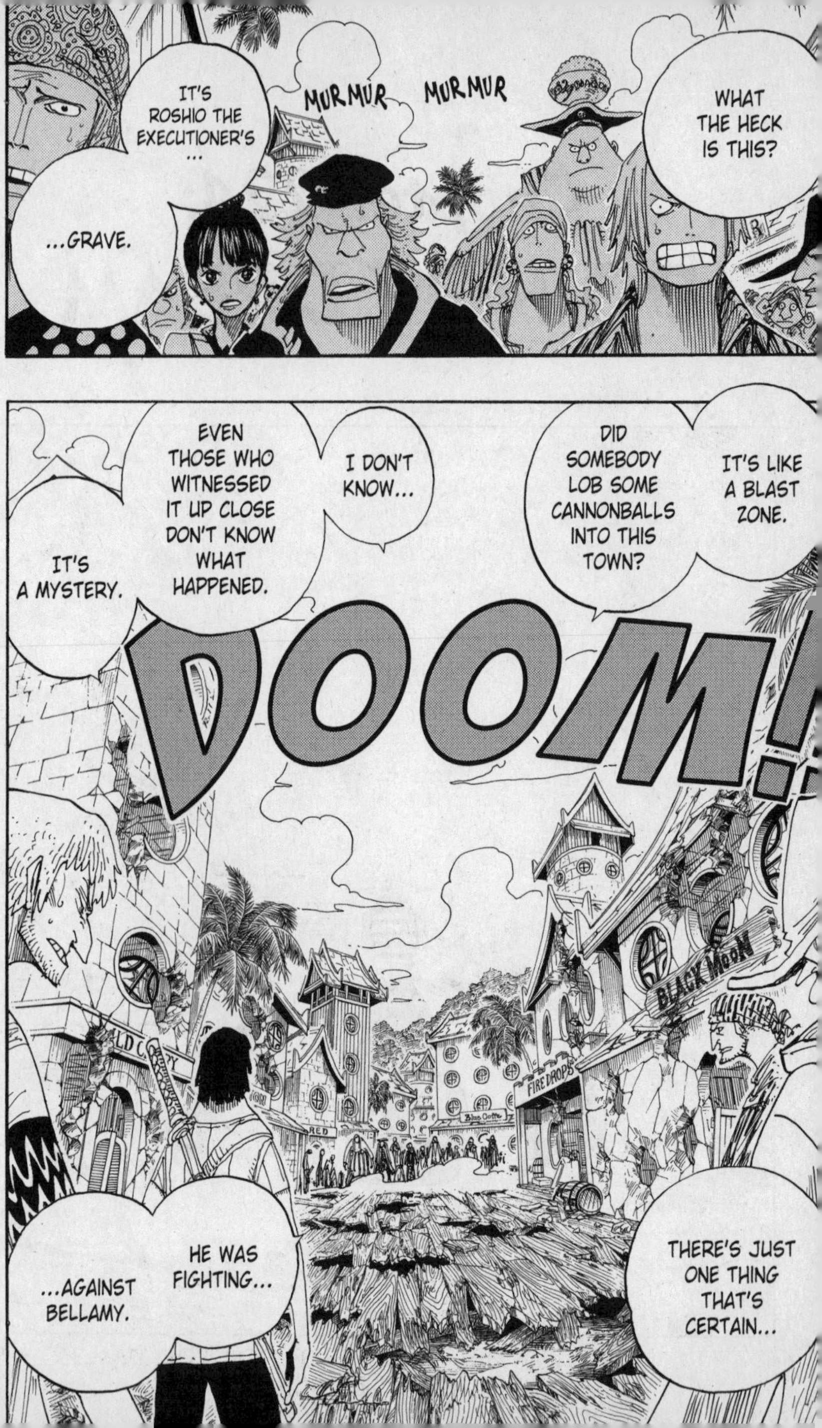
WHAT THE HECK IS THIS?
MURMUR
MURMUR
IT'S ROSHIO THE EXECUTIONER'S ...
...GRAVE.
IT'S LIKE A BLAST ZONE.
DID SOMEBODY LOB SOME CANNONBALLS INTO THIS TOWN?
I DON'T KNOW...
EVEN THOSE WHO WITNESSED IT UP CLOSE DON'T KNOW WHAT HAPPENED.
IT'S A MYSTERY.
DOOM!!
BLACK MOON
FIREDROP
THERE'S JUST ONE THING THAT'S CERTAIN...
HE WAS FIGHTING...
...AGAINST BELLAMY.

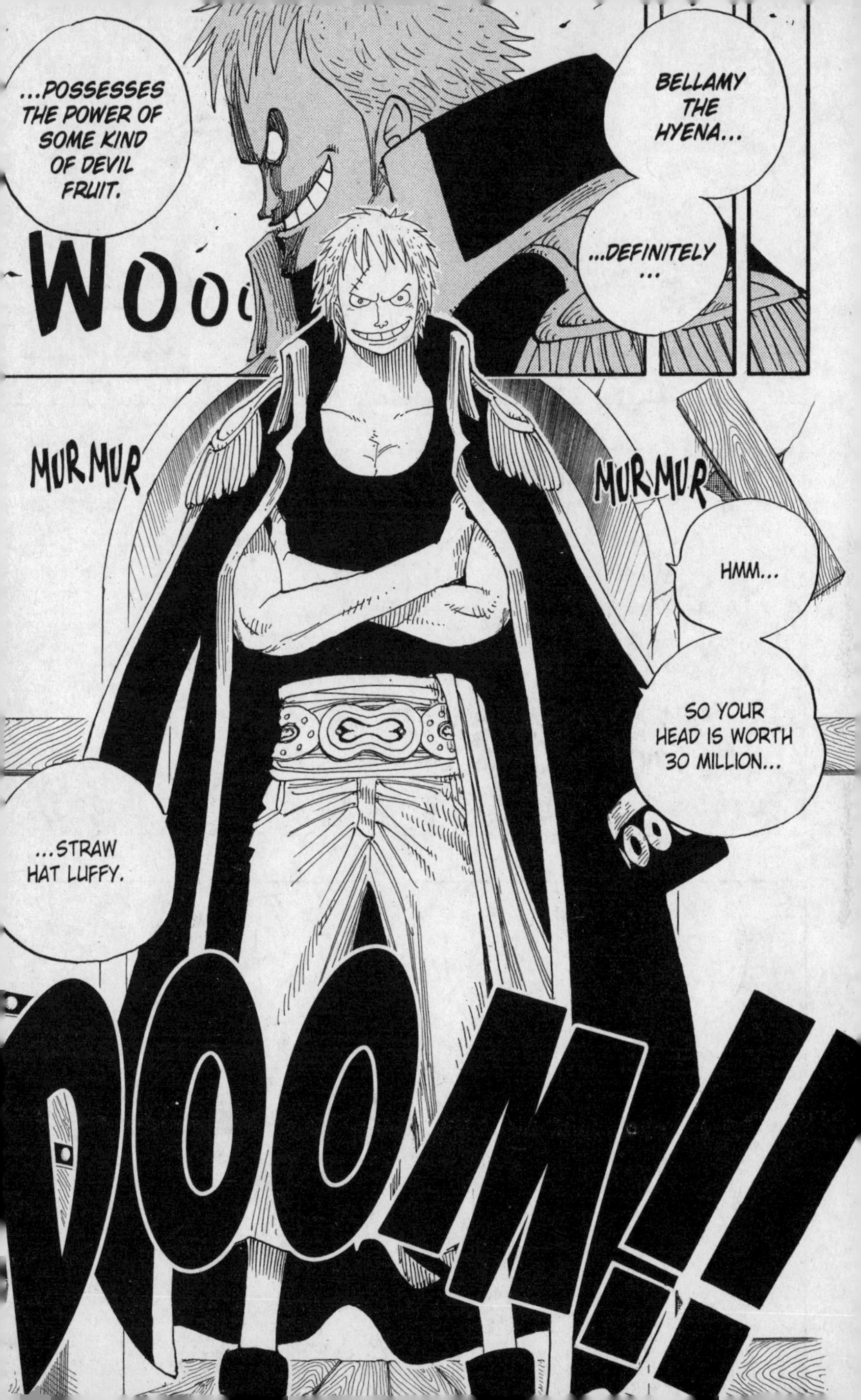
BELLAMY THE HYENA...
...DEFINITELY ...
...POSSESSES THE POWER OF SOME KIND OF DEVIL FRUIT.
WOOO
MUR MUR
MUR MUR
HMM...
SO YOUR HEAD IS WORTH 30 MILLION...
...STRAW HAT LUFFY.
DOOM!!

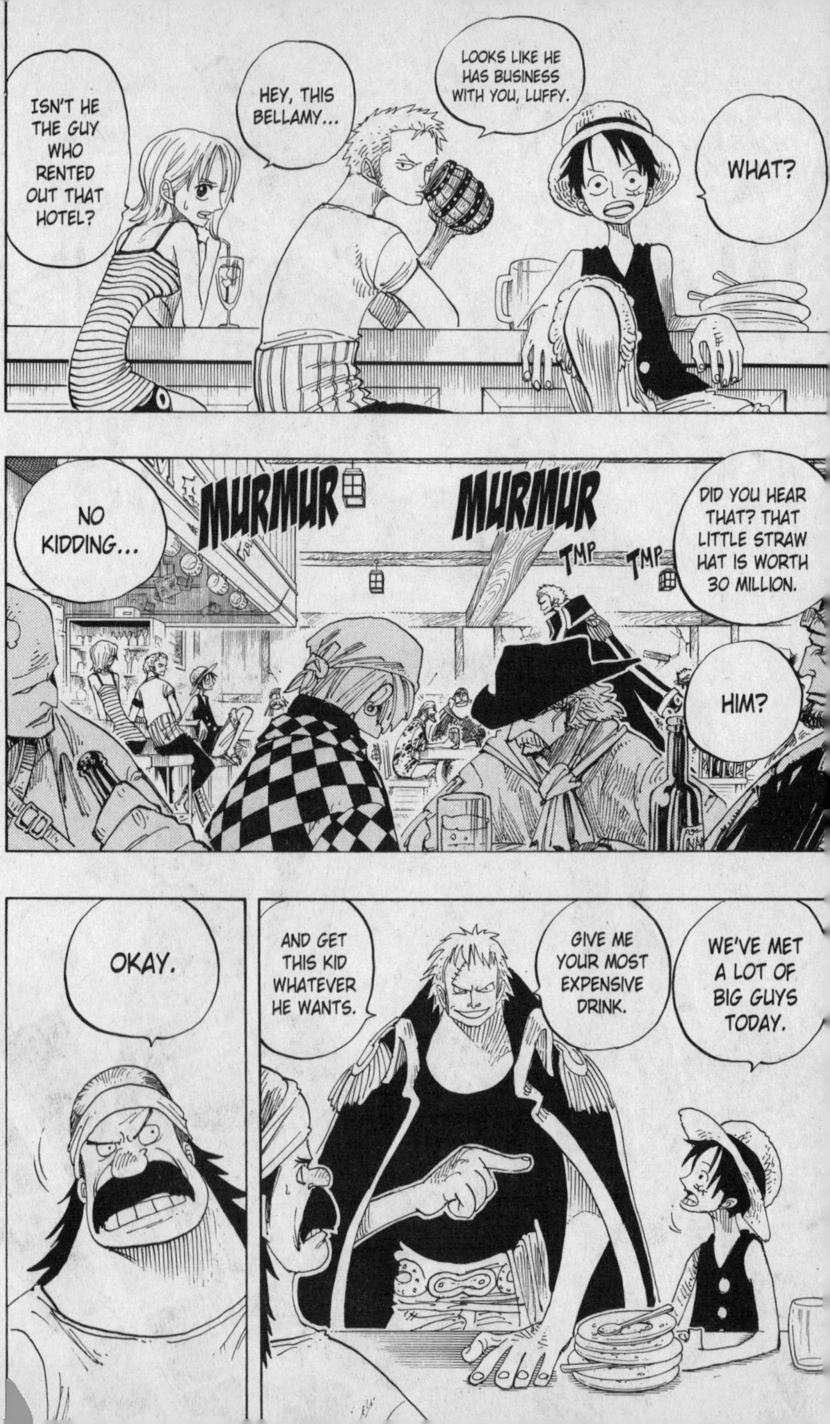
WHAT?
LOOKS LIKE HE HAS BUSINESS WITH YOU, LUFFY.
HEY, THIS BELLAMY...
ISN'T HE THE GUY WHO RENTED OUT THAT HOTEL?
DID YOU HEAR THAT? THAT LITTLE STRAW HAT IS WORTH 30 MILLION.
MURMUR
MURMUR
TMP
TMP
HIM?
NO KIDDING...
WE'VE MET A LOT OF BIG GUYS TODAY.
GIVE ME YOUR MOST EXPENSIVE DRINK.
AND GET THIS KID WHATEVER HE WANTS.
OKAY.

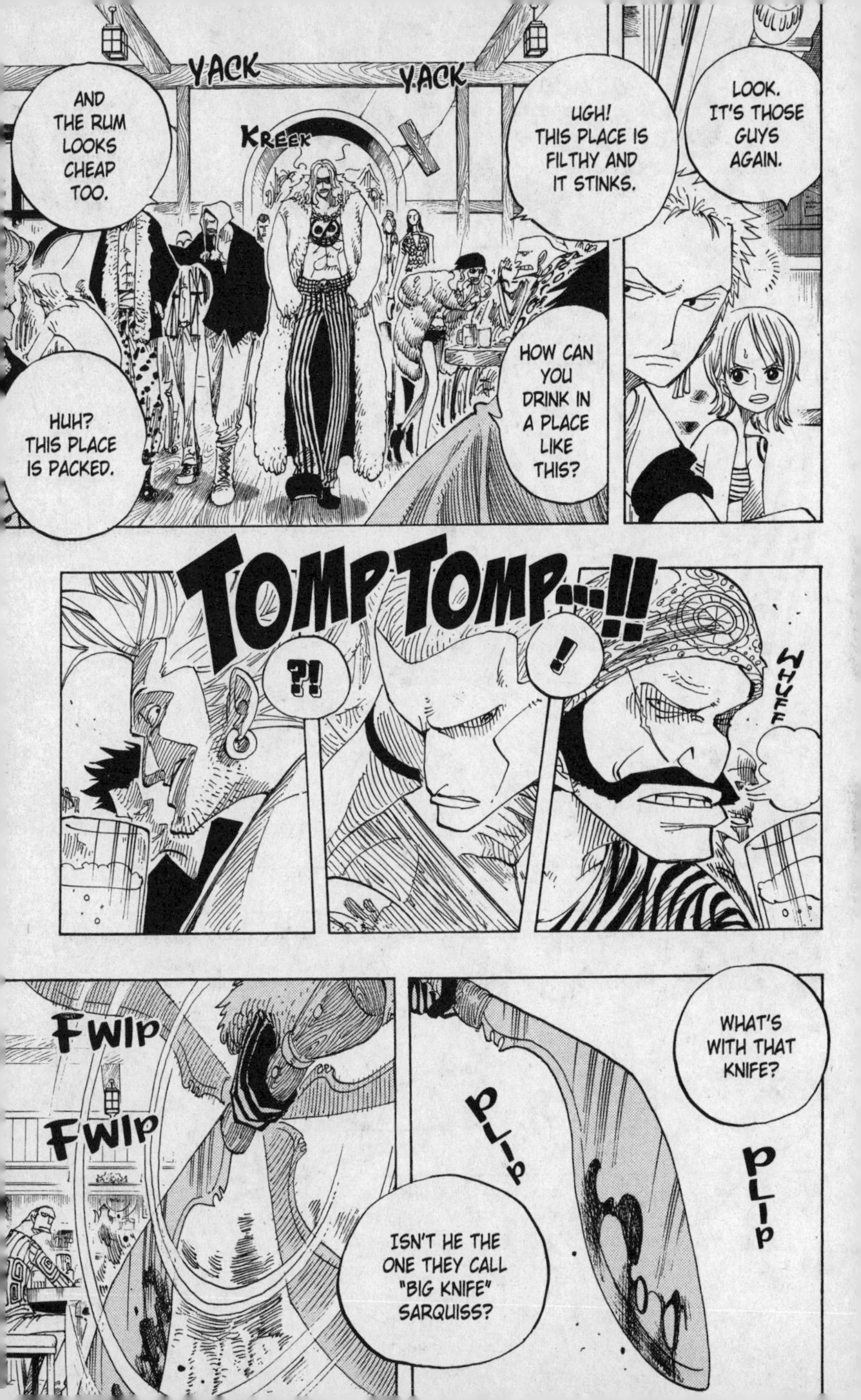
LOOK. IT'S THOSE GUYS AGAIN.
YACK
YACK
UGH! THIS PLACE IS FILTHY AND IT STINKS.
KREEK
AND THE RUM LOOKS CHEAP TOO.
HOW CAN YOU DRINK IN A PLACE LIKE THIS?
HUH? THIS PLACE IS PACKED.
TOMP TOMP...!!
WHUFF
!
?!
WHAT'S WITH THAT KNIFE?
PLIP
PLIP
ISN'T HE THE ONE THEY CALL "BIG KNIFE" SARQUISS?
FWIP
FWIP

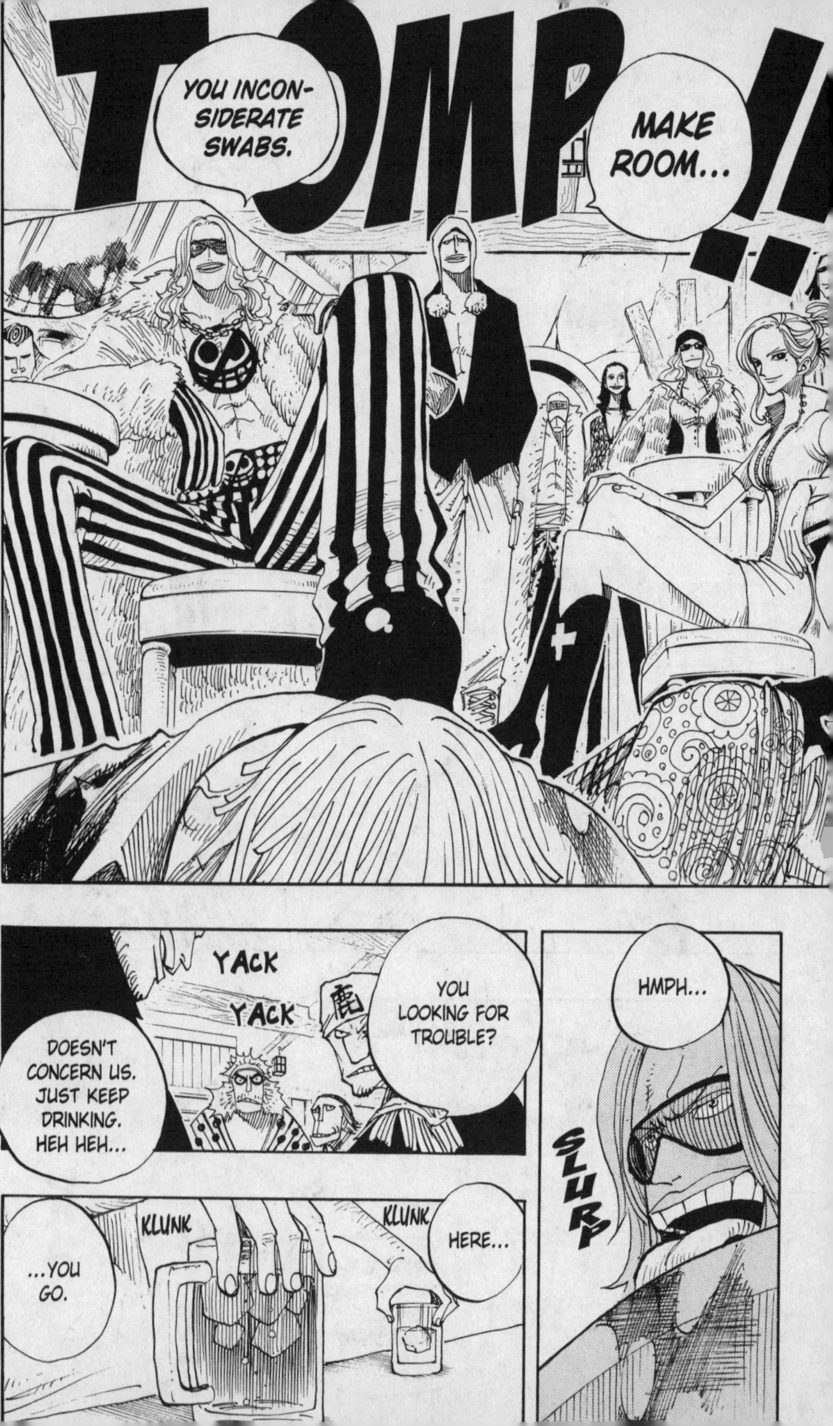
TOMP!!
MAKE ROOM...
YOU INCONSIDERATE SWABS.
HMPH...
SLURP
YOU LOOKING FOR TROUBLE?
YACK
YACK
DOESN'T CONCERN US. JUST KEEP DRINKING. HEH HEH...
KLUNK
HERE...
KLUNK
...YOU GO.

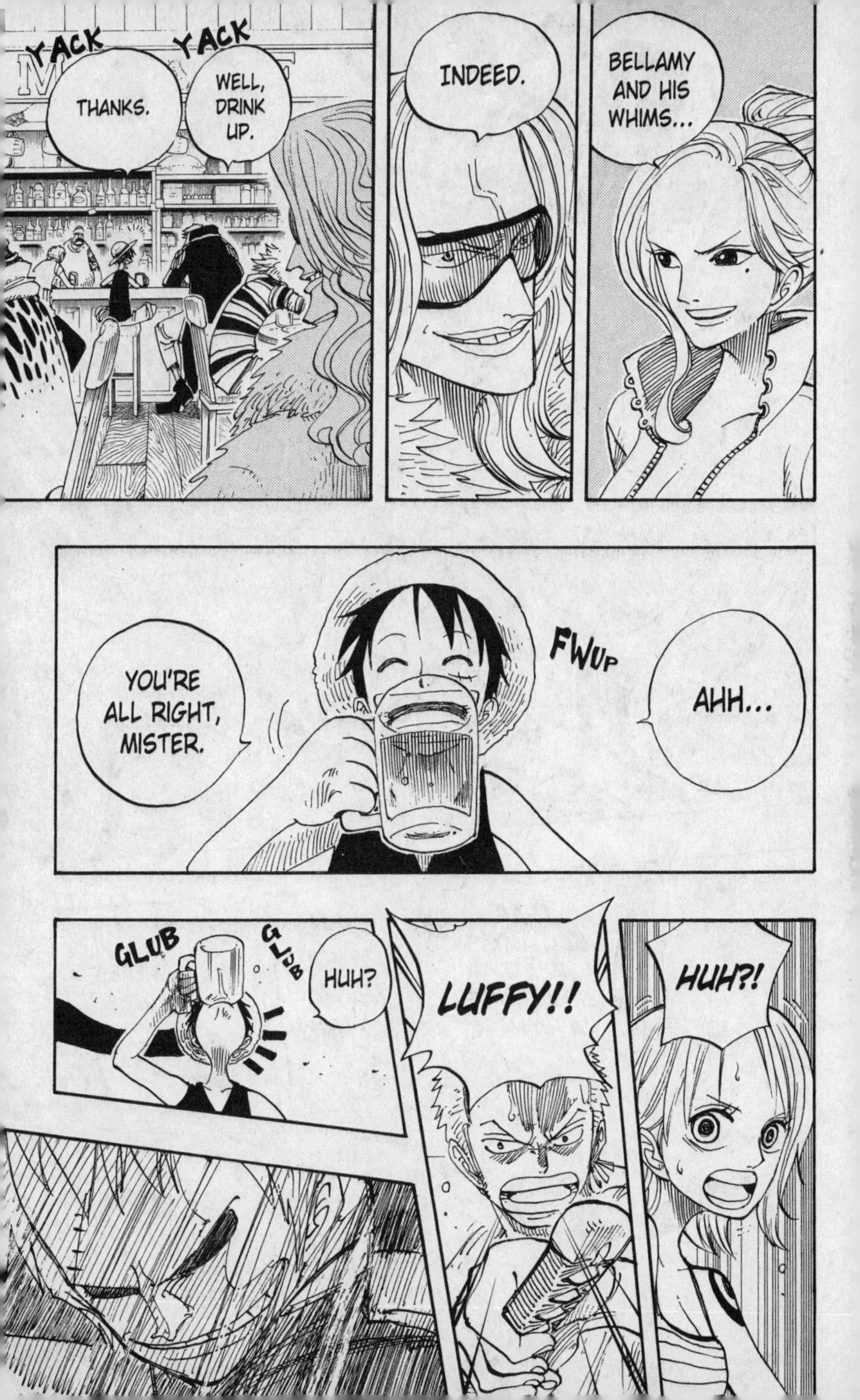
BELLAMY AND HIS WHIMS...
INDEED.
YACK
YACK
WELL, DRINK UP.
THANKS.
AHH...
FWUP
YOU'RE ALL RIGHT, MISTER.
HUH?!
LUFFY!!
HUH?
GLUB
GLUB

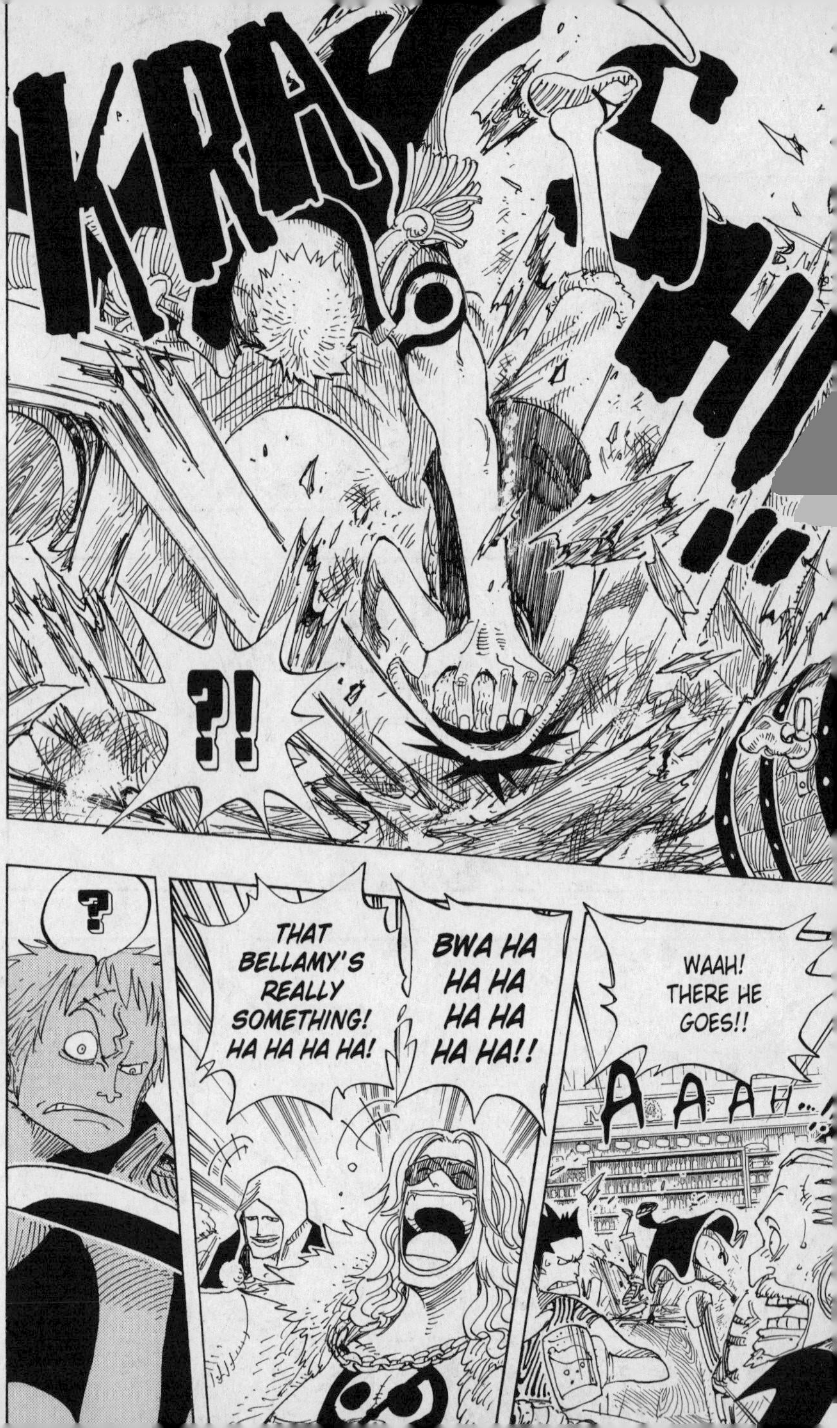
KRASSH!!
?!
WAAH! THERE HE GOES!!
AAAH...
BWA HA HA HA HA HA HA HA!!
THAT BELLAMY'S REALLY SOMETHING! HA HA HA HA!
?

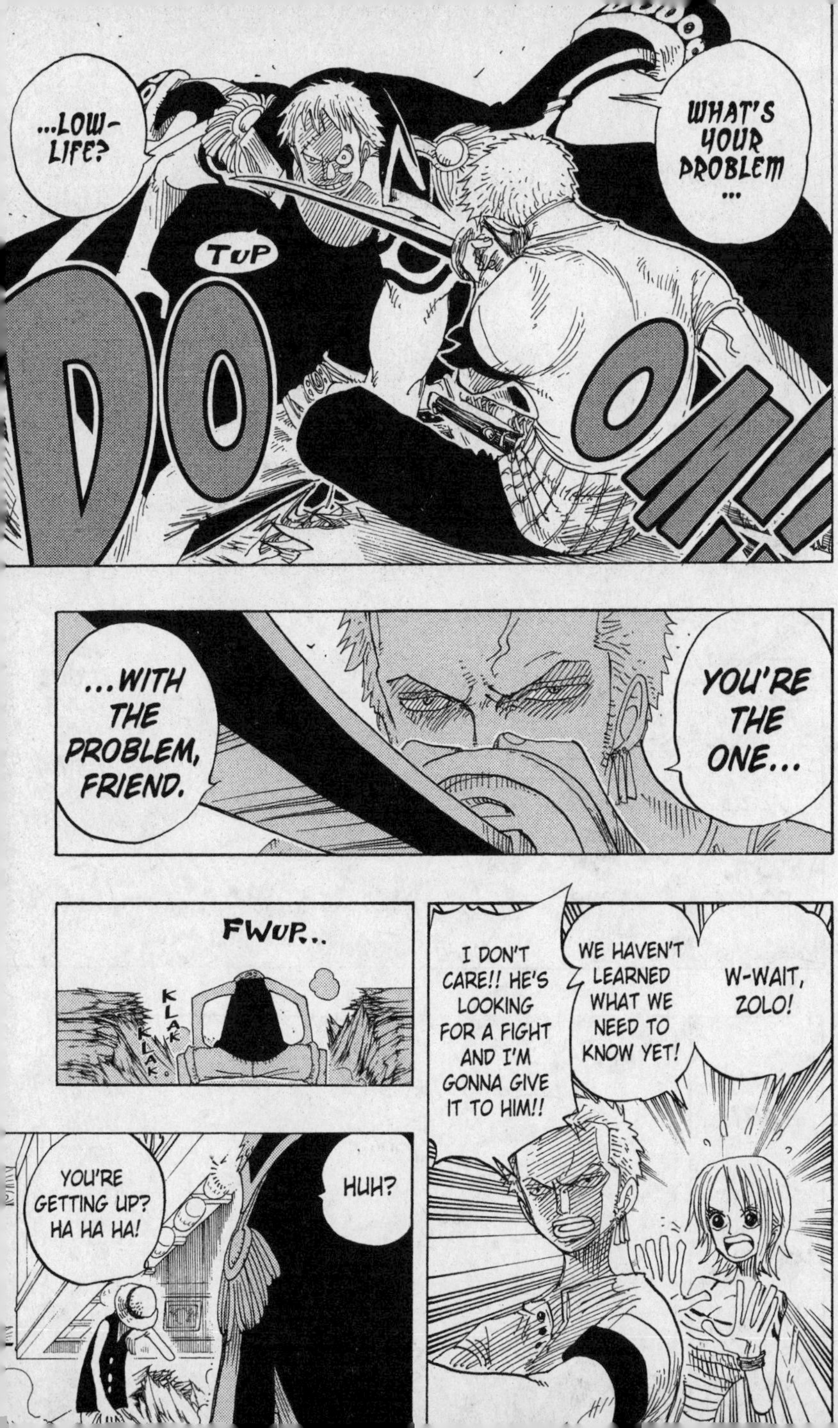
WHAT'S YOUR PROBLEM ...
...LOW-LIFE?
TUP
DOOM
YOU'RE THE ONE...
...WITH THE PROBLEM, FRIEND.
W-WAIT, ZOLO!
WE HAVEN'T LEARNED WHAT WE NEED TO KNOW YET!
I DON'T CARE!! HE'S LOOKING FOR A FIGHT AND I'M GONNA GIVE IT TO HIM!!
FWUP..
KLAK KLAK
HUH?
YOU'RE GETTING UP? HA HA HA!

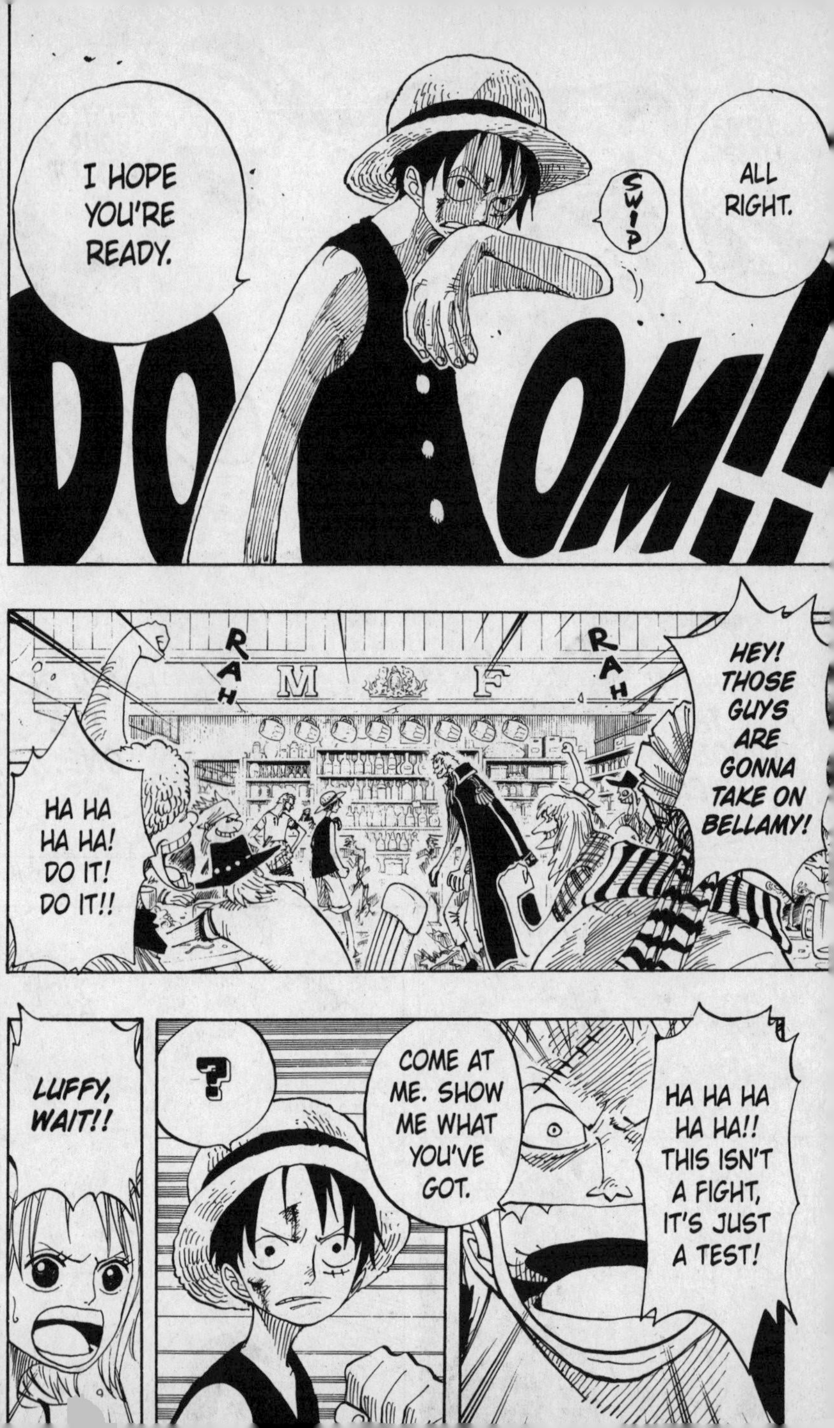
ALL RIGHT.
SWIP
I HOPE YOU'RE READY.
DO OM!!
HEY! THOSE GUYS ARE GONNA TAKE ON BELLAMY!
RAH
RAH
HA HA HA HA! DO IT! DO IT!!
HA HA HA HA HA!! THIS ISN'T A FIGHT, IT'S JUST A TEST!
COME AT ME. SHOW ME WHAT YOU'VE GOT.
?
LUFFY, WAIT!!

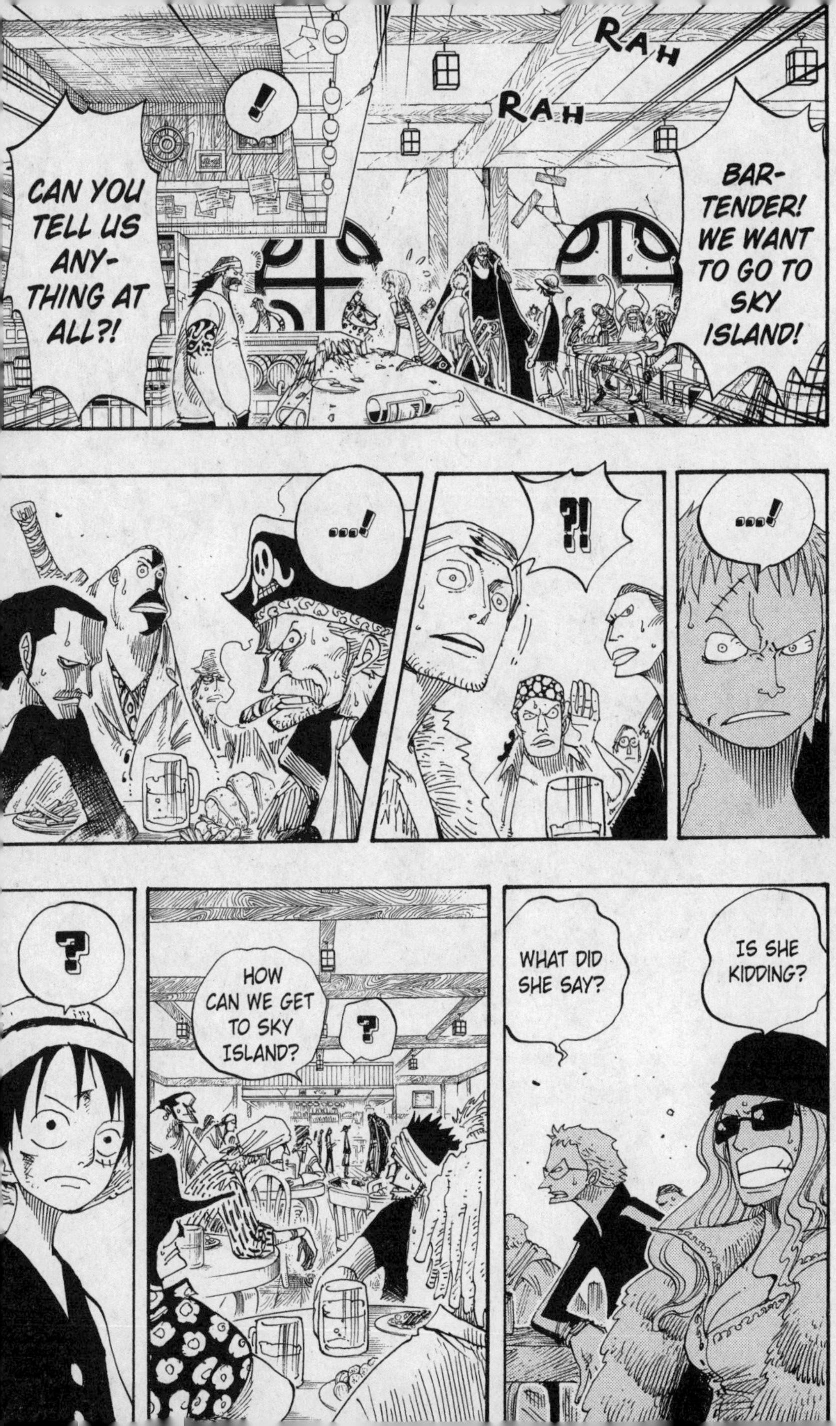
RAH
RAH
BAR-TENDER! WE WANT TO GO TO SKY ISLAND!
!
CAN YOU TELL US ANY-THING AT ALL?!
...!
?!
...!
IS SHE KIDDING?
WHAT DID SHE SAY?
?
HOW CAN WE GET TO SKY ISLAND?
?

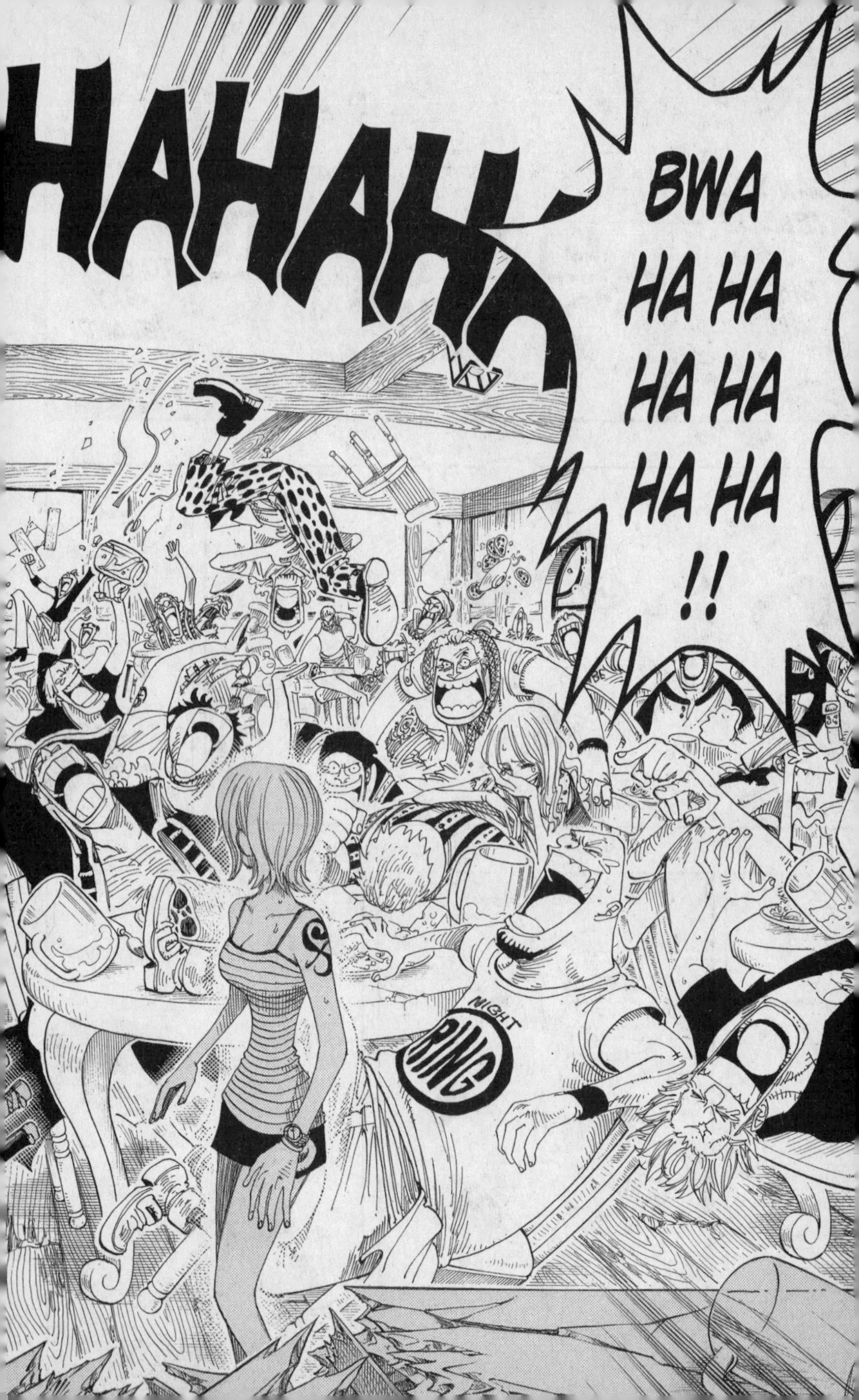
BWA HA HA HA HA HA HA !!
HAHAH
NIGHT
RING

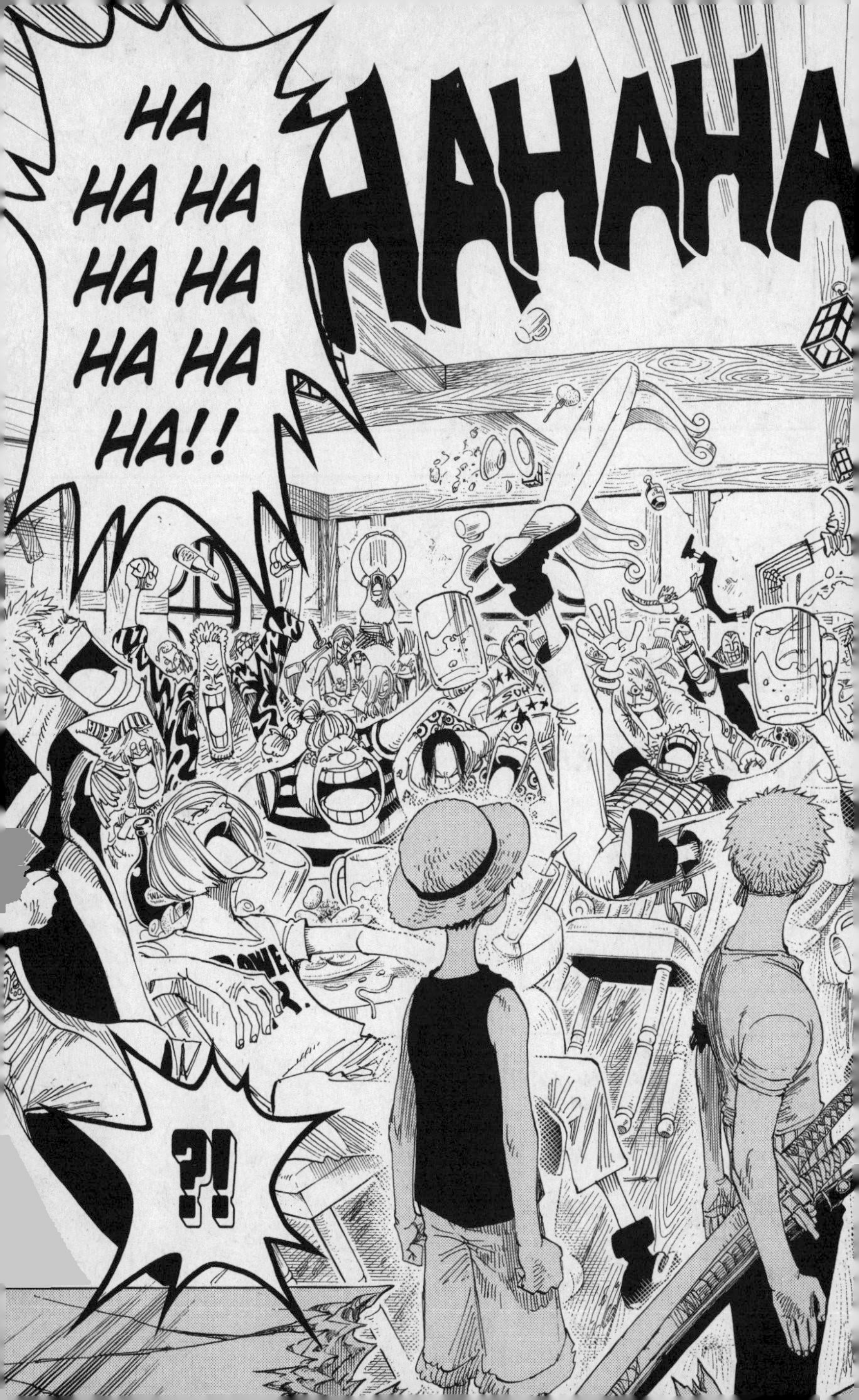
HAHAHA
HA HA HA HA HA HA HA HA HA!!
?!

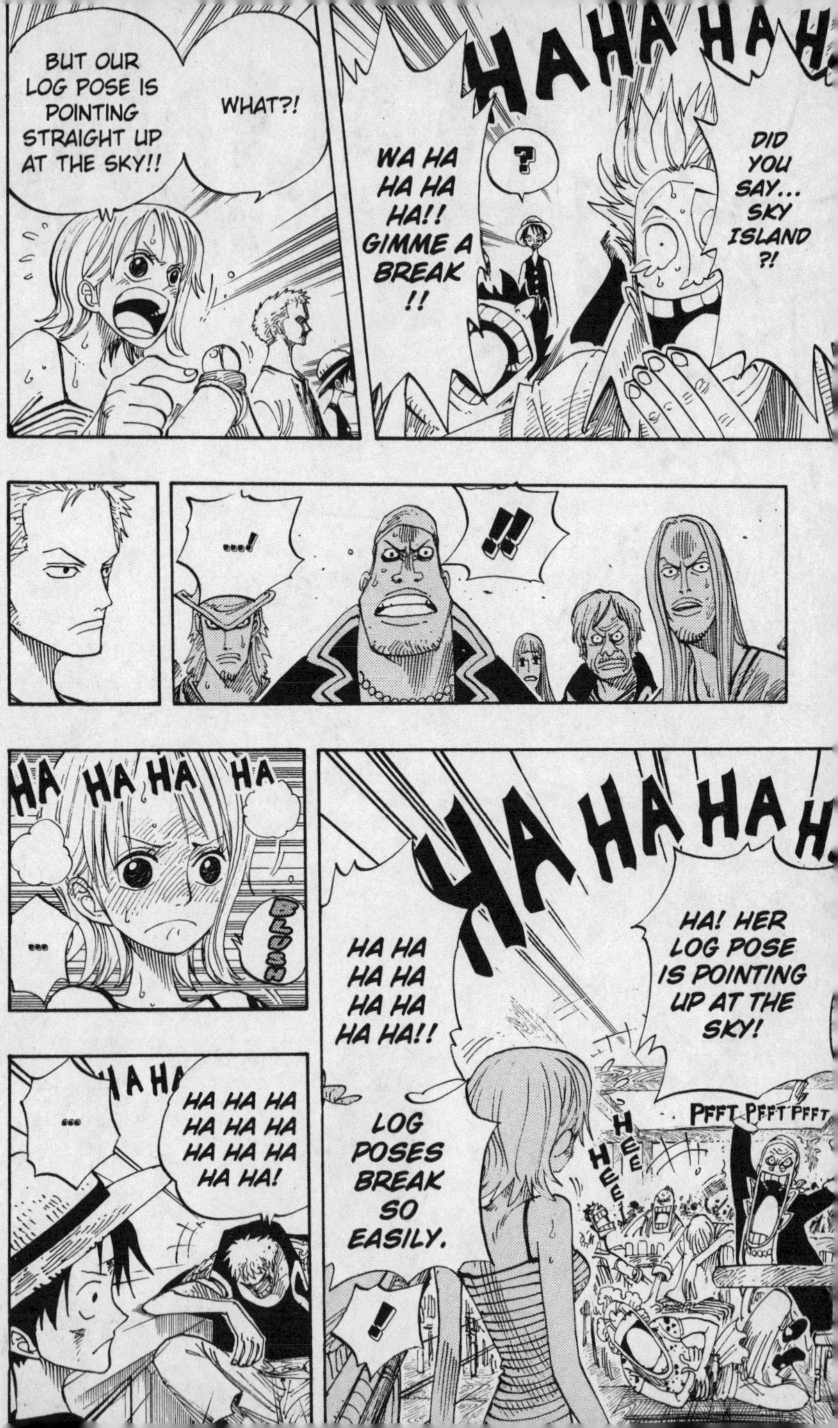
HAHAHAHAH
DID YOU SAY... SKY ISLAND?!
?
WA HA HA HA HA!! GIMME A BREAK!!
WHAT?!
BUT OUR LOG POSE IS POINTING STRAIGHT UP AT THE SKY!!
!!
...!
HAHAHAHAH
HA! HER LOG POSE IS POINTING UP AT THE SKY!
HA HA HA HA HA HA HA HA!!
PFFT PFFT PFFT
HEE HEE HEE
LOG POSES BREAK SO EASILY.
!
HA HA HA HA
BLUSH
...
HAHAH
HA HA HA HA HA HA HA HA HA HA HA!
...

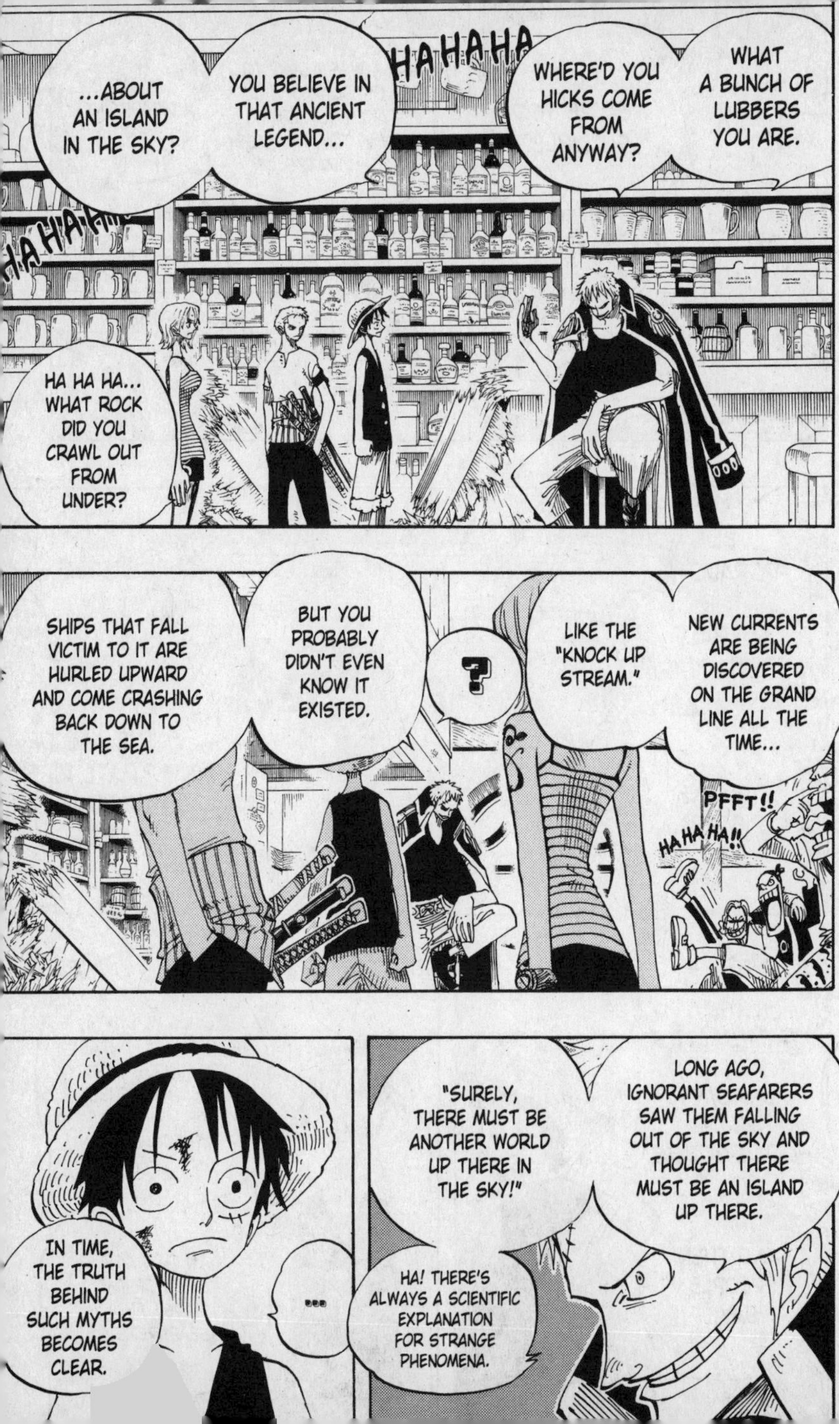
WHAT A BUNCH OF LUBBERS YOU ARE.
WHERE'D YOU HICKS COME FROM ANYWAY?
HAHAHA
YOU BELIEVE IN THAT ANCIENT LEGEND...
...ABOUT AN ISLAND IN THE SKY?
HAHAHA
HA HA HA... WHAT ROCK DID YOU CRAWL OUT FROM UNDER?
NEW CURRENTS ARE BEING DISCOVERED ON THE GRAND LINE ALL THE TIME...
LIKE THE "KNOCK UP STREAM."
PFFT!!
HA HA HA!!
?
BUT YOU PROBABLY DIDN'T EVEN KNOW IT EXISTED.
SHIPS THAT FALL VICTIM TO IT ARE HURLED UPWARD AND COME CRASHING BACK DOWN TO THE SEA.
LONG AGO, IGNORANT SEAFARERS SAW THEM FALLING OUT OF THE SKY AND THOUGHT THERE MUST BE AN ISLAND UP THERE.
"SURELY, THERE MUST BE ANOTHER WORLD UP THERE IN THE SKY!"
HA! THERE'S ALWAYS A SCIENTIFIC EXPLANATION FOR STRANGE PHENOMENA.
...
IN TIME, THE TRUTH BEHIND SUCH MYTHS BECOMES CLEAR.

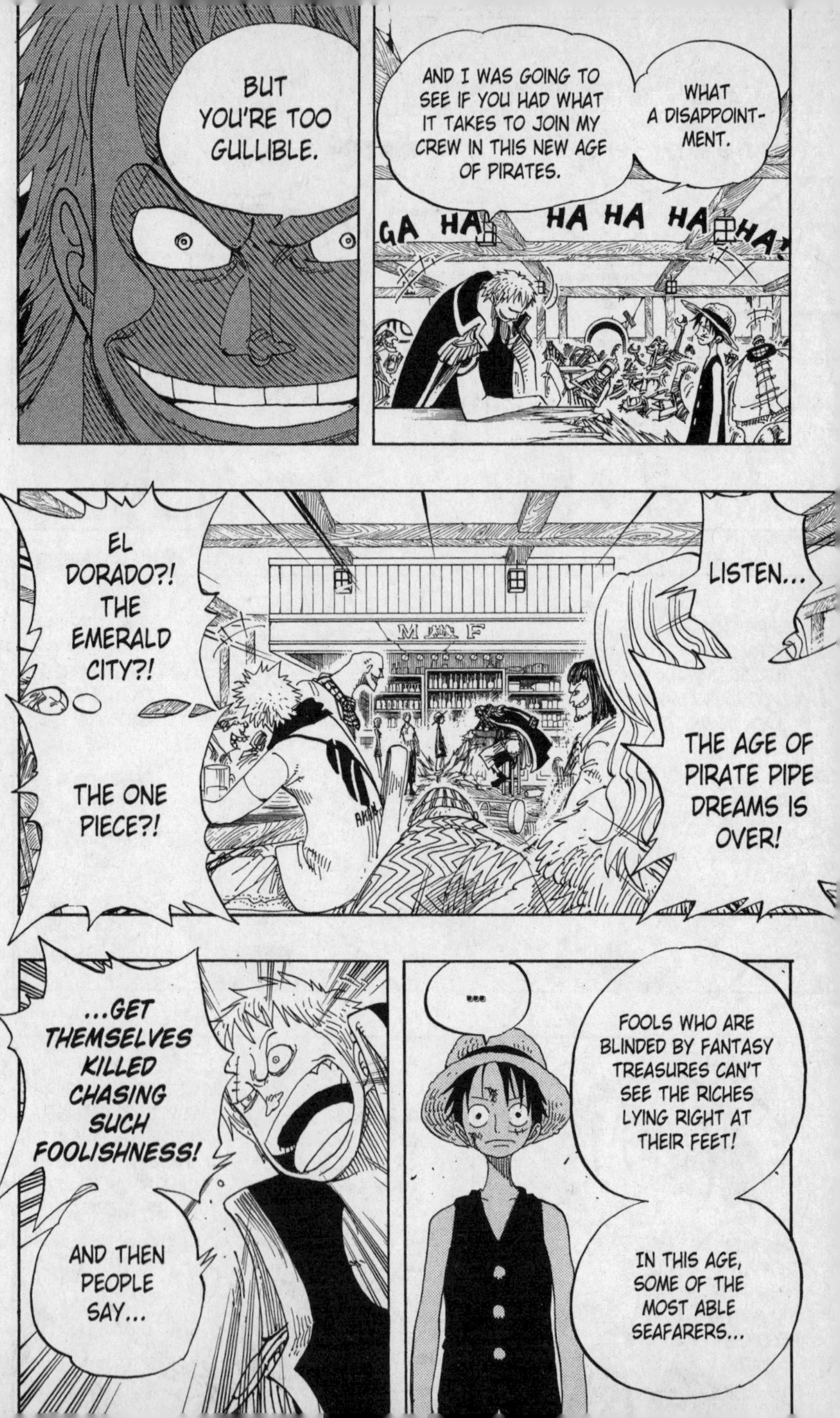
AND I WAS GOING TO SEE IF YOU HAD WHAT IT TAKES TO JOIN MY CREW IN THIS NEW AGE OF PIRATES.
WHAT A DISAPPOINTMENT.
GA HA HA HA HA HA
BUT YOU'RE TOO GULLIBLE.
LISTEN...
THE AGE OF PIRATE PIPE DREAMS IS OVER!
EL DORADO?! THE EMERALD CITY?!
THE ONE PIECE?!
FOOLS WHO ARE BLINDED BY FANTASY TREASURES CAN'T SEE THE RICHES LYING RIGHT AT THEIR FEET!
...
IN THIS AGE, SOME OF THE MOST ABLE SEAFARERS...
...GET THEMSELVES KILLED CHASING SUCH FOOLISHNESS!
AND THEN PEOPLE SAY...

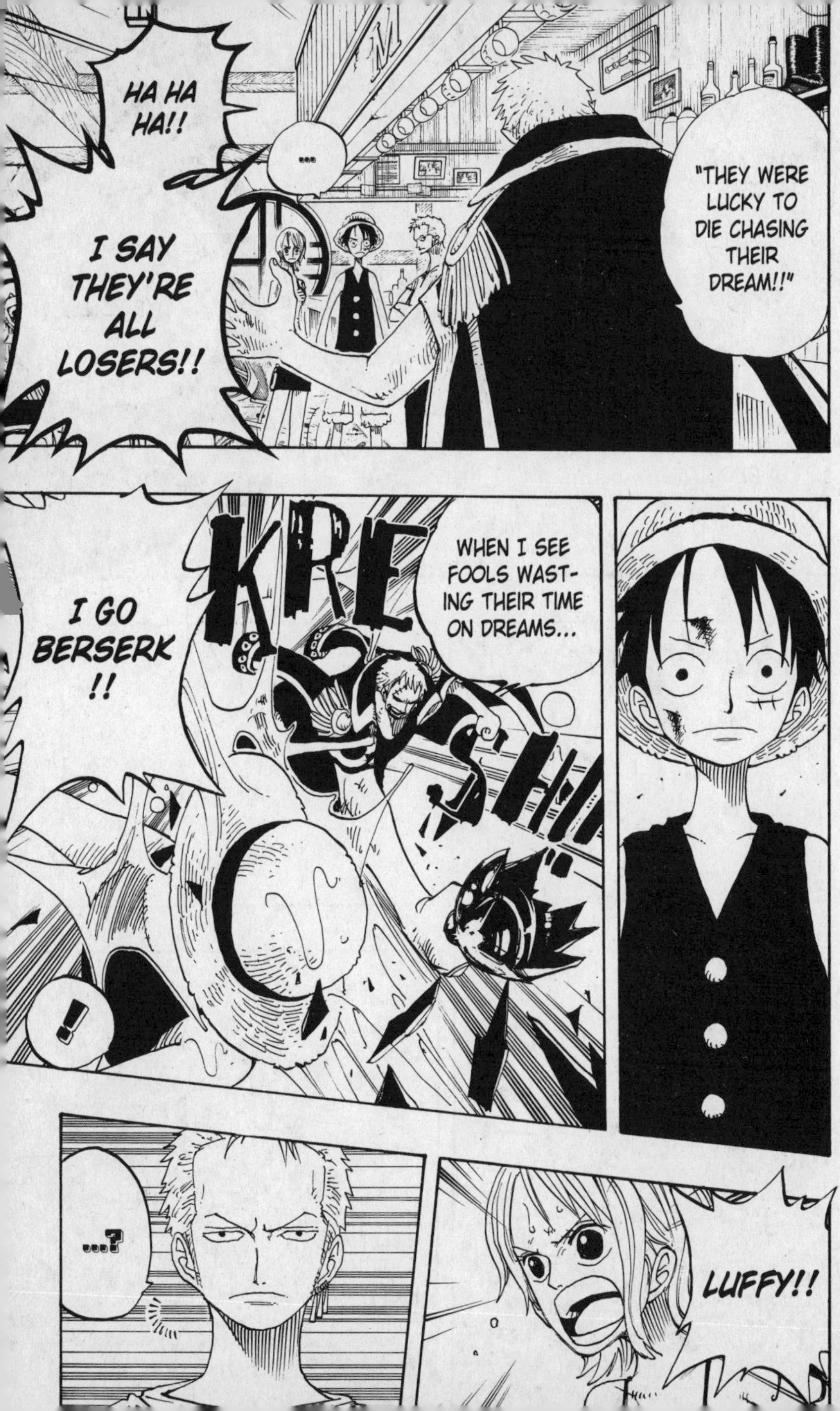
"THEY WERE LUCKY TO DIE CHASING THEIR DREAM!!"
...
HA HA HA!!
I SAY THEY'RE ALL LOSERS!!
WHEN I SEE FOOLS WAST-ING THEIR TIME ON DREAMS...
KRE
SSHH
I GO BERSERK !!
!
LUFFY!!
...?

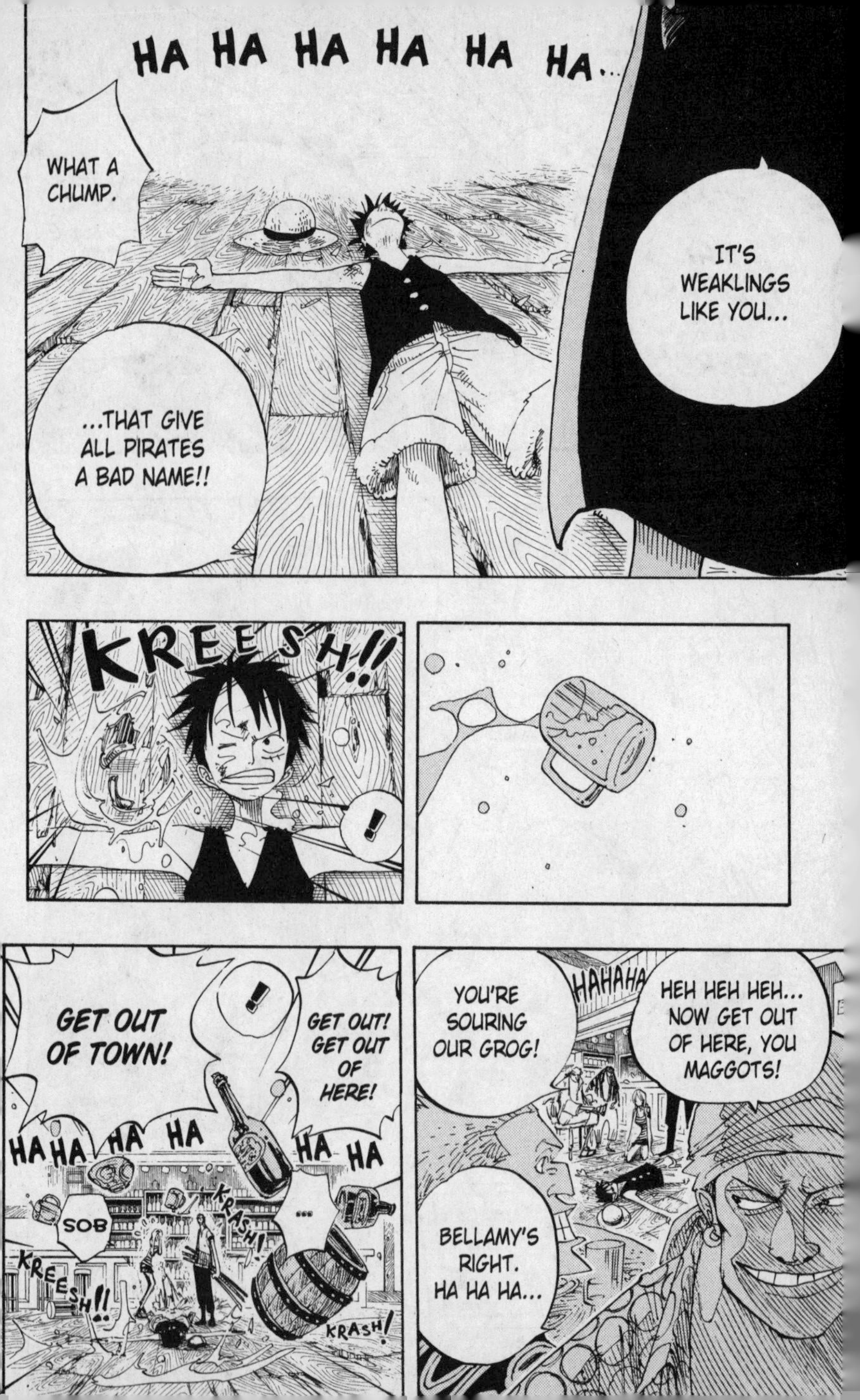
HA HA HA HA HA HA...
WHAT A CHUMP.
IT'S WEAKLINGS LIKE YOU...
...THAT GIVE ALL PIRATES A BAD NAME!!
KREESH!!
!
HEH HEH HEH... NOW GET OUT OF HERE, YOU MAGGOTS!
HAHAHA
YOU'RE SOURING OUR GROG!
BELLAMY'S RIGHT. HA HA HA...
GET OUT! GET OUT OF HERE!
!
GET OUT OF TOWN!
HA HA
HA HA HA HA
KRASH!
...
SOB
KREESH!!
KRASH!

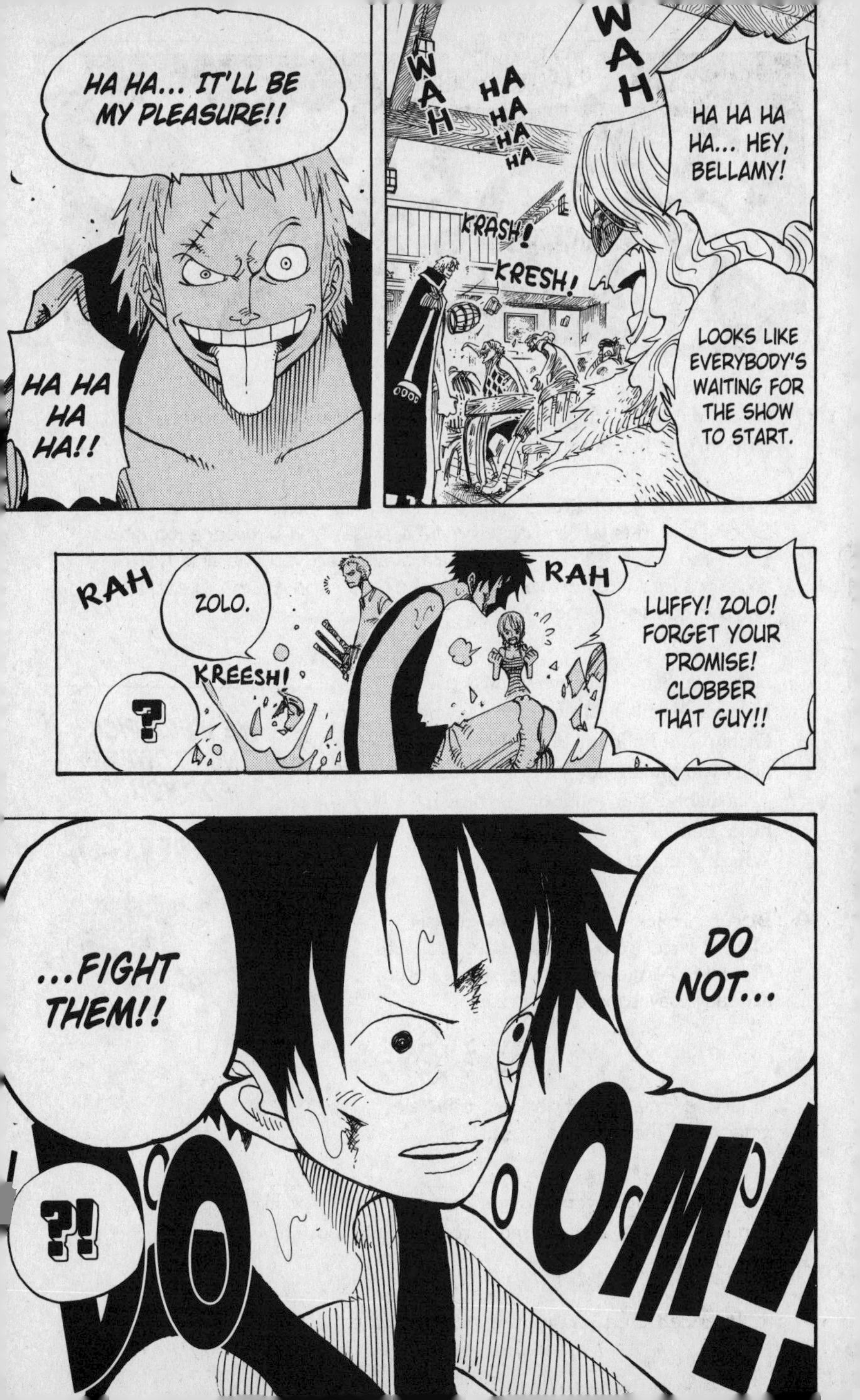
WAH
HA HA HA HA HA
WAH
HA HA HA HA... HEY, BELLAMY!
KRASH!
KRESH!
LOOKS LIKE EVERYBODY'S WAITING FOR THE SHOW TO START.
HA HA... IT'LL BE MY PLEASURE!!
HA HA HA HA!!
LUFFY! ZOLO! FORGET YOUR PROMISE! CLOBBER THAT GUY!!
RAH
ZOLO.
RAH
KREESH!
?
DO NOT...
...FIGHT THEM!!
?!

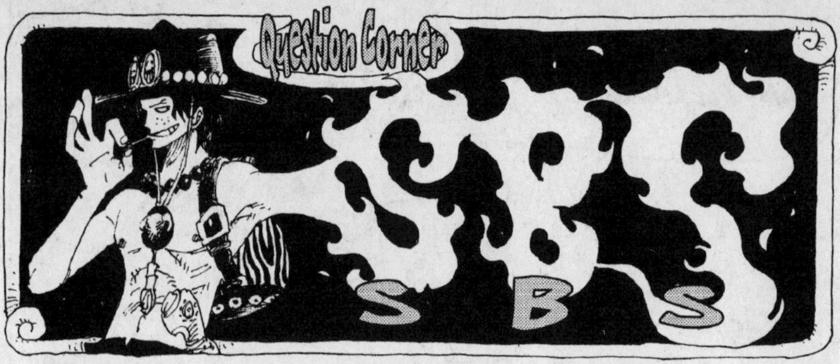
Question Corner
SBS

Q : When Ms. Doublefinger uses her Spike-Spike Fruit powers, how come it doesn't rip her clothing to pieces?

A : What? Are you suggesting she shred her outfit with her spikes? Sorry, but this isn't that kind of manga! And if I were to draw that, you know I'd put it on the cover. Can you imagine how embarrassed people would be if they saw something like that on the cover?! Should I do it?!

Q : Hello. I'm Sam's daughter. Oda Sensei! I have a complaint! In volume 23, when Django and Fullbody bring flowers to Hina, don't you think Django's flowers looked a bit shabby? But you took the time to make Fullbody's flowers look like roses! What's going on?!

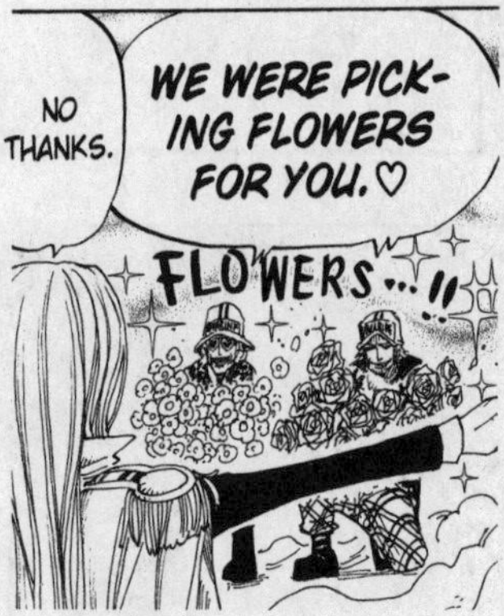
WE WERE PICK-ING FLOWERS FOR YOU.♡
NO THANKS.
FLOWERS...!!

A : Don't nitpick! I put equal (minimal) effort into both of those bouquets! (Ta dah!) All right, let me show you an easy way to draw a rose.

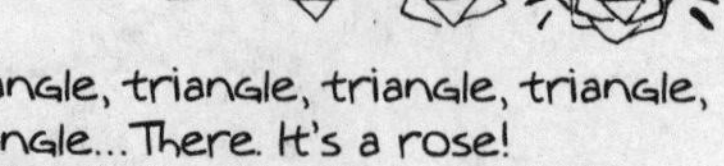

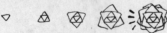

Triangle, triangle, triangle, triangle, triangle... There. It's a rose!

Q : Oda Sensei, you're very mischievous, aren't you? You like to draw things like Panda Man a lot. Then let me have a little fun too. The Question Corner is over! Nyah!

A : It...It ended. See you in the next volume.

Chapter 225:
PEOPLE'S DREAMS

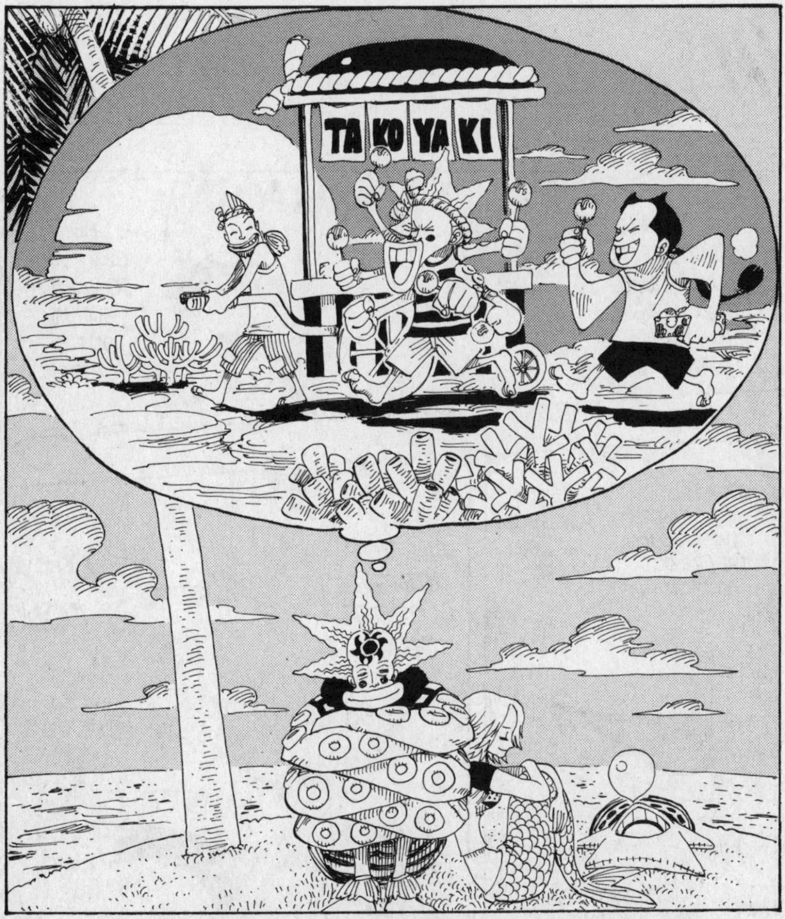
TA KO YA KI

HACHI'S WALK ON THE SEAFLOOR, VOL. 38:
"SUNSET DREAMING—REMEMBERING A CHILDHOOD DREAM TO HAVE AN OCTOPUS FRITTER CART"

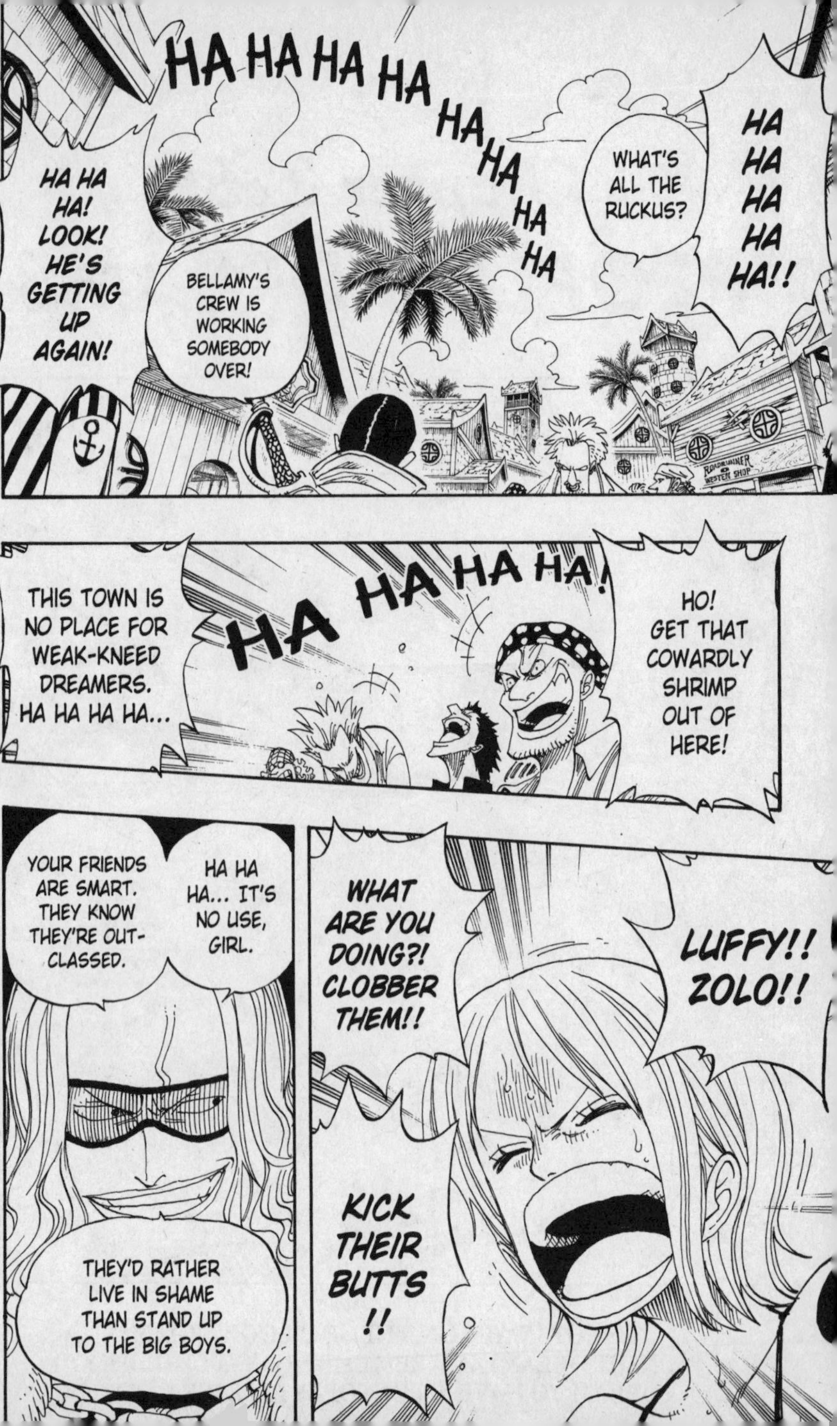
HA HA HA HA HA!!
WHAT'S ALL THE RUCKUS?
HA HA HA HA HA HA HA HA HA
BELLAMY'S CREW IS WORKING SOMEBODY OVER!
HA HA HA! LOOK! HE'S GETTING UP AGAIN!
HO! GET THAT COWARDLY SHRIMP OUT OF HERE!
HA HA HA HA HA!
THIS TOWN IS NO PLACE FOR WEAK-KNEED DREAMERS. HA HA HA HA...
LUFFY!! ZOLO!!
WHAT ARE YOU DOING?! CLOBBER THEM!!
KICK THEIR BUTTS !!
HA HA HA... IT'S NO USE, GIRL.
YOUR FRIENDS ARE SMART. THEY KNOW THEY'RE OUT-CLASSED.
THEY'D RATHER LIVE IN SHAME THAN STAND UP TO THE BIG BOYS.

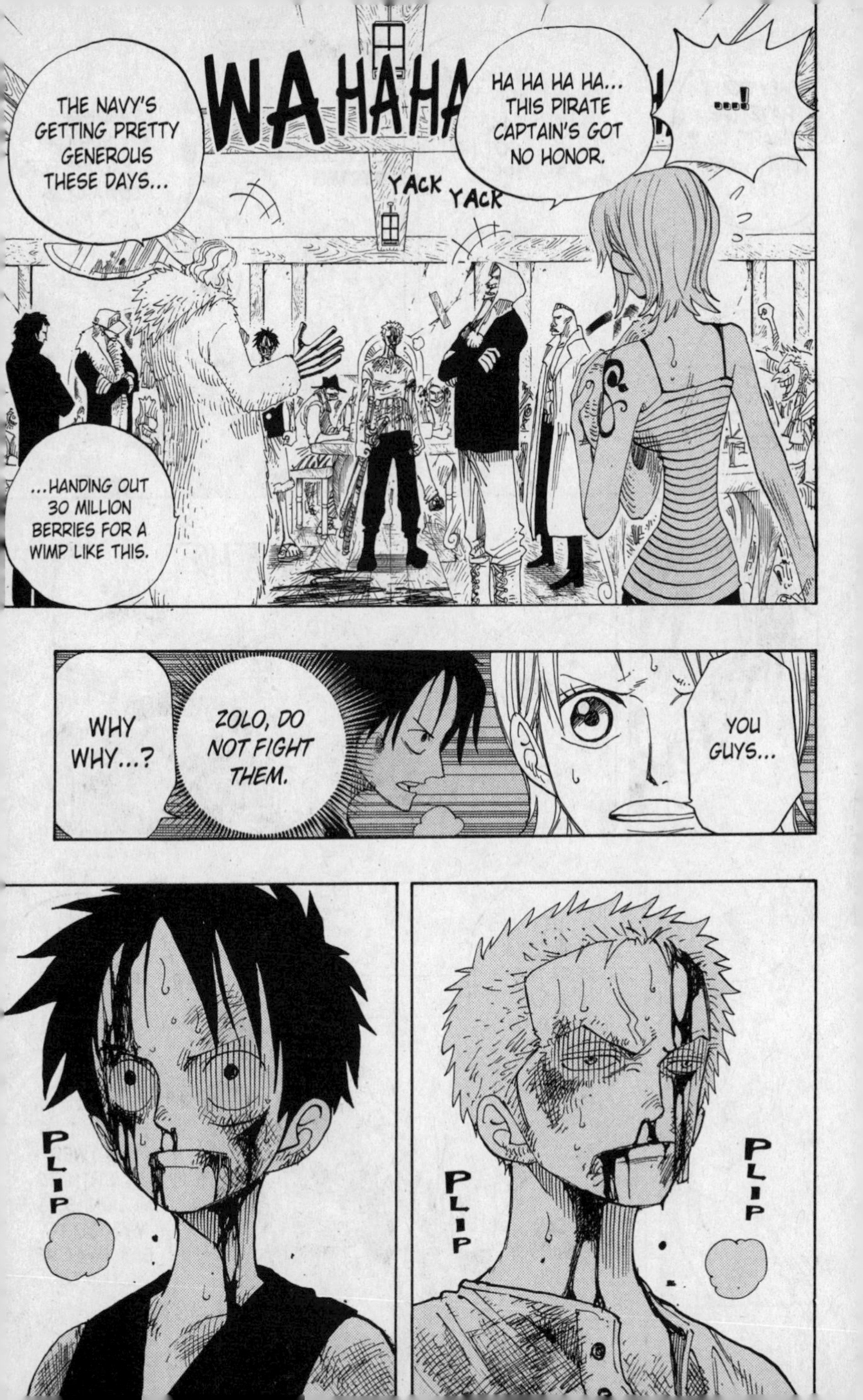
...!
HA HA HA HA... THIS PIRATE CAPTAIN'S GOT NO HONOR.
WAHAHA
THE NAVY'S GETTING PRETTY GENEROUS THESE DAYS...
YACK YACK
...HANDING OUT 30 MILLION BERRIES FOR A WIMP LIKE THIS.
YOU GUYS...
ZOLO, DO NOT FIGHT THEM.
WHY WHY...?
PLIP
PLIP
PLIP

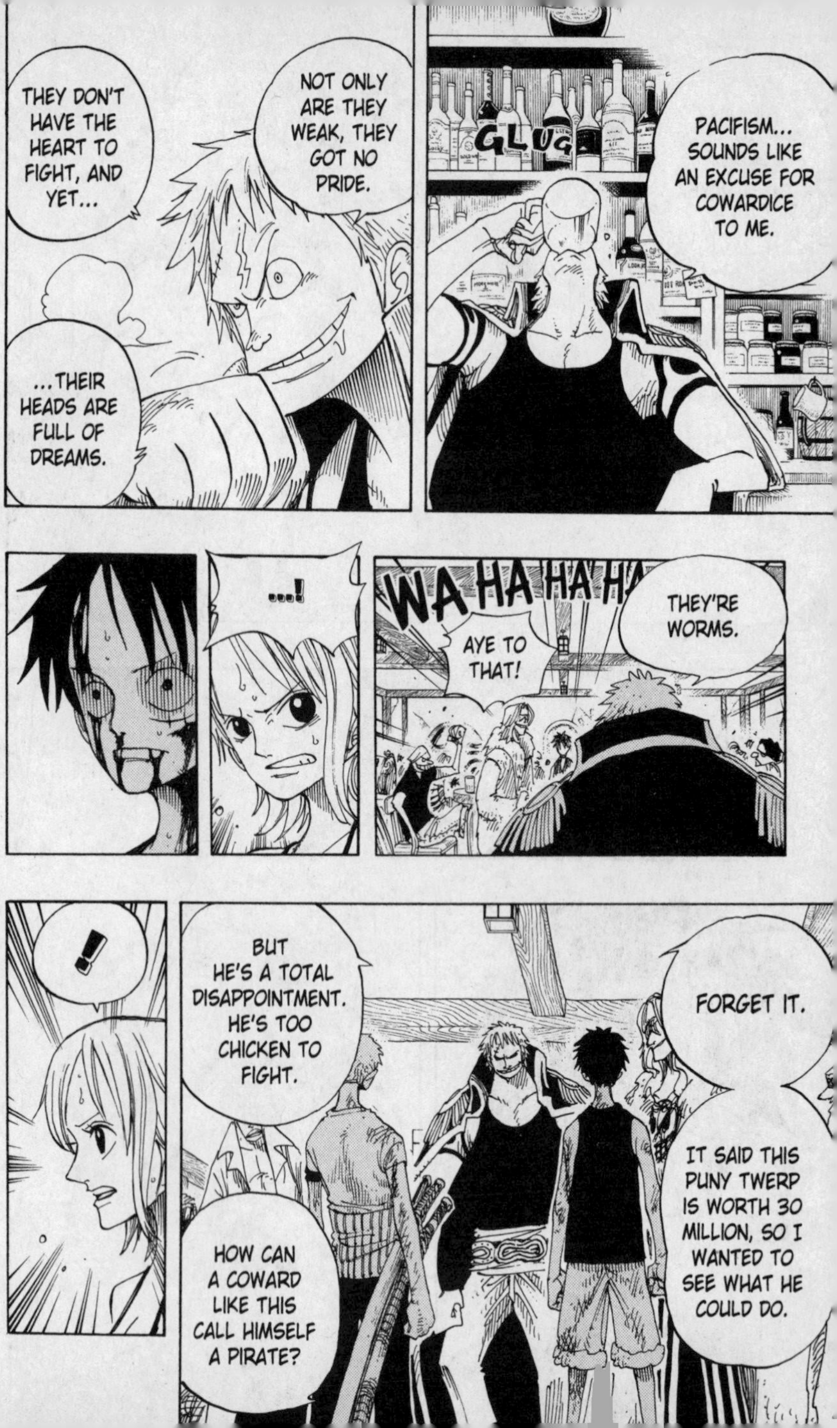
PACIFISM... SOUNDS LIKE AN EXCUSE FOR COWARDICE TO ME.
GLUG
NOT ONLY ARE THEY WEAK, THEY GOT NO PRIDE.
THEY DON'T HAVE THE HEART TO FIGHT, AND YET...
...THEIR HEADS ARE FULL OF DREAMS.
THEY'RE WORMS.
WA HA HA HA
AYE TO THAT!
...!
FORGET IT.
IT SAID THIS PUNY TWERP IS WORTH 30 MILLION, SO I WANTED TO SEE WHAT HE COULD DO.
BUT HE'S A TOTAL DISAPPOINTMENT. HE'S TOO CHICKEN TO FIGHT.
HOW CAN A COWARD LIKE THIS CALL HIMSELF A PIRATE?
!

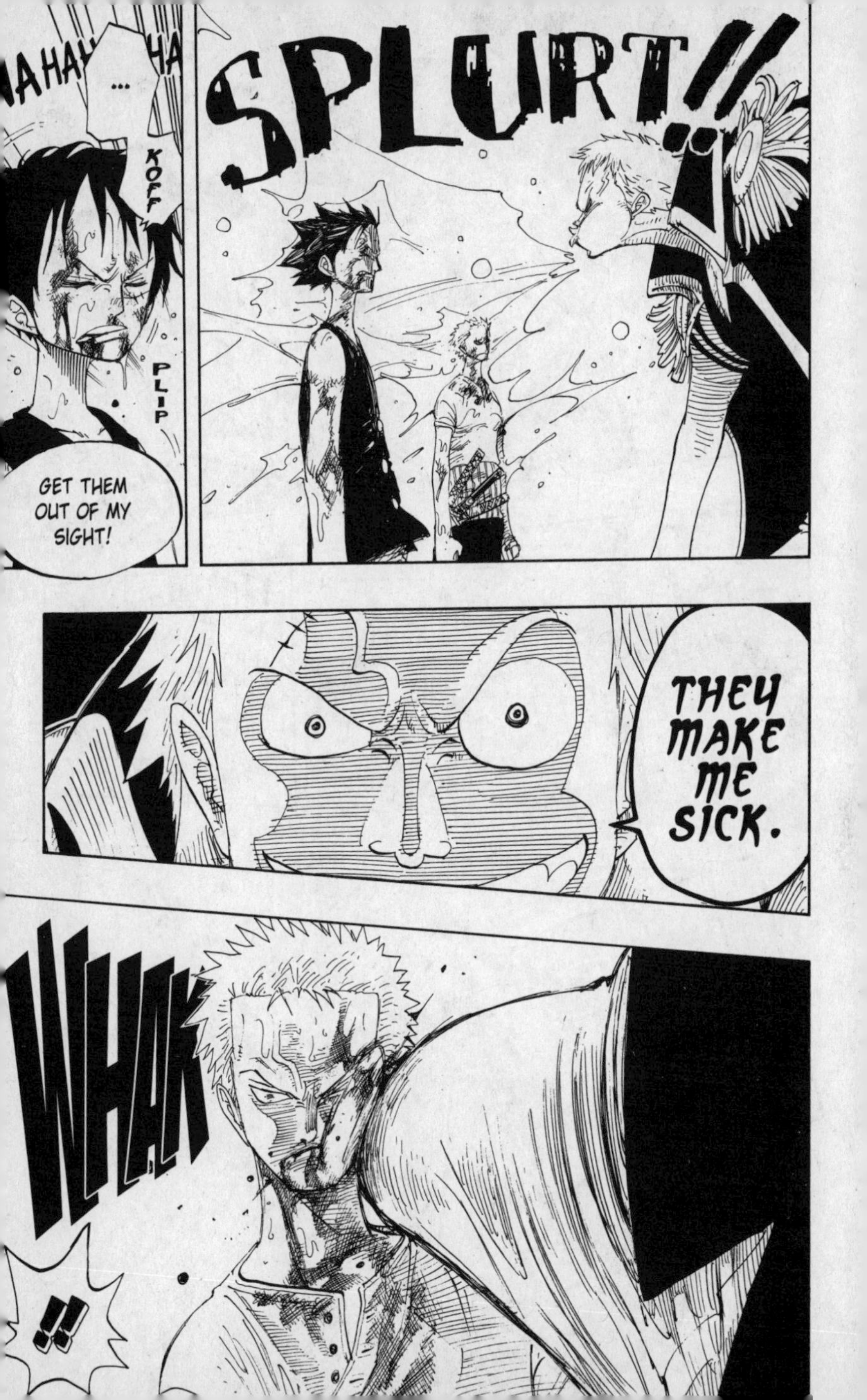
SPLURT!!
HAHAHA HA
...
KOFF
PLIP
GET THEM OUT OF MY SIGHT!
THEY MAKE ME SICK.
WHAK
!!

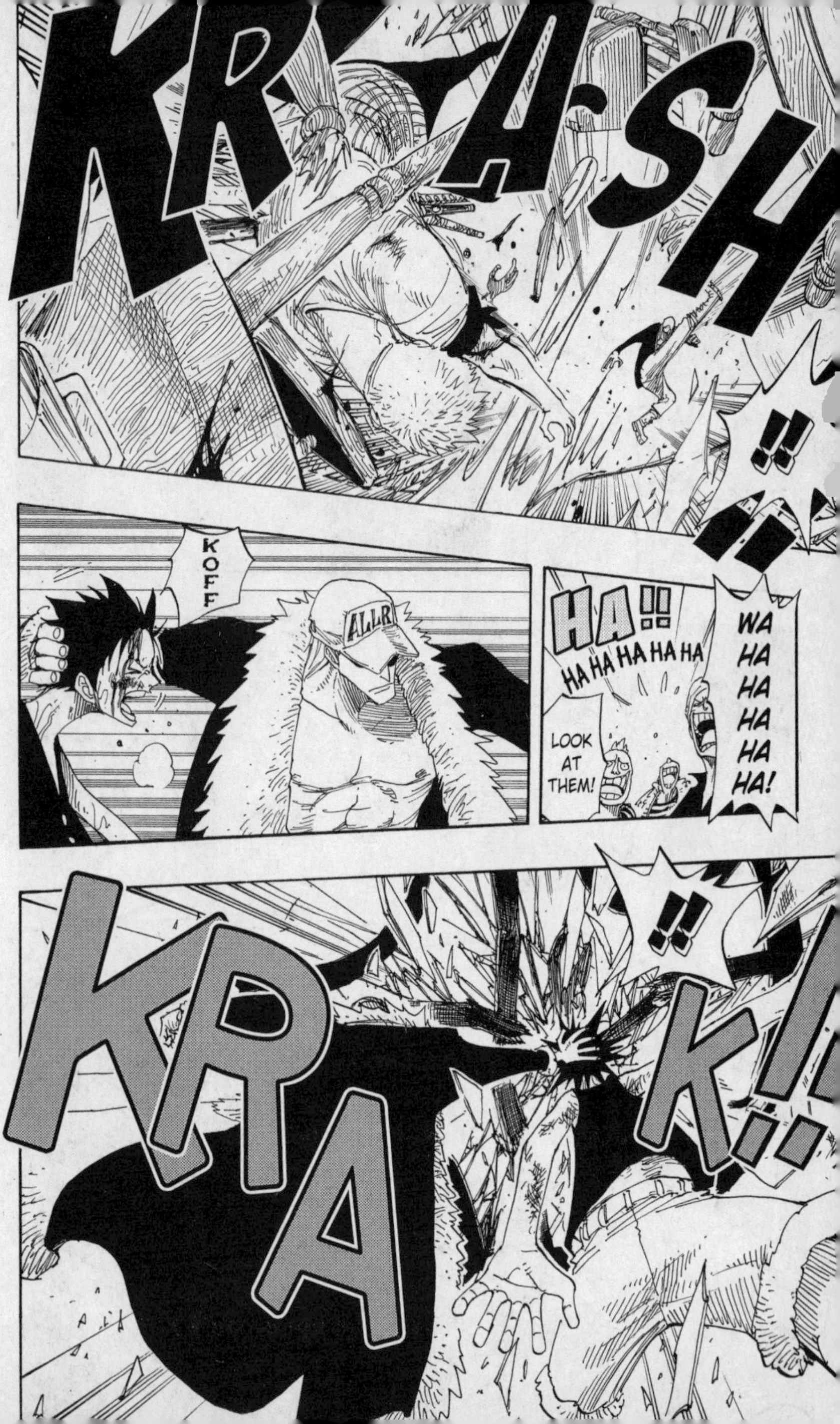
KRASH!!
!!
WA HA HA HA HA HA HA!
HA!! HA HA HA HA HA
LOOK AT THEM!
KOFF
!!
KRAKK!!

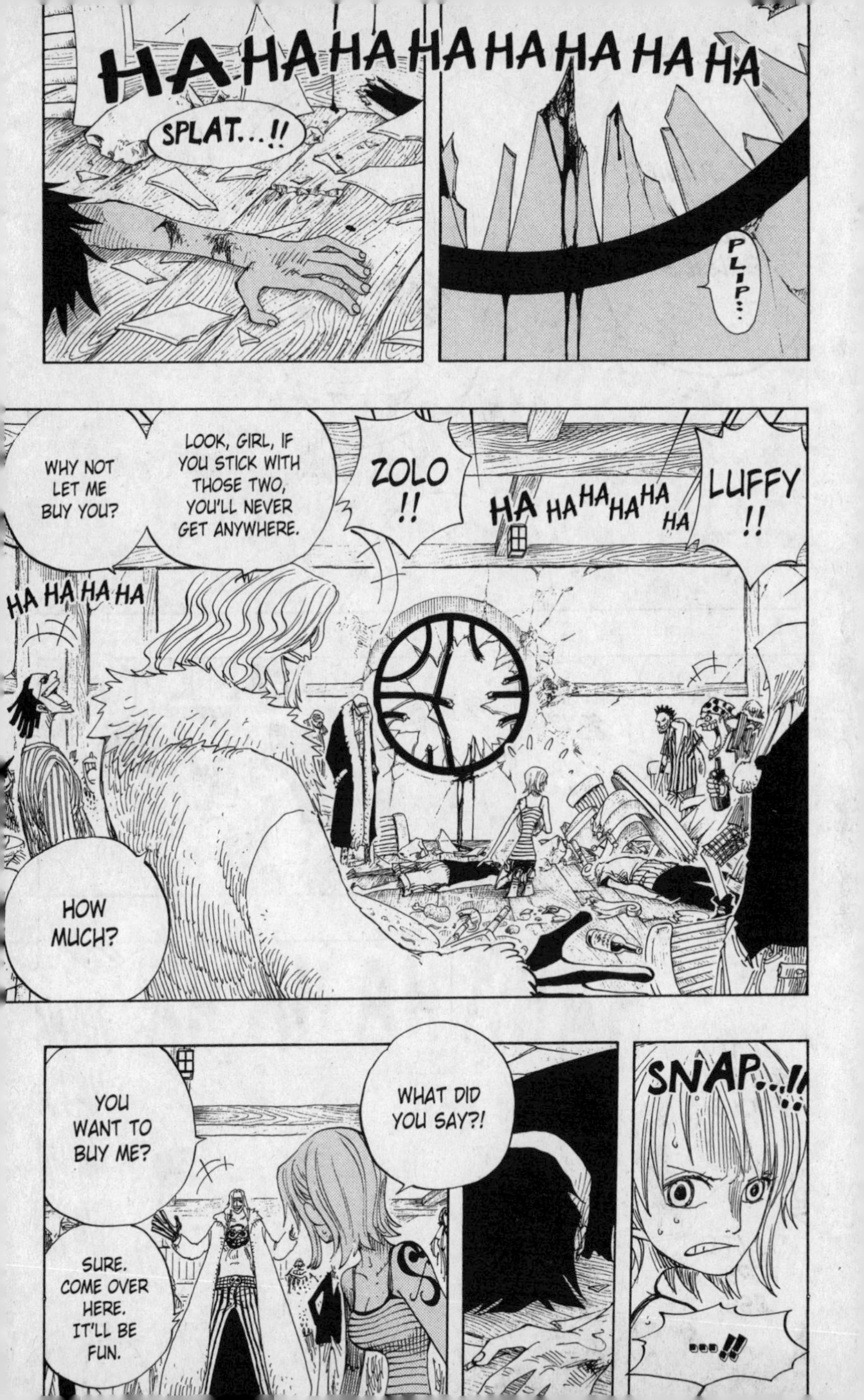
HA HA HA HA HA HA HA HA HA
PLIP...
SPLAT...!!
LUFFY!!
HA HA HA HA HA HA
ZOLO!!
LOOK, GIRL, IF YOU STICK WITH THOSE TWO, YOU'LL NEVER GET ANYWHERE.
WHY NOT LET ME BUY YOU?
HA HA HA HA
HOW MUCH?
SNAP...!!
...!!
WHAT DID YOU SAY?!
YOU WANT TO BUY ME?
SURE. COME OVER HERE. IT'LL BE FUN.

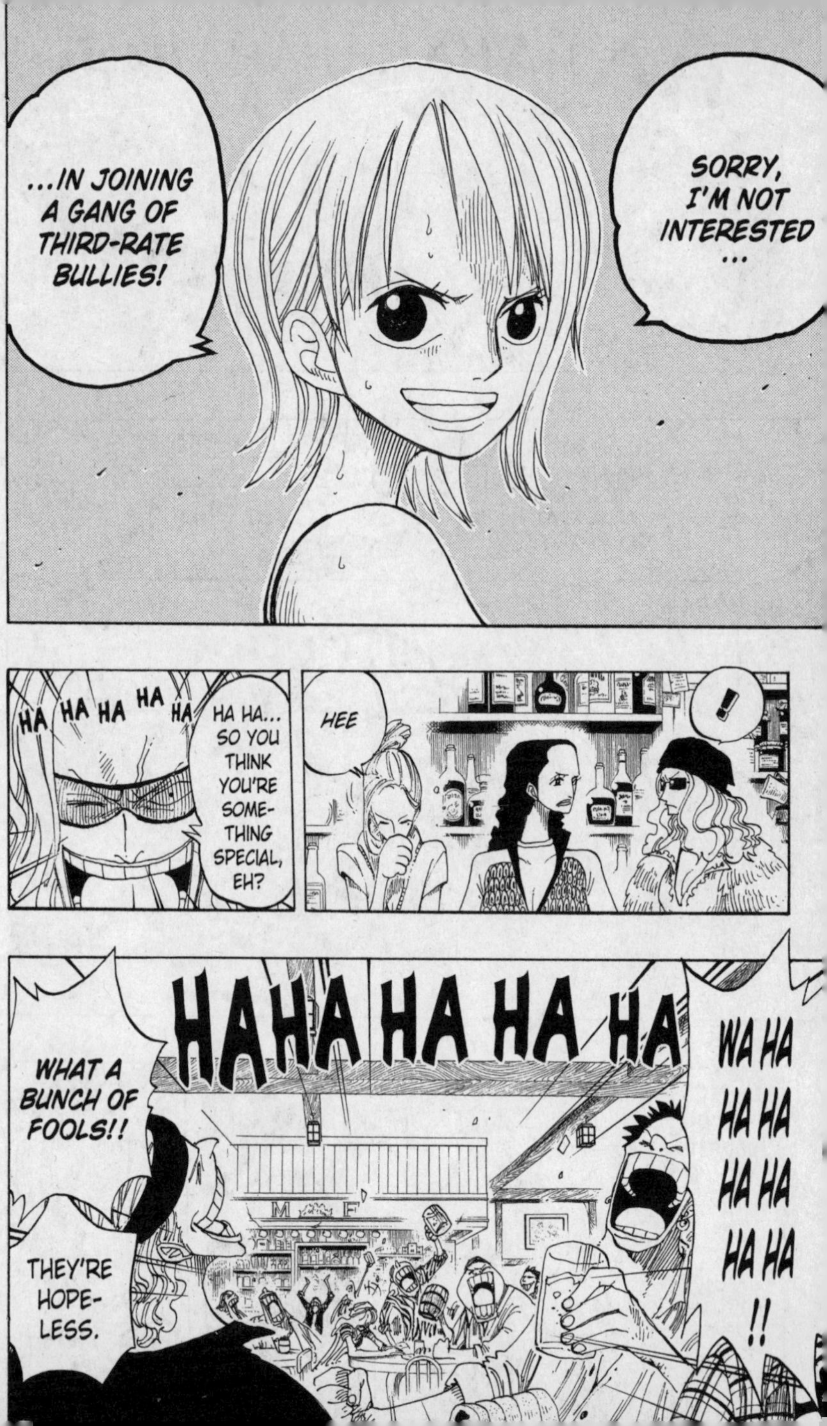
SORRY, I'M NOT INTERESTED ...
...IN JOINING A GANG OF THIRD-RATE BULLIES!
!
HEE
HA HA... SO YOU THINK YOU'RE SOME-THING SPECIAL, EH?
HA HA HA HA HA HA
WA HA HA HA HA HA HA HA !!
HAHAHA HA HA HA
WHAT A BUNCH OF FOOLS!!
THEY'RE HOPE-LESS.

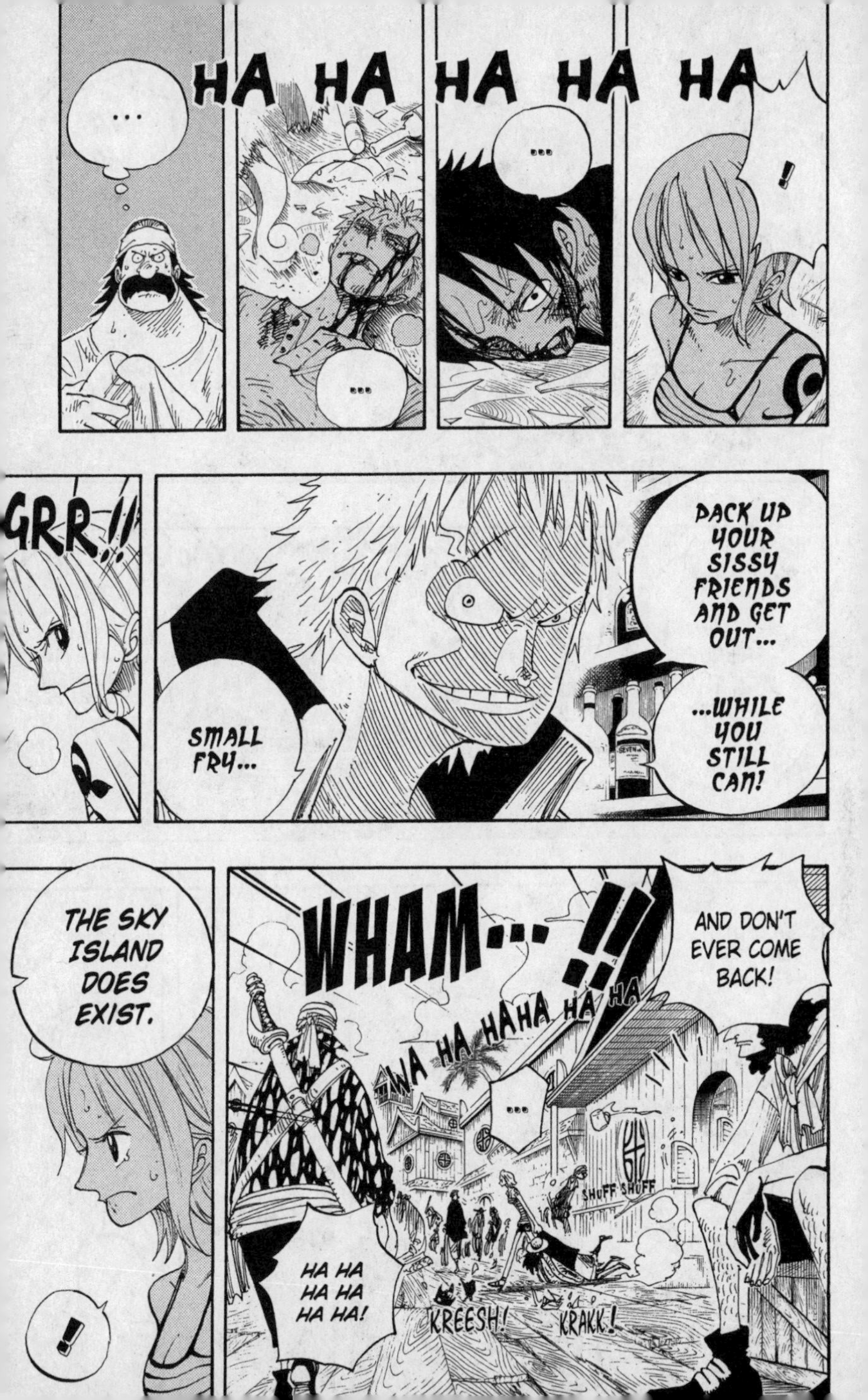
HA HA HA HA HA
!
...
...
...
...
PACK UP YOUR SISSY FRIENDS AND GET OUT...
...WHILE YOU STILL CAN!
SMALL FRY...
GRR!!
AND DON'T EVER COME BACK!
WHAM...!!
HA HA HAHA HA HA
...
SHUFF SHUFF
HA HA HA HA HA HA!
KREESH!
KRAKK!
THE SKY ISLAND DOES EXIST.
!

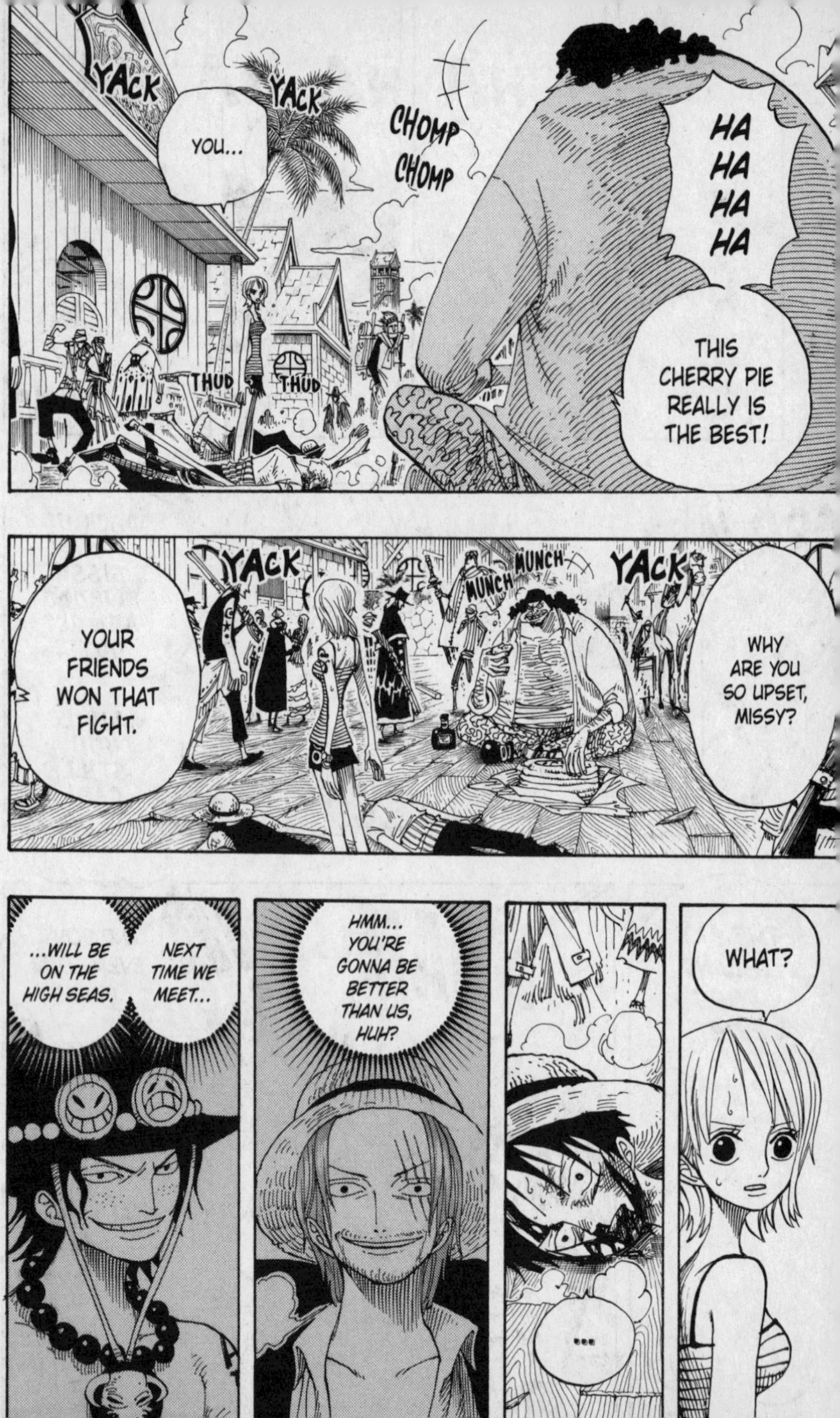
HA HA HA HA
THIS CHERRY PIE REALLY IS THE BEST!
CHOMP CHOMP
YACK
YOU...
YACK
THUD
THUD
WHY ARE YOU SO UPSET, MISSY?
YACK
MUNCH MUNCH
YACK
YOUR FRIENDS WON THAT FIGHT.
WHAT?
...
HMM... YOU'RE GONNA BE BETTER THAN US, HUH?
NEXT TIME WE MEET...
...WILL BE ON THE HIGH SEAS.

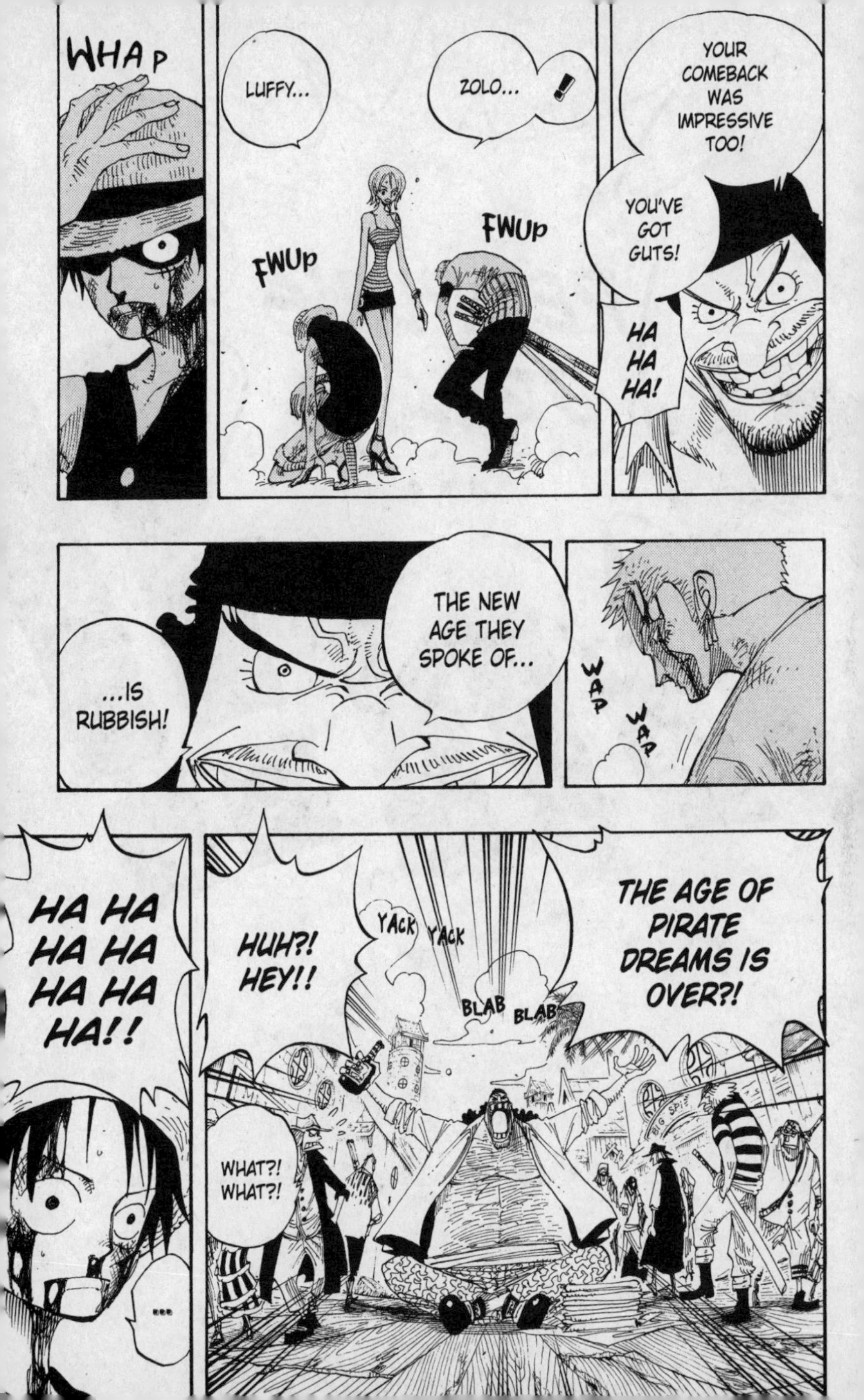
YOUR COMEBACK WAS IMPRESSIVE TOO!
YOU'VE GOT GUTS!
HA HA HA!
ZOLO...
!
FWUP
LUFFY...
FWUP
WHAP
WAP
WAP
THE NEW AGE THEY SPOKE OF...
...IS RUBBISH!
THE AGE OF PIRATE DREAMS IS OVER?!
YACK YACK
BLAB BLAB
HUH?! HEY!!
WHAT?! WHAT?!
HA HA HA HA HA HA HA!!
...

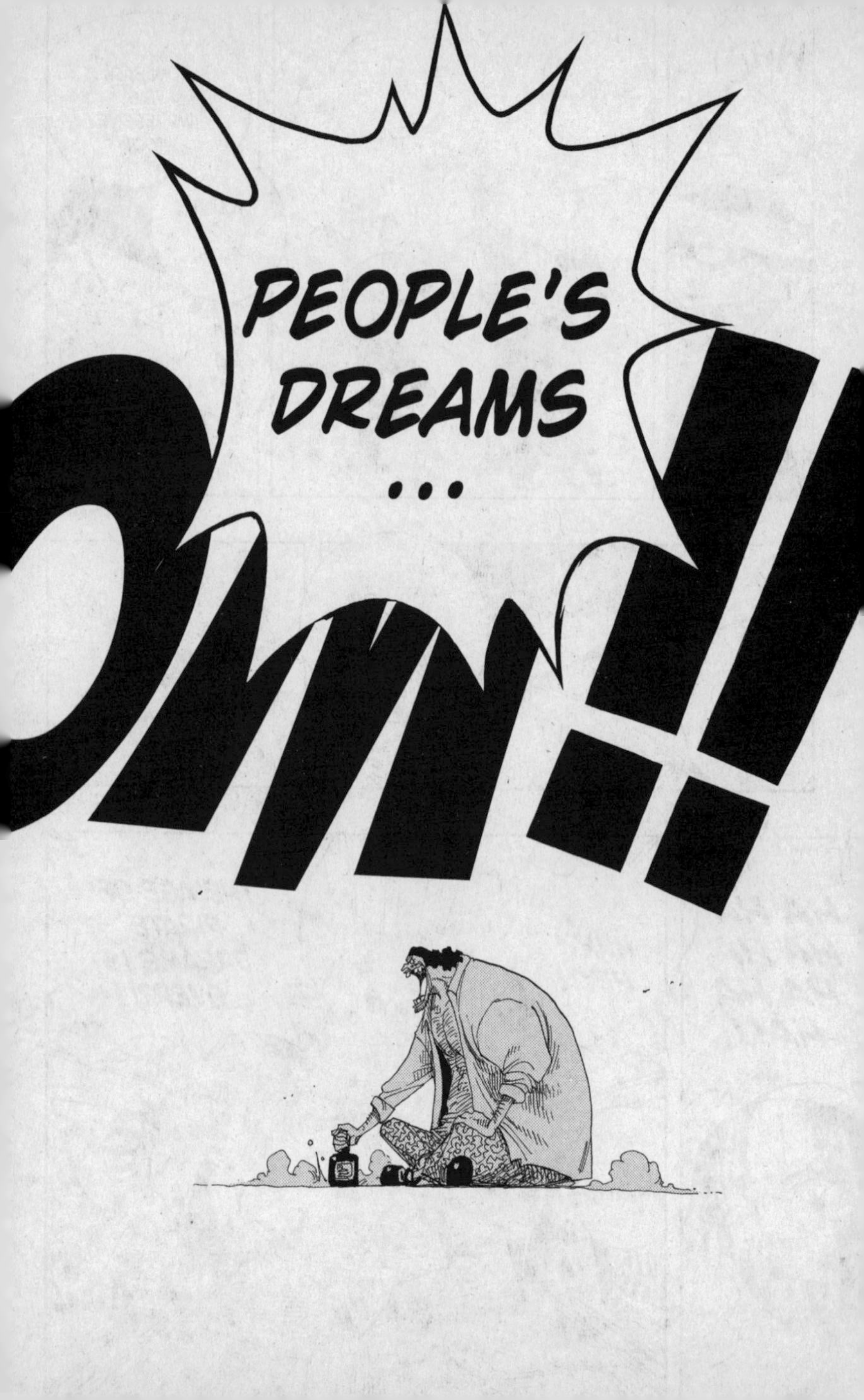
PEOPLE'S DREAMS ...

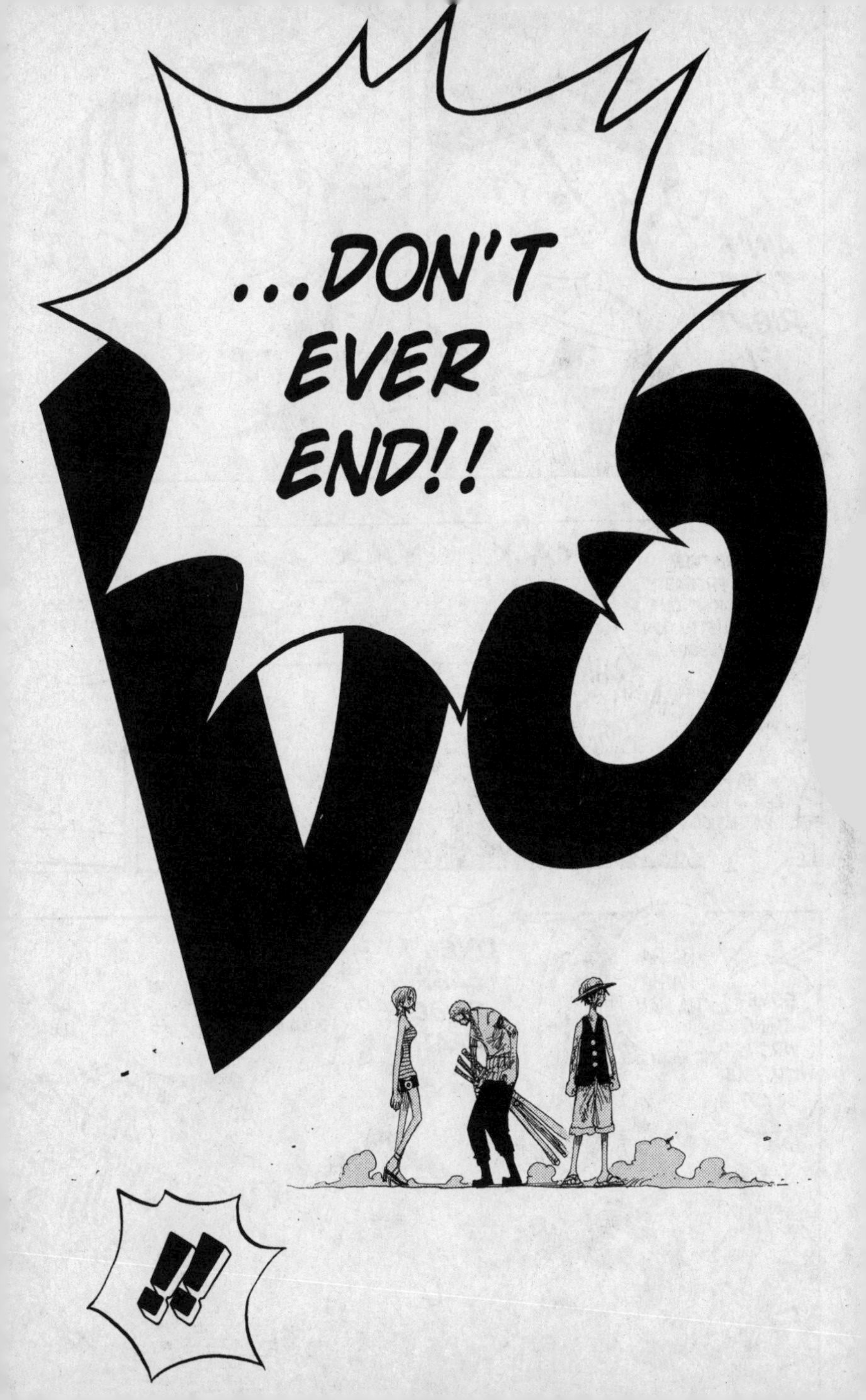

...DON'T EVER END!!
!!

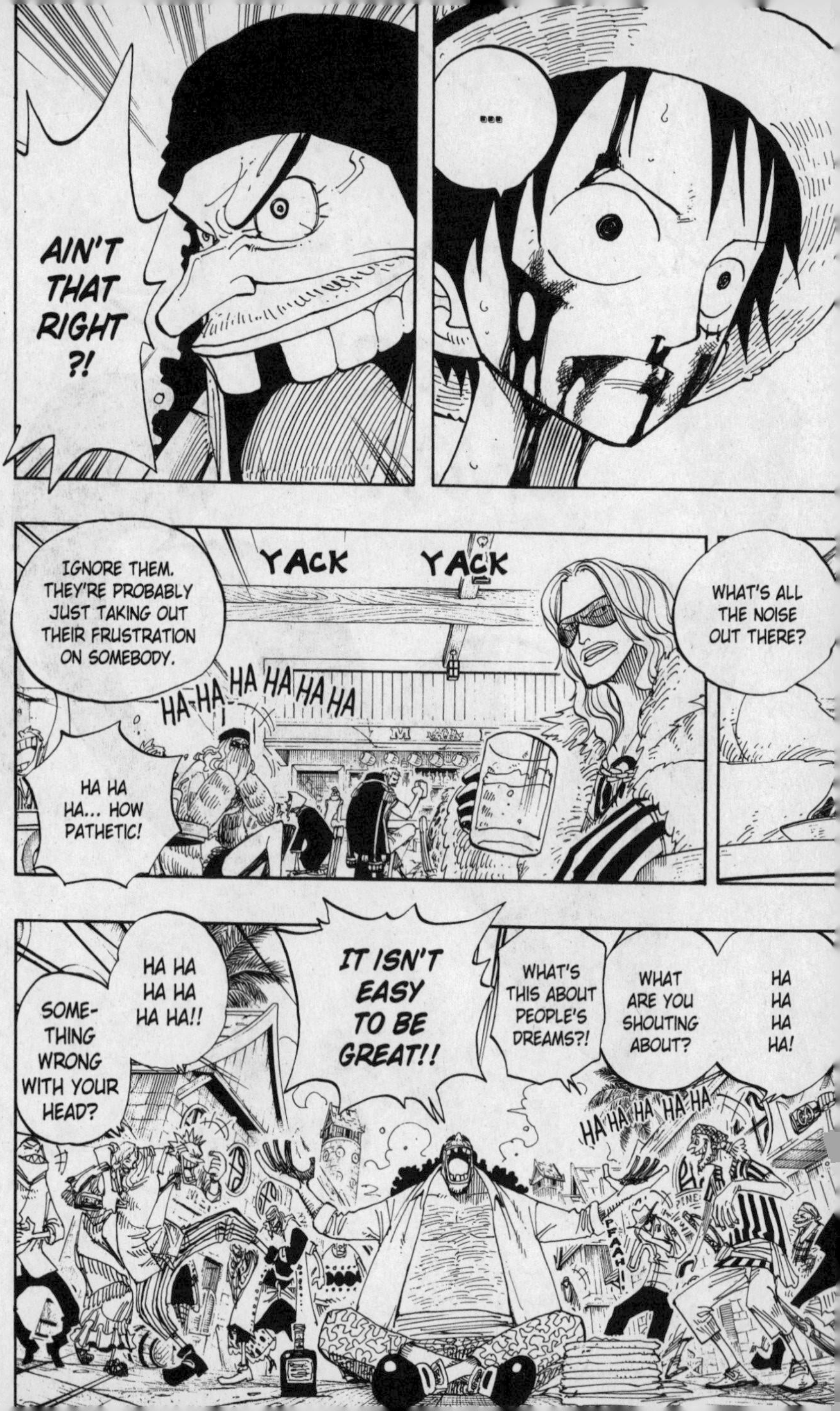
...
AIN'T THAT RIGHT?!
WHAT'S ALL THE NOISE OUT THERE?
YACK YACK
IGNORE THEM. THEY'RE PROBABLY JUST TAKING OUT THEIR FRUSTRATION ON SOMEBODY.
HA-HA HA HA HA HA
HA HA HA... HOW PATHETIC!
HA HA HA HA!
WHAT ARE YOU SHOUTING ABOUT?
WHAT'S THIS ABOUT PEOPLE'S DREAMS?!
IT ISN'T EASY TO BE GREAT!!
HA HA HA HA HA HA!!
SOME-THING WRONG WITH YOUR HEAD?
HA HA HA HA HA HA
PFAAH!

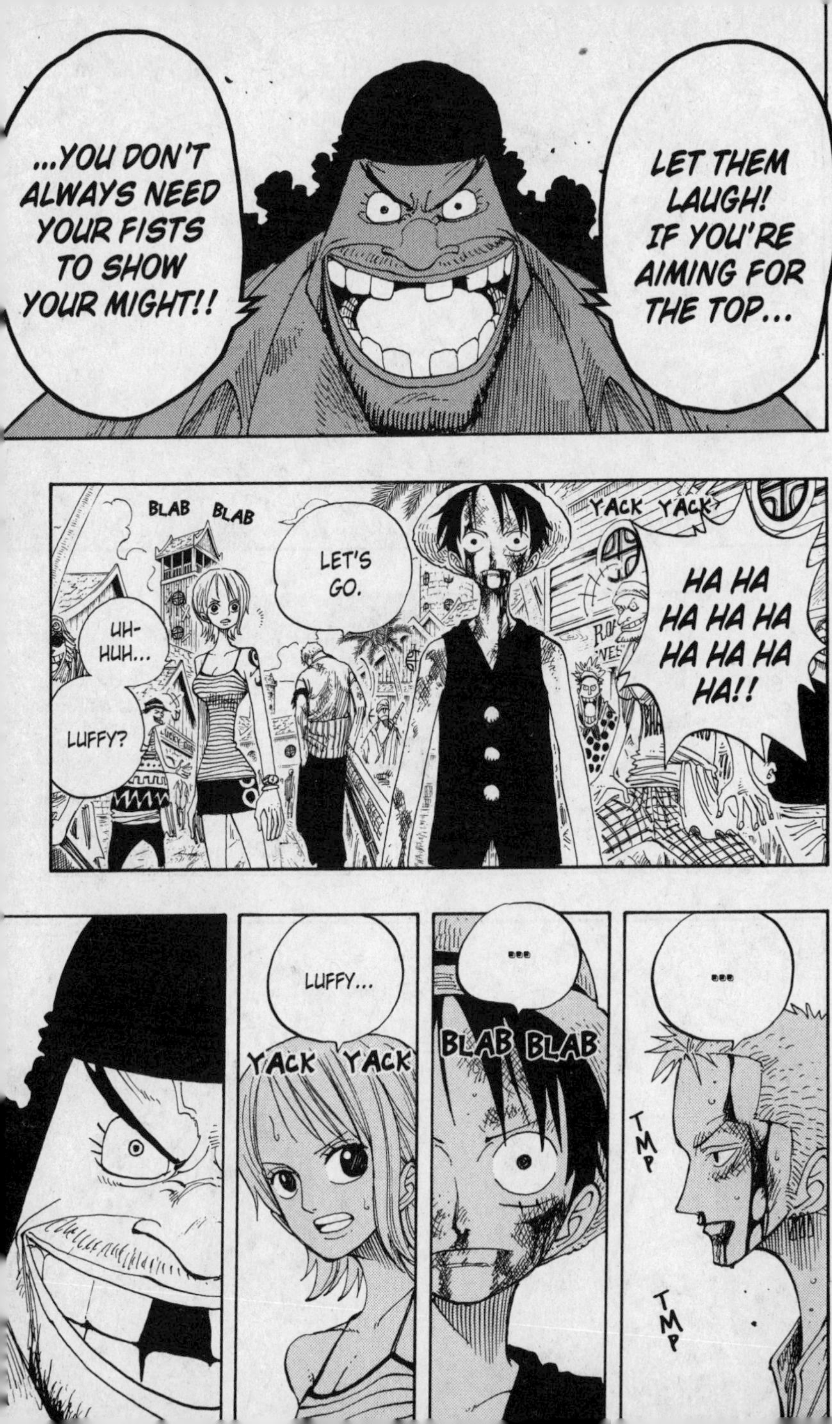
LET THEM LAUGH! IF YOU'RE AIMING FOR THE TOP...
...YOU DON'T ALWAYS NEED YOUR FISTS TO SHOW YOUR MIGHT!!
YACK YACK
HA HA HA HA HA HA HA HA HA!!
LET'S GO.
BLAB BLAB
UH-HUH...
LUFFY?
...
TMP
TMP
...
BLAB BLAB
LUFFY...
YACK YACK

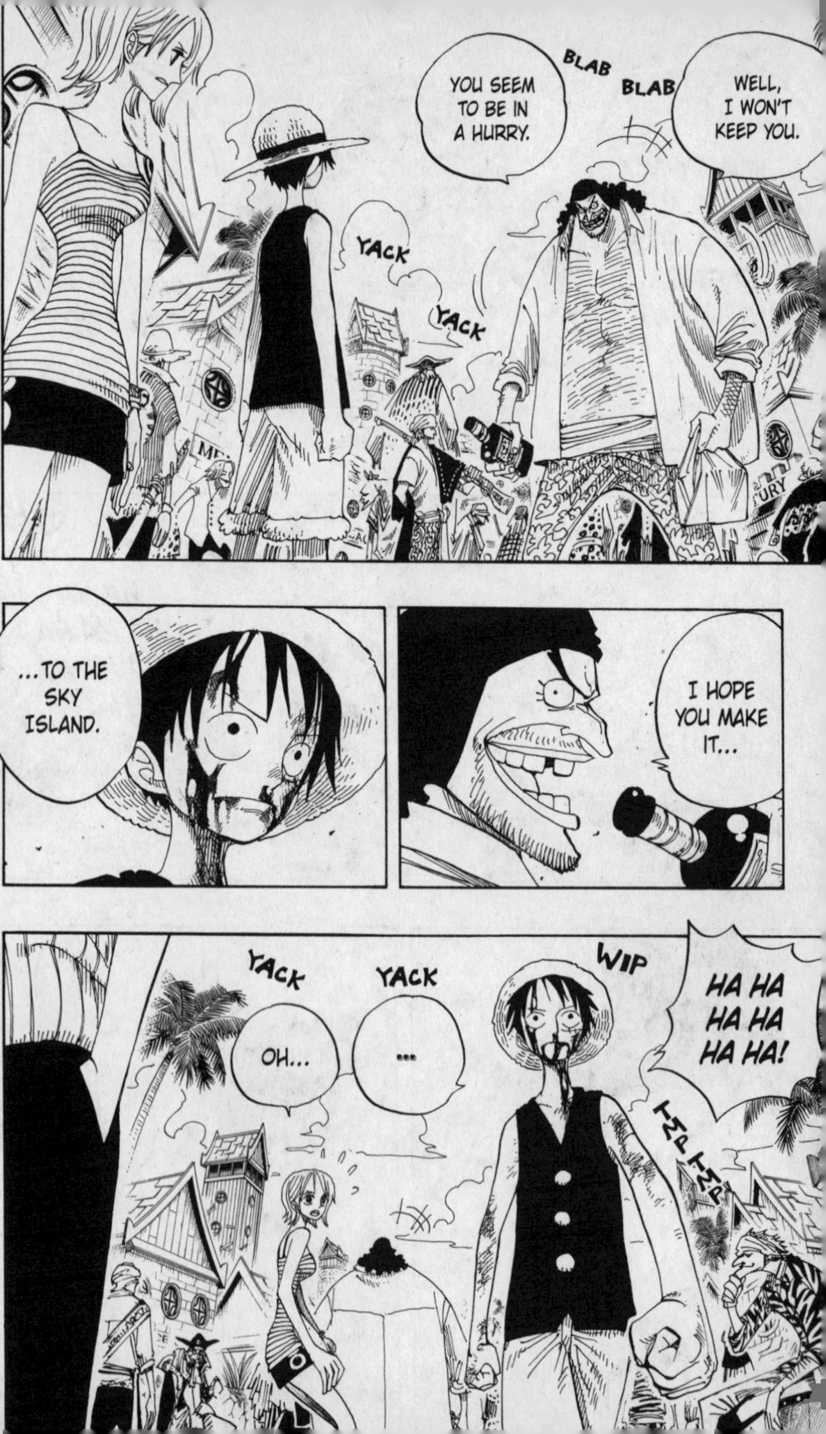
WELL, I WON'T KEEP YOU.
BLAB BLAB
YOU SEEM TO BE IN A HURRY.
YACK
YACK
I HOPE YOU MAKE IT...
...TO THE SKY ISLAND.
HA HA HA HA HA HA!
WIP
TMP TMP
YACK
YACK
...
OH...

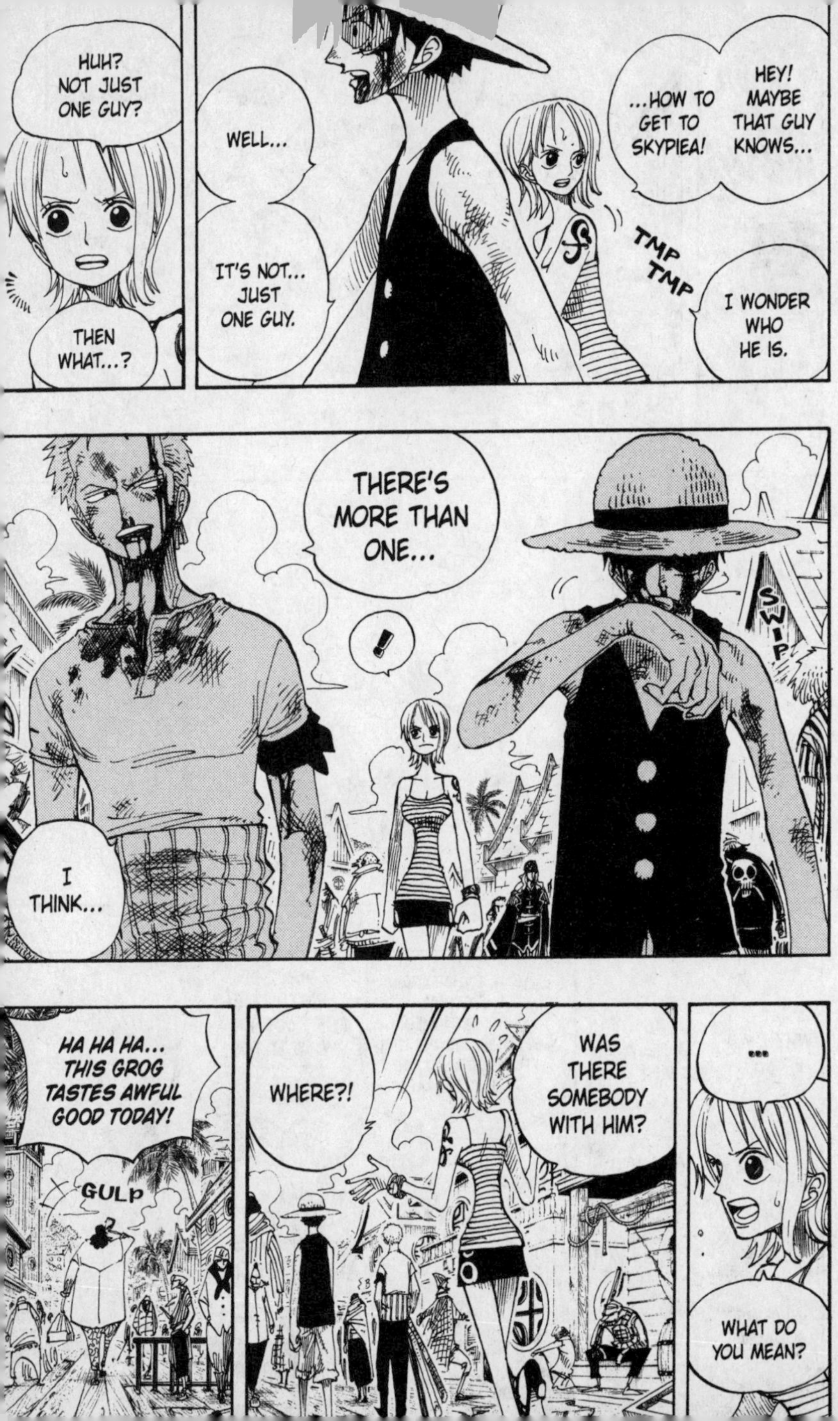
HEY! MAYBE THAT GUY KNOWS...
...HOW TO GET TO SKYPIEA!
TMP TMP
I WONDER WHO HE IS.
WELL...
IT'S NOT... JUST ONE GUY.
HUH? NOT JUST ONE GUY?
THEN WHAT...?
SWIP
THERE'S MORE THAN ONE...
!
I THINK...
...
WHAT DO YOU MEAN?
WAS THERE SOMEBODY WITH HIM?
WHERE?!
HA HA HA... THIS GROG TASTES AWFUL GOOD TODAY!
GULP

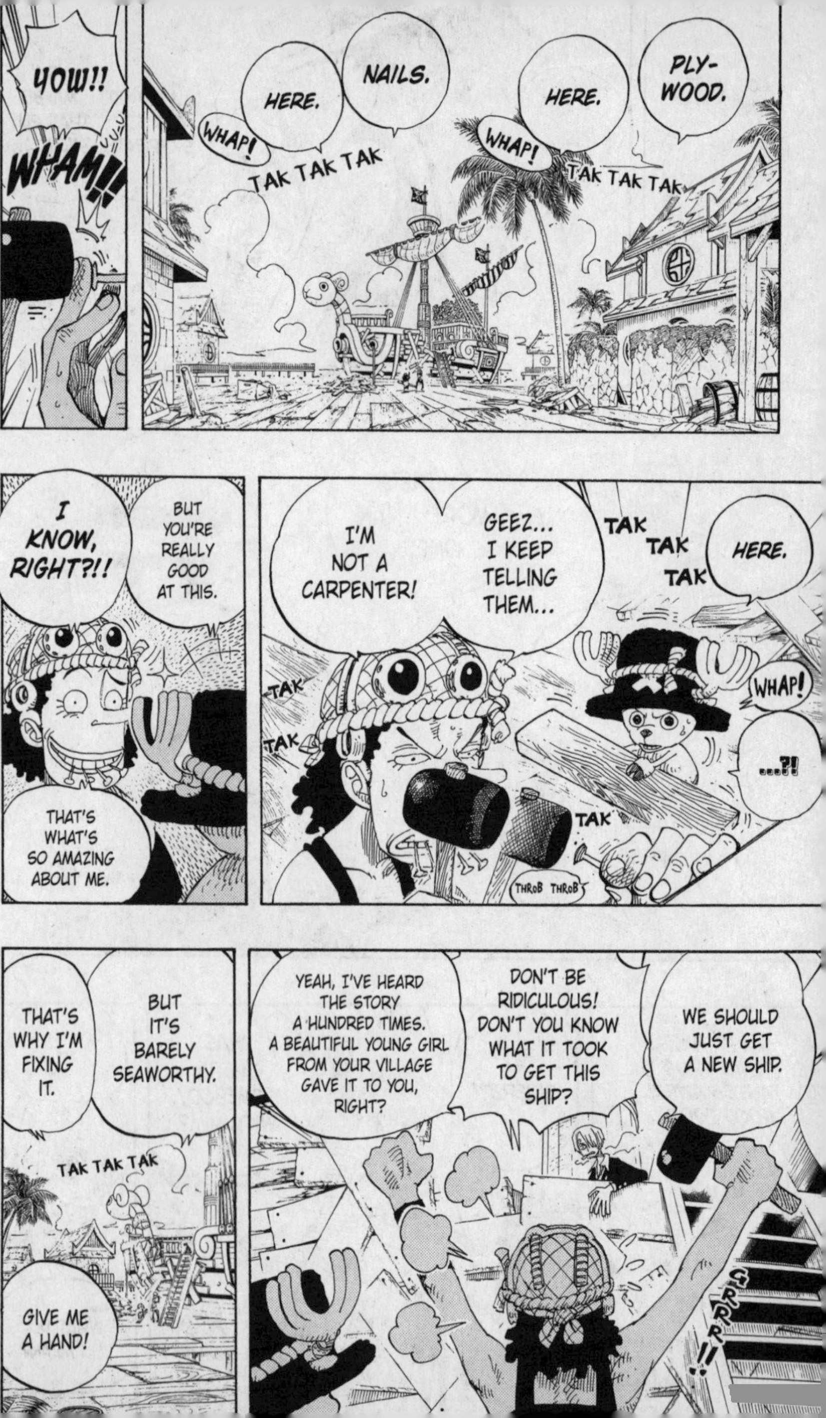
PLY-WOOD.
HERE.
WHAP!
TAK TAK TAK
NAILS.
HERE.
WHAP!
TAK TAK TAK
YOW!!
WHAM!!
HERE.
TAK
TAK
TAK
GEEZ... I KEEP TELLING THEM...
I'M NOT A CARPENTER!
WHAP!
...?!
TAK
TAK
TAK
THROB THROB
BUT YOU'RE REALLY GOOD AT THIS.
I KNOW, RIGHT?!!
THAT'S WHAT'S SO AMAZING ABOUT ME.
WE SHOULD JUST GET A NEW SHIP.
DON'T BE RIDICULOUS! DON'T YOU KNOW WHAT IT TOOK TO GET THIS SHIP?
YEAH, I'VE HEARD THE STORY A HUNDRED TIMES. A BEAUTIFUL YOUNG GIRL FROM YOUR VILLAGE GAVE IT TO YOU, RIGHT?
GRRR!!
BUT IT'S BARELY SEAWORTHY.
THAT'S WHY I'M FIXING IT.
TAK TAK TAK
GIVE ME A HAND!

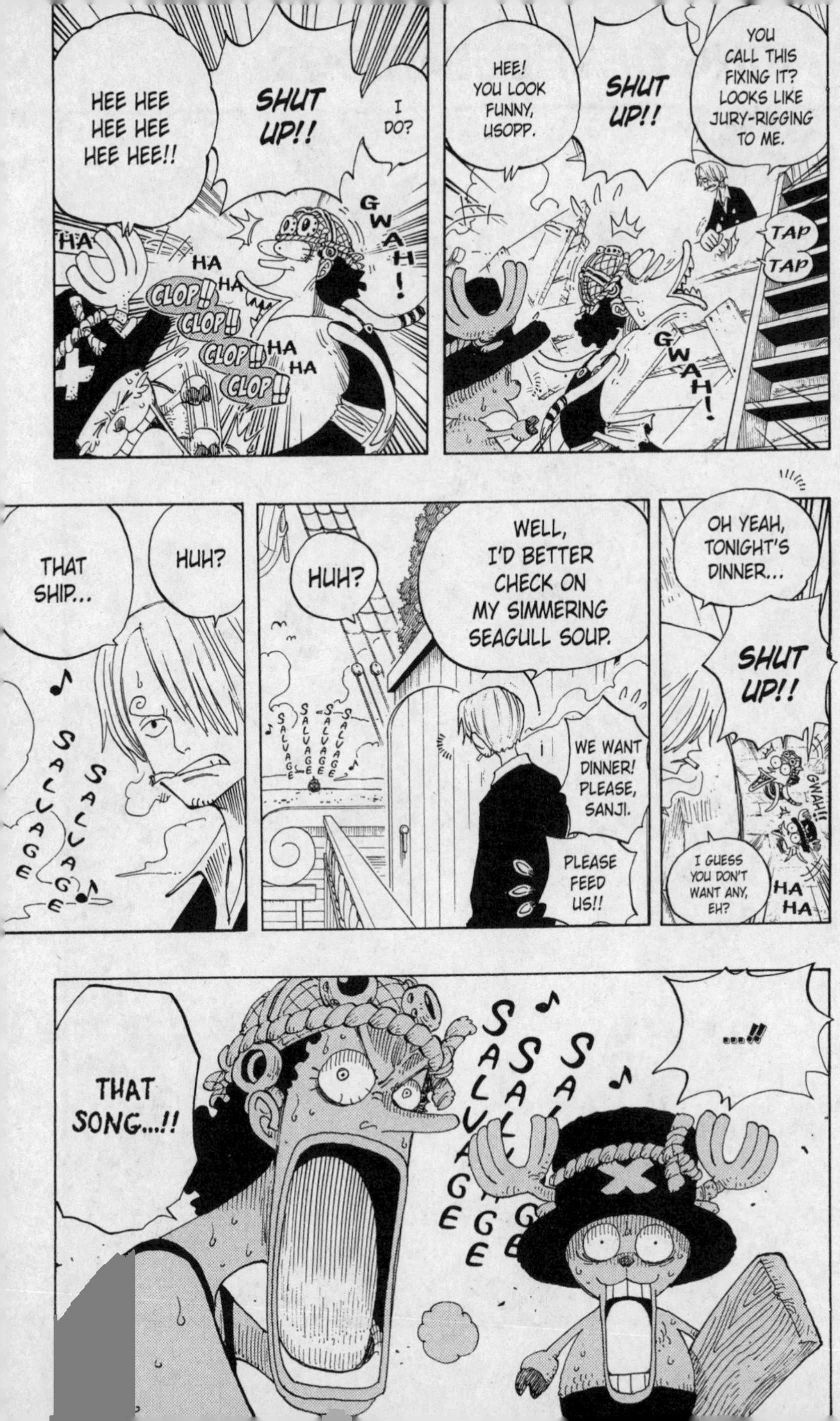
YOU CALL THIS FIXING IT? LOOKS LIKE JURY-RIGGING TO ME.
SHUT UP!!
HEE! YOU LOOK FUNNY, USOPP.
TAP
TAP
GWAH!
I DO?
SHUT UP!!
HEE HEE HEE HEE HEE HEE!!
GWAH!
HA
HA
HA
CLOP!! CLOP!! CLOP!! CLOP!!
HA
HA
OH YEAH, TONIGHT'S DINNER...
SHUT UP!!
GWAH!!
I GUESS YOU DON'T WANT ANY, EH?
HA HA
WELL, I'D BETTER CHECK ON MY SIMMERING SEAGULL SOUP.
WE WANT DINNER! PLEASE, SANJI.
PLEASE FEED US!!
HUH?
SALVAGE SALVAGE SALVAGE SALVAGE
HUH?
THAT SHIP...
SALVAGE SALVAGE
...!!
SALVAGE SALVAGE SALVAGE
THAT SONG...!!

KING OF THE SEAFLOOR

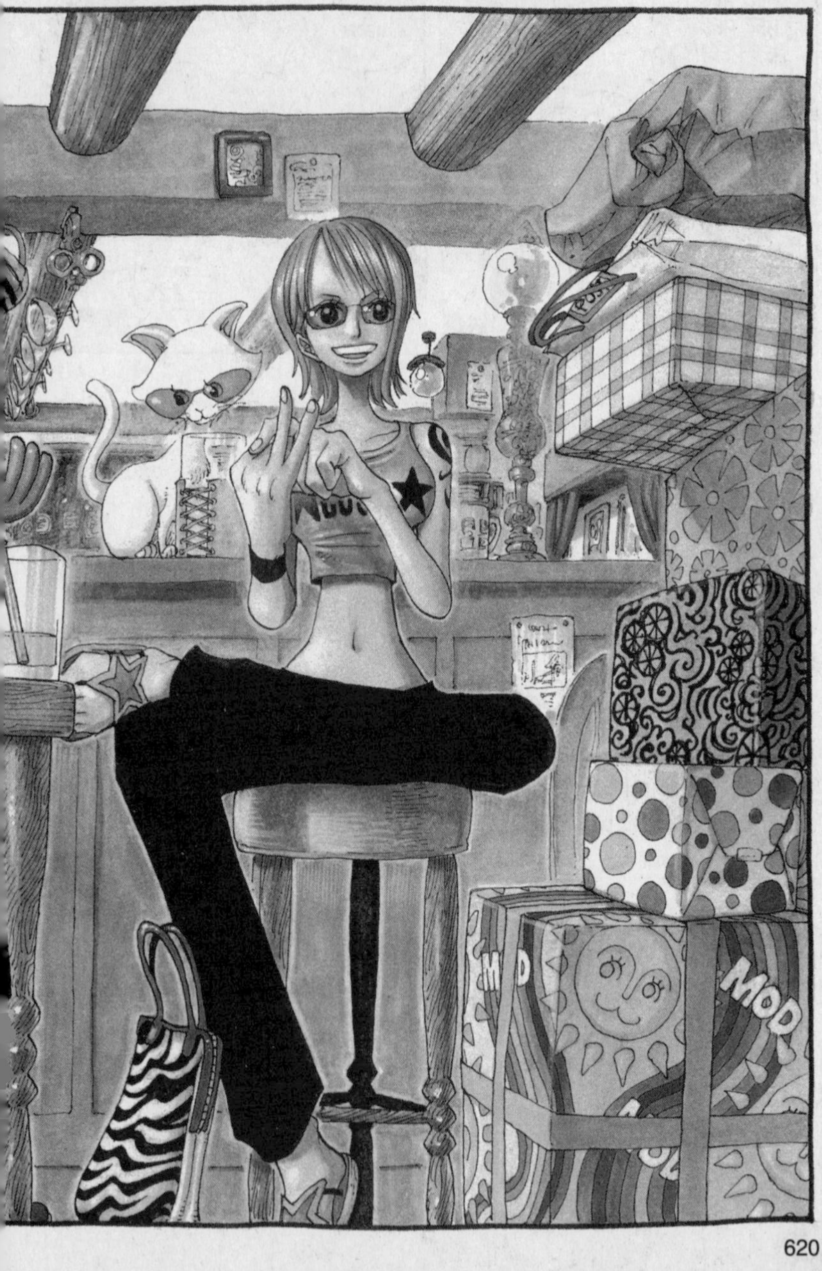
MOD
MOD

Chapter 226: SHOUJOU, THE SALVAGE

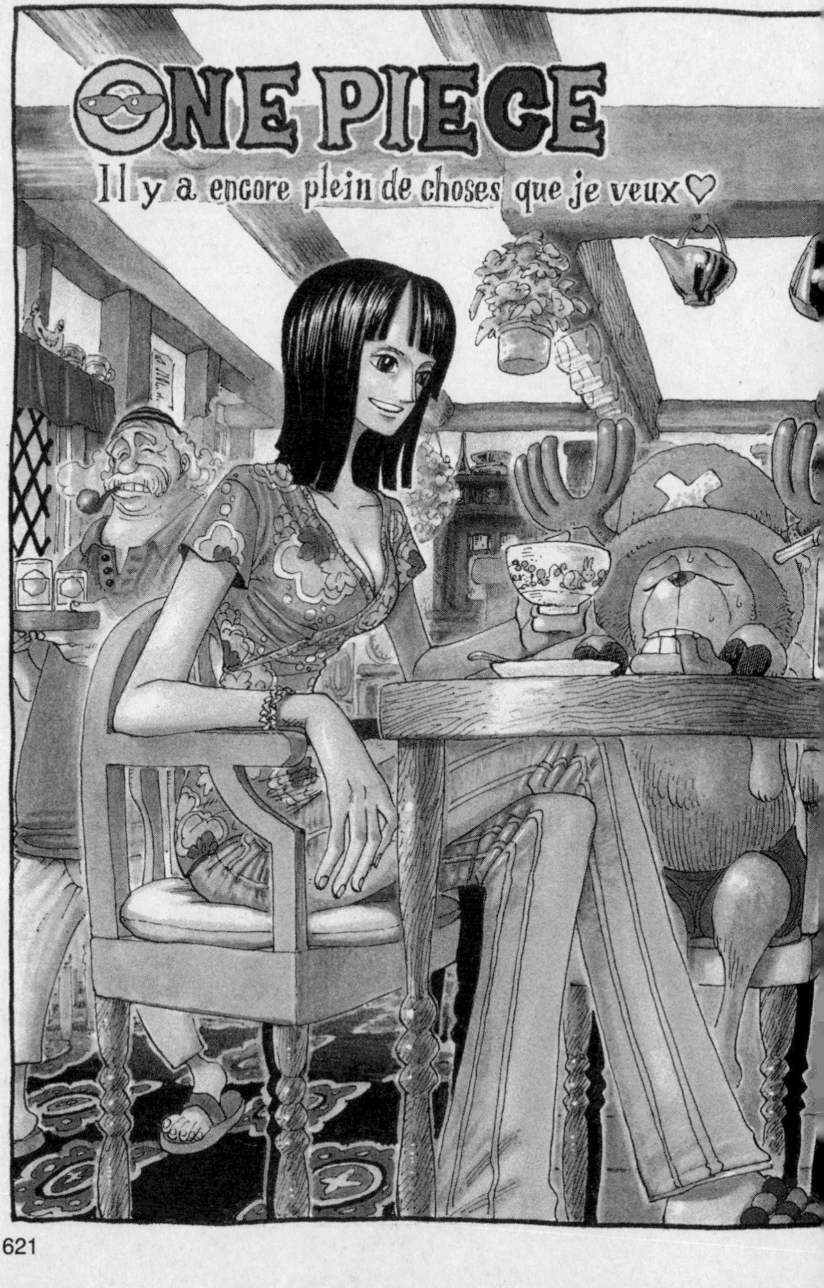
ONE PIECE
Il y a encore plein de choses que je veux♡

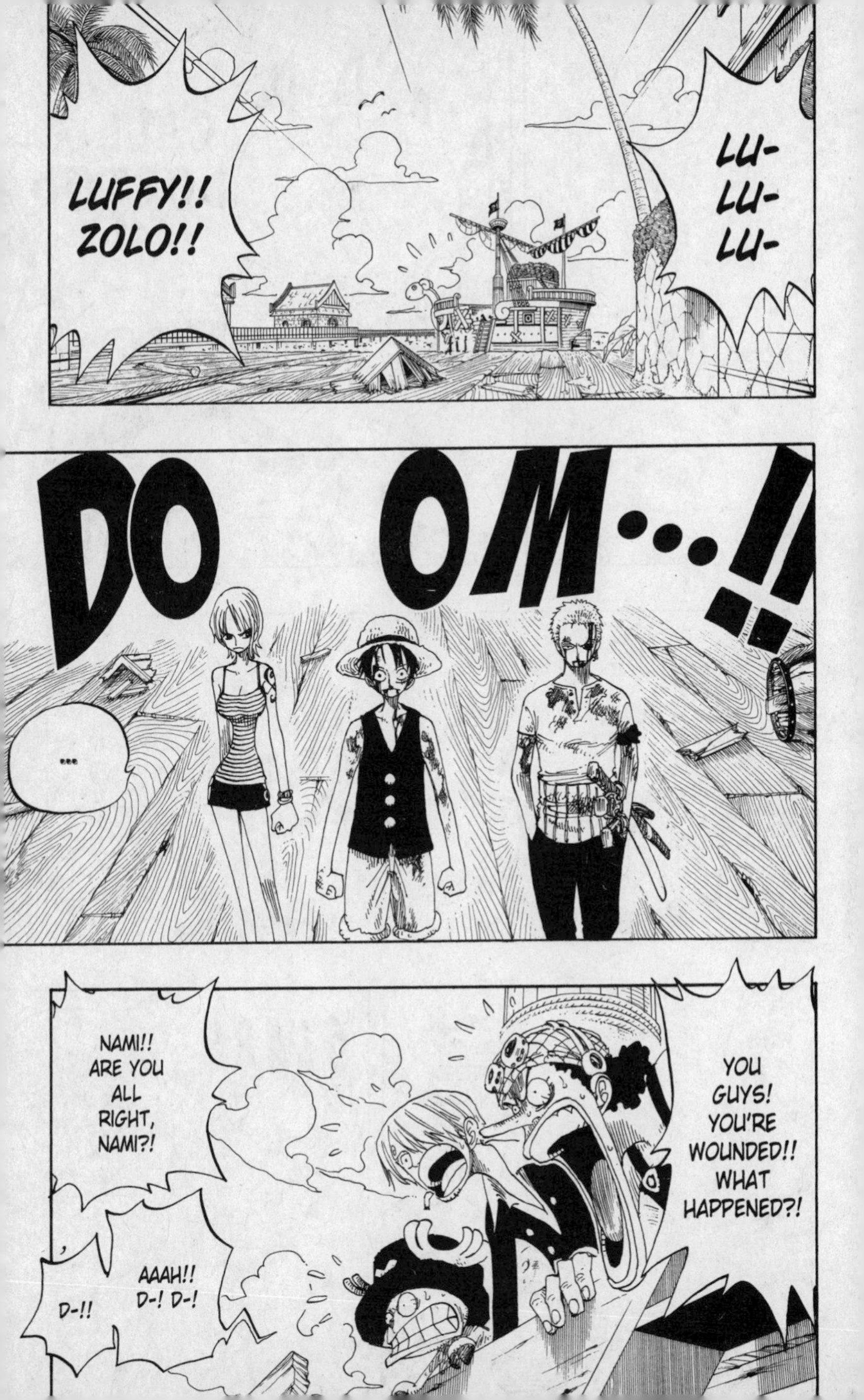
LU- LU- LU-
LUFFY!! ZOLO!!
DO OM...!!
...
YOU GUYS! YOU'RE WOUNDED!! WHAT HAPPENED?!
NAMI!! ARE YOU ALL RIGHT, NAMI?!
AAAH!! D-! D-!
D-!!

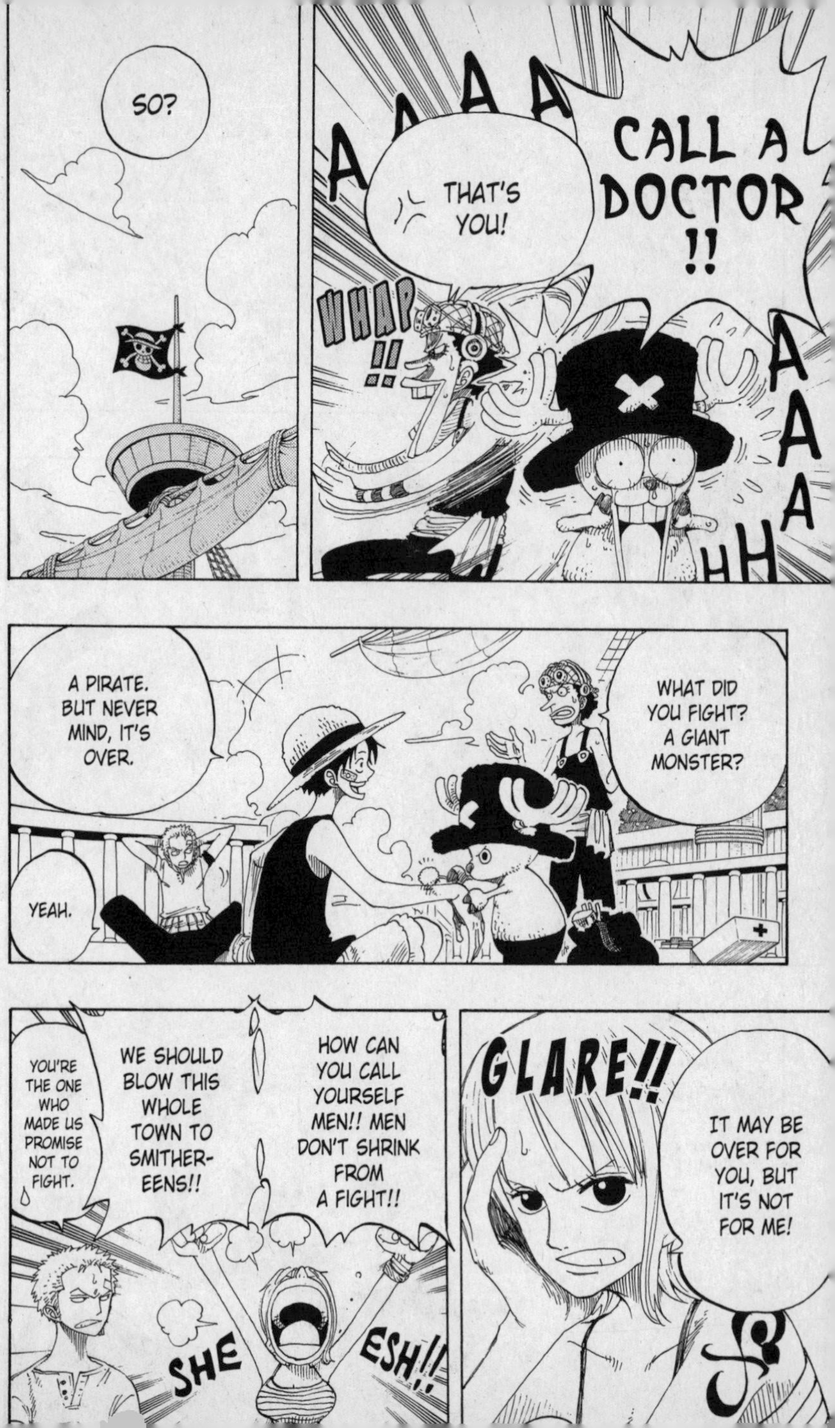
CALL A DOCTOR!!
AAAAAAAHH
THAT'S YOU!
WHAP!!
SO?
WHAT DID YOU FIGHT? A GIANT MONSTER?
A PIRATE. BUT NEVER MIND, IT'S OVER.
YEAH.
GLARE!!
IT MAY BE OVER FOR YOU, BUT IT'S NOT FOR ME!
HOW CAN YOU CALL YOURSELF MEN!! MEN DON'T SHRINK FROM A FIGHT!!
WE SHOULD BLOW THIS WHOLE TOWN TO SMITHEREENS!!
YOU'RE THE ONE WHO MADE US PROMISE NOT TO FIGHT.
SHEESH!!

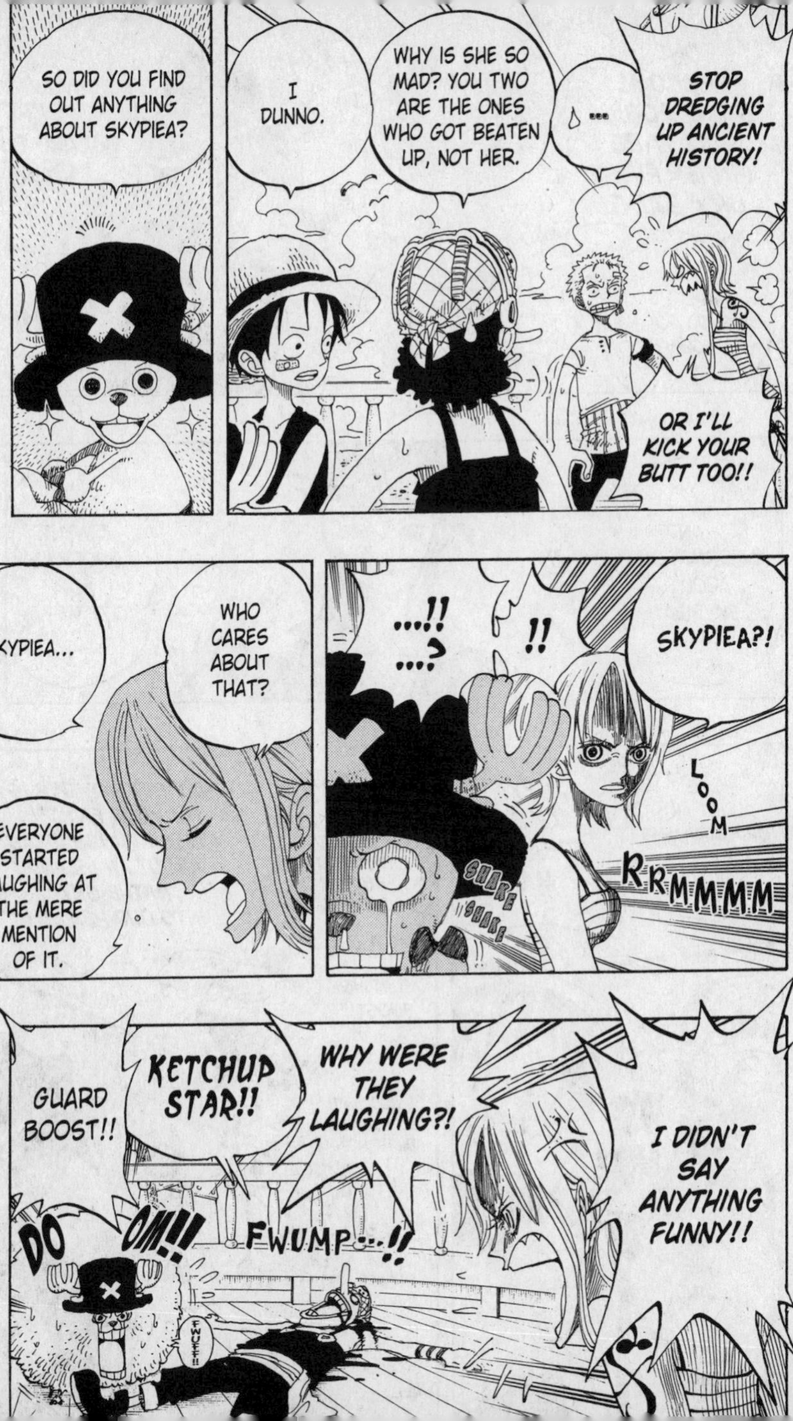
STOP DREDGING UP ANCIENT HISTORY!
...
OR I'LL KICK YOUR BUTT TOO!!
WHY IS SHE SO MAD? YOU TWO ARE THE ONES WHO GOT BEATEN UP, NOT HER.
I DUNNO.
SO DID YOU FIND OUT ANYTHING ABOUT SKYPIEA?
SKYPIEA?!
!!
...!!
...?
LOOM
RRMMMMM
SHAKE SHAKE
WHO CARES ABOUT THAT?
SKYPIEA...
EVERYONE STARTED LAUGHING AT THE MERE MENTION OF IT.
I DIDN'T SAY ANYTHING FUNNY!!
WHY WERE THEY LAUGHING?!
KETCHUP STAR!!
GUARD BOOST!!
DOOM!!
FWUMP...!!
FWUFF!!

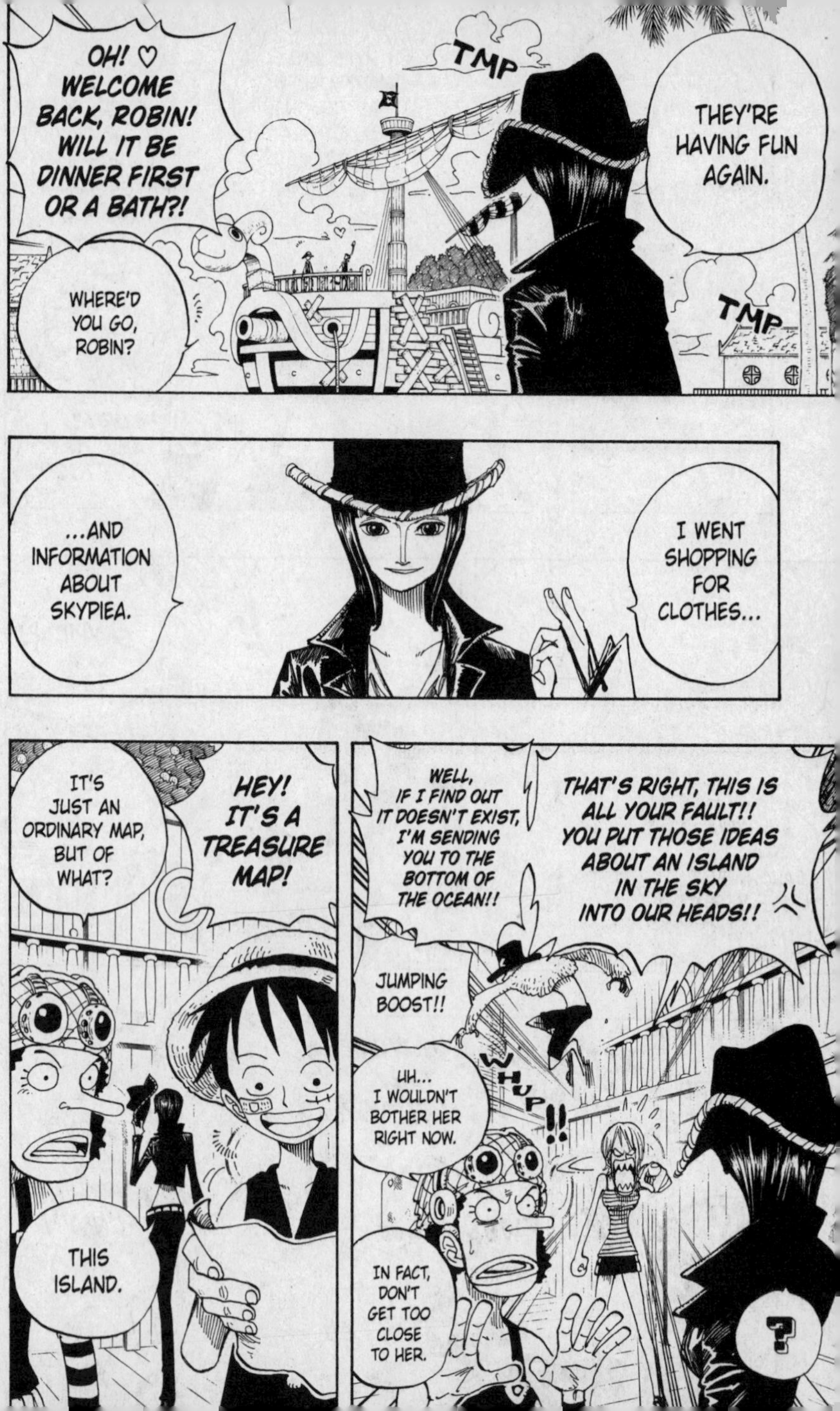
THEY'RE HAVING FUN AGAIN.
TMP
OH! ♡ WELCOME BACK, ROBIN! WILL IT BE DINNER FIRST OR A BATH?!
TMP
WHERE'D YOU GO, ROBIN?
I WENT SHOPPING FOR CLOTHES...
...AND INFORMATION ABOUT SKYPIEA.
THAT'S RIGHT, THIS IS ALL YOUR FAULT!! YOU PUT THOSE IDEAS ABOUT AN ISLAND IN THE SKY INTO OUR HEADS!!
WELL, IF I FIND OUT IT DOESN'T EXIST, I'M SENDING YOU TO THE BOTTOM OF THE OCEAN!!
JUMPING BOOST!!
WHUP!!
UH... I WOULDN'T BOTHER HER RIGHT NOW.
IN FACT, DON'T GET TOO CLOSE TO HER.
?
HEY! IT'S A TREASURE MAP!
IT'S JUST AN ORDINARY MAP, BUT OF WHAT?
THIS ISLAND.

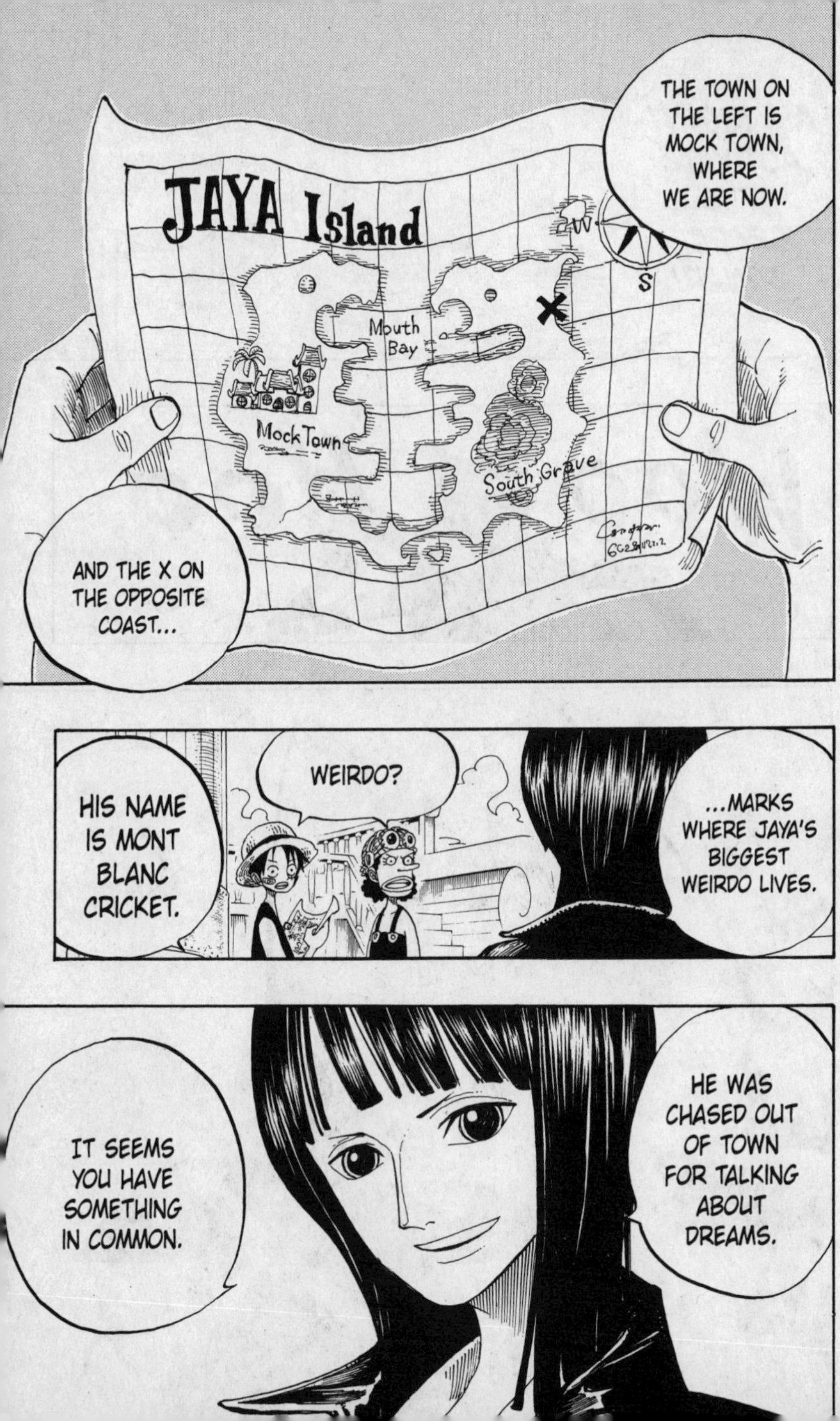
THE TOWN ON THE LEFT IS MOCK TOWN, WHERE WE ARE NOW.
JAYA Island
S
Mouth Bay
Mock Town
South Grave
AND THE X ON THE OPPOSITE COAST...
...MARKS WHERE JAYA'S BIGGEST WEIRDO LIVES.
WEIRDO?
HIS NAME IS MONT BLANC CRICKET.
HE WAS CHASED OUT OF TOWN FOR TALKING ABOUT DREAMS.
IT SEEMS YOU HAVE SOMETHING IN COMMON.

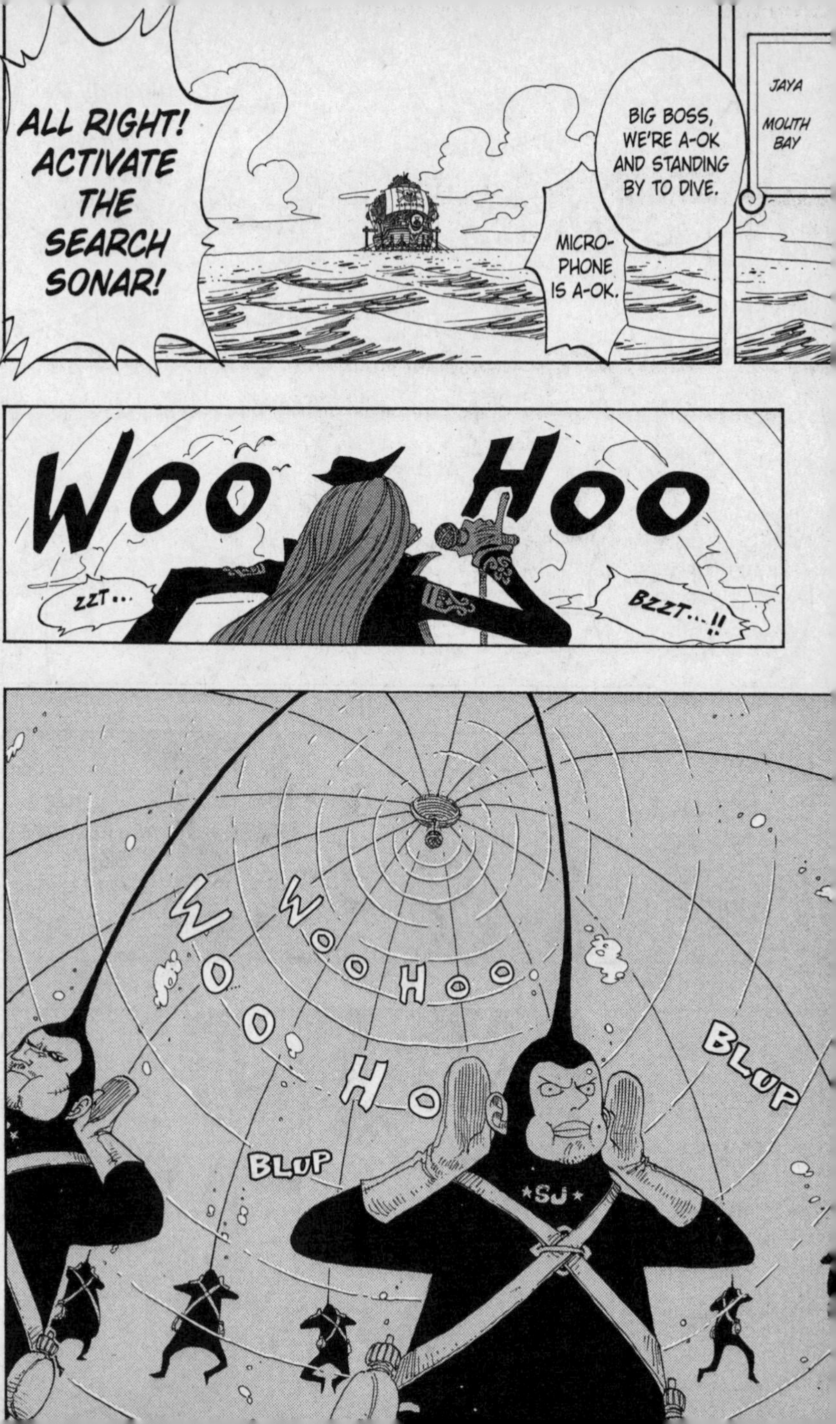
JAYA
MOUTH BAY
BIG BOSS, WE'RE A-OK AND STANDING BY TO DIVE.
MICROPHONE IS A-OK.
ALL RIGHT! ACTIVATE THE SEARCH SONAR!
WOO HOO
BZZT...!!
ZZT...
WOO HOO
WOO HOO
BLUP
BLUP

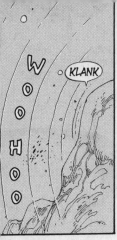

WOOOHOOO
WOOOHOOO
BZZT...
WOOOHOOO
KLANK
WOOOHOOO
BZZT...
!
UTAN DIVER NO. 27!
SONAR REVERBERATION CONFIRMED! LARGE SCHOOL OF FISH DETECTED AT 0900! THEIR SWIMMING SPEED IDENTIFIES THEM AS SAUREL!
!
SPLASH!!
ALL RIGHT! GRILLED FISH FOR DINNER!
DIVER NO. 4! SONAR REVERBERATION CONFIRMED!
SPLASH
A SMALL SAILING VESSEL HAS BEEN DETECTED!!

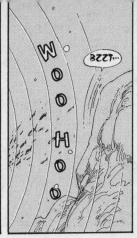

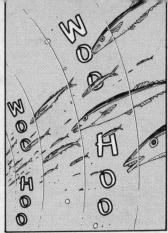

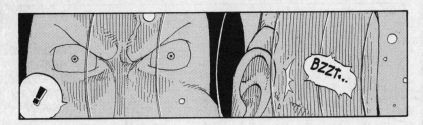

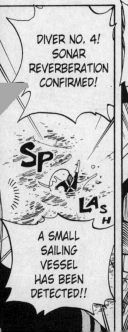

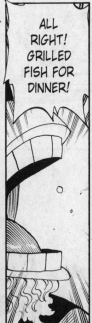

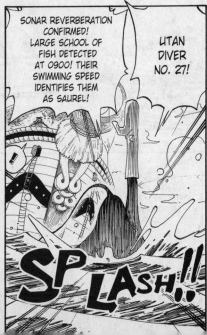

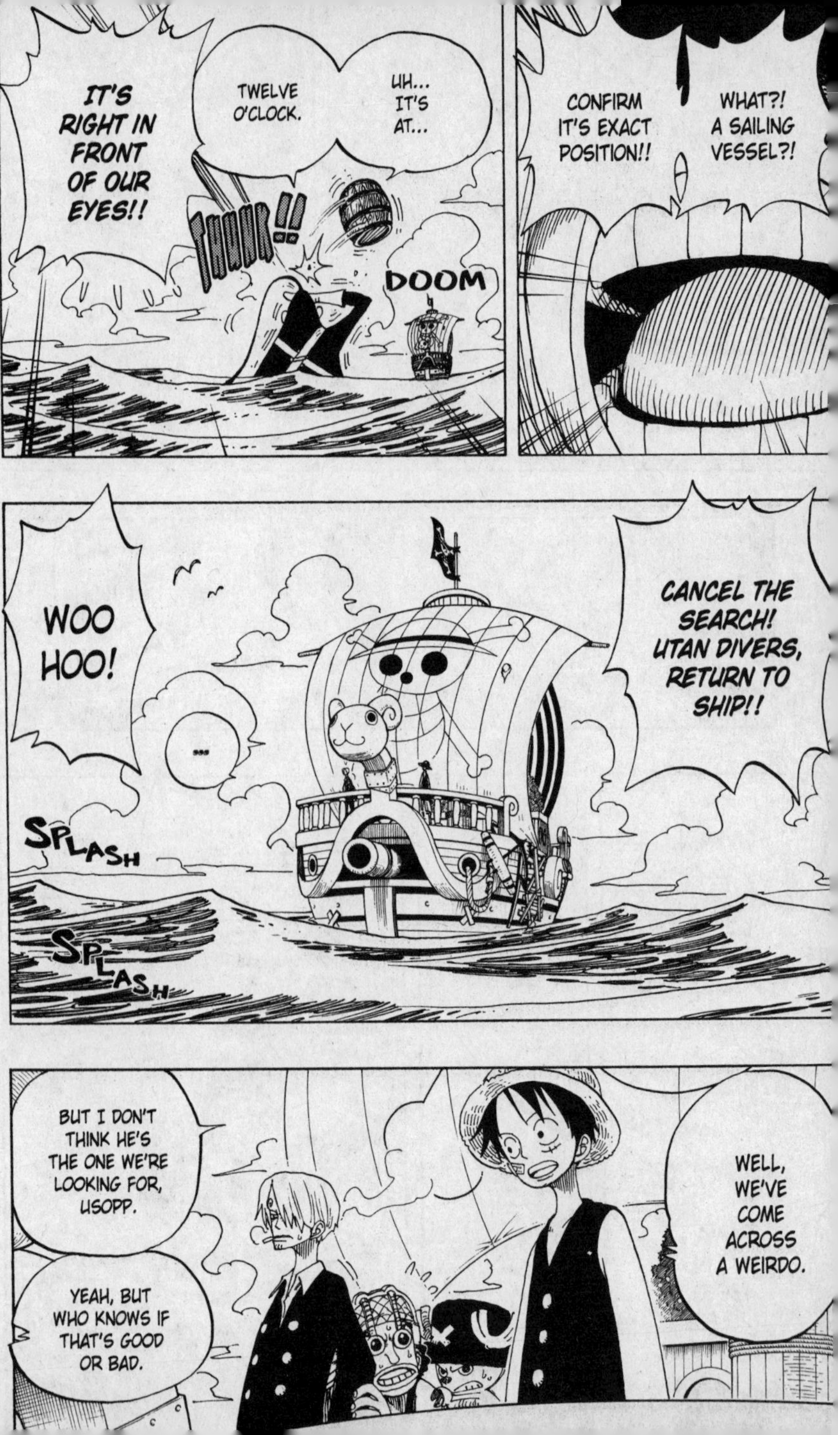
WHAT?! A SAILING VESSEL?!
CONFIRM IT'S EXACT POSITION!!
UH... IT'S AT...
TWELVE O'CLOCK.
IT'S RIGHT IN FRONT OF OUR EYES!!
DOOM
CANCEL THE SEARCH! UTAN DIVERS, RETURN TO SHIP!!
WOO HOO!
SPLASH
SPLASH
WELL, WE'VE COME ACROSS A WEIRDO.
BUT I DON'T THINK HE'S THE ONE WE'RE LOOKING FOR, USOPP.
YEAH, BUT WHO KNOWS IF THAT'S GOOD OR BAD.

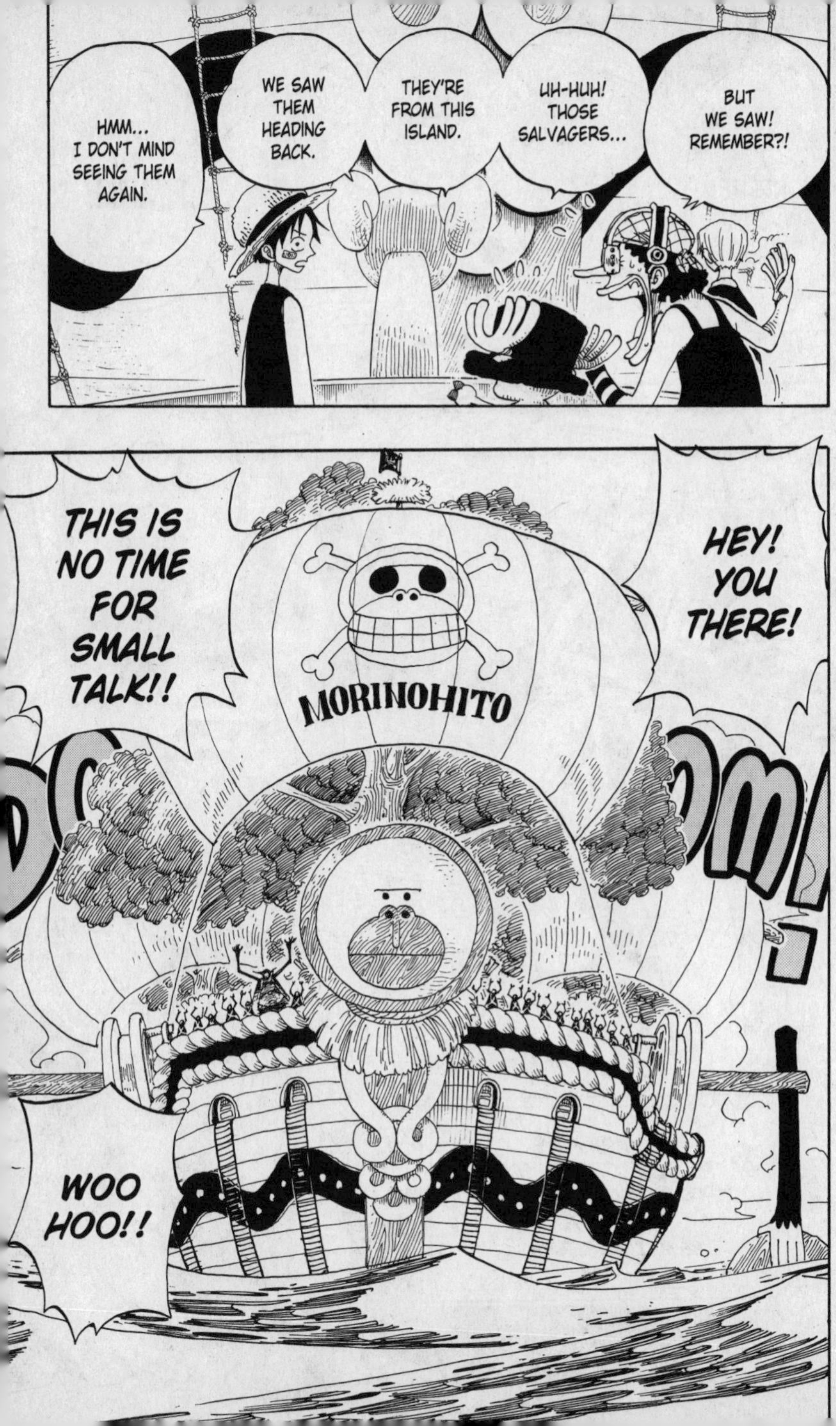
BUT WE SAW! REMEMBER?!
UH-HUH! THOSE SALVAGERS...
THEY'RE FROM THIS ISLAND.
WE SAW THEM HEADING BACK.
HMM... I DON'T MIND SEEING THEM AGAIN.
HEY! YOU THERE!
THIS IS NO TIME FOR SMALL TALK!!
MORINOHITO
WOO HOO!!

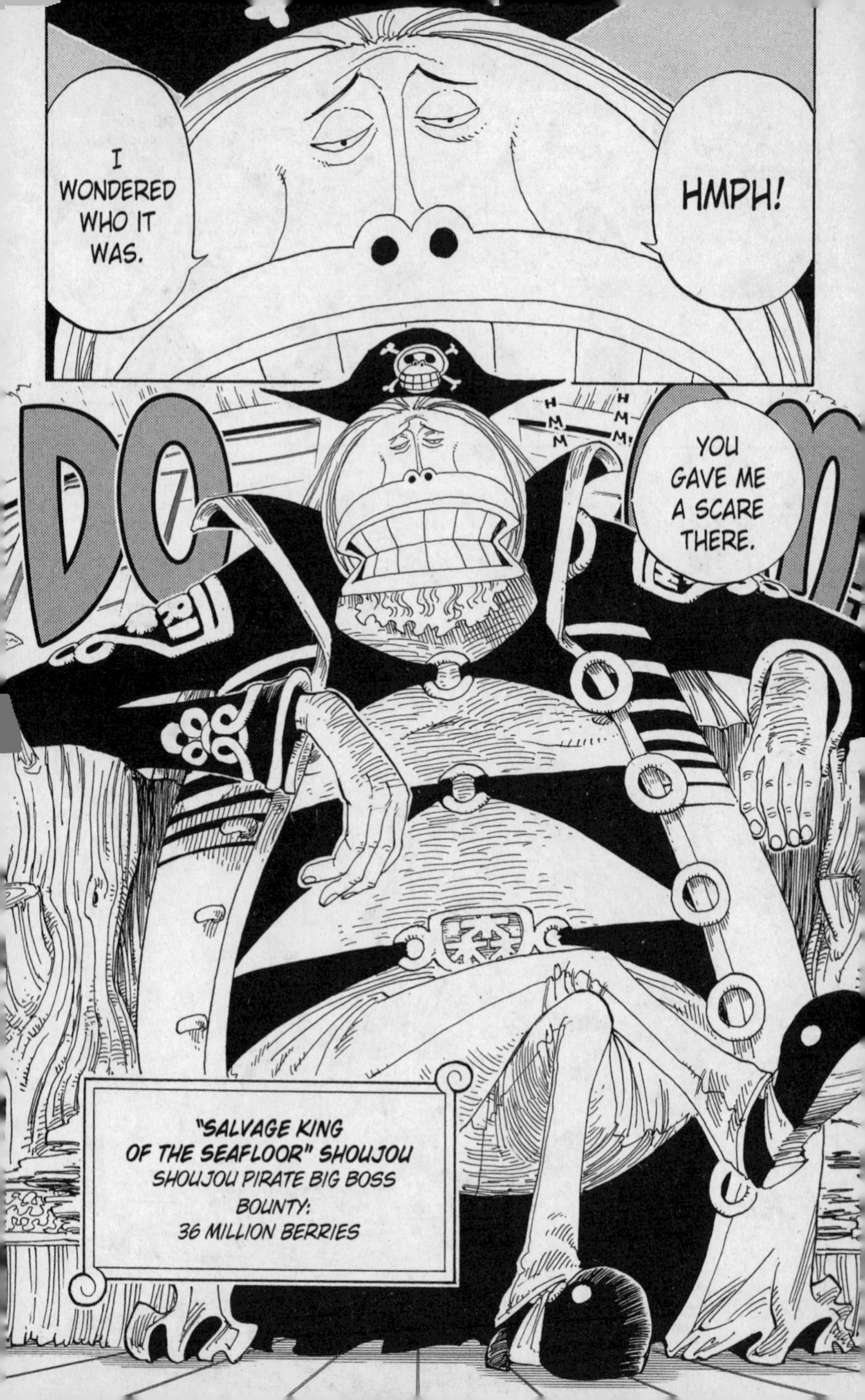
HMPH!
I WONDERED WHO IT WAS.
YOU GAVE ME A SCARE THERE.
HMMM
HMMM
DOM
"SALVAGE KING OF THE SEAFLOOR" SHOUJOU
SHOUJOU PIRATE BIG BOSS
BOUNTY:
36 MILLION BERRIES

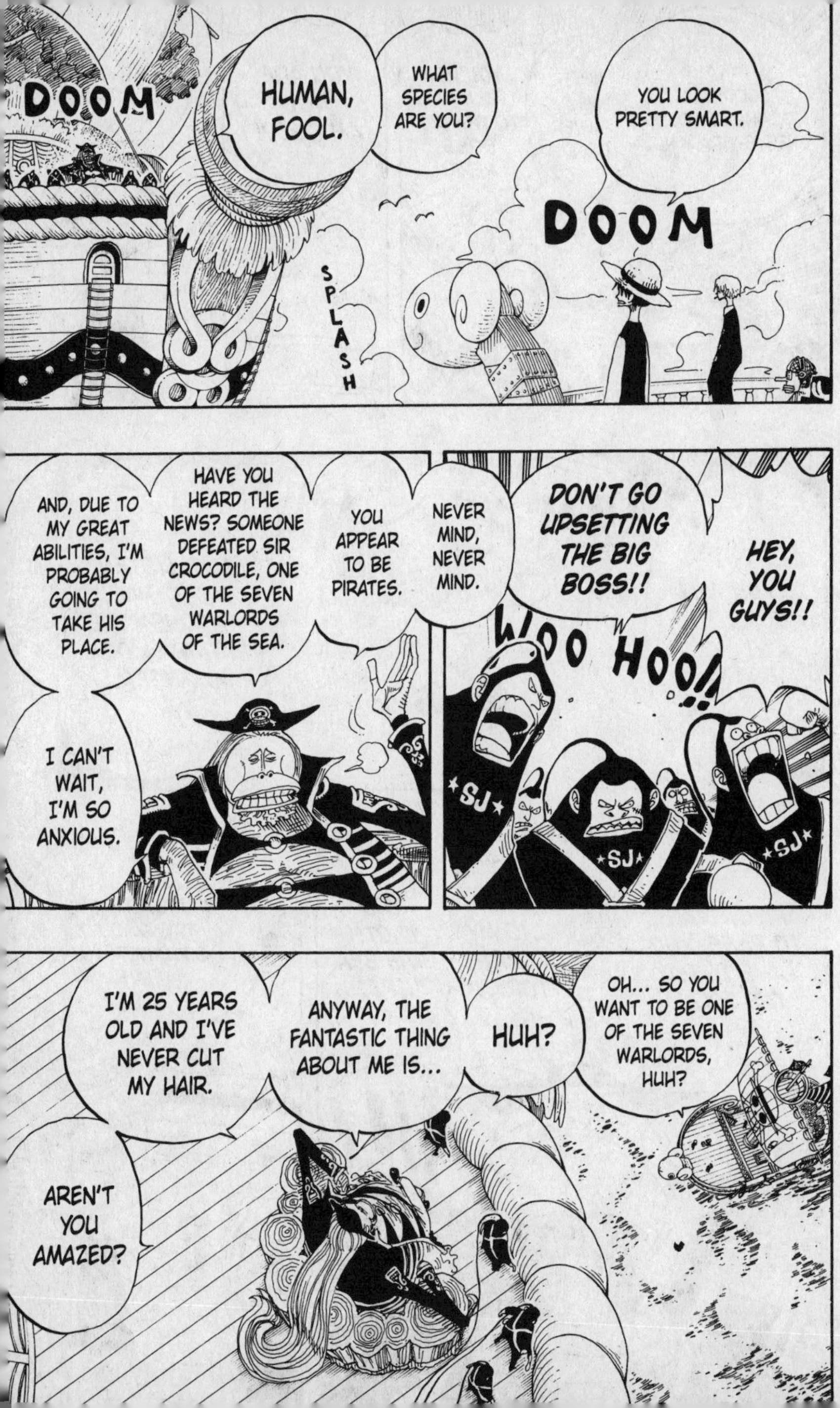
YOU LOOK PRETTY SMART.
DOOM
WHAT SPECIES ARE YOU?
HUMAN, FOOL.
DOOM
SPLASH
HEY, YOU GUYS!!
DON'T GO UPSETTING THE BIG BOSS!!
WOO HOO!!
NEVER MIND, NEVER MIND.
YOU APPEAR TO BE PIRATES.
HAVE YOU HEARD THE NEWS? SOMEONE DEFEATED SIR CROCODILE, ONE OF THE SEVEN WARLORDS OF THE SEA.
AND, DUE TO MY GREAT ABILITIES, I'M PROBABLY GOING TO TAKE HIS PLACE.
I CAN'T WAIT, I'M SO ANXIOUS.
OH... SO YOU WANT TO BE ONE OF THE SEVEN WARLORDS, HUH?
HUH?
ANYWAY, THE FANTASTIC THING ABOUT ME IS...
I'M 25 YEARS OLD AND I'VE NEVER CUT MY HAIR.
AREN'T YOU AMAZED?

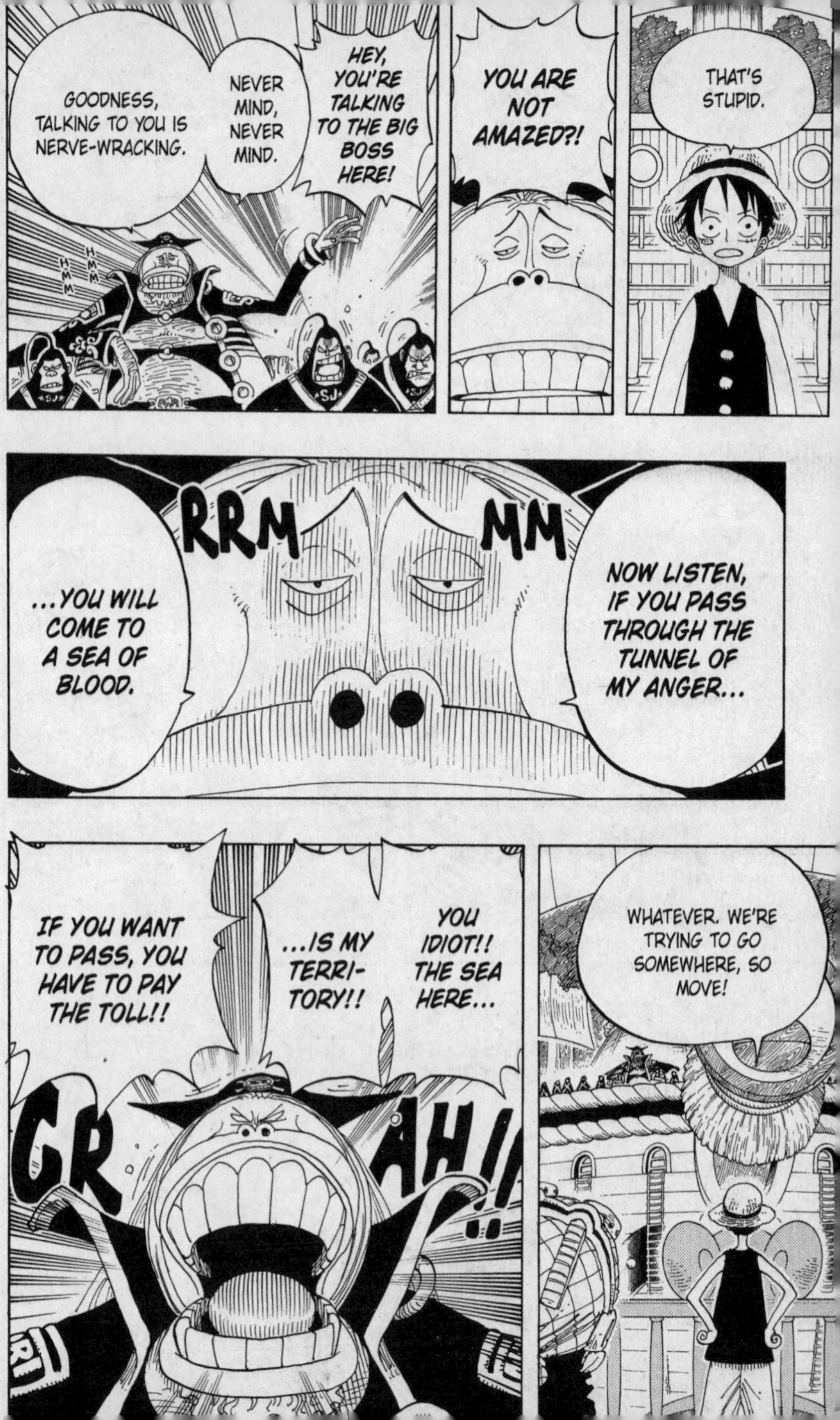
THAT'S STUPID.
YOU ARE NOT AMAZED?!
HEY, YOU'RE TALKING TO THE BIG BOSS HERE!
NEVER MIND, NEVER MIND.
GOODNESS, TALKING TO YOU IS NERVE-WRACKING.
HMM HMM
NOW LISTEN, IF YOU PASS THROUGH THE TUNNEL OF MY ANGER...
RRM MM
...YOU WILL COME TO A SEA OF BLOOD.
WHATEVER. WE'RE TRYING TO GO SOMEWHERE, SO MOVE!
YOU IDIOT!! THE SEA HERE...
...IS MY TERRITORY!!
IF YOU WANT TO PASS, YOU HAVE TO PAY THE TOLL!!
CR AH!!

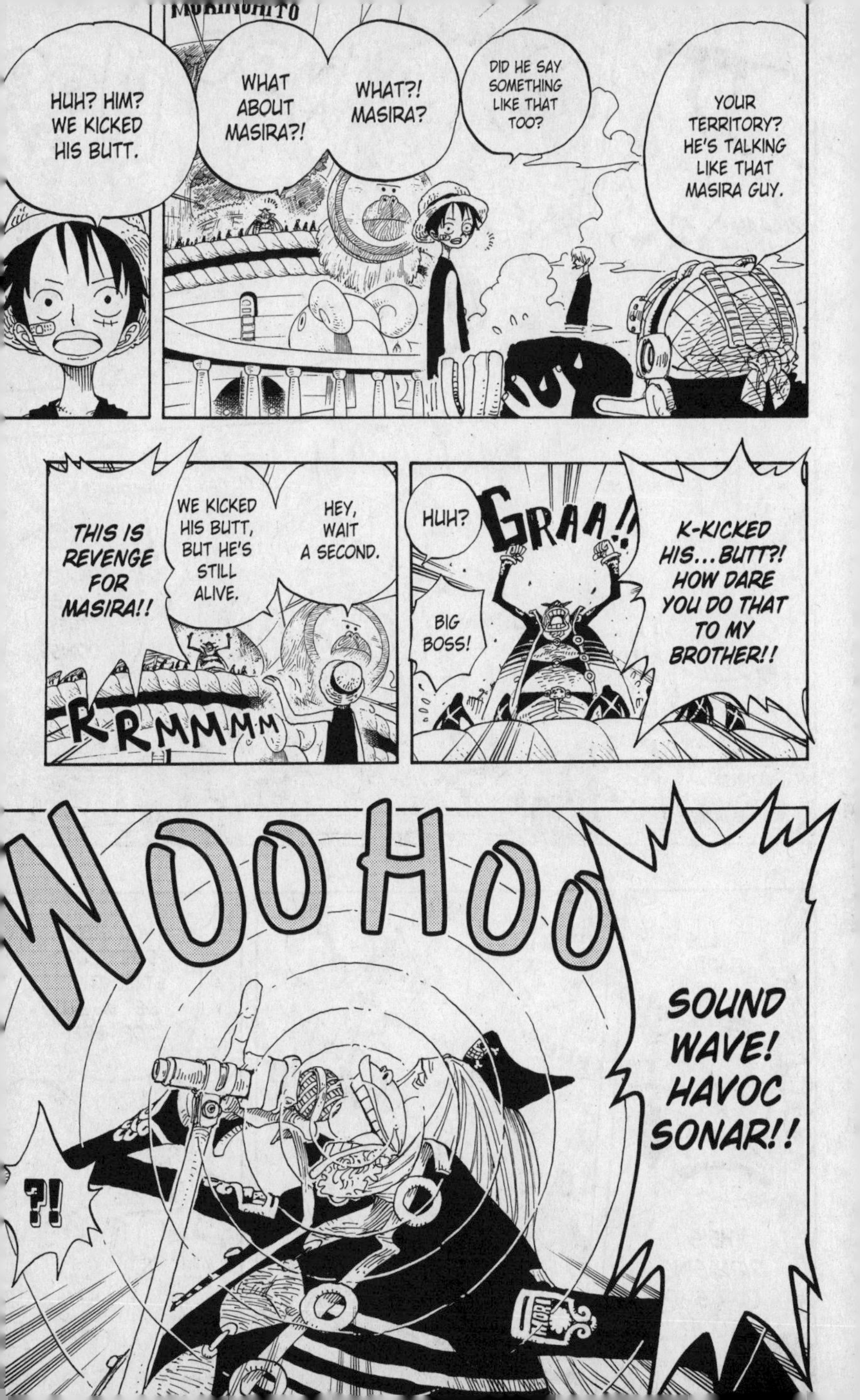
YOUR TERRITORY? HE'S TALKING LIKE THAT MASIRA GUY.
DID HE SAY SOMETHING LIKE THAT TOO?
WHAT?! MASIRA?
WHAT ABOUT MASIRA?!
HUH? HIM? WE KICKED HIS BUTT.
K-KICKED HIS...BUTT?! HOW DARE YOU DO THAT TO MY BROTHER!!
GRAA!!
HUH?
BIG BOSS!
HEY, WAIT A SECOND.
WE KICKED HIS BUTT, BUT HE'S STILL ALIVE.
THIS IS REVENGE FOR MASIRA!!
RRMMMM
SOUND WAVE! HAVOC SONAR!!
WOOHOO
?!

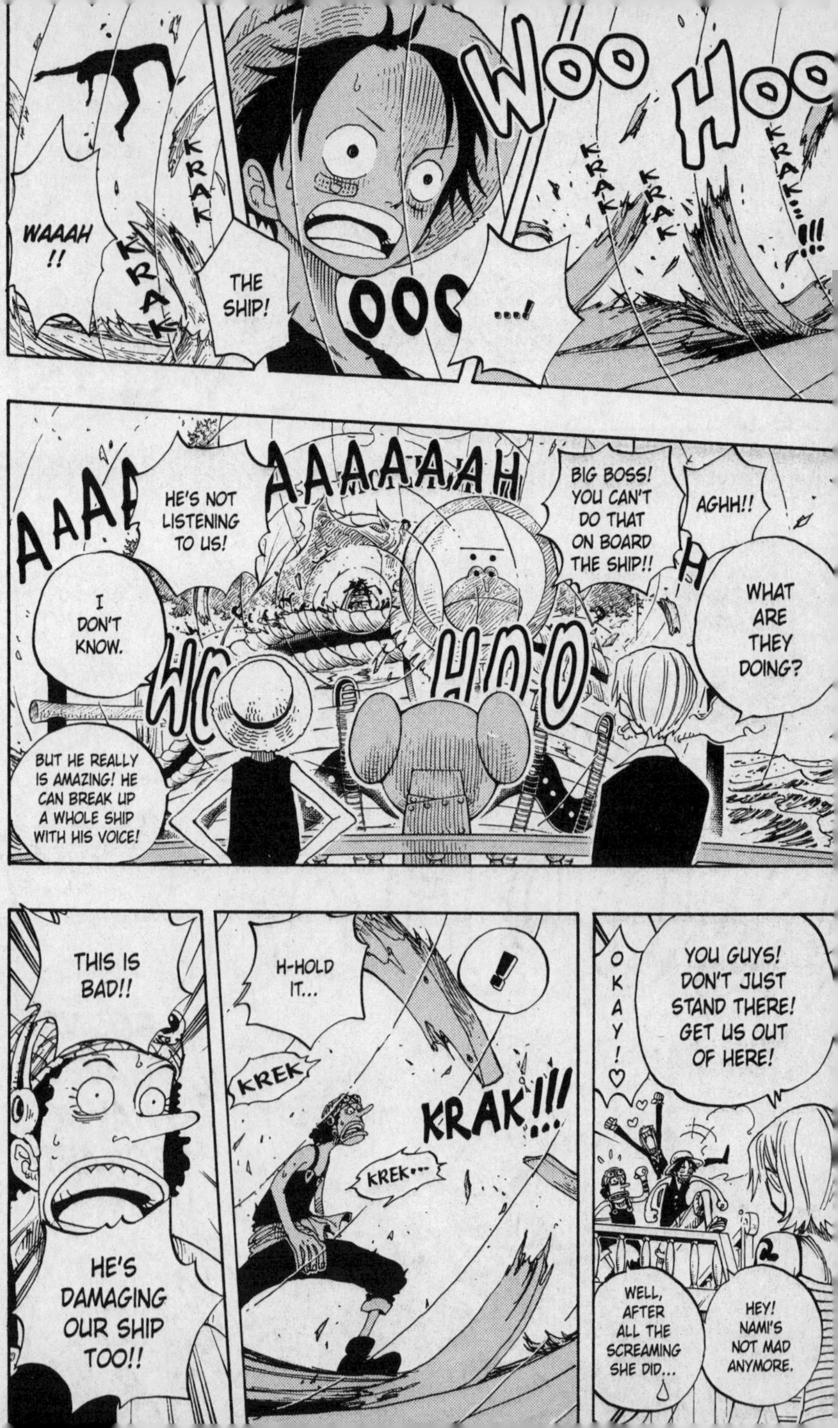
WOO HOO
KRAK...!!!
KRAK
KRAK
OOO
...!
THE SHIP!
KRAK
KRAK
WAAAH!!
AGHH!!
WHAT ARE THEY DOING?
BIG BOSS! YOU CAN'T DO THAT ON BOARD THE SHIP!!
AAAAAAH
HE'S NOT LISTENING TO US!
AAAH
I DON'T KNOW.
WO HOO
BUT HE REALLY IS AMAZING! HE CAN BREAK UP A WHOLE SHIP WITH HIS VOICE!
YOU GUYS! DON'T JUST STAND THERE! GET US OUT OF HERE!
OKAY!♡
HEY! NAMI'S NOT MAD ANYMORE.
WELL, AFTER ALL THE SCREAMING SHE DID...
!
H-HOLD IT...
KRAK!!!
KREK
KREK...
THIS IS BAD!!
HE'S DAMAGING OUR SHIP TOO!!

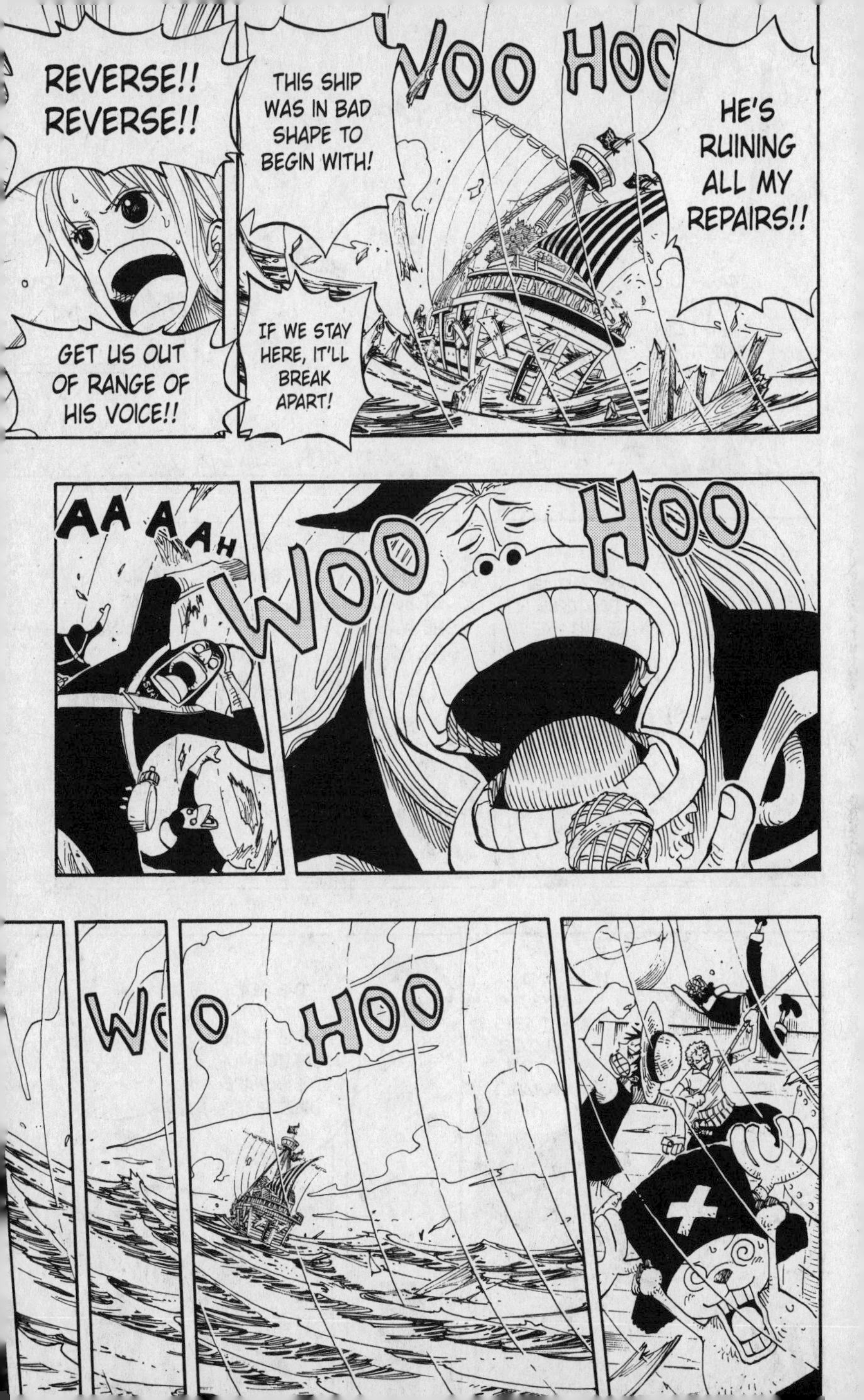
VOO HOO
HE'S RUINING ALL MY REPAIRS!!
THIS SHIP WAS IN BAD SHAPE TO BEGIN WITH!
IF WE STAY HERE, IT'LL BREAK APART!
REVERSE!! REVERSE!!
GET US OUT OF RANGE OF HIS VOICE!!
WOO HOO
AA AAAH
WOO HOO

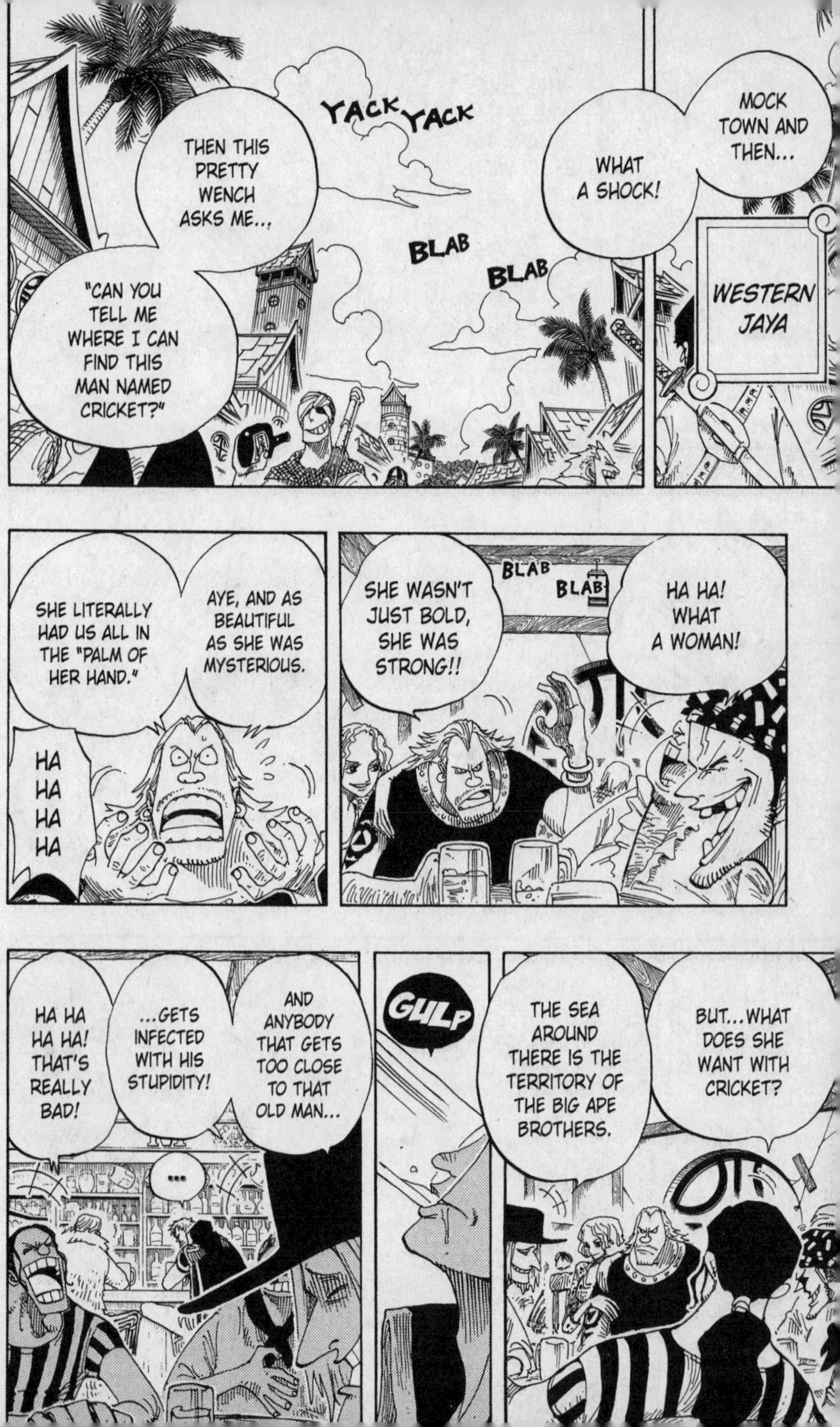
WESTERN JAYA
MOCK TOWN AND THEN...
WHAT A SHOCK!
BLAB
BLAB
YACK YACK
THEN THIS PRETTY WENCH ASKS ME...
"CAN YOU TELL ME WHERE I CAN FIND THIS MAN NAMED CRICKET?"
HA HA! WHAT A WOMAN!
BLAB
BLAB
SHE WASN'T JUST BOLD, SHE WAS STRONG!!
AYE, AND AS BEAUTIFUL AS SHE WAS MYSTERIOUS.
SHE LITERALLY HAD US ALL IN THE "PALM OF HER HAND."
HA HA HA HA
BUT...WHAT DOES SHE WANT WITH CRICKET?
THE SEA AROUND THERE IS THE TERRITORY OF THE BIG APE BROTHERS.
GULP
AND ANYBODY THAT GETS TOO CLOSE TO THAT OLD MAN...
...GETS INFECTED WITH HIS STUPIDITY!
HA HA HA HA! THAT'S REALLY BAD!
...

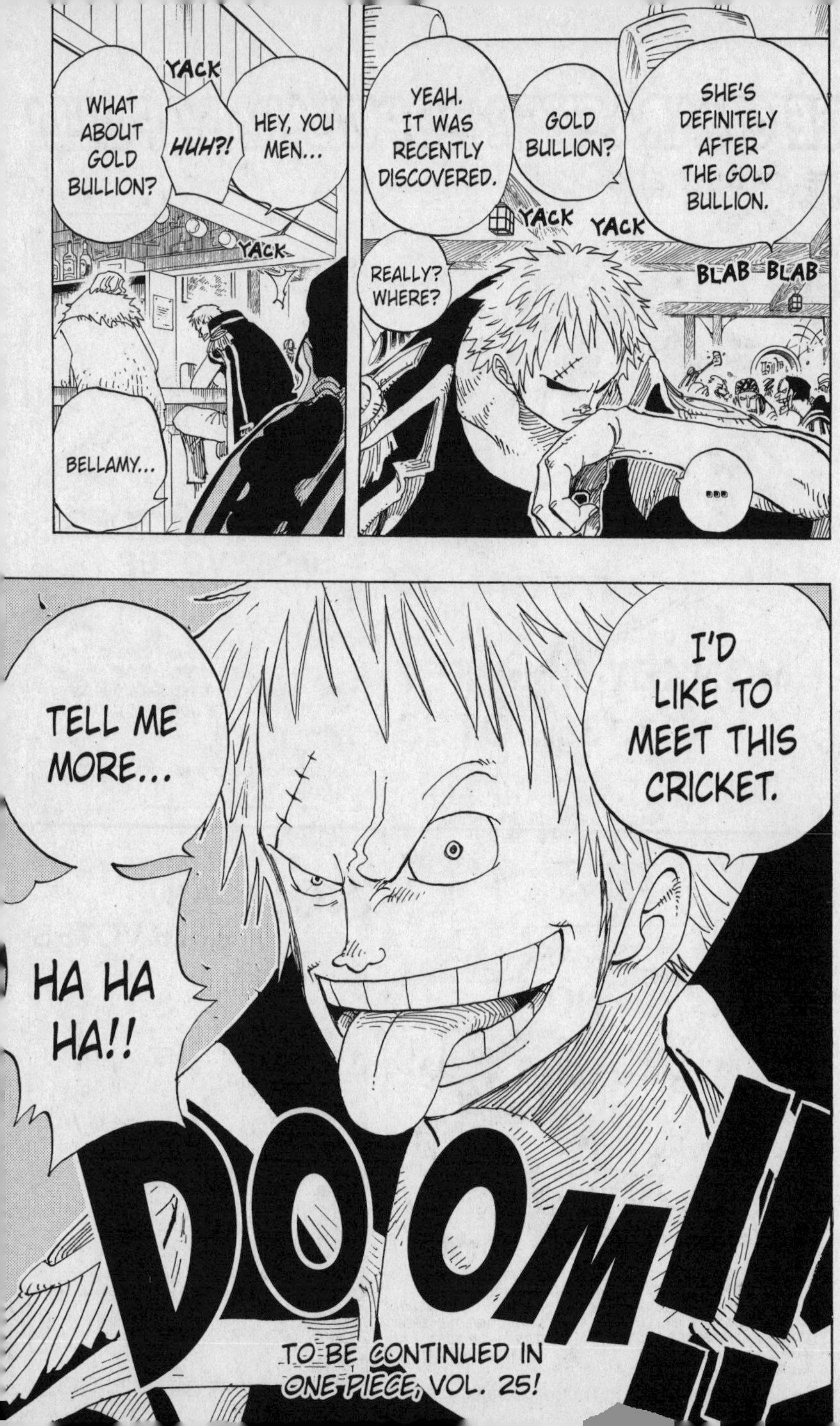
SHE'S DEFINITELY AFTER THE GOLD BULLION.
GOLD BULLION?
YEAH. IT WAS RECENTLY DISCOVERED.
YACK YACK
BLAB BLAB
REALLY? WHERE?
...
YACK
HEY, YOU MEN...
HUH?!
WHAT ABOUT GOLD BULLION?
YACK
BELLAMY...
I'D LIKE TO MEET THIS CRICKET.
TELL ME MORE...
HA HA HA!!
DOOM!!
TO BE CONTINUED IN ONE PIECE, VOL. 25!

ECE CHARACTER POPULARITY POLL!

RITE CHARACTERS DO?!

NO.1

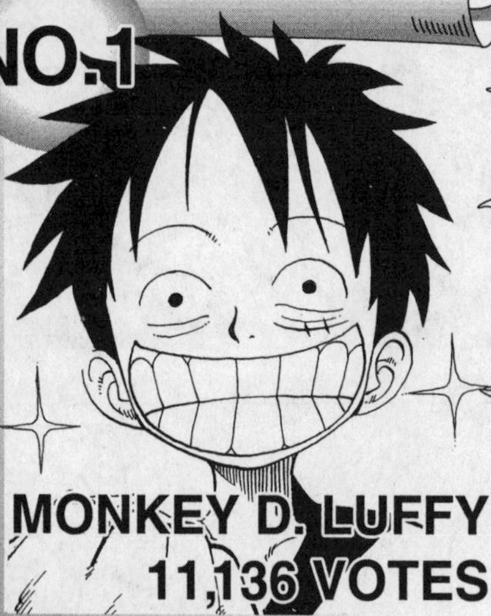

MONKEY D. LUFFY

11,136 VOTES

"HE'S BEEN COOL FROM HIS VERY FIRST APPEARANCE." "SEEING HIM MAKES ME HAPPY." HE GOT THE MOST VOTES AS WELL AS COMMENTS LIKE THESE. IT JUST PROVES THAT EVERYONE LOVES HIM!

NO.2

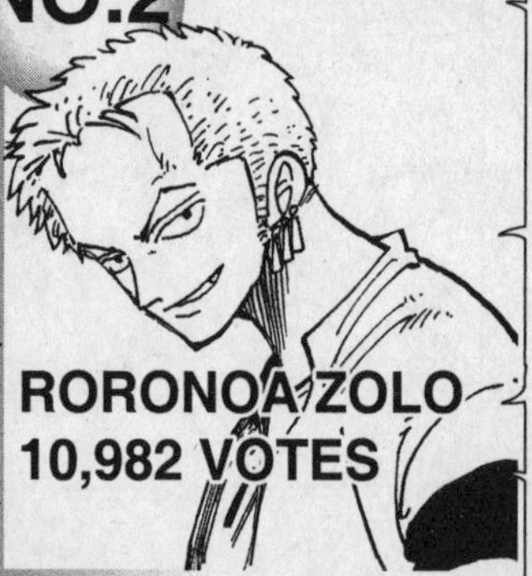

RORONOA ZOLO

10,982 VOTES

"HE'S SO COOL!" "HE'S AWESOME WHEN HE SHOWS OFF HIS FULL STRENGTH!" "I LOVE THE CASUAL WAY HE TELLS HIS ZINGERS." AND THAT'S WHY HE GOT MORE THAN 10,000 VOTES!

NO.3 SANJI

9,676 VOTES

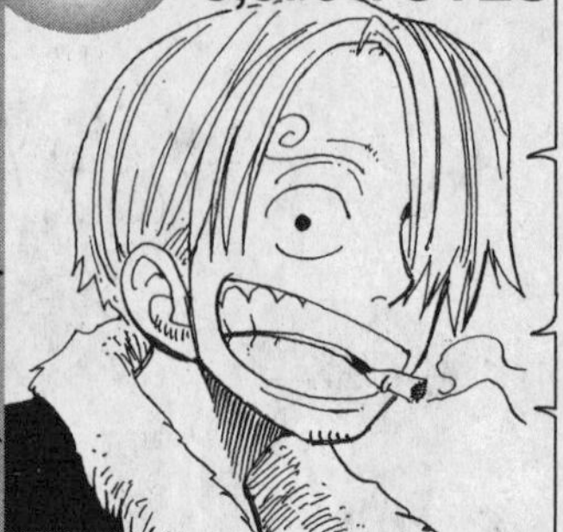

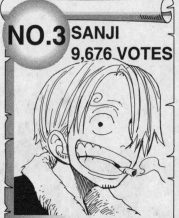

"HE'S SO CRAP-COOL!" "HE'S COOL-HEADED, BUT PASSIONATE!" THAT'S WHY HE WAS SO POPULAR WITH FEMALE VOTERS! NATURALLY, HE'S AIMING FOR NO. 1 NEXT TIME.

NO.4

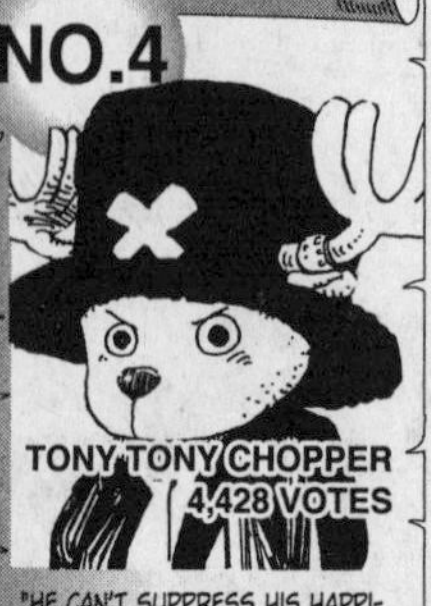

TONY TONY CHOPPER

4,428 VOTES

"HE CAN'T SUPPRESS HIS HAPPINESS, AND THAT'S SO CUTE!"♡ "HIS SEVEN-STAGE TRANSFORMATION IS SO FUN!" HE'S THE NEWEST CHARACTER WITH THE MOST VOTES, PUTTING HIM IN FOURTH PLACE!

NO.5

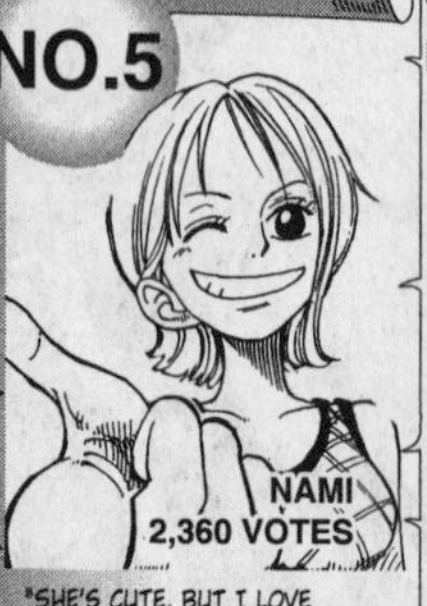

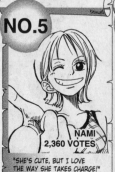

NAMI

2,360 VOTES

"SHE'S CUTE, BUT I LOVE THE WAY SHE TAKES CHARGE!" "SHE HAS AN INCREDIBLE BODY!" "I LOVE IT WHEN SHE USES HER CLIMATE BATON." SHE'S POPULAR WITH BOTH MALE AND FEMALE READERS!

51,873 TOTAL VOTES CAST

RESULTS OF THE 2ND ONE P

THANK YOU FOR VOTING! HOW DID YOUR FAV

No.6 1,957 VOTES
USOPP
"USOPP REALLY MAKES ME LAUGH!" "HE'S SO HAPPY-GO-LUCKY." HE WENT UP TWO RANKS HIGHER THAN THE LAST TIME!

No.7 1,880 VOTES
SHANKS
"I CAN'T WAIT TILL HE APPEARS AGAIN!" "HE'S THE GROWN-UP I ADMIRE MOST." HE'S A POPULAR CHARACTER WHO LEAVES A STRONG IMPRESSION WITH READERS.

No.8 1,735 VOTES
PORTGAZ D. ACE
"HE'S A GREAT BIG BROTHER!" "HIS FIRE FIST IS SUPER COOL!" THAT'S LUFFY'S POPULAR BIG BROTHER FOR YOU!

No.9 811 VOTES
MR. 2 BON CLAY
"HE'S SO FUNNY. REALLY, THIS AIN'T NO JOKE!" "HIS CLONE-CLONE TRICK IS TOPS!" HIS POPULARITY AIN'T NO JOKE!

No.10 748 VOTES
NEFELTARI VIVI
"HER DEVOTION TO HER COUNTRY IS ADMIRABLE!" "YOU CAN'T HELP BUT ROOT FOR HER." HER DIGNITY MAKES HER VERY POPULAR WITH THE VOTERS.

No.11 722 VOTES
NICO ROBIN (MS. ALL SUNDAY)

No.12 720 VOTES
CAPTAIN SMOKER

No.13 564 VOTES
"HAWK-EYE" MIHAWK

No.14 476 VOTES
SGT. TASHIGI

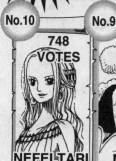

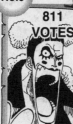

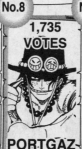

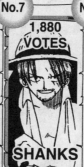

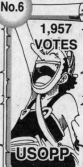

No.15 307 VOTES
CROCODILE

No.16 288 VOTES
KOZA

No.17 218 VOTES
BENN BECKMAN

No.18 216 VOTES
JOHNNY

No.19 215 VOTES
PANDA MAN

No.20 179 VOTES
BUGGY

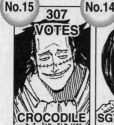

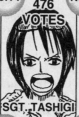

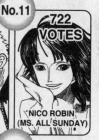

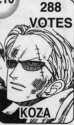

NO.21 CONTINUES ON THE NEXT PAGE, ALONG WITH USOPP'S OVERALL CRITIQUE.

THE SECOND ONE PIECE CHARACTER POPULARITY POLL RESULTS!! CONTINUED

NO.26	NO.25	NO.24	NO.23	NO.22	NO.21
 DR. KUREHA 95 VOTES	EIICHIRO ODA 97 VOTES	 KURO 111 VOTES	 GIN 120 VOTES	KAROO 170 VOTES	PELL 173 VOTES

NO.32	NO.31	NO.30	NO.29	NO.27	NO.27
GAIMON 60 VOTES	 ZEFF 62 VOTES	DR. HIRILUK 69 VOTES	 KUINA 74 VOTES	 MR. 9 81 VOTES	KUNG FU JUGONS 81 VOTES

NO.38	NO.37	NO.35	NO.35	NO.34	NO.33
 DJANGO 38 VOTES	BELLE-MERE 41 VOTES	MS. GOLDEN WEEK 45 VOTES	 MARIA ONION BEAR 45 VOTES	LABOON 47 VOTES	LT. FULL-BODY 56 VOTES

NO.38	NO.38
 MR. 1 38 VOTES	MS. VALENTINE 38 VOTES

USOPP'S ... OVERALL CRITIQUE!

WHAT HAPPENED, MY 8,000 HENCHMEN?! OH WELL, AT LEAST I'M TWO RANKINGS HIGHER THAN LAST TIME, AND I BEAT OUT MY RIVAL (?) BON CLAY. NEXT TIME I'LL WIN IT ALL!

SO LOOK FORWARD THE NEXT POPULARITY POLL!

THAT'S RIDICULOUS!

MR. MINA-TOMO THE CARPENTER

NO.51

AND EVEN ...

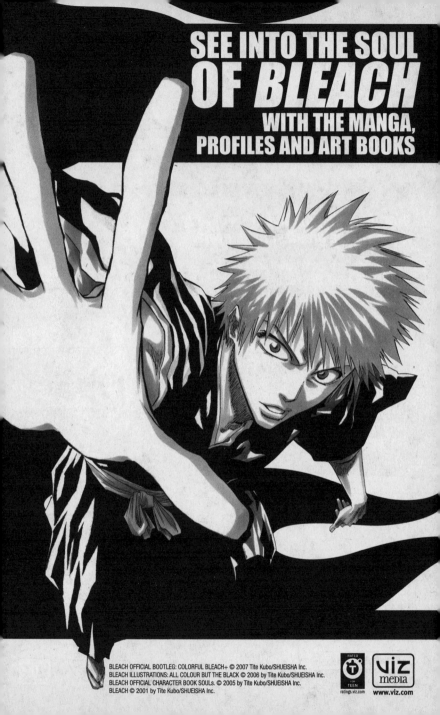

SEE INTO THE SOUL
OF *BLEACH*
WITH THE MANGA,
PROFILES AND ART BOOKS

BAKUMAN.

STORY BY TSUGUMI OHBA
ART BY TAKESHI OBATA

From the creators of *Death Note*

The mystery behind manga making REVEALED!

Average student Moritaka Mashiro enjoys drawing for fun. When his classmate and aspiring writer Akito Takagi discovers his talent, he begs to team up. But what exactly does it take to make it in the manga-publishing world?

Bakuman. Vol. 1
ISBN: 978-1-4215-3513-5
$9.99 US / $12.99 CAN *

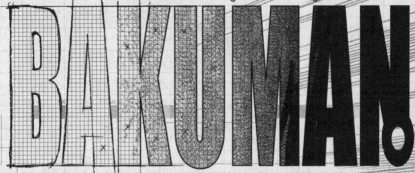

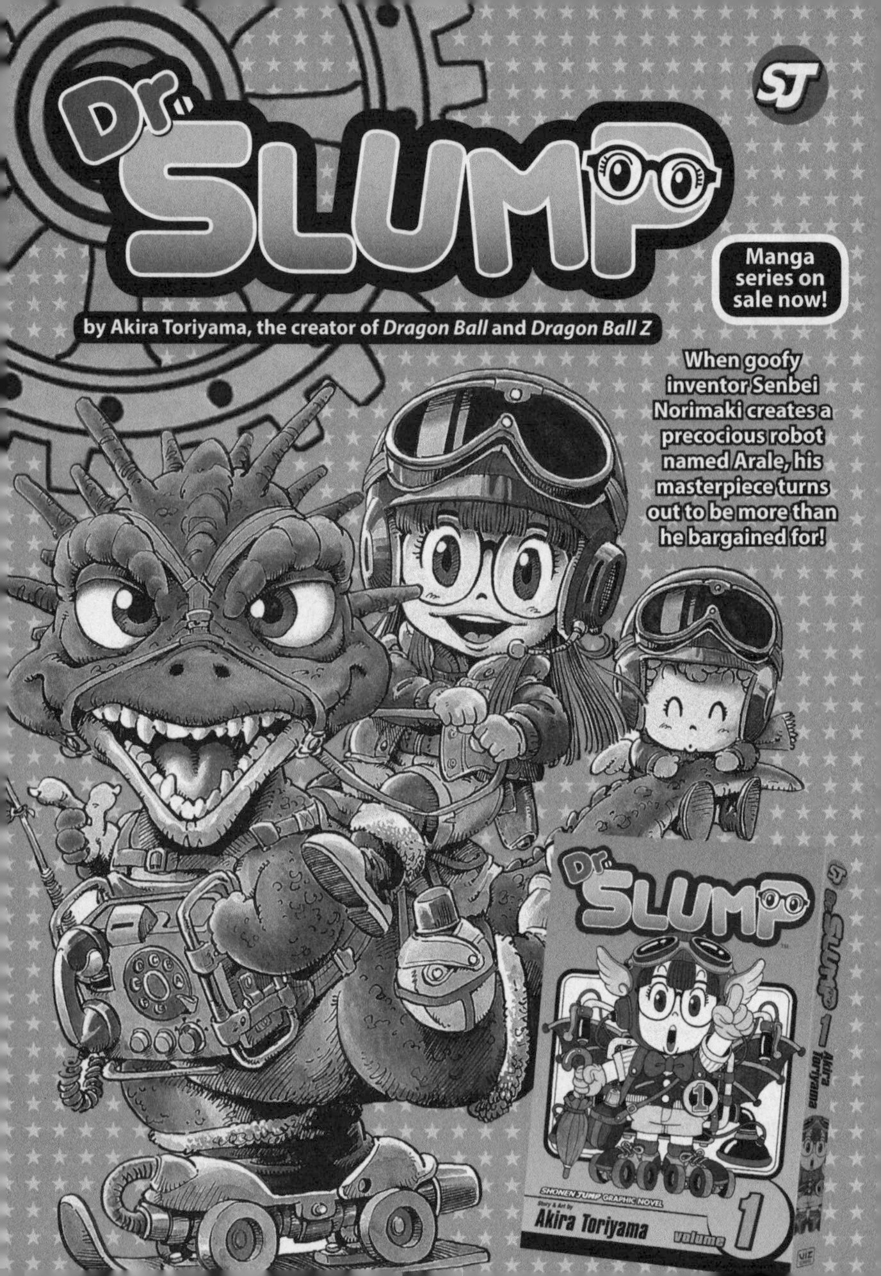
SJ
Dr. SLUMP
Manga series on sale now!
by Akira Toriyama, the creator of *Dragon Ball* and *Dragon Ball Z*
When goofy inventor Senbei Norimaki creates a precocious robot named Arale, his masterpiece turns out to be more than he bargained for!
Dr. SLUMP
SHONEN JUMP GRAPHIC NOVEL
Story & Art by
Akira Toriyama
volume 1
SJ Dr. SLUMP 1 Akira Toriyama

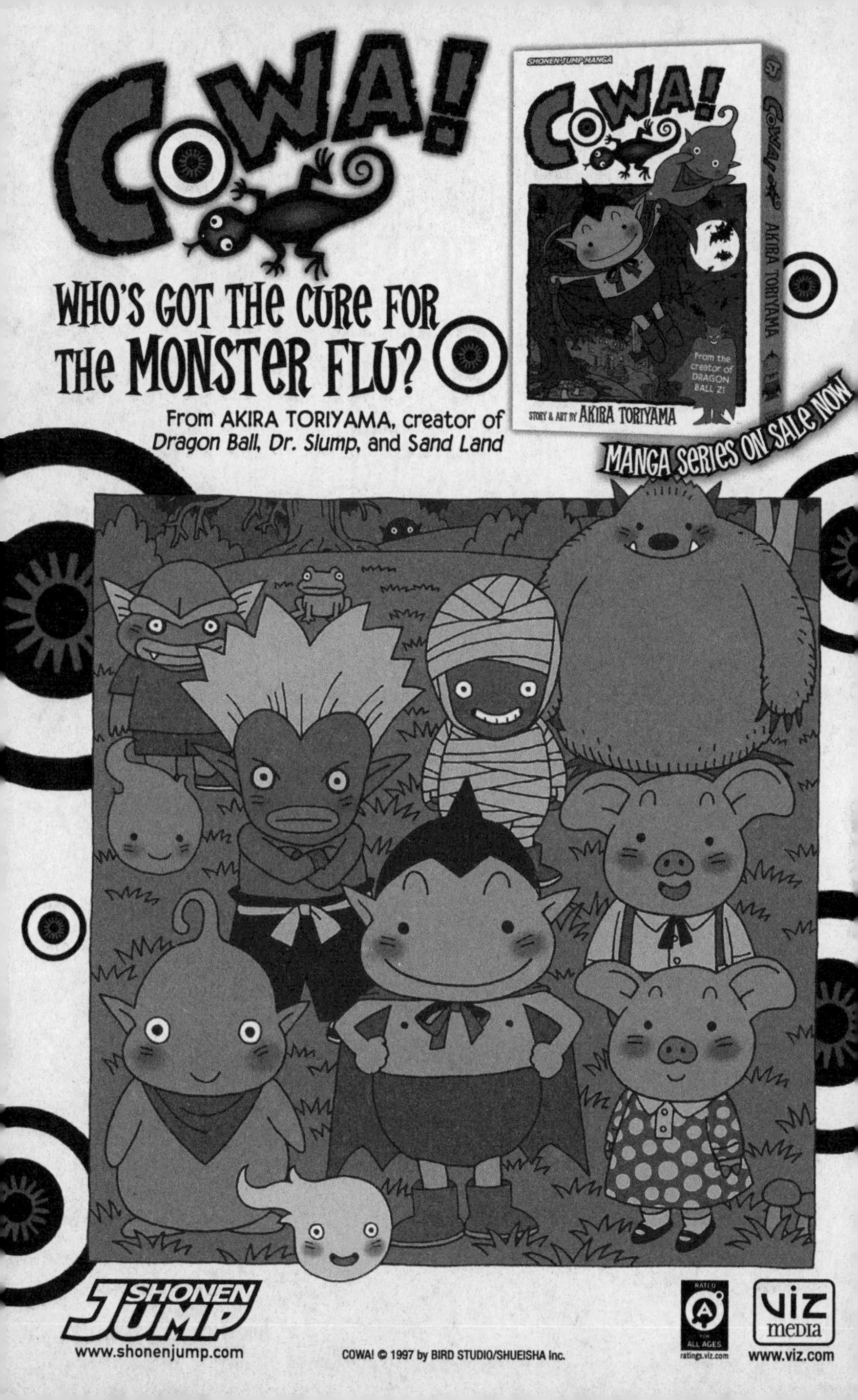
COWA!
WHO'S GOT THE CURE FOR THE MONSTER FLU?
From AKIRA TORIYAMA, creator of *Dragon Ball, Dr. Slump,* and *Sand Land*
SHONEN JUMP MANGA
COWA!
From the creator of DRAGON BALL Z!
STORY & ART BY AKIRA TORIYAMA
AKIRA TORIYAMA
MANGA SERIES ON SALE NOW
SHONEN JUMP
www.shonenjump.com
COWA! © 1997 by BIRD STUDIO/SHUEISHA Inc.
RATED A FOR ALL AGES
ratings.viz.com
VIZ media
www.viz.com

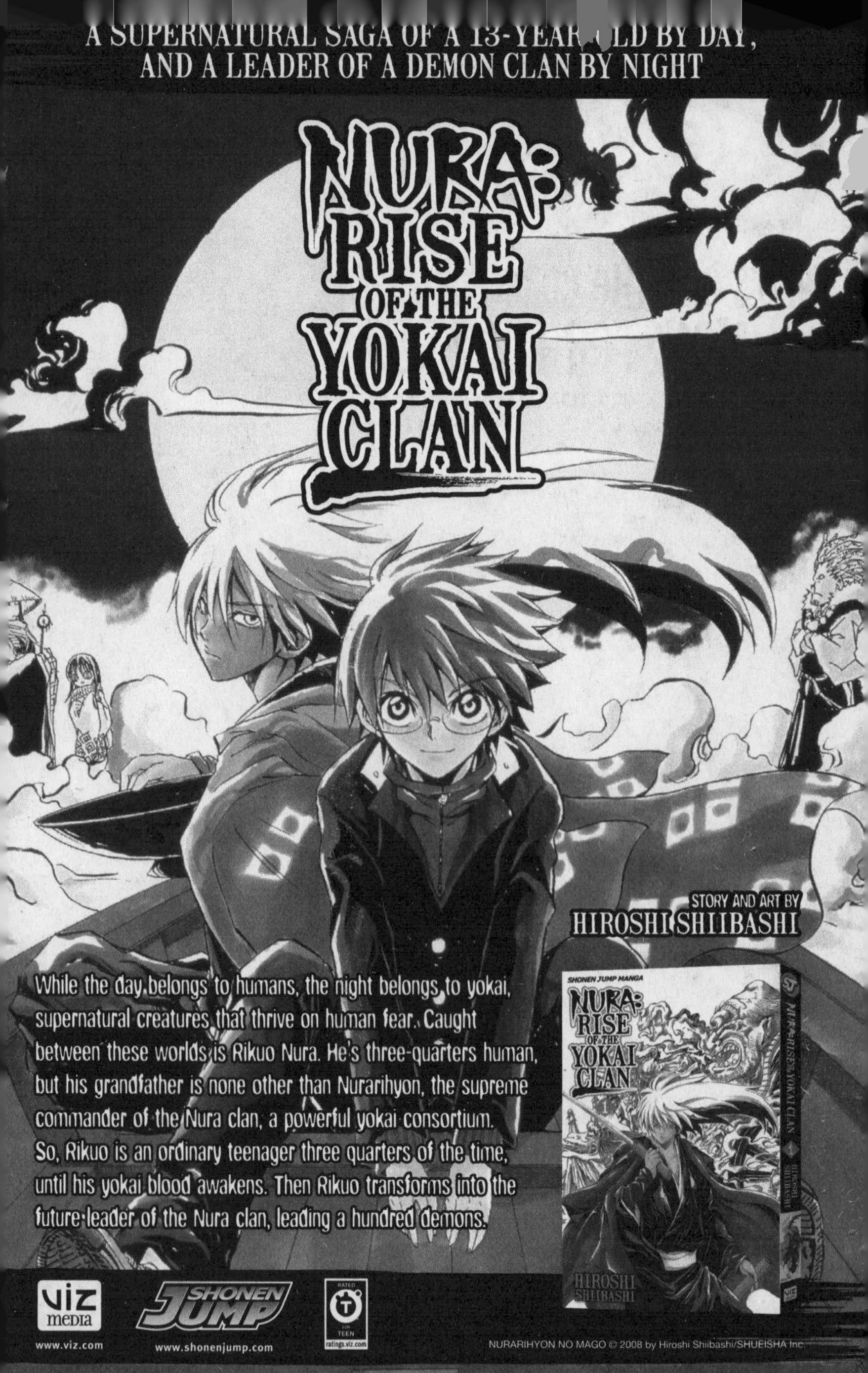

A SUPERNATURAL SAGA OF A 13-YEAR-OLD BY DAY,
AND A LEADER OF A DEMON CLAN BY NIGHT
NURA: RISE OF THE YOKAI CLAN
STORY AND ART BY
HIROSHI SHIIBASHI
While the day belongs to humans, the night belongs to yokai, supernatural creatures that thrive on human fear. Caught between these worlds is Rikuo Nura. He's three-quarters human, but his grandfather is none other than Nurarihyon, the supreme commander of the Nura clan, a powerful yokai consortium. So, Rikuo is an ordinary teenager three quarters of the time, until his yokai blood awakens. Then Rikuo transforms into the future leader of the Nura clan, leading a hundred demons.
SHONEN JUMP MANGA
NURA: RISE OF THE YOKAI CLAN
HIROSHI SHIIBASHI
viz media
SHONEN JUMP
RATED T TEEN
www.viz.com
www.shonenjump.com
ratings.viz.com
NURARIHYON NO MAGO © 2008 by Hiroshi Shiibashi/SHUEISHA Inc.